ENCYCLOPEDIA OF
Protestantism

ENCYCLOPEDIA OF WORLD RELIGIONS

ENCYCLOPEDIA OF
Protestantism

J. Gordon Melton

J. Gordon Melton, Series Editor

Facts On File, Inc.

Encyclopedia of Protestantism

Copyright © 2005 by J. Gordon Melton

Facts On File, Inc.
132 West 31st Street
New York NY 10001

Library of Congress Cataloging-in-Publication Data
Encyclopedia of Protestantism/[edited by] J. Gordon Melton.
  p. cm.—(Encyclopedias of world religions)
Includes bibliographical references and index.
ISBN 0-8160-5456-8 (alk. paper)
1. Protestantism—Encyclopedias. I. Melton, J. Gordon. II. Series.
BX4811.3.E54 2005
280'.4'03—dc22   2004016792

Facts On File books are available at special discounts when purchased in bulk quantities for businesses, associations, institutions, or sales promotions. Please call our Special Sales Department in New York at (212) 967-8800 or (800) 322-8755. You can find Facts On File on the World Wide Web at http://www.factsonfile.com.

Text design by Erika Arroyo
Cover design by Cathy Rincon

Printed in the United States of America

VB FOF 10 9 8 7 6 5 4 3 2 1

This book is printed on acid-free paper.

CONTENTS

ABOUT THE EDITOR

Series editor J. Gordon Melton is the director of the Institute for the Study of American Religion in Santa Barbara, California. He holds an M.Div. from the Garrett Theological Seminary and a Ph.D. from Northwestern University. Melton is the author of *American Religions: An Illustrated History* and author of *The Encyclopedia of American Religions: Religious Creeds; Religious Leaders of America;* and several comprehensive works on Islamic culture, African-American religion, cults, and alternative religions. He has written or edited more than three dozen books and anthologies as well as numerous papers and articles for scholarly journals. He is the series editor for Religious Information Systems, which supplies data and information in religious studies and related fields. Melton is a member of the American Academy of Religion, the Society for the Scientific Study of Religion, the American Society of Church History, the Communal Studies Association, and the Society for the Study of Metaphysical Religion.

LIST OF ILLUSTRATIONS

PREFACE

The Encyclopedias of World Religions series has been designed to provide comprehensive coverage of six major global religious traditions—Buddhism, Hinduism, Islam, Judaism, Roman Catholicism, and Protestant Christianity. The volumes have been constructed in an A-to-Z format to provide a handy guide to the major terms, concepts, people, events, and organizations that have, in each case, transformed the religion from its usually modest beginnings to the global force that it has become.

Each of these religions began as the faith of a relatively small group of closely related ethnic peoples. Each has, in the modern world, become a global community, and, with one notable exception, each has transcended its beginning to become an international multiethnic community. Judaism, of course, largely defines itself by its common heritage and ancestry and has an alternative but equally fascinating story. Surviving long after most similar cultures from the ancient past have turned to dust, Judaism has, in this century, regathered its scattered people into a homeland while simultaneously watching a new diaspora carry Jews into most of the contemporary world's countries.

Each of the major traditions has also, in the modern world, become amazingly diverse. Buddhism, for example, spread from its original home in India across southern Asia and then through Tibet and China to Korea and Japan. Each time it crossed a language barrier, something was lost, but something seemed equally to be gained, and an array of forms of Buddhism emerged. In Japan alone, Buddhism exists in hundreds of different sect groupings. Protestantism, the newest of the six traditions, began with at least four different and competing forms of the religious life and has since splintered into thousands of denominations.

At the beginning of the 19th century, the six religious traditions selected for coverage in this series were largely confined to a relatively small part of the world. Since that time, the world has changed dramatically, with each of the traditions moving from its geographical center to become a global tradition. While the traditional religions of many countries retain the allegiance of a majority of the population, they do so in the presence of the other traditions as growing minorities. Other countries—China being a prominent example—have no religious majority, only a number of minorities that must periodically interface with one another.

The religiously pluralistic world created by the global diffusion of the world's religions has made knowledge of religions, especially religions practiced by one's neighbors, a vital resource in the continuing task of building a good society, a world in which all may live freely and pursue individual visions of the highest values the cosmos provides.

In creating these encyclopedias, the attempt has been made to be comprehensive if not exhaustive. As space allows, in approximately 800 entries, each author has attempted to define and explain the basic terms used in talking about the religion, make note of definitive events, introduce the most prominent figures, and highlight the major organizations. The coverage is designed to result in both a handy reference tool for the religious scholar/specialist and an understandable work that can be used fruitfully by anyone—a student, an informed lay person, or a reader simply wanting to look up a particular person or idea.

Each volume includes several features. They begin with an introductory essay that introduces the particular tradition and provides a quick overview of its historical development, the major events and trends that have pushed it toward its present state, and the mega-problems that have shaped it in the contemporary world.

A chronology lists the major events that have punctuated the religion's history from its origin to the present. The chronologies differ somewhat in emphasis, given they treat two very ancient faiths that both originated in prehistoric time, several more recent faiths that emerged during the last few millennia, and the most recent, Protestantism, that is yet to celebrate its 500-year anniversary.

The main body of each encyclopedia is constituted of the approximately 800 entries, arranged alphabetically. These entries include some 200 biographical entries covering religious figures of note in the tradition, with a distinct bias to the 19th and 20th centuries and some emphasis on leaders from different parts of the world. Special attention has been given to highlighting female contributions to the tradition, a factor often overlooked, as religion in all traditions has until recently been largely a male-dominated affair.

Geographical entries cover the development of the movement in those countries and parts of the world where the tradition has come to dominate or form an important minority voice, where it has developed a particularly distinct style (often signaled by doctrinal differences), or where it has a unique cultural or social presence. While religious statistics are amazingly difficult to assemble and evaluate, some attempt to estimate the strength of the tradition on the selected countries has been made.

In some cases, particular events have had a determining effect on the development of the different religious traditions. Entries on events such as the St. Bartholomew's Day Massacre (for Protestantism) or the conversion of King Asoka (for Buddhism) place the spotlight on the factors precipitating the event and the consequences flowing from it.

The various traditions have taken form as communities of believers have organized structures to promote their particular way of belief and practice within the tradition. Each tradition has a different way of organizing and recognizing the distinct groups within it. Buddhism, for example, has organized around national subtraditions. The encyclopedias give coverage to the major groupings within each tradition.

Each tradition has developed a way and a vocabulary of encountering and introducing individuals to spiritual reality. It has also developed a set of concepts and a language to discuss the spiritual world and humanity's place within it. In each volume, the largest number of entries explore the concepts, the beliefs that flow from them, and the practices that they have engendered. The authors have attempted to explain these key religious concepts in a nontechnical language and to communicate their meaning and logic to a person otherwise unfamiliar with the religion as a whole.

Finally, each volume is thoroughly cross-indexed using small caps to guide the reader to related entries. A bibliography and comprehensive index round out each volume.

—J. Gordon Melton

INTRODUCTION
THE PROTESTANT MOVEMENT

Defining the Subject Matter

Encyclopedia of Protestantism deals with a movement within the larger Christian community that began in Europe in the 16th century, established itself in opposition to the Roman Catholic Church, subsequently spread around the world, and in the present day lives on in literally thousands of individual denominations and PARACHURCH ORGANIZATIONS. Using an A-to-Z format, the work covers the primary people, events, groups, and theological issues that emerged at the movement's origin; the main individuals, concerns, and movements that shaped it in subsequent centuries; and a representative sample of the movement as it now exists around the world. A special effort has been made to include coverage of those parts of the world in which Protestantism did not appear until the 19th century, regions that are now home to the growing edge of the movement (Asia, Africa, and Oceania).

In constructing this volume, the author had to confront the ambiguity of the term *Protestantism,* which can be used in both a broad and a narrow sense. Most narrowly, it denotes a movement that began within the Roman Catholic Church in Europe in the 16th century and the churches that come directly out of it. In this narrow sense, Protestantism would include the Lutheran, Reformed or Presbyterian, and Anglican (Church of England) churches, and by extension the churches of the British Puritan movement, which sought to bring the Church of England into the Reformed/Presbyterian camp. Most recently, scholars have argued quite effectively that the churches of the radical phase of the 16th-century Reformation, the Anabaptist and Mennonite groups, also belong within this more narrow usage.

While each gave slightly different meanings to some of the main ideas of the Reformation, the original Protestant churches generally agreed upon certain basic points: the sole authority of the Bible as the source of doctrine and church practice (*sola scriptura*), salvation by grace through faith in Jesus Christ (*sola fide*), and the priesthood of all believers. They also shared a rejection of certain Roman Catholic beliefs, for example, transubstantiation (the transformation of the elements of the Eucharist into the actual body and blood of Christ), purgatory (an intermediate place for the dead during which a final cleansing takes place before entering heaven), and the authority of the pope (the head of the Roman Catholic Church). Protestants also rejected the idea of a celibate priesthood and encouraged their clergy to marry.

While agreeing that there were only two sacraments (and not seven as maintained by the Roman Catholic Church), Protestants disagreed among themselves concerning the nature of those two sacraments. As regards the Eucharist, which Protestants generally call the Lord's Supper, Lutherans proposed the idea of consubstantiation, rejecting the notion of a change in the elements of bread and wine but maintaining that the substance of Christ coexists in these elements. Anglicans suggested that Christ was really present in the sacrament but left open the nature of that presence. Swiss reformer John CALVIN suggested that Christ was spiritually present in the elements and only perceived by the eye of faith.

Beginning with Swiss reformer Ulrich ZWINGLI, some Protestant spokespersons suggested that the Lord's Supper (and baptism) were not sacraments at all, thus denying any special sacredness to the elements. Zwingli, and following him, the Radical Reformers, suggested that the Lord's Supper and baptism were simply "ordinances" that were to be performed because they (1) were commanded by Scripture, (2) recalled to memory important events in the life of Christ, (3) were acts that constituted church fellowship, and (4) reminded people of a range of teachings affirmed by the church.

A slightly broader use of the term *Protestantism* would include all those groups that, though not in organizational continuity with one of the 16th-century Reformation churches, were/are in substantive agreement with the core doctrines of the early Protestant movement. This broader definition brings into the Protestant camp a set of churches that actually predated the Reformation. These churches had proposed some of the basic ideas later championed by the Protestants, and eventually accepted all of the other core Protestant beliefs and practices. Most prominent among such groups are the MORAVIAN CHURCH, which grew in response to the work of John HUS (in what is now the Czech Republic), and the Waldensians of Italy. In like measure, people such as John Hus (c. 1373–1415), Peter Waldo (d. c. 1217), and British biblical scholar John WYCLIFFE (c. 1329–84) are now seen as heralds of Protestantism.

A still more expanded definition of Protestantism would include a variety of groups that largely agree with Protestantism but that, on various grounds, frequently define themselves as outside the movement. Such are the Baptists. At first glance, they appear to be a Protestant movement. Few today would disagree that they were part of British Puritanism—if its most radical wing. Emerging at the beginning of the 17th century, Baptists disagreed with the Lutheran, Reformed, and Anglican churches over several new and vital issues. They considered any close relationship between churches and the state to be illegitimate, and they denied biblical authority for baptizing infants (the two positions being closely linked).

Doctrinally, the Baptists appeared most like the Calvinists. They affirmed the great majority of what, for example, Presbyterians affirmed, and even though they professed the Bible alone as their creed, like the Reformation churches they offered statements of belief (confessions of faith) to sum up their teachings. Their differences with other Protestants concerned matters that had not been emphasized in 16th-century debates, though many had been raised by the Anabaptists at that time.

Baptists were a relatively small group in 17th-century England. Often dismissed as fringe Puritans, they denied that they were Protestants at all. They claimed to be members of the true church through which the authority of Christ had been passed, and which throughout the centuries had always dissented from the corrupt alignment with the secular state. They suggested that they derived from a lineage of Christians who had always practiced adult (or believers) baptism.

The Baptists were eventually joined by an ever-growing number of churches that for various reasons separated from state and other established churches. Throughout the 19th and 20th centuries these "Free Churches" multiplied, usually as the result of movements protesting the organization within the parent body or calling for doctrinal or other changes. They often aimed at reviving a spirituality that the more staid and proper older Protestant bodies had lost, in their opinion. Such Free Churches often rejected the Protestant label; however, it should be noted that during the Reformation, Free Churches sided with the Protestants on every issue.

Among the Free Churches are such groups as the Swedish Mission Covenant Church, the Plymouth Brethren, the Holiness churches, and the modern Pentecostal and Charismatic churches. Also included would be the churches of the Restorationist movement that developed on the American frontier in the 19th century and that continued under such names as the Churches of Christ and the Christian Church (Disciples of Christ).

Encyclopedia of Protestantism consistently uses this broader definition of Protestantism, which includes the Reformation churches, the Protestant-like churches that predated them, and the Free Churches.

Finally, popular discourse often defines Protestantism more loosely to include a whole spectrum of groups that originated within the Protestant movement but that have deviated considerably from its tenets, in some cases even from the Christian consensus. Such movements as the Unitarians (and other non-Trinitarian groups), the CHURCH OF JESUS CHRIST OF LATTER-DAY SAINTS, the JEHOVAH'S WITNESSES, and CHRISTIAN SCIENCE have formally distanced themselves from the Christian and Protestant tradition. Some of them have ascribed to additional revelatory books and materials the authority that Protestants give to the Bible alone. Amid the great diversity that is the Protestant movement, Protestants as this book defines them would consider these groups as beyond the boundaries.

However, it is appropriate to treat these groups in a book on Protestantism. They are a product of the larger Protestant world, and in some cases they identify with it. For our purpose, they most clearly identify the boundaries of what can properly be called Protestant.

An Outline History of Protestantism

The Early Churches

Protestantism emerged in the first half of the 16th century in a set of geographically separate locations and in a variety of forms—most important were the German Lutheran, Swiss Reformed, and British Anglican. The Radical Reformation significantly expanded this variety through groups such as the Swiss Brethren, the Mennonites, the Schwenckfelders, and the followers of Sebastian Franck, though the Mennonites were the only major group that thrived and continued into the contemporary era. The 16th century also saw any number of would-be leaders and alternative movements that were pushed to the fringe and died out.

Protestantism represented not only a religious but also a political disruption of Europe. The movement succeeded only because it was able from its beginning to align itself with previously existing political powers. In England, Henry VIII (1491–1547) broke with Rome during the process of trying to gain a suitable heir to the throne. In Geneva, John Calvin (1509–64) had the backing of the magistrates to carry through reforms, and in Germany Martin LUTHER (1483–1546) won support from the Elector of Saxony and subsequently other German princes. The Anabaptists, persecuted because they had no friends in high places, survived only after they could find tolerant rulers who provided protection, if not agreement.

The political divisions opened by the Reformation in the 1520s had the effect of throwing the whole of Europe up for grabs. The Lutheran phase of the Reformation spread from Germany to gain the support of rulers throughout Scandinavia and the Baltic states. From Geneva, Calvin's brand of reform took hold in various Swiss cantons, Scotland, the Low Countries, parts of France, and faraway Transylvania. It also penetrated Germany, where in some areas it competed with Lutheranism.

The Roman Catholic Church and its political allies did not go away quietly, but fought to reestablish hegemony over northern and western Europe. A variety of wars small and large broke out, perhaps the most important between 1546 and 1555, culminating in the Peace of Augsburg (*see* AUGSBURG, PEACE OF). The peace gave the various German rulers the right to choose the religion of their land, be it Catholic or Lutheran (with the Reformed only included at a later date).

In England, Catholicism and Reformed Christianity vied for control. The attempt to protestantize the country moved forward during the five-year reign of Edward VI (1547–53), followed by a five-year attempt under Mary I (1553–58) to reassert Roman Catholic hegemony. Finally, Elizabeth I imposed the VIA MEDIA between the Calvinist Protestantism of Geneva and Roman Catholicism, the result being the unique Anglican way. Though constantly facing attempts to undermine her decision, Elizabeth's defeat of the Spanish Armada in 1588 blunted the Catholic challenge.

Among the last places to decide for or against the Reformation were France and the Low Countries. In the Low Countries, Protestantism became identified with the effort to overthrow the rule of Spain. Independence was declared in 1581, though the region remained contested until 1648. Meanwhile, Protestantism grew strong in France, even winning a degree of tolerance in 1570. That was undone two years later when Catholics fell upon Protestants (Huguenots), massacring many on St. Bartholomew's Day. The survivors took up the cause, ensuring an additional generation of hostilities. The EDICT OF NANTES (1598) finally resolved the dispute, granting Protestants a number of rights as a minority dissenting community. By 1600, the basic shape and structure of the Protestant community in Europe had been established, and the stage was set for its first significant expansion, across the Atlantic to the British American colonies.

Protestantism in North America

Immediately after the European discovery of a new land across the Atlantic (and not long after European circumnavigation of Africa), the pope, in consultation with the rulers of Spain and Portugal, drew a line down the middle of the Atlantic, dividing rights of colonization between the two major Catholic powers. Spain was assigned the territory to the west, hence most of North and South America. Portugal was to operate east of the line, leaving it only Brazil in the New World, but all of Africa. France and England, left out of negotiations, did not recognize the results. The former moved to establish itself in Canada, while England (along with Holland and Sweden) claimed land along the Atlantic coast of North America. England and Denmark challenged Spain's exclusive rights in the Caribbean.

Permanent settlement of the territory claimed by Britain began at Jamestown, Virginia, in 1606. Its short-lived Anglican minister, Robert Hunt (c. 1568–1608), was followed by Alexander Whitaker (1585–c. 1616) whose ministry established worship according to the Church of England. In 1619, Anglicanism was formally named the colony's official religion. Though getting a head start in Virginia, the church did not fare as well elsewhere in the English colonies.

Instead, several American colonies became home for groups that had lost out in the religious conflicts of the Elizabethan era. First to arrive were the Pilgrims, a small separatist group from the most radical wing of the Puritan movement, with no interest in government ties. They settled at Plymouth, Massachusetts, in 1620, after having spent a generation in Holland. They were followed by the Puritans, who wanted to build a society in which a congregational form of Reformed Christianity reigned supreme. After settling Boston in 1630, the Puritans spread across New England in an attempt to model what the Church of England could be if it adopted the Reformed faith of John Calvin along with a congregational polity. As Congregationalism emerged, it became as religiously intolerant as the ecclesiastical powers in England who had provoked the Puritan leaders to forsake their homeland in the first place.

Other British dissenters obtained grants to establish two additional colonies in North America, the Catholics (Maryland) and the Quakers (Pennsylvania). Under the guidance of Lord Baltimore, a rather free and open society was created in Maryland in which Catholics and others could coexist. However, toward the end of the century, forces from neighboring Virginia marched into Maryland, overthrew the government, and recreated Maryland along the lines of Virginia. In 1692, the authorities declared the Church of England the established church of Maryland. William Penn's experiment fared somewhat better, and Pennsylvania became a haven for dissidents not only from England but also from across Europe.

Initially, Pennsylvania was bordered north and south by a Dutch (New Amsterdam) and a Swedish (Delaware) colony. In 1624, the Dutch had begun a permanent settlement on Manhattan from which additional settlements were made in what is now New Jersey, on Long Island, and northward along the Hudson River. The first congregation of the Reformed Church of the Netherlands was opened in New Amsterdam (now New York City) in 1628. That congregation, the Collegiate Church of the City of New York, continues today as the oldest continuously active Protestant church in North America. Swedes settled along the Delaware River in 1638 where Fort Christina (now Wilmington) was erected. Swedish Lutheranism was formally constituted following the arrival of Rev. Reorus Torkillsu two years later.

In 1664, the British moved to consolidate their claims to America's Atlantic seaboard by forcing both the Swedes and the Dutch to turn over their lands to British control. Thus, by the end of the century, the outline of Protestant life in the American colonies was evident. To the north, in New England, a strong Congregational establishment was thoroughly ensconced in power, though it had a cancerous growth on its fringe in Rhode Island, where a dissenting Puritan minister, Roger Williams (c. 1603–c. 83), had created a colony not unlike Pennsylvania—it tolerated a variety of religious expression.

To the south, Anglicanism reigned supreme, though the establishment was weak and a spectrum of dissenting groups (Roman Catholic, Lutheran, Reformed, Quaker, Baptist) operated quite openly. Like Rhode Island in New England, Pennsylvania was the exception to the south. Here Anglicanism was present, but as a distinct minority.

While the initial Protestant structures were being erected in America, Britain was experiencing equally important changes within its Protestant community. During Elizabeth's reign (1558–1603), Anglicanism was firmly established in the beliefs and practices of the Church of England. However, it continually faced challenges from those who wanted to further purify the church by making its doctrine conform more closely to that of Geneva and replacing its episcopal polity with leadership by elders (Presbyterianism) or congregations (Congregationalism). Presbyterianism (already established in Scotland) proved to be the greater threat.

In the mid-17th century, dissatisfaction with the rule of Charles I (r. 1625–49) gave the Puritans an opening they were quick to seize. In several steps during the 1640s they introduced Reformed worship into England's churches and took complete control of the government. They reorganized the Church of England without bishops and replaced the monarchy with a commonwealth, but the opportunity to demonstrate the superiority of their way lasted less than two decades. The monarchy was restored in 1660, and Anglicanism resumed its dominance in the church. However, the 1689 Act of Toleration assured a place for those who continued in good conscience to dissent from the established order.

New Movements Arise

By the beginning of the 18th century, Protestantism was a settled reality in Europe. While a few contested spaces remained, as a whole it was clear that Protestantism had established itself and would remain a viable part of European life for the foreseeable future. Protestant lands were not likely to fall to internal or external pressures. The time had come to turn some attention from the issues that defined the movement in the 16th century, including the establishment of reform churches, to the spiritual needs of individuals, many of whom were not being adequately served by the Protestant churches. These churches, many complained, did not provide an environment that could nurture personal religious growth. In addition, it was said, their failure to call members to the ethical life had resulted in rampant immorality.

Taking the lead in exploring ways to revitalize the spiritual life of the churches was Lutheran pastor Philipp Jacob Spener (1635–1705). In 1694, Spener founded the University of Halle, which became the great dissemination point for his movement, popularly known as PIETISM. The university, a training school for future Lutheran ministers, came to be dominated by August Hermann Francke (1663–1727), a man who by precept and practice exemplified the Pietist life of personal devotion and service. He was also one of the first Protestants to develop a vision for missionary work around the world.

Soon aligning themselves with the Pietists were the Moravians, whose movement was founded a century before the Lutheran Reformation. The Moravians fled Bohemia and Moravia (now the Czech Republic) when Roman Catholicism reasserted hegemony there in the 1620s. Hounded from place to place, in 1722 they finally found some protection and acceptance on the estate of Nicolas von ZINZENDORF (1700–60), a German nobleman. At the village of Herrnhut, which they created on Zinzendorf's land, they reorganized and emerged as the Moravian Church. As the situation allowed, they soon opened other centers of activity in the Protestant countries of Europe.

In England, the kind of personal religion represented by the Pietists and the Moravians gave birth to Methodism. Challenged by Moravians like Bishop August Spangenberg (1704–92) and future missionary Peter Böhler (1712–75),

Methodist founder John WESLEY (1703–91) explored a new depth of Christian experience that led him to launch an effort to revitalize religious life in the British Isles.

Among Wesley's associates was a former classmate at Oxford, George WHITEFIELD (1714–70). Like Wesley, he became an Anglican minister, but while Wesley itinerated through England, Whitefield traveled to America. His preaching trips throughout the colonies beginning in 1739 led to a revival known as the Great Awakening. The revival not only affected religion; it has been understood as the first significant unifying event shared by people across the different colonies, helping to make them into a nation. The revivalism that Whitefield initiated became a hallmark of American religion in the centuries after the American Revolution.

Global Spread

The North American colonies and the initial beachheads established in the Caribbean gave Protestants their first vision of life beyond the borders of Europe, though the Dutch were also carrying Protestantism into new territories in the 17th century as a result of their colonial adventures in Southeast Asia and Oceania. The emergence of a global consciousness, however, came slowly. Thomas BRAY (1656–1730), sent by the Anglican Church to the American colonies in the 1690s to observe the church situation, returned to England and became the instigator of the first two Protestant foreign mission agencies, the SOCIETY FOR THE PROPAGATION OF THE GOSPEL IN FOREIGN PARTS, to recruit ministers for the American colonies, and the SOCIETY FOR PROMOTING CHRISTIAN KNOWLEDGE, to publish the materials they would need for their work.

The Dutch established Reformed churches in their colonial centers, but did not expect their ministers serving abroad to do much more than serve the expatriate community. The first Protestant church to be established with the goal of evangelizing the host country was initiated by King Frederick IV of Denmark, who in 1705 commissioned his chaplain to recruit missionaries for India, where Denmark had a trading post. The Pietists at Halle quickly supplied two young candidates, Bartholomew Ziegenbalg (1682–1719) and Heinrich Plütschau (1677–1747). They arrived in India in 1706. For a generation, the men who led the Danish-Halle Mission in India were the only Protestant missionaries to the non-Christian world.

That would change in 1731, after Moravian leaders met with a slave visiting Copenhagen with his master from the Danish West Indies. The slave, ANTHONY, urged the Moravians to send missionaries to work among his suffering brothers and sisters. His plea catalyzed the Brethren into action. Two missionaries arrived on St. Thomas in 1732, and within a few years the first Protestant global missionary program had begun. Missionaries were soon sent to Greenland (1733), the British American colonies (1736), and South Africa (1737), and, shortly after, to Labrador, South America, and Egypt.

The Moravians would bear further missionary fruit by inspiring John Wesley to found the Methodist movement, which produced the second expansive Protestant missionary effort. Methodism developed a concern for the conversion of the world through its encounter with African Americans who came to Methodism with no Christian background. That concern grew with the travels of Methodist bishop Thomas COKE, who at Wesley's behest organized a separate American Methodist Episcopal Church after the American Revolution, and then traveled to the Caribbean.

Even before his 18 transatlantic voyages, Coke had developed a vision for the worldwide Methodist missionary expansion. In 1784, he presented Wesley a *Plan of the Society* [of Methodists] *for the Establishment of Missions among the Heathen.* The plan first targeted the Caribbean, and then Gibraltar and Sierra Leone. It culminated in the commissioning of a team to begin work in India.

Following the Moravian and Methodist lead, William CAREY and Andrew FULLER began to mobilize the Baptists. Baptists had no central authority structure of the kind that had allowed the Moravians and Methodists to respond quickly to the missionary call, but in 1792 Carey issued his booklet, *An Enquiry into the Obligation of Christians, to Use Means for the Conversion of the Heathen,* while Fuller took the lead in founding the Baptist Foreign Missionary Society as the organizational vehicle to develop a global evangelizing outreach. Carey led the first Baptist missionary team to India in 1783.

The Moravians, Methodists, and Baptists thus provided the models Protestants could use to expand into the non-Christian world in the next century. Within a few decades other groups also responded to the missionary imperative. An interdenominational LONDON MISSIONARY SOCIETY (LMS) was founded in 1795. After the evangelical Anglicans formed their own CHURCH MISSIONARY SOCIETY in 1799, the LMS became primarily a Congregational body with some Presbyterian support. The Church of Scotland joined the missionary effort in 1824.

The Reformed Church in the Netherlands joined the effort in 1797 with the formation of the Netherlands Missionary Society. Similar efforts were organized by the French Reformed (Paris Mission, 1822), and in the German-speaking Reformed and Lutheran communities (Basel, 1815; Barmen, 1815; Berlin, 1824; Rhenish, 1828), in both Switzerland and Germany.

America was slower in sending missionaries abroad, as the frontier itself presented a huge mission field to American churches, one that was very close to home. Early debates on foreign missions were weighed against responsibilities to supply the frontier and evangelize Native Americans. However, in 1810 the American Commissioners for Foreign Missions was formed with the primary support of the Congregationalists, the strongest church in the United States at the time. Other Calvinist churches supported it for a period, but they all eventually formed their own mission boards. As in England, missions were the catalyst for the organization of national structures for the

Baptists, following the conversion to the Baptist faith by some of the original American Board missionaries in India.

By the early decades of the 20th century, Protestant missionary agencies had transformed Protestantism from a religion largely confined to northern and western Europe and North America into a worldwide faith. With the exception of the Muslim-controlled countries across North Africa and the Middle East, a significant Protestant presence developed in most of the world's countries and territories. Protestantism's very success left its leaders with significant issues of how to relate to this new body of Christians.

The Twentieth-Century Shift

The global church has remained the great question for the Protestant movement. Protestantism had divided into a number of denominations with substantive disagreements that reappeared on the mission field, despite early attempts to keep the squabble at home. Missionaries from different churches entered comity agreements to stay out of one another's way—at best a temporary solution. Eventually, the problems created by denominational competition led to the Ecumenical movement, in which like-minded but competing churches tried to overcome past differences and find a new affirmation of oneness. That movement eventually led to the merger of closely related churches and to cooperation and positive feelings even among churches that did not merge.

The creation of a host of local and national councils of churches culminated in 1948 with the WORLD COUNCIL OF CHURCHES. A parallel set of international bodies arose to provide contact among national churches of a single denominational family or with similar beliefs, sometimes out of a feeling that the larger church bodies had undercut their doctrinal integrity. Associations such as the WORLD EVANGELICAL ALLIANCE and the INTERNATIONAL COUNCIL OF CHRISTIAN CHURCHES provide ecumenical contacts for more theologically conservative segments of the Protestant community.

The Ecumenical movement provided the framework for confronting the crisis created by mid-century changes—World War II, the Chinese Revolution, the independence of India, the foundation of the United Nations (with its subsequent decolonization policy), and the emergence of a host of new nations out of the old European colonial empires. The churches faced one crisis after another beginning with the forced merger of all the Protestant churches by the Japanese government in 1940. The war brought both the disruption of the missionary field as Japan expanded the war and the destruction and loss of leadership by churches across Europe. For example, the new Communist government of China expelled all foreign missionaries. It was the largest displacement of missionary personnel ever and a portent of actions by other new Asian and African governments eager to resist foreign ideological influence.

Post–World War II realities brought to the fore an old debate within missionary circles: the status of the churches created by the missionaries. Most denominations had been content to leave them in a perpetually subordinate mission status. Now the major European and North American churches rapidly moved to grant them autonomy and to reorient them toward a relationship as equals. Many of the newly independent churches became members of the World Council of Churches.

While the majority of Protestants worldwide are represented in the member bodies of the World Council of Churches, mainstream Protestantism is now facing a challenge from its more conservative wing, the global Evangelical movement. Rejecting what they see as increasing secularization in mainstream churches and far too much acceptance of doctrinal divergences and innovations, Evangelical Protestants have become a potent force everywhere, challenging liberal Protestant hegemony. While still a minority in Europe, they have become the majority in some countries, as a result of zealous and creative evangelism programs and a willingness to contextualize their outreach efforts. They have found a major asset in the rapidly spreading CHARISMATIC MOVEMENT. EVANGELICALISM appears to be in a growth phase that should allow it to have an even greater voice in defining Protestantism in the decades immediately ahead.

An Encyclopedia Approach

In the pages that follow, *Encyclopedia of Protestantism,* in some 800 entries, explores the world of Protestantism from its origins to the present. It focuses on the most significant leaders (especially the often neglected women and non-Westerners),

the doctrinal concerns and controversies, and the structures that have been its vehicles for growth.

As is often the case, even in a work that seeks to be comprehensive, not every topic is mentioned, not every significant person is profiled, nor, possibly, is every theological concept given its due consideration. Choices had to be made. However, *Encyclopedia of Protestantism* aims to provide a representation of the events, unique people, and central concepts that have molded the Protestant world and turned Protestantism into a world religion.

—J. Gordon Melton

CHRONOLOGY

1517

- October 31, Martin Luther launches the Protestant Reformation by nailing the Ninety-five Theses to the door of the Church at Wittenberg, Germany.

1521

- April 17–18, Luther defends his view before the emperor and the leaders of the Holy Roman Empire at the Diet of Worms.

1523

- Zwingli leads the Reformation of the church in Switzerland with the publication of the Sixty-seven Articles.

1525

- William Tyndale publishes his translation of the New Testament in English.

1527

- Schleitheim Confession summarizes the major beliefs of the Swiss brethren but is unable to stop the persecution of the Anabaptists.

1529

- Colloquy at Marburg between Lutheran and Reformed leaders fails to resolve major differences concerning the Lord's Supper.

1530

- Publication of the Augsburg Confession, early statement of the Lutheran position.

1531

- Zwingli killed in battle between Reformed and Catholic forces at Kappel, Switzerland.

1535

- Miles Coverdale publishes Old Testament in English.

1536

- Subsequent to the publication of the *Institutes of the Christian Religion*, John Calvin arrives in Geneva. He would leave two years later but return in 1541 and lead the city in becoming the center of the French-speaking segment of the Reformation.

1540

◆ Pope Paul III approves the formation of the Society of Jesus (the Jesuits) by Ignatius Loyola (1491–1556).

1545

◆ The Council of Trent opens deliberations. It will meet sporadically to 1563.

1547

◆ With the death of Henry VIII, his young son, Edward VI, becomes king of England, and his Protestant advisers move to establish the Reformation throughout the land.

1553

◆ Calvin approves the execution of Michael Servetus, who had published antitrinitarian volume, *The Restoration of Christianity*.

◆ The Catholic Queen Mary I begins her attempt to reverse the Protestantization of the Church of England. Many Protestant leaders are arrested, and during her short reign they become martyrs.

1555

◆ Peace of Augsburg legalizes Lutheranism in those countries ruled by a Lutheran prince.

1558

◆ Elizabeth I begins her lengthy rule in England. Through a series of actions, she will institute the modern Anglican tradition as a *via media* between Puritanism (Calvinist Protestantism) and Roman Catholicism.

1563

◆ John Fox Publishes his *Book of Martyrs* that recounts the deaths of Protestant leaders during the reign of Mary I. Periodically reissued,

Foxe's book will negatively affect Protestant-Catholic relations for centuries.

1572

◆ Numerous Protestants are killed in the St. Bartholomew's Day Massacre.

1588

◆ Defeat of the Spanish Armada assures Anglican dominance of England for the next century.

1598

◆ Edict of Nantes provides toleration for Protestants (Huguenots) in France.

1607

◆ Virginia settled. Church of England founded in Virginia, its first establishment outside of England.

1611

◆ Publication of the King James Version of the Bible.

1618–1619

◆ Synod of Dort.

1620

◆ The Pilgrims, separatist independent Protestants, land at Plymouth, Massachusetts.

1630

◆ Puritans migrate to Massachusetts, where they will establish the Congregational Church.

1643

◆ Roger Williams publishes *The Bloody Tenant of Persecution*, an early tract on religious liberty.

1648

◆ The assembly of church leaders at Westminster publish a new Presbyterian confession and catechism. Presbyterianism will dominate the religious landscape in England until the Restoration (of the monarchy) in 1666.

1649

◆ King Charles I is executed and Oliver Cromwell becomes the ruler of England as the Lord Protector.

1666

◆ Restoration of the monarchy in England leads to the reestablishment of Anglicanism as the primary church of England.

1678

◆ John Bunyan publishes the Protestant classic *The Pilgrim's Progress*.

1685

◆ Revocation of the Edict of Nantes.

1689

◆ The Act of Toleration grants legal status to dissenting Protestant groups (but not Roman Catholicism) in England.

1701

◆ Founding of the Society for the Propagation of the Gospel in Foreign Parts, an Anglican missionary organization.

1706

◆ Bartholomaus Ziegenbalg and Heirich Plutschau, with the support of the Danish government, arrive in India, thus initiating the modern Protestant global missionary enterprise.

1737

◆ First missionary assigned to Africa, Moravian George Schmidt, settles near Cape Town.

1738

◆ John Wesley's "heart-warming" experience becomes the seminal event leading to the establishment of Methodism.

1739

◆ George Whitefield's preaching throughout the American colonies becomes a catalyst for the initiation of the First Great Awakening.

1748

◆ The Pennsylvania Ministerium is established by Henry Melchior Muhlenberg and others as the first Lutheran denominational structure in North America.

1781

◆ Bill of Rights guaranteeing religious freedom and separating religious groups from the national government is added to the Constitution of the United States.

1784

◆ John Wesley consecrates Thomas Coke as a superintendent (bishop) and gives him Articles of Religion (a statement of faith) to take to the newly founded United States. In America, Coke will lead in the establishment of an independent Methodist Episcopal Church.

1789

◆ The Bill of Rights, added to the United States Constitution, proscribes the national government from establishing any religion and prevents its interference with the free exercise of religion.

1792

♦ More than 1,000 former slaves who sided with the British in the American Revolution leave Halifax, Nova Scotia, for Sierra Leone. Once settled in Freetown, they will found the first Methodist and Baptist congregations on the continent of Africa.

1793

♦ William Carey arrives in India as the first missionary of the Baptist Missionary Society (England).

1793

♦ Congregationalists and others found the London Missionary Society.

1799

♦ Anglicans found the Church Missionary Society to supplement the effort of the older Society for the Propagation of the Gospel in Foreign Parts.

1804

♦ British and Foreign Bible Society founded.

1807

♦ With the support of the London Missionary Society, Robert Morrison becomes the first Protestant missionary to reside in China.

1810

♦ Founding of the American Board of Commissioners for Foreign Missions with primary support of New England Congregationalists.

1813

♦ Adoniram Judson, the first missionary supported by American Baptists, arrives in Burma (Myanmar).

1816

♦ American Bible Society founded.

1833

♦ John Keble's sermon at Oxford on national apostasy leads to the formation of the Oxford Movement and the development of the Anglo-Catholic faction of the Church of England.

1834

♦ Peter Parker, the first medical missionary, begins work in China under the auspices of the American Board.

1835

♦ German scholar David Friedrich Strauss publishes his *Life of Jesus*, which attacks many of the historical claims of Christianity.

1844

♦ Founding of the Young Men's Christian Association in London.
♦ John Ludwig Krapf, with the support of the Church Missionary Society, settles in Kenya as the first Protestant missionary in East Africa.

1845

♦ Southern Baptists separate from the national Baptist organization. The Southern Baptist Convention would become the largest Protestant body in the United States by the end of the 20th century.

1848

♦ The first Women's Rights Convention convenes in the Wesleyan Methodist church in Seneca Falls, New York.

1853

◆ Antoinette Brown, first woman ordained by a Protestant church body, is ordained by the Congregational Church (in the United States).

1855

◆ As a result of his exploration of the Zambezi River, David Livingstone becomes the first European to find Victoria Falls.

1859

◆ As a result of a treaty concluded the year before, two Episcopalian missionaries, John Liggins and Channing M. Williams, enter Japan and are allowed to stay.

1865

◆ Hudson Taylor founds the China Inland Mission, later to become the largest Protestant missionary agency working in China.

1875

◆ Alliance of the Reformed Churches throughout the world holding the Presbyterian System (now the World Alliance of Reformed Churches) is founded.

1881

◆ First of the Ecumenical Methodist Conferences is held. They would lead to the formation of the World Methodist Council.

1884

◆ Horace N. Allen, a physician, becomes the first Protestant missionary to reside in Korea.

1890

◆ William Booth's *In Darkest England and the Way Out* becomes the manifesto of the newly formed Salvation Army.

1906

◆ A revival begun among a small African-American congregation based on Azusa Street in Los Angles becomes the catalyst for the worldwide spread of Pentecostalism.

1907

◆ Having received the baptism of the Holy Spirit, Charles H. Mason and his supporters form the Church of God in Christ, the largest Pentecostal church in North America.

1909

◆ The first volume of *The Fundamentals,* a 12-volume collection of essays by 64 conservative British and American Protestants, offers a founding perspective to the Fundamentalist movement.

1910

◆ World Missionary Conference in Edinburgh launches the modern Ecumenical movement.

1925

◆ Scopes Monkey trial in Dayton, Tennessee.

1934

◆ Confessing Church in Germany issues the Barmen Declaration to counter the positions taken by the larger body of Lutherans in support of the Nazis.

1936

◆ United Church of Canada begins to ordain women.

1942

◆ Anglicans in Hong Kong ordain Florence Li Tim Oi on an "emergency basis."

1947

- The Lutheran World Federation holds its first meeting in Lund, Sweden.

1948

- World Council of Churches founded in Amsterdam, the Netherlands.

1951

- World Evangelical Fellowship (now Alliance) founded.

1956

- Presbyterians in Taiwan begin ordaining women.

1957

- United Church of Christ founded by merger of General Council of Congregational Christian Churches with the Evangelical & Reformed Church.

1961

- World Missionary Council merges into the World Council of Churches.

1962

- Vatican II, a council of the Roman Catholic bishops, opens in Rome. During the years of its sessions (1962–65), it will pass important statements that will make possible a vigorous Roman Catholic–Protestant dialogue in subsequent decades.

1968

- United Methodist Church formed by merger of the Methodist Church and the Evangelical United Brethren.

1970

- November, Elizabeth Platz becomes the first woman ordained by an American Lutheran church body, following the approval of female ordination by the Lutheran Church in America several months earlier.

1972

- William Johnson is ordained by the United Church of Christ, thus becoming the first openly homosexual person ordained in modern times to the ministry by a historic or "mainline" Christian church.

1973

- Supreme Court ruling on *Roe v. Wade* legalizes abortion in the United States.

1973

- Anglican Church in Wales approves ordination of women.

1977

- Anne Holmes becomes the first openly lesbian woman ordained in the United Church of Christ.

1997

- David Bromell is "received into full connexion" with the Methodist Church of New Zealand in spite of his being openly gay.

1980

- Marjorie S. Matthews becomes first woman elected as a bishop of the United Methodist Church.

1988

- January 1, the Evangelical Lutheran Church in America, formed the previous year by the merger of the Association of Evangelical Lutheran Churches, the American Lutheran Church, and the Lutheran Church in America, officially begins operation.

1989

♦ Barbara Harris of the Episcopal Church (U.S.) becomes the first Anglican woman consecrated as a bishop.

2003

♦ The Episcopal Church consecrates openly gay Rev. Gene Robinson as bishop of the Diocese of New Hampshire.

ENTRIES A TO Z

A

Abeel, David (1804–1846) *Reformed Church minister and pioneer missionary to China*

David Abeel was instrumental in establishing American Protestant missions in China. His travels and his writings also helped establish and strengthen missionary organizations in the United States and England.

Abeel was born in New Brunswick, New Jersey, on June 12, 1804. He had decided on a career as a doctor, but a religious experience sent him into the ministry. He attended Rutgers College (now University) and completed his studies at the Theological Seminary of the Reformed Church in New Brunswick. Ordained in 1826, his first call to the pastorate was from Athens, New York. After two years, his health failed, and he moved to the West Indies.

Abeel had felt a growing call to foreign missions, and once he had recovered his health, he applied to the Seaman's Friend Society for a position. They appointed him a chaplain and sent him to China in 1829. He sailed on the same ship that took Elijah Coleman BRIDGMAN, the first American missionary to China, and arrived in Canton early in 1830. He worked with the society for a year, then traveled widely in Southeast Asia picking up some knowledge of Malay, Tahi, and Fukienese. In 1832, he received an appointment, from the AMERICAN BOARD OF COMMISSIONERS FOR FOREIGN MISSIONS as their second missionary to China after Bridgman.

Poor health soon overtook him, and in 1833 he returned to the West. Stopping in England, he became a cofounder of the Society for Promoting Female Education in the East. As health allowed, he continued to promote foreign missions, especially in his own Reformed Church in America, in no small part through his books *The Claims of the World to the Gospel, Journal of a Residence in China,* and *The Missionary Convention at Jerusalem.*

He returned to Asia in 1839 just as the Opium War was heating up. In 1842, he settled in Amoy, one of five ports newly opened to Westerners, and made it the center of Reformed Church activity in China. After three years, ill health again forced him home. He died in Albany, New York, on September 4, 1846. The first Protestant church erected in China was dedicated in 1848 by the Reformed Church in Amoy.

Further reading: David Abeel, *Journal of a Residence in China* (New York: Leavitt, Lord, 1834); ———, *The Missionary Convention at Jerusalem* (New York: John S. Taylor, 1838); G. R. Williamson, *Memoir of the Reverend David Abeel, D.D.: Late Missionary to China* (1849; reprint, Wilmington, Del.: Scholarly Resources, 1972).

abortion

The intensive debate over abortion is a relatively new phenomenon in Christian history. Nevertheless, it is a major divisive issue among Protestant churches around the world.

Though rarely a major topic of concern, abortion has generally been opposed by Christians. The earliest statement is from the *Didache,* a popular second-century instructional manual, which states, "You shall not kill the fetus by abortion or destroy the infant already born." St. Augustine, an important church father in the eyes of early Protestants, considered the topic in the *Enchiridion.* As with the philosopher Aristotle, who preceded him, and the theologian Thomas Aquinas, who followed, Augustine believed that the fetus became fully human at some point during pregnancy (males attaining their humanity quicker than females). However, in the 16th century Pope Sixtus V (1521–90) declared abortion at any stage to be homicide. His decision was directly tied to the increased role of the Virgin Mary in Catholic devotion.

Three years later Sixtus's successor Gregory XIV (1535–91) returned to the Thomist position, which was once more overturned by Pius IX (1792–1878) in 1869. Sidestepping the question of when a fetus attains full humanity, he noted that the unborn child was potentially human. Any abortion might thus be homicide, and he prohibited them all; that remains the current Catholic position.

Protestants did not begin to deal with abortion definitively until the 19th century. Abortion was legal in the United States in the decades prior to the Civil War. In the postwar years, however, the American Medical Association, as part of a general program to assume hegemony over issues of birth, began a campaign against abortion. Only a few churches responded, the AMA being a relatively controversial organization at the time. However, in 1869, the same year of Pius IX's statement, the Presbyterians issued a brief declaration against abortion, a unique pronouncement for the era.

The modern American debate on abortion reflected the convergence of two trends—the development of medicine and the rise of the feminist movement. By the time of the AMA campaign, which by the 1880s had succeeded in making abortion illegal in most American states, doctors were quite aware of basic techniques for safe abortions. The campaign against abortion was thus not a medical issue but a political one. Early in the 20th century, advocates for women's rights supported birth control and ultimately abortion as part of their demand that women assume control of their own bodily functions.

The new phase of the women's movement, popularly dated from the 1963 publication of *The Feminine Mystique* by Betty Freidan, placed the question of abortion on the public agenda. During the next decade, a move to decriminalize abortion culminated in the 1973 Supreme Court decision, *Roe v. Wade,* which reversed most state laws against abortion. In the years since, women's rights advocates fought to maintain and extend the rights articulated by the Court in 1973. Leading the antiabortion fight were such groups as Operation Rescue, Concerned Women for America, and the National Right to Life Committee. *Roe v. Wade* established a context in which abortion counseling centers and abortion clinics could emerge, and they became the focus of demonstrations that on occasion turned violent.

Through the early 1990s, verbal encounters often turned into physical assaults, bomb threats, and actual explosions. Some antiabortion activists even began to suggest that killing those who facilitated abortions was justified as they were murderers. Most famously, former Presbyterian minister Paul Hill (1954–2003), director of an antiabortion group, Defensive Action, killed a doctor and his escort. Hill was subsequently convicted and in 2003 executed.

In the face of charges that it tacitly condoned such tactics, the main body of the antiabortion movement denounced violence; by the end of the 1990s, the number of incidents had radically (though not completely) decreased.

Those who found abortion acceptable dubbed themselves prochoice. In their view, they were fighting traditional male controls over females. They said decisions about abortions should be made on a case-by-case basis by pregnant women and their physicians. They generally viewed the unborn fetus as not yet fully human and hence not enjoying the same rights as those of a baby following childbirth. They tended to stress individual rights over those of groups (especially the family). They deplored the high number of illegal abortions that occurred before 1973, the number of deaths attributed to such abortions, and the likelihood of their return should *Roe v. Wade* be reversed.

Those favoring a ban on abortion called themselves prolife. They viewed the unborn as fully human and hence saw abortion as homicide. They have also tended to identify with traditional family structures. Protestant prolifers made common cause with Roman Catholics in this issue.

Following the decision in *Roe v. Wade,* prochoice advocates founded the Religious Coalition for Abortion Rights. Its support has been drawn from the larger liberal Protestant churches such as the UNITED METHODIST CHURCH and the PRESBYTERIAN CHURCH (USA). In 1987, the UNITED CHURCH OF CHRIST adopted a resolution that spoke for many liberal Protestants, stating that the church "Encourages persons facing unplanned pregnancies to consider giving birth and parenting the child or releasing the child for adoption before considering abortion; [and] Upholds the right of men and women to have access to adequately funded family planning services, and to safe, legal abortions as one option among others."

More conservative Protestant groups, allying themselves with the Roman Catholic Church and most Eastern Orthodox bodies, took up the prolife cause. Typical of their stance is the 1984 statement of the Conservative Baptist Association (now CBAmerica): "WHEREAS, the most abused, defenseless, and un-cared-for segment of our society is composed of the unborn infants who are ripped from the womb by induced abortion; and

WHEREAS, it has become socially acceptable for men to repudiate their paternal responsibilities by acquiescing to the destruction of their own unborn children . . . [we] urge that Conservative Baptists protest by every legitimate method this wanton attack upon human life."

The great majority of Protestant individuals and churches find themselves on a spectrum between those two opposite positions. Many conservative Protestants leave a door open for abortions on some occasions, as when a pregnancy results from a rape or threatens the life of the mother. The CHURCH OF THE NAZARENE, for example, would allow abortions when based on "sound medical reasons" suggesting the life of the mother was in danger. Most Protestants, both conservative and liberal, oppose abortion as a rule but differ on the number and type of exceptions to that general rule.

Further reading: Charles and Stacey Tipp Cozic, eds., *Abortion: Opposing Viewpoints* (San Diego, Calif.: Greenhaven Press, 1991); Anne Eggebroten, ed., *Abortion—My Choice, God's Grace: Christian Women Tell Their Stories* (Pasadena, Calif.: New Paradigm Books, 1994); Richard L. Ganz, ed., *Thou Shalt Not Kill: The Christian Case Against Abortion* (New Rochelle, N.Y.: Arlington House, 1978); J. Gordon Melton, *The Churches Speak on Abortion* (Detroit: Gale Research, 1989); Denyse O'Leary, *The Issue Is Life: A Christian Response to Abortion in Canada* (Burlington, Ontario: Welch Publishing, 1988); Robert N. Wennberg, *Life in the Balance: Exploring the Abortion Controversy* (Grand Rapids, Mich.: William B. Eerdmans, 1985).

Adventism

Adventism is belief in the imminent Second Coming or Advent of Jesus Christ, seen as the climactic moment in history. In the more limited sense used in this volume, it refers to the movement that originated in the teachings of William MILLER (1782–1849), a Baptist lay minister who became well-known throughout the United States in the 1830s for his prediction that Jesus would return in

1843 (later adjusted to 1844). Though Miller later withdrew with apologies for his errors, the movement continued into the 20th century and flourished through a number of new Christian bodies that became large international denominations—most notably the SEVENTH-DAY ADVENTIST CHURCH, the JEHOVAH'S WITNESSES, and the Worldwide Church of God.

Miller's speculation centered on Bible PROPHECY. Starting from easily dated biblical events, and a belief that days and years may be interchanged in prophetic Bible passages (Job 10:5; Psalms 90:3; II Peter 3:8), Miller laid out a complicated but logical argument for Christ's imminent return. Following the failure of his predictions (termed the Great Disappointment in Adventist history), Millerites regrouped and several organizations emerged. One group continued to pose new dates for Christ's return. Others believed the date was imminent but could not be predicted exactly.

The most successful group took the position that Miller's date had been correct, except that it referred only to the start of the process of cleansing the heavenly sanctuary (a task believed to be described in Hebrews 9). In the very near future, the heavenly work would be completed and become visible. Church founders James and Ellen G. WHITE had also come to believe in SABBATARI-ANISM, and proposed that Saturday, the true Sabbath, be restored as the day of worship. Propounding their ideas through the 1850s and 1860s, the Seventh-day Adventist movement emerged as the largest surviving segment of the Adventist cause.

In the wake of Christ's failure to return in 1874, as some Adventists predicted, a young Pittsburgh Bible student, Charles Taze RUSSELL, proposed a new version of Ellen G. White's idea. The year 1874 was indeed the time of Christ's *parousia* (the Greek word commonly translated as *coming*), but *parousia*, said Russell, actually meant *presence*. Christ had become invisibly present for the final harvest of believers; he would actually appear a generation later, around 1914. The millennium in which Christ would rule on Earth was dawning. Russell's Millennium Dawn movement underwent vast changes following his death, eventually emerging as the Jehovah's Witnesses in the 1930s. It would be further distinguished from the rest of the Protestant community by its harsh criticism of other churches, its denial of popularly held beliefs concerning the Trinity and hell, and its willingness to proselytize the members of other churches.

One small segment of Millerites accepted Ellen G. White's teaching on sabbatarianism, but not her understanding of the heavenly sanctuary. Reforming as the seventh-day Church of God, it divided into even smaller groups, some of them promulgating what became known as the Sacred Name Message. SACRED NAME groups believed that the Hebrew name of God (usually written as Yahweh) and of Jesus (Yeshua) should be used in all church discourse and the words God and Jesus dropped from their vocabulary. The Jehovah's Witnesses adopted some Sacred Name perspectives in its use of Jehovah (another spelling of the Hebrew name of God).

In the 1930s, the most successful of the sabbatarian Church of God groups emerged out of the broadcast ministry of Herbert W. ARMSTRONG (1892–1986) as the Radio Church of God. After World War II, Armstrong relocated to Pasadena, California, and changed the name to the Worldwide Church of God, using radio and then television. As an integral part of its teachings, it adopted BRITISH ISRAELISM, the idea that the legendary Ten Lost Tribes of Israel are to be identified with the modern Anglo-Saxon peoples. The church also developed a modern version of the ancient Hebrew festivals, practiced a system of tithing, and separated itself from other Christian churches.

After Armstrong's death, his successor, Joseph Tkach Sr., and his son, Joseph Tkach Jr., led a reformation in the church and dropped all of Armstrong's distinct ideas from sabbatarianism to the British Israel theory, and moved the church to an orthodox Evangelical position. The majority of the church membership defected into three groups—the Living Church of God, the United Church of God, and the Philadelphia Church of God—and a number of smaller groups that more or less continue Armstrong's teachings.

Both the Seventh-day Adventists and the Jehovah's Witnesses enjoyed spectacular success, having joined the short list of religious groups that have worshipping communities in more than 200 countries. The Witnesses are now the second- or third-largest denomination in all of the European countries save Switzerland, where a Witness splinter group, the Church of the Kingdom of God, is the third-largest denomination. Some disrepute came to the larger movement in 1993 with the incident at Waco, Texas, involving the deaths of members of a small Seventh-day Adventist splinter group, the BRANCH DAVIDIANS.

Further reading: Gary Land, ed., *Adventism in America: A History* (Berrien Springs, Mich.: Andrews University Press, 1998); James M. Penton, *Apocalypse Delayed: The Story of Jehovah's Witnesses* (Toronto: University of Toronto Press, 1985); Michael J. St. Clair, *Millenarian Movements in Historical Context* (New York: Garland, 1992); Joseph Tkach, *Transformed by Truth* (Sisters, Ore.: Multnomah Books, 1997).

Africa, sub-Saharan

Brought to sub-Saharan Africa largely as a by-product of British imperialism, Protestantism today counts more than 170 million followers. A huge variety of Protestant churches together account for half the Christian population of the continent.

Protestant missionary work began as early as 1737 in South Africa with George Schmidt (1709–85) of the MORAVIAN CHURCH. A century earlier (1652), Dutch settlers had brought the Netherlands Reformed Church with them and prohibited the establishment of any other faith, including rival forms of Christianity, but the church operated almost exclusively among the European settlers who saw no need to convert the local population. Schmidt found the Dutch treatment of blacks shocking. They in turn looked

down upon his attempt to work with them, and they expelled him in 1743, when he converted and baptized six blacks. The Moravians were allowed back in 1792.

A Congregationalist missionary, John Theodore Vanderkemp, arrived in South Africa in 1799 as an agent of the LONDON MISSIONARY SOCIETY. However, the opening of the Cape to a wide range of Protestant missionaries only came after the British takeover in 1806, as the Dutch (now called AFRIKANERS) moved inland. Through the first half of the 19th century, a variety of organizations sent missionaries, including the METHODIST CHURCH, the Glasgow Missionary Society, the PARIS EVANGELICAL MISSIONARY SOCIETY, and the AMERICAN BOARD OF COMMISSIONERS FOR FOREIGN MISSIONS. By the 1830s, Anglicans as well had begun missionary activity directed toward the non-European population.

The most important figure in the early 19th century was undoubtedly Robert Moffat (1795–1883), who arrived in Africa in 1817 and worked there for the next half century. His first accomplishment was the translation of the New Testament into Tswana, a language used across southern Africa. Back home for a visit in 1840, one of his speeches deeply affected a young David LIVINGSTONE, who would five years later marry Moffat's daughter. Livingstone used the area pioneered by Moffat as a base for two decades of exploring the interior of Africa; he was the first European to see many of its more interesting features, and he provided the knowledge used by later missionaries. Among the most important of these was George GRENFELL (1849–1906), who in 1877 launched explorations of the Congo River that would lead both to widespread missionary endeavors and the establishment of Belgium as a colonial power in the region.

Meanwhile, the expanding slave trade along the West African coast (largely controlled by the Portuguese) provided the impetus for a second Protestant thrust. In the 1780s, British abolitionists purchased a plot of land, which they named Freetown, as a place to settle repatriated slaves.

The first settlers arrived in 1787, followed five years later by a group of former American slaves who had been transported by the British to Nova Scotia after the American Revolution. Unused to the cold, they welcomed the opportunity to move to Freetown, where they established the first Methodist and Baptist congregations in all of Africa.

From Sierra Leone, British missionaries extended Protestantism along the coast toward Nigeria. Prominent in that endeavor was Thomas Birch FREEMAN (1809–90). Born in England to a freed African slave (hence his name), he converted to Methodism and was sent to Ghana (then called the Gold Coast) in 1838. Unlike most of his colleagues, he survived quite well in the climate. He began to evangelize the coast region and to train some of his converts as preachers. His efforts led to the continuing Methodist presence in Ghana, Nigeria, and Benin.

Protestant access to much of West Africa expanded along with British control. Because of its alignment with the government, the CHURCH OF ENGLAND had a distinct advantage. Its CHURCH MISSIONARY SOCIETY (CMS) emerged to prominence in Freetown in the 1820s with the founding of Fourah Bay College. Both the CMS and the SOCIETY FOR THE PROPAGATION OF THE GOSPEL IN FOREIGN PARTS established work across West Africa. As the French began to move into West Africa, the PARIS MISSION sent Reformed ministers to French-controlled territory, but they were in a distinct minority relative to their Roman Catholic competitors.

The CMS pioneered work in East Africa, focusing on Kenya. As early as 1844, a CMS-sponsored German missionary, John Ludwig Krapf (1810–81) settled in Mombasa. He had actually arrived in the region seven years earlier to begin work in Ethiopia but had been expelled following complaints by the Ethiopian Orthodox Church. He was the first to envision a chain of linked missions across Africa, an idea that later influenced a number of missionary efforts.

The pattern of missionary activity in Africa, and especially in East Africa, was altered by the Berlin Conference of 1884–85, where (with later supplemental agreements), 14 European nations agreed to partition African territory for colonization. New German territories (lost after World War I) gave scope to Lutheran missionaries, while France conquered large blocks of the western Sahara and the territory immediately south. British hegemony in Uganda and Kenya led to a major push inland. By the end of the second decade of the 20th century, the overall pattern of Protestant development across Africa was set.

Within the Protestant area, the denominational breakup began to change, in ways that would become especially evident toward the end of the century. PENTECOSTALISM was introduced to the continent by 1908, when John G. Lake (1870–1935) and Thomas Hezmalhalch (1848–1934) arrived in Cape Town. Their visit led to the founding of the Apostolic Faith Mission of South Africa, an independent African-based denomination, in 1913. Pentecostalism soon spread to every area of the continent where it was not officially denied access. Besides being the basic teaching of a set of churches, it is now the religious experience of many members of other churches not otherwise in the Pentecostal camp.

The spread of Pentecostalism is intimately connected with the other significant movement in Africa, the emergence of numerous independent AFRICAN INITIATED CHURCHES (AICs). Beginning among the Methodists in Freetown early in the 19th century, Christian Africans often broke from the European and American missionaries who had originally brought the gospel message to them, and founded black-led churches. The rejection of white leadership was exacerbated by the slowness of the missionary churches in developing African ministerial leadership.

However, additional factors have clearly encouraged the emergence of the new churches. Most important has been the unique religious experience of mission church founders and members, a factor that even in Europe often led to new Protestant communities. Such experiences often included elements of traditional African religions.

The AICs can be seen as existing along a spectrum from those who most closely resemble the European mission churches to those that include significant elements of the older African faiths. The end of colonialism in the decades following World War II stimulated the appearance of still more AICs.

As the 21st century began, Christianity had become the largest religion of Africa, though only slightly ahead of Islam. Of the 360 million Christians, approximately 173 million were affiliated with the thousands of Protestant and Free Church denominations. Protestantism is strongest in the former British colonies and weakest in those countries where the religious and political authorities are Muslim. Protestantism did emerge in North Africa in the 20th century during the days of French rule, but with the end of colonialism, not only did the great majority of Protestants (who were European) leave, but postcolonial governments have shown a distinct hostility to foreign missionaries and have reinstituted laws against the conversion of Muslims to other faiths. The total Protestant community in North Africa (the great majority of whom reside in Sudan) constituted less than 2 percent of the population.

See also ANGOLA; CONGO; GAMBIA; IVORY COAST; KENYA; LIBERIA; NIGERIA; SENEGAL; SIERRA LEONE; SOUTH AFRICA; UGANDA; ZIMBABWE.

Further reading: Gerald H. Anderson, ed., *Biographical Dictionary of Christian Missions* (Grand Rapids, Mich.: William B. Eerdmans, 1998); David Barrett, *The Encyclopedia of World Christianity,* 2nd ed. (New York: Oxford University Press, 2001); Patrick Johnstone and Jason Mandryk, *Operation World, 21st Century Edition* (Carlisle, Cumbria, U.K.: Paternoster, 2001); J. Herbert Kane, *A Global View of Christian Missions* (Grand Rapids, Mich.: Baker Book House, 1971); J. Gordon Melton and Martin Baumann, eds., *Religions of the World: A Comprehensive Encyclopedia of Beliefs and Practices* (Santa Barbara, Calif.: ABC-CLIO, 2002); A. Scott Moreau, ed., *Evangelical Dictionary of World Missions* (Grand Rapids, Mich.: Baker Book House, 2000).

Africa Evangelical Fellowship

The Africa Evangelical Fellowship (AEF), one of the early independent faith missions, was founded in 1889 in Cape Town, South Africa. AEF traces it history, however, to 1879, when a wealthy South African–born widow in England returned to Cape Town, set on opening a home for the soldiers. From this idea, a decade later the Cape General Mission began with Andrew MURRAY, Spencer Walton, and George Howe as leaders. Their original goal to minister to sailors on their way to and from Asia expanded to encompass evangelism all across southern Africa and beyond, including peoples in Angola, Botswana, Gabon, Madagascar, Mauritius, Reunion, Mozambique, Namibia, Swaziland, Tanzania, Zambia, and Zimbabwe.

In 1998, AEF merged into SIM International (formerly SUDAN INTERIOR MISSION).

Further reading: J. du Plessis, *A History of Christian Missions in South Africa* (Cape Town: C. Struik, 1911, 1965); ———, *The Life of Andrew Murray of South Africa* (London: Marshall Brothers, 1919).

Africa Inland Church

The Africa Inland Church is a conservative Evangelical church whose membership extends across Central Africa. It dates to the 1890s and the creation of an independent missionary agency by Peter Cameron Scott (1867–96), an American then residing in Kenya. He aimed to found a set of missionary stations extending from Mombasa, Kenya, to Lake Chad, as a barrier to the spread of Islam. To actualize his goal, in 1895 he founded the Africa Inland mission. After his death, his task was picked up by Charles E. Hurlburt (1860–1936). During the next 30 years under Hurlburt's leadership the mission pushed westward to the Central African Republic, south to Uganda, and north to Sudan. Schools were built and an indigenous leadership created. The self-governing Africa Inland Church superseded the missions in 1943. Since that time, the mission (now AIM International) has served a largely supporting role.

The African Inland Church has more than a million members in Kenya, where it is second in size only to the Roman Catholic Church. It also has significant support in Tanzania, the Democratic Republic of the Congo, Sudan, and the Central African Republic. AIM now has some 300 support personnel in Kenya.

Further reading: Dick Anderson, *We Felt Like Grasshoppers: The Story of the Africa Inland Mission* (Nottingham, U.K.: Crossway Books, 1994); Kenneth Richardson, *Garden of Miracles: History of the Africa Inland Mission* (London: Victory Press, 1968).

African-American Baptists

From the days of slavery, the majority of African-American Christians have been Baptists. While many have always affiliated with the wider Baptist community, a rich community of independent African-American Baptist churches, organizations, and institutions emerged; they continue to play a unique and important role in Protestant life in the United States.

The Baptist movement initially spread among African Americans during the First Great Awakening of the 18th century. The first African-American Baptist church was founded around 1774 at Silver Bluff, South Carolina, its members drawn from residents of John Galphin's plantation. A similar church was formed at Williamsburg, Virginia, and a third in Charleston, South Carolina, the latter's membership including both slaves and free blacks. One of the founders of the Silver Bluff and Charleston congregations, David George (1742–1810), would later found churches in Nova Scotia and Sierra Leone. His colleague George Lisle (c. 1750–1820) founded the Baptist movement in Jamaica.

Similar congregations in the northern states did not form until the beginning of the 19th century, prominent among them the Jay Street Church in Boston and the Abyssinian Church in New York, both founded by the Rev. Thomas Paul (1773–1831). In subsequent years, members of these congregations would find the colonization movement a ready vehicle for the initiation of missionary activity, and in 1824, Lott Carey (c. 1780–1828) and Collins Teague became the first African-American foreign missionaries.

Most of the few African-American Baptist churches of that era joined white-led pan-congregational associations. After the American Civil War (1860–65) one of these groups, the American Baptists (now the American Baptist Churches in the U.S.A.) initiated a variety of efforts to assist the recently freed slaves, especially in areas of education and Christian literature. But some black leaders felt the need to control efforts to evangelize and educate their own people, and in 1880 they created the first of a series of African-American church organizations, the Foreign Mission Baptist Convention of the U.S.A. Other organizations focusing on publishing and education evolved into the National Baptist Convention in the U.S.A. in 1895.

The latter remained the dominant organization among African-American Baptists throughout the 20th century, although internal tensions led to the formation of several important rival bodies—the National Baptist Convention of America (1915), the Progressive National Baptist Convention (1961), and the National Missionary Baptist Convention of America (1988). Many African Americans remained affiliated with the American Baptist Churches, fully a third of whose members are African American.

The Progressive Baptists originated out of differences over the convention's role in the Civil Rights movement led by Martin Luther KING, Jr. Black Methodists and Baptists formed the core of King's support and of the leadership of the Southern Christian Leadership Conference. Prominent Baptists supporting King included Ralph D. Abernathy (1926–90), Jesse Jackson (b. 1941), and Fred Lee Shuttlesworth (b. 1922).

Today the majority of African Americans identify themselves as Baptist; through the several conventions they support major Baptist institutions such as Shaw University (North Carolina),

Morehouse School of Religion (in cooperation with the Interdenominational Theological Center in Atlanta, Georgia), and the Central Baptist Theological Seminary (Indiana).

Further reading: Leroy Fritts, *A History of Black Baptists* (Nashville, Tenn.: Broadman Press, 1985); J. H. Jackson, *A Story of Christian Activism: The History of the National Baptist Convention, USA, Inc.* (Nashville, Tenn.: Townsend, 1980); Sandy D. Martin, *Black Baptists and African Missions: The Origins of a Movement 1880–1915* (Macon, Ga.: Mercer University Press, 1989); Owen Pelt and Ralph Lee Smith, *The Story of the National Baptists* (New York: Vantage, 1960).

African-American gospel music

While absorbing American Protestant religious music, African Americans molded it to fit their own needs. In the process, they created a unique and influential art form that has influenced religious music around the world.

The spirituals sung by black slaves had a double meaning, combining traditional Christian themes of salvation and life after death with a longing for freedom from slavery and life outside of the slave culture. To the slave, the Promised Land could be heaven—or the states across the Jordan (Ohio) River. A typical lyric says: "O, blow your trumpet, Gabriel/Blow your trumpet louder/And I want dat trumpet to blow me home/To my new Jerusalem."

In the decades after the Civil War, with the emergence of black Methodist and Baptist denominations, a complex interaction developed between the largely segregated Protestant churches. Whites borrowed from African Americans to create white spirituals, largely devoid of the immediate physical references in their black counterparts. (Even in the slave era, especially at camp meetings, whites had observed the enthusiastic singing by black participants, often accompanied by hand clapping, dancing, and body movements. Spontaneous improvisation on older songs would transform them, often to the consternation of the whites.)

At the same time, black churches borrowed heavily from the dominant European tradition of hymnody, often mediated through the music programs within the new African-American colleges. However, black churches could often not afford such tools of European hymnody as organs and hymnbooks. Besides, the dominant white community identified Euro-American culture with civilization; their attempt to "civilize" as well as Christianize African Americans was not always welcome. Instead, African-American colleges celebrated spirituals as a valued illustration of ethnic creativity, and nourished them through choral performances.

By the end of the 19th century, an African-American style of worship and religious music had emerged. "Gospel music" developed within the black HOLINESS and Pentecostal churches (often called the Sanctified churches), adding to the earlier spirituals a strong beat (provided by hand clapping and foot stomping) and the beginnings of instrumental accompaniment—drums, pianos, guitars, and (at a later date) organs. This music eventually found its way into the older, more conservative denominations, in small doses.

Gospel music was taken in a different direction by Baptist musician Thomas Dorsey (1899–1993). Heavily influenced by secular black music from the blues to ragtime, he created an African-American urban gospel music designed to be performed by professionals, or at least accomplished amateurs (the church choir). Other outstanding practitioners such as Mahalia Jackson (1911–72) and James Cleveland (1931–91) left their own marks on the tradition.

Today, gospel music in all its variety may be found in all segments of the black church. It exists not only as a means of worshipping God but of preserving African-American identity.

Further reading: Mellone Burnim, *The Black Gospel Music Tradition: Symbol of Ethnicity* (Bloomington: Indiana University, M.A. thesis, 1980); Sherry Sherrod DuPree, *African-American Good News (Gospel) Music* (Washington, D.C.: Middle Atlantic Regional

Press, 1993); Michael W. Harris, *The Rise of Gospel Blues: The Music of Thomas Andrew Dorsey in the Urban Church* (New York: Oxford University Press, 1992); Joan R. Hillsman, *Gospel Music: An African American Art Form* (Washington, D.C.: Middle Atlantic Regional Press, 1990); Eileen Southern, *The Music of Black Americans*, 2nd. ed. (New York: W. W. Norton, 1983).

African-American Methodists

African Americans have played an essential role in American Methodism from its origins. The various independent black Methodist churches and organizations still maintain a significant position in African-American religious life today.

The Short Street United Methodist Church in Baltimore, Maryland, is one of the oldest African-American congregations in existence. *(Institute for the Study of American Religion, Santa Barbara, California)*

METHODISM emerged in America in the 1760s. From the first classes in Maryland and New York City, African Americans were an integral presence, comprising one-fourth to one-third of its adherents. All-black classes were soon formed, and class leaders and local preachers were drawn from their ranks. However, when the Methodist Episcopal Church (MEC) was formed in 1784, blacks were not admitted to the ordained ministry, though several were licensed to preach.

Reacting to these discriminatory practices, in the 1790s some members, mostly free blacks in the urban centers, moved to found all-black congregations. Such churches included Bethel and Zoar in Philadelphia, Ezion in New York City, the African Union Church in Wilmington, Delaware, and Sharp Street in Baltimore.

In the 19th century, some of these same churches became organizational centers for independent black denominations. The African Union Church in Wilmington became the first congregation of the African Union Methodist Protestant Church. Bethel Church under Richard ALLEN became the center of the African Episcopal Church (AME). Ezion church became the mother church of the African Methodist Episcopal Zion Church (AMEZ). The strength of these three organizations was found in the free black communities located in most of America's urban centers.

Many free blacks and most of the slaves who became Methodists continued their membership in the MEC, and congregations such as Zoar and Sharp Street became prominent MEC congregations. In the 1820s, the MEC launched a special mission to slaves living on large plantations. This effort brought many black members into the church, especially in South Carolina, where they became the majority. Most of these members became part of the Methodist Episcopal Church, South (MECS) when the MEC voted to split in 1844 after northern leaders objected to slave-owning bishops. Black membership continued to grow through the 1850s in all branches of Methodism.

After the Civil War, the MECS moved to assist its newly freed black members in forming the predominantly Black Colored Methodist Episcopal Church (CME), now the Christian Methodist Episcopal Church. However, many MECS members chose instead to join the AME or the AMEZ, both of which attempted to recruit members among former slaves. The MEC also attempted to invite former slaves back, with some success.

The three major African-American Methodist bodies, the AME, the AMEZ, and the CME all retained the doctrines and practices of their parent bodies. They, together with African-American MEC members, all participated in the Methodist Ecumenical Conferences that began to be held in the 1880s.

The first African-American Methodist missionary program in Africa was launched in the 1820s as part of the colonization program, an effort in England and America to send free blacks to Africa. In 1827, the AMEs also sent a missionary to work in Haiti. Missions spread to various African nations and around the Caribbean. The AMEZ initiated work in the Caribbean in the 1850s and in Liberia in Africa in 1878. The CMEs began their missionary effort following World War I, but permanent work was not established until the 1940s. As the 21st century begins, all three churches include affiliated conferences in Africa and in the Caribbean.

In the 1860s, black members in the MEC were organized into all-black conferences (the Methodist equivalent of a diocese). In 1939, when the MEC and MECS united to form the Methodist Church, the predominantly white conferences were organized into five geographical jurisdictions, while the all-black conferences were put together in the nongeographical Central Jurisdiction. Debate focused on whether the benefits (guaranteed black leadership over black programs) outweighed the evils of segregation.

Four years after the merger of the Methodist Church into the UNITED METHODIST CHURCH (UMC) in 1968, the Central Jurisdiction was disbanded, and its black conferences were gradually merged into the geographical conferences. For the first time, black bishops were assigned to predom-

inantly white conferences and black superintendents were assigned to predominantly white districts. The church has subsequently worked to rid itself of racism at all levels of church life.

Some regret was expressed that the AME, AMEZ, and CME churches did not participate in the 1968 merger. Since that time, several plans have surfaced whose goal is an ultimate merger of the four bodies.

As the 21st century began, the AME reported 2.3 million members, the AMEZ 1.5 million, and the CME 850,000. There are an estimated 300,000 African American members in the UMC. All four churches hold membership in the WORLD METHODIST COUNCIL and the WORLD COUNCIL OF CHURCHES.

Further reading: Lewis V. Baldwin, *"Invisible" Strands in African Methodism* (Metuchen, N.J.: Scarecrow Press, 1983); Howard D. Gregg, *History of the African Methodist Episcopal Church* (Nashville, Tenn.: A.M.E. Church Publishing House, 1980); Othal Hawthorne Lakey, *The History of the CME Church* (Memphis, Tenn.: CME Publishing House, 1985); Larry G. Murphy, J. Gordon Melton, and Gary L. Ward, *Encyclopedia of African American Religions* (New York: Garland, 1993); Grant S. Shockley, ed., *Heritage and Hope: The African-American Presence in United Methodism* (Nashville, Tenn.: Abingdon Press, 1991); William J. Walls, *The African Methodist Episcopal Zion Church: Reality of the Black Church* (Charlotte, N.C.: A.M.E. Zion Publishing House, 1974).

African Initiated Churches

African Initiated Churches (AIC) are the churches and organizations founded by Christian converts in Africa independent of the colonial Christian churches. Today they comprise a significant minority of the sub-Saharan Christian population on the continent.

Even in the early phases of the Protestant effort to establish missions in sub-Saharan Africa, there were converts who rejected the continued oversight of European and American missionaries, preferring to use the knowledge and skills they acquired in colonial churches in new, independent churches. As early as 1703, an African woman, Donna Beatrice, had led a short-lived schism from the Roman Catholic Church in the Congo. Among the first successful AIC bodies was the West African Methodist Church. It was founded in 1844 in Sierra Leone by Africans denied the right to preach by the European missionaries who had assumed control of the Methodist movement there. Other schisms cropped up in the following decades in direct proportion to the overall success of Protestant missionary activity. Observers noticed AICs flourished in the areas where Protestant missions first developed (South Africa, the Congo Basin, central Kenya, and West Africa), and that a connection existed between the number of different contending Protestant missions and the subsequent emergence of AICs.

By the beginning of the 20th century, enough new AIC had arisen to provoke concern among other Christians, who used labels such as nativistic, messianic, and syncretist to describe their programs. As they attempted to build an indigenous Africanized Christianity, AICs often integrated a range of religious and nonreligious elements from indigenous cultures.

Several independent missionary initiatives from abroad led to still more groups of AICs. In South Africa, the Christian Catholic Church, a small body headed by charismatic healer John Alexander Dowie (1847–1907) began work in Johannesburg in the 1890s. Then in 1908, the first Pentecostal missionaries arrived, and as in America, the ZIONISTS (named for the headquarters town of Dowie's church) proved fertile ground for the development of the Apostolic Faith Church. The Christian Catholic Church and the Apostolic Faith Church then became the foundation from which a host of new denominations developed. Among them, the Zion Christian Church, founded by Engenas Lekganyane (c. 1880–1948), is now the largest Protestant denomination in South Africa. In Kenya, the spread of independent churches began with the founding of the Nomiya

Luo Church by members of the CHURCH OF ENGLAND mission in 1914 and greatly increased in the 1920s and 1930s; by the end of the 20th century more than 200 separate AICs had been documented in Kenya alone. Efforts to network the different AICs in ecumenical fellowships emerged and spread to the rest of the continent, the most important being the ORGANIZATION OF AFRICAN INITIATED CHURCHES.

In West Africa, Liberian prophet William Wade Harris (1865–1929) received a prophetic call while in prison and began preaching in Ghana and the Ivory Coast in 1913. In the face of repression by the authorities and antagonism from the older Methodist and Catholic churches (Harris accepted polygamy), a separate HARRIST CHURCH emerged, becoming one of the largest churches in the region. Harris's work also contributed to the formation of "new spiritual" or ALADURA CHURCHES that emphasized prayer and healing.

The revelation vouchsafed to Simon KIMBANGU (c. 1887–1951), a contemporary of Harris, gave the greatest impetus to AICs in the Congo. Belgian authorities attempted to suppress the movement, and Kimbangu spent his last 30 years in prison, but Africans revered him as a nationalist leader. The movement he initiated has become the largest of the many AICs in that country.

AICs come in all varieties. They draw on all of the different European churches that established missions and from the many different indigenous African religions. Some closely resemble the mission churches; others are primarily African in belief and practice. The largest numbers of AICs, like the DEEPER LIFE BIBLE CHURCH, are rooted in Pentecostal belief and practice, in part because Pentecostalists are willing to confront local beliefs in multiple deities and a demonic world, rather than dismissing such beliefs as pure superstition.

With the coming of independence in recent decades, the older Protestant churches seemed more willing to turn their missions over to local leadership, and to show new respect toward the AICs. Groups such as the Church of the Lord

Aladura, the Kimbanguist Church, and the AFRICAN ISRAEL CHURCH, NINEVEH have led the way for AICs into the WORLD COUNCIL OF CHURCHES. The larger Pentecostal community has welcomed the newer Pentecostal and Charismatic churches, and other AICs have affiliated with the WORLD EVANGELICAL ALLIANCE.

The rate of growth of the AICs has accelerated. It has been estimated that by the end of the 20th century AICs had some 60 million adherents, more than 20 percent of the total Christian population of Africa.

Further reading: Allan H. Anderson, *African Reformation: African Initiated Christianity in the Twentieth Century* (Trenton, N.J.: Africa World Press, 2001); David B. Barrett, *Schism and Renewal in Africa: An Analysis of Six Thousand Contemporary Religious Movements* (Nairobi: Oxford University Press, 1968); David B. Barrett and T. John Padwick, *Rise Up and Walk! Conciliarism and the African Indigenous Churches, 1815–1987* (Nairobi: Oxford University Press, 1989); Harold W. Turner. *Religious Innovation in Africa* (Boston: G. K. Hall, 1979).

African Israel Church, Nineveh

The Kenya-based African Israel Church Nineveh (AICN), also known as the African Israel Nineveh Church, is one of the most prominent of the 20th-century AFRICAN INITIATED CHURCHES (AIC). It was founded in western Kenya in 1942 by evangelist Daudi Zakayo Kivuli (1896–1974) of the Luyia people. As early as 1925, Kivuli had associated with the Pentecostal Assemblies of Canada, eventually becoming supervisor of mission schools. Kivuli had a dramatic experience of the BAPTISM OF THE HOLY SPIRIT in 1932 and began an evangelistic and healing ministry, which was officially authorized by a Canadian missionary in 1939. When other African leaders failed to support him, in 1942 Kivuli founded his own church and assumed the title of High Priest. Pilgrims began to arrive at his home, called Nineveh, which became the headquarters of the church.

As in other African Pentecostal churches, AICN members wear white robes and turbans, engage in singing and dancing, emphasize spirit possession, observe many Old Testament and other dietary and purification rules (eschewing alcohol, tobacco, pork, or fish without scales), and have a holy place where their leader resides. The AICN has become known for its joyful and colorful processions and open air meetings in which flags, drums, staffs, bells, and trumpets are used to accompany traditional African singing. Members gather for Friday worship, in remembrance of Christ's crucifixion, in addition to Sunday, the day of his resurrection. They make open confession of sins and rise at dawn for daily prayers. The church accepts polygamists, but leaders are expected to remain monogamous and unmarried members to refrain from sex. Sexual intercourse on Fridays is forbidden.

Kivuli died in 1974 and was succeeded by his widow, Rebecca Jumba Kivuli (1902–88), who led the church until her retirement in 1983. She was followed by the present leader, John Mweresa Kivuli II (b. 1960), Kivuli's grandson. Possessing a degree in theology, Kivuli assumed the title archbishop in 1991, after he came to believe in the PRIESTHOOD OF ALL BELIEVERS, and that Christ was the only High Priest.

The African Israel Church, Nineveh claimed more than 800,000 members in Kenya alone in the early 1990s, drawing members from across Kenya's native population. Unlike other Pentecostal churches, it has participated in the larger ecumenical community, joining the National Council of Churches of Kenya. In 1975, it was admitted to the WORLD COUNCIL OF CHURCHES.

Further reading: John M. Kivuli, II, "The Modernization of an African Independent Church," in Stan Nussbaum, ed., *Freedom and Independence* (Nairobi: Organization of African Instituted Churches, 1994); Peter Wilson Kudoyi, *African Israel Nineveh Church: A Theological and Socio-Historical Analysis* (Nairobi: M.A. thesis, Kenyatta University, 1991); F. B. Welborn, and B. A. Ogot, *A Place to Feel at Home* (London: Oxford University Press, 1966).

African Methodist Episcopal Church

See AFRICAN-AMERICAN METHODISTS.

Afrikaners

Descendants of Dutch settlers who began arriving in South Africa in 1652, Afrikaners constitute the majority of the white Christian population of that country. Their Reformed faith has spread to many in the black population as well.

From a small beginning, the Dutch colony at the Cape of Good Hope attracted increasing numbers of settlers, many of them refugees from the protracted conflict between Catholics and Calvinists in Holland. Joining the migrants were a number of HUGUENOTS who had fled France for Holland following the revocation of the EDICT OF NANTES in 1685. By this time the Dutch Reformed Church had been established in the new colony, and the Huguenots shared its faith.

The 1795 French invasion of the Netherlands allowed the English to take over and colonize Cape Town. The number of English settlers steadily increased over the next decades. When in the 1830s the British passed laws abolishing discrimination on the basis of color, the Dutch Boers (farmers), who had had some broader disputes with the native Africans, decided to leave the Cape. In 1835, Afrikaners (people of Africa), as the Dutch had become known, began to head inland, where they fought a number of battles with Zulus and other peoples over control of the land. Following the second Boer War (1899–1901), all the Afrikaners surrendered to British authority. Nevertheless, their superior numbers gave them political control by the late 1940s in the whites-only government, and they were able to impose stringent segregation between whites and the other racial groups.

The independent Dutch Reformed Church was integral to Afrikaner culture. Adherence to its Calvinist creed further set the Afrikaners apart from British South Africans, most of whom were Anglicans or Methodists. Although divided into three denominations due to doctrinal differences, the Dutch Reformed churches all shared an unusual racial theology, similar to the ideas used by some white Christian Americans in defense of slavery before the Civil War. Drawing on selected strains of CALVINISM, they declared that nationality was one of the God-ordained "orders of creation" and concluded that South Africa should enforce apartheid, the strict segregation of its various nations, all white people constituting one such nation. Furthermore, God had foreordained certain nations to be the chosen people.

While the Afrikaners were implementing apartheid, Dutch Reformed church leaders were reconnecting with the worldwide Reformed and Protestant communities. The two larger branches (known by their Afrikaner names as the Nederduitse Gereformeerde Kirj and the Nederduitse Herformde Kerk) affiliated with the WORLD COUNCIL OF CHURCHES (WCC) and the WORLD ALLIANCE OF REFORMED CHURCHES (WARC). In the 1950s, the member churches of the WCC began an intense debate over the compatibility of apartheid and Christianity, which intensified, following the Sharpsville Massacre in 1960. In response, the two South African churches withdrew from the council, an action that has affected South African church relations ever since. The churches remained in the WARC but were suspended in 1982 when the WARC's General Council declared apartheid a sin and its theological justification a heresy. One of the churches broke completely with the alliance, while the other maintained a dialogue and was received back into full membership in 1997.

Meanwhile, the Dutch Reformed Mission Church, established in 1881 for Africans who had converted to Reformed Christianity, issued a new statement of faith, the BELHAR CONFESSION (1986). It affirmed that "separation, enmity and hatred between people and groups is sin" and rejected "any doctrine which absolutises either natural diversity or the sinful separation of people . . . or breaks the visible and active unity of the church."

Following the end of apartheid and whites-only government, South African churches have been engaged in an ongoing struggle with their past, looking for ways to repent racism, offer and accept forgiveness, and move toward a healing of the fissures that divided Protestants along racial, cultural, and linguistic lines via barriers that all now affirm were illegitimate.

Further reading: Allan Boesak, *Black and Reformed: Apartheid, Liberation and the Calvinist Tradition.* (Maryknoll, N.Y.: Orbis Books, 1984); John W. de Gruchy, *The Church Struggle in South Africa* (Grand Rapids, Mich.: William B. Eerdmans, 1979); T. Dunbar Moodie, *The Rise of Afrikanerdom: Power, Apartheid and the Afrikaner Civil Religion* (Berkeley: University of California Press, 1975); Tracy Kuperus, *State, Civil Society and Apartheid in South Africa: An Examination of Dutch Reformed Church-State Relations* (Houndmills, Basingstoke, U.K./New York: Macmillan/St. Martin's, 1999).

Aglipay, Gregorio (1860–1940) *founder of the Philippine Independent Church*

Gregorio Aglipay was born in Bathe, Ilocos Norte, the Philippines, on May 8, 1860. Orphaned in his second year, he was raised by his maternal granduncles and grandaunts. Much of his boyhood was spent working in the tobacco fields. At the age of 14 he was arrested and interrogated for failing to meet his work quota, stoking his resentment of the islands' Spanish rulers.

In 1876, Aglipay moved to Manila to further his meager education, eventually graduating from the Colegio de San Juan de Letran. In 1883, he entered the Vigan Seminary to study for the Roman Catholic priesthood. He was ordained in 1889 and served in various parishes over the next decade. His assignment to the parish at Victoria, Tarlac, in 1896 led him to take part in the Philippine revolution.

As the representative of his home province, Ilocos Norte, he attended the 1898 meeting that established a revolutionary government, and signed the constitution of the hoped-for independent country. General Emilio Aguinaldo (1869–1964) appointed Aglipay military vicar general and assigned him the task of building an indigenous church in the Philippines. His call to the Filipino clergy to take control of the Catholic Church in the Philippines occasioned his formal excommunication. He soon emerged as the supreme bishop of the new Philippine Independent Church (PIC), a body that was Catholic in every way except in its ties to the Roman hierarchy.

Aglipay took up arms during the Spanish-American War, but in 1901, realizing it was a lost cause, he surrendered to the American forces. He continued to lead the Philippine Independent Church following the war, though most of its millions of members left when all of its property was returned to the Catholic Church. He rebuilt the church, which soon returned to prominence as the second-largest church in the country. During the remaining years of his life, Aglipay worked for Philippine self-governance and for a strong PIC, the two efforts often interrelated.

During the years of American rule of the islands, a number of Protestant churches took root, and some were quite successful. After World War I, Aglipay was attracted to Unitarianism, and during the 1930s, he openly rejected traditional Trinitarian views. In 1939, when Louis Cornish, then president of the American Unitarian Association (now the Unitarian Universalist Association) visited the Philippines, Aglipay had him named honorary president of the PIC. The PIC began to deviate from Catholicism in other ways, too, among them by rejecting a celibate priesthood. Aglipay himself married in 1939, when he was nearly 80 years old.

Aglipay died in Manila on September 1, 1940. After his death, his successor in the PIC dropped the non-Trinitarian theology and the relationship with the Unitarian Association, instead establishing ties with the Episcopal Church (based in the United States). It was subsequently accepted as a full member of the worldwide Anglican Communion.

In the 1980s, the PIC became involved in battles in the United States between the Episcopal

Church establishment and conservative traditionalists. Several PIC bishops consecrated bishops for the breakaway factions. This led to a split in the PIC in the 1990s, with almost half the membership leaving to form the Philippine Independent Catholic Church. Both churches now claim the Aglipay heritage. With more than 2 million members each, they remain the largest church bodies in the Philippines apart from the Catholic Church.

Further reading: Pedro S. de Achutegui, S.J., *Religious Revolution in the Philippines: The Life and Church of Gregorio Aglipay 1860–1960,* 2 vols. (Manila: Ateneo de Manila, 1960); Ambrocio M. Manaligod, *Gregorio Aglipay: Hero or Villain?* (Manila: Communication Foundation for Asia, 1977); *Our Heritage Our Response* (Manila: Iglesia Filipina Independiente, 1993); Apolonio M. Ranche, ed., *Doctrine and Constitutional Rules, Important Documents, Various Articles and Chronology of the Iglesia Filipina Independiente* (Quezon City: St. Andrew's Seminary, 1996); William Henry Scott, *Aglipay before Aglipayanism* (Quezon City: National Priest Organization, 1987).

Aladura churches (Nigeria)

The Aladura churches constitute a movement of Pentecostal-like AFRICAN INITIATED CHURCHES (AICs) in West Africa.

Largely in reaction to the paternalism of European missions in West Africa, in the decades after World War I a new group of AICs arose that became known as the Aladura or "prayer" people. They drew on Pentecostal themes but remained independent of parallel efforts by Pentecostalists. The largest group of Aladura churches is in the area dominated by the Yoruba people. The major bodies are the Christ Apostolic Church, the Church of the Lord (Aladura), the Eternal Sacred Order of the Cherubim and Seraphim, and the CELESTIAL CHURCH OF CHRIST. In the 1950s, the movement spread to Ghana, Liberia, and Sierra Leone, primarily by traveling Nigerian preachers such as the Apostles Oduwole and Adejobi of the Church of the Lord (Aladura). In Ghana, new

independent Aladura churches arose. As early as 1964, Nigerian immigrants brought Aladura churches to Great Britain; they later spread to other countries in Europe.

Rejected by the Christian Council of Nigeria, the Aladura churches formed the Nigerian Association of Aladura Churches, which began in 1964 with 95 denominations representing some 1.2 million members. The association has grown steadily, accepting other AICs and individual autonomous congregations. The Church of the Lord, Aladura was finally accepted into the WORLD COUNCIL OF CHURCHES, which has in recent years made a concerted effort to respond to the AICs.

Further reading: Allan H. Anderson, *African Reformation: African Initiated Christianity in the Twentieth Century* (Lawrenceville, N.J.: Africa World Press, 2000); J. D. Y. Peel, *Aladura: a Religious Movement among the Yoruba* (Oxford: Oxford University Press, 1968); Harold W. Turner, *History of an African Independent Church (1) The Church of the Lord (Aladura)* (Oxford: Clarendon Press, 1967).

Albania

Albania, a small, primarily Muslim country on the Adriatic Sea northwest of Greece, has had a tumultuous religious history. After the 11th-century split between Roman Catholics and Eastern Orthodox, it fell under the influence of the Eastern church, but it was close enough to Italy for Catholics to reach out regularly for Albanian disciples.

In the 15th century, the country was overrun by Turkish Muslim forces. Though Christianity was not totally suppressed, the majority of Albanians became Muslims. The Orthodox Church in Albania operated under the direct authority of the Ecumenical Patriarchate in Istanbul until 1920, but an independent Albanian Orthodox Church emerged when the country itself became independent following the collapse of the Ottoman Empire.

A few Protestant groups had started to put down roots from the end of the 19th century: Methodists (1890s) from Yugoslavia, Seventh-day Adventists (1903) from Greece, and Baptists (1939) from Italy. The Jehovah's Witnesses launched a mission in the 1920s.

The Marxist state established in 1944 under Enver Hoxha (1908–85) was extremely hostile to religion. Hoxha officially declared Albania an atheist country and moved to dismantle the Orthodox Church. He closed the seminary, stopped ordination, and then moved on to close churches and arrest priests. The church barely survived the 40 years of his rule. The Roman Catholic Church, which had survived in an enclave in the north of the country, suffered equally. All the Protestant efforts were lost.

The fall of the Marxist regime at the end of the 1980s provided a context for the rebirth of the older religious communities and an opportunity for many new ones, including a spectrum of Protestant groups, to enter the country. Methodists from Germany, for example, began work in several predominantly Muslim villages in 1992. They provided humanitarian aid and helped rebuild schools. There are now four small Methodist churches attached to the United Methodist Church's Central and Southern Europe Central Conference.

More than 100 Protestant churches and missionary organizations began work in the 1990s. Pentecostalism has been widely received and now accounts for more than half of the Protestant community. The largest group apart from the Orthodox and Catholic churches are the Jehovah's Witnesses, with some 10,000 members. Pentecostals and Charismatics may have numbered as high as 100,000 as the 21st century began. The largest Pentecostal group appears to be the Word of Life Church, with more than 8,000 members in 1995.

Among the Albanian Christians, only the Albanian Orthodox Church and the Methodists (affiliated with the United Methodist Church) are members of the World Council of Churches. A majority of the Protestant and Free Church groups

that began work in the 1990s have joined the Albanian Encouragement projects, a cooperative endeavour. Some of them also joined the Albanian Evangelical Alliance, which is affiliated with the World Evangelical Alliance.

Further reading: David Barrett, *The Encyclopedia of World Christianity,* 2nd ed. (New York: Oxford University Press, 2001); Patrick Johnstone and Jason Mandryk, *Operation World, 21st Century Edition* (Carlisle, Cumbria, U.K.: Paternoster, 2001).

Albury conferences

The Albury conferences were a series of private religious discussions among a small group of British Protestants between 1826 and 1830. They helped develop ideas that contributed to the premillenial and Pentecostal movements.

In December 1826, Presbyterian minister Edward Irving (1792–1834), the pastor of the Scottish congregation in London, opened his home at Albury Park, a village in rural Surrey, to a group of some 20 individuals for an extended discussion of Christian eschatology. Included in the select coterie were Rev. Lewis Way, one of the founders of the London Society for the Promotion of Christianity. Among the Jews, Joseph Frey, one of its missionaries, Rev. Hugh McNeile, an Anglican who had written a book on prophecy, and banker Henry Drummond (1786–1860), not to be confused with his later contemporary of the same name who lectured on science and religion.

These conferences were held annually until 1830, by which time Irving had published a number of books, including several on prophetic issues: *For Judgment to Come* (1823) and *Babylon and Infidelity Foredoomed* (1826). His multivolume collection of *Sermons, Lectures and Occasional Discourses* appeared in 1828, and a new *Exposition of the Book of Revelation* three years later. As his colleagues read his books and heard of the strange occurrences associated with him, he was rejected by the London Presbytery in 1830. His ideas were condemned by the ministers in Scotland in 1831.

Apart from his controversial new ideas on ESCHATOLOGY, a form of what would later be termed PREMILLENNIALISM, by 1828 Irving had become convinced that the gifts of the spirit so evident in the biblical church had fallen away due to lack of faith and were ready to be reborn. In 1830, he learned of an outbreak of spiritual manifestations in a remote part of Scotland. Soon those attending Irving's church in London reported similar events, extraordinary "manifestations of the spirit" including speaking in tongues, prophecies, healings, and even raising of the dead.

Irving, Drummond, and other supporters planned a new church that would follow what they saw in the Bible as the apostolic model. The fivefold ministry described in Ephesians (4: 11–14) suggested to them that apostles, prophets, evangelists, pastors, and teachers should be ongoing officers in the church. These ministers were to help dispense the gifts of the Holy Spirit to church members. The return of the gifts of the spirit anticipated the return of Christ. A crucial feature of the new church would be the calling of 12 new apostles. The Catholic Apostolic Church was officially founded in 1832. The next year, the Presbytery of Annan of the Church of Scotland deposed Irving from the ministry; he died the following year.

The Albury conferences and Irving's brief ministry were later seen as important steps in the emergence of premillennialism as a significant view among conservative Protestants. The spiritual manifestations at Irving's church were seen as precursors to PENTECOSTALISM. The Catholic Apostolic Church left no provisions for replacing the original apostles; without apostolic leadership it dwindled into nonexistence in the 20th century. But before the church lost all of its apostles, some of the German members founded the NEW APOSTOLIC CHURCH. That church calls new apostles as old ones die, and has also radically increased their number as the church itself has grown. The New Apostolic Church is now a global community with more than 8 million members in some 190 countries.

Further reading: Arnold A. Dallimore, *The Life of Edward Irving: The Fore-Runner of the Charismatic Movement* (Carlisle, Pa.: Banner of Truth, 1983); A. L. Drummond, *Edward Irving and His Circle* (London: James Clarke, n.d.); Edward Irving, *The Collected Works of Edward Irving,* ed. by Gavin Carlyle, 5 vols. (London: Alexander Strahan, 1864–65); C. Gordon Strachan, *Pentecostal Theology of Edward Irving* (London: Darton, Longman & Todd, 1973).

Algeria

A predominantly Muslim country in North Africa, Algeria's Protestant history rose and fell with the arrival and departure of French rule.

Algeria had been predominantly Muslim since the eighth century C.E. Only in the 1830s, following the establishment of a small Roman Catholic enclave, did Protestant missionaries attempt to begin work. Efforts made little impact until the influx of hundreds of thousands of French settlers in the 1870s, at which time the Reformed Church of France was able to open churches. In 1881, the U.S.-based North Africa Mission (now Arab World Ministries), an interdenominational sending agency, sponsored the work launched by Edward H. Glenny in Algiers. He found his greatest success among the Kabyle Berber people. A third effort was launched in 1888 by British representatives of the Algiers Mission Band.

American Methodists entered Algeria after two female missionaries already in the country joined the Methodist Episcopal Church (now an integral part of the UNITED METHODIST CHURCH) and in 1909 brought their work under its charge. That work grew slowly but was eventually capped with the opening of a hospital in 1966, by which time centers had been established throughout the country. The work then came to an abrupt end in 1969, when most missionaries were accused of working with the American Central Intelligence Agency and expelled from the country.

Muslim Algerians had begun active resistance to French colonial rule in the 1920s, which grew after World War II. Following the independence accord in 1962, a massive exodus of French expatriates began. Most Protestants, whether French Reformed or members of the other missionary churches, came from the French community, and their exodus devastated church activity. Among the groups hardest hit was the ASSEMBLIES OF GOD. Others such as the JEHOVAH'S WITNESSES, known for their door-to-door evangelism, were totally expelled.

Upon gaining full independence, Algeria declared Islam the state religion, though it did not declare itself an Islamic state. It outlawed religious discrimination but also strongly discouraged Christian attempts to proselytize among Muslims. The government has allowed various Protestant and FREE CHURCH groups to remain, but they are quite small.

In 1964, the Protestant community reorganized its ecumenical group, the Evangelical Mission Council, as the Association of Protestant Churches and Institutions of Algeria, but many of the more theologically conservative groups withdrew in protest over the association's relationship with the WORLD COUNCIL OF CHURCHES. In 1972, the Methodists (now affiliated with the United Methodist Church [UMC]), the Reformed Church of France, and several other groups merged to form the Protestant Church of Algeria, which at present has only eight congregations. It functions as a district in UMC's Switzerland/France annual conference. It is a member of the World Council of Churches.

Among the other surviving Protestant groups, the largest are the North African Mission (with some 1,000 members), the SALVATION ARMY (with 300 members), and the Mission Rolland (with 300 members). The Evangelical Coptic Church serves approximately 500 Egyptian expatriates residing in Algeria. Some 20 additional groups work in Algeria, each with a small following.

Further reading: David Barret, *The Encyclopedia of World Christianity,* 2nd ed. (New York: Oxford University Press, 2001); Patrick Johnstone and Jason Mandryk, *Operation World, 21st Century Edition* (Carlisle, Cumbria, U.K.: Paternoster, 2001); World Methodist Council, *Handbook of Information* (Lake Junaluska, N.C.: World Methodist Council, 2003).

Allen, Horace Newton (1858–1932)
pioneer Protestant missionary to Korea

Horace Newton Allen was born in Delaware, Ohio, on April 23, 1858. He attended Ohio Wesleyan College and Miami Medical College in Oxford, Ohio, from which he graduated in 1883. He married soon after graduation and moved to China as a medical missionary under the auspices of the Foreign Mission Board of the Presbyterian Church in the U.S.A. The Allens did not like China, where they first settled, and asked for reassignment. They were relocated to Korea in 1884.

Korea did not permit missionary activity at the time, but Allen was free to introduce Western medicine. He founded a hospital and began educating Koreans in Western medicine. Several months after his arrival, the queen's nephew, Young Il Min, was wounded during a revolt. Under Allen's treatment he recovered. Allen was subsequently appointed the physician to the king and his family. This opened the way for fellow Presbyterian J. Heron and Methodist W. Scranton to join him at the Kwanghewon (Extended Grace Clinic) the following year.

As had been the case in China, Allen was unable to work cooperatively with other missionaries. Happily for all concerned, in 1887 the king named him foreign secretary to the Korean legation to Washington, and he devoted the next two years trying to block China's assertion of hegemony over Korea. He also had time to write his first book, *Korean Tales (1889).* When he returned in 1889, the U.S. government made him secretary of the American consulate in Korea. He was later appointed assistant consul and finally consul in 1901. His determination to work against Japanese hegemony in Korea increasingly alienated him from Washington. In 1905, he resigned and moved back to Ohio, where he practiced medicine in Toledo. He died in Toledo on December 11, 1932.

The clinic he founded continued to serve tens of thousands of patients. Korea subsequently received hundreds of missionaries and became home to one of the strongest Protestant communities in Asia.

See also MEDICAL MISSIONS.

Further reading: Horace Newton Allen, *Korea: Fact and Fancy: Being a Republication of Two Books Entitled "Korean Tales" and "A Chronological Index"* (Seoul: Methodist Publishing House, 1904); ———, *Things Korean: A Collection of Sketches and Anecdotes Missionary and Diplomatic* (New York: Fleming H. Revell, 1908); George Lak Geoon Paik, *The History of Protestant Missions in Korea, 1832–1910,* 2nd ed. (Seoul: Yonsei University Press, 1971).

Allen, Richard (1760–1831) *founder of the African Methodist Episcopal Church*

Richard Allen was born a slave in Philadelphia on February 14, 1760, and grew up on the Sturgis family plantation near Dover, Delaware.

Around the age of 18, Allen responded to the message of Methodist circuit riders, and his master subsequently encouraged his participation in Methodist meetings. He soon learned to read and write and began preaching. Eventually, Sturgis himself converted; he soon concluded that slavery was incompatible with his faith, and he worked out an arrangement for Allen to buy his freedom, which occurred in the early 1780s.

Allen preached in Delaware and the surrounding states and finally settled in Philadelphia, where he became active at St. George's Church. He attended the 1784 conference at which the Methodist Episcopal Church (now an integral part of the UNITED METHODIST CHURCH) was organized. He preached to meetings of blacks and whites in Maryland, Delaware, New York, New Jersey, and Pennsylvania. He was requested to serve at St. George's, where he quickly increased the black membership. Early on, he and colleague Absalom Jones (1746–1818) saw the need for a separate place of worship for Africans, but they were

opposed by a number of black and white members. In 1787, they organized the Free African Society to oppose slavery and assist blacks in Philadelphia, the first such independent black organization in the country.

Later that year, responding to discrimination at St. George's, Allen, Jones, and some other black members left to form an independent congregation. Those black members who did not follow Allen would later form the Zoar Church, currently affiliated with the United Methodist Church. The Free African Society assisted in raising funds for the Allen-Jones group. The majority of members of the new congregation, "The African Church of Philadelphia," decided to affiliate with the Episcopal Church. Allen, however, wished to remain a Methodist, and along with his supporters he founded the Bethel African Church. The congregation was affiliated with the predominantly white Methodist Episcopal Church, whose bishop, Francis ASBURY (1745–1816), dedicated their building in 1794. In 1799, Asbury ordained Allen as a deacon.

The association with the Methodist Episcopal Church continued for two decades, but in 1815 problems arose over the ownership of the Bethel property. Similar problems confronted free black Methodists in other cities. In 1816, Allen organized a meeting of representatives of the several black congregations at which the African Methodist Episcopal Church was organized. Allen was immediately ordained elder, and on April 11, 1816, consecrated as the church's first bishop. He continued to serve as the senior minister at Bethel, but made his living from a small boot and shoe business he oversaw.

Over his years, Allen made numerous contributions to the development of Philadelphia's African-American community. He was a cofounder of the African Masonic Lodge (1798); he promoted a series of education initiatives; and he opposed the American Colonization Society's plans to send free blacks to Africa. His autobiography is a classic of early American black literature. A statue of Allen, the first erected by African

Americans to celebrate the career of one of their leaders, stands in Fairmount Park in Philadelphia. *See also* AFRICAN-AMERICAN METHODISTS.

Further reading: Richard Allen, *The Life, Experience, and Gospel Labors of the Rt. Rev. Richard Allen* (1793; reprint, Philadelphia: Lee & Yoakum, 1888); Absalom Jones and Richard Allen, *A Narrative of the Proceedings of the Black People During the Late Awful Calamity in Philadelphia in 1793, and a Refutation of Some Censures, Thrown Upon Them in Some Late Publications* (Philadelphia: William W. Woodard, 1794); Marcia M. Matthews, *Richard Allen* (Baltimore: Helicon, 1963); Charles H. Wesley, *Richard Allen: Apostles of Freedom* (1935; rev. ed., Washington, D.C.: Associated Publishers, 1969).

Allen, Young J. (1836–1907) *American Methodist missionary in China*

Born on January 3, 1836, in Burke County, Georgia, Young J. Allen was orphaned as a child and raised by Primitive Baptist relatives. He converted to Methodism as a teenager. He later attended Emory and Henry College in Virginia and Emory College in Georgia. Upon his graduation in 1858, he sold his plantation and slaves, married, and was admitted on trial (probationary membership) in the Methodist's Georgia Conference. He also applied for missionary service. In 1860, amid rumors of war, he sailed for China.

The American Civil War erupted while he was en route. As a result, he (and the several missionaries who had preceded him) heard nothing from church leaders for the next five years. Allen settled in Shanghai, the center of Southern Methodist activity, quickly learned Chinese, and took a job as a teacher and translator for the Chinese government. He is said to have learned Chinese so well that when he gave his first sermon from the text "Arise, and let us go hence" (John 14:31), the entire Chinese congregation arose and headed for the church door.

Allen quickly became convinced that the major task before the missionary community was breaking down the hostility of the Chinese toward Westerners. He saw education as the major tool, and to that end began to found several small schools and later the Anglo-Chinese College, where he served as president for a decade. The college later merged into Soochow University (also founded by the Southern Methodist Mission).

Allen established a Methodist press, translated numerous books into Chinese, edited a Chinese newspaper, *The Review of the Times*, and wrote three books. By the end of the century, he had won the confidence of many Chinese leaders, who called him Lin Lo Chih, and had become a force for change in Chinese society in general.

Allen occasionally returned to the United States as the representative for the China Conference to the Methodist General Conference. His last visit to the States was in 1907 to attend the Centennial Conference on Missions in China, held to commemorate the pioneering work of Robert MORRISON. Allen died in Shanghai on May 30, 1907.

Further reading: Young J. Allen, *Diary of a Voyage to China, 1859–1860* (Atlanta, Ga.: Emory University, 1953); Adrian Arthur Bennett, III, *Missionary Journalism in Nineteenth-century China: Young J. Allen and the early "Wan-Kuo Kung-Pao," 1868–1883* (Davis: University of California, Ph.D. diss., 1970); ———, "Missionary Journalist in China: Young J. Allen and His Magazines." *Georgia Historical Quarterly* 67 (1983): 574–76; Walter N. Lacy, *A Hundred Years of China Methodism* (Nashville, Tenn.: Abingdon-Cokesbury Press, 1964); Akin Candler Warren, *Young J. Allen: The Man Who Seeded China* (Nashville, Tenn.: Abingdon-Cokesbury Press, 1931).

Alliance World Fellowship

The Alliance World Fellowship is a network of Evangelical missions and independent churches in some 100 countries.

The CHRISTIAN AND MISSIONARY ALLIANCE (CMA) can be traced to the 1883 formation of the

Missionary Union for the Evangelization of the World by Presbyterian minister Albert Benjamin SIMPSON (1843–1919). Two years earlier, Simpson had been healed of a heart disorder at the camp meeting at Old Orchard Beach, Maine. Several months later, he was rebaptized by immersion in a Baptist chapel in New York City, following which he resigned from the Presbyterian Church and began an independent evangelistic ministry focused on evangelism, the promotion of holiness of life, Christian healing, and missionary activity around the world. In 1887, those who had been attracted to his work created two organizations, the Christian Alliance and the Evangelical Missionary Alliance; they later merged as the Christian and Missionary Alliance.

The CMA sent out its first missionaries in 1887, the Cassidys to China and Helen Dawley to India. Over the next several years 20 additional missionaries were commissioned. It was to become one of the most expansive missionary programs of any Protestant denomination. In the 20th century, missions were started in more than 100 countries. In recent debates, the CMA, like most successful Western missionary churches, began a process of transforming its missions into autonomous churches under indigenous leadership. Out of that transformation came the Alliance World Fellowship (AWF), a network of evangelical churches raised up through the ministry of the Christian and Missionary Alliance. The Division of Overseas Ministries of the CMA took the lead in 1975 by bringing national leaders of former CMA churches to a meeting at Nyack, New York, where the AMF was formally established. In 1979, the CMA reported that it supported 890 missionaries and was in fellowship with 4,453 overseas local churches with 332,443 baptized church members.

The AWF meets quadrennially. It provides much needed leadership education and the exchange of specialists in ministry. The fellowship also promotes the common theological heritage that all the churches share and works toward keeping the unity of belief they have come to appreciate. The AMF is headed by an executive committee with an elected president. In response to appeals from member churches, the group hired a full-time executive director in 1991, and began setting up theological and mission commissions to help member churches. As the new century began, the AMF claimed some 2 million members in churches in 50 countries.

Further reading: Alliance World Fellowship. Available online. URL: http://www.allianceworldfellowship.org; H. D. Ayer, *The Christian and Missionary Alliance: An Annotated Bibliography of Textual Sources* (Lanham, Md.: Scarecrow Press, 2001); G. P. Pardington, *Twenty-five Wonderful Years* (New York: Garland, 1984).

American Baptist Churches U.S.A.

One of the larger Baptist bodies in the United States, the American Baptist Churches in the U.S.A. continues the history begun by Roger WILLIAMS with the founding of the first Baptist congregation in America at Providence, Rhode Island. In colonial times, Baptists were strongest in Pennsylvania, and it was in Philadelphia that the first association of Baptist churches was formed (1707). The Philadelphia Association had leanings toward Calvinist theology and adopted the LONDON CONFESSION OF FAITH.

The call to support foreign missions was the occasion for several Baptist associations to come together in 1814 to organize the General Missionary Convention of the Baptist Denomination in America. After the initial gathering, the convention met every three years, became known as the Triennial Convention, and served as a model for additional conventions that supported education, home missions, and the publication of literature. These four conventions tended to meet at the same time and place and gradually the lines of distinction became blurred.

In 1845, a split developed over slavery issues. The great majority of the congregations in the southern states withdrew and created the SOUTHERN BAPTIST CONVENTION. The Triennial Convention evolved in subsequent decades and was known for a period as the Northern Baptist Convention, assuming its present name in 1972.

The group won the loyalty of many AFRICAN-AMERICAN BAPTISTS in the years after the American Civil War, as it poured large sums into education and publishing for its African members. However, many blacks felt the need for an autonomous, black-led organization, and separate groups were eventually formed. Still, about one-third of the American Baptist membership remains African American.

Missionary zeal has led the American Baptists around the world. Beginning with the initial mission of Adoniram JUDSON (1788–1850) in India, during its first generation the Triennial Convention sent more than 100 missionaries to Europe, Africa, Asia, and the American West. In the 20th century, the missions they founded matured into 100 different Baptist bodies around the world.

The American Baptists witnessed some of the most heated verbal battles during the fundamentalist-modernist controversy of the 1920s and 1930s. Many of the more conservative ministers and churches withdrew to found new fundamentalist and Evangelical denominations. Leaders with liberal leanings gained control of the denominational agencies and educational institutions, though many with conservative leanings remain in the membership. The American Baptist Churches is among the few Baptist bodies that are ecumenically oriented; it belongs to both the BAPTIST WORLD ALLIANCE and the WORLD COUNCIL OF CHURCHES.

In 2001, the American Baptist Churches reported a membership of 1.5 million members. Its partner churches around the world have an additional 2.6 million adherents.

See also BAPTISTS.

Further reading: William H. Brackney, ed., *Baptist Life and Thought, 1600–1980: A Source Book* (Valley Forge, Pa.: Judson Press, 1983); H. Leon McBeth, *The Baptist Heritage: Four Centuries of Baptist Witness* (Nashville, Tenn.: Broadman Press, 1987); Robert G. A. Torbet, *A History of the Baptists* (Philadelphia: Judson Press, 1963).

American Board of Commissioners for Foreign Missions

The American Board of Commissioners for Foreign Missions was the first American Protestant agency to send missionaries to serve in foreign lands. It continued its venerable role well into the 20th century, when it was merged into a larger body as part of the ecumenical activities of its parent Congregational churches.

The American Board grew directly out of the legendary "haystack prayer meeting" in which five Williams College students caught the missionary spirit and organized the secret Society of Brethren, dedicated to the missionary cause. The group's leader, Samuel Mills Jr., had come to Williams very much aware of missionary efforts already launched in Europe.

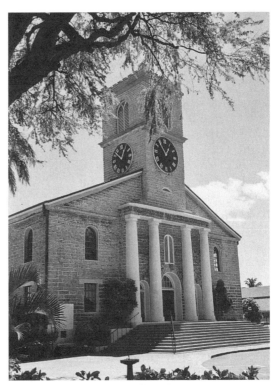

The Kawaihao Church is the original church established in Hawaii. *(Institute for the Study of American Religion, Santa Barbara, California)*

Members of the Society of Brethren, including Mills, Luther RICE, and Gordon Hall, recruited additional members while continuing their education at Andover Theological Seminary. In 1810, they took their concern to the annual meeting of the General Association of the Congregational Churches of Massachusetts, New England (now a constituent part of the UNITED CHURCH OF CHRIST). It approved the formation of the American Board, which was formally incorporated in 1812, at which time it commissioned its first missionaries. The Indian mission had unexpected consequences as two of the original group, Adoniram JUDSON and Luther Rice, converted to the Baptist faith and went on to found the competing American Baptist missionary endeavor. Still, the American Board mission was successful in India; a few years later, Dr. John SCUDDER founded the first MEDICAL MISSION there under the board's auspices.

In 1819, the American Board initiated what would become its most famous endeavor when it sent Hiram Bingham Sr. and a group of fellow missionaries and their wives to the Sandwich Islands (aka Hawaii). The mission was sparked by the appearance of Henry OBOOKIAH (c. 1792–1818) in New England in 1808. Obookiah, who developed a written Hawaiian language, joined the first class at the Foreign Mission School founded by the American Board in 1817, but he died of typhus before the mission to Hawaii set out.

The mission had great success winning over Hawaiian leaders, though it was later criticized for destroying much of Hawaii's history and culture in the process; Bingham was later caricatured in James Michener's popular novel *Hawaii*. Some of the Hawaiian converts were instrumental in the board's mission to other Pacific island groups. Bingham's son Hiram Jr. (1831–1908) began a mission to the Gilbert Islands in the 1850s. Throughout the 19th century, the American Board sponsored one of the largest Protestant missionary endeavors in the world.

The American Board attracted the interest of other groups that shared the Congregationalists' Calvinist theological perspective. Until they set up

their own missionary organizations, the American Presbyterians (1812–70), the Dutch Reformed Church (now the Reformed Church in America) (1826–57), and the German Reformed Church (now a constituent part of the United Church of Christ) (1839–1866), used the services of the American Board. After 1870, the American Board operated as an exclusively Congregational agency and cooperated with the National Council of Congregational Churches.

The American Board was considerably altered in 1961, as part of the merger of the Congregationalists into what became the United Church of Christ. The American Board was subsumed as the largest component of the new United Church Board for World Ministries. The new United Church Board participated in the transformation of the missionary endeavor in most Protestant churches. After World War II, under the impetus of the United Nations and the WORLD COUNCIL OF CHURCHES, missions were turned over to indigenous leadership and became autonomous bodies; the Western sending agencies became but one of their resources for engaging in ministry, often supplying both financial assistance and personnel.

Still further changes occurred in 1995, when the United Board of World Ministries of the United Church of Christ merged with the Division of Overseas Ministries of the CHRISTIAN CHURCH (DISCIPLES OF CHRIST) to form a common Global Ministries Board. The Global Ministries Board officially began to function on January 1, 1996, out of offices in New York City, Cleveland, and Indianapolis.

Further reading: Global Ministries Board. Available online. URL: http://www.globalministries.org; Alfred DeWitt Mason, *Outlines of Missionary History* (New York: Hodder & Stoughton, 1912); Clifton Jackson Phillips, *Protestant America and the Pagan World: The First Half Century of the American Board of Commissioners for Foreign Missions, 1810–1860* (Cambridge, Mass.: East Asian Research Center/Harvard University, 1969); LaRue W. Piercy, *Hawaii's Missionary Saga: Sacrifice and Godliness in Paradise* (Honolulu: Mutual

Publishing, 1992); William E. Strong, *The Story of the American Board* (New York: Pilgrim Press, 1910).

amillennialism

Since the Reformation era, most Protestant churches have subscribed to some version of amillennialism, a spiritualized view of the Christian promise of the kingdom of God.

Amillennialism had been articulated by St. Augustine (354–430) in the fifth century. Augustine approached the promises concerning the kingdom of God in a somewhat allegorical or spiritualized sense. He suggested that the kingdom was inaugurated by Christ's ministry, death, and resurrection and continues through this present age along with the worldly kingdom of Babylon. When this age ends at some unknowable point in the future, the church will begin to enjoy the fruits of the fullness of eternal life.

Both Martin Luther, himself an Augustinian friar, and John Calvin accepted this view and passed it along to their followers. It reigned supreme in Protestant circles until challenged in the 17th century by POSTMILLENNIALISM, which suggested that history was moving toward an earthly kingdom of peace and brotherhood, and in the 19th century by a rebirth of PREMILLENNIALISM, which suggested that God was going to intervene in the presently downward spiraling course of human events and establish his kingdom.

Amillennialism retains the acceptance of the majority of Protestants (including most liberal Protestants and many conservative ones). Contemporary amillennialism has been strengthened by the collapse of the postmillennialist view; in the face of the tremendous evil experienced in World Wars I and II, people lost confidence in the progress of human goodness. Holiness and faith, unlike technology, do not seem to be traits that can be passed down from generation to generation and improved upon. Premillennialism, too, has been weakened, as the repeated delays in the fulfillment of its expectations have been experienced by the Christian community. Most Protestants would suggest that time spent predicting the world's future by deciphering biblical passages only distracts from the responsibilities of living in the real world.

In the 20th century, liberal Protestants have developed a renewed stress in Jesus as the announcer of the kingdom of God, which is both present and future. That emphasis has been separated from any consideration of a literal millennium, a thousand-year period of Christ's rule on earth. The millennium, in contrast to the kingdom of God, is mentioned only once in the Bible, in Revelation 20:1–6. Amillennialism often leads to a lack of interest in prophecy and related topics, and thus has produced considerably less literature than its two major competitors.

See also ESCHATOLOGY.

Further reading: Darrell L. Bock, ed., *Three Views of the Millennium and Beyond* (Grand Rapids, Mich.: Zondervan, 1999); William E. Cox, *Amillennialism Today* (Phillipsburg, Pa.: Presbyterian and Reformed Press, 1966); Charles Feinberg, *Premillennialism or Amillennialism* (Grand Rapids, Mich.: Zondervan, 1936); Kim Riddlebarger, *Case for Amillennialism: Understanding the Endtimes* (Grand Rapids, Mich.: Baker Book House, 2003).

Amish

The Amish are an ANABAPTIST group that has become well known for its efforts to maintain its separatist agricultural life in small enclaves in the United States, resisting involvement with the state and, more recently, with modern technology.

The Amish trace their history to Jacob Amman (b. c. 1644), a Swiss Mennonite leader who called for a strict interpretation of the writings of Menno SIMONS (the founder of the MENNONITES) and of the Dordrecht Confession of Faith (1632), a widely acknowledged statement of belief for Mennonites. The Dordrecht text includes an important paragraph on banning (disfellowshipping) and SHUNNING. As members are expected not to eat, drink, or even converse on nonreligious matters

An Amish bookstore in central Pennsylvania *(Institute for the Study of American Religion, Santa Barbara, California)*

with a banned person, shunning can have severe consequences, even in relations between spouses.

Amman's strict interpretation of church discipline eventually led him to place all who disagreed with him under the ban. The harsh feelings so generated resulted in separation between the Amish and other Mennonites, and the schism was never healed. Over time, as Mennonites accommodated in many ways to changes in modern life, other issues intruded to keep the two groups apart.

The Amish have attempted to keep the common clothing of the 17th century, as a sign of the life of humility and separation from the world they espouse. Their garb is further distinctive in having no buttons, a fashion adopted out of the memory of the large buttons decorating the uniforms of soldiers that killed many Anabaptists.

After marriage, men grow beards (for which there are many biblical precedents) but not mustaches, which are also associated with the military. Women wear bonnets and aprons.

After more than a century of persecution in Europe, the Amish migrated to America in the 18th century and largely disappeared from their homeland. They established themselves in Pennsylvania, and as their fellowship grew, expanded to Ohio and Illinois. Being close to major urban areas has made them objects of curiosity, and they have increasingly moved to more isolated regions of North America and, most recently, Central America.

There are an estimated 150,000 Amish, of which approximately half are members of the Old Order Mennonite Church. Amish organization is congregationally based, and there are no central headquarters for the various groups. Splits have occurred over accommodations made by some Amish (such as allowing members who work away from their farms to use automobiles). They also periodically find themselves in court in attempts to maintain customs that conflict with local laws.

Old Order Amish worship in the homes of the members, with each family hosting the congregation on a rotating basis. The construction of church buildings by some smaller groups has been a source of schism. The Mennonite Information Center, 2209 Millstream Road, Lancaster, PA 17602, has assumed part of the task of interpreting Amish life to the many tourists who visit Lancaster County.

Further reading: A. Martha Denlinger, *Real People: Amish and Mennonites in Lancaster, Pennsylvania* (Scottdale, Pa.: Herald Press, 2000); John A. Hoestetler, *Amish Society* (Baltimore: Johns Hopkins University Press, 1968, 1993); Donald B. Kraybill and Carl F. Bowman. *On the Backroad to Heaven: Old Order Hutterites, Mennonites, Amish, and Brethren* (Baltimore: Johns Hopkins University Press, 2001); William R. McGrath, *Why We Wear Plain Clothes* (Cattolton, Ohio: Amish Mennonite Publication, 1980).

Anabaptists

One of the four major dissenting groups that emerged during the Reformation, the Anabaptists were unique in rejecting the idea of an inclusive state church. Fiercely independent and combative, Anabaptists were unable to prevent repeated schisms and were eventually far less successful than Lutherans, Anglicans, or Reformed Protestants.

The first Anabaptist fellowship was the Swiss Brethren of Zurich, who emerged in the mid-1520s. The movement spread through the German-speaking lands within a few years, and expanded to the other Protestant regions soon after.

Anabaptists argued that the church should consist only of those who were old enough to make a conscious commitment to faith in Christ and a life derived from that faith. They refused to baptize infants. Rejecting any alliance with the secular government, they had no means of coercing members, apart from the tool of disfellowshipping (usually called "banning").

The movement soon became home to a wide variety of opinions. It was greatly embarrassed by the violence associated with the followers of Thomas MUNZER and with the communalists who attempted to build an end-time society of MUNSTER, Germany. In reaction to the violence, the authorities killed many Anabaptists, who responded by adopting statements opposed to any violent activity; in fact, most of them became pacifists. The states defined the role of the magistrate as the keeper of the social order and reaffirmed their belief in core Christian principles.

Many first-generation Anabaptist leaders became martyrs; most believers left their homes to seek havens in the Netherlands and a few tolerant German states. In the late 1530s, Menno SIMONS welded the majority of the Anabaptists into the major surviving group, the MENNONITES. Only a few other small groups, such as the Schwenkfelder Church, continue in the contemporary world.

See also RADICAL REFORMATION.

Further reading: Cornelius Krahn, *Dutch Anabaptism: Origin, Spread, Life, and Thought (1450–1600)* (The Hague: Martinus Nijhoff, 1968); C. Arnold Snyder, *Anabaptist History and Theology: An Introduction* (Kitchener, Ontario: Pandora Press, 1995); J. Denny Weaver, *Becoming Anabaptist: The Origin and Significance of Sixteenth-Century Anabaptism* (Scottdale, Pa.: Herald Press, 1987); George H. Williams, *The Radical Reformation* (Kirksville, Mo.: Sixteenth Century Journal, 1992).

Anglican Communion/Anglican Consultative Council

The worldwide Anglican Communion includes those national and regional churches that emerged from the international spread of the CHURCH OF

ENGLAND and today continue in a formal communion with that church and its primary official, the archbishop of Canterbury. The Church of England itself traces its origins to the emergence of Christianity in the British Isles, though modern Anglicanism is generally defined with regard to the 16th-century split between the British church and the Roman Catholic communion.

Modern ANGLICANISM emerged from the compromises proposed by ELIZABETH I in the late 16th century, reaffirmed after the Puritan episode in the 17th century. This was the era when England began to build a global presence, initially with colonies in North America. The colonial enterprise moved on to include many Caribbean islands, Australia, New Zealand, various South Pacific island groups, much of Africa, and most of southern Asia from India to Hong Kong. The Church of England eventually established foreign branches in all these territories.

Efforts to grow and develop the church in lands outside of the British Isles began with the SOCIETY FOR PROMOTING CHRISTIAN KNOWLEDGE (1698) and the SOCIETY FOR THE PROPAGATION OF THE GOSPEL IN FOREIGN PARTS (1701) but received a significant boost from the CHURCH MISSIONARY SOCIETY (1799). The first bishop to establish his residence outside of England, Charles INGLIS, was sent to Canada in 1787. By that time, the United States had been created, an independent Protestant Episcopal Church in the U.S. organized, and three bishops consecrated: Samuel Seabury (1784), William White (1787), and William Provost (1787). As the church grew around the world, additional bishops were consecrated, but it was the establishment of the episcopacy in Australia in 1842 that really began the process of normalizing the hierarchy in British lands around the world.

In the 19th century, the number of independent Anglican churches increased, administratively separate but otherwise in communion with the Church of England. In 1867, the Canadian bishops requested a gathering of Anglican leadership. The idea led to the Lambeth conferences, now held every 10 years. These conferences provide a time for discussion and debate on the issues facing the communion. The Lambeth Conference of 1888 clarified the basic doctrinal commitments of the Anglican Communion.

The considerable latitude of belief and practice in the Anglican Communion tended to make it an inclusive body. Nevertheless, in the 19th century, the Reformed Episcopal Church (United States) and the Church of England in South Africa were both established independently outside the communion.

In 1897, the bishops created the Consultative Body of the Lambeth Conference to provide for continuity between conferences. The body evolved into the Anglican Consultative Council, now headquartered at Lambeth Palace in London. The council brings together clergy and lay people to work on common problems, meeting biannually at different locations around the world. The Anglican Communion Secretariat serves the Consultative Council as well.

In the middle of the 20th century, the various branches of the Church of England in different countries matured into autonomous provinces, each with their own bishops and archbishops. The move to grant autonomous status to different national and regional churches was spurred by the post–World War II drive toward independence in former colonies. Through the postwar era, some 40 provinces spread across more than 160 countries have been recognized. These provinces remain in communion with the See of Canterbury and find a degree of unity as the Anglican Communion through the Anglican Consultative Council. The bishops meet every 10 years for the Lambeth Conference.

Many of the churches in older British colonies remain the dominant religious community of the now independent country. Several provinces, such as the Church of the Province of the West Indies and the Anglican Province of the Southern Cone of America, cover a vast territory where Anglican membership is relatively sparse. Among the more interesting churches are the Church of South

India and the Church of North India, both products of a merger of several Protestant churches, but still able to meet the minimal requirements to be considered Anglican.

The Anglican provinces range from the more theologically liberal bodies such as the EPISCOPAL CHURCH (in the United States), which has taken the lead in consecrating females and most recently a homosexual to the episcopacy, to staunchly traditional conservative churches such as the Anglican Provinces of Singapore and Rwanda.

The communion has been hard pressed by changes in its member churches through the latter half of the 20th century, including attempts to alter/update the liturgy of the Prayer Book. In several countries, independent conservative churches claiming Anglican orders have arisen to challenge the legitimacy of the Episcopal Church and, more recently, any other churches that remain in communion with it. The Episcopal Church's acceptance of women priests in 1976 precipitated a schism in the United States, though the groups that left were unable to agree among themselves and splintered into more than 50 jurisdictions. Traditionalists were reenergized by the 2003 consecration of a bishop who is a practicing homosexual. In 2000, Archbishops Kolini of Rwanda and Yong of the Province of South East Asia consecrated Chuck Murphy and John Rodgers as bishops of an Anglican Mission to America to raise up conservative churches outside the jurisdiction of the Episcopal Church, but having status in the communion through the archbishops who appointed them.

Meanwhile, several of the more substantial conservative Anglican groups have formed the Traditional Anglican Communion to resist what they see as the continuing secularization of the church. As the new century began, the communion reported 14 member churches with a total of 300,000 members spread over six continents.

Further reading: Richard Holloway, *The Anglican Tradition* (Wilton, Conn.: Morehouse-Barlow, 1984); Stephen Neill, *Anglicanism* (London: A. R. Mowbrays, 1977); Andrew Wingate, et al., eds., *Anglicanism: A Global Communion* (London: A. R. Mowbrays, 1998); John Whale, *The Anglican Church Today: The Future of Anglicanism* (London: A. R. Mowbrays, 1988).

Anglicanism

Anglicanism is the name given to the gestalt of beliefs and practices brought together in the CHURCH OF ENGLAND in the post-Reformation era. Prior to the Reformation, the British Isles were united religiously by the Roman Catholic Church. From the pre-Reformation period, Anglicanism continues its adherence to the Bible, the Apostles and Nicene Creeds, the sacraments of the LORD'S SUPPER and BAPTISM, and an episcopal leadership with apostolic succession. During the 16th century, it underwent vast changes, veering from its

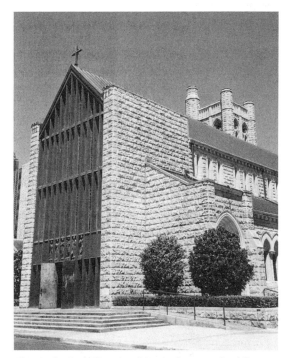

The Cathedral Church of St. Andrew resulted from the archbishop of Canterbury's establishing an Anglican mission in Hawaii in 1816. *(Institute for the Study of American Religion, Santa Barbara, California)*

most Protestant era during the reign of EDWARD VI (1547–53) to its near return to the Catholic fold during the reign of MARY I (1553–58). During the lengthy reign of ELIZABETH I (1558–1603), the policy of *via media* between the two extremes was articulated. The essence of the *via media* was embodied in the Prayer Book, the guide to worship, and in the ARTICLES OF RELIGION adopted in 1563.

Protestant elements of the *via media* include an emphasis on biblical authority; a rejection of all sacraments apart from baptism and the Lord's Supper; and repudiation of a variety of Roman Catholic beliefs and practices as delineated in the church's 39 ARTICLES OF RELIGION. Roman Catholic elements include the three-fold ministry (deacon, priest, and bishop) and the emphasis on a formal liturgy and church tradition.

This new form of Christianity was severely challenged by Puritanism in the middle of the 17th century, but solidified its position following the restoration of the monarchy in 1660. Anglicans have always taken pains to ensure their status as bearers of an unbroken succession of bishops from Jesus' apostles. As a result of efforts to Protestantize the church during the 16th century, Roman Catholics have frequently questioned Anglican claims of retaining an apostolic succession.

With the growth of the British Empire, Anglicanism took root in countries around the world. The many autonomous Anglican churches are united in the ANGLICAN COMMUNION.

The Lambeth Conference of 1888 proposed the most commonly cited doctrinal commitments of the Anglican Communion—the CHICAGO-LAMBETH QUADRILATERAL. The Quadrilateral affirmed four basic principles: the Holy Scriptures of the Old and New Testaments as the revealed Word of God "containing all things necessary to salvation" and as the rule and ultimate standard of faith; the Apostles' Creed as the symbol of baptism and the Nicene Creed as the sufficient statement of the Christian Faith; the two sacraments of baptism and the Eucharist as administered with the unfailing words and elements used by Christ; and the

historic episcopate locally adapted in the methods of its administration to the varying needs of Christian peoples. This faith finds expression in the BOOK OF COMMON PRAYER, which includes the liturgical text for Sunday worship and the 39 Articles of Religion. These principles could, it was believed, facilitate union with other churches.

In the last decades of the 20th century, Anglicans have been plagued with controversies over issues such as the ordination of female priests, changes in the liturgy, and the status of homosexuals in the church and in the priesthood.

Further reading: John Booty and Stephen Sykes, eds., *The Study of Anglicanism* (Minneapolis Minn.: Fortress Press, 1988); *The Church of England Yearbook* (London: Church Publishing House, published annually); William L. Sachs, *The Transformation of Anglicanism: From State Church to Global Communion* (Cambridge: Cambridge University Press, 1993); Andrew Wingate, et al., eds., *Anglicanism: A Global Communion* (London: A. R. Mowbrays, 1998).

Angola

Angola is a large, predominantly Roman Catholic country in southern Africa. Protestant and AFRICAN INITIATED CHURCHES have won many members in the 20th century.

For nearly 500 years after its discovery by Europeans in the 15th century Angola was a colony of Portugal. Roman Catholic missionaries had free reign to spread Christianity, which eventually became the dominant religion. Protestantism only entered in the last half of the 19th century. Drawing on a prior agreement, the different groups selected different target peoples for missionary work. British Baptists arrived in 1878 and made their base among the Bakongo people. Congregationalists from America (working through the AMERICAN BOARD OF COMMISSIONERS FOR FOREIGN MISSIONS) cooperated with Presbyterians from Canada to evangelize the Ovimbundu people. William TAYLOR, the missionary bishop of the Methodist Episcopal Church, brought a team of 45 people to Angola in 1885 to establish a mission among the Kinbundi people. The Evangelical Church of Central Angola (the result of the Congregationalist work) and the UNITED METHODIST CHURCH remain among the largest Protestant groups in the country.

The entire Christian community was strongly affected by the independence struggle against Portugal, a war that lasted from 1961 to 1975. Fighting persisted long after independence, as rival groups contended for control of the new government. Peace came in 1994 with the signing of the Lusaka Protocol, but some fighting was still going on as late as 2003.

The civil war, combined with the government's relatively pro-Catholic tendencies, hindered Protestant church development. In 1975, the authorities expelled several churches, including the CHURCH OF GOD (CLEVELAND, TENNESSEE) and the Pentecostal ASSEMBLIES OF GOD. The Church of Jesus Christ on Earth by His Messenger Simon KIMBANGU (the Kimbangu Church) was persecuted for many decades. The Marxist government that came to power in 1975 was openly hostile to religion, and in 1976 it expelled a number of Catholic and Protestant missionaries. In 1978, a new process of registering churches was put in place and tax-exemption withdrawn. In 1986, it was announced that 12 churches had been approved for registration and 19 churches denied approval and thus banned from operation.

Approved churches included the Evangelical Church of Southwest Angola, the Evangelical Congregational Church of Angola, the Catholic Church, the United Methodist Church, the Evangelical Baptist Church, the Evangelical Reformed Church, the Kimbangu Church, the (formerly expelled) Pentecostal Assemblies of God, the SEVENTH-DAY ADVENTIST CHURCH, the Angola Baptist Convention, and the Union of Evangelical Churches. These churches form the backbone of the Angolan Christian community, though after the government eased its approach to religion in the 1990s, a variety of older groups have revived and new ones have entered the country.

The Kimbangu Church, which came into Angola from Zaire in the 1920s, is the largest of several African Initiated Churches. The Tocoist Church and the Church of Our Savior Jesus Christ (founded by former Baptists in 1949) are its largest competitors. Pentecostalism arrived in 1938 with Edmond and Pearl Mabel Stark of the Church of God; though Edmond soon died, Pearl revived the mission in 1948 with help from Brazilian Assemblies of God missionaries. Thus began what became the largest Pentecostal church in the country, the Pentecostal Assemblies of God of Angola. Since 1975, several additional Pentecostal churches have been founded, and the Pentecostal revival has entered several of the older Protestant bodies. One Pentecostal body, the Evangelical Pentecostal Mission of Angola, is notable for its membership in the WORLD COUNCIL OF CHURCHES.

The Protestant missions formed the Evangelical Alliance of Angola in 1922. Tensions within this body became evident in the mid-1970s, when it went through a schism and reorganization. In 1974, six member groups reorganized the alliance as the Association of Evangelicals of Angola, which linked up to the Association of Evangelicals of Africa and Madagascar and the WORLD EVANGELICAL ALLIANCE. Three years later, eight of the older denominations formed the Angolan Council of Evangelical Churches and aligned with the All-Africa Council of Churches and the World Council of Churches.

As the 21st century begins, less than 5 percent of the population still practice traditional African religions, and secularism is now viewed as the primary challenge to church life. Some 94 percent of the public profess Christianity, of which the great majority (85 percent) are Roman Catholic.

See also AFRICA, SUB-SAHARAN.

Further reading: David Barrett, *The Encyclopedia of World Christianity,* 2nd ed. (New York: Oxford University Press, 2001); L. W. Henderson, *The Church in Angola: A River of Many Currents* (Cleveland, Ohio: Pilgrim Press, 1992).

Anthony (fl. 1730s) *African slave who helped spark worldwide Protestant missionary activity*

Little is known of Anthony's early life. He was converted to Christianity while a slave on St. Thomas. In 1731, he traveled with his master to Copenhagen, where he had the opportunity to tell his story and that of the African population on St. Thomas to Count Nicolas von Zinzendorf and the Moravian brothers in Denmark at the time. The slaves were in need of the church's ministrations, he said, but it was not being provided by the Lutheran ministers in St. Thomas. He argued that it would take a slave to reach them, as they worked long, exhausting hours.

The Moravians became enthusiastic about responding to Anthony's request. They commissioned two of their members, Leonhard Dober (1706–66) and David Nitschmann (1696–1772) (chosen by lots, as was their custom), as the first Moravian foreign missionaries. They reached St. Thomas at the end of 1732. Dober returned to Europe in 1734, bringing his first and only convert, a former slave named Carmel Oly, to the Moravian center at Herrnhut (on Zinzendorf's estate).

Over the decades, the Moravians had lost their episcopal leadership, which meant they could not ordain, and thus had no one who could baptize. Faced with the need to baptize Oly, they reorganized and selected a bishop (again by lots), David Nischmann, who was consecrated in 1735. Among his first actions of the reconstituted church was the baptism of Carmel Oly.

After his encounter with the Moravians, Anthony slipped back into obscurity, and his eventual fate is unknown. However, he is remembered for his pivotal role in launching the spread of Protestantism around the world.

See also Moravian Church.

Further reading: J. Taylor Hamilton and Kenneth G. Hamilton, *History of the Moravian Church: The Renewed Unitas Fratrum, 1722–1957* (Bethlehem, Pa./Winston-Salem, N.C.: Interprovincial Board of Christian Education, Moravian Church in America, 1967).

Antiburghers

The Antiburghers were a faction among the Presbyterians of Scotland in the 1730s who refused to take an oath they interpreted as requiring loyalty to the Church of Scotland.

More than a century of Scottish Presbyterian history was marked by a series of controversies that caused the proliferation of independent churches. The first conflict concerned choosing ministers for vacant parishes.

At the time of the Reformation, most parish church buildings had been built and were still maintained by the head of the local noble family. It was common for the nobleman to choose, or at least assume veto power over, the local minister, whose salary he would be paying. In 1690, when William of Orange was chosen to be the new king of Great Britain, the right of choosing their own ministers was granted to the Scottish congregations. However, in 1717 Parliament passed what was known as the Patronage Act, which returned that privilege to those nobles who operated as patrons (i.e., financially supported their local church).

While the Patronage Act angered many, a real crisis did not occur until the beginning of the 1730s. When one local patron neglected his duty of securing a new pastor, a group of landowners and church elders assumed the task and made a choice. When other members of the congregation demanded a voice, they were ignored. In 1731, under the leadership of Ebenezer Erskine (1680–1754), the congregation seceded from the Church of Scotland and formed what became known as the Associate Presbytery.

Within the Associate Presbytery, a subsequent issue arose over the oath required of all citizens (i.e., burghers), which stated, "I profess . . . the true religion presently professed within this realm . . . renouncing the Roman religion called papistry." Most in the Presbytery saw the operative phrase to be the rejection of Roman Catholicism. However, some saw the oath as expressing loyalty to the Church of Scotland (as the "true religion professed within the realm") and hence refused to take it. The dispute between Burghers and Antiburghers (those who refused to take the oath) led to a split in the Associate Presbytery. The two factions continued through the end of the century.

In the 1790s, a new issue arose among both the Burgher and Antiburgher churches over the role of the state. One group in each faction rejected any role for the state in maintaining the church, especially in paying the minister. The other group approved state assistance. At this point, four churches (denominations) existed.

In the 1840s, the issue of the congregational right to choose its minister surfaced again within the larger Church of Scotland. After years of wrangling, those who opposed ministers being assigned to parishes against the wishes of the congregation pulled out of the Church of Scotland and formed the Free Church of Scotland. In the 20th century, most of these issues lost resonance, and both the Associate Presbytery and the Free Church reunited with the Church of Scotland, though small factions remained outside.

The Burgher/Antiburgher controversy was carried overseas to the British colonies, especially to North America, where some Presbyterian churches aligned with various factions of the Associate Presbytery. They, too, eventually lost the rationale for a separate existence and eventually merged into larger Presbyterian bodies, although remnants continue to the present.

See also UNITED KINGDOM.

Further reading: Randall Balmer and John R. Fitzmier, *The Presbyterians* (Westport, Conn.: Greenwood Press, 1994); Lefferts A. Loetscher, *A Brief History of the Presbyterians* (Philadelphia: Westminster Press, 1978); Robert Benedetto, Darrell L. Guder, and Donald K. McKim. *Historical Dictionary of Reformed Churches* (Lanham, Md.: Scarecrow Press, 1999); James H. Smylie, *A Brief History of the Presbyterians* (Louisville, Ky.: Geneva Press, 1996).

anti-Catholicism

Intense criticism of the Roman Catholic Church has been a persistent theme in Protestant writings at all levels since the Reformation of the 16th century. Protestantism's Roman Catholic origins, and the intensity of the break between them, may explain this persistent criticism.

The very first Protestant documents are essentially criticisms of Catholic practice and pointed comments on the church's hierarchy and its monarch, the pope. Martin LUTHER, in a 1520 letter to Pope Leo X, wrote: "But thy See, which is called the Roman Curia, and of which neither thou nor any man can deny that it is more corrupt that any Babylon or Sodom ever was, and which is, as far as I can see, characterized by a totally depraved, hopeless and notorious wickedness—that See I have truly despised, and I have been incensed to think that in thy name and under the guise of the Roman Church the people of Christ are Mocked."

The Reformation was more than a war of words; it resulted in the disruption of the unity of the Catholic Church. The threat to remove Switzerland, Germany, Scandinavia, and the British Isles from the Catholic realm led to almost continual warfare through most of the 16th century. For Protestants, the struggle was punctuated by several instances of martyrdom that inflamed opinions against the Catholic Church. During the reign of MARY I (r. 1553–58), a number of Protestant leaders were executed in an attempt to swing the CHURCH OF ENGLAND back into the Roman Catholic camp. In 1572, tens of thousands of French Protestants were murdered in what became known as the ST. BARTHOLOMEW'S DAY MASSACRE, and authorities in Rome added insult to injury by striking a medal to commemorate the event.

John Foxe (1516–87), one of the MARIAN EXILES, waited out Mary's regime by compiling a book initially published in England in 1563. In its many editions (which continued to appear after his death, updated with new atrocities as they occurred), FOXE'S BOOK OF MARTYRS documented Catholic acts against Protestants (and proto-Protestants such as John HUS), thus keeping alive Protestant anti-Catholic feelings for many years.

The Catholic minority in England, supported by the Spanish king, repeatedly tried to overthrow or assassinate ELIZABETH I (r. 1558–1603); the Jesuit order was banned for backing these attempts. James I (r. 1603–25) continued Elizabeth's policy after a series of plots against his life were thwarted, including the still celebrated Guy Fawkes Plot (1605) to blow up Parliament. Perhaps for these reasons, William III's 1689 Toleration Act specifically excluded Roman Catholics from its provisions.

Protestant leaders developed a theology that portrayed Roman Catholicism in starkly negative images, often drawing from the emotive imagery of the biblical Book of Revelation, itself originally directed at the Roman Empire. The pope was often identified with the beast of Revelation 13 who had seven heads and 10 horns and who spoke blasphemy. The Catholic Church created a similar set of observations on Protestantism that were integrated into theology texts and popular literature.

Anti-Catholic feelings were transferred to the British American colonies. They led to the 1702 Protestant takeover of Maryland, established as a haven for British Catholics. Over the next few years, a series of anti-Catholic laws were enacted in the colonies. Catholics were denied the right to vote and to hold public office, and they were not allowed to found schools. Most colleges would not admit Catholic students.

The First Amendment to the United States Constitution excluded no one from its promise of religious freedom, and Catholicism prospered in the new nation. In 1844, when the Methodists split, the Roman Catholic Church became the largest church in America, a position it still maintains (though the total Protestant community continues to dominate American religious life). Fear of Roman Catholic gains motivated Protestant evangelistic activity; following the Civil War, Protestant churches mobilized to evangelize the recently freed slaves on the grounds that they might otherwise become Roman Catholics. Anti-Catholic feelings flared at the time of the Know-Nothing movement in the 1840s and again toward the end of the century in reaction to large-scale immigration from Roman Catholic countries such as Italy and Poland.

Protestant missionary efforts in the 19th century gave added impetus to anti-Catholic feelings. When Protestants, citing religious freedom, tried to established churches in Roman Catholic countries across South America and in Europe (especially Spain and Italy), they always met intense resistance from Catholic authorities. Protestants were in worldwide competition with Catholic missionaries in Africa, Asia, and the South Pacific—a competition increased by the entry of France and Belgium into the quest for empire.

The Protestant Ecumenical movement of the 20th century paradoxically helped mitigate anti-Catholic feelings, as the vision of unity led to overtures to Eastern Orthodoxy and then to Roman Catholicism. The breakthrough in attitudes occurred during the papacy of John XXIII (r. 1958–63). In 1960, he created a Secretariat for Christian Unity, which sent official observers to the WORLD COUNCIL OF CHURCHES gathering at New Delhi in 1961. Then in 1962, he invited official Protestant observers to a bishops' council at the Vatican, where important new statements on Protestant-Catholic relationships were presented. John XXIII's successor, Paul VI, oversaw an era of good feelings between the two communities that found expression at every level of church life.

Following Vatican II (1962–66), official consultations were set up between the Catholic Church and both the World Council of Churches and the major branches of Protestantism. At the national and local levels, Protestants and Catholics worked together as members of church councils. Catholics and Protestants now appear together regularly in services designed to commemorate important events in modern religiously plural countries. Meanwhile, a significant step in overcoming anti-Catholic feeling in the predominantly Protestant United States was made in 1960 with the election of the first Catholic American president, John F. Kennedy (1917–63).

Elements of anti-Catholicism remain in the Protestant community, especially among the more conservative denominations, which are generally less tolerant of doctrinal differences. They have continued to reprint classic anti-Catholic books and perpetuate anti-Catholic patterns of Bible interpretation. In recent years, some Evangelical Protestants have tried to replace polemics with dialogue, perhaps a sign of the movement's growing power.

Protestant-Catholic tensions remain strong and politically important in a few countries. Most notably, violence continued in Northern Ireland through the last decades of the 20th century.

See also ROMAN CATHOLIC–PROTESTANT DIALOGUE.

Further reading: Ray Allen Billington, *The Protestant Crusade, 1800–1860, A Study of the Origins of American Nativism* (New York: Macmillan, 1938); Philip Jenkins, *The New Anti-Catholicism: Hating the Church in Modern America* (New York: Oxford University Press, 2003); Robert P. Lockwood, ed., *Anti-Catholicism in American Culture* (Huntington, Ind.: Our Sunday Visitor, 2000); E. R. Norman, *Anti Catholicism in Victorian England* (New York: Barnes and Noble, 1968).

Antigua

Antigua is a small island country in the Caribbean. The majority of the inhabitants are descendants of Africans brought to work sugar plantations.

The British brought the CHURCH OF ENGLAND with them at the end of the 17th century, after the French abandoned the island. Both Moravians and Methodists arrived in the middle of the 17th century. These three churches remain the three largest Protestant groups on the island, although the 22,000-member Anglican Church is by far the largest. Among groups that arrived in the 20th century are the WESLEYAN CHURCH (an American Holiness body) and the SEVENTH-DAY ADVENTIST CHURCH. Though split among several groups, PENTECOSTALISM has gained a significant foothold.

Two ecumenical organizations have arisen. The Anglican, Methodist, and Moravian churches and the SALVATION ARMY have formed the Antigua Christian Council, associated with the WORLD COUNCIL OF CHURCHES. More conservative groups have formed the United Evangelical Association associated with the WORLD EVANGELICAL ALLIANCE.

See also CARIBBEAN.

Further reading: David Barrett, *The Encyclopedia of World Christianity,* 2nd ed. (New York: Oxford University Press, 2001); Patrick Johnstone and Jason Mandryk, *Operation World, 21st Century Edition* (Carlisle, Cumbria, U.K.: Paternoster, 2001).

apocalyptism

Apocalyptism is an approach to the future that sees history, culture, and society to be in unavoidable decline and heading for a catastrophic end. According to this view, only a small group of people, often called a remnant, has or will have advance knowledge of the end-time and can prepare for it; only they will be delivered from the catastrophe, through supernatural means. In the Christian tradition, the remnant will be saved by the intervention of Jesus, whose return will coincide with the end of history.

Apocalyticism in some form appears in most of the major world religions, a prominent source for Christian apocalypticism being the book of Daniel in the Jewish Bible (the Christian Old Testament). In the modern world, non-Christian apocalyptic groups, such as the Aum Shinrikyo group that released poison gas in the Tokyo train system in 1995, have absorbed their view from Christian apocalyptic literature.

Apocalytic groups appeared soon after the beginning of the Reformation. The violent strain in the apocalyptic teachings of Thomas Münzer and at the community of Münster did much to discredit the approach, but it has reappeared in every generation in Protestant regions, despite the failure of earlier predictions of catastrophic change. Its popularity is frequently seen as a sign of alienation from the dominant culture, often among poorer elements of the population.

Apocalyticism attained a new life in the 19th century with the development of various forms of DISPENSATIONALISM beginning with Irish minister John Nelson DARBY (1800–82) and William MILLER (1782–1849), the founder of ADVENTISM. Each proposed a system of world history based on the Bible that suggested that contemporary believers were living in the last days. Both Darby's and Miller's system invited date setting; Millerites were especially prone to engage in projecting dates for end-time events.

Darby's dispensational theology energized one wing of the Fundamentalist movement of the late 19th century, shaping a series of Bible conferences that began in the United States soon after the Civil War. Beginning with the Believers' Meeting for Bible Study in 1868 in New York, these annual gatherings of ministers affected by Darby's teachings covered a wide range of Bible topics, including ESCHATOLOGY. In 1878, a group of eight dispensationalists, most of them active in the Bible conferences, issued a call for a prophecy conference to discuss the imminent return of Christ to inaugurate a 1,000-year reign of peace. More than 100 bishops, professors, and ministers endorsed the call for a First American Bible and Prophetic Conference, to meet at the Church of the Holy Trinity in New York City. The conference was successful enough that a second was held in 1886 in Chicago; subsequent conferences met periodically over the next three decades.

The Bible and prophetic conferences helped to establish dispensationalism and its belief in the imminent return of Christ and in the Baptist, Presbyterian, and Congregational movements, including most of those who favored aligning with the Fundamentalist movement in the decades after World War I. Dispensationalism also shaped a number of schools such as the Moody Bible Institute and Dallas Theological Seminary, which perpetuate the theology to the present. The SEVENTH-DAY ADVENTIST CHURCH, the JEHOVAH'S WITNESSES, and the Worldwide Church of God all promulgate apocalypticism in their highly successful movements.

The success of dispensational PREMILLENNIALISM and Adventism has made apocalyptic thought one of the most popular religious expressions in the United States. It received an additional boost from the formation of the state of Israel in 1948. Integral to the dispensational worldview was a belief in the end-time reemergence of Israel. Many dispensationalists became convinced that the founding of the state of Israel marked the beginning of the final generation before the return of Christ. A generation being roughly 40 years, Christ was expected before 1988. This belief provided the foundation for the most popular book on prophecy in the 20th century, Baptist minister Hal Lindsey's *The Late Great Planet Earth,* published in 1970. The failure of Lindsey's predictions has not deterred believers. More recently, Baptist minister Tim LaHaye and writer Jim Jenkins have collaborated on a series of highly successful novels based upon the present dispensational understanding of the end-time, suggesting that Christ will return to gather all true believers in the air. The rest will be "Left Behind," the name of the series. The series has led to a movie and a number of spin-off nonfiction books on eschatology.

The end of the second millennium since the ministry of Jesus Christ gave an additional push to Protestant apocalypticism. In this case, the primary impetus for speculation was a glitch in computer clocks as 1999 became 2000. Many thought that the *Y2K problem,* as the glitch was termed, would lead to a massive disruption of the computer systems upon which all the advanced nations relied.

A primary concern with apocalypticism has been its image as condoning violence, which dates back to some isolated incidents at the very beginning of the Reformation. In fact, for centuries most apocalyticists have avoided violence. However, in the 1990s several unconnected violent events revived the image, involving such unrelated (and mostly non-Christian) groups as the Branch Davidians near Waco, Texas, the Aum Shinrikyo in Japan, the Solar Temple in Switzerland and Canada, and the Heaven's Gate group in suburban San Diego, California.

Further reading: Paul Boyer, *When Time Shall be No More: Prophecy Belief in Modern American Culture* (Cambridge, Mass.: Harvard University Press, 1992); Tim LaHaye and Jim Jenkins, *Left Behind: A Novel of the Earth's Last Days* (Carol Stream, Ill.: Tyndale House, 1996); Hal Lindsey, *The Late Great Planet Earth* (Grand Rapids, Mich.: Zondervan, 1970); Tom McIver, *The End of the World: An Annotated Bibliography* (Jeffersonville, N.C.: McFarland, 1999); James H. Morehead, *World Without End: Mainstream American Protestant Visions of the Last Things, 1880–1925* (Bloomington: Indiana University Press, 1999); George H. Williams, *The Radical Reformation* (Kirksville, Mo.: Sixteenth Century Journal, 1992).

Apocrypha

The term *Apocrypha* generally refers to those ancient Hebrew books that were originally included in the Latin Vulgate Bible compiled and edited by St. Jerome (c. 347–419/420), even though they were not considered canonical by most Jews at the time.

In Christian Bibles the Apocrypha is generally placed following the Old Testament. It includes the books of 1 and 2 Esdras, Tobit, Judith, Additions to Esther, Wisdom of Solomon, Ecclesiasticus, Baruch, Letter of Jeremiah, Prayers of Azariah and Song of the Three Young Men, Susanna, Bel and the Dragon, Prayer of Mannasseh, and 1 and 2 Maccabees. As the Vulgate became the official Bible translation for the Roman Catholic Church, the Apocrypha took on canonical authority as sacred text. In 1546, at the Council of Trent, the Catholic Church named the works of the Apocrypha, with the exception of the prayer of Mannasseh and 1 and 2 Esdras, as part of the Old Testament canon.

Early Protestants had to decide whether to accept the Apocrypha. In its favor, it had been included in the Septuagint, the Hebrew Bible as translated for Greek-speaking Jews, and it was accepted by Augustine, possibly the most influential Catholic theologian for Protestants. Furthermore, it was found in the Bible translations available to 16th-century reformers when they began their work.

When Martin LUTHER translated the Old Testament into German, he included the Apocrypha, but also posted a statement explaining he did not believe these books to be canonical, merely "good and useful for reading." Luther's reticence concerning the Apocrypha was clearly influenced by its support for several practices he condemned, such as prayers for the dead (Tobit 12:12, 2 Maccabees 12:39–45 ff.; cf. 1 Corinthians 15:29), intercession of the saints (2 Maccabees 15:14), and intermediary intercession of angels (Tobit 12:12, 15). Interestingly, Luther did not include in his translation the books of 1 and 2 Esdras.

The CHURCH OF ENGLAND followed Luther's lead, rejecting the canonicity of the Apocrypha, but considering it worthy to be read as an "example of life and for instruction in manners." The books are included in the standard cycle of readings in the churches.

The Reformed and Presbyterian church leaders also followed Luther and, for example, included the Apocrypha in the Geneva Bible (1560), Bishop's Bible (1568) and the KING JAMES VERSION (1611), which was prepared by British Puritans. However, in the WESTMINSTER CONFESSION (1647), the Puritan leaders declared it to have no authority in the church.

A controversy over the Apocrypha developed in the 1820s concerning the British and Foreign Bible Society, an early ecumenical organization dedicated to publishing the Bible text for common distribution by all Protestant (and in some countries Eastern Orthodox and Roman Catholic) churches. In 1826, Protestant churches forced the society to abandon any future publication of the Apocrypha; from that point, the Bible societies were generally seen as solely a Protestant enterprise.

In more recent years, Bibles published by Protestants generally do not include the Apocrypha.

During the 19th and 20th centuries, when Protestants made massive efforts to translate the Bible into all of the languages spoken on earth, they rarely included the Apocrypha. Increasingly, the Apocrypha has been ignored in the Protestant and Free Churches.

In 1964 and 1966 respectively, the American Bible Society and the British and Foreign Bible Society removed all restrictions against the Apocrypha. In the post–Vatican II spirit of cooperation, they have begun again to work with Roman Catholics on the publication of acceptable Bible texts.

See also BIBLE SOCIETIES; BIBLE TRANSLATIONS.

Further reading: L. H. Brockington, *A Critical Introduction to the Apocrypha* (London: Duckworth, 1961); Bruce M. Metzger, ed., *The New Oxford Annotated Apocrypha: The Apocrypha/Deutero-canonical Books of the Old Testament* (New York: Oxford University Press, 1991); J. Roe, *History of the British and Foreign Bible Society* (London: British and Foreign Bible Society, 1965).

apologetics

Apologetics is a branch of THEOLOGY concerned with the elucidation and defense of the Christian religion. A technical term derived from a Greek root for defense, the word *apologetics* is confusing to modern English speakers and is often confused with the word *apology*. In the theological world, the term is closer to Plato's use in the *Apology*, in which Socrates presents his defense in the face of his Athenian accusers.

Different Christian apologists might concentrate upon the rationale for theism within the broad field of religion; or the rationale for Christianity within theistic religion; or the rationale for choosing any of the various forms of Christianity over the others. The apologist will present truth claims and offer reasoned discourse to the end that the listener or reader will accept those truths. In general, apologists have had two audiences—the unbeliever whom one hopes might convert

and the believer whom one hopes will be confirmed in the faith.

In the first centuries of the Protestant era, Protestant apologetics were almost entirely directed to the continuing challenge of the Roman Catholic Church. The border between simple Protestant-Catholic polemic literature and apologetic literature is often difficult to draw. In the 18th century, apologetics that answered the challenge of secularism, atheism, and non-Christian theism (deism) began to appear and became a more significant element in subsequent centuries. Crucial to the apologetic task relative to nontheist philosophies have been a set of "proofs" of the existence of God. British philosophical theologian William Paley (1743–1805), for example, became known for his advocacy of the argument from design, namely that the orderliness of the universe proved the existence of a creator. In the 20th century, the appeal of such arguments persists but has significantly waned.

At the end of the 19th century, conservative Protestants developed apologetics to answer the challenges of both the new sciences (symbolized in the the theory of evolution as an alternative to a more literal reading of the early chapters of Genesis) and the modernist form of Protestantism that evolved out of accepting those sciences (biology, geology, and sociology). By contrast, liberal Protestants attempted to revise theology as a discipline more open to the ever-changing findings of science. Increasingly, the dialogue with science has become a very specialized branch of apologetics. Apologists must deal not only with the challenge of scientific method as a better way to knowledge of the cosmos, but with atheistic philosophies that have grown out of speculations on science.

Swiss Reformed theologian Karl BARTH rejected both the conservative and liberal approaches, abandoning apologetics as a theological task. He criticized the defensive tone that apologists were forced to adopt, which allowed the nonbelievers to set the issues for any discussion. According to Barth and his colleagues, the best course for the Christian is the clear statement of the churches' teachings.

Emil BRUNNER, one of Barth's associates, argued for a continued if reduced role for apologetics. While it might appear thankless to develop rational arguments for Christianity, theologians should strive to present a Christianity that is intellectually acceptable to combat the popular opinion in academic circles that the religion was not intellectually defensible.

Barth and Brunner were in fact continuing an old theme in Protestant theology. Martin LUTHER disdained the role philosophers played in defending what he saw as a corrupt Catholic establishment. Later Protestant leaders, noting how well people responded to the preaching and proclamation of the Gospel message, justified their neglect of apologetics in favor of a clear and forceful presentation of the Christian message. Such would be typical of the Pietist tradition as expressed in METHODISM. Spokespersons of this tradition doubt the value of human arguments in winning over the unbeliever, though they were willing to argue strongly against what are seen as erroneous positions. They stress instead the power of presenting the good news of salvation and emphasizing the personal encounter with God through the action of the Holy Spirit. While not necessarily anti-intellectual, this school of thought sees reason, science, and philosophy to be of limited value to the church.

A second school of Protestantism, which can be traced to John CALVIN, utilizes the full range of rational and philosophical tools in the presentation of the faith. Instead of emphasizing metaphysical arguments, Calvin's apologetics placed priority on epistemology (understanding the nature of knowledge/truth). He argued that self-knowledge leads to a desire to know God. The search lets us see that only in knowing God can we in fact know ourselves fully and truthfully. In this approach, the Bible is seen as the central source of our knowledge of God. This approach to apologetics has been most frequently, though not exclusively, associated with Reformed theology.

In the 17th century, some Protestant apologists rediscovered the classical proofs of God (ontological, cosmological, teleological, and moral); over the years they have added new ones. The classical arguments became a prolegomena to the more familiar Calvinist approach. Examining these proofs remains an important task for philosophers of religion.

As Christianity was confronted by a variety of non-Christian belief systems in the 19th and 20th centuries, detailed arguments in support of traditional Christianity have developed around such issues as the New Testament fulfillment of Old Testament prophecies, the existence of miracles (as God's intervention in nature and history), the superiority of the person of Christ, and the preeminence of Christian teachings of love.

One older theme that has largely dropped out of contemporary apologetics is the benign influence of Christianity on the people and cultures among whom it has spread. Christianity's support of European colonialism, racism, and female subjugation, and its inability to oppose the Jewish Holocaust, have vitiated this argument.

Protestant belief has been so centered on the Bible as the source of revelation and truth that apologists have been particularly concerned with advances in biblical scholarship in the last century. Critical tools unleashed by modern biblical scholars have often provided a platform from which to argue against the revelatory status of the Bible, emphasizing instead the human aspects of its origin. In the face of such attacks, Protestants have spent considerable energy defending the Bible as the Word of God. Liberal theologians have developed views of the Bible that attempt to reclaim it as an authority within the church, while at the same time acknowledging the insights of contemporary biblical scholars. More conservative Protestants tend to reject modern biblical scholarship. They try to argue for the Bible's integrity, authenticity, and truthfulness in all matters (sometimes stated as its infallibility and INERRANCY).

Conservative evangelical Christian apologists have been most concerned with the emergence of new forms of Christianity in the 20th century, which they feel deny essential affirmations of the church, especially the Triune God, the deity of Jesus Christ, and Christ's substitutionary atonement. The task of defending tradition against modern innovations in theology has led Evangelicals to elevate the importance of apologetics. For example, Baptist theologian Gordon R. Lewis argues, "Theology presupposes the primary tenets of Christianity and sets forth their implications in systematic detail. Apologetics, on the other hand, examines Christianity's most basic presuppositions. It considers why we should start with Christian presuppositions rather than others."

Among the groups singled out for special treatment within Evangelical circles have been the "cults," as they call the new religions that arose in 19th- and 20th-century America, such as the CHURCH OF JESUS CHRIST OF LATTER-DAY SAINTS, Christian Scientists, the JEHOVAH'S WITNESSES, The Family (Children of God), and New Age or Esoteric Christianity. These groups often use Christian symbols and words but pour very different meanings into them. In the late 20th century, an apologetic concern about all these different forms of Christianity produced a countercult movement with an extensive literature. This popular movement has more recently worked to counter the growth in the West of older non-Christian religious traditions (Buddhism, Hinduism, Islam, etc.).

The ECUMENICAL MOVEMENT has tended to operate against the development of apologetics, at least between Christian denominations. The Ecumenical movement has relied upon dialogue and a search for commonality, understanding, and mutual respect in place of rigid adherence to a particular perspective on Christian teachings. Ecumenical theologians have attempted to reconcile differences between different churches and to develop common affirmations as the bedrock of cordial relationships.

Interfaith dialogue has been explored as well, especially in post-Holocaust conversations with Jewish leaders and post-Israel conversations with Muslims. In each case, shared monotheism is emphasized as a basis for continued conversations and cooperation. Dialogue does not do away with issues, nor discard concern for truth, but it does place an individual's, church's, or movement's position into a relationship with other positions that make a similar claim on truth and provides a more positive approach to resolving differences.

See also ORTHODOX-PROTESTANT DIALOGUE; ROMAN CATHOLIC–PROTESTANT DIALOGUE.

Further reading: Edward John Carnell, *An Introduction to Christian Apologetics: A Philosophic Defense of the Trinitarian-Theistic Faith,* 2nd ed. (Grand Rapids, Mich.: William B. Eerdmans, 1953); Cky J. Carrigan, "Contemporary Evangelical Approaches to Apologetics," 1997. Available online. URL:http://ontruth.com/apologetics.html. Accessed on November 18, 2003; Avery Dulles, *History of Apologetics* (Philadelphia: Westminster, 1971); Norman Geisler, *Christian Apologetics* (Grand Rapids, Mich.: Baker Book House, 1976); Gordon R. Lewis, *Testing Christianity's Truth Claims* (Chicago: Moody, 1976; rpt.: Lanham, Md.: University Press of America, 1990); William Paley, *A View of the Evidences of Christianity* (Dublin: Printed by John Pasley, for J. Milliken, 1794); Bernard Ramm, *Varieties of Christian Apologetics* (Grand Rapids, Mich.: Baker Book House, 1962); Konrad Raiser, "The Nature and Purpose of Ecumenical Dialogue," *The Ecumenical Review* (July 2000). Available online. URL:http://www.findarticles.com/cf_0/m2065/3_52/6 6279069/p1/article.jhtml; Elton Trueblood, *Philosophy of Religion* (New York: Harper & Brothers, 1957); Cornelius Van Till, *Christian Apologetics* (Phillipsburg, N.J.: Presbyterian and Reformed Press, 1976).

apostles

The biblical apostles were the leaders of the first generation of the Christian movement. In more recent times, various Protestant and other religious leaders have claimed the title as well.

The exalted status of the original apostles in the geographically expanding church was based on having known and followed Jesus prior to his crucifixion and resurrection. Paul claimed apostolic status based on his encounter with Jesus on the road to Damascus (Acts 9; I Corinthians 15:8–10).

Through the centuries, the church claimed that authority had been passed to it from the original 12 apostles (minus Judas and plus Matthias) and Paul. The Apostles' Creed was seen as a summary of what the apostles taught. The apostles had passed authority to the bishops through the laying on of hands during their consecration service. The bishops in turn passed authority to congregational leaders through their ordaining the priests.

Reformation-era churches held differing views on apostolic authority. The Anglican and some Lutheran churches continued to claim apostolic succession for their episcopacy. Within the Roman Catholic Church, the pope was seen as the "successor to the apostles," and his position as bishop of Rome of the Apostolic See. Catholics use the adjective *apostolic* to describe a variety of individual officials and offices deriving their authority directly from Rome. However, almost all Christians at that time (and today) assumed that the title *apostle* was retired with the death of the last of the 12.

The position of apostle was revived in the 1820s following the visions claimed by Joseph Smith Jr., which led to the founding of the Church of Jesus Christ of Latter-day Saints. In one vision, the apostles Peter, James, and John gave Joseph Smith and Oliver Cowdery the authority to organize the church anew. The two were ordained as modern-day apostles. Eventually, the new church established a self-perpetuating Quorum of the Twelve (apostles).

An analogous movement emerged in England when a group of Bible students intently focused on the imminent return of Jesus Christ concluded that this event would not occur until certain biblical signs appeared, including the emergence of the charismatic gifts such as healing and prophecy, and the reestablishment of a 12-fold apostolate. They moved to designate a group of 12 apostles, who in 1835 assumed leadership over what was called the Catholic Apostolic Church. Because they believed the end-time was imminent, they made no provision for replacing any of the 12, and as they died off, the movement languished and has all but disappeared. Another group in Germany in the 1860s also set up a new apostolic core group, whose members could be replaced and whose number was not limited to 12. In the 20th century, this New Apostolic Church has become a significant international body.

In the 20th century, a number of newer movements have claimed a form of apostolic authority for their founders/leaders. The term usually connotes the founding of new churches, but also usually implies a larger cosmic role—often prophesies of the end-time. For example, Herbert W. Armstrong, founder of the Worldwide Church of God, was seen as an apostle. It was the belief of the Worldwide Church that at particular moments, God chooses to do a new work in history and commissions an individual to accomplish it. Armstrong assumed the power to pass his office to a successor; when the church splintered in the 1990s, some leaders claimed to have inherited the title.

Various Pentecostals and Charismatics have also used the term. Several years after the founding of Pentecostalism, a non-Trinitarian perspective arose which was known as the "Jesus Only" movement. Its followers took the name "apostolic." While divided into different denominations, the "apostolic" churches have come together ecumenically in the Apostolic World Christian Fellowship.

In the 1940s, the Latter-Rain movement appeared among Canadian Pentecostals, who adopted a church organization based on Ephesians 5:11–12, centered around a five-fold ministry of apostles, prophets, evangelists, pastors, and teachers. An apostle was someone called and given authority by Christ, endowed with gifts of leadership, and assigned the special task of founding and overseeing local churches. In the second half of the 20th century, the Pentecostal/

Charismatic movement has seen the emergence of a number of new denominations and congregational associations who each accept a particular leader as apostle. In the late 1990s, Peter Wagner, a professor at Fuller Theological Seminary in Pasadena, California, who had become impressed with the new apostolic groups as the present work of God, organized the International Coalition of Apostles to provide contact and coordination among the new generation of apostles.

See also PENTECOSTALISM.

Further reading: R. Brown, *The Churches the Apostles Left Behind* (New York: Paulist Press, 1984); David Cannistraci and Peter Wagner, *Apostles and the Emerging Apostolic Movement* (Ventura, Calif.: Regal Books, 1998); M. Kraus, *Completion Work in the New Apostolic Church* (Waterloo, Ontario: New Apostolic Church, 1978); James S. Prothro, *Apostles: The Missing Link of the Five-Fold Ministry* (Marietta, Ga.: Robot Publishing, 1998); Wilburn D. Talbot, *The Duties and Responsibilities of the Apostles of the Church of Jesus Christ of Latter-day Saints, 1835–1945* (Provo, Utah: Brigham Young University, Ph.D. diss., 1978).

Apostolic World Christian Fellowship

The Apostolic World Christian Fellowship was founded in 1970 to promote and provide fellowship for churches that follow the doctrine of the apostles, which in this case means the non-Trinitarian perspective of the Oneness or "JESUS ONLY" movement within the larger Pentecostal movement. The idea for such an organization was originally put forth by Bishop W. G. Rowe.

The Jesus Only position was first advocated at a Pentecostal camp meeting in 1913, but quickly gained adherents in the still emerging Pentecostal movement. Eventually, it would divide along racial lines with groups such as the UNITED PENTECOSTAL CHURCH INTERNATIONAL emerging as the largest predominantly white group and others such as the Bible Way Church of Our Lord Jesus Christ World Wide and the Church of the Lord Jesus Christ of the Apostolic Faith as the larger predominantly black groups. The PENTECOSTAL ASSEMBLIES OF THE WORLD is the only group to remain functionally integrated.

The fellowship emphasizes the unity of the larger apostolic community, the need for individual churches to share their successes programmatically with one another, the need to prepare and utilize the hidden resources of the lay membership, and support for both home and world missions.

As of 2003, some 135 denominations and organizations representing more than 3 million believers were affiliated with the fellowship. Strength is primarily in North America, Asia, and the Caribbean. International headquarters is in Evansville, Indiana.

Further reading: Apostolic World Christian Fellowship. Available online. URL:http://www.awcf.org. Accessed on November 15, 2004.

Appasamy, Aiyadurai Jesudasen
(1891–1975) *Indian Protestant leader and bishop*
Aiyadurai Jesudasen Appasamy was born on September 3, 1891. He grew up in India, but received his college education in America and the United Kingdom (1915–22). He wrote his Oxford doctoral dissertation on "The Mysticism of the Fourth Gospel and Its Relation to Hindu Bhakti Literature." Bhakti is the devotional approach to the Hindu deities, commonly known in the West from its centrality to the Hare Krishna Movement (the International Society for Krishna Consciousness). Appasamy created what amounted to a commentary of the Gospel of John using many citations to the Tamil-speaking poets of southern India. Appasamy believed that there was a direct and fruitful connection between the teachings of the biblical Gospel of John and the bhakti tradition that could serve as a basis of conversation and some reconciliation between Indian Christianity and the Hindu community. While at Oxford, he met his countryman SADHU SUNDAR SINGH, with whom he shared an appreciation of Indian religious literature.

Appasamy returned to India in 1922. In 1929, he published the first of several books developing themes from his doctoral dissertation, *Christianity as Bhakti Marga,* followed three years later with *What Is Moksha? Moksha* is an Indian term roughly defined as liberation. He tried to explain how sin and karma are related, and how Christ releases/liberates the believer from both.

In 1947, the Church of South India was created by the merger of the Anglicans, the Wesleyan (British) Methodists, and the South India United Church (continuing the Presbyterian and Congregationalist missionary efforts). Three years later, following a quarter of a century as a leading Anglican priest, Appasamy was elected bishop and called to serve the Coimbatore Diocese. He died on May 2, 1975.

While most remembered for his appropriation of bhakti insights, Appapamy was strongly influenced in that direction by Sundar Singh, about whom he wrote two books.

See also INDIA.

Further reading: A. J. Appasamy, *Christianity as Bhakti Marga: A Study in the Mysticism of the Johannine Writings.* (London: Macmillan, 1927);————, *A Bishop's Story* (Madras: Christian Literature Society, 1969);————, *The Johannine Doctrine of Life: A Study of Christian and Indian Thought* (London: Society for Promoting Christian Knowledge, 1934);————, *Sundar Singh: A Biography* (London: Lutterworth Press, 1958); B. H. Streeter and A. J. Appasamy. *The Message of Sadhu Sundar Singh: A Study in Mysticism on Practical Religion* (New York: Macmillan, 1921).

Argentina

Spanish settlers and Roman Catholic missionaries entered Argentina set upon wresting political and religious control from the native peoples. Four centuries later, the church reported that it had been 99 percent effective.

Beginning early in the 19th century, Protestantism began to enter the country via immigrants from northern and western Europe. In 1818, Scots-man James Thompson, an agent of the British and Foreign Bible Society, became the first Protestant missionary. He distributed Bibles as he worked to create public education in Buenos Aires (1818–21). The CHURCH OF ENGLAND and the (Presbyterian) Church of Scotland began missionary programs in the expatriate communities. Protestants began to address the larger population when Methodists opened a church in Buenos Aires (1836) and Anglicans began a mission among the native people in Patagonia (in the far south) and among the Chaco in the north. The Christian Brethren (1882) were among the first of several groups to begin evangelistic efforts to the ethnic Spanish population.

Protestant growth was facilitated by the ambiguous relationship between the government and the Catholic Church. The government viewed the church as both an ally and an obstacle during the independence struggle and more recently in terms of government policies.

A spectrum of Protestant groups entered Argentina throughout the 20th century, usually starting with ethnic churches among the expatriates from the missionaries' own homelands. This included Lutheran denominations of German, Danish, and Swedish heritage, the Waldensian church (Italian), and the Reformed churches founded by believers from Holland, Switzerland, Scotland, Hungary, and, most recently, Korea.

Though Pentecostals arrived as early as 1908 (from Norway and Canada), real growth did not occur until after World War II. An important impetus came from Chile, where PENTECOSTALISM had thrived from early in the century. Postwar growth can be dated from 1948, when several of the smaller Pentecostal groups came together in the Union of the Assemblies of God. In 1954, evangelist Tommy Hicks appeared to have healed President Juan Peron's skin condition; Peron gave Hicks access to Argentinean radio and allowed him to rent a large stadium in Buenos Aires. During his two months in Argentina, several hundred thousand attended Hicks's meetings, and a national Pentecostal movement was created. Besides the ASSEMBLIES OF GOD, the Evangelical Pentecostal

Church of Argentina and the Svenska Fria Mission received the primary benefit from the revival.

At present, more than 20 Pentecostal denominations operate across Argentina. The largest are the two Assemblies of God, one with American and one with Swedish roots, the Evangelical Pentecostal Church of Argentina, and the Evangelical Pentecostal Church of Chile. Noteworthy in the larger Pentecostal community is the Miracles of Jesus Renewed Christian Church, more popularly known by its radio show, "Waves of Love and Peace." Founded in 1983 by Hector Gimenez, an ex-drug addict and gunfighter, it has become the largest church in Buenos Aires. Its 70,000 members and additional visitors fill the 2,500-seat church for eight daily services emphasizing salvation and healing held every day of the week.

Ecumenically, some 28 denominations are members of the Argentina Federation of Evangelical Churches, which grew out of the older Confederation of Evangelical Churches of the River Platte (that also included churches in Uruguay and Paraguay). The federation is affiliated with the WORLD COUNCIL OF CHURCHES. A number of the more conservative groups have formed the Argentine Alliance of Evangelical Churches, which is affiliated with the WORLD EVANGELICAL ALLIANCE. The several Pentecostal churches cooperate through a Pentecostal Federation.

See also SOUTH AMERICA.

Further reading: Arno W. Enns, *Man, Milieu and Mission in Argentina* (Grand Rapids, Mich.: William B. Eerdmans, 1971); Norberto Saracco, ed., *Directorio y Censo de Iglesias Evangélicas de la Ciudad de Buenos Aires* (Buenos Aires: Fundación Argentina de Educación y Acción Communataria, 1992); Waldo Luis Villapando, ed., *La Iglesias del Transplante: Protestantismo de Immigración en la Argentina* (Buenos Aires: Centro de Estidios Cristianos, 1970).

Armageddon

In the book of Revelation, Armageddon is the site of the battle of the "great day of God." (Rev. 16:15–16). It is widely identified with the ancient biblical city of Megiddo (mentioned in Judges 4–5 and II Kings 9), currently the site of archaeological digs from King Solomon's days. In conservative Christian circles, including Protestant Evangelicals, Armageddon is the site of the final battle between the forces of good and evil at the end of the temporal order as we know it.

The literal interpretation of Armageddon as the site of actual future events has gained impetus since World War II, as mass destruction through modern weaponry appears to be a realistic possibility. Those who approach the book more allegorically have suggested that Armageddon should be seen as a symbol of the continual battles between good and evil into which humanity has been drawn in the modern era. In countries with a strong Christian tradition, the word *Armageddon* has been secularized to refer to any imaginable worldwide catastrophe, whether of astronomic, environmental, or other cause.

The literature about Armageddon that circulates as APOCALYPTISM spread within the Protestant community tends to view the coming battle as a literal event, often focused around the state of Israel as a new Jewish nation in the old Holy Land.

See also PREMILLENNIALISM.

Further reading: Paul Boyer, *When Time Shall Be No More: Prophecy Belief in Modern American Culture* (Cambridge, Mass.: Belknap Press/Harvard University Press, 1992); Edgar C. James, *Armageddon and The New World Order,* rev. ed. (Chicago: Moody Press, 1981); Grant R. Jeffrey, *Armageddon: Appointment With Destiny* (New York: Bantam Books, 1988); Walvoord, *Armageddon, Oil and The Middle East Crisis,* rev. ed. (Grand Rapids, Mich.: Zondervan, 1990).

Arminianism

Arminianism is a moderate theological revision of the doctrine of predestination in CALVINISM. It seeks to reconcile God's sovereignty with human free will. Jacob Arminius (1560–1609), a minister in the Netherlands Reformed Church and a professor of theology at the University of Leiden, believed that a strict Calvinist view would make God the author of sin and humans mere automatons. The controversy he stirred continued after his death.

The followers of Arminius were known as the Remonstrants. They soon proposed five statements that affirmed (1) that before the foundation of the world, God willed the salvation of those who would through faith in Christ turn to him; (2) that Christ died for all though only those who turn to faith will find salvation; (3) that humans are in a state of apostasy and sin and have no saving grace of themselves, hence it is needful that they be redeemed; (4) that humans may resist God's grace; and (5) that those who have been saved may find victory over sin and not fall back into apostasy.

The publication of the Remonstrants' ideas created a major controversy in the Dutch church. It led to the SYNOD OF DORT (1618–19), which condemned the Arminian position by asserting in its own famous five points: the TOTAL DEPRAVITY of humankind, God's unconditional election of those whom He would save, a LIMITED ATONEMENT (i.e., Christ died only for the elect), the irresistibility of grace, and the perseverance of the saved.

This had the effect of driving the Remonstrants out of the Netherlands Reformed Church into a dissenting body that continues today. Their ideas were later picked up by John WESLEY and became integral to METHODISM, from where they passed to the HOLINESS movement and PENTECOSTALISM. Wesley chose to name his early periodical *The Arminian Magazine*. Arguments over free will versus predestination fueled popular polemics between Protestant groups throughout the 18th and 19th centuries. It would also find favor among many Baptists in the General or Free-Will segment of the movement.

Arminian views took on even more relevance as Protestants prepared to evangelize beyond Europe. The Baptist theologian Andrew Fuller (1754–1806) developed a modified Calvinism, informed by Arminian thought, that was more compatible to the missionary enterprise.

Further reading: Carl Bangs, *Arminius* (Nashville, Tenn.: Abingdon Press, 1971); George L. Curtiss, *Arminianism in History Or the Revolt From Predestinationism* (Nashville, Tenn.: Carnston & Curts, 1894); O. Glenn McKinley, *Where Two Creeds Meet: a Biblical Evaluation of Calvinism and Arminianism* (Kansas City, Mo.: Beacon Hill Press, 1959); Richard Alfred Muller, *God, Creation, and Providence in the Thought of Jacob Arminius* (Grand Rapids, Mich.: Baker Book House, 1991); Carl H. Pinnock, *The Grace of God, the Will of Man: A Case for Arminianism* (Grand Rapids, Mich.: Zondervan, 1989).

Armstrong, Annie Walker (1850–1938)
American Baptist missionary executive

Lottie MOON, the missionary to CHINA, is largely credited with opening the SOUTHERN BAPTIST CONVENTION to the value of women in its missionary program, However, Moon's challenges to the convention were largely implemented through the efforts of her American counterpart, Annie Walker Armstrong.

Born in Baltimore, Armstrong was described by acquaintances as independent, outspoken, and opinionated. Those who worked with her came to value her organizational skills.

As she lacked formal education, the church became the primary vehicle for Armstrong's formidable talents. In 1870, she helped form the Maryland Baptists Woman's Mission to Women. It was in place when the first women missionaries (other than spouses of male missionaries) were appointed under the auspices of the Southern Baptist Convention. Over the next years, a number of local women's missionary societies were formed.

In 1887, Lottie Moon, one of the original 1872 missionaries, challenged Southern Baptist women to unite in a week of prayer for foreign missions. Armstrong stepped forward as the champion of Moon's cause. She also took the lead in organizing

Annie Armstrong (1850–1938), Southern Baptist missionary executive *(Southern Baptist Historical Society)*

the many local societies and Baptist women in general into the Women's Missionary Union (WMU), and she became its first executive. She served unpaid for the next 16 years.

Armstrong set the focus for the WMU in a three-point program of education, prayer for missions, and fund-raising. The first annual Christmas offering was held in 1888. Over the next 100 years, the offering raised a cumulative total of more than $1 billion for missions. It became the largest lay organization within the Southern Baptist Convention and went on to become the largest Protestant women's missionary organization in the world.

Armstrong retired in 1906 but lived another three decades. She remained an active Southern Baptist, never marrying.

Further reading: Jacqueline Durham, *Miss Strong Arm: The Story of Annie Armstrong* (Nashville, Tenn.: Broadman Press, 1966); Elizabeth Marshall Evans, *Annie Armstrong* (Birmingham, Ala.: Woman's Missionary Union, 1963); Bobbie Sorrill, *Annie Armstrong: Dreamer in Action* (Nashville, Tenn.: Broadman Press, 1984); Ruth Tucker, *Guardians of the Great Commission.* (Grand Rapids, Mich.: Zondervan, 1988).

Armstrong, Herbert W. (1892–1986)
founder of the Worldwide Church of God

Herbert W. Armstrong, founder of the WORLDWIDE CHURCH OF GOD, developed a variant form of Adventist teachings that became quite popular internationally in the last decades of his life. While the church survived his death, it abandoned many of his ideas.

Armstrong was born on July 31, 1892, in Des Moines, Iowa, and raised as a Quaker. After dropping out of high school, he went through a series of job changes and a business failure. With his wife, Loma Dillion, he moved to Oregon, where Dillon began to study the Bible and became convinced that Saturday was the true Sabbath (a position known as SABBATARIANISM). Armstrong himself began to change his opinion on a spectrum of issues from BAPTISM to evolution. The end result was his ordination as a minister in a small Sabbatarian church, the Oregon Conference of the Church of God, in 1931.

The most important idea Armstrong accepted at this time was BRITISH ISRAELISM, which held that the Anglo-Saxon people were the modern descendants of the Ten Lost Tribes of Israel (those Israelites who had been taken captive by the Assyrians in the eighth century B.C.E.), and that the Anglo-Saxon people were the real recipients of God's promises to the Israelites, not the modern-day Jews. British Israelism had gained a following through the English-speaking world in the 19th century, but Armstrong became its major 20th-century advocate.

In 1934, Armstrong began a broadcast ministry on an Oregon radio station. Following World

War II, he moved to Pasadena, California, where the ministry blossomed. His following, known as the Radio Church of God, in 1968 became the Worldwide Church of God. He founded Ambassador College to train ministers and developed an international following. Congregations arose in the United Kingdom, Australia, New Zealand, South Africa, and the Caribbean.

Armstrong's son Garner Ted Armstrong (1930–2003) played a major role in developing the church; a charismatic speaker, he became one of the most familiar faces on television prior to his fall from grace due to illicit sexual affairs. The younger Armstrong founded his own rival group, the Church of God International.

Armstrong faced a number of controversies in the years after his son left. In 1979, his church was placed in receivership for a short period. Following his death on January 16, 1986, the relatively unknown Joseph W. Tkach Sr. (1927–95) was appointed to succeed him as Pastor General.

Under Tkach, who was himself succeeded by his son, Joseph W. Tkach Jr. (b. 1951), the Worldwide Church of God repudiated all of Armstrong's teachings on British Israelism, tithing, the Sabbath, and others issues. By the mid-1990s, the church had moved to an orthodox Evangelical Protestant theology, and by the end of the decade had been admitted as a member of the National Association of Evangelicals, whose members had previously condemned the church as a cult. In the process, a significant number of members withdrew, the majority realigning in three new church bodies, the Living Church of God, the United Church of God, and the Philadelphia Church of God.

See also APOCALYPTISM; PREMILLENNIALISM.

Further reading: Herbert W. Armstrong, *Autobiography,* 2 vols. (Pasadena, Calif.: Worldwide Church of God, 1986, 1987);———, *The United States and Britain in Prophecy* (Pasadena, Calif.: Worldwide Church of God, 1980); J. Michael Feazell, *The Liberation of the Worldwide Church of God.* (Grand Rapids, Mich.: Zondervan, 2001); George Mather and Larry Nichol, *Rediscovering the Plain Truth* (Downers Grove, Ill.: InterVarsity Press, 1997); Joseph Tkach, Jr., *Transformed by Truth* (Sisters, Ore.: Multnomah Books, 1997).

Articles of Religion

The Articles of Religion is a set of documents that established the beliefs of the CHURCH OF ENGLAND in the 16th century and then were edited by John WESLEY in the 18th century for use by the Methodists.

Following the passing of the Act of Supremacy (1534) that established the English monarch as the head of the church in the lands over which he ruled, it seemed necessary to publish a statement of church beliefs. After all, the Lutherans with whom the Church of England was associated had in 1530 published their AUGSBURG CONFESSION OF FAITH.

An initial set of articles was drawn up, approved by church authorities, and published in 1536 as The Articles of Our Faith, described as "Articles devised to establish Christian quietness and unity among us and to avoid contentious opinions." They were commonly referred to as the Ten Articles. They were Catholic in tone, the primary doctrinal concession to the Protestants being a statement that the pope did not control the church.

The next year, Archbishop Thomas CRANMER, in spite of HENRY VIII's known allegiance to Roman Catholic beliefs, authored a new set of articles, the Thirteen Articles. These were thoroughly Protestant in tone, Cranmer having drawn his inspiration from the Augsburg Confession.

Henry was not pleased. In 1539, he issued a supplementary document, the so-called Six Articles. Clearly Roman Catholic in perspective, they affirmed the real presence in the Eucharist, denied communion in both kinds, upheld clerical celibacy, and continued the practice of private masses and confession of one's sins to a priest. Lack of conformity to these articles carried heavy penalties. A commentary on the Ten Articles and the Six Articles was issued in 1543 under the title A Necessary

Doctrine and Erudition for any Christian Man, popularly known as the King's Book.

The Ten Articles, the Six Articles, and the King's Book remained authoritative in England until 1552, when they were superseded by the Forty-two Articles. Cranmer served as the primary author of the Forty-two Articles, but they were subsequently approved by the other church leaders and by King EDWARD VI and his advisers and published in English and in Latin. All these were suppressed during the reign of MARY I. In 1562, the bishops revised the Forty-two Articles, which ELIZABETH I later approved. Scottish Presbyterian John KNOX helped write these articles, which included phrases reflecting his Calvinist (Reformed Church) orientation. These Thirty-nine Articles have remained unchanged within the Anglican tradition and are frequently printed as an appendix to the BOOK OF COMMON PRAYER, though they were not included in its earliest editions.

The Methodist movement began as a revitalization movement within the Church of England in the 1740s. In the 1760s, it began to spread internationally. Most important, Methodists gathered in small groups called classes in the American colonies. Following the American Revolution, it was decided to allow the American Methodists to organize as a separate denomination. Methodist founder John Wesley set about the task of preparing materials for the new church. In the process he edited the Thirty-nine Articles and arrived at Twenty-four Articles of Religion, which in 1784 were adopted by the Americans as the statement of faith for the Methodist Episcopal Church (with the addition of a 25th article on the church's relation to the new American government). That statement of faith was carried in the Book of Discipline of the church and the several bodies that broke from it and remained in the discipline through the several mergers in the 20th century that led to the founding of the UNITED METHODIST CHURCH in 1968. The Twenty-five Articles were also passed around the world by American Methodists missions and have been retained (with appropriate local alterations) by most Methodist bodies internationally.

Both the Anglican and Methodist versions of the Articles of Religion affirm the ancient teachings of the church, including the triune god, salvation in Christ, the authority of the scriptures, original sin, and the sacraments. They also include Protestant emphases on justification by faith, the distribution of both bread and wine in the Lord's Supper, and the marriage of clergy. They contain specifically Reformed (as opposed to Lutheran) teachings on, for example, the nature of the church, which is defined as "a congregation of faithful men, in which the Word of God is preached and the sacraments be duly administered . . ." Both sets of articles carry specific refutations of certain Roman Catholic teachings, such as purgatory, transubstantiation, and lifting up the elements during the Lord's Supper.

Among the items deleted by Wesley as unnecessary for Methodists were articles on Of Works Before Justification, which in Calvinism are largely discounted, but in Methodism lauded; Of Predestination and Election, which Wesley felt would be understood in a Calvinist manner that the Methodists rejected; and Of the Traditions of the Church, which Wesley felt to be no longer at issue. Among the most popular items added to the 25 articles by groups that separated from the Methodists in America were statements on the doctrine of sanctification and holiness.

See also ANGLICANISM; METHODISM.

Further reading: J. H. Benton, *The Book of Common Prayer: Its Origin and Growth* (Boston: the author, 1910); Thomas F. Chilcoate, *The Articles of Religion* (Nashville, Tenn.: Cokesbury Press, 1960); J. Gordon Melton, ed. *The Encyclopedia of American Religions: Religious Creeds.* (Detroit: Gale Research, 1988); Kenneth N. Ross, *The Thirty-nine Articles* (London: A. R. Mowbray, 1957).

Aruba

In 1648, by the treaty of Westphalia, Holland took control of the Caribbean island of Aruba from Spain, which was grouped with the nearby islands of Curacao and Bonaire to form the Netherlands

Antilles. Raising horses and cattle became the dominant industry, rather than plantation agriculture, and the need for slave labor never developed as it did elsewhere in the region. People of African heritage constitute some 12 percent of the island's population. It separated from the Netherlands Antilles in 1986, but remains a Dutch dependency.

From its pre-Dutch days, a majority of the islands residents (over 80 percent currently) have been Roman Catholic. The Dutch introduced the Reformed Church, which is still the largest Protestant body, and the United Protestant Church of Aruba (having absorbed the small Lutheran movement that also came to the island from Holland).

A spectrum of Protestant and Free Church groups arrived in the 20th century, mostly after World War II. Of these groups, the JEHOVAH'S WITNESSES and the ASSEMBLIES OF GOD (a Pentecostal body) are the only groups to attract as many as 1,000 members.

See also CARIBBEAN.

Further reading: David Barrett, *The Encyclopedia of World Christianity,* 2nd ed. (New York: Oxford University Press, 2001); Patrick Johnstone and Jason Mandryk, *Operation World, 21st Century Edition* (Carlisle, Cumbria, U.K.: Paternoster, 2001).

The Francis Asbury statue in Washington, D.C. *(Institute for the Study of American Religion, Santa Barbara, California)*

Asbury, Francis (1745–1816) *first bishop of the Methodist Episcopal Church*

Francis Asbury, first bishop of the Methodist Episcopal Church (now a constituent part of the UNITED METHODIST CHURCH), was born at Handsworth, Staffordshire (near Birmingham), England, on August 20, 1745. His parents were members of the relatively new Methodist movement. At 13, Francis had his first religious experience and at 16 he left an apprenticeship to become a local Methodist preacher. He was 22 when he began to travel as a Methodist minister.

In 1771, Asbury was one of the preachers sent to America by John WESLEY, the founder of METHODISM, to oversee the fledgling movement that had emerged in the 1760s. Richard Wright accompanied him to Philadelphia. The next year,

Wesley named Asbury his "general assistant in America" to supervise the preachers then functioning in the colonies and the few societies that had been founded. He served until Thomas Rankin, one of the older preachers, arrived in 1773.

Following the outbreak of the American Revolution, Asbury was the only one of Wesley's preachers who remained in America. Because of Wesley's Tory sympathies, Methodists were distrusted and Asbury worked to have them accepted, first as an apolitical group, and then as loyal Americans. An opponent of all oaths, he was arrested on June 20, 1776, and fined five pounds for refusing to take Maryland's oath of allegiance. In March 1778, he retired to the Delaware home of his friend Judge Thomas White, where he remained for the next 10 months. Only in 1780 did he resume his wide-ranging travels, by which time most people had come to accept the Methodists.

After the colonists won their independence, Wesley decided to put American Methodist work on an independent basis. Unable to get help from the Anglican authorities to ordain the lay preachers then in America, he assumed the role of bishop himself and designated Thomas COKE (1747–1814) and Richard Whatcoat (1736–1806) as "superintendents" with the authority to act in his stead. Upon their arrival in America in 1784, they met with Asbury, who called the meeting at Barrett's Chapel in rural Maryland where, over the Christmas holidays, the Methodist Episcopal Church was organized. On three successive days, Asbury was ordained a deacon and an elder (minister) and consecrated as a bishop.

For the next 30 years Asbury traveled the length and breadth of America (averaging around 6,000 miles a year on horseback), encouraging preachers and assisting as he could in building the work. He kept an extensive journal, which became a basic record of the church's growth and an important document of the first generation of the national life. He decided not to marry, that he not be distracted from his primary task.

He made up for his lack of education by reading and study, even acquiring a working knowledge of Greek and Hebrew. He devoted much attention to developing the church's educational program. He left the church with some 700 fully ordained ministers (itinerants, who traveled at his direction to various assigned territories), 2,000 local preachers, and more than 214,000 members. He died in Spottsylvania, Virginia, on March 31, 1816, a week after preaching his last sermon. In 1924, a statue of Bishop Asbury on horseback was unveiled in Washington, D.C., in recognition of his role in building the United States.

See also AFRICAN-AMERICAN METHODISTS.

Further reading: Francis Asbury, *The Journal and Letters of Francis Asbury,* ed. by Elmer T. Clark, 3 vols. (Nashville, Tenn.: Abingdon Press, 1958); Frank Baker, *From Wesley to Asbury: Studies in Early American Methodism* (Durham, N.C.: Duke University Press, 1976); Emory Bucke, ed., *The History of American Methodism* (New York: Abingdon Press, 1964); Russell Richey, *Early American Methodism* (Bloomington: Indiana University Press, 1991); J. C. Rudolph, *Francis Asbury* (Nashville, Tenn.: Abingdon Press, 1966).

ashrams, Christian

Christian ashrams are spiritual retreats designed to speak to Christian converts in India. The ashram was an old feature of Hindu culture that was reborn at the end of the 19th century as part of the Hindu renaissance. Mohandas K. (Mahatma) Gandhi (1869–1948) and Rabindranath Tagore (1861–1941) established ashrams in the early 1920s. Built around an enlightened teacher (guru), the ashram was a place for retreat and intense focus upon the spiritual life. Participants could learn methods of meditation, hear teachings from sacred texts, and learn the duties of the religious life. Additionally, they could be instructed in daily living and the performance of family or occupational duties.

In the early 20th century, Christian leaders around the world were eager to mold the Christian movement, so much based in Western forms and customs, into more indigenous forms in non-Christian countries, so as not to separate converts from their family, society, and history. In the 1920s, Methodist missionary E. Stanley JONES (1884–1973), one of the more important students of Christianity and Indian culture who had spent time at both Gandhi's and Tagore's ashrams, began to explore using the form to organize the converts received into the Christian faith.

The ashram was to be a local community living together over an extended period of time. In 1930, Jones met with Rev. Yunas Sinha and Ethel Turner to initiate the first ashram at Sat Tal, India. Theologically, the ashram would evolve from the perspective laid out in Jones's classic work, *The Christ of the Indian Road.* Jesus was pictured as an Indian holy man (a *sadhu*) who placed his hands upon the lepers and brought hope to the masses, eventually dying alone but rising to walk the roads of India again. Life at the ashram was thoroughly Indian and consciously identified with Gandhi and the nationalist movement. Clothing was made of homespun khaddar cloth, a symbol of the movement. Jones help found a second ashram in 1935 in Lucknow, hoping that community could model the kingdom of God. From these two centers, ashrams sprung up across India and even in the West.

The original ashram founded by Jones evolved into an international retreat ministry, United Christian Ashrams International, whose centers conduct a set of retreats each year, most of them lasting three to seven days. As such, the ashrams serve as an interdenominational revitalization force within Protestantism in India and the 20 other countries in which they operate. A Catholic version of the Christian ashram was founded in 1950 by Jules Monchanin (1895–1957), Swami Abhishiktananda (Dom Henri Le Saux, 1910–73), and Bede Griffiths (1906–93). The Saccidanda Ashram Santivanam became the motherhouse of some 80 presently existing ashrams of Catholic initiative.

See also INDIA.

Further reading: E. Stanley Jones, *The Christ of the Indian Road* (New York: Abingdon Press, 1925); Charles Wesley Mark, *A Study in the Protestant Christian Approach to the Great Tradition of Hinduism with Special Reference to E. Stanley Jones and P. D. Devanandan* (Princeton, N.J.: Princeton Theological Seminary, Ph.D. diss., 1988); Michael O'Toole, *Christian Ashrams in India* (Indore, India: Satprakashan Sanchar Kendra, 1983); Richard W. Taylor, *The Contribution of E. Stanley Jones* (Madras, India: CLS/CISRS, 1973).

Asia

While Christianity penetrated Asia from the Middle East quite early, according to some legends even in the first century, organized Protestant missionary work only began early in the 18th century. The worldwide missionary impulse that was to become such an important part of 19th- and 20th-century Protestantism was initiated with the arrival of Bartholomew Ziegenbalg and Heinrich Plutschau at Tranquebar on July 9, 1706. They started the DANISH-HALLE MISSION, the origin of the Lutheran movement in India. The mission welcomed the first Asian converts to Protestantism, one of whom, a wealthy widow named CLORINDA, helped build the first Protestant church in Asia.

In the 1790s, as other missionary agencies were founded in England, India was considered a natural first target. In 1793, British Baptist William CAREY arrived in India with the support of the newly founded Baptist Missionary Society. The work expanded with the arrival of John and Hannah MARSHMAN, the latter being particularly helpful in gathering financial support.

Congregationalists took the lead in the 1795 founding of the LONDON MISSIONARY SOCIETY (LMS) (which also attracted support from Presbyterians and low-church Anglicans), which sent Nathaniel Forsyth as its first missionary to India in 1798. The CHURCH MISSIONARY SOCIETY (CMS), an Anglican sending agency, commissioned missionaries for India in 1813, and the British Methodists sent their first team the following year. Unable to settle in India, the group redirected their attention to Sri Lanka (then called Ceylon) returning to India in 1819.

In the meantime, the AMERICAN BOARD OF COMMISSIONERS FOR FOREIGN MISSIONS (ABCFM), founded in 1810, sent its first contingent of missionaries to India in 1812. Two of the ministers, Adoniram JUDSON and Luther RICE, converted to the Baptist faith and became key promoters of American Baptist missionary work—Rice back in the United States and Judson in Burma (now Myanmar) as its first Protestant missionary.

The second focal point for Protestants in Asia was China. Robert MORRISON, with the backing of the LMS, arrived at Macao on February 20, 1809;

he secured a post as translator and thus the right to remain. He translated the Bible into Chinese and compiled a Chinese dictionary. Among his early converts, Tsae A-ko was the first to be baptized (1814) while his first convert, LEONG FUNG FA (1787–1855), became the first Chinese minister, ordained in 1823.

As a way to get around Chinese resistance to foreigners, early German missionary Karl Gützaff (1803–51) suggested that Christian physician/evangelists be sent into the country. In 1824, Peter PARKER arrived as the first medical missionary; four years later, the Medical Missionary Society in China was established. Medical missions would subsequently spread across China, India, Korea, Japan, and then throughout Asia (not to mention other parts of the world). The spread of medical missions provided an important opportunity for women to assume leadership roles in the mission field.

The LMS developed an early interest in Malaysia, sending missionaries in 1815. At the suggestion of Robert Morrison, an Anglo-Chinese school was opened at the key trading center of Malacca in 1818. The school served the Chinese community of Malacca for the next generation.

Japan began receiving Protestant missionaries in 1859, a result of American pressure to open the country to the rest of the world. Within the first year, Episcopalian, Presbyterian, and Reformed church missionaries began work. In 1878, all restrictions on missionary activity were lifted, and both the number of missionaries and the number of churches they represented shot up dramatically.

Protestant efforts in Korea were blocked until Horace Newton ALLEN, a Presbyterian, settled in Seoul as physician to the American legation. After saving the life of a royal prince in 1884, Allen won an opening for missionaries. Within a year both Presbyterian and Methodist missionaries had arrived; in 1887, the first congregations were established. The first Korean Protestant was the young man who served as Allen's interpreter.

Through the first half of the 20th century, the early missions grew into ever larger subunits of Western denominations. Little effort was made to create indigenous churches, and as in other locations, new denominations independent of Western missions arose. Several such churches in China, like the Local Church and the True Jesus Church, grew to be substantial bodies. China also became an early target of the Pentecostal movement. In 1907, Mr. and Mrs. T. J. McIntosh, Rev. and Mrs. Alfred G. Garr, May Law, and Rosa Pittman arrived in Hong Kong, ready to spread the message of the BAPTISM OF THE HOLY SPIRIT.

World War II brought immense changes to Asian Protestantism. For example, in 1940, the Japanese government insisted that all Protestant churches merge into a single organization, the United Church of Christ of Japan. Several churches, including the SALVATION ARMY and the Anglican Church, refused and were officially nonexistent for the duration of hostilities. After the war, General Douglas MacArthur, head of American forces, called for a thousand missionaries to come to Japan. Many hundreds did arrive, but Protestantism still claims less than 2 percent of Japan's population.

Christianity was even more disrupted in those lands captured by Japanese forces. In China, for example, many Christians abandoned their homes in the coastal regions and moved far inland. Japanese forces also overran Thailand, Malaysia, and Burma.

Korea suffered from brutal Japanese rule between 1910 and the end of World War II, when the country was divided in two. The North Korean government has reduced Christianity to a token presence. In contrast, Protestantism, especially the Presbyterian Church, has thrived in the South. Seoul is now also home to the largest single Christian congregation in the world, the YOIDO FULL GOSPEL CENTRAL CHURCH, which counts its members in the hundreds of thousands.

The most significant postwar change in Asia occurred in China, where civil war brought an antireligious Communist government to power in 1949. In 1950, it expelled all foreign missionaries and moved to suppress the various indigenous churches. As a first step, it forced all of the Protestant churches into one organization, the Church of Christ of China, which was mandated to operate under what was known as the THREE-SELF PRINCIPLES. The church was expected to be self-governing, self-supporting, and self-propagating. Christianity would have to survive without the leaders and financial support of any foreign religious bodies. In addition, the church was expected to support the new government. Attempts to suppress the church in China reached their apex during the years of the Cultural Revolution (1966–76), when churches were ordered closed and religious activity forbidden altogether. That policy proved unworkable and in the late 1970s was replaced by limited toleration.

The missionaries expelled from China were redistributed to other nearby lands, many becoming active in diaspora Chinese communities. Most affected was Taiwan. Taiwan had received Protestant missionaries since the middle of the 19th century, with Presbyterians having the most success. Only the Presbyterians were able to develop significant work during the 1915–45 Japanese occupation. The Republic of China on Taiwan was initially hostile to Christian missions, but gradually moved toward a more tolerant policy.

As the 21st century begins, Asia remains the area of the world with the smallest percentage of Christians (about 8.5). The total Protestant population is about 200,000,000 or 5.5 percent. South Korea is the most Christianized of Asian countries, about 35 percent Protestant. Hong Kong, the longtime British colony and now a Special Administrative Region of the Peoples Republic of China, has taken on a special role. The site to which many Christians fled following the Chinese revolution, Hong Kong is known for its free religious environment. It is now home to a multitude of Christian denominations and the staging area for missionary organizations throughout southeastern Asia.

See also BANGLADESH; BHUTAN; CENTRAL ASIA; INDIA; INDONESIA; JAPAN; KOREA, PEOPLES REPUBLIC OF (NORTH); KOREA, REPUBLIC OF (SOUTH); RUSSIA; SINGAPORE; SRI LANKA.

Further reading: Gerald H. Anderson, ed., *Biographical Dictionary of Christian Missions* (Grand Rapids, Mich.: William B. Eerdmans, 1998); David Barrett, *The Encyclopedia of World Christianity,* 2nd ed. (New York: Oxford University Press, 2001); Donald Hoke, ed., *The Church in Asia* (Chicago: Moody Press, 1975); Patrick Johnstone and Jason Mandryk, *Operation World, 21st Century Edition* (Carlisle, Cumbria, U.K.: Paternoster, 2001); J. Herbert Kane, *A Global View of Christian Missions* (Grand Rapids, Mich.: Baker Book House, 1971); J. Gordon Melton and Martin Baumann, eds., *Religions of the World: A Comprehensive Encyclopedia of Beliefs and Practices* (Santa Barbara, Calif.: ABC-CLIO, 2002); A. Scott Moreau, ed., *Evangelical Dictionary of World Missions* (Grand Rapids, Mich.: Baker Book House, 2000).

Assemblies of God

The Assemblies of God, an American-based Pentecostal denomination, has emerged as one of PENTECOSTALISM's most globally important organizations.

Pentecostalism spread quickly during and after the famous AZUSA STREET REVIVAL in Los Angeles, which began in 1906. While in general agreement with the teachings of mainstream Protestant Christianity, the early exponents had also been associated with the HOLINESS movement that grew out of Methodism. Holiness teachings emphasized the possibility of becoming sanctified or perfect in love in this life. Within Holiness churches, the experience of sanctification, a gift of the Holy Spirit to the believer, actually became the norm. Pentecostal believers shifted the emphasis from the experience of sanctification to the BAPTISM OF THE HOLY SPIRIT, which evidenced itself by the believer speaking in unknown tongues.

Very early in the movement, as the revival progressed, a difference of opinion developed. The founders of the movement taught that the baptism of the Holy Spirit was a third experience for the believer, available only to those who had first experienced salvation (become a believer) and then sanctification. However, some teachers, most notably William H. Durham (1873–1912), rejected the idea of Wesleyan sanctification and argued that Christ's finished work becomes available to the believer immediately after they accept Christ as savior.

The earliest Pentecostal organizations, such as the CHURCH OF GOD (CLEVELAND, TENNESSEE) and the INTERNATIONAL PENTECOSTAL HOLINESS CHURCH, continued the Wesleyan emphasis and taught three experiences of justification, sanctification, and baptism of the Holy Spirit. The Assemblies of God brought together those who came out of the FINISHED WORK CONTROVERSY in basic agreement with Durham's position (though Durham passed away prior to its formation).

In April 1914, leaders of the many independent Pentecostal congregations met in Hot Springs, Arkansas, and created the Assemblies of God congregational fellowship to promote cooperation and coordination. Wishing to avoid the strong central authority associated with the Methodists or Presbyterians, the participants appointed a General Council without any constitution or doctrinal statement.

Nevertheless, the assemblies were forced to take doctrinal position when it was discovered that some of the leaders had adopted a non-Trinitarian theology, popularly known as the Apostolic or "Jesus Only" teachings. In 1916, the assemblies adopted a Statement of Fundamental Truth and disfellowshipped the JESUS ONLY PENTECOSTALS. The ordination of women (*see* WOMEN, ORDINATION OF) became another controversial issue. Though the assemblies always accepted women as evangelists and missionaries, only in 1935 were they fully accepted into the ordained ministry.

Pentecostals always favored world evangelism. Most believed that the revival at Azusa signaled the end-time descent of the Holy Spirit that heralded a significant spread of Christianity in the last days before Christ's return. One of the primary motivations for forming the Assemblies of God was to support missionary activity. The mission program was impressive even in its first generation. Assemblies churches and indigenous Pentecostal movements emerged in many countries. In the last decades of the 20th century, however, the growth of the assemblies was spectacular; it spearheaded the spread of Pentecostalism around the world.

In the late-1980s, the U.S. church was forced to deal with scandal as two prominent televangelists connected to the assemblies, James Bakker and Jimmy Swaggart, were charged with sexual misconduct and defrocked. Swaggart's ministry, in particular, had been a major source of mission funds. In the 1990s, the assemblies also took some initial steps to face its history of racial division, primarily by supporting the formation of the interracial ecumenical Pentecostal/Charismatic Churches of North America.

The assemblies currently report 1.5 million members in the United States and 41 million members worldwide. The spectacular growth has fueled an extensive program of higher education based in 19 universities, colleges, and seminaries in the United States. Missionary personnel are now supported in more than 190 countries. Globally, the American-based Assemblies of God should not be confused with the many national Assemblies of God movements that originated in the PENTECOSTAL/FILADELPHIA CHURCH in Sweden.

Further reading: Edith Blumhoffer, *Assemblies of God: A Chapter on the Story of American Protestantism,* 2 vols. (Springfield, Mo.: Gospel Publishing House, 1989); ———, *Restoring the Faith: the Assemblies of God, Pentecostalism, and American Culture* (Champaign: University of Illinois Press, 1993); William W. Menzies, *Anointed to Serve* (Springfield, Mo.: Gospel Publishing House, 1971); Vinson Synan, *The Century of the Holy Spirit* (Nashville, Tenn.: Thomas Nelson, 2001).

Assemblies of God in Great Britain and Ireland (AGGBI)

Like the ASSEMBLIES OF GOD in the United States, the Assemblies of God in Great Britain and Ireland (AGGBI) was organized by previously existing Pentecostal congregations. In February 1924, John

Nelson Parr (1886–1976) invited representatives to a meeting in Birmingham. Promising to honor local autonomy, he proposed a united fellowship of assemblies sharing the same Fundamental Truths, who would maintain fellowship through district presbyteries and a General Presbytery composed of local pastors and elders. The formal organization took place at a second gathering in London in May with 80 people in attendance, including Donald Gee (1891–1966) and John (1893–1981) and Howard Carter (1891–1971). In the first year, 76 assemblies in England, Wales, and Northern Ireland joined.

The Fundamental Truths resembled those of the American assemblies concerning such issues as the Trinity, the authority of the Bible, the need for a personal experience of conversion, and water BAPTISM by immersion. It affirmed that healing comes only through Jesus' atonement, by means of the BAPTISM OF THE HOLY SPIRIT, the first sign of which is speaking in tongues (glossolalia). The Holy Spirit was seen as empowering the ordinary believer for Christian service.

At the end of 1925, the Pentecostal Missionary Union (PMU), formed in 1909, merged with the assemblies as its missionary arm. It had already established work in China and India and has subsequently come to operate in more than 30 countries, primarily by supporting indigenous national Pentecostal churches.

The Assemblies of God grew steadily in its first generation (200 affiliated assemblies by the end of the 1920s, 500 in the mid-1950s), thanks in part to the healing ministry of evangelist Stephen Jeffreys (1876–1943). In response to slower growth, a new constitution was adopted in the 1980s, grouping congregations into districts and providing for regional and national superintendents. In 1947, Donald Gee helped create the PENTECOSTAL WORLD FELLOWSHIP; he subsequently emerged as an important voice of Pentecostalism internationally.

The international headquarters of the assemblies is located at Nottingham, England. It supports a Bible college, Mattersey Hall, for training leaders.

Further reading: Donald Gee, *Wind and Flame* (Nottingham, U.K.: Assemblies of God Publishing House, 1967); *A Sound and Scriptural Union: An Examination of the Origins of the Assemblies of God in Great Britain and Ireland 1920–25*; W. K. Kay, *Inside Story* (Mattersey, U.K.: Mattersey Hall, 1990); ———, *Pentecostals in Britain* (Carlisle, U.K.: Paternoster, 2000); R. Massey, (Birmingham, U.K.: University of Birmingham. Ph.D. dissertation, 1987).

Augsburg, Peace of

By the mid-16th century, Lutheran leaders were firmly in control of Scandinavia and most of northern Germany. While the Catholic Holy Roman emperors had at times scored marked successes against Protestant strongholds, all their victories proved temporary. Three decades of war and the deaths of tens of thousands had had almost no impact. One attempt to resolve the issues, the Augsburg Interim of 1548, had proved a failure.

In 1554, Charles V, unable to resolve the situation by either war or religious diplomacy, turned the problem over to the Imperial Diet. The timing proved bad for the Roman Catholic Church. Pope Julius III died just a month after it began. His successor lived only a month, and the diet's work was largely concluded before Paul IV (1555–59), who would eventually emerge as a forceful leader of the Counter-Reformation, could make his presence felt.

Thus the German princes hammered out an agreement on their own. Promulgated in September 1555, it allowed each of the many rulers to choose freely between Lutheranism or Catholicism. The main provision read: "In order to bring peace to the Holy Roman Empire of the Germanic Nation . . . let neither his Imperial Majesty nor the Electors, Princes, etc., do any violence or harm to any estate of the empire on the account of the Augsburg Confession, but let them enjoy their religious belief, liturgy and ceremonies as well as their estates and other rights and privileges in peace."

Each ruler would be considered head of the local church and would choose the people's religion. Those who disagreed could move to another land. CALVINISTS (centered in Switzerland), SOCINIANS, and ANABAPTISTS were not included in the accord.

The Peace of Augsburg, limited though it was, was an important step in the development of religious toleration and then religious freedom in Europe and was the first time Protestants received legal recognition from Catholics. It would not be until the Peace of Westphalia in 1648 that the Calvinists would receive such recognition.

The Peace of Augsburg did not end religious conflict in Europe. The Counter-Reformation was soon fighting to reclaim territory from Protestants where possible; it managed to stop the Protestant advance in many countries. Protestants on their part worked to win over isolated Catholic territories within Germany. But the Peace did establish a time of relative calm during which Lutherans could concentrate on nurturing church life rather than merely surviving as a movement.

See also LUTHERANISM.

Further reading: Roland H. Bainton, *The Reformation of the Sixteenth Century.* (Boston: Beacon Press, 1952); Harold J. Grimm, *The Reformation Era,* 2nd ed. (New York: Macmillan, 1973); Hans J. Hillerbrand, *The Reformation: A Narrative History Related by Contemporary Observers and Participants* (Grand Rapids, Mich.: Baker Book House, 1981).

Augsburg Confession of Faith

The Augsburg Confession of Faith of 1530 was the first major Protestant creedal statement. It aimed to reconcile differences between reformers, and find common ground with Roman Catholics as well. At least that was the hope of Holy Roman Emperor Charles V, who came to Germany with the stated goal of resolving the Lutheran-Catholic split that had developed in the previous decade. At that time, Muslim Turkish forces still threatened central Europe, and Charles hoped to create a united Christian front.

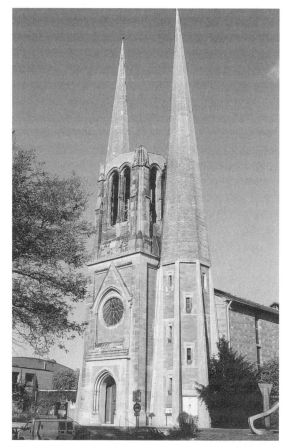

The Lutheran Church at Augsburg *(Institute for the Study of American Religion, Santa Barbara, California)*

A more limited Protestant statement had been drafted in 1529, called the Schwabach Articles. It was designed as a common Protestant position around which a political union of German princes could be created. In the interim, Roman Catholic theologian John Eck had circulated a document accusing the Lutherans of more than 400 heretical positions, and a response was deemed necessary. At Augsburg, Philip MELANCTHON assumed the tasks of reconciling positions adopted by different reformers; affirming Protestant allegiance to the faith of the ancient church as articulated by the ecumenical councils of the fourth through seventh centuries; clarifying what was distinctive in

Protestant beliefs (and hence Reformation demands); and mollifying Roman Catholics as much as possible. The text was prepared in Latin and German and was read before the imperial court on June 30.

The confession opens with an affirmation of the Nicene Creed and a condemnation of the recognized heresies. An early paragraph strongly affirms justification by faith. The real presence of Christ in the Eucharist is supported, but not the sacrificial nature of the Mass. Toward the end, the document presents the Lutheran positions on clerical celibacy, giving the cup to the laity during the Eucharist, and the disregard of monastic vows. There is no mention of purgatory or the universal priesthood of believers. In effect, the confession separated Lutherans from both the Anabaptists and the followers of Ulrich ZWINGLI in Zurich, Switzerland.

There is no separate article on the authority of the Bible, but every Lutheran position is justified by biblical references. "Article 28 On Ecclesiastical Power" attacks the development of tradition beyond biblical sources.

Following the reading of the Augsburg Confession, the emperor had Catholic authorities, including Eck, draw up a counterstatement, which was read on August 3, 1530. At that point, the emperor rejected the Protestant position. Though he ordered that the confession not be published, copies were already in circulation. In addition, Melancthon wrote a lengthy *Apology* answering the Roman Catholic attack on the confession. Charles gave the Protestants until February 1531 to return to the Catholic fold.

The Augsburg Confession is still definitive to LUTHERANS and Lutheran churches worldwide. In 1580, the confession, Melancthon's *Apology,* and some subsequent doctrinal statements were gathered together with the ancient creeds of the Ecumenical Church into the *Book of Concord,* the ultimate statement of Lutheran belief. Today, Lutherans disagree on the literalness with which one must accept the Augsburg Confession and the *Book of Concord.*

Further reading: *The Book of Concord: The Confessions of the Evangelical Lutheran Church,* trans. from German and Latin and ed. by Theodore G. Tappert in collaboration with Jaroslav Pelikan, Robert H. Fischer, and Arthur C. Piepkorn (Philadelphia: Fortress Press, 1959)—one of several English editions available; Eric Gritschand and Robert Jenson, *Lutheranism: The Theological Movement and Its Confessional Writings* (Philadelphia: Fortress Press, 1976); Wilhelm Maurer, *Historical Commentary on the Augsburg Confession* (Philadelphia: Fortress Press, 1986); J. Gordon Melton, *The Encyclopedia of American Religions: Religious Creeds,* 2 vols. (Detroit: Gale Research, 1988, 1994); David Scaer, *Getting into the Story of Concord: A History of the* Book of Concord (St. Louis: Concordia, 1977).

Australia

Protestantism came to Australia along with CHURCH OF ENGLAND chaplains assigned to tend to the religious need of the original colonists, most of whom were convicts. Rev. Richard Johnson sailed with the first fleet of ships to Australia in 1788, which brought 1,100 convicts, soldiers, and settlers to what is now Sydney. Rev. Samuel Marsden arrived five years later; he played a commanding role through the end of the 1820s, though he was joined after the turn of the century by Presbyterians, Congregationalists, Baptists, and Methodists. New settlers swelled the ranks of the Church of England most of all; the church also benefited from Australia's status as part of a global network of British colonies. Methodists were the second-largest group through the 19th century.

In 1824, the Anglicans were reorganized as an archdeanery in the Diocese of Calcutta. The first archdeacon, Thomas Scott, arrived in 1825. He was succeeded in 1829 by William Grant Broughton. In 1836, Broughton was consecrated as bishop with jurisdiction over the entire country. During his tenure, the land was divided into several dioceses.

Methodists, Presbyterians, and Congregationalists all established work early in the 19th century.

The Methodists formed their Australian conference in 1855, which divided into multiple conferences in 1873. Several Methodist groups that had split from the main body over the years merged back into the Methodist Church in 1902.

Presbyterians organized a synod aligned with the Church of Scotland in 1840. Almost immediately the split then occurring in Scotland was imported to Australia; the synod split into two factions over issues of congregational vs. synod and state power. Presbyterians representing other Presbyterian bodies in Great Britain also came to Australia, but most Australian Presbyterians merged into the Presbyterian Church of Australia in 1901.

Congregationalists came to Australia as a part of the larger movement by the LONDON MISSIONARY SOCIETY to evangelize throughout the South Pacific.

In the 1970s, all three churches began to seek unity. In 1977, they merged into the Uniting Church of Australia (though a third of the Presbyterians refused to adhere). The Uniting Church remains the third-largest in Australia after Roman Catholics and Anglicans. The Lutheran Church, which had begun work in 1838, did not join in the merger.

In the 20th century, Australia became home to the same kind of religious pluralism that was common to most Western countries, with more than 100 different Protestant and Free Church groups. Among the more interesting are the Two-by-twos or Go-Preachers, who oppose denominationalism to such a degree that they refuse to have a name for the group. The movement was founded in England by William Irvine (1863–1947). Irvine appointed itinerant ministers to travel in pairs, just as Jesus had done with his disciples. In the early years of the 20th century, he began to preach that the end of the dispensation of grace would come in 1914. His followers rejected that idea and with it Irvine as general overseer. Since that time, the movement has had a collective leadership in each country. It has been particularly successful in Australia, relative to the size of the population, and now counts more than 100,000 members.

Australia was for many years the home of John Alexander Dowie (1847–1907), who as a Congregational minister in 1875 began a divine healing ministry. Three years later, he resigned from the church to start an independent movement. He was an important independent religious voice in Australia through the 1880s, in spite of unsuccessful attempt at politics. In 1888, he moved his flamboyant and controversial ministry to the United States, where he founded the Christian Catholic Church.

Australian PENTECOSTALISM had but the slimmest of ties to the movement in the United States. In 1906, Methodist Sarah Jane "Jeannie" Lancaster (1858–1934) received some Pentecostal literature from England, which directed her attention to the BAPTISM OF THE HOLY SPIRIT. She had an intense experience in 1908 that included speaking in tongues. The following year she opened the Good News Hall in North Melbourne, from where Pentecostalism spread across the country. Those associated with her took the name Apostolic Faith Mission. Today, the largest Pentecostal movement is the ASSEMBLIES OF GOD, which counts more than 100,000 adherents, but numerous Charismatic revival movements have been launched in the last generation, a few of which, such as the Christian Life Churches, International and the Christian Outreach Center have become international movements.

Many of the older Protestant churches are members of the National Council of Churches in Australia, which is affiliated with the WORLD COUNCIL OF CHURCHES. More conservative groups are affiliated with the Australian Evangelical Alliance, which is in turn a member of the Evangelical Fellowship of the South Pacific and the WORLD EVANGELICAL ALLIANCE.

See also NEW ZEALAND; SOUTH PACIFIC.

Further reading: I. Breward, *A History of the Australian Churches* (St. Leonards, Australia: Allen & Unwin, 1993); I. Gillman, *Many Faiths, One Nation: A Guide to the Major Faiths and Denominations in Australia* (Sydney: Collins, 1988); R. A. Humphries and

R. S. Ward, eds., *Religious Bodies in Australia: A Comprehensive Guide* (Wantirna, Australia: New Melbourne Press, 1995); S. Piggin, *Evangelical Christianity in Australia: Spirit, Word, and World* (New York: Oxford University Press, 1996).

Austria

LUTHERANISM spread into Austria from neighboring Germany very quickly, reaching both Salzburg and Vienna in the 1520s. At the same time, the mountainous western part of the country became a refuge for the Swiss BRETHREN, who had been driven out of Zurich. The Habsburg royal family, though staunchly Roman Catholic, did little to suppress the Protestants, granting Lutherans a limited legal status in 1552. The situation changed following the 1620 arrival in Vienna of Jesuits eager to spread the Counter-Reformation. By the end of the Thirty Years' War (1618–48), Protestantism's legal status was revoked in an attempt to impose Roman Catholic uniformity.

When the Lutherans were granted recognition in 1552, the Reformed believers were excluded. Eventually the two communities united as the Evangelical Church of the Augsburg and Helvetic Confessions in Austria (with each church retaining internal autonomy), which henceforth carried the Protestant tradition in the country. After surviving as an underground movement for more than a century, Protestants found new life during the reformist reign of Emperor Joseph II (1780–90). Though a pious Roman Catholic, Joseph proclaimed an Edict of Tolerance in 1781 that gave the Evangelical Church a legal status similar to that of Catholicism.

While there was some religious differentiation during this period, the proliferation of Protestant sects did not really begin until new laws on religious freedom were passed in 1867 and 1874. State approval was granted to both the Moravians (who today have no active congregations in Austria) and the Methodists (related to the UNITED METHODIST CHURCH). After World War I, further efforts were made to separate church and state.

A wide spectrum of Protestant and Free Church groups become active in 20th-century Austria. Among the more prominent are the JEHOVAH'S WITNESSES (founded in 1910), the SALVATION ARMY (1927), and the SEVENTH-DAY ADVENTIST CHURCH (1947). One of the largest groups, the Evangelical Association of Congregations of Austria, with 10,000 members, was not founded until 1991. There is relatively little sign of Pentecostal activity in Austria.

The Evangelical Council of Churches in Austria includes the Evangelical Church, by far the largest member, as well as the Baptist, Methodist, Anglican, Old Catholic, and Orthodox churches. It is affiliated with the WORLD COUNCIL OF CHURCHES. Conservative Evangelicals are associated in the Oesterreichische Evangelische Allianz, which is affiliated with the WORLD EVANGELICAL ALLIANCE. The Protestant and Free Church community in Austria consists of fewer than a half million believers or about 5 percent of the population. Of that number, 350,000 are members of the Evangelical Church.

Further reading: M. Lawson, ed., *Christliches Handbuch für Österreich: Kirchen und Missionen* (London: MARC Europe, 1991); *Religions in Austria. Austria documentation.* (Vienna: Federal Press Service, 1990).

Azariah, Vedanayagam Samuel
(1874–1945) *first Indian Anglican bishop*

Vedanayagam Samuel Azariah was born in Vellalavilai in southern India on August 17, 1874, the son of an Anglican pastor. Azariah was educated at Madras University and Madras Christian College. He began working with the Y.M.C.A. and helped found the Indian Missionary Society of Tinnevelly in 1903 and the National Missionary Society in 1905. He obtained ordination in 1909 in order to become a missionary.

In 1910, he attended the World Missionary Conference in Edinburgh, where he impressed attendees by advocating that missionaries adopt a more Asian view of life. Two years later, though only 38, he was consecrated as the first Anglican bishop of Dornakal.

Church union was high on his list of priorities as bishop; he prepared the ground for the Church of South India, though he died two years before it actually came into existence. In response to mass conversions of Indians who had not fully learned the faith and life of Christianity, he proposed that the new Christians be allowed to retain some aspects of the caste system in the short term, with the goal of eventually abandoning it.

Azariah wrote a number of books on subjects such as BAPTISM, marriage, and stewardship. He died on January 1, 1945.

See also ANGLICANISM; INDIA.

Further reading: Vedanayagam Samuel Azariah, *Christian Giving* (Madras, India: Christian Literature Society for India, 1941); Carol Graham, *Azariah of Dornakal* (London: S. C. M. Press, 1946); Susan B. Harper, *In the Shadow of Mahatma: Bishop V. S. Azartiah and the Travails of Christianity in British India* (Grand Rapids, Mich.: William B. Eerdmans, 2000).

Azusa Street revival

A Pentecostalist revival broke out in a church on Azusa Street in Los Angeles in 1906, which became one of the more important events in 20th-century Protestantism.

PENTECOSTALISM can be traced to the Topeka, Kansas, Bible school led by Charles Fox PARHAM. There, in 1901, Agnes Oznam became the first person in modern times to pray for and receive the BAPTISM OF THE HOLY SPIRIT with the expectation that the baptism would manifest in her speaking in tongues. The experience soon spread to the other students and to Parham.

Parham eventually settled in Houston, Texas, where he introduced his new teaching to an African-American Holiness minister, William J. SEYMOUR. Seymour was subsequently invited to become the pastor of a small congregation in Los Angeles in February 1906. His preaching about the Pentecostal experience was rejected, so he

moved his ministry to the home of supporters on Bonnie Brae Avenue. On April 9, Edward Lee and Jamie Evans Moore became the first of the group to experience the baptism of the Holy Spirit and to speak in tongues. Others soon followed, including Seymour himself on April 12.

Crowds at the Bonnie Brae home soon forced a move to larger facilities. A former African-American Methodist church building, then used as a stable, was rented at 312 Azusa Street. A makeshift pulpit and seating area were put together, and a meeting was held every night. While the original group was largely African-American, the new audience included many whites and Latinos. The congregation took the name Apostolic Faith Mission.

On April 18, a Los Angeles newspaper ran an article critical of Seymour and the meetings. That same day, the San Francisco earthquake occurred. Frank Bartleman, an itinerate evangelist, then published a tract tying together the revival, the earthquake, and the end of the world. Tens of thousands of copies were distributed all along the West Coast. Thousands soon flocked to the small building. A periodical was begun, *The Apostolic Faith,* whose circulation soon climbed into the tens of thousands.

Services were held thrice daily. Seymour continued to lead the group, which gradually became predominantly white. People from across North America came to Azusa Street, experienced the baptism, and returned home to found new Pentecostal churches or to convince older groups to accept the new teachings. Others, believing that speaking in tongues would give them facility in foreign languages, left Azusa for the mission field.

The Azusa Street revival fed a desire for interracial harmony in the Pentecostal movement. Over the next few decades, however, the movement became segregated, with only a few exceptions, most notably the Pentecostal Assemblies of the World. The Azusa Street experience bore fruit in the largely African-American CHURCH OF GOD IN CHRIST and the major white Pentecostal bodies, the ASSEMBLIES OF GOD and the CHURCH OF GOD (CLEVELAND, TENNESSEE).

By the end of the decade, Seymour was somewhat isolated from the movement, though he continued to lead the more permanent congregation at the Lost Angeles Mission and traveled for a national African-American Pentecostal denomination. Because he was black, his role in the revival was largely forgotten by several generations of white Pentecostal leaders, but he became more widely known in the post–civil rights era of Pentecostalism.

Further reading: Frank Bartleman, *How Pentecost Came to Los Angeles* (Los Angeles: the author, 1928)—this small work reprinted under variant titles; Larry Martin, *Holy Ghost Revival on Azusa Street: The True Believers* (Joplin, Mo.: Christian Life Books, 1998); Cheryl J. Sanders, *Saints in Exile: The Holiness-Pentecostal Experience in African American Religion and Culture* (New York: Oxford University Press, 1996); Vinson Synan, *The Century of the Holy Spirit: 100 Years of Pentecostal and Charismatic Renewal, 1901–2001* (Nashville, Tenn.: Thomas Nelson, 2001).

B

Baba, Panya (b. 1932) *international Evangelical missionary leader*

Panya Baba was born in Karu, Nigeria. He developed a personal faith in Christ as a teenager and attended Kagoro Bible College. He completed his studies at All Nations Christian College in the United Kingdom and the Fuller Theological Seminary in the United States.

Returning to Nigeria, he held both pastoral and administrative posts with the Evangelical Churches of West Africa, one of Nigeria's largest church bodies, an outgrowth of the Sudan Interior Mission of the 1890s. In 1970, he became director of his denomination's Mission Society. In that capacity, in 1980 he persuaded the Nigerian Evangelical Fellowship to form a coordinating agency for the various indigenous missionary bodies in the country—the Nigeria Evangelical Missions Association, founded in 1982. The association included initially his own organization, plus the Calvary Ministries, His Grace Evangelical Movement, the Christian Missionary Foundation (CMF), Christ Ambassador Evangelical Team, and the Community Missions Board of the Church of Christ in Nigeria. Baba became the first chairperson, a position he retained for seven years.

In 1988, he became president of the Evangelical Churches of West Africa. After the completion of his second term, he became the group's foreign missions director and missions consultant.

Apart from his official positions, Baba emerged as an important international voice in the global Evangelical community for indigenous missions. He urged cooperation among indigenous mission agencies and between them and Western-based agencies. In particular, he has advocated the development of partnership models for cooperation between independent churches in former foreign mission fields and Western sending agencies. He networked 12 daughter churches of the Sudan Interior Missions into the Evangelical Fellowship Missions Association, which he served as first coordinator. He was active through the last half of the 20th century in the WORLD EVANGELICAL ALLIANCE and served on the board of the AD 2000 Movement, which sought to place a missionary among all the peoples of the earth who had yet to hear a Christian witness in their own language.

See also AFRICA, SUB-SAHARAN; NIGERIA.

Further reading: Panya Baba, "Cross-cultural evangelism," in J. D. Douglas, ed., *Proclaim Christ Until He Comes* (Minneapolis, Minn.: World Wide, 1990), 170–76; ———, "The Seriousness of the Task," *International Journal of Frontier Missions* 11, 1 (January

1994), 1–4—Available online. URL: http://www.ijfm.org/PDFs_IJFM/11_1_PDFs/ijfm_11_1.pdf.

Babylonian Captivity of the Church, The

The Babylonian Captivity of the Church was a pamphlet written by Martin LUTHER calling for reform of the church's sacramental system. It was one of three pamphlets he issued at the end of 1520 in response to the papal bull *Exurge Domin.* The pope had given Luther 60 days to recant his earlier statements or face excommunication. Instead, Luther's pamphlets made a significant break with Rome, leading directly to his appearance before the Diet of Worms.

In *The Babylonian Captivity,* Luther wrote that just as Israel had been taken captive to Babylon in the sixth century B.C.E., the Christian sacraments had been taken captive by Rome.

Luther argued that the Bible authorized only two of the church's seven sacraments, BAPTISM and the LORD'S SUPPER (or Eucharist). The others—holy orders, confirmation, marriage, penance, and extreme unction—should be done away with (though he was open to further consideration of penance). Turning to the Eucharist, he wrote that the cup of wine should be shared with the laity, just like the wafer. He charged that the doctrine of TRANSUBSTANTIATION, the doctrine that the real presence of Christ enters the sacramental elements once the words of consecration are spoken, was a 12th-century innovation. He then argued that baptism did not by itself, apart from faith, impart any spiritual blessing.

Though he completely rejected Catholic teachings on the sacraments, Luther never came to his own clear understanding of them.

Further reading: Martin Luther, *Martin Luther's Basic Theological Writings,* ed. by Timothy F. Lull (Philadelphia: Fortress Press, 1989); ———, *Three Treatises* (Philadelphia: Fortress Press, 1970); "A Prelude on The Babylonian Captivity of the Church (6 October 1520) by Martin Luther, 1483–1546." Available online. URL: http://www.ctsfw.edu/etext/luther/baby-

lonian; E. Gordon Rupp, *Luther's Progress to the Diet of Worms* (New York: Harper & Row, 1964).

Bahamas

Spain first discovered the Bahamas, a set of islands more than 500 miles southeast of Miami, but they were first settled by the British, who brought the CHURCH OF ENGLAND with them. Methodists arrived in 1786, loyalists from the losing side of the American Revolution. The Methodist community gained new strength in the 1870s with help from the African Methodist Episcopal Zion Church, which had expanded rapidly following the American Civil War and launched its own international missionary program.

Though growing in absolute numbers, the Anglican community became a smaller percentage of the Protestant community as rival churches grew. Being so close to the United States, the islands saw missionaries from many different North American churches. British Baptists sent their first representative in the 1830s. The Bahamas National Baptist Union is now the second-largest church on the islands.

Among 20th-century arrivals, the fastest-growing have been the SEVENTH-DAY ADVENTIST CHURCH, which began work in 1909, and the CHURCH OF GOD (ANDERSON, INDIANA). As in many of the Caribbean islands, PENTECOSTALISM has flourished, especially in the decades since World War II; its followers are scattered among a variety of churches such as the ASSEMBLIES OF GOD, the CHURCH OF GOD (CLEVELAND, TENNESSEE), and the CHURCH OF GOD OF PROPHECY.

Ecumenically, the Bahamas Christian Council is notable for its broad base. It includes Pentecostals, Methodists, the Brethren, Baptists, Catholics, Greek Orthodox, and the SALVATION ARMY. It is associated with the WORLD COUNCIL OF CHURCHES.

See also CARIBBEAN.

Further reading: V. M. Prozan, *A Religious Survey of the Bahamas Islands* (Columbia, S.C.: Columbia Bible

College, M.A. thesis, 1961; David Barrett, *The Encyclopedia of World Christianity,* 2nd ed. (New York: Oxford University Press, 2001); Patrick Johnstone and Jason Mandryk, *Operation World, 21st Century Edition* (Carlisle, Cumbria, U.K.: Paternoster, 2001).

Bakht Singh (1902–2000) *Indian Christian evangelist*

Bakht Singh was born in Punjab (in what is now Pakistan) and raised as a Sikh. He graduated from Punjab University and studied engineering at King's College, London. On a trip to Canada in 1928, he met a group of evangelical Christians, read through the New Testament several times, and was baptized on February 4, 1932. He returned to India in 1933, determined to be an evangelist, but with a clear understanding that he would not affiliate with any existing church organization. Among his first converts were his parents.

As he began his evangelical endeavors, first in northern India and then in Madras, his oratorical abilities were quickly recognized. From his evangelistic meetings, congregations began to form. As a result of his first major revival in Madras in 1941, he founded the first such church, Jehovah Shammah, which grew to include several thousand believers. After World War II, he concentrated his work in the state of Andhra Pradesh, where he helped found 1,300 congregations. He also founded assemblies, as the congregations were called, in western Europe, North America, Australia, and New Zealand. He led the first American Holy Convocation in Syracuse, New York, in 1974 and returned annually for the next decade. Similar convocations were begun in Sarcelles, France, in 1977.

Bakht Singh was, like his contemporary in China, Watchman NEE, very much influenced by the PLYMOUTH BRETHREN movement and particularly one of its leading spokespersons, Anthony Norris GROVES, who advocated the development of new churches in new lands without the apparatus of foreign missionary control or even the need for ordained ministers. These ideas had originally been put to effective use in India by John Aurlappen. Singh also agreed with Watchman Nee that there should be only one Christian church in each city, where people from varied backgrounds and speaking different languages in a single Christian gathering could become an impressive demonstration of church unity.

In the assemblies raised up by Bakht Singh, Sunday worship would begin with an all-night prayer vigil. The morning service would begin with singing and last for several hours, punctuated by the celebration of the LORD'S SUPPER and up to three sermons. A meal would follow the service; then the congregation would go into the surrounding neighborhoods to conduct open-air evangelistic services.

Bakht Singh and some of his associates moved to Elim, Hyderabad, in 1950. They later established facilities to house the local ministry and train coworkers. This center, which Singh called Hebron, became the focal point for the fellowship of assemblies. Singh also led mass meetings, called holy convocations, for members and potential converts.

Bakht Singh taught a conservative evangelical faith and was a popular speaker for interdenominational evangelical missionary gatherings, especially the annual conferences held in Urbana, Illinois, by Inter Varsity Christian Fellowship. He authored a number of books, many transcripts of his sermons and training messages, and articles in the movement's periodical, the *Hebron Messenger.*

Bakht Singh died on September 17, 2000. His funeral brought hundreds of thousands of mourners to Hyderabad. The assemblies related to Bakht Singh's work included more than 200,000 members at the beginning of the 21st century.

See also INDIA; LOCAL CHURCH.

Further reading: Bakht Singh, *Behold I Will Do a New Thing,* 4th ed. (Hyderabad, India: Hebron, 1994). Available online. URL:http://www.brother bakhtsingh.org/Behold.pdf.; ———, *The Greatest Secret.* (Hyderabad, India: Hebron, 1975); ———,

How to Find God's Will. (Hyderabad, India: Hebron, n.d.); T. E. Koshy, "Brother Bakht Singh—a Saint of God: An Overview of His Life and Ministry." Available online. URL:http://www.brotherbakhtsingh.org/biography.html.

Baltic States

The Protestant faith in Lithuania, Latvia, and Estonia dates to the first years of the Reformation. Andreas Knopcken (1468–1539) came to Latvia in 1521 to spread Lutheran ideas using the Church of Saint Peter in Riga as his platform. Latvian leaders signed the Peace of Augsburg (*see* AUGSBURG, PEACE OF) in 1555; Lutheranism subsequently became the majority religion.

Lithuanian nobles studying at Wittenberg and Leipziz in the 1520s returned home eager to institute reforms. Lutheranism spread quickly through the countryside, and by the middle of the century the country was predominantly Lutheran; the Reformed church had also made its appearance and was growing. Progress came to a radical halt in 1564, however, when Polish-Lithuanian King Sigismund II (1520–72) instituted the Counter-Reformation at various levels in the country. The subsequent entry of the Jesuits in force pushed Protestantism into the western and northern parts of the country.

Lutheranism reached Estonia in 1524. Its rise to dominance was aided by the publication of a prayer book and catechism in 1535 and a new Bible translation in 1539. Over the centuries, other Protestant groups arrived. Moravians began to migrate into Estonia in 1727. Though the German contingent was expelled in 1745, they made some converts who later played important roles in the development of the Moravian movement as well as the development of Estonia.

A spectrum of Protestant groups arrived in the region in the mid-19th century—Baptists, Methodists, and Seventh-day Adventists. The first Baptist congregation was established in Riga in 1860; a union of Baptists churches was formed in 1879.

After the Russian annexation of Lithuania at the end of the 18th century, the Lutheran and Reformed Churches aided the struggle for cultural and linguistic survival alongside the Catholic Church. Russian rule did not stop the arrival of a variety of churches. By the time Lithuania regained its independent status in 1918, the NEW APOSTOLIC CHURCH and PENTECOSTALISM had established their initial congregations. The Roman Catholic Church resumed its privileged position, with Russian Orthodoxy as its most prominent rival.

Following World War II, Latvia, Estonia, and Lithuania were incorporated into the Soviet Union. All three countries suffered from Soviet policies that included the repression of religion and the attempt at Russification. In 1990–91, the three countries withdrew from the disintegrating Soviet Union. They all now have constitutions that recognize religious pluralism. Lutheranism currently vies with Roman Catholicism for dominance in Latvia and with Orthodoxy for dominance in Estonia. It remains a small but important church in Lithuania, where Roman Catholicism and Orthodoxy predominate. Tallinn, Estonia, has become the center of the United Methodist Church in the region and the site of its new seminary. Pentecostalism has had it greatest response in Latvia, where it reports some 10,000 members.

See also ESTONIA; LATVIA; LITHUANIA.

Further reading: Ilmo Au and Ringo Ringvee, *Kirkud ja kogudused Eestis* (Tallinn, Estonia: Ilo, 2000); David Barrett, *The Encyclopedia of World Christianity,* 2nd ed. (New York: Oxford University Press, 2001); Nikandra Gillis, *Religija, Vesture, Dzive: Religiska dzive Latvija* (Riga: Institute of Philosophy and Sociology, Latvian Academy of Sciences, 1993); Donatas Glodenis and Holger Lahayne, eds., *Religijos Lietuvoje* (Šiauliai: Nova Vita, 1999); D. Krueger, *Lutherans in Latvia and Estonia* (Lansing, Ill.: the author, 1984); A. Musteikis, *The Reformation in Lithuania: Religious Fluctuation in the Sixteenth Century* (Boulder, Colo.: East European Monographs, 1988); *World Methodist Council, Handbook of Information* (Lake Junaluska, N.C.: World Methodist Council, 2003).

Bangladesh

Bangladesh became independent from Pakistan in 1971. The new nation declared itself an Islamic state in 1973, and in 1988 added a clause to the constitution making Islam the state religion. An attempt to evict all foreign missionaries in 1978 was stopped in the face of international pressure.

The early Baptist effort in India, usually associated with William CAREY (1761–1834), spread to Dinajpur, East Bengal, by 1795. By 1816, the church was established in Dacca, now Bangladesh's capital. Mass conversions took place around Mymensingh, among peoples who were neither Hindu nor Muslim. Baptists from Australia, Great Britain, the United States, and New Zealand have supported the work over the years, which has resulted in three denominations, the Baptist Sangha, the Bangladesh Baptist Fellowship, and the Mymensingh Garo Baptist Convention.

Soon after the Baptists, missionaries from the CHURCH OF ENGLAND, British Presbyterians, and Lutherans of various national backgrounds arrived. The Lutheran work is now carried by the Bangladesh Evangelical Lutheran Church. Presbyterians and Anglicans united in the 1970s to become the Diocese of Dacca of the Church of Pakistan. After independence, the diocese reorganized as the Church of Bangladesh.

Though a Muslim country, Bangladesh has been relatively open to Christian missionaries, and new missions have continued to arrive. Some relatively recent groups such as the German-based NEW APOSTOLIC CHURCH have built substantial followings.

PENTECOSTALISM came to Bangladesh after World War II. The ASSEMBLIES OF GOD, with 15,000 members, is by far the largest Pentecostal fellowship, but the movement has produced a variety of smaller groupings and the Pentecostal message has spread into some of the older churches.

Bangladesh is home to one of the most interesting Christian movements in the world, the Messianic Mosques. Similar to the Messianic Judaism movement in the West, believers accept Jesus as savior but refuse to leave Muslim culture or their Muslim families. They have developed a style of worship that resembles that of a mosque. There are an estimated 100,000 Messianic believers. Some Western missionaries have tried to adopt a similar approach as a means of reaching Muslims.

The Church of Bangladesh and the Bangladesh Baptist Sangha are members of the WORLD COUNCIL OF CHURCHES. They have joined with other Bangladesh churches to form the Bangladesh National Council of Churches. Other groups have formed the National Christian Fellowship of Bangladesh, affiliated with the WORLD EVANGELICAL ALLIANCE. In spite of two centuries of activity, the Protestant-Free Church community in Bangladesh constitutes less than 1 percent of the country's population.

See also ASIA; INDIA; PAKISTAN.

Further reading: David Barrett, *The Encyclopedia of World Christianity,* 2nd ed. (New York: Oxford University Press, 2001); J. C. Hefley and M. Hefley, *Christ in Bangladesh* (London: Coverdale House, 1973); J. Herbert Kane, *A Global View of Christian Missions* (Grand Rapids, Mich.: Baker Book House, 1971); G. Soddy, *Baptists in Bangladesh: An Historical Sketch of More Than One Hundred Years' Work in the Baptist Missionary Society in Bengal* (Khulna, Bangladesh: Literature Committee, National Council of Churches, Bangladesh, 1987).

baptism

At the time of the Reformation, the SACRAMENTS, those ceremonial acts that dramatized biblical events even as they served as a sign of God's presence, became a key issue between Roman Catholics and Protestants and among Protestants themselves. Protestants dropped five of the seven Roman Catholic sacraments and moved to bring the remaining two, the LORD'S SUPPER (Eucharist) and baptism, into line with their new theological perspective. During the 16th century, the Lord's Supper received the bulk of attention, as the major issue dividing Lutherans, Reformed, and Anglicans. Each continued the Roman Catholic practice of baptizing infants.

The Roman Catholic Church maintained that through baptism, one is freed from original sin (and other sins committed prior to baptism), reborn as a child of God, and admitted into the church. Lutherans and Anglicans had similar beliefs. The Lutheran AUGSBURG CONFESSION OF FAITH stated that the grace of God is offered through baptism. Calvinists (including Arminians) generally considered baptism as an outward and visible sign of an inward and spiritual grace. Baptism paralleled the act of God in washing the sins from the soul of the person being baptized.

A small group of dissenters in Switzerland, known as the Swiss Brethren, raised the issue of baptism as essential to their vision of a reformed church. They rejected the idea of a state church including all of the population. Instead, the church should welcome and baptize only those who made a profession of faith after they reached the age of accountability, that is, adulthood (which occurred at a much earlier age than now).

Infant baptism was invalid. The founding members of the Swiss Brethren rebaptized each other, thus becoming known as ANABAPTISTS (rebaptizers). An early Anabaptist statement, the SCHLEITHEIM ARTICLES, explained: "Observe concerning baptism: Baptism shall be given to all those who have learned repentance and amendment of life, and who believe truly that their sins are taken away by Christ. . . . This excludes all infant baptism, the highest and chief abomination of the pope."

The Anabaptist position would be passed on to MENNONITES and the BAPTISTS. The Baptists emerged as the most radical wing of the Puritan movement in England. They accepted a congregational form of church governance, separation of the church from the state, and the practice of believer's baptism (only those who had first professed faith could be baptized). The first Baptist church appears to have been formed by dissenters from the CHURCH OF ENGLAND who had taken

Methodist minister Steven Peralta baptizes an infant by sprinkling, the common mode in the Wesleyan tradition. *(Institute for the Study of American Religion, Santa Barbara, California)*

refuge in Holland at the beginning of the 16th century.

Believer's (adult) baptism was a distinctly minority position among Protestants until the 19th century, when the Baptist movement experienced a dramatic spread across Europe and North America and assumed a leading role in the world Protestant missionary movement. In those areas in which Protestantism was first being established, adult baptism became a major issue.

From the start, Baptists also differed with other churches over how to perform baptism. The Catholic Church used affusion, pouring water over the head, especially for infants, though immersion was allowed for those of older years. This practice was commonly continued in the

Anglican, Lutheran, Presbyterian, and Reformed churches.

Some Anabaptists practiced baptism by immersion, but only Baptists made it the exclusive method, starting in the 1630s at the London congregation headed by John Spilsbury. As stated in the London Confession of Faith of 1644, immersion symbolized "the washing the whole soul in the blood of Christ," and was "a confirmation of our faith, that as certainly as the body is buried under water, and riseth again, so certainly shall the bodies of the Saints be raised by the power of Christ in the day of the resurrection."

The Bible itself does not clearly specify which mode of baptism is preferable. Baptists pointed to Romans 6:4, where Paul speaks of being buried with Christ in baptism, and Matthew 3:16, in which Jesus comes up out of the water after being baptized by John. Methodists, who favored sprinkling, stressed Ezekiel 36:24–29 or I Peter 1:2. Those who practice pouring compared it with God's pouring out His Spirit on the day of Pentecost (Acts 2). Whatever their preference, most Protestants accepted any mode of baptism as legitimate, while Baptists accepted only immersion.

In later years, some Baptists found an essential connection between baptism and salvation. They cited biblical passages such as Acts 2:38, which quotes Peter: "Repent, and be baptized every one of you in the name of Jesus Christ for the remission of sin." Baptism, they now believed, was a necessary step in the process of salvation. This view, termed *baptismal regeneration,* was popular in the American frontier Restoration Movement, most notably in the Churches of Christ and the Christian Church (Disciples of Christ), from which it passed to a variety of other new denominations, including the Church of Jesus Christ of Latter-day Saints. Most Baptists rejected this position.

Other novel approaches to baptism remain the preserve of small groups. German Baptist Brethren (today the Church of the Brethren and related groups) still practice triune immersion. They dip new believers three times, once each for the three persons of the Trinity. Other churches identify baptism with the Baptism of the Holy Spirit and have discontinued water baptism. A few groups, such as the Salvation Army, have discontinued the practice of baptism altogether.

Baptists, most other Protestants, and Roman Catholics all agreed on the trinitarian formula found in the Great Commission (Matthew 28:19): "Go ye therefore, and teach all nations, baptizing them in the name of the Father, and of the Son, and of the Holy Spirit." But starting in 1913, some Pentecostals have interpreted Acts 2:38 and other passages as calling for baptism "in the name of the Lord Jesus Christ" alone, in line with their rejection of the traditional doctrine of the Trinity. To these Pentecostals, Jesus is the only God. Referring to Matthew 28:19, they argued that Jesus was the name of the Father, the Son, and the Holy Spirit. These apostolic or Jesus Only Pentecostals have subsequently become a significant minority voice within the Pentecostal community.

In the 20th-century Ecumenical movement, mutual recognition of baptism became an important issue. While progress between Protestants, Eastern Orthodox, and Roman Catholics has been limited, that within the Protestant movement has been significant, leading to intercommunion agreements between Protestant churches and the formation of the Leuenberg Church Fellowship. Today, only a minority of Protestant churches, mostly in the Baptist or Restoration Movement traditions, insist that new members be rebaptized.

See also Babylonian Captivity of the Church, The.

Further reading: Jay E. Adams, *The Meaning and Mode of Baptism* (Phillipsburg, N.J.; Presbyterian and Reformed Press, 1975); Rollin S. Armour, *Anabaptist Baptism: A Representative Study* (Scottdale, Pa.: Herald Press, 1966); *Baptism, Eucharist and Minister 1982–1990. Report on the Process and Responses.* Faith and Order Paper No. 149 (Geneva: World Council of Churches, 1990); Alexander Carson, *Baptism . . . Its Mode and Subjects* (Grand Rapids, Mich.: Kregel Publications, 1981); Nicholas Lossky, et al., eds., *Dictionary of the Ecumenical Movement* (Geneva/Grand

Rapids, Mich.: WCC Publications/William B. Eerdmans, 1991); J. Gordon Melton, *The Encyclopedia of American Religions: Religious Creeds,* 2 vols. (Detroit: Gale Research, 1988, 1994); W. H. Murk, *Four Kinds of Water Baptism* (St. Paul, Minn.: Northland, 1947); John R. Rice, *Bible Baptism* (Murfreesboro, Tenn.: Sword of the Lord, 1943); Thomas O. Summers, *Baptism* (Nashville, Tenn.: Southern Methodist, 1882).

baptism of the Holy Spirit

The term *baptism of the Holy Spirit* derives from several biblical passages, the most important being Acts 1:5, in which the risen Christ tells the apostles to wait for the promise of the Father, about which He had spoken, "John, as you know, baptized with water, but you will be baptized with the Holy Spirit, and within the next few days." The phrase also appears in Acts 1:8 and 2:32–33. All four Gospels quote John the Baptist as saying, "I indeed baptize you with water unto repentance: but He that cometh after me . . . shall baptize you with the Holy Ghost and with fire" (Matt. 3:11; Mark 1:8; Luke 3:16; John 1:26–27).

The Roman Catholic Church believes the Holy Spirit is bestowed during the sacrament of confirmation. The Lutheran, Reformed, and Anglican churches continued the practice of confirmation, but they did not consider it a sacrament; any connection to a baptism of the Holy Spirit was largely neglected.

The issue was raised anew in the 19th-century HOLINESS MOVEMENT. Believers who had experienced a saving faith in Jesus Christ were led to expect a second similar experience in which they would be sanctified, made perfect in love. Many Holiness leaders associated full sanctification with the baptism of the Holy Spirit.

Late in the 19th century, some Holiness people began to speak about a third experience—a baptism of fire. The Fire-Baptized movement influenced those who were present at the founding event of the Pentecostal and Charismatic movements, which occurred at Charles Fox PARHAM's new school in Topeka, Kansas, in 1901. Searching the New Testament for accounts of the reception (or baptism) of the Holy Spirit, students concluded that it was always associated with speaking in tongues (glossolalia). On January 1, 1901, one of the students received the Spirit and spoke in tongues. Since that time, the baptism of the Holy Spirit evidenced by speaking in tongues has been the defining event of Pentecostal life.

In Pentecostal thought, those who have faith in Jesus Christ as savior have their sins forgiven and are destined for heaven. However, they often lack the joy, power, and motivation to live the Christian life and be active disciples. The baptism of the Spirit conveys those qualities and equips the believer with gifts (I Corinthians 12) that assist their personal ministry and lead to a life of fruitfulness (Galatians 5:22–23).

In the early Pentecostal movement, those with a Holiness background insisted that the baptism of the Spirit was reserved for those who had already been sanctified, while others suggested that it was an experience immediately available to everyone. Pentecostal founders Charles Parham and William J. SEYMOUR advocated the first position, while Baptist minister William H. Darham was the first to deny it.

Later believers, especially in the Charismatic movement, tended to downplay the connection between baptism of the Holy Spirit and speaking in tongues. The baptism could be manifested though the reception of any one of the gifts of the Spirit—healing, prophecy, and so forth.

As the Charismatic movement spread within the Roman Catholic Church, the hierarchy refused to abandon the old tradition relating the baptism of the Holy Spirit to confirmation. Catholic Charismatics now speak of the "release" of the Holy Spirit, previously conveyed during confirmation.

See also PENTECOSTALISM.

Further reading: Dennis Bennett, *How to Pray for the Release of the Holy Spirit. What the Baptism or Release of the Holy Spirit Is and How to Pray for It* (South Plainfield, N.J.: Bridge, 1985); Stephen B. Clark, *Confirmation and the "Baptism of the Holy Spirit"*

(Plainfield, N.J.: Logos International, 1971); Richard Gilbertson, *The Baptism of the Holy Spirit. The Views of A. B. Simpson and His Contemporaries* (Camp Hill, Pa.: Christian Publications, 1993); Kilian Mcdonnell, *Christian Initiation and Baptism in the Holy Spirit: Evidence from the First Eight Centuries* (Collegeville, Minn.: Liturgical Press, 1991); Oral Roberts, *The Baptism with the Holy Spirit (and the Value of Speaking in Tongues Today)* (Tulsa, Okla.: Oral Roberts Evangelistic Association, 1964).

Baptists

Baptists constitute one of the largest Free Church movements within the Protestant community. Their theological origins can be traced back to

Baptists took the lead in bringing Protestantism to Mexico City. *(Institute for the Study of American Religion, Santa Barbara, California)*

ANABAPTISTS/MENNONITES of the early Reformation, but their history really begins as a small fringe of the Puritan movement in 17th-century England.

Puritanism arose early in the reign of ELIZABETH I (r. 1558–1603). Elizabeth had imposed the VIA MEDIA (middle way) on the CHURCH OF ENGLAND as a compromise between what she perceived to be the best of Roman Catholicism and Calvinist Protestantism, appointing bishops to govern the state church. In reaction, many Protestants who would accept nothing less than complete reform set up their own independent movements to pursue the goal of a "purified" church (hence the name *Puritans*). The largest group favored PRESBYTERIANISM—the leadership of the church by elders (presbyters). Another group advocated CONGREGATIONALISM, which favored a church built of autonomous congregations. One radical faction of Puritans advocated complete separation from the state; the church, they believed, should be composed only of adults who made a profession of faith and were subsequently baptized.

The first person to publicly advocate this position was John Smyth (c. 1570–1612), a graduate of Cambridge and an Anglican priest. After his views got him into trouble in England, he founded a Baptist church in the Netherlands (1609). Thomas Helwys, who was with Smyth in Holland, established the first Baptist church in England three years later. These churches were not Calvinist in doctrine. They agreed with Jacob Arminius that Christ's death had atoned for everyone's sins, not just those of the elect; furthermore, everyone was free to believe in Christ. The Smyth and Helwys congregations are generally looked upon as the parents of the General or Free Will Baptists.

The Calvinist Baptists, on the other hand, grew out of a separatist Calvinist congregation founded in 1616 by Henry Jacob in the Southwark section of London. Sometime in the next two decades, the congregation split over the issue of infant BAPTISM. It appears that a church of Calvinist faith practicing adult baptism was operating in London by 1634. It was called a Particular Baptist church for its belief that Christ offered a particular atonement, that is, he died just for the elect, who were predestined to believe in him. The label *Baptist* was coined by critics of the movement, but by the late 17th century believers were calling themselves by that name.

Both the General and Particular Baptists came to believe that baptism should be by immersion. This was an English innovation; their Mennonite associates in Holland generally baptized by sprinkling or pouring.

Quite early in their history, General Baptists began to form regional associations for fellowship between congregations; in 1654 they created a National Assembly with limited authority over local congregations. The assembly experienced a schism in 1699 over the Unitarian views of some leaders (denying the deity of Christ and hence the Trinity). The more conservative believers formed the General Baptist Association. A reunion occurred in 1731, but General Baptists were in decline until Dan Taylor (1738–1816), a convert from METHODISM (which held similar theological views), brought new life to the movement, helping to found the New Connection of General Baptists in 1770, which absorbed many General Baptist churches (others moving into the Unitarian fold).

Particular Baptists were much slower in creating national organs, although they were able to unite over doctrinal issues. In 1644, seven Particular Baptist congregations in the London area published an initial Confession of Faith. By 1677, after the movement had spread throughout England, a second London Confession was printed, anonymously. Immediately following the Act of Toleration of 1689, some 107 congregations gathered to formally adopt the Confession of 1677. It has become the most popular statement worldwide of the Calvinist Baptist position.

The emergence of a hard-line Calvinist (sometimes called hyper-Calvinist) minority got in the way of any further unity. These Baptists understood God's election to mean they should not address the Gospel to anyone outside the church, who might not be of the elect. Andrew FULLER (1754–1815) revived the evangelistic impulse among Particular Baptists, which eventually led to the founding of the Baptist Missionary Society (1792). The enthusiasm generated by the missionary endeavor led in 1813 to the formation of the BAPTIST UNION OF GREAT BRITAIN, the first national organization of Particular Baptists.

Over the 19th century, Particular and General Baptists cooperated on a growing number of endeavors; in 1891, they merged, and the Baptist Union continued as the agency of both. Meanwhile, through the Baptist Missionary Society, the movement had been carried worldwide, especially throughout the British Empire.

The Baptist movement in North America goes back to Roger WILLIAMS, the New England dissenter. Williams adopted Baptist views after leaving Massachusetts and founding his separatist colony in Providence, Rhode Island. The first Baptist church in what became the United States was established there in 1639. Though Williams remained a Baptist for only a short time, the church continued under other pastors.

A second Baptist congregation, in Newport, Rhode Island, emerged among the followers of Anne HUTCHINSON, who first set up a church in Newport in 1639. Hutchinson withdrew two years later in a doctrinal dispute—she argued for the authority of the inner light, while fellow Massachusetts exile John Clarke stressed the authority of Scripture. Through the 1640s, Clarke's church became distinctly Baptist in faith and practice; it split along Particular-General lines in the 1660s, with one group leaving to found the first General Baptist Church in America.

In 1688, Elias Keach formed a Baptist church in an Irish suburb of Philadelphia. An earlier Pennsylvania Baptist congregation did not survive. Keach became the major evangelist for the Baptist cause in the region for the next generation. Baptists appeared in South Carolina about this time, though evidence is sparse. Recorded Baptist history in the South begins when a group from Maine moved to Charleston around 1696.

Both General and Particular Baptists drew strength from the First Great Awakening in the 1740s, sparked largely by the preaching of George WHITEFIELD. As the revival proceeded, the growing

Particular Baptist community divided into Regular Baptists, many from Congregational backgrounds, who rejected the emotional displays characteristic of the revival meetings, and Separate Baptists, who embraced the revivals. Isaac Backus (1724–1806) emerged as the leading spokesperson of the Separate Baptists. General Baptists tended to divide into Free-Will Baptists and Six-Principle Baptists; the latter emphasized the six principles they found in Hebrews 6: 1–2.

In the 19th century, both General and Particular Baptists, who had already formed a number of regional associations, moved toward national association. Foreign missionary zeal was the catalyst among Particular Baptists, especially following the conversion of two Congregationalist missionaries to the Baptist faith. In 1814, one of the missionaries returned to America and organized the General Missionary Convention of the Baptist Denomination in America. Subsequently, a publishing unit and a Home Missionary Society were created. What became the AMERICAN BAPTIST CHURCHES U.S.A. developed when these three organizations began meeting jointly in the 1820s. In 1845, the Baptists split over the slavery issue, and the Southern churches formed the SOUTHERN BAPTIST CONVENTION, whose central offices would assume most of the functions of those agencies that remained in the hands of the Northern Baptists. By the last half of the 20th century, the Southern Baptist Convention had become the largest Protestant body in North America.

Almost all the 50-plus Baptist denominations in America are outgrowths of either the American Baptist Churches U.S.A. or the Southern Baptist Convention. Several of those emerged as a result of the Fundamentalist/Modernist controversy of the 1920s and 1930s. Older groups include the Primitive Baptists, who emerged in the 1820s in opposition to the organizations then being formed. Even earlier, in the 17th century, a few Baptists in New England had accepted SABBATARIANISM and formed a Seventh-day Baptist fellowship.

The great majority of Baptist churches worldwide can trace their existence to either the Baptist Missionary Society of Britain or the two major Baptist fellowships headquartered in the United States. German Baptists, inheritors of a different tradition, were responsible for the spread of Baptist churches through eastern Europe and the lands of the former Soviet Union.

Most Baptist churches worldwide are members of the BAPTIST WORLD ALLIANCE.

Further reading: W. L. Lumpkin, *Baptist Confessions of Faith,* rev. ed. (Valley Forge, Pa.: Judson Press, 1969); H. Leon McBeth, *The Baptist Heritage: Four Centuries of Baptist Witness* (Nashville, Tenn.: Broadman Press, 1987); Albert W. Wardin, ed., *Baptists Around the World: A Comprehensive Handbook* (Nashville, Tenn.: Broadman and Holman, 1995).

Baptist Union of Great Britain

In the 17th and 18th centuries, Baptists in England were organized around independent congregations, with some regional associations emerging in the 1700s. The first national organization was the Particular Baptist Society for the Propagation of the Gospel among the Heathen (or more popularly, the Baptist Missionary Society), founded by William CAREY (1761–1834) and Andrew FULLER (1754–1815).

In light of the society's success, London pastor Joseph Ivimey called for a union of congregations that would support Sunday schools, help build church buildings, and send preachers to the more remote parts of the country. An initial meeting held in 1812 led to a more formal meeting in 1813, at which time the Baptist Union was formed.

At the time, Baptists were divided between CALVINIST ideas of predestination and the ARMINIAN emphasis on free will. The Baptist Union tended to be supported by the Calvinist (or Particular) Baptists. In 1816, the Armenian or General Baptists formed the Foreign Baptist Mission, patterned on the Baptist Missionary Society; they had already formed the Connection of General Baptists in 1770. In 1891, the General Baptist organizations merged into the Baptist Union and Baptist Missionary Society.

The Baptist Union has been among the most ecumenically oriented of Baptist groups. It hosted the organizing meeting of the BAPTIST WORLD ALLIANCE in 1905, and it subsequently joined the WORLD COUNCIL OF CHURCHES. As the 20th century came to an end, the Baptist Union reported some 140,000 members in the United Kingdom. Though relatively small, it has had a significant role in the spread of Baptist church life globally.

See also BAPTISTS.

Further reading: H. Leon McBeth, *The Baptist Heritage: Four Centuries of Baptist Witness* (Nashville, Tenn.: Broadman Press, 1987); A. C. Underwood, *A History of Baptists* (London: Carey Kingsgate Press, 1947).

Baptist World Alliance

The idea for a Baptist World Alliance can be traced to a 1904 article written by Archibald T. Robertson (1863–1934), a professor at the Southern Baptist Theological Seminary in Louisville, Kentucky. Robertson sent the article to a host of global contacts, including British Baptist J. H. Shakespeare, editor of the *Baptist Times and Freeman* in London. At Shakespeare's invitation, delegates from Baptist churches in 23 countries gathered in London July 11–19, 1905, and created the Baptist World Alliance. The delegates chose the word *alliance* to avoid any appearance of competition with existing Baptist denominational fellowships (variously known as unions, associations, or conventions).

The new organization set as its main goal the promotion of fellowship between the world's Baptists. In the previous century, the Baptists had been transformed from a largely English-speaking community in the United Kingdom and North America into a worldwide fellowship with Baptists on every continent and in most countries of the world. The alliance also hoped to speak on issues of mutual concern such as world peace and religious freedom—many Baptist groups were struggling to survive in predominantly Roman Catholic countries. Increasingly after World Wars I and II, the alliance accepted its role as a coordinator for distributing relief funds in response to emergencies.

Shakespeare became the first general secretary, a post he held for 20 years. Headquarters remained in London until 1941, when the German bombing forced a transfer to the United States, its current home. After the war, a European headquarters, now located in BULGARIA, was established. Other regional offices have been opened in ARGENTINA, Ghana, INDIA, and the BAHAMAS.

The alliance has identified with the WORLD COUNCIL OF CHURCHES (WCC) but avoided formal affiliation in order to maintain support from many conservative Baptist bodies who consider the council anathema. The SOUTHERN BAPTIST CONVENTION, a prominent founding member of the alliance, is notably absent from the National Council of Churches and the WCC.

In 2003, the alliance reported 206 Baptist unions and conventions in membership, representing some 47 million baptized believers.

See also BAPTISTS.

Further reading: Baptist World Alliance. Available online. URL: http://www.bwanet.org; H. Leon McBeth, *The Baptist Heritage: Four Centuries of the Baptist Witness* (Nashville, Tenn.: Broadman Press, 1987).

Barclay, Robert (c. 1648–1690) *early Quaker apologist*

Robert Barclay was born around 1648 at Gordonstown, Morayshire, Scotland. Sent by his father to study in France, Barclay almost became a Roman Catholic, but eventually he joined his father in adhering to the recently formed Society of Friends (QUAKERS). In 1670, he married a Quaker, Christian Millison.

His learning and bent for theology quickly pushed Barclay to the fore in the still fragile movement. He came to public notice in the mid-1670s in a controversy with the Quakers' opponent William Mitchell. His book *Theses Theologiae* (1676) sparked a public debate in Aberdeen. Most controversial was his claim that the inner light, which according to Quakers everyone possesses as a natural link with God, is superior to reason or even Scripture.

Barclay is most remembered today as the author of *An Apology for the True Christian Divinity*, published in Latin in 1676 and in English two years later. He traveled widely for the Quaker cause. Like his contemporary George FOX (1624–91), Barclay was arrested and imprisoned on several occasions for his views.

During the last years of his life, he was able to turn his acquaintance with the future King James II to use. With his help, a group of Quakers including William PENN purchased half the island of Jersey in 1681; they elected Barclay as their governor. He died on October 3, 1690.

Further reading: Robert Barclay, *An Apology for the True Christian Divinity: as the Same is hold forth, and Preached, by the People, called Scorn, Quakers; Being a full Explanation and Vindication of their Principles and Doctrines . . . Written in Latin and English by Robert Barclay, and son* (Newport, R. I.: James Franklin, 1729);———, *A Catechism and Confession of Faith* (Philadelphia: Joseph James, 1788); D. Elton Trueblood, *Robert Barclay: A Portrait of the Life and Times of a Great Quaker Intellectual Leader* (New York: Harper & Row, 1968).

Barmen Declaration

Following Hitler's rise to power in Germany in 1933, the Nazi Party put pressure on German Protestants to restate their faith in a manner that would ideologically support Nazi claims. A "Faith movement" arose within these churches (Lutheran, Reformed, and Evangelical), advocating "positive Christianity." Their program included uniting the churches in each of the 29 German states into a single body under a bishop,

active opposition to Marxism, and a denunciation of pacifism. The German Christians, as they were generally called, wanted to end any missions to Jews, fire all pastors of Jewish ancestry, and disavow intermarriage between Christian Germans and ethnic Jews. Their program amounted to an allegiance to Hitler and his racial ideas.

In summer 1933, the German Christians scored a decisive victory in the elections of the state churches, and a national bishop for the German Protestants was designated. A minority of church leaders led an opposition force called the Confessing Church movement. At its first synod, at Wuppertal-Barmen on May 29–31, 1934, it issued a statement written mainly by theologians Karl BARTH (Reformed) and Hans Asmussen (Lutheran). This Theological Declaration of Barmen refuted the program of the German Christians.

While not mentioning Hitler and the Nazis explicitly, the declaration stated clearly, "We reject the false doctrine that the Church could and should recognize as a source of its proclamation, beyond and besides this one Word of God, yet other events, powers, historic figures, and truths as God's revelation. . . . We reject the false doctrine that. . . . the Church could . . . allow itself to be given special leaders [Führer, a reference to Hitler] vested with ruling authority."

The Barmen Declaration was not accepted by the German Church, but it became the basis for the anti-Nazi activity of individuals such as Dietrich BONHOEFFER, who became a participant in an assassination attempt on Hitler, for which he was executed.

In the aftermath of World War II, the Confessing Church has become an important model for Protestants in approaching the political complexities of the contemporary world. Several churches have added the Barmen Declaration to their doctrinal statements, among the first being the United Presbyterian Church in the U.S.A. (now a constituent part of the PRESBYTERIAN CHURCH [U.S.A.]) in 1967. Barmen also became the basis for the BELHAR CONFESSION, drafted in 1982 and adopted in

1986 by the then Dutch Reformed Mission Church, as it moved to end apartheid in South Africa.

See also CREEDS/CONFESSIONS OF FAITH.

Further reading: R. Ahlers, "The Barmen Theological Declaration of 1934." *Toronto Studies in Theology,* vol. 34 (Lewiston: The Edwin Mellen Press): 39–42; Victoria Barnett, *For the Soul of the People: Protestant Protest against Hitler* (Oxford: Oxford University Press, 1992); A. C. Cochrane, *The Church's Confession under Hitler* (Philadelphia: Westminster Press, 1962); Ernst Christian Helmreich, *The German Churches under Hitler: Background, Struggle, and Epilogue* (Detroit: Wayne State University Press, 1979); J. Gordon Melton, *The Encyclopedia of American Religions: Religious Creeds,* 2 vols. (Detroit: Gale Research, 1988, 1994).

Barth, Karl (1886–1968) *German Protestant theologian*

Karl Barth, one of the most important Protestant theologians of the 20th century, was the leading proponent of NEO-ORTHODOXY, a conservative, biblically oriented theology that became prominent after the collapse of liberal Protestant theology following World War I.

Barth was born in Basel, Switzerland, on May 10, 1886, the son of Swiss Reformed minister and New Testament scholar Fritz Barth. Karl studied successively at the universities of Bern, Berlin, Tübingen, and Marburg, though he never completed his doctoral studies. He became a pastor in Switzerland in 1909 and married in 1913. During World War I, Barth became a critic of many of his former professors, among them some of the most outstanding exponents of liberal theology, which promoted an optimistic vision of Christianity's steady progress toward the Kingdom of God. Barth came to believe that liberal theology had sold out to modern culture and began to stress the gap between true Christianity and the world.

Barth became a professor at Göttingen in 1923 and at Münster shortly thereafter. In 1930, he accepted an appointment as professor of systematic theology at the University of Bonn. During the 1930s, he opposed the rise of Hitler; he was chief author of the BARMEN DECLARATION, which defined Christian opposition to the Nazis. Expelled from Germany in 1934, he moved to Switzerland, where in 1935 he began his long tenure at the University of Basel.

Barth began attracting attention with the first edition of *The Letter to the Romans* (1918), which showed a fresh appreciation for the wholly-otherness of God. He revived the approach of the medieval theologian Anselm, who believed that the basic theological task was a systematic exposition of church teachings. This led to his multivolume *Church Dogmatics* (1932–68), the writing of which consumed the rest of his life. The last volume was published posthumously.

Barth's renewed emphasis on the Bible went beyond the traditional treatment of Scripture as the simple Word of God. The Bible was the record of God's revelation; it can become the Word of God only when it functions as the means for humans to confront the gospel. God is the Wholly Other who is revealed through the Bible and who, because of his transcendence, can only be known by the revelation in Christ. The task of the church is the proclamation of the good news of Jesus Christ.

In the decades following World War II, Protestant theology experienced an unprecedented flowering; the international crisis of liberal theology led many to find inspiration and direction from Barth and colleagues such as Emil BRUNNER, Rudolf BULTMANN, and Paul TILLICH. In America, ethicist Reinhold NIEBUHR articulated an American Neo-Orthodoxy.

Barth died at Basel on December 10, 1968. At the height of his fame and influence, Barth inspired a generation (even those who disagreed with him) and left behind a number of students, most notably Jürgen Moltmann, Wolfhart Pannenberg, and Eberhard Jüngel. One of his most famous students, Deitrich BONHOEFFER, was killed by the Nazis during World War II.

Further reading: Karl Barth, *Church Dogmatics* [*Kirchliche Dogmatik*], trans. by T. H. L. Parker, W. B. Johnston, Harold Knight, and J. L. M. Haire, ed. by G. W. Bromiley and G. T. Thomson (Edinburgh: T & T Clark, 1936–75); ———, *The Epistle to the Romans,* trans. from the sixth German edition [*Römerbrief*] by Edwyn C. Hoskyns (London; Oxford; New York: Oxford University Press, 1968); G. W. Bromiley, *Introduction to the Theology of Karl Barth* (Grand Rapids, Mich.: William B. Eerdmans, 1979); Eberhard Busch, *Karl Barth: His Life from Letters and Autobiographical Texts* (Philadelphia: Fortress Press, 1976); George Hunsinger, *How to Read Karl Barth: The Shape of His Theology* (New York/Oxford: Oxford University Press, 1991).

Baur, Ferdinand Christian (1792–1860)
founder of the historical critical method of biblical study

Ferdinand Christian Baur, who helped introduce historical critical methods into the study of Scripture, church history, and theology, was born at Schmiden, Germany, on June 21, 1792. He was educated at Blaubeuren and Tübingen. He taught for nine years at Blaubeuren, during which time he wrote the three-volume *Symbolik and Mythologie* (1824–25), which earned him an appointment with the theological faculty at the University of Tübingen, where he spent the rest of his life.

A student of Hegel's historical dialectic, he strove to understand past events in the context of their time and place. Church documents, he believed, had to be understood as a part of a stream of development. His work on such topics as the atonement, Trinity, and incarnation helped create the modern discipline of historical theology.

In the 1830s, especially after the publication of the landmark *Life of Jesus* by David Friedrich STRAUSS, Baur began to concentrate on biblical history. His use of Hegel's historical dialectic helped define what became known as the Tübingen School.

Baur initially used the Pastoral Epistles (Timothy and Titus) and the works ascribed to the Apostle Paul to construct a history of the early church and the factions that vied for control. Further study convinced him that Paul was to be credited with writing only Galatians, I and II Corinthians, and Romans, and he was one of the first to question the authorship of the Pastoral Epistles.

Baur's view that the Roman Catholic Church was simply the product of the quarrels and controversies of early Christianity was cutting-edge for its time. Historical inquiry, now so integral to Christian studies, was at the time considered a destructive enterprise that questioned traditional assumptions about biblical texts and church teachings at every step.

Turning to the Gospels in the 1840s, Baur questioned the authenticity (ascribed authorship) of the Gospel of John. By this time, Baur had trained a number of students, most notably Albert Schwegler, Karl Christian Planck, and Albrecht RITSCHL (1822–89). In the late 1840s some of Baur's students took more secular teaching positions, convinced that their work was incompatible with church membership and employment. Baur himself remained convinced that his work would eventually lead to a positive view of the development of Christianity. To that end, he capped his intellectual life with a multivolume survey of the church's history, the first two volumes appearing before his death, the last one issued posthumously by his faithful associate Edward Zeller.

In the end, Baur located what he considered the essence of Christianity and its superiority in Jesus' ethical teachings, expressed in his doctrine of the Kingdom of God and the conditions of membership in it. Baur's students held to this perspective on Jesus' teachings and became leading voices of the liberal Christianity that dominated continental European Protestantism until World War I. His own historical work was quickly superseded, but Baur is still honored as a pioneer of the historical critical method. He died at Tübingen on December 2, 1860.

See also BIBLICAL CRITICISM.

Further reading: Ferdinand Christian Baur, *The Church History of the First Centuries,* 2 vols. (London/Edinburgh: Williams and Norgate, 1878–79); ————, *Paul, the Apostle of Jesus Christ: His Life and Work, His Epistles and His Doctrine, a Contribution to a Critical History of Primitive Christianity* (London/Edinburgh: Williams and Norgate, 1875–76); George Park Fisher, *Essays on the Supernatural Origin of Christianity, With Spec. Ref. to the Theories of Renan, Strauss, and the Tübingen School* (New York: Charles Scribner's Sons, 1877); Horton Harris, *The Tübingen School: A Historical and Theological Investigation of F. C. Baur and Colleagues* (Ada, Mich.: Baker Book House, 1990).

Beecher family

In the 19th century, few names were as important in American Protestantism as Beecher. The family's rise began with Lyman Beecher (1775–1863). Educated at Yale and ordained as a Presbyterian, in 1799 he became a minister of the Presbyterian church at East Hampton, Long Island, and in 1810 was called to the Congregationalist parish in Litchfield, Connecticut. A quickly won reputation landed him a church post in Boston, where he vigorously defended orthodoxy and opposed UNITARIANISM, Roman Catholicism, intemperance, and dueling (which he helped outlaw across the United States).

In 1832, Beecher became president of Lane Theological Seminary, a new Presbyterian school in Cincinnati, Ohio, which aimed at educating ministers in what was then the American West. Soon after his arrival, the faculty and student body split over slavery. When in 1834 Beecher and the faculty tried to curb abolitionist activism among students, many left for the more liberal atmosphere at Oberlin College. Beecher was later accused of being a Calvinist and charged with heresy by a conservative colleague. Though ultimately acquitted, he had to undergo the humiliation of a heresy trial.

All Beecher's seven sons became ministers. His well-educated daughters made their marks in literature.

In 1851, Beecher returned to Boston and in 1856, went to live his last years in Brooklyn, New

York, with his son Henry Ward Beecher, then a rising star.

Henry (1813–87) attended Amherst College and Lane Theological Seminary. He ministered to congregations in Indiana for a decade before becoming pastor of Plymouth Congregational Church in Brooklyn, New York, in 1847.

At Plymouth, Beecher emerged as one of the most well-known preachers in America. His sermons were noted for their power, their use of humor, and their originality, and he was frequently called upon to give lectures and after-dinner talks. In 1863, he traveled to England on a lecture tour supporting the Union cause at a time when England appeared to favor the Confederacy. Beecher began to publish his sermons in *The Plymouth Pulpit* as early as 1859; he founded a periodical, *The Christian,* in 1870 and authored a number of books.

Beecher became a leading spokesperson for the new liberal Protestantism, supporting both BIBLICAL CRITICISM and biological evolution. He formally resigned from the Congregational Church and became an independent minister, though remaining at Plymouth Church.

At the very height of his career, Beecher was almost undone by accusations of adultery with the wife of a church member. A lengthy trial in 1875 resulted in a hung jury, but the church found him innocent, and he remained its pastor until his death in 1887.

The Beecher most remembered today is Henry's sister Harriet (1811–96), born on June 14, 1811. As a young adult, she became a teacher and wrote a book on geography. In 1836, she married Calvin Stowe, with whom she had seven children, all the while writing poems, travel books, children's books, and novels.

She was lifted from obscurity by her novel *Uncle Tom's Cabin,* which provoked a national controversy when it was serialized in the *National Era,* a controversy that intensified when the book version appeared in 1852. Stowe wrote *A Key to Uncle Tom's Cabin* (1853), which extensively documented the book's realism, which had been challenged by pro-slavery critics. Now deeply involved in the antislavery cause, in 1856 she authored a second novel, *Dred,* in reaction to the infamous Dred Scott decision by the Supreme Court. Stowe continued to write until her death in 1896.

Lyman Beecher's other children also made their marks. Catherine Esther Beecher (1800–78) became a prominent educator; Edward Beecher (1803–95) pastored the prestigious Park Street Church in Boston and was a college president in Illinois; Isabella Beecher Hooker (1822–1903) became a leading suffragette. The year of Lyman's death, leading Congregationalist minister Leonard Bacon observed, "This country is inhabited by saints, sinners and Beechers."

See also CONGREGATIONALISM.

Further reading: Henry Ward Beecher, *Autobiographical Reminiscences of Henry Ward Beecher,* ed. by Truman, J. Ellinwood (New York: Stokes, 1898); ———, *Evolution and Religion* (New York: Fords Howard & Hulbert 1886); ———, *Sermons by Henry Ward Beecher Plymouth Church Brooklyn. Selected from published and unpublished discourses and revised by their author,* 2 vols. (New York: Harper, 1869); Barbara M. Cross, *The Autobiography of Lyman Beecher* (Cambridge, Mass.: The Belknap Press of Harvard University Press, 1961); Joan Hedrick, *Harriet Beecher Stowe: An American Woman's Life* (New York: Oxford University Press, 1994); Paxton Hibben, *Henry Ward Beecher: An American Portrait* (New York: Doran, 1927); Robert Shaplen, *Free Love and Heavenly Sinners: The Henry Ward Beecher Scandal* (London: Andre Deutsch, 1956); Harriet Beecher Stowe, *The Writings of Harriet Beecher Stowe,* 16 vols. (Boston: Houghton Mifflin, 1896).

Belgic Confession

The Belgic Confession is the basic doctrinal statement of Reformed Protestants in the Netherlands and Dutch Reformed churches overseas.

While Lutherans in different countries share a common set of doctrinal documents as compiled in the *Book of Concord* (1580), the various national Reformed and Presbyterian churches have tended to issue their own confessional documents.

By the middle of the 16th century, both Lutherans and ANABAPTISTS had emerged in the NETHERLANDS, and both came under severe attack by the Roman Catholic authorities when Holy Roman Emperor Charles V introduced the Inquisition. Nevertheless, under Charles's successor, Philip II (1555–98), the Reformed faith spread rapidly among the Dutch.

Around 1561, Guido De Bräs (Guy de Brès) (d. 1567), who had recently returned to the Netherlands after a period of training in Geneva, prepared a statement of the Reformed faith. A copy was sent to Philip in 1562, along with a letter in which de Bräs and his colleagues cited their desire to remain within the law if possible, and their willingness to be martyred if necessary. De Bräs was indeed eventually put to death.

A synod of Reformed elders held at Antwerp in 1566 accepted a modified version of de Bräs's statement as their confession of faith. The 1566 text was reaffirmed by several additional national synods held over the next three decades. After minor changes were made, the SYNOD OF DORT in 1618–19 proclaimed the confession one of the doctrinal standards that anyone holding office in the Reformed Church of the Netherlands had to affirm.

De Bräs's confession drew on a 1559 statement published by John CALVIN in Geneva just before de Bras's departure, but it is far more than a mere revision of Calvin's work. It includes a very strong statement concerning biblical authority, noting Peter's statement that God "himself wrote with his own finger the two tables of the law." After rejecting the Apocrypha, the confession adds, "We believe that this Holy Scripture contains the will of God completely and that everything one must believe to be saved is sufficiently taught in it."

Rejecting the role of the pope in conferring legitimacy, the Belgic Confession maintains that the true church "engages in the pure preaching of the gospel; it makes use of the pure administration of the sacraments as Christ instituted them; it practices church discipline for correcting faults . . . [and recognizes] Jesus Christ as the only Head. By these marks one can be assured of recognizing the true church."

The document recognizes only two sacraments, BAPTISM and the LORDS'S SUPPER, both of which are outward signs of God invisibly working in the believer. To distinguish the Reformed position from that of the Anabaptists, the confession affirms the public (inclusive) rather than sectarian (exclusive) nature of the church, infant baptism, and God's sanction of the civil government.

The Belgic Confession remains the basic statement of faith of the several Reformed churches that now exist in the Netherlands and those around the world derived from them, most notably in South Africa and the United States (including the Reformed Church in America and the Christian Reformed Church of North America).

See also CREEDS/CONFESSIONS OF FAITH.

Further reading: Joel R. Beeke and Sinclair B. Ferguson, eds., *Reformed Confessions Harmonized: With an Annotated Bibliography of Reformed Doctrinal Works* (Grand Rapids, Mich.: Baker Book House, 1999); P. J. S. De Klerk, *Reformed Symbolics* (Pretoria: Van Schaik, 1954); J. Gordon Melton, *The Encyclopedia of American Religions: Religious Creeds*, 2 vols. (Detroit: Gale Research, 1988, 1994); M. Eugene Osterhaven, *Our Confession of Faith* (Grand Rapids, Mich.: Baker Book House, 1964).

Belhar Confession

The Belhar Confession was adopted in 1986 by the Nederduitse Gereformeerde Sendingkerk of Suid Afrika (Dutch Reformed Mission Church of South Africa [DRMC]) as a response to apartheid. The DRMC was established in 1880 as a separate Reformed church for the Black African members of the Dutch Reformed Church of South Africa.

In the 1970s, the institution of apartheid led some South African blacks to adopt a form of LIBERATION THEOLOGY, which applied the biblical theme of liberation to those suffering from political oppression. Christian opposition to the oppressive situation increased after Steve Biko (1946–77), the founder of the black consciousness movement, died violently while in police custody. Among the voices raised were those of Manas Buthelezi (Lutheran), Desmond TUTU (Anglican), Alan Boesak (Reformed), Frank Chikane (Pentecostal), and Albert Nolan (Roman Catholic). Boesak, a theologian with the DRMC, assumed a leading role in speaking out against the Dutch Reformed Church and its support of apartheid. He brought the case to the WORLD ALLIANCE OF REFORMED CHURCHES in 1982. In response, the alliance suspended the two AFRIKANERS Reformed churches, declared apartheid a heresy, and elected Boesak their new president.

Insisting that the very essence of Christianity was at stake, Boesak's church took a traditional Reformed approach by issuing a new confession of faith. Its model was the BARMEN DECLARATION of 1934, which had opposed the growing Nazi power in Germany. The resulting Belhar Confession affirmed the unity of the church (as against the racially divided churches under apartheid), asserted the central role in the Gospel message of reconciliation between peoples, and declared justice and peace as basic to the nature of God.

The Belhar Confession became a landmark document that rallied churches in South Africa and around the world to the antiapartheid cause, together with the 1985 Kairos Document, in which ecumenical leaders convened by the Institute for Contextual Theology called for repentance and reconciliation as the means of getting beyond apartheid. The Belhar Confession and the Kairos Document were subsequently adopted by the South African Council of Churches, which selected as its general secretaries a series of liberation (or in South Africa, contextualizing) theologians: Desmond Tutu (1978–85), Beyers Naude (1985–88), and Frank Chikane (1988–95).

The Belhar Confession was one of the creedal statements officially adopted by the Uniting Reformed Church in Southern Africa (formed in 1994 by the merger of the DRMC with the Dutch

Reformed Church in Africa). Other churches such as the Reformed Church of America have commended it to member congregations for study and enlightenment.

See also CREEDS/CONFESSIONS OF FAITH.

Further reading: Alan Boesak, *Farewell to Innocence* (Maryknoll, N.Y.: Orbis Books, 1977); Richard Elphick and Rodney Davenport, eds., *Christianity in South Africa* (Berkeley: University of California Press, 1997).

Believer's Baptism *See* BAPTISM.

Belize

The tiny nation of Belize was an English enclave when Spain controlled most of Central America. Pirates used its protected coast as a base to launch raids against Spanish ships. It evolved into the colony of British Honduras, and since attaining independence in 1981 has remained in the British Commonwealth. Until recently, it was the only Central American country where Protestantism prevailed.

The SOCIETY FOR THE PROPAGATION OF THE GOSPEL IN FOREIGN PARTS commissioned the first Anglican clergymen in the 1770s. Their primary task was to tend to the spiritual needs of British citizens, and not much attention was paid to evangelizing the indigenous population. METHODISM was imported in the early 1800s by the layman William Jeckel, who organized several churches. The first Methodist preacher came in 1824.

In 1822, British Baptists commissioned Joseph Bourne and his wife to evangelize the resident Africans both slave and free. At the time, all but 300 of the colony's 4,500 recorded inhabitants were African, about half of them freemen. The early Methodist and Baptist churches both suffered from periodic fires and hurricanes. The British Baptists withdrew support in 1850, leaving the work to the one man who chose to stay, Alexander Henderson, who toiled for the next 25 years until failing health forced retirement. A thin thread of leadership continued the church until the Jamaican Baptists took responsibility for Belize. Robert Cleghorn arrived in 1889 to begin a half century of distinguished service.

The SEVENTH-DAY ADVENTIST CHURCH arrived in 1927, eventually overtaking the Anglicans as the second-largest religious group. PENTECOSTALISM has done quite well, though its work is scattered among a half dozen groups, the ASSEMBLIES OF GOD being the largest with some 3,000 members.

Beginning in the 1950s, Mennonites from across North America began to arrive and establish agricultural colonies. Most represented either the Old Colony Mennonites (Reinlanders) or the Kleinegemeinde (Little Brotherhood), who had retained their use of German. The 1961 hurricane that devastated Belize brought in other Mennonites as relief workers, and some stayed to create a permanent presence in Belize City and support an outreach effort among the native population.

The Belize Christian Council includes the more liberally minded Protestant churches along with the Roman Catholics (who represent 60 percent of the population). It is affiliated with the WORLD COUNCIL OF CHURCHES. As with other countries relatively close to the United States, Belize has welcomed into its land representatives of the whole spectrum of Protestant and Free Church life.

See also CENTRAL AMERICA.

Further reading: Robert Cleghorn, *A Brief History of Baptist Missionary Work in British Honduras (1822–1939)* (London: Kingsgate Press, 1939); Clifton L. Holland, ed., *World Christianity: Central America and the Caribbean* (Monrovia, Calif.: MARC-World Vision, 1981); W. R. Johnson, *A History of Christianity in Belize: 1776–1838* (New York: University Press of America, 1985).

Benin

Several different African peoples occupied the land of present-day Benin in centuries past. The Fon people had established Ouidah as a major

West African seaport that in the 18th century was a frequent calling point for slave ships.

Benin remained in African hands until the 1890s, when the French turned it into a colony known as Dahomey. In the process, they destroyed the economic base of the land, palm oil and agriculture. Having run the colony into bankruptcy, in 1960 they abandoned it, and the present nation of Benin emerged.

Benin became a religious battleground with Islam expanding from the north and west, while Catholics and Protestants launched missions in the 19th century. African Methodist convert and missionary Thomas Birch FREEMAN (1809–90) began the Protestant work. It has persisted steadily for a century and a half, and the Methodist Protestant Church of Benin remains the largest non-Catholic Christian body.

There has been no Lutheran, Presbyterian, Congregational, or even Baptist work of note. Instead, Benin has become a haven for many of the AFRICAN INITIATED CHURCHES (AIC), most of which have spread there from neighboring countries. Only a very few, the Celestial Church of Christ being the most prominent example, originated in Benin (as the Heavenly Christianity Church). The United Native African Church, a split from the Anglican Church, was apparently the first AIC to establish itself in Dahomey, in 1895.

The African Initiated Churches have had a resonance with American PENTECOSTALISM, which appears to have been introduced in the 1930s. The ASSEMBLIES OF GOD, with a reported 50,000 members, is by far the largest, and work is also proceeding under the auspices of the INTERNATIONAL CHURCH OF THE FOURSQUARE GOSPEL, the CHURCH OF GOD OF PROPHECY, and the UNITED PENTECOSTAL CHURCH.

Ecumenical work has not progressed in Benin as in other countries. The Methodist Protestant Church of Benin is the only group that belongs to the WORLD COUNCIL OF CHURCHES. Most recently, some of the more conservative bodies have formed the Féderation des Eglises et Missions Evangéliques du Benin, which is affiliated with the WORLD EVANGELICAL ALLIANCE. Benin is now approximately 20 percent Muslim, 20 percent Catholic, and 10 percent Protestant-Free Church. About 50 percent of the population continue to follow one of several traditional religions.

See also AFRICA, SUB-SAHARAN.

Further reading: Samuel Decalo, *Historical Dictionary of Benin* (Metuchen, N.J.: Scarecrow Press, 1995); M. C. Merlo, "Les sectes du Dahomey" in *Devant les sectes nonchrétiennes* (Louvain, Belgium: Desclée de Brouwer, 1961); *World Methodist Council, Handbook of Information* (Lake Junaluska, N.C.: World Methodist Council, 2003).

Bermuda

Bermuda, a set of some 150 islands in the Atlantic due east of the state of Georgia, was uninhabited when in 1609 British shipwreck survivors arrived. Deciding to stay, they invited others to join them. A group of Scottish Presbyterians accepted the invitation and became the majority party on the island. Their church at Warwick is believed to be the oldest Presbyterian church in the former British colonies. St. Peter's, erected in St. George in 1612, is the oldest Anglican church in continuous use in the Western Hemisphere.

In the early 18th century, the Anglicans won their current place as the largest group in the islands, holding the allegiance of some 35 percent of the population. A bishop resides in St. George; the church is unique as one of only a few extraprovincial dioceses directly tied to the archbishop of Canterbury.

During the American Revolution, Bermuda developed close ties with Canada, its fellow loyalist colony. A number of Canadian churches took root, including the United Church of Canada, the Pentecostal Assemblies of Canada, and the Presbyterian Church of Canada. Once the hostile feeling generated by the Revolution and the later War of 1812 subsided, Bermuda's proximity to the United States ensured the eventual arrival of a spectrum of U.S. Protestant groups.

British Methodists built a significant work that was tripled by the African Methodist Episcopal Church mission starting in the 1870s. Other prominent American-based groups are the SEV-ENTH-DAY ADVENTIST CHURCH and the New Testament Church of God that originated from the CHURCH OF GOD (CLEVELAND, TENNESSEE). The latter group is the largest Pentecostal body.

Several Protestant groups began to meet together in 1957. When joined by the Catholics in 1966, the Joint Committee of Churches emerged as the major expression of ecumenism in Bermuda. Most of the churches operating in Bermuda are related to the international ecumenical bodies through their denominational affiliates in England, Canada, or the United States.

See also CARIBBEAN.

Further reading: Barrett, David. *The Encyclopedia of World Christianity,* 2nd ed. (New York: Oxford University Press, 2001).

Beza, Theodore (1519–1605) *French Protestant reformer*

Theodore Beza was born in Burgundy, France, in 1519. Beza was honored as a Latin poet and wit. His family secured him an income as a clergyman, but he had become sympathetic to Protestantism and secretly married. Shortly thereafter, he had a spiritual crisis during an illness. He left France and moved to Geneva, where he became a close friend and confidant of John CALVIN. In 1549, Beza assumed the post of professor of Greek at Lausanne. While there, he wrote *De haereticis a civili magistratu puniendis* (1554), defending Calvin and the Geneva authorities for executing Michael SERVETUS on charges of heresy. In 1558, he returned to Geneva as professor of Greek. Following Calvin's death in 1564, he succeeded to his mentor's chair in theology.

While CALVINISM reigned supreme in Geneva, it faced hard times in France. Beza emerged as the chief defender of the French Protestants (Huguenots). He served as a chaplain in their army, advocated their cause in the courts of Europe, and on several occasions traveled into Catholic-dominated territory on their behalf. His most famous encounter with Catholic authorities occurred at the Colloquy of Poissy, a conference set up by the French queen Catherine de' Medici in 1561 in hopes of reconciling the factions that were tearing her kingdom apart. Beza and Peter Martyr Vermigli (1500–62) of Zurich represented the Reformed Church. Beza's opening presentation was well received until he began to discuss the Eucharist (LORD'S SUPPER), provoking the Catholic cardinal of Lorraine to take the stand to refute what he called a blasphemous position. The colloquy did not succeed in its goal.

Beza worked to perfect the Greek and Latin versions of the New Testament. In 1581, he gave Codex D (also known as Codex Bezae), one of the important manuscript copies of the Bible, to CAMBRIDGE UNIVERSITY. Beza died in Geneva on October 13, 1605.

See also REFORMED/PRESBYTERIAN TRADITION.

Further reading: Henry Martyn Baird, *Theodore Beza. The Counsellor of the French Reformation* (New York: G. P. Putnam's Sons, 1899); Theodore Beza, *The Christian Faith,* trans. by James Clark (East Sussex, U.K.: 1992); ———, *A Little Book of Christian Questions and Responses,* trans. by K. M. Summers (Allison Park, Pa.: Pickwick, 1986); John S. Bray, *Theodore Beza's Doctrine of Predestination* (Nieuwkoop: Bibliotheca Humanistica & Reformatorica XII, 1975); Jill Raitt, *The Eucharistic Theology of Theodore Beza* (Atlanta: Scholars Press, 1972).

Bhutan

Bhutan is about 75 percent Buddhist. Some 25 percent of the country are Nepalese, traditionally Hindu, and their presence and religion are recognized in law. Strict laws against proselytizing have made it difficult for Christianity to gain a foothold.

As early as 1892, the Scandinavian Alliance Mission began working among Bhutanese who resided or did business in Indian communities just across the Bhutanese border. Then, early in the 20th century, the Church of Scotland founded several schools in Bhutan. Those schools are now maintained by the Church of North India (into which the Church of Scotland's Indian mission merged). The Church of North India is the only Christian church with personnel living and working in Bhutan.

The work among Bhutanese in the border communities has yet to show much visible result. Several Christian congregations have appeared in the Nepalese section of the country.

See also ASIA; INDIA; NEPAL.

Further reading: David Barrett, *The Encyclopedia of World Christianity,* 2nd ed. (New York: Oxford University Press, 2001); Patrick Johnstone and Jason Mandryk, *Operation World, 21st Century Edition* (Carlisle, Cumbria, U.K.: Paternoster, 2001).

Bible

The Protestant Bible includes both the Hebrew Old Testament (the Jewish scriptures) and the Greek New Testament, though it is almost always read in translation in the vernacular of each national church. To understand Protestantism, one must consider its special reverence for the Bible, as compared with that of other Christians. The Bible's role in challenging Roman Catholic practices in the 16th century helped give it its unique role in Protestant life.

Crucial to the Reformation was a widespread perception that the Roman Catholic Church had wandered from the teachings of the Bible by promoting an unbiblical system of salvation and by maintaining practices that had no foundation in the teachings of Jesus and the apostles. Martin LUTHER used the Bible to refute what he saw as the errors of popes and church councils; he was thus forced to challenge the exclusive authority of the church in interpreting the Bible. He summarized his stand at the DIET OF WORMS: "Unless I am convinced by Scripture or by right reason (for I trust neither

To emphasize the role of the Bible, most Protestant churches will at some point present their youths with a copy. *(Institute for the Study of American Religion, Santa Barbara, California)*

popes nor councils, since they have often erred and contradicted themselves)—unless I am thus convinced, I am bound by the texts of the Bible, my conscience is captive to the word of God."

The position would later be reflected in various Lutheran and Reformed creedal statements. For example, the Second HELVETIC CONFESSION (1561) opens: "We believe and confess the canonical Scriptures of the holy prophets and apostles of both Testaments to be the true Word of God, and to have sufficient authority of themselves, not of men. For God himself spoke to the fathers, prophets, apostles, and still speaks to us through the Holy Scriptures."

The 39 ARTICLES OF RELIGION of the CHURCH OF ENGLAND echoed this idea, stating: "Holy Scripture containeth all things necessary to salvation: so that whatsoever is not read therein, nor may be proved thereby, is not to be required of any man, that it should be believed as an article of the Faith. . . . In the name of the Holy Scripture we do understand those canonical Books of the Old and New Testament, of whose authority was never any doubt in the Church."

At the time of the Reformation, the text of the Bible was also called into question. Luther denied canonicity to the books of the APOCRYPHA, a set of books found in the Latin Vulgate Bible apparently written in the centuries just prior to the Christian era. He found these books of disputed and questionable authority, though he conceded they were "good and useful." At times, he also expressed questions about other biblical texts including James, Jude, Hebrews, and Revelation. As the Catholic Church continued to affirm the canonicity of the Apocrypha, Protestant statements of faith frequently included a list of what they considered to be the canonical books.

In the 19th century, the Bible's authority was questioned from a variety of sources. Geologists rejected a literal reading of the timetable of Genesis, asserting that the earth was much older than the Bible suggested. Biologists claimed that species evolved out of other species and were not created separately by God as the Bible told. Biblical critics claimed that the Bible's text had gone through a complicated editing process, and they challenged the traditional authorship of many sections. They also rejected the historicity of many of the events recorded in the Bible. A variety of skeptical voices challenged belief in the miracles revealed in the pages of the Scripture.

Christian modernists tried to absorb the criticisms in a positive manner and to adjust their understanding of biblical authority accordingly. Approaches varied greatly, especially as BIBLICAL CRITICISM grew more sophisticated. Some developed an evolutionary approach to the Bible, seeing it as an evolving tradition that developed an increasingly insightful understanding of God. They often spoke of the Bible as containing Word of God along with other material.

The popular Neo-Orthodox view expounded by Swiss theologian Karl BARTH saw the Bible as analogous to any other book, but set apart by the regular action of the Holy Spirit in revealing truth to those who read it. That is, the believer (and occasionally the unbeliever) can encounter God through the Bible, both individually and collectively through the church. Such a view conforms with the findings of biblical criticism, while continuing to hold a high view of the Bible and its authority.

Other equally sophisticated Protestants developed an apology for its authority, in an attempt to defend traditional Protestant creeds. These attempts paralleled the conservative Roman Catholic defense of papal authority with claims to infallibility and INERRANCY. The most popular statement of this view was in the PRINCETON THEOLOGY developed late in the 19th century by people such as A. A. Hodge (1823–86), Benjamin Warfield (1851–1921), and J. Gresham MACHEN (1881–1937). Hodge and Warfield wrote a seminal book on biblical inerrancy in 1881.

In the 20th century, a language of biblical authority based on Princeton theology has become common in Fundamentalist and Evangelical circles. Believers are asked to affirm the infallibility and inerrancy of the Bible, the former referring to the biblical statements on faith and morals and the latter to statements on other matters such as science and history. The Bible is seen as possessing verbal plenary inspiration, which means that every word is God-given and that every passage is equally authoritative.

The Princeton position was often attacked by biblical critics who pointed out "errors" in the text, for example discrepancies between different accounts of the same event such as the Flood, for which two distinct accounts appear in Genesis 6–9. Some writers attempted to explain away all the discrepancies; others suggested that errors had entered as ancient texts were copied; only the original texts (which no longer exist) were inerrant.

The debates have continued. Thus, the Affirmation of Faith of the Baptist General Conference

(1951) reads: "We believe the Bible is the word of God, fully inspired and without error in the original manuscript, written under the inspiration of the Holy Spirit, and that it is the supreme authority in all matters of faith and conduct."

In 1932, the conservative LUTHERAN CHURCH– MISSOURI SYNOD summarized its position thusly: "We teach that the Holy Scriptures differ from all other books in the world in that they are the Word of God. . . . We teach also that the verbal inspiration of the Scriptures is . . . taught by direct statements of the Scriptures . . . [the Scriptures] contain no errors or contradictions, but . . . they are in all their parts and words the infallible truth, and also in those parts which treat of historical, geographical, and other secular matters."

Churches in the Wesleyan Methodist tradition, though often equally conservative, have generally stayed away from the Princeton theology approach to Scripture and have argued instead for the sufficiency of the traditional statement found in the Methodist Article of Religion that Scripture contains all things necessary to salvation. Typical is the affirmation of the SALVATION ARMY: "We believe that the scriptures of the Old and New Testaments were given by inspiration of God and that they only constitute the divine rule of Christian faith and practice."

In 1967, the United Presbyterian Church [now a constituent part of the Presbyterian Church (U.S.A.)], showed its movement away from Princeton theology by its primary affirmation of Christ as the Word of God to which the Scripture bears witness. It affirmed: "The one sufficient revelation of God is Jesus Christ the Word of God incarnate, to whom the Holy Spirit bears unique and authoritative witness through the Holy Scriptures, which are received and obeyed as the word of God written. . . . The church has received the books of the Old and New Testaments as prophetic and apostolic testimony in which it hears the word of God and by which its faith and obedience are nourished and regulated."

While Protestants have differed on how they understand the Bible and its authority, their consensus on its centrality has inspired a vast litera-ture to assist believers in understanding the Bible, whose books are several thousand years old and written in archaic forms of Hebrew and Greek. The Bible is the product of cultures that are vastly different from those in which most Christians now live. Scholars have produced a huge number of Bible commentaries, expositions, theological word studies, and historical critical interpretations.

See also BIBLE SOCIETIES; BIBLE TRANSLATION; INSPIRATION OF THE BIBLE; KING JAMES VERSION OF THE BIBLE; REVISED STANDARD VERSION OF THE BIBLE; SOLA SCRIPTURA.

Further reading: Paul J. Achtemeier, *The Inspiration of Scripture: Problems and Proposals.* (Philadelphia: Westminster Press, 1980); Robert Gruse, *The Authority of the Bible: Theories of Inspiration, Revelation, and the Canon of Scripture* (Mahwah, N.J.: Paulist Press, 1985); J. Gordon Melton, *The Encyclopedia of American Religions: Religious Creeds,* 2 vols. (Detroit: Gale Research, 1988, 1994); John W. Haley, *Alleged Discrepancies of the Bible* (Nashville, Tenn.: Gospel Advocate, 1974); Benjamin B. Warfield, *Inspiration and Authority of the Bible,* ed. by Samuel G. Craig (Philadelphia: Presbyterian and Reformed Press, 1970).

Bible Sabbath Association

The Bible Sabbath Association is the largest North American fellowship of believers in SABBATARIANISM, the belief that the Jewish Sabbath (Saturday) is the proper day for Christians to set aside for worship, rather than the more commonly observed Sunday. Sabbatarianism remains a significant and growing minority opinion within the Protestant community.

The idea was brought to America and introduced to the Baptists in the 1660s by Stephen Mumford. It was found exclusively among Baptists until the middle of the 19th century, when Ellen G. WHITE, the founder of the SEVENTH-DAY ADVENTIST CHURCH (SDA), proposed it to the ADVENTISTS who had survived the Great Disappointment when Christ did not return in 1844. The issue split the Adventist movement, but White's following emerged as the most successful segment. In the 20th century, more than half of all

Sabbatarian Christians around the world were members of the SDA.

One group of Adventists who accepted Sabbatarianism but not the particular revelations of Ellen White formed the Church of God (Seventh Day). Through the 20th century, this relatively small group splintered in more than a dozen factions, one of which, the WORLDWIDE CHURCH OF GOD, emerged as the second-largest Sabbatarian Adventist group, though far smaller than the SDA. A number of Sabbatarian Church of God congregations regrouped around a second idea, the importance of calling God by his correct name. These churches collectively constituted the SACRED NAME MOVEMENT.

By 1940, there were several dozen Sabbatarian groups, almost all of Baptist or Adventist origin. In 1943, people affiliated with the smaller groups founded the Bible Sabbath Association (BSA) to provide mutual support. They tried to change the laws found in many Western nations (including the United States) that restricted commerce on Sunday, and to end discrimination against Sabbatarians (especially people who refused to work on Saturday).

Since that time, many Sabbath laws have been repealed or modified for Sabbatarians, though the fight to end Sabbath discrimination continues. In recent decades, Christians outside of the Adventist lineage have accepted Sabbatarianism, including several splinters of the CHURCH OF JESUS CHRIST OF LATTER-DAY SAINTS.

The BSA has set as its goal to unite "all believers in the Bible Sabbath, regardless of sect, creed or denomination for the sole purpose of spreading knowledge of, belief in, and observance of God's Holy Day." While primarily operating in the United States, there are now member churches around the world. At the beginning of the 21st century, BSA reported some 400 Sabbatarian groups with some 1,600 congregations. BSA headquarters are in Gillette, Wyoming. It publishes *The Sabbath Sentinel* bimonthly.

Further reading: Bible Sabbath Association. Available online. URL: http://www.biblesabbath.org; George

Dellinger, *A History of the Sabbath Resurrection Doctrine* (Westfield, N.J.: Sabbath Research Center, 1982); *Directory of Sabbath-Observing Groups* (Fairview, Okla.: Bible Sabbath Association, revised periodically); Carlyle B. Haynes, *From Sabbath to Sunday* (Washington, D.C.: Review and Herald Publishing, 1928).

Bible societies

Bible societies are devoted to distributing Bibles as widely as possible, and to that end, support their translation into more and more languages.

From its beginning, Protestantism has supported publication of the Bible in the languages of its believers, starting with Martin LUTHER's translation and the publication of the German-language Bible and continuing with new BIBLE TRANSLATIONS into most European languages. In the American British colonies, efforts to translate the Bible into the various Native American tongues began in the 17th century.

The 18th-century Evangelical Awakening in England gave birth to the word missions movement and concomitantly to a new type of organization, the Bible society, whose only work was the translation, publication, and distribution of Bibles. The pioneer Naval and Military Bible Society, founded in 1779, was later superseded by the British and Foreign Bible Society (BFBS), founded in 1804. This type of work generated widespread approval among Protestants of all denominations, and the BFBS eventually won support from both the CHURCH OF ENGLAND and the several Dissenting churches.

The BFBS worked to reprint English Bibles (KING JAMES VERSION) and to produce biblical texts in other languages with a demonstrated need. The society acted as publisher and distributor, relying upon others to do the actual translations. Bibles were often distributed free or at less than cost. Supporters organized into local auxiliaries to raise funds and to distribute the society's publications.

Overseas, the BFBS consigned Bibles to missionaries and interested lay people (colporteurs) who would distribute them for a small fee or free will offering. In some areas, such as South America, where Protestant missionaries and ministers were not allowed, Bible distributors were able to roam with relative freedom, distribute Bibles and other Christian literature, and seed what would later become Protestant churches.

In other countries with active Protestant populations, societies similar to the BFBS soon began to form. In the British colonies, these new societies served as BFBS auxiliaries. The Hivernian Bible Society in Ireland (1806) and the American Bible Society (1816) were among the independent organizations. The Scottish auxiliaries broke with the BFBS in 1826 over the publication of the APOCRYPHA, and in 1861 created a national organization now known as the Scottish Bible Society. The continental societies also broke with the BFBS over the Apocrypha; thereafter the British society employed its own agents to continue its work throughout Europe. A century after its founding, the BFBS had some 2,000 affiliated Bible societies throughout the empire with approximately 5,000 local auxiliaries in England and Wales.

The formation of many more national Bible societies in the early 20th century led in 1946 to the formation of a coordinating agency, the United Bible Societies. As of 1993, the UBS had 137 affiliated societies/offices working in more than 200 countries and territories.

Further reading: William Canton, *A History of the British and Foreign Bible Society,* 5 vols. (London: John Murray, 1904–10); Creighton B. Lacy, *The Word Carrying Giant: The Growth of the American Bible Society, 1816–1966* (Pasadena, Calif.: William Carey Library, 1977); James Moulton Rice, *A History of the British and Foreign Bible Society, 1905–1954* (London: British and Foreign Bible Society, 1965); Ethel Emily Wallis and Mary Angela Bennett, *Two Thousand Tongues to Go: The Story of the Wycliffe Bible Translators* (New York: Harper & Row, 1964).

Bible translations

The Protestant Reformation believed that the Bible was the property of every believer. The successful effort to translate the Bible into the spoken language of Christians (using the best Hebrew and Greek texts for sources) was instrumental in the spread of the movement.

In deciphering the Hebrew and Greek originals, Protestants benefited from the work of the humanist movement, which emphasized classical Hellenic studies, and from the revival of Hebrew learning, in part a product of the dispersion of the Jewish communities expelled from Spain and Portugal beginning in the 1490s. For Protestants, HUMANISM culminated in the publication of a Greek text of the New Testament by ERASMUS in 1516 and Johannes REUCHLIN's efforts to make the Hebrew text of the Jewish Bible (the Old Testament) more available in Germany. The wider distribution of the Bible was also facilitated by the practical use of moveable type and parallel improvements in the printing and publishing industries.

Using Erasmus's Greek text, commonly referred to as the Textus Receptus, Martin LUTHER began work on his German translation of the New Testament as the Reformation was beginning. It was published in 1522. The complete Bible appeared in 1534. As would be the case in a number of other languages, his translation had a marked effect on the evolution of the German language. Throughout the 16th century, translations followed the spread of the Reformation.

The Textus Receptus, which went through various revisions (including Erasmus's own corrected edition of 1519) remained the basic source for translations for several hundred years. It underlay the various English editions beginning with that of William TYNDALE (1525). French reformer Theodore de BEZA (1519–1605) issued several editions of the Textus Receptus beginning in 1565; they were used by the translators of the KING JAMES VERSION OF THE BIBLE (1611) early in the 17th century. Like Luther's text, the King James Version helped shape the evolving English language.

Native Americans were among the first non-Europeans for whom the Bible was translated. These peoples were preliterate; their languages usually had to be rendered in writing before the translations could be made. John Eliot's Bible for the "praying communities" of Massachusetts Natives, published in 1663 in Algonquin, was the first such translation and the first complete Bible published in North America. Eliot's work called attention to the convergence of Bible translation and missionary activity.

Many pioneering 19th-century Protestant missionaries had to learn the language of the people among whom they had chosen to work, reduce that language to a written format, produce a lexicon, and then translate Scripture. Where a written language existed, translation of the New Testament became a primary goal. The first missionary to India, Bartholemew Ziegenbalg (1682–1719), published a New Testament in Tamil in 1714. The Old Testament was not published until 1796. William CAREY (1761–1834) completed the first Bengali New Testament in 1801 and went on to build a team that initiated translation work in Sanskrit, Marathi, Khasi, Pashto (Afghanistan), and, interestingly, Chinese (Wenli).

In CHINA, Robert MORRISON (1782–1834) saw his first translation (the book of Acts) published in Wenli in 1810. The first full Wenli New Testament appeared in 1814, followed by various dialect editions: Foochow (1856), Mandarin (1857), Nanking (1857), and Cantonese (1877).

In Burma, Baptist Adoniram JUDSON (1788–1850), assisted by his wife, Ann Hasseltine Judson (1789–1826), worked for two decades to produce an English-Burmese dictionary and a Burmese Bible (finally published in 1834). Ann Judson also did the first translation of a book of the Bible into Thai. In Tahiti, the first of the South Sea Islands colonized by Protestant missionaries, the publication of a vernacular translation had to await the arrival of a printing press; progress began with the 1812 conversion of the king, and the Bible was finally published in 1838.

All these efforts and others like them were assisted throughout the early 19th century by the new BIBLE SOCIETIES, the first being the British and Foreign Bible Society in 1804. More than 100 associations for the printing and distribution of Bibles were founded in the United States, the first

in 1809. Many of them united in 1816 in the American Bible Society. The first such society in the mission field itself was formed in Calcutta, India, in 1811. As the number of translations increased, the societies assumed the task of publishing them.

The next significant step forward in Bible translation occurred in Central America when missionary William Cameron Townsend (1896–1982) offered a Bible in Spanish to a native Guatemalan who only spoke his people's language, Cakchiquel. Townsend and his wife spent the next 12 years mastering Cakchiquel, reducing it to writing, and translating the New Testament, which in 1929 became the first book published in the Cakchiquel language. Townsend subsequently founded the Wycliffe Bible Translators (1942) and its affiliated Summer Institute of Linguistics, now one of the largest Protestant missionary organizations in the world. Wycliffe personnel began a systematic process of approaching the more than 6,000 peoples of the world who had as yet no Bible in their language. Once a group is selected, a Wycliffe team usually settles among them, learns the language, reduces it to writing, prepares a grammar, and translates the New Testament. The process usually takes more than a decade. At the beginning of the 21st century, Wycliffe Bible. Translators launched Vision 2025, whose goal is to have a New Testament translation at least in progress among every language group that needs it by the year 2025. The work of the Wycliffe Bible Translators has possibly the broadest support among the different segments of the Protestant and Free Church community of any ecumenical activity.

By the start of the 21st century, complete Bibles existed in about 400 languages, New Testaments in an additional 1,000 languages, and portions of the New Testament in over 2,000 languages.

In the meantime, the English Bible was undergoing revisions, spurred by the expanding knowledge of the biblical text. Numerous manuscript fragments of the New Testament had been found and dated. Linguists called attention to changes in modern speech that called for new translations into contemporary English. Finally, a century of BIBLICAL CRITICISM had produced new understandings of the development of the biblical text. A consensus emerged among Protestant Bible scholars that there were numerous defects in the King James Version and it was time for a new translation.

Important contemporary translations appeared in Britain in 1885 (Revised Version) and the United States in 1901 (American Standard Version). The development of the ECUMENICAL MOVEMENT in the early 20th century provided support for what became the most important of the new translations, the REVISED STANDARD VERSION. It was published in two stages, the New Testament in 1946 and the entire Bible in 1951. The final publication was authorized (and copyrighted) by the National Council of Churches of Christ in the U.S.A. That fact alone became the spur to many new translations by segments of the Protestant community that rejected any cooperation with the National Council. The council's limited granting of publication rights also prompted some publishing houses to produce editions of their own.

Not all new translations were products of committees. Individual scholars, such as Edgar J. Goodspeed (1871–1962) of the University of Chicago, produced translations that highlighted particular insights on the Bible. Popular individual translations have been made by Robert Moffat (1795–1883), J. B. Philips (1906–82), and Kenneth J. Taylor (*The Living Bible,* 1971).

In addition, various churches have offered translations in line with their own sectarian understandings of the text. Thus, in the last two centuries Bibles have been published that appear to substantiate Baptist theology (baptism by immersion), Sacred Name Bibles (that transliterate the Hebrew names for God and Jesus), and the JEHOVAH'S WITNESSES's New World Translation (that emphasizes non-Trinitarian theology).

Further reading: H. W. Hoare, *The Evolution of the English Bible: An Historical Sketch of the Successive Versions from 1382 to 1885* (New York: E. P. Dutton, 1901); Sakae Kubo and Walter Specht, *So Many Versions? Twentieth Century English Versions of the Bible* (Grand Rapids, Mich.: Zondervan, 1975); Jack P. Lewis, *The English Bible from KJV to NIV: A History and Evaluation,* 2nd ed. (Grand Rapids, Mich.: Baker Book House, 1991); Bruce Metzger, *The Bible in Translation: Ancient and English Versions* (Grand Rapids, Mich.: Baker Academic, 2001); H. W. Robinson, *The Bible in Its Ancient and English Version* (Oxford: Clarendon Press, 1940); Ethel Emily Wallis and Mary Angela Bennett, *Two Thousand Tongues to Go: The Story of the Wycliffe Bible Translators* (New York: Harper & Row, 1964).

biblical criticism

The work of scholars such a ERASMUS on the biblical text and publication of more accurate Bible translations in the 16th century, coupled with Martin LUTHER's idea that the Bible's meaning was plain to any commonsense reader, led in the next century to the first suggestions that the Bible could (and should) be read much like any other ancient text, and understood like any other document that attempts to communicate information, that is, in light of its historical context and cultural setting. Understanding the biblical text, it was said, begins with asking how a reader at the time of its writing understood it.

At the same time, challenges began to appear to the accuracy of the commonly used Masoretic text of the Hebrew Bible (the Christian Old Testament). In the early 16th century, Elijah ben Asher (1424–1549) demonstrated that the vowel points were later additions to the text (Hebrew having no vowels). In the next century, scholars noting differences between the Hebrew Masoretic and the Greek Septuagint text called the Masoretic text into question. Meanwhile, variant readings of New Testament texts from ancient manuscripts then available led to continual attempts to reconstruct the best text possible.

Richard Simon (1638–1712), a Catholic scholar, was among the first who challenged the traditional attribution of authorship of the Old Testament books. He suggested that those books that tell the story of ancient Israel were written not by a single author but by schools of scribes working over decades, possibly centuries. In 1753, Jean Astruc (1684–1766) suggested that Genesis had been constructed from two main and several lesser sources (based upon the variant words used for God throughout the text). Simon's and Astruc's work would lead directly to modern critical studies.

In the relatively freer atmosphere of the 19th century, these suggestions would be taken more seriously. Scholars pondered the problems presented by the belief that the Pentateuch was written by a single author, namely Moses, and was an accurate account of the history of ancient Israel. Major thinking and research was carried out by Karl Heinrich Graf (1815–69) and Julius Wellhausen (1844–1918), who developed what has come to be known as the Graf-Wellhausen Hypothesis or the Documentary Hypothesis. It assumes that the Pentateuch was composed of four major documents, combined in stages. The first two documents were given the name "J" and "E" based upon their use of the name Jehovah (i.e., Yahweh) or Elohim for God. The third document was named "P" as representing the views of the priestly class, and the last was called "D" or Deuteronomic, covering most of the book of Deuteronomy, which these scholars believed was the book of the law found during the reign of Josiah, as recounted in 2 Kings 22:3–23:25.

The theory dates the J document to around 900 B.C.E. and the E document to a century later. The opening chapter of Genesis is considered a typical example of the E document. The J document picks up in Genesis 2:4, where the name of God changes. The P document is seen in chapter 7 of Genesis, where God for a second time instructs Noah about the animals to be taken into the ark and makes a clear distinction between clean and unclean animals, an important consideration for priests who were responsible for animal sacrifices, and a matter ignored in the first set

of instructions (Genesis 6:14–22), attributed to E. The final document, D, includes most of the book Deuteronomy.

The Documentary Hypothesis gained popularity in the late 19th century along with the theory of evolution (which also contradicted a literal reading of the Genesis text). It explained many of the contradictions and peculiarities in the text of the Pentateuch, very evident to those who studied the Bible in any detail. The theory was accepted by a majority of biblical scholars by the early 20th century and became the basis of most future work on the Old Testament.

Meanwhile, New Testament scholars began to approach the four Gospels (Matthew, Mark, Luke, and John) in the same spirit, focusing on similar problems of apparent contradictions and peculiarities of the texts. Scholars proposed what has become known as the two-source theory for the Gospels, namely the Gospel of Mark (the first written Gospel) and a lost source named "Q." In this reconstruction, Matthew and Luke began their Gospels with Mark and then added material from Q (consisting of the material common to Luke and Matthew but not found in Mark). Q consists largely of sayings of Jesus (as opposed to accounts of his actions). In addition Matthew and Luke each had unique sources of his own. John is largely based on other independent sources.

Contemporary Catholic and liberal Protestant scholars see the Bible as the product of a communal activity involving a number of editors and scribes. Two new subdisciplines have arisen, FORM CRITICISM (focusing on the literary forms that appear in Scripture such as poetry, parables, and letters) and redaction criticism (focusing on the work of the editors of the final biblical text).

The Documentary Hypothesis became an additional bone of contention between fundamentalists and modernists in the 1920s. Conservative Protestants believed it undermined the authority and INSPIRATION OF THE BIBLE. In reaction, many intensified their advocacy of the infallibility and INERRANCY of the Bible. Some Evangelical scholars have found a way to accommodate their view of the Bible with biblical criticism, but many have not, including some outstanding Evangelical scholars who have attempted to refute the documentary hypothesis while defending a more traditional approach.

One artifact of modern biblical criticism is the Jesus Seminar, begun in 1985. It brings together Bible scholars to examine what is known about the historical Jesus in light of the critical work on the texts. Over the years, some 200 scholars have participated. Issues are debated and decided by votes. The often controversial results, representing the most liberal perspectives of modern scholarship, have been widely reported in the media and have resulted in several books.

Differences over the Documentary Hypothesis sometimes overshadows other, less controversial achievements of modern scholarship. For example, a large number of ancient New Testament manuscripts (from complete codices to small fragment of different books) have been found over the last few hundred years. Much work has been done in classifying them and developing a history of the copying of the New Testament in the centuries prior to modern printing. This work has yielded growing agreement on a critical text of the New Testament books that more closely approaches the original.

See also CREATIONISM.

Further reading: John Dominic Crossan, *The Historical Jesus: The Life of a Mediterranean Jewish Peasant* (San Francisco: HarperSan Francisco, 1991); Richard Elliott Friedman, *Who Wrote the Bible?* (New York: Summit Books, 1987); Stephen R. Haynes and Steven L. McKenzie, eds., *To Each Its Own Meaning: An Introduction to Biblical Criticisms and Their Application* (Louisville, Ky.: Westminster/John Knox Press, 1993); William Sanford Lasor, David Allan Hubbard, and Frederic William Bush, *Old Testament Survey: The Message, Form, and Background of the Old Testament* (Grand Rapids, Mich.: William B. Eerdmans, 1982); Ernest Nicholson, *The Pentateuch in the Twentieth Century: The Legacy of Julius Wellhausen* (Oxford: Clarendon Press, 1998).

bishops

The office of bishop (Greek *episcopos*) emerged slowly over the first centuries of the Christian church. In New Testament times, a bishop was hardly distinct from what is termed elsewhere an *elder* (Greek *presbyteros*). By the 16th century, the episcopacy collectively, with its visible head in the pope (the bishop of Rome), was seen as carrying the apostolic lineage of the church. That lineage was passed on by the laying on of hands by a bishop who stood in apostolic succession with Christ and the apostles. Any bishop was, in theory, able to trace his (the bishopric had become an entirely male occupation) lineage backward through a series of consecrations to one of the apostles. As one approached the early centuries, the lines of consecration tended to become ever more difficult to verify.

The office of bishop was called into question by John CALVIN and the Reformed Church. Calvin argued for a church led by elders, whose authority would be based on preaching the Word and the proper administration of the sacraments. The leaders of the Radical Reformation likewise rejected apostolic successions and bishops. Seventeenth-century Baptists and Congregationalists had no use for bishops.

Episcopacy survived in the CHURCH OF ENGLAND (and its lesser known parallel community in Scotland). Though the Roman Catholic Church has at times questioned the legitimacy of the Church of England's orders, Anglicans have staunchly defended them and worked to keep them intact. Martin LUTHER seemed personally indifferent to apostolic succession, but branches of the Lutheran Church, most notably the Church of Sweden, preserve episcopal leadership and apostolic succession. Other Lutheran churches have presbyterial or congregational organizations. Among other Protestants that claim apostolic succession is the Moravian Church.

As the Protestant community continued to divide, the question of bishops came up once more. John WESLEY, himself an Episcopal minister, tried to have the Anglican bishop of London consecrate a bishop for American Methodists in the years immediately after the American Revolution. Failing in that approach, Wesley suggested that the office of bishop was primarily a functional one; since he had himself functioned as a bishop in calling forth and overseeing the Methodist movement for several decades, he was in fact a bishop and thus had the power to consecrate (set apart) some of his ministers as bishops (he called them superintendents), most notably Thomas COKE. In 1784, Coke consecrated Francis ASBURY as the general superintendent of the American work, and the ministers collectively chose to call Asbury a bishop.

In the 19th century, with the emergence of new churches such as the Reformed Episcopal Church, the title "bishop" lost even more of its traditional meaning; it could simply mean the person or persons chosen to act as the leaders of a church or a major division thereof. Most of the new 20th-century churches that call their leaders bishops make no claim to apostolic succession. Traditional divisional terms such as *diocese* have been replaced with modern organizational terms—*district, conference, territory,* and so forth. Often the designation of a leader as a bishop is simply an attempt by a new sectarian group to claim legitimacy within the larger church community.

African Americans lobbied for entrance into the episcopacy in the older churches at the beginning of the 20th century. The first African American admitted to such orders was Richard ALLEN, who after leaving the Methodist Episcopal Church and establishing the African Methodist Episcopal Church, was elected as its first bishop and consecrated by several black ministers. A similar event occurred a few years later with the founding of the African Methodist Episcopal Zion Church.

Both Methodists and Episcopalians admitted African Americans to their episcopal orders, but in each case the bishops were designated for service outside the United States. In 1858, the Methodist Episcopal Church (now part of the United Methodist Church) selected Francis Burns (1809–63) to superintend the work in Liberia. He served for five years and was succeeded by John

W. Roberts (1812–75). Not until 1920 were black bishops selected to serve the predominantly African-American Methodist conferences in the Methodist Episcopal Church—Robert Edward Jones (1872–1960) and Matthew Wesley Clair Jr. (1865–1943).

The first African-American Episcopal bishop was James Theodore Holly (1929–91), who was assigned to minister in Haiti, where he raised up a French-speaking church, Église Orthodoxe Apostolique Haitienne. In 1874, the Episcopal Church recognized the Haitian jurisdiction and authorized the consecration of Holly as a missionary bishop to Haiti. Meanwhile, in 1864, Samuel A Crowther was consecrated in England as the first Anglican bishop of African descent.

The drive for an African-American bishop within the Episcopal Church become focused in the 1920s on the figure of George A. McGuire, a prominent priest. In 1918, two African Americans, Edward Demby (1859–1967) and Henry Delany (1858–1928) were named suffragan (assistant) bishops in Arkansas and North Carolina, respectively. However, there was little prospect of a black being named to lead a diocese. In 1921, McGuire left the church and founded the African Orthodox Church, over which he came to preside as archbishop. It would not be until 1970 that John Burgess (b. 1909) was consecrated as the bishop of Massachusetts.

The episcopacy became a major bar to modern plans for church union, especially involving Anglicans. Only in a few cases, for example, the Church of South India, was a consensus reached between supporters and opponents of apostolic succession.

The issue of admitting women ministers to the episcopacy became the major topic of the 1970s, and it has continued to plague the Anglican community to the present. The UNITED METHODIST CHURCH, the largest American Protestant church with episcopal leadership, elected their first female bishop in 1980. Marjorie Swank Matthews (d. 1986) served a single four-year term in Wisconsin before retiring. Since that time, United Methodism has elected a number of women to the office.

Within the Anglican Communion, Barbara Clementine HARRIS of the Episcopal Church (in the United States) was the first woman elected to the episcopacy (and incidentally the first African-American woman). While other Anglican churches, including the Church of England, continue to debate the issue, most of the churches of the Anglican Communion have copied the American example. Several Anglican provinces, most notably Singapore and Uganda, have strongly opposed females in the ministry.

The Episcopal Church raised an even more divisive issue for fellow Anglicans in 2003, when it approved the election and consecration of Rev. Gene Robinson, a homosexual priest living with a gay partner, as the suffragan bishop of New Hampshire.

See also DEACONS; ELDERS.

Further reading: Ivar Asheim and Victor R. Gold, eds., *Episcopacy in the Lutheran Church? Studies in the Development and Definition of the Office of Church Leadership* (Philadelphia: Fortress Press, 1970); Gerald Moede, *The Office of Bishop in Methodism: Its History and Development* (New York: Abingdon Press, 1964); Jack M. Tuell and Roger W. Fjeld, eds., *Episcopacy: Lutheran-United Methodist Dialogue II* (Minneapolis, Minn.: Augsburg, 1991); *Women in the Anglican Episcopate: Theology, Guidelines, and Practice,* The Eames Commission and the Monitoring Group Reports (Toronto: Anglican Book Centre [for the Anglican Consultative Council], 1998); William L. Wright, *The Anglican Concept of Episcopacy* (Toronto: Hart House, 1964).

Blackmore, Sophia (1857–1945)
Methodist missionary and educator
Sophia Blackmore, the first female missionary of the Methodist Church in Singapore, was born in Goulburn, Australia, on October 18, 1857. A chance encounter with Isabella Leonard, an American evangelist, led her to accept a call to the missionary's life. Australian Methodists at that time did not support unmarried females as missionaries.

Nevertheless, Blackmore accompanied Leonard to India. There they met Bishop William F. Oldham (1854–1937), who at the time needed someone to work among the women and children who attended the Anglo-Chinese School in Singapore. Blackmore offered herself and was accepted.

She arrived in Singapore in 1887. Within a month, she founded the Tamil Girl's School there at the request of several Indian businessmen, and one year later she opened the Fairfield Girls' School. These two schools expanded to serve young women of every ethnic community on the island, and seeded a series of girls' schools in neighboring Malaysia. In her first year in Singapore, Blackmore also opened the Nind Home, a hostel for women named for the Minneapolis woman who had raised much of the financial support for Blackmore's work. Similar hostels were established in Malaysia.

Blackmore also worked at evangelizing the Baba Chinese women, her efforts resulting in the formation of a Baba church, now Kampong Kapor Methodist Church, which grew to be the largest Methodist congregation in the region.

After 40 years of work, Blackmore retired and went back to Australia, where she lived until her death on July 3, 1945. The institutions she founded have served Singaporeans ever since, with a brief hiatus during the Japanese occupation of World War II. Today, the Kampong Kapor Methodist Church and over a dozen schools carry on the effort initiated by Blackmore in the 1880s.

See also FEMINISM, CHRISTIAN; SINGAPORE.

Further reading: Theordore R. Doraisamy, *Forever Beginning, One Hundred Years of Methodism in Singapore* (Singapore: Methodist Church in Singapore, 1985); ———, *Sophia Blackmore in Singapore* (Singapore: Methodist Book Room, 1987); Ernest Lau, "Sophia Blackmore." Available online. URL: http://www.trac-mcs.org.sg/discipleship/pdf/sb1.pdf.

black theology
Black theology, a form of LIBERATION THEOLOGY, developed in the United States in the context of

the 1960s Civil Rights movement and the changes wrought by Martin Luther KING JR. Christian thinkers within the African-American community developed a particular appreciation for the insights of liberation theologians, beginning with the notion that the Christian message is shaped by one's location in life and that most Christian theology has been done by elite white males of European heritage. Traditional theological affirmations have been shaped to reflect the experience and practice of this relatively small group.

Black theology was designated to reflect the reality of the African-American community, whose members struggle under the oppression of white racism. Racism expresses itself not only as direct hatred of African Americans and violence (or the threat of violence), but also in the institutionalized power held by people of European heritage that denies people of color the chance to participate as equals in the society.

The idea of a black theology was initially articulated by James H. Cone, a minister in the African Methodist Episcopal Church and a professor of systematic theology at Union Theological Seminary. Cone received his Ph.D. as the Civil Rights movement was peaking in the mid-1960s. Like his South American counterparts, he found his basic themes in the New Testament Gospel texts, especially in Luke 4:18–19, where the youthful Jesus announces his mission: "The Spirit of the Lord is upon me, because he has anointed me to preach the good news to the poor. He has sent me to proclaim release to the captives and recovering of sight to the blind, to set at liberty those who are oppressed, to proclaim the acceptable year of the Lord." Cone concluded that as God through Jesus entered the affairs of humanity, he took sides, identifying with the oppressed. Their suffering becomes his divine despair. Cone found new force in Jesus' condemnations of the rich, and his pronouncement of blessing on the poor, who he understood as completely ready to receive the kingdom of God.

Cone's initial statement of his position, *Black Theology and Black Power* (1969), appeared simultaneously with the major texts of liberation theology, and drew very mixed reviews, many older theologians interpreting it as youthful and immature. However, it struck a cord among many black Christian intellectuals and became a foundation upon which both Cone and a host of peers have built a mature theological structure. Following Cone's leadership have been, among others, J. Deotis Roberts, James H. Evans, Cornel West, and Dwight Hopkins.

Over time, black theologians gained the respect of their colleagues and watched as the ideas seeded a set of reactions and responses. Not the least of these were conscious attempts within black congregations to embody Christianity in African-American forms, the most famous being the foundation of the Black Christian Nationalist Movement by former UNITED CHURCH OF CHRIST minister Albert B. Cleage Jr. (now known as Jaramogi Abebe Agyeman). Black theology has also taken root in Africa and in African communities in Europe. In the United States, Cone and his colleagues have been critiqued as somewhat blind to the oppression of women, and two additional movements—FEMINIST THEOLOGY and Womanist Theology—have emerged in partial response to black theology.

Further reading: James H. Cone, *Black Theology and Black Power* (New York: Seabury Press, 1969); James H. Evans, comp., *Black Theology: A Critical Assessment and Annotated Bibliography* (Westport, Conn.: Greenwood Press, 1987); Dwight Hopkins, *Shoes That Fit Our Feet: Sources for a Constructive Black Theology* (Maryknoll, N.Y.: Orbis Books, 1993); J. Deotis Roberts, *Black Theology in Dialogue* (Philadelphia: Westminster Press, 1987); Cornel West, *Prophesy Deliverance! An Afro American Revolutionary Christianity* (Philadelphia: Westminster Press, 1982).

Blackwell, Antoinette Brown
(1825–1921) *pioneer woman minister*
Antoinette Brown, the first female Protestant minister to be ordained with the approval of a church

judicatory, was born in Henrietta, New York, on May 20, 1825. She began to speak publicly during worship services at her local Congregational church when only nine years old. She attended Oberlin College, one of the first colleges to open its classes to women, from which she graduated in 1847. She completed her seminary work at Oberlin in 1850 but was denied a divinity degree. She was also refused ordination, though she did become the pastor of a Congregational church in South Butler, New York, where she was finally ordained on September 15, 1853. She left the parish the following year and eventually became a Unitarian.

Two years after leaving the pastoral ministry, Brown married Samuel L. Blackwell, the brother of college mate Lucy Stone's husband. The Blackwell brothers were both supportive of Stone's outstanding work as a women's rights activist. Antoinette moved to New Jersey with her husband and began preaching at Unitarian churches (though never returning to the pastor's role). She authored several books and frequently lectured on women's rights. She was a founding member of the New Jersey Woman's Suffrage Association in 1867. Oberlin eventually recognized Brown with an honorary M.A. in 1878 and an honorary doctorate in 1908.

Brown led an active life into her 90s, her last sermons delivered during World War I. She died in Elizabeth, New Jersey, on November 5, 1921, after participating in the first national election in which women could vote.

See also FEMINISM, CHRISTIAN; WOMEN, ORDINATION OF.

Further reading: Antoinette Brown Blackwell, *Sea Drift* (New York: James Wright, 1902); ———, *The Sexes throughout Nature* (New York, 1875); ———, *The Social Side of Mind and Action* (New York: 1915); Elizabeth Cazden, *Antoinette Brown Blackwell: A Biography* (Westbury, N.Y.: The Feminist Press, 1983); Carol Lasser and Marlene Merrill, eds., *Friends and Sisters: Letters Between Lucy Stone and Antoinette Brown Blackwell, 1846–93* (Urbana: University of Illinois Press, 1987).

Blake, Eugene Carson (1906–1985)
major ecumenical leader

Eugene Carson Blake is considered one of the 20th century's primary ecumenical visionaries. He was born on November 7, 1906, in St. Louis, Missouri. After graduating from Princeton in 1928 with a philosophy degree, he spent a year teaching at the Forman Christian College in Lahore, India. He completed his ministerial degree at Princeton Theological Seminary (1932) and served for 20 years as a Presbyterian pastor in New York City, Albany, New York, and Pasadena, California. During his decade in Pasadena, he was regularly heard in the broadcast ministry over the station his congregation owned and operated.

Also at Pasadena, in 1948, he attended the first assembly of the WORLD COUNCIL OF CHURCHES, where his speaking and organizations skills were initially recognized internationally. Two years later, he was invited to preach at the service culminating the organization of the National Council of Churches of Christ in the U.S.A. In 1951, he was elected as the stated clerk of the United Presbyterian Church (now a constituent part of the PRESBYTERIAN CHURCH [USA]).

Retaining his Presbyterian post, Blake also served as president of the National Council of Churches between 1954 and 1957. He continued on the national board of the Presbyterian General Assembly until 1966, when he became general secretary of the World Council of Churches. Blake had worked with the World Council of Churches starting in 1954, serving in a succession of key posts.

Blake was instrumental in formulating an ambitious plan to unite some of the larger Protestant churches in the United States, which resulted in the Consultation on Church Union. In 1960, Blake invited representatives of the Episcopalian, Presbyterian, and Methodist churches and the United Church of Christ, along with several other groups to engage in conversation looking toward the creation of a united Protestant church. The consultation began meeting in 1962. Over the years, it has presented several proposals for overcoming differences between the major participants, though none of the plans received more than modest support from denominational authorities.

Blake traveled widely on behalf of church union. He earned the enmity of the more conservative elements in the Protestant community who protested the attempts to build a super denomination and to establish relations with Christian churches in Communist countries, most notably the Russian Orthodox Church. Blake retired from the World Council in 1972. He went on to work with Bread for the World, an antihunger organization. He died in Stamford, Connecticut, on July 13, 1985.

See also ECUMENICAL MOVEMENT.

Further reading: Eugene Carson Blake, *The Church in the Next Decade* (New York: Macmillan, 1966); ———, *He is Lord of All* (Philadelphia: Westminster Press, 1958); R. Douglas Brackenridge, *Eugene Carson Blake: Prophet with Portfolio* (New York: Crossroad Books, 1978); Paul A. Crow, "Eugene Carson Blake: Apostle of Christian Unity," *The Ecumenical Review* 38/2 (April 1986): 228–236; Martin Niemller, Eugene Carson Blake, and Marlene Maertens, *The Challenge to the Church: The Niemoller-Blake Conversations, Lent, 1965* (Philadelphia: Westminster Press, 1965).

Blaurock, Georg (c. 1492–1529) *founding Anabaptist leader*

Little is known of the early life of Georg Blaurock. In the 1520s, he was a monk at St. Lucius Church in Chur, Switzerland, where he was known as Georg from the House of Jacob (he got his surname from the blue coat or *blauer rock* he wore during a later disputation). In 1524, he joined up with Ulrich ZWINGLI, who as pastor of the main church in Zurich, Switzerland, had begun his reformation activities. He became part of the study/discussion group that included Conrad GREBEL and Feliz MANZ, who decided that infant BAPTISM was not biblical and should be abandoned.

Infant baptism was an issue for ANABAPTISTS. Traditionally, Christians saw the church as co-

terminus with the state. Through baptism, an infant was formally made a member of the church and a citizen. By arguing against infant baptism, Blaurock was also calling for a new form of church limited to adults who had made a public profession of faith. In January 1525, after a public discussion of infant baptism and related issues, the church council decided to continue the practice.

Nevertheless, the day after the decision, on January 18, 1525, Blaurock was the first person to receive the new adult baptism. His baptism by Conrad Grebel is seen as the initiation event of the Anabaptist movement. He then baptized Grebel, Manz, and the others present. The small group began to evangelize from door to door in Zurich.

As the authorities became aware of this activity contravening the council decision, they moved to arrest the three men. Blaurock fled to the Austrian Tyrol but was eventually captured and burned at the stake at Clausen in 1529. Prior to his death, he made one significant convert, Jacob Hutter. Hutter emerged as leader of a local Anabaptist community, which developed a communal existence. They eventually moved to Russia and then the United States, where they live on through several groups of Hutterites.

Further reading: George Blaurock, "The Beginnings of the Anabaptist Reformation, Reminiscences of George Blaurock: An Excerpt from the *Hutterite Chronicle* (1525)," in George H. Williams, ed., *Spiritual and Anabaptist Writers: Documents Illustrative of the Radical Reformation* (Philadelphia: Westminster Press, 1957), The Library of Christian Classics, vol. 25; C. Arnold Snyder, *Anabaptist History and Theology: An Introduction* (Kitchener, Ontario: Pandora Press, 1995); J. Denny Weaver, *Becoming Anabaptist: The Origin and Significance of Sixteenth-Century Anabaptism* (Scottdale, Pa.: Herald Press, 1987); George H. Williams, *The Radical Reformation* (Kirksville, Mo.: Sixteenth Century Journal, 1999).

Bloody Mary *See* MARY I, QUEEN OF ENGLAND.

Bonhoeffer, Dietrich (1906–1945) *theologian and martyr of the Nazis*

German Lutheran theologian Dietrich Bonhoeffer became an inspiration to many Christian activists in the later 20th century through his resistance to the Nazi regime in Germany and his eventual martyrdom. He was born in Berlin on February 4, 1906, one of fraternal twins. His father, Karl, was an outstanding professor of psychiatry and neurology at Berlin University.

Bonhoeffer also attended Berlin University, where he lectured and earned his doctorate in 1927. He was ordained as a Lutheran minister in 1931, and subsequently lectured in theology at the university. In 1933, he moved to London, where for two years he served as pastor of two German Lutheran churches.

In 1934, a large group of Lutheran pastors organized what became known as the Confessing Church in opposition to the state church, which had been taken over by the Nazis. Upon his return to Germany, Bonhoeffer became head of the Confessing Church seminary at Finkenwalde. When the government closed the seminary in 1937, he became more active in the anti-Nazi cause. In 1940, shortly after World War II began, he was recruited to the resistance.

Bonhoeffer took part in a conspiracy to assassinate Adolf Hitler. Fellow conspirators included Bonhoeffer's brother-in-law Hans von Dohnanyi, special projects chief in German military intelligence, Admiral Wilhelm Canaris, and General Hans Oster. The bomb plot of July 20, 1944, failed, and the major conspirators, including Bonhoeffer, were arrested.

If the plot had been successful, Bonhoeffer's role was to go to England, activate his network of friends and acquaintances, and assist the process of suing for peace. During his months in jail, Bonhoeffer kept notes and corresponded with friends, the papers later becoming the property of his friend Eberhard Bethge. Much of Bonhoeffer's postwar fame resulted from the publication of his *Letters and Papers from Prison* by Bethge.

On April 9, 1945, Bonhoeffer, Canaris, Oster, and von Dohnanyi were executed. Several weeks later, Bonhoeffer's brother, Klaus, and brother-in-law Rudiger Schleicher were also executed.

Bonhoeffer was just getting started on his theological career when he became involved in the resistance. His major writing during this period is his work on ethics. His revised ethical system was remarkably similar to what would in the 1970s become known as situational or contextual ethics. A major issue was the role of the ethical person in extreme circumstances, where the ethical thing to do might be breaking the law—as in assassinating Hitler.

See also Evangelical Church of Germany.

Further reading: Eberhard Bethge, *Dietrich Bonhoeffer: A Biography* (Minneapolis, Minn.: 1999); Dietrick Bonhoeffer, *Ethics,* ed. by Eberhard Bethge. (New York: Macmillan, 1955); ———, *Letters and Papers from Prison,* ed. by Eberhard Bethge (New York: Macmillan, 1968); Theodore A. Gill, *Memo for a Movie: A Short Life of Dietrich Bonhoeffer* (New York: Macmillan, 1971); Charles Marsh, *Reclaiming Dietrich Bonhoeffer: The Promise of His Theology* (New York: Oxford University Press, 1996).

Book of Common Prayer

The Book of Common Prayer, the liturgical text most identified with the Anglican tradition, was the first complete book of church liturgy endorsed by both a church hierarchy and a government body. It was prepared by Protestant clerics who came to power after Henry VIII broke with the Roman church (1534 Act of Supremacy), and who gained additional power under the child-king Edward VI (r. 1547–53).

In 1543, Archbishop of Canterbury Thomas Cranmer declared that by Henry's wish all references to the pope should be removed from all prayer books in his realm, as should all "apocryphas, feigned legends, superstitions, orations, collects, versicles, and responses . . . [and] all saints which be not mentioned in the Scripture or authentic doctors." The service "should be made out of the Scripture and other authentic doctors." Two years later, Henry ordered that the English language be introduced into worship in place of Latin.

The first Parliament under Edward passed an act already approved by church convocation requiring that the sacrament of the LORD'S SUPPER be publicly administered under both kinds (bread and wine) and in the English language. Parliament approved the new prayer book on January 21, 1549, and ordered that all ministers in the jurisdiction ruled by Edward VI "be bounden to say and use the Mattens, Evensong, Celebration of the Lord's Supper, commonly called the Mass, and administration of each of the Sacraments, and all their common and open Prayer in such order and form as is mentioned in the same book, and none other or otherwise." In 1550, Parliament ordered all the old mass books destroyed, as the Book of Common Prayer was the only legal form of worship in England.

MARY I (r. 1553–58) tried to reestablish Roman Catholic prayer; her successor, ELIZABETH I, reinstituted the Edwardian prayer book in 1559, with a few alterations. The Book of Common Prayer, with some minor additions and changes under Elizabeth and James I, was used until 1645, when it was replaced by the Puritan *Presbyterian Directory;* the Puritans tried to destroy all copies of the Book of Common Prayer.

With the restoration of the monarchy, the prayer book was reinstituted in British churches. Parliament, in accord with church authorities, issued a revision in 1662, which for the first time included the Psalter. Scriptural quotes were revised to conform to the text of the 1611 KING JAMES VERSION of the Bible. This prayer book has remained in force, with only minor changes in 1871, 1872, and 1880. As individual ministers and congregations are authorized to use the liturgy as a base from which variations can be made (most noticeably by high-church Anglo-Catholics and low-church Evangelicals), demands for changes have been considerably reduced.

The prayer book was carried to the new English colonies in the 17th century. After the American Revolution, the newly independent Episcopal Church published a prayer book in 1790. It was adapted from the 1662 edition, with changes reflecting the political autonomy of the new country; it also included a Psalter/Hymnal. The American edition of the Book of Common Prayer was the product of the church alone, without any role by the secular government. As such, it can be changed relatively easily, and revisions have been introduced periodically. The 1928 edition was used through much of the 20th century.

In the 1970s, the Episcopal Church went through a period of turmoil over issues such as ordaining women as ministers. The church proposed a new prayer book eventually approved in 1979. Many believers criticized it for breaking too much from the 1928 edition. A significant number of conservative members withdrew from the church and established what they described as traditional Anglican churches. While divided into several episcopal jurisdictions, they all agreed to continue using the 1928 prayer book.

Elsewhere in the world, the 1662 edition was used in the missions established by the CHURCH MISSIONARY SOCIETY and the SOCIETY FOR THE PROPAGATION OF THE GOSPEL IN FOREIGN PARTS. As these mission churches matured, the new jurisdictions adapted the Church of England Book of Common Prayer to guide their worship.

The Book of Common Prayer in its several editions illustrates the role of the Anglican tradition as a bridge between the Protestant community and the Roman Catholic Church. Anglicans are the most liturgically oriented Protestants and thus the ones most open to the possibilities of reconciliation with the Roman tradition.

See also ANGLICANISM; CHURCH OF ENGLAND.

Further reading: J. H. Benton, *The Book of Common Prayer: Its Origin and Growth* (Boston: the author, 1910); David N. Griffiths, *The Bibliography of the*

Book of Common Prayer 1549–1999 (New Castle, Del.: Oak Knoll Press, 2002); William Muss-Arnolt, *The Book of Common Prayer among the Nations of the World* (New York: E. S. Gorham, 1914).

Booth, Catherine (1829–1890) *cofounder of the Salvation Army*

Catherine Mumford Booth was born on January 17, 1829, and grew up in Ashbourne, Derbyshire, England. In 1844, her family moved to London. She joined a Methodist church in Brixton, but in 1844 was excommunicated for siding with the group that left the church to form the New Connexion Methodist Church. In 1855, she married William BOOTH, a New Connexion preacher. In 1860, she wrote and published a pamphlet defending the rights of women to preach, a pamphlet that would be frequently quoted in the late 20th century. She preached for the first time in her husband's church.

In 1861, the Booths left the New Connexion and began an independent evangelistic ministry. In 1865, they settled in the Whitechapel section of East London and began to minister to the area's poor. Over the next decade, this work grew into what is now known as the SALVATION ARMY. She remained active in the Whitechapel ministry while working as a lobbyist for women and children, an author, and a public speaker. In 1886–87, she toured England, speaking on behalf of the Salvation Army and its causes. Catherine Booth died of cancer on August 20, 1890.

Further reading: Catherine Booth, *Aggressive Christianity.* (Boston: The Christian Witness, 1899); ———, *Female Ministry: Woman's Right to Preach the Gospel* (New York: Salvation Army Supplies, 1859; rpt., London: Salvation Army, 1975); F. St. G. de L. Booth-Tucker, *The Life of Catherine Booth* (New York: Fleming H. Revell, 1892); Catherine Bramwell-Booth, *Catherine Booth, the Story of Her Loves* (London: Hodder & Stoughton 1970); Roy Hattersley, *Blood and Fire: William and Catherine Booth and Their Salvation Army* (London: Little, Brown, 1999).

Booth, William (1829–1912) *cofounder of the Salvation Army*

William Booth was born on April 10, 1829, into a CHURCH OF ENGLAND family residing near Nottingham, England. As a youth, he experienced conversion in a Methodist meeting and felt a call to evangelism and missions. He began to visit the ill and practice street preaching. His lack of formal education blocked his entrance into the Wesleyan Connexion (then the largest of the Methodist churches), but he spent a decade (1850–61) preaching for the New Connexion Methodist Church, where he was ordained in 1858. He objected to his church's system of appointing ministers, and he continually wandered from his assigned posts.

In 1861, Booth and his wife Catherine BOOTH (1829–90), became involved in the HOLINESS MOVEMENT, which had been brought from America, and both experienced the Second Blessing, which the movement taught makes one perfect in love. They withdrew from the New Connexion to begin independent evangelistic work. By 1865, they had found their way to East London's Whitechapel neighborhood and launched a mission among the poor. They founded the East London Christian Revival Society which grew into the SALVATION ARMY, which organized workers in the growing mission on a military model.

In 1890, Booth published his most important book, *In Darkest England and the Way Out.* His wife died the same year. He spent the rest of his life as the Army's general, preaching, traveling, and promoting his plan to help society's most destitute. By his death on August 21, 1912, the Army had spread into more than 50 countries. He was succeeded as general by his son, Ballington Booth (1857–1940), who eventually left the Army to found the rival group Volunteers of America. His daughter, Evangeline Cory Booth, headed the Army in America before becoming its worldwide general in 1934.

Further reading: Harold Begbie, *Life of William Booth, the Founder of the Salvation Army,* 2 vols. (London:

Macmillan, 1920); William Booth, *In Darkest England and the Way Out* (London: International Headquarters of the Salvation Army, 1890); Richard Collier, *The General Next to God. The Story of William Booth and the Salvation Army* (London: Collins, 1965); Roy Hattersley, *Blood and Fire: William and Catherine Booth and Their Salvation Army* (London: Little, Brown, 1999).

born again

Born again is a phrase used by many Protestants to describe the phenomenon of gaining faith in Jesus Christ. It is an experience when everything they have been taught as Christians becomes real, and they develop a direct and personal relationship with God. The phrase derives from an incident in the Gospel of John, when Jesus tells Nicodemus, who is undergoing conversion: "I tell you the truth, unless a man is born again, he cannot see the kingdom of God" (John 3:3).

The experience is accompanied by a sense of God's forgiveness and an opening to the power and presence of the Holy Spirit. While often associated with Evangelical Christianity, the phenomenon is common across the entire spectrum of Protestant churches. In churches that emphasize evangelism, the "born again" experience tends to become the norm, and everyone is expected to be able to recount such an experience.

Most Protestants place the born again experience within the process of entering the Christian life. In this view, the beginning of faith should be followed by water BAPTISM and joining a church (becoming active in a worshipping community), if these have not been done previously.

Because many who experience being "born again" were already churchgoers, some critics compare the life of an ordinary church member unfavorably with the life of faith. In a minority of cases, this can lead to a rejection of church life, though most Protestants would point out that such a conclusion is unbiblical.

Some Protestants who note that Jesus also told Nicodemus that unless someone is "born of water and of the Spirit, he cannot see the kingdom of

God" believe that baptism is a necessary part of the born again experience, and that the absence of baptism negates its salvific effect. This idea is called baptismal regeneration and is rejected by most Protestants.

See also EVANGELICALISM.

Further reading: Charles "Chuck" Colson, *Born Again* (Old Tappan, N.J.: Chosen Books, 1978; Richard D. Dixon, Diane E. Levy, and Roger C. Lowery, "Asking the Born-Again Question," *Review of Religious Research* 30 (1988): 33–39; Billy Graham, *How to Be Born Again* (Waco, Tex.: Word, 1977).

Bosnia and Herzegovina

Bosnia and Herzegovina has been predominantly Muslim since the Ottoman Muslim conquest of the 15th century. Christianity had some presence, thanks largely to Catholic Croatia to the north and west and Orthodox Serbia to the east, but there was little room for Protestantism, the closest enclave being in more distant Transylvania.

A Lutheran church was formed in the 1750s. In 1865, Franz Tabor, a Baptist, moved to Sarajevo. His work was supplemented in the next decade by the arrival of representatives of the CHURCH OF THE NAZARENE. The small amount of Protestant work was totally disrupted by World War II and the subsequent establishment of a Marxist Yugoslavian regime under Marshal Josip Tito (1892–1980). With the fall of Marxism and the dismantling of Yugoslavia, Bosnia emerged as an independent nation. In 1992, it declared its intention to become the first Islamic state in Europe. Moves to implement the declaration resulted in civil war (a third of the country being ethnic Serbs, with another large minority of Croats). Forces from Croatia and Serbia were soon involved in the fighting. Both sides became known for their brutality and actions against civilians. A fragile peace was brought to the region toward the end of the decade.

The raging conflicts kept missionaries away, in contrast to other post-Marxist countries such as Romania and Hungary. The older churches, by now thoroughly indigenous in character, have only begun to recover. The largest work was reported by the JEHOVAH'S WITNESSES, with more than 1,300 members, followed closely by the SEVENTH-DAY ADVENTIST CHURCH, the only Protestant church with more than 1,000 members. Several other groups have initiated work, including the CHRISTIAN BRETHREN and the New Apostolic Church. Some of the Evangelical organizations worked together to found the Bosnia and Herzegovina Bible Society in 1999 to coordinate the publication of the Bible and Christian literature.

Further reading: David Barret, *The Encyclopedia of World Christianity,* 2nd ed. (New York: Oxford University Press, 2001); Patrick Johnstone and Jason Mandryk, *Operation World, 21st Century Edition* (Carlisle, Cumbria, U.K.: Paternoster, 2001).

Branham Tabernacle and related assemblies

In the 1940s, a movement grew up around the healing ministry of William Marion Branham (1909–65), an independent Pentecostal minister. While healing evangelists such as John G. Lake (1870–1935) had been active in previous decades, Branham's ministry inspired other Pentecostal evangelists to coordinate their activities. The movement coalesced around a magazine, *The Voice of Healing,* edited by Branham associate Gordon Lindsay (1906–1973).

The movement flourished in the 1950s with evangelists such as Oral Roberts (b. 1918), Morris Cerullo (b. 1932), and Velmer Gardner. Toward the end of the decade, Branham became distanced from most of his former associates. He began to preach against the Trinity, and denounced denominationalism as the mark of the Beast (Rev. 13:17). Many heard that as a call to leave even the loose denominational associations operating among the Pentecostals and join independent Pentecostal assemblies.

In 1963, Branham began to speak about God's promise to send Elijah as a messenger. He allowed others to identify him as the Elijah messenger (mentioned in Malachi 4:5), though he never made the claim himself. Two years later, Branham died. Those ministers and congregations who had come to accept the Elijah message and believed Branham was the messenger began acting on that belief. The Branham Tabernacle in Jeffersonville, Indiana, began publishing audio and print copies of all of Branham's sermons and books. Led by Branham's relatives, the William Branham Evangelistic Association and The Voice of God (the publishing concern) worked to disseminate the message.

By the end of the 20th century, Branham's writings were being translated into more than 30 languages and distributed worldwide by an estimated 700,000 believers. Congregations are loosely associated and avoid denominational labels, but are tied together by Branham's non-Trinitarian theology and belief in his prophetic role. The Branham movement exists as a major dissenting community in world Protestantism.

See also ESCHATOLOGY; PENTECOSTALISM.

Further reading: William Branham, *Footprints in the Sands of Time* (Jeffersonville, Ind.: Spoken Word Publications, n.d.); Gordon Lindsay, *William Branham, A Man Sent from God* (Jeffersonville, Ind.: William Branham, 1950); C. Douglas Weaver, *The Healer Prophet, William Marion Branham: A Study in the Prophetic in American Protestantism* (Macon, Ga.: Mercer University Press, 1987).

Bray, Thomas (1656–1730) *early founder of missionary organizations*

Thomas Bray, cofounder of two of the oldest Protestant missionary organizations, was born on February 15, 1656, in Shropshire, England. He attended Oxford and was ordained a priest in the CHURCH OF ENGLAND. He served a parish in Warwickshire, where he wrote a popular book of catechetical lectures that brought him to the attention of the bishop of London, who was responsible for the slowly emerging work in the American colonies.

In 1695, the governor of Maryland asked the bishop to appoint a commissary (assistant) to guide the development of the Church of England there. Bray was appointed to the post in 1696. It would be almost three years before he left for the New World. He used the time to try to recruit other missionaries but discovered only young and hence relatively poor ministers were willing to join the adventure.

On March 8, 1698, Bray met with four influential laymen who were convinced of the need to help Bray "counteract the growth of vice and immorality" by combating the widespread public ignorance of Christian teachings. Bray suggested education and the publishing of Christian literature as the solution. The five men founded the SOCIETY FOR PROMOTING CHRISTIAN KNOWLEDGE (SPCK). Among other programs, the society aimed to provide deanery libraries throughout the church. Bray eventually founded 39 libraries in America and some 80 in England.

Bray spent only 10 weeks in Maryland, in 1699. Back in England, he worked to create an agency to support foreign missions. In 1701, he obtained a charter from the king and moved swiftly to incorporate the SOCIETY FOR THE PROPAGATION OF THE GOSPEL IN FOREIGN PARTS (SPG), understood at the time as the American and Caribbean colonies. The SPG took on the search for ministers for the American colonies, while the SPCK undertook to supply them with a basic library.

In 1806, Bray became the priest in charge of St. Botolph without Aldgate. He used his pulpit to advocate for a wide variety of causes including the care of prisoners and the plight of African slaves in the Americas. He helped convince James Oglethorpe to found the Georgia colony, designed to provide those in debtors' prison with a second chance.

See also ANGLICANISM; UNITED STATES OF AMERICA.

Further reading: William D. Houlette, "Parish Libraries and the Work of the Reverend Thomas Bray,"

Library Quarterly 4 (October 1934): 588–609; Charles F. Pascoe, *Two Hundred Years of the SPG: An Historical Account of the Society for the Propagation of the Gospel in Foreign Parts, 1701–1900* (London: Society for the Propagation of the Gospel, 1901); Bernard C. Steiner, "The Reverent Thomas Bray and His American Libraries," *American Historical Review* 2 (1896–1897): 59–75; Henry P. Thompson, *Into All Lands: The History of the Society for the Propagation of the Gospel in Foreign Parts, 1701–1950* (London: SPCK, 1951); ———, *Thomas Bray* (London: SPCK, 1954).

Brazil

Protestantism had a first beginning in Brazil when the Dutch briefly occupied Recife (1630–54), but it really took root in 1819, when the CHURCH OF ENGLAND established a small parish for English expatriates in São Paulo. A few years later, a German Lutheran church was opened for immigrants who had settled outside of Rio de Janeiro. Over the next century, Germans continued to immigrate and form a number of relatively homogeneous communities, most in southern Brazil. There are now more than a million Brazilian Lutherans, divided between the Evangelical Church of the Lutheran Confession of Brazil (a member of the WORLD COUNCIL OF CHURCHES) and the Evangelical Lutheran Church of Brazil (aligned with the LUTHERAN CHURCH–MISSOURI SYNOD).

In 1859, an American Presbyterian minister arrived in Brazil and founded the first Presbyterian church in the country in Rio de Janeiro in 1865. It would eventually spawn three different Presbyterians bodies, the Presbyterian Church of Brazil, the Independent Presbyterian Church, and the Conservative Presbyterians Church, which between them now include approximately 700,000 members.

Baptists were next to arrive; they have had spectacular results in the 20th century. The Brazilian Baptist Convention (affiliated with the SOUTHERN BAPTIST CONVENTION) has approximately 1.5 million members.

Methodism had small beginnings in 1835, but only flourished after the arrival in 1876 of Rev.

Junias Eastham Newman, a missionary with the Methodist Episcopal Church, South (now a part of the UNITED METHODIST CHURCH). Today the Methodist Church of Brazil numbers approximately 130,000 members.

Toward the end of the 19th century, the SEVENTH-DAY ADVENTIST CHURCH entered Brazil; it already claims almost 1 million members. However, within the larger Protestant community, the older groups have been completely overwhelmed by the growth of PENTECOSTALISM. The ASSEMBLIES OF GOD of Brazil began when two Swedish missionaries who had encountered the movement in William H. Durham's church in Chicago settled in Belém, where their initial audience included members of the Baptist church.

From their initial effort, Pentecostalism gradually spread, and by 1940 had only some 400,000 members. In the years immediately following World War II, the growth rate picked up considerably. By 1970, the Assemblies had become the largest non-Catholic church in the country, and by the end of the century reported in excess of 7 million members. It has also become the parent to several other large churches, the most important being the Christian Congregation of Brazil (a movement among Italian immigrants with more than 3 million members) and the UNIVERSAL CHURCH OF THE KINGDOM OF GOD, with more than 4 million members. The latter has become an international body with churches in 50 or more countries.

Pentecostalism has thus become the majority group of the Protestant community. Several newer churches have also experienced spectacular growth, especially the Evangelical Pentecostal Church of Brazil for Christ, the Cornerstone Gospel Church, and the God Is Love Pentecostal Church, which together have more than a million members. With the spectacular spread of Pentecostalism, the growth of the other Evangelical churches, including some Holiness churches, has largely been ignored.

The ecumenical scene has been somewhat chaotic, with several competing councils. Many of the older Protestant churches belong to the National Council of Churches in Brazil, itself affil-iated with the World Council of Churches. Several major denominations belong to the World Council independently of the Brazil Council. There is also an affiliate of the WORLD EVANGELICAL ALLIANCE, the Brazil National Alliance, to which a spectrum of more conservative churches belong. Counting Protestants in Brazil is difficult because of the high number of doubly affiliated Christians.

See also SOUTH AMERICA.

Further reading: R. G. Frase, *A Sociological Analysis of the Development of Brazilian Protestantism: A Study in Social Change* (Princeton, N.J.: Princeton Theological Seminary, thesis, 1975); E. P. Velasco, *A History of the Christian Evangelical Church in Brazil* (Jackson, Miss.: Reformed Theological Seminary, Th.M. thesis, 1992); W. Wedemann, *A History of Protestant Missions in Brazil, 1850–1914* (Louisville, Ky.: Southern Baptist Theological seminary, thesis, 1977); E. Willems, *Followers of the New Faith: Culture, Change and the Rise of Protestantism in Brazil and Chile* (Nashville, Tenn.: Vanderbilt University Press, 1967).

Brethren

Within the Protestant movement, several distinct groups have at different times assumed the name Brethren; the name implied the closeness and intimacy they saw as a feature of their fellowship and also allowed them to distinguish themselves without assuming a sectarian name. All these groups opposed the state church system, advocating a return to the beliefs, organization, and practices of the church as they saw it portrayed in the Bible.

In Zurich, Switzerland, in the 1520s, Conrad GREBEL (1498–1526), Feliz MANZ, and others initiated the movement that became known as the Swiss Brethren by performing the first adult BAPTISMS in 1525. Persecuted in Switzerland, believers scattered to Germany, Austria, and the Netherlands. All but destroyed in the German-speaking countries, the Brethren found relative safety in the Netherlands. A new leader emerged there, Menno SIMONS, who transformed the remnants of the Brethren into the MENNONITES. The heritage of the Swiss Brethren is periodically recalled when new

Mennonite groups add the word *Brethren* to their name, more significant ones being the Mennonite Brethren Church and the Brethren in Christ.

At the beginning of the 18th century, a similar FREE CHURCH impulse grew up in the Palatinate (western Germany) when a group decided to separate from the dominant Lutheran Church and found a group centered on personal piety. In 1708, Alexander Mack became the leader of the small company of eight individuals covenanted together in a "church of Christian believers." They rebaptized one another. However, Germany was no more accepting than Zurich had been two centuries before. Fortunately, there was one land that not only accepted them, but also recruited them as settlers—the Pennsylvania colony in British North America. Many migrated and eventually organized as the Church of the Brethren. The German Baptist Brethren, as they were commonly known, eventually splintered into a number of different groups, most of which retained the word *Brethren* in their name—Fellowship of Grace Brethren Churches, Old Brethren Church, and so forth. Like the Quakers, the Brethren and Mennonites have remained relatively small, but they have had an impact as spearheads of the modern peace movement.

A new group emerged in the British Isles in the mid-19th century that wished to separate from the state church (the several Anglican bodies) and to return to what it saw as the simple life of the biblical church. The group refused to adopt any "denominational" label, and they were commonly referred to as "the brethren." There was no headquarters. Periodicals were published by individuals and survived on subscriptions. Leadership was charismatic and arose out of the local assemblies. Those who distinguished themselves by writing or preaching soon became informally known as the "chief men among the brethren." An early congregation at Plymouth, England, became known to outsiders as the "Plymouth Brethren," and the name stuck.

Standing out in the first generation was John Nelson DARBY (1800–82). A former priest in the Church of Ireland (Anglican), he left the church in 1827, and with a small group in Dublin formed the first Brethren fellowship. Darby evangelized widely through Europe and North America. He developed a new way of understanding the Bible called DISPENSATIONALISM. Dispensationalists divided biblical and world history into a series of periods, in each of which God acted differently toward humanity and made different demands. Early dispensations were seen as hinting at and leading to Christ, whose death and resurrection initiated a new dispensation, that of grace. The dispensation of the kingdom was yet to come, but was imminent.

In the middle of the century, Darby and one of the leaders in Plymouth, B. W. Newton, pursued a controversy over several issues, the most important being the relationship of the Brethren to other Christians. Those who would relate only to true believers in separated Brethren congregations were called the Exclusive Brethren, as opposed to the Open Brethren, who related to true believers in non-Brethren fellowships.

Over the next century, the Open Brethren supported a vigorous missionary program and continued to grow internationally. In the late 20th century, they became known as the Christian Brethren. Controversies split the Exclusive Brethren into as many as a dozen mutually exclusive factions, the largest falling under the leadership successively of F. E. Raven, James Taylor Sr., and James Taylor Jr. The Raven-Taylor Brethren became increasingly separatist by the late 20th century.

The Brethren movement launched by John Nelson Darby has had a significant impact on contemporary EVANGELICALISM. In North America, beginning with evangelist Dwight L. MOODY, many conservative Protestants adopted dispensationalism and its belief in the imminent return of Christ. Dispensationalism became prominent, if not dominant, among Fundamentalists in the 1920s and continues as an important theological force in contemporary Evangelicalism, being identified with such leading institutions as the Dallas Theological Seminary and Moody Biblical Institute.

See also RADICAL REFORMATION.

Further reading: Roy Coad, *A History of the Brethren Movement* (Exeter, U.K.: Paternoster Press, 1968); Donald F. Durnbaugh, *The Brethren Encyclopedia* (Philadelphia: Brethren Encyclopedia, 1983); Hy Pickering, *Chief Men among the Brethren* (London: Pickering & Inglis, 1918); Bryan R. Wilson, *The Brethren: A Current Sociological Appraisal* (Oxford: All Souls College, 1981).

Bridgman, Elijah Coleman (1801–1861)
first American missionary to China

E. C. Bridgman was born at Belchertown, Massachusetts, on April 22, 1801. He attended Amherst College and graduated from Andover Theological Seminary in 1829. Almost immediately, he responded to the call for help in China and accepted an appointment from the AMERICAN BOARD OF COMMISSIONERS FOR FOREIGN MISSIONS. Sailing on the same ship that brought fellow American Board missionary David ABEEL to China, early in 1830, he arrived in Canton, where he met Robert MORRISON, began to learn Chinese, and purchased a press, where he began issuing the *Chinese Repository* in 1832.

Bridgman attempted both to inform Westerners of the realities of Chinese life and to change overly negative opinions of the West among Chinese by teaching them about Western learning and culture. To accomplish the former goal, he wrote home voluminously; to advance the latter end, he founded the Society for the Diffusion of Useful Knowledge in 1834.

The *Chinese Repository* anchored much of Bridgman's life while he mastered Chinese and engaged in other endeavors. In 1838, he founded the Medical Missionary Society in China. For a period he edited the journal of the North China Branch of the Royal Asiatic Society. He spent two years working on a Chinese chrestomathy, a tool to help foreigners learn Chinese. He served as a translator during the negotiations that led to further opening of China to the Americans in the 1840s.

In 1847, Bridgman moved to Shanghai, where his wife, Mary Jane Gillet, an Episcopalian missionary, opened a girl's school and ran it for the next 15 years. Bridgman spent the rest of his life working on a Bible translation, which was published posthumously. In 1858, he founded the Shanghai Literary and Scientific Society, modeled on the Royal Asiatic Society. Following Bridgman's death on November 2, 1861, his wife moved to Beijing, there founded the Bridgman Academy, and continued her work in female education.

Like Morrison, Bridgman made few converts, but is honored for his work in opening the Chinese to the growing Christian missionary effort throughout China.

See also CHINA; CONGREGATIONALISM.

Further reading: Elijah C. Bridgman, *Chinese Chrestomathy in the Canton Dialect* (Macau: S. Wells Williams, 1841); Eliza Jane Bridgman, *The Life and Labors of Elijah Coleman Bridgman* (New York: Anson D. F. Randolph, 1864); Murray A. Rubenstein, *The Origin of the Anglo-American Missionary Enterprise in China, 1807–1840* (London: Scarecrow Press, 1996).

Brief Statement of Faith (Presbyterian)

In 1983 in the United States, the United Presbyterian Church and the Presbyterian Church, separated since before the American Civil War, merged to form the PRESBYTERIAN CHURCH (U.S.A.). In adopting the Plan for Reunion, the new church called for a new brief statement of the Reformed faith, to be included in the church's *Book of Confessions*.

In 1967, the United Presbyterian Church adopted a new statement of faith, in the face of opposition from conservatives who said that it departed from the traditional standards set forth at Westminster in the 17th century. In place of the one WESTMINSTER CONFESSION, the church (much as the Lutherans had done in the 16th century) adopted a set of confessional statements that were placed in a *Book of Confessions*. Ministers and other leaders were not asked to "subscribe" to the confessions, but to receive them and operate out of the context that they set.

Those who supported the new confession, finally presented in 1991, insisted that it was not to be seen as a stand-alone document or a complete statement of beliefs. It was to affirm some important contemporary themes and be placed alongside the other confessions that the church affirmed. Like the ancient Nicene Creed, the new confession was written in a format that suggested its use in public worship as a statement to be read aloud by the gathered congregation.

The new confession emphasizes themes affirmed in common in the ecumenical church, represented most visibly by the WORLD COUNCIL OF CHURCHES. It stresses the church's work in the world and some contemporary concerns that have become the focus of liberal Protestantism, such as the inclusiveness of the Christian community and the need to reach out to the poor, the captive, and the suffering. Toward the end, it affirms the activity of the Holy Spirit by noting that: "the Spirit gives us courage / to pray without ceasing, / to witness among all peoples to Christ as Lord and Savior, / to unmask idolatries in church and culture, / to hear the voices of peoples long silenced, / and to work with others for justice, freedom, and peace."

See also CREEDS/CONFESSIONS OF FAITH.

Further reading: Clifton Kirkpatrick and William H. Hopper, Jr., *What Unites Presbyterians: Common Ground for Troubled Times* (Louisville, Ky.: Geneva Press, 1997); J. Gordon Melton, *The Encyclopedia of American Religions: Religious Creeds,* 2 vols. (Detroit: Gale Research, 1988, 1994); Jack Bartlett Rogers, *Presbyterian Creeds* (Louisville, Ky.: Westminster/John Knox Press, 1991); ———, *Reading the Bible and the Confessions: The Presbyterian Way* (Louisville, Ky.: Geneva Press, 1999).

British Israelism

British Israelism (also known as Anglo-Israelism) is a pandenominational movement advocating the notion that the people of northern and western Europe, especially Great Britain, are the literal descendants of the ancient Israelite people, specifically the fabled Ten Lost Tribes of Israel. The Anglo-Saxon nations were thus the inheritors of God's promises to the ancient Israelites and destined to rule the world. While a number of similar ideas were expressed as early as the 17th century, it was first presented as a full-blown concept by Richard Brothers (1757–1824), who also claimed direct descent from King David of Israel.

A more sober treatment of the idea emerged in 1840, when John Wilson (1779–1870) published his lectures on *Our Israelitish Origin*. Wilson had gathered as much supporting data as was then available from linguistic, archaeological, and historical sources. His book circulated throughout the English-speaking world and drew support from among various Protestant bodies. Later in the century, Edward Hine (1825–91) tied British Israelism to pyramidology, a belief that the Great Pyramid of Giza conceals secret meanings in its design and measurements.

Hine formed the British Israel Identity Corporation in 1878, which in 1919 merged into the British Israel World Federation in the United Kingdom. Canadian affiliates were organized as early as 1907. The oldest American group seems to be the Anglo-Saxon Federation of America formed in 1928 by Howard Rand. Other groups appeared in Australia, New Zealand, and South Africa.

British Israelism found confirmation in the 19th century expansion of the British Empire. By the beginning of the 20th century, it was finding further confirmation in various racist and white supremacist theories. In the latter half of the 20th century, it became associated with some of the more radical racist and anti-Semitic groups in North America.

In the 1930s, British Israelism was adopted by evangelist Herbert W. ARMSTRONG, whose Worldwide Church of God became in the 1980s the most successful organization ever to advocate the idea, circulating hundreds of thousands of copies of Armstrong's book, *The United States and Britain in Prophecy.* The Worldwide Church disavowed

British Israelism, but it is still taught in successor groups such as the Living Church of God, the United Church of God, and the Philadelphia Church of God.

The more racist and violent trend within the world of British Israelism is called the Identity movement, which is generally traced to the scurrilous anti-Semite Gerald L. K. Smith (1898–1976) and his follower Wesley Swift, who brought SACRED NAME teachings into the movement. Swift founded the Church of Christ Christian (later adding the words *of Aryan Nations*).

Mainstream Protestant leaders began to distance themselves from British Israelism in the 19th century and made serious efforts to refute it at the beginning of the 20th. They condemned its non-Trinitarian theology, but focused even more on the bad science and history behind claims for a physical relationship between Anglo-Saxons and the ancient Israelites. British Israelism has suffered greatly from the demise of the British Empire and the findings of modern archaeology, which clearly refute their ideas. The Identity movement has been additionally discredited by its association with racial violence.

See also CHRISTIAN IDENTITY MOVEMENT.

Further reading: Herbert W. Armstrong, *The United States and Britain in Prophecy* (Pasadena, Calif.: Worldwide Church of God, 1981), various editions; Michael Barkun, *Religion and the Racist Right: The Origins of the Christian Identity Movement* (Chapel Hill: University of North Carolina Press, 1994); Anton Drams, *The Delusion of British-Israelism* (New York: Loizeaux Brothers, n.d.); Reginald Horsman, *Race and Manifest Destiny: The Origins of American Racial Anglo-Saxonism* (Cambridge, Mass.: Harvard Press, 1981); John Wilson, *Our Israelish Origins* (Philadelphia: Daniels & Smith, 1950).

British Virgin Islands

The British Virgin Islands comprise 36 islands on the northeast edge of the Caribbean Sea. They were successively inhabited by the Carib and Arawak peoples, the Spanish, the Dutch and finally, in the 17th century, the British, who introduced sugar plantations and brought in African slaves as cheap labor. Descendants of the slaves constitute the majority of the population. Local citizens elect their own legislature, but London still appoints the governor and has responsibility for foreign relations, defense, and internal security.

Methodists arrived in 1780. They took pains to evangelize the Africans and at one point claimed 70 percent of the population as their members. With 4,000 members, they still claim the allegiance of half of the islands' churchgoers.

The CHURCH OF ENGLAND, based in the white population, became the second-largest church in the islands. Early in the 20th century, the care of the islands' Anglicans was turned over to the EPISCOPAL CHURCH (of the United States), whose Diocese of the Virgin Islands is based in the neighboring American Virgin Islands.

More than a dozen Protestant-Free Church groups have arrived in the British Virgin Islands over the past 100 years, the largest being the SEVENTH-DAY ADVENTIST CHURCH and the CHURCH OF GOD (ANDERSON, INDIANA). The Anglicans, Methodists, and Catholics cooperate in the Tortola Interchurch Council (Tortola being the principal island in the territory).

See also CARIBBEAN.

Further reading: F. W. Blackman, *Methodism: Two Hundred Years in the British Virgin Islands* (Bridgetown, Barbados: Methodist Church of the British Virgin Islands, 1989); D. G. Mason, *The Church in the Process of Development in the British Virgin Islands* (Madison, N.J.: Drew University, STM thesis, 1874).

Brotherhood of the Cross and Star

The Brotherhood of the Cross and Star is an AFRICAN INITIATED CHURCH founded in Nigeria in 1956 by Olumba Olumba Obu (b. 1918). Raised in a non-Christian environment, Obu was a somewhat precocious child and is claimed to have performed miracles when only five years old. He claims to know the Bible but asserts that most of it, apart from the Book of Revelation, is closed to modern readers and hence useless. He is believed to be the eighth and final incarnation of God (Jesus having been the seventh), a belief he acknowledged in 1977. Known for his healing and miracles (done in the powerful name of Obu), Obu's initials are frequently written on homes and automobiles as a protective sign.

Obu teaches a variety of ideas that draw on Protestantism as well as other sources. For example, his idea of God is monistic; he reveres Jesus but believes him to have been fallible; and he teaches reincarnation. He emphasizes healing and material prosperity but promises deliverance from witchcraft. Among traditional practices that Obu denounces are magic, divining, and polygamy. Members are baptized by immersion, and prior to Sunday worship, FOOT WASHING is often practiced.

The church has grown significantly with estimates as high as 1 million members. Concentrated in Nigeria and Ghana, it now has members scattered through West Africa, Europe (especially the United Kingdom), and even the United States.

See also AFRICA, SUB-SAHARAN.

Further reading: Roselind I. J. Hackett, *Religion in Calabar* (Berlin: Mouton de Gyuter, 1989); *The Handbook of the Brotherhood and Star* (Calabar, Nigeria: Brotherhood Press, n.d.); Friday M. Mbon, *Brotherhood of the Cross and Star: A New Religious Movement in Nigeria* (Frankfurt am main: Peter Lang, 1992).

Brown, Antoinette   *See* BLACKWELL, Antoinette Brown.

Browne, Robert *(c. 1550–1633) early English radical reformer*

Claimed by both BAPTISTS and CONGREGATIONALISTS, Robert Browne was the founder of an independent church movement in Elizabethan England notable for its rejection of church-state connections. Born into a well-to-do family near Stamford, England, about 1550, he attended CAMBRIDGE UNIVERSITY, graduating from Corpus Christi College in 1572. He became a schoolmaster at Southwark and also began to preach at Islington, where he first espoused some of his separatist, Puritan notions.

At the end of the 1570s, he returned to Cambridge, where he lived with a Puritan clergyman, Richard Greenham; loyal to the CHURCH OF ENGLAND, Greenham was known for his simplicity in both dress and worship. Here, Browne's ideas were nurtured, and he concluded that the voice of the church rested with the people, not with bishops. When Browne was placed in charge of the Benet Church in Cambridge, he refused to seek the legitimizing authority of the local bishop, refused his stipend, and used his pulpit to attack episcopal authority. The city council and the bishop moved to stop his preaching.

Now unemployed, Browne visited Holland, then the most religiously tolerant nation in Europe, where he probably made contact with ANABAPTIST leaders. He returned to settle in Norwich, known as a refugee center of Dutch who had earlier fled from Spanish rule. With a friend, Robert Harrison, he formed the first British independent congregation around 1580. The structuring of the congregation included instruction in Browne's basic understanding of church life and the adoption of a covenant in which believers joined themselves to God and elected their leaders, to whom they promised obedience. They adopted procedures for receiving new members and for removing any who proved unworthy. Officers included the pastor, the teacher, the elders, the deacons, and the widows. Anticipating other such congregations, Browne made provisions for associative fellowships of congregations.

Browne became an enthusiastic propagandist for separatism and soon faced the first of his many imprisonments. In 1581, the congregation as a group relocated to Middleburg, which brought him up against Thomas CARTWRIGHT, who had been fired from his position at Cambridge for advocating

Presbyterianism, which opposed bishops but still wanted formal ties with the government.

Browne lived two tumultuous years at Middleberg, during which time he published three works outlining his position. In the end, his conflicts with other Puritans and his brash manner turned the church at Middleberg against him as an "unlawful pastor." He withdrew and went to Scotland, Harrison inheriting leadership of the congregation, which dispersed in the 1590s. In 1593, ELIZABETH I condemned Browne and had the two men who attempted to distribute his works executed.

After failing in 1584 to bring the Presbyterians of Scotland into the Independents' camp, he returned to England. Two years later, he relented, offered his assent to the Church of England, and returned to his old occupation as a schoolmaster. Five years later, he became rector of Achurchcuin-Thorpe in Northamptonshire, where he lived quietly for the next 40 years, married twice, having outlived his first wife, and fathered nine children. In 1633, he died in jail after assaulting a local constable.

In later centuries, the Baptists would see in him a precursor, though he did not voice opinions on adult BAPTISM. He was also claimed by the Congregationalist Puritans, who arose in the next century, though he argued for complete disconnection from the state. Closest to his approach were the Pilgrims, the small band that left England for Holland and eventually settled in Plymouth, Massachusetts.

Further reading: Stephen Brachlow, *The Communion of Saints: Radical Puritan and Separatist Ecclesiology 1570–1625* (Oxford, New York: Oxford University Press, 1988); A. Peel and L. H. Carlson, eds., *The Writings of Robert Harrison and Robert Browne* (London: George Allen & Unwin, 1953); Fredericke J. Powicke, *Robert Browne: Pioneer of Modern Congregationalism* (London: Congregational Union, 1910); R. B. White, *The Development of the Doctrine of the Church among English Separatists with Special Reference to Robert Browne and John Smyth* (Oxford: Oxford University, Ph.D. diss., 1961); ———, *The English Separatist Tradition from the Marian Martyrs to the Pilgrim Fathers* (London: Oxford University Press, 1971).

Bruderhof

The Bruderhof is a Christian communal group inspired largely by the Hutterites, a communal Anabaptist group. It began in 1920, when Eberhard Arnold (1883–1935) and his wife, Emmy, opened a Christian commune in a rented German farmhouse. Reading ANABAPTIST history led to a fascination with the Hutterites, and in 1930 Arnold spent a year visiting the colonies in Canada.

To escape the Nazis, in 1933 Bruderhof members moved first to Liechtenstein and then to England, where Arnold died in 1935, to Paraguay at the start of World War II, and finally to the United States, where they settled initially at Rifton, New York, still the informal headquarters. Further growth, largely from members of other communal groups, led to the founding of eight additional hofs in the U.S., England, and Australia. Internal discord has led to desertions at several important points, most recently in the 1980s, when charges of child abuse were leveled at some of the leaders. Ties with the Hutterite movement were broken in the 1990s. In 2000, the Bruderhof reported some 3,000 members.

Further reading: Eberhard Arnold, *Why We Live in Community* (Farmington, Pa.: Plough, 1995); Emmy Arnold, *Torches Together: The Beginning and Early Years of the Bruderhof Communities* (Rifton, N.Y.: Plough, 1964); Benjamin Zablocki, *The Joyful Community* (Chicago: University of Chicago Press, 1971).

Brunei

Brunei is a small country on the island of Borneo, the remnant of a sultanate that at one time controlled the entire island. The British formed a protectorate in 1888 that lasted until independence in 1984. Some two-thirds of the population are Malaysian, almost all of whom are Muslim.

Another 11 percent follow traditional ethnic religions, and 9 percent are Buddhists.

The British introduced Christianity and the CHURCH OF ENGLAND. Today, Anglicans and Catholics, each 3,000-strong, are the largest Christian groups. The Evangelical Church of Borneo is an outgrowth of the Borneo Evangelical Mission, an independent Protestant missionary agency founded in 1928 with Methodist roots. Missionary personnel left with the departure of British rulers, but the church continued with indigenous leadership.

In the decades since World War II, other churches have established work, primarily among non-Malaysians. Of these, the SEVENTH-DAY ADVENTIST CHURCH has been by far the most successful. The growth of the Christian community has been checked by government regulations against proselytizing and any activities that might infringe upon the peace of society. The country has lived under an official state of emergency since 1962.

In December 2000, three members of the Evangelical Church of Borneo were arrested and charged with "cultlike" activities that included attempting to convert Muslims and importing Indonesian Bibles. The church has remained under intense scrutiny.

See also MALAYSIA.

Further reading: David Barrett, *The Encyclopedia of World Christianity,* 2nd ed. (New York: Oxford University Press, 2001); Shirley P. Lees, *Jungle Fire* (Lawas: Borneo Evangelical Mission, 1967).

Brunner, Emil (1889–1966) *Neo-Orthodox Protestant theologian*

Emil Bruner was born on December 23, 1889, at Winterthur, Switzerland. He studied at the universities at Berlin and Zurich, receiving his doctorate in 1913. He then spent a year in England (1913–14) teaching high school in Leeds, before returning to his homeland, where he was ordained in the Swiss Reformed Church and became a pastor. In 1924, he joined the faculty of the University of Zurich, where he remained for almost three decades.

Trained by professors steeped in classical liberal Protestantism, with its promise of progress into the kingdom of God, Brunner began to reject his teachers even before World War I, which so decisively killed liberalism for most Europeans. His early work *Das Symbolische in der Religiösen* (1914) criticized the views of Friedrich SCHLEIERMACHER (1768–1834), the early voice of German liberalism. In the 1920s, Brunner became part of the theological network around fellow Swiss theologian Karl BARTH. The NEO-ORTHODOXY they developed looked much more closely to the biblical text in creating a theology based on the traditional affirmations of the church.

Brunner's multivolume *Church Dogmatics* reexamined the doctrines of God, creation, redemption, and the church. Christ was the focus of books such as *The Mediator,* and ethics were discussed in *The Divine Imperative.*

During the 1920s and early 1930s, Barth and Brunner had an ongoing exchange on some basic theological issues including knowledge of God and the role of apologetics in Christian theology. Their differences culminated in a short work by Brunner entitled "Nature and Grace" and the famous reply by Barth entitled "No!" They broke in 1934, despite basic agreement on most issues. Brunner capped his career with two years as a professor at the new International Christian University in Tokyo (1953–55). He died on April 6, 1966, in Zürich.

Further reading: Emil Brunner, *The Divine Imperative: A Study in Christian Ethics,* trans. by Olive Wyon. (London: Lutterworth Press, 2002); ———, *Dogmatics I–III,* trans. by Olive Wyon (James Clarke, 2002); Emil Brunner and Karl Barth, *Natural Theology: Comprising "Nature and Grace" by Professor Dr. Emil Brunner and the Reply "No!" by Dr. Karl Barth,* trans. by Peter Frankel (Eugene, Ore.: Wipf & Stock, 2002); Mark G. McKim, *Emil Brunner: A Bibliography,* American Theological Library Association Bibliography Series (Scarecrow Press, 1997); René de Visme Williamson, *Politics and Protestant Theology: An Inter-*

pretation of Tillich, Barth, Bonhoeffer, and Brunner (Baton Rouge: Louisiana State University Press, 1976).

Bucer, Martin (1491–1551) *unifying church leader in the Reformation era*

As a leader of the 16th-century Reformation, Martin Bucer became known for his efforts to reconcile the opposing views of Swiss reformer Ulrich ZWINGLI and Martin LUTHER. Bucer was born on November 11, 1491, at Schlettstadt, Alsace, and became a Dominican monk at age 14; he eventually graduated from the University of Heidelberg in 1517. The following year, he heard Luther speak for the first time and soon became an enthusiastic supporter of the Reformation. He left the Dominicans in 1521. While serving as a parish priest in Landstuhl (1522), he married Elizabeth Silbereisen, a former nun.

In 1523, he moved to Strasburg, where he soon became the dominant voice of the Reformation in the region. His efforts to mediate between Zwingli and Luther, whose ideas on the LORD'S SUPPER diverged considerably, brought him criticism from both camps. Zwingli and Luther met personally to attempt a reconciliation, but the MARBURG COLLOQUY of 1529 failed. Bucer tried again in 1530, when he presented the Confession of the Four Cities (Strasburg, Constance, Memmingen, and Lindau), which mediated the two positions but proved acceptable to neither. Later that year, he gave up and simply adhered to the Lutheran AUGSBURG CONFESSION OF FAITH.

Though now committed to the Lutherans, in 1536 he led in the "Concordia of Wittenberg," a last attempt to unite German-speaking Protestants. He also tried to further the Protestant cause among Roman Catholics by attending the 1540 Catholic-Protestant conference at Hagenau, Lower Alsace, and the 1541 Diet of Ratisbon. He worked with Philip MELANCHTHON to introduce Lutheran ideas into the Archdiocese of Cologne in 1542, though the effort had little effect.

For three years (1538–41), John CALVIN lived in Strasburg and absorbed much of his thinking

about church organization and the nature of the ideal Christian society from Bucer. Bucer is seen as the fountainhead of the Book of Church Order that later became a standard document in the Reformed tradition.

In 1548, the diet at Ausburg proclaimed a temporary doctrinal agreement (the Augsburg Interim) between Catholics and Protestants in Germany. Though it permitted the marriage of priests and the offering of the Eucharist in both kinds, on most issues it accepted the Roman Catholic stance. Bucer emerged as one of its most outspoken opponents, and his position at Strasburg became untenable. In 1549, he accepted an invitation extended from Archbishop Thomas CRANMER to move to England, where he was offered a position as Regius Professor of Divinity at CAMBRIDGE UNIVERSITY. He died in Cambridge a scant two years later on February 28, 1551.

In 1556, Catholic queen MARY I (1553–58) had Bucer's remains exhumed and burned and his tomb demolished. The tomb was reconstructed in 1560 under ELIZABETH I. In 1577, the first of a projected 10-volume set of his writings appeared under the title *Tomas Anglicanus*, a reflection of the high-church content.

Further reading: W. P. Stephens, *The Holy Spirit in the Theology of Martin Bucer* (Cambridge: Cambridge University Press, 1970); D. F. Wright, *Martin Bucer: Reforming Church and Community* (Cambridge: Cambridge University Press, 1994).

Bulgaria

Bulgaria is relatively close to the center of the Eastern Orthodox Church in Constantinople (Istanbul), and the Orthodox Church came to dominate its Christian community. Its position was shaken during four centuries of Ottoman Turkish rule, but reinforced with independence in 1878 under a king related to the Russian czar. Communist rulers (1945–91) tended to persecute Catholics and Protestants more than the Orthodox.

The Muslims allowed Orthodoxy to stand during the centuries of Turkish rule, but approximately 11 percent of the public today are Muslim believers. Periodically, Roman Catholicism attempted to gain a foothold, the majority of present-day Catholics deriving from a Franciscan mission set up in the 18th century.

Protestants began their mission in 1850 with the arrival of Congregationalists from the AMERICAN BOARD OF COMMISSIONERS FOR FOREIGN MISSIONS. Methodists soon followed, but their work was small compared to that begun by BAPTISTS (1865), the SEVENTH-DAY ADVENTIST CHURCH (1891), and Pentecostals from Russia (1921). By World War II, the Pentecostals had become the largest segment of the Protestant community.

Like the Catholics, the Protestants suffered greatly during the years of Communist rule, though the situation improved some in the 1960s and 1970s. Since the coming of a post-Marxist government in 1991, a spectrum of conservative Protestant churches have initiated evangelistic activity. Pentecostals remain by far the largest of the new groups, with the Pentecostal Union of Bulgaria and the CHURCH OF GOD claiming the allegiance of almost 50 percent of the Protestant community between them.

Protestants number several hundred thousand, as compared with the 6-million-member Bulgarian Orthodox Church. In the face of charges that they constituted a cult (in Europe a "sect"), in 1993 a number of the Protestant and Free Church groups banded together as the United Evangelical Churches. The government accorded them some recognition and allowed members to take official days off on several church-designated holidays. Some of the more conservative churches and organizations formed the Bulgarian Evangelical Alliance, which is aligned internationally with the WORLD EVANGELICAL ALLIANCE.

Further reading: David Barrett, *The Encyclopedia of World Christianity,* 2nd ed. (New York: Oxford University Press, 2001); P. B. Mojzes, *A History of the Congregational and Methodist Churches in Bulgaria and Yugoslavia* (Boston: Boston University Ph.D. dissertation, 1965); P. Stoynov, *Churches and Religions in the Peoples Republic of Bulgaria* (Sofia: Synodal Publishing House, 1975).

Bullinger, Heinrich (1504–1575) *leading first-generation Swiss reformer*

The successor of Ulrich ZWINGLI as leader of the Reformation in Zurich, Heinrich Bullinger moved to consolidate the gains that had been made during Zwingli's short career. He was born on July 18, 1504, in Bremgarten near Zurich. He was guided to the priesthood and sent for training at Emmerich and Cologne. As the Reformation began, he absorbed its teachings from his father, an early sympathizer. Bullinger taught at the Cistercian monastery near Kappel (1523–29).

He later became the pastor in his hometown, where he remained until he succeeded Zwingli as pastor of the Grossmünster in Zurich following the latter's death in 1531. He held that position for the rest of his life, more than four decades. He published more than 100 religious titles, many of which were translated, reprinted, and circulated widely throughout Europe.

Bullinger tried to foster Protestant unity, especially between the Swiss Reformed and the Lutherans. To that end, with two colleagues he authored the "First Helvetic Confession," the classic early confession of faith issued in 1536. However, while Bullinger's effort found broad support among the German-speaking Swiss Protestants, it found little favor in Germany.

A decade later, John CALVIN emerged as the new leader of the French-speaking Protestants based in Geneva. Meanwhile, Bullinger worked on the "Consensus Tigurinus," a statement of agreement between what had become two wings of the Swiss Reformed movement. In 1566, Bullinger composed the "Second Helvetic Confession," which found support from all the Swiss Protestant centers except Basel. He never composed a systematic theology, but came close in his *Decades* (1549), a collection of 50 sermons that covered the major theological themes. He died on September 17, 1575.

Immensely influential in his own day and through the end of the 16th century, Bullinger was later overshadowed by Zwingli and Calvin in the Protestant tradition. In the 20th century, his important role was more favorably acknowledged.

See also REFORMED/PRESBYTERIAN TRADITION.

Further reading: J. W. Baker, *Bullinger and the Covenant: The Other Reformed Tradition.* (Athens: University of Ohio Press, 1980); J. W. Baker and Charles S. McCoy, *Fountainhead of Federalism: Heinrich Bullinger and the Covenantal Tradition* (Louisville, Ky.: Westminster John Knox Press, 1991); Pamela Biel, *Doorkeepers in the House of Righteousness: Heinrich Bullinger and the Zurich Clergy 1535–1575* (Bern, N.Y.: P. Lang, 1991); Ulrich Gabler and Erland Herkenrath, *Heinrich Bullinger 1504–1575, Gesammelte Aufsatze zum 400, Todestag* (Zurich: Theologische Verlag Zurich, 1975). Bruce Gordon, *Clerical Discipline and the Rural Reformation. The Synod in Zurich, 1532–1580* (Bern, N.Y.: P. Lang, 1992).

Bultmann, Rudolf (1884–1976) *German theologian and biblical scholar*

Rudolf Karl Bultmann was born on August 20, 1884, in Wiefelstede, Oldenburg, Germany, the son of a Lutheran pastor. He attended the Universities of Tübingen, Berlin, and Marburg, where he absorbed the liberal German theology that dominated higher education at the beginning of the 20th century. He received his doctorate in 1910 at Marburg and taught there briefly before moving to Breslau in 1916. He returned to Breslau a year later to occupy the chair in New Testament, where he remained for the rest of his career.

Bultmann began to move beyond the liberalism of his teachers soon after receiving his doctorate. He believed their theology treated Christianity as simply one religion among many, and made one's knowledge of and relationship to God a matter of an internal search. To Bultmann, such an approach left God out of the picture and made religion a merely human affair.

From his colleague Rudolf Otto (1869–1937), Bultmann took the term *Wholly Other* to describe God. Bultmann argued that because of sin, humankind is unable to relate to God. Any God that sinful humanity could relate to would be a mere idol. God reveals "Godself" only on God's own terms, not on human ones. That is, the encounter with God is a justification by faith, without regard for any accomplishments (works) of humankind.

Bultmann also came to draw a sharp distinction between faith and theology. Faith referred to the individual's decision at any moment to accept a new self-understanding. By contrast, theology was the attempt to reflect upon and understand the meaning of faith. Theology, however, requires an appropriate framework for reflection; Bultmann used an existentialist model dependent somewhat on the thinking of philosopher Martin Heidegger (1889–1976). That philosophy played so crucial a role in his theology led to his eventual break with Karl BARTH.

Although active for several decades in the world of theological NEO-ORTHODOXY, Bultmann is best remembered for his work on biblical interpretation and his introduction of the term *demythologizing*. The term itself was offensive to many who refused to consider the idea that the Bible contained mythology, even in the rather limited and technical sense implied by Bultmann. To him, demythologizing was simply the removal of the more transient elements of the narrative (mythology) from the text so one could find the Christian *kerygma* or proclamation. New Testament mythology included, for example, the particular worldview of first-century Christians and their manner of objectifying concepts and images in order to understand the transcendent. Demythologization thus attempts to remove thinking about God as object or for that matter any interpretation that would not begin with God as Wholly Other. It rejects any attempt to ascribe ultimate significance to images of God.

Bultmann also emphasized, though on this point he was often ignored, that demythologizing was only the first half of the interpretive process. The more positive half, exposition, begins once the *kerygma* is recognized.

Among the tools Bultmann developed for his biblical interpretation was FORM CRITICISM. He noticed that certain types of material in the first three Gospels of the New Testament followed a formula in their telling. The existence of such "forms" implied their use in ritualized activity, hence their later date of composition. Form criticism led to the development of redaction criticism, which assumes that different editors altered the biblical texts to make them conform to the editor's idea of true religion.

Bultmann died on July 30, 1976.

See also BIBLICAL CRITICISM.

Further reading: Rudolf Bultmann, *Faith and Understanding,* trans. by Louise Pettibone Smith (Philadelphia: Fortress Press, 1987); ———, *Jesus and the Word,* trans. by Louise Pettibone Smith and Erminie Lantero (New York: Scribner, 1958); ———, *Theology of the New Testament,* 2 vols. (New York: Scribner, 1955); David Fergusson, *Bultmann* (London: George Chapman, 1992); Roger A. Johnson, *Introduction to Rudolf Bultmann: Interpreting Faith for the Modern Era* (Minneapolis, Minn.: Fortress Press, 1991).

Bulu, Joeli (c. 1810–1877) *cofounder of the Methodist church in Fiji*

Joeli Bulu was born on Tonga and converted by Methodist missionaries during a great revival that swept the island in 1833–34. He was deeply affected by a letter sent by missionary David Cargill, then working in Fiji, and developed a call to missionary work there. In 1838, he was sent as part of a Tongan-based team to evangelize the islands. After learning the Fijian language, he began work in the printing establishment set up by British missionaries. A decade of zealous missionary endeavor led to his ordination as the first South Sea Islander Methodist minister in 1850.

For the remaining 27 years of his life, Bulu pioneered new mission stations, often in areas too dangerous for Europeans, trained indigenous leadership, and served as chaplain to Tahkombau, the Fijian high chief. From 1863 to 1866, he was the principal of the training college for catechists. His last years were spent on Bau, the royal island, where he died.

Bulu worked for the indigenization of the METHODIST CHURCH in Fiji, though his efforts were set back at one point by a massive epidemic of measles that claimed a large percentage of the church members as its victims.

See also FIJI ISLANDS; SOUTH PACIFIC.

Further reading: Charles W. Forman, "Joeli Bulu," in Gerald H. Anderson, ed., *Biographical Dictionary of Christian Missions* (Grand Rapids, Mich.: William B. Eerdmans, 1998); Joeli Bulu, *The Autobiography of Joeli Bulu, Tongan Missionary to Fiji,* ed. by Alan R. Tippett and Tomasi Kanailagi. (Pasadena, Calif.: Fuller Theological Seminary, thesis, 1976).

Bunyan, John (1628–1688) *inspirational author of* The Pilgrim's Progress

Baptist minister and author of the Protestant classic *The Pilgrim's Progress,* John Bunyan was born at Elstow, Bedfordshire, England, in November 1628. His father was a whitesmith, a maker and mender of pots and kettles, and Bunyan continued professionally in his father's footsteps. He received some primary education locally, but did not attend college. Following his mother's death and his father's remarriage, in 1644, he left home for the army, the civil war that would bring Oliver Cromwell to power having already begun. After two years of service, he returned to his home and married. His wife influenced a turn toward religion—he gave up a number of bad habits and began to attend church regularly. He also began a spiritual search that led to a personal understanding of Christianity. In 1653, he joined an independent nonconformist (Baptist) church. He would later describe the change in his life in his second most famous text, "Grace Abounding to the Chief of Sinners."

Moving to Bedford around 1655 after his wife died, he became more active in church, first as a deacon and then as a preacher. In 1657, he was ordained as a nonconformist minister. He began to travel and win a reputation as a speaker, attracting large audiences that caught the attention of the authorities. He also began to write, his first publications being attacks upon the beliefs and practices of the QUAKERS. He married again in 1659.

Bunyan's life took a new direction after the monarchy was restored in England in 1660. The nonconformist meeting houses were closed and nonconformist worship outlawed. People were required to attend worship at the local parish of the CHURCH OF ENGLAND. Nonconformists continued to meet in barns and other buildings, and Bunyan continued to travel and preach. He was arrested on November 12, 1660. He remained in jail after confessing to his preaching activity and to his determination to continue if freed. He refused all compromises offered him, including an agreement that he would preach only in small private gatherings.

He remained in prison for 12 years, ministering to his fellow prisoners, not infrequently his cobelievers. He also found time to write both poetry and religious tracts. His autobiographical "Grace Abounding to the Chief of Sinners" appeared in 1666. Shortly before his release in 1672, he penned the "Confession of my Faith and Reason of my Practice," an apologetic of his ministry.

Even before his release, Bunyan was called to pastor the Baptist church in Bedford, which was meeting in a barn. From Bedford he traveled through the countryside, founding churches and nurturing believers. He also kept up his production of books and pamphlets. His most famous book, *The Pilgrim's Progress,* was probably written during a brief second imprisonment in 1675, and first appeared in print in 1678. It was an immediate success, and a second edition appeared before the year was out. The allegorical book recounts the course through life of the hero, Christian, who along the way meets various types of worldly people who try to tempt him from the successful completion of his course.

By the time *The Pilgrim's Progress* was published, the acts against nonconformists had been reinstituted (1675). However, acting more circumspectly, Bunyan was able to continue to travel and preach, drawing large crowds, and was not again molested by the authorities. He died in 1688. His works remained popular for several centuries, though more recently only his two most important works continue to be widely read.

See also BAPTISTS; PURITANISM.

Further reading: John Brown, *John Bunyan (1628–1688): His Life, Times and Work,* rev. ed. (London: Hulbert, 1928); John Bunyan, *The Pilgrim's Progress* (New York: Columbia University Press for the Facsimile Text Society, 1934). Numerous editions and reprints exist; Frank Mott Harrison, *A Bibliography of the Works of John Bunyan* (London: Bibliographical Society, 1932); Roger Sharrock, *John Bunyan* (London: Hutchinson, 1954); Ola Elizabeth Winslow, *John Bunyan* (New York: Macmillan, 1961).

C

Calvin, John (1509–1564) *founder of the Reformed stream of Protestantism*

One of the principle intellectual and organizational leaders of the 16th-century Protestant Reformation, John Calvin was the fountainhead of one of the two major streams of Reformation life. His thought helped define the Reformed, Presbyterian, Congregational, and Baptist churches. Calvin can also be viewed as the inspiration for ARMINIANISM, ultimately leading to METHODISM.

Calvin was born on July 10, 1509, in Noyon, France. His father directed him toward a career in the church and sent him to Paris to be schooled. After he completed his bachelor's degree, his father decided that law was better and sent him to Orleans and then to Bourges, where he completed work in 1531. He became an enthusiastic student of the Christian humanists of his day, and after his father's death in 1531 moved back to Paris to study with the likes of Jacques LeFevre d'Etaples.

In 1533, Calvin was identified with a speech given by his friend Nicolas Cop espousing Protestant ideas for reform. The pair took refuge in Basel, Switzerland, where Calvin set to work on his monumental *Institutes of the Christian Religion* (1536), the first systematic book-length presentation of Protestantism. Later that year, he moved to Geneva and accepted the offer of William FAREL to assist in the reform of the city, but negotiations with the city council quickly came to a standstill. Calvin left for Strasbourg, where reformer Martin BUCER was leading the Reformation cause. While there, he wrote a commentary on the book of Romans, and developed his characteristic ideas on PREDESTINATION for the second edition of the *Institutes*.

In 1541, he accepted the invitation to return to Geneva, which would be his home for the rest of his life. The cathedral became his pulpit, and he preached twice every Sunday. His insistence on a strict moral code was popular, and his followers were elected to city offices. He aimed to work with the government, while keeping control of the church out of state hands. He placed the administration of the church into the hands of presbyters (ELDERS), of which there were two kinds, preaching elders (ministers) and ruling elders (laypeople).

The most important challenge to Calvin's authority came from Michael SERVETUS (1511–53). Calvin was offended by Servetus's attack on the Trinity and saw to his arrest and execution. This has remained the major blemish on his character from the historical viewpoint.

The crucial points in Calvin's theology were the affirmation of the authority of the Bible, the sovereignty of God, salvation as God's gift, and the predestination and election of the saved. He worked out a position on the LORD'S SUPPER that mediated between the Lutheran understanding of the real presence and Ulrich ZWINGLI's understanding of a memorial meal. Most of the Reformed church leaders of Calvin's time accepted his position. Calvin's legal background is reflected in his concept of the three uses of the law. In the hands of the state, the law constrains evil. In the hands of the church, it convicts people of sin and calls for repentance. In the hands of the regenerated Christian, it provides guidance for living the Christian life.

Calvin wrote voluminously, including a set of biblical commentaries. He opened Geneva to many Protestant leaders who had fled persecution in their homeland, providing a place for them to learn and prepare for their return when a more favorable climate dawned. By harboring many of the MARIAN EXILES, Calvin was an important force in the development of English Puritanism and in the eventual import of Reformed ideas and practices into ELIZABETH I's *VIA MEDIA*, the platform of Anglicanism.

Calvin died on May 27, 1564, and was buried in an unknown plot, on his own instructions.

Calvin's writings have gone through many editions, and works about him are voluminous. The H. Henry Meeter Center for Calvin Studies at Calvin College/Calvin Theological Seminary, Grand Rapids, Michigan, has since 1998 posted a running bibliography on new Calvin material at its Web page, http://www.calvin.edu/meeter.

See also CALVINISM; PURITANISM; REFORMED/ PRESBYTERIAN TRADITION.

Further reading: William J. Bouwsma, *John Calvin: A Sixteenth Century Portrait* (New York: Oxford University Press, 1988); Alexandre Ganoczy, *The Young Calvin,* trans. by David Foxgrover and Wade Provo (Philadelphia: Westminster, 1987); W. Stanford Reid, *John Calvin: His Influence in the Western World* (Grand Rapids, Mich.: Zondervan, 1982); David C. Steinmetz, *Calvin in Context* (New York: Oxford University Press, 1995); François Wendel, *Calvin: Origins and Development of His Religious Thought* (New York: Harper & Row, 1963; reprint, Durham, N.C.: Labyrinth Press, 1987).

Calvinism

Calvinism is the theological current derived from the works and writings of John CALVIN (1509–64). Key documents are Calvin's *Institutes of the Christian Religion* (1536), the 16th- and 17th-century Reformed confessions of faith (such as the HELVETIC CONFESSION, the HEIDELBERG CATECHISM, the Canons of the SYNOD OF DORT, and the WESTMINSTER CONFESSION OF FAITH), and the words of theologians and church leaders of the world's Reformed, Presbyterian, Congregationalist, and Baptist churches. Calvin believed he was articulating a Christian perspective in line with the Bible and the early church fathers, while stripping away the many accretions of the intervening centuries that characterized the Roman Catholic Church.

Several basic affirmations are key to understanding Calvinism. The Bible is the written Word of God and hence the final authority for Christian life and thought. It is the self-revelation of God in nature and history. God is intimately connected to his world as creator and sustainer. He has also decreed a plan for the world and his creatures.

In stark contrast, humans are neither God nor divine entities; they are God's creation. God created humans in his own (spiritual) image and pronounced them good. As God rules over creation, so humans must serve God and rule over the world as God's representatives. Humans, desiring to be independent, broke faith with God, and went their own way. Thus, sin entered the world, and humans are now in slavery to sin. The sin of the first human to fall from grace is now passed to all; all have sinned and can do nothing on their own to reestablish a relationship with God.

The sovereign God foresaw the fall of humanity and made provision for many to return to a positive relationship to him. He sent Christ into the world to make atonement for sin and release God's grace into the world. God has elected some humans, apart from any consideration of human logic effort, or desire, for this renewed relationship and freely gives them his grace so that they might repent of their sin, be regenerated, and have faith in Jesus Christ. Calvin assumed a society in which everyone was baptized into the church as infants and grew up in a community dominated by the church and by secular authorities who were professing Christians. At the same time, it was obvious that many did not live a life of Christian values and virtue.

Calvinism faced a defining challenge in the person of Jacob Arminius (1560–1609), a Reformed theologian residing in Holland. A student of Calvin's colleague Theodore BEZA (1519–1605), Arminius came to believe that Reformed thought had stressed God's sovereignty to such an extent that Christ's saving work was overshadowed. The key biblical passage for Arminius was Romans 8: 28–30, "And we know that all things work together for good to them that love God, to them who are called according to his purpose. For whom He did foreknow, he also did predestinate to be conformed to the image of His Son, that he might be the firstborn among many brethren. Moreover, whom he did predestinate, them he also called: and whom he called, them he justified: and whom he justified, them he also glorified." The question became, in what logical order did God foreknow and predestine to justification.

Arminius's position, termed *infralapsarianism* (literally, after the fall), suggested that when God established the process of redemption, he did so with fallen humanity in mind, and he chose those who by his foreknowledge he knew would turn in faith to him. The Calvinist position, termed *supralapsarianism* (literally, before the fall), suggested that God in his sovereignty, without reference to the merits or lack of merits of any person, had chosen and predestined them to grace and salvation.

In reaction to Arminius and his followers, the Remonstrants, Calvinist leaders in the NETHERLANDS (one of the leading centers of Reformed thought), called the Synod of Dort. The synod issued a set of statements accepting the supralapsarian position and condemning ARMINIANISM.

The Calvinist position has been summarized as holding to five doctrines: total depravity, unconditional election, LIMITED ATONEMENT, irresistible grace, and the perseverance of the saints. (In English, the first letters of these five points spell out the word *tulip,* a convenient tool for remembering them.) Calvinists thus believe that human beings are totally depraved and hence unable of themselves to turn to and believe the Gospel. From humanity, God has, of his own will, chosen to elect some. To that end, he sent his son, Jesus, to die and atone for the sins, not of all, but of the elect. God has shared his grace with the elect, and grace once shared is irresistible. Those who are given grace will remain in a state of grace for all eternity.

The churches that arose out of the Reformed Protestant movement separated themselves out on the basis of this Calvinist/Arminiam divide. Calvinists believed they were protecting the Reformation's core belief in salvation by grace rather than by works of merit, which they understood the Roman Catholic system to uphold. Arminians believed they were proclaiming the grace of God given to the whole world. What began as an argument about free grace turned in the 19th century into an argument about free will. Were human beings free to turn and have faith in Christ? Overall, among Protestants, free will appears to have carried the day.

Among Calvinists, other arguments flowed from the logic of the position adopted at Dort. For example, if God elected some to salvation, then God in his sovereignty and foreknowledge must have also elected some to damnation. This position, termed *double-edged* PREDESTINATION, was adopted by the most conservative wing of the Calvinists, but is only rarely found among believers at the present time.

The Calvinist tradition has also been identified with a tradition of church POLITY or government, which gave its name to PRESBYTERIANISM (rule by elders); with a particular view of the SACRAMENTS (which in the 16th century constituted its chief disagreement with Lutheranism); and with a style of worship emphasizing simplicity and order.

See also REFORMED/PRESBYTERIAN TRADITION.

Further reading: John Calvin, *The Institutes of the Christian Religion,* ed. by J. T. McNeill, trans. by Ford Lewis Battles, Library of Christian Classics (Philadelphia: Westminster, 1960); Donald McKim, ed., *Encyclopedia of the Reformed Faith.* (Louisville, Ky.: Westminster/John Knox, 1992); John T. McNeill, *The History and Character of Calvinism* (London, New York: Oxford University Press, 1954); Henry H. Meeter, *The Basic Ideas of Calvinism,* rev. ed. by Peter A. Marshall (Grand Rapids, Mich.: Baker Book House, 1990).

Cambridge Platform

The Cambridge Platform was a presentation of the Congregational form of church POLITY developed by Puritan leaders in Massachusetts toward the end of their first generation, and published in 1648. As New England Puritanism spread and new churches and towns were established, England was in the throes of political and religious revolution. Reformed Protestants not unlike the New Englanders had overturned the episcopal polity of the CHURCH OF ENGLAND, and the Westminster Assembly had issued the several documents that largely define PRESBYTERIANISM in the English-speaking world. While the WESTMINSTER CONFESSION OF FAITH (1646) is the most well known of these documents, of almost equal significance was the "Form of Presbyterian Church Government" of 1645.

The New England Puritans had little problem with the Westminster Confession, as they were fully in accord with its Calvinist theology. However, they rejected the vision of a church led by elders (presbyters) gathered in presbyteries and synods with legislative power. True, they were not BAPTISTS, and they did in fact support the idea of an exclusive church aligned with the state with hegemony on religious teaching in any given location—that was their practice in New England. But for them, as they affirmed in the platform, the focus of church government was in the local congregation, with ultimate authority resting in the vote of a majority of members. When a local problem could not be resolved, the congregation could seek guidance from a pan-congregational assembly.

The Cambridge Platform recognized the office of ruling elder (lay leaders who handle temporal affairs), who had the authority to ordain ministers. Such elders, and other officers who might be designated, operated with the guidance of the congregation, who could vote them out of office.

The Cambridge Platform also recognized the need for local congregations to have communion with other congregations, but it also stated that pan-congregational synods were not absolutely necessary to the existence of the church; they only become necessary due to the iniquity of humans. The platform concluded that synods should not exercise ecclesial authority or jurisdiction over local churches. Any gathering of ruling and preaching (ministerial) elders carried weight, but its decisions would not become operative in the local church unless the membership approved them.

The Cambridge Platform called for the state to align itself with the church and see to certain religious matters. The civil authority was to "restrain and punish" any "Idolatry, blasphemy, heresy, venting corrupt and pernicious opinions . . . profanation of the Lord's Day, disturbing the peaceable administration and exercise of the worship and holy things of God."

This form of church government worked in New England through the colonial period and for several decades after the formation of the United States. It was modified in Connecticut in 1708 (the Saybrook Platform) to allow for some pan-congregational associations, a step toward Presbyterianism. The system finally fell apart in the early 19th century, when all connections to the government were severed, and the state ceased to uphold the hegemony of the Congregational Church. At that point, the congregational system evolved into a form of free church polity similar to that operating among the Baptists. Having lost the state's backing, Congregationalists lost many churches to Unitarianism, which captured congregations where its non-Trinitarian theology was accepted by a majority of members.

See also CONGREGATIONALISM; CREEDS/CONFESSIONS OF FAITH.

Further reading: *The Cambridge Platform: A New Edition of the Historic Puritan Congregational Church Order,* ed. by Darrell Todd Maurina (Lawrence, Mich.: Reformed Tract Publication Committee, 3rd corrected printing, 1993); Perry Miller, *Errand into the Wilderness* (New York: Harper & Row, 1964); Williston Walker, *The Creeds and Platforms of Congregationalism* (New York: Scribner, 1893, rev. ed., New York: The Pilgrim Press, 1991).

Cambridge University

In the 16th and 17th centuries, Cambridge University became associated with the Protestant and then the Puritan cause. The university dates to the 13th century, when several monastic orders settled in the area. In 1231, King Henry III granted it a writ of governance. As with all European universities, theology was always a key subject in the curriculum.

Early in the 16th century, a number of the future leaders of the Reformation in England studied at Cambridge, including William TYNDALE, Miles COVERDALE, Thomas CRANMER, Hugh Latimer, and Nicolas Ridley. Among Continental Protestant figures, Martin BUCER taught at Cambridge and ERASMUS disseminated many of his humanist ideas from Cambridge during his lengthy professorship.

In 1569–70, Cambridge became the focal point for a Presbyterian form of PURITANISM advocated by Thomas CARTWRIGHT (1535–1603), who held a professorship there. Cartwright left the university after being deprived of his fellowship in 1571, but his influence helped bring a new wave of CALVINISM to England, as a new generation of graduates, many of whom entered the church (such as Richard Rogers, John Dod, and Arthur Hildersham), began to influence the intellectual life of the country. One of Cartwright's students, Robert BROWNE, is generally seen as the founder of Puritan CONGREGATIONALISM.

The Puritan movement became more firmly established at Cambridge in 1584 with the foundation of Emmanuel College by Sir Walter Mildmay. He saw the college producing many ministers "fit for the administration of the Divine Word and Sacraments." Emmanuel was led by a series of outstanding Puritan spokespersons such as Laurence Chaderton (c. 1546–1640), the first master, and John Preston (1587–1628).

The vacuum caused by Cartwright's departure was filled by William Perkins (1558–1602). Perkins became a student at Christ's College, Cambridge, in 1577, where he experienced a great religious transformation, At age 24, he was made a fellow of his college; his preaching at St. Andrew's Church in Cambridge had enormous influence. Among those directly affected by Perkins was William Ames, who later wrote one of the most influential Puritan works, *A Marrow of Sacred Theology* (1623).

By the end of the 16th century, Cambridge was the major disseminating point for Puritan thinking, through its colleges and the ministers they trained. In the early 17th century, Thomas Hooker, John Winthrop, Peter Hobart, and Roger WILLIAMS, among the leaders of the New England Puritan colonists, were all trained at Cambridge. They named one of their new towns Cambridge and located Harvard University there. John Harvard had himself attended Emmanuel College, Cambridge.

The English Civil War brought Cambridge to center stage. Oliver CROMWELL, Lord Protector of a Puritanized England, was a graduate of Sidney Sussex College and was also the local member of Parliament from Cambridge. Among the Cambridge graduates he would appoint to important positions in his government was the Puritan poet John MILTON.

After the Restoration, the great era of Cambridge Puritanism slowly died away, though the tendency never completely disappeared. Charles Simeon (1759–1836), an Anglican influenced by the EVANGELICAL AWAKENING (Methodism), graduated from Cambridge in 1782 and became the priest in charge of Trinity Church in Cambridge. During his 50 years of tenure, he encouraged a number of men to enter foreign missions work, and he became one of the founders of both the CHURCH MISSIONARY SOCIETY and the Society for Promoting Christianity Among the Jews, and he established a fund to assist young men going into the ministry.

See also UNITED KINGDOM.

Further reading: Stephen Foster, *The Long Argument: English Puritanism and the Shaping of New England Culture, 1570–1700* (Chapel Hill: University of North Carolina Press, 1996); William Haller, *The Rise of Puritanism; or The Way to New Jerusalem as Set Forth in Pulpit and Press from Thomas Cartwright to John Lilburne and John Milton, 1570–1643.* (New York: Harper, & Row 1957); Elisabeth Leedham-Green, *A Concise History of the University of Cambridge* (Cambridge: Cambridge University Press, 1996).

Campbell, Alexander (1788–1866) *founder of the Restoration movement*

Alexander Campbell was one of the founders of the 19th-century RESTORATION MOVEMENT, which produced three large international Christian communities—the Churches of Christ, the Christian Church (Disciples of Christ), and the Churches of Christ and Christian Churches. He was born on September 12, 1788, at Ballymena, Antrim County, Ireland, the son of Thomas Campbell (1763–1854), a Presbyterian minister. Alexander's father had left the Church of Scotland and affiliated himself with one of the factions of Successionists, Presbyterians opposed to the patronage system in the state church. Thomas Campbell saw to his son's education at the University of Glasgow, where Alexander was strongly influenced by the HALDANE BROTHERS.

Thomas Campbell moved to America in 1807, and Alexander followed two years later. They lived in western Pennsylvania. Originally working among the American Presbyterians, they eventually withdrew out of dislike for their creedal demands. They also began to doubt the validity of infant BAPTISM.

In 1811, the Campbells organized the independent First Christian Association of Washington, Pennsylvania, the so-called Brush Run church. The following year, Alexander was ordained to the ministry, and both he and his father were rebaptized by immersion by Matthias Luce, a Baptist minister. Alexander became leader of the little church, which in 1813 became affiliated with the Redstone Baptist Association. Alexander's 1826 translation of the Bible rendered the Greek word *baptizo* as *immerse,* rather than the usual *baptize,* and the name John the Baptist became John the Immerser.

Campbell refined his views in a series of public debates with leaders from various Christian churches. In 1823, he began the *Christian Baptist* (1823–30). He became increasingly critical of the Baptists, who also had creedal standards. He wanted to abandon any activities without a biblical base, such as creeds or theology, and "restore" the church to the model of the biblical church—simple worship, the LORD'S SUPPER, and the autonomy of local congregations. His approach to the Bible assigned higher inspirational value to the New Testament than to the Old.

Campbell came to advocate an informal fellowship of congregations that chose to worship according to the New Testament pattern. By 1830, he had left the Baptists; he discontinued the *Christian Baptist* in favor of a new periodical, the *Millennial Harbinger.* In 1832, he and Barton Stone, who had reached similar conclusions, united the movements that had developed around their ideas. They wanted to be known only as Christians, but soon the designation Disciples of Christ was common.

In 1840, Campbell founded and became president of Bethany College in what is now West Virginia. He continued to edit the *Millennial Harbinger* and head Bethany until his death on March 4, 1866.

See also BAPTISTS; FREE CHURCH.

Further reading: Alexander Campbell, *Christian Baptism With Its Antecedents and Consequences* (Bethany, Va.: Alexander Campbell, 1853); Selina Huntington Campbell, *Home Life and Reminiscences of Alexander Campbell By His Wife* (Joplin, Mo.: College Press, 1882); *Debate on the Evidences of Christianity; containing an examination of the social system, and of all the*

The Des Plaines Campgrounds is an old "Camp Meeting" site that is still in use outside Chicago. *(Institute for the Study of American Religion, Santa Barbara, California)*

systems of scepticism of ancient and modern times, held in the city of Cincinnati, for eight days successively, between Robert Owen, of New Lanark, Scotland, and Alexander Campbell, of Bethany, Virginia. With an appendix by the parties (Bethany, Va.: Alexander Campbell, 1829); Bill J. Humble, *Light from Above: The Life of Alexander Campbell* (Nashville, Tenn.: Gospel Advocate, 1988); Eva Jean Wrather, *Creative Freedom in Action: Alexander Campbell on the Structure of the Church* (St. Louis: Bethany House, 1968).

camp meetings

Camp meetings were a unique form of religious gathering developed on the American frontier at the beginning of the 19th century. Each meeting offered a week or more of religious activity, including preaching, services, music prayer meetings, Bible study, and counseling sessions for those in the process of converting. Attendees brought food, bedding, and other necessities for camping out.

The camp meeting is generally traced to summer 1800, when members of three congregations pastored by Rev. James McGready in rural Kentucky gathered to await an outpouring of the Holy Spirit. Others heard about the meeting and came to see; many converted in the sea of expectant emotion. As news of the event spread, other ministers organized similar gatherings. At one such

meeting the next year at Cane Ridge, Kentucky, more than 25,000 people showed up. At first, ministers from many denominations cooperated in the camp meetings, but over the next years most of the Baptists and Presbyterians dropped out, uncomfortable with the emotional atmosphere and the loose theology. Methodists, Free Will Baptists, and Cumberland Presbyterians (who had split with their parent group over support for the camp meetings) remained the primary supporters. The journals and memoirs of Methodist ministers include many accounts of their visits to and participation in camp meetings.

The Methodists used the camp meetings for the rest of the century as a primary tool for growth in rural areas, though they increasingly became routine affairs that served more to nurture current church members than convert new ones. In the decades after the Civil War, the HOLINESS movement found the Methodist camp meetings fertile ground for their work; their first national organization was the National Camp Meeting Association for the Promotion of Holiness, founded in 1867. Holiness churches and the first Holiness denominations grew out of camp meetings.

The camp meeting structure eventually passed to the Pentecostals, who through the early 20th century used it to strengthen their new movement. Once again, however, the institution became routine and was used more to nurture members rather than to find new ones. Most Holiness and Pentecostal denominations continue to maintain one or more campgrounds, at which summer preaching and recreational programs are held for members who wish to take their vacation in a Christian camp setting.

See also REVIVALISM.

Further reading: Kenneth O. Brown, *Holy Ground: A Study of the American Camp Meeting* (New York: Garland, 1992); Dickson D. Bruce Jr., *And They All Sang Hallelujah: Plain-Folk Camp-Meeting Religion, 1800–1845.* (Knoxville: University of Tennessee Press, 1974); Charles A. Johnson, *The Frontier Camp Meeting* (Dallas, Tex.: Southern Methodist University Press, 1955); Wallace Thornton Jr., ed., *Sons of*

Thunder: Camp Meeting Sermons by Post-World War II Holiness Revivalists (Salem, Ohio: Schmul, 1999).

Campus Crusade for Christ

Campus Crusade for Christ, a ministry to college students begun in the 1950s by Bill and Vonette Bright, has grown into one of the largest Evangelical organizations in the world. Bill Bright (1921–2003), a California businessman, had experienced a conversion in 1945. He attended Fuller Theological Seminary in Pasadena, California, but left in 1951 before finishing his degree. He sold his business and began a ministry to college students at the University of California, Los Angeles. The couple began with a simple plan: convert college students, train them to convert others, and place Christian ministries on all of the campuses in the United States.

To implement that vision, in 1956, Bright wrote a small booklet entitled *The Four Spiritual Laws.* A new attempt to capsulize the essence of Evangelical Christianity, it became a simple, valuable tool that almost anyone could use in evangelical work. By the end of the 20th century, it had been translated into some 200 languages, and millions of copies had been distributed. It is considered the most widely disseminated piece of Christian literature apart from the Bible. Some critics accused the book and the crusade with its concentration on the beginning of the Christian life of perpetuating a shallow Christianity and being irresponsible in neglecting new converts.

While continuing its work on college campuses, the organization began to expand its vision into other ministries. An early 1970s campaign proposed to visit every home in the United States, arousing negative reactions, especially from the Jewish community. The New Life 2000 program, launched in 1987, was aimed at evangelizing every person on Earth by the year 2000. Though falling far short, the program motivated many people to increase their evangelistic endeavors. Meanwhile, the crusade backed some very successful subsidiary ministries, including the Josh McDowell ministry, Athletes in Action, and the Man's Authentic Nature program. Possibly its most successful program began in 1979 with the filming of the life of Christ. Subsequently translated into almost 400 languages, the *Jesus* film has been shown to almost a billion people, and in some countries has become the backbone of national evangelism programs.

As the new century began, the aging Bright named longtime colleague Steve Douglass as his successor. By that time, Campus Crusade had the word's largest Evangelical Christian ministry, with operations in 191 countries, a staff of 26,000 full-time employees, and more than 225,000 active volunteers. It greatly extended its reach through widespread networking with other Evangelical organizations. In 1991, the center of operations, located since its beginning in California, was moved to Orlando, Florida.

See also EVANGELICALISM.

Further reading: Bill Bright, *Believing God for the Impossible: A Call to Supernatural Living* (San Bernardino, Calif.: Here's Life Publishers, 1979); ———, *Come Help Change the World* (Neptune, N.J.: Fleming H. Revell. 1970); ———, *A Handbook for Christian Maturity* (San Bernardino, Calif.: New Life, 1992); Judy Douglass, ed., *Until Everyone Has Heard: Campus Crusade for Christ International* (Orlando, Fla.: Campus Crusade For Christ International, 2001); Michael Richardson, *Amazing Faith: The Authorized Biography of Bill Bright* (Colorado Springs, Colo.: WaterBrook Press, 2000).

Canada

Ignoring the papal document assigning most of the New World to Spain, France began settling Canada at the beginning of the 17th century. Quebec was settled in 1608; the entire colony was named New France in 1663. Canada remained exclusively Roman Catholic territory until it was ceded to Britain in 1763. In the next decade, it received many loyalist immigrants fleeing the American Revolution.

An important step in British control had been the founding of Halifax, Nova Scotia, in 1749 and its settlement with British and German colonists. Within a few years the CHURCH OF ENGLAND and a spectrum of Lutheran, Presbyterian, and Congregationalist churches took root. Anglicanism had been present marginally after an initial parish was opened in St. John's, Newfoundland, in 1699. However, the Church of England was formally established in 1758 in Nova Scotia and in 1784 in New Brunswick. The first Anglican bishop assigned to territory outside the British Isles was Charles INGLIS (1734–1816), the first bishop of Halifax, who took up office in 1787.

The 1774 Quebec Act ensured the rights of the French citizens of Canada, and thus guaranteed the privileges of and support for the Catholic Church. That act in effect limited the privileges of the established Church of England. In the mid-19th century, the Canadian government withdrew most Anglican privileges, nationalized Anglican schools, and seized some church lands. Canadian Anglicans began to reorganize for self-governance, including autonomy from the Church of England, which was achieved in the 1860s as Canada became an autonomous dominion. In 1893, the church reorganized as a national body, the Church of England in Canada; it adopted its present name, the Anglican Church of Canada, in 1955.

After the British takeover, the wide spectrum of Protestant groups already present in the British American colonies began to flood into the country. Through the 1760s and 1770s, the BAPTISTS, QUAKERS, Moravians, and Methodists arrived. Ontario (formerly Upper Canada) became the center of Canadian population and the Protestant community.

Further growth in the Protestant community was spurred by the completion of the transcontinental railroad in 1885. With the western provinces now open for settlement, a number of new groups arrived, especially ANABAPTISTS (MENNONITES) from Russia. Many Hutterites joined them in 1917 to avoid the military draft in the United States.

In 1925, most Methodists, Congregationalists, and Presbyterians united into the UNITED CHURCH OF CANADA (UCC), which replaced the Anglicans

as the largest Protestant church in the country. A half century of negotiations failed to bring the Anglicans into the new church. The Fundamentalist-Modernist controversy did not disturb Canadians the way it did their neighbors to the south, though it did split the Baptist community, leading to the formation of the conservative Fellowship of Evangelical Baptist Churches in Canada. Thomas Todhunter Shields (1873–1955) was the primary Fundamentalist voice.

PENTECOSTALISM spread quickly to Canada in 1906 after the outbreak of the AZUSA STREET REVIVAL in Los Angeles. In 1909, Canadians organized a congregational fellowship, the Pentecostal Missionary Union, superseded in 1917 by the Pentecostal Assemblies of Canada. Robert McAleister (1880–1953), who had originally brought the revival to Canada, was also responsible for one of its major schisms when he promoted the biblical (non-Trinitarian) formula of BAPTISM. His ideas were later developed by the JESUS ONLY PENTECOSTALS. In the middle of the century, the Latter-Rain Revival began in western Canada and then spread to the United States, condemning the lack of vitality in Pentecostal worship and introducing a new organizational pattern based on the five-fold ministry of Ephesians 4:11, headed by APOSTLES.

As the new century begins, the United Church of Canada is the largest Protestant church, with 3,700 congregations, a membership of 640,000, and a constituency of more than 3 million. The UCC is the epitome of liberal Protestantism. It began ordaining women in 1936, and in 1988 admitted openly gay and lesbian ministers to ordination. It is the leading member of the Canadian Council of Churches. Among other Canadian churches that also belong the the WORLD COUNCIL OF CHURCHES are the Anglican Church of Canada, Canadian Yearly Meeting of the Religious Society of Friends, the Christian Church (Disciples of Christ), the Estonian Evangelical Lutheran Church Abroad, the Evangelical Lutheran Church in Canada, and the Presbyterian Church in Canada. Evangelical churches support the Alliance Francophone des Protestants Evangeliques du Quebec and the Evangelical Fellowship of Canada, both associated with the WORLD EVANGELICAL ALLIANCE. Pentecostals are active in the Pentecostal/Charismatic Churches of North America.

Several hundred smaller Protestant denominations exist. Most of the larger churches became independent of their American counterparts during the 20th century, but the overwhelming majority of the remaining churches have members in both countries. Roman Catholicism remains the largest religious community in Canada with slightly more than 40 percent of the population.

Further reading: John Webster Grant, *The Church in the Canadian Era* (Vancouver: Regent College Publishing, 1998); John S. Moir, *The Church in the British Era* (Toronto: McGraw-Hill Ryerson, 1972); R. O'Toole, "Religion in Canada: Its Development and Contemporary Situation." *Social Compass* 43, 1 (1996): 119–134; Douglas J. Wilson, *The Church Grows in Canada* (Toronto: Canadian Council of Churches, 1966).

Carey, Lott (1780–1828) *early African-American foreign missionary*

Lott Carey, the second African American to serve as a foreign missionary, was born in 1780 as a slave in rural Virginia on a farm 30 miles from Richmond. Though his parents were members of the local Baptist church, young Lott did not take to religion. Carey was hired out to work in a tobacco warehouse in Richmond. While there in 1807, he was converted and joined the local Baptist church. He learned to read, which allowed him to improve his position at the warehouse and eventually led to his being licensed by the church to preach.

Carey married and had two children, though his wife died in 1813. Over the next years, with money he saved from his work, he purchased his and his children's freedom, bought a home, and saw to his children's education. He also became one of the organizers of the Richmond African Missionary Society, dedicated to raising support for missionary activity in Africa. The society, in cooperation with the Triennial Convention (the recently organized national association of BAP-

TISTS) and the American Colonization Society, selected Carey and Collin Teague as their first missionaries to Africa.

Before leaving, Carey, Teague, and their families formally organized the First Baptist Church. The group sailed for Africa in 1821. Lott's second wife died soon after they landed in Sierra Leone. In 1822, Carey moved to Monrovia, Liberia, where the Baptist church organized in Richmond became a reality. Today, it continues as the Providence Baptist Church. Carey worked primarily in the town with repatriated former slaves, but he also reached out to native Liberians in the surrounding countryside. He founded a weekday school in Monrovia and a second one in Big Town in the Cape Mount region.

Carey was eventually named vice agent for Liberia, responsible for the needs of the former slaves who were swelling the colony's population. Many of the new residents were Africans recently captured for the slave trade and then released.

In 1828, Carey became temporary head of the colony, but was killed in an accident in the munitions depot. He died on November 10, 1828.

In the years after the Civil War, AFRICAN-AMERICAN BAPTISTS established the Lott Carey Baptist Foreign Missionary Convention, in memory of his pioneering efforts. The convention continues to focus the missionary efforts of African-American Baptists.

See also LIBERIA.

Further reading: Miles Mark Fisher, "Lott Carey, The Colonizing Missionary," *Journal of Negro History* 7, 4 (October 1922): 380–418.; Leroy Fitts, *Lott Carey: The First Black Missionary to Africa* (Valley Forge, Pa.: Judson Press, 1978); ———, *The Lott Carey Legacy of African American Missions* (Baltimore: Gateway Press, 1994).

Carey, William (1761–1834) *pioneer of the Protestant missionary movement*

William Carey was born in Paulerspury, Northamptonshire, England, on August 17, 1761, the son of a schoolmaster. He was raised in the

CHURCH OF ENGLAND, but following a conversion experience in his 18th year he joined a Congregational church. While making his living as a shoemaker, he began preaching as opportunity allowed. He married Dorothy Plackett in 1781.

In 1783, Carey joined a nearby Particular (Calvinist) Baptist church and was rebaptized. In 1785, he moved to Moulton, where he assumed a job as schoolmaster. He became a Baptist minister the following year, though possessing little formal education. An avid reader, he eventually mastered several classical and modern languages.

Carey traced his interest in the world and in missionary activity to his reading of the *Last Voyage of Captain Cook* and other books about foreign countries, including accounts of Moravian and Lutheran missionary activity and the outreach efforts to Native Americans by New England Congregationalists. After several years of contemplation, he concluded that it was the duty of Christians to spread the Christian message to all nations. He faced resistance from fellow ministers who reasoned that it was God's responsibility and not their own to convert the unbelieving nations, a reasonable position from the Calvinist perspective of PREDESTINATION.

Carey persisted, and in 1792 wrote a booklet, *An Enquirey into the Obligation of Christians, to Use Means for the Conversion of the Heathen*. This brief work convinced many of his colleagues to organize the Particular Baptist Society for Propagating the Gospel amongst the Heathen in 1792, the first such organization in the English-speaking world. A short time later, John Thomas, a Baptist who had spent time in Bengal, made an appearance in Northamptonshire, and along with Carey was chosen to begin missionary activity in India. Carey sailed in June 1793.

Not particularly welcomed by the East India Company, which controlled Calcutta, Carey and his family settled in the Dutch settlement at Serampore farther inland. During his first six years, he mastered some local languages, but was beset with the mental deterioration of his wife. He was joined in 1799 by Joshua Marchman and William Ward. In 1801, the British governor-general appointed him to a teaching position in Calcutta that later evolved into a professorship at Fort William College. He used his position to secure government protection for the mission and assistance in their publication of Bibles and Christian literature. Carey's wife finally passed away in 1807. Six months later, he married Charlotte Rumohr, a Danish convert, with whom he lived until her death in 1821.

Though the mission did not make many converts, its success in translating the New Testament into various languages and its assistance to the initial wave of British missions in India from across the Protestant spectrum, inspired many in England to support the emerging missionary endeavor. The Baptist Missionary Society would provide a model for others that would be established by the other British Protestant bodies.

In 1827, Carey and his colleagues broke with the Baptist Missionary Society, in part over ownership issues. In the 1830s, the mission suffered financial instability, and after the death of Carey (June 9, 1834), and then Marshman (1837), the mission collapsed, and the college Carey founded at Serempore closed.

See also BAPTISTS; FULLER, Andrew; INDIA.

Further reading: William Carey, *Letters from the Rev. Dr. Carey* (London, 1828); Mary Drewery, *William Carey: Shoemaker and Missionary* (London: Hodder and Stoughton, 1978); John Clark Marshman, *The Life and Times of Carey, Marchman, and Ward, Embracing the History of the Serampore Mission*, 2 vols. (London: Longman, Brown, Green, Longmans & Roberts, 1859); A. Christopher Smith, "William Carey, 1761–1834: Protestant Pioneer of the Modern Mission Era," in Gerald H. Anderson et al., eds. *Mission Legacies: Biographical Studies of Leaders of the Modern Missionary Movement* (Maryknoll, N.Y.: Orbis Books, 1998): 245–54.

Caribbean

Protestantism entered the Caribbean as part of the Dutch and English attempt to challenge Spanish hegemony. The elimination of most of the native inhabitants (Caribs, Arawaks) in the 16th century and their replacement by African slaves, and later Hindu Asians, forms the backdrop for the religious history of the region.

Spanish colonists established Roman Catholicism wherever they settled, at first on Jamaica and Cuba. The Dutch challenge began with the takeover of Curaçao in 1634 and Bonaire in 1648. The Dutch brought the Reformed Church of the Netherlands in the 1650s, though it largely served only the European settlers. The Lutheran Church of the Netherlands arrived a short time later.

British attention to the Caribbean increased after the destruction of the Spanish Armada in 1588. British privateers roamed the area, harassing Spanish ships. The Bahamas became an early haven for the privateers. Real settlement began in the 17th century, starting with previously uninhabited Bermuda in 1609. The real push came after the Restoration of the monarchy in the 1660s; the loss of North American colonies in the American Revolution provided a renewed incentive a century later. The need for slaves to work the plantations in Jamaica (taken from Spain in 1655) and the Bahamas was an important factor involving the British in the slave trade.

The Danish placed settlements in the western Virgin Islands in the 17th century, and later joined in developing the slave culture. Although Denmark never played a major political role in the Caribbean, its settlement of the Virgin Islands was a key factor in the emergence of the Protestant missionary movement. With its New World outlook, Denmark funded the first Protestant foreign mission at the start of the 18th century—the DANISH-HALLE MISSION in India. In 1731, in Copenhagen, Nicolas von ZINZENDORF, the leader of the MORAVIAN CHURCH, had a chance meeting with ANTHONY, a slave who had become a Christian. Anthony's call for someone to bring the Gospel to his fellow slaves received an enthusiastic response. In 1732, the Moravians commissioned Leonhard Dober (1706–66) and David Nitchmann (1696–1772) as missionaries to the island of St. Thomas, as a first step in the Moravian missionary drive that took them in the next few decades to India, North America, and Africa, and brought about the chance encounter between missionary Peter Böhler (1712–75) and John WESLEY that so influenced the founding of METHODISM.

The work on St. Thomas soon spilled over to St. Croix and St. John, and grew in spite of the opposition of most of the plantation owners and the other ministers, one of whom eventually had the Moravian missionaries arrested. Nevertheless, the mission thrived and moved on to Jamaica (1754), Barbados (1765), Antigua (1771), St. Kitts (1777), and Tobago (1790). The church did well in the next century among freed slaves, who remembered it to be one of the few groups who identified with them during the slave era. The other church Africans looked to favorably was the Methodist.

In the meantime, with the spread of British hegemony over an increasing number of the Islands, the CHURCH OF ENGLAND was becoming a powerful force at least among British settlers.

Methodist international expansion had been focused on the British North American colonies. Following the independence of the United States, Bishop Thomas COKE helped develop a new missionary vision for the church with his 1784 "Plan of the Society for the Establishment of Works among the Heathen," and his subsequent trip to the Caribbean two years later. Methodism had an earlier start on Antigua at the plantation of Nathaniel Gilbert, who had worked to convert his slaves. Coke would make several visits to the Caribbean, and the movement spread through the islands in the 1790s. The early efforts of the Anglicans, Moravians, and Methodists were eventually consolidated in several denominational churches: the Church of the Province of the West Indies; the Moravian Church, East Indian Province; the Moravian Church of Jamaica; and the Methodist Church in the Caribbean and the Americas.

The BAPTISTS came to the Caribbean as a result of the American Revolution. George Lisle (c. 1750–1828), who had helped organize African-American Baptists in South Carolina, left his home when the British pulled out of South Carolina and made his way to Jamaica. There, in 1783, he founded the first Baptist congregation. In the 1890s, British Baptists were inspired by William CAREY's *An Enquiry into the Obligations of Christians to use Means for the Conversion of the Heathens* (1792). While the Baptist Missionary Society was drawn to India initially, in 1814 it sent John Rowe (in spite of the law against preaching to the slaves, passed in 1806). The work of Lisle and Rowe continues in the Jamaica Baptist Union. The spread of the Baptist church through the Caribbean was greatly assisted by the formation of the Jamaica Baptist Missionary Society in 1843. It, in turn, would send missionaries to Africa and Central America.

The Anglicans, Moravians, Methodists, and Baptists dominated the religious life of those Caribbean islands included in the British Empire, with both Reformed and Lutheran churches active in the islands under Dutch and Danish authority. Roman Catholicism dominated in those islands that continued under Spanish or French control. Protestantism came to the French islands along with French citizens who moved to the islands, and the Reformed Church they founded was usually confined to the French population. Protestants entered Haiti after the Haitian government gained control of the whole of the island of Hispanola (1822) and encouraged blacks from the United States to migrate there. The coming of Protestants to Cuba occurred in the wake of the Spanish-American War (1898).

That war focused the attention of American churches not just on Cuba, but on the Caribbean as a whole. In its wake, the number of groups targeting Caribbean islands, including several large African-American denominations, rose sharply. The nearness of the islands allowed some of the newer and smaller groups to support missionary work there while building strength for Africa and Asia. Early in the 20th century, several Holiness groups—the CHURCH OF GOD (ANDERSON, INDIANA), the CHURCH OF THE NAZARENE, the Pilgrim Holiness Church (now part of the WESLEYAN CHURCH), the SALVATION ARMY—began their spread through the Caribbean.

By the middle of the century, the Holiness churches began to be overshadowed by Pentecostal churches. The ASSEMBLIES OF GOD, the CHURCH OF GOD (CLEVELAND, TENNESSEE), and the CHURCH OF GOD OF PROPHECY took the lead, but others soon followed. Paralleling the growth of PENTECOSTALISM, a variety of independent indigenous churches and movements emerged.

Among notable efforts by independent Evangelical missions is the Evangelical Church of the West Indies begun in Cuba in 1928. The group's work spread to Haiti in 1936 and then to the Dominican Republic (1939), Jamaica (1945), and Guadaloupe (1947). In 1949, it began a concerted effort to reach the islands of the eastern Caribbean. The original mission effort has evolved into World-Team, with a focus far beyond the West Indies, while the work in the West Indies evolved into the Evangelical Church of the West Indies.

As the 21st century begins, the older Protestant churches in the Caribbean have associated together in the Caribbean Conference of Churches, itself associated with the WORLD COUNCIL OF CHURCHES. Some of the newer Evangelical groups now cooperate with the WORLD EVANGELICAL ALLIANCE and its affiliate, the Evangelical Association of the Caribbean (which has chapters on many of the islands). Recent estimates suggest that about 80 percent of the residents of the Caribbean islands are Christians, with about three-fourths of them belonging to the Roman Catholic Church.

Through the 20th century, the progress of Christianity has been affected by the relative poverty of the region, as well as by the difficulties in travel imposed by the island environment. One response to the poverty has been the formation of a variety of new competing religions such as the Rastafarians and the Spiritual Baptists, which draw heavily on Protestantism. The JEHOVAH'S WITNESSES and the CHURCH OF JESUS CHRIST OF LATTER-DAY SAINTS have also developed a presence throughout the Caribbean.

See also ANGUILLA; ANTIGUA; BAHAMAS; BERMUDA; CUBA; GRENADA; GUADALOUPE; GUYANA; HAITI; JAMAICA; PUERTO RICO.

Further reading: David Barrett, *The Encyclopedia of World Christianity,* 2nd ed. (New York: Oxford University Press, 2001); Patrick Johnstone and Jason Mandryk, *Operation World, 21st Century Edition* (Carlisle, Cumbria, U.K.: Paternoster, 2001); J. Herbert Kane, *A Global View of Christian Missions* (Grand Rapids, Mich.: Baker Book House, 1971); J. Gordon Melton and Martin Baumann, eds., *Religions of the World: A Comprehensive Encyclopedia of Beliefs and Practices* (Santa Barbara, Calif.: ABC-CLIO, 2002); A. Scott Moreau, ed., *Evangelical Dictionary of World Missions* (Grand Rapids, Mich.: Baker Book House, 2000).

Cartwright, Thomas (1535–1603)
Puritan leader who helped found Presbyterianism
Thomas Cartwright was born in Hertfordshire, England. He attended CAMBRIDGE UNIVERSITY, where in 1569 he was appointed as Lady Margaret Professor of Divinity at Cambridge. Almost immediately, he began to advocate the Presbyterian brand of Puritanism in his classes, and was dismissed the following year. He then journeyed to Geneva, the center of Reformed/Presbyterian teachings and conferred with Theodore de BEZA and others. Upon his return to England, he presented the "Admonitions to Parliament" (1570, 1571) calling for the adoption of the presbyterian system of church government. He was opposed by Bishop John Wright (c. 1530–1604), later archbishop of Canterbury, the prominent defender of the Anglican system.

Ordered to appear before an ecclesiastical court, in 1574 he returned to Geneva. Upon his return to England, he settled among the Puritans at Middleburg. Here, in 1580, he fought against the teachings of Robert BROWNE (who advocated a congregational system of church governance and separation of the church from state authority), forcing Browne to withdraw from Middleburg.

In 1583–84, Cartwright worked with Walter Travers (c. 1548–1635) to construct the Book of Discipline for the Presbyterian Puritans. The book found enough support by the end of the decade that the authorities moved against Cartwright and attempted to destroy all copies.

In 1590, Cartwright was imprisoned but released in 1592 in poor health and allowed to retire peacefully to the island of Guernsey. He died at Warwick in 1603.

See also PURITANISM; REFORMED/PRESBYTERIAN TRADITION.

Further reading: Stephen Brachlow, *The Communion of Saints: Radical Puritan and Separatist Ecclesiology 1570–1625.* (Oxford: Oxford University Press, 1988); Patrick Collinson, *The Birthpangs of Protestant England: Religious and Cultural Change in the Sixteenth and Seventeenth Centuries* (New York: St. Martin's, 1988); William Haller, *The Rise of Puritanism; or The Way to New Jerusalem as Set Forth in Pulpit and Press from Thomas Cartwright to John Lilburne and John Milton, 1570–1643* (New York: Harper, 1957); A. F. Scott Pearson, *Thomas Cartwright and Elizabethan Puritanism, 1535–1603.* (Cambridge: Cambridge University Press, 1925).

Central America
Central America includes the predominantly Roman Catholic former colonies of SPAIN: GUATEMALA, HONDURAS, EL SALVADOR, Nicaragua, Costa Rica, and Panama. BELIZE, the former British Honduras, was a predominantly Protestant country until immigration tipped the balance toward Roman Catholicism in the 20th century.

The CHURCH OF ENGLAND was the first Protestant group to emerge in Central America with settler congregations along the Miskito Coast of Nicaragua as early as the 17th century. In the 1770s, the SOCIETY FOR THE PROPAGATION OF THE GOSPEL IN FOREIGN PARTS commissioned chaplains for British Honduras, centered primarily on Belize City.

Methodists arrived soon after the beginning of the 19th century. A British merchant founded Methodist societies at Belize City, Burrell Boom, and Freetown, which provided a base for the first missionary, who arrived in 1824. Work began at Bluefields, Nicaragua, around 1830. Meanwhile, African Methodists (former slaves in Jamaica) settled in Panama. Through the rest of the century, the Methodist presence expanded, primarily through immigration from the islands. In 1880, for example, Methodist missionaries came to Costa Rica to work among English-speaking workers who had come from various Caribbean islands to build the railroad from San José to the Caribbean coast.

A Baptist missionary arrived in British Honduras in 1822 and a Presbyterian minister in 1825, but the real movement among the native population did not begin until the 1840s and the arrival of the representatives of the MORAVIAN CHURCH. Beginning at Bluefields, Moravians reached out to the Miskitos and the other peoples in rural Nicaragua, the Creoles (people of European descent who had been born in the region), and the Garífunas (people of African heritage brought from St. Vincent).

These early missionaries, most of European heritage, suffered greatly from the hot and humid climate, but churches were planted throughout the century. The British and Foreign Bible Society began distributing a Spanish edition of the Christian Scriptures in Costa Rica in the 1840s, partly with the support of Jamaican Methodists and BAPTISTS. Adding to the diversity of the Protestant community in Central America prior to World War I were the SEVENTH-DAY ADVENTIST CHURCH and the SALVATION ARMY.

In Guatemala in 1873, the liberal (and somewhat anti-Catholic) president, Justo Rufino Barrios (r. 1873–85) invited the Presbyterian Church in the United States to send missionaries. Barrios hoped they would help counter the opposition of the Catholic Church to the reforms he had proposed. (A short-lived Baptist mission in the 1840s had been quickly expelled.)

Protestant growth was stimulated in 1903 by the takeover of the Panama Canal project from the French by the United States. As Americans flocked to the Canal Zone, congregations of a number of American denominations were opened, which provided a base for probings into the predominantly Catholic countryside. Over the next decade, the SOUTHERN BAPTIST CONVENTION, the Methodist Episcopal Church, the CHURCH OF GOD (ANDERSON, INDIANA), the National Baptist Convention U.S.A., the FREE METHODIST CHURCH, and

the CHRISTIAN BRETHREN established Panamanian congregations.

The first interdenominational faith mission to target the region was the Central American Mission (now CAM International), founded in 1890 by fundamentalist leader Cyrus I. SCOFIELD and associates. By focusing its attention entirely on Central America, it was able to send missionaries first to Costa Rica (1891) and then successively into El Salvador (1896), Guatemala (1899), Nicaragua (1900), and Panama (1944). Sizeable denominational bodies later emerged, especially in Guatemala and El Salvador.

PENTECOSTALISM, apparently introduced in 1912 by independent Pentecostals visiting Nicaragua, has become a dominant element of the non-Catholic religious community. With more than 200,000 members, for example, the ASSEMBLIES OF GOD of Guatemala is the largest Protestant body in the country; the larger Pentecostal community includes the INTERNATIONAL CHURCH OF THE FOURSQUARE GOSPEL, the Elim Christian Mission, the Full Gospel Church of God, Calvary Christian Evangelical Church, and the Prince of Peace Evangelical Church, all of which have in excess of 100,000 members. Only the CAM International affiliated Central American Evangelical Church and the Seventh-day Adventist Church have won comparable support. The situation is similar in Panama and Costa Rica, where the Assemblies of God is the only Protestant church with more than 100,000 members. In Honduras, where the Christian Brethren remains the largest Protestant body, the Assemblies of God is a close second. Only Belize seems out of step with this trend, the Seventh-day Adventists and Methodists being the largest Protestant denominations.

The original Pentecostal mission in Nicaragua was absorbed by the Assemblies of God in 1936. In 1916, Charles T. Furman and Thomas A. Pullin, representing the CHURCH OF GOD (CLEVELAND, TENNESSEE) settled in Guatemala. Through the 1920s, they devoted most of their time to the Quiche people, one of several groups descended from the ancient Mayans.

Ecumenically, the WORLD COUNCIL OF CHURCHES has a national affiliated council only in Belize, but member churches include the Baptist Association of El Salvador, the Baptist Convention of Nicaragua, the Evangelical Methodist Church of Costa Rica, the Moravian Church in Nicaragua, and the Salvadorean Lutheran Synod. In contrast, the WORLD EVANGELICAL ALLIANCE has national affiliated associations in all of the Central American countries except Belize.

See also BELIZE; BRITISH VIRGIN ISLANDS; MEXICO.

Further reading: David Barrett, *The Encyclopedia of World Christianity.* 2nd ed. (New York: Oxford University Press, 2001); Clifton L. Holland, ed., *World Christianity: Central America and the Caribbean* (Monrovia, Calif.: MARC-World Vision, 1981); J. Herbert Kane, *A Global View of Christian Missions* (Grand Rapids, Mich.: Baker Book House, 1971); William R. Read, *Latin American Church Growth* (Grand Rapids, Mich.: William B. Eerdmans, 1969).

Central Asia

In the 1990s, the Asian countries absorbed into the Russian Empire and ruled by the Soviet Union became independent as all emerged as autonomous nations. Georgia and Armenia were predominantly Eastern Orthodox in faith, while the others were predominantly Muslim. Throughout the region, Protestantism exists as an extremely small group with roots in the former Russian Empire. The Protestant presence can be traced to the early 19th century, when Russia conquered the Caucasus region and forced Molokans, a Russian Free Church group (and later some DOUKHOBORS), to relocate into undeveloped areas of Transcaucasia.

In 1862, a German Baptist, Martin Kalweit (1833–1918), moved to Georgia, eventually settling in Tiflis (now Tbilisi), where he began to hold services for other German-speaking people. Among his early converts was Nikita I. Voronin (1840–1905), a Molokan, who helped recruit Vasilii G. Pavlov (1854–1924) to the Russian-speaking Baptist contingent. In the 1880s, Pavlov

studied at the Hamburg seminary established by Johann Oncken (1800–84). From Georgia, primarily through Pavlov's efforts, the Baptist Church spread to neighboring countries such as Azerbaijan, and also into Russia proper. Georgia became a center uniting BAPTISTS throughout the Caucasus and Ukraine.

As early as 1890, some members of the Evangelical Christian movement (similar to Baptists) settled in Turkmenistan, and a community began to develop reinforced by Mennonite and Baptist migrants. In 1892, they formed their own settlement, called Kuropatkinsky, not far from Ashkhabad. An Evangelical movement began among both German- and Russian-speaking residents of Uzbekistan in 1898, and a first congregation was organized in Tashkent in 1902. CHRISTIAN BRETHREN missionaries worked in the region for several decades but withdrew in 1928, their fruits absorbed by the Evangelical Christians. An initial Evangelical church was founded in Petropavlosk, Kazakhstan, in 1908; it served the scattered German-speaking community. In 1912, a Russian Baptist, Rodion G. Bershadskii, moved to Bishkek and built the first church in Kyrgyzstan.

These initial churches, scattered and disconnected, survived until the 1928 law that withdrew legal status from all religious groups in the Soviet Union. Some congregations, such as in Tiflis and Ashkhabad, continued to meet underground. Some revived in 1944 in time to join the new Union of Evangelical Christians and Baptists, created by the merger of Baptists and Evangelical Christians.

These churches received new life in the 1990s with the fall of the Soviet Union, but they have subsequently found themselves the targets of governments that have allied themselves with the respective majority religious communities. Neither the Eastern Orthodox groups (such as the Georgian Orthodox Church) nor the Muslims have a history of religious tolerance, and reports are regularly filed of both official and unofficial discriminatory acts against the Baptist and other Protestant churches that have arisen since the 1990s.

In 1992, churches in Turkmenistan, Tajikistan, and Uzbekistan formed the Union of Evangelical Christians-Baptists of Central Asia. It has several thousand members. The largest community of Evangelicals is found in Kazakhstan (some 10,000) and Georgia (around 4,000). Recently, Baptists and Pentecostal evangelists from South Korea have entered Central Asia. YOIDO FULL GOSPEL CENTRAL CHURCH, the large Pentecostal center in Seoul, for example, reports five affiliated churches in Uzbekistan with a total membership of more than 2,000.

See also GEORGIA; TURKMENISTAN.

Further reading: David Barrett, *The Encyclopedia of World Christianity,* 2nd ed. (New York: Oxford University Press, 2001); Steve Durasoff, *The Russian Protestants: Evangelicals in the Soviet Union, 1944–1964* (Rutherford, N.J.: Fairleigh Dickinson University Press, 1969); Albert W. Wardin, ed., *Baptists Around the World* (Nashville, Tenn.: Broadman & Holman, 1995).

Chad

Islam was introduced to Chad, a landlocked country south of Libya, in the 11th century and came to predominate by the 17th century, though many followers of traditional African religions in the southern part of the country never became Muslims. The 1885 Berlin Treaty gave France hegemony over Chad, but the French were slow to move in. In the 1920s, the French Foreign Legion overpowered the local rulers, but independence was granted in 1960.

In 1925, Baptist Mid-Missions, a fundamentalist sending agency based in the United States, sent the first Protestant/Free Church missionaries to Chad. Three years later, an interdenominational sending agency, the Sudan United Mission, and the CHRISTIAN BRETHREN joined the effort. Through the years, the French Mennonites, the Worldwide Evangelism Crusade, the Church of the Brethren, and the Lutheran Brethren (from America) also established work. Eventually, the Sudan United Mission, the Mennonites, and the Worldwide Evangelism Crusade united to form the Evangelical Church of Chad. With 330,000 members, it is the largest Protestant body. It is followed by the Christian Brethren with 230,000 members. Together, they make up 75 percent of the Protestant community, assuring dominance to a conservative form of Protestantism. They have taken the lead in the Entente des Eglises et Missions Evangéliques au Tchad, a national church council affiliated with the WORLD EVANGELICAL ALLIANCE.

Other Evangelical churches, with beginnings in the 1920s, are the Baptist Mid-Mission mission, now the Baptist Churches of Chad, the African Inland Mission work (now the Central African Evangelical Church), the Evangelical Church of the Brethren, the Evangelical Lutheran Church, and the Union of Elim Evangelical Churches (a Pentecostal group with Swiss roots). All measure their membership in the tens of thousands.

Possibly the largest of the AFRICAN INITIATED CHURCHES is the Central African Evangelical Baptist Association of Churches, which in 1973 was founded by former members of the Baptist Churches of Chad. Several groups such as the Church of Jesus Christ on Earth by His Messenger Simon Kimbangu, a large international church that originated in the Democratic Republic of the Congo (Zaire), have started to take root.

The entire Christian community went through a crisis in 1973, when Chad's president, Ngarta Tombalbaye, of the Sara people, ordered all citizens to undergo the traditional initiation rites of his people as part of a program of verifying national authenticity. This was accompanied by an attack on the Baptist community, the expulsion of 18 Baptist missionaries, the arrest of 13 Chadian pastors, and the closing of all Baptist churches and schools. More than 130 Christian leaders were killed in the next 12 months, often for refusing to undergo the suspect ceremony. The president also created an independent church, the Evangelical Church of Chad, to serve Sara Protestants. Persecution ended with Tombalbaye's assassination on April 13, 1975.

Chad was first established with a secular government, and both Christian and Muslim holidays were recognized. Following Tombalbaye's death, his successors reaffirmed the secular nature of the state and withdrew all laws restricting religious freedom.

Further reading: David Barrett, *The Encyclopedia of World Christianity,* 2nd ed. (New York: Oxford University Press, 2001); Patrick Johnstone and Jason Mandryk, *Operation World, 21st Century Edition* (Carlisle, Cumbria, U.K.: Paternoster, 2001).

Charismatic movement

During the 1970s, a movement characterized by the appearance of the gifts of the Spirit (I Corinthians 12)—healing, prophecy, discernment, working of miracles, and so forth—swept through Roman Catholicism and the older Protestant churches. While similar to PENTECOSTALISM, including experiences of speaking in tongues, the movement did not necessarily accept the Pentecostal belief that the BAPTISM OF THE HOLY SPIRIT was always accompanied with speaking in tongues.

The new tendency, generally called the Charismatic movement (from *charis,* Greek for gifts), has been traced to a Spirit outpouring among some Episcopalians in California in 1959 including two Episcopal priests, Frank Maguire and Dennis Bennett (1917–91). On April 3, 1960, Bennett shared what had happened to him to his congregation at St. Mark's Episcopal Church in Van Nuys, and shortly thereafter resigned and moved to an Episcopal church in Washington state. Jean Stone, a laywoman in Bennett's parish, then organized the Holy Trinity Society based in Van Nuys, and sent its periodical to ministers across the country.

Stone found support from the FULL GOSPEL BUSINESS MEN'S FELLOWSHIP INTERNATIONAL (FGBMFI), led by California layperson Demos Shakarian (1913–93). FGBMFI's primary activity had been holding prayer luncheons to introduce the Pentecostal experience to Christians from a variety of backgrounds. The FGBMFI periodical, *Voice,* became the major instrument for spreading the emergent Charismatic movement.

Through the 1960s, local Charismatic groups appeared within all the major Protestant denominations, gradually creating denominationally oriented national Charismatic fellowships. Simultaneously, Roman Catholics were rapidly discovering the Charismatic experience and reaching out to Protestant Charismatics in the Vatican II ecumenic spirit. With the assistance of Belgian cardinal archbishop Leon-Joseph Suenens (1904–96), the Catholic Charismatic movement quickly spread worldwide.

The larger Protestant denominations responded to the new trend with a range of reactions from open hostility to benign neglect, but showed little sign of fully accepting and approving it. Several denominations, beginning with the American Lutheran Church (now part of the EVANGELICAL LUTHERAN CHURCH IN AMERICA), officially discouraged its members and ministers from participating. Through the 1970s, many Charismatics left their home churches to form new congregations and denominationlike fellowships. Most of the new denominations avoided centralized forms of governance. They included such groups as the Evangelical Presbyterian Church, the Charismatic Episcopal Church, and the United Network of Christian Ministers and Churches.

Influenced by Roman Catholic Charismatics, many Protestant Charismatics came to accept that the Holy Spirit could empower people to manifest various gifts of the Spirit, not just tongues. Simultaneously, the findings of psychologists concerning speaking in tongues were being integrated into new theological understandings.

In the 1980s and 1990s, Fuller Theological Seminary in Pasadena, California, the leading ministerial training school of Evangelicalism, developed a new openness to Pentecostalism. In 1985, it invited David du PLESSIS (1905–87) to set up the du Plessis Center for Christian Spirituality there. At the same time, John Wimber (1934–98) began teaching classes at Fuller about the normal status of miraculous activity ("signs and wonders") in evangelism. His classes provided the intellectual basis for his Vineyard movement, which as the Association of Vineyard Churches grew into an international denomination.

Fuller was also home to Peter Wagner (b. 1930) who became famous for his studies on church growth. Wagner joined Wimber as the co-teacher of the "signs and wonders" courses and became an enthusiastic supporter of what he termed the *third wave* of EVANGELICALISM—Christians who were not Charismatics but who believed that miracles would accompany the proclamation of the Gospel. He also worked to network the various Charismatic groups and fellowships that had emerged from the Latter-Rain Movement of the 1950s, a Pentecostalist outgrowth that preached the five-fold ministry of apostles, prophets, evangelists, pastors, and teachers (Ephesians 4:11).

Outside of the United States, the majority of Charismatics appear to have remained in their former churches, but the movement has reached literally millions of believers, and brought a sizable minority into independent Pentecostal and Charismatic denominations. In the United States, more than a hundred new Charismatic denominations have emerged, while the older Pentecostal churches have experienced significant membership growth. The two national Christian cable-television networks have facilitated this growth.

In Europe, despite strong opposition from Protestant state churches, the Pentecostal/Charismatic movement has become the largest non-established religious community in SWEDEN, NORWAY, FINLAND, and ITALY, while making a strong showing in FRANCE, the NETHERLANDS, and SPAIN.

The movement has had its most dramatic impact in Latin America, where new churches have sprung up almost overnight. In BRAZIL, five different Charismatic denominations, each with more than 2 million members, came to the fore late in the 20th century. One, the ASSEMBLIES OF GOD OF BRAZIL, is now the largest Protestant body in the country. In MEXICO, the 5-million-member LIGHT OF THE WORLD CHURCH is reaching out to Spanish-speaking communities worldwide. Similar dramatic growth has been documented from GUATEMALA to ARGENTINA.

The Charismatic movement is also remaking the complexion of Christianity in sub-Saharan Africa (*see* AFRICA, SUB-SAHARAN). Africa is now home to literally thousands of independent churches, which exist in the space between the older missionary bodies and the traditional African religions. The majority of these AFRICAN INITIATED CHURCHES incorporated elements of Pentecostalism and the Charismatic movement. In many countries, Pentecostalism is the dominant religious force, though no individual churches have assumed the same dominant position as in SOUTH AMERICA.

The Charismatic movement launched Pentecostalism on a new worldwide growth phase that continues as the 21st century begins. It is difficult to judge how far it will go in building and changing the Protestant community.

See also BAPTISM OF THE HOLY SPIRIT; PENTECOSTALISM.

Further reading: Dennis Bennett, *Nine O'Clock in the Morning* (Plainfield, N.J.: Bridge, 1970); Cecil David Bradfield, *Neo-Pentecostalism: A Sociological Assessment* (Washington, D.C.: University Press of America, 1979); Stanley M. Burgess and Eduard M. Van der Maas, eds., *International Dictionary of Pentecostal Charismatic Movements*, rev. exp. ed. (Grand Rapids, Mich.: Zondervan, 2002); Patrick Johnstone and Jason Mandryk, *Operation World, 21st Century Edition* (Carlisle, Cumbria, U.K.: Paternoster, 2001); David Martin, *Tongues of Fire: The Explosion of Protestantism in Latin America* (Cambridge, Mass.: Basil Blackwell, 1990); Vinson Synan, *The Century of the Holy Spirit: 100 years of Pentecostal and Charismatic Renewal* (Nashville, Tenn.: Thomas Nelson, 2001).

Chicago-Lambeth Quadrilateral

The Chicago-Lambeth Quadrilateral is a four-point statement of beliefs presented by various Anglican groups in the late 19th century as the basis for possible Protestant unity. In 1870, Episcopal priest William Reed Huntington's book *The Church Idea* searched for a minimum doctrinal basis for uniting Protestantism across denominational lines. He proposed four points: the Holy Scriptures as the Word of God, the Apostles' and Nicene Creeds as the rule of Faith; the two sacraments commonly accepted within Protestantism (BAPTISM and Holy Communion), and the historical episcopate. Most Protestants agreed on the first three points, but only Anglicans and some Lutherans retained an episcopate in apostolic succession.

Huntington's four points, now called the quadrilateral, were raised and endorsed at the 1886 Chicago meeting of the Episcopal Church's House of Bishops in response to the recent creation of the Joint Commission on Christian Reunion. The four points were further supported at the 1888 session of the Lambeth Conference, the decennial worldwide gathering of Anglican bishops.

Subsequently, the Episcopal Church's house of deputies adopted what was now known as the Chicago-Lambeth Quadrilateral. The brief statement often served as a handy tool in 20th-century ecumenical discussions. Discussion on these issues in the 1970s under the auspices of the WORLD COUNCIL OF CHURCHES led to the 1982 publication *Baptism, Eucharist, and Ministry*.

See also ANGLICANISM; CHURCH OF ENGLAND.

Further reading: G. Richmond Bridge, ed., *Rebuilding the House of God, The Lambeth Quadrilateral of 1888. Report of the 1987 Theological Conference* (Charlottetown, S.C.: St. Peter Publications, 1988); George Carey, *Sharing a Vision* (London: Darton, Longman and Todd, 1993); William Reed Huntington, *The Church Idea: An Essay Towards Unity* (New York: Charles Scribner's Sons, 1899); Stephen Sykes and John Booty, eds., *The Study of Anglicanism* (London: SPCK, 1988).

China

China was one of the most prominent targets of Protestant missionary activity in the 19th century, though progress was slow for many decades. The first missionary, Robert MORRISON (1782–1834), was a British Presbyterian minister commissioned by the LONDON MISSIONARY SOCIETY. At the time he arrived in China in 1809, the Chinese allowed only limited contact with the West, all funneled through the Portuguese settlement at Macau and the British trading warehouses in Canton (now Guangzhou). To attain legal residency status, Morrison took a job with the East India Company. His work was always confined by official Chinese policy that discouraged informal contacts between Chinese citizens and Westerners.

Nevertheless, Morrison accomplished much. He translated the New Testament into Chinese (1813), cofounded the Anglo-Chinese College in Malacca, Malaysia, for training missionary personnel (1818), with William Milne (1785–1907) completed the translation of the Old Testament (1819), and compiled a massive Chinese-English dictionary.

Morrison's baptized his first convert in 1814; his second convert, LEONG KUNG FA (also spelled Liang Afa) became the first Chinese person ordained as a minister (1827). By that time, Leong already had a significant career as a lay evangelist; he built the initial Christian community in the Guangzhou region. Morrison baptized fewer than a dozen Chinese Christians. His successors, confined to Macau and Canton, used creative means of getting the Word out. Some set up schools, but the most successful innovation was the MEDICAL MISSIONS idea, pioneered by Dr. Peter PARKER, a Presbyterian physician. German missionary Karl Friedrich August Gützlaff (1803–51) suggested the idea as a way to reach large numbers of Chinese, with Christian literature to be dispensed along with prescriptions. Parker, originally sent by the AMERICAN BOARD OF COMMISSIONERS FOR FOREIGN MISSIONS, founded the Medical Missionary Society of China in 1838.

The 1842 Treaty of Nanking, which was imposed on China following the Opium War, opened new ports for trade, ceded Hong Kong to England, and ended the ban on the opium trade. Missionaries were in demand because of their linguistic abilities, and many took permanent positions with Western governments. The churches gained access to China, but at the cost of being identified with Western aggression and the opium trade.

The ports of Canton (Guangzhou), Amoy (Xiamen), Foochow (Fuzhou), Ningpo, and Shanghai were now available for missionary activity and became the focus of outreach into China. Even today, the overwhelming majority of Chinese Christians live in the coastal provinces between Shanghai and Guangzhou. Among the many groups to begin work in this era was the Methodist Episcopal Church, which established its first center in Foochow (Fuzhou) in 1847. The following year, the Southern Methodists established theirs in Shanghai.

After the Taiping Rebellion (1851–64), a peasant uprising put down with the aid of Western troops, the Chinese granted further concessions to the West, including the opening of most of China to missionary activity. Shanghai became the center of Western mercantile activity and eventually the center of Protestant church life.

Through the last half of the 19th century, a wide variety of Protestant missionary activity emerged, supported by most of the larger European and North American denominations from the CHURCH OF ENGLAND to the Seventh-day Baptists (which introduced SABBATARIANISM to China in 1847). Efforts to prevent denominational competition led in 1877 to the First General Conference of Protestant Missionaries in China.

The CHINA INLAND MISSION, founded in 1865 by James Hudson TAYLOR (1832–1905), used unusual means to achieve considerable success. Taylor decided to build his organization on the basis of a set of faith principles: missionaries would make no public appeals for funding, would not draw a salary but rely on free-will offerings, would integrate into Chinese society as far as possible, and would focus on the essentials of the faith and avoid sectarian squabbles. The mission became the most successful Protestant missionary endeavor in China through the 1930s.

The identification of Christian missionaries with Western aggression provoked numerous incidents against their work and even their very presence. During the Boxer Rebellion in 1900, a large number of Christians, including some 200 missionaries, were killed. Anti-Christian activities

continued through the 1930s. Nevertheless, by 1920 China had become the largest mission field in the world. Schools and hospitals were opened and maintained, including the Society for the Diffusion of Christian and General Knowledge, founded in 1887 to publish Western books in Chinese, the Peking Union Medical College, opened in 1906, and 13 colleges and universities for general higher education.

PENTECOSTALISM appears to have been introduced by Mr. and Mrs. T. J. McIntosh, who arrived in Macau and Hong Kong in 1907 and found their first success among leaders of the CHRISTIAN AND MISSIONARY ALLIANCE. The first church grew from the work of Alfred G. (1874–1944) and Lillian Garr (d. 1916), who were quickly followed by two women, May Law and Rosa Pittman. Lillian Garr had been convinced that the tongues she spoke following her BAPTISM IN THE HOLY SPIRIT included Chinese and Tibetan. Their first convert, Mok Lai Chi, became the group's translator. Mok would arise as the effective leader of the small group. He also founded the first Pentecostal periodical in Chinese, *Pentecostal Truths*. By this time Pentecostalism had spread to northern China, where work was begun by Bernt Bernstein. Subsequently, British Pentecostals in China tended to affiliate with the Pentecostal Missionary Union and Americans with the ASSEMBLIES OF GOD.

The spread of Pentecostalism highlighted the emergence of indigenous Protestant groups. Among the first leaders was Zou Liyou, who broke with the Presbyterian Church to found an independent thanksgiving meeting. In 1911, a group within that meeting founded the China Independent Church.

One important independent movement was begun in the 1920s by Watchman NEE (aka Nee To-shang, 1903–72), a former Methodist who had associated with the exclusive Plymouth BRETHREN. In the early 1920s, Nee, the editor of an independent Christian periodical, *Revival*, concluded that denominational competition was wrong and that there should be only one church in any city. He founded the first such congregation in Shanghai in 1927. He also operated under the THREE-

SELF PRINCIPLES, that churches should be self-governing, self-sustaining, and self-propagating. He took DISPENSATIONALISM from the Brethren and developed a unique Chinese theology. His movement took no name, but variously became known as the LOCAL CHURCH, the Little Flock, and the Assembly Hall churches.

At about the same time, three Beijing Christians, Paul Wei, Ling-Shen Chang, and Barnabas Chang, who had all received the baptism of the Holy Spirit in 1917, began the TRUE JESUS CHURCH. It was distinguished by its sabbatarianism, its non-Trinitarian "Jesus Only" theology, its unique inclusion of speaking in tongues in the Sabbath services, and the bodily movements that frequently accompanied the manifestation of tongues. Like the Local Church, the True Jesus Church gathered hundreds of thousands of followers throughout China.

The spread of Protestant Christianity peaked in the mid-1930s, by which time rumors of war became a factor. The Japanese invasion in 1937 unleashed forces that would dramatically alter the church. While church growth in the old fields came to standstill, refugees moving westward to escape the Japanese introduced Christianity into regions heretofore neglected. The Christian community in the coastal regions felt the full brunt of World War II, while the Chinese Revolution (1947–49) brought more fighting and the rise to power of a government that was opposed to the West, to religion in general, and to the alignment of Christian churches with Western political and economic forces.

In 1950, the new government expelled the Western missionary agencies and missionaries. The remaining churches had to cut their ties with the West immediately, educational and medical centers were nationalized, and seminary education was largely curtailed. Chinese denominational leaders were pushed aside and replaced with state-appointed officials. Churches were merged into a single Church of Christ of China.

In 1954, the Three-Self Patriotic movement (TSPM) of Protestant Churches in China was established at the First National Christian Representative Conference. It became the national expression of Protestantism in China, and all churches were required to affiliate. The three-self movement had been revived in 1950 by Wu Yaozong (aka W. T. Wu, 1893–1979). Active in social and political affairs in the 1940s, he had become interested in Marxism and accused Protestants of collaborating with capitalism. Wu became the chairman of the TSPM in 1954 and was reelected in 1961.

The reduced size of the visible Christian community allowed the TSPM to launch the Church Union movement, which consolidated many congregations and nationalized the property of defunct congregations. The uneasy peace between the government and the Christian community in the early 1960s came to an end in 1966 with the Cultural Revolution. The government declared religion incompatible with the new order and ordered the closing of all religious institutions (including the Three-Self Patriotic Movement). The burning of many Bibles and religious books and the arrest of pastors and other church leaders followed. Christian practice went underground.

The Cultural Revolution came to an end in the late 1970s. In 1979, Chinese president Deng Xiaoping declared an open-door policy that allowed some churches to reopen. In 1980, the Third National Christian Conference organized the China Christian Council (CCC), a second attempt at a single recognized Protestant movement in China (the Church of Christ of China ceased to exist in 1954). The TSPM handled government relations while the CCC was to handle internal ecclesiastical matters. Together, they now publish *Tian Feng,* a national Protestant periodical. Leadership is selected every five years at a national Christian representatives conference.

The CCC established headquarters in Shanghai with Bishop K. H. TING (aka Ding Guangxum, b. 1915) as president. Ting enjoyed a lengthy tenure as head of both the CCC and the Three-Self Association. He supervised the reopening of the Nanjing Union Theological Seminary and the founding of the Amity Foundation, which has worked to reintegrate the church into Chinese life and build ties to Christians outside of China. The CCC joined the World Council of Churches in 1991. Ting was succeeded in 1997 by Dr. Han Wenzao, who was in turn succeeded by Rev. Cao Shengjie in 2003.

In the decades following the founding of the CCC, Protestantism has blossomed in China as never before. From a few hundred thousand believers in 1979, it begins the 21st century with a government-estimated 20 million adherents. All these Protestants are considered to be members of the one official Protestant church. However, pre-World War II denominations survive as active traditions in different congregations and as recognized federations. Thus, for example, the True Jesus Church survives as a group within the CCC, and its members meet on Saturday in the local church building. The existence of these fellowships within the larger single church has often caused tensions within the Chinese Christian community.

Much of the growth of Protestantism in China has been channeled into the house church movement, which takes its name from the practice of meeting in members' homes. These fellowships disagree with the teachings of the CCC (which tends toward liberal Protestantism), reject the organization of the church, or mistrust its ties to the government. As they are unaffiliated, they are denied access to the local authorized church building and, under present Chinese law, are not allowed to construct their own meeting facilities. The movement tends to be conservative in its theology, though it includes a great variety of beliefs, some quite extreme. While some house churches are disconnected local assemblies, others have affiliated in regional and even national fellowships.

It is difficult to estimate the number of house church members. Enthusiastic estimates of tens of millions remain unsubstantiated. However, the radical growth of Protestant Christianity in the last several decades has certainly been accompanied by the spread of Christian beliefs far beyond the walls of the established church. Outside of house churches, there are probably millions of individuals who identify as Christians but who keep their beliefs private. As China evolves, it is expected that Christianity, now adhered to by only 2 percent of the population, will continue to grow.

China itself has emerged as a significant exporter of religion. The displacement of large numbers of refugees from the turmoil of 20th-century China into receiving countries in Southeast Asia and the West brought various forms of Chinese Protestant Christianity to other countries, while the Chinese residing in different countries have themselves been the target for missionary concern. Today, a complex relationship exists between Chinese Christian communities in China and in the diaspora.

See also Asia; China: Hong Kong; China: Macau.

Further reading: David Barrett, *The Encyclopedia of World Christianity,* 2nd ed. (New York: Oxford University Press, 2001); Alan Hunter and Kim-Kwong Chan, *Protestantism in Contemporary China* (Cambridge: Cambridge University Press, 1993); Donald F. MacInnis, *Religion in China Today: Policy and Practice* (Maryknoll, N.Y.: Orbis Books, 1989); J. Gordon Melton and Martin Baumann, eds., *Religions of the World: A Comprehensive Encyclopedia of Beliefs and Practices* (Santa Barbara, Calif.: ABC-CLIO, 2002); A. Scott Moreau, ed., *Evangelical Dictionary of World Missions* (Grand Rapids, Mich.: Baker Book House, 2000); Scott W. Sunquist, ed., *A Dictionary of Asian Christianity* (Grand Rapids, Mich.: William B. Eerdmans, 2001); Luo Zhufeng, ed. *Religion under Socialism in China,* trans. by Donald A. MacInnis and Zheng Xi'an (Armonk, N.Y.: M. E. Sharpe, 1919).

China: Hong Kong

Under British rule from the mid-1800s, Hong Kong was returned to the People's Republic of China in 1997. It now exists as a Special Administrative Region and as such operates under Hong Kong Basic Law regarding religion. Hong Kong possesses a high degree of religious freedom, and because of its strategic location has become the point of dissemination of many religious groups, including Protestant and Free Churches. Buddhism and traditional Chinese religion remain the dominant religious forces among the population.

When the British took control of Hong Kong in 1841, ANGLICANISM in the form of the CHURCH OF ENGLAND was established. An initial chapel was erected and opened for worship the next year. In 1849, the first bishop, George Smith, was consecrated. The work was integrated into the larger field of missionary endeavor in China and Japan. The Anglican diocese survived 20th-century turmoils, but it was not attached to any provincial structure. In 1997, as the governmental changeover became imminent, the new Province of Hong Kong Sheng Kung Hui (aka the Anglican Church of Hong Kong and Macau) was created with three dioceses and a missionary area (Macau). The Anglican Church remains one of the larger Protestant groups in Hong Kong.

As Hong Kong grew through the 19th century, other churches—the Methodists, BAPTISTS, Congregationalists, Presbyterians—arrived and established congregations. The American Baptists actually erected their building before the first Anglican church was completed, and the Congregationalists (represented through the LONDON MISSIONARY SOCIETY [LMS]) followed quickly. James Legge (1815–97), a prominent LMS minister/scholar, opened a school in 1843. He played an important role in the development of public education. Those groups that arrived during the first generation of British rule were assisted by government land grants and even some financial assistance, but that came to an end in 1881.

The older Protestant churches controlled Christian religious life in the years prior to World War II. The Baptist Convention of Hong Kong has survived as the largest Protestant body, and the only one with more than 50,000 members. The Hong Kong Council of the Church of Christ in China (which continues the Presbyterian and Congregationalist churches), the Methodists, and the Lutherans also retain a substantial following. More recently, they have been joined by the CHRISTIAN AND MISSIONARY ALLIANCE, which began work in Hong Kong in 1933 and now reports more than 30,000 adherents.

Since 1950, Protestantism has grown both by migration from mainland China (bringing several indigenous Christian groups) and by the establishment of more than 100 new missionary works. Among the indigenous groups now established in Hong Kong are the TRUE JESUS CHURCH (a non-Trinitarian Pentecostal body) and the LOCAL CHURCH founded by Watchman NEE (which in Hong Kong has given birth to several additional groups). Among the more interesting of the new groups is the Spiritual Bread Worldwide Evangelical Mission, which grew out of the Local Church in the 1950s, and has become a global body with members in more than 20 countries.

The older liberal Protestant groups have affiliated in the Hong Kong Christian Council (aligned with the WORLD COUNCIL OF CHURCHES), and some of the more conservative churches and organizations have come together in the Hong Kong Chinese Christian Church Union. The Christian Conference of Asia, which coordinates those national ecumenical councils in Asia related to the World Council of Churches, is headquartered in Hong Kong.

The SEVENTH-DAY ADVENTIST CHURCH, the CHURCH OF JESUS CHRIST OF LATTER-DAY SAINTS, and the JEHOVAH'S WITNESSES have been active in Hong Kong, the former two reporting some 10,000 members each, and the latter around 2,500.

Though a minority community, Protestants view Hong Kong as extremely important. It symbolizes a hoped-for return to religious freedom in China as a whole, and it has become an organizational center and a launching pad for many missionary-minded outreach efforts both inside China and throughout Southeast Asia.

See also ASIA; CHINA.

Further reading: Gail V. Coulson with Christopher Herlinger and Camille S. Anders, *The Enduring Church: Christians in China and Hong Kong* (New York: Friendship Press, 1996); G. B. Endacott, *A History of Hong Kong* (New York: Oxford University Press, 1973); Nai-wang Kwok, *Hong Kong 1997: a Christian Perspective* (Kowloon: Christian Conference of Asia, 1991).

China Inland Mission

The China Inland Mission (CIM) was the most geographically expansive Protestant missionary endeavor in pre–World War II China. It was founded in 1865 by James Hudson TAYLOR (1832–1905), who had previously served in China with Karl Gutzlaff's short-lived society. Taylor won some support in England with his 1865 book, *China's Spiritual Needs and Claims*. Later that year, with the assistance of William Thomas Berger (d. 1872) but with little financial backing, he created the CIM.

The CIM was to operate under a unique set of rules. It would not make public appeals for financial support but rely on voluntary offerings. Those in service would not be guaranteed a salary. They were expected to integrate themselves into Chinese life and culture, and they were to concentrate on the essentials of the Protestant faith and avoid interdenominational controversies. Taylor returned to China in 1866. The initial missionary station was established at Hangchow (Hangzhou) in Chekiang (Zhejiang); in its first years, work centered on the coastal regions south of Shanghai.

Berger remained behind in London to administer the affairs and finances of the mission. Following his demise in 1872, a council was set in place to select future missionaries, and promote the work in England. Councils were later established in AUSTRALIA (1890), NEW ZEALAND (1894), SOUTH AFRICA (1943), North America (1888), and SWITZERLAND (1950).

Taylor instituted a course of study for newly arrived missionaries, which included mastering Chinese and gaining basic knowledge of local geography, government, and etiquette. In addition, they were given instruction in Chinese religion and advised how best to communicate the Gospel in a new context. Recent arrivals were then usually posted to a station where they could be supervised by an experienced associate.

The China Inland Mission grew steadily through the first half-century of its operation. It began with 24 workers, and peaked in 1934 with 1,368 workers at 364 mission stations all across China and in Manchuria, Mongolia, Tibet, and Burma. Women were integral to the CIM's success. In 1878, Taylor braved possible negative reactions by assigning single women to the mission field. By 1882, Taylor had assigned 95 single women and 56 wives of missionaries to official posts.

After the turn of the century, Taylor's health began to fail, and he was affected by the loss of colleagues during the Boxer Rebellion. He resigned as general director in 1903 and died two years later.

The Japanese invasion in 1937 and the Communist victory in 1949 devastated the CIM. In 1950, all CIM missionaries were ordered to leave the country, with the last missionary reaching Hong Kong in 1953. As personnel withdrew from China, the leadership gathered in England and decided to redirect the work to the Chinese communities outside of the People's Republic. Personnel were restationed throughout Southeast Asia, and headquarters moved to Singapore.

In 1964, a new name, Overseas Missionary Fellowship (OMF), signified a major redirection. For the first time non-Western Christians were welcomed into full membership, and home councils were established in Asian countries to support the work. Also, OMF now moved to include non-Chinese in their missionary efforts.

See also CHINA; FAITH MISSIONS.

Further reading: Marshall Broomhall, *The Jubilee Story of the China Inland Mission* (Philadelphia: China Inland Mission, 1915); Leslie T. Lyall, *A Passion for the Impossible: The China Inland Mission 1865–1965* (Chicago: Moody Press, 1965); John Charles Pollock, *Hudson Taylor and Maria: Pioneers in China* (New York: McGraw-Hill, 1962); Dr. and Mrs. Howard Taylor, *Hudson Taylor and the China Inland Mission* (London: Morgan and Scott, 1919); J. Hudson Taylor, *China's Spiritual Need and Claims* (London: Morgan and Scott, l887).

China: Macau

Macau, a former Portuguese colony, was returned to the People's Republic of China in 1990. The Macau Basic Law, agreed upon prior to the return, includes guarantees of religious freedom.

The population of Macau is primarily Buddhist of Chinese background. The Portuguese government, until the late 20th century, favored the Roman Catholic Church, which dominates the Christian community. Out of a population of 450,000, the Roman Catholics claim 23,000 of 34,000 Christians. The Baptist Church, the Chinese Evangelical Church, an indigenous body, and the SEVENTH-DAY ADVENTIST CHURCH, each with more than 1,000 members, are the only Protestant bodies of any size.

Though Protestants are a distinct minority in Macau, an important chapter in their history occurred there. It was in Macau that Robert MORRISON (1782–1834) launched the Protestant mission to China. The Church of Christ in China in Macau, which continues his work, reports only a few hundred members. In 1997, the small Anglican presence was incorporated into the new Anglican Church of Hong Kong and Macau as a missionary area.

See also CHINA.

Further reading: Y. M. Cheng and K. S. Haung, *Religioes De Macau* (Macau: Macau Foundation, 1994); R. D. Cremer, *Macau: City of Commerce and Culture* (Hong Kong: UEA Press, 1987).

A congregation of the Presbyterian Church of Taiwan, the largest Christian body in Taiwan *(Institute for the Study of American Religion, Santa Barbara, California)*

China: Taiwan

Taiwan (also known as Formosa), a large island some 90 miles off the coast of the China, did not have a significant Protestant presence until after 1949, when the defeated government of the mainland Republic of China arrived with 2 million supporters, an important minority of them Christians. Despite the country's uncertain political future, its economic success, democratic progress, and ties with the United States have created the conditions for rapid growth of a variety of Protestant communities.

Several indigenous groups, some of Malay extraction, others Chinese, settled Taiwan over the centuries. Both the Dutch and the Spanish established colonies in the 1620s but were pushed aside by new Chinese immigrants later in the century.

The first lasting Protestant communities were a British Presbyterian mission on the southern part of the island founded in 1865 and a Canadian effort led by George L. MACKAY in the north beginning in 1872. During 50 years of Japanese colonial rule, no other groups were allowed access. The two Presbyterian synods merged in 1951, and the Presbyterian Church in Taiwan (PCT) remains the largest Protestant group, with a bit more than 200,000 members.

Following World War II, missionaries from a host of Western Protestant and Free Church groups arrived, and groups reached Taiwan from both the Chinese mainland and Hong Kong. Refugees from China brought not only the older mission churches but also several indigenous

Chinese Christian groups, such as the LOCAL CHURCH. For a few decades, Christian growth was limited by martial law regulations, and Christians constituted only about 6 percent of the population. Apart from the Presbyterians, other important churches include the TRUE JESUS CHURCH (Pentecostal) and the Local Church (both indigenous Chinese groups), the Chinese Baptist Convention, and the Taiwan Holiness Church.

The Presbyterian Church of Taiwan (PCT), the only local member of the WORLD COUNCIL OF CHURCHES, has held a unique position in the Protestant community. It led the way in church growth with its Doubling Movement (1954–65) that spearheaded growth in other churches, too. In the 1970s, based upon its understanding of Taiwan's role in God's plan, the PCT issued three statements that called for political reform, asked the nations of the world (especially the United States and the People's Republic of China) to refrain from unilateral decisions determining Taiwan's future, and issued a call for Taiwanese self-determination. The Presbyterians became one of the first Asian churches to call for the CONTEXTUALIZATION of Christianity in Asia, and one of its leaders, NG CHOING HUI, played an important role in the spread of that idea through the former mission churches.

See also ASIA; CHINA.

Further reading: Donald Hoke, ed. *The Church in Asia* (Chicago: Moody Press, 1975); Douglas H. Mendel Jr., *The Protestant Community on Modern Taiwan: Mission, Seminary, and Church* (Armonk, N.Y.: M. E. Sharpe, 1991); Allen J. Swanson, *Taiwan: Mainline versus Independent Church Growth* (South Pasadena, Calif.: William Carey Library, 1970); Hollington Tong, *Christianity in Taiwan: A History* (Taipei: China Post Publishing, 1961).

Christadelphians

The Christadelphians are a decentralized Protestant community deriving from 19th-century American revivalism that has spread throughout the world. Some of their doctrines depart significantly from the Protestant mainstream.

In the 1840s, physician John Thomas (1805–71) of Richmond, Virginia, left the Churches of Christ (the revivalist RESTORATION MOVEMENT that began on the American frontier) as a result of doctrinal disputes with church leader Alexander CAMPBELL (1788–1866). Thomas came to believe that the Holy Spirit was not a third "person" of a triune God, but God's power; this led to a complete revision of his understanding of God and salvation. He also maintained that believers would remain unconscious from the time of their death until the general resurrection, at which time they would be judged and enter the kingdom. Unbelievers, rather than being confined in eternal torment, would simply be annihilated.

For a while, Thomas and his followers refused to give their movement a name. As supporters of PACIFISM, however, they needed some way to identify themselves in order to be considered for conscientious objector status during the American Civil War. The name Christadelphian means "Brethren in Christ."

Their doctrinal divergence separated Christadelphians from the larger community of Protestant and FREE CHURCH Christians, who published a considerable amount of anti-Christadelphian literature over the years. Opposition did not stop the movement, however, and it spread to CANADA, England, AUSTRALIA, and NEW ZEALAND. Periodicals kept the autonomous Christadelphian congregations (called ecclesias) in contact. A split developed in the 1890s over issues of resurrection, resulting in two international fellowships. Most of the British Christadelphians maintained that among unbelievers, only those who had heard the Gospel and been called to repentance could be considered responsible, while unbelievers who had never heard of Christ would have a place in God's kingdom. Robert Roberts, editor of *The Christadelphian*, was the leading British exponent of this position, while J. J. Andrew championed the more conservative older position. Those who accepted Roberts's position became known as the Amended Christadelphians, and those who followed Andrew's lead were the Unammended Christadelphians. Efforts to overcome the division proved unsuccessful.

The movement has no national or international headquarters, and is instead represented by periodicals and publishing houses, separate ones for each of the two branches of the movement. In the 20th century, the movement has spread beyond the English-speaking world, and ecclesias may now be found in more than 100 countries.

Further reading: *A Declaration of the Truth Revealed in the Bible* (Birmingham, U.K.: Christadelphian, 1967); J. J. Andrew, *Jesus Christ and Him Crucified, or, The Truth Concerning Jesus as a Prophet, Priest, and King Shown to Be Subversive of Popular Views* (Sydney, Arthur Norwood, 1913); *One Hundred Years of the Christadelphian* (Birmingham, U.K.: Christadelphian, 1964); Robert Roberts. *A Guide to the Formation and Conduct of Christadelphian Ecclesias* (Birmingham, U.K.: Christadelphian, 1922).

Christian and Missionary Alliance

The Christian and Missionary Alliance (CMA) grew out of the ministry of Canadian-born Presbyterian minister Albert Benjamin SIMPSON (1843–1919). Simpson's ministry was shaped by an experience of healing at a HOLINESS CAMP MEETING and his own zeal for evangelism. He left the Presbyterian Church in 1882 to found an independent congregation and start a magazine devoted to missionary concerns. The work blossomed into the Christian Alliance, consisting of like-minded independent congregations, and the Missionary Alliance, which sponsored missionaries overseas. In 1887, the two organizations merged.

Simpson adopted a version of the Holiness theology in which sanctification made the believer holy as part of the Christian life. He also developed a Christocentric theology that centered on Christ as Savior, Sanctifier, Healer, and Coming King—popularly known as the Four-fold Gospel.

The alliance was a growing evangelistic church in North America, but its real spirit was channeled into support for missions. During its first decade it sent out more than 200 missionaries. In the 20th century, it developed work in some 50 countries. Many of the mission churches later became autonomous bodies and were reorganized as a set of partnership churches through the ALLIANCE WORLD FELLOWSHIP. In 1974, the alliance, which had operated as a fellowship of independent congregations, reorganized and declared itself a denomination.

In 2003, the CMA reported some 350,000 affiliated believers worshipping in approximately 2,000 churches in the United States. One-fourth of the congregations predominantly serve new immigrants and minority groups. The alliance supports around 700 missionaries. The World Alliance community numbers more than 2 million people.

See also INTERNATIONAL CHURCH OF THE FOURSQUARE GOSPEL; MONTGOMERY, Carrie Judd.

Further reading: H. D. Ayer, *The Christian and Missionary Alliance* (Metuchen, N.J.: Scarecrow Press, 2001); J. H. Hunter, *Beside All Waters: The Story of Seventy-Five Years of World-Wide Ministry: The Christian and Missionary Alliance* (Harrisburg, Pa.: Christian Publications, 1964); Robert L. Niklaus, *To All Peoples: Missions World Book of the Christian and Missionary Alliance* (Camp Hill, Pa.: Christian Publications, 1990); ———, John S. Sawin and Smuel J. Stoesz, *All for Jesus: God at Work in the Christian and Missionary Alliance Over One Hundred Years* (Camp Hill, Pa.: Christian Publications, 1986): Lindsay Reynolds, *Footprints; the Beginnings of the Christian & Missionary Alliance in Canada* (Toronto: Christian & Missionary Alliance, 1981).

Christian Brethren

The name Christian Brethren designates the Free Church movement originally associated with John Nelson DARBY (1800–82), an Anglican priest serving with the Church of Ireland who came to reject the idea of a state church as well as much of the denominational and ritual trappings of the Anglican tradition. In the 1820s, Darby began to meet with a small group of like-minded people in Dublin. As the movement spread, an assembly began to meet at Plymouth (whence the often-used name Plymouth Brethren).

At Plymouth, Benjamin W. Newton (1807–99) challenged Darby on a series of issues. Newton emphasized the autonomy of the local assembly as opposed to the unity of the Brethren as a whole. He also called for an inclusive fellowship with other Evangelical Protestants, as opposed to Darby's more exclusive concept. At first, the exclusive side of the movement prevailed. In England, George MÜLLER (1805–98), head of a large assembly and of an orphanage in Bristol, was a prominent, open-minded Brethren leader. Darby would go on to develop DISPENSATIONALISM.

The Brethren accepted the traditional Protestant beliefs of the one God, Jesus Christ, and salvation. They tended to practice CLOSED COMMUNION and believer BAPTISM. They were distinctive in their affirmation of Christian unity, as demonstrated by the weekly observance of the LORD'S SUPPER, i.e., the "breaking of bread," a regular reminder that Christ created one body; the avoidance of distinctive denominational labels (like Presbyterian or Lutheran) in favor of the informal designation "brethren"; and the avoidance of pan-denominational structures and headquarters. Specialized service agencies (camps, missionary sending organizations, and Bible colleges) came to be seen as acceptable.

The Brethren are not very visible on the religious landscape. A local congregation does not even use the name Brethren but exists as a "Gospel Hall," "Bible Chapel," or "Christian Assembly." In some countries, the Brethren have organized in conformity with government regulations, but frequently without using the Brethren name. Many Brethren have been leaders in the Evangelical world without stressing their Brethren affiliation. Prominent Brethren include ministers George MÜLLER and Harry A. IRONSIDE, biblical scholars F. F. Bruce and H. H. Rowdon, hymn writers Francis Trevor and Joseph Scriven, evangelist Luis PALAU, and missionaries A. N. Groves and Jim Eliot.

By the end of the 19th century, the Exclusive Brethren had splintered into five major groups,

later consolidated into two. The so-called Taylor Brethren were the most significant group in the United Kingdom and its former colonies, while the Reunited Brethren (also called the Continental or Grant Brethren) are most numerous on the European continent and in North America. But most of the movement now identifies with the Open (meaning open to fellowship with non-Brethren Christians) or Christian Brethren, which has developed a spectrum of opinion without openly fracturing.

The Christian Brethren are now a global movement, due to vigorous support of foreign missions. They are found throughout most of Europe, Latin America and the Caribbean, Africa (notably ANGOLA, CHAD, CONGO, EGYPT, and Zambia), and much of South and East Asia (especially INDIA and Malaysia). Worldwide membership is estimated between 1 and 1.5 million adults in some 20,000 congregations. Contact with the movement may be made through one of its service agencies such as Christian Missions in Many Lands in Spring Lake, New Jersey, Echoes of Service in Bath, England, or MSC Canada in Markham, Ontario.

See also PREMILLENNIALISM.

Further reading: Robert H. Baylis, *My People: The History of those Christians Sometimes Called Plymouth Brethren* (Wheaton, Ill.: Harold Shaw, 1995, rev. ed., 1997); F. Roy Coad, *A History of the Brethren Movement* (Exeter, England: Paternoster, 1968, 2nd ed., 1976); Harold H. Rowdon, *The Origins of the Brethren* (London: Pickering & Inglis, 1967); Frederick A. Tatford, *That the World May Know,* 10 vols. (Bath, England: Echoes of Service, 1982–86).

Christian Church (Disciples of Christ)
See RESTORATION MOVEMENT.

Christian Churches and Churches of Christ *See* RESTORATION MOVEMENT.

Christian Holiness Partnership

The Christian Holiness Partnership (CHP) is the cooperative fellowship of HOLINESS churches and organizations. The Holiness movement, which had developed in the early 19th century, enjoyed a period of heightened growth following the Civil War. It found its primary organizational expression in a set of CAMP MEETINGS that operated independently of the Methodist church groups to which most Holiness people belonged. In the meetings, Methodists mingled with Holiness people from across the American denominational spectrum. The National Camp Meeting Association for the Promotion of Holiness was founded in 1867 to coordinate the work. By the 1880s, Methodist bishops and district superintendents were beginning to look askance at the movement.

By 1894, the first Holiness denominations had been formed, and numerous independent Holiness churches had come into existence. The words *Camp Meeting* were dropped from the name, and the organization became known as the National Holiness Association. To accommodate Canadian members, in 1971 it became the Christian Holiness Association. Its present name, reflecting the changing relationship between North American churches and their many mission churches around the world, was adopted in 1997.

The partnership, headquartered in Clinton, Tennessee, includes 21 member denominations, three missionary agencies, 48 colleges and seminaries, six Holiness publishing houses, and some 2,000 camp meetings. The CHP also allows local churches (many from non-Holiness denominations) to affiliate. Approximately 10 percent of these local churches are from the UNITED METHODIST CHURCH.

Further reading: Myron F. Boyd and Merne A. Harris, compilers, *Projecting Our Heritage: Papers and Messages Delivered at the Centennial Convention of the National Holiness Association* (Kansas City, Mo.: Beacon Hill Press, 1969); Charles Edwin Jones, *A Guide to the Study of the Holiness Movement* (Metuchen, N.J.: Scarecrow Press, 1974); ———, *Perfectionist Persuasion: The Holiness Movement and American Methodism, 1867–1936* (Metuchen, N.J.: Scarecrow Press, 1974).

Christian Identity Movement

The Christian Identity Movement, born out of the belief system known as BRITISH ISRAELISM, takes its name from the supposed identity of modern white Anglo-Saxon peoples: they are the Ten Lost Tribes of Israel, taken captive in 740 B.C.E. by the Assyrians.

British Israelism was a relatively benign philosophy in the 19th century, although it drew a sharp distinction between ancient Israelites of the Northern Kingdom and modern Jews as descendants of the Southern Kingdom. In the mid-20th century, the theory became wedded to virulent racism and was used to denigrate both Jews and African Americans. Jews were seen as an inferior race, subhuman and of Satanic origin, while Israelites were seen as a godly race of superior beings.

The emergence of the Identity Movement is usually traced to the career of Gerald L. K. Smith (1898–1976), a minister in the Christian Church (Disciples of Christ) and founder of the Christian Nationalist Crusade. Smith passed his teachings to Wesley Swift (1919–70), his onetime bodyguard and chauffeur, who in the mid-1940s opened a church in Lancaster, California, which eventually became the Church of Jesus Christ Christian of Aryan Nations, headed by former Swift associate Richard Butler (b. 1918).

Swift allied his church with militant hate groups such as the Ku Klux Klan (a chapter of which he founded in Los Angeles). Butler welcomed association with various neo-Nazi groups. The Identity Movement thrived in the 1980s under leaders such as William Potter Gale (d. 1988) and Pete Peters (b. 1946). The movement, never large, consisted of independent congregations, each funded with a mail order and/or broadcast ministry. The Aryan Nations group developed an effective prison outreach ministry.

The movement suffered a major setback in 2000 when a civil court handed down a $6-million judgment against Butler and his church, forcing it into bankruptcy, but it carries on through its dozen branches.

Identity is primarily an American fringe movement with little actual membership, drawing much of its strength from a loose alignment with other small racial groups in the United States and northern Europe. It continues to cause concern because of the pervasive violent rhetoric and the occasional acts of violence traced to it.

Further reading: James Aho, *The Politics of Righteousness* (Seattle: University of Washington Press, 1990); Michael Barkun, *Religion and the Racist Right* (Chapel Hill: University of North Carolina Press, 1997); Jeffrey Kaplan, *Encyclopedia of White Power* (Walnut Creek, Calif./Lanham, Md.: AltaMira Press, 2000).

Christian Reconstructionism   *See* RECON-
STRUCTIONIST MOVEMENT.

Christian Science

Christian Science is a metaphysical religion that emerged in New England in reaction to the spiritual healing experienced by founder Mary Baker Eddy (1821–1910). Eddy was a semi-invalid for most of her life until she met Phineas Parkhurst Quimby (1802–66), a mesmerist and mental healer, in Belfast, Maine. She improved dramatically under his care and began to ponder the nature of healing. Shortly after Quimby's death, Eddy had an accident in 1866, slipping on some ice, and was confined to bed seriously ill. She reported that while reading her Bible she received a revelation about divine healing. She was immediately able to get up and walk.

Her struggle to understand the world based on the healing experience led her to a period of teaching and writing, culminating in her major treatise, *Science and Health* (later expanded as *Science and Health with Key to the Scriptures*), initially published in 1875. Her students came to accept the book as a companion volume to the Bible.

In 1870, Eddy began to train others how to heal in silence using her methodology. She started the Christian Science Association for students near Boston in 1876, and in 1879, she organized the Church of Christ, Scientist, in Lynn, Massachusetts, moving it to Boston in 1881. She allowed her students to ordain her as the sole pastor. In 1882, she founded the Massachusetts Metaphysical College, where for the next seven years she continued to teach future Christian Science practitioners and teachers.

Although Eddy's attempt to wed healing with Christianity had parallels in the healing experiences so central to Jesus' ministry, her teachings radically departed from Protestant tradition. God was seen as a Principle, not as a person, and that principle was described as Life, Truth, Love, Substance, and Intelligence. Eddy also advanced an allegorical interpretation of the Bible; the *Key to the Scriptures* she appended to *Science and Health* was a dictionary to assist in that interpretation. The very fact that *Science and Health* was a new revelation challenged the authority that Protestants ascribed to the Bible alone.

Eddy reorganized the church in 1892 and later developed the *Church Manual* containing the rules for governing the church. A five-person governing board administers the Mother Church and issues charters for branch churches. The Christian Science Publishing Society, with its own board of directors, is responsible for several periodicals, including *The Christian Science Monitor, The Herald of Christian Science* (published in 12 languages and Braille), *The Christian Science Journal, the Christian Science Sentinel,* and the *Herald of Christian Science Quarterly.*

There are approximately 3,000 churches worldwide. Membership is unknown. Headquarters are in Boston. Several of Eddy's students left her to found independent churches and schools. Emma Curtis Hopkins (1853–1925) opened the Christian Science Theological Seminary in

Chicago in the 1880s, became the fountainhead of the movement later called New Thought, and ordained many of the first generation of its leaders, such as Myrtle and Charles Fillmore, the founders of the UNITY SCHOOL OF CHRISTIANITY.

Further reading: *Christian Science: A Sourcebook of Contemporary Materials* (Boston: Christian Science Publishing Society, 1990); Gillian Gill, *Mary Baker Eddy* (Reading, Mass.: Perseus Books, 1998); Stephen Gottshalk, *The Emergence of Christian Science in American Religious Life* (Berkeley: University of California Press, 1978); Robert Peel, *Mary Baker Eddy,* 3 vols. (New York: Holt, Rinehart & Winston, 1971).

Churches of Christ   *See* RESTORATION MOVEMENT.

Church Missionary Society

The Church Missionary Society (CMS) was the prominent force behind the worldwide spread of ANGLICANISM in the 19th century.

As knowledge of the world's peoples grew toward the end of the 18th century, John Venn, a CHURCH OF ENGLAND minister at Chapham, challenged his colleagues to find ways to "more effectively . . . promote the knowledge of the gospel among the heathen." Several ministers responded in 1799 by founding the Society for Missions in Africa and the East, which evolved in 1812 into the Church Missionary Society.

The society can be seen as a product of the Evangelical Awakening that produced METHODISM. The movement influenced many who remained in the Church of England, stimulating interest in Christian evangelization of the world. The older SOCIETY FOR THE PROPAGATION OF THE GOSPEL IN FOREIGN PARTS was identified with high-church Anglicanism, while support for the CMS was decidedly low church and evangelical. In most fields, the two agencies worked side by side. The CMS became an important link between Protestant/Free Churches and the larger Anglican community as well as with secular officials in the British colonies.

The CMS began its work in CANADA, CHINA, and the SOUTH PACIFIC, but decade by decade increased its presence globally, especially within the growing British Empire. They pioneered in developing indigenous leadership, commissioning Samuel Adjai CROWTHER for work in Niger. Crowther was later consecrated as the first Anglican bishop of African background.

In countries pioneered by the CMS, conflict would often erupt later on, when the Church of England created the necessary episcopal structures. Society leaders felt undermined by bishops who tried to incorporate CMS missions into their dioceses. Later still, as autonomous jurisdictions became the almost universal form of Anglican church life around the world, CMS missions were incorporated into the new independent Anglican provinces.

Over time, new social service projects built in cooperation with the local provinces took the place of the old mission centers. Since the early 20th century, the CMS had worked closely with the Zenana Missionary Society, another Church of England sending agency, on education and medical care for women. Zenana and CMS merged in 1957. The CMS also took a leading role in ecumenical concerns. It championed cooperation between Protestant missionaries and helped build several new churches that united Anglicans in a single ecclesiastical community with Methodists, Presbyterians, Congregationalists and others, most notably the Church of South India, the Church of North India, and the Church of Sri Lanka.

The CMS, now known as the Church Mission Society, continues an active global program from its headquarters in London.

See also INDIA.

Further reading: Kevin Ward and Brian Stanley, *The Church Missionary Society and World Christianity, 1799–1999* (Richmond, Surrey, U.K.: Curzon Press, 2000).

Church of Christ (Philippines) *See*
IGLESIA NI CHRISTO.

Church of England
The Church of England, still the established religion of the United Kingdom, traces its history back to Christian missionaries who came to the British Isles in the Roman era. The archbishopric of Canterbury was established under Augustine (d. c. 605), who was consecrated in 597. As England expanded its territorial hegemony over Scotland and Ireland, so the church in those areas came under Canterbury's jurisdiction.

Early in the 16th century, Protestantism gained support within the church and among the nobility, but King HENRY VIII (r. 1509–47) at first resisted. However, when he later quarreled with the pope over divorcing his first, barren wife, Henry had a set of laws passed in 1533 and 1534, which made him the supreme authority over the Church in England. Several notables, including Sir Thomas More (1478–1535), were executed for refusing to acknowledge Henry's new role.

In 1536, while negotiating an alliance with Protestant countries against the Holy Roman Emperor, Henry came close to accepting Protestantism, but he backed away when the alliance failed. However, the new archbishop of Canterbury, Thomas CRANMER, had come to accept much of Protestantism and used his office to further its cause.

During the brief reign of Henry's son, EDWARD VI (r. 1547–53), Protestantism became the faith of the Church of England, and the first edition of the BOOK OF COMMON PRAYER was introduced. After Edward's death, the fiercely Roman Catholic MARY I (r. 1553–58) tried to undo the changes. She abolished the prayer book and arrested and executed Protestant leaders who failed to leave the country, including Cranmer.

Mary was soon succeeded by ELIZABETH I (r. 1558–1603), who early in her reign imposed what became known as the VIA MEDIA, or middle way, on the Church of England. The prayer book was reinstituted but revised to lessen the objections of Roman Catholics. A Protestantized statement of belief, the Thirty-nine ARTICLES OF RELIGION, was issued in 1563. The episcopacy was maintained, but Elizabeth assumed supremacy over the church, and in 1570 the pope had her excommunicated. In the meantime, the *via media* became the rule for the church in Wales and Ireland, though not in Scotland, where Presbyterianism was supreme.

Die-hard Catholics tried to assassinate or overthrow Elizabeth, which pushed her further into an alignment with Protestants. At the same time, she faced dissent from a new movement, the Puritans, a spectrum of diverse voices that wished to further "purify" the Church of England. The first challenge concerned clerical vestments. When Puritan ministers refused to don the prescribed garb, Elizabeth had them removed from their congregations. When Thomas CARTWRIGHT (1535–1603) of CAMBRIDGE UNIVERSITY advocated a presbyterial polity for the church, he lost his teaching post.

Puritans at first made little headway, apart from gaining the acceptance of a new translation of the Bible, the KING JAMES VERSION, in 1611. Some formed separate congregations, and some left for Holland or the American colonies. However, by the 1640s, Presbyterians had gained the majority in Parliament and rebelled against Charles I (r. 1625–49). In 1645, it replaced the Book of Common Prayer with a Presbyterian Directory (for worship). In 1648, it called together a group of Presbyterian clergymen who authored the WESTMINSTER CONFESSION OF FAITH (to replace the Thirty-nine Articles) and two new catechisms. In 1549, Oliver Cromwell, leader of the Protestant forces, had Charles executed and assumed leadership of the new British Commonwealth. The Westminster documents were the standard of faith for the Church of England for the next decade.

The country's brief flirtation with Presbyterianism came to an abrupt end in 1660 with the restoration of the monarchy. BISHOPS were returned to their posts, the prayer book reappeared in the pews, and the Thirty-nine Articles resumed their status as a guiding statement of belief. A series of laws were passed to discourage

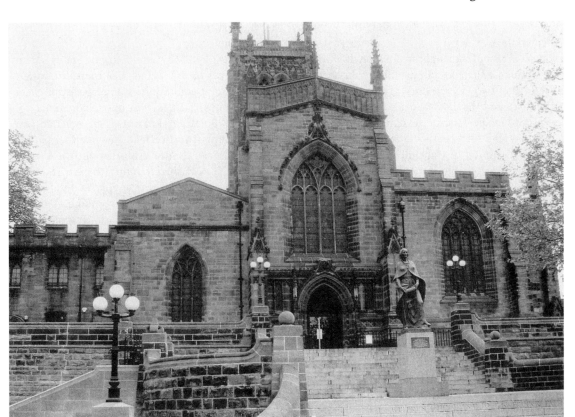

The Collegiate Church of St. James, Wolverhampton, is one of the older parishes of the Church of England in northern England. *(Institute for the Study of American Religion, Santa Barbara, California)*

Puritan gatherings, and persecution continued until the Act of Toleration of 1689. From that time, Puritans ceased their efforts to change the Church of England and organized their own set of dissenting churches.

By this time, the restored church could not ignore the growing numbers of British citizens living in the overseas colonies and began to feel a need to supply them with clergy. This led, at the start of the 18th century, to the formation of the SOCIETY FOR THE PROPAGATION OF THE GOSPEL IN FOREIGN PARTS (which sent ministers) and the SOCIETY FOR PROMOTING CHRISTIAN KNOWLEDGE (which supplied them with Christian literature).

The spread of the church to other lands led some Anglicans to launch missionary work directed at the native populations of the different colonies. The CHURCH MISSIONARY SOCIETY took the lead, later joined by several other organizations. In the course of time, literally millions of non-British people became Anglicans.

Bishops were needed in the new region to confirm new members and ordain priests, but it was not until 1787 that the bishop of London consecrated the first Church of England bishop assigned to a post outside of the British Isles, Charles INGLIS, bishop of Halifax, Nova Scotia. No other bishopric would be established until 1842 (AUSTRALIA), though a number were set up in successive decades. However, it was not until after World War II that native people from the British colonies were integrated into the episcopacy.

The first global meeting of the bishops occurred in 1867, giving birth to the regular Lambeth conferences every decade. In 1888, the bishops accepted the CHICAGO-LAMBETH QUADRILATERAL as a valid statement of the Anglican position. It affirmed the church's adherence to the Bible, the Nicene Creed, the two sacraments (BAPTISM and the Eucharist), and the historic episcopate (leadership by bishops in apostolic succession).

In the mid-20th century, a move to dismantle the global Church of England prevailed. One by one, archdioceses around the world have reorganized as autonomous jurisdictions with local leadership; the international Church of England was reborn as the ANGLICAN COMMUNION, a fellowship of churches in communion with the archbishop of Canterbury. The communion includes more than 40 churches.

The Church of England is now largely confined to England proper; Anglicans in other parts of the United Kingdom are cared for by the Church of Wales, the Church of Ireland (Anglican), and the Scottish Episcopal Church. There is a diocese of Europe, which has oversight of some widely separated Anglican churches in various countries of Europe that primarily serve expatriates. There are also a few isolated dioceses around the world that remain directly under the archbishop of Canterbury.

See also PURITANISM; UNITED KINGDOM.

Further reading: *The Church of England Yearbook* (London: Church Publishing House, published annually); John R. H. Moorman, *A History of the Church in England* (Harrisburg, Pa.: Morehouse, 1986); Stephen C. Neill, *Anglicanism* (Harmondsworth, U.K.: Penguin, 1965); John William Charles Wand, *What the Church of England Stands For: A Guide to Its Authority in the Twentieth Century* (Westport, Conn.: Greenwood Press, 1972); Andrew Wingate, et al., eds., *Anglicanism: A Global Communion* (London: Mowbray, 1998).

Church of God

Variations of the name Church of God are used by many Protestant denominations in the United States, as an expression of their founders' desire to reconstitute the simple church of the New Testament.

In the 19th-century United States, many believers began to rebel against the splintering of the Protestant community into a spectrum of sectarian groups, each known for its adherence to a particular doctrine (Reformed) or practice (BAPTISM by immersion) or its allegiance to a particular historical figure (Martin LUTHER, John WESLEY). They wished to return to New Testament simplicity and be known simply as followers of Jesus Christ and a part of his church. The only term they could find in the New Testament was *church of God*, as in Acts 20:28. Hence, a host of different groups with varied perspectives have taken the name Church of God.

Possibly the first to call themselves by that name were the followers of John Winebrenner (1797–1860), a former pastor in the German Reformed Church residing in Harrisburg, Pennsylvania. He began a movement in the 1820s to reinvigorate the Reformed church by adopting many of the NEW MEASURES, practices at Methodist and Baptist revivals and CAMP MEETINGS. The first congregation to adopt Winebrenner's lead was formed in 1825. After a scriptural search, they chose the name Church of God to proclaim that all true faithful were members of one church. In the process, they created yet another new denomination, now known as the Churches of God, General Conference.

Later in the century, a different group that emerged from the HOLINESS MOVEMENT within the Methodist Episcopal Church chose the same name. Though it was led by Daniel Warner (1842–95), a former member of the Winebrenner fellowship, the new fellowship of congregations was not part of Winebrenner's Church of God. The Warner group became known for the location of their headquarters in Anderson, Indiana: CHURCH OF GOD (ANDERSON, INDIANA). Over the next generation, several other groups followed Warner's example. One small group that spread across Kansas, Missouri, and Iowa and went through several name changes emerged as the Church of God (Holiness).

In the 1880s, during a Holiness revival in the mountains of eastern Tennessee, a group led by R. G. Spurling, took the name Church of God. It emerged as a significant pioneering Pentecostal fellowship in the next century and gave birth to many additional groups. It became known as the CHURCH OF GOD (CLEVELAND, TENNESSEE).

The multiplication of church bodies with the same name caused public confusion and legal problems. Quite apart from the Winebrenner, Holiness, and Pentecostal Churches of God, various independent congregations had long used the name, including some who were caught up in the Adventist movement launched by William Miller in the 1830s. In the years following the Great Disappointment (1844) (when Christ failed to return), two fellowships of such churches emerged. One became known as the Church of God General Conference with an additional tag, "of the Abrahamic Faith." The second group, which worshiped on Saturday, became known as the General Conference of the Church of God (Seventh-Day).

The original Churches of God have given birth to more than 200 Christian denominations, all of which use a variation of the original name, often with the addition of tags referring to their headquarters location or theological uniqueness. Thus today, one will find the Biblical Church of God, the Church of God (Guthrie, Oklahoma), the Original Church of God, the Apostolic Church of God, and the Twentieth Century Church of God, to name a few. Most of these remain relatively small, with membership confined to a few states within the United States, although the CHURCH OF GOD IN CHRIST (a Pentecostal body) has become one of the 10 largest religious bodies in the United States. A few of the older groups have become large international bodies—the Church of God (Anderson, Indiana), the Church of God (Cleveland, Tennessee), and the CHURCH OF GOD OF PROPHECY (from the Tennessee group).

The motivations behind the name Church of God led many other Protestant groups to adopt variations of the name: Church of Christ, Church of Jesus Christ, Church of the Living God, ASSEMBLIES OF GOD, House of God, Christian Church, and so on. The 19th-century RESTORATION MOVEMENT associated with evangelists Barton Stone and Thomas and Alexander Campbell, who all wanted to be known only as Christians, gave rise to the Christian Church (Disciples of Christ), the Churches of Christ, and the Christian Churches and Churches of Christ.

Some of the newer groups have been forced to assume longer, distinguishing names. Possibly the longest is the House of God Which is the Church of the Living God, the Pillar and Ground of Truth Without Controversy (Keith Dominion).

Further reading: J. Gordon Melton, *Encyclopedia of American Religion,* 7th ed. (Detroit, Mich.: Gale Group, 2002); Milburn H. Miller, *"Unto the Church of God."* (Anderson, Ind.: Warner Press, 1968); S. G. Yahn, *History of the Church of God in North America* (Harrisburg, Pa.: Central Publishing House, 1926).

Church of God (Anderson, Indiana)

The Church of God with headquarters in Anderson, Indiana, was one of the earliest independent HOLINESS denominations. It was founded by Daniel Warner (1842–1925), who had been a member of the original CHURCH OF GOD General Council. Warner had come to believe in the holiness experience of sanctification, in which the believer is thought to be made perfect in love. He was expelled from the Church of God General Council and in 1880 founded a new Church of God. It is a noncreedal church distinguished by its Holiness perspective and the practice of FOOT WASHING as a third ordinance beside BAPTISM and the LORD'S SUPPER.

Warner had a zeal for evangelism and missions, and his church began to sponsor missionaries soon after its formation. The majority went to the Caribbean and Spanish-speaking countries in CENTRAL and SOUTH AMERICA. The Church of God also sponsors workers in EGYPT.

In line with its noncreedal and antidenominational perspective, there is no formal affiliation.

Adherents are assumed to be members if they evidence personal conversion and their life suggests the reality of that conversion experience. As of 2003, the church reports an average weekend attendance in its 2,300 North American congregations of some 235,000 people. The missionary program has planted 7,340 churches in 90 countries with some 750,000 believers in attendance.

Further reading: Barry L. Callen, ed. *The First Century,* 2 vols. ((Anderson, Ind.: Warner Press, 1979); ————, ed., *A Time to Remember: Milestones in the Growth of the Church of God Reformation Movement* (Anderson, Ind.: Warner Press, 1978); Milburn H. Miller, *"Unto the Church of God"* (Anderson, Ind.: Warner Press, 1968).

Church of God (Cleveland, Tennessee)

One of the original Pentecostal churches, the Church of God with headquarters in Cleveland, Tennessee, has grown into a large international association of churches with a significant role in the emergence of the global Pentecostal movement. The church traces its beginning to 1886 and the small group that grew up around Baptist minister R. G. Spurling Sr. He wanted to start a movement centered on the holiness of life. Spurling was eventually succeeded by his son, R. G. Spurling Jr. (1858–1935), as leader of the group known as the Christian Union.

In the 1890s, three laymen in the union had an experience that they described as similar to that of John WESLEY (the founder of METHODISM). As a result they began to speak of sanctification as a second work of grace for the believer. This new teaching included an experience of speaking in tongues. A short time later, the group came into contact with an agent of the American Bible Society, Ambrose J. Tomlinson (1865–1943). In 1903, Tomlinson became the pastor of the group, and persuaded them to adopt the name CHURCH OF GOD.

By 1908, the church had several congregations; Tomlinson presided at the Cleveland, Tennessee, headquarters. That year, the group encountered G.

B. Cashwell (1860–1916), an evangelist who had been introduced to the Pentecostal experience of the AZUSA STREET REVIVAL. Tomlinson received the BAPTISM OF THE HOLY SPIRIT and spoke in tongues. Over the next year the church followed him. In 1909, he was selected the general overseer of the church, a post he would hold until 1922.

The Church of God accepted the Azusa teachings, namely that the baptism of the Holy Spirit was available as a third experience of grace to those who had previously been saved and sanctified. The church also believed in BAPTISM by immersion and practiced FOOT WASHING.

The Church of God's reach beyond the United States began in 1909 in the Bahamas. After a CAMP MEETING in Florida, where they received the baptism of the Holy Ghost, Rebecca and Edmond S. Barr returned to their native Bahamas to spread the word. From that beginning, the Church of God has grown into a global fellowship that includes work in 161 countries serving some 6 million members. It was a significant force in introducing PENTECOSTALISM to several countries, especially in the Caribbean.

A. J. Tomlinson ran the Church of God until 1922, when he was driven from office following charges of financial mismanagement. With his supporters, he organized the CHURCH OF GOD OF PROPHECY. Following his death, his son Milton Tomlinson (1906–1995) proved an effective leader of the church, while his brother Homer, one of the more colorful characters in the Protestant world, founded another church, which proved less successful. As the church grew, it spawned a variety of new movements, many of which took some form of the name Church of God as their own, but none of which developed an important international ministry.

The Church of God (Cleveland, Tennessee) has a worldwide membership of 5,766,000 members, of whom 850,000 reside in the United States. It actively supports the PENTECOSTAL WORLD FELLOWSHIP. In 2003, the Church of God (Cleveland, Tennessee) announced a new joint global evangelistic initiative to be untaken with the Church of God of Prophecy.

Further reading: Charles W. Conn, *Like A Mighty Army: A History of the Church of God,* definitive edition, 1886–1995 (Cleveland, Tenn.: Pathway Press, 1996); R. Hollis Gause, *Church of God Polity: With Supplement* (Cleveland, Tenn.: Pathway Press, 1985); Ray H. Hughes, *Church of God Distinctives* (Cleveland, Tenn.: Pathway Press, 1989); David G. Roebuck, "Restorationism and a Vision for World Harvest: A Brief History of the Church of God (Cleveland, Tennessee)." *Cyberjournal for Pentecostal-Charismatic Research,* vol. 5. Available online. URL: http://www.pctii.org/cyberj/index.html; James L. Slay, *This We Believe* (Cleveland, Tenn.: Pathway Press, 1963).

Church of God in Christ

The largest Pentecostal church in the United States, the Church of God in Christ is a predominantly African-American church that in the late 20th century became a significant international force. The church has its origin in the HOLINESS MOVEMENT in Mississippi, the first congregation being founded in 1897. Crucial to its history was the visit of Charles Harrison Mason (1861–1961) and two other clergy to meetings at the AZUSA STREET REVIVAL in Los Angeles in 1907. There they received the Pentecostal blessing complete with speaking in tongues. The Pentecostal message was not well received among their former colleagues, and the three men and a small following left. Originally an interracial group, most (but not all) of its white members would later become part of the ASSEMBLIES OF GOD.

The church was led by Mason for 44 years and is now led by an elected presiding bishop. It is a Holiness Pentecostal fellowship, preaching that the Christian life is punctuated with three main experiences: JUSTIFICATION, sanctification, and BAPTISM OF THE HOLY SPIRIT.

The church became an international body in the 1920s with affiliated congregations in CANADA, MEXICO, Panama, Costa Rica, and several Caribbean islands. The spread to Latin America was assisted by leadership from Latino congregations in the United States. In the years since World War II, the church has developed an extensive presence in Asia, the largest membership being in India. It developed in Europe following the migration of American members to England, Germany, ITALY, and BULGARIA. The church now has some 6 million members in 60 countries, of which 4 million reside in the United States.

See also PENTECOSTALISM.

Further reading: Ithiel C. Clemmons, *Bishop C. H. Mason and the Roots of the Church of God in Christ* (Bakersfield, Calif.: Pneuma Life, 1997); Lucille J. Cornelius, compiler, *The History of the Church of God in Christ* (n.p.: 1975).

Church of God of Prophecy

The Church of God of Prophecy resulted from a schism in the CHURCH OF GOD (CLEVELAND, TENNESSEE) when in 1922 many questioned the leadership of longtime general overseer Ambrose J. Tomlinson (1865–1943). Tomlinson left with his supporters and founded what later became known the Church of God of Prophecy. Following Tomlinson's death in 1943, his son Milton A. Tomlinson (1906–1995) succeeded him as general overseer.

The Church of God of Prophecy was quite similar to its parent body except in its POLITY, though a more democratic order developed after the aging Tomlinson resigned in 1990. The church is notable for the number of women in its ministry. It is a Holiness Pentecostal body and sees the Christian life as punctuated with the three notable experiences of JUSTIFICATION, sanctification, and the BAPTISM OF THE HOLY SPIRIT. Living a holy life is emphasized.

The Church of God began with a substantial membership and has grown to include more than 150,000 members in the United States. It became international soon after its founding and now has affiliated congregations in more than 100 countries, with a worldwide membership of 400,000. It actively supports the PENTECOSTAL WORLD FELLOWSHIP.

In 2003, the Church of God of Prophecy announced a new cooperative missionary program with the Church of God (Cleveland, Tennessee), a first step in healing an 80-year break.

Further reading: C. T. Davidson, *Upon This Rock,* 3 vols. (Cleveland, Tenn.: White Wing Press, 1973–76); Raymond M. Pruitt, *Fundamentals of the Faith* (Cleveland, Tenn.: White Wing Press, 1981); James Stone, *The Church of God of Prophecy: History and Polity* (Cleveland, Tenn.: White Wing Press, 1977); Vinson Synan, *The Century of the Holy Spirit* (Nashville, Tenn.: Thomas Nelson, 2001).

Church of Jesus Christ of Latter-day Saints

The Church of Jesus Christ of Latter-day Saints (popularly called Mormons), with more than 5 million members in the United States and more than 6 million in some 200 other countries, is one of the fastest-growing religious communities in the modern world. It cannot be understood apart from its Protestant heritage, however, its unique doctrines have taken it far beyond the Protestant fold, and many would argue, in spite of its name, beyond the Christian community.

The church grew out of revelations to Joseph Smith Jr. (1805–44), which began in the 1820s near his home at Palmyra, New York. His encounter with God the Father and Jesus Christ led him to a set of golden plates, which, with supernatural help, he was able to translate. The translated material was then published as the *Book of Mormon,* viewed by Mormons as an additional revelation concerning Jesus Christ and the ancient Hebrew people, who they say lived in the Americas during his ministry.

The publication of the *Book of Mormon* and several lesser works that also have scriptural authority (the *Doctrines and Covenants* and the *Pearl of Great Price*), led to the founding of the church. Members believe the church is a restoration of true Christianity, with an apostolic organization that had been lost over the centuries. Temples were organized for weddings and crucial ceremonies that affect the believers' status in heaven.

The church became quite controversial in the mid-19th century for advocating polygamy, which was abandoned starting in 1890 as a condition for the entry of Utah as a state. Remnants of the teaching survive in the belief that marriage is for not only this life but all eternity. The church continues to place a strong emphasis on family life and on tightly integrated community life, although the original communal economy has long since disappeared.

The church is led by the First Presidency that includes the President-Prophet, who has the power to receive new revelation and add to the open-ended *Doctrines and Covenants.* The First Presidency is assisted by the Quorum of the Twelve, the Quorum of the Seventy (who oversee the missions of the church), and the Presiding Bishopric (which handles temporal affairs).

The church has positioned itself as a new form of Christianity that is related to other Christian churches as they are related to Judaism. Many Evangelical Protestants consider the Latter-day Saints to be a non-Christian body and have created organizations to counter its growth.

Following the martyrdom of its founder in Nauvoo, Illinois, in 1844, the majority of the church members moved to Utah and settled the Rocky Mountain region from Idaho to Arizona. As a majority or large minority in a number of western states, the church has achieved a national presence in American politics in the decades since World War II, and with it a reduction in hostility from outsiders.

Further reading: James B. Allen and Glen M. Leonard, *The Story of the Latter-day Saints* (Salt Lake City, Utah: Deseret Book, 1992); Francis Beckwith, Carl Mosser, and Paul Owen, eds. *The New Mormon Challenge* (Grand Rapids, Mich.: Zondervan, 2002); Terryl Givens, *By the Hand of Mormon: The American Scripture That Launched a New World Religion* (New York: Oxford University Press, 2003).

Church of South India *See* INDIA.

Church of the Nazarene

The Church of the Nazarene, an American-based HOLINESS church, was founded in 1895 by Phineas F. Bresee (1838–1915), a former pastor in the Methodist Episcopal Church. In 1894, Bresee asked church leaders to appoint him to an independent mission in downtown Los Angeles that had requested his services. They refused him, and he simply resigned from the ministry. The mission soon grew into the First Church of the Nazarene. In 1897, Bresee founded a second congregation in Berkeley, and after several other congregations emerged, he decided to organize a new denomination to operate along America's West Coast.

The first delegated assembly of churches in 1898 named Bresee its superintendent. By this time, the church had sent five missionaries to India. The church became a national organization through a series of mergers with other regional Holiness associations, beginning in 1907 with the absorption of the Association of Pentecostal Churches of America. Further mergers were negotiated with the Holiness Church of Christ (1908), the Pentecostal Church of Scotland (1915), the Pentecostal Mission of Nashville (1915), the Laymans Holiness Association (1922), the International Holiness Mission (1952), the Calvary Holiness Church (1955), the Gospel Workers Church of Canada (1958), and the Church of the Nazarene (Nigeria) (1988).

The Church of the Nazarene is headquartered in Kansas City, Missouri. Some 600,000 of its 1.1 million members reside in the United States, with the remainder scattered around the globe. Work is divided into districts under a district superintendent. The General Assembly elects the General Superintendents (who function somewhat like BISHOPS) and the General Board, the primary executive body. The church is affiliated with the CHRISTIAN HOLINESS ASSOCIATION and the National Association of Evangelicals, through which it is additionally related to the WORLD EVANGELICAL FELLOWSHIP.

Further reading: Russel D. Bredholt, Joseph. F. Nielson, and G. Ray Reglin, *A Great Commission Movement: the Church of the Nazarene in the 21st Century*

First Church of the Nazarene, Washington, D.C.
(Institute for the Study of American Religion, Santa Barbara, California)

(Kansas City, Mo.: Beacon Hill Press, 1993); J. Fred Parker, *Mission to the World: A History of Missions in the Church of the Nazarene Through 1985* (Kansas City, Mo.: Nazarene Publishing House, 1988); W. T. Purkiser, *Called Unto Holiness, II* (Kansas City, Mo.: Beacon Hill Press, 1983); M. E. Redford, *The Rise of the Church of the Nazarene* (Kansas City, Mo.: Beacon Hill Press, 1948); Timothy Smith, *Called Unto Holiness* (Kansas City, Mo.: Nazarene Publishing House, 1962).

Clorinda (c. 1766–1806) *early Indian convert and supporter of Protestantism*

Clorinda, a well-to-do Brahmin convert to Christianity, gave the money to erect the first Protestant church building in India. She was a Maratta Brahmin and the wife of a government employee. Following the death of her husband, she was expected to throw herself on his funeral pyre, but she was brought under protection to the British military camp in Tanjore. She later moved, having begun a relationship with a British officer, to Palayamcottah, where in the 1770s she met Lutheran missionary Christian Friedrich SCHWARTZ.

Kokila, as she was then known, asked Schwartz to baptize her, but he refused until she ended her affair with the officer. Shortly thereafter, the officer became ill and died. On February 25, 1778, she was baptized, and afterward became known as Clorinda. She began to evangelize in Palayamcottah and quickly gathered a small worshipping community; some 40 people participated in the first baptismal service.

Relatively wealthy, Clorinda paid for Schwartz's assistant Sathiyanandan to come as pastor of the growing church. She herself gave money to build a sanctuary, dedicated in 1785. The building, known locally as the Brahman Lady's church, remains in use today. It became the center of a large movement of people into Christianity. Clorinda founded the first school in the area, which eventually evolved into St. John's College.

Clorinda died in 1806 and is buried in Palayamcottah. The work she helped start is now part of the United Evangelical Lutheran Churches of India.

See also INDIA.

Further reading: Franklyn J. Balasundaran, "Clorinda" in *A Dictionary of Asian Christianity,* ed. Scott W. Sunquist (Grand Rapids, Mich.: William B. Eerdmans, 2001); William H. Price, *The Life and Labors of the Rev. Christian Frederick Schwartz, the Great Lutheran Missionary to India* (Columbus, Ohio: Lutheran Book Concern, 1895).

closed communion

Closed communion is the practice of limiting the LORD'S SUPPER to members in good standing of the church. In denominations with an episcopal or presbyterial POLITY, communion may be limited to members of the denomination. In those with a congregational polity, participation is often limited to members of the local congregation. In the Roman Catholic Church, in those countries where citizenship and church membership were almost the same thing, one's first communion following confirmation was a significant event in a person's life, and excommunication, the withdrawal of the privilege of taking communion, was a serious matter. During the Reformation, the papacy issued many widely heralded pronuncia-

tions of excommunication of those who broke with Rome.

Closed communion became a serious issue for Protestants as the movement split into various factions, and as congregations arose whose members saw themselves as formal converts to Christianity with a different status from those who had merely been born into the church. Within the ANABAPTIST movement, denial of participation in the communion service was an important means of discipline, short of full disfellowshipping.

Most churches continued some form of closed communion into the 19th century, but it was often discarded on the mission field, to avoid the appearance of competition among various denominations working in the same area. Later in the century, as the ECUMENICAL MOVEMENT emerged, closed communion was discarded by many groups in a spirit of harmony. Many churches have made formal agreements to be open to one another's members, a practice often tied to pulpit fellowship, in which ministers of one church are allowed to preach in the others. Still other churches have discarded closed communion as impractical in the highly pluralistic environment of the modern West.

However, a number of denominations have continued the practice of closed communion, basing their arguments on 1 Corinthians 11:17–34, in which Paul warns against partaking of the Lord's Supper unworthily. It continues especially among churches that have grown out of the RADICAL REFORMATION (MENNONITES, AMISH, BRETHREN), and in many BAPTIST churches.

Further reading: Abraham Booth, *An Apology for the Baptists: in which they are vindicated from the imputation of laying an unwarrantable stress on the ordination of baptism: and against the charge of bigotry in refusing communion at the Lord's Table to Pedobaptists* (London: W. Button, 1812); J. W. Kesner Sr., *Credenda: (Being a Treatise of Thirteen Bible Doctrines) Fundamental or Basic Beliefs of Missionary Baptists,* ed. by L. D. Foreman (Little Rock, Ark.: Seminary Press, 1950), see chapter on "Restricted Communion"; Paul T. McCain, *Communion Fellowship: A Resource for Understanding, Implementing, and Retaining the Practice of Closed Com-*

munion in a Lutheran Parish (Waverly, Iowa: The International Council for Lutheran Confessional Research, 1992); Elert Werner, *Eucharist and Church Fellowship in the First Four Centuries,* trans. by Norman E. Nagel (St. Louis: Concordia Publishing House, 1966).

Coke, Thomas (1747–1814) *early Methodist missionary leader*

Methodist leader Thomas Coke initiated the worldwide spread of METHODISM in the decades after the American Revolution. He was born in Brecon, Wales, on September 9, 1747. He attended Jesus College at Oxford University and following completion of his work was ordained as a deacon (1770) and priest (1772) in the CHURCH OF ENGLAND. As curate in South Petherton, Somerset, he encountered Methodism and in 1776 he met Methodist founder John WESLEY. In 1777, he was expelled from his parish, and he joined the Methodists.

As one of the few ordained ministers among the Methodists, Coke quickly became a trusted assistant, used by Wesley for important affairs outside of England. In 1782, he went to Ireland to preside over the first annual conference meeting of the Methodists. In 1784, having been "set apart" as a superintendent, he traveled to the United States, where he helped organize the Methodist Episcopal Church, and was designated a BISHOP.

Also in 1784, Coke published a *Plan of the Society* [of Methodists] *for the Establishment of Missions among the Heathen.* He led the British Methodists to sponsor missionary activity first in Antigua and then on the remaining Caribbean islands, dedicating much of his own inheritance to that cause. He also helped Methodists open centers on GIBRALTAR and in SIERRA LEONE.

During the early years of the 19th century, Coke's vision became increasingly focused on India. Following the opening of the subcontinent to missionaries in 1813, he organized the first team. He died en route on May 3, 1814, and his body was buried at sea. Shortly after his death, the British Methodists organized the Missionary Society to continue his pioneering efforts. That society

Thomas Coke (1747–1814) *(Drew University Library)*

would take British Methodism around the world during its first century of activity.

See also CARIBBEAN; METHODISM.

Further reading: Warren A. Candler, *Life of Thomas Coke* (New York: Abingdo-Cokesbury Press, 1923); Samuel Drew, *The Life of the Rev. Thomas Coke, Ll. D. Including in Detail His Various Travels and Extraordinary Missionary Exertions, in England, Ireland, America, and the West-Indies* (New York: J. Soule & T. Mason, 1818); John Vickers, *Thomas Coke Apostle Of Methodism* (Nashville, Tenn.: Abingdon Press, 1969).

Comenius, John Amos (Jan Amos Komensky) (1592–1670) *educator and Moravian Church leader*

John Comenius was born in 1592 in Nivnice, Moravia, in what is now the Czech Republic. He studied theology at Herborn and Heidelberg and became pastor of the Protestant church at Prerau.

The MORAVIAN CHURCH, also known as the Unitas Fratrum or United Brethren, had been organized by the followers of John HUS after his martyrdom in 1414. In spite of persecution, it survived and in the 16th century aligned with the Reformation cause. By 1517, the Unitas Fratrum had some 200,000 members in more than 400 congregations. A new effort to suppress the church was launched in 1547, and many of the members fled to Poland.

Comenius emerged as a leader early in the 17th century as the Thirty Years' War (1618–48) spread to Czech lands and persecution of Protestants began. After a Protestant defeat at White Mountain in 1620, Comenius and many of his co-religionists were expelled from Bohemia. He first moved to Lissa, Poland, but as Catholicism had reasserted itself in that country he was forced to keep on the move. Meanwhile, the Unitas Fratrum was being systematically suppressed in Bohemia.

While serving as bishop of the Unitas Fratrum (the last to serve until the group reorganized in GERMANY in the next century), Comenius became known throughout Europe for his advocacy of various progressive educational ideas. He pioneered the use of pictures in textbooks and promoted what today would be seen as a more holistic concept of education. He believed that education was a lifelong process that began in childhood and continued into one's last years. He called for the formal education of women. Comenius developed a system termed Pansophism, which integrated theology, philosophy, and education, in the belief that learning, spiritual progress, and emotional growth occurred together. His union of spiritual enlightenment with education was termed the *via lucis* or way of light.

He responded to calls from England, Transylvania (1650–54), and SWEDEN, where he was asked to restructure the school system. There is some evidence that he was offered the presidency of Harvard University, then just beginning in Massachusetts, but declined to move too far from the center of the struggling Unitas Fratrum.

The Unitas Fratrum survived as a small, largely underground movement. Comenius died in Amsterdam in 1670. The church passed through a period without a bishop, but Comenius's grandson Daniel Jablonsky later received episcopal orders which he would pass along to the revived Unitas Fratrum early in the 18th century.

Comenius wrote more than 150 books, including *Pansophiae Prodromus*, the most important statement of his educational views, and the pictorial *Orbis Sensualium Pictus* (*The Visible World In Pictures*, 1658).

Further reading: Eduard Benes, et al., *The Teacher of Nations: Addresses and Essays in Commemoration of the Visit to England of the Great Czech Educationalist Jan Amos Komensky Comenius 1641–1941.* (Cambridge: Cambridge University Press, 1942); Johann Amos Comenius, *Selections,* intro. by Jean Piaget. In commemoration of the third centenary of the publication of Opera didactica omnia, 1657–1957. (Paris: UNESCO, 1957); S. S. Laurie, *John Amos Comenius: Bishop of the Moravians—His Life and Educational Works* (Cambridge: Cambridge University Press, 1893); Will S. Monroe, *Comenius and the Beginnings of Educational Reform* (New York: Scribner, 1900); Matthew Spinka, *John Amos Comenius: That Incomparable Moravian* (Chicago: University of Chicago, 1943).

common sense

Among the most influential philosophical approaches in 19th- and 20th-century Protestant theology has been the common sense realism of Scottish philosopher Thomas Reid (1710–96). Reid, who taught at both King's College in Aberdeen and the University of Glasgow, developed his philosophical, ethical, and religious ideas in reaction to the views of philosophers David Hume and George Berkeley. Both men believed that humans related to the world via perceptions, ideas, and the mind. Reid championed common sense, that ordinary people (as well as intellectuals) could gain a reliable perception of the world through the use of their senses. Individuals, he posited, also have an innate moral sense. Theologically, Reid's approach suggested that anyone could grasp the meaning of the Bible by a simple and somewhat literal reading. Reid published his view in several books, the most important being *An Inquiry into the Human Mind on the Principles of Common Sense* (1764), *Essays on the Intellectual Powers of Man* (1785), and *Essays on the Active Powers of Man* (1788).

Reid found an early champion in the United States in John Witherspoon (1723–94), long-term president of the College of New Jersey (Princeton University). The ideas were incorporated into what is called PRINCETON THEOLOGY, with its emphasis on the literal reading of the biblical text.

While Reid remains popular in some Fundamentalist and Evangelical circles, common sense philosophy suffered in modern times from the apparent failure of anthropologists to document a common moral sense in their observation of different cultures, and as subatomic physics revealed a world not previously available to sensory perception or understandable through common sense.

Further reading: Melvin Dalgarno, *The Philosophy of Thomas Reid* (Dordrecht, Netherlands: Kluwer Academic Publishers, 1989); Norman Daniels, *Thomas Reid's Inquiry: The Geometry of Visibles and the Case for Realism* (Stanford, Calif.: Stanford University Press, 1989); John Haldane, *The Philosophy of Thomas Reid: A Collection of Essays* (Oxford: Blackwell, 2003); Thomas Reid, *The Works of Thomas Reid,* 4 vols. (Charlestown, U.K.: Samuel Etheridge, 1813) Various editions.

Company of Pastors

The Company of Pastors was a corporate body of ministers in Geneva who played a major theological and practical role in the early Reformed Church. In the 1530s, William FAREL helped reorganize church governance in Geneva by organizing Reformed ministers into a body replacing the BISHOP. This new organization was approved by John CALVIN in 1541. The basic plan of rule by teaching ELDERS persisted for several decades. The company held frequent discussions on theology, and began to exercise authority especially in the selection and ordination of additional ministers. The company elected a moderator to preside over its meetings and a secretary to keep records.

The idea of the company passed on to various Reformed and Presbyterian churches, where it survived as the classis or presbytery. The original Company of Pastors survives to the present in Geneva. In 2001, the Geneva body made history when it elected Rev. Dr. Isabelle Graesslé as its first female moderator. In November 2002, she in turn presided at the annual celebration at the Reformation monument, as the names of four precursors to the Reformation were added to the wall: Peter VALDES, John WYCLIFF, John HUS and Marie DENTIÈRE. Dentière was the first female figure to be so recognized.

Further reading: Philip Edgcumbe Hughes, trans., *The Register of the Company of Pastors in the Times of Calvin* (Grand Rapids, Mich.: William B. Eerdmans, 1966); E. William Monter, *Studies in Genevan Government, 1536–1605* (Geneva: Librairie E. Droz, 1964).

Confessing Church *See* EVANGELICAL CHURCH IN GERMANY.

Congo

Congo is the name of two countries located on either side of the Congo River in Central Africa, the Republic of the Congo being a former French colony, the Democratic Republic of the Congo, a former Belgian colony. The Roman Catholic Church was introduced to the Congo River basin in 1491, and in both Congos, the Roman Catholic Church represents about half of the population.

Protestantism arrived in 1878, when George GRENFELL and Thomas Comber (1852–87), two British Baptist missionaries, made some initial exploration up the Congo River. Grenfell soon resigned from the Baptist Missionary Society (BMS) but Comber persevered. Despite the loss of several family members, he continued working to establish the Baptist Church's mission among the Bakongo people. His first convert, Mbanza Kongo, was baptized in 1886.

In 1880, Grenfell reconciled with the BMS and oversaw the construction of *Peace,* a ship designed to navigate the upper Congo. Returning to Africa, he made the exploration of the river his life's work. Over the next 15 years, a string of mission stations were opened from modern Kinshasa to near Kisangani. Unfortunately, Grenfell played into the hands of Belgian King Leopold II, who in 1885 was acknowledged by the European powers as ruler of the lands south and west of the river. Ignoring the growing catalogue of abuses by Belgian colonists, Grenfell worked with Leopold and refused to blame him for what was occurring until near the end of his life.

Following the British Baptists were the American Baptists, Presbyterians, and Christian Church (Disciples of Christ), and the Swedish Evangelical Covenant Church. In 1885, Methodist bishop William TAYLOR came to the Congo and set up the first Methodist work. All of the 19th-century work operated on the south side of the river in Belgian territory. It would not be until 1990 that a Protestant group, the Swedish Mission Covenant Church, would enter the former French territory.

The Belgian Congo became a popular target for missionaries in the early 20th century, and a spectrum of churches set up missions. Most successful were the CHRISTIAN BRETHREN, the MENNONITES, and the SEVENTH-DAY ADVENTIST CHURCH. The most important movement of the early 20th century, however, was an AFRICAN INITIATED CHURCH (AIC) founded by Simon KIMBANGU. Kimbangu began preaching and healing in 1921. In a short time, worried Belgian authorities arrested him, and he spent the rest of his life in jail. Nevertheless, he attracted a following that grew into a multimillion-member international church, the first of the AICs to become a member of the WORLD COUNCIL OF CHURCHES. Through the rest of the century, hundreds of AICs sprouted in the Congo, though none with the appeal of the Kimbanguists.

PENTECOSTALISM came to the Congo in 1915 through the Congo Evangelistic Mission based in England. By the end of the decade, representatives of the ASSEMBLIES OF GOD IN GREAT BRITAIN AND IRELAND and the Assemblies of God in the United States had also arrived.

In the decades after World War II, the mission churches hurried to complete the process of indigenization. Both Congos became independent in 1960 and established their capitals across the river from each other in Brazzaville and Kinshasa. After several years of instability, Sese Seko Mobutu (1930–97) came to power in the former Belgian Congo, changed the country's name to Zaire, and led an increasingly repressive regime.

In 1970, the Mobutu government demanded that all of the Protestant churches unite into one body, the Church of Christ in Zaire, using the previously existing Congo Protestant Council as the starting point for the new organization. In 1971, eight churches tried to withdraw from the merged body and set up an alternative church, but were forced by the government to drop their quest. The Kimbanguists were allowed to exist as a separate body (along with the Catholic and Orthodox churches). Denominations were allowed to maintain a separate identity as a "community." Outside of Zaire, each church was still recognized as a separate body, a number of which joined the World Council of Churches. Those churches that refused to join the united church were denied recognition and many ceased to exist. A few were able to survive the Mobutu era, including the JEHOVAH'S WITNESSES, ideologically opposed to government ties. The government blocked the attempt of conservative churches to organize a local affiliate of the WORLD EVANGELICAL ALLIANCE.

The total Protestant community is approximately 22 million, some 45 percent of the Democratic Republic of the Congo (the post-Mobutu country name).

In the Republic of Congo (Brazzaville), there is a Council of Churches with three members—the Evangelical Church (from the original Swedish work), the SALVATION ARMY, and the Kimbaguists; the council is affiliated with the World Council of Churches.

See also AFRICA, SUB-SAHARAN; KIMBANGU, Simon.

Further reading: Kenneth Lee Adelman, "The Church-State Conflict in Zaire," *African Studies Review*, 18, no. 1, April 1975: 103–16; E. Anderson,

Churches at the Grass-Roots: A Study in Congo-Braz-zaville (London: Lutterworth, 1968); E. M. Braekman, *Historie du Protestantisme au Congo* (Brussels: Eclaireurs Unionistes, 1961); Peter Forbath, *The River Congo: The Discovery, Exploration, and Exploitation of the World's Most Dramatic River* (Boston: Houghton Mifflin, 1977); Cecilia Irvine, *The Church of Christ in Zaire* (Indianapolis, Ind.: Christ Church, 1978).

Congregationalism

Congregationalism is a Protestant movement that grew out of the Reformation in England and evolved into several major denominations. It has always stressed a church POLITY that keeps power in the individual congregation.

Congregationalism emerged in the 17th century as a branch of PURITANISM. Most Puritans wanted to replace the episcopal organization of the CHURCH OF ENGLAND with government by elders (lay ruling elders and clergy teaching elders) who would meet in presbyteries and synods, thus providing a more democratic and collective leadership to the church.

A more radical critique began to emerge in the 16th century. In the 1580s Robert BROWNE (c. 1550–1633) argued for a church organized around autonomous congregations. Each congregation would start with a covenant agreement in which members joined themselves to God and then to one another. Members would then elect their own leaders: a pastor, one or more teachers, the ELDERS, the deacons, and the widows, and convey to them the authority to act. Browne also developed procedures to receive new members and disfellowship recalcitrant members. Congregations would associate with other congregations through regional synods, whose power would be largely advisory.

Congregationalists believed that it was possible for the entire Christian community to be reorganized along this pattern, but it was not until the Puritans landed in New England in the 1630s that they had a chance to put their program into operation. Here they worked out problems of organization, controversy, the status of nonchurch members, and the relationship with the state.

Bethany Congregational Church, Santa Barbara, California *(Institute for the Study of American Religion, Santa Barbara, California)*

As the Puritans came to power in England in the 1640s, Congregationalists seized the opportunity to state their case. Following the promulgation of the Westminster "Form of Presbyterian Church Government" in 1645, Congregationalists on both sides of the Atlantic moved to publish their alternative program for church governance while affirming their general acceptance of the Puritans' theological affirmations. In 1648, the New Englanders issued the CAMBRIDGE PLATFORM and the British leadership the SAVOY DECLARATION. These two documents have become the classic statements of the Congregational perspective.

Following the restoration of the monarchy in England and the separation between church and state in the United States after the American Revolution, classical Congregationalism became a moot issue. The goal of a Congregationalist establishment relying on government support, with a single Christian congregation in each community, could not be achieved. Instead, Congregationalism evolved into a form of the Free Church operating as a minority in a religiously pluralistic culture. It retained its theological heritage as a would-be state church, most visibly demonstrated in its continued practice of infant BAPTISM.

American Congregationalists experienced several mergers in the 20th century that eventually resulted in the UNITED CHURCH OF CHRIST. The main branches of British Congregationalism merged into the UNITED REFORMED CHURCH, though several groups, including the Scottish Congregational Church and the Union of Welsh Independents, stayed out of the merger.

Congregationalism made major contributions to the 19th-century Protestant missionary movement. It was the primary supporter of the AMERICAN BOARD OF COMMISSIONERS FOR FOREIGN MISSIONS and the LONDON MISSIONARY SOCIETY (now the Council on World Missions). Through these two organizations, Congregational churches have emerged around the world. Most are now members of the WORLD ALLIANCE OF REFORMED CHURCHES, a reaffirmation of a shared Reformed theological heritage, though some of the more conservative Congregational churches now constitute the INTERNATIONAL CONGREGATIONAL FELLOWSHIP.

Further reading: Jean-Jacques Bauswein and Lukas Vischner, eds. *The Reformed Family Worldwide: A Survey of Reformed Churches, Theological Schools, and International Organizations* (Grand Rapids, Mich.: William B. Eerdmans, 1999); John Von Rohr, *The Shaping of American Congregationalism, 1620–1957* (New York: Pilgrim Press, 1994); Williston Walker, ed. *Creeds and Platforms of Congregationalism* (New York: Pilgrim Press, 1991).

consistory

The term *consistory* designates certain ruling bodies in various churches. In the Reformed tradition the consistory is the authority in the local church, generally made up of all of the teaching ELDERS (ministers) and the ruling elders (lay leaders). It governs the congregation, implements the policies of the SYNOD and/or assembly of which it is a part, and provides for discipline of church members where necessary. In Geneva in the 16th century, John CALVIN oversaw the formation of the consistory, whose members were assigned the duty of visiting households and checking upon the conduct of the citizenry.

The Geneva consistory met weekly to examine people accused of misbehavior. If the charges proved of substance, it had a range of options including referring the person for counseling or, in more severe matters, to the civil courts. In 1555, excommunication was added to its powers. As much as Calvin's theology, the consistory gave Geneva in particular and the Reformed church its unique lifestyle.

In the Lutheran Church, the consistory is a district, regional, or national organization that either serves the congregations in its geographical area (in churches with a congregational polity), or governs them (in more centrally organized Lutheran churches). The consistory had great powers when it operated within a state church under the authority of the government.

In Anglican churches, the consistory is the diocesan court, usually presided over by the bishop's chancellor or commissary. It deals with a variety of issues at the diocesan level, and its decisions may be appealed to higher courts in the national church.

Further reading: Robert McCune Kingdon, "Calvin and the Family: The Work of the Consistory in Geneva," in Richard Craig Gamble, ed., *Calvin's Work in Geneva* (New York: Garland, 1992), 93–106; Raymond A. Mentzer, *Sin and the Calvinists: Morals Control and the Consistory in the Reformed Tradition* (Kirksville, Mo.: Sixteenth Century Journal, 1994).

consubstantiation

The term *consubstantiation* designates the Lutheran understanding of the status of the elements in the communion service, which Protestants call the LORD'S SUPPER and Catholics call the Eucharist.

The Roman Catholic theory of transubstantiation held that when the words of consecration (or institution) were spoken, the substance (true reality) of the elements of bread and wine were literally changed into the substance of Jesus Christ. At the same time, the various accidental attributes of the bread and wine (color, smell, taste, texture, and so forth) remained the same.

Protestants in general rejected this idea, but Martin LUTHER wanted to retain the idea of Christ's real presence in the sacrament. It appears that Philip MELANCTHON, Luther's associate and a New Testament scholar at WITTENBERG, initially suggested the solution that Luther later advocated, namely consubstantiation. Drawing on the same Aristotelian philosophical ideas, Luther suggested that neither the substance nor the accidents of the bread and wine are changed, but that the substance of Christ coexists in the elements of bread and wine. This coexistence occurs by the power of the word of God, not by the actions of the officiant. Luther suggested an analogy: if one sticks an iron rod into fire, the two substances (iron and fire) are united in the heated rod, but the substance of neither is altered.

In 1529, Luther's teaching was opposed by Ulrich ZWINGLI. At their meeting at Marburg, Zwingli suggested a doctrine of the Lord's Supper that denied the real presence. John CALVIN would later suggest a compromise built around the idea of the spiritual presence of Christ in the sacrament, which most members of the Reformed and Presbyterian churches found acceptable. Lutherans and most Anglican continued to speak of the real substantive presence of Christ.

See also SACRAMENTS.

Further reading: Paul Althaus, *The Theology of Martin Luther* (Philadelphia: Fortress Press, 1986); Hermann Sasse, *This Is My Body: Luther's Contention for the Real Presence in the Sacrament of the Altar* (Minneapolis, Minn.: Augsburg, 1959); Theodore G. Tappert, *The Lord's Supper* (Philadelphia: Fortress Press, 1961).

contextualization

Contextualization is the general label under which the long-term move to de-Westernize the global Protestant movement has proceeded in recent decades. As originally defined in 1972 by the Theological Education Fund of the WORLD COUNCIL OF CHURCHES, *contextualization* is the ability to respond to the Gospel out of one's own situation—with a stress on situations outside Europe and North America. While originally referring to theology, the term was soon picked up by missiologists, theoreticians of the missionary enterprise.

There had been a growing belief that non-Western churches should become autonomous of the missionary agencies that had originally worked to found them. The call for indigenous leadership had been made by, for example, Henry Venn (1796–1873) of the CHURCH MISSIONARY SOCIETY (the THREE-SELF PRINCIPLES), and Methodist William TAYLOR (1821–1902). However, they did not gain a serious hearing until post–World War II decolonialization forced missionaries to turn over control of most churches, and a major shift of power occurred within the Protestant community.

Almost immediately, new voices arose to articulate long-felt concerns. The first manifestation was LIBERATION THEOLOGY, which arose in SOUTH AMERICA at the end of the 1960s, and spread in the next two decades to disenfranchised groups in the West (African Americans, women) and to churches in Africa and Asia. At first, the movement focused on removing European-based male leadership, which some perceived as a threat to traditional Protestant structures. Later on, the emphasis in the new Asian, African, and South American theological texts shifted to a call for creative and responsible appropriation of the Gospel message by non-Western Christians. This trend was supported by grants released through the Theological Education Fund.

The call for contextualization was also heard among Evangelicals who launched the Lausanne Movement, which aimed to focus on unreached peoples. As early as 1978, Lausanne leadership sponsored a conference to examine the cultural contexts in which they hoped to plant new churches. Evangelicals have generally seen the spread of the Gospel as the start of a conversation between new believers and the Bible that takes into account their own milieu. The effort has stimulated new Bible studies that emphasize the

St. Luke Episcopal Church serves Korean-Americans in Honolulu, Hawaii. *(Institute for the Study of American Religion, Santa Barbara, California)*

original context and message of the Bible as well as each particular cultural context.

Further reading: John W. De Gruchy, John W. Charles Villa-Vicencio, and Charles Villa-Vicencio, eds., *Doing Theology in Context: South African Perspectives* (Maryknoll, N.Y.: Orbis Books, 1994); Virginia Fabella and Mercy Amba Oduyoye, eds., *With Passion and Compassion: Third World Women Doing Theology* (Maryknoll, N.Y.: Orbis Books, 1988); Dean Gilliland, "Contextualization," in Moreau, ed. *Evangelical Dictionary of World Missions*, ed. A. Scott Moreau (Grand Rapids, Mich.: Baker Book House, 2000); John S. Mbiti, *Bible and Theology in African Christianity* (Nairobi: Oxford University Press, 1986).

covenant

The covenant has been a popular metaphor in Protestant thought. It found its most thorough expression in what was termed *covenant theology* within the Reformed tradition.

The idea of covenant makes particular reference to the Abrahamic covenant (Genesis 17), in which God takes the Hebrew people as his people and promises to bless them, while in return they will live in obedience to God. In the 17th century, federal theology (a form of covenant theology) became dominant in British and American Puritanism. It maintained that God made an initial covenant with Adam as the "federal" head of the human race, which bound humanity to obey moral law (summarized in the Ten Commandments). Humanity fell into sin, thus denying the possibility of salvation via this initial covenant. Hence, God established a new covenant of grace in Christ who by fulfilling the law and atoning for sin became the new federal head of the race.

In federal theology, everyone is viewed as living under the covenant of works (which requires obedience to the law), and condemned by the inability to keep the law. However, the elect are also under the covenant of grace. Thus, Christians experience the law not as condemnation, but as a guide to living a devout life. The logical conclusion was that God demands that Christian and non-Christian alike abide by the law, and the church has the obligation to call society to righteousness. The covenant also kept central the idea that God continued to interact with his people. Covenant theology underlay the WESTMINSTER CONFESSION OF FAITH (1646–47), and was spelled out in detail in Chapter VII, "Of God's Covenant with Man."

In the 20th century, federal theology came into conflict with DISPENSATIONALISM, a form of theology that divided Bible history not into two covenants, but into seven dispensations. During each dispensation, God chooses to act differently toward humankind and demands different responses from people, both individually and collectively. Dispensationalism proved very popular in those churches (Presbyterian, Baptist) traditionally rooted in Calvinism.

See also REFORMED/PRESBYTERIAN TRADITION.

Further reading: E. M. Emerson, "Calvin and Covenant Theology," *Church History* 25 (1956): 136–44; Renald E. Showers, *There Really Is a Difference!: A Comparison of Covenant and Dispensational Theology* (Bellmawr, N.J.: Friends of Israel Gospel Ministry, 1990); Geerhardus Vos, *The Covenant in Reformed Theology* (Philadelphia: K. M. Campbell, 1971); David A. Weir, *The Origins of the Federal Theology in Sixteenth-Century Reformation Thought* (Oxford: Clarendon Press, 1990).

Covenanters

The Covenanters were the most militant faction of Scots who resisted the imposition of English Anglican control in the 17th-century Church of Scotland.

When James I (r. 1603–25) ascended to the English and Scottish thrones, he attempted to bring the Church of Scotland (which since the Reformation had been Presbyterian in belief and organization) to conform to the Anglican principles of the CHURCH OF ENGLAND. In 1612, having largely succeeded in reintroducing BISHOPS into Scottish church life, he tried to have the church adopt a brief document known as the Five Articles of Perth. In the context of the times, they were seen as a major step toward Anglicanism, if not Catholicism. It called for bishops to bless children following their catechetical instruction, and for the church to commemorate the days designated in the Western liturgical calendar for Christ's birth, passion, resurrection, and ascension, and for the descent of the Holy Spirit (Pentecost). The articles were passed by the assembly of the Church of Scotland in 1618, and by the Parliament in 1621.

Charles I (r. 1625–49) reaffirmed the Five Articles. A short time later, he moved to increase the powers of the bishops by naming them to powerful civil posts. His attempt in 1637 to impose a new book of worship services, prepared by Archbishop William LAUD (1573–1645), on all the Scottish congregations was apparently the last straw and led to a riot in Edinburgh and other locations.

Opponents of the prayer book wrote up a national covenant pledging continued loyalty to the Presbyterian church while still defending the person and authority of the king. Issued on February 28, 1638, the covenant met with popular support, and the great majority of Scots signed it. An assembly in the fall moved to depose the bishops, withdraw the prayer book, and annul the Five Articles of Perth. Charles sent an army to quell what he saw as open revolt, but it was defeated.

In 1643, the Scots sided with Parliament in the Civil War against the king and entered into the Solemn League and Covenant to establish true (i.e., Protestant) religion in the land. The Scots, however, broke with their English allies following the execution of Charles I, and while Oliver CROMWELL ruled in England, the Scots set Charles

II on their throne. Charles quickly reneged on his promise to acknowledge the covenants of 1638 and 1643 and moved to reintroduce bishops into Scotland. Those most opposed to supporting the Church of Scotland under such conditions began to meet separately in their homes and in the open air. The struggle continued until James II finally allowed a Presbyterian church order to be reestablished in the 1680s.

By the time William II and Mary ascended the throne of England in 1689, the dissenting Covenanter party, which had come to see the Church of Scotland, even with its new Presbyterian order, as corrupted, was reduced to a small lay following until joined in 1706 by minister John McMillan (c. 1669–1753) and in 1743 by Thomas Nairn. That year they founded the Reformed Presbytery, the mother organization of the Reformed Presbyterian Church.

Some Covenanters moved to North America (in some cases after being banished by the government), where they established Reformed Presbyterian presbyteries in the 1700s. The largest branch survives as the Reformed Presbyterian Church of North America.

In Scotland, the Reformed Presbyterians grew rapidly for more than a century. In 1863, the great majority united with the Free Church of Scotland. The surviving Reformed Presbyterian Church has been reduced to four congregations. It enjoyed somewhat greater success in Northern Ireland, where work was established in the 1740s. The Irish Covenanters, though only a few thousand strong, support mission work in Ethiopia, Syria, Lebanon, and Cyprus, and supply ministers for the Scottish congregations.

See also REFORMED/PRESBYTERIAN TRADITION; UNITED KINGDOM.

Further reading: Jean-Jacques Bauswein and Lukas Vischer, eds. *The Reformed Family Worldwide: A Survey of Reformed Churches, Theological Schools, and International Organizations* (Grand Rapids, Mich.: William B. Eerdmans, 1999); Robert Benedetto, Darrell L. Guder, and Donald K. McKim, *Historical Dictionary of Reformed Churches* (Lanham, Md.: Scarecrow Press, 1999); James H. Smylie, *A Brief History of the Presbyterians* (Louisville, Ky.: Geneva Press, 1996).

Coverdale, Miles (1488–1568) *British reformer and Bible translator*

Miles Coverdale was born in Coverham, Yorkshire, educated at CAMBRIDGE UNIVERSITY, ordained as a Roman Catholic priest in 1514, and later joined the Augustinian monastic order. He absorbed a Protestant perspective in the 1520s and in 1528 left his order and moved to the Continent, where he began his long career as a Bible translator. He initially worked with William TYNDALE, who had already published an English New Testament, on a translation of the Pentateuch. Following his mentor's arrest and execution in 1535, he continued the effort, and in 1538 brought out a new English translation of the entire Bible, based on both the Latin and Martin LUTHER's German version.

He later worked with Thomas CROMWELL on a revised translation, known as the Great Bible or (after additional editing) Cranmer's Bible (1540), and then pastored a Lutheran church near STRASBOURG. He remained in France until HENRY VIII died, then returned in 1548 amid great fanfare. EDWARD VI named him his chaplain, and in 1551 he became bishop of Exeter.

Coverdale was targeted by Queen MARY I as part of her program to return England to the Roman Catholic fold. He was arrested but saved from the fate of many of his colleagues probably through the intervention of the Lutheran king of Denmark. Mary allowed him to accept exile, eventually in Geneva. Surviving Mary, he returned to England, but ELIZABETH I did not restore his episcopal position. Her new Anglican way did not have room for those perceived to be too Reformed or too much tied to Roman Catholicism.

In 1564, he received a parish, St. Magnus, in London, but was forced out two years later for being too attached to the beliefs and practices he absorbed in Geneva. He died two years later at the age of 81. His body was eventually (1840) interned at St. Magnus.

See also BIBLE TRANSLATIONS.

Further reading: Miles Coverdale, *Memorials of the Right Reverend Father in God Myles Coverdale* (London: S. Bagster, 1838); William Dallmann, *Miles Coverdale* (St. Louis, Mo.: Concordia Publishing House, 1925); Francis Fry, *The Bible of Coverdale* (London: Willis & Sotheran, 1867); James F. Mozley, *Coverdale and his Bibles* (London: Lutterworth, 1953); George Pearson, ed., *Remains of Myles Coverdale, Bishop of Exeter* (Cambridge: Cambridge University Press, 1846).

Cranmer, Thomas (1489–1556) *martyred author of the Book of Common Prayer*

Chief author of the Anglican BOOK OF COMMON PRAYER, Thomas Cranmer was remembered even more for his martyrdom during the reign of MARY I, which helped win her the name "Bloody Mary."

Cranmer was born at Aslockton, Nottinghamshire, in 1489. He attended Jesus College at CAMBRIDGE UNIVERSITY. Ordained a Roman Catholic priest in 1523, he remained in Cambridge as a campus preacher. Recruited as a diplomat in 1527, he worked on the issue of annulling the marriage of HENRY VIII to Catherine of Aragon, who had not produced a male heir.

Cranmer's theological colleagues sided with Henry, and Cranmer began to rise. Four years later, he was named archbishop of Canterbury and thus head of the CHURCH OF ENGLAND. Among his first acts was a declaration annulling the marriage to Catherine and legitimizing Henry's marriage to Anne Boleyn.

By this time, Cranmer had absorbed a variety of Protestant ideas and had begun instituting reforms, suppressing masses for the dead, prayers to the saints, and pilgrimages. He worked with Miles COVERDALE on a revised translation of the Bible.

Cranmer was able to survive Henry's vacillating demands, but he reached the pinnacle of power only after Henry's death in 1547, when he was named one of the regents who would govern England in the name of the new child king, EDWARD VI. He was the chief voice in dictating changes that were instituted throughout the British church.

Cranmer produced two editions of the Book of Common Prayer (1549, 1552) containing the order of worship that would replace the Roman Catholic Mass. The prayer book, though subsequently revised, remains an essential item defining the Anglican tradition. He authored the new doctrinal statement, the Forty-two Articles, which under Elizabeth was edited to become the Thirty-nine ARTICLES OF RELIGION still found in Anglican prayer books.

Following the coronation of Mary as queen of England, Cranmer was arrested, partially for his acquiescence in the unsuccessful attempt to place Lady Jane Grey on the throne. He was condemned for treason (1553) and then of heresy (1554). In an attempt to avoid execution, he signed several statements recanting his Protestant views, but these did not save him from the stake. He made a last public recantation of his statements before being burned on March 21, 1556.

See also ANGLICANISM; UNITED KINGDOM.

Further reading: P. Ayris and D. Selwyn, eds. *Thomas Cranmer, Churchman and Scholar.* (Woodbridge, Suffolk, U.K.: The Boydell Press, 1999); Peter Brooks, *Thomas Cranmer's Doctrine of the Eucharist,* 2nd ed. (Houndmills, Basingstoke, Hampshire, U.K.: Palgrave Press, 1992); Thomas Cranmer, *Miscellaneous Writings and Letters of Thomas Cranmer, Archbishop of Canterbury, Martyr, 1556,* ed. by John Edmund Cox. (Cambridge: Cambridge University Press, 1846); ———, *Works,* 2 vols., ed. by John Edmund Cox (Cambridge: Cambridge University Press, 1844); Diarmaid MacCulloch, *Thomas Cranmer* (New Haven, Conn.: Yale University Press, 1996).

creationism

Creationism is the belief that the universe and the creatures within it were were created by God. It has been especially reasserted, among some Protestant groups, in opposition to the theory of evolution.

The publication of Charles DARWIN's books *On the Origin of Species* (1859) and *The Descent of Man* (1871) challenged the traditional belief that God created the Earth, each of the different animal species, and by a special additional act, humanity. Most Christians held to the traditional view through the early 20th century; intellectuals such as Henry DRUMMOND and Louis Agassiz (1807–73) responded to Darwin by restating their beliefs in greater detail and in a great variety of modern scientific and philosophical terms. The most liberal thinkers in the church were theistic evolutionists, who accepted a form of evolution as descriptive of how God created and sustained the world and its life-forms.

In their disputes with the modernists in the years after World War I, American Fundamentalists labeled evolution an attack on Christianity as a whole, as subverting belief in the veracity of the Bible. A campaign to ban the teaching of evolution in the public schools was successful in three states—Tennessee, Mississippi, and Arkansas. The Tennessee law became the focus of the 1925 "Monkey Trial" in Dayton, Tennessee. A local high school teacher agreed to stand trial for teaching evolution to test the law. Presbyterian layman William Jennings Bryan (1860–1925) served as prosecutor, and skeptical lawyer Clarence Darrow (1857–1938) as defense lawyer. He was convicted (though the conviction was later overturned on a technicality), but afterward the evolution debate gradually faded from public attention. In the 1960s, as a footnote to the debate, the U.S. Supreme Court ruled that the Arkansas law was unconstitutional.

Through the middle of the 20th century, conservative Christians generally held one of two understandings of creation. The "gap theory" dates back to 1814, when Scottish Presbyterian minister Thomas Chalmers (1780–1847) developed the idea that the Bible referred to two cre-

ations, the one described in the first chapter of Genesis that occurred in the distant past, and a second one centered on the Garden of Eden in relatively recent times. The gap between the two creations appears between verses 25 and 26 in Genesis 1. The gap theory was advocated by Cyrus I. SCOFIELD in the *Scofield Reference Bible;* Chinese Christian leader Watchman NEE; Fundamentalist journalist Arno Gaebelein (1861–1945); conservative Presbyterian Harry Rimmer (1890–1952), founder and head of the Science Research Bureau; and radio evangelists Martin R. DeHaan (1891–1965) and J. Vernon McGee (1904–88). It remains a popular theory for Fundamentalists and Evangelicals.

The "day-age theory" interpreted the "days" spoken of in Genesis 1 as the long geological ages that intervened after God, in a single act, created the earth and the natural laws that prepared it for the creation of humanity. This approach had much in common with the gap theory, both suggesting multiple creations. Major advocates included Fundamentalist Baptist preacher William Bell Riley (1861–1947) and William Jennings Bryan.

In the early 20th century, George McCready Price (1870–1963), a member of the SEVENTH-DAY ADVENTIST CHURCH with no particular training in science, began to advocate a third approach, the young-Earth theory. He suggested that a literal reading of Genesis was correct, that God had created the world in one week some 6,000 years ago and that the Flood described in Genesis 7 and 8 was an actual global deluge that occurred around 2000 B.C.E., during which all of the many fossil-bearing rocks were deposited.

Price won little support until Old Testament scholar John C. Whitcomb Jr. and engineer Henry M. Morris published *The Genesis Flood* in 1961. Two years later, they pulled together a small group of supporters, most of whom had scientific credentials, to found the Creation Research Society (CRS). They began to call their approach "creation science." Morris and his supporters have produced a number of books that have made their approach a serious rival to old-Earth creationism in Fundamentalist and Evangelical circles. In the 1980s, they began a renewed campaign directed at state legislators to have creation science taught concurrently with scientific evolution. They succeeded in Louisiana and Arkansas, but in 1987 the Supreme Court overturned the Arkansas law as unconstitutional.

While a generation of creation science has brought most Fundamentalists into the young-Earth camp, many Evangelicals still support the old-Earth approach, which retains the favor of the American Scientific Affiliation, a professional association for scientists who identify themselves as Evangelicals. Both views are now advocated by a number of Christian organizations, but a newer approach has captured the imagination of many. Termed "intelligent design theory," it was initially advocated by University of California law professor Philip Johnson in two books, *Darwin on Trial* (1991) and *Reason in the Balance: The Case against Naturalism in Science, Law and Education* (1995). Johnson has challenged the basic naturalism of the sciences, which starts from the assumption that scientific explanations should not appeal to God or the supernatural. In contrast, intelligent design theorists argue that God is a necessary element in understanding the patterns found in the natural world.

See also FUNDAMENTALISM.

Further reading: Robert B. Fischer, *God Did It, But How?*, 2nd ed. (Ipswich, Mass.: American Scientific Affiliation, 1997); Willard B. Gatewood Jr., *Controversy in the Twenties: Fundamentalism, Modernism and Evolution* (Nashville, Tenn.: Vanderbilt University Press, 1969); Philip Johnson, *Darwin on Trial* (Chicago: Regnery, 1991); J. P. Moreland and John Mark Reynolds, eds., *Three Views on Creation and Evolution* (Grand Rapids, Mich.: Zondervan, 1999); Henry M. Morris, *The Genesis Flood* (Grand Rapids, Mich.: Baker Book House, 1963); Ronad Numbers, *Darwinism Comes to America* (Cambridge, Mass.: Harvard University Press, 1998.); George McCready Price, *Genesis Vindicated* (Washington, D.C.: Review & Herald, 1941); Harry Rimmer, *Modern Science and the Genesis Record* (Grand Rapids, Mich.: William B. Eerdmans, 1945).

creeds/confessions of faith

Creeds (derived from the Latin *credere,* to believe) are summary statements of Christian beliefs, whether overall affirmations of Christianity or clarifications on a particular issue or set of issues. Several creeds became authoritative in the early centuries of the church as the "orthodox" stance was hammered out against alternative understandings of the nature of God and the salvation offered by Christ. These decisions were reached at the seven ecumenical councils that met between 325 and 787 C.E. The most widely used is the Nicene Creed promulgated by the first council that met at Nicaea in 325 and revised at Constantinople in 381. It superseded the earlier widely used Apostles' Creed, and was itself supplemented by the Chalcedonian Creed of 451, with its greater definition of the divine and human nature of Christ.

The Western church also recognized the so-called Athanasian Creed. Named after Athanasius (293–373 C.E.), the statement is actually of later origin and is not recognized by the Eastern Orthodox churches. It deals primarily with the doctrines of the Trinity, the Incarnation, and the nature of Christ.

The first generations of Protestantism affirmed their acceptance of the Apostles', Nicene, and Athanasian Creeds as a basis for discussions with Roman Catholics. Their texts were included in the Lutheran Book of Concord, and both the Apostles' and the Nicene Creeds were widely used in Protestant worship services.

Protestants also produced a new set of creedal statements, usually termed *confessions* in Lutheran and Reformed churches, by which they attempted to define their position in contrast to Roman Catholicism and later to one another. These confessions affirmed the traditional orthodox consensus, and added Protestant distinctions on the authority of the Bible, salvation by grace through faith, and the nature of the church.

Lutherans issued the Augsburg Confession in 1530, followed by the Smalcald Articles in 1537 and additional confessional statements through the century. All of these documents, together with the longer and shorter catechisms written by Martin LUTHER, were collected in 1580 as the Book of Concord; they are still the defining theological documents of Lutheranism.

Reformed Church confessions begin with the Sixty-seven Articles issued by Ulrich ZWINGLI in 1523, but became authoritative in the post-John CALVIN era with the issuance of the Gallican Confession in 1559. Subsequently, different confessions would emerge in different segments of the Reformed Church, including the BELGIC CONFESSION (Holland and Belgium, 1561), the Second HELVETIC CONFESSION (Switzerland, 1566), the Second Scottish Confession (Scotland, 1580), the Canons of Dort (Holland, 1619), and finally the Puritan WESTMINSTER CONFESSION (England, 1643).

Among radical reformers, the SCHLEITHEIM ARTICLES of 1527 and the Mennonite Dordrecht Confession (1632) stand out. Anglicans sought to define their wavering positions via a series of documents including the Thirteen Articles (1537), the Six Articles (1539), the Forty-two Articles (1553), and finally the Thirty-nine ARTICLES OF RELIGION (1563).

Following the promulgation of the Westminster Confession, Congregationalists (who dissented from the Presbyterian form of church government) issued the SAVOY DECLARATION (1658), and the BAPTISTS, who dissented on a variety of issues from the SACRAMENTS to the church's ties to the state, issued the First and Second LONDON CONFESSIONS OF FAITH (1646 and 1689).

As the Protestant movement splintered over the centuries, each new group has promulgated a creedal or confessional statement to affirm its ties to historical affirmations, to clarify its unique doctrinal position for its members, and to define it as a separate body from other Protestant denominations. A few of these creedal statements, such as the Methodist Articles of Religion developed by John WESLEY for the Methodists in the United States, have become widely used, often with variations.

As Free Churches developed, the very idea of a creed was called into question. A number of groups saw them as divisive, and suggested that the Bible was a sufficient rule for faith and practice. The Baptists adopted a middle ground, affirming the Bible as their only authoritative creedal document, but issuing confessions and statements of doctrine over the years as useful summaries of their consensus of belief.

In the 20th century, many Protestant churches found that their inherited statements no longer represented the consensus of belief among members and, more important, ministers. Different churches debated the authority that should be ascribed to creedal documents and whether or not they had to be affirmed by and adhered to by ministers and others in teaching positions (such as seminary professors). Many groups have refrained from changing the older statements, but have added new statements that place the old ones in a historical context that effectively limits their authority. Following the merger that produced the UNITED METHODIST CHURCH in 1968, the church's general conference placed the doctrinal statement of the merging groups into its Discipline, and adopted a statement affirming theological pluralism. In 1967, the United Presbyterian Church adopted a new confession and then published a Book of Confessions that included a selection of ancient creeds and Reformation-era confessions. Future ministers were instructed to "receive and adopt the essential tenets of the Reformed faith as expressed in the confessions of our Church as authentic and reliable expositions of what Scripture leads us to believe and do." This stance was continued in the new PRESBYTERIAN CHURCH (USA), enhanced by an additional Brief Statement of Faith representing the consensus of the merging churches. A new statement was also promulgated in 1960 by the recently formed UNITED CHURCH OF CHRIST.

In the 1930s, the Evangelical Church in Germany split into two factions over their response to Nazism. One faction, the Confessing Church, issued the BARMEN DECLARATION, expressing their dissent against the majority position of cooperation with the Nazis and setting forth a rationale for their action at the moment, given their new situation. The Barmen Declaration became a model for later statements dealing not so much with doctrinal teachings but with how a body of Christians must act in a crisis. The most notable post-Barmen statements are the KAIROS DOCUMENT and the BELHAR CONFESSION, both issued during the last days of apartheid in South Africa.

Today, almost every Protestant and Free Church denomination and para-church organization has adopted a creedal statement at least minimally defining its doctrinal position. Given the rise of a pluralistic setting within the Protestant community and the existence of many Christian groups that deny what are seen as essential doctrines, the Evangelical community consistently asks groups who wish to join in fellowship to be upfront about their orthodoxy. Given that so many liberal Protestant groups continue to publish traditional statements of belief while allowing a wide range of interpretation or dissent, Evangelicals often look for additional affirmations such as beliefs about the authority or INSPIRATION OF THE BIBLE.

See also BRIEF STATEMENT OF FAITH (PRESBYTERIAN); CAMBRIDGE PLATFORM; FORMULA OF CONCORD; HALFWAY COVENANT; LAUSANNE STATEMENT.

Further reading: Bruce A. Demarest, "The Contemporary Relevance of Christendom's Creeds," *Themelios* 7, 2 (1982): 9–16; Sinclair B. Ferguson and Joel R. Beeke, *Reformed Confessions Harmonized* (Ada, Mich.: Baker Book House, 1999); J. Gordon Melton, ed., *The Encyclopedia of American Religions: Religious Creeds,* 2 vols. (Detroit: Gale Research, 1988, 1994); Jaroslav Pelikan and Valerie Hotchkiss, eds., *Historical and Theological Guide to Creeds and Confessions of Faith in the Christian Tradition* (New Haven, Conn.: Yale University Press, 2003); Jack Bartlett Rogers, *Presbyterian Creeds: A Guide to the Book of Confessions* (Louisville, Ky.: Westminster / John Knox, 1992).

Cromwell, Oliver (1599–1658) *ruler of England during the Puritan Revolution*

Oliver Cromwell, who as Lord Protector of the Commonwealth ruled England through the 1640s until his death, was born in Huntingdon in 1599. He was educated in his hometown by a strict adherent of PURITANISM and then studied at Sidney Sussex College at CAMBRIDGE UNIVERSITY. In 1628, he was elected to Parliament, where he first made an impression by his advocacy of freedom for the Presbyterians and Independents.

He rose to prominence during the Short Parliament (April 1640) and Long Parliament (August 1640 through April 1660). King Charles I, who favored a return to Roman Catholicism, had tried to force a new prayer book on Scotland. British forces were badly beaten in the resulting conflict, and the settlement created a financial crisis. Charles was forced to summon Parliament to raise funds, but delegates at the Long Parliament seized power from the king.

In 1642, Parliament removed the BISHOPS who headed the CHURCH OF ENGLAND and put the army and navy directly under its own authority. Charles left London to rally support, and England entered a period of civil war. As the first battles were being fought, Parliament called for an assembly of "learned, godly, and judicious divines" to meet at Westminster for the purpose of reforming the church. A total of 30 laymen, a few Scottish observers, and 125 ministers (mainly Presbyterian) took the opportunity to create a set of documents, including the WESTMINSTER CONFESSION OF FAITH, the Westminster Catechism (subsequently published in both a longer and shorter version), and a Directory of Worship designed to order church life in Scotland, Ireland, and England. These documents came to define Presbyterianism internationally.

Following an initial defeat of forces loyal to Parliament (termed *Roundheads*), Cromwell set about the task of building a professional cavalry. He subsequently proved himself a capable military leader. His leadership proved decisive in the Roundhead victory at Marston Moor in 1644, and he led the final Roundhead victory at Naseby the next year. Shortly thereafter, Charles surrendered and was placed in custody. Cromwell ordered his execution in 1649.

Power was now in the hands of Cromwell's army. In November 1648, Cromwell expelled all opponents from Parliament. The remaining Rump Parliament formally abolished the monarchy and those government departments most loyal to the king. The Parliament and an executive Council of State constituted the new government. Favoring the Puritan factions, Cromwell then moved to crush other opposition groups that remained including the Levellers (who sought extensive economic reform). In 1649, he moved against the Irish, suppressing a revolt in a bloody campaign, and then turned to quell the opposition in Scotland.

On April 21, 1653, Cromwell disbanded the Rump Parliament, which had alienated the army. He later dissolved an unsuccessful new Parliament of Puritan leaders, assumed the title of Lord Protector of the Commonwealth, and ruled as a virtual dictator.

Cromwell died on September 3, 1658. He left his son Richard Cromwell in control, but Richard proved unable to deal with the antagonistic forces in the country, and in 1660, the monarchy was restored under Charles II. The episcopally led Church of England was also restored, and the Puritans were suppressed until the Act of Toleration of 1689 allowed them some freedom of action.

See also REFORMED/PRESBYTERIAN TRADITION; UNITED KINGDOM.

Further reading: Barry Coward, *Cromwell.* (London: Longman, 1991); Oliver Cromwell, *Writings and Speeches of Oliver Cromwell,* ed. by Wilbur Abbott (Cambridge, Mass.: Harvard University Press, 1937); Christopher Hill, *God's Englishman: Oliver Cromwell and the English Revolution* (New York: Harper & Row, 1970); Derek Hirst, *Authority and Conflict: England,*

1603–1658 (Cambridge, Mass.: Harvard University Press, 1986); John Morrill, *Oliver Cromwell and the English Revolution* (London: Longman, 1990).

Cromwell, Thomas (c. 1485–1540)
Lord Chancellor who helped establish Protestantism in England

As a top government official, Thomas Cromwell helped advance the Protestant cause in England during the reign of HENRY VIII. Cromwell was born in London around 1485 and raised in a humble environment as the son of a blacksmith. Of limited education, he moved to France, served in the French army, and made a small fortune as a moneylender.

Back in England around 1513, he worked as a lawyer and was eventually taken as adviser by Cardinal Wolsey. After Wolsey's untimely death in 1530, Cromwell ran for Parliament, where he attracted the attention of the king. Following the fall of Thomas More, Henry tapped Cromwell as the new Lord Chancellor.

As the close adviser/confidant of Henry, he was able, in concert with Thomas CRANMER, the archbishop of Canterbury, to push for a variety of reforms. He supported Henry in his move to break with the pope and have the king declared the head of the CHURCH OF ENGLAND. He was also responsible for the report to Parliament that led to the 1536 law that allowed Henry to sell 376 monasteries to replenish state coffers. Two years later, Cromwell helped close down a number of shrines, including one honoring St. Thomas à Becket, which occasioned Henry's formal excommunication by the pope in 1538.

Cromwell's great mistake was supporting Henry's marriage to Anne of Cleves in 1540, as part of a push to align England with the German reformers. In his anger, Henry turned on Cromwell, charged him with treason, and had him beheaded on July 28, 1540.

Further reading: B. W. Beckingsale, *Thomas Cromwell, Tudor Minister* (Totowa, N.J.: Rowman & Littlefield, 1978); A. G. Dickens, *Thomas Cromwell* and the English Reformation (London, English Universities Press 1959); G. R. Elton, *Policy and Police: the Enforcement of the Reformation in the Age of Thomas Cromwell* (New York: Cambridge University Press, 1972); Christopher Haigh, *English Reformations: Religion, Politics, and Society under the Tudors* (New York: Oxford University Press, 1993); John N. King, *English Reformation Literature, the Tudor Origins of the Protestant Tradition* (Princeton, N.J.: Princeton University Press, 1986).

Crosby, Fanny (1820–1915) *American hymn-writer*

Fanny Crosby was the pen name of Frances Jane Van Alystyne, one of the most famous and prolific of American hymn-writers. She was representative of the post–Civil War writers who were under contract to produce a steady supply of hymns week by week. She eventually authored 8,000 hymns, many published under pseudonyms. Though most are now forgotten, a few remain popular in Evangelical circles, such as "Blessed Assurance," "Pass Me Not, O Gentle Saviour," "I Am Thine, Oh Lord," "To God Be the Glory," "Near the Cross," and "Saviour More than Life to Me."

Crosby was born in Putnam County, New York, on March 24, 1820. She became blind during childhood and later attended the New York City Institution for the Blind (1835–47), where she taught after completing her studies. In 1851, she joined the Methodist Episcopal Church, and in 1858, she married Alexander Van Alstyne (d. 1902), a music teacher.

Crosby published her first collection of poetry in 1844, "A Blind Girl and Other Poems," and further volumes followed. She wrote her first hymns in the 1850s. Set to music by George F. Root, some became quite popular at the time. Most of her life she wrote under contract to Bigelow & Main, and she was expected to produce new songs on a regular basis. She also became closely associated with songleader Ira Stankey and his boss, evangelist Dwight L. MOODY.

Crosby died on February 12, 1915.

See also HYMNS/MUSIC.

Further reading: Fanny J. Crosby, *Fanny J. Crosby: Memories of Eighty Years. Her Own Story of Her Life and Hymns* (London: Hodder & Stoughton, 1908); Sandy Dengler, *Fanny Crosby: Writer of 8,000 Songs* (Chicago: Moody Press, 1985); S. Trevena Jackson, *Fanny Crosby's Story of Ninety-Four Years* (New York: Fleming H. Revell, 1915); John Loveland, *Blessed Assurance: The Life and Hymns of Fanny J. Crosby* (Nashville, Tenn.: Broadman & Holman, 1978).

Crowther, Samuel Ajayi (c. 1807–1891) *first African Anglican bishop*

Bishop Samuel Ajayi Crowther was born into a Yoruba family around 1807 in present-day Nigeria. In 1820, his hometown was raided by Muslim people who lived to the north of the Yoruba. He was captured and sold into slavery and eventually fell into the hands of Portuguese merchantmen. The ship that was to take him to the Americas was intercepted by the British in 1822, and he was taken to SIERRA LEONE and freed. Like most other freedmen, Crowther knew of no way to return home; instead he adapted to his new life.

Three years later, Crowther became a Christian. At his baptismal ceremony (conducted by a member of the CHURCH MISSIONARY SOCIETY [CMS]) he took the name of a prominent British clergyman, Samuel Crowther. He later attended Fourah Bay College, the first Western institution of higher learning in sub-Saharan Africa. While learning English, he nurtured knowledge of his own tongue and learned Temne, a local language.

Crowther's impressive abilities led to an 1841 invitation to England to study for the Anglican priesthood. He was ordained there in 1843, there being no bishop who could ordain priests in Africa. Upon his return to Africa, he was recruited for a new mission among the Yoruba people at Abeokuta, an agricultural colony created to keep the area out of the slave economy. Crowther also had an emotional reunion with his family, who became Christians. In 1851, he went to England on behalf of the mission and impressed all he met.

Back in Africa, he worked on the Yoruban translation of the Bible.

In 1854, Crowther joined an expedition up the Niger River to establish a string of mission stations, during which he added languages to his repertoire. He emerged as a champion of using Africans as primary missionaries, then a relatively new idea. He found an ally in Henry Venn (1796–1873), who headed the CMS in London and had been among those impressed with Crowther in 1851. Although the majority of the British missionaries did not believe Africans capable of self-governance, Venn was able to secure the consecration of Crowther as a BISHOP in 1864. His designated diocese was "the countries of Western Africa beyond the limits of the Queen's dominions."

His territory was in essence a mission, designed to be self-supporting with little financial support from the CMS. The "Niger mission" grew spectacularly, but after Venn's death there was no champion in England to advocate the consecration of a bishop successor. In his last years, Crowther had to watch as white missionaries took over his diocese. He was succeeded by a white bishop, though Crowther's son, Archdeacon Dandeson Crowther (1844–1938), was able to remain head of one relatively autonomous structure within the diocese, the Niger Delta Pastorate Church. It would be some time before another African bishop was named and before the example of his work would be followed elsewhere.

See also AFRICA, SUB-SAHARAN; ANGLICANISM; NIGERIA.

Further reading: J. F. A. Ajayi, *Christian Missions in Nigeria: 1841–1891* (London: Longmans, 1965); Samuel A. Crowther, *Journal of an Expedition up the Niger and Tshadda Rivers* (1855; rpt., London: Frank Cass, 1970); ———— and John Christopher Taylor, *The Gospel on the Banks of the Niger: Journals and Notices of the Native Missionaries Accompanying the Niger Expedition of 1857–1859* (London: Dawsons, 1968); Jesse Page, *The African Bishop* (London: Hodder & Stoughton, 1908); J. B. Webster, *The African*

Churches among the Yoruba (Oxford: Clarendon Press, 1964).

Cuba

From a Protestant perspective, Cuba's history is divided by the Spanish-American War (1898). Prior to this time, the country was dominated overwhelmingly by Roman Catholicism, which is still the largest denomination in the country. A small Protestant presence began as early as 1741, when the CHURCH OF ENGLAND began to hold services for expatriates; then, after some of the Cubans who migrated to the United States found their way to the Episcopal Church, that church placed a pastor in Havana in 1871.

In 1873, the Methodist Episcopal Church, South, began work among Cuban expatriates in Florida. By 1883, two Cuban Methodist preachers had been ordained—Enrique B. Someillan and Aurelio Silvera—and they returned to Cuba to begin the spread of METHODISM. About this same time, a Baptist minister recruited by BAPTISTS working in Florida also returned to Cuba.

The American authorities who took power after the Spanish-American War imposed religious freedom on the island. A spectrum of churches arrived in the next few years to reproduce the denominational spectrum of the United States. In 1941, the Cuban Council of Protestant Churches (now the Ecumenical Council of Cuba) was founded. It is now affiliated with the WORLD COUNCIL OF CHURCHES. Through the middle of the century, several HOLINESS churches and more than 25 different Pentecostal churches arrived.

Protestant churches initially welcomed Castro, whose 1958 revolution replaced a harsh dictator, but he became increasingly repressive toward religious groups. In the 1960s, more than half a million Cubans, many of them Protestants, left the country and relocated to the United States, which had the effect of further weakening the churches. The Castro government was especially harsh on JEHOVAH'S WITNESSES, the SEVENTH-DAY ADVENTIST CHURCH, and Bando Evangelisto Gedéon, which were all declared to be bearers of a reactionary anti-Marxist ideology; they subsequently ceased to have any visibility in Cuba. During the early years of the regime, Castro banned public religious celebration and confiscated a significant amount of church property.

At the beginning of the 21st century, Protestantism had the allegiance of only 3 percent of the population. Most of the churches that were present in 1958 have survived, but in a greatly weakened state. The Evangelical Theological Seminary at Matanzas serves a spectrum of the Protestant churches and shortly after the turn of the century reported 125 resident students and slightly more than that in extension programs.

A loosening of repression in the 1990s allowed significant growth in various Protestant faiths, especially PENTECOSTALISM. The independent Evangelical Pentecostal Church of Cuba has led the way, followed closely by the ASSEMBLIES OF GOD, currently the two largest non-Catholic churches in the country.

See also CARIBBEAN.

Further reading: S. J. Bazdresch and E. S. Sweeney, "The Church in Communist Cuba: Reflections on the Contemporary Scene," *Thought* 63, 250 (September 1988); Leslie Dewart, *Christianity and Revolution: The Lessons of Cuba.* (New York: Herder & Herder, 1963); M. A. Ramos, *Protestantism and Revolution in Cuba* (Research Institute for Cuban Studies, University of Miami, 1989); Jason M. Yaremko, *U.S. Protestant Missions in Cuba: From Independence to Castro* (Gainesville: University Press of Florida, 2000).

D

Danish-Halle Mission

The modern Protestant missionary movement began with a joint project of the Lutheran king of Denmark and the Pietists of the University of Halle in Germany.

In 1705, King Frederick IV of Denmark asked the court physician to recruit some men to go to INDIA as missionaries, working from Tranquebar, the Danish colony on India's east coast. When no Danes volunteered for what was then a novel idea, the king sought support from the Pietists at Halle. PIETISM was a movement in the Lutheran Church that called for spiritual transformation in the lives of Christians via prayer and Bible study. Its enthusiasm provided the energy for the missionary endeavor.

The university recommended former students Bartholomew Ziegenbalg (1682–1719) and Heinrich Plütschau (1677–1747). Lutheran authorities balked at ordaining the men, and church leaders across Europe protested when they set sail in 1705. The Lutheran chaplains serving the Danish residents viewed the missionaries as competitors, and the governor of Tranquebar resented their presence.

Plütschau remained in India for five years and Ziegenbalg for 15. They learned Tamil and completed a translation of the New Testament. In 1715, Ziegenbalg toured Europe to build support for the mission work. He eventually won the support of two Anglican agencies, the SOCIETY FOR PROMOTING CHRISTIAN KNOWLEDGE and the SOCIETY FOR THE PROPAGATION OF THE GOSPEL IN FOREIGN PARTS, both originally established to support Anglican ministers in the American colonies.

Ziegenbalg was succeeded by Benjamin Schultze (1689–1760) who carried the work into Telugu- and Hindi-speaking communities. The work among the Tamil was carried on by Johann Philip Fabricius (1711–91), who spent 50 years in southern India, completed the Bible translation, and translated a number of hymns and Lutheran liturgical materials. Arriving in 1750, Christian Friedrich SCHWARTZ spent 48 years laying the foundation for the present Lutheran Church of India.

The mission languished in the 19th century, and the CHURCH MISSIONARY SOCIETY, a British-based Anglican agency, assumed the support. Eventually, church members were absorbed into the various Lutheran churches that were created to serve the different Indian language groups.

See also DENMARK.

Further reading: E. Theodore Bachmann and Mercia Brenne Bachmann, *Lutheran Churches in the World: A*

Handbook (Minneapolis, Minn.: Augsburg Press, 1989); J. Herbert Kane, *A Global View of Christian Missions* (Grand Rapids, Mich.: Baker Book House, 1971); Arno Lehmann, *It Began at Tranquebar: The Story of the Tranquebar Mission and the Beginnings of Protestant Christianity in India* (Madras, India: Christian Literature Society on Behalf of the Federation of Evangelical Lutheran Churches in India, 1956); William H. Price, *The Life and Labors of the Rev. Christian Frederick Schwartz, the Great Lutheran Missionary to India* (Columbus, Ohio: Lutheran Book Concern, 1895); C. H. Swavely, ed., *The Lutheran Enterprise in India 1706–1952* (Madras, India: Federation of Evangelical Lutheran Churches in India, 1952); H. M. Zorn, *Bartholomaeus Ziegenbalg* (St. Louis, Mo.: Concordia Publishing House, 1933).

Darby, John Nelson   (1800–1882) *founder of the Plymouth Brethren*

Darby was born in London, England, on November 18, 1800. In 1815, his family moved to their ancestral home in Ireland. Darby studied law at Trinity College in Dublin and was admitted to the bar in 1822, but he soon renounced his legal career in favor of a spiritual vocation and was admitted to deacon's orders in the Church of Ireland (Anglican). He was assigned curate at Calary, County Wicklow. However, he began to examine the biblical church and contrast it to the established church in which he served.

In 1827, he withdrew from the Church of Ireland, and joined with a small religious group in Dublin that shared a common rejection of denominationalism, formal church membership, and nonscriptural church names. They would meet on the Sabbath (Sunday) to show their unity by breaking bread together. A similar group emerged at Plymouth, England, which gave the movement its common name.

For the next 15 years, Darby wrote voluminously to promote the Brethren cause and traveled extensively in England and in FRANCE and SWITZERLAND, where strong Brethren movements emerged. Shortly after his return to England in the mid 1840s, a controversy broke out at Plymouth that would split the movement into the Exclusive Brethren (supported by Darby), who would receive into communion only full members of a separated assembly, and the Open (now called CHRISTIAN BRETHREN), who would break bread with all they perceived to be a true Christians. Darby and the Exclusive Brethren received no one who was not a member of a fully separated assembly.

In the years after the controversy, Darby continued his travels. In the last decades of his life, he made three trips to Germany, six to CANADA and the United States, and various tours to ITALY, NEW ZEALAND, and the West Indies.

Darby originated the system of biblical theology called DISPENSATIONALISM. It approaches the Bible as the story of God's interaction with humanity, over a series of historical periods. In each era or dispensation, God reveals himself ever more clearly and alters his expectation of how humans should respond. The process culminates in the incarnation of Jesus and the present age of grace. This system, which has continued to evolve since Darby's death, spread among Evangelical Protestants during the last decades of the 19th century. It was accepted by many Fundamentalists in the 1920s and continues to influence the current Evangelical movement. The Brethren, now in more than 100 countries, have also helped spread dispensationalism.

Darby died on April 29, 1882, at Bournemouth. Over the next decades, the Exclusive Brethren would be shaken by a series of controversies and splits, but Darby's approach to theology and the Bible, as explicated in the notes to the popular *Scofield Reference Bible,* have spread among BAPTISTS and Presbyterians and helped shape conservative Protestantism through the 20th century.

See also PREMILLENNIALISM.

Further reading: F. Roy Coad, *A History of the Brethren Movement Its Origins Its Worldwide Development and Its Significance for the Present Day* (Sydney: Paternoster Press, 1968); John Nelson Darby, *Collected Writings,*

34 vols. (Oak Park, Ill.: Bible Truth, 1971); ———. *Letters of J. N. Darby,* 3 vols. (Sunbury, Pa.: Believers Bookshelf, 1971); W. G. Turner, *John Nelson Darby* (London: C. A. Hammond, 1944); Max S. Werenchuk, *John Nelson Darby: A Biography* (Neptune, N.J.: Loizeaux Brothers, 1992).

Darwin, Charles (1809–1882) *naturalist who developed the theory of evolution*

Charles Robert Darwin, whose theories concerning biological evolution sparked a revolution in Protestant thought, was born on February 12, 1809, at Shrewsbury, Shropshire, England, and was raised in the family's CHURCH OF ENGLAND background. In 1827, his father arranged for him to attend Christ's College, CAMBRIDGE UNIVERSITY, to prepare for the clergy. There he met Rev. John Stevens Henslow (1796–1821), who taught him botany. In 1831, he passed his final exams, and prepared for a career as a pastor.

Before Darwin settled down, however, Rev. Henslow arranged for him to travel as a naturalist aboard the H.M.S. *Beagle* on a two-year survey voyage around the coast of SOUTH AMERICA, where he collected specimens of living plants and animals and fossil forms. Back in England, his thoughts about his observations led to doubts about the commonly held idea that species were all individual miraculous creations by the deity; he also began to question popular arguments for the existence of God. He published his findings and pursued speculations through correspondence with animal breeders. Realizing the heretical nature of his speculations (in both the theological and scientific communities and in the mind of his pious wife, Emma Wedgwood), he delayed publishing for a number of years.

By 1842, he had worked out the basics of evolution. By this time, Darwin had become a deist, believing that God had established the laws of nature at the time of creation, and then stepped back and allowed the world to evolve.

Darwin spent the next 15 years refining his ideas with the help of a selection of trusted colleagues. Finally in 1858, at a meeting of the Linnean Society in London, he went public with his ideas on the evolution of species, which he recently learned had been independently arrived at by his colleague Alfred Russel Wallace (1823–1913). His groundbreaking 1859 book, *On the Origin of Species by Means of Natural Selection,* explained how new species had evolved over time.

The book created a heated controversy. Some churchmen, such as Anglican Bishop Samuel Wilberforce (1805–73), charged that his approach led natural science away from its primary role as an investigator of God's creation. He won wide support from scientists and even some clergy. Naturalist Thomas Henry Huxley (1825–95) began years of very effective work to defend and advance Darwinism (a term he coined). Huxley's 1863 book, *Evidence on Man's Place in Nature,* broached the notion that humans were related to apes.

In 1871, Darwin published *The Descent of Man.* Though the majority of scientists and many laymen now supported the idea of evolution, in the eyes of many church leaders, especially in the United States, the new book drew a line across which they could not move.

Darwin died on April 19, 1882. He was buried at Westminster Abbey.

For decades after, in North American Protestant circles, evolution (even married to theism) was seen as a sign of modernism and a departure from the literal interpretation of the Bible. Heated arguments over evolution raged throughout the first decades of the 20th century, culminating in the so-called Monkey Trial of 1925 in Dayton, Tennessee, where CREATIONISM clashed with popular versions of evolutionary thought. In the 1920s, American Protestantism split into two communities: the Fundamentalists (who opposed evolution) and the Modernists (who supported it). The latter gained control of most of the larger DENOMINATIONS and the leading seminaries. FUNDAMENTALISM evolved over the rest of the century and developed a spectrum of views on creation, including various attempts to build scientific support for a literal reading of the opening chapters of Genesis.

Further reading: Peter J. Bowler, *Charles Darwin: the Man and his Influence* (Cambridge: Cambridge University Press, 1990); Charles Darwin, *The Autobiography of Charles Darwin. 1809–1882. With Original Omissions Restored. Edited with Appendix and Notes by His Grand-daughter Nora Barlow* (New York: Harcourt, Brace, 1959); ———, *The Descent of Man* (London: John Murray, 1871); ———, *On the Origin of the Species by Means of Natural Selection* (London: John Murray, 1859); Francis Darwin, ed., *The Life and Letters of Charles Darwin,* 2 vols. (London: John Murray, 1887); James R. Moore, *The Post-Darwinian Controversies: A Study of the Protestant Struggle to come to Terms with Darwin in Great Britain and America, 1870–1900* (Cambridge: Cambridge University Press, 1979); Ronald L. Numbers, *The Creationists: The Evolution of Scientific Creationism* (New York: Alfred A. Knopf, 1992).

deaconess

Deaconesses are women who perform the functions of a DEACON in many Protestant churches. The modern Protestant deaconess movement began as a small ministry within the MORAVIAN CHURCH in 1745. That movement inspired a German Lutheran pastor, Theodor Fliedner (1800–64), to begin the Rhenish-Westphalian Deaconess Society to operate the hospital and deaconess training center he had opened in Kaiserswerth in 1836. Fliedner was initially assisted in this effort by his wife, Friedericke Munster, and a nurse, Gertrude Reichardt. At the center, women went through an ordination service in which they committed themselves to the care of the poor, the sick, and the young. Their commitments were not for life, and they could leave the order whenever they chose.

In 1838, the first deaconess was sent to serve away from Kaiserswerth. Fliedner authorized a foreign deaconess motherhouse in Pittsburgh, Pennsylvania, in 1849, followed by one in Jerusalem in 1851. Others soon appeared in Paris and Berlin. By the mid-1860s, there were 30 motherhouses and 1,600 deaconesses serving in locations around the world.

The move to the United States was facilitated by William A. Passavant (1821–94), who brought four of Fliedner's deaconesses to Pittsburgh to manage the first Protestant hospital in the United States. That work grew to include hospitals in Milwaukee, Chicago, and elsewhere, as well as several orphanages. Philadelphia businessman John Lankenau in 1884 brought seven deaconesses to run the German hospital there. His actions encouraged other deaconesses to initiate new ministries in several cities with large Lutheran populations. In the 20th century, three main centers of deaconess work emerged in the Lutheran community; they merged in 1988 to form the present Deaconess Community of the Evangelical Lutheran Church in America.

The Lutheran deaconesses inspired the creation of a similar movement in the Methodist Episcopal Church. In 1885, Lucy Rider Meyer (1849–1922) opened the Chicago Training School (now part of Garrett-Evangelical Theological Seminary in Evanston, Illinois) for women who wished to enter full-time Christian work, and in 1887 she proposed the creation of a deaconess order to employ the graduates. The proposal was approved by her church's general conference in 1888.

A deaconess movement was born within the Episcopal Church in the United States in 1852, when William A. Muhlenberg of New York City organized the Sisterhood of the Holy Communion to provide nursing care at St. Luke's Hospital. Three years later, Bishop W. R. Whittingham ordained deaconesses in Baltimore, Maryland, to serve destitute women and orphans. These efforts served as a catalyst for William Pennefather to organize the Anglican "Mildmay Deaconesses," an order of teachers and nurses, for work in London. The following year, the bishop of London moved unilaterally to revive the Order of Deaconesses in the CHURCH OF ENGLAND.

The movement emerged among Presbyterians in the 1890s in diverse locations from Toronto, Ontario, to New Zealand. The Ewart Missionary Training Home in Toronto opened in 1897. The first deaconess in NEW ZEALAND completed her training as the decade ended, and began work at a church in Dunedin. In 1903, Jeanetta Blackie became the first superintendent of a training center in that city, the first step toward a New Zealand Presbyterian deaconess order.

The deaconess movement spread worldwide in the 20th century. In 1947, the Diakonia World Federation was established to promote ecumenical relationships among the different female diaconal associations and communities.

See also FEMINISM, CHRISTIAN; WOMEN, ORDINATION OF.

Further reading: Myra Blyth and Wendy S. Blyth, *No Boundaries to Compassion: An Exploration of Women, Gender and Diakonia* (Geneva: World Council of Churches, 1998); Christian Golder, *History of the Deaconess Movement in the Christian Church* (Cincinnati, Ohio/New York: Jennings & Pye/Eaton & Main, 1903); Janet Grierson, *The Deaconess* (London: CIO, Church House, 1981); Lucy Rider Meyer, *Deaconesses. Biblical, Early Church, European, American, With the Story of the Chicago Training School, for City, Home and Foreign Missions, and the Chicago Deaconess Home* (Chicago: Message Publishing, 1889); Karyn-Maree Piercy, *"Presbyterian Pioneers": The Deaconess Movement, Dunedin, 1900–1920.* (Dunedin, New Zealand: University of Otago, B.A. honors thesis, 2000).

deacons

The office of deacon is common to most churches, tracing back to the early church at Jerusalem. Acts 6:1–6 describes their role as providing for the widows and managing the communal meals, freeing the ELDERS for their ministerial duties—prayer, teaching, preaching.

Deacons over the ages were usually seen as practical assistants to the priests in the SACRAMENTS, especially BAPTISM and the Eucharist. It evolved into an order of the ordained ministry, used primarily as a step toward becoming a priest. Within the Catholic Church, the office of permanent lay deacon was reestablished during Vatican II (1962–65). Catholic lay deacons may marry.

The office of deacon was accepted by Protestants. Among Anglicans (and later Methodists) the role remained close to the Roman tradition. Deacons are primarily ordained as a step toward a second ordination as priest (Anglican) or elder (Methodist). In each case, the deacon receives his/her orders from the BISHOP by the LAYING ON OF HANDS.

John CALVIN included the office of deacon when he reappraised church order. In the REFORMED/PRESBYTERIAN TRADITION, deacons serve alongside the elders. Their duties include (but are not limited to) helping members in need, distributing gifts of money, food, clothing, and so forth, and training members in stewardship. Deacons operate primarily at the local church level.

Within the Lutheran Church, deacons are primarily members of a congregation who assist the pastor(s) to lead worship. They may also extend their duties to assist in matters of instruction, finance, visitation, and support for members and others with any physical or emotional distress.

The Free Church tradition radically reassessed the office of deacon. In the ANABAPTIST tradition, the deacon operates primarily in the local church. Duties include receiving church alms for distribution to the needy; helping any estranged members to return to full fellowship; and assisting ministers in administering the ordinances. If no minister is present for a worship service, it may fall upon the deacon to preach.

BAPTISTS put particular emphasis on the office of deacon. At first, deacons' primary function was to oversee the benevolent activity (charity) in the local congregation. As the Baptist movement spread in the 18th century, they assumed additional duties as local church administrators. In the 19th century, when pastoral leadership was often uncertain and sporadic, deacons (organized into a board) won a considerable amount of power in running a local congregation. The churches of the RESTORATION MOVEMENT

(Churches of Christ, Disciples of Christ) follow a very similar pattern.

In late 19th-century Protestantism, the issue of women's ministry began to effect the concept of deacon. As far back as 1745, the MORAVIAN CHURCH had instituted a DEACONESS order. In 1836, Pastor Theodor Fliedner (1800–64) of Kaiserswerth, Germany, founded a hospital and deaconess training center, which became the Rhenish-Westphalian Deaconess Society. Fliedner was joined by a nurse, Gertrude Reichardt. From their efforts, the modern deaconess movement in the Lutheran and Methodist churches emerged.

In the 1990s, the UNITED METHODIST CHURCH moved to establish the ministry of nonordained deacons (full-time salaried lay ministers) as an important part of church life.

Further reading: James D. Bales, *The Deacon and His Work.* (Shreveport, La.: Lambert, 1967); Gunnel Borgegård, and Christine Hall, eds, *The Ministry of the Deacon,* 2 vols., Anglican-Lutheran Perspectives (Uppsala, Sweden: Nordic Ecumenical Council 1999, 2000); John N. Collins, *Diakonia. Reinterpreting the Ancient Sources* (New York: Oxford University Press 1990); Charles W. Deweese, *The Emerging Role of Deacons* (Nashville, Tenn.: Broadman Press, 1979); Ben L. Hartley and Paul E. Van Buren, *The Deacon. Ministry Through Words of Faith and Acts of Love* (Nashville, Tenn.: General Board of Higher Education and Ministry, United Methodists, 1999).

Deeper Life Bible Church

The Deeper Life Bible Church is one of the leading examples of the success of PENTECOSTALISM and the CHARISMATIC MOVEMENT in sub-Saharan Africa (*see* AFRICA, SUB-SAHARAN) in the last decades of the 20th century. It was founded in Lagos, Nigeria, in 1973 as the Deeper Christian Life Ministry by William Folorunso Kumuyi (b. 1941), a former Anglican who joined the Apostolic Faith Church after receiving the BAPTISM OF THE HOLY SPIRIT. In 1975, he was expelled from that church for preaching without being credentialed. He contin-

ued his independent ministry, which in 1982 became the Deeper Life Bible Church.

The church experienced spectacular growth, drawing in half a million members during its first decade. Much of this growth can be attributed to the support of the Yoido Full Gospel Church in Korea, and the adoption of its model of intimate home-based fellowships. Kumuyi's congregation is the largest in all of Africa. Deeper Life is a Holiness-Pentecostal church with an emphasis on holy living.

The church has spread throughout sub-Saharan Africa and then to the United Kingdom, from where branches were developed in western Europe, RUSSIA, INDIA, and North America.

See also NIGERIA.

Further reading: Allan H. Anderson, *African Reformation: African Initiated Christianity in the Twentieth Century* (Trenton, N.J.: Africa World Press, 2001); Matthews A. Ojo, "Deeper Life Bible Church of Nigeria," in Paul Gifford, ed., *New Dimensions in African Christianity* (Nairobi, Kenya: All Africa Conference of Churches, 1992).

Deng, Guangun   *See* TING, K. H.

Denmark

Reformation propaganda reached Denmark in the 1520s and won early support. An evangelical hymn book in the vernacular appeared in 1528, and in 1530 a group of ministers in Copenhagen promulgated the Confessio Hafniensis (Copenhagen Confession). Hans Tavsen (1494–1561) emerged as the leading Lutheran advocate. In the mid-1530s, King Christian II was won to the Lutheran cause. After suppressing the main opponents, he declared the state church to be Lutheran (1537). BISHOPS who remained loyal to Rome were dismissed from their posts and imprisoned. A national assembly held in Copenhagen in October 1536 officially removed them from office, and the next year they were replaced by seven Protestant superintendents. The king was named head of the church, and he took possession of all church lands.

The Protestantizing of the Danish church proceeded in stages. A church order introduced worship in the vernacular, built around preaching and congregational singing. A Danish-language Bible was published in 1550, and an authorized hymn book in 1569. Emerging as prominent second-generation leaders were Bishop Peder Palladius (d. 1560), Wittenberg-trained theologian Niels Hemmingsen, and hymn-writer Hans Christensen Sthen.

The role of the king was strengthened in 1665, when a new law gave him the right to make all decisions concerning the church. A 1683 law defined the church as "the King's religion," characterized by conformity to the Bible, the three creeds of the ancient church, the AUGSBURG CONFESSION OF FAITH, and Martin LUTHER's Small Catechism.

At the beginning of the 18th century, PIETISM, with its emphasis on personal religion and small informal gatherings, spread at the courts of Kings Frederick IV and Christian IV. The movement was strengthened by the arrival of Moravian Brethren, who found a level of tolerance and acceptance in Denmark.

Frederick IV turned to the Pietists at Halle University in Germany for recruits for his planned mission to INDIA. Two Halle graduates, Bartholomew Ziegenbalg (1682–1719) and Heinrich Plütschau (1677–1747), answered the call. The Danish church leadership resisted, but the king managed to get the men ordained. They arrived at the Danish colony at Tranquebar in India in July 1706. Their work, known as the DANISH-HALLE MISSION, is now seen as the beginning of the modern Protestant global missionary enterprise.

The Danish-Halle Mission inspired Count Nicolaus von ZINZENDORF, the Moravian leader, to develop the first diverse missionary endeavor by a Protestant church body. In Copenhagen in 1730, Zinzendorf met two Greenland Eskimos and an African slave from the West Indies named ANTHONY who were seeking missionaries to work among their peoples. Zinzendorf presented their request to his Moravian colleagues; they responded by initiating work in the Danish West Indies in 1732 and in Greenland in 1733. Within a decade they extended their endeavors to North and SOUTH AMERICA and SOUTH AFRICA.

The influence of Pietism in the Danish court led to an extensive reform of church discipline, confirmation, and schooling. The many hymns by Hans Adolph Brorson introduced Pietism to the laity.

Through the 19th century, various movements initiated work in Denmark including the BAPTISTS, Methodists, SEVENTH-DAY ADVENTIST CHURCH, QUAKERS, and JEHOVAH'S WITNESSES. The Baptists eventually formed the Baptist Union of Denmark. The Methodists remained connected to their American parents and are now an integral part of the UNITED METHODIST CHURCH. The Witnesses are the largest FREE CHURCH movement in the country. PENTECOSTALISM has established itself, but has not enjoyed the success it has manifested in other Scandinavian countries.

In 1953, Denmark adopted a new constitution. It recognizes the Lutheran Church as the national church, or more popularly stated, the People's Church (Danske Folkekirke), to which the great majority of the Danish public belongs. The relationship is confirmed in the church tax, which the government collects for support of the church. All citizens pay this tax; the small number who are members of other religious communities pay an equivalent amount for their support. In 1975, the law was modified to allow non-Lutherans to be buried in church-controlled cemeteries. Most non-Lutheran groups now have official recognition, the most important benefit being that their ministers may conduct legal marriages.

The Danish Lutheran Church includes Greenland and the Faeroe Islands as well. In 1919, church leaders created the Danish Church Abroad, a structure that oversees congregations of expatriate Danes in countries around the world.

In Denmark, 4.6. million of the 5.2 million citizens are considered members of the Folkekirke, yet church participation by the citizenry is among the lowest in Europe. Denmark is noted for its high levels of secularization and indifference to religion.

The Folkekirke is the leading member of the Ecumenical Council of Denmark, which includes a number of the smaller Protestant bodies (and the Roman Catholics). The council is affiliated with the WORLD COUNCIL OF CHURCHES.

Further reading: H. Fledelius and B. Jull, *Freedom of Religion in Denmark* (Copenhagen: Danish Centre for Human Rights, 1992); P. Hartling, *The Danish Church,* trans. by S. Mammen (Copenhagen: Danish Institute, 1965); L. S. Hunter, *Scandinavian Churches: a Picture of the Development of the Churches of Denmark, Norway, Finland, Iceland, and Sweden* (London: Faber & Faber, 1965).

denominations

Very early in the Reformation, the Protestant movement divided into several factions, each distinguished by a peculiarity of belief and/or practice. The different factions came to be denominated by labels, some self-chosen, others imposed by outsiders, mostly critics. There were the Lutherans (followers of Martin LUTHER), the BAPTISTS (who demanded BAPTISM by immersion limited to adults), the Methodists (named for John WESLEY's methodical habits), and the Presbyterians (whose churches were led by presbyters or ELDERS). The factions eventually congealed into the competing denominations.

The fracturing of the Protestant community into ever more denominations, many formed for what some considered frivolous and ephemeral reasons, provoked a variety of reactions in the 19th century. There were attempts, for example, to call the movement back to a predenominational state by dropping all peculiar names in favor of biblical names—Church of God or Church of Christ. Toward the end of the century, the ECU-MENICAL MOVEMENT began to call for a resolution of denominational differences and a merger of Protestant bodies. They were inspired by the missionary experience, where denominational differences originating in Europe and North America seemed far less important.

In the last half of the 20th century, many newer Christian fellowships began to describe themselves as interdenominational, nondenominational, or even postdenominational. At times, the use of such designations papered over what were in effect new denomination traditions, especially the Pentecostal/Charismatic denominational family, which includes many "nondenominational" churches. Each of these churches must still decide how to organize (POLITY), how to observe SACRAMENTS and ordinances, and how to respond to theological issues from the Trinitarian nature of God to the nature of salvation in Christ.

At the height of the Ecumenical movement in the middle of the 20th century, obituaries were written on denominational life. However, denominations have shown a remarkable resiliency and continue as the vital center of the Protestant community as the 21st century begins.

Further reading: Samuel G. Dawson, *Fellowship: With God and His People: The Way of Christ Without Denominationalism* (Amarillo, Tex.: Gospel Themes Press, 1988); H. Richard Niebuhr, *Social Sources of Denominationalism* (New York: Henry Holt, 1929); Russell E. Ritchie and Robert B. Mullin, eds., *Reimagining Denominationalism: Interpretive Essays* (New York: Oxford University Press, 1994).

Dentière, Marie (d. c. 1561) *early Protestant writer and apologist*

At the time of the Protestant Reformation, religious life in Europe was still largely managed by men. Marie Dentière was one of the few women to break through and make a visible contribution to further the cause. Prioress of an Augustinian convent in Belgium, Marie quickly accepted the ideas of fellow

Augustinian Martin LUTHER, and left the convent in 1521. She moved to STRASBOURG, where she married, and the couple settled in Aigle, Switzerland. After her husband's death, she married Antoine Froment (1509–81), and they settled in Geneva.

During the next decade, Dentière wrote three pieces that established her place in Reformation history. In 1535, she authored an account of the Reformation in Geneva, the first to treat the events in a favorable light. In 1539, she wrote an apology for William FAREL and John CALVIN, when they were asked to leave the city; she included an argument for women becoming more involved in church life. Published anonymously as *A Very Useful Letter written and composed by a Christian woman from Tournai, sent to the Queen of Navarre, sister of the King of France, Against the Turks, Jews, Infidels, False Christians, Anabaptists, and Lutherans,* this second work did not meet with the approval of the authorities in Geneva, and copies were confiscated and destroyed. Only two copies have survived to the present.

Finally, in 1561, she wrote the preface to Calvin's *Sermon on Female Apparel,* to which she appended some observation's from Cyprian (c. 200–258), one of the church fathers, which she had translated into French. Dentière died around 1561.

In 2002, her name was added to the Reformation Monument in Geneva in belated recognition of her contributions.

Further reading: Marie Dentière, *Epistle to Marguerite de Navarre and Preface to a Sermon by John Calvin,* ed. by Mary B. McKinley (Chicago: University of Chicago Press, 2004); Katherina M. Wilson, ed., *Women Writers of the Renaissance and Reformation* (Athens: University of Georgia Press, 1987).

Devanandan, Paul David (1901–1962)
Indian theologian and ecumenist
Paul David Devanandan was born in Madras on July 8, 1901. He grew up in a Christian family, and attended Nizam College (Hyderabad) and Presidency College (Madras). During his college years,

he became acquainted with K. T. Paul (1876–1931), a prominent Indian Christian statesman and Y.M.C.A. leader. Paul helped Devananda travel to the United States, where he attended the Pacific School of Religion (B.D.) and Yale University (Ph.D. in comparative religions).

Upon his return to India in 1931, he became a professor at the United Theological College at Bangalore. He began a long career as a scholar and Y.M.C.A. worker (1949–56). Through most of his career, he operated as a layman, but in 1954 he was ordained in the recently formed Church of South India (a union of a number of Indian Protestant DENOMINATIONS).

In 1956, Devanandan was appointed director of the new Center for the Study of Hinduism (now the Christian Institute for the Study of Religion and Society). His work, including his talk at the WORLD COUNCIL OF CHURCHES Assembly in 1961, caught the attention of the larger ecumenical church. Recognition has been slow in coming as he had spent most of his career fighting the missionary establishment. His views on how the Indian Christian community could fit into the national ethos became influential in the postmissionary era. He initiated dialogues with leaders in the other Indian religious communities, based in a faith that Christ did not limit his work to the church alone.

Devanandan authored a number of books; he died on August 10, 1962.

See also ECUMENICAL MOVEMENT; INDIA.

Further reading: P. D. Devanandan, *The Concept of Maya* (London: Lutterworth Press, 1950); ———, *The Dravida Kazagham: A Revolt against Brahmanism* (Bangalore: Christian Institute for the Study of Religion and Society, 1960); ———, and M. M. Thomas, *Preparation for Dialogue: Collection of Essays on Hinduism and Christianity in New India* (Bangalore: Christian Institute for the Study of Religion and Society, 1964); Charles Wesley Mark, *A Study in the Protestant Christian Approach to the Great Tradition of Hinduism with Special Reference to E Stanley Jones and P. D. Devanandan* (Princeton, N.J.: Princeton Theological Seminary, Ph.D. diss., 1988); Joachim Wietzke, ed., *Paul D. Devanandan,* 2 vols. (Madras: Christian Literature Society, 1983, 1987).

Dharma Angkuw, Margaritha
(b. 1925) *Indonesian ecumenist and social activist*
Margaritha Dharma Angkuw was born on October 11, 1925, in Bogor, West Java. After completing secondary school, she became one of only two female students at the theological seminary in Bogor (now the Sekolah Tinggi Theologia Jakarta). Following graduation in 1955, she was ordained, and she assumed a position in the synod office of the Protestant Church in Western Indonesia.

At the synod office, she began two tasks that dominated the rest of her life. First, as a pioneering female minister, she promoted the status and role of women throughout the church. Second, she promoted diakonal service and popularized the notion that the church's ministrations were not just for church members but for whoever was in need.

In 1962, she became head of the spiritual-care commission at Cikini Hospital in Jakarta, a facility sponsored by the national ecumenical association, the Indonesian Commission of Churches. She became a member of the commission's executive committee, using her position to promote various health services and family planning. In 1958, she was one of the founders of the Asian Women's Christian Conference (later attached to the East Asia Christian Conference). She represented the commission at the WORLD COUNCIL OF CHURCHES Assemblies in New Delhi (1961) and Uppsala (1968).

See also INDONESIA.

Further reading: Scott W. Sunquist, ed., *A Dictionary of Asian Christianity* (Grand Rapids, Mich.: William B. Eerdmans, 2001).

Diet of Worms
Martin LUTHER's trial at a session of the Imperial Diet (council) of the Holy Roman Empire at Worms in 1521, and the diet's decision to condemn him, was a turning point in the historic split between the Roman Catholic Church and the Reformation movement.

At that time, central Europe, and especially Germany, was divided into a large number of small countries. They were united in a loose confederacy termed the *Holy Roman Empire,* led by an emperor and held together in part by its allegiance to Roman Catholicism and to the the pope. Its highest legislative body, weak by any standard, was the Imperial Diet (*Reichstag*). The diet included the leaders of the various political entities in the empire, and it met at different places and times.

Martin Luther's challenge to papal authority was gathering support just as the empire faced a severe military crisis. Turkish Islamic forces had marched out of Budapest and were heading for Vienna a short distance away. The Reformation was creating a division in the empire at the very point that all its strength was needed to resist the Muslim advance.

The pope had excommunicated Luther for publicizing his NINETY-FIVE THESES in 1517 and other declarations and pamphlets accusing the popes and church councils of error. Luther had won protection from various German princes, some who agreed with him ideologically and some who simply did not want money from their lands flowing to Rome.

The pope pressured the emperor to outlaw Luther. In 1521, Luther was summoned to appear before the diet to defend himself. If the diet declared him an outlaw, he could be arrested and jailed. Precedents were not auspicious—Bohemian reformer John HUS, who had faced similar charges a century before, had been found guilty at the Council of Constance and burned at the stake. Unlike Hus, Luther had the backing of several powerful German princes, most importantly the Elector Frederick of Saxony; Luther also enjoyed much popular support in Germany, including Worms.

At the diet, Luther defended his views vigorously, drawing upon biblical authority and reason.

He is reported to have concluded, "Unless I am convinced by Scripture and plain reason—I do not accept the authority of the popes and councils, for they have contradicted each other—my conscience is captive to the Word of God. I cannot and I will not recant anything for to go against conscience is neither right nor safe. God help me. Amen." He is also quoted as having said, "Here I stand. I cannot do otherwise," but these words appear to be apocryphal.

After the emperor and the diet found against him, Luther left Worms, making use of his temporary safe conduct. After 21 days, anyone could kill him as an outlaw without threat of reprisal from the authorities. On his way home, Luther was "kidnapped" and taken to the castle at Wartburg, where he remained for 11 months. The Diet of Worms marked a watershed, after which any compromise between Luther and the Catholic Church was all but impossible.

Further reading: David V. N. Bagchi, *Luther's Earliest Opponents: Catholic Controversialists 1518–1525* (Minneapolis, Minn.: Augsburg Fortress, 1991); Martin Brecht, *Martin Luther: Shaping and Defining the Reformation 1521–32* (Minneapolis, Minn.: Fortress Press, 1990); Gordon Rupp, *Luther's Progress to the Diet of Worms* (New York: Harper & Row, 1964).

Disciples of Christ *See* RESTORATION MOVEMENT.

discipling/shepherding movement

Discipling is the practice among some Pentecostals in which each member is counseled by a shepherd, a more senior member of the congregation or larger fellowship. As the CHARISMATIC MOVEMENT spread in the 1960s to traditional non-Pentecostal Protestant churches (as well as the Roman Catholic Church), new congregations emerged among people who withdrew from their former churches but did not wish to affiliate with one of the older Pentecostal churches. Such inde-

pendent and unattached congregations, some led by people with little formal training, faced the problem of how to lead young converts to a mature life as a Christian disciple.

In response, a group of older Pentecostal leaders—Don Basham (1926–89), Ern Baxter (1914–93), Bob Mumford (b. 1930), Derek Prince (1915–2003), and Charles Simpson (b. 1937)—founded the Holy Spirit Teaching Mission (later known as Christian Growth Ministries) in Fort Lauderdale, Florida. There, through the early 1970s, they developed a program called shepherding or discipling, for building leadership and nurturing church members. They promoted the idea through books, tapes, and a monthly magazine, *New Wine.*

The discipling program assigned each church member to a more senior member; they in turn would be discipled by a pastor, who might have a shepherd in another city or state. Shepherds were expected to meet frequently with those they were discipling to discuss their progress in the faith and counsel them on important life matters, including school, work, and even choosing a mate. Depending on personalities, such counseling could become authoritarian and demanding.

As discipling spread, it threatened the unity and cordial feeling that dominated the early Charismatic movement. Opponents charged that shepherds were asking for a form of submission that belonged only to God. The Fort Lauderdale group was charged with building a rigid new denominationalism. In 1976, the Fort Lauderdale Five issued a "Statement of Concern and Regret," promising to correct any abuses.

After several conferences, the leadership of the Charismatic movement agreed to allow discipling to continue among those who accepted it. It continued to spread quietly, reappearing among various Evangelical groups such as the Christian Crusade and, more recently, the Promise Keepers.

The INTERNATIONAL CHURCHES OF CHRIST (ICC) can be traced to the introduction of the shepherding/discipling movement into the Church of Christ congregation in Gainesville, Florida, by its pastor Charles Lukas, and into a Lexington, Massachusetts, church led by Kip McKean. McKean integrated the practice into his idea that all church members should be actively committed to evangelism and nurturing new members. He also developed a plan for world evangelism, and member churches sprang up across the United States and internationally. ICC congregations were usually the largest Church of Christ in any given location; many attracted thousands of members. In the 1980s, the ICC became a target of the anticult movement, and a number of members were deprogrammed. As the churches did much of their recruitment on college campuses, their relationships with campus authorities were often strained.

In the 1990s, the ICC moved toward a less authoritarian style of discipling and ended those practices that had attracted most complaints. Meanwhile, discipling has spread worldwide and is no longer limited to Charismatic and independent Evangelical churches. While few people object to a mild form of discipling, watchdogs remain who quickly call attention to overly authoritarian practices.

Further reading: Bob Buess, *Discipleship Pro and Con* (Van, Tex.: Sweeter Than Honey, 1974); Gordon Ferguson, *Discipling: God's Plan to Train and Transform His People* (Woburn, Mass.: Discipleship Publications International, 1997); Derek Prince, *Discipleship, Shepherding, Commitment* (Ft. Lauderdale, Fla.: Derek Prince Publications, 1976); Charles Simpson, *The Challenge to Care* (Ann Arbor, Mich.: Servant Publications, 1986); Flavil Yeakley, *The Discipling Dilemma: A Study of the Discipling Movement among Churches of Christ* (Nashville, Tenn.: Gospel Advocate, 1988).

dispensationalism

Dispensationalism is one of the most popular schools of theology and biblical interpretation among conservative Evangelical and Fundamentalist Protestants. It is grounded in the belief that Scripture and human history are divided into a number of successive periods, in each of which God acts in a special way with his covenant people. The theory is usually traced to John Nelson DARBY (1800–82), one of the founders of the Plymouth Brethren. It spread with the growth of the BRETHREN, in the British Isles and then in continental Europe and North America. It also spread beyond the Brethren, attracting such notables as evangelist Dwight L. MOODY. Dispensational views underlay much of the discussions at the popular Prophetic conferences at the end of the 19th century and helped fuel the Fundamentalist-Modernist controversy in the 1920s.

The great exponent at the beginning of the 20th century was Cyrus I. SCOFIELD (1843–1921). An associate of Moody, Scofield became a Congregationalist minister and in that capacity authored his first book on dispensationalism, *Rightly Dividing the Word of Truth,* in 1888. Between 1902 and 1908, Scofield prepared a reference Bible annotated from a dispensationalist viewpoint. He later edited a correspondence course that built on the notes.

In the years after World War I, many Fundamentalists identified with dispensationalism, and it became integral to the curriculum of such places as Moody Bible Institute, Dallas Theological Seminary, Philadelphia Bible College, and the Bible Institute of Los Angeles (BIOLA). As PENTECOSTALISM began to influence BAPTISTS and Presbyterians, dispensationalism came along with it, especially teachings about future end-time events. Toward the end of the 20th century, dispensationalist writers such as Hal Lindsey (b. 1929) and Tim LaHaye (b. 1926) helped to extend its popularity.

Dispensationlists make a sharp distinction between Israel and the church. Prior to the resurrection and ascension of Christ, God dealt primarily with the nation of Israel. Since that time, God has dealt with the church fellowship that includes both Jews and Gentiles united into one spiritual body. God gave language to humanity for the purpose of communication, and he reveals himself in language in its most understandable way. Hence, the Bible is to be interpreted literally, giving to each word of the text the meaning it would have in ordinary usage (with proper attention to different usages of language as symbols or in figures of speech).

The group believes the Bible clearly designates seven dispensations. The first, Innocence, begins with the creation of Adam and Eve and continued until the Fall. The second, Conscience, when God ordained that humans follow the dictates of conscience, lasted until the time of Noah and the Flood. The third, Human Government, lasted from the Flood until the covenant with Abraham. With Abraham, a fourth dispensation began, that of Patriarchal Rule, and lasted until the giving of the law of Moses. The dispensation of Law covered the greater part of Israel's history up until the events culminating in Christ's crucifixion and the inauguration of the church.

We currently live in the dispensation of Grace, when God offers salvation to all through his grace. When Christ returns, he will establish the last dispensation, the Millennium, his thousand-year reign, during which he will personally rule on Earth.

Dispensationalists concerned with the future (especially those who believe that the end of the dispensation of Grace is near) have created detailed outlines of what will happen in the last days of the current dispensation. During the Rapture (I Thessalonians 4:13–18), believers will be caught up in the air with the returning Jesus Christ during a seven-year period of Tribulation (Revelation 20:7–9).

Dispensationalists disagree over the relative placement of the Rapture and the Tribulation. Pre-tribulationists believe that the Rapture will come first, while post-tribulationists reverse the order. There are also a few mid-tribulationists who believe that the two will take place at the same time, and some who foretell a partial Rapture; a sanctified group of Christians, who are already living righteously, will be raptured immediately, while the rest go through the tribulation as a means of perfecting them.

As the end of the second millennium C.E. passed without significant events, dispensationalists came in for criticism. Many of them had viewed the reestablishment of the state of Israel as an end-time event. Some, like Hal Lindsey, suggested that 1948 was the beginning of the last generation (40 years).

The failure of dispensationalism to predict history has been the major argument against its biblical interpretation. Nevertheless, dispensationalists have continued into the 21st century riding the wave created by the very successful "Left Behind" fictional series of James Jenkins and Tim LaHaye.

See also ESCHATOLOGY; PREMILLENNIALISM.

Further reading: Mal Couch, ed., *Dictionary of Premillennial Theology* (Grand Rapids, Mich.: Kregal, 1996); Charles C. Rulie, *Dispensationalism* (Chicago: Moody Press, 1995); Wesley R. Willis and John R. Master, eds., *Issues in Dispensationalism* (Chicago: Moody Press, 1994).

Ditt (fl. late 19th century) *Indian evangelist*
Ditt, an untutored pioneer evangelist in eastern INDIA, is one of a few 19th-century native evangelists still remembered amid the host of western Protestant missionaries. He was a farmer and a member of the Chuhra caste, a lower caste whose members were not, for example, allowed to drink from wells belonging to recognized Hindus, Muslims, or Sikhs, nor enter their places of worship. He was small of stature and lame in one leg. He could neither read nor write. He was about 30 years old when he encountered a Christian convert named Nattu. Ditt converted and accepted BAPTISM.

Living 40 miles from the nearest mission station, Ditt managed to convert four people within two months—his wife, his daughter, and two neighbors. He continued to witness among his neighbors and was soon recognized as a valued evangelist, and he was later supplied with a small salary so he could work full-time. Though unlettered, he mastered the Bible and Christian teachings and developed an ability to share the basics of the faith with his peers.

Ditt's efforts inspired a MASS MOVEMENT in southeast Uttar Pradesh; the results of his work continue in several churches now operating in eastern India and Bangladesh. His story was recorded in a book by American Presbyterian missionary Andrew Gordon, *Our India Mission* (1886), one of the few books of the era to celebrate the native leadership developed by the missionaries of the period. Ditt was typical of such leadership, which greatly expanded the work initiated by Western missionaries and prepared the way for the rise of an indigenous ordained Protestant ministry in the next century.

Further reading: Andrew Gordon, *Our India Mission, 1855–1885* (Philadelphia: by author, 1886).

doctrine

A doctrine is a principle or statement of belief (or by extension, a set of principles/beliefs) presented for acceptance and/or assent by an individual, group, or organization. Protestantism was largely identified by the doctrines it adhered to that contradicted Roman Catholicism, and was subsequently divided by differences of doctrine among the various branches of Protestantism.

Protestantism affirmed the traditional doctrines of the ancient church stated in the common creedal statements, especially the Nicene Creed, but added its own doctrines on salvation by grace alone, the ultimate authority of the Bible in matters of faith and practice, and the priesthood of all believers. It affirmed two SACRAMENTS as opposed to the seven affirmed in Roman Catholicism. It denied belief in the authority of the pope, the existence of purgatory, and the practice of indulgences.

The set of doctrines held by various Protestants groups often found expressions in formal confessional documents, with some attaining broad acceptance: AUGSBURG CONFESSION OF FAITH, Dordrecht Confession, WESTMINSTER CONFESSION OF FAITH, the SAVOY DECLARATION, the Canons of Dort, and the ARTICLES OF RELIGION (Anglican, Methodist), among others.

Early disagreements among Protestants concerned the doctrines of the SACRAMENTS, church POLITY, and the church's relationship to the state. Unitarians dissented on the doctrine of God, unable to affirm the Trinity.

Over the centuries, some groups drew sharp distinctions between the ultimate authority of the Bible and the particular man-made statements of doctrine of the churches. In the 19th century, churches emerged that opposed the idea of creedal statements. They rejected the normative value often assigned to creedal statements, which short-circuited creativity and new insights in Bible study. However, those same groups often saw the need to summarize what they had learned and agreed upon from their study of the Bible and issued documents that looked very much like doctrinal statements.

The overwhelming majority of the thousands of DENOMINATIONS that now exist have issued statements of the primary doctrines they expect members to affirm, though with widely differing expectations about the level of homogeneity they demand.

See also CREEDS/CONFESSIONS OF FAITH; DOGMATICS.

Further reading: L. Berkhof, *The History of Christian Doctrines* (Edinburgh: Banner of Truth Trust, 1969); Jubert Cunliffe-Jones and Benjamin Drewery, *A History of Christian Doctrine* (Philadelphia: Fortress Press, 1980); Walter Elwell, ed., *Dictionary of Evangelical Theology* (Grand Rapids, Mich.: Baker Book House, 1984); J. Gordon Melton, *The Encyclopedia of American Religions: Religious Creeds,* 2 vols. (Detroit: Gale Research, 1988, 1994); Alan Richardson and John Bowden, eds., *The Westminster Dictionary of Christian Theology* (Philadelphia: Westminster, 1983).

dogmatics

Dogmatics is a branch of theology that attempts to expound in a coherent way the teachings (dogma) of the church. In the Protestant context, dogmatics attempts to lay out more or less systematically the teachings of the Protestant tradition, a particular Protestant family tradition (Lutheran, Reformed, Methodist, Baptist), or a particular denomination.

Dogmatics will typically treat such central Christian ideas as God, the Trinity, Jesus Christ, the Holy Spirit, the human situation, salvation, ECCLESIOLOGY, and ESCHATOLOGY. Most of this work is done in the context of a seminary where a new generation of church leaders are being trained.

Increasingly in the post-Enlightenment world, dogmatics has attempted to relate church teachings to contemporary reality by discussing church teachings that no longer seem relevant or even possible to affirm, and highlighting the problems that demand the attention of the church. In the 19th century, new theologies have accommodated the findings of science (especially the idea of evolution). In the 20th century, some theologians announced their inability to affirm traditional beliefs from the virgin birth of Jesus to the afterlife. Some have called for a reworking of theology in the name of various groups who had been excluded from its work (LIBERATION THEOLOGY).

No dogmatics can claim to speak for more than a minority of Protestant churches, which is itself only a part of the Christian communion. Each dogmatic exposition becomes part of an ongoing theological conversation that slowly moves the church in one direction or another. The modern context demands a heightened degree of self-consciousness from the individual theologian, who speaks out of a particular context while attempting to be aware of different contexts and true to the universal implications of Christianity.

Dogmatics should not be confused with dogmatism, which refers to the narrow-minded way opinions are sometimes asserted. Dogmatic conclusions may be asserted dogmatically, and on many occasions theologians have done so. However, dogmatism is by no means a necessary correlate of the theological disciplines.

See also DOCTRINE.

Further reading: Karl Barth, *Dogmatics in Outline* (London: SCM, 1958); Walter Elwell, ed., *Dictionary of Evangelical Theology* (Grand Rapids, Mich.: Baker Book House, 1984); Justo Gonzales, *A History of Christian Thought*, 3 vols. (Nashville, Tenn.: Abingdon Press, 1987); Donald K. McKim, *Westminster Dictionary of Theological Terms* (Louisville, Ky.: Westminster/John Knox, 1996); Alan Richardson and John Bowden, eds., *The Westminster Dictionary of Christian Theology* (Philadelphia: Westminster, 1983).

Dort, Synod of

The affirmations approved by Reformed church delegates from the NETHERLANDS, Belgium, England, and FRANCE at the Synod of Dort (Holland) in 1619 are considered among the clearest, most abiding summations of Calvinist belief. The synod had been called to deal with the challenge of ARMINIANISM; it succeeded in pushing the Remonstrants to the margins of Reformed Protestantism.

Jacob Arminius (1560–1609), professor of theology at the University of Leyden, began in 1603 to reject what he saw as an extreme form of PREDESTINATION as articulated by his Leyden colleague Francis Gomar (1563–1641). He tried to develop a view that would not, as he put it, make God the author of sin or turn humans into mere automatons.

Arminius died in 1609, but his views were championed by Johan Wtenbogaert (1577–1644), who summarized Arminianism in a 1610 document called the Remonstrance. He argued that (1) From eternity, God determined to save those he foresaw would believe and persevere to the end in their faith; (2) Jesus' act of atonement was for all humankind but is applicable only to those with faith; (3) Humans are in a state of sin and have no saving grace of themselves, thus they need to be renewed in Christ by the Holy Spirit; (4) Apart from grace, humankind can do nothing, but this grace can be resisted by the unbeliever; (5) Believers can win over sin through God's grace, and all who are willing will be kept from falling back into a sinful state (falling from grace).

In Dortrecht, visitors may see this reproduction of the Synod of Dort that includes mannequins in 17th-century dress. *(Institute for the Study of American Religion, Santa Barbara, California)*

The debate climaxed at a church SYNOD held at Dort, the center of counter-Remonstrant sentiment, over the winter of 1618–19. In the end, the ultra-Calvinist position was put aside, and what was considered a more centrist approach adopted. The synod adopted a five-point document known as the Canons of Dort. The canons affirmed that (1) The election to salvation is determined solely by the will of God; (2) Christ died only for the elect; (3) Humankind is so corrupted by the fall, humans have nothing to contribute to their salvation; (4) God's grace is irresistible, hence all of the elect will be saved; and (5) God's elect are assured of their state and will persevere to the end. This position, sometimes referred to as the five points

of Calvinism, is often stated in English using a mnemonic device referring to the Dutch national flower: T—Total depravity; U—Unconditional election; L—LIMITED ATONEMENT; I—Irresistible grace; and P—Perseverance of the saints.

Following the synod, the Arminians were forced underground for several years, many leaving the country. Not a few settled in England. They were able to return after Frederick Henry of Orange (r. 1625–47) ended the strict enforcement of the decisions of Dort. They subsequently opened a seminary at Amsterdam, and supporters were allowed to attend churches with Remonstrant ministers. Arminianism had its greatest success by influencing John WESLEY and METHODISM.

See also CALVINISM; DOCTRINE; REFORMED/PRES-
BYTERIAN TRADITION.

Further reading: Carl Bangs, *Arminius* (Nashville,
Tenn.: Abingdon Press, 1971); Horatius Bonar, *The
Five Points of Calvinism* (Evansville, Ind.: Sovereign
Book Club, 1957); Peter Y. DeJong, ed., *Crisis in the
Reformed Churches; Essays in Commemoration of the
Great Synod of Dort, 1618–1619* (Grand Rapids,
Mich.: Reformed Fellowship, 1968); Pieter Geyl, *The
Netherlands in the Seventeenth Century* (New York:
Barnes & Noble, 1961); Thomas Scott, trans., *The
Articles of the Synod of Dort* (Philadelphia: Presbyter-
ian Board of Publication, 1841).

Doukhobors

The Doukhobors are a group of religious dissenters who originated in 18th-century RUSSIA.
They drew ideas from other Russian sectarian
groups and from Polish Unitarianism. By the
1730s, they had emerged under the leadership of
Sylvan Kolesnikoff, who formed the original community in Nikolai, Russia. The name Doukhobor
was given to them as a derisive term by a Russian
bishop, but they accepted it as denoting "Spirit
Wrestlers" struggling against lust and spiritual
pride.

After periods of persecution, in part because of
their pacifism, in 1895 they engaged in a massive
demonstration in which they burned their
weapons to illustrate their refusal to serve in the
army. In 1899, most Doukhobors moved to
CANADA.

The Doukhobors practice a non-Trinitarian
form of Christianity that emphasizes Jesus' role as
a teacher and exemplar, not a deity. They also dispensed with priests, liturgy, and church buildings.
They recognize the symbolic value of bread, salt,
and water as the basic elements needed to sustain
life, and these elements are prominently displayed
at their meetings. At times, Doukhobors have
lived communally, but at present most do not. The
Bible has largely been replaced by a set of Russian
psalms and hymns, compiled over the last two
centuries in The Living Book and sung at their
meetings.

Canadian Doukhobors have had ongoing conflicts with Canadian authorities. They are known
for their unorthodox ways of resisting Canadian
regulations, including burning their own barns
and disrobing in the midst of court proceedings.

Today, there are between 30,000 and 40,000
Doukhobors in Canada and some 30,000 in Russia. In Canada, they have divided into several
groups, the Union of Spiritual Communities of
Christ being the oldest and largest, and the Sons
of Freedom, the group most ready to confront
government authorities.

Further reading: Sam George Stupnikoff, *Historical
Saga of the Doukhobor Faith, 1750–1990s* (Saskatoon,
Saskatchewan: Apex Graphics, 1992); Koozma J.
Tarasoff and Robert Klymasz, eds., *Spirit Wrestlers:
Centennial Papers in Honour of Canada's Doukhobor
Heritage* (Hull, Quebec: Canadian Museum of Civi-
lization, 1995); George Woodcock and Ivan Avaku-
movic, *The Doukhobors* (Toronto, Ontario:
McClelland & Stewart, 1977).

Dow, Lorenzo (1777–1834) *popular
American Methodist preacher*

Lorenzo Dow, known for his eccentric ways and
his wide travels, was born in Coventry, Connecticut, on October 16, 1777, and was converted in
1791 under the ministry of Hope Hull
(1763–1818), a Methodist preacher. Dow began to
preach in 1794. He was admitted on trial as a
preacher in 1798 by Bishop Francis ASBURY.

After a two-year stay in England, trying to
overcome poor health, he returned in 1801 and
was appointed to a circuit in New England. Six
months later, he left the circuit, effectively sever-
ing his ties to organized METHODISM, and he began
a life of itinerant preaching.

Dow was tall and thin, with a long, red beard.
His harsh, raspy voice and jerky movements and
gestures while preaching became famous, along
with numerous anecdotes of odd and humorous

incidents. However, he was acknowledged to be a serious evangelist, creative in devising methods of reaching his audiences. Early in his ministry, he met Samul K. Jennings, who had written about CAMP MEETINGS, and he became an advocate of them. In 1804, he published the first of many editions of his *Life and Travels,* recounting his evangelistic work. In 1805, he traveled to England, where he met Peters Phillips (1778–1853), later the founder of the Independent Methodists, and Hugh Bourne (1772–1852), who joined Dow in introducing camp meetings into England. Bourne later helped found the PRIMITIVE METHODIST CHURCH.

Though cut off from the main body of Methodists, Dow's travels did much to spread Methodism in the United States and England in the early 19th century. He died in Washington, D.C., on February 2, 1834.

Further reading: Lorenzo Dow, *The Dealings of God, Man, and the Devil, As Exemplified in the Life, Experience, and Travels of Lorenzo Dow, in a Period of Over Half a Century, Together with His Polemic and Miscellaneous Writings, To Which Is Added the Vicissitudes of Life,* by Peggy Dow (New York: Sheldon, Lamport & Blakeman, 1849); ———, *History of Cosmopolite, Or the Four Volumes of Lorenzo Dow's Journal* (Wheeling, Va.: 1848); ———, *The Eccentric Preacher* (Lowell, Mass.: E. A. Rice, 1841); Charles Coleman Sellers, *Lorenzo Dow: The Bearer of the Word* (New York: Minton, Balch & Company, 1928).

doxology

Literally, a short verse praising God; doxologies may be traced to the New Testament and became part of the Roman Catholic liturgy, from whence they passed to Protestantism. By the fourth century, two doxologies had achieved special status in Western Christianity. The lesser doxology, spoken or sung, was called the *Gloria Patri:* "Glory be to the Father, and to the Son, and to the Holy Spirit; as it was in the beginning, is now, and ever shall be, world without end. Amen." The greater doxology, "Gloria in excelsis Deo," is based on the song of the angels recorded in Luke 2:1; it is less used by Protestants.

Most common of all in Protestantism is the last stanza of the "Morning and Evening Hymn," written by Anglican Bishop Thomas Ken (1637–1711), commonly thought of as simply "The Doxology" in many Protestant congregations. Most frequently sung as a response following the taking of the offering, it reads: "Praise God from whom all blessings flow; / Praise Him, all creatures here below; / Praise Him above, ye heavenly host. / Praise Father, Son and Holy Ghost."

See also LITURGY.

Further reading: Hugh A. L. Rice, *Thomas Ken. Bishop and Non-juror* (London: SPCK, 1958).

Drummond, Henry (1851–1897)
Christian writer and philosopher of science

Henry Drummond, a Christian scientist who attempted to respond positively to the scientific findings of the mid-19th century in a number of best-selling books, was born at Stirling, Scotland, on August 17, 1851. He attended the University of Edinburgh and the New College, Edinburgh, where he studied theology in preparation for the ministry of the Free Church of Scotland, a more conservative alternative to the Church of Scotland.

In 1877, Drummond, though never having received a formal degree, became a lecturer in natural science at the Free Church College in Glasgow. In 1884, he became a full professor and was ordained as a minister in the Free Church. A set of lectures given at a local Free Church, in which he tackled the controversial subject of evolution, were later compiled as Drummond's first major book, *Natural Law in the Spiritual World* (1883). He defended science, arguing that the scientific study of natural law led to the discovery of spiritual laws and conformed with Calvinist views in particular. He argued that evolution was no danger to Christianity.

Lectures in London were later compiled into what may be his most enduring book, *The Greatest Thing in the World* (1880), his commentary on I Corinthians 13. He asserted his belief that "To love abundantly is to live abundantly, and to love forever is to live forever." He suggested that reproduction, the struggle of life not just for the self but for others, was the missing consideration in evolutionary theory. Altruism sits beside the survival of the fittest as a factor in the upward movement of humanity. The lectures satisfied neither his scientific nor his religious colleagues.

Shortly after the publication of his last book, *The Ascent of Man,* Drummond became ill, and he died on March 11, 1897. (The Scottish Henry Drummond is not to be confused with the British Henry Drummond (1786–1860), who was active in the Catholic Apostolic Church.)

See also CREATIONISM; DARWIN, Charles.

Further reading: Henry Drummond, *The Greatest Thing in the World* (London: Hodder & Stoughton, 1880), frequently reprinted; ———, *The Lowell Lectures on the Ascent of Man* (London: Hodder & Stoughton, 1894; ———, *Natural Law in the Spiritual World* (London: Hodder & Stoughton, 1883); George A. Smith, *The Life of Henry Drummond* (London: Hodder & Stoughton, 1898).

Duff, Alexander (1806–1878) *Scottish missionary and educator*

A pioneering Church of Scotland missionary to INDIA, Alexander Duff developed the theories that helped shape the Protestant global missionary endeavor throughout the 19th century. Duff was born into a farming family in Moulin, Perthshire, in Scotland. An early experience of nearly drowning left him with a sense that God had a special mission for him.

Duff entered St Andrews University in 1821, and founded a missionary society as a student. In 1829, Duff became the first missionary officially appointed by the church's general assembly. He was to superintend an educational facility in Calcutta. He and his wife arrived in India in 1830, but only after experiencing two shipwrecks and the loss of his entire library.

The institute was designed to provide a Western education and produce an intellectual elite who would guide India with Western values. Duff was assisted by famed Hindu reformer Ram Mohan Roy, who provided access to the upper levels of Calcutta society, from whom Duff hoped to draw students. Duff's school provided a religious-based education, but he actively engaged both Hindu and atheist intellectuals. Also on Roy's advice, Duff chose to keep instruction in English, which had the effect of integrating students from different Indian linguistic backgrounds. He was one of the first in India to include women in his education program.

Duff, never at ease with Calcutta's climate, returned home in 1834 to find that interest in missions had flagged. While traveling across Scotland to rebuild support, he thought through a systematic approach to the missionary enterprise that included the development of indigenous leadership, active engagement with cultural elites, and an understanding of the church as essentially a missionary enterprise.

Back in India in 1840, he found that his school was successfully producing a generation of Christian leaders. However, when he and his fellow missionaries took sides with the new, dissident Free Church of Scotland, the established Church of Scotland took over the school's property. Duff and his associates had to start over. He established a new college, also founding additional branches in other locations. Instruction concentrated on literature, science, and the Christian religion. He was among those who drew up a constitution for Calcutta University, and until his return to Scotland in 1851, he led the university's senate.

After another interval working to increase support for missionaries back in Scotland and in the United States, he returned to India. While there, he wrote a book criticizing the British government's handling of the 1857 rebellion of Indians against British control. Upon his return to Scotland, Duff became head of the Free Church's foreign missions committee. In 1867, he was appointed to a chair in missions at the New College, Edinburgh. He died on February 12, 1878.

Further reading: Alexander Duff, *India and Indian Missions* (Edinburgh: J. Johnstone, 1839); ———. *The Indian Rebellion: Its Causes and Results. In a Series of Letters.* (London: Nisbet, 1857): W. P. Duff, *Memorials of Alexander Duff* (London: Nisbet, 1890); Michael A. Laird, "Alexander Duff, 1806–1878: Western Education as Preparation for the Gospel," in Gerald H. Anderson, et al., eds., *Mission Legacies: Biographical Studies of the Modern Missionary Movement* (Maryknoll, N.Y.: Orbis Books, 1998), 271–76; Thomas Smith, *Alexander Duff, D.D., L.D.* (London: Hodder & Stoughton, 1888).

du Plessis, David J. (1905–1987) *South African Pentecostal leader*

David J. du Plessis emerged in the years after World War II as ambassador of PENTECOSTALISM to ecumenical Protestantism and the Roman Catholic Church. Du Plessis was born near Cape Town on February 7, 1905. During his childhood, his family became Pentecostal under John G. Lake (1870–1935) and Thomas Hezmalhalch (1848–1934), whose work led to the development of the Apostolic Faith Mission in 1913. Du Plessis joined the mission in 1917 and received the BAPTISM OF THE HOLY SPIRIT the next year. He attended Grey University and became a pastor in the Apostolic Faith Mission. He served as general secretary of the denomination between 1936 and 1947.

In 1947, du Plessis attended the World Pentecostal Conference in Zurich, SWTIZERLAND, and remained there to work as organizing secretary for what became the WORLD PENTECOSTAL FELLOWSHIP. He traveled to America in 1948 and worked closely with the CHURCH OF GOD (CLEVELAND, TENNESSEE), including a period as a teacher at Lee College. He later affiliated with the ASSEMBLIES OF GOD.

In the mid-1960s, du Plessis opened a dialogue with the Roman Catholic Church while attending the third session of Vatican II. His efforts led to the establishment of a Roman Catholic-Pentecostal Dialogue, at a time when the Charismatic movement was spreading rapidly through the Catholic Church.

Shortly before his death, Fuller Theological Seminary in Pasadena, California, invited du Plessis to deposit his papers at the school, where he became Resident Consultant for Ecumenical Affairs. The David J. du Plessis Center for Christian Spirituality opened on February 7, 1985. He died in August 1987.

See also ECUMENICAL MOVEMENT; SOUTH AFRICA.

Further reading: David J. du Plessis, *A Man Called Mr. Pentecost* (Plainfield, N.J.: Logos International, 1977); ———, *Simple and Profound* (Orleans, Mass.: Paraclete, 1986); ———, *The Spirit Bade Me Go: The Astounding Move of God in the Denominational Churches* (Plainfield, N.J.: Logos International, 1970); Walter J. Hollenweger, "Two Extra-Ordinary Pentecostal Ecumenists: The Letters of Donald Gee and David du Plessis," *Ecumenical Review* 52, 3 (July 2000): 391–402; Martin Robinson, *To the Ends of the Earth: The Pilgrimage of an Ecumenical Pentecostal, David J. du Plessis* (Birmingham, U.K.: University of Birmingham, Ph.D. diss., 1987).

E

Ebina Danjo (1856–1937) *Japanese liberal Protestant leader*

Ebina Danjo was born in Chikugo Province (now Fukuoka). He studied at the nearby Kumamoto Yogakko, a school designed to introduce Western learning to Japan. While there, he fell under the influence of Reformed Church teacher Leroy Lansing Janes (1838–1909). He was one of 40 students who on January 30, 1876, climbed Mount Hanaoka and pledged their loyalty to Jesus Christ. After the school was closed later that year, most of the group, which became known as the Kumamoto Band, moved to Kyoto to attend the recently opened Doshisha College (now Doshisha University). He was part of the first graduating class of 1879.

When in 1874 the Japanese government lifted its ban on Christianity, the Kumamoto Band, together with a few other similar groups, joined forces with the Congregational Church mission to create the Congregational Church of Japan. Ebina served in a series of pastorates starting in 1879. He later served (1891–93) as president of the Japan Christian Mission Company and as chancellor of Doshisha (1920–28)

As a pastor, Ebina worked out a theology that resonated with liberal Protestantism in the United States. A universal religious consciousness, he suggested, had produced older religions such as Shinto or Confucianism before culminating in Christianity, the ultimate religious consciousness. He came to see Shintoism as parallel to Judaism, which in the Christian view was a preparation for receiving the Gospel. His debates with more conservative Protestant leaders such as Uemura Masahira and UCHIMURA KANZO led to his 1902 break with the Evangelical Alliance.

In 1930, Ebina became the pastor of Hongo Church (Congregational) in Tokyo, serving until his death on May 30, 1937.

See also JAPAN.

Further reading: Scott W. Sunquist, ed., *A Dictionary of Asian Christianity* (Grand Rapids, Mich.: William B. Eerdmans, 2001).

ecclesiology

Ecclesiology (from the Greek *ecclesia*) is the division of theology that studies the church, its organization, and its relation to the state. It begins with biblical references to the church as the body of Christ or the bride of Christ, examines the church as it exists in the present and in different times and places, and prescribes how it should be changed or preserved.

Ecclesiology was at the center of many Reformation debates about POLITY (governance) and church-state relations. Anglicans, for example, retained an episcopal polity (leadership by BISHOPS) and a close relation to the state. John CALVIN replaced bishops with ELDERS (presbyters) in his state church. The RADICAL REFORMATION favored a congregational polity, with only a distant relationship to the state. ANABAPTISTS and other FREE CHURCHES wanted to be free of any entanglement with the state and exist as a fellowship of the committed.

Another key issue was church membership. State churches tended to retain BAPTISM of infants, a sign of their induction into the church. They would later be confirmed. Among Free Churches, only believers committed to a godly life could join the fellowship of members.

The multiplying Protestant denominations confronted another question: was the church (or the true church) one's own denomination, or possibly a spectrum of DENOMINATIONS holding similar views? Some Protestants made distinctions between the true church, consisting of all those who have a saving faith in Jesus Christ whatever their denomination, and the visible church, which consists of both believers and nonbelievers. Some tried to put aside denominational divisions, and formed new churches with nondenominational names such as the CHURCH OF GOD, the Churches of Christ, the Disciples of Christ, and the Brethren. Chinese preacher Watchman NEE tried to revive what he saw as the New Testament pattern of one church per city. Each of the churches he founded was simply known as the Church in whatever city it was located. The movement became known as the LOCAL CHURCH.

A more overt attempt to reconcile the differences among Protestants resulted in the 20th-century ECUMENICAL MOVEMENT. After only limited success in merging denominations, the goal became the mutual recognition of different churches, often through pulpit fellowship and recognition of SACRAMENTS. A major embodiment is the LEUENBERG CHURCH FELLOWSHIP.

This Church of Christ congregation, in agreement with most Protestants, emphasizes that the church is to be identified with the people of God, not a building. *(Institute for the Study of American Religion, Santa Barbara, California)*

Many 20th-century church leaders have jettisoned ecclesiology as a search for a single model of church life or organization. Any church polity is acceptable if it brings people to faith and nurtures Christian fellowship. A variety of innovative forms of church life, each with New Testament credentials, have been proposed, including communal homes, house churches, and cell churches.

Further reading: Paul D. L. Avis, *The Church in the Theology of the Reformers* (Atlanta: John Knox Press, 1981); Ernest Best, *One Body in Christ: A Study in the Relationship of the Church to Christ in the Epistles of the Apostle Paul* (London: SPCK, 1955); John Calvin, *Institutes of the Christian Religion*, 2 vols., trans. by Ford Lewis Battles, ed. by John T McNeill. (Philadelphia: Westminster, 1960); James Leo Garrett, *The Concept of the Believers' Church* (Scottdale, Pa.: Herald Press, 1969); William Robinson, *The Biblical Doctrine of the Church* (St. Louis: Bethany, 1948).

Ecuador

Ecuador became independent in 1830. By that time, Roman Catholicism had come to dominate, though the religions of the native peoples survived, especially in remote regions.

Protestantism first came in 1824 through James Thompson (1788–1854), the ubiquitous agent of the British and Foreign Bible Society. Permanent work had to wait until Ecuador repudiated its concordat with the Vatican. Three missionaries of the Gospel Missionary Union (GMU) arrived in 1896, joined the next year by representatives of the CHRISTIAN AND MISSIONARY ALLIANCE (CMA). The GMU work evolved into the Evangelical Missionary Union Church, the largest Protestant body in the country. In 1931, CMA layman Clarence Jones launched HCJB, the Voice of the Andes, the first religious radio station outside of the United States. The station, under the care of the independent World Radio Missionary Fellowship, now serves all of Latin America with programming in a number of languages.

Mainstream Protestant churches neglected Ecuador, resulting in its development as a bastion of EVANGELICALISM. PENTECOSTALISM has made headway, led by the ASSEMBLIES OF GOD, the INTERNATIONAL CHURCH OF THE FOURSQUARE GOSPEL, the CHURCH OF GOD (CLEVELAND, TENNESSEE), and the UNITED PENTECOSTAL CHURCH INTERNATIONAL. Ecuador has also been responsive to the efforts of the SEVENTH-DAY ADVENTIST CHURCH, the CHURCH OF JESUS CHRIST OF LATTER-DAY SAINTS, and the JEHOVAH'S WITNESSES, who are second in size only to the Evangelical Missionary Union Church among non-Catholics. Of the several indigenous churches, the Iglesia Independiente National, with more than 35,000 members, is the largest. In recognition of the maturing of the mission field, the early Inter-Mission Fellowship was replaced in 1965 by the Ecuador Evangelical Fellowship, now affiliated with the WORLD EVANGELICAL ALLIANCE.

In 1945, four of the older DENOMINATIONS (the Evangelical and Reformed Church, the United Brethren, the PRESBYTERIAN CHURCH USA, and the United Presbyterian Church) created a joint effort, the United Andean Indian Mission, now known as the United Evangelical Church of Ecuador; it remains a minuscule part of the Protestant scene.

See also SOUTH AMERICA.

Further reading: K. Carpenter, *Religion in Ecuador: From Paganism to Protestantism* (Minneapolis, Minn.: Bethany Theological Seminary, Th.D. diss., 1992); A. M. Goffin, *The Rise of Protestant Evangelism in Ecuador, 1895–1990* (Gainesville: University Press of Florida, 1994).

Ecumenical movement

The Ecumenical movement emerged early in the 20th century in an attempt to reverse the splintering of Protestantism into so many competing DENOMINATIONS. It has been a major force in Protestant church life ever since.

Protestantism began as a set of national churches representing Lutheran, Reformed, and Anglican approaches to the Christian faith, plus some smaller bodies that emerged from the RADICAL REFORMATION. The 17th-century Puritans added BAPTISTS, Congregationalists, and Presbyterians to the denominational mix in England, and later centuries saw the rise of Methodists, Adventists, various BRETHREN groups, HOLINESS churches, and several European FREE CHURCHES. Splintering of denominations occurred at an ever-increasing rate as religious liberty became a reality in Europe and North America.

As Protestantism spread globally in the 18th century, the denominational differences were carried to the mission field, where such differences seemed irrelevant, giving rise to calls for unity in the late 19th century. Various 19th-century revitalization movements had already denounced denominationalism, but their naive programs only resulted in still more new denominations.

A first step toward unity was taken in 1846 with the formation in Europe of the WORLD EVANGELICAL ALLIANCE. The alliance tried to unite individuals (as opposed to delegates from church bodies) around a core of Protestant beliefs, but the refusal of American attendees to allow a resolution barring slaveholders effectively blocked the formation of a single international body. The alliance became a loose fellowship of national organizations in England, CANADA, SWEDEN, INDIA and Turkey; it held several international conferences on missionary concerns.

Denominational leaders also launched efforts to create fellowship structures within denominational families. Reformed and Presbyterian leaders organized the Alliance of Reformed Churches in 1875, and the Methodists held the first Ecumenical Methodist Conference in 1881. Baptists held their first international gathering in London in 1905; Lutherans did the same in 1923. These initial efforts led to the present-day WORLD ALLIANCE OF REFORMED CHURCHES, WORLD METHODIST COUNCIL, BAPTIST WORLD ALLIANCE, and LUTHERAN WORLD FEDERATION, and similar bodies in other denominations.

The Federal Council of Churches was organized in the United States in 1908, when the United States had some 300 different Christian denominations, the largest number of any country. As the century progressed, other Western countries formed similar councils, and missionary councils were organized in countries around the world.

Many contemporary historians date the modern Ecumenical movement to the 1910 Missionary Conference at Edinburgh. The conference became a potent force in spreading the ecumenical ideal in the English-speaking world, at the time the backbone of the global missionary effort. The work at Edinburgh bore fruit with the formation of the LIFE AND WORK MOVEMENT, which concentrated on the church's interaction with society, and the FAITH AND ORDER MOVEMENT, which dealt with doctrine and church structure. The Life and Work movement held its first conference in Stockholm, Sweden, in 1925; it brought European church leaders outside the United Kingdom into prominent leadership roles, and it included Eastern Orthodox churches in the dialogue. Two years later, when the Faith and Order conference met in Lausanne, Switzerland, 108 church bodies were represented. Also emerging from Edinburgh was the INTERNATIONAL MISSIONARY COUNCIL in 1921.

During the same era, the Fundamentalist-Modernist controversy in the United States, focusing upon BIBLICAL CRITICISM, social ministries, and theological dissent, tended to work against unity. A number of denominations split, especially the Baptists and Presbyterians, and the more conservative denominations tended to reject cooperation with the more liberal ones that happened to dominate the ecumenical scene.

The WORLD COUNCIL OF CHURCHES (WCC) was formed after World War II, encompassing the Faith and Order and Life and Work movements and eventually including the International Missionary Council. It would soon grow to include most of the larger denominations in most countries of the world and take its place beside the Roman Catholic Church as an important voice of the Christian community.

The WCC wielded significant power in the international Protestant community. It played an important role in the transformation of missions into autonomous churches, but its primary effect was to encourage the merger of like-minded churches. Protestant mergers were already occurring; notable milestones were the formation of the UNITED CHURCH OF CANADA and the Church of South India. The merger forced on Protestant churches in Japan as World War II approached helped churches discover the many elements they had in common.

In the second half of the 20th century, numerous mergers occurred. A few managed to overcome denominational family lines, prominent being the United Church of Zambia (1965), the Church of North India (1970), the Church of Pakistan (1970), the Uniting Church in Australia (1977), and the United Protestant Church of Belgium (1978). More typical were the mergers that reunited churches within a single denominational family, such as the UNITED METHODIST CHURCH (1968), the United Reformed Church of the United Kingdom (1972), and the Uniting Reformed Church in South Africa (1994). By the

1980s, the goal of creating one united Protestant church was largely abandoned. Instead, the movement shifted energies toward improving relationships among denominations.

The two movements that emerged from the Fundamentalist-Modernist controversy in the United States—conservative EVANGELICALISM and conservative separatist FUNDAMENTALISM—both saw the value of cooperative ecumenical action and organization. The Fundamentalists organized first, creating the American Council of Christian Churches (ACCC) in 1941 to oppose the Federal Council of Churches. Under the guidance of its energetic leader, Presbyterian minister Carl McIntire (1906–2003), the ACCC took the lead in creating the INTERNATIONAL COUNCIL OF CHRISTIAN CHURCHES (ICCC).

American Evengelicals organized the National Association of Evengelicals (NAE) in 1942. It upheld conservative theological standards, but was willing to cooperate with Evangelicals who remained within the larger liberal denominations. In 1951, following the merger of the remnant of the American branch of the old Evengelical Alliance into the new National Council of Churches of Christ in the U.S.A., NAE leaders called a meeting in Europe that established the World Evangelical Fellowship (WEF). Though much smaller than the WCC, the WEF, now known as the World Evangelical Alliance (WEA), has created a global alternative to the WCC. In several countries, Evangelicalism has become the dominant segment of the Protestant community.

PENTECOSTALISM has always presented itself as a unifying movement with an emphasis on basic Protestant doctrines and the experience of the BAPTISM OF THE HOLY SPIRIT. Pentecostal leaders, however, found their message unacceptable to the older churches and were pushed into founding their own denominational bodies. Pentecostals were accepted into the NAE and later into the WEA.

As the CHARISMATIC MOVEMENT spread among older churches in the 1970s, several Pentecostal leaders, most prominently South African David du PLESSIS, began a long dialogue with the World Council of Churches. Simultaneously, ecumenical relationships were growing between Pentecostal churches. These efforts have led to regular World Pentecostal Conferences; as the new century began, the WORLD PENTECOSTAL FELLOWSHIP was formed.

Ecumenism has succeeded in raising the level of cordiality among the larger Protestant communities and among Protestant, Eastern Orthodox, and (since Vatican II) Roman Catholic churches. That cordiality finds expression in the WCC, its regional and national affiliate councils, and numerous local councils. It has significantly reduced the amount of polemics among Christian communities and created structures in which differences can be discussed. Those churches that do not feel able to cooperate with the WCC and its allies have been able to unite with the ICCC and the WEA and their cooperating regional and national organizations. In those denominational families that have split, a set of parallel denominational associations have arisen. For example, Lutherans who reject the Lutheran World Federation may join the INTERNATIONAL LUTHERAN COUNCIL and those from the Reformed tradition who reject the World Alliance of Reformed Churches may associate with the INTERNATIONAL ASSOCIATION OF REFORMED AND PRESBYTERIAN CHURCHES or the REFORMED ECUMENICAL COUNCIL.

Further reading: Michael Kinnamon and Brian Cope, eds., *The Ecumenical Movement: An Anthology of Key Texts and Voices* (Geneva: World Council of Churches, 1997); Nicholas Lossky, et al., eds., *Dictionary of the Ecumenical Movement* (Geneva: WCC Publications/Grand Rapids, Mich.: William B. Eerdmans, 1991); J. Gordon Melton, *Encyclopedia of American Religions,* 7th ed. (Detroit: Gale Research Company, 2002); Ans J. Van der Bent, ed. *Handbook/Member Churches/World Council of Churches* (Geneva: World Counci] of Churches, 1985); *Yearbook* (Geneva: World Council of Churches, issued annually).

Edict of Nantes

The Edict of Nantes, issued by King Henry IV in 1598, granted tolerance to Protestants in FRANCE. The Reformation in France grew in the 1550s and began to penetrate the ranks of the nobility, most significantly the Coligny family. However, under Francis II increasingly harsh measures were enacted to suppress the HUGUENOTS, as Protestants were termed in France. One edict in 1559, for example, decreed that houses in which unlawful (Protestant) assemblies were held would be leveled and those responsible executed. There was some relief during the reign of Charles IX, but for three decades France became embroiled in a series of civil wars. Each side scored significant victories at different times and places. The most horrendous incident was the notorious ST. BARTHOLOMEW'S DAY MASSACRE in 1572, when almost 100,000 Protestants were killed in one week; many others were imprisoned. Many survivors went into exile.

In 1598, King Henry IV issued the Edict of Nantes, which had the effect of granting French Protestants a high degree of toleration. Protestants allowed Catholics to repossess property they had lost and reestablish Catholicism in places that had been under Protestant control. The Huguenots were granted the right to practice their faith wherever they lived at that time and were allowed to attend state-owned universities and hold public office. The government granted them support out of the public treasury similar to that the Roman Catholics enjoyed. The edict brought most fighting to an end for a period, though a number of local conflicts over property and worship facilities ensued, and the Catholic Church did launch an aggressive proselytization campaign aimed at returning Protestants to the fold.

During the time of Cardinal Richelieu (who became prime minister in 1624), Hugenots found political access cut back, and they lost their right to hold public office. Their position then took a decided downturn under Louis XIV. In 1660, he forbade them to hold a national synod, the first of a set of orders that began to whittle away at the Edict of Nantes. In 1685, the Edit of Nantes was formally revoked. Protestants were barred from gathering for public worship, even in their homes. Protestant pastors were banished from France, and Protestant children ordered to be baptized as Catholics and sent to Catholic schools. A significant number of Protestants left the country; those who remained formed an underground movement that was strongest in the southern half of the country.

Over the next century, a more tolerant attitude grew among the public, and in 1787 a new Edict of Toleration granted non-Catholics the right to practice their faith unmolested. It included the right to be legally married before a magistrate and to have the births of children officially recorded. While not specifically part of the new edict, from that time Protestant churches were again open for public worship.

Further reading: Euan Cameron, *The European Reformation* (Oxford: Clarendon Press, 1991); Barbara B. Diefendorf, *Beneath the Cross: Catholics and Huguenots in Sixteenth-Century Paris* (New York/Oxford: Oxford University Press, 1991); Robert M. Kingdon, *Myths about the St. Bartholomew's Day Massacres, 1572–1576* (Cambridge, Mass.: Harvard University Press, 1988); George A. Rothrock, *The Huguenots: A Biography of a Minority* (Chicago: Nelson Hall, 1979).

Edward VI (1537–1553) *child king of England under whom Protestantism flourished*

The boy king (r. 1547–1553) who became the instrument of the Reformation in England, Edward VI, the son of HENRY VIII and his third wife, Jane Seymour, was born on October 12, 1537. He became king in 1547 at the age of nine.

The Council of Regency that ruled on Edward's behalf was dominated by Edward Seymour, duke of Somerset. Together with the Protestant-leaning archbishop Thomas CRANMER, Seymour worked to further the Reformation cause. He ordered a royal visitation of all the parishes, distributing to each priest a copy of Cranmer's Book of Homilies, Erasmus's Paraphrase of the New Testament, and most important, the new BOOK OF COMMON PRAYER written by Cranmer, which supplied an order of worship to replace the Roman Catholic Mass. Parliament repealed the Six Articles, Henry's Roman Catholic statement of belief, ordered all relics and images removed from parish sanctuaries, dropped rules on fasting, and released priests from their vows of celibacy. Cranmer recruited Protestant intellectuals from the Continent to take up residence at British universities. Their Calvinist beliefs influenced the Forty-two Articles issued by Cranmer toward the end of Edward's reign.

Edward died on July 6, 1553. His sister and successor, MARY I, systematically reversed all the Protestant reforms undertaken during his five-year reign.

Further reading: Arther G. Dickens, *The English Reformation,* rev. ed. (University Park: Pennsylvania State University Press, 1991); Christopher Haigh, *English Reformations: Religion, Politics, and Society under the Tudors* (New York: Oxford University Press, 1993); C. S. Knighton, ed. *Calendar of State Papers, Domestic Series Edward VI 1547–1553* (London: Public Record Office, 1992); Alison Weir, *The Children of Henry VIII* (New York: Ballantine Books, 1996).

Edwards, Jonathan (1703–1758)
American Congregational theologian and preacher
Jonathan Edwards was the greatest American theologian of his day. He is remembered for his theological writings and for his participation in and observations about the period of religious excitement known as the GREAT AWAKENING.

Edwards was born on October 5, 1703, in East Windsor, Connecticut. He entered Yale University at age 13; at 17 he moved to New York City to pastor a Presbyterian church. He came back to Yale in 1724 as a tutor, but illness forced his resignation. In 1729, Edwards became the pastor of the church in Northampton, Massachusetts, which his grandfather Solomon Stoddard (1643–1729) had led for many years.

In his preaching at Northampton, Edwards defended traditional Calvinist affirmations against growing dissent within the Congregational fellowship. He argued that faith implied a conversion of the heart away from sin; it was a total response of the heart to God, an experience of the divine that he likened in one of his most famous sermons, "A Divine and Supernatural Light," to the tongue's tasting honey.

Edwards's preaching was a catalyst for an outbreak of religious enthusiasm in the mid-1730s, which Edwards promoted, defended, and analyzed in his book *A Faithful Narrative of the Surprising Work of God* (1737). The book helped prepare the way for the EVANGELICAL AWAKENING that had come to America with George WHITEFIELD. Edwards continuing to write about the Great Awakening, which now spread to the whole of the American colonies, in three books: *The Distinguishing Marks of the Work of the Spirit of God* (1741), *Some Thoughts Concerning the Present Revival* (1743), and his classic study, *A Treatise Concerning Religious Affections* (1746).

In 1750, Edwards moved his family to Stockbridge, Massachusetts, and for the next seven years worked to evangelize the Native Americans in the area. In 1758, he was invited to head the new Presbyterian school at Princeton, but he died of smallpox a few months later, on March 22, 1758.

Edwards holds a unique position in American religious history. He stands at the beginning of the great tradition of Calvinist theological work that would flow from the Congregational and Presbyterian schools. He also represents the beginning of REVIVALISM, which became so much a part of the American Methodist and Baptist traditions. He has therefore been honored by both major branches of American Protestantism, those who followed CALVINISM and those who adhered to ARMINIANISM. Edwards's studies continue to thrive among American religious scholars.

See also POSTMILLENNIALISM.

Further reading: Leon Chai, *Jonathan Edwards and the Limits of Enlightenment Philosophy* (New York: Oxford University Press, 1998); Robert W. Jenson, *America's Theologian: A Recommendation of Jonathan Edwards* (New York: Oxford University Press, 1988); *The Life and Character of the Late Reverend Mr. Jonathan Edwards, President of the College at New Jersey. Together with a number of his sermons on various important subjects* (Boston: S. Kneeland, 1765); Gerald R. McDermott, *Jonathan Edwards Confronts the Gods: Christian Theology, Enlightenment Religion, and Non-Christian Faiths* (New York: Oxford University Press, 2000); Michael J. McClymond, *Encounters with God: An Approach to the Theology of Jonathan Edwards* (New York: Oxford University Press, 1998).

Egypt

Egypt, a majority Muslim country, is also home to two ancient Christian churches, the Coptic Orthodox Church and the Greek Orthodox Patriarchate of Alexandria and All Africa. Of approximately 9.5 million Christians in Egypt, more than 8.5 million are members of the Coptic Church.

Anglicans initiated activity early in the 19th century, but substantial Protestant work did not begin until 1854, when American representatives of the Associate Reformed Presbyterian Church began proselytizing Coptic Christians. Their efforts resulted in the founding of the Coptic Evangelical Church, now known as the Evangelical Church-Synod of the Nile. As in other Middle Eastern countries, Protestant growth has been at the expense of Orthodox churches rather than the Muslim community. The Evangelical Church split in 1869, with one offshoot now associated with the Exclusive Plymouth Brethren.

The Free Methodist Church began supporting missionaries in Egypt in 1899. Pentecostals made Egypt an early target; their work, now under the ASSEMBLIES OF GOD, dates to 1907. For most of the 20th century, missionary success has been largely limited to the expatriate communities. The government expelled foreign missionaries after the 1956 and 1967 wars, causing disruption and a transfer of control to local leadership.

The largest Protestant church by far is the Evangelical Church. The Assemblies of God is the only other group with more than 100,000 members. The Free Methodists and the Plymouth Brethren are also active. The Evangelical Church is a member of the WORLD COUNCIL OF CHURCHES, and cooperates with Anglican, Catholic, and Orthodox churches in the Middle East Council of Churches. Several churches have united in the Fellowship of Evangelicals of Egypt, which is affiliated with the WORLD EVANGELICAL ALLIANCE.

Further reading: Jean-Jacques Bauswein and Lukas Vischer, eds., *The Reformed Family Worldwide: A Survey of Reformed Churches, Theological Schools, and International Organizations* (Grand Rapids, Mich.: William B. Eerdmans, 1999); O. F. A. Meinardus, *Christian Egypt: Ancient and Modern* (Cairo: American University in Cairo Press, 1977).

elders

The office of presbyter, commonly translated as elder, appears in the New Testament church. In Acts 15 the elders meet with the apostles to make decisions. In Acts 14:23, Paul and Barnabas designate elders to lead each of the churches they organize. The biblical elder evolved into the ordained minister/priest over the next centuries. In the Catholic Church, three orders of ministry developed—deacon, elder or priest (which also derives from presbyter), and BISHOP.

The early Protestants went to the Bible to resolve questions over the nature and function of elders/ministers. They all agreed that the biblical elder and the common church minister were the same. In the Anglican Church, the elders/priests constituted the second order of ministry, below the bishops. American Methodists followed the Anglican structure by having a bishop, but for them a bishop was considered merely an elder with a different job assignment.

John CALVIN did away with the bishopric and proposed two orders of elders, the teaching elder (minister) and ruling elder (lay leader). Baptists also did away with bishops, but did not accept Calvin's distinction between elders. Ministers were the elders spoken of in the Scriptures. In most Protestant churches, the biblical elders are equated with modern ordained ministers. The more radical of modern groups have done away with the idea of ordained and/or salaried ministers and operate with a lay leadership entirely.

See also DEACONS.

Further reading: Eugene Carson Blake and Edward Burns Shaw, *Presbyterian Law for the Presbytery, a Manual for Ministers and Ruling Elders* (Philadelphia: Office of the General Assembly, 1959); Loren S. Bowman, *Power and Polity among the Brethren: A Study of Church Governance* (Elgin, Ill.: Brethren Press, 1987); John E. Harnish, *The Orders of Ministry in the United Methodist Church* (Nashville, Tenn.: Abingdon Press, 2000); Waymon D. Miller, *The Role of Elders in the New Testament Church* (Tulsa: Oklahoma Plaza Press, 1980); Alexander Strauch, *Biblical Eldership: An Urgent Call to Restore Biblical Church Leadership* (Littleton, Colo.: Lewis & Roth, 1995).

Elim Pentecostal Church

The Elim Pentecostal Church was one of the first Pentecostal church fellowships in the British Isles; it has now expanded to some 35 countries around the world. It was founded in Ireland in 1915 by Welsh-born revivalist George Jeffreys (1889–1962). At first an opponent of PENTECOSTALISM, Jeffreys received the BAPTISM OF THE HOLY SPIRIT and was ordained in 1912. He and his brother Stephen (1876–1943) evangelized for the new movement throughout the British Isles. George's revivals were known for the healings that occurred.

In 1915, George and a group of supporters in Ireland founded the Elim Pentecostal Alliance (later Church), and established the first congrega-

tion the next year in Belfast. A congregation was started in England in 1921, and the church grew rapidly thanks to Jeffreys's preaching. Though Jeffreys left the church in 1939 in a dispute over church POLITY, Elim continued to grow, with 500 new congregations by the end of the century.

In the 1920s, the church adopted the four-fold gospel concept of Albert Benjamin SIMPSON, as revised by American evangelist Aimee Semple MCPHERSON. The doctrine honored Christ as Savior, Healer, Baptizer in the Spirit, and coming King.

The church became international in 1920, when it sent missionaries to Africa. In 1934, the Jeffreys brothers preached successfully in SWITZERLAND, their efforts leading to the formation of the Eglise Evangélique du Réveil. Today, the Elim Church has affiliated bodies in some 35 countries. Its Bible college, originally founded in 1925, has become part of Nantwich-Regents Theological College, which has accredited status through Manchester University. It offers both B.A. and M.A. degrees.

In England, Elim is best known through its lead congregation, Kensington Temple in London. Elim was a founding member of the Pentecostal Churches of the United Kingdom, an alliance of the primary Trinitarian Pentecostal denominations in the country.

See also UNITED KINGDOM.

Further reading: E. C. W. Boulton, *George Jeffreys: A Ministry of the Miraculous,* 1928, rpt. (Ventura, Calif.: Gospel Light Publications, 1999); D. W. Cartwright, *The Great Evangelists—The Remarkable Lives of George & Stephen Jeffreys* (Basingstoke, U.K.: Marshall Pickering, 1986); W. J. Hollenweger, *The Pentecostals* (London: SCM, 1972).

Elizabeth I, Queen of England
(1533–1603) *consolidated the Church of England around the* via media

During her long reign (1558–1603), Elizabeth I consolidated the Protestant character of England. She refashioned the CHURCH OF ENGLAND as a compromise between Roman Catholic and Reformed practices; this Anglican VIA MEDIA (middle way) has persisted to the current day.

Elizabeth was born on September 7, 1533, the child of HENRY VIII and Anne Boleyn, the second of Henry's wives. Her mother's marriage was considered illegitimate by the pope. Elizabeth was three years old when Anne was beheaded.

Elizabeth inherited a country that was divided by fierce religious passions after the reigns of her siblings EDWARD VI and MARY I. She leaned toward Protestantism due to threats to her rule from Catholic SPAIN, FRANCE, and Scotland, but she wanted to reconcile her Catholic subjects at home as well. Her approach became known as the *via media,* or middle way. Following Henry's precedent she had herself named Supreme Governor of the Church of England. She modified some elements of the prayer book for the sake of Roman Catholics but not enough to prevent the Catholic BISHOPS from resigning. The very Protestant Forty-two Articles (of Religion) written by Thomas CRANMER were revised, and the resultant Thirty-nine Articles were adopted in 1563. They remain the doctrinal statement of the Anglican tradition.

Elizabeth was excommunicated by the pope after putting down a Catholic uprising in the north in 1569. She expelled the Jesuits in 1585 for encouraging her assassination. When Mary Queen of Scots was implicated in the so-called Babington conspiracy, Elizabeth had her executed in 1587. In 1588, Pope Sixtus V helped finance an armada of Spanish ships to crush England. The British defeated the Spanish Armada in 1588 to emerge as the world's greatest naval power.

Elizabeth faced opposition from some Protestants (mostly Presbyterians) as well. When they refused to wear priestly vestments, she had them removed from their parish posts. Presbyterians, BAPTISTS, and QUAKERS called for further purification of the Church of England. Puritan leaders opposed to a church led by bishops were arrested by Elizabeth. Some fled to the Netherlands, then the most religiously tolerant country in Europe.

Nevertheless, Elizabeth enjoyed broad popularity for establishing England as a leading world power. Her support for explorers such as Sir Francis Drake also set the stage for the global spread of the Church of England over the next centuries as England began to build a colonial empire.

See also UNITED KINGDOM.

Further reading: Carolly Erickson, *The First Elizabeth* (New York: St. Martin's Griffin, 1997); Richard L. Greaves, *Society and Religion in Elizabethan England* (Minneapolis: University of Minnesota Press, 1981); Leah Marcus, Janel Mueller, and Mary Beth Rose, eds., *Elizabeth I: Collected Works* (Chicago: University of Chicago Press, 2000); Susan Watkins, *In Public and Private: Elizabeth I and Her World* (London: Thames and Hudson, 1998); Neville Williams, *The Life & Times of Elizabeth I,* ed. by Antonia Fraser (London: Weidenfeld & Nicolson, 1972).

El Salvador

For more than 400 years, the Roman Catholic Church was the only Christian group operating in what is now El Salvador. Catholicism is still the religion of the large majority. Catholic hegemony was unchallenged until the end of the 19th century, with the arrival of representatives of the Central American Mission (now CAM International).

The beachhead established by the CAM missionaries was expanded by the California Friends Missions (1902), American Baptists (1911), and the SEVENTH-DAY ADVENTIST CHURCH (1915). They quickly won a substantial response among both the native population (descendants of the Aztec and Mayan peoples) and the *mestizos* (those of mixed Spanish and native lineage).

PENTECOSTALISM had a unique beginning in El Salvador. In 1904, an independent Canadian minister, Frederick Mebius, began a movement called the Apostolic Churches of the Apostles and Prophets, a non-Trinitarian Pentecostal church that preceded a similar movement in the United States. He founded several independent assemblies that later affiliated with the ASSEMBLIES OF

GOD when that church entered the country in 1929. The Assemblies of God was the first non-Catholic church to surpass 200,000 members. Large followings have also adhered to the Elim Christian Mission (a Pentecostal movement from GUATEMALA), the Church of the Prince of Peace (also from Guatemala), the Apostolic Church of the Apostles and Prophets, the CHURCH OF GOD (CLEVELAND, TENNESSEE), and the UNITED PENTECOSTAL CHURCH INTERNATIONAL. Pentecostalism has somewhat overwhelmed the original missionary efforts by the CAM and the Friends.

El Salvador has also seen steady work by the Seventh-day Adventists and newer work by the JEHOVAH'S WITNESSES and CHURCH OF JESUS CHRIST OF LATTER-DAY SAINTS. The older Protestant bodies are represented by several Baptist associations (the largest of which is affiliated with the National Baptist Convention, an African-American church) and the Evangelical Lutheran Church (based in Costa Rica).

While several of the churches operating in El Salvador (all based in other countries) are members of the WORLD COUNCIL OF CHURCHES, there is no local council of churches. Some of the conservative churches have joined together in the Confraternidad Evangélica Salvadorena affiliated with the WORLD EVANGELICAL ALLIANCE. It appears that more than 20 percent of the population adheres to one of the Protestant churches.

See also CENTRAL AMERICA.

Further reading: Clifton L. Holland, ed., *World Christianity: Central America and the Caribbean* (Monrovia, Calif.: MARC World Vision, 1981); Everett A. Wilson, "Sanguine Saints: Pentecostalism in El Salvador," *Church History* 52 (June 1983) 186–98.

Equatorial Guinea

Equatorial Guinea, a small West African country, is over 80 percent Roman Catholic as a result of two centuries of Spanish rule. Indigenous religions appear to be waging a losing battle for survival.

Presbyterians began work on the island of Corisco in 1858 and moved onto the mainland in the 1860s. Methodists arrived in 1870. The first substantial non-Catholic activity dates to the 1930s, when the Worldwide Evangelism Crusade (now WEC International) began to evangelize the Fang people, the largest native group in the country. The WEC, the Presbyterian Church, and the Methodists merged to form the Reformed Church of Equatorial Guinea. In the 1990s, the name was changed to the Council of Evangelical Churches in Equatorial Guinea. The council, currently the largest Protestant body, is a member of the WORLD COUNCIL OF CHURCHES.

Over the course of the 20th century, a spectrum of Protestant churches began work in the relatively small country. Of these, the German-based NEW APOSTOLIC CHURCH has had the most success, followed by the Free Protestant Episcopal Church, an import from NIGERIA and SIERRA LEONE, and the JEHOVAH'S WITNESSES; they are the only bodies with more than 2,000 members.

Further reading: David Barrett, *The Encyclopedia of World Christianity,* 2nd ed. (New York: Oxford University Press, 2001); Jean-Jacques Bauswein and Lukas Vischer, eds., *The Reformed Family Worldwide: A Survey of Reformed Churches, Theological Schools, and International Organizations* (Grand Rapids, Mich.: William B. Eerdmans, 1999).

Erasmus, Desiderius (1466–1536)
humanist philosopher and supporter of moderate reform

One of the most respected philosophers and scholars of his era and the greatest exponent of HUMANISM, Erasmus helped refine some of the ideas and approaches that led to the emergence of the Protestant faiths. However, he also became a powerful intellectual opponent of Martin LUTHER and worked hard to prevent the religious schisms and wars that accompanied the Reformation.

Erasmus was born in Rotterdam, the Netherlands, around 1466. At the age of nine, he was sent to a school at Deventer run by the humanist Hegius. Humanism was a movement that placed secular studies (the humanities) on a par with theology, focusing on the recovery of classical Greek and Latin learning. Most humanists celebrated the critical spirit, believing that educated individuals could use reason to improve their world, even to reform church and society.

Erasmus was spurred by poverty to enter a monastic order in 1486 as the only way to pursue his studies. From 1491, he served as secretary of the bishop of Cambrai, who paid for his education at the University of Paris and allowed him to travel. John Colet of Oxford introduced him to Bible study as a means of reconciling faith to his humanistic learning.

His first major work was the "Enchiridion militis christiani" of 1502, which explored true religion and piety while aiming some biting criticism at the church. His satirical *The Praise of Folly* (1509) was also filled with critical comments on ecclesiastical life. Originally meant for limited private circulation, it was quickly reprinted and made Erasmus famous. He subsequently carried on a vast correspondence with intellectuals across the Continent.

Among his many works, he is most remembered for his scholarly edition of the Greek New Testament, "Novum Instrumentum omne," published in Basle in 1516. It included a new, more accurate Latin translation, which he hoped would replace the Vulgate version then in use. His text later became the standard for Protestants trying to learn the authentic sources of Christianity. His elevation of Scripture to greater authority than theological tradition also influenced Protestant thought. Furthermore, he believed that individuals could interpret the Scriptures on their own. He discounted the value of pilgrimages, the veneration of saints, celibacy, and religious orders.

Though his ideas might be seen as putting him in the Protestant camp, he argued for limited, gradual reform that would not antagonize the church leadership. Nevertheless, he opposed Luther's excommunication, and suggested that a panel of scholars be established to mediate his disagreements with the church. When he was attacked by Catholics, he argued that while he was against church abuses, he had always adhered to orthodox teachings and the authority of the pope.

In 1524, Erasmus criticized Luther for disparaging free will, thus beginning a series of polemics both public and private between the two. After his break with Luther, some Roman Catholics welcomed him as a friend of the church, while others distrusted him. Pope Paul III offered him a cardinal's hat, but Erasmus refused, citing old age. He died on July 12, 1536.

Erasmus devoted years to the preparation of improved editions of the classics and the writings of the ancient Church Fathers—Irenæus, Ambrose, Augustine, Epiphanius, and Chrysostom. He also authored a number of theological works. A biography and complete edition of Erasmus's works was issued in 1540–41. However, in 1559 his works were placed on the Index of Forbidden Books by the Council of Trent. His reputation was revived in the 18th century, and later historians came to view him as a major intellectual source for the Reformation.

See also BIBLE TRANSLATIONS.

Further reading: Cornelius Augustijn, *Erasmus: His Life, Works, and Influence,* trans., G. C. Grayson (Toronto: University of Toronto Press, 1991); Léon-E. Halkin, *Erasmus: A Critical Biography* (Cambridge, Mass.: Blackwell, 1993); James McConica, *Erasmus,* Past Masters Series (New York: Oxford University Press, 1991); Alister E. McGrath, *The Intellectual Origins of the European Reformation* (Cambridge, Mass.: Blackwell, 1986).

Eritrea

Eritrea gained its independence from Ethiopia in 1993. Most of the population is divided equally between Islam and the Ethiopian Orthodox Church.

As early as 1866, the Swedish Evangelical Mission opened work among the Kunama. They were later joined by the Swedish Mission of True Bible Friends; the two missions continue today as the Evangelical Church of Eritrea and the Lutheran Church of Eritrea, respectively. Ethiopia also received Lutheran missionaries from Germany, the other Scandinavian countries, and the United

States. The scattered and competing efforts united in 1959 as the Ethiopian Evangelical Church Mekane Yesus. With approximately 15,000 members, the three Lutheran churches account for the bulk of Eritrea's Protestants.

Further reading: J. S. Trimingham, *The Christian Church and Mission in Ethiopia* (London: World Dominion Press, 1950).

eschatology

Eschatology is the part of theology that deals with last things, including the future destiny of humankind both individually and collectively. On the individual level, it treats life after death, heaven and hell. On the collective level, it treats the coming kingdom of God and the transformation and/or transcendence of the present historical context. Protestant eschatology concerning the destiny of humankind has centered upon the idea of the Millennium, the thousand-year reign of Christ mentioned in Revelation 20:6.

At the time of the Reformation, the position known as AMILLENNIALISM was the dominant view. Amillennialism approached the kingdom of God in an allegorical sense. The kingdom was inaugurated during Christ's earthly ministry and will continue into the foreseeable future. At some unknowable future point, Christ will return, and the fullness of the kingdom will be inaugurated. Martin LUTHER and John CALVIN inherited this view and passed it along to the Lutheran and Reformed church movements. It continues to be the dominant view in Protestant circles.

POSTMILLENNIALISM emerged in the 18th century. While amillennialism sees an ongoing conflict between good and evil until the end of this age, postmillennialism sees the gradual triumph of Christianity and the development of a more righteous society progressing into the millennial age. Among its champions were Jonathan EDWARDS and evangelist Charles G. FINNEY. Its optimism was severely challenged by the horror of the American Civil War and World Wars I and II,

but it has survived in the SOCIAL GOSPEL and the more recent movement called Christian reconstructionism.

A third view came into prominence in the 19th century among conservative Protestants—PREMILLENNIALISM. Premillennialists suggest that Christ will return at the end of this church age, which they generally hold is imminent, and establish his millennial kingdom. They have developed rather detailed pictures of future events. Premillennialist views have been especially identified with DISPENSATIONALISM. Dispensationalists view history as divided into a set of periods in each of which God has made specific demands. This present dispensation, the dispensation of Grace, is the sixth such period; it will soon end with a period of Intense Tribulation to be followed by the seventh dispensation, the Millennium.

Within liberal Protestantism, eschatology became a hotly contested issue in the 20th century, beginning with a renewed emphasis upon the kingdom of God as seen in the ministry and message of Jesus. The kingdom of God was identified variously as a more just and loving social system (as in the Social Gospel) or an individual appropriation of the Gospel message. In recent decades, eschatological speculations have centered on a new appreciation of Christian hope, notably in the writings of German theologian Jürgen Moltmann.

See also APOCALYPTISM.

Further reading: R. H. Charles, *A Critical History of the Doctrine of a Future Life* (London: Adam & Charles Black, 1899); Mal Couch, ed., *Dictionary of Premillennial Theology* (Grand Rapids, Mich.: Kregal, 1996); Millard J. Erickson, *A Basic Guide to Eschatology: Making Sense of the Millennium* (Grand Rapids, Mich.: Baker Book House, 1998); Stanley J. Grenz, *The Millennial Maze: Sorting Out Evangelical Options* (Downers Grove, Ill.: InterVarsity Press, 1992); Jon R. Stone, *A Guide to the End of the World: Popular Eschatology in America: The Mainstream Evangelical Tradition* (New York: Garland, 1993).

Estonia

The Roman Catholic Church became the dominant force in Estonia between the 10th and the 13th centuries, though the Eastern Orthodox presence is almost as ancient.

Estonia's geographical position near Germany ensured that Lutheranism would spread there. From its introduction in 1524, it quickly became the dominant faith. The subsequent publication of an Estonian prayer book (1535), catechism (1535), and Bible (1539) helped establish the country's national identity and culture. Lutheranism remained dominant until World War II, though its role was challenged in the 19th century by Baptists, the Seventh-day Adventist Church, the Methodist Episcopal Church, and Pentecostals.

Estonia was incorporated into the Russian Empire in the 18th century. The collapse of the empire in 1917 occasioned the formal organization of the Estonian Evangelical Lutheran Church. Russia retook the country in 1940 and kept it after German occupation during World War II. The Soviet government banned the Jehovah's Witnesses, and it forced the various Free Churches—Pentecostal, Baptist, independent Evangelical, and so forth—to merge into a single Union of Baptist and Evangelical Christians. The activity of all Christian groups was severely curtailed.

By 1939, about 20 percent of Lutheran pastors (who were of German ancestry) had moved to Germany. Other Lutheran pastors were among the 70,000 Estonians who fled to the West before the returning Russian army. Expatriate Estonians residing in Sweden formed the Estonian Evangelical Lutheran Church Abroad. Though now realigned with its parent body, it remains a separate organization.

Since independence in 1991, the Lutheran Church has remained the largest ecclesiastical body, though supported by only 16 percent of the population. Its main competitor is Estonian Orthodoxy, now divided into two rival churches. All the older churches have reasserted their presence, though none claim as much as 1 percent of the population.

The Methodists, now an integral part of the international United Methodist Church, have experienced a resurgence, and in 1994 opened a new mission center and seminary in Tallin.

See also Baltic states.

Further reading: Ilmo Au and Ringo Ringvee, *Kirikud ja kogudused Eestis* (Tallin, Estonia: Ilo, 2000); *We Bless You from the House of the Lord. The Estonian Evangelical Lutheran Church Today* (Tallin, Estonia: Consistory of the EELC, 1997).

Evangelical Awakening

The Evangelical Awakening was a burst of religious fervor that emerged in the 1730s, generally focused in the Methodist movement that permeated England in the following two decades. The Awakening can be traced to the spread of Pietism late in the 17th century from its center at the University of Halle in Germany. Making common cause with the Pietists were the Moravian Church followers at Herrnhut. Pietism promoted personal religion and a life of devotion and charity.

In England and the American colonies, Pietism became a mass movement through the efforts of Moravian missionaries, the preaching of Jonathan Edwards, the travels of George Whitefield, and the development of the Methodist movement by John Wesley and his brother Charles. Hymnody was a significant part of the Awakening; it had been passed from the Moravians to Charles Wesley and Whitefield.

The Awakening in the American colonies (generally called the first Great Awakening) was absorbed by the existing churches. In England, it led to the formation of the Wesleyan Connexion, led for many years by the long-lived John Wesley, and to several Calvinist Methodist churches overseen by Whitefield and now part of the United Reformed Church in the United Kingdom. Methodist global missionary work may be seen as the most significant long-term result of the Evangelical Awakening.

See also revivalism.

Further reading: Edwin Scott Gaustad, *The Great Awakening in New England* (New York: Harper & Brothers, 1957); William Warren Sweet, *Religion in Colonial America* (New York: Scribner, 1951); W. Reginald Ward, *The Protestant Evangelical Awakening* (New York: Cambridge University Press, 1992).

Evangelical Church in Germany

The Evangelical Church in Germany, by far the largest Protestant church in the country, embodies the legacy of Martin LUTHER, tracing its roots to the very beginning of the Reformation in 1517.

Most of the early German Protestants attended one of a large number of state churches that were gradually brought together as Germany united. Eventually, 24 Protestant state churches came into being, one for each of the 24 states that currently constitute the Federal German Republic. The orientation was primarily Lutheran, with some admixture of Reformed ideas that came into Germany along with supporters of John CALVIN of Geneva.

In 1613, the ruler of Prussia adopted the Reformed faith, and a number Reformed congregations were organized, some of them made up of French Protestants fleeing persecution. In 1817, the Prussian king forced a merger of the Reformed and Lutheran churches into what became known as the Evangelical Church. In the state of Lippe, the Reformed church became the dominant body.

In 1918, SEPARATION OF CHURCH AND STATE was proclaimed, and authority over the established churches passed from political rulers to synods in each church. All 24 autonomous churches, the majority of them Lutheran and a minority Reformed, adopted new constitutions. They also continued to receive financial support from the government. Four years later, they banded together into the German Evangelical Church Federation. The preexisting German Evangelical Lutheran Conference continued to manage relationships with other Lutheran churches around the world.

One force uniting the German churches was the missionary work performed by several agencies that arose in the 19th century. Among the most productive were the Leipzig, Gossmer, and North German missionary societies, the RHENISH MISSION, and the Bethel Mission. In 1971, the latter two merged to form the United Evangelical Mission-Community of Churches on Three Continents.

The rise of Nazism in the 1930s split the leadership between those more or less supportive of the government and the Confessing Church that opposed Nazism. Church leaders who supported the government worked to create a united German Evangelical Church. World War II left the German church in disarray. The surviving leadership of the Confessing Church, most notably Pastor Martin NIEMOLLER, emerged to lead in the formation of a reorganized Evangelical Church in Germany. Within that church, the Lutheran majority formed a fellowship, the United Evangelical Lutheran Church of Germany.

When Germany divided into two hostile states in the 1940s, both the Evangelical Church and the Lutheran fellowship split along national boundaries. These two factions were reunited following the country's unification in 1990.

Today, the Evangelical Church in Germany exists as a federation of the 24 autonomous churches, each of which has considerable latitude in doctrine, administration, and local programming. The national church carries out a variety of functions, especially the representation of the churches within various ecumenical bodies such as the WORLD COUNCIL OF CHURCHES, the LUTHERAN WORLD FEDERATION, and the WORLD ALLIANCE OF REFORMED CHURCHES.

The Evangelical Church in Germany has approximately 27 million members. Its member churches are the parents of a number of German Lutheran, Reformed, and Evangelical (united Lutheran/Reformed) churches around the world. Among these are the UNITED CHURCH OF CHRIST (USA), which includes within it the former Evangelical and Reformed Church.

Further reading: E. Theodore Bachmann and Mercia Brenne Bachmann, *Lutheran Churches in the World: A Handbook* (Minneapolis, Minn.: Augsburg Press,

1989); Jean-Jacques Bauswein and Lukas Vischer, eds., *The Reformed Family Worldwide: A Survey of Reformed Churches, Theological Schools, and International Organizations* (Grand Rapids, Mich.: William B. Eerdmans, 1999).

Evangelicalism

Evangelicalism is a stream that emerged among conservative Protestants in the United States in the 1940s who opposed the modernism that prevailed in many older churches but refused to join Fundamentalists in separating themselves from the larger Protestant world.

In the 1940s, conservative leaders in the American (and to a lesser extent Canadian) Protestant community, most of whom belonged to Presbyterian, Baptist, and Congregationalist churches, divided into two groups. One group demanded that all conservatives separate themselves from liberal Protestants and refuse to cooperate with liberal churches, ministers, or members. These separatists formed the core of the Fundamentalist community.

A second group, who also had left the liberal DENOMINATIONS, did not wish to withdraw from the wider Protestant culture and intellectual world, and wanted to maintain ties with conservatives who still remained members of those denominations. They hoped to build a large coalition including denominations committed to traditional Christian affirmations as well as individuals and churches within more liberal denominations who shared their conservative faith. They wanted to be

Wheaton College, Wheaton, Illinois, a bastion of Evangelicalism in the Midwest *(Institute for the Study of American Religion, Santa Barbara, California)*

aggressively evangelistic and keep a global perspective. This group came to be known as Evangelicals; they followed a path distinct from both Modernism and FUNDAMENTALISM.

Evangelicalism did not break with Fundamentalism over doctrine. Both groups continued to find common ground in the doctrines of biblical authority, the Trinity, the deity of Christ, sinful humanity in need of salvation through faith, and holy living. Both saw a miraculous element in Christianity symbolized in the virgin birth, and both talked of God's intervention in human affairs, often in answer to prayer. Both opposed textual BIBLICAL CRITICISM and biological evolution, though many Evangelicals came to a limited accommodation with both ideas. Both groups upheld the INERRANCY and infallibility of the Bible, language developed at Princeton Theological Seminary in the 19th century. Evangelicals would later accommodate conservatives who acknowledged the authority of the Bible but were uncomfortable with the particular formulations of the Princeton theology.

Evangelicalism coalesced in the 1940s around several structures, most notably the National Association of Evangelicals. The association welcomed Evangelical denominations as well as congregations, ministers, and individuals of Evangelical perspective in other churches. The Fuller Theological Seminary was founded in Pasadena, California, in 1947 to train Evangelical ministers. Conservative scholars formed the Evangelical Theological Society in 1949, and a national voice was launched with the first issue of *Christianity Today* in 1956. A key role was played by one individual, evangelist Billy GRAHAM, who led the way in creating broad-based Evangelical coalitions first in North America and later around the world.

The first generation of Evangelicalism concentrated on building structures to make up for the loss of access to seminaries, mission boards, and parachurch organizations. By the 1970s the movement had become a significant force in American religious life. Institutionally, Evangelicalism's

broad coalition included not only Presbyterian, Baptist, and Congregational churches, but conservatives in African American churches, churches with roots in the Radical Reformation such as Mennonites and Brethren, Wesleyan Holiness churches, and most importantly, Pentecostal churches.

Evangelicals, unlike the liberal Protestant churches, saw the potential of RELIGIOUS BROADCASTING. Leading the way were Pentecostal healing evangelist Oral ROBERTS (b. 1918) and Billy Graham (b. 1918). In the 1960s, Pat Robertson (b. 1930) founded the Christian Broadcasting Network (CBN) to provide a full day of Evangelical programming. CBN would later be joined by the Trinity Broadcasting Network.

A certain distaste of centralized authority has made for a very decentralized movement built around a number of independent organizations, each performing one or more of the tasks previously assumed by the large denominational apparatuses in other churches. PARACHURCH ORGANIZATIONS support missionaries, provide Christian higher education, publish Evangelical materials, and advocate various social causes. Among the more important new parachurch organizations were CAMPUS CRUSADE FOR CHRIST, WORLD VISION, and Focus on the Family.

Evangelicalism sought to enter national debates on issues of primary importance to them, such as U.S. Supreme Court decisions abolishing prayer in public schools (1963) and allowing abortion (1973). A major step in mobilizing conservative Christians, both Evangelicals and Fundamentalists, was taken in 1979 with the formation of the Moral Majority, which worked on the 1980 presidential campaign that swept Ronald Reagan into the White House. In the process, Evangelical political activists came to be identified with the Republican Party, which was seen as supportive of Evangelical perspectives on public acknowledgment of God and opposition to abortion and to the extension of rights to the homosexual community. The coalition of Evangelicals and conservative politicians was labeled the radical right by its critics. The Christian Coalition, founded in 1989 by Pat Robertson superseded the Moral Majority in the 1990s as the primary organization articulating the conservative Christian political agenda.

Evangelicals have also focused upon world evangelism, often with the belief that the larger denominations had redefined missions as mere social work. Many older missionary parachurch organizations came to identify with the Evangelical cause, and many new missionary organizations were formed. The issues that led to the emergence of the American Evangelical community took on a global aspect as Evangelicals around the world critiqued the WORLD COUNCIL OF CHURCHES. In many countries, the more conservative churches separated from their liberal sister communities and reorganized as Evangelicals, and countrywide alliances were formed that affiliated with the WORLD EVANGELICAL ALLIANCE, an Evangelical counterpart of the World Council of Churches (WCC). While still far smaller than the WCC, the alliance is growing at a rapid rate.

By the end of the 20th century, Evangelicals had emerged as the second force beside liberal Protestantism as a voice of American Protestantism. As it has grown, it has become a much more diverse community, welcoming variant interpretations of the core beliefs it was created to defend.

Further reading: Randall Balmer, *Encyclopedia of Evangelicalism* (Louisville, Ky.: Westminister John Knox Press, 2002); Mark Ellinsen, *The Evangelical Movement: Growth, Impact, Controversy, Dialog* (Minneapolis, Minn.: Augsburg Press, 1988); George Marsden, ed., *Evangelicalism and Modern America* (Grand Rapids, Mich.: William B. Eerdmans, 1984); Mark A. Shibley, *Resurgent Evangelicalism in the United States: Mapping Cultural Change since 1970* (Columbia: University of South Carolina Press, 1996); Glen H. Utter and John W. Storey, *The Religious Right* (Santa Barbara, Calif.: ABC-CLIO, 2001); David F. Wells and John D. Woodbridge, *The Evangelicals: What They Believe, Who They Are,* *Where They Are Changing* (Nashville, Tenn.: Abingdon, 1975).

excommunication

Excommunication is the action of a church to deny spiritual benefits to a member, often including its sacramental offices such as the LORD'S SUPPER and last rites. The excommunicated person is also barred from participation in the church's fellowship (disfellowshipping). When church membership was universal, excommunication carried much more serious consequences than it does in religiously pluralistic societies.

Excommunication usually requires a judicial process, which varies widely from church to church, to determine whether the person has broken a church law or refused to participate in the judicial process itself. The act of excommunication aims to limit the person's negative influence among the membership and tries to elicit repentance, which will allow the ultimate restoration of communion.

Excommunication played an important role in transforming Protestantism from an attempt to reform the Roman Catholic Church into a separate movement consisting of different denominations. The pope excommunicated Martin LUTHER in 1521, and the weapon was used against other reformers and their supporters.

Among the Radical Reformers, who were attempting to build a small disciplined fellowship without state support, excommunication (often called SHUNNING or banning) became a major means of maintaining order and calling straying members back to the fold. Excommunication was imposed at the family level and often led to the alienation of a member from a believing spouse.

Further reading: Francis Edward Hyland, *Excommunication: Its Nature, Historical Development and Effects* (Washington, D.C.: Catholic University of America, 1928); Jung-Sook Lee, *Excommunication and Restoration in Calvin's Geneva, 1555–1556* (Princeton, N.J.: Princeton Theological Seminary, Ph. D. diss., 1997);

The Order of Excommunication and Public Repentance (Church of Scotland, 1569; rpt., Dallas, Tex: Presbyterian Heritage Publications, 1993); Ulrich Stadler, "Cherished Instructions on Sin, Excommunication, and the Community of Goods (c. 1537)," in George H. Williams, ed., *Spiritual and Anabaptist Writers: Documents Illustrative of the Radical Reformation.* (Philadelphia: Westminster Press, 1957), 274–84; Elizabeth Vodola, *Excommunication in the Middle Ages* (Berkeley: University of California Press, 1986).

exhorter

The exhorter was an unordained lay preacher. The office appears in the MORAVIAN CHURCH but found its greatest use among 19th-century Methodists. Methodist founder John WESLEY, who had been ordained in the CHURCH OF ENGLAND, was reluctant to assume the office of BISHOP or ordain any of his assistants. Instead, they remained unordained lay preachers; such preachers helped build METHODISM into a large, vibrant movement. Eventually, ministers were ordained, often traveling between churches, but Methodism still had more congregations than ministers, and churches where ministers were stationed often had more services than one person could lead.

To meet this need, American Methodists developed the office of licensed lay preacher or exhorter. An exhorter supplied continuous leadership to a congregation during the frequent absences (and changes) of the ordained minister. If a traveling ordained minister delivered one of his stock sermons on general themes, the exhorter was expected to speak after the minister and apply the message to the particular local situation and audience.

From its founding until the Civil War, the Methodist Episcopal Church (and after 1845, the Methodist Episcopal Church, South) generally refused to ordain African Americans, and most of the few blacks who were ordained left to found independent churches. The churches were, however, quite willing to give exhorters' licenses to black men, many of whom became the virtual preachers in charge of predominantly black congregations.

In the 20th century, the office of licensed preacher continued in Methodism, in both the United Methodist Church and a number of its offshoots. However, it is usually held as a first step for young ministers on their way to the ordained ministry.

Further reading: Nolan B. Harmon, *Encyclopedia of World Methodism,* 2 vols. (Nashville, Tenn.: United Methodist Publishing House, 1974).

exorcism

Exorcism is the act of freeing persons from the influence of, or possession by, what are believed to be demons or evil spirits. It played almost no role in the Protestant movement until the emergence of PENTECOSTALISM in the 19th century; the practice has subsequently attracted increased interest in those circles, especially in the missionary field.

The Bible depicts various cases of exorcism, most clearly in the ministry of Jesus (Matthew 8:28–34) and the apostles (Acts 16: 16–18). In the Roman Catholic Church, acts of exorcism were included in the ministrations leading to the BAPTISM of a new member. One of the offices to which a priest is ordained is that of exorcist; however, over the centuries, the ministry to people who exhibited behaviors ascribed to evil spirits became restricted to BISHOPS or to specially designated priests appointed by bishops.

Martin LUTHER kept some abbreviated references to exorcism in the baptismal rite, but in the 17th century they fell into disuse. Reformed and Radical Reformation churches discarded such references from the beginning. They were also dropped by Anglicans.

Under the impact of rationalism, the belief in demons and the practice of exorcism slowly withered away, though in the 20th century they have made significant return. Exorcism has reemerged in the context of literal biblical interpretation, belief in God's intervention in worldly affairs in answer to prayer, and belief in a personal devil and his demonic domain. Over the centuries many missionaries came to see the deities of the people whom they hoped to evangelize as demons, a view that provided an excuse to destroy non-Christian places of worship.

Exorcisms cropped up very early in the history of the Pentecostal movement; its practice increased steadily through the 20th century, especially on the mission field, where it was seen as a valuable tool in the expansion of the church into "areas of darkness." In the last generation, via the CHARISMATIC MOVEMENT, exorcism has been placed in the context of SPIRITUAL WARFARE. A number of "deliverance" ministries have been created that specialize in casting out demons. They point to Mark 16:17, where Jesus tells his disciples to preach the Gospel around the world, and says that the casting out of demons will be a sign of their work.

Most Pentecostals/Charismatics assume that a believer who has been baptized and filled with the spirit cannot be possessed by a demon, yet they can still be harassed or victimized by demon obsession or oppression. They often assume that nonbelievers are demon possessed; some observers of the mission field credit exorcisms as a key element in the rapid spread of Pentecostalism in developing countries.

Pentecostal churches vary widely in the incidence of exorcism and demonic possession. In some, it is almost absent, in others, an occasional presence. Some groups invite specialized deliverance evangelists as guests to their congregations. In a few churches, the issue plays a central role.

Further reading: George A. Birch, *The Deliverance Ministry* (Camp Hill, Pa.: Horizon House, 1988); Noel Gibson and Phyl Gibson, *Evicting Demonic Intruders and Breaking Bondages* (Chichester, U.K.: New Wine, 1993); Michael Green, *I Believe in Satan's Downfall* (Grand Rapids, Mich.: William B. Eerdmans, 1981); Derek Prince, *They Shall Expel Demons: What You Need to Know about Demons—Your Invisible Enemy* (Grand Rapids, Mich.: Chosen Book, 1998); Swartley Willard Swartley, *Essays on Spiritual Bondage and Deliverance* (Elkhart, Ind.: Institute of Mennonite Studies, 1988).

F

Faith and Order movement

The Faith and Order movement has been one of the most diverse ongoing church dialogues in the 20th century, with significant participation from Protestant, Catholic, and Orthodox churches. A permanent commission (now part of the WORLD COUNCIL OF CHURCHES) and conferences have dealt with both theological issues and questions of church structure and polity.

In 1910, the convention of the Episcopal Church (in the United States) issued a call for a commission across church boundaries to consider questions of "Faith and Order." Such a commission would facilitate theological dialogue as a means of overcoming the differences that had historically divided Protestants into many denominations. After other churches passed similar resolutions, a commission was selected to plan an international conference. World War I intervened, and the conference was not held until 1920.

Some 80 churches were represented at the 1920 meeting in Geneva, each presenting its own vision of church unity. A continuation committee was established to plan for the next meeting, which occurred in 1927, at which some 400 participants represented Eastern Orthodox churches and a wide spectrum of Protestant bodies. Charles

H. Brent (1862–1929), the key person nurturing the process, presided.

The 1927 conference and a subsequent conference in 1937 discussed how to reach agreements on the issue of church union, and spotlighted areas of most profound disagreement. The 1937 conference also agreed to a proposal for union with the LIFE AND WORK MOVEMENT, which eventually led to the creation of the World Council of Churches in 1948. The Faith and Order concerns were carried forth after 1948 by a commission within the World Council.

The Faith and Order Commission has debated the issues of the SACRAMENTS, the ordained ministry, the nature of the church, the nature and role of Scripture, and controversial questions such as the ordination of WOMEN. The work of the commission has helped build respect between communions though differences remain. It has also nurtured the establishment of more formal fellowship among closely related groups within the council.

Like the ECUMENICAL MOVEMENT with which it overlaps, the Faith and Order movement began with the hope that its efforts would lead to the emergence of a united church, at the very least a united Protestant church. To date, that goal has had only moderate success, most notably in INDIA,

AUSTRALIA, and SOUTH AFRICA. Denominational differences seem important to the way people express their life in the church. The movement has also had to contend with the celebration of diversity by the world's different peoples and the assertion of national rights in the former European colonies. Throughout the 20th century, the multiplication of Protestant DENOMINATIONS became a new challenge to any attempts at unity.

Further reading: Ruth Rouse and Stephen Neill, eds., *A History of the Ecumenical Movement, 1517–1948* (Geneva: World Council of Churches, 1986); John E. Skoglund and J. Robert Nelson, *Fifty Years of Faith and Order: An Interpretation of the Faith and Order Movement* (New York: Committee for the Interseminary Movement of the National Student Christian Federation, 1963); Lukas Vischer, ed., *A Documentary History of the Faith and Order Movement, 1927–1963* (St. Louis: Bethany, 1963)

faith missions

The global missionary agencies that emerged in the last half of the 19th century to serve the expanding Protestant community across denominational lines were called faith missions. By keeping their focus on the essentials of Protestantism, they were able to draw support from people in different churches who shared a common interest in a particular region of the world. They also tried to avoid exporting European and American denominational issues to other continents.

The term *faith mission* derived in large part from the approach used by Hudson TAYLOR (1832–1905), founder of the CHINA INLAND MISSION. With faith that God would provide the needed resources, he never solicited funds and did not guarantee salaries for missionaries, who had to live off whatever they received.

Faith missions arose at a time when the model of centrally structured denominations was losing favor with many new church movements. Only limited structures for fellowship were allowed by the Plymouth BRETHREN, the RESTORATION MOVE-

MENT (the Churches of Christ, the Disciples of Christ, and the Churches of Christ and Christian Churches), and many Baptist groups; the absence of central bodies created a need for specialized mission societies. In addition, in the years between the American Civil War and World War II, HOLINESS churches and Pentecostal churches with a missionary zeal emerged faster than denominational organizations could respond; both movements spawned independent agencies to structure their missionary imperative.

One of the first faith missions was the CHRISTIAN AND MISSIONARY ALLIANCE (1887), which would not be the last missionary agency that began as an interdenominational work and later evolved into a new denomination. Some of the later interdenominational missions pioneered heretofore neglected fields—the AFRICA EVANGELICAL FELLOWSHIP (1889), the Arabian Mission led by Samuel M. ZWEMER (1890), the SUDAN INTERIOR MISSION (1893), and the Africa Inland Mission (now the AFRICA INLAND CHURCH) (1895). At the same time, new agencies facilitated missions for the Holiness churches, the ORIENTAL MISSION SOCIETY (1901) being the most successful. As early as 1909, Pentecostals in Great Britain and the United States formed two missionary organizations, both named the Pentecostal Missionary Union (PMU). The short-lived American PMU was followed by such agencies as the Pentecostal Mission in South and Central Africa (1910) and the Russian and Eastern European Mission (1927).

Charismatic evangelist Dwight L. MOODY played a major role in energizing support for such activity. Moody's student Frederik Franson founded THE EVANGELICAL ALLIANCE MISSION (TEAM) in 1990. Possibly the most important organization initiated and nurtured by Moody was the Student Volunteer Movement (SVM), which began in 1888 at a student conference held at Moody's Northfield, Massachusetts, headquarters. SVM would mobilize thousands of young adults to missionary service, including such notables as John R. MOTT, Robert E. SPEER, and Samuel Zwemer.

In 1917, a number of the faith missions joined together in the Interdenominational Foreign Mission Association of North America (IFMA), standing against the perceived liberal trends in the International Missionary Council. In 1945, the Evangelical Foreign Missions Association was created for American-based missions by the National Association of Evangelicals, with a wider base than the IFMA.

In the post–World War II era, relationships soured between agencies based in the newer Evangelical, Holiness, and Pentecostal churches on the one hand and representatives of denominations affiliated with the WORLD COUNCIL OF CHURCHES and the INTERNATIONAL MISSIONARY COUNCIL on the other. The more conservative churches, who believed the older Protestant churches had largely abandoned missionary work, initiated a series of world conferences reaffirming their commitment to traditional missionary endeavors. The most important of these was the 1974 Lausanne Congress on World Evangelism called by evangelist Billy GRAHAM. The congress adopted the LAUSANNE COVENANT, which remains a guiding document for Evangelical missions work. At this conference, Ralph D. WINTER introduced the idea of frontier missions, calling for missions to hitherto unreached ethnic-linguistic groups.

Two years later, Winter established the United States Center for World Mission and the William Carey International University (1977) to research the unreached people and mobilize Evangelical churches to carry out the task. The center became a breeding ground for programs and agencies that have remade the face of the contemporary missionary endeavor—the Adopt-a-People program, AD2000 and Beyond (especially active in the 1990s), and global mapping research. Combined with the work of David B. Barrett and Todd M. Johnson at the World Evangelization Research Center (now the Center for the Study of Global Christianity at Gordon-Conwell Theological Seminary) and World Vision's Missions Advanced Research and Communications Center, a vast database on the status of Christianity globally has

been made available and is having a profound effect in guiding the work of missionary agencies worldwide.

See also EVANGELICALISM.

Further reading: David Barrett, *The Encyclopedia of World Christianity,* 2nd ed. (New York: Oxford University Press, 2001); E. L. Frizen Jr., *75 Years of IFMA, 1917–1992: The Non-denominational Missions Movement* (Pasadena, Calif.: William Carey Library, 1993); Patrick Johnstone and Jason Mandryk, *Operation World, 21st Century Edition* (Carlisle, Cumbria, U.K.: Paternoster, 2001); J. H. Kane, *A Concise History of the Christian World Mission* (Grand Rapids, Mich.: Baker Book House, 1995). A Scott Moreau, ed., *Evangelical Dictionary of World Missions* (Grand Rapids, Mich.: Baker Book House, 2000); Ralph Winter and Steve Hawthorne, eds. *Perspectives on the World Christian Movement: A Reader;* 3rd ed. (Pasadena, Calif.: William Carey Library, 1999).

Farel, William (1489–1565) *Protestant preacher and Reformed church pioneer in Switzerland*

Though somewhat overshadowed by his friend and colleague John CALVIN, William Farel was a pioneer of the Reformation in Geneva and all of French-speaking SWITZERLAND. He was born into a noble family near Gap, Dauphiné. He studied in Paris with Jacobus Faber (Jacques Lèfevre d'Étaples), the reform-minded scholar and champion of biblical authority. In 1521, Lefevre's former student Bishop Briçonnet invited Farel to Meaux to assist his initial efforts at reform. Briçonnet wanted to keep reform within Catholic boundaries, and in 1523 instituted a ban on all Lutheran literature. Farel decided to leave the increasingly hostile atmosphere of FRANCE; he settled briefly in Basel, where ERASMUS lived and where Johannes OECOLAMPADIUS was leading a reform effort. His welcome wore thin when in 1524 he promulgated 13 theses contra Catholic doctrine.

After a term as an unordained preacher in Montbéland in eastern France, Farel settled at Aigle (near Bern) in 1525; in 1528, he was granted a license to preach anywhere in the canton of Bern; he worked in the neighboring cantons of Neuchâtel and Vaud as well. In 1532, he visited Waldensian leaders in ITALY, and on his return to Switzerland fatefully stopped in Geneva. He found a city divided, with secular authorities issuing reform decrees while the church leadership resisted.

Farel stayed on to support reform, but was expelled by church leaders, only to return when the reformists were granted liberty in March 1533. Over the next two years, he helped win over the great majority of Genevans to the reform cause. When the bishop of Geneva tried to halt his preaching, public debates were scheduled, giving him an even broader audience. On August 27, 1535, the Catholic Mass was officially suppressed and the Reformed faith established.

John Calvin was just visiting Geneva at that time, and Farel convinced him to take over the leadership of the Reformed movement. Over the next two years, the pair imposed a set of stringent reform measures that brought a sharp reaction, but after two years in exile they were invited back in 1541. Farel stayed for only a few months, moving on to Metz in 1542 and to Neuchâtel in 1544. He continued to work for the Reformed cause in Switzerland for the rest of his life. He remained in close contact with Calvin and mourned his passing in 1564. Farel died at Metz on September 13, 1565.

Further reading: Francis Bevan, *The Life of William Farel* (Edinburgh: Pickering & Inglis, n.d.); Wm. M. Blackburn, *William Farel and the Story of the Swiss Reform* (Philadelphia: Presbyterian Board of Publications, 1865); Bruce Gordon, *The Swiss Reformation* (Manchester, England: Manchester University Press, 2002); William G. Naphy, *Calvin and the Consolidation of the Genevan Reformation* (Manchester, U.K.: Manchester University Press, 1994).

fasting

Fasting is the practice of abstaining from food or drink for religious purposes, usually for a specified period of time. It passed into Protestantism from its Catholic and Jewish roots, but only in an attenuated form as a voluntary, occasional discipline.

Fasting is found in both the Jewish Bible (Old Testament) and the New Testament, as when Paul established his leadership credentials by citing his fasts (II Corinthians 6:5; 11:27). Jesus extolled fasting by his example in the wilderness following his BAPTISM, and by telling the apostles (Matthew 17:21) that demons could not be cast out without prayer and fasting.

Martin LUTHER, who had fasted as a Catholic monk, continued the practice in later life. John CALVIN refers to fasting in the *Institutes of the Christian Religion* while discussing repentance. He emphasized the need for inward change, not just outward actions, and implied that public fasting should be reserved "for times of calamity" and grief. As for individuals, "the life of the godly ought to be tempered with frugality and sobriety that throughout its course a sort of perpetual fasting may appear."

Calvin attacked the fixed fasts of the Roman Catholic tradition, such as during Lent, but supported the practice of public days of fasting when leaders felt it appropriate. For example, during the Salem witchcraft hysteria in the 1690s in Massachusetts, Salem pastor Rev. Samuel Parris led times of prayer and fasting to bring an end to the crisis.

Fasting continues to be extolled by some Protestant leaders as an occasional valuable tool. In 1994, Bill Bright, founder of CAMPUS CRUSADE FOR CHRIST, summoned believers to participate in a 40-day fast accompanied with prayer, revival, and the fulfillment of the Great Commission (to go into all the world and preach the Gospel). Bright cited the examples of great Protestant leaders of the past who included fasting as part of their Christian witness, from Luther and Calvin to John KNOX, Jonathan EDWARDS, Matthew Henry, Charles Finney Andrew MURRAY, and D. Martyn Lloyd-Jones. In 1995, the National Council of Churches of Christ in the U.S.A. held its first annual period of prayer and fasting during Holy Week (the week prior to Easter Sunday), with prayer especially directed to lawmakers and those most affected by legal changes: the young, the marginalized, the poor, and the otherwise vulnerable.

Most Protestant denominations have made fasting optional, but some officially support it. For example, the ASSEMBLIES OF GOD have adopted a statement extolling the virtue of fasting, as a way to "heighten focus, intensify fervor, and gain control over one's fleshly cravings and human will." It can be helpful in many unusual circumstances, but it should be "carried out in secret only before God."

The practice remains less popular in Protestant circles than among Roman Catholics.

Further reading: Jerry Falwell, *Fasting* (Wheaton, Ill.: Tyndale House, 1984); Richard J. Foster, *Celebration of Discipline* (San Francisco, Calif.: Harper, 1978); J. Oswald Sanders, *Prayer Power Unlimited* (Chicago: Moody Bible Institute, 1977); Arthur Wallis, *God's Chosen Fast* (Fort Washington, Pa.: Christian Literature Crusade, 1968).

Fellowship of Reconciliation

The Fellowship of Reconciliation (FOR) is an international Protestant interfaith group that has worked to support PACIFISM and other political causes in line with its view of Christianity.

The group originated in one of several Protestant efforts to prevent World War I. British Quaker Henry Hodgkin (1877–1933) and German Lutheran Friedrich Sigmund-Schultze manifested their concern at an ecumenical conference in SWITZERLAND that was cut off by the outbreak of the war. Before leaving Switzerland, Hodgkin and Sigmund-Schultze agreed to stay in touch.

In December that year, Hodgkin helped found the Fellowship of Reconciliation to continue the effort against war. An American branch was started the next year. Among its early accomplishments was the formation of the National Civil Liberties Bureau, later reorganized as the American Civil Liberties Union. The bureau worked for the legal recognition of conscientious objectors and later for the rights of those arrested for actively opposing the war. In the 1920s, it helped organize the National Conference of Christians and Jews.

In 1919, an International FOR organization was formed to network the autonomous national groups that sprouted up after the war. FOR has involved itself in a wide variety of issues and causes. During World War II, it sought ways to oppose the war, lobbied against the internment of Japanese-Americans, and helped rescue people fleeing the Nazis. In the 1960s, FOR staff supported the movement begun by Martin Luther KING Jr., staging workshops to train people in nonviolent resistance. It has consistently opposed the successive wars that have plagued humankind, worked to pose alternatives to war, and assisted people in postwar situations.

FOR has come to include people from a wide variety of faith communities. It has branches in more than 40 countries. The United States organization is headquartered in Nyack, New York, and the international headquarters at Alkmaar, the NETHERLANDS.

Further reading: *40 Years for Peace: A History of the Fellowship of Reconciliation 1914–1954* (New York: Fellowship of Reconciliation, 1954); William R. Miller, *Martin Luther King, Jr.: His Life, Martyrdom and Meaning for the World* (New York: Weybright & Talley, 1968); Jill Wallis, *Valiant for Peace: A History of the Fellowship of Reconciliation 1914–1989* (London: Fellowship of Reconciliation, 1991); Walter Wink, ed., *Peace Is the Way: Writings on Nonviolence from the Fellowship of Reconciliation* (Maryknoll, N.Y.: Orbis Books, 2000).

feminism, Christian

Christian feminism deals with issues of women's roles within the church and society from the perspective of Christian beliefs and practices. Protestant churches have been intimately connected with the efforts of women to improve their status and role from the very beginning of the women's rights movement in the 19th century. The first convention on the rights of women, called by Elizabeth Cady Stanton in 1848, met at the Wesleyan Methodist Chapel in Seneca Falls, New York. Among the points discussed was Stanton's complaint that women were generally barred from participation in church affairs.

A key goal of 19th-century Christian feminists was entrance into the ordained ministry. Such notables as Phoebe PALMER and Catherine BOOTH wrote books promoting that goal. Although a few such as Antoinette Brown BLACKWELL and Olympia BROWN achieved the goal, it would take a century before most barriers to the ordination of WOMEN were lifted. In the first half of the 20th century, a number of denominations, mostly HOLINESS and Pentecostal groups, ordained women. Women such as Alma White of the Pillar of Fire and Aimee Semple MCPHERSON of the INTERNATIONAL CHURCH OF THE FOURSQUARE GOSPEL emerged as the founding leaders of their own DENOMINATIONS.

The missionary enterprise brought additional obstacles and opportunities. Women sometimes found openings there that were not available in the United States and Europe. Women were commissioned as medical missionaries, starting with Clara SWAIN in India in 1870; they were able to build and head quite significant medical establishments. Missionary women were able to found and head schools, which sometimes grew into modern universities.

A new wave of feminism emerged in the 1960s, the new movement generally traced to the appearance of *The Feminine Mystique* by Betty Friedan (1963). Feminists charged that women had been systematically barred from full participation in all the social arenas and institutions of modern society. They claimed that by changing that situation, they could revolutionize society; outdated assumptions about the nature of social relationships would disappear; and the equality of women would come to be seen as the norm.

The movement had an immediate impact in Protestant churches, with interdenominational efforts arising to change the status and role of women in the churches. A new enterprise, FEMINIST THEOLOGY, explored female perspectives in theology and called for an end to male domination of the field. Church feminists called for opening the ordained ministry to women, reorganizing denominational bodies to give women greater access, and appointing women to policy-making positions in the denominational administration, teaching posts at church-sponsored colleges and seminaries, and roles in church judicatories.

Among the first denominations to respond was the UNITED METHODIST CHURCH, founded in 1968 by a merger of the Evangelical United Brethren and the Methodist Church (1939–68). In 1972, the new Commission on the Status and Role of Women was created; in 1976, the general conference approved a requirement that women make up 30 percent of membership on boards, commissions, and committees of the national church and its regional conferences. The church already ordained women, but a new recruitment drive was begun, and seminaries were revamped to be more welcoming to female students. In 1980, Marjorie Matthews became the first woman elected to the bishop's office. Other liberal Protestant churches (and ecumenical organizations) followed a parallel course.

Slowest to respond among the major Protestant groups around the world were the various Anglican churches. The Episcopal Church took the lead with the ordination of women in 1976 and the consecration of the first female bishop, Barbara C. HARRIS, in 1989. Since then, a number of other Anglican churches have begun ordaining female ministers, but very few have approved the admission of females to bishop's order.

Women's concerns were also addressed in the ECUMENICAL MOVEMENT. As early as 1948, Kathleen Bliss addressed women's issues at the first assembly of the WORLD COUNCIL OF CHURCHES (WCC). Her text on the status and role of women in the churches became the major resource for the commission set up by the WCC at that assembly. The WCC commission, which has changed names several times, has taken a somewhat more conservative stance than some of its member churches, as it has had to reflect the life of its more conservative Protestant and Orthodox members. It has concentrated more on women's role in secular society than in the church. In 1988, it proclaimed a Decade of the Churches in Solidarity with Women, and asked member churches to work toward freeing themselves from centuries of sexist practices and teachings.

Women's groups in the mainline Protestant bodies have called attention to gender references in the text of liturgies, hymns, and even the Bible. They have called for inclusive language, so that texts that obviously refer to both men and women should no longer read as if they referred only to men. Thus, for example, the Christmas hymn "Good Christian Men Rejoice" might be rendered as "Good Christian Folk Rejoice."

Women in liberal Protestant churches have also been active in the ABORTION controversy, often identifying with the Religious Coalition for Reproductive Rights, which supports legal abortion. In contrast, feminist women in more conservative churches have tended to distance themselves from the abortion issue.

The conservative Fundamentalist and Evangelical movements reacted somewhat differently to Christian feminism. The SOUTHERN BAPTIST CONVENTION has strongly opposed the admission of women to the ordained ministry, and other conservative Baptist churches have concurred. They have tended to take literally those New Testament passages that appear to suggest a subordinate position for women in the home and church (for example, I Timothy 2:11, I Corinthians 14:34, Ephesians 5:24). On the other hand, conservative churches in the Calvinist tradition were building relationships with Pentecostal and Holiness churches that admitted women to the ministry.

While Fundamentalists have generally dismissed the new feminism, Evangelicals have responded more positively. A 1973 workshop issued the influential Chicago Declaration of Societal Concern, and in 1974 the Evangelical Women's Caucus was formed. The most important Evangelical response to the new feminism appeared that same year: *All Were Meant to Be: A Biblical Approach to Women's Liberation* by Letha Scanzoni and Nancy A. Hardesty.

Four years later, caucus leaders Letha Scanzoni and Virginia Ramey Mollenkott issued a call for gay rights in *Is the Homosexual My Neighbor?* Many feared that the women's movement would lose any chance for success if it became identified with lesbianism. When the caucus passed a resolution supporting gay rights in 1986, more feminists withdrew and founded a new organization, Christians for Biblical Equality. The caucus also itself assumed a new name, the Evangelical and Ecumenical Women's Caucus, and it has continued to make common cause with liberal Roman Catholic and Protestant feminists.

In 1988, a group of Fundamentalist and Evangelical leaders formed the Council on Biblical Manhood and Womanhood, and issued the Danvers Statement in an effort to block the spread of feminism in their churches. The council assumed that males are called by God to bear the primary teaching authority in the church as ELDERS or pastors, and that marriage implies that the husband will bear the primary responsibility of leadership in the home.

African-American women and their churches also participated in the movement. The African Methodist Episcopal Zion Church began ordaining women in the 1890s, though other churches took much longer to follow suit. Black churches have tended to be more conservative on this issue than their white counterparts. Black female theologians have also complained of the inadequacy of feminist theology to meet their needs and have launched a Womanist theology movement looking toward their own liberation as African-American females.

See also LIBERATION THEOLOGY; WOMEN, ORDINATION OF.

Further reading: Kathleen Bliss, *The Service and Status of Women in the Churches* (London: SCM Press, 1952); Rosemary Radford Reuther and Rosemary Keller, eds., *Women and Religion in America,* (New York: Harper & Row, 1981); Letty M. Russell, *Church in the Round. Feminist Interpretation of the Church* (Louisville, Ky: Westminster/John Knox Press, 1993); Letha Scanzoni and Nancy A. Hardesty, *All Were Meant to Be: A Biblical Approach to Women's Liberation* (Waco, Tex.: Word Books, 1975); ———, and Virginia Ramey Mollenkott, *Is the Homosexual My Neighbor?* (San Francisco: Harper & Row, 1978).

feminist theology

Feminist theology is a blend of the secular feminism that emerged in the 1960s and LIBERATION THEOLOGY. Modern feminism is a massive critique of male-dominated structures in Western society; it was built on several centuries of women's activism that took organized form in the United States in the 1840s. In the intervening years, Christian feminism worked to open leadership roles in the church for women, especially in the ordained ministry.

When African-American theologians began exploring the theological implications of the 1960s Civil Rights movement, Christian feminists were inspired to relate their issues to this liberation theology. Galatians 3:28, where Paul tells the church that there is neither male nor female within the fellowship, but all one in Christ Jesus, became the most frequently quoted scripture of the movement.

Like liberation theology, feminist theology claimed that all theology was created at a particular location in time and space. They argued that the church emerged in a patriarchal society dominated by males and that Christian theology had been dominated by males. In fact, they claimed, both liberation theology and BLACK THEOLOGY perpetuated male dominance and did not really deal with women's issues.

During the 1970s, a host of books began to call for a revision of theology with feminist insights.

Among the outstanding Protestant voices who joined the debate were Sheila Collins, Virginia R. Mollenkott, and Letty Russell. Of particular importance was Rosemary Ruether, a Roman Catholic who taught theology at the UNITED METHODIST CHURCH's Garrett-Evangelical Seminary. She was the author of a series of books starting with *Liberation Theology: Human Hope Confronts Christian History and American Power* in 1972.

Ruether's position as a Catholic teaching at a Protestant seminary was symbolic of the pluralistic atmosphere within which Protestant feminist theology developed. Women were exploring the question of a female aspect to God and thus paid attention to pagan and Wiccan feminism and the development of a new community of Goddess worshippers. They read the writings of Mary Daly, a Roman Catholic theologian whose radical critique led her into conflict with the Catholic university in which she taught and eventually led her out of the church altogether. They made common cause with Jewish women who were simultaneously seeking to open Reform, Reconstructionist, and Conservative Jewish communities to the acceptance of female rabbis. They also debated the role of lesbians within the church and ministry.

It was widely recognized that the initial phase of feminist theology was somewhat negative. It focused on demonstrating how patriarchal structures had oppressed women, distorted the picture of women in biblical literature and church history, and generally denied them their rightful place in God's kingdom.

Mary Daly's *Beyond God the Father* discussed the male gender language by which most Christians addressed God, and the maleness of Jesus Christ. She claimed that "God talk" led to male rule in society and that the male gender of Jesus was used to justify male-dominated family life. The use of male pronouns in the Bible when the reference clearly included women as well as men obscured the female presence in the Gospel story. This early critique led to demands for a new translation of the Bible, new liturgies, and revised hymnbooks. In 1989, the National Council of the

Churches of Christ in the U.S.A. authorized the publication of the New Revised Standard Version of the Bible, notable for its attempt to replace masculine nouns and pronouns when both males and females were indicated by the text. The New RSV, while not granting all that feminists wanted, represented a singular triumph of the first two decades of work.

Meanwhile, within the Evangelical Protestant community, a feminist community emerged around organizations such as the Daughters of Sarah and Christians for Biblical Equality. These conservative feminists insisted that the Bible, correctly interpreted, supports the fundamental equality of men and women, a position outlined in the early text by Letha Scanzoni and Nancy Hardesty, *All We're Meant To Be* (1974).

Feminist theology found an immediate response in Protestant churches internationally. One result has been a steadily growing number of denominational bodies admitting women to ordination and a full spectrum of lay leadership roles. As the 21st century begins, a new generation of formally trained female theologians have taken their place within the theological community and have begun the work of producing a new theology that integrates feminist insights. Female church historians have picked up the task of documenting the neglected story of leadership by women through the ages of the church, and female biblical scholars are presenting their findings from considerations of the biblical text. In the meantime, some black feminists, perceiving the lack of an African-American voice in feminist theology, have begun to explore what they call womanist theology.

Further reading: Sheila Collins, *A Different Heaven and Earth.* (Valley Forge, Pa.: Judson Press, 1974); Mary Daly, *Beyond God the Father: Toward a Philosophy of Women's Liberation* (Boston: Beacon, 1973); Virginia R. Mollenkott, *Women, Men and the Bible* (Nashville, Tenn.: Abingdon Press, 1977); Rosemary Ruether, *Liberation Theology: Human Hope Confronts Christian History and American Power* (New York: Paulist Press, 1972); ———, *Sexism and God-Talk: Toward a Feminist Theology* (Boston: Beacon Press, 1983, rev. ed., 1993); Letty M. Russell, *Human Liberation in a Feminist Perspective—A Theology* (Philadelphia: Westminster Press, 1974); Letha Scanzoni and Nancy Hardesty, *All We're Meant to Be* (Waco, Tex.: Word, 1974).

Fifth Monarchy Men

The Fifth Monarchy Men was a powerful millennial movement that emerged in the 1640s during the tumultuous times of the Puritan Commonwealth in England. They hoped to reform Parliament in preparation for the return of Christ toward the end of the century. The name "Fifth Monarchy" is derived from the dream of King Nebuchadnezzar (Daniel 2), a crucial text for most Christian millennialists; it speaks of five successive kingdoms, the last one initiating the kingdom of God.

Drawing on popular millennial writings of the period, the Fifth Monarchy movement found its greatest strength among BAPTISTS and Congregationalists (or Independents). It also made common cause with the New Model Army (a Puritan force led by Oliver CROMWELL) and the so-called Levellers, a popular political movement that advocated among other things religious toleration, legal reforms, a bill of rights, and a popularly elected government. The Fifth Monarchy Men initially supported Cromwell, but turned against him after he established the Commonwealth and took the title Lord Protector.

Thomas Harrison (1610–60), a former army officer and former close friend of Cromwell, became the group's leading spokesman in the mid-1650s. Cromwell had him arrested on questionable charges of subversion. Harrison was executed at the time of the restoration of the monarchy (1660). His execution provoked a short-lived violent attempt to unseat the new king. The effort failed and the leaders were executed, while several thousand supporters (many QUAKERS) were imprisoned. This action killed the movement, in part by associating millennial speculation and violence in the popular imagination.

See also ESCHATOLOGY; PREMILLENNIALISM.

Further reading: B. S. Capp, *The Fifth Monarchy Men: A Study in Seventeenth-Century English Millenarianism* (London: Faber & Faber, 1972); Norman Cohn, *The Pursuit of the Millennium, Revolutionary Millenarians and Mystical Anarchists of the Middle Ages* (New York: Oxford University Press, 1990); R. L. Greaves, *Deliver Us from Evil: The Radical Underground in Britain, 1660–1669* (New York: Oxford University Press, 1986).

Fiji Islands

The first Christian missionaries found their way to the Fiji Islands in 1830. Five years later, due to an agreement dividing responsibility in the SOUTH PACIFIC, the original LONDON MISSIONARY SOCIETY personnel turned over their work to the British Methodists. The METHODIST CHURCH was the only Protestant church in the islands until the Anglicans arrived in 1860, and it has remained the largest religious group in the islands, though the Roman Catholic Church, which launched its mission in 1844, has almost overtaken it. The Methodist effort, which relied heavily on Tongan converts, made slow progress until 1854, when Thakombau, the principal chief in the islands, converted. After the British authorities began to bring Indians (primarily from Kerala and Madras) into Fiji to work the plantations, the Methodists began an Indian mission. The mission developed into the present-day Methodist Church in Fiji and Rotuma, the only Fiji-based church in the WORLD COUNCIL OF CHURCHES.

The Anglicans were followed by the Presbyterians (1876) and the SEVENTH-DAY ADVENTIST CHURCH (1889). Important efforts were launched in the 20th century by the CHRISTIAN BRETHREN and the ASSEMBLIES OF GOD. The latter group has had spectacular growth in the last two decades. While PENTECOSTALISM has spread rapidly, most adherents have not separated from their former churches. The CHURCH OF JESUS CHRIST OF LATTER-DAY SAINTS, which has a special role for South Sea Islanders in its schema of salvation, has done well in the islands, along with its sister church, the Reorganized Church of Jesus Christ of Latter Day Saints (now the Christian Community).

In 1924, the older Protestant churches founded the Fiji Council of Churches. This cooperative effort facilitated the founding of the Pacific Theological School (jointly sponsored by the Methodists, Anglicans, Presbyterians, and Congregationalists), which now serves a number of the South Sea Island nations. Fiji has also provided the headquarters site for the Pacific Conference of Churches. Meanwhile, the more conservative churches have come together in the Evangelical Fellowship of Fiji, affiliated with the WORLD EVANGELICAL ALLIANCE.

Fiji has seen a variety of indigenous church movements, mostly offshoots of the Methodists. The Vessel of Christ movement, which emerged during World War II, was suppressed by the government. The Messiah Club, which continues to exist, is focused upon the higher standard of living that members expect their messianic leader to bring to the islands in the near future.

Further reading: J. Garrett, *Footsteps in the Sea: Christianity in Oceania to World War II* (Suva: University of the South Pacific, Institute of Pacific Studies in association with the World Council of Churches, 1992); *Methodist Church in Fiji, 1835–1985: 150th Anniversary Celebration* (Suva: Lotu Pasifika Production, 1985).

Finished Work controversy

The Finished Work controversy was a dispute that arose in the early Pentecostal movement in America. At the AZUSA STREET REVIVAL in Los Angeles (1906–08), the seminal event in PENTECOSTALISM, leader William J. SEYMOUR preached sanctification according to the understanding of the Methodist HOLINESS movement, from which he came. A Christian's life moved from JUSTIFICATION (or conversion) as one phase, to God's promise to cleanse the heart and sanctify the believer fully as the next. The experience of the BAPTISM OF THE HOLY SPIRIT, and its accompanying sign of speaking in tongues, was only for the sanctified believer.

William H. Durham (1873–1912), who did not come from a Holiness background, began to criticize this view from his base in Chicago. He followed the general Lutheran and Reformed view that Christ's "finished work" of atonement provided for both justification and sanctification. Sanctification was not a second instantaneous work of the Holy Spirit; it was a gradual process of acquiring in one's life all that had been accomplished at Calvary. Durham lobbied for his views in Los Angeles in 1911 and as people aligned with Durham, the Pentecostal movement split into two camps.

Those who had previously been Methodists and/or Holiness people rejected Durham's views. They founded such groups as the CHURCH OF GOD (CLEVELAND, TENNESSEE), the INTERNATIONAL PENTECOSTAL HOLINESS CHURCH, and the CHURCH OF GOD IN CHRIST. Those who followed Durham's view founded the ASSEMBLIES OF GOD, the INTERNATIONAL CHURCH OF THE FOURSQUARE GOSPEL, and the Pentecostal Assemblies of Canada.

Further reading: Frank Bartleman, *How Pentecost Came to Los Angeles* (Northridge, Calif.: Voice Christian, 1968); Vinson Synan, *The Century of the Holy Spirit: 100 Years of Pentecostal and Charismatic Revival* (Nashville, Tenn.: Thomas Nelson, 2001); A. C. Valdez, Jr., *Fire on Azusa Street* (Costa Mesa, Calif.: Gift Publications, 1980).

Finland

At the time the Reformation was launched in Germany, the Roman Catholic Church held religious hegemony in Finland, though pockets of paganism could be found. The first Lutheran writings reached Finland in the 1520s, helping to win the allegiance of Mikael Agricola (c. 1510–57), bishop of Turku and representative of the Finns at the Royal Council of Sweden. Turku is considered to be the father of Finnish literature, and in 1538 wrote the first book in the Finnish language. In 1548, he translated and published the New Testament (1548) into Finnish. Thus Protestantism became ultimately connected with literary Finnish.

The move to LUTHERANISM involved relatively little rancor, following the lead of its western neighbor and ruler SWEDEN. The church abandoned Latin, priestly celibacy, and all of the SACRAMENTS except BAPTISM and the Eucharist. It remained in episcopal hands, though the king took ownership of much former Roman Catholic property.

The 1809 transfer to Russian rule did little to disturb the Lutheran establishment. In 1869, the church gained some independence at the cost of losing some of its ties to the state. As a result of the change, a national synod was created to decide on queries and administer policies.

Lutheranism dominated life in the 19th century to the exclusion of rival DENOMINATIONS, though a variety of revival movements swept the country and created pockets of dissent. In 1844, Lars Levi Laestadius (1800–60), a Lutheran pastor, converted to a pietistic form of Lutheranism emphasizing personal faith and moral uprightness. He emerged as a charismatic evangelist whose earthy language and attacks against worldly, elitist church leaders appealed to the people of northern Sweden and Finland. Transferred to America, his movement would emerge as an independent denomination, the Apostolic Lutheran Church.

Taking the opportunity offered by the revolution in Russia, Finland declared independence in 1917. Subsequently, in 1923, religious freedom was adopted, and a variety of groups separated from the Lutheran Church of Finland. Among the first were the Orthodox, who had existed as a revitalization group within the Church of Finland that had been strongly influenced by Russian Orthodoxy. Most of the new groups, however, originated in the 19-century revivalist movements.

North American missionaries invaded Finland in the second half of the 19th century and helped establish a spectrum of Protestant denominations. Swedish branches of the Baptist Church, the UNITED METHODIST CHURCH, the SALVATION ARMY, the JEHOVAH'S WITNESSES, and the SEVENTH-DAY ADVENTIST CHURCH all date from this period.

PENTECOSTALISM was introduced by Norwegian pastor Thomas B. Barrett (1862–1940). It found an immediate response among the existing revivalist groups within the Lutheran Church that had already experienced manifestations such as speaking in tongues, visions, and prophecies. Barrett explained the role of the Holy Spirit in fostering these signs. Today, Pentecostalism constitutes the largest Christian community independent of the Lutheran Church. Still, non-Lutheran Protestants constitute fewer than 1 percent of the total population.

The Evangelical Lutheran Church of Finland still plays some state roles. It maintains local population registers, and most non-Lutherans are buried in the cemeteries maintained by Lutheran parishes. As of the beginning of the 21st century, 85 percent of the population were registered as members of the Evangelical Lutheran Church of Finland.

The Lutheran Church is a member of both the LUTHERAN WORLD FEDERATION and the WORLD COUNCIL OF CURCHES.

Further reading: *The Churches of Finland* (Helsinki: Evangelical Lutheran Church of Finland, 1992); L. S. Hunter, *Scandinavian Churches: a Picture of the Development of the Churches of Denmark, Norway, Finland, Iceland, and Sweden* (London: Faber & Faber, 1965); G. Sentzke, *Finland: Its Church and Its People* (Helsinki: Lutheran-Agricola Society, 1963); Fred Singleton, *A Short History of Finland* (Cambridge: Cambridge University Press, 1998).

Finney, Charles G. (1792–1875) *early American frontier revivalist and educator*

Charles Grandison Finney, evangelist, theologian, and social activist, emerged as an important voice of frontier revivalism in early 19th-century America. He was born on August 29, 1792, in Warren, Connecticut, and grew up in Oneida County, New York. He studied law and was admitted to the bar in 1818. While serving as a lawyer in 1821, he experienced an intense religious experience, and shortly thereafter left the practice of law to preach.

He was ordained as a minister by the St. Lawrence Presbytery in 1824, and then began traveling and conducting revival meetings. He developed creative "new measures" to encourage people to accept the Christian message. He summarized these in a series of talks delivered in 1835 and subsequently published as *Lectures on Revivals of Religion.* Beginning in 1832, he pastored the Second Free Presbyterian Church in New York City.

In 1836, Finney resigned from the presbytery to assume the leadership of the seminary at the new antislavery Oberlin Collegiate Institute (now Oberlin University); he considered himself a Congregationalist from then on. Finney accepted the position on condition that black students would be admitted. He also opened a place for women in worship and let women study for degrees at Oberlin. Finney was named professor of systematic theology and of pastoral theology, and served as pastor of Oberlin Congregational Church. He became president of Oberlin in 1851. He also founded the *Oberlin Evangelist.*

Finney was strongly influenced by Wesleyan views on sanctification and the idea of a second work of grace that made one perfect in love. His wedding of Calvinist and Wesleyan perspectives, shared by fellow Oberlin theologian Asa Mahan (1800–89), was called the Oberlin theology. It favored the Methodist view that individuals are always ready to accept Christ and that Christians have a capacity for holy living. Among his many works were his *Lectures to Professing Christians* (1837); *Skeletons of a Course of Theological Lectures* (1840); and the *Systematic Theology* (1846), the latter being one of the first theologies to offer an apology for the kind of revolution that brought the United States into existence.

Finney taught well into his 80s, though he resigned the presidency in 1865. He died in Oberlin on August 1875 of heart problems.

See also HOLINESS MOVEMENT; REVIVALISM.

Further reading: David B. Chesebrough, *Charles G. Finney: Revivalistic Rhetoric* (Westport, Conn.: Greenwood Press, 2001); Charles G. Finney, *An Autobiography* (New York: Fleming H. Revell Company, 1908); ———, *Lectures on Systematic Theology* (Grand Rapids, Mich.: William B. Eerdmans, 1953); ———, *Sermons on Gospel Themes* (New York: Dodd, 1876); Keith Hardman, *Charles Grandison Finney 1792–1875: Revivalist and Reformer* (Syracuse, N.Y.: Syracuse University Press, 1987).

foot washing

In the 13th chapter of the Gospel of John, Jesus washes the feet of the disciples at the Last Supper, usually the task of a servant. He says in verse 14, "If I then your Lord and Master have washed your feet, you also ought to wash one another's feet." In the Roman Catholic tradition, priests wash the feet of several representatives of their congregation during Maundy Thursday, when the events of the Last Supper are remembered and ritually reenacted.

The CHURCH OF ENGLAND continued the practice, but over the centuries it fell into disuse. Martin LUTHER had problems with the practice, and over the years, Lutherans have tended to substitute sermons on the meaning of Christ's foot washing.

However, the ANABAPTISTS, who tended to take admonitions such as that of John 13:14 literally, revived foot washing as an integral part of church life. It was considered a third ordinance besides that of BAPTISM and the LORD'S SUPPER, and mandated in the Dordrecht Confession of 1632. The practice passed from the MENNONITES to the BAPTISTS and various FREE CHURCH groups in Europe. Some chose to practice it as an ordinance, some to practice it but not consider it an ordinance, and some did not adopt the practice. In the modern world, the practice is most identified with the various Mennonite and Amish groups, the Church of the BRETHREN (and related groups), the Primitive Baptists, the Free-Will Baptists, some Adventist groups, and many Pentecostal groups.

In recent years, as part of a movement to explore new Christian rituals, new and innovative foot washing practices have appeared for optional use in various churches and informal Christian fellowships. Examples may be found in the EPISCOPAL CHURCH's *Book of Occasional Services* and in the UNITED METHODIST CHURCH's *Book of Worship*.

See also SACRAMENTS/ORDINANCES.

Further reading: Elam J. Daniels, *Footwashing by the Master and by the Saints* (Orlando, Fla.: Christ for the World Publishers, n.d.); Martin Connell, "*Nisi Pedes,* Except for the Feet," *Worship* 70 (1996) 517–530; J. Gordon Melton, *The Encyclopedia of American Religions: Religious Creeds*, 2 vols. (Detroit: Gale Research, 1988, 1994); John Christopher Thomas, *Footwashing in John 13 and the Johannine Community* (London: Sheffield Academic Press, 1991).

form criticism

Form criticism is a modern method of biblical interpretation based upon the understanding that the Bible contains a variety of types of literature, from poetry to proverbs to accounts of events to sermons. The form that a narrative takes has significant importance in how it is interpreted by form critics. One popular form identified in the New Testament, for example, is the healing story.

Form criticism invites the comparison of different examples of texts that have the same or similar form, to compare their differences and likenesses. This study encourages the search for possible older stories upon which the biblical stories might be based. The introduction of form criticism is largely attributed to German biblical scholar Rudolf BULTMANN (1884–1976).

In the late 20th century, form criticism became popular among Protestant Bible scholars who were already familiar with textual criticism. As is the case with other types of BIBLICAL CRITICISM,

Evangelical and Fundamentalist Protestants have tended to reject form criticism as an attack upon the sacredness of the Bible.

Further reading: Rudolf Bultmann, *Form Criticism: A New Method of New Testament Research,* trans. by Frederick C. Grant (Chicago: Willett, Clark, 1934); E. T. Guttgemans, *Candid Questions Concerning Gospel Form Criticism: A Methodological Sketch of the Fundamental Problematics of Form and Redaction Criticism* (Pittsburgh, Pa.: Pickwick, 1979); Edgar V. McKnight, *What Is Form Criticism?,* in *Guides to Biblical Scholarship,* ed. by Dan O. Via, Jr. (Philadelphia: Fortress, 1969); W. A. Maier, *Form Criticism Reexamined* (St. Louis: Concordia, 1973).

Formula of Concord

The Formula of Concord was a doctrinal confession issued by the second generation of Lutherans after the deaths of Martin LUTHER in 1546 and Philip MELANCTHON in 1560. The formula deals with theological questions that arose after the founders were no longer present.

In the 1560s, two parties became evident among the Lutheran leadership. One generally accepted Melancthon's attempts to find common ground with other Christians on such issues as the LORD'S SUPPER; the other party was dismissive of such efforts, and in particular condemned the Leipzig Interim, which Melancthon had accepted, an attempted compromise with Roman Catholics that had been imposed by Emperor Charles V.

A new generation of scholars, including James Andreae, Martin Chemnitz, David Chytraeus, and Nikolaus Selnecker, after years of dialogue, completed the formula in 1577, and won the support of 86 German states, including Saxony, Brandenberg, and the Palatinate. The 12 articles of the formula focused on a number of newer issues such as original sin (in which total depravity is affirmed); the necessity of preaching the law in the Christian community, even though it has no role in individual salvation; the Lord's Supper (maintaining

Lutheran emphasis on the real presence); and the denunciation of some heretical positions including Anabaptism, Schwenckfeldianism, and Neo-Arianism.

The formula was published along with a set of other Lutheran confessional documents and ancient creeds in the *Book of Concord* (1580). The *Book of Concord* includes the Apostles' Creed, Athanasian Creed, Nicene Creed, AUGSBURG CONFESSION OF FAITH, Apology of the Augsburg Confession, Schmalkald Articles, and Luther's Larger and Smaller Catechisms. The *Book of Concord* has served as the sourcebook for Lutheran teachings for generations.

See also CREEDS/CONFESSIONS OF FAITH; LUTHERANISM.

Further reading: Friedrich Bente, *Historical Introductions to the Book of Concord* (St. Louis: Concordia, 1921, 1965); *The Book of Concord* (Fortress Press: Philadelphia, 1959); Eric Gritsch and Robert Jenson, *Lutheranism: The Theological Movement and its Confessional Writings* (Philadelphia: Fortress Press, 1976); Robert Kolb, *Andreae and the Formula of Concord* (St. Louis: Concordia, 1977); Edmund Schlink, *Theology of the Lutheran Confessions.* (Philadelphia: Fortress Press, 1961); Louis W. Spitz and Wenzel Lohff, eds., *Discord, Dialogue, and Concord: Studies in the Lutheran Reformation's Formula of Concord* (Philadelphia: Fortress Press, 1977).

Fox, George (1624–1691) *founder of the Quaker movement*

George Fox, the founder of the Society of Friends, popularly known as the QUAKERS, was born in July 1624 in Fenny Drayton, Leicestershire, England. During his teen years, as an apprentice shoemaker, his religious speculations led him to withdraw from the CHURCH OF ENGLAND. As early as 1643, he was traveling around England speaking against grand church buildings and ordained ministers as irrelevant to one's personal relationship with God. His preaching took on a more positive tone after a divine revelation in 1646. He became

Representation of an early Quaker meeting *(Institute for the Study of American Religion, Santa Barbara, California)*

convinced that God dwelled within each person, and that communication with God was possible. Christ communicated to people through what Fox termed the *Inner Light*.

Fox organized an initial group, the Friends of Truth, which became the core group for the Society of Friends. The Friends withdrew from the Anglican community and refused to pay their church tithes. They were first called Quakers, originally a derisive label, by Justice Bennet of Derby, in reference to Fox's call to tremble before the word of the Lord.

By 1660, the movement had acquired some 20,000 adherents, but Fox and the Quakers did not fare well under the Restoration. More than 300 were killed in assaults or died in prison;

another few hundred were sent into slavery, and more than 13,000 were imprisoned. The persecution slowed but did not stop their growth.

Among Fox's early converts was Margaret Fell (1614–1702), wife of the vice-chancellor of the Duchy of Lancaster. She provided a haven in Britain for Quakers at her estate, Swarthmore Hall. As a widow, she married Fox in 1669. Women were to play a prominent role in the developing movement.

Fox visited Germany and Holland in this period, and then crossed the Atlantic to visit the American colonies, Barbados, and Jamaica. William PENN, his close associate and founder of two havens for Quakers in America, frequently accompanied Fox. Fox traveled until his death in 1691.

Fox worked out the Quaker organization, which relied on a set of monthly (congregational), quarterly (district), and annual (national) meetings. The movement appointed ELDERS to care for ministry, and overseers to care for the poor and provide for the education of children. They adopted a simple lifestyle; their meetings consisted of waiting for communications from the Inner Light to prompt witnesses to speak.

Penn asssumed leadership of a group that gathered and published Fox's *Journal,* his major literary output, which appeared in 1694.

Further reading: T. Canby Jones, *George Fox's Attitude toward War* (Richmond, Ind.: Friends United Press, 1984); George Fox, *The Journal of George Fox,* ed. by John L. Nickalls (Philadelphia: Philadelphia Yearly Meeting of the Religious Society of Friends, 1995); Philip F. Gura, *A Glimpse of Sion's Glory: Puritan Radicalism in New England 1620–1660* (Middletown, Conn.: Wesleyan University Press, 1984); H. Larry Ingle, *First among Friends: George Fox and the Creation of Quakerism* (New York: Oxford University Press, 1994).

Foxe's *Book of Martyrs*

The *Book of Martyrs* is a famous Protestant text documenting the persecution of Christians through the ages, with a special focus on Protestants executed during the reign of Queen MARY I (r. 1553–58) of England. Written at the time of the Protestant breakaway from the Roman Catholic community, it was both a record of the intensity of the controversy and a means in later years to keep the enmity between the two communities alive.

The author, John Foxe (1516–87), was born in Boston, Lincolnshire, England. He was expelled from Oxford University for his Protestant ideas, then worked as a tutor until the beginning of Mary's reign. Shortly thereafter, he left for the Continent. At Basel, he began his multivolume history of Christianity with particular attention to the theme of martyrdom. As Protestant leaders were being executed by Mary, he accepted a sug-

gestion to add current material to his history, which was first published in Latin in 1554, with the material on Mary appearing in 1559.

Following the coronation of ELIZABETH I, Foxe returned to England and set about the task of translating his book. The English edition appeared in 1563 under various titles, including *Acts and Monuments.* The book was ordered to be placed in every cathedral church in England. It enjoyed widespread sales, going through four editions during Foxe's life, and confirming Protestant opinion of the cruelty of Catholics in general and "Bloody Mary" in particular. It would help mold Protestant-Catholic relations in the English-speaking world into the 20th century.

Foxe's text recounts the history of martyrdom in Western Christianity, squarely placing much of the blame at Rome's door. About half of the text concerns the trials that began with proto-Protestants such as John HUS and John WYCLIFFE. Foxe died on April 18, 1587. His book has gone through numerous editions (under various titles), and new material was added on Protestant martyrs in the post-Reformation era.

See also MARIAN EXILES; PURITANISM.

Further reading: John Foxe, *The New Foxe's Book of Martyrs,* rewritten and updated by Harold J. Chadwick (Gainesville, Fla.: Bridge-Logos, 2001)—one of many editions; Christopher Highley and John N. King, ed., *John Foxe and His World* (Aldershot, Hampshire, U.K.: Ashgate, 2001); D. M. Loades, ed., *John Foxe: An Historical Perspective* (Aldershot, Hampshire, U.K.: Ashgate, 1999); James Frederic Mozley, *John Foxe and His Book* (London: SPCK: 1940); V. Norskov Olsen, *John Foxe and the Elizabethan Church* (Berkeley: University of California Press, 1973).

France

During the Reformation, Protestantism spread rapidly and forcefully in France, and it took 150 years for the Roman Catholic Church to reestablish complete control. Tolerance was not achieved until the late 18th century, and the country's

Christian community remains predominantly Catholic until today.

The Protestant movement that began in German-speaking countries—Saxony and Zurich—soon spread to French-speaking lands. The ground was laid by the HUMANISM that had spread from ITALY in the mid-15th century. The first prominent humanist was Guillaume Budé (1467–1540), who became librarian to King Francis I (r. 1515–47). His contemporary Jacques Lefèvre d'Estaples (1455–1536) produced a French translation of the New Testament (1523–25). In his commentaries on the Scripture, he relied on his own reading of the text, while ignoring the medieval Catholic commentaries. Lefèvre had significant influence on Catholic bishop Guillaume Briçonnet (1470–1533), who turned his diocese of Meaux into a humanist center that thrived through the crucial decade of the 1520s; another of his students was William FAREL, among the founders of the Reformed church in Geneva.

Lutheran writings began to filter into France soon after their issuance. In April 1521, the faculty at the University of Paris condemned some 100 propositions that it claimed had been found in Martin LUTHER's writings. In 1523, Briçonnet felt compelled to ban Lutheran pamphlets from his diocese. However, his own milder calls for reforms were blunted in 1525, when the Paris faculty, well on their way to assuming leadership in the anti-Protestant battle, declared that Lefèvre's French Bible fostered heresy. The reform-minded leaders at Meaux subsequently dispersed, and even Lefèvre moved to STRASBOURG, then a free city. Francis I, though personally favoring the humanists, was drawn into the conservative camp by his need for their support. As Protestant sympathies grew in France, his policies wavered between active suppression and benign neglect, the latter an attempt to pacify his Protestant neighbors in Germany. Periods of suppression would generally come in reaction to some flagrant attack upon Roman Catholic sensitivities.

In the meantime, Protestant activists, most notably Farel and John CALVIN, had fled to French-speaking SWITZERLAND and had gained considerable support in Geneva. In 1536, Calvin released his *Institutes of the Christian Religion*, destined to become the leading statement of the Reformed theological position. In absentia, Calvin became the titular leadere of French Protestants. In 1540, Francis took a definite stand and issued the Edict of Fontainebleau calling for the repression of Protestantism. Two years later, the Sorbonne faculty issued their attack on the *Institutes*. The first group to feel the severity of systematic persecution were the Waldensians of the Durance Valley, in Provence (near the Italian border). The following year, a group of 14 reformers from Meaux were executed.

The Protestant movement moved underground. Francis's successor, Henry II, in 1548, set up a special court to try heretics; years later, he issued the Edict of Chateaubriand to codify all the anti-Protestant laws and regulations. However, Protestantism continued to grow and to gain support among influential and noble families. Converts included those of royal blood. In 1561, the French Protestant leadership gathered in Paris to compose their statement of faith, the Gallican Confession.

Various parties tried to work out compromises that would allow some degree of toleration for the HUGUENOTS (as the Protestants were now known). In 1561, Catherine de' Medici (1519–89), mother of the new boy king, Charles IX (r. 1561–74), invited Protestant leaders to a colloquy at the town of Poissey. It failed to budge either group. In 1562, a series of violent incidents, including the massacre of a group of Protestants who had gathered near Vassy in a barn for worship, set off a civil war. An initial peace was reached in 1570, in which toleration was granted to the Huguenots, but it did not last long. On August 24, 1572 (*see* ST. BARTHOLOMEW'S DAY MASSACRE), Catherine and her supporters launched a sudden attack on the Huguenots, some 20,000 of whom were killed in the next few days. France was once again beset with a series of wars between the various factions, that continued until Henry IV (r. 1589–1610) assumed the throne in 1589. He slowly settled with each group and finally brought the wars to an end in 1598 with the EDICT OF NANTES. The edict proclaimed the Catholic Church as the state church of France, but granted religious and civil rights to the estimated 1.25 million Huguenots.

The Huguenots were able to rebuild a strong community, and some of their leaders were appointed to high government positions. However, under Louis XIII and Louis XIV their favored position began to erode. Cardinal Richelieu, who became prime minister of France in 1624, began the process of denying public offices to Huguenots. In 1660, they were forbidden to hold their national synods. Over the next 25 years, Louis step by step abrogated all the provisions of the Edict of Nantes, which he abruptly revoked in 1685. Protestants were not allowed to gather for public worship, even in their homes. Protestant ministers were ordered out of France, and the Catholic Church took charge of baptizing and schooling Protestant children. Those who did not leave the country reverted to the underground. Those who did flee were largely artisans, craftsmen, and/or professional people, who were usually welcomed by other countries.

Only in 1787, under Louis XVI, was a new Edict of Toleration granted. For the first time in over a century, Protestants were allowed to be legally married before a magistrate and to have the births of children officially recorded. Shortly thereafter, Protestant churches were again opened for public worship, and the Protestant community took its place on the French religious landscape.

Today, the Protestant community in France is represented by the Reformed Church of France (the primary descendants of the Huguenots), the Evangelical Lutheran Church of France, the Reformed Church of Alsace and Lorraine, and the Church of the Augsburg Confession of Alsace and Lorraine (all members of the WORLD COUNCIL OF CHURCHES). While the Reformed Church of France carries much of the history of persecution and survival, that history is also shared by the much smaller Lutheran community.

One section of the country is unique, Alsace and Lorraine. Protestantism gained an early foothold in Strasbourg, and Alsace became predominantly Protestant. The region was ceded to France in 1648. The two Protestant churches in the region have remained autonomous.

In the early 19th century, the missionary enthusiasm in England and Switzerland spread to France. Protestants began to organize informal prayer groups that led in 1822 to the founding of the PARIS MISSION (the Sociétée de missions évangéliques des Paris). It established branches in Italy, Holland, and French-speaking Switzerland, and in 1829 commissioned its first missionary, who was sent to SOUTH AFRICA. As France joined its European neighbors in founding a global empire, the Paris Mission took the lead in evangelizing the residents of the colonies. Many of its missions have resulted in the emergence of new Reformed bodies in other parts of the world.

In the 19th and 20th centuries, the dominance of the Reformed and Lutheran Churches in the French Protestant community has been challenged by the introduction of a spectrum of Protestant bodies primarily from North America. Among the newer groups are the Federation of Evangelical Baptist Churches, the CHRISTIAN BRETHREN, the SALVATION ARMY, the ASSEMBLIES OF GOD (and its sister ministry among the Gypsies, the Eglises Tziganes), the SEVENTH-DAY ADVENTIST CHURCH, and the JEHOVAH'S WITNESSES, the latter group now being one of the largest religious bodies in the country.

A number of Protestant groups have banded together in the Protestant Federation of France, founded in 1913. At the beginning of the new century, the Protestant community includes approximately 1.5 to 2 percent of the population.

In the 1990s, following the suicide of members of a small esoteric group, the Solar Temple, the French government moved against what it saw as a number of dangerous sect groups (or cults), and a potentially repressive law was passed in 2001. Included in a list of dangerous groups were several of the newer Protestant groups, including the Evangelical Pentecostal Church of Besançon, and the Neo Apostolic Church of France as well as some of the post–World War II groups such as the INTERNATIONAL CHURCHES OF CHRIST in France and the Jehovah's Witnesses. The older Protestant churches joined with human rights organizations to oppose these measures.

Further reading: *Annuaire de la France* (Paris: Fédération Protestante de France, issued annually); Frederic Baumgartner, *France in the Sixteenth Century* (New York: St. Martin's, 1995); Jean-Jacques Bauswein and Lukas Vischer, eds., *The Reformed Family Worldwide: A Survey of Reformed Churches, Theological Schools, and International Organizations* (Grand Rapids, Mich.: William B. Eerdmans, 1999); Mack P. Holt, *The French Wars of Religion 1562–1629* (Cambridge: Cambridge University Press, 1995); George A. Rothrock, *The Huguenots: A Biography of a Minority* (Chicago: Nelson Hall, 1979).

Francken, August Hermann *See* PIETISM.

Free Churches

The term *free church* was initially used to refer to those Protestant Christian churches that separated themselves from the state governments of Europe. Free Churches originally emerged in strength at the time of the Protestant Reformation when leaders of the Swiss Brethren called for a more RADICAL REFORMATION of the church than that being asked for by Martin LUTHER, Ulrich ZWINGLI, and later John CALVIN. They wanted a pure church consisting of adults who had been converted to Christianity and who made a conscious decision to affiliate with it. By definition, such a church could not align with the state nor include all of the nation's citizens. In the Free Churches, ecclesiastical discipline operated only among church members, the most extreme discipline being the expulsion of a member from the church's fellowship.

Free Churches practiced adult BAPTISM. State churches (including the Lutheran, Reformed, and Anglican) baptized the children of members soon after their birth. The Free Churches waited to baptize persons only after they had reached an age at which they could make a personal confession of faith. Free Church members previously baptized in one of the state churches as an infant were as a matter of course rebaptized. Concern for the true exercise of baptism led to a secondary concern about the proper mode of baptism, with many following the lead of the BAPTISTS in opting for immersion. A few, including the Church of the Brethren, advocated triune immersion. Free Churches also divided over the necessity of the act of baptism for individual salvation, a concept called baptismal regeneration.

Today, Free Churches include in Europe the MENNONITES, Baptists, QUAKERS, the Mission Covenant Church of Sweden, the Evangelical Lutheran Free Church of Norway, and the Free Church of Scotland. In North America, the churches of the RESTORATION MOVEMENT (i.e., the Churches of Christ, the Christian Churches and Churches of Christ, and the Christian Church [Disciples of Christ]) are among the most prominent of Free Church groups.

The idea of a Free Church also came to mean being free of creeds (other than the Bible) or lacking various forms of ecclesiastical hierarchy. Most Free Churches have adopted a modified congregational POLITY. Groups such as the Churches of Christ and the Primitive Baptists have adopted an ultracongregational polity that limits any governance functions by structures above the local congregations. Other Free Churches, such as the SOUTHERN BAPTIST CONVENTION and the Christian Church (Disciples of Christ), grant denominational structures considerable power to build and control programs operated for the denomination as a whole.

Further reading: Horton Davies, *The English Free Churches,* 2nd ed. (Oxford: Oxford University Press, 1963); Paul M. Harrison, *Authority and Power in the Free Church Tradition* (Princeton, N.J.: Princeton University Press, 1959); Franklin H. Littell, *The Free Church* (Boston: Starr King Press, 1957); Earnest A. Payne, *The Free Church Tradition in the Life of Eng-*

land (London: SCM Press, 1951); Gunnar Westin, *The Free Church through the Ages* (Nashville, Tenn.: Broadman Press, 1958).

Freeman, Thomas Birch (1809–1890)
pioneer Methodist missionary in Africa

An African who became a pioneer Methodist missionary in West Africa, Thomas Birch Freeman was born at Twyford, Hampshire, England, in 1809, the son of an English mother and a freed African slave, Thomas Freeman. As a young man, he joined the Methodists while working as a gardener. In the mid-1830s, he lost his job because of his religion, and he applied to the Wesleyan Methodist Missionary Society to become a missionary in West Africa. He sailed for the Gold Coast (now Ghana) in 1837, arriving early the next year. Several English missionaries had preceded him there, but their work had failed to bear fruit.

Freeman built a church at Cape Coast, which served as a base from which he moved up and down the coastal plain. He became acquainted with William deGraft, a Fanti, whom he recruited as a colleague in the ministry. Freeman's real breakthrough came from a visit inland to Kusami, the capital of the Ashanti kingdom, where he developed friendships with the head of the nation and a number of chiefs. At the end of the decade, he returned to England for a visit with de Graft. In 1841, he published his journals, which, along with his lectures, made him a celebrity. He was able to increase his support and returned to the Gold Coast with several missionary recruits.

Upon his return to Africa, he again visited Kusami. He next went to SIERRA LEONE, where some Yorubans had requested assistance from the Wesleyans. He expanded the older Wesleyan work at Freetown to the Yoruban territory. He later opened work in Dahomey (now Benin) and in the heart of Yoruba territory in NIGERIA (Lagos and Abeokuta). His ability to work was constantly hampered by British attempts to colonize the African coast, and by the limited financial resources available from the Wesleyans in England.

His far-flung missionary endeavor came to end in 1857. While Freeman was a most capable diplomat, he spent money far beyond his budget. He was accused of financial mismanagement and forced out as superintendent. To repay the mission, he took a government job in Accra. Beginning in 1860, he lived in the Gold Coast as a farmer, and preached as he was able. In 1873, he and the Wesleyan Missionary Society reconciled, and he assumed duties as a missionary at Anamabu (Nigeria), where he served for six years. For the last six years of his working life he preached in Accra, where he died in 1890.

Freeman led in the spread of Protestantism in general and METHODISM in particular throughout West Africa. He is now given credit for establishing their presence throughout West Africa.

See also AFRICA, SUB-SAHARAN.

Further reading: Allen Birtwhistle, *Thomas Birch Freeman* (London: Cargate Press, 1950); Thomas Birch Freeman, *Journal of Various Visits to the Kingdoms of Ashanti, Aku and Dahomi in West Africa* (London: John Mason, 1843); ———, *Missionary Enterprise No Fiction* (1871); F. Deaville Walker, *Thomas Birch Freeman: The Son of an African* (London: Student Christian Movement, 1929).

Free Methodist Church of North America

The Free Methodist Church was founded in an attempt to bring American Methodists back to their roots, by emphasizing modest living and sanctification. The church was formally organized in Pekin, New York, in 1860, but its origins can be traced back to a decade-old call for reform within the Genesee Conference of the Methodist Episcopal Church (now a constituent part of the UNITED METHODIST CHURCH). Ministers such as Benjamin Titus Roberts (1823–93) called for a renewed emphasis on traditional Methodist doctrines such as sanctification, and an end to the worldliness they saw among the increasingly affluent Methodists. They rejected the selling of pews, denounced secret societies, and advocated abolitionism, which most Methodists saw as an unworkable solution to the slavery question.

Roberts and others were expelled from the conference, and following an unsuccessful appeal to the 1860 General Conference, they moved to set up the Free Methodist Church. One of the first congregations was in St. Louis, Missouri, then in slaveholding territory.

In the decades after the Civil War, the church was an enthusiastic supporter of the HOLINESS movement. It added an article on entire sanctification to the common ARTICLES OF RELIGION used by most Methodist groups. In 1874, the church adopted a new doctrinal statement. The church found its greatest strength in the Midwest, and also planted churches on the West Coast. By the 1880s, it was ready to join the world Protestant missionary movement, and in 1881 the first Free Methodist missionaries, Rev. and Mrs. E. F. Ward, established work in India. Subsequently, work has been established in more than 35 countries. The Free Methodists are unusual for their affiliated work in Egypt, a predominantly Muslim country. The work originated in 1899, when Herbert E. Randall, a Canadian missionary with the Holiness Movement Church, settled in Asyut, Egypt. In 1959, the Holiness Movement Church merged into the Free Methodist Church, bringing the Egyptian conference with it.

The Free Methodist Church is headquartered in Indianapolis, Indiana. As the new century began, the church reported 74,170 members in 900 congregations in the United States, and a total world membership of 400,000. The church is a member of the CHRISTIAN HOLINESS PARTNERSHIP.

See also HOLINESS MOVEMENT; METHODISM.

Further reading: Wilson T. Hogue, *History of the Free Methodist Church* (Chicago: Free Methodist Publishing House, 1915); David L. McKenna, *A Future with a History* (Indianapolis, Ind.: Light and Life Communications, 1997); Leslie Marston, *From Age to Age a Living Witness* (Winona Lake, Ind.: Life and Light Press, 1960); Louis A. Mussio, "The Origins and Nature of the Holiness Movement Church: A Study in Religious Populism," *Journal of the Canadian Historical Association,* New Series 7 (1996).

French Polynesia

Catholics began the process of Christianizing the islands that are now French Polynesia in 1659, but Protestant efforts that began in the 19th century have won over the majority of the population.

In 1797, a group of missionaries arrived in Tahiti from the recently founded LONDON MISSIONARY SOCIETY (LMS). The first breakthrough came in 1815, when the local ruler, King Pomare, requested BAPTISM. At his urging, most of the Tahitians converted, and he oversaw the building of a large church. The development of French colonial rule in the SOUTH PACIFIC in the latter half of the 19th century led the LMS to withdraw from Tahiti and turn their work over to the PARIS EVANGELICAL MISSIONARY SOCIETY (sponsored by the Reformed Church of France). The resulting church, formally established in 1963 as the Église Evangelique de Polynésie Française, is the largest ecclesiastical body in French Polynesia, with close to 100,000 adherents. It is a member of the WORLD COUNCIL OF CHURCHES.

Second only to the Catholic Church and the French Protestant church is the CHURCH OF JESUS CHRIST OF LATTER-DAY SAINTS (LDS). LDS missionaries arrived in 1844, motivated by their belief in the unique role of Polynesians in world history. It was the first effort by Mormon missionaries in a non-English-speaking area of the world. The French authorities expelled them in 1852, but they were allowed to reopen in 1892. Together with the Reorganized Church of Jesus Christ of Latter-day Saints (recently renamed the Christian Community), which began work in 1884, the LDS claims 10,000 Mormons in the islands. The only additional churches with as many as a thousand members are the SEVENTH-DAY ADVENTIST CHURCH and the JEHOVAH'S WITNESSES.

Further reading: S. G. Ellsworth and K. C. Perrin, *Seasons of Faith and Courage: The Church of Jesus Christ of Latter-day Saints in French Polynesia, A Sesquicentennial History, 1843–1993* (Sandy, Utah: Yves R. Perrin, 1994); Daniel Mauer, *Protestant Church at Tahiti* (Paris: Nouvelles Editions Latines, 1970).

French West Africa

Most of the countries that make up the former French West Africa are predominantly Muslim, with a large presence of Roman Catholicism and indigenous religions. The small Protestant communities that were planted by missionaries have maintained a sometimes precarious existence in the region.

France entered the European competition to colonize Africa with the conquest of ALGERIA in 1830. Between 1851 and 1895, the country took over a vast stretch of territory it called French West Africa, which today comprises eight independent countries: BENIN (formerly Dahomey), GUINEA, IVORY COAST, Mauritania, Niger, SENEGAL, Mali (French Sudan), and Burkina Faso (Upper Volta). For Europeans, this vast region included some of the most inhospitable lands on earth, from arid desert to humid rainforest. France also added Tunisia (1881) and MOROCCO (1912) to its North African territories.

With the French came Roman Catholicism, which in the early 20th century became the second-largest religious community in most of the French territories.

Protestantism was introduced into Dahomey by Methodist missionary Thomas Birch FREEMAN (1809–90) in 1843 and has maintained its existence to the present. The Reformed Church of France came to Algeria in 1873 with the first wave of French settlers, but its growth was primarily limited to the expatriate community. Its missionary arm, the PARIS EVANGELICAL MISSIONARY SOCIETY, launched work in Senegal, but its missionaries were little able to deal with the equatorial climate. Then in 1881, the newly formed North Africa Mission (NAM), led by Edward H. Glenny, launched missionary activity in Algeria among the Berber and Arab populations. NAM pushed on into Tunisia the next year, where it encountered the small Anglican mission established in 1829 to evangelize the Jewish population. In 1888, NAM's work was supplemented by the arrival of missionaries from a small British sending agency, the Algiers Mission Band.

In the 20th century, the opening of new missions in the region was a spotty affair. The Paris Mission sent as many people as it was able, but its resources were limited. Significant work was launched by the CHRISTIAN AND MISSIONARY ALLIANCE in Guinea (1918), Mali (1923), Burkina Faso (1923), and the Ivory Coast (1930); the Gospel Missionary Union in Mali (1919); the World Evangelization Crusade in the Ivory Coast (1934); and the SUDAN INTERIOR MISSION in Niger (1934).

PENTECOSTALISM first entered the region in 1912 in the person of Josephine Planter, who settled in Tunisia. She was not allowed to hold public gatherings, but she did establish a Bible distribution center and carried on a personal ministry for more than four decades. She was supported by the CHURCH OF GOD (CLEVELAND, TENNESSEE), though the first official Church of God missionary, Margaret Gaines, did not arrive until some years later. The first Pentecostal church was opened in Tunisia in 1957. The ASSEMBLIES OF GOD spread the Pentecostal message to Burkina Faso (1921), Benin (1945) and Senegal (1956), though its success has been limited.

One of the AFRICAN INITIATED CHURCHES did play an important role in French West Africa. In 1913–15, William Wade HARRIS, a Christian prophet from Liberia, preached in the region and founded a number of prayer groups. He baptized more than 100,000 people. Many later became Catholics, and some 25,000 joined the Methodists, who entered the area in 1924. However, the majority formed an independent church. Today, the Harrist Church is the largest non-Catholic church in the region, with some 350,000 members. It is a member of the WORLD COUNCIL OF CHURCHES.

The effect of independence on the Protestant community was disastrous, especially in those countries dominated by Islam. With the French expatriates returning to their homeland in the 1960s and 1970s, only a token Protestant presence was left. The churches survived somewhat better in the more southerly lands. However, in Guinea in 1961, the secular Marxist government nationalized all church schools and began deporting all foreign missionary personnel, both Catholic and Protestant. Following the overthrow of the government in 1984, some stability returned. Today, the largest Protestant body is the Evangelical Protestant Church, an outgrowth of the Christian and Missionary Alliance work.

Much of the region falls within what modern Evangelicals call the 10/40 Window, which includes the most unevangelized nations of the world. The 10/40 Window, lands between 10° and 40° north of the equator in Africa, Asia, and the Middle East, are among the most resistant to Christian missionary endeavors. What Protestant presence remains in Muslim North and West Africa consists mostly of support for schools and hospitals and maintenance of expatriate congregations. Ecumenical activity is limited to an Association of Evangelical Churches and Missions in Guinea and the Evangelical Federation of the Ivory Coast, both related to the WORLD EVANGELICAL ALLIANCE. Apart from the Harrist Church, only the Methodist Church in Benin and the Ivory Coast are members of the WORLD COUNCIL OF CHURCHES.

See also EQUATORIAL GUINEA; FRENCH GUINEA; GABON; GUINEA-BISSAU.

Further reading: David Barrett, *The Encyclopedia of World Christianity*, 2nd ed. (New York: Oxford University Press, 2001); Patrick Johnstone and Jason Mandryk, *Operation World, 21st Century Edition* (Carlisle, Cumbria, U.K.: Paternoster, 2001); J. Herbert Kane, *A Global View of Christian Missions* (Grand Rapids, Mich.: Baker Book House, 1971); Sheila Suzanne Walker, *The Religious Revolution in the Ivory Coast: The Prophet Harris and His Church*

(Chapel Hill: University of North Carolina Press, 1983); *World Methodist Council, Handbook of Information* (Lake Junaluska, N.C.: World Methodist Council, 2003).

Friends *See* QUAKERS.

Friends United Meeting

The Friends United Meeting, based in the United States, is the largest Friends (QUAKERS) association in the world.

The Friends movement in North America began in the colonial era, when William PENN (1644–1718) created Pennsylvania as a haven for persecuted groups, including his own Quaker fellowship. The Friends accepted the basic beliefs of Christianity concerning God as Father, the Lordship of Jesus Christ, and salvation by faith, but were distinguished by their radical separation from the state and their commitment to a life of nonviolence and PACIFISM.

As the movement in the United States grew, two dissenting groups emerged. One, led by Elias HICKS (1748–1830), emphasized the work of the Inner Light and tended to reject all external authority in worship. Another, led by Joseph John Gurney (1788–1847), became attracted to the Wesleyan HOLINESS MOVEMENT. These two branches eventually separated from the main body of Quakers to form what is now known as the Friends General Conference (Hicksite) and Evangelical Friends International (Holiness). Efforts to form a national organization for the remaining Friends began in the 1880s, resulting in the Five Years Meeting in 1902, known since 1965 as the Friends United Meeting.

In the 19th century, Friends began evangelistic work in other countries, with notable success in CUBA, JAMAICA, MEXICO, Israel, and Africa. Today, 100,000 of the 150,000 members of the Friends United Meeting reside outside of the United States, of which more than 60,000 are in Kenya. The Friends United Meeting actively cooperates with the FRIENDS WORLD COMMITTEE FOR CONSULTATION.

Further reading: Francis B. Hall, ed. *Friends in the Americas* (Philadelphia: Friends World Committee, Section of the Americas, 1976); *Quakers Around the World* (London: Friends World Committee for Consultation, 1994).

Friends World Committee for Consultation

The Friends World Committee for Consultation (FWCC) is the major agency uniting the various bodies of QUAKERS (Society of Friends) around the world. It was organized at the Second World Conference of Friends held in 1937 at Swarthmore, Pennsylvania. Through the early 20th century, Quaker leaders had been calling for greater unity to overcome the splits in the movement. Quakers had united in resistance to World War I, which gave many hope that unity was possible.

The FWCC reorganized after World War II. At the 1952 World Conference in Oxford, England, the top agenda item was a proposal for creating a united voice for Quaker witness on social issues, especially issues related to peace and social justice. Over the next decade, most of the yearly (district and national) meetings around the world affiliated with the committee. The committee divided its work into four arenas—Africa, the Americas, Asia and the western Pacific, and Europe and the Middle East. Its work focuses on maintaining lines of communication with Friends worldwide, and providing a voice for the Quaker community to the outside world, both the larger Christian community and the secular world.

The committee reviews its work every three years in a large international meeting. Between the triennial meetings, an Interim Committee and an executive staff administer its affairs from its headquarters in London, England.

Further reading: George Peck, *What Is Quakerism? A Primer* (Wallingford, Pa.: Pendle Hill Publications, 1988); *Quakers Around the World* (London: Friends World Committee for Consultation, 1994).

Fuller, Andrew (1754–1815) *founder of the worldwide Protestant missionary endeavor*

English Baptist minister Andrew Fuller helped lay the theological and practical groundwork for the first Baptist missionary efforts in the late 18th century. Fuller was born on a farm on February 5, 1754, at Wicken, Cambridgeshire, England. He had a conversion experience in 1769 and the following year was baptized and joined a Baptist church at Solam. Self-educated, in 1775 he was ordained and assumed the pastorate of the Solam church. In 1782, he moved to Kettering, Northamptonshire, and served the Baptist church there until his death.

Fuller's Baptist community was dominated by an extreme Calvinist doctrine of PREDESTINATION, and thus evangelism was not a priority. At the same time, the growing Wesleyan Methodist movement derived from ARMINIANISM was teaching that God's free grace had been planted in the hearts of all people. Fuller, mindful of his own youthful conversion and of the biblical command to preach the Gospel to all people, began to modify his CALVINISM to make a place for preaching to the unbelieving public. He explored these ideas in his 1781 book, *The Gospel of Christ Worthy of All Acceptation*. Though he was careful to distinguish his Calvinism from an explicit Arminian approach, his views sparked intense controversy among his Baptist colleagues.

In 1787, Fuller baptized William CAREY, who five years later published his pamphlet *An Enquiry into the Obligations of Christians to Use Means for the Conversion of the Heathens*. Carey pressed his views at Fuller's church, where in 1793 the Baptist Missionary Society (BMS) took shape. The BMS was the first of a set of British denominational missionary societies that emerged in that era, and which became the backbone of the global spread of Protestantism.

While Carey left for India as the BMS's first missionary, Fuller stayed behind to build support.

He served as secretary of the BMS until his death from tuberculosis on May 7, 1815.

See also BAPTISTS.

Further reading: George M. Ella, *Law & Gospel in the Theology of Andrew Fuller* (Eggleston, Colo./Durham, Ireland: Go Publications, 1996); Andrew Fuller, *Complete Works of the Rev. Andrew Fuller,* 2 vols. (Boston: Lincoln, Edmands, 1833; new ed.: Harrisonburg, Va.: Sprinkle Publications, 1988); Timothy George and David S. Dockery, eds., *Baptist Theologians* (Nashville, Tenn.: Broadman Press, 1990); Gilbert Laws, *Andrew Fuller* (London: Carey Press, 1942).

Full Gospel Business Men's Fellowship International

The Full Gospel Business Men's Fellowship International (FGBMFI) is an organization of laymen that promotes Pentecostal beliefs and practices among members and has helped spread PENTE-COSTALISM among members of other DENOMINA-TIONS. Since its founding in 1951, it has spread to countries all over the world.

The fellowship was conceived by Demos Shakarian (1913–93), a successful businessman and lay supporter of evangelistic programs. Shakarian grew up in an Armenian Pentecostal congregation in Southern California. He received the BAPTISM OF THE HOLY SPIRIT as a youth of 13, after which a hearing problem was healed. In 1951, during an Oral ROBERTS revival in Los Angeles that he helped arrange, he won Roberts's support for his idea of an interdenominational group where businessmen could gather to share their faith in Christ. Roberts spoke at the first gathering of what would become the FGBMFI.

Some 3,000 people attended the first conference, representing a handful of chapters. The group began issuing a periodical, *Voice,* to spread the message, and by 1965 there were 300 groups meeting weekly around the United States.

The FGBMFI was very successful in spreading the Pentecostal message into mainline Protestant churches. People attending a meeting for the first time were often unaware of the Pentecostal orientation, but many experienced the baptism of the Holy Spirit and others were healed. Some invited their pastors, who also had similar experiences. The FGBMFI and the *Voice* became major sources for the CHARISMATIC MOVE-MENT that emerged in the 1960s. Between the mid-1960s and mid-1980s, the organization grew tenfold and spread to more than 80 countries. A television program that ran in the late 1970s and early 1980s, based around the extraordinary experiences of its members, was a factor in this growth. FGBMFI also had a role in the emergence of the Word Faith movement, whose early exponents, Kenneth Hagin Sr. and Kenneth Copeland, were popular speakers at Fellowship gatherings.

After Demos Shakarian had a stroke in 1984, his son Richard Shakarian emerged as the new international president. As of 2004, the fellowship is active in 132 countries.

Further reading: David E. Harrell Jr., *All Things Are Possible* (Bloomington: Indiana University Press 1975); Demos Shakarian, as told to John and Elizabeth Sherrill, *The Happiest People on Earth* (Old Tappan, N.J.: Chosen Books, 1975); Vinson Synan, *The Century of the Holy Spirit: 100 Years of Pentecostal and Charismatic Renewal* (Nashville, Tenn.: Thomas Nelson, 2001).

Fundamentalism

Fundamentalism is a 20th-century movement within American Protestantism that defends the continued validity of traditional Christian beliefs in the face of a spectrum of modern ideas that have won acceptance in older DENOMINATIONS. Strictly speaking, Fundamentalism calls for an adversarial relation with church bodies that support these nontraditional ideas. In popular and journalistic use, the term is also used to refer to EVANGELICALISM; recently, it has become used as a label to cover conservative movements and tendencies in non-Protestant and non-Christian religions as well.

By the early 20th century, many leaders in major Protestant denominations, including administrators, prominent preachers, and seminary professors, had come to support one or more nontraditional concepts such as the theory of evolution, modern BIBLICAL CRITICISM, rejection of the deity of Christ or the Trinity, and the priority of the social gospel over against traditional evangelism. Conservative leaders believed the new ideas threatened the very roots of church life and would make the church unrecognizable. Christianity, they insisted, was not incompatible with true science.

At first, conservatives tried to fight the new ideas with a series of trials of ministers and seminary professors. A prominent example was Charles A. Briggs (1814–1913), whose 1891 address on the occasion of his assuming a teaching post at Union Theological Seminary was rejected by PRESBYTERIAN CHURCH leadership. The church's assembly in 1893 defrocked him from the ministry. As a result, Union broke its relationship with the Presbyterians, and Briggs joined the Episcopal Church.

The conservative cause was strongest in the Methodist HOLINESS tradition, the Presbyterian Church's Princeton Theological Seminary, and among independent Bible students, many influenced by evangelist Dwight L. MOODY. The Presbyterian Church in 1910 passed a position paper called the Five Point Deliverance, which required ministers to affirm five essential doctrines: the inspiration and INERRANCY of the Bible, Christ's virgin birth, Christ's death as a sacrifice to satisfy divine justice, Christ's bodily resurrection, and Christ's performance of miracles during his earthly ministry.

In the next phase, as modern ideas spread in several of the older churches, conservative Christians from a wide range of theological perspectives and denominational allegiances began to come together to affirm their faith. In 1909, brothers Lyman and Milton Stewart, both wealthy oilmen, underwrote the production and distribution of a 12-volume set of conservative Christian essays titled *The FUNDAMENTALS: A Testimony of Truth.* More than 3 million individual volumes were mailed out free of charge to ministers throughout the English-speaking world.

By World War I, the several hundred Protestant denominations, who had always differed from one another over theological issues often dating back to the Reformation, were now increasingly divided internally over how much to tolerate the new ideas. Many conservatives were beginning to develop a self-conscious identity as a pandenominational movement united to oppose further inroads by the modernists. One sign was the formation of the World Christian Fundamentals Association. Credit for giving Fundamentalists their name is generally ascribed to Curtis Lee Laws (1868–1946), a Baptist editor who seems to have coined the term *fundamentalist* in an editorial he penned in 1920.

Churches with a more decentralized structure (BAPTISTS, Congregationalists) had more difficulty keeping a consensus of theological opinion than Episcopalians, already used to differences, thanks to the earlier endeavor to include both low-church evangelicals and high-church Anglo-Catholics. The primary focus of the 1920s battle between fundamentalists and modernists was in the Presbyterian Church and the Northern Baptist Convention (now the AMERICAN BAPTIST CHURCHES U.S.A.). The battle raged on two fronts, a fight for control of the denominational machinery, and a struggle for the hearts and minds of the members.

The struggle for hearts and minds came to focus on the theory of evolution as a scientific explanation of human origins. It reached a critical point in the so-called Monkey Trial in Dayton, Tennessee, in 1925. Though Fundamentalist politician William Jennings Bryan (1860–1925) officially won the case, there was widespread belief that his opponent, Clarence Darrow (1857–1938), had the better arguments and that evolution would eventually carry the day (which it has done).

On the denominational front, the two factions fought over credentialing new ministers and missionaries, and control of the seminaries where these clergy were trained. Power seemed to change hands in the Presbyterian Church by 1925, when the Five Points Deliverance was replaced with the Auburn Affirmation, which opened the church to a variety of views on key doctrines. Among the Northern Baptists in the early 1920s, the fundamentalist position was also rejected; the church affirmed a statement that the Bible was the only rule in faith and practice, a statement that left the door open for a wide variety of interpretation.

Through the 1920s, both conservatives and modernists scored victories and defeats as different issues came before the several church judicatories. However, by the 1930s it was obvious that the modernists were gaining the upper hand. In 1929, a group of Princeton professors left to found the independent Westminster Theological Seminary. From their new base, under the leadership of J. Gresham Machen (1881–1937), they fought a final battle over Presbyterian missions. Machen led in the formation of the Independent Board of Foreign Missions, asking Presbyterians to support it in order to guarantee the orthodoxy of the missionaries they were paying for. When the church formally censured Machen, he left to found the Orthodox Presbyterian Church. A similar move had already led Fundamentalist Baptists to establish the General Association of Regular Baptist Churches (GARBC). Through the 1930s, a number of other fundamentalist denominations were founded, including the Independent Fundamental Churches of America (IFCA).

At this juncture, people of differing theological perspectives who had previously made common cause against the modernists now found themselves divided and unable to work with one another. The major division was between the dispensationalists, such as Carl McIntire (1906–2003), and those like Machen who followed the older Princeton theology. McIntire broke with the Orthodox Presbyterian Church and founded the Bible Presbyterian Church. Other bodies advocating DISPENSATIONALISM included the GARBC and IFCA.

Fundamentalist leaders now faced another issue: how to relate to their colleagues who had chosen to remain in the liberal-controlled churches for career and other reasons. One group remained in contact with their colleagues and were willing to work with anyone who retained a conservative faith. This group would in the 1940s became known as Evangelicals or Neo-Evangelicals. The other group, probably a minority, demanded separation from all apostasy and unbelief and remained determined to carry on the battle against modernism in all its forms. This group continued to be known as the Fundamentalists.

In the 1940s, the Evangelicals came together in the National Association of Evangelicals. Fundamentalists founded the American Council of Christian Churches, and in 1948 the INTERNATIONAL COUNCIL OF CHRISTIAN CHURCHES (ICCC). Carl McIntire took the lead in both fundamentalist organizations.

In the decades since World War II, the Evangelical movement has thrived through religious broadcasting, campus ministries, involvement in national politics, and missionary work. Fundamentalism also grew, though to a far lesser extent, limited by its separatism. Its largest organizations were found within the Baptist community—the Bible Baptist Fellowship International, the Independent Baptists, and the World Baptist Fellowship. The latter group was associated with the outstanding if controversial Fundamentalist minister J. Frank Norris (1877–1952).

In the last generation, Fundamentalism received a boost from the ministry of televangelist Jerry Falwell (b. 1932), pastor of the Thomas Road Baptist Church in Lynchburg, Virginia, founder of Liberty University, and head of Liberty Baptist Fellowship. His Baptist colleague Tim LaHaye (b. 1926) contributed by coauthoring the hugely popular "Left Behind" novels about end-time events. LaHaye and his wife, Beverley LaHaye (b. 1930), are major personalities in the RELIGIOUS RIGHT, which has attracted support from both Fundamentalists and Evangelicals. Meanwhile, the ICCC gained its largest member when the Korean Presbyterian Church split into two denominations, the more conservative branch with more than 2 million members.

See also CREATIONISM.

Further reading: George W. Dollar, *A History of Fundamentalism in America* (Greenville, S.C.: Bob Jones University Press, 1973); Jerry Falwell, *The Fundamentalist Phenomenon: The Resurgence of Conservative Christianity* (Garden City, N.Y.: Doubleday-Galilee Original, 1981); George Marsden, *Fundamentalism and American Culture.* (New York: Oxford University Press, 1980); Ernest R. Sandeen, *The Roots of Fundamentalism* (Chicago: University of Chicago Press, 1970); Glen H. Utter and John W. Storey, *The Religious Right* (Santa Barbara, Calif.: ABC-CLIO, 2001).

Fundamentals, The

The Fundamentals: A Testimony to Truth was a 12-volume set of essays published starting in 1909 and purporting to set forth the fundamentals of the Protestant Christian faith. It was a response to the spread of opinions among American Protestant leaders that were seen by conservatives as departures from the historic faith. They included BIBLICAL CRITICISM, evolutionary theory in biology and geology, reinterpretations of traditional Christian affirmations, and the social gospel, which sought the rehabilitation of society rather than the evangelization of individuals.

Oil millionaires Lyman Stewart (1840–1923) and his brother Milton Stewart (1838–1923), devout Presbyterians, funded the publication and free distribution of 3 million copies of the book to ministers throughout the English-speaking world.

The volumes were edited by Amzi C. Dixon (1854–1925), R. A. Torrey (1856–1928), and Louis Meyer. The authors were drawn from various churches and theological perspectives, but were united in their affirmation of traditional Protestant teachings. Included were James Orr (1844–1913), W. J. Erdman, H. C. G. Moule, James M. Gray (1851–1935), Jessie Penn-Lewis (1861–1927), Arno C. Gaebelein (1861–1945), and Benjamin B. Warfield (1851–1921). Two themes running through the volumes were the compatibility of Christian supernaturalism with modern science and confirmation of Christian truth in personal experience.

The Fundamentals was rather conciliatory in tone and represented a first stage of what would become FUNDAMENTALISM after World War I. By the 1920s, many of the writers were either retired or deceased, but they raised the issues that would become the substance of the Fundamentalist movement a decade later.

Further reading: S. G. Cole, *History of Fundamentalism* (Westport, Conn.: Greenwood Press, 1931); A. C. Dixon, Louis Meyer, and R. A. Torrey, eds., *The Fundamentals: A Testimony to the Truth* (rpt., Grand Rapids, Mich.: Baker Book House, 2003); Norman Furniss, *The Fundamentalist Controversy, 1918–1931* (New Haven, Conn.: Yale University Press, 1954); George Marsden, *Fundamentalism and American Culture* (New York: Oxford University Press, 1980); Ernest R. Sandeen, *The Roots of Fundamentalism* (Chicago: University of Chicago Press, 1970).

G

Gabon

Roman Catholicism was founded in Gabon in the 1600s by members of the Capuchin Order from ITALY and later promoted by Portuguese priests and other Catholic orders. Libreville, founded as a town for freed slaves, became the capital of a French colony in the 19th century.

Missionaries from the AMERICAN BOARD OF COMMISSIONERS FOR FOREIGN MISSIONS arrived in 1842. Their work was turned over to American Presbyterians in 1870 and then to the PARIS EVANGELICAL MISSIONARY SOCIETY (of the Reformed Church of France). The mission became independent in 1960, when the country became independent, and is now called the Evangelical Church of Gabon. The Paris Mission, which operated primarily in the northern half of Gabon, encouraged the CHRISTIAN AND MISSIONARY ALLIANCE to begin work in the south, beginning in 1934. The CMA mission became autonomous as the Evangelical Church of South Gabon. The South Gabon church is now the larger of the two; together they dominate Protestant efforts. The Evangelical Church of Gabon is a member of the WORLD COUNCIL OF CHURCHES.

The Church of the Initiates (the Bwiti movement) mixes Christianity and the traditional religion of the Fang people and encourages the use of the mood-altering drug eboga. It has claimed more than 100,000 adherents.

Since independence, the country has gone through several transitions regarding religious freedom, beginning with the conversion of the president to Islam in 1973. Several groups were officially banned in the 1980s, including the SALVATION ARMY, the JEHOVAH'S WITNESSES, the Church of the Cherubim and Seraphim (an AFRICAN INITIATED CHURCH), and the Bethany Church. By 1991, governmental changes led to the lifting of all the bans.

Further reading: Patrick Johnstone and Jason Mandryk, *Operation World, 21st Century Edition* (Carlisle, Cumbria, U.K.: Paternoster, 2001); E. Kruger, "Le gabon," in R. Blanc, J. Blocher and E. Kruger, eds., *Historie des missions protestantes françaises* (Flavion, Belgium: Editions la Phare, 1970).

Gambia

Britain's African presence began with the purchase of European rights to Gambia in 1618. The centuries of British rule coincided with the influx of Islam in the area, and today the country remains overwhelmingly a Muslim nation. Christianity arrived only in the 19th century, and it remains a distant third behind Islam and traditional Gambian religions.

In 1816, a chaplain with the CHURCH OF ENGLAND settled in the country and soon afterward was joined by missionaries of the SOCIETY FOR THE PROPAGATION OF THE GOSPEL IN FOREIGN PARTS. British Methodists arrived in 1821 and Roman Catholics in the 1840s. For the next century, these three churches provided the sole Christian presence. They constitute the Christian Council of Gabon, affiliated with the WORLD COUNCIL OF CHURCHES.

Evangelical groups began to arrive in the 1950s. The German-based New Apostolic Church entered the country in 1970; by 1999, it had 5,000 members, twice as many as any other non-Catholic body.

See also AFRICA, SUB-SAHARAN.

Further reading: Patrick Johnstone and Jason Mandryk, *Operation World, 21st Century Edition* (Carlisle, Cumbria, U.K.: Paternoster, 2001); J. R. C. Laughton, *Gambia: Country, People and Church in the Diocese of Gambia and the Rio Pongas* (London: SPG, 1938); B. Prickett, *Island Base: A History of the Methodist Church in the Gambia* (Bo, Sierra Leone: Bunumbu Press, 1969).

Gaussen, Louis (1790–1863) *champion of biblical inerrancy*
François Samuel Robert Louis Gaussen, a Swiss minister in the conservative Evangelistic Society, is considered the fountainhead of the contemporary belief in the INERRANCY of the Bible.

He was born in Geneva on August 25, 1790. He attended college and seminary there and became pastor of a Swiss Reformed congregation in nearby Satigny in 1816. While there, he became influenced by members of the FREE CHURCHES founded by the HALDANE BROTHERS.

In 1819, Gaussen published a commentary on the Second HELVETIC CONFESSION, strongly advocating its use by the Federation of Swiss Protestant Churches. He thought the federation was drifting from his doctrinal moorings. In 1830, when he attacked its catechism as being weak on essentials such as the divinity of Christ, original sin, and grace, he was censured, and the next year he helped found the Evangelical Society (Sociéte Evangélique), which set up a new conservative theological college. He pastored a Free Church congregation for several years, and in 1834 became a professor at the new college, where he remained until his retirement in 1857.

He published his most memorable work in 1840, *Theopneustia: The Plenary Inspiration of the Holy Scriptures*. Originally published in France, it was translated into English in 1841. This was the spark that ignited the theologians at Princeton University, who were also perceiving a similar doctrinal drift in American PRESBYTERIANISM. They used Gaussen as a foundation for their more detailed approach to the INSPIRATION and authority of the Bible in what is known as the PRINCETON THEOLOGY.

Gaussen died in Geneva on June 18, 1863.

Further reading: Louis Gaussen, *Theopneustia: The Plenary Inspiration of the Holy Scriptures*, 1841 (rpt., Chicago: The Bible Institute Colportage, n.d.).

General Baptists *See* PARTICULAR BAPTISTS.

Georgia
Christianity entered Georgia in the first century C.E., and an autonomous Georgian Orthodox Church emerged in the fifth century. The Armenian Orthodox Church also dates to ancient times, serving a large population of ethnic Armenians in Georgia. Roman Catholics began missionary work in the 13th century. In the course of the 19th century, czarist Russia annexed the country, eventually moving to incorporate the Georgian church into the Russian Orthodox Church. An independent Georgian church reappeared in 1917.

The first Protestants in Georgia were Molokans exiled by the Russian authorities. In 1862, a German Baptist, Martin Kalweit (1838–1918), settled in Tbilisi, Georgia's capital, and began work among German-speaking residents. One of his converts, Vasilov G. Pavlov (1854–1924), studied in Germany and returned to become the leading force in building the Baptist church. BAPTISTS organized in 1919, but after the Soviet conquest were integrated into the larger Russian Baptist movement. In the Stalinist 1930s, all Baptist churches were closed. Some were allowed to reopen in 1944, though all FREE CHURCHES were forced into a single organization, the All-Union Council of Evangelical Christians-Baptists. Only after the collapse of the Soviet Union in 1991 were the Georgian Baptists able to revive their own organization.

Among other Protestant groups are the Lutherans (primarily German-speaking), Pentecostals, and JEHOVAH'S WITNESSES, who with upwards of 15,000 members have emerged as possibly the largest of the Free Church groups.

Opposition among the Orthodox majority to prosetylizing by the Free Churches turned violent in the 1990s; the local press reports church burnings and mass assaults against worshippers. As a result, Georgia and the Orthodox Church of Georgia have come under sharp criticism from human rights spokespersons.

See also CENTRAL ASIA; RUSSIA.

Further reading: David Barrett, *The Encyclopedia of World Christianity,* 2nd ed. (New York: Oxford University Press, 2001); Patrick Johnstone and Jason Mandryk, *Operation World, 21st Century Edition* (Carlisle, Cumbria, U.K.: Paternoster, 2001).

Gibraltar

Gibraltar has been a British colony since 1704, but most residents are of Italian, Portuguese, Spanish, and Maltese descent and are predominantly Roman Catholic, despite early British attempts to suppress the church. The CHURCH OF ENGLAND has had little impact, its 2,000 adherents being primarily British expatriates and their descendants; it is part of the diocese of Europe based in London. The only other group making any impact is the JEHOVAH'S WITNESSES, which has been actively evangelizing since 1959 and has several hundred adherents.

Further reading: H. J. C. Knight, *The Diocese of Gibraltar: A Sketch of Its History, Work, and Tasks* (London: SPCK, 1917); *Upon This Rock, 1969–1969: a Short History of Methodism in Gibraltar* (Gibraltar, 1969).

Gideons International

Gideons International is a business and professional men's association devoted primarily to distributing Bibles in hotels and other public institutions. It was founded in 1899 by two traveling businessmen, John H. Nicholson (1859–1946) and Samuel E. Hill (1867–1936), who met, discovered their shared Christian faith, and decided to create an organization to bring together traveling businessmen for fellowship, service, and evangelism. They were soon joined by William J. Knights (1853–1940).

In order to witness in the hotels at which they stayed, they decided to present hotel desks with a BIBLE that could be borrowed by any guest. In 1908, the growing movement decided to furnish a Bible in each bedroom of every hotel in the United States.

As of 2004, the Gideons reported 236,000 members working in 179 countries. The organization annually distributes in excess of 50 million Bibles, including replacement copies. Recipients include jails and prisons, the military, youths, college campuses, and medical facilities. The program has been copied by the CHURCH OF JESUS CHRIST OF LATTER-DAY SAINTS, which distributes the Book of Mormon in hotels, and by the Society for the Promotion of Buddhism (Japanese), which now distributes a small volume, *The Teaching of the Buddha,* to hotels. Gideons International is headquartered in Nashville, Tennessee.

Further reading: *The Gideons International Guide Book* (Nashville, Tenn.: Gideons International 2001); M. A. Henderson, *Sowers of the Word: A 95-Year History of the Gideons International, 1899–1994* (Nashville, Tenn.: The Gideons International, 1995).

Gore, Charles (1853–1932) *advocate of the social gospel and ecumenicalism*

Charles Gore, Anglican bishop, liberal theologian, and ecumenical leader, was born in Wimbledon, England, in 1853, and educated at Harrow school and Oxford University. He was named a fellow of Trinity College in 1875 and ordained as a priest of the CHURCH OF ENGLAND in 1878. Two years later, he was named vice-principal of Cuddesdon Theological College.

In 1883, following the death of Edward Pusey (1800–82), a leader of the high-church Tractarian movement, Gore was made principal of Pusey House, the library established at Oxford in his honor. This appointment brought some controversy as Gore was an advocate of the new BIBLICAL CRITICISM, which Pusey had opposed. As part of his work at Pusey House, Gore wrote two books on the priestly office in the early church, defending the Church of England's Anglican orders against Roman Catholic challenges. Gore's social activist views led him to cofound the Christian Social Union in 1889 and become its vice president. The union attempted to apply Christian perspectives toward the reform of society, with the problems of trade unions being of primary concern. Gore was heavily criticized for his leanings toward socialism. He later became a harsh critic of British policy in the Boer War.

In 1889, he edited *Lux Mundi: A Series of Studies in the Religion of the Incarnation,* which called for a revision of traditional Christian affirmations in light of scientific findings and biblical research. His own essay, on the "Inspiration of the Holy Scriptures," suggested that the books of the Bible be valued not for historical or scientific information, but for their information on God's nature and his dealings with humanity. Gore also expressed his views on Christology by advocating what is generally referred to as the Kenotic (emptying) Theory of the Incarnation, which draws on Philippians 2:7, where Jesus is said to have emptied himself and to have taken on the nature of a servant. Gore interpreted this passage to suggest that Jesus, in taking on the limitations of humanity, also assumed the limitations of human knowledge of his first-century surroundings. Therefore, his words should be interpreted in light of his ignorance of modern science.

In an attempt to reassure his colleagues and the public, Gore presented what amounted to an apology at the annual Bampton lectures in 1891. His papers were later published as *The Incarnation of the Son of God.* Some years later, he argued strongly against Anglican clergy who publicly denied the virgin birth and physical resurrection of Christ. In 1887, Gore privately founded the Society of the Resurrection, an association for deepening the spiritual life of priests. The society evolved into the Community of the Resurrection order in 1892, with Gore as its senior.

In 1894, Gore was made a canon of Westminster. His lectures there became the basis of several additional books. In 1902, Gore was consecrated bishop of Worcester, and was ordained the first bishop of Birmingham in 1905. Six years later, he became bishop of Oxford, where he earned wide support for the workers of Reading who were seeking to improve their living conditions. His final years as a bishop were spent laying plans for the quick repair of relations between the opposition sides in World War I. He retired in 1919 but continued to travel, lecture, and teach. He worked with the FAITH AND ORDER MOVEMENT, which became one of the foundations of the WORLD COUNCIL OF CHURCHES. At the end of the 1920s, he gave the famous Gifford lectures, published in 1930 as *The Philosophy of the Good Life.* He lectured across India in 1930–31 and died on January 17, 1932.

Further reading: Charles Gore, *The Incarnation of the Son of God* (New York: Scribner, 1891); ———, ed., *Lux Mundi: A Series of Studies in the Religion of the*

Incarnation (London: Murray, 1891); ———, *Philosophy of the Good Life* (London: John Murray, 1930); G. L. Prestige, *The Life of Charles Gore* (London: William Heinemann, 1935); Hugh A. Lawrence Rice, *The Bridge Builders: Biographical Studies in the History of Anglicanism* (London: Darton, Longman & Todd, 1961).

Gospel music *See* AFRICAN-AMERICAN GOSPEL MUSIC.

Graham, William Franklin "Billy"
(b. 1918) *prominent international evangelist*
Billy Graham was born on November 7, 1918, at Charlotte, North Carolina, a child of conservative Presbyterians. He was converted to a personal faith in fall 1934 by Baptist evangelist Mordecai Ham (1878–1959) at a revival in Charlotte. Graham subsequently attended Bob Jones University and Florida Bible Institute (now Trinity College). He was ordained by the SOUTHERN BAPTIST CONVENTION in 1939 and graduated from Wheaton College in 1943. While at Wheaton, he met his future wife, Ruth McCue Bell, who was the daughter of a medical missionary in China.

Graham became associated with Youth for Christ, for whom he held revival meetings, and he became president of the Northwestern schools in Minneapolis founded by William Bell Riley (1861–1947). Then in 1949, he led a set of revival services in Los Angeles that proved so popular they were extended for more than eight weeks of overflow crowds. Within a few years, the structures that were to carry him for most of his life were set in place.

In 1950, he founded the Billy Graham Evangelistic Association and launched a radio show, *The Hour of Decision,* which was broadcast across the United States and around the world for more than 50 years. The next year, he resigned from his school presidency to become a full-time evangelist, and in 1952, he began his nationally syndicated daily newspaper column, "My Answer," which still

has a readership of 5 million. In 1953, he released his first book, *Peace with God.* The Evangelistic Association, headquartered in Minneapolis, Minnesota, sponsors World Wide Pictures, which has produced more than 125 motion pictures, some translated into as many as 40 languages. Graham has continued to preach in his senior years.

As Graham's reputation grew, he became the confidant of American presidents and a well-known public figure worldwide. His evangelistic services were broadcast on television as popular special events several times annually. He has preached in most of the world's 240 countries, usually accompanied by songleader George Beverley Shea (b. 1909). In 1974, Graham convened the Lausanne Congress on World Evangelism, which issued the LAUSANNE COVENANT, one of the more definitive statements of modern EVANGELICALISM.

Graham has authored some 25 books, including *Angels: God's Secret Agents* (1975), *How to Be Born Again* (1977), *Approaching Hoofbeats: The Four Horsemen of the Apocalypse* (1983), and his best-selling autobiography, *Just As I Am,* which is also the title of the song often played as participants are called for decision at the close of Graham's preaching services.

In his senior years, Graham was honored with a Congressional Gold Medal and the Ronald Reagan Presidential Foundation Freedom Award. He was also honored by the Anti-Defamation League of the B'nai B'rith and the National Conference of Christians and Jews for his contributions to understanding between faiths (a unique recognition for a Christian evangelist); he was made an Honorary Knight Commander of the order of the British Empire (KBE).

Graham's son, Franklin Graham (b. 1952), has emerged as the heir apparent of the Billy Graham Evangelistic Association and also serves as the head of the SAMARITAN'S PURSE, an international Christian aid association. Anne Graham Lotz, Graham's daughter, though not ordained, has founded Angel Ministries and serves as an evangelist and Bible teacher, with her father's blessings.

See also REVIVALISM.

Further reading: Lewis A. Drummond, *The Evangelist* (Nashville, Tenn.: World, 2001); Billy Graham, *Just As I Am: The Autobiography of Billy Graham* (San Francisco: HarperSanFrancisco, 1997); ———, *My Answer* (Garden City, N.Y.: Doubleday, 1960); ———, *World Aflame* (Garden City, N.Y.: Doubleday, 1965); John Pollock, *Billy Graham: The Authorized Biography* (New York: McGraw-Hill, 1966).

Great Awakening

The term *Great Awakening* has been applied to two periods of enthusiastic religious revival: in the American colonies of the 1740s and on the frontier of the United States in the early decades of the 19th century. Both were periods of religious ferment, creativity, and initiative and gave birth to new churches and to changes in existing denominations.

In the 1720s, voices were heard decrying the state of religion in the American colonies. It was difficult for the churches to keep up with the population as it moved westward. Established churches had grown weak, and ministers seemed unable to perpetuate traditional patterns of church participation—the population was fleeing from the churches.

The first effort at revival is usually traced to Theodore Jacob Frelinghausen (1691–1720), who came from Holland to begin work among the Dutch settlers of New Jersey. As revivals broke out under his ministry, he influenced Scotch-Irish Presbyterian Gilbert Tennent (1703–64), who soon discovered that revivals were spreading to his people as well. In 1737, Massachusetts Congregational minister Jonathan EDWARDS published an influential account of a revival that broke out in his Northampton ministry in the winter of 1734–35.

All this activity prepared the way for George WHITEFIELD's travels through America, which began in 1735. One of the great orators of the century, he preached from Charleston to Boston; at every stop crowds gathered, people were converted, and revival followed. A wave of religious concern swept the American colonies through the early 1740s and to a lesser extent in the following decades. This first Great Awakening revived the sagging faith of many and converted many others, and it had a marked effect in creating an American national consciousness. Whitefield was the major connecting point between the American revival and similar events in Europe, which together constitute what is generally termed the EVANGELICAL AWAKENING.

A second wave of religious enthusiasm began as settlers began pushing across the Allegheny Mountains early in the 19th century. New groups, primarily Methodists and BAPTISTS, set about the task of churching the West. They developed two very successful tools: CAMP MEETINGS, where farmers could take a religious vacation when farm work was least demanding, and protracted meetings, where evangelists would keep a revival going in a particular location as long as need and interest persisted.

This second Great Awakening made the Methodists and Baptists the largest religious communities in the country and spawned several new denominations—the Cumberland Presbyterians and the churches of the RESTORATION MOVEMENT—whose founders had left the more slow-moving DENOMINATIONS behind.

The second Great Awakening received a new boost in the 1830s from Charles G. FINNEY, who refined the revivals and camp meetings even more. Finney carried the evangelistic activity of the frontier churches through the 1850s and fed the development of the new urban evangelism that would characterize the decades after the Civil War.

See also REVIVALISM.

Further reading: Richard L. Bushman, ed., *The Great Awakening: Documents on the Revival of Religion, 1740–1745* (New York: Atheneum, 1970); Roger Finke and Rodney Stark, *The Churching of America, 1776–1990: Winners and Losers in Our Religious Economy* (New Brunswick N.J.: Rutgers University Press, 1994); Frank Lambert, *Inventing the Great Awakening*

(Princeton, N.J.: Princeton University Press, 1999); William G. McLoughlin, *Revivals, Awakening, and Reform: An Essay on Religion and Social Change in America, 1607 to 1977* (Chicago: University of Chicago Press, 1978); Darrett B. Rutman, *Great Awakening: Event and Exegesis* (New York: John Wiley, 1970).

Great Disappointment

The Great Disappointment refers to the letdown felt by the followers of William MILLER'S ADVENTISM when Christ did not return as predicted in 1844. Miller, a Baptist preacher from New York, had suggested, based on his study of the Bible, that Christ was to return around 1843 or 1844. Later, Miller confessed his error and left his own movement. The Great Disappointment resulted in a period of chaos and the division of the Adventist movement into a number of factions. From the Millerite movement would come the SEVENTH-DAY ADVENTIST CHURCH, the JEHOVAH'S WITNESSES, and the worldwide CHURCH OF GOD.

Further reading: Gary Land, *Adventism in America* (Grand Rapids, Mich.: William B. Eerdmans, 1986); Francis D. Nichol, *The Midnight Cry* (Takoma Park, Md.: Review & Herald, 1944).

Grebel, Conrad (c. 1498–1526) *Protestant martyr and advocate of adult baptism*

A writer and religious activist in Zurich, Switzerland, at the very start of the Reformation, Conrad Grebel was one of the first advocates of adult BAPTISM; he helped lay the groundwork for the RADICAL REFORMATION. Grebel was born around 1498 into a prominent family of Zurich. He was educated at Basel, Vienna, and Paris, where he studied the humanities. In 1522, following a religious awakening, he aligned himself with Ulrich ZWINGLI, leader of the Reformation in his hometown.

Grebel was among a small group of Bible students who concluded that the Reformation should oppose the practice of infant baptism. Baptism, Grebel argued, should be reserved for adults who make a profession of faith. In January 1525, at a small meeting at the home of Felix MANZ in Zurich, Grebel baptized George BLAUROCK, who then baptized the others present. Following a public disputation held shortly thereafter, the city council ordered the brethren to either conform or go into exile. Grebel left Zurich. Later, during the summer, Grebel, Blaurock, and Manz were arrested in Grüningen and returned to Zurich, where following two trials they were sentenced to life imprisonment for rebelling against the state's authority.

In March 1526, the three escaped from their cell in the tower of Zurich. In the meantime, Zurich had instigated the punishment of drowning for their crime. When recaptured, Manz was drowned, but Grebel took ill with the plague and died before he could be captured.

The more radical phase of the Reformation is generally dated from Grebel's baptism of Blaurock. Grebel is also acknowledged as the intellectual leader of the original ANABAPTISTS, who articulated the ideal of a free church consisting exclusively of those who freely commit themselves to living a godly life. His views would have led to the abandonment of a state church, a concept quite foreign to most Reformation leaders. Grebel's approach survives primarily in the Mennonite Church. His chief literary legacy is a set of letters that were published in the 20th century.

Further reading: Harold Bender, *Conrad Grebel: The Founder of the Swiss Brethren, Sometimes Called Anabaptists* (Scottdale, Pa.: Herald Press, 1950); Conrad Grebel, *The Sources of Swiss Anabaptism: The Grebel Letters and Related Documents,* ed. by Leland Harder. Classics of the Radical Reformation (Scottdale, Pa.: Herald Press, 1985); C. Arnold Snyder, *Anabaptist History and Theology: An Introduction* (Kitchener, Ontario: Pandora Press, 1995); J. Denny Weaver, *Becoming Anabaptist: The Origin and Significance of Sixteenth-Century Anabaptism* (Scottdale, Pa.: Herald Press, 1987); George H. Williams, *The Radical Reformation* (Kirksville, Mo.: Sixteenth Century Journal, 1992).

Greece

Protestantism was first introduced in 1828 to Greece, a land dominated by Eastern Orthodoxy, when Jonas King (1792–1869) arrived as a representative of the AMERICAN BOARD OF COMMISSIONERS FOR FOREIGN MISSIONS. Staying on for decades in a rather hostile environment, King organized the first congregation in 1866; his assistant Michael Kalopothakis, a young convert, built the first Protestant church. In 1885, a synod was formed by the three congregations that had come into being by that time.

Meanwhile, other missionaries were active in Turkey, where many Greeks lived. Following the Greek-Turkish War of 1922, Greeks who had responded to the missionaries relocated to Greece, and the Protestant movement experienced a spurt of growth.

The Greek Evangelical Church was the only Protestant church in Greece for many years, but other groups arrived in the 20th century. The JEHOVAH'S WITNESSES began work in 1900 and have subsequently become the largest non-Orthodox group in the country; the SEVENTH-DAY ADVENTIST CHURCH arrived in 1903. More than 20 other groups now have one or more congregations, though progress overall has been slow, given the aggressive efforts of the Orthodox Church of Greece to retain its hegemony. The Free Evangelical Churches of Greece (1908), the CHURCH OF GOD OF PROPHECY (1927), and the SOUTHERN BAPTIST CONVENTION (1969) have garnered some support. There were approximately 200,000 Protestants in Greece as the 21st century began.

Further reading: David Barrett, *The Encyclopedia of World Christianity,* 2nd ed. (New York: Oxford University Press, 2001); Jean-Jacques Bauswein and Lukas Vischer, eds., *The Reformed Family Worldwide: A Survey of Reformed Churches, Theological Schools, and International Organizations* (Grand Rapids, Mich.: William B. Eerdmans, 1999); S. L. Burch, *The Beginning of Protestant Mission to the Greek Orthodox in Asia Minor and Pontos* (Pasadena, Calif.: Fuller Theological Seminary, M.A. thesis, 1977).

Grenada

French control of Grenada, established in the 18th century, was replaced by British control in the next century. Grenada attained independence in 1974.

Roman Catholicism was established in Grenada under French rule and remains the religion of more than half the population. In 1784, following the British takeover, the CHURCH OF ENGLAND established its first parish. The Anglicans in 1878 established the Diocese of the Windward Islands, now part of the Church of the Province of the West Indies. Some 15 percent of the population are Anglicans.

The remaining 25 percent of the population who are Christians are spread among a spectrum of groups, most of which originated in the United States. British Methodists arrived in 1789 and the SEVENTH-DAY ADVENTIST CHURCH in 1903; the latter now has the largest following after the Anglicans. Of the several Pentecostal churches, the Pentecostal Assemblies of the West Indies, whose roots can be traced to the Pentecostal Assemblies of Canada, is the largest.

A number of the churches participate in the Grenada Council of Churches. While the council is not directly related to the WORLD COUNCIL OF CHURCHES, most of its member churches are.

See also CARIBBEAN.

Further reading: David Barrett, *The Encyclopedia of World Christianity,* 2nd ed. (New York: Oxford University Press, 2001); Patrick Johnstone and Jason Mandryk, *Operation World, 21st Century Edition* (Carlisle, Cumbria, U.K.: Paternoster, 2001).

Grenfell, George (1849–1906) *Baptist missionary leader in Africa*

British Baptist missionary George Grenfell is most remembered for introducing Protestantism to the Congo River basin. Roman Catholics had developed a presence at the mouth of the Congo as early as the 15th century.

George Grenfell was born on August 21, 1849, in Cornwall, England. He became interested in the exploits of explorer David LIVINGSTONE (1813–73), and following his graduation from Bristol Baptist College he applied for service through the Baptist Missionary Society (BMS). He left for Cameroon in December 1874 with Alfred Sakar, who had pioneered Baptist work there. While there, he developed a facility for exploration and made several trips to the interior.

In 1877, the BMS invited Grenfell to join a feasibility study on opening work in the CONGO. His explorations led to the start of Baptist work the next year. However, after marrying his pregnant Jamaican housekeeper in 1878, he resigned from the BMS and ceased missionary activity.

In 1880, the BMS asked Grenfell to resume his work. He oversaw the construction of the *Peace,* a ship that made exploratory trips up the Congo River and its many branches over the next six years. In the next decade, he established a string of mission stations from near Kinshasa (then Leopoldville) to modern Kisangani (Stanleyville) a thousand miles away. These stations were designed to connect up with another string of stations being established by the CHURCH MISSIONARY SOCIETY (British Anglicans), who were simultaneously moving across Kenya and Uganda, but the Belgians thwarted the attempt to push farther upriver. Grenfell had come to believe that the region north and west of Stanleyville would witness a great competition between Protestantism and Islam, a belief that has been confirmed in the 20th century.

Grenfell's accomplishments have been somewhat overshadowed by his misplaced faith in King Leopold. He saw the Belgians as benevolent rulers and ignored evidence of widespread atrocities. Late in the 1890s, he admitted that the abuses were occurring, and in 1904 he admitted Leopold's role in them.

Grenfell died in the Congo at Basoka on July 1, 1906.

See also AFRICA, SUB-SAHARAN.

Further reading: George Hawker, *The Life of George Grenfell: Congo Missionary and Explorer* (New York:

Fleming H. Revell, 1909); Harry Johnston, *George Grenfell and the Congo* (London: Hutchinson & Company, 1908); David Lagergren, *Mission and State in the Congo* (Uppsala, Sweden: University of Uppsala, Ph.D. diss., 1970).

Grenfell, Wilfred Thomason
(1865–1940) *pioneer British medical missionary*
Wilfred Thomason Grenfell was born on February 28, 1865, at Parkgate, Cheshire, England, the son of a clergyman in the CHURCH OF ENGLAND. After graduating with a medical degree from the University of London, he affiliated with the Royal National Mission to Deep Sea Fisherman, a demonstration of the influence that evangelist Dwight L. MOODY (1837–89) had made on his life.

In 1892, Grenfell joined the crew of a hospital ship on its way to Labrador. The next year, he assembled his own medical team and left for Labrador and Newfoundland, where he spent the rest of his active life serving the medical and other needs of residents and fishermen.

Grenfell wrote a number of books and gave lecture tours in England and North America. In 1912, he established the International Grenfell Association, headquartered in St. Anthony, Newfoundland. The association would be responsible for founding and maintaining a set of hospitals, orphanages, cooperative stores, and other facilities. He was knighted in 1927. He remained active until ill health forced his retirement in 1935. He lived his last years in Vermont, where he died on October 9, 1940.

See also MEDICAL MISSIONS.

Further reading: Wilfred Thomason Grenfell, *Adrift on an Ice Pan* (Boston: Houghton Mifflin, 1926); ———, *Forty Years for Labrador* (Boston: Houghton Mifflin, 1932); ———, *The Story of a Labrador Doctor: The Autobiography of Wilfred Thamason Grenfell* (London: Hodder & Stoughton, 1919); Ronald Rompkey, *Grenfell of Labrador: A Biography* (Toronto: University of Toronto Press, 1991).

Groves, Anthony Norris (1795–1853)
founder of the faith mission model

Anthony Norris Groves, missiologist and a leader of the Plymouth BRETHREN, was born at Newton, Hampshire, England, in 1795. After a successful career as a dentist, he developed a desire to become a foreign missionary and applied to the CHURCH MISSIONARY SOCIETY (an agency of the CHURCH OF ENGLAND). In 1825, he and his wife moved to Dublin, where he entered Trinity College to prepare himself.

While at Trinity, he met John Nelson DARBY and the small group of believers who were to inaugurate the Plymouth Brethren movement. Groves withdrew from the Church of England and the Church Missionary Society. In 1829, he became the first missionary representative of the Brethren. He spent his first years (1829–33) in Iraq, but given the hostile atmosphere he was relatively unproductive there. His wife died during these years.

In 1825, Groves wrote a booklet, "Christian Devotedness," which made the case that Jesus' words to his disciples were applicable to all Christians, including such commands as "Sell all that you have and give to the poor, . . . and come follow me." He and his wife tried to live by such standards, and he preached them to his colleagues and audiences. He also shunned traditional ways of raising funds, including the denominational sending agencies. He advocated that missionaries rely solely on prayer and trust in God. He himself engaged in farming and business to provide funds for his ministry.

Groves moved to India in 1833 to implement his ideas of independent "faith" missions. He worked for 20 years there, leaving behind a small following and one major disciple, John Aurlappen. He also influenced many through his books and his work, most notably Chinese missionary leader Watchman NEE, and Indian evangelist BAKHT SINGH. When the Brethren split into Exclusive and Open factions in 1848, Grove adhered to the Open Brethren, now known as the CHRISTIAN BRETHREN.

Groves retired to England and died in May 1853.

Further reading: Anthony N. Groves, *Christian Devotedness* (Kansas City, Kans.: Walterick Publishers, 1993); G. H. Lang, *Anthony Norris Groves, Saint & Pioneer: A Combined Study of a Man of God & of the Original Principles & Practices of the Brethren with Applications to the Present Conditions* (London: Paternoster, 1949); Harriet Groves, *Memoir of the Late A.N. Groves, Containing Extracts from His Letters and Journals. By His Widow* (London, 1856), rpt. as *Memoir of the Late Anthony Norris Groves* (Sumneytown, Pa.: Sentinel Publications, 2003); Hy Pickering, *Chief Men among the Brethren* (London: Pickering & Inglis, 1961).

Guadeloupe

Following the establishment of French rule, Roman Catholicism became the dominant religious influence on the island, whose main population are descendants of African slaves.

Protestant influence came to Guadeloupe with the arrival of Moravian missionaries in the 1750s. More substantial response was accorded the Reformed Church of France, though both churches were eclipsed by the JEHOVAH'S WITNESSES and SEVENTH-DAY ADVENTIST CHURCH in the last half of the 20th century. The former now claims more than half of those professing religion outside of the Roman Catholic Church in Guadeloupe.

See also CARIBBEAN.

Further reading: David Barrett, *The Encyclopedia of World Christianity,* 2nd ed. (New York: Oxford University Press, 2001); Patrick Johnstone and Jason Mandryk, *Operation World, 21st Century Edition* (Carlisle, Cumbria, U.K.: Paternoster, 2001).

Guatemala

Guatemala, the ancient center of Mayan civilization, was conquered by Spain in the 16th century. Roman Catholicism remains the religion of the majority of descendants of both the Mayan and the Spanish colonists.

The struggle for independence in the 19th century was accompanied by anti-Catholic sentiment.

Anticlerical legislation had the side effect of allowing the introduction of Protestantism. In 1882, President Justo Rufino Barrios (1835–85) invited the PRESBYTERIAN CHURCH (USA) to come into Guatemala, ostensibly to counter the Roman Catholic Church's opposition to his reform policies. The Presbyterians sent John Clark Hill, who with a Spanish-speaking assistant in 1885 opened the first Protestant church in Guatemala City. Numerous schools were soon established.

In 1899, the Central American Mission (now CAM International) opened work in Guatemala City. Its work grew even faster than the Presbyterians, and in its first generation CAM founded an average of two congregations per year. In 1926, CAM founded the Central American Bible Institute (now the Central American Theological Seminary), which became the major educational institution for Evangelical groups in Guatemala and neighboring countries. The 20th century saw the founding of numerous missions from the whole spectrum of American Protestantism. Guatemala became an attractive site for the operation of missionary agencies, the founding of indigenous Protestant/FREE CHURCHES denominations, and the exportation of Christianity to other Latin American countries.

PENTECOSTALISM began in 1934 with the conversion of a primitive Methodist minister, Charles Furman, who then brought 14 Methodist congregations into the CHURCH OF GOD (CLEVELAND, TENNESSEE). Over the next half century, the church planted over 650 additional congregations. The ASSEMBLIES OF GOD opened work in Guatemala in 1937, and eventually outstripped the Church of God. In the 1950s, the cause benefited from evangelist T. L. Osborn's healing revival. The Assemblies of God experienced a major schism in 1956, when José María Muñoz organized the Prince of Peace Church. These three churches, the Church of God, the Assemblies of God, and the Prince of Peace Church, with a combined membership of more than 600,000, spearheaded a Pentecostal CHARISMATIC MOVEMENT that now includes more than 2

million Guatemalans, though many (especially Roman Catholics) remain members of their non-Pentecostal denominations.

Non-Pentecostal Protestant churches have also grown, including a variety of indigenous Evangelical bodies. Alone among liberal Protestant churches, the Presbyterian Church (USA) remains an active force. No Guatemalan-based church is a member of the WORLD COUNCIL OF CHURCHES, and there is no national council of churches. The Evangelical Alliance of Guatemala, affiliated with the WORLD EVANGELICAL ALLIANCE, includes approximately 20 church bodies.

A major obstacle to Protestant growth was Efraín Ríos Montt. A brutal dictator, Ríos Montt massacred thousands of citizens of native extraction. His brief reign (1982–83), coupled with his public self identification as an Evangelical, blemished the image of Evangelical groups, even though prominent Evangelical leaders had distanced themselves from Ríos Montt as his crimes became known. He has remained a power in Guatemalan politics in the years since his removal from office, and is pastor of the Word of God Evangelical Association, a denomination affiliated with the American-based Pentecostal sending agency Gospel Outreach (aka Verbo Ministries), based in Eureka, California.

See also CENTRAL AMERICA.

Further reading: Clifton L. Holland, ed., *World Christianity: Central America and the Caribbean* (Monrovia, Calif.: MARC-World Vision International, 1981); William R. Read, et al., *Latin American Church Growth* (Grand Rapids, Mich.: William B. Eerdmans, 1969); *Reporte Preliminar: El Estado de la Iglesia Evagélica en Guatemala, 2001* (Guatemala City: Servicio Evagelizadora para América Latina [SEPAL], 2001).

Guinea

The French conquered the land now called Guinea in the late 19th century. Since then, Islam, Christianity, and traditional African religions have vied for the hearts of the people. As the 20th century came to an end, Islam had approximately 5 million adherents, compared with 2 million followers of traditional religions. Christians, most of whom are Roman Catholics, number less than 300,000 adherents.

In 1918, the CHRISTIAN AND MISSIONARY ALLIANCE (CMA) was the first Protestant group to begin work, which included the building of two schools at Telekoro and Mamou. Arriving later in the century were the Anglicans, the PARIS EVANGELICAL MISSIONARY SOCIETY (of the Reformed Church of France), and the Church of the Open Door, a Pentecostal church. In 1967, all foreign missionaries were ordered to leave the country. The CMA negotiated a deal whereby some of their missionaries could remain as staff for the two schools. All the churches quickly appointed indigenous leadership to carry on their work, but the CMA was able to concentrate on leadership training and continue their work in Bible translation. The Evangelical Protestant Church, which grew from the CMA missions, is by far the largest Protestant church in Guinea.

The New Apostolic Church entered from Germany around 1970. In three decades it built a work of some 20,000 members. During the 1990s, PENTECOSTALISM, brought to the country by French members of the ASSEMBLIES OF GOD, had also begun to attract a sizable following. The visit to the country in 1992 of Evangelist Richard Bonnke had a marked effect; he became the catalyst for the organization of the Association des Eglises et Missions Evangélique en Guinea. Most of the Protestant/Free Church bodies operating in Guinea are members of this association, which is affiliated with the WORLD EVANGELICAL ALLIANCE. No Guinea-based church is affiliated with the WORLD COUNCIL OF CHURCHES.

See also FRENCH WEST AFRICA.

Further reading: David Barrett, *The Encyclopedia of World Christianity,* 2nd ed. (New York: Oxford University Press, 2001); Patrick Johnstone and Jason Mandryk, *Operation World, 21st Century Edition* (Carlisle, Cumbria, U.K.: Paternoster, 2001).

Guinea-Bissau

Although Portugal ruled the region for several hundred years, Islam predominates. In addition, traditional African religions have remained strong, especially among the peoples of the southeastern part of the country. As the 21st century begins, traditional religions claim 45 percent of the population, Islam 40 percent, and Roman Catholics around 12 percent.

Protestantism came in 1939, when the World Evangelism Crusade (now WEC International) established a mission. The resultant Evangelical Church of Guinea has built a significant ministry, which includes a number of medical programs. Entering the country in the 1970s, the New Apostolic Church of Germany emerged in the 1990s as the largest non-Catholic Christian body in the land, with more than 25,000 members.

See also FRENCH WEST AFRICA.

Further reading: David Barrett, *The Encyclopedia of World Christianity,* 2nd ed. (New York: Oxford University Press, 2001); Patrick Johnstone and Jason Mandryk, *Operation World, 21st Century Edition* (Carlisle, Cumbria, U.K.: Paternoster, 2001); H. Willis, *The Light Shines in the Darkness: The Story of the Evangelical Church of Guinea-Bissau, 1940–1974* (Balstrade, U.K.: WEC, 1996).

Guyana

European settlement in Guyana was initiated by the Dutch, and Protestantism arrived with their rule. The first ministers were of the Netherlands Reformed Church. They erected a church in 1720, but banned Africans or native Guyanese from becoming members. The Lutherans, who arrived a short time later, also devoted their attention to the European settlers.

Britain won control in 1814. METHODISM had already arrived in 1802 with a small group of freed slaves from Nevis. The LONDON MISSIONARY SOCIETY (Congregationalists) arrived in 1807, and the CHURCH OF ENGLAND, soon to become the government church, in 1810. With the loss of government subsidies, Netherlands Reformed Church ministers gave way to the Church of Scotland (a Presbyterian body). The Church of England, eventually evolving into the Diocese of Guyana within the Church of the Province of the West Indies, became the largest of these churches by the end of the 19th century.

The SEVENTH-DAY ADVENTIST CHURCH, which began work in 1887, is now the fourth-largest church in the country, with more than 20,000 members. It has been surpassed by the ASSEMBLIES OF GOD, a Pentecostal church that only began work in the 1950s. Among the 50 DENOMINATIONS with congregations in Guyana, a set of indigenous churches have arisen, the most successful being the Hallelujah Church and the Jordanites, the latter a Pentecostal body.

The Guyana Council of Churches, which includes the Roman Catholic Church and most of the older Protestant bodies, dates to 1937. It is affiliated with the WORLD COUNCIL OF CHURCHES. The more conservative Evangelical churches have formed the Guyana Evangelical Fellowship, which is affiliated with the WORLD EVANGELICAL ALLIANCE.

Today almost one-third of Guyana's population follows one of several forms of Hinduism, thanks to the import of Indian workers.

Guyana became the scene of a singular event in church history in 1978, when most of the members of the PEOPLES TEMPLE, a congregation of the Christian Church (Disciples of Christ) that had relocated from the United States, committed mass suicide and murder. The incident had little effect on the local religious community.

See also CARIBBEAN; SOUTH AMERICA.

Further reading: Henry B. Jeffrey and Colin Baber, *Guyana: Politics, Economics, and Society—Beyond the Burnham Era* (Boulder, Colo.: Rienner, 1986); Thomas J. Spinner, Jr., *A Political and Social History of Guyana, 1945–1983* (Boulder, Colo.: Westview Press, 1984); Michael Swan, *British Guiana: The Land of Six Peoples* (London: HMSO, 1957).

Gypsies *See* ROMA PEOPLE.

H

Haiti

During the years of French and Spanish colonial rule, Roman Catholicism became the dominant religion in Haiti. However, West African religion remained a strong influence among the descendants of African slaves who make up almost the entire population. These religions reemerged as voodoo (Vodun) at the end of the 18th century. The revolt that led to independence in 1804 was started at a voodoo ceremony held in 1791. At various times, the Catholic Church has launched anti-voodoo campaigns; the last, in 1941–42, led to the destruction of a number of voodoo worship sites. Since the 1960s, the Catholic Church has attempted to arrive at some accommodation with voodoo.

Protestantism was initially brought to Haiti by British Methodists who first visited in 1807, attracted by the growing community of English-speaking blacks who had migrated to Haiti after siding with the British during the American Revolution. The Methodists are remembered for their literacy work. The wave of American Protestant and FREE CHURCH missionaries began in 1823 with the arrival of the American Baptists and the African Methodist Episcopal Church. They were joined later in the century by the CHURCH OF GOD (ANDERSON, INDIANA) and the SEVENTH-DAY ADVEN-TIST CHURCH. In 1861, a group of African Americans set up the independent Eglise Orthodoxe Apostolique Haitian, which early in the next century would formally affiliate with the Episcopal Church in the United States.

A new surge of Protestantism accompanied the American occupation (1915–34). The most important new churches to establish work during this period were the CHURCH OF GOD OF PROPHECY and its parent body, the CHURCH OF GOD (CLEVE-LAND, TENNESSEE). Together, they introduced PEN-TECOSTALISM in the early 1930s; it has shown spectacular growth. The ASSEMBLIES OF GOD and the two Churches of God together have in excess of 300,000 adherents. BAPTISTS have had some success as well, represented by the several associations of Baptist congregations affiliated with the Baptist Convention of Haiti, the Baptist Mission of Haiti, and the Baptist Mission of South Haiti.

At least 200 different Protestant groups are operating in Haiti today, including a number of small indigenous churches. There is no national council of churches in Haiti, and no Haitian-based church is a member of the WORLD COUNCIL OF CHURCHES, though several churches whose international headquarters are located in other countries are members. Some of the more conservative groups have formed the Council of Evangelical

Churches of Haiti, which is affiliated with the WORLD EVANGELICAL ALLIANCE.

See also CARIBBEAN.

Further reading: F. J. Conway, *Pentecostalism in the Context of Haitian Religion and Health Practice* (Washington, D.C.: American University, Ph.D. diss., 1978); L. Griffiths, *History of Methodism in Haiti* (Port-au-Prince: Imprimerie Methodiste, 1991); I. T. Heneise, *A History of Baptist Work in Haiti* (Rochester, N.Y.: Colgate Rochester Divinity School, D.Min. thesis, 1974); E. A. Jeanty, *La Christianisme en Haiti* (Port-au-Prince: Librairie de la Presse Evangélique, 1990); H. A. Johnson, *The Growing Church in Haiti* (Coral Gables, Fla.: West Indies Mission, 1970).

Haldane brothers *Scottish Baptist leaders*

Though not the first BAPTISTS in Scotland, the brothers Robert Haldane (1764–1842) and James Alexander Haldane (1768–1851) did much to promote the Baptist cause there in the first half of the 19th century.

Robert was born on February 28, 1764, in London. After three years in the navy beginning at age 16, Haldane left the service, toured Europe, married, and settled in the family castle at Stirling. James Alexander was born on July 14, 1768; he too went to sea, making four voyages to India. During this time, he had begun a study of the Bible and received council from David Bogue (1750–1825), one of the founders of the LONDON MISSIONARY SOCIETY. He turned down an offer to captain a ship and returned to Scotland determined to lead a life of Christian service. Around 1796, he associated himself with Charles Simeon (1759–1836), with whom he traveled around Scotland distributing tracts and trying to awaken people to the spiritual life.

About this time, Robert sold the family home with plans to devote the money to the spread of Christianity, and the brothers cofounded the Society for Propagating the Gospel at Home. They began to preach wherever they could find an audience. Their independent efforts soon brought

them to the attention of the authorities of the Church of Scotland, the Presbyterian body that dominated Scottish religious life, and they separated from the church.

In 1799, James was ordained and became the pastor of an independent Congregationalist congregation in Edinburgh, which in 1801, with money from Robert, built a huge church seating 3,000 people. James came to profess Baptist perspectives, and the church subsequently became a leading Baptist congregation, which James pastored into the 1840s.

Meanwhile, Robert laid plans to use the society to erect chapels for independent congregations, support foreign missionaries, and create institutions for training evangelists. In 1816, he visited the Continent and taught for a time at Geneva. In 1817, he moved to Montauban, the main French Protestant center. His helped found a small French Baptist movement. Upon his return to Scotland in 1819, he continued his philanthropic activities and joined his brother in speaking out on the major issues of the day. He died on December 12, 1842. James died on February 8, 1851.

Robert published a number of books, among the most popular being *Evidences and Authority of Divine Revelation* (1816), *On the Inspiration of Scripture* (1828), and an *Exposition of the Epistle to the Romans* (1835). Today, the Haldanes are claimed by a variety of movements, from the Christian Church (Disciples of Christ) to the Plymouth BRETHREN.

Further reading: Alexander Haldane, *Memoirs of R. and J. A. Haldane* (1852; rpt., Edinburgh: Banner of Truth Trust, 1990); Robert Haldane, *Exposition of the Epistle to the Romans* (1835; rpt., Edinburgh: Banner of Truth Trust, 1996).

Haldeman, I. M. (1845–1933) *leading Fundamentalist Baptist preacher*

Isaac Massey Haldeman, a prominent Fundamentalist and pastor of First Baptist Church of New

York City, was born in Concordville, Pennsylvania, on February 13, 1845. He was ordained as a minister in the Northern Baptist Convention and served several churches before being called in 1884 to First Baptist, where he remained for the rest of his life, gradually making a name for his oratorical skills.

His career in New York spanned the emergence of FUNDAMENTALISM and its major battles with Modernism in the Northern Baptist Convention. Haldeman became a leading spokesperson for the Fundamentalist cause. He was also an early convert to premillennial DISPENSATIONALISM. In 1910, he wrote *Signs of the Times,* one of the early surveys of the end-time from a dispensational perspective. He later wrote a defense of the *Scofield Reference Bible* and its editor, C. I. SCOFIELD.

Haldeman tackled the ideas of the more liberal voices in the convention, including Walter Rauschenbush (1861–1918), who championed the SOCIAL GOSPEL, and Harry Emerson Fosdick (1878–1969), the prominent liberal Baptist pastor in New York City. He also battled inroads of new religions such as CHRISTIAN SCIENCE and Spiritualism.

Haldeman died in New York City on September 27, 1933.

Further reading: I. M. Haldeman, *Christian Science in the Light of Holy Scripture* (New York: Fleming H. Revell, 1909); ———, *The Coming of Christ—Pre-Millennial & Imminent* (New York: Charles C. Cook, 1906); ———, *The Signs of the Times* (New York: Charles C. Cook., 1912); George Marsden, *Fundamentalism and American Culture* (New York: Oxford University Press, 1980).

Halfway Covenant

The Halfway Covenant was a compromise measure adopted by Massachusetts Congregationalists on questions of BAPTISM and the LORD'S SUPPER.

In 17th-century New England CONGREGATIONALISM, the church was supposed to consist only of individuals identified as the elect, the true Christians in each community. In order to verify that candidates for membership were among the elect, local churches asked for a testimony of their religious life.

The testimony was part of the membership process that included accepting a church COVENANT. In general, the children of full church members were admitted to membership in the Congregational Church (which also entailed voting and officeholding rights in the secular community), in the assumption that as children of the elect they would undoubtedly experience conversion and become full members of the church on their own. However, that proved not always to be the case. Many such children did not profess a conversion experience.

By the 1660s, the problem of the third generation arose. Should children of second-generation members who had not professed a personal experience of God be admitted to the church?

Patriarch Richard Mather proposed a solution: children of the third generation would be baptized as infants and admitted to a limited church membership. However, they were not to be admitted to the Lord's Supper and full membership until they were at least 14 years old and offered personal testimony of conversion. Supported by the likes of Edward Taylor and Richard's son Increase Mather, the Halfway Covenant was approved in 1662 and generally adopted throughout New England.

Samuel Stoddard, the minister of the Northampton, Massachusetts, church, criticized this solution. Mather assumed that all who partook of the Lord's Supper should have certain knowledge and assurance of salvation. However, Puritan theology did not allow of such assurance of salvation. Stoddard offered a simple solution. He suggested that any otherwise fit churchgoer who wanted to partake of the Lord's Supper be allowed the elements irrespective of personal assurance of salvation. If some who were not yet among the saved communed at the Lord's table, such action might be a positive influence leading to their conversion. He put this policy into effect at Northamption in 1677. Other ministers, especially in western Massachusetts, began to follow suit. Over the next generation, the practice, which came very close to a policy of open communion, was largely accepted by Congregationalists.

See also CREEDS/CONFESSIONS OF FAITH.

Further reading: Edward H. Davidson, *Jonathan Edwards: The Narrative of a Puritan Mind* (Cambridge, Mass.: Harvard University Press, 1968); Horton Davies, *The Worship of the American Puritans, 1629–1730* (New York: Peter Lang, 1990); Richard P. Gildrie, *The Profane, the Civil, and the Godly* (University Park: Pennsylvania State University Press, 1994); Perry Miller, *The New England Mind: From Colony to Province* (Boston: Beacon Press, 1953).

Harnack, Adolf von (1851–1930) *liberal German theologian and New Testament scholar*

Adolph von Harnack, the leading German theologian and church historian of his time, was a powerful proponent of using historical methods to clarify the Christian message. Harnack was born in 1851. His father taught homiletics and church history, and Harnack developed an early interest in the field. At the University of Dorpat, he first learned to pursue theology with historical insight. He also became fascinated with Gnosticism and the career of the heretic Marcion. Von Harnack accepted the historical methodology and the liberal theology of Ferdinand C. BAUR (1792–1860) and Albrecht RITSCHL (1822–89).

In 1874, Harnack received his Ph.D. and joined the faculty at the University of Leipzig. He began work on a multivolume *History of Dogma*. Its publication made Harnack the focus of theological debate in German-speaking lands. Some accused Harnack of using the New Testament as a historical source, rather than as a norm for shaping faith. Harnack's personal charisma, however, kept him a popular lecturer.

In 1888, Harnack moved to the University of Berlin, where in 1901 he wrote *What Is Christianity?* The book tried to separate the teachings of

Jesus from the church's teachings about Jesus. Harnack concluded that Christian thought had been reshaped by Greek philosophy into something quite alien to Jesus and his simple message. After stripping away the layers of theology, he believed the core of what Jesus taught was: 1) the coming Kingdom of God; 2) God the Father and the infinite value of the human soul; and 3) the commandment to love, which is to be lived out in a social context.

Harnack's conclusions were startling for his time and alienated many conservative Lutherans. He created more opponents when in 1892 he proposed removing the Apostles' Creed from public worship, and offered a briefer creed that reflected his historical conclusions.

In addition to his writing and lecturing, Harnack edited the *Theologische Literaturzeitung* for 29 years, served as rector of the university, was director of the Royal Library, and was the first president of the Kaiser-Wilhelm Foundation. He died in Berlin in 1930.

Most of Harnack's writings were translated into English, including the *History of Dogma* (1896–99); *The Mission and Expansion of Christianity in the First Three Centuries* (1962); *Outlines of the History of Dogma* (1957); *Thoughts on the Present Position of Protestantism* (1899); and preeminently, *What is Christianity?* (1957). Though both theology and church history have moved beyond Harnack, he is remembered as a significant force in changing the discipline of church history by bringing the life of Jesus and the early church into the realm of critical historical investigation.

Further reading: G. Wayne Glick, *A Study of Adolf von Harnack as Historian and Theologian: The Reality of Christianity* (New York: Harper & Row, 1967); Adolf von Harnack, *The Expansion of Christianity in the First Three Centuries,* 2 vols. (New York: G. P. Putnam, 1908); ———, *History of Dogma,* 7 vols. (Peter Smith, 1976); ———, *What Is Christianity?* (Philadelphia: Fortress Press, 1986); Martin Rumscheidt, *Adolf Von Harnack: Liberal Theology at Its Height* (London: Collins Liturgical Publications, 1989).

Harris, Barbara Clementine (b. 1930)
pioneer female Episcopal bishop

Barbara Harris, the first woman consecrated as a BISHOP in the worldwide ANGLICAN COMMUNION, was born on June 12, 1930, in Philadelphia, Pennsylvania. As a child she attended the predominantly African-American St. Barnabas Episcopal Church in Germantown, where she emerged as a youth leader.

While pursuing a successful business career, Harris became active in the Civil Rights struggle through the Church of the Advocate in northern Philadelphia, and participated in the Selma march led by Martin Luther KING JR. in 1965. Her pastor supported her call to the ministry at a time when the Episcopal Church had yet to ordain women as priests.

In 1974, Harris led a march of Episcopal laywomen to an unauthorized service at which 11 women were ordained as priests. Two years later, the church authorized the ordination of women, and she began to study for the ministry. After completing work at the Episcopal Divinity School in Cambridge, Massachusetts, she was ordained a deacon in 1979 and a priest a year later. She left Sun Oil, where she had been head of community relations, to become a priest at St. Augustine of Hippo Church in Philadelphia and chaplain at Philadelphia County Prison.

In 1984, she was appointed executive director of the Episcopal Church Publishing Company, and as editor of the church journal *Witness* Harris assumed a platform and maintained a degree of notoriety throughout the church. Her articles on racism in the church and President Ronald Reagan's policies provoked a strong reaction, but more liberal factions in the church promoted her candidacy for the episcopacy. Despite opposition from those who opposed her stands on various issues and those who opposed the idea of women bishops, in February 1989 she was consecrated suffragan bishop of the Diocese of Massachusetts, thus becoming the first woman to become a bishop in the history of the worldwide Anglican Communion.

Harris continued to criticize the church for what she contended was an insufficient number of female bishops—only 10 others (out of hundreds of men) were serving in the Anglican Communion by 1999. She also criticized her Episcopal colleagues for continuing to question the efficacy of female priests and bishops.

At the mandatory retirement age, Harris officially left her post in 2002. In the summer of 2003, she agreed to become the assisting bishop in the Diocese of Washington (D.C.).

See also EPISCOPAL CHURCH; WOMEN, ORDINATION OF.

Further reading: Mark Francisco Bozzuti-Jones, *The Miter Fits Just Fine: A Story about the Rt. Rev. Barbara Clementine Harris, Suffragan Bishop, Diocese of Massachusetts* (Cambridge, Mass.: Cowley Publications, 2003); Pamela W. Darling, *New Wine: The Story of Women Transforming Leadership and Power in the Episcopal Church* (Cambridge, Mass.: Cowley Publications, 1994).

Harrist Church

The Harrist Church is one of the more important AFRICAN INITIATED CHURCHES in West Africa. In 1910, William Wadé Harris (1865–1929), imprisoned in Liberia on treason charges, received a call from God. Upon his release in 1913, he began traveling through Ghana and the IVORY COAST, preaching and healing the sick. Accompanied by two women disciples who sang with the accompaniment of calabash rattles, he was a striking figure in a long white robe, turban, and black bands across his chest. He walked barefooted and carried a Bible, a staff shaped like a cross, and a gourd rattle. He preached a simple message—turn to the one true God, accept forgiveness from the Savior, and be baptized. He organized those who accepted his message into prayer groups and taught them to give up their traditional religious practices, follow God's commandments, and live in peace. He found a positive reception throughout West

Africa, except from Roman Catholic priests. The older churches attempted to suppress his ministry, and Harris spent most of the 1920s in LIBERIA.

Harris sent his converts to the local Methodist and Catholic churches for Sunday worship, though they also formed prayer groups that used African hymns and dances. Where there were no other Christian churches, they built their own. Harris refrained from attacking polygamy, which helped create a break with the Methodists. Shortly before his death, Harris seemed to be calling for a separate church; he passed along the symbols of his authority (his cane cross and a Bible) to John Ahui, the Harrist Church's first leader.

In the Ivory Coast, where Harris's largest following was located, the movement faced continual repression; it was first officially organized only in 1955. By 1964, it was recognized as one of the country's four official religions. With a membership in excess of 350,000, the Harrist Church is the largest Protestant fellowship in the Ivory Coast, second in size only to Roman Catholicism. It is a member of the WORLD COUNCIL OF CHURCHES.

Further reading: Gordon Mackay Haliburton, *The Prophet Harris* (London: Longmans, 1973); Casely Hayford, *William Waddy Harris: The West African Reformer* (London: C. M. Phillips, 1915); David A. Shank, *Prophet Harris, the "Black Elijah" of West Africa* (Leiden: E. J. Brill, 1994); Sheila Suzanne Walker, *The Religious Revolution in the Ivory Coast: The Prophet Harris and His Church* (Chapel Hill: University of North Carolina Press, 1983).

Haystack Prayer Meeting

A single prayer meeting under a Massachusetts haystack is believed by historians to have been a focal point in America's transition from a missionary target region to a missionary-sending country. On an afternoon in August 1806, five students at Williams College, Samuel J. Mills

(1783–1818), Harvey Loomis (1785–1825), Byram Green (1786–1865), Francis L. Robbins (1787–1850), and James Richards (1784–1822), assembled for a regular outdoor prayer session. When it began to rain, they sought shelter under a haystack. Mills persuaded the group to pray in support of his dream for a missionary effort overseas, especially in Asia, though Loomis believed the American West should take priority as a missionary field.

The idea bore fruit two years later when a student society was formed called the BRETHREN, to promote a mission to the "Heathen." The society moved to Andover Theological Seminary in 1810 where new members joined, including Adoniram JUDSON (1788–1850), Samuel Newall (1784–1821), and Samuel Nott (1788–1869). Judson presented the Brethren's ideas before the General Association of Congregational Ministers of Massachusetts, which in response founded the first organization to send missionaries overseas from the United States, the AMERICAN BOARD OF COMMISSIONERS FOR FOREIGN MISSIONS. At the time of the ministerial conclave, Mills's family was hosting Henry OBOOKIAH (c. 1792–1818), a Hawaiian convert who symbolized the fertile missionary field Mills hoped to reach.

The American Board took the lead in sending missionaries around the world, first to INDIA and Ceylon and then to Hawaii and the Pacific Islands. They would soon be joined by American BAPTISTS (to whom Judson quickly shifted his allegiance) and the Methodists.

Further reading: Calvin Durfee, *A History of Williams College* (Boston: A. Williams, 1860); "The Haystack Prayer Meeting." Available online. URL: http://wso.williams.edu/~dchu/MissionPark/meeting.html. Accessed on February 15, 2004; *Haystack Prayer Meeting—The 100th Anniversary of the Haystack Prayer Meeting* (Boston: American Board of Commissioners for Foreign Missions, 1907); LaRue W. Piercy, *Hawaii's Missionary Saga: Sacrifice and Godliness in Paradise* (Honolulu: Mutual Publishing, 1992).

Heck, Barbara (1734–1804) *founder of Methodism in the United States and Canada*

Barbara Heck was born Barbara von Ruckle in County Limerick, IRELAND, to German parents who had fled Napoleon's forces in 1709. The family was deeply moved by John WESLEY, who visited Ireland on several occasions and was able to preach in German.

Barbara converted at the age of 18. In 1760, she married Paul Hescht (later anglicized to Heck) (d. 1795). Evicted by their Irish landlord, the family settled in New York City that same year.

Cut off from the church structures in Ireland, Heck pressed her cousin, Philip Embury (1728–73), to begin preaching services, offering to gather people to meet in his home. The initial group, which began to meet in 1766, consisted of four people including Heck's African-American servant. Growth followed the arrival of a British soldier, Thomas Webb, who assumed preaching duties. In need of a building for the growing group, Heck drew up the building plans. A larger building was erected in 1768.

To escape the threatening war, the Hecks and other German-speaking families moved to the Camden Valley near Lake Champlain in 1770. However, in 1778 they were burned out by neighbors who did not like their Tory views. The Hecks moved to Montreal and then to Augusta township, near present-day Brockville, Ontario. Here Barbara Heck convened the first Methodist class in Canada.

The Hecks moved to a home on the St. Lawrence River in 1799, where she lived until her death on August 17, 1804.

See also METHODISM; UNITED METHODIST CHURCH.

Further reading: G. Lincoln Caddell, *Barbara Heck: Pioneer Methodist* (Cleveland, Tenn.: Pathway Press, 1961); Blanche Hume, *Barbara Heck* (Toronto: Ryerson Press, 1930); Abel Stevens, *The Women of Methodism: Its Three Foundresses, Susanna Wesley, the Countess of Huntingdon and Barbara Heck* (New York: Carlton & Porter, 1866); W. H. Withrow, *Barbara Heck, a Tale of Early Methodism* (Toronto: Methodist Mission Rooms, 1895).

Heidelberg Catechism

The 1563 Heidelberg Catechism is still the most popular catechism for use by the Reformed churches around the world. It was initiated by Frederick III, the elector of the Palatinate, who like all German princes held the right under the 1555 Peace OF AUGSBURG to choose the state religion. It was composed primarily by Zacharius Ursinus (1534–83) and Caspar Olevianus (1536–87), with help from the theological faculty at the University of Heidelberg, following the standard format of question and answer on the basic subjects of the Christian Faith. A church synod in Heidelberg in January 1563 approved the document; before the end of the year, two slightly revised editions and a Latin translation were published. Resourceful church leaders divided it into 50 sections so that it could be taught Sunday by Sunday through a calendar year.

The large Lutheran minority in the Palatinate complained to the German imperial diet that the new catechism, written from a Reformed perspective, was heretical. Frederick was brought before the diet in 1566, but was able to exonerate himself with the assistance of Heinrich BULLINGER, the Swiss Reformed leader from Zurich.

Subsequently, the catechism spread throughout Europe, getting it biggest boost from the SYNOD OF DORT (1618–19). As the Reformed Church became global in the 19th century, the catechism was translated into a number of Asian and African languages.

The Christian Reformed Church of North America adopted "a modern and accurate [English] translation" as an official document in 1975.

See also CREEDS/CONFESSIONS OF FAITH.

Further reading: Karl Barth, *The Heidelberg Catechism for Today* (Richmond, Va.: John Knox Press, 1964); *The Heidelberg Catechism* (Grand Rapids, Mich.: Christian Reformed Church, 1975); Herman

Hoeksema, *Triple Knowledge, An Exposition of the Heidelberg Confession* (Grand Rapids, Mich.: Kregel Publications, 1972); George W. Richards, *The Heidelberg Catechism: Historical and Doctrinal Studies* (Philadelphia: Reformed Church in the U.S., 1913); Zacharias Ursinus, *Commentary on the Heidelberg Catechism,* trans. and ed. by G. Willard (Philipsburg, Pa.: Presbyterian & Reformed Press, 1985).

Helvetic Confessions (Reformed)

The two Helvetic Confessions were a 16th-century attempt to define the common beliefs of the various Swiss Reformed churches. The second confession was eventually adopted by other Reformed churches throughout Europe, and remains part of the Reformed heritage even today.

The early Reformed churches in SWITZERLAND had no common confession of faith. The first attempt at such a doctrinal statement, the Basel Confession of 1534, was accepted only in Basel and Muhlausen. In 1536, Heinrich BULLINGER, Oswald Myconius, Simon Grynaeus, Leo Jud, and others gathered in Basel to revise the earlier confession. Their First Helvetic Confession retained the perspective of Zurich reform leader Ulrich ZWINGLI. This attempt won wider acceptance, but its attempts to reconcile Lutheran and Zwinglian positions on the Eucharist satisfied neither camp, and the 27 articles were rejected by Lutherans and other Protestants at the important centers of STRASBOURG and Constance.

In 1549, John CALVIN, William FAREL, and Bullinger worked out the Zurich Consensus, which satisfied all the Reformed churches in German- and French-speaking Switzerland. In 1561, Bullinger quietly composed a personal statement of faith based on the First Helvetic Confession of 1536, as an attachment to his will. It took on a public role when Bullinger sent it to Frederick III, the elector of the Palatinate, to use in his defense of the HEIDELBERG CATECHISM in 1566. Frederick was exonerated, and Bullinger's confession was published. As the Second Helvetic Confession, it was officially adopted by the Protestant Swiss cantons in 1566.

The lengthy document covers the authority of the Bible, the Triune God, the salvation offered in Christ, creation, the fall, human redemption, and the church. It carefully distinguishes the Protestant from the Catholic position, and the Reformed position from that of the ANABAPTISTS. It incorporated the Zurich Consensus on the SACRAMENTS, stating, "Sacraments are mystical symbols, or holy rites, or sacred actions, instituted by God himself consisting of his Word, of signs, and of things signified."

The confession was subsequently adopted by the Reformed churches in FRANCE (1571), HUNGARY (1567), and POLAND (1571). In 1566, though already having a confession of its own, the Church of Scotland (Presbyterian) gave the Helvetic Confession its approval; it was informally received in Holland and England. It remains the official doctrinal statement of the Reformed Churches of Eastern Europe (and their foreign affiliates). In 1967, it was added to the Book of Confessions of the United Presbyterian Church in the U.S.A., which brought it into the 1983 merger that produced the PRESBYTERIAN CHURCH (U.S.A.).

See also CREEDS/CONFESSIONS OF FAITH.

Further reading: Joel R. Beeke and Sinclair B. Ferguson, eds., *Reformed Confessions Harmonized: With an Annotated Bibliography of Reformed Doctrinal Works* (Grand Rapids, Mich.: Baker Book House, 1999); A. C. Cochrane, *Reformed Confessions of the 16th Century* (Philadelphia: Westminster Press, 1985); Jack Rogers, *Presbyterian Creeds: A Guide to the Book of Confessions* (Philadelphia: Westminster Press, 1985); J. Gordon Melton, *The Encyclopedia of American Religions: Religious Creeds,* 2 vols. (Detroit: Gale Research, 1988, 1994).

Henry VIII, king of England
(1491–1547) *founder of the independent Church of England*

The instigator of the Protestant Reformation in England, King Henry VIII was born on June 28,

1491, the son of Henry VII. He ascended the throne in 1509 and immediately married Catherine of Aragon (1485–1536), the widow of his deceased elder brother.

Henry owed much of his early success as a ruler to his counselor Thomas Wolsey (c. 1474–1530), who helped maintain Henry's cordial alliance with the papacy. Henry helped Wolsey become archbishop of York and a cardinal in 1515. He also found time to write a book, the *Assertio Septem Sacramentorum,* attacking Martin LUTHER and defending the church against his demands for change. Among other topics, Henry insisted on the supremacy of the papacy, for which Leo X granted him the title of Fidei Defensor (Defender of the Faith).

At this time, Henry was trying to divorce Catherine, who had failed to produce a male heir. Turned back by the pope, Henry asked Wolsey to justify the divorce. Wolsey's failure led to his fall and the rise of Thomas CRANMER and Thomas CROMWELL. In 1529, Cranmer suggested that Henry appeal the question of his marriage to the university scholars of Europe, who concluded that the marriage was null and void. Eventually, the pope gave in. Wolsey was accused of treason and died in 1530 awaiting trial.

Apparently with Cromwell's advice, Henry decided to drop his allegiance to the papacy and have himself declared the supreme head of the church in his domain. In 1531, he forced the clergy to present him with a gift of £100,000 and a statement recognizing his supremacy. The following year a convocation of the clergy renounced papal authority and acknowledged Henry's leadership over the church. The annual offering to Rome was now deposited into the king's coffers.

In 1533, Henry secretly married Anne Boleyn (c. 1501–36) and then pushed through the selection of Cranmer as archbishop of Canterbury. When Pope Clement (r. 1523–34) threatened Henry with excommunication, Parliament made the agreements between Henry and the church part of English law. Parliament also passed the Act of Succession, declaring Catherine's daughter,

Mary, illegitimate, and naming Anne Boleyn's daughter, Elizabeth, heir apparent. Nonacceptance of the Act of Succession was later declared a capital crime. Sir Thomas More (1478–1535) was the most famous person to lose his life for that crime.

Henry next ordered a survey of all monasteries on the grounds that they were beds of corruption. He took ownership of most of them and sold them off to raise money.

In 1536, Catherine died and Anne Boleyn was beheaded for treason. Henry married Jane Seymour (c. 1509–37), who bore him Edward. In the meantime, both Cranmer and Cromwell had developed sympathies with the Reformation and tried to move Henry in that direction. Following the death of Jane Seymour, Henry agreed to Cromwell's advice and married Anne of Cleaves (1515–57), sister-in-law to the Protestant Frederick of Saxony's wife. However, he soon annulled the marriage; the unhappy experience solidified Henry's anti-Protestant views. He remained Catholic in all matters except his allegiance to the pope. In 1539, he published the Six Articles, opposing Cranmer's recently published Ten Articles, a work quite sympathetic to Lutheranism. He then had Thomas Cromwell beheaded and married a Roman Catholic, Catherine Howard (1521–42).

Henry died on January 28, 1547. He was succeeded by his son, EDWARD VI, who was himself succeeded by both of his two sisters, MARY I and ELIZABETH I.

See also ANGLICANISM; CHURCH OF ENGLAND: UNITED KINGDOM.

Further reading: Antonia Fraser, *The Wives of Henry VIII* (New York: Alfred A. Knopf, 1993); Christopher Haigh, *English Reformations: Religion, Politics, and Society under the Tudors* (New York: Oxford University Press, 1993); J. J. Scarisbrick, *Henry VIII* (Berkeley: University of California, 1968); Lacey Baldwin Smith, *Henry VIII, The Mask of Royalty* (Boston: Houghton Mifflin, 1971); Neville Williams, *Henry VIII and His Court* (New York: Macmillan, 1971).

hermeneutics

Hermeneutics is the art and science of interpreting the Bible. The Protestant emphasis on biblical authority made hermeneutics an essential task for church leaders.

The dominant Christian hermeneutics of the Middle Ages, developed by Origen, Anselm, and Thomas Aquinas, used allegorical interpretations of the Bible to support various Catholic notions and practices. The pope retained final authority as to how any passage should be interpreted.

Early in his career, Martin LUTHER found the allegorical method inadequate, as it could be used to make Scripture say anything. He suggested instead that Scripture had a simple meaning conveyed by the historical and grammatical context of the passage under discussion. He came to believe that Scripture was accessible to the common believer—an idea called the perspicuity of Scripture.

Luther recognized that some passages were less clear than others; he believed they could be interpreted in light of the clearer ones. He also advocated that the Bible be read in light of one's faith, believing that the Holy Spirit would confirm the meaning for the individual and allow its personal appropriation.

Luther's readings relied in part on the new Greek text of the New Testament prepared by ERASMUS, and the effort of Hebraicist Johann REUCHLIN and others to make the Old Testament text readily available as well. Their work allowed him to ignore the Latin translation then used by the Catholic Church. His hermeneutics also suggested that the Bible should be translated into the language(s) of the people. John CALVIN basically agreed, and like him supported new BIBLE TRANSLATIONS.

In the course of the 16th and 17th centuries, the promulgation of creedal statements by the various Protestant groups tended to reduce the scope of permissible biblical interpretation. In some situations, adherence to a creed became more important than an individual's appropriation of the Bible's teachings. In reaction, supporters of PIETISM such as Methodist founder John

WESLEY revived the Lutheran idea of the perspicuity of the Bible.

During the 18th century, the Pietists' desire to understand and apply Scripture to their lives was confronted by a new trend: rationalists began to set up reason as a judge of Scripture. A rational search of the Bible, they said, should yield a set of basic religious affirmations. In its more skeptical form, the approach reduced Christianity to a deistic affirmation of God, the need for prayer, the existence of an afterlife, and the centrality of the moral life. It jettisoned much of Christian orthodoxy, especially the teachings on Christ and salvation, and denied God's role in history and the existence of miracles.

Science buttressed this rationalist approach in the 19th century. The findings of geology and biology in particular led many Christians to doubt the accuracy of the Bible on matters of history, the origin of the earth, and the nature of humanity. Whereas previously Protestants had differed on their interpretation of specific passages of Scripture, this new approach tended to challenge the basic Protestant consensus about the authority of the Bible.

Some Protestants now started with the assumption that the Bible can be read, as any other text, in light of its historical context and with its stated purpose. Scholars began to read the Pentateuch (the first five books of the Hebrew Bible) as a set of independent documents that had been edited together to create a single narrative. This approach became known as the Documentary Hypothesis, and it became the foundation for modern BIBLICAL CRITICISM.

Today, the great majority of biblical scholars treat other biblical books the same way. Thus, they say, the Gospel of Matthew was created by blending material from the Gospel of Mark, a supposed text called "Q" (which contained the material common to Matthew and Luke), and an additional source (or sources) unique to Matthew. Such an understanding yields a very different interpretation of the Bible than the more traditional Protestant understanding, though it is by no means incompatible with a high view of the authority and INSPIRATION OF THE BIBLE.

More conservative Protestants, Fundamentalists and Evangelicals among them, have tended to reject the modern critical methods in favor of a more traditional literal reading that emphasizes historical context and purpose. They tend to affirm the integrity and unity of each book and respect the traditional authorships. In their view, the authority of Scripture is greatly compromised if St. Paul did not write the letter to Titus, for example, or if the book of Genesis was compiled from separate and contradictory texts.

Some Evangelicals have used the language of PRINCETON THEOLOGY to affirm their opinion of Scripture. They suggest that the Bible is infallible (relative to moral and spiritual matters) and inerrant (relative to other matters such as history and science). They affirm that every word of the Bible is inspired.

Conservative scholars have developed a sophisticated hermeneutic of their own, usually termed the historical-grammatical approach: the text should be interpreted in light of its historical and cultural context and its language and syntax. Without compromising the integrity or authenticity of the text, such an approach has greatly expanded the possibilities for interpretation, and has been able to incorporate insights from new methodological tools such as FORM CRITICISM.

Some conservative Protestants have used DISPENSATIONALISM as a hermeneutical tool, accepting its division of history into different ages or dispensations of divine and human action. Dispensationalism is compatible with another hermeneutical approach, the typological, in which the Old Testament characters and stories are seen as foreshadowing the New. Thus, the priest Melchizedek becomes a type of Christ. These and other additional hermeneutical principles allow for a further expansion of the believer's ability to appropriate the text.

At the other extreme, a more radical use of biblical criticism has been adopted by the group of scholars who organized the Jesus Seminar in the 1980s. They attempted a rigorous use of the critical tools to discern how much can be known about the historical Jesus.

Further reading: Louis Berkhof, *Principles of Biblical Interpretation* (Grand Rapids, Mich.: Baker Book House, 1950); Gerald L. Burns, *Hermeneutics Ancient and Modern.* Yale Studies in Hermeneutics (New Haven, Conn.: Yale University Press, 1992); Millard J. Erickson, *Evangelical Interpretation: Perspectives on Hermeneutical Issues* (Grand Rapids, Mich.: Baker Book House, 1993); Robert W. Funk, Roy W. Hoover, and the Jesus Seminar, *The Five Gospels: The Search for the Authentic Words of Jesus* (New York: Scribner/Polebridge, 1996); Norman L. Geisler, *Explaining Hermeneutics: A Commentary on the Chicago Statement on Biblical Hermeneutics* (Oakland, Calif.: International Council on Biblical Inerrancy, 1983).

Hicks, Elias (1748–1830) *American liberal Quaker leader*

Elias Hicks, a leader of the most liberal faction of the Society of Friends, was born on March 10, 1748, at Rockaway, New York. As a young carpenter, he was introduced to and became a member of the Society of Friends (QUAKERS). In 1771, he married Jemina Seaman, at whose family home he lived for the rest of his life.

Hicks had become an extremely popular Quaker preacher, venturing as far as Philadelphia, the center of the Quaker world. Later in life, he traveled across the United States and into Canada. Hicks's sermons called into question some commonly accepted Quaker beliefs that tied them to orthodox Christianity—the divinity and virgin birth of Jesus Christ, his saving work, and the authority of the Bible, which he opposed to the authority of the spirit within each person.

Hicks's popularity made his views a matter of widespread debate, which resulted in an 1827 split in the American branch of the society, as many congregations (weekly meetings) divided.

Hicksite congregations were most numerous on his native Long Island, but he found some support in most regions of the country into which the Quakers had spread—New York, Philadelphia, Baltimore, Ohio, and Indiana. British Quakers remained in touch with the orthodox groups and did not initiate correspondence with the Hicksites. Hicks had no quarrel with Quaker dress or lifestyle, which his supporters carried on. The Hicksite faction continues today as the Friends General Conference, based in Philadelphia.

Hicks died on February 27, 1830.

Further reading: Robert W. Doherty, *The Hicksite Separation: A Sociological Analysis of Religious Schism in Early Nineteenth Century America* (New Brunswick, N.J.: Rutgers University Press, 1967); Bliss Forbush, *Elias Hicks, Quaker Liberal* (New York: Columbia University Press, 1956); Elias Hicks, *Journal of the Life and Religious Labours of Elias Hicks, written by himself* (New York: F. T. Hooper, 1832); Homer Larry Ingle, *Quakers in Conflict: The Hicksite Reformation* (Knoxville: University of Tennessee Press, 1986).

Hocking, William Ernest (1873–1966)
American theologian and missiologist

William Ernest Hocking was a philosopher and theologian whose controversial ideas on the SOCIAL GOSPEL and the global spread of Christianity had a substantial impact on the Protestant missionary endeavor.

Hocking was born in Cleveland, Ohio. He received his B.A., M.A., and Ph.D. (1904) degrees from Harvard University, where he taught from 1914 until his retirement in 1943. As a teenager, he had experienced conversion at a Methodist gathering, and as a philosopher he devoted considerable attention to personal perceptions of the divine, the subject of his first book, *The Meaning of God in Human Experience* (1912). He returned to the issue in later writings as well.

His early METHODISM also left Hocking with an interest in the missionary enterprise. He wrote about the commonalities of religious experience between Christians and followers of other faiths. In an early work, *Human Nature and Its Remaking* (1918), he argued for a need to reshape human consciousness, and saw the Christian world mission as the means to accomplish that task. In his 1932 volume, *Re-Thinking Missions*, he criticized the exclusive claims of Christianity, and tried to address the challenges presented by secular worldviews. He also suggested that missionaries should deemphasize the search for converts and put more emphasis on social and medical needs.

Hocking's approach provoked considerable controversy in ecumenical circles, and finally prompted a response from missiologist Hendrick KRAMER, whose 1938 volume *The Christian Message in a Non-Christian World* criticized syncretism (mixing Christianity with elements from other religions). Kramer emphasized the discontinuity with one's religious past that came with the decision of faith in Christ.

Within more conservative circles, Hocking became a symbol of all that was bad in modernism and liberal Protestantism. For example, his name surfaced in the controversy over missions that so engaged the PRESBYTERIAN CHURCH (USA) in the 1930s. On the other hand, in 1966 Kramer contributed to a volume honoring Hocking, writing that the two had moved closer since their views were published in the 1930s.

In 1957, Hocking produced one of his last studies on religious life, *The Meaning of Immortality in Human Experience*. He died in 1966.

Further reading: William Ernest Hocking, *Human Nature and Its Remaking* (New Haven, Conn.: Yale University Press, 1918); ———, *Living Religions and a World Faith* (New York: Macmillan, 1940); ———, *Re-Thinking Missions: A Layman's Inquiry after One Hundred Years* (New York: Harper & Brothers, 1932); Leroy S. Rouner ed., *Philosophy, Religion and the Coming World Civilization: Essays in Honor of William Ernest Hocking* (The Hague: Martinus Nijhoff, 1966); ———, *Within Human Experience: The Philosophy of William Ernest Hocking* (Cambridge, Mass.: Harvard University Press, 1969).

Hodge, Charles (1797–1878) *conservative Presbyterian founder of the Princeton Theology*

Charles Hodge is generally considered the originator of the ideas that became known as the PRINCETON THEOLOGY. He was born on December 27, 1797 in Philadelphia. He graduated from Princeton University in 1815, and in 1819 completed his studies at Princeton Theological Seminary, where he worked with Archibald Alexander (1772–1851). He joined the seminary faculty the following year, when he was also ordained as a Presbyterian minister.

Hodge became an apologist for traditional CALVINISM and a critic of revivalism, BIBLICAL CRITICISM, and Darwinism. One of his more effective tools in promoting his views was the *Biblical Repertory and Princeton Review,* which he launched in 1825 and edited for 45 years.

His reputation began to rise with the publication of his early exegetical work, *A Commentary on the Epistle of the Romans* (1835). Latter publications, including the two-volume *Constitutional History of the Presbyterian Church in the United States of America* (1839, 1840) and *The Way of Life: A Handbook of Christian Belief and Practice* (1841), culminated in his monumental *Systematic Theology* (1871–73).

Hodge actively participated in the denominational leadership of the Presbyterian Church, and served as moderator of the Old School (anti-revivalist) General Assembly in 1846. He also served on both the missionary and education boards.

He died on June 19, 1878.

Further reading: Charles Hodge, *The Constitutional History of the Presbyterian Church in the United States of America* (1851, rpt., Wrightstown, N.J.: American Presbyterian Press, 1984); ———, *Systematic Theology* (1871–73, rpt., Grand Rapids, Mich.: William B. Eerdmans, 1993); ———, Mark A. Noll and David N. Livingstone, eds., *What Is Darwinism? And Other Writings on Science & Religion,* (Grand Rapids, Mich.: Baker Book House, 1994); W. Andrew Hoffecker, *Piety and the Princeton Theologians: Archibald Alexander, Charles Hodge, and Benjamin Warfield* (Grand Rapids, Mich.: Baker Book House, 1981); David F. Wells, ed., *The Princeton Theology* (Grand Rapids, Mich.: Baker Book House, 1989).

Hoffmann, Melchior (c. 1500–1543) *Millennarian leader of the Radical Reformation*

One of the radical voices of the RADICAL REFORMATION, Melchior Hoffmann's apocalyptic or millennarian views did much to discredit the ANABAPTISTS in their first decade. Hoffman was born in Schwäbisch-Hall, Württemberg, in southern Germany. He began working as a leather dresser, but after he became an enthusiastic supporter of the Reformation, he moved to Livonia, Balticum, in 1523 and became a parish priest, despite his lack of training. He soon moved beyond LUTHERANISM, and ran into popular opposition after preaching against the use of images in the church. He developed an emphasis on prophetic and eschatological themes, which tended to isolate him from the main body of reformers.

In 1526, Hoffmann was offered a post in SWEDEN, preaching in a German-speaking community, but King Gustavus I soon felt the need to stop his sermons. Martin LUTHER asked him to leave the ministry, but he continued to preach, first in Denmark, and then in STRASBOURG, which he became convinced would be the New Jerusalem predicted in the book of Revelation. He predicted Christ's return in 1533 to take the seat of his new universal kingdom. He attacked Luther, whom he had once called the apostle of the third stage of history, but whom he now considered a traitor to the cause; he himself assumed the apostolic mantle.

When he demanded equal status for Anabaptists in Strasbourg, the city council, concerned by his increased following, ordered him arrested. Hoffman spent the last decade of his life in jail. He died in 1543. However, two of his many followers, Jan Matthys and Jan Beuckelsz (Jan of Leiden), established themselves in Münster, Westphalia, and moved to create a "new Jerusalem" based upon their literalistic reading of the Bible. The structure of their communal society became increasingly bizarre; polygamy was introduced, and brutality and torture were used to maintain conformity. After a long siege, Catholic forces overran the city and killed the leadership. Münster presented the European public with a very negative image of the Anabaptists, which they never outlived. The surviving remnant eventually re-emerged as a pacifist community.

See MENNONITES.

Further reading: Norman Cohn, *Pursuit of the Millennium* (Oxford: Oxford University Press, 1971); K. Deppermann, *Melchior Hoffmann* (Edinburgh, Clarke Press, 1987); R. Po-Chia Hsia "Münster and the Anabaptists," in R. Po-Chia Hsia, ed., *The German People and the Reformation* (Ithaca, N.Y.: Cornell University Press, 1988); W. Klaassen, *Living at the End of the Ages: Apocalyptic Expectations in the Radical Reformation* (Lanham, Md.: University Press of America, 1992); George H. Williams, *The Radical Reformation* (Philadelphia: Westminster Press, 1962).

Holiness movement

The Holiness movement, an offshoot of American Methodist REVIVALISM, aimed to achieve a life of perfect love for each Christian through the gift of sanctification.

Methodist founder John WESLEY (1703–91) had taught a doctrine of Christian perfection, in which believers could aim to become perfect in love in this life. In Wesley's view, the sinner begins in repentance and salvation, then embarks on a life of striving to integrate Christian virtues into one's behavior, a process Wesley called growing in grace. This can culminate in sanctification, the attainment of perfection or holiness. Sanctification was an encounter with God, not unlike conversion. It depended on God's grace, not on the Christian's striving.

In America, given the primary task of evangelizing a largely unchurched nation, the doctrine of perfection was neglected in the decades immediately after the American Revolution. By the 1830s, it had been rediscovered by a new generation,

including some non-Methodists. It was a key to the conversion and call to the ministry of evangelist Charles G. FINNEY (1792–1875), whose revivals and writings contributed greatly to the new movement.

Some Methodists in America, reasoning that sanctification was an act of God and not an accomplishment of the believer, concluded that it was a second work of grace immediately available to the serious Christian, and a goal that they should seek as soon as they were converted. These Holiness teachers tended to deemphasize the life of growth in grace, and focused instead on the believer's immediate attainment of perfection by God's action. The result was a fellowship in which the sanctified life became the norm in the church.

Holiness attracted a growing following in the 1840s and 1850s. Timothy Merritt, editor of the *Guide to Christian Perfection,* led the way. He found support from future BISHOPS Randolph S. Foster (1820–1903) and Jesse T. Peck (1811–83), and most notably from female lay evangelist Phoebe PALMER (1807–84) and her husband, Walter (1804–83). The Holiness revival that broke out in New York City just prior to the Civil War picked up as soon as hostilities ceased and permeated the various branches of METHODISM. In 1866, Walter Palmer purchased Merritt's periodical (now the *Guide to Holiness*), which he used to spearhead a national revival that reached many non-Methodists, too. Holiness poured new life into the CAMP MEETING culture already favored by Methodists; the meetings were a way for the movement to spread despite church leaders who might oppose it.

In the years immediately after the war, both the Methodist Episcopal Church and the Methodist Episcopal Church, South, elected Holiness advocates as bishops. However, by the 1880s, many bishops and superintendents found themselves unable to handle the excesses that were ever more frequently reported from the camp meetings; their attempts to moderate the movement caused resentment among Holiness supporters from Quaker and Baptist backgrounds.

As conflicts emerged, beginning in the 1880s, many Holiness advocates left the Methodists and formed the first independent Holiness churches, Bible colleges, and associations. In the early 20th century, these churches began to coalesce into the major Holiness denominations such as the CHURCH OF THE NAZARENE, the Pilgrim Holiness Church (now a constituent part of the Wesleyan Church) and the CHURCH OF GOD (ANDERSON, INDIANA). These churches picked up support from several older Methodist bodies, especially the Wesleyan Methodists (now a constituent part of the Wesleyan Church) and the Free Methodists. At the same time, those larger Methodist churches that later made up the UNITED METHODIST CHURCH backed away from Holiness emphases.

Through the 20th century, Holiness churches have given birth to affiliate congregations in the majority of the world's countries. In North America, they banded together in a fellowship now known as the CHRISTIAN HOLINESS PARTNERSHIP.

Some Holiness writers identified sanctification as the BAPTISM OF THE HOLY SPIRIT. That particular presentation provided the foundation for PENTECOSTALISM.

Further reading: Melvin Easterday Dieter, *The Holiness Revival of the Nineteenth Century,* Studies in Evangelicalism, no. 1 (Metuchen, N.J.: Scarecrow Press, 1980); J. Kenneth Grider, *A Wesleyan-Holiness Theology* (Kansas City, Kans.: Beacon Hill, 1994); Charles E. Jones, *A Guide to the Study of the Holiness Movement,* ATLA Bibliography Series no. 1 (Metuchen, N.J.: Scarecrow Press/American Theological Library, 1974); William C. Kostlevy, ed., *Historical Dictionary of the Holiness Movement* (Lanham, Md.: Scarecrow Press, 2001); Charles Edward White, *The Beauty of Holiness: Phoebe Palmer as Theologian, Revivalist, Feminist, and Humanitarian* (Grand Rapids, Mich.: Zondervan, 1986).

Honduras

The many years of Spanish rule has left the great majority of Honduras's citizens Roman Catholics, except along the Miskito coast to the north, which the British seized in the 17th century.

As early as 1739, the Miskito people asked for someone to instruct them in the teachings of the CHURCH OF ENGLAND, and several of them later traveled to JAMAICA to study. The first British missionary, Christian Frederick Post, arrived in 1768 under the sponsorship of the SOCIETY FOR THE PROPAGATION OF THE GOSPEL IN FOREIGN PARTS. Methodists established their initial mission on the Bay Islands, off the Miskito coast and also controlled by the British. The first congregation was formed in 1844. Toward the end of the century, Methodists from neighboring Belize entered the Spanish-speaking part of Honduras, establishing congregations among English-speaking expatriates.

BAPTISTS came to the Bay Islands from BELIZE in 1846, and also began working among expatriates. They were joined by the SEVENTH-DAY ADVENTIST CHURCH (1891), the Central American Mission (CAM International), which directed their work to Spanish speakers in the more central and rural part of the country (1896), the CHRISTIAN BRETHREN, and the QUAKERS (1902). PENTECOSTALISM was introduced in the 1930s by the ASSEMBLIES OF GOD. The initial work was supplemented with the arrival of the CHURCH OF GOD (CLEVELAND TENNESSEE) (1945) and the CHURCH OF GOD OF PROPHECY (1952). Pentecostalism thrived in the late 20th century and now has more than 100,000 adherents, though the Christian Brethren appears to be the largest Protestant FREE CHURCH body in the country. The largest indigenous church is the Church of the Prince of Peace, brought to the country from neighboring Guatemala.

Since the end of World War II, several more Protestant missionary organizations have initiated work, representing the full range of conservative Protestant churches. Many participate in the Honduras Evangelical Alliance, affiliated with the WORLD EVANGELICAL ALLIANCE. No church based in Honduras is affiliated with the WORLD COUNCIL OF CHURCHES, and there is no national council of churches.

The oldest Protestant church, now the Honduras Episcopal Church, retained its affiliation with the Church of England until 1957, when it was incorporated into the Episcopal Church based in the United States. In the 1930s, the English-speaking Methodist work was turned over to the African Methodist Episcopal Church, which in turn passed it to the Methodist Church in the Caribbean and the Americas.

See also CENTRAL AMERICA.

Further reading: Clifton L. Holland, ed., *World Christianity: Central America and the Caribbean* (Monrovia, Calif.: MARC-World Vision, 1992); E. F. Mathews, *Planting the Church in Honduras: The Development of a Culturally Relevant Witness* (Pasadena, Calif.: Fuller Theological Seminary, M.A. thesis, 1970); William R. Reed, *Latin American Church Growth* (Grand Rapids, Mich.: William B. Eerdmans, 1986).

Hong Kong *See* CHINA: HONG KONG.

Hoover, Willis Collins (1856–1936)
American Pentecostalist missionary in Chile
Willis Collins Hoover, the father of PENTECOSTAL-ISM in Chile, was born in Freeport, Illinois, and grew up as a Methodist with strong HOLINESS leanings. His wife, Mary Louise Hilton, shared his Holiness beliefs. After becoming a physician, he had a call to the mission field and found support from the William Taylor Building and Transit Fund. William TAYLOR had spurred the missionary cause within the Methodist Episcopal Church by arguing for self-supporting missions. Chile had been one his chosen targets.

Hoover joined the staff of the English College in Iquique, Chile, in 1889, and was soon pastoring the nearby Methodist congregation. When the newly created South American Conference in 1893 disenfranchised the female workers and the Chilean native workers who had previously worked as equals with the American male missionaries, Hoover remained one of the most indigenized of the missionaries.

In 1907, Hoover first learned of the Pentecostal revival from a friend of his wife. Two years later, the couple experienced the BAPTISM OF THE HOLY SPIRIT and the accompanying speaking in tongues. Hoover introduced the baptism to his own congregation and several closely related ones. Opposition to his Pentecostalism led to his withdrawal in 1910; with his supporters he founded the Methodist Pentecostal Church of Chile. Hoover left that church in a 1932 controversy and founded the Evangelical Pentecostal Church. The original body would go on to seed two other groups, the Pentecostal Church of Chile and the Pentecostal Mission Church. Between them, the four churches that arose from Hoover's original work claim more than 1 million members in Chile.

Hoover remained active until his death in 1936. Shortly before his death, he published an account of his life and ministry (1934).

Further reading: M. G. Hoover, *Willis Collins Hoover: History of the Pentecostal Revival in Chile* (Santiago, Chile: Imprenta Eben-Ezer, 2000); Willis Collins Hoover, *Historia del Avivamiento Pentecostal en Chile* (Valparaiso, 1934); Jean Baptists August Kessler Jr., *A Study of the Older Protestant Missions and Churches in Peru and Chile* (Goes, The Netherlands: Oostervaan & Le Cointre, 1967).

Hübmaier, Balthasar (1481–1528)
martyred Anabaptist leader
Balthasar Hübmaier was born in Freiburg, Bavaria, in 1481. He earned his M.A. at the University of Freiburg in 1511. His gifts were soon recognized with a position teaching theology at the University of Ingolstadt, where in 1515 he was named vice-rector. He later became a priest at the cathedral at Ratisbon.

In the early 1520s, Hübmaier was attracted to the Reformation, and in 1523 he made his first visit to Zurich, where he met Ulrich ZWINGLI, who was just beginning his reform of the city. Hübmaier became the priest of the church at Waldshut, Austria, where he tried to institute reforms.

He became convinced that infant BAPTISM should be replaced with adult baptism; unfortunately, Zwingli had already encountered that idea in Zurich, among a group who challenged the church's authority.

The concept of the church as a communion of believers rather than of all citizens was far beyond what Zwingli could accept. The Zurich group was banned. After inviting others to join their fellowship, Zurich authorities arrested them.

Meanwhile, Hübmaier was facing opposition from the bishop at Constance after he began to offer the Eucharist in both kinds (bread and wine) to his parishioners. He had to leave Waldstadt in August 1524. Settling at Schaffhausen, he penned his small work *Heretics and Those Who Burn Them,* the first call for religious toleration in the modern era. In January 1525, he publicly repudiated infant baptism in his book *The Christian Baptism of Believers,* and had himself rebaptized on Easter Sunday.

When the Austrian army moved against Schaffhausen at the end of 1525, Hübmaier fled to Zurich. Hoping to find a haven with his former friend, he discovered instead that Zwingli was aware of the direction of his thought and had Hübmaier arrested immediately. He recanted under torture and was allowed to leave Zurich. For some months he moved about German-speaking lands, raising up churches, including one at Augsburg. Anabaptism had gained a foothold in Nikolsburg, Moravia (now in the Czech Republic), and here Hübmaier finally settled. Through 1527, he authored many Anabaptist tracts that circulated throughout Europe.

Authorities caught up with him and his wife toward the end of 1527, and both were taken to Vienna. In jail, he now resisted torture. Finally tried for heresy, he was condemned to the stake. Prior to his execution, he was paraded through the streets to the public square. In the presence of his wife, he was burned alive, gunpowder being rubbed into his beard before the pyre was ignited. Three days later, his wife was drowned in the Danube, a large stone tied around her neck.

In spite of Hübmaier's execution, Nikolsburg remained a center of the ANABAPTISTS.

Further reading: William Roscoe Estep, *The Anabaptist Story: An Introduction to Sixteenth-Century Anabaptism* (Grand Rapids, Mich.: William B. Eerdmans, 1996); Balthasar Hübmaier, *Balthasar Hübmaier: Theologian of Anabaptism,* ed. by H. Wayne Pipkin and John H. Yoder, Classics of the Radical Reformation, vol. 5 (Scottdale, Pa.: Herald Press, 1989); *The Writings of Balthasar Hübmaier,* compiled by G. D. Davidson, 3 vols. (Liberty, Mo.: reproduced by microfilm, William Jewell College, 1939); Henry C. Vedder, *Balthasar Hübmaier, The Leader of the Anabaptists* (New York: Knickerbocker Press, 1905); George H. Williams, *The Radical Reformation* (Philadelphia: Westminster Press, 1962).

Huguenots

Protestantism came to FRANCE immediately after its emergence in neighboring Germany and SWITZERLAND. When strong opposition arose, two of the leading Protestant thinkers, John CALVIN and William FAREL, moved to Geneva, which became the center of the French-speaking Protestants. Calvin developed the theology and ecclesiology that would dominate the Reformed church (as opposed to the Lutheran Church based in Germany). French Protestants overwhelmingly sided with Calvin, their position being summarized in the Gallican Confession of 1561.

Opposition became persecution during the ST. BARTHOLOMEW'S DAY MASSACRE, when some 20,000 Huguenots (French Protestants) were killed. (The term *Huguenot* is of disputed origin, though it may have derived from Bezanson Hugues, one of their early leaders. It was originally a term of opprobrium, but it long ago came into common use.) A period of civil war ended with the EDICT OF NANTES in 1598, which granted toleration. Persecution resumed in the next century; the edict was revoked in 1685, and Protestant ministers were ordered to leave the country. Only in 1787 was a final edict of toleration enacted in France.

After the revocation of the Edict of Nantes, an estimated 100,000 Huguenots left France. French Protestant churches were founded in relatively tolerant countries in both Europe and the Americas.

Within France, the Huguenots survived underground and formed what is today the Reformed Church of France. It was reorganized during the reign of Napoleon, at which time it had an estimated 430,000 adherents. The law of 1806 dictated local churches to be organized around a consistory composed of its pastor and the leading laymen (ELDERS), who would manage local affairs. There would be one consistorial church for every 6,000 believers. Originally, 76 consistories served by 171 pastors were formed. Every five churches would unite into a synod. The synod (comprising one pastor and one elder from each of the five churches) supervised public worship and religious education. Its enactments had to be approved by government authorities, a provision that ended with the separation of church and state in France in 1905.

A national organization was formed during the reign of Louis Napoleon in reaction to divisions that had appeared. Two groups split off in the 1830s and 1840s, one representing a pietistic tendency, and the other supporting a strictly confessional faith.

Despite their conflicts, the Reformed churches were able to build one of the most active foreign missionary agencies, the PARIS MISSION ("Societe des missions évangéliques de Paris"), which began in SOUTH AFRICA and spread around the world, especially in the French colonial empire.

In the 20th century, most Huguenot churches in other countries disappeared, as members adapted to local languages and merged into likeminded Reformed and Presbyterian churches. In the United States, for example, most former Huguenot congregations have been integrated into the fellowship of the PRESBYTERIAN CHURCH (U.S.A.). The former works of the Paris Mission have become autonomous church bodies and continue to exist throughout the former French colonies.

See also REFORMED/PRESBYTERIAN TRADITION.

Further reading: Jean-Jacques Bauswein and Lukas Vischer, eds., *The Reformed Family Worldwide: A Survey of Reformed Churches, Theological Schools, and International Organizations* (Grand Rapids, Mich.: William B. Eerdmans, 1999); Mack P. Holt, *The French Wars of Religion 1562–1629* (Cambridge: Cambridge University Press, 1995); George A. Rothrock, *The Huguenots: A Biography of a Minority* (Chicago: Nelson Hall, 1979).

humanism

In the context of the Reformation, humanism refers to a scholarly movement during the Renaissance that placed secular studies (the humanities) on a par with theology. Humanists worked to revive classical Greek and Latin learning. They wanted to foster a critical spirit, believing that educated individuals could use reason to improve their world, even to reform church and society. By the 16th century, many humanists felt that their learning, especially their knowledge of Greek, could be used to bring much-needed reform to the church.

Humanism's first major success was a book by Lorenza Valla (1405–57) that proved that the Donation of Constantine (which had been used to justify the pope's temporal power) was a fake. Valla also discovered a number of errors in the Latin Vulgate Bible.

Humanists used their new linguistic expertise to correct the available Greek texts of the New Testament, from which new translations could be produced. In SPAIN, for example, the University of Alcalá, founded in 1500, became a humanistic center. Under the guidance of Cardinal Archbishop Francisco Ximenes de Cisneros (c. 1436–1517), the first printed Greek New Testament appeared in 1520, followed by a polyglot Bible (multiple texts printed side by side) two years later.

French humanist Jacobus Faber (Jacques Lefèvre d'Étaples) (1455–1536) paired a study of the ancient texts with an interest in mysticism (including Jewish forms). Through the 1520s, as the Reformation flowered in Germany, he worked on commentaries and a new translation of the New Testament. Putting aside medieval commentaries, he studied the Greek text directly and found in it a simple message of love and faith that had strong resonance with Reformation themes. Faber's student Guillaume Briçonnet (1470–1533) went on to become the bishop of Meaux and turned the city into a humanist center. John Colet (c. 1467–1519) and Sir Thomas More (1478–1535) were the leading humanists in England. From his base at Oxford, Colet's lectures on Paul's epistles earned him the post of dean of St. Paul's Cathedral in London, which he turned into another center of humanist learning. More went from Oxford to a career in politics, rising to the post of lord chancellor under HENRY VIII. He is remembered for his novel *Utopia*, picturing an ideal society. A devout Catholic, he refused to support Henry's supremacy of the church in England, and was executed in 1533.

The most famous of the humanists, however, was the Dutch scholar Desiderius ERASMUS of Rotterdam (c. 1469–1536). Through his studies, he developed a vision of the simple Christian life lived out of what he termed the "philosophy of Christ." He believed that purifying the New Testament as it then existed would promote such a life. His Greek text became the basis of Martin LUTHER's German translation.

As a whole, the humanists remained loyal to the Roman Catholic Church. Many did show sympathy with Reformation concerns, having themselves long been seeking reforms in the church. Whatever their loyalties, their work to create accurate, readable biblical texts made plausible the reliance on biblical authority that was to become the hallmark of the Protestant movement.

Some humanists, especially in Germany, did openly support the reformist cause. Ulrich von Hutten (1488–1523), for example, became an outspoken critic of the papacy, monasticism, and Catholic scholarship in general. Possibly more important was Johannes REUCHLIN (1455–1522), one of the most widely traveled and linguistically adept of the German intellectuals. Reuchlin introduced the study of Hebrew into Germany (thus preparing the way for Luther's Old Testament translation), and fought the Dominicans, who were trying to have a variety of Jewish books destroyed.

Further reading: Cornelius Augustin, *Erasmus: His Life, Works, and Influence;* trans. by G. C. Grayson (Toronto: University of Toronto Press, 1991); John D'Amico, *Renaissance Humanism in Papal Rome: Humanists and Churchman on the Eve of the Reformation* (Baltimore: Johns Hopkins Press, 1983); Steven Ozment, *The Age of Reform, 1250–1550: An Intellectual and Religious History of Late Medieval and Reformation Europe* (New Haven, Conn.: Yale University Press, 1980); Charles Trinkhaus, *The Scope of Renaissance Humanism* (Ann Arbor: University of Michigan Press, 1983).

Hungary

In the Reformation era, Hungary was divided into three parts: the western region ruled by the Austrian Habsburgs, the central area ruled directly by the Ottoman Turks, and Transylvania, an autonomous region under Ottoman suzerainty.

Transylvania was home to a large Saxon community. Under the influence of Johann Honter (1498–1549), Transylvania's German-speaking population became largely Protestant. After a Magyar translation of the New Testament appeared in 1541 and of Martin LUTHER's *Small Catechism* in 1550, some Hungarian-speaking people became Lutheran. The 1557 Edict of Torda in Transylvania granted religious tolerance to the various groups then active in the countryside.

Reformed churches arose in the 1550s and eventually fared much better than the Lutherans. A third form of Protestantism appeared right after the Edict of Torda, UNITARIANISM, which by the end of the century had some 425 parishes.

After the battle of Zenta in 1697, Hungary was absorbed into the Habsburg Empire, and the new government launched a campaign to return

Hungary, including Transylvania, to the Catholic Church. Nevertheless, the three Protestant churches survived until Emperor Joseph II took the Austrian throne. In 1781, Joseph issued his famous Edict of Toleration, which granted free practice of the Protestant faith in any community where at least 100 families professed it.

In 1848, Hungary disestablished the Roman Catholic Church and declared the equality of all "legally recognized" DENOMINATIONS. At the time, there were only four, but others would be "recognized" at later dates. In 1895, three different levels of legal recognition were introduced. The Catholic, Lutheran, Reformed, and Orthodox churches were placed in the highest category (received) along with Judaism. Smaller and newer churches and religious groups were also "recognized." A third category of "tolerated" churches included the Seventh-day Adventists, the Methodists, and the Mormons. After the JEHOVAH'S WITNESSES became active, a fourth category of "banned" groups was created, later to include the Pentecostals and the CHURCH OF THE NAZARENE.

In the 19th century, the Baptist Church was established by three Hungarian workers who had briefly settled in Germany. Johann Gerhard Onchen (1800–84), the man most responsible for the spread of the Baptist Church across Europe, had met them there and sent them back to organize the first Baptist congregation, the seed for what would become the Baptist Union of Hungary. METHODISM spread initially among German-speaking residents. As the work grew in the first decade of the 20th century, it was incorporated into the Northern Germany Conference of the Methodist Episcopal Church (now the UNITED METHODIST CHURCH).

After World War I, Transylvania was ceded to Romania, along with its German-speaking Protestants. After World War II, the Marxist government drastically repressed religious life. The harsh conditions were only slightly relieved during the 1960s. Protestant churches survived partly underground, but experienced a rebirth after the fall of the Berlin Wall. The coming of religious freedom in the 1990s found the Reformed Church of Hungary claiming some 20 percent of the population; Lutherans have about 5 percent. The FREE CHURCH community has only 1 or 2 percent, but is experiencing significant growth.

The older Protestant churches are members of the Ecumenical Council of Churches, which is in turn affiliated with the WORLD COUNCIL OF CHURCHES. Some of the smaller and newer churches have formed the Magyar Evangeliumi Aliancz, affiliated with the WORLD EVANGELICAL ALLIANCE. The Unitarians, not aligned with either organization, have associated with the larger Unitarian global fellowship.

See also ROMANIA.

Further reading: *Churches, Denominations and Congregations in Hungary* (Budapest: Ministry of Foreign Affairs, 1991); J. Craig, *History of the Protestant Church in Hungary: From the Beginning of the Reformation to 1850; with Reference to Transylvania* (London: James Nisbet, 1864); B. Dercsényi, *Calvinist Churches in Hungary* (Budapest: Hegyi, 1992); *Hungarian Protestantism: Its Past and Present* (Budapest: Ecumenical Council of Churches, 1956).

Hus, John (Jan Hus) (1373–1414) *reforming churchman and forerunner of the Reformation*

John Hus's views on theology and church practice prefigured much of later Protestant theory. Though he was martyred, his followers kept his ideas alive for 150 years until they were adopted by millions during the Reformation.

Hus was born in 1373 in Husinec, a small town in Bohemia (in what is now the Czech Republic). His peasant parents saw the priesthood as the best means of escaping their life and supported his clerical studies. In 1390, he entered the University of Prague, where he completed his B.A. in 1393, his M.A. in 1396, and his bachelor of divinity in 1404. He became one of the most popular of the university's instructors.

While continuing to study for the priesthood, in 1402 he was appointed rector and preacher at the Chapel of the Holy Infants of Bethlehem in Prague. His appointment coincided with a conversion experience, about which he began to preach. Hus also began to absorb the ideas on church reform and biblical authority advocated by John WYCLIFFE, as conveyed to him by Jerome of Prague, a former student at Wycliffe's Oxford. Hus began by advocating the moral reform of the clergy, but was calling for changes in church teachings and practices, including the distribution of both elements of the Eucharist to the laity.

Hus was calling commonly accepted church doctrines heresy, and his support at the university eroded. A total of 45 statements identified with Hus were condemned by his colleagues, after which he was forbidden to preach. Finally, he was excommunicated by the archbishop of Prague. Summoned to Rome, he refused to go, after which the pope ratified his excommunication. When the pope placed Prague under an interdict, meaning that no religious services could be held in the city, Hus moved back to his hometown.

In 1414, a church council was called at Constance (Germany) to decide between rival claimants to the papal throne. Hus was also summoned to appear before the council and promised safe-conduct by Sigismund (r. 1411–37), emperor of the Holy Roman Empire.

A month after his arrival in Constance, Hus was arrested and kept in prison for almost a year. When he was finally brought before the council, Hus was denied the opportunity to speak for himself. He was defrocked and condemned to be burned at the stake. In the face of the church leadership gathered at Constance, Sigismund felt powerless to keep his promise of safe-conduct.

Hus's ashes were thrown into the Rhine River in an attempt to prevent him from being venerated. However, when news of his betrayal and death reached Prague, it led to further popularization of his ideas. They are carried on by the Czechoslovak Hussite Church in his homeland and the MORAVIAN CHURCH, established by Czech immigrants in Germany in the 18th century.

A portrait of John Hus (1373–1415) preaching to his congregation at the church at Prague *(Institute for the Study of American Religion, Santa Barbara, California)*

Further reading: Heiko A. Oberrman, *The Dawn of the Reformation* (Edinburgh: T & T Clark, 1986); Edward Peters, ed., *Heresy and Authority in Medieval Europe* (Philadelphia: University of Pennsylvania Press, 1980); Matthew Spinka, *John Hus at the Council of Constance* (New York: Columbia University Press, 1965).

Hutchinson, Anne (1591–1643) *religious dissident in colonial New England*

Anne Hutchinson, a leading dissenter in early 17th-century Puritan Massachusetts, has been recognized in the 20th century as a pioneer Christian feminist. Hutchinson was born Anne Marbury in Alford, Lincolnshire, England. Her father, a Puritan minister, had been arrested on several occasions for expressing dissenting opinions. She married William Hutchinson in 1612.

Anne Hutchinson's unorthodox views prompted the Antinomian Controversy and led to her banishment from the Massachusetts Bay Colony. *(Library of Congress)*

In 1634, the Hutchinsons took up residence in Boston, Massachusetts. Hutchinson had been impressed by John Cotton's ministry in London the previous year, but she found the atmosphere in Boston considerably less free than in London. Only the male members of the church were invited to meet after Sunday services to discuss the sermon. In reaction, she invited the women to her home. These meetings provided an opportunity for her to inject her dissenting views into the community. The meetings became quite popular, eventually drawing men as well as women. She emphasized personal religion and also questioned the faith of many of the ministers, at one point claiming that only John Cotton and John Wheelwright (her brother-in-law) showed signs of being among the elect.

Hutchinson's real troubles began when former governor John Winthrop blocked the appointment of Wheelwright as pastor to one of the Boston churches. Her dissent now became a public issue, and she was branded as an antinomian (against the law).

As a result of the controversy, Winthrop resumed his former post and placed a ban on private meetings. His supporters had a list of reputed heresies read out at a SYNOD meeting. When Hutchinson continued to hold her meetings, she and Wheelwright were tried for heresy. Hutchinson proved an articulate defendant and answered all the charges against her. However, in the process, she also revealed that she had received a private revelation. Winthrop branded it a delusion, and the court banished her from Massachusetts. She was put under house arrest to await a church trial.

In March 1638, Hutchinson was tried by the ELDERS of the church of Boston. By this time, John Cotton had joined her opponents and accused her of teaching free love. She was excommunicated. Hutchinson, her family, and some followers left Massachusetts to settle on an island purchased from the Narragansett people in what is now Rhode Island. Her husband died in 1642, and she moved to a settlement just north of present-day New York City, where she and several of her children were killed in 1643 in an Indian war.

Further reading: Robert Rimmer, *The Resurrection of Anne Hutchinson* (Amherst, N.Y.: Prometheus Books, 1987); Winnifred King Rugg, *Unafraid: A Life of Anne Hutchinson* (Boston/New York: Houghton Mifflin, 1930); Jared Sparks, *In Defiance of the Law: From Anne Hutchinson to Toni Morrison* (New York: Peter Lang, 2001); Selma R. Williams, *Divine Rebel: The Life of Anne Marbury Hutchinson* (New York: Holt, Rinehart & Winston, 1981).

hymns/music

Hymns and other music have been integral to shaping and expressing the beliefs and practices of Protestantism. For Protestants, hymns took the place of important parts of the Roman Catholic liturgy. Simplified Protestant worship, lacking the ritual drama of the Mass, was energized by music; it became one of Protestantism's defining elements within the larger Christian community.

Protestant hymnody begins with Martin LUTHER, author of "A Mighty Fortress is our God," the anthem of the Reformation that was sung as the Protestant princes presented their affirmation of faith at the 1529 Diet of Speyer. Luther advocated the writing of many hymns; they could be learned by the masses as a tool for spreading and establishing Protestantism. Over a dozen hymnals were published in Germany by 1550, and Lutheran parishes gradually accustomed themselves to congregational singing. Congregational singing in the Lutheran Church, which declined along with the early enthusiasm, was revived by the Pietists toward the end of the 17th century. PIETISM extolled singing as an essential part of personal devotion.

Meanwhile, among French-speaking Protestants, the singing of PSALMS set to contemporary music emerged as the dominant musical practice. John CALVIN advocated modest, simple church singing without instrumental accompaniment. This perspective, embodied in the *Geneva Psalter* of 1562, was passed to Geneva's English Protestant refugees; when they returned to England after the death of MARY I, they established psalmody as the dominant form of music among the Elizabethan Puritans.

Radical reformers also developed an extensive hymnody. They included metrically arranged Psalms, as well as many hymns that embodied their particular beliefs and referred to their ever-present persecution and martyrdom. The primary collection of hymns, the *Ausbund,* was published around 1565.

The MORAVIAN CHURCH, an independent pre-Reformation Protestant group, published its first hymnal in 1501. Its leader in the early 18th century, Count Nicolas von ZINZENDORF (1700–60), himself authored some 2,000 hymns, many of which were included in the Moravians 1736 hymnal, a massive volume with 999 songs.

British hymnody experienced a watershed with the career of Isaac WATTS (1674–1748), a Puritan who challenged the dominance of Psalm singing by arguing that the church's music should more directly reflect its New Testament message. His first volume of *Hymns and Spiritual Songs* in 1707 proved very popular; such songs as "When I Survey the Wondrous Cross" are still often sung in Protestant circles. Some of his more popular new hymns were directly based on the Psalms, including "Joy to the World" (Ps. 98) and "Oh God, Our Help in Ages Past" (Ps. 90). Watts also wrote the first Protestant children's songbook.

Methodist hymnody begins with the encounter of John WESLEY (1703–91) with Moravian hymns on his voyage to Georgia in 1735. He began to learn German in order to understand and translate them into English. Wesley himself wrote a few hymns for his first hymnal, published in South Carolina in 1737. It included some hymns of Watts, some translations from the German, and Wesley's own songs, the first Christian hymns to be penned on American soil.

As the Wesleyan movement grew in England, a new hymnody, largely the product of John's brother, Charles WESLEY (1707–88), defined the movement. During John's life, more than 50 hymn collections were published to serve the needs of the rapidly expanding movement. Among Charles's 6,500 hymns are the still-popular "Christ the Lord Is Risen Today," "Hark the Herald Angels Sing," "Love Divine, All Love's Excelling," and "O For a Thousand Tongues to Sing."

The Wesleyan hymns contrasted the songs written for congregational singing and indoctrination with the great church music that was pouring from the organs and choirs of the leading churches of the European urban centers. Musicians of every generation, a prime example being

Johann Sebastian Bach (1685–1750), composed music to be performed rather than sung; such music always competed for attention with congregational singing in the Lutheran and Anglican churches.

The first hymnal in America, the *Bay Psalm Book,* was published by the Massachusetts Puritans. Wesleyan-style music spread in the 18th century, initially through the efforts of George WHITEFIELD (1714–70). Though he broke with Wesley over the issue of free grace, Whitefield heartily approved of Wesley's hymnody and freely borrowed from Charles's hymns (which he changed to conform to his own theology). His major hymnal was published in 1753 as *Hymns for Social Worship.* The singing of hymns apart from the Psalms would be a factor in the split of the Presbyterians in the 1740s into Old School and New School factions.

The hymns of Watts, the Wesleys, and Whitefield reached into the African-American community as well. There, especially among the slaves, a new hymnology emerged that would give rise to AFRICAN-AMERICAN GOSPEL MUSIC.

Wesleyan hymn singing became institutionalized in the frontier CAMP MEETINGS. People such as Bostonian Lowell Mason (1792–1872) were encouraged to begin schools to improve the quality of congregational music. Musical training became part of the revival movement, especially the new urban revivalism of the post–Civil War era.

The last decades of the 19th century saw the rise of a new hymnody, characterized by a somewhat repetitive restatement of basic Protestant affirmations, ease of singing, and a sentimental emotional content. These new hymns became known as "gospel songs," a reference to Philip P. Bliss's 1874 volume, *Gospel Songs.* The last quarter of the century was marked by the emergence of great evangelical musician/evangelist teams, most notably Ira Sankey (1840–1908) and Dwight L. MOODY, and the spread of gospel songs through the revivals and the emerging SUNDAY SCHOOLS movement.

The 1831 copyright law gave the new music publishing houses a stake in securing popular hymn writers. Fannie CROSBY, the most popular hymn writer of the period, was under contract to the Biglow & Main Company. Philip P. Bliss (1838–76) worked for Root and Candy and later the John Church Company. These companies had a stake in the regular introduction of new hymns; new songbooks gave rise to special musical events within the revival campaigns. Singing conventions emerged, where the new gospel songbooks were distributed and the latest songs introduced.

The rise of popular gospel songs created a problem for denominations. They could not pay the royalties demanded by the publishing houses to include the gospel hymns in their denominational hymnals. Beginning in the late 19th century, many local churches supplemented their denominational songbook with a gospel hymnal as a means of accessing the new music.

As Protestantism spread around the world, the religious music of Europe and North America spread with it, through denominational hymnals and gospel songbooks. The songs were often translated. More recently, they have served as the base for various national Protestant hymnologies.

In the 20th century, church music continued to thrive. Though the most popular hymns are usually associated with the more conservative and evangelistic churches, the liberal movements produced music that emphasized their own concerns for building the kingdom of God through the SOCIAL GOSPEL, a global perspective, and modernist theology. Some of the most well-known liberal Protestant hymns are: "O Master, let me walk with Thee" (Washington Gladden); "God of Grace and God of Glory" (Harry Emerson Fosdick); "This is my Father's world" (Maltbie D. Babcock); "Where cross the crowded ways of life" (Frank M. North); "Joyful, joyful we adore thee" (Henry van Dyke); "Rise up, O men of God" (William P. Merrill); and "O God of every nation" (William W. Reid Jr.).

One 20th century trend was the professionalization of gospel music. The singing conventions gave way to gospel singing events featuring quartets, family groups, and soloists. These groups became even more important with the rise of religious broadcasting on radio and television. Early singing stars such as the Stamps Quartet gave way to such groups as the Blackwood Brothers and Hovie Lister and the Statemen Quartet after World War II.

By the end of the 20th century, a Christian music industry had developed around a set of superstars whose fans followed their careers like their secular counterparts. Included among the outstanding contemporary stars are Bill and Gloria Gaither, Keith Green, Amy Grant, and Kirk Franklin. Christian musical artists have adopted every form of music from bluegrass to rock and rap.

The communities created by the CHARISMATIC MOVEMENT also produced a new hymnody, associated with such organizations as the Association of Vineyard Churches (and the associated Vineyard Music USA) and Integrity Incorporated. This music, with its emphasis on praise and worship, spread far beyond Charismatic circles into the large DENOMINATIONS by the start of the 21st century.

Further reading: Robert Anderson and Gail North, *Gospel Music Encyclopedia* (New York: Sterling Publishing, 1979); Millar Patrick, *The Story of the Church's Song*, rev. ed. by James Rawlings Sydnor (Richmond, Va.: John Knox Press, 1962); William Jensen Reynolds and Milburn Price, *A Survey of Christian Hymnody* (Carol Stream, Ill.: Hope Publishing, 1987); Erik Routley, *The Music of Christian Hymnody* (London: Independent Press, 1957); W. J. Limmer Sheppard, *Great Hymns & Their Stories* (Fort Washington, Pa.: Christian Literature Crusade, 1979).

Hyper-Calvinism

Hyper-Calvinism is a form of Calvinist theology that emphasizes the sovereignty of God and God's eternal decrees to the point that it negates the necessity of any human action to achieve salvation, especially evangelism. To those whom God has elected, God's grace is irresistible; their acceptance of the Gospel is not related to any other activity.

The emergence of Hyper-Calvinism is generally attributed to Cambridge Congregational minister Joseph Hussey in England, author of *God's Operations of Grace but No Offers of Grace*, published in 1707. Its most gifted exponent was John Gill (1697–1771), who presented his perspectives in *A Body of Divinity* (1767). Gill, one of the most learned British BAPTISTS of his day, presented his theology as in part an attack on Methodist ARMINIANISM. It gained considerable support among Baptists at the end of the century and was used by opponents of the Baptist Missionary Society. Andrew FULLER emerged as the major opponent of Hyper-Calvinist views, which he countered in his *The Gospel Worthy of All Acceptance; or, The Obligation of Men Fully to Credit and Cordially Approve Whatever God Has Made Known* (1785).

Hyper-Calvinism continues to have some support among Strict Baptists in the United Kingdom and Primitive Baptists in the United States, and it is the dominant position of the Protestant Reformed Church. However, it is opposed by most Calvinists, who see it as a theological error as grave as Arminianism.

See also CALVINISM; PREDESTINATION.

Further reading: David Jack Engelsma, *Hyper-Calvinism & the Call of the Gospel: An Examination of the "Well-Meant Offer" of the Gospel* (Grand Rapids, Mich.: Reformed Free Publishing Association, 1994); John Gill, *A Body of Doctrinal Divinity: Or, A System of Evangelical Truths, Deduced from the Sacred Scriptures* (London: Printed for the author, 1769); Herman Hoeksema, *Reformed Dogmatics* (Grandville, Mich.: Reformed Free Publishing Association, 1966); John R. Rice, *Hyper-Calvinism: A False Doctrine* (Murfreesboro, Tenn.: Sword of the Lord Publishers, 1970).

I

Ibiam, Francis Akanu (1906–1955)
Nigerian medical missionary and ecumenical leader

In 1927, Francis Akanu Ibiam became the first African to attend the medical school at the University of St. Andrews in Scotland. Following graduation, he returned to Nigeria, and in 1936 founded Abiriba hospital, where he served as director for many years. In 1957, he added duties as a physician at the Church of Scotland's mission hospital at Itu.

Ibiam established the Student Christian Movement in Nigeria in 1937, served a term as president of the Nigerian Council of Churches (1955–58), and became a member of the standing committee of the INTERNATIONAL MISSIONARY COUNCIL (1957–58). He chaired the provisional committee that established the All Africa Conference of Churches. By the time he addressed the WORLD COUNCIL OF CHURCHES (WCC) assembly in New Delhi in 1961, he had earned a reputation as a critic of Western missions. Most missionaries, he said, were "guardians of white supremacy." He was elected one of the presidents of the WCC that year.

In the 1960s, the British appointed him governor of Eastern Nigeria, and he was knighted for his accomplishments. When the Biafrian War broke out, he sided with the rebels and was forced into exile in Geneva, though he was later invited back to participate in the reconstruction and reconciliation process. In protest against the British taking sides against the Biafrans, he renounced his knighthood.

See also AFRICA, SUB-SAHARAN.

Further reading: D. C. Nwafo, *Born to Serve: The Biography of Dr. Akanu Ibiam* (Lagos, Nigeria: Macmillan, 1988); Donald K. Smith, "Sir Francis Akanu Ibiam," in A. Scott Moreau, ed., *Evangelical Dictionary of World Missions* (Grand Rapids, Mich.: Baker Book House, 2000).

Iceland, Protestantism in

Iceland was under Danish rule at the time of the Reformation, and most of the country accepted the decision of Denmark's rulers to adhere to the Lutheran cause. After the defeat of a minor rebellion, when Jón Arason, the bishop of Hólar, refused to break with Rome, there was a gradual transition to Lutheran practice. In the short term, the most important impact was the closing of the monasteries. In the long term, worship in Icelandic (rather than Latin or Danish) meant that the church became the center of the developing Icelandic identity.

When Iceland obtained home rule in 1874, the new constitution, while granting religious freedom, maintained the Evangelical Lutheran Church as "a national church . . . supported by the State." This was reaffirmed in the 1944 constitution of the new independent Republic of Iceland. Democratic reforms were adopted early in the 20th century that allowed for some independent decision making in parish councils, and let congregations choose their own pastors. Under a 1998 law, the church became largely autonomous, though it is still the designated established church, supported by government taxes. At the end of the 19th century, Lutherans who wanted freedom from the state church founded the Evangelical Lutheran Free Church of Iceland, which now has in excess of 7,000 members.

The majority of Icelanders are members of the state church. Almost all children are baptized as Lutheran and more than 90 percent are subsequently confirmed. The church conducts 75 percent of all marriages and 99 percent of all funerals. At the same time, participation and church attendance is low. Liberal theology and BIBLICAL CRITICISM are pursued at the Department of Theology of the University of Iceland, although there is still a large conservative core that opposes many of these innovations.

Iceland's relative isolation and small population (about 250,000) have made it a low priority for the international Free Church movements. In the 1890s, the SALVATION ARMY and the SEVENTH-DAY ADVENTIST CHURCH established work, followed in the 20th century by the CHRISTIAN BRETHREN, the Pentecostalists, the JEHOVAH'S WITNESSES, and the BAPTISTS.

The Evangelical Lutheran Church in Iceland is a member of the LUTHERAN WORLD FEDERATION and the WORLD COUNCIL OF CHURCHES.

See also DENMARK.

Further reading: Jón R. Hjálmarsson, *History of Iceland: From the Settlement to the Present Day* (Reykjavik Iceland Review, *1993*); L. S. Hunter, *Scandinavian Churches: A Picture of the Development of the Churches of Denmark, Norway, Finland, Iceland, and Sweden* (London: Faber & Faber, 1965); Karl Sigurbjörnsson, *The Church of Iceland: Past and Present* (Reykjavik: Church of Iceland, 1998).

Identity Movement　*See* CHRISTIAN IDENTITY MOVEMENT.

Iglesia ni Cristo (Church of Christ)

The Iglesia ni Cristo, or Church of Christ, is an indigenous 20th-century Protestant church that has become one of the largest and most controversial churches in the Philippines. It was founded by Felix Manalo Isugan (1886–1963) after leaving behind his childhood Roman Catholic Church and several Protestant churches along the way. In 1913, he felt a calling from God to found his own church. Following World War II, the church grew; it now has more than 1,750,000 members.

The Church of Christ is staunchly anti-Catholic. It rejects the Trinity in favor of a strict monotheism: Christ is not God, though he did have a messianic role. Manalo is venerated as the *sugo* or last prophet of God, and identified with the angel in the seventh chapter of Revelation. Like the equally successful JEHOVAH'S WITNESSES, Iglesia ni Cristo members take literally the biblical injunction against eating the blood of animals, which in the Philippines means they refuse to consume a popular food known as *dinuguan*, prepared with cooked animal blood.

The Iglesia ni Cristo has appeared in various countries of western Europe and the United States, primarily within the Filipino expatriate communities. It now publishes a journal in English, *God's Message,* and has opened a world mission headquarters in California.

Further reading: A. Leonard Tuggi, *Iglesia ni Cristo: A Study in Independent Church Dynamics* (Quezon City: Conservative Baptist Publishing, 1976); ———, "Iglesia ni Cristo: An Angel and His Church," in David J. Hesselgrave, ed., *Dynamic Religious Move-*

ment: *Case Studies of Rapidly Growing Religious Movements around the World.* (Grand Rapids, Mich.: Baker Book House, 1978): 85–101.

India

When the Protestant world missionary endeavor began in the 18th century, India was among the first targets. The DANISH-HALLE MISSION began work in Tranquebar in 1706. The mission, which eventually evolved into the United Evangelical Lutheran Church in India, was the lone Protestant presence for most of the century.

British expansion in India in the 18th century piqued the interest of English missionaries, but the powerful East India Company was hostile to religion in general and Christianity in particular, and even Anglicans were unable to establish operations. In 1792, William CAREY, the first representative of the Baptist Missionary Society, arrived in Bengal. His work in Serampore attained legendary status in Protestant church history. He was joined six years later by Congregationalist missionaries sent by the LONDON MISSIONARY SOCIETY. Calcutta became the early center of Indian Protestantism.

In subsequent decades, a wide variety of Protestant churches established their initial missions. Among the more interesting were the American Congregationalists operating through the AMERICAN BOARD OF COMMISSIONERS FOR FOREIGN MISSIONS. Their first group included Adoniram JUDSON, his wife, Anne Hesseltine, and Luther RICE. On their way to India, the three converted to the Baptist cause. They set up the original American Baptist mission in India (later relocated to Burma), and catalyzed the formation of the American Baptist Foreign Mission Society, the first national Baptist body in America. The following year, the CHURCH OF ENGLAND established its first independent mission under the supervision of the CHURCH MISSIONARY SOCIETY. The CMS's arrival in India also signaled the formal end of the company's opposition to missions. Among the first to benefit from the change were the Methodists, who

had set up shop in Ceylon (Sri Lanka) while waiting for an opening.

A growing number of churches from England and increasingly the United States were now arriving in Calcutta. Often British churches found themselves competing with sister churches from the United States. The competition grew intense as denominational bodies and Evangelical sending agencies launched missions. Further competition came from the indigenous Indian MASS MOVEMENTS, in which large numbers of people, usually from one caste or subgroup, would convert to Christianity together.

India received modern PENTECOSTALISM even before parts of the United States. In 1908, George E. Berg, who had been in India for seven years, visited the AZUSA STREET REVIVAL in Los Angeles. Appropriating the experience of speaking in tongues, he returned to India to launch a new work there. In 1915, former African missionary Mary Weems Chapman settled in Madras; the ASSEMBLIES OF GOD trace their presence in the country to her ministry. Robert F. Cook, an Assemblies missionary who arrived in 1913, withdrew from the movement in 1929 and joined the CHURCH OF GOD (CLEVELAND, TENNESSEE) in 1936. In 1930, his former assistant, K. E. Abraham, founded the first indigenous Pentecostal movement, the Indian Pentecostal Church. These churches together number a million adherents.

The CHARISMATIC MOVEMENT swept through the Indian Christian world toward the end of the 20th century; it claims to affect as much as half of the Christian community across DENOMINATIONS. A number of new Charismatic churches have cropped up, too, such as the Manna Full Gospel Churches and the Nagaland Christian Revival churches. The non-Trinitarian Pentecostals are also well represented; the UNITED PENTECOSTAL CHURCH INTERNATIONAL has more than 200,000 members.

Today, the Christian community in India includes approximately 62 million people, about 6 percent of the population. Of these, 14 million are Roman Catholic and 3 million are Orthodox. The remainder are scattered among several hundred Protestant and Free Church denominations, including the Church of South India (3 million members), the Council of Baptist Churches in northeast India (1.6 million), the United Evangelical Church of India (1.5 million), the Church of North India (l.3 million), the Saora Association of Baptist churches (1.2 million), and the Methodist Church in India (1.1 million).

In the 1850s, a movement emerged to create an Indian-based Christianity using Indian cultural forms, culminating in the Hindu Church of the Lord Jesus (1858), the first of a number of indigenous Christian groups. Among the more radical of these was the Subba Row movement formed during World War II. It refused to organize congregations or practice BAPTISM, and built its life around informal prayer meetings and large healing crusades. The Assemblies that grew from the ministry of Indian Christian leader BAKHT SINGH drew much of their inspiration from the Plymouth BRETHREN and the LOCAL CHURCH movement founded by Watchman NEE in China.

The modern ECUMENICAL MOVEMENT had one of its greatest successes in India. In 1912, various Protestant and Orthodox churches formed a unified Missionary Council, which matured through several steps into the National Council of Churches of India (affiliated with the WORLD COUNCIL OF CHURCHES). The Missionary Council became the meeting ground for those groups that wished to go beyond close working relationships to form unified Protestant churches. Methodists, Presbyterians, Congregationalists, Brethren, and Anglicans engaged in numerous ecumenical contacts culminating in the formation of the Church of South India (1947), the Church of North India (1970), and the United Evangelical Churches of India (Lutheran 1926). Approximately a hundred groups participate in the Evangelical Fellowship of India, affiliated with the WORLD EVANGELICAL ALLIANCE.

A growing Christianity has encountered resistance from the Hindu nationalist movement. Radical nationalists have committed a number of violent acts against Christians, including the murder of missionaries and the burning of church facilities. Several states attempted to pass anticonversion laws, making it a punishable offense to "induce" people to convert, but these laws have been declared unconstitutional. This new tension between Hindus and Christians has grown simultaneously with heightened tensions between Hindus and Muslims, as well as the periodic clashes between India and Pakistan, a predominantly Muslim nation. Hindus constitute approximately 75 percent of the Indian citizenry.

Christianity can be found across India, but is strongest in South India, in the area north and east of Calcutta, and in some of the larger northern cites such as Lahore and Lucknow.

See also ASIA; PAKISTAN; SRI LANKA.

Further reading: *The Churchman's Handbook, 1989* (Christian Literature Society, 1988); Herbert E. Hoefer, *Churchless Christianity* (Madras, India: Gurukul Lutheran Theological College and Research Institute, 1991); S. Co. Neill, *A History of Christianity in India,* 2 vols. (Cambridge: Cambridge University Press, 1984–85); S. D. Ponraj and Sue Baird, eds., *Reach India 2000* (Madhupur: Mission Education Books 1996); O. M. Rao, *Focus on North East Indian Christianity* (Delhi, India: ISPCK, 1994).

Indonesia

Protestantism was brought to Indonesia by the Dutch, who in 1605 established their first outpost in the island country. The Dutch East India Company soon forced the 150,000 native Catholics in the Moluccas (converted by the Portuguese) to become Protestants, but they allowed new missions to develop only where they judged it in the company's interest. Among the pioneer missionaries was Justus Heurnius (1587–1652). He organized the Reformed Church at Batavia, translated the HEIDELBERG CATECHISM into Chinese, and later assisted in the translation of the Bible into Malay. His attempts to reach out to the Chinese in Batavia led to his banishment to Ambon for the last years of his missionary endeavors.

In 1806, due to the Napoleonic influence over Holland, freedom of religion was proclaimed throughout Indonesia. Roman Catholics reentered, and the older Protestant churches and missions were reorganized as the Protestant Church of the Netherlands Indies. Beginning in 1797, a new wave of missionaries supported by the Nederlandsch Zendeling Genootschap moved into Java and some of the eastern islands.

The 19th century saw significant expansion of the missionary effort. Back in Holland, several independent denominations split off from the Reformed, and some of them sponsored their own missionaries. British and American sending agencies began to open mission stations in the region as well. The result was a diversity of DENOMINATIONS, only a few of which reached beyond a single island or island group; many were confined to a single ethnic group.

The Indies missionaries were among the last to ordain indigenous clergy. The first theological seminaries opened late in the 19th century. Hendrik KRAMER (1888–1965), a Reformed Church missiologist who worked in Indonesia for 14 years, became a major voice calling for the native ministerial leadership, the maturing of the missions into autonomous churches, and the de-Westernization of the churches.

There were about 1.7 million Protestants in the country when the Japanese occupation began. The churches and missions were totally reorganized, though the arrival of Christian leaders from Japan softened the blow. The internment of almost all foreign missionaries forced the churches to mature quickly. The end of the war brought Indonesia's independence. In spite of a Muslim majority, the country was organized on a multifaith basis and a Protestant political party was created, but the churches faced periodic difficulties and national instability both under Sukarno (1901–70) and after.

A particular challenge came in 1984, when the government imposed the principle of Pancasila on all organizations, including churches. Pancasila asserts that the republic is founded on five principles—belief in God, humanity, national unity, consultative democracy, and social justice. Pancasila has allowed Christmas, Good Friday, and Ascension Thursday to be declared national holidays. It also dictates penalties against anyone who offends or insults, either verbally or in writing, any of the country's recognized religions.

Prominent among the several hundred Christian groups are the Moluccan Protestant Church, the oldest Protestant church body in Asia; the 2.5-million-member Protestant Church in Indonesia, which continues the legacy of Dutch Protestant missionary activity; the Batak Christian Protestant Church (Lutheran), which dates back to the RHENISH MISSION to Sumatra in the 1860s and also has more than 2 million members; and the Pentecostal Church of Indonesia, dating back to the work of two ethnic Dutch families from Seattle, Washington, in the 1920s, with more than a million members. There are more than 20 additional denominations with over 100,000 members.

More than 50 Indonesian churches, 25 of them Indonesian-based, belong to the Council of Churches of Indonesia, which is affiliated with the WORLD COUNCIL OF CHURCHES. A number of newer, more conservative churches have affiliated with the Persekutuan Injili Indonesia, which is associated with the WORLD EVANGELICAL ALLIANCE. The total population of Protestant and Free Church Christians in Indonesia is about 20.5 million, or 10 percent of the total population.

As the new century began, Indonesia and its Christian community were rent by the war over the separation of East Timor, a predominantly Catholic region, into a separate state.

See also ASIA.

Further reading: F. L. Cooley, *The Growing See: The Christian Church in Indonesia* (Jakarta: Christian Publishing House, 1981); G. P. Harahap, *Christianity in the Batak Culture: The Making of an Indigenous Church* (Columbus, Ohio: Trinity Lutheran Seminary, M.S.Th. thesis, 1982); Douglas G. McKenzie with I. Wayna Mastra, *The Mango Tree Church, The Story of the Protestant Christian Church in Bali* (Boolarong Publications,

1988); Edward 0. V. Nyhus, *An Indonesian Church in the Midst of Social Change: The Batak Protestant Christian Church, 1942–1957* (Madison: University of Wisconsin, Ph.D. diss., 1987).

indulgences

The Catholic practice of "selling" indulgences to sinners helped provoke the Protestant Reformation. In Roman Catholic theology, the church was said to possess a storehouse of grace built up from the lives of the saints, which it could dispense to sinners through indulgences. Indulgences could release people from punishments in purgatory; plenary indulgences could release people from temporal punishments as well.

In traditional understandings of the Christian faith, God forgives sin but demands some action that manifests sorrow and makes retribution for harm done. In the Roman Catholic Church, this action was accomplished by the sacrament of penance. By medieval times, the priest was seen as having the authority to absolve individuals of guilt if they confessed their sins and performed penance, which might include saying prayers, fasting, performing acts of charity, or other actions. The average person would have to finish penance after death, in the form of suffering and pain; that penance might be lessened or avoided by an indulgence.

Indulgences could be granted for going on a pilgrimage, engaging in a specified devotional practice, or contributing to a worthy cause such as endowing a church. The latter practice meant, in effect, that indulgences could be bought, and the "selling" of indulgences became a means of raising money for the church or its agents.

A massive campaign to sell indulgences to finance the construction of St. Peter's in Rome provoked biting reactions from church critics. They denounced the sellers for making extravagant claims for the indulgences, even promising to release loved ones already in purgatory. Martin LUTHER, in the NINETY-FIVE THESES, questioned the legitimacy of the idea itself, suggesting that indul-

gences could not relieve guilt. If they could, the pope should use them to empty purgatory for the sake of love, rather than money.

At the Council of Trent, which opened in 1545, Catholic leadership tried to make reforms in the practice. However, the modified use of indulgences continues to the present day in the Roman Catholic Church.

Further reading: Alexius M. Lepicier, *Indulgences: Their Origin, Nature, and Development* (London: Kegan Paul, 1906); Bernhard Lohse, *Martin Luther, An Introduction to His Life and Work* (Philadelphia: Fortress Press, 1986); Nicolaus Paulus, *Indulgences as a Social Factor in the Middle Ages,* trans. by J. Elliott Ross (New York: Devin-Adair, 1922).

inerrancy

The doctrine of inerrancy, propounded for the past 150 years by many conservative Protestants, maintains that the entire BIBLE contains no errors of fact from a scientific, historical, or any other standpoint. Together with the doctrine of infallibility on matters of faith or morality, inerrancy is a response to the challenge of modern BIBLICAL CRITICISM.

Nearly all Protestants place the Bible at the center of their faith and ascribe to it an authority not claimed in either Catholic or Orthodox churches. However, over the centuries, disagreements as to the nature of that authority have arisen. In the 19th century, Bible critics questioned the authorship of biblical texts, theologians began to use the Bible as a historical text to be read much as other ancient texts, and scientists suggested that the creation accounts in the book of Genesis could not be taken literally, since they conflicted with scientific findings on the age of the earth and the process of evolution.

In reaction, the main body of Protestant intellectuals tried to revise their understanding of biblical authority. Some came to view the present text of the Bible as the end of a long process of development from oral tradition through a series of written documents. The different books of the Bible were often seen as witnessing a progressively more enlightened view of God, or as mundane texts that can become the instruments through which the word of God speaks to us (NEO-ORTHODOXY).

Many conservative scholars rejected the new direction. They began to argue for the integrity of the text as it stood, and to suggest that it was infallible on issues of faith and morality and inerrant on fact. In the 20th century, inerrancy became the crucial point.

The first of these conservative voices was Swiss Free Church professor Louis GAUSSEN (1790–1863), who in 1840 published a defense of traditional biblical authority, *Theopneustia: The Plenary Inspiration of the Holy Scriptures*. The book found an appreciative readership, especially at Princeton Theological Seminary, where it inspired several landmark books. In the 1880s, Princetonians A. A. Hodge (1823–86) and Benjamin B. Warfield (1851–1921) published *Inspiration,* which was followed in 1888 by Baptist Basil Manly Jr.'s volume *The Bible Doctrine of Inspiration* (1888). Warfield was followed at Princeton by J. Gresham Machen, who left Princeton in 1929 to teach at the new Westminster Theological Seminary.

Though other issues assumed center stage in the disputes between Fundamentalists and the Modernists in the 1930s, inerrancy continued to be upheld. Important later works were *The Infallible Word,* edited by Ned Stonehouse and Paul Woolley (1946), E. J. Young's *Thy Word is Truth* (1957), and J. I. Packer's *"Fundamentalism" and the Word of God* (1958). More recently, a new generation of scholars such as F. F. Bruce (1910–90) have taken up the cause.

In the 1960s, Fuller Theological Seminary, the flagship of EVANGELICALISM, dropped its requirement that faculty and students ascribe to inerrancy. Many intellectuals who identified with Evangelicalism came to accept Neo-Orthodoxy as a suitable substitute. However, within a few years Evangelical leaders (especially those from Presbyterian and Baptist backgrounds) seemed to have second thoughts. In 1973, a number of them

drafted the "The Ligonier Statement," which affirmed inerrancy.

The debate has raged in Evangelical circles ever since. In 1976, former Fuller professor Harold Lindsell (1913–98) published an attack on his former colleagues, *The Battle for the Bible* (Zondervan, 1976). Lindsell warned against what he saw as significant drift in both the SOUTHERN BAPTIST CONVENTION and the LUTHERAN CHURCH-MISSOURI SYNOD. The most important statement by his opponents was Jack Roger and Donald McKim's *The Authority and Interpretation of the Bible: An Historical Approach* (1979).

In 1978, a gathering of Evangelical leaders issued "The Chicago Statement on Biblical Inerrancy," which in turn lead to the formation of the INTERNATIONAL COUNCIL ON BIBLICAL INERRANCY. During its 10-year existence, the council held conferences and published books and papers advocating inerrancy. In the meantime, the Missouri Synod experienced a schism as its more liberal members left to become part of what is now the EVANGELICAL LUTHERAN CHURCH IN AMERICA. A similar split among Southern Baptists led to the founding of the Cooperative Baptist Fellowship by more moderate members.

As the 21st century begins, Evangelicals remain divided on the issue of inerrancy, though its supporters are more vocal than its opponents. Wording that supports inerrancy has been added to several denominational statements, such as those of the Evangelical Mennonite Brethren Church and the Bible Baptist Fellowship International. Many other Fundamentalist and Evangelical churches have not seen the need to alter their older statements.

See also FUNDAMENTALISM; INSPIRATION OF THE BIBLE.

Further reading: Mark Dever, "Inerrancy of the Bible: An Annotated Bibliography." Available online. URL: http://www.9marks.org/partner/Article_Display_Page/0,,PTID314526|CHID626244|CIID15527 1 6,00.html, Accessed on January 15, 2004; Louis Gaussen, *Theopneustia: The Plenary Inspiration of the*

Holy Scriptures (1841; reprint, Chicago: The Bible Institute Colportage, n.d.); Harold Lindsell, *The Battle for the Bible* (Grand Rapids, Mich.: Zondervan, 1976); J. I. Packer, *"Fundamentalism" and the Word of God* (Downers Grove, Ill.: InterVarsity, 1958); Ned Stonehouse and Paul Woolley, ed., *The Infallible Word* (Philadelphia: Westminster Theological Seminary, 1946); E. J. Young, *Thy Word is Truth* (Grand Rapids, Mich.: William B. Eerdmans, 1957).

Inglis, Charles (1734–1816) *first Anglican bishop to serve outside the United Kingdom*

Charles Inglis was born at Glencolumbkille, County Donegal, Ireland, the son of an Anglican minister. At age 20, Inglis moved to Lancaster, Pennsylvania, where he taught school until 1758, when he returned to England to be ordained as a priest in the CHURCH OF ENGLAND. He was appointed as a "missionary" to Dover, Pennsylvania (now Delaware), and assumed his post in 1759.

In December 1765, Inglis became assistant rector at Trinity Church in New York City. A loyalist, he wrote a refutation of Thomas Paine's revolutionary pamphlet *Common Sense*. On the eve of the war, he called colonists to reconcile with England rather than revolt. During the conflict, he remained in New York, which was in British hands, returning to England in 1783 with the departing British troops.

In 1787, Inglis was consecrated bishop by the archbishop of Canterbury and assigned to Nova Scotia. He settled in Halifax and set about his work with notable enthusiasm. He founded a number of churches and helped create what became King's College, originally intended for training ministers.

He continued in his duties for more than a quarter of a century and died on February 24, 1816.

See also ANGLICANISM; CANADA.

Further reading: Brian Cuthbertson, *The First Bishop: A Biography of Charles Inglis* (Halifax: Waeg-woltic Press, 1987); Reginald V. Harris, *Charles Inglis: Missionary, Loyalist Bishop* (Toronto: General Board of Religious Education, 1937); Charles Inglis, "The True Interest of America Impartially Stated" (1776), available online. URL: http://odur.let.rug.nl/~usa/D/1776-1800/libertydebate/inglis.htm.

inspiration of the Bible

Most Protestants affirm that the Bible is authoritative in religious matters and not a book like any other, but they differ as to its nature and the manner in which it was inspired. The most popular traditional Protestant approach is to describe the Bible as the inspired Word of God; in other words, the human authors or editors of

A frequent sight in rural America—Bible verses placed on signs for passing travelers to absorb *(Institute for the Study of American Religion, Santa Barbara, California)*

the biblical books were influenced by God as they went about their work. Modern-day Protestants offer an array of different explanations as to how the authors were inspired and in exactly what sense the Bible is properly labeled the Word of God.

The Reformation raised the authority of Scripture over that of the church and the clergy; Martin LUTHER's belief in SOLA SCRIPTURA (Scripture alone) is representative of the movement. In reaction, the Roman Catholic Church eventually clarified its own ideas about the exalted nature of Scripture as having been dictated by God. The First Vatican Council (1871) modified the Dogmatic Constitution on Divine Revelation to say that "the books of the Old and New Testaments in their entirety, with all their parts, are sacred and canonical because, having been written under the inspiration of the Holy Spirit, they have God as their author and have been handed to the Church herself."

The early Protestants did little to spell out the nature of biblical inspiration, though affirmations about Scripture were often the first item in confessions of faith. The Second HELVETIC CONFESSION states that "God himself spoke to the fathers, prophets, apostles, and still speaks to us through the Holy Scriptures."

In the 19th century, as geology, biology, archaeology, and BIBLICAL CRITICISM began to undermine the traditional view of the truth of the Bible, modernist theologians tried to find ways to remain confident in the Bible while accepting the challenges to the traditional view. Some theologians suggested that the Bible was the product of inspired individuals and suggested that their inspiration was similar in kind to that of an artist or poet. It was religious genius, not God's action, that produced the Bible. Those who adopted such a view could still speak of the Bible as *containing* the Word of God as well as other material. Such a view also allowed the proponent to dismiss questionable stories in which biblical heroes behaved unethically—killed, committed adultery, acted dishonestly, and so forth.

In the face of both skeptical and modernist voices, traditional believers began to reassert the theory of biblical inspiration and authority and to define the nature of such authority in much greater detail. Conservative Evangelicals adopted a theory of divine influence: God did not dictate the Bible but oversaw the writing process, so that while the individuality, peculiar vocabulary, and historical situation of each author comes through, the message is what God intended to convey. The truth and trustworthiness of Scripture are thus ensured.

The PRINCETON THEOLOGY, developed in the late 19th and early 20th centuries by writers such as Charles HODGE, Benjamin B. Warfield, and A. A. Hodge, used a terminology to define the nature of Scripture that became widely popular: infallibility, INERRANCY, and plenary verbal inspiration. Plenary verbal inspiration suggests that the very words chosen by the writers were inspired, not just the basic concepts and teachings.

In response to discoveries of early biblical texts that differ in many small details with the standard versions, the Princeton theologians introduced the idea that full inerrancy belonged only to the original written versions, and not to later copies or to translations by the average believer. It is important to arrive at the most accurate Hebrew and Greek texts possible, and to translate them into different languages as accurately as possible.

The views and the language of the Princeton theologians are widely reflected in contemporary statements by Evangelical churches. For example, the New Testament Association of Independent Baptists affirms that the Bible's "author was God using Spirit-Guided men, being thereby verbally and plenarily inspired."

In the midst of the arguments between modernists and conservatives over biblical authority, the movement called NEO-ORTHODOXY emerged, its primary spokesperson being Swiss Reformed theologian Karl BARTH. Neo-Orthodoxy sees the Bible as the witness to the Word of God. Scripture becomes the authoritative written Word of

God when it is read and becomes the instrument of the believers' encounter with God. Neo-Orthodoxy became quite popular in the mainline Protestant churches in the last half of the 20th century.

While agreement about the inspiration and authority of Scripture provides a common basis for biblical study and reflection, it has not served the cause of unity of belief. That is, the assertion of the inspiration of the Bible does not solve the problem of interpretation, HERMENEUTICS.

See also BIBLE.

Further reading: William J. Abraham, *The Divine Inspiration of Holy Scripture* (New York: Oxford University Press, 1981); David S. Dockery, *Christian Scripture: An Evangelical Perspective on Inspiration, Authority, and Interpretation* (Nashville, Tenn.: Broadman & Holman, 1995); Carl F. H. Henry, *God, Revelation and Authority,* vol. 4, *The God Who Speaks and Shows* (Waco, Tex.: Word Books, 1979); Bruce Vawter, *Biblical Inspiration* (Philadelphia: Westminster, 1972); Benjamin Breckinridge Warfield, *The Inspiration and Authority of the Bible* (Phillipsburg, N.J.: Presbyterian & Reformed Publishing, 1948).

International Association of Reformed and Presbyterian Churches

The International Association of Reformed and Presbyterian Churches (IARPC) is one of several ecumenical bodies within the worldwide Reformed/Presbyterian community. It serves the most conservative fundamentalist segment of that community. It was founded in 1962 by delegates attending the meeting of the fundamentalist INTERNATIONAL COUNCIL OF CHRISTIAN CHURCHES (ICCC) in Amsterdam, the NETHERLANDS. Rev. Carl McIntire (1906–2003), a Presbyterian and the dominant leader of the ICCC, took the lead in forming the international association along with Dr. A. B. Dodd of Taiwan and Dr. J. C. Maris of the Netherlands.

The IARPC offers itself as an alternative to the more liberal WORLD ALLIANCE OF REFORMED CHURCHES (WARC). In fact, it was the visit to Rome of the Church of Scotland's moderator, a prominent member of WARC, that provoked the founding of IARPC. The group affirms the infallibility and INERRANCY of the Bible and demands separation from all apostasy and heresy (which it believes has infected the liberal REFORMED/PRESBYTERIAN TRADITION).

The IARPC began with those Reformed and Presbyterian churches that were already affiliated with the ICCC. It has its headquarters in Collingswood, New Jersey, in the same building that houses the ICCC in America and the Bible Presbyterian Church, founded by Carl McIntire.

See also ECUMENICAL MOVEMENT.

Further reading: Margaret C. Harden, comp., *A Brief History of the Bible Presbyterian Church and Its Agencies* (privately published, 1968).

International Churches of Christ

The International Churches of Christ emerged as a movement within the older Churches of Christ, one of the main branches of the RESTORATION MOVEMENT that began on the American frontier in the early 1800s. The Churches of Christ were similar to BAPTISTS concerning congregational POLITY and BAPTISM by immersion, but chose a name reflecting their attempt to transcend denominationalism, eschewed the use of instrumental music in worship, and included the LORD'S SUPPER as part of their weekly worship. The Churches of Christ developed their major strength in the American South.

In the 1970s, the Church of Christ congregation adjacent to the University of Florida at Gainesville began the practice of what was called discipling in its campus ministry. The DISCIPLING/SHEPHERDING MOVEMENT sought to turn nominal church members into active disciples of Christ, by assigning each new church member to an older more mature member. This mentoring process involved regular contacts between the discipler and the new disciple. With this program in place, the Gainesville church grew significantly.

Influenced by the Gainesville example, Kip McKean (b. 1954) introduced discipling to a small congregation in Lexington, Massachusetts. The true church of Christ, argued McKean, consisted entirely of disciples. Eventually relocating to Boston and spreading his message through the network of already existing Churches of Christ, McKean articulated a program for world evangelization by building churches in the key cities of the world.

As the "Boston movement" grew, it created a heated controversy within Churches of Christ congregations over the practice of discipling. Other churches criticized what they saw as aggressive proselytization among college students. A group of former members called the movement a destructive cult; they were backed by the secular cult awareness movement. In the wake of the intensive criticism, the fellowship removed several key leaders and modified its discipling program to make it less intrusive.

In the meantime, the church continued to grow. In 1994, an Evangelism Proclamation was issued declaring an intention to plant a church in every nation with a city that had 100,000 residents by the year 2000. Beginning with 146 congregations, over the next years 246 new congregations were begun around the world. In the 1990s, the International Churches of Christ gradually separated itself from the parent body. McKean's evangelism program required a degree of centralized authority that was alien to the traditions of the Churches of Christ. The new body has introduced some instrumental music and has given women an unprecedented degree of leadership, though not yet admitting them to the ordained ministry. HOPE Worldwide was created as a social service delivery agency.

In 2002, Kip McKean left his post as World Missions Evangelist, and the organization moved toward a more collective leadership. The International Churches of Christ is headquartered in Los Angeles, California.

Further reading: *The Disciple's Handbook* (Los Angeles: Discipleship Publications International, 1977); Gordon Ferguson, *Prepared to Answer* (Los Angeles: Discipleship Publications International, 1995); Robert Nelson, *Understanding the Crossroads Controversy* (Fort Worth, Tex.: Star Bible Publications, 1981).

International Church of the Foursquare Gospel

The International Church of the Foursquare Gospel is a Pentecostal church that was founded by noted evangelist Aimee Semple MCPHERSON (1890–1944). McPherson's message, the foursquare gospel, was a Pentecostal variant of the fourfold gospel of Benjamin Albert SIMPSON, founder of the CHRISTIAN AND MISSIONARY ALLIANCE. In her version of this Christ-centered theology, MacPherson emphasized Jesus Christ as Savior, Baptizer with the Holy Spirit, Healer, and Coming King. Over the years, the church has made common ground with the other large Pentecostal bodies in the United States.

Even before World War II, the church began to develop a global missionary program. Today, less than 10 percent of the membership is found in the United States. The church now includes 3,331,561 members in 26,139 churches and meeting places in 107 countries.

The church actively supports the PENTECOSTAL WORLD FELLOWSHIP. Rolf McPherson (b. 1913) followed his mother as president of the church from 1944 to 1988. He was succeeded by John R. Holland (1988–97), Paul C. Risser (1997–2004), and Jack Hayford (2004–   ).

See also PENTECOSTALISM.

Further reading: Edith L. Blumhofer, *Aimee Semple McPherson: Everybody's Sister* (Grand Rapids, Mich.: William B. Eerdmans, 1993); Daniel Mark Epstein, *Sister Aimee. The Life of Aimee Semple McPherson* (New York: Harcourt Brace Jovanovich, 1993); Aimee Semple McPherson, *This Is That* (New York: Garland, 1985).

Angelus Temple, the lead church of the International Church of the Foursquare Gospel *(Institute for the Study of American Religion, Santa Barbara, California)*

International Conference of Reformed Churches

The International Conference of Reformed Churches (ICRC) is one of several ecumenical bodies that serve various segments of the worldwide Reformed Presbyterian community. These organizations operate on a spectrum: the larger and more liberal churches are part of the WORLD ALLIANCE OF REFORMED CHURCHES, and many fundamentalists belong to the INTERNATIONAL ASSOCIATION OF REFORMED AND PRESBYTERIAN Churches. The ICRC represents more conservative Reformed churches.

The ICRC was founded in 1982, when representatives of nine Reformed and Presbyterian DENOMINATIONS assembled at Groningen, Netherlands, at the invitation of the Reformed Churches (Liberated), a relatively new church that had broken with the Netherlands Reformed Church during World War II. Its founder, Professor K. Schilder (1890–1952), had been ousted from the ministry for refusing to accept innovative theological statements as binding on teaching ELDERS. The

church quickly grew into a substantial denomination and developed a close relationship with the Christian Reformed Churches in the Netherlands.

At the founding meeting, Schilder and his followers and allies maintained that an attack was under way within the larger Reformed world against traditional standards of faith—the Bible and the Reformed confessions of the 16th century. The new ICRC adopted the Bible, the "Three Forms of Unity" (BELGIC CONFESSION, HEIDELBERG CATECHISM, Canons of Dort), and the Westminster documents (WESTMINSTER CONFESSION, Larger and Shorter Catechisms) as the basis of its fellowship.

The Free Church of Scotland hosted the first assembly of the ICRC in Edinburgh in 1985. Subsequent meetings have been held in Langley, British Columbia, Canada (1989), Zwolle, Netherlands, and Seoul, South Korea. Prominent among the ICRC's more than 20 members are the Orthodox Presbyterian Church (United States), the Canadian Reformed Churches, the Presbyterian Church of Korea (KoShin), and the Christian

Reformed Churches in the Netherlands. Headquarters are now in Edmonton, Alberta.

See also ECUMENICAL MOVEMENT.

Further reading: Jean-Jacques Bauswein and Lukas Vischner, eds., *The Reformed Family Worldwide. A Survey of Reformed Churches, Theological Schools, and International Organizations* (Grand Rapids, Mich.: William B. Eerdmans, 1999).

International Congregational Fellowship

The International Congregational Fellowship is a coordinating body between Congregationalists in various countries that refused to merge with other Reformed church bodies during the ecumenical activity of the 1960s and 1970s.

As early as the 1890s, churches within the British Puritan lineage that advocated a congregational POLITY (system of governance) had created a structure, the International Congregational Council (ICC), to facilitate communication and fellowship. By 1966, however, the majority of members had come to think that the beliefs and heritage they shared with non-Congregational Reformed churches was more important than church polity, and the ICC merged into the WORLD ALLIANCE OF REFORMED CHURCHES, the majority of whose members follow a Presbyterian rather than Congregationalist polity. That high-level merger was facilitated by the merger of the largest individual ICC member, the Congregational-Christian Churches in the United States, with the Evangelical and Reformed Church to form the UNITED CHURCH OF CHRIST. A short time later (1972), the Congregational Church in England and Wales merged into the United Reformed Church.

Many member churches of the Congregational-Christian Churches rejected the mergers. Asserting their Congregational heritage, they formed the National Association of Congregational Christian Churches. In England, congregations staying out of the United Reformed Church formed the Congregational Federation of England.

Called together by David Watson in England and John Alexander in the United States, people from six countries met in 1975 to form a new ecumenical body, the International Congregational Fellowship. At its first conference, two years later, delegates signed a document called "The Chiselhurst Thanksgiving," affirming their allegiance to the Congregational way.

The fellowship operates as a gathering of individuals concerned with the promotion of the Congregational form of church life and has rejected the model of a council of DENOMINATIONS. Rather than competing with the World Alliance of Reformed Churches, the fellowship runs quadrennial conferences to promote CONGREGATIONALISM. The fellowship's program has found a response from the many churches around the world with Congregational roots, and in the 1990s regional secretaries were established for central Europe, AFRICA, CENTRAL and SOUTH AMERICA, and the Pacific and AUSTRALIA. The fellowship now has affiliates in more than 50 countries, with headquarters in both London, England, and Royal Oak (suburban Detroit), Michigan. It publishes the *International Congregationalist Journal*.

See also ECUMENICAL MOVEMENT.

Further reading: International Congregational Fellowship. Available online. URL: http://www.congregationalist.org.uk and http://congregationlist.org; Jean-Jacques Bauswein and Lukas Vischner, eds. *The Reformed Family Worldwide: A Survey of Reformed Churches, Theological Schools, and International Organizations* (Grand Rapids, Mich.: William B. Eerdmans, 1999).

International Congress for World Evangelism

Held in Lausanne, Switzerland, in 1974, the International Congress for World Evangelism helped spark renewed missionary enthusiasm in the Evangelical Protestant community. The organizational and theological framework that emerged from the congress has played an important role in world evangelism over the past several decades.

In 1966, a World Congress on Evangelism was held in Berlin. In 1974, a new, broader congress was convened by evangelist Billy GRAHAM and 164 other leaders from around the world. Its goal was to promote strategic planning, inspiration, and fellowship.

During the 10-day meeting, 2,300 participants signed the LAUSANNE COVENANT, a statement defining the necessity of spreading the Christian Gospel in the modern world. The congress also set up the Lausanne Committee for World Evangelization, chaired by evangelist Leighton Ford (Billy Graham's brother-in-law), with Ghanaian Bible teacher Gottfried Osei-Mensah as executive secretary. The committee has run many conferences on themes developed at the 1974 congress. Large international congresses were held in 1980 in Pattaya, Thailand, in 1989 in Manila, the Philippines, and in 2004, again in Thailand.

The committee has had a significant role in shaping and coordinating the missionary outreach of the cooperating Evangelical churches and has been instrumental in the dramatic spread of EVANGELICALISM as a global phenomenon at the end of the 20th century. Many of the committee's working papers have now been placed on the Internet at its Web site, http://www.gospelcom.net/lcwe.

Further reading: *Christian Witness to Secularized People* (Wheaton, Ill.: Lausanne Committee for World Evangelization and World Evangelical Fellowship, 1980); *Evangelism and Social Responsibility* (Wheaton, Ill.: Lausanne Committee for World Evangelization and World Evangelical Fellowship, 1982); *The Thailand Report on Large Cities. Report of the Consultation on World Evangelization Mini-Consultation on Reaching Large Cities* (Pattaya, Thailand: Lausanne Committee for World Evangelization, 1980).

International Council of Christian Churches

The International Council of Christian Churches (ICCC) is a worldwide ecumenical body serving conservative fundamentalist Protestant churches. FUNDAMENTALISM arose in American Protestantism as a protest against Modernism, which many considered to be a departure from essential Christian beliefs. One group of Fundamentalists demanded complete separation from the modernists who controlled the major DENOMINATIONS. This group retained the name Fundamentalist. Those who continued their fellowship with conservative Christians who remained in the larger denominations came to be known as Evangelicals.

In 1941, the separatist Fundamentalists founded the American Council of Christian Churches (ACCC), as an alternative to the Federal Council of Churches, then controlled by the modernists. Immediately after World War II, when most large American denominations joined with their European counterparts to create the WORLD COUNCIL OF CHURCHES (WCC), ACCC leaders called Fundamentalist churches from around the world to found an alternative. The first gathering of the ICCC was held in Amsterdam in 1948 within days of the opening assembly of the WCC.

The ICCC has continued to affirm the infallibility and INERRANCY of the Bible and the need for a complete separation from heresy and apostasy, as represented by the World Council of Churches and the WORLD EVANGELICAL ALLIANCE.

The ICCC faced a significant crisis in 1970. A year earlier, the ACCC had removed Carl McIntire (1906–2003), an American Presbyterian minister who had dominated the ICCC from the beginning, as its leader. The ICCC chose to continue its support of McIntire, and the ICCC and the ACCC parted company. Subsequently, McIntire led in the creation of the ICCC in America, and the ACCC led in the formation of the World Council of Bible Believing Churches.

At its 1998 meeting, the ICCC reported 700 denominations from more than 100 countries represented in its membership. Headquarters are located in Collingswood, New Jersey.

See also ECUMENICAL MOVEMENT.

Further reading: Margaret C. Harden, comp., *A Brief History of the Bible Presbyterian Church and Its Agencies* (privately published, 1968).

International Council on Biblical Inerrancy (ICBI)

The International Council on Biblical Inerrancy was created in 1978 and given the task of preparing books and other materials to shore up the belief in biblical INERRANCY and to keep the issue in the forefront among Evangelical Christians.

For most of the 20th century, Evangelicals all tended to accept the language of PRINCETON THEOLOGY to defend traditional views of the Bible, including its inerrancy in all matters of historical or scientific fact. Then, in the 1970s, some Evangelical leaders and scholars seemed to be drifting away from the idea of inerrancy, often by adopting NEO-ORTHODOXY instead. In the early 1970s, for example, Fuller Theological Seminary had abandoned official support for the idea. In 1976, Harold Lindsell, then on the staff of *Christianity Today,* the leading Evangelical journal, wrote his famous volume, *The Battle for the Bible,* calling attention to widespread abandonment of the idea. Lindsell's book alerted many Evangelical leaders to what they now saw as an urgent problem.

In reaction, R. C. Sproul (b. 1939) called a conference on the authority of Scripture, which was held at Mt. Hermon, California, in February 1977. Plans were laid for a national council of theologians, Bible scholars, and Evangelical leaders who could work out a theological affirmation of the full inerrancy of the Bible. Jay Grimstead, who had been active in the process from the beginning, emerged as executive of the new International Council on Biblical Inerrancy. At a meeting in Chicago in October 1978, the 300 attendees signed a Chicago Statement on Biblical Inerrancy. Many Evangelical seminaries and schools responded positively to the Chicago statements and the work of the council, though Fuller and other faculties did not.

The council was designed to do its work and then disband. In the 10 years of its existence, it supported the publication of a host of books on the subject and succeeded in placing it once again at the forefront of the agenda for Evangelical groups (though those from the Methodist-Holiness tradition were reluctant to engage in what they saw as a Presbyterian Baptist issue). As an outgrowth of the council's work, advocates were identified who have continued to carry on the work from their various academic positions.

See also INSPIRATION OF THE BIBLE.

Further reading: James Montgomery Boice, ed., *The Foundations of Biblical Authority* (Grand Rapids, Mich.: Zondervan, 1978); D. A. Carson and John D. Woodbridge, eds., *Scripture and Truth* (Grand Rapids, Mich.: Zondervan, 1983); Norman Geisler, ed., *Inerrancy* (Grand Rapids, Mich.: Zondervan, 1980); Kenneth Kantzer, ed., *Applying the Scriptures* (Grand Rapids, Mich.: Zondervan, 1987); Harold Lindsell, *The Battle for the Bible* (Grand Rapids, Mich.: Zondervan, 1976).

International Federation of Free Evangelical Churches

The International Federation of Free Evangelical Churches is an association of churches that grew out of PIETISM and the EVANGELICAL AWAKENING of the 18th century. It includes member churches from Europe, North America, AFRICA, SOUTH AMERICA, and Asia.

The Free Church movement (Protestant in faith but free of state churches) grew through the 19th century in SWITZERLAND from its early bases in Berne, Basel, and Zurich despite official opposition. It was characterized by strong personal faith and piety and the absence of creeds apart from the Bible. As early as 1834, these churches attempted to make common cause with similar congregations in FRANCE and northern ITALY. In 1910, the Swiss congregations came together as the Union of Free Evangelical Churches in Switzerland.

A similar revivalist impulse in SWEDEN gave birth to the Mission Covenant Church, which spread to DENMARK and NORWAY and was brought by immigrants to the United States. In the 20th century, the church also developed a strong mission program in Africa and Latin America, which led to autonomous churches in those regions in close association with their parent body.

Leaders from several European free churches met in the years after World War I and were joined in the 1930s by American leaders of Mission Covenant Church. In 1948, the International Federation of Free Evangelical Churches emerged. The federation has held international gatherings at irregular intervals since that time.

Further reading: Walter Persson, *Free and United: The Story of the International Federation of Free Evangelical Churches* (Chicago: Covenant Publications, 1998); Gunar Westin, *The Free Church through the Ages* (Nashville, Tenn.: Broadman Press, 1958).

International Fellowship of Evangelical Students

The International Fellowship of Evangelical Students (IFES) is a worldwide group of Protestant students that aims to enlist other students in spreading its theologically conservative Christian message.

In 1910, a group of Protestant student leaders in England withdrew from the WORLD STUDENT CHRISTIAN FEDERATION (WSCF) to found the more conservative Inter-Varsity Fellowship. The movement spread to Canada in the 1920s and to the United States as World War II began. After the war, members of 10 national evangelical campus fellowships in CHINA, AUSTRIA, NEW ZEALAND, North America, and several European countries met at Harvard University in Cambridge, Massachusetts, in 1947 to form the International Fellowship of Evangelical Students. The American-based InterVarsity Christian Fellowship was the largest national affiliate of the new group.

By the end of the 20th century, IFES included members from 145 countries. It has become a training ground for Evangelical leadership; students originally associated with IFES have gone on to work for groups such as the Lausanne Committee for World Evangelism and the EVANGELICAL WORLD ALLIANCE.

The IFES affirms the "divine inspiration and entire trustworthiness of Holy Scripture, as originally given." The organization has a primary goal of training students to reach other students with the Christian message. Since the mid-1990s, IFES has focused on reaching students in the Muslim world.

IFES has been served by three executive secretaries: C. Stacey Woods (1947–75), Chua Wee Huen (1975–91), and Lindsey Brown (1991–present). Its international headquarters is located in Harrow, England.

Further reading: International Fellowship of Evangelical Students. http://www.ifesworld.org; Nicholas Lossky, et al., eds., *Dictionary of the Ecumenical Movement* (Geneva: WCC Publications/Grand Rapids, Mich.: William B. Eerdmans, 1991); A. Scott Moreau, ed. *Evangelical Dictionary of World Missions* (Grand Rapids, Mich.: Baker Book House, 2000).

International Lutheran Council

The International Lutheran Council (ILC) is a fellowship of church bodies that seeks to maintain the original Lutheran doctrines and practices unmixed with either Reformed Church influences or liberal modernist trends.

Through the 19th and 20th centuries, a variety of Lutheran bodies had distanced themselves from the larger Lutheran community, which, they claimed, had become watered down doctrinally and infused with modern secular philosophies. They demanded strict allegiance to the Lutheran confessional documents, especially the AUGSBURG CONFESSION OF FAITH. This "confessional movement" opposed the blending of Lutheran and Reformed theologies such as they saw in Germany, where states were creating united "Evangelical" churches in areas where both Lutheran and Reformed churches existed in strength. In the United States, the bedrock of the confessional movement was the LUTHERAN CHURCH–MISSOURI SYNOD; in Europe, the Evangelical Lutheran Free Church in DENMARK and the Confessional Lutheran Church of FINLAND played important roles.

Early meetings of confessional Lutheran churches from different countries took place in Uelzen, Germany (1952), Oakland, California (1959), and Cambridge, England (1963). After more than two decades of dialogue and fellowship, in the early 1990s a constitution (including a statement of faith) for a formal ecumenical organization was agreed upon.

Delegates gathered in 1993 in Antigua, Guatemala, to found the International Lutheran Council. Many of the autonomous churches that arose from the missionary work of the Missouri Synod joined the council. Doctrinally, ILC member churches affirm Scripture as the inspired and infallible Word of God, and the Lutheran confessions as contained in the *Book of Concord* as the true and faithful exposition of the Word of God.

The ILC serves its member churches primarily in areas of communication, fellowship, mutual encouragement, and mutual assistance. Its headquarters is located in St. Louis, Missouri.

See also ECUMENICAL MOVEMENT.

Further reading: International Lutheran Council. Available online. URL: http://www.ilc-online.org. Accessed on October 1, 2001.

International Missionary Council

The International Missionary Council was a pioneer ecumenical Christian body, which fostered cooperation in missionary work between DENOMINATIONS for half of the 20th century.

As the Protestant missionary enterprise expanded globally in the 19th century, the division into many different denominations caused many problems. Early missionaries tried to avoid competition on the mission field by agreeing to stay out of one another's territory, but as the work expanded, such agreements became woefully inadequate. Attempts were made to find a more comprehensive organizational and theological solution that would affirm the church as the One Body of Christ, and respond faithfully to the Great Commission to go into all the world and preach the Gospel.

The groundwork was laid by leaders trained in the YMCA, YWCA, WORLD STUDENT CHRISTIAN FEDERATION, and Inter-Varsity Fellowship, organizations that focused on evangelism with an international perspective. Several small conferences prepared the way for the memorable international gathering at Edinburgh in 1910. The conference had 1,200 participants, and is usually cited as the beginning of the modern international ECUMENICAL MOVEMENT. Methodist and YMCA executive John R. MOTT chaired the meeting.

The conference established a continuation committee, which inaugurated the quarterly journal, the *International Review of Mission*. The experiences of World War I convinced the committee that a more permanent structure was needed to facilitate dialogue and cooperative action, and in 1921 the International Missionary Council (IMC) was created.

The new IMC agreed not to speak on matters of doctrine or POLITY, and to focus instead on uniting Christians in a search for justice in international and interracial relationships. This later goal spoke directly to European and North American domination of the missionary enterprise, and to missionary compromises with colonial powers and racist attitudes, which had brought discredit to the church. One early study commissioned by the IMC and written by J. H. Oldham (1874–1969) was published in 1924 as *Christianity and the Race Problem*.

The first IMC conference was held in 1928 in Jerusalem; it focused on the relation of Christianity to competing worldviews, both religious and secular. It was followed 10 years later with a conference in Madras that affirmed the close relationship between world peace and world evangelism. World War II devastated the missionary enterprise, but it also made Christian leaders aware of the inherent strength of the Asian and African churches. At its next gathering (Dec. 1957–Jan. 1958), the IMC voted to merge into the WORLD COUNCIL OF CHURCHES. The IMC continued as the Division on World Mission and Evangelism (DWME) of the WCC.

The IMC/WCC merger highlighted a profound transformation in missionary activity. Protestant churches around the world now thought of themselves as partners in one mission.

The DWME has held discussions with Eastern Orthodox churches and Roman Catholic observers about past Protestant evangelizing in both communities, as if they were not Christians, and about religious freedom.

Further reading: W. R. Hogg, *Ecumenical Foundations: A History of the International Missionary Council* (New York: Harper, 1952); Leslie Newbigin, *The Gospel in a Pluralistic Society* (Geneva: World Council of Churches, 1989); Ruth Rouse and Stephen Neill, eds. *A History of the Ecumenical Movement, 1517–1948* (Geneva: World Council of Churches, 1986).

International Pentecostal Holiness Church

The International Pentecostal Holiness Church emerged when followers of the HOLINESS MOVEMENT were exposed to PENTECOSTALISM in the early 20th century. The church views the Christian life as punctuated by three important moments—justification by faith, sanctification, in which the believer is made perfect in love (a Holiness belief), and the BAPTISM OF THE HOLY SPIRIT, which is confirmed by speaking in tongues (a Pentecostal belief).

The original followers of the Holiness movement tended to follow a legalistic life based on a lengthy set of rules. In reaction, the Fire-Baptized movement postulated a baptism with fire (power) that energized one for service and brought joy to life. The Fire-Baptized Holiness Association was founded in 1898. Two years later, J. H. King (1869–1946) became its general overseer and the editor of its periodical.

In 1906–07, A. B. Crumbler and G. B. Cashwell (d. 1916), Holiness preachers in the Carolinas, received the Pentecostal experience of speaking in tongues and led their church into the Pentecostal camp. In 1911, the Pentecostal Holiness Church, in which Crumbler and Cashwell were leading ministers, absorbed the Fire-Baptized Holiness Association. The word *International* was added in 1975.

Even before the 1911 merger, the two churches had begun foreign missionary work, with women taking a leading role. Early missions were opened in Hong Kong by Anna Dean in 1909 and in India by Della Gaines in 1910. In 1913, J. O. Lehman went to SOUTH AFRICA and Amos Bradley to CENTRAL AMERICA. In the 1960s, close working relationships were forged with sister Pentecostal bodies including the Pentecostal Methodist Church of Chile (1967) and the Wesleyan Methodist Church of Brazil (1983). Today, the church has a presence in more than 90 countries with a global membership of slightly more than 1 million. There are 184,000 members in the United States. An initial World Conference of Pentecostal Holiness churches met in 1990 in Jerusalem, Israel.

The church is a member of the National Association of Evangelicals, associated with the WORLD EVANGELICAL ALLIANCE. It is also active in the WORLD PENTECOSTAL FELLOWSHIP. World headquarters are located in Oklahoma City, Oklahoma.

Further reading: Joseph E. Campbell, *The Pentecostal Holiness Church, 1898–1968* (Franklin Springs, Ga.: Publishing House of the Pentecostal Holiness Church, 1951); Vinson Synan, *Old Time Power: A Centennial History of the International Pentecostal Holiness Church* (Franklin Springs, Ga.: LifeSprings Resources, 1998).

Ireland

The Republic of Ireland acknowledges the special role the Catholic Church occupies in Irish life. The 90 percent of the population who belong to the church participate in worship at higher rates than in other Catholic countries.

In 1171, the Synod of Cashell established British supremacy over the Irish church. The Church of Ireland was gradually incorporated into the CHURCH OF ENGLAND, and followed it in separation from Rome in the 16th century. However, opposition to British control went hand in hand with support for the Catholic Church, which was finally given legal status in 1829. The Church of Ireland, the Anglican Church in Ireland, was disestablished in 1869; today, it has only 300,000 members, two-thirds of whom live in Northern Ireland, part of the United Kingdom.

In the 16th and 17th centuries, the British government encouraged large-scale immigration of Scots (mostly Presbyterian) into Ireland. While most settled in the north, some managed to introduce PRESBYTERIANISM into what is now the Republic of Ireland. METHODISM was introduced to Ireland during its first generation in the 18th century. In 1827, John Nelson DARBY left the Church of Ireland and launched his radically anticlerical movement, the Plymouth BRETHREN, in Dublin. The JEHOVAH'S WITNESSES date to the 1890s and are second in size only to the Church of Ireland among non-Catholic churches.

PENTECOSTALISM came to Ireland in the first decade of the 20th century with the ASSEMBLIES OF GOD from England providing the major leadership. During the last decades of the century, the movement expanded and a number of new independent charismatic churches were formed.

There is an Irish Council of Churches that serves member bodies in both the Republic of Ireland and Northern Ireland. It is affiliated with the WORLD COUNCIL OF CHURCHES. More conservative local congregations in Ireland may affiliate with the Association of Irish Evangelical Churches.

Further reading: Jean Blanchard, *The Church in Contemporary Ireland* (Dublin: Clonmore & Reynolds, 1963); *Irish Christian Handbook* (Eltham, London: Christian Research, 1994).

Ironside, Harry A. (1876–1951) *American preacher and champion of Fundamentalism*

Henry Allen (Harry) Ironside was born on October 14, 1876, and raised in Toronto, Ontario, in a pious Plymouth BRETHREN home. The family moved to Los Angeles in 1888, and at age 11 Harry organized and taught a SUNDAY SCHOOL. That year he attended revival services led by evangelist Dwight L. MOODY. After a personal conversion experience a year later, he preached his first sermon.

He joined the SALVATION ARMY, in which he was commissioned a lieutenant in 1892, but later questioned the army's HOLINESS theology, and by 1896 he returned to the Plymouth Brethren. He married, settled in the Bay Area, and began three decades of preaching wherever he was invited, locally and later around the country. In 1900, he published a volume of expository notes on the book of Esther, and commentaries on other biblical books followed. His 1912 book, *Holiness, the False and the True,* explained his differences with the Holiness movement.

In 1924, Ironside began a relationship with the Moody Bible Institute. Moody had accepted much Brethren teachings as his own, especially their dispensational theology; Ironside also began visiting the Dallas Theological Seminary, another dispensational school. In 1929, he was called as pastor of Moody Memorial Church, the large congregation on Chicago's Northside. Among his duties at Moody would be delivering the funeral sermon for prominent evangelist Billy Sunday (1862–1935).

The self-taught Ironside emerged as one of the great preachers of his age. He traveled and preached tirelessly for most of his adult life and was an effective force through his speaking and writing in spreading a conservative Fundamentalist faith. Operating as he did within the Brethren movement and then in the independent Moody Church, he was able to avoid the polemics that typified other Fundamentalists, who belonged to the large modernist-controlled denominations in the 1920s and 1930s. Nevertheless, by his later years he was considered their ally.

In 1938, Ironside began writing the weekly International Sunday School Lessons, published in the *Sunday School Times.* In 1942, he became

Harry Ironside was one of the prominent pastors of Chicago's Moody Memorial Church, constructed in the memory of evangelist Dwight L. Moody. *(Institute for the Study of American Religion, Santa Barbara, California)*

president of the Africa Inland Mission. For most of his time in Chicago, he also taught at Moody Bible Institute.

He retired in 1948 and died two years later while on a visit to NEW ZEALAND.

See also DISPENSATIONALISM; FUNDAMENTALISM.

Further reading: E. Schuyler English, *H. A. Ironside. Ordained of the Lord* (New York: Loizeaux Brothers, 1976); Arthur Hoke, *Life Story of Harry Ironside* (Chicago Sunday Magazine, n.d.); Harry A. Ironside, *Except Ye Repent* (New York: American Tract Society, 1937); ———, *The Only Two Religions and Other Gospel Papers* (New York: Loizeaux Brothers, n.d); ———, *The Unchanging Christ and Other Sermons* (New York: Loizeaux Brothers, 1942).

Italy

Italy was not historically known as a welcoming community for Protestantism, but it played a vital role in early Protestant history. The Waldensian valleys, in the mountains to the west of Turin, were home to an independent group of dissenting believers centuries before the Protestant Reformation. While the origins of the WALDENSIANS remains unclear, in the 16th century they identified with the Protestant movement. Reformer William FAREL traveled from Geneva to a Waldensian Synod at Chanforan in 1532, and official contacts were never lost. The northwest has been the center of Protestant life in Italy ever since.

A radical Protestant community existed at Venice, an early, if short-lived, transmission point

Waldensian Church, Turin, a major Protestant center in Italy *(Institute for the Study of American Religion, Santa Barbara, California)*

for Protestant ideas picked up by Venetian merchants in Germany. A secret anti-Trinitarian society existed in the 1540s. Among its members were George Blandrata (1515–90); Lelio Socinius (1525–62), a priest of Siena and friend of prominent Protestant leaders such as Heinrich BULLINGER, John CALVIN, and Philip MELANCTHON; and Fausto Socinius (1539–1604), Lelio's nephew. When this group split up, it took its UNITARIANISM to POLAND and Transylvania, from where Unitarianism found its way to England.

Naples became a second important Protestant center. Juan de Valdés (c. 1500–40) was the first leader, later joined by former vicar general of the Capuchins, Bernardino Ochino (1487–1565). Following a summons to Rome in 1536, Ochino went into exile in Geneva, where he worked with Italian

expatriates. Peter Martyr the Younger (1500–62) was another member of the Valdés circle, who like Ochino moved to SWITZERLAND and worked among Italian immigrants. For a while he lived in England, but left during the reign of MARY I.

After the church suppressed the Venice and Naples centers, Protestantism survived primarily in the Waldensian valleys. In the 19th century, Protestant missionaries entered Italy as it was undergoing unification and moving toward a modern secular state. The early groups, including Methodists (1859), BAPTISTS (1863), and Seventh-day Adventists (1864), supported unification, which endeared them to the the new government, but did not help them acquire many new members.

Several hundred Protestant and Free Churches worked in Italy in the 20th century. Pentecostals arrived soon after their emergence in the United States (1908), and the ASSEMBLIES OF GOD would eventually attract several hundred thousand adherents. The JEHOVAH'S WITNESSES (founded in the 1890s) became and remain the largest non-Catholic group in the country. Other relatively successful groups include the Churches of Christ, the Free Pentecostals, and the International Evangelical Church.

Altogether, the Protestant and Free Church community includes only about a half-million adherents in Italy. The Evangelical Baptist Union, the Evangelical Methodist Church, and the Waldensian Church (the latter two in a working union) belong to the WORLD COUNCIL OF CHURCHES and are leading members of the Federation of Protestant Churches of Italy. More conservative Protestant churches are affiliated with the WORLD EVANGELICAL ALLIANCE through the Alleanza Evangelica Italiana. The majority of Italian Protestant groups, many of which operate exclusively among various expatriate communities, are members of neither the Protestant Council nor the Evangelical Alliance.

Further reading: Harold J. Grimm, *The Reformation Era* (New York: Macmillian, 1954); R. E. Hedlund,

The Protestant Movement in Italy: Its Progress, Problems, and Prospects (South Pasadena, Calif.: William Carey Library, 1970); Massimo Introvigne, PierLuigi Zoccatelli, Nelly Ippolito Macrina, and Verónica Roldán, *Enciclopedia delle Religioni in Italia* (Leumann (Torino): Elledici, 2001).

Ivory Coast

Contemporary Ivory Coast (Côte d'Ivoire) is almost equally divided into three religious communities—Christians, Muslims, and followers of traditional African religions. The Christian community of about 5 million members is almost equally divided between Roman Catholics and Protestants.

Protestantism was not introduced until after World War I. In 1924, British Methodists opened a mission that became the Protestant Methodist Church in Côte d'Ivoire. They were soon followed by BAPTISTS from FRANCE and the American based CHRISTIAN AND MISSIONARY ALLIANCE. Representatives of the World Evangelism Crusade (now WEC International) came in 1934. To avoid competition, as each group entered, it worked out an agreement over where and among whom it would concentrate its missionary efforts. These agreements are now reflected in the regional spread and tribal constituency enjoyed by the four pioneering churches.

Beginning in the 1930s, a host of groups arrived from the United States including the JEHOVAH'S WITNESSES, the SEVENTH-DAY ADVENTIST CHURCH, and the newly formed Conservative Baptists (now CBAmerica). As early as 1924, the ASSEMBLIES OF GOD introduced PENTECOSTALISM.

Most important, new AFRICAN INITIATED CHURCHES began to establish themselves in Côte d'Ivoire, which became the originating point of two of the most interesting and influential new religions. William Wade Harris experienced a call

from God to preach while in prison in Liberia in 1910. In 1913 and 1914, he traveled through Ghana and the Ivory Coast, preaching and directing hearers to previously established churches. His simple message of one God and opposition to traditional magic did not seem at first to necessitate a new church. However, he developed a following and eventually designated disciples to expand the reach of his message, and he counseled followers, many of whom had no access to a Christian church, to create prayer houses and designate ministers. The HARRIST CHURCH subsequently emerged as one of the country's largest churches with more than 350,000 members.

Equally interesting is the Deima Church (Ashes of Purification Church) founded by Lalou, a female prophetess who claimed to be the heir of William Wade Harris. Rejecting both the traditional deities and the missionaries, and espousing a role for female leaders, Lalou organized her movement in 1942. It became the seedbed of several other female-led churches. Today, African Initiated Churches claim more than a million members in the Ivory Coast.

The METHODIST CHURCH is the only Ivory Coast-based group that is a member of the WORLD COUNCIL OF CHURCHES. A number of the churches, including those that grew from the CBA, WEC, French Baptist, and Free Will Baptist missions, are members of the Evangelical Federation of the Ivory Coast (Féderation Evangélique de la Côte d'Ivoire) which is affiliated with the WORLD EVANGELICAL ALLIANCE.

See also AFRICA, SUB-SAHARAN.

Further reading: David Barrett, *The Encyclopedia of World Christianity,* 2nd ed. (New York: Oxford University Press, 2001); G. M. Haliburton, *The Prophet Harris: A Study of an African Prophet and His Mass-Movement in the Ivory Coast and the Gold Coast* (London: Longmans, 1971).

J

Jamaica

Protestant Christianity was introduced to Jamaica following the British takeover from SPAIN in the 1650s. By then, the number of native Jamaicans had been radically reduced; over the next century, they were replaced with African slaves.

The CHURCH OF ENGLAND came with the original British authorities, as with other colonies, but the island was unique in that the second group to arrive was the Society of Friends (QUAKERS), who were a persecuted group in both England and the American colonies. The Anglicans have remained a substantial movement, but they have fallen behind a number of more recently introduced Evangelical churches and even the Roman Catholic Church, which was reintroduced to Jamaica in 1837. The Quakers have remained a small movement in spite of an infusion of energy from the United States toward the end of the 19th century.

Jamaica was one of the early targets for 18th-century Protestant evangelism. The Moravians arrived in 1754 and the Methodists in 1789. Both churches developed among the plantation slaves, benefiting from their opposition to slavery. George Lisle (c. 1750–1828), a former slave who worked with the British in South Carolina and was repatriated to Jamaica after the American Revolution, began the local Baptist movement.

A spectrum of Protestant and Free Church groups launched work in Jamaica in the 19th century. Of these, the SEVENTH-DAY ADVENTIST CHURCH, whose work dates from the 1880s, has been the most successful. It is second in size only to the Catholic Church. PENTECOSTALISM was introduced early in the 20th century, and the New Testament Church of God, associated with the CHURCH OF GOD (CLEVELAND, TENNESSEE), is now the third-largest church.

Contemporary Jamaica is quite pluralistic, its 2.5 million residents scattered among more than 100 DENOMINATIONS. More than 50 indigenous Christian groups have appeared; a few such as Revival Zion and the New Testament Church of Christ the Redeemer have a substantial presence. Several of the older Protestant bodies (Presbyterian, Congregational, Disciples of Christ) merged in 1956 to form the United Church in Jamaica and the Cayman Islands.

A few of the older Protestant mission churches have reorganized with local control, including the Church of the Province of the West Indies (Anglican) and the Methodist Church in the Caribbean and the Americas. These along with the Jamaica Baptist Union, the MORAVIAN CHURCH, and the United Church are members of the WORLD COUNCIL OF CHURCHES, and make up the backbone of the Jamaica Council of Churches. The more conservative bodies have united in the Jamaica Association of Evangelicals aligned with the WORLD EVANGELICAL ALLIANCE.

Among the more interesting groups in Jamaica is the SPIRITUAL BAPTISTS, an indigenous Caribbean movement that originated in Trinidad. It mixes Protestant beliefs with African practices and emphasizes spiritual healing. Operating in that same space between Protestantism and traditional African religion are the Rastafarians, most known for their hair (grown to resemble a lion's mane, called dreadlocks), Rasta music, and their ingestion of ganja (marijuana). Identified with the black liberation cause in the 1920s, the movement has gone on to become an international phenomenon.

See also CARIBBEAN.

Further reading: S. C. Gordon, *God Almighty Make Me Free: Christianity in Preemancipation Jamaica* (Bloomington: Indiana University Press, 1996); D. A. McGasvran, *Church Growth in Jamaica* (Lucknow, India: Lucknow Publishing House, 1961); R. J. Stewart, *Religion and Society in Post Emancipation Jamaica* (Knoxville: University of Tennessee Press, 1992).

Japan

The growth of Christianity in Japan was stymied by the country's isolationist policies following the arrival of Catholicism in the 16th century. That isolation ended in 1854, when the United States forced an opening of the country to foreign trade and cultural influence. The 1858 Townsend Harris Treaty provided an opening for Protestants, and a spectrum of groups initiated work beginning the next year.

The Episcopal Church, the Presbyterian Church, and the Reformed Church in America were the first to take advantage of the new opportunity; they were able to react quickly by drawing personnel from CHINA. They began translating the Bible and other Christian materials into Japanese and developed strategies to respond to Japanese

hostility to "un-Japanese" culture. During their first decade, work was confined to Nagasaki and Yokohama, where the first permanent Protestant church was built in 1872.

The early missionaries tried to keep American sectarian differences out of Japan, and the first groups of converts were brought together in congregations simply called the Church of Christ. A united Protestant seminary was opened in 1877, and that same year the churches of the Calvinist tradition merged their work as the United Church of Christ of Japan.

In 1878, the Japanese government removed all of the restrictions that had limited access by missionaries, and a new wave of missionaries representing different churches flocked to the country. Many churches established schools and hospitals. By the end of the century, there were almost 100,000 Japanese Protestants, mostly affiliated with DENOMINATIONS that had originated in the United States.

In 1940, the Japanese government ordered all Protestant and Free Church groups to merge into a single United Church of Christ of Japan. A few churches, including the Anglicans, the Seventh-day Adventists, and most of the HOLINESS bodies (such as the SALVATION ARMY) refused to join. Their existence as legal entities ended, though they survived the war years underground and were able to reestablish themselves after the war. After the declaration of religious freedom by the American occupation authorities, many of the denominations decided to continue as the United Church of Christ of Japan, while others withdrew to reestablish their separate work.

In the generation after the war, more than 2,500 Western missionaries arrived, most of them representing the hundreds of smaller Evangelical church bodies in the United States. The number of Christian denominations in Japan rose sharply (while at the same time the number of new Buddhist groups also rapidly increased).

Today, some 300 separate Protestant and Free Church groups operate in Japan, though most remain quite small. The total Christian community

A Japanese Christian diaspora congregation in Salt Lake City, Utah *(Institute for the Study of American Religion, Santa Barbara, California)*

includes around 3 percent of the Japanese citizenry. Among the older Protestant bodies, the United Church of Christ of Japan and the Japan Holy Catholic Church (Anglican) are among the larger ones; they are the backbone (along with the Holy Orthodox Church of Japan) of the National Christian Council of Japan, which is affiliated with the WORLD COUNCIL OF CHURCHES. Some of the more conservative churches are affiliated with the Japan Evangelical Association affiliated with the WORLD EVANGELICAL ALLIANCE.

Since World War II, Japan has also been the target of missionary work from countries other than the United States. Most notably, a number of Korean churches have emerged in the country.

David Yonghi Cho's large center in Seoul has spurred the formation of the Japan Full Gospel Church, and Korean expatriates have formed the Korean Christian Church in Japan. The Little Flock (the LOCAL CHURCH) has come to Japan from China, and a variety of groups have developed from Scandinavian missionary efforts. Several of the churches more on the fringe of Protestantism—the UNIFICATION MOVEMENT, the JEHOVAH'S WITNESSES, and the CHURCH OF JESUS CHRIST OF LATTER-DAY SAINTS—have also enjoyed great success.

People who accepted Christianity but rejected the foreignness of the missionaries formed the No-Church movement (*mukyokai*) under the leadership of a former Methodist, UCHIMURA KANZO (1861–1930), in the 1920s. The Spirit of Jesus Church, formed by former members of the ASSEMBLIES OF GOD in 1937, now reports more than 400,000 members, making it the largest Protestant church in the country. Christians throughout the West have been deeply affected by the example of the independent social activist Toyohiko KAGAWA (1888–1960), who became an exemplar of the Christian SOCIAL GOSPEL message.

See also ASIA; CHINA: TAIWAN; KOREA.

Further reading: J. Breen and M. Williams, eds., *Japan and Christianity: Impacts and Responses* (New York: St. Martin's, 1995); Otis Cary, *History of Christianity in Japan, Roman Catholic and Greek Orthodox Missions* (Rutland, Vt./Tokyo: Charles E. Tuttle, 1982); A. Lande, *Meiji Protestantism in History and Historiography: A Comparative Study of Japanese and Western Interpreters of Early Protestantism in Japan* (Frankfurt am Main: Peter Lang, 1989); P. J. Patterson, *The Way of Faithfulness: Study Guide to Christians in Japan* (New York: Friendship Press, 1991); K. Yoshinobu and D. C. Swain, *Christianity in Japan, 1971–1990* (Tokyo: Kyo Bun Kwan [Christian Literature Society], 1991).

Jehovah's Witnesses

One of the most successful and one of the most controversial religious bodies, the Jehovah's Witnesses have spread their ADVENTISM to large numbers of people all around the world. The group emerged from within the Adventist community in America in the 1880s.

Following the GREAT DISAPPOINTMENT in 1844, when Christ failed to return as predicted, Adventists divided into several groups. One of them proposed a date of 1874 for Christ's coming or *Parousia*. In 1879, Charles Taze RUSSELL (1852–1916), who led an independent Bible study group in Allegany, Pennsylvania, suggested that the 1874 date had been correct, but that the nature of the event was misunderstood—*Parousia* should be translated not as *coming* but as *presence*. He suggested that the end-time had arrived and

would culminate in a generation, possibly around 1914.

To that end, he founded a periodical, *Zion's Watch Tower and Herald of Christ' Presence* and in 1884, an organization, the Watch Tower Bible and Tract Society of Pennsylvania. He presented a systematic treatment of his perspective in a set of books, *Studies in the Scripture*. Groups formed to study his writings, and the movement soon spread across North America and Europe.

Russell died in 1916, and leadership of the Bible students movement passed to Joseph F. Rutherford (1869–1942), who guided the movement through the disappointment that World War I did not bring substantive change to society. He began to mold the followers into what would in 1931 be renamed the Jehovah's Witnesses. He introduced kingdom halls, regular places for Witnesses to gather.

Rutherford also introduced new ideas that pushed the Witnesses beyond the fringe of Christianity, according to many Protestants. Russell had adopted an Arian understanding of God and salvation that denied the divinity of Christ, though still calling Jesus the Son of God and Redeemer.

The Jehovah's Witnesses grew with an aggressive program of literature distribution and door-to-door visits. They became targets of the Nazi party in Germany, which sent many of them to concentration camps. In the United States, attempts were made to halt their proselytizing activities, but they were sustained in a number of landmark U.S. Supreme Court cases.

The Witnesses decried what they saw as the evil systems of the world, including governments. Members refused to salute the flag of any nation, an act they considered idolatrous. They also were pacifists and refused induction in the armed forces. The Witnesses believe that biblical admonitions against drinking blood prohibit any medical procedures that include blood transfusions, and they have been challenged in the courts in cases that involve minors. They have promoted surgical techniques that do not require transfusions, procedures that were widely adopted in the 1990s following scares about tainted blood supplies.

In the years after World War II, the Witnesses adopted a concerted program of lay evangelism that led to spectacular global expansion. Each kingdom hall is responsible for contacting all the residents in its assigned area. Those who wish to become full-time missionaries may attend the movement's school, Watchtower Bible School of Gilead, now located at Patterson, New York.

The Witnesses affirm the entire Bible as the Word of God and they await the arrival of the millennium of Christ's rule on earth. By the end of the 20th century, some 6 million Witnesses were meeting in more than 85,000 kingdom halls in more than 200 countries of the world, with almost twice that number attending their annual memorial of Christ's death. They are either the second- or third-largest religious group in most of the countries of Europe, and have about 1 million members in the United States.

World headquarters is located in Brooklyn, New York. There is also a strong anti-Witness movement in America supported largely by Evangelical Protestants.

Further reading: *Jehovah's Witnesses in the Divine Purpose* (Brooklyn, N.Y.: Watchtower Bible and Tract of New York, 1959); M. James Penton, *Apocalypse Delayed: The True Story of Jehovah's Witnesses* (Toronto: University of Toronto Press, 1997); *Yearbook of Jehovah's Witnesses* (Brooklyn, N.Y.: Watchtower Bible and Tract of New York, issued annually).

Jesus Only Pentecostals

Jesus Only or Oneness Pentecostalism rejects Trinitarian ideas. It stresses the oneness of God, who reveals himself in three aspects; Jesus, the name of the One God, is the only name needed for BAPTISM and salvation. The movement arose as an extension of the FINISHED WORK CONTROVERSY, in which Chicago Baptist minister William Durham tried to reorient PENTECOSTALISM toward a simpler emphasis on the complete saving work of Jesus Christ.

Founder Frank J. Ewart (1876–1947) began developing a new non-Trinitarian theology that emphasized Jesus' name, after hearing a 1913 sermon by Canadian evangelist R. E. McAlister (1880–1953). McAlister equated the phrase "Lord Jesus Christ," which frequently appears in Acts, with "Father, Son and Holy Spirit," the baptismal formula in Matthew (28:19).

Ewart came to view Trinitarian theology as advocating tri-theism (three gods). In contrast, Jesus Only believes that the one God reveals himself in three aspects or modes—as Father through creation, as Son through redemption, and as Spirit by empowering humans. Jesus is the name whereby humans can be saved (Acts 4:12), and baptism should be in the name of Jesus Christ (Acts 2:38).

Ewart began to spread the doctrine through his periodical *Meat in Due Season.* Among his early converts was Glenn A. Cook (1867–1948), who in turn brought African-American leader Garfield T. Haywood (1880–1931) into the cause. The fledgling ASSEMBLIES OF GOD became a major battleground as E. N. Bell (1866–1923) used his two periodicals, *Weekly Evangel* and *Word and Witness,* to defend Trinitarian thought. J. Roswell Flower (1888–1970) soon emerged as the leading voice of Trinitarianism.

When the Assemblies approved a new statement of belief in 1916, including a strongly worded Trinitarian affirmation, "Jesus Only" believers formed a spectrum of new Oneness Pentecostal churches, some using the name "Apostolic" to distinguish them from the Trinitarian churches. The older PENTECOSTAL ASSEMBLIES OF THE WORLD emerged as the first significant "Jesus Only" denominational body.

In 1924, the Pentecostal Assemblies of the World split. Most white members withdrew and eventually formed the United Pentecostal Church in 1945 (now the UNITED PENTECOSTAL CHURCH INTERNATIONAL). It is currently the largest "Jesus Only" church in the world. Over the years, both African Americans and whites have formed a host of "Jesus Only" DENOMINATIONS. The APOSTOLIC WORLD CHRISTIAN FELLOWSHIP is an effort to bring these many churches into a common ecumenical association, though the United Pentecostal Church has declined affiliations.

See also LIGHT OF THE WORLD CHURCH; TRUE JESUS CHURCH.

Further reading: Arthur L. Clanton and Charles E. Clanton, *United We Stand, Jubilee Edition* (Hazelwood, Mo.: Word Aflame Press, 1995); Frank Ewart, *Revelation of Jesus Christ* (St. Louis: Pentecostal Publishing House, n.d.); Fred Foster, *Their Story: 20th Century Pentecostals* (Hazelwood, Mo.: Word Aflame Press, 1986); James L. Tyson, *The Early Pentecostal Revival* (Hazelwood, Mo.: Word Aflame Press, 1990); Andrew Urshan, *The Almighty God in the Lord Jesus Christ* (Portland, Ore.: Apostolic Book Corner, 1919).

Jewish missions

Protestants first began to evangelize Jews systematically at the end of the 18th century. While many DENOMINATIONS abandoned the mission by the end of the 20th century, some efforts continued.

The first Christians were Jews; Christianity established itself as a new religion in part by separating itself from the Jewish community. By the fourth century, most Christians of Jewish heritage had been integrated into the larger Gentile Christian community.

Christians made repeated attempts to force Jews to abandon Judaism, often through acts of discrimination and persecution that remain a blot on Christian history. Shortly before the Reformation, both SPAIN (1492) and PORTUGAL (1496) banished Jews who would not convert. The anti-Semitism that had become institutionalized in Roman Catholic countries passed to Protestantism. The relatively liberal policies of Napoleon, embodied in the Civil Code of 1804, was followed late in the 19th century by a new wave of anti-Semitism that emanated from Germany, which would culminate in the Jewish Holocaust during World War II.

A new interest in evangelizing Jews was born at the end of the 18th century, in the context of the Protestant community's global missionary endeavor. The London Society for Promoting Christianity Among the Jews (popularly referred to as the London Jews Society) was founded in 1809 by Joseph Samuel Christian Frederick Frey (1773–1850), who had formerly worked with the LONDON MISSIONARY SOCIETY. A scandal forced Frey to resign; the real work of the London Jews Society would fall on a later associate, Joseph Wolff (1795–1862).

Wolff, the son of a German rabbi, was educated at Protestant and Roman Catholic universities. He was baptized as a Catholic, but after moving to England in 1919, he affiliated with the CHURCH OF ENGLAND and with the London Jews Society. In 1821, he left England to begin a career as a missionary to Jews from the Mediterranean to Russia, founding missions in several countries. In 1838, he was ordained as a priest in the Church of England, and a decade later he settled in a British parish and wrote books on his adventures. The London Jews Society continues to operate, though a number of new societies began to form in the last half of the 19th century. The Midmay Mission to the Jews was founded in 1876 and the Scripture Gift Mission in 1888.

In America, as in England, real interest in the mission began only in the decades following the Civil War, especially in the 1880s, when a new wave of Jewish immigration began, primarily from RUSSIA and POLAND. New interdenominational societies and denomination agencies were established to further the effort. In addition, various churches funded missionaries who targeted Jewish communities in eastern Europe. By far the most important effort was the American Board of Missions to the Jews (ABMJ) founded in 1894 by Leopold Cohn (d. 1937). Through the 20th century, it established mission stations across the United States. Joined by other groups such as the Chicago Hebrew Mission (later the American Messianic Fellowship) and the Biblical Research Society, as well as denominationally supported missionaries, a significant effort to evangelize the Jewish community was established. It remained somewhat invisible, as converts were rarely organized into separate Jewish Christian congregations, which were opposed by the agencies.

Following World War II, most major Protestant denominations withdrew their support. Jewish evangelism, which had regularly been a part of the program at international missionary conferences earlier in the century, completely dropped out of consideration by the time the WORLD COUNCIL OF CHURCHES was founded in 1948. The reduction of support for Jewish missions was eased by their lack of success relative to other missionary activity.

On the other hand, a new generation of evangelists who had been born Jewish emerged in the 1970s. Moshe Rosen, a staff member of the ABMJ, who was caught up in the Jesus People movement in California, broke with the organization over the issue of maintaining those elements of Jewish culture and religious practice that did not conflict with the Christian faith. Rosen insisted that he was still a Jew, and wished to keep his culture in spite of his faith in Jesus as the Messiah. Like the ABMJ, the Jews for Jesus founded by Rosen and others in 1973 continued to direct their converts toward existing congregations, but in their self-identification as Jews and their use of Jewish religious forms (such as using Passover ritual in the LORD's SUPPER), they set the stage for the most significant development in modern Jewish missions—MESSIANIC JUDAISM.

The growth of Messianic Judaism was spurred in no small part by the establishment of the state of Israel and the speculation among conservative Evangelicals that the last generation before the return of Christ had begun in 1948, a view popularized in Hal Lindsey's best-selling *The Late Great Planet Earth* (1970).

The spectacular growth of Jews for Jesus occurred at a time when other ethnic groups within the American Protestant community were discussing how their particular cultures could be used as tools for expressing their faith. Christians who had been raised as Jews also discussed whether they should abandon their distinctive culture (thus cutting themselves off from family and friends). At the time, Jewish Christians were integrated into congregations where their Jewish past was not acknowledged. In the 1970s, young Jewish converts began to call for new Christian centers that were Jewish in every way possible, even to the point of being called synagogues.

In 1975, the old Hebrew Christian Alliance of America was renamed the Messianic Jewish Movement. Shortly thereafter, "Messianic synagogues" emerged and united into new Christian denominations. By the end of the century, several denominations (reflecting differences between Reform and Orthodox Jewish practice and Pentecostal and non-Pentecostal forms of Christianity) had been formed, including the International Alliance of Messianic Congregations and Synagogues, the Union of Messianic Jewish Congregations, the Fellowship of Messianic Jewish Congregations, and the Association of Torah-Observant Messianics.

The Jewish community has protested against Protestant missionary activity and raised the issue through its programs of dialogue with Christian organizations. It has been quite successful among Roman Catholics and those churches connected to the WORLD COUNCIL OF CHURCHES in winning declarations against Jewish missionary activity. It has been less successful among conservative Protestants, who, interestingly, are among the key advocates of continued American support for the state of Israel. The Jewish community has been particularly offended by the rise of Jews for Jesus and the Messianic synagogues, both of which perpetuate what they believe is a lie—that one can be Jewish and Christian at the same time. Several organizations, such as the Los Angeles–based Jews for Judaism, have been founded in the last generation to counter the work of Jewish missionary groups.

See also EVANGELICALISM.

Further reading: David Berger and Michael Wyschograd, *Jews and Jewish Christianity* (New York: Ktav, 1978); Leopold Cohn, *To an Ancient People: The*

Autobiography of Dr. Leopold Cohn (Charlotte, N.C.: Chosen People Ministries, 1996); Arnold G. Fruchtenbaum, *Hebrew Christianity: Its Theology, History, and Philosophy* (Washington, D.C.: Canon, 1974); Carol Harris-Shapiro, *Messianic Judaism: A Rabbi's Journey through Religious Change in America* (Boston: Beacon Press, 1999); Baruch Maoz, *Judaism Is Not Jewish: A Friendly Critique of the Messianic Movement* (U.K.: Mentor: Christian Focus Publications and CWI, 2003); J. Gordon Melton, *Encyclopedia of American Religions*, 7th ed. (Detroit: Gale Research, 2002); Karl Pruter, *Jewish Christians in the United States: A Bibliography* (New York: Garland, 1987); David A. Rausch, *Messianic Judaism: Its History, Theology, and Polity* (Lewiston, N.Y.: Edwin Mellen, 1982).

John, Griffith (1831–1912) *popular Congregationalist missionary to China*

Griffith John was born in Swansea, Wales. He was educated in Wales and England at colleges sponsored by the Union of Welsh Independents (Congregationalist), and then offered himself as a missionary for the LONDON MISSIONARY SOCIETY (LMS, now the Council for World Mission), founded by Congregationalists. John had been inspired by the work of missionary David Griffiths, whose daughter Jane became his wife.

John sailed for Shanghai in 1855. Once there, he proved himself an energetic worker, known for enthusiastic preaching, many writings, and journeys inland. In 1861, he relocated from Shanghai to Hankow in central CHINA, which became his headquarters for the next 50 years.

John spoke to large audiences assisted by his fluency in several dialects of Chinese. He trained and motivated a number of Chinese evangelists. He was a prolific writer, and he translated the New Testament into both Mandarin and Wen-li. He chaired the Central China Tract Society and wrote numerous tracts and pamphlets for use by those he had trained. From his center in Hankow, he traveled extensively, creating new centers of activity.

He made only a few trips back to Wales. He died during his last visit in 1912.

Further reading: Nelson Bitton, *The Life of Griffith John* (London: The Sunday School Union, 1920); Noel Gibbard, *Griffith John: Apostle to Central China* (Bryntirion, Wales: Bryntirion Press, 1998); Griffith John, *A Voice from China* (London: James Clarke, 1907); Ralph Wardlaw Thompson, *Griffith John: The Story of 50 Years in China* (London: Religious Tract Society, 1906).

Jones, E. Stanley (1884–1973) *Methodist missionary to India*

Jones was possibly the best-known and respected Western Christian leader in INDIA in the mid-20th century. His efforts to integrate elements of Indian culture into Christianity helped ease Indian resentment of the missionary endeavor.

Jones was born on January 3, 1884, in Baltimore. A call to the ministry during his high school

E. Stanley Jones (1884–1973), noted Methodist missionary in India *(Drew University Library)*

years ended plans to become a lawyer. He attended Asbury College beginning in 1903. In 1907, though lacking ordination, he became the pastor of the Lal Bagh Methodist Episcopal Church in Lucknow, India. In January 1908, he was ordained first a deacon and immediately thereafter an ELDER. While serving various charges over the next years, he became popular as an outstanding speaker.

During the years after World War I, Jones began to seek methods of creating a more indigenous church. He visited the ashrams established by Mahatma Gandhi (1869–1948) and Rabindranath Tagore (1861–1941). He also began to hold Round Table Dialogues in which Christians and Hindus would talk as equals, on practical rather than abstract issues.

In 1928, the Methodist Episcopal Church (now part of the UNITED METHODIST CHURCH) elected Jones as a BISHOP, but he turned down the honor as it was in conflict with his true calling as a missionary. The church responded by naming him "Evangelist-at-large for India and the world."

His experiences led in 1930 to the formation of the first of the Christian ASHRAMS. The small ashram at Sat Tal led to a second in Lucknow in 1935. The Ashram movement would spread to some 20 countries, and in the 1950s was picked up by several Roman Catholic priests. The first American ashram was created in Harlem in the 1940s. As a model for the kingdom of God, members worked for racial justice, Puerto Rican self-determination, peace, and Indian independence.

Jones's life and thought became the subject of a set of books in the 1920s and 1930s, beginning with *The Christ of the Indian Road* (1925). His last book, a sympathetic treatment of Gandhi, followed the martyrdom of the Indian leader in 1948.

The integrity and trust placed in Jones by both the Protestant community in the West and the Indian people, who had shown some hostility over the activity of missionaries in general, was demonstrated by *Time* magazine's naming him the world's greatest missionary (1938) and the Indian

government's presenting him with the Gandhi Peace Prize in 1964.

Further reading: E. Stanley Jones, *The Choice before Us* (New York: Abingdon Press, 1937); ———, *Christ at the Round Table* (New York: Abingdon Press, 1928); ———, *The Christ of the Indian Road* (New York: Abingdon Press, 1925); Charles Wesley Mark, *A Study in the Protestant Christian Approach to the Great Tradition of Hinduism with Special Reference to E. Stanley Jones and P. D. Devanandan* (Princeton, N.J.: Princeton Theological Seminary, Ph.D. diss., 1988); Richard W. Taylor, *The Contribution of E. Stanley Jones* (Madras, India: CLS/CISRS, 1973).

Jordan

Jordan's rich religious history is punctuated by the entrance of Christianity in the first century C.E. and the establishment of Muslim dominance in the seventh century.

Thanks to the weakening of the Ottoman Empire, Protestantism was introduced in 1860 by Anglicans associated with the CHURCH MISSIONARY SOCIETY. Today, the church supports several schools and a home for the aged. About the same time, Lutherans (with German and American support) began work in the region, and a single congregation was established in what is now Jordan. The Society of Friends (QUAKERS) also began a small work in the 1860s.

The CHRISTIAN AND MISSIONARY ALLIANCE was the first of several groups to enter following World War I, as the Ottoman Empire collapsed. The ASSEMBLIES OF GOD, which initiated work in 1929, has become the second-largest Protestant church, next to the Anglicans. The SEVENTH-DAY ADVENTIST CHURCH arrived in 1932. The SOUTHERN BAPTIST CONVENTION has supported a small work begun in 1943.

The Protestant/Free Church community in Jordan remains small, with fewer than 20,000 believers. There is no council of churches, though the Anglicans, as part of the Episcopal Church in Jerusalem and the Middle East, and the Jordanian

Lutherans participate in the Middle East Council of Churches. Since the 1990s, Evangelicals have reported more freedom to openly proselytize and have been allowed to offer free Bibles. However, Muslim converts to Christianity (as opposed to Catholic or Orthodox converts to Protestantism) face penalties from the government, as it is against the law for a Muslim to convert to Christianity.

See also MIDDLE EAST.

Further reading: David Barrett, *The Encyclopedia of World Christianity,* 2nd ed. (New York: Oxford University Press, 2001); J. Herbert Kane, *A Global View of Christian Missions* (Grand Rapids, Mich.: Baker Book House, 1971).

Judson, Adoniram (1788–1850) *pioneer of American Baptist missions*

Adoniram Judson was born in Malden, Massachusetts, the son of a Congregationalist minister. He attended Brown University and Andover Theological Seminary, where he helped organize a Society of Inquiry, a study group on missions. Following his graduation in 1810, he was among the first group commissioned by the Congregationalist AMERICAN BOARD OF COMMISSIONERS FOR FOREIGN MISSIONS for service in South Asia.

On their voyage to India in 1812, Judson and his wife decided that the Baptist position on BAPTISM was correct, and they were rebaptized by British Baptist William CAREY on their arrival. Shortly thereafter, another Congregationalist missionary, Luther RICE, took the same step. Rice returned home to rally American Baptists to the foreign mission cause. Judson, forced by the British East India Company to leave the country, moved to Rangoon, Burma (now Myanmar). Rice succeeded in organizing the General Missionary Convention of the Baptist Denomination in the United States for Foreign Missions (the first national Baptist organization in the United States). At its initial gathering in 1814, it accepted the Judsons as its first missionary appointments.

Adoniram Judson (1788–1850), pioneer Baptist missionary *(Southern Baptist Historical Society)*

Judson set about the work of evangelism. He and his wife, Ann, mastered Burmese, compiled a dictionary, and began to translate the Bible. Ann went on to learn Thai; her translation of the Gospel of Matthew was the first part of the Bible to appear in that language. Adoniram was jailed in 1824 for 21 months on charges of spying. He was exonerated, but the ordeal sapped the strength of Ann, who died a few months after his release.

Judson completed the Burmese Bible in 1834, and an enlarged Burmese dictionary in 1849. He died at sea in 1850.

See also BAPTISTS.

Further reading: Courtney Anderson, *To the Golden Shore: The Life of Adoniram Judson* (Valley Forge, Pa.: Judson Press, 1987); Joan Jacobs Brumberg, *Mission for Life: The Story of the Family of Adoniram Judson,* *the Dramatic Events of the First American Foreign Mission, and the Course of Evangelical Religion in the Nineteenth Century* (New York: Free Press-MacMillan, 1980); Edward H. Fletcher, *Records of the Life, Character, and Achievements of Adoniram Judson* (New York: Edward H. Fletcher, 1854); Howard B. Grosse and Fred P. Hagard, *The Judson Centennial 1814–1914: Celebrated in Boston, Mass., June 24–25 in Connection with the Centenary of the American Baptist Foreign Mission Society* (Philadelphia: American Baptist Publication Society, 1914).

justification by faith

One of the defining ideas of the Protestant reformers was that humans are justified in God's eyes by grace working through faith alone. Martin LUTHER wrote that justification "is the head and the cornerstone. It alone begets, nourishes, builds, preserves, and defends the church of God." In 1530, the AUGSBURG CONFESSION OF FAITH, written to explain the Protestant position to the Roman Catholic community, affirmed, "that men cannot be justified before God by their own strength, merits, or works, but are freely justified for Christ's sake, through faith. . . . This faith God imputes for righteousness."

For Luther, the doctrine grew out of his Bible study in the context of his objections to the selling of INDULGENCES. He rejected the idea that human acts, such as the purchase of an indulgence, could become the agent of attaining salvation. Instead, faith (trust) in the Gospel message of the saving acts of Jesus Christ was alone the necessary and sufficient condition of salvation. His arguments were put forth in writings such as the early "Treatise on Christian Liberty" (1520) and became a theme to which he frequently returned.

Trained as a lawyer, John CALVIN explained justification in his *Institutes of the Christian Religion* (1536), "A man will be justified by faith when, excluded from the righteousness of works, he by faith lays hold of the righteousness of Christ, and clothed in it appears in the sight of God not as a sinner, but as righteous."

Justification by faith does not deny the importance of good works. However, for the Reformers, such works were not the basis of one's relationship to God, but an outgrowth of that relationship. Gratitude for salvation should lead to a life of goodness that manifests in outward actions—devotion, kind acts, obedient behavior, and so forth.

Protestants, born in conflict with Roman Catholicism, tended to accuse Catholics of preaching a salvation by works. Although Protestantism (as derived from Luther and Calvin) and Catholicism teach different schemas of the Christian life, 20th-century theological explorations by Protestant and Catholic scholars have tended to see that difference in far less divisive terms than those of the 16th century.

Protestants and Free Church believers have also argued among themselves on the meaning of the doctrine. The tendency to reduce faith to mere verbal or intellectual assent to Protestant doctrines began even in the 16th century and has been a perennial temptation. At the same time, elevation of justification by faith has occasionally led to a disparagement of piety, good works, and/or obedience to the law. In addition, church leaders have often accused other DENOMINATIONS and movements of denying, distorting, or subverting the doctrine. In the 18th century, for example, Presbyterians accused Methodists, who preached a doctrine of manifesting faith in activity, of reverting to a Pelegian or works righteousness teaching. Methodists responded by accusing Presbyterians of antinomianism—so emphasizing God's election of the faithful as to discount the need to follow God's law.

In the 20th century, the doctrine of justification by faith has been challenged by various theologians, who have proposed radically different understandings of the Christian life and the nature of salvation. In some of these schemes, Christ is viewed basically as an exemplar to which human beings should conform their lives in an attempt to improve natural human goodness and godliness.

With the popularity of various forms of individualism, the church has confronted the tendency to view salvation in purely essentialist and individual terms. Popular forms of Protestant teachings have emphasized the nature of faith as establishing the individual's personal relationship with God in such terms as to suggest that the role of the church is secondary. Protestant teachings have, however, always assumed that salving faith also serves as an entrance into the community of believers, that is, that faith also manifests as life in a worshipping fellowship.

Both liberal and conservative Protestants, however, would affirm that faith is essential to their understanding of Christianity. Such faith is contrasted to a simple assent to the church's teachings or submission to its behavioral demands.

The major branches of Protestantism have seen faith as a response of the whole person, including the mind. Faith not only leads to piety and action, but also to a reasoned understanding of its intellectual underpinnings, which should engage the believer through Bible study, theological reflection, and a comprehension of one's place in history.

Further reading: H. George Anderson, T. Austin Murphey, and Joseph Burgess, eds., *Justification by Faith: Lutherans and Catholics in Dialogue VII* (Minneapolis, Minn.: Augsburg, 1985); D. A. Carson, *Right with God: Justification in the Bible and the World* (Exeter, U.K.: Paternoster, 1992); Don Kistler, ed., *Justification by Faith Alone* (Morgan, Pa.: Soli Deo Gloria, 1994); Alister McGrath, *Iustitia Dei: A History of the Christian Doctrine of Justification,* 2 vols., (Cambridge: Cambridge University Press, 1986); Elsa Tamez, *The Amnesty of Grace: Justification by Faith from a Latin American Perspective* (Nashville, Tenn.: Abingdon Press, 1993).

K

Kagawa, Toyohiko (1888–1960) *Japanese Christian social activist*

Toyohiko Kagawa was born on July 10, 1888, in Kobe, JAPAN. He was born into affluent circumstances but was orphaned as a child and raised by a stepmother. Kindness expressed by a Christian led to his conversion during his teen years, and he disowned his remaining family.

He attended the Presbyterian College in Tokyo for three years. He felt a calling to help the poor and reasoned that helping them effectively meant living with them. In 1910, he moved to one of the poorest sections of Kobe, helping individuals as best he could. He launched his activist career with efforts to unionize the shipyard workers in 1912. In 1914, he moved to the United States and studied at Princeton University, developing his study program around a quest for ways to relieve poverty.

Upon his return to Kobe, he resumed his program of organizing Japanese workers. He concentrated on factory workers (1918) and farmers (1921), organizing their first unions. He helped the campaign for universal male suffrage (gained in 1925), and facilitated the establishment of credit unions, schools, hospitals, and churches.

Kagawa developed a theological perspective that resonated with the American SOCIAL GOSPEL movement, including a favorable opinion of socialism. He wrote and spoke on the application of Christian principles to the ordering of society, and his writings found their way to the desks of some Japanese government officials. In 1923, he was asked to supervise social work in Tokyo. American missionary Helen Topping became his English secretary and organizer in America in 1925.

In the 1930s, Kagawa founded an Anti-War League, and in 1940 made a public statement apologizing to CHINA for Japan's invasion, for which he was briefly arrested. In 1941, he came to the United States in an unsuccessful attempt to head off the impending conflict between the two countries.

After the war, Kagawa saw a need to reconcile the new democratic ideals that were being imposed on Japan with traditional Japanese culture. He also faced criticism from many Japanese Christian leaders over his activist career.

Kagawa wrote a best-selling autobiographical novel, *Across the Death Line,* as well as more than 150 books and pamphlets. He donated all of his royalties to assist the poor.

He died in Tokyo on April 23, 1960. The Japanese emperor posthumously bestowed the Order of the Sacred Treasure, Japan's highest honor, on him. Internationally, Christian leaders have recognized the groundbreaking nature of his work, and his writings now serve as basic source materials for the development of Asian Christian theology.

Further reading: William Axling, *Kagawa* (New York: Harper Brothers, 1946); Toyohiko Kagawa, *Brotherhood Economics* (New York: Harper Brothers, 1936); ———, *Across the Death-Line*. Ichiji Fukumoto and Thomas Satchell, trans. (Kobe, Japan: Chronicle Office, 1922), rev. ed. as *Before the Dawn* (New York: George H. Doran, 1924); Robert Schildgen, *Toyohiko Kagawa: Apostle of Love and Social Justice* (Berkeley, Calif.: Centenary Books, 1988).

Kairos Document

In the 1985 Kairos Document, South African theologians and lay people, mostly from the Reformed Church tradition, condemned the government for imposing apartheid and the church for cooperating with it. It presented a Christian justification for revolutionary change.

As the level of violent resistance to apartheid intensified in SOUTH AFRICA in June 1985, a large number of leaders from South African Protestant churches came together to draft a Christian response to the crisis. An initial text circulated informally for broader feedback and support. The finished document, formally published in September, took its name from its opening affirmation, "It is the Kairos or moment of truth not only for apartheid but also for the Church."

The document criticized the government for using the Bible and traditional theological themes to justify its oppressive policies and actions, and for commissioning chaplains in the army to support its position. It then criticized the Protestant churches. Though they had championed praiseworthy themes—reconciliation, justice, nonviolence—the weakness of their social analysis allowed them to conform to oppression. The churches had taken a quasi-Gnostic position that divorced theological affir-

mations from life in the mundane world. Spirituality had become individualistic and lost its social dimension.

The theologians analyzed the South African situation as one of oppressor and oppressed. In such a condition, the government loses any moral right to govern and (picking up a theme from LIBERATION THEOLOGY) the biblical God always comes out on the side of the oppressed as Liberator. They concluded, "To say that the Church must now take sides unequivocally and consistently with the poor and the oppressed is to overlook the fact that the majority of Christians in South Africa have already done so. By far the greater part of the Church in South Africa is poor and oppressed." The church was called upon to "mobilize its members in every parish to begin to think and work and plan for a change of government in South Africa . . . and [it] will have to be involved at times in civil disobedience."

The original publication of the Kairos Document carried 156 names of leaders from some 20 South African Protestant denominations. The document helped push the Nederduitse Gereformeerde Sendingkerk of Suid Afrika [Dutch Reformed Mission Church of South Africa (DRCM)] into adopting the BELHAR CONFESSION in 1986. Together, the Kairos Document and the Belhar Confession initiated a process of negotiations to heal the racial divisions in the Reformed Church community that culminated a decade later in the merger of the predominantly black Dutch Reformed Mission Church of South Africa and the predominantly white Dutch Reformed Church in Africa into the Uniting Reformed Church in Southern Africa.

The Kairos Document has become a model for theological activity based upon the concept of *Kairos* as a moment of grace and opportunity in which God issues a challenge to decisive action. The *Kairos* concept has subsequently inspired Christian groups involved in liberation struggles from Europe to the Philippines. In 1998, a group in ZIMBABWE issued a similar document denouncing the government for replacing the old white colonial regime with an African-led regime that continued oppression and corruption.

See also CREEDS/CONFESSIONS OF FAITH; REFORMED/PRESBYTERIAN TRADITION.

Further reading: Kairos Document, Available online. URL: http://www.bethel.edu/~letnie/AfricanChristianity/SABelhar.html; *The Kairos Document: Challenge to the Church,* foreword by John W. de Gruchy (Grand Rapids, Mich.: William B. Eerdmans, 1986); Louise Kretzschmar, *The Voice of Black Theology in South Africa* (Athens: Ohio University Press, 1986).

Karthak, Robert (b. 1926) *pioneer Protestant missionary in Nepal*

Robert Karthak was born into a Christian family in Kalimpong, India, on January 10, 1926. As a young adult, he served as a youth leader at the MacFarlane Memorial Church, a Scottish Presbyterian congregation in his hometown. The church had developed a ministry over the years to Nepali immigrants. In 1956, Karthak moved to Kathmandu, along with some young people who became the nucleus of a new Christian congregation.

In 1951, the predominantly Hindu country had begun to open to the outside world. By the time Karthak arrived, several churches had been opened in Nepal. In 1957, he founded the Gyaneswor Church in Kathmandu, and he emerged as a dominant leader in the expanding Protestant community. He was a cofounder of the Nepal Christian Fellowship and served as its president for 15 years starting in 1963. During that time, he also served on the committee that helped bring the Bible society to Nepal. The fellowship aimed at avoiding the denominational differences that had been so much a part of Protestantism elsewhere, but it subsequently aligned with the Evangelical Fellowship of Asia and the WORLD EVANGELICAL ALLIANCE.

Karthak traveled across the country assisting new churches, and he represented the Nepalese Christian community at international gatherings.

Under his pastoral leadership, Gyaneswor Church's membership exceeded 1,000. Adjacent to the church, Presbyterians support Bethany Ashram, a multipurpose center that serves as a hospice, nursing home, and old people's home.

See also ASIA.

Further reading: Jonathan Lindell, *Nepal and the Gospel of God* (Kathmandu: United Mission to Nepal, 1979); Scott W. Sunquist, ed., *A Dictionary of Asian Christianity* (Grand Rapids, Mich.: William B. Eerdmans, 2001).

Kelly, Leontine T. C. (b. 1920) *pioneer African-American female bishop*

Leontine Turpeau Current Kelly was born on March 5, 1920, in Washington, D.C. Her father, David Turpeau, was a minister in the Methodist Episcopal Church (now a constituent part of the UNITED METHODIST CHURCH), and her brother also become a Methodist preacher.

After returning to college after a divorce, she completed her B.A at Virginia Union University in 1960. She subsequently married J. David Kelly, a licensed lay minister, and taught school near the church that he pastored. He died in 1969, and she was asked to hold his pulpit for an interim. During this period, she experienced a call to the ministry. She subsequently attended Wesley Theological Seminary and Union Theological Seminary in Richmond, Virginia, from which she graduated in 1976. She was age 56 when ordained as an ELDER in the United Methodist Church.

Kelly pastored Asbury-Church Hill United Methodist Church in Richmond for seven years (1977–83) and then joined the staff of the United Methodist General Board of Discipleship in Nashville, Tennessee. She was with the board in 1984, when the church's western jurisdiction elected her to the bishopric, only the second female so recognized, the first being Marjorie Swank MATTHEWS. Kelly was appointed to lead the Northern California and Nevada Conferences.

Leontine Kelly (1920–   ), the first African-American woman to be selected as a bishop in the United Methodist Church *(Drew University Library)*

She retired in 1998 and subsequently served as a visiting professor of evangelism and witness at Pacific School of Religion, Berkeley, California. In October 2000, she was inducted into the National Women's Hall of Fame in Seneca Falls, New York.

See also AFRICAN-AMERICAN METHODISTS; WOMEN, ORDINATION OF.

Further reading: Angella Current, *Breaking Barriers: An African American Family and the Methodist Story* (Nashville, Tenn.: Abingdon Press, 2001); Martha Henegar, "Pioneering Women," *Interpreter* 48, 2 (February–March 2004) 15–16; Jessie Carney Smith, ed., *Epic Lives: One Hundred Black Women Who Made a Difference* (Detroit: Visible Ink Press, 1993).

Kenya

When Protestants first arrived in the territory comprising modern Kenya, they found a land inhabited by a variety of African peoples, most notably the Masai and the Kikuyu. A weakened Muslim culture, previously ravaged by Portuguese forces, still existed along the Indian Ocean coast.

Johann Ludwig Krapf (1810–81), a German Lutheran missionary sponsored by the CHURCH MISSIONARY SOCIETY, led the establishment of the CHURCH OF ENGLAND in Kenya beginning in 1844. Following his retirement in 1855, he published an account of his pioneering efforts, and briefly returned to Kenya to assist Charles New (1840–75) in starting the Methodist mission in 1862. Representatives arrived from the Church of Scotland in 1891 and the African Inland Mission in 1895.

British hegemony of the region grew in the late 19th century, and in 1895 British East Africa was established as a protectorate. The British quickly built a railroad connecting UGANDA (which it also controlled) with the coast. Its completion across the country in 1901 facilitated the further entrance of a variety of missionaries.

Protestantism in Kenya has been marked by the emergence of numerous AFRICAN INITIATED CHURCHES. Among the first to succeed was the Nomiya Luo Church, created by former Anglicans in 1914. Prominent Kenyan AICs include the African Church of the Holy Spirit (1927), the Kenyan Foundation of the Prophets Church (1927), the National Independent Church of Africa (1929), and the Gospel Furthering Church (1936). AICs were quick to respond to PENTECOSTALISM, after missionaries arrived in 1910 from the Pentecostal Assemblies of Canada. The African Independent Pentecostal Church of Africa, formed in 1925 with indigenous leadership, emerged late in the century as the third-largest church in the country. The Friends movement (*see* QUAKERS) has been successful, too; the East Africa Yearly Meeting of Friends is now the largest Quaker body outside of North America.

Kenya is one of the most Christianized countries in the world, with approximately 75 percent of the population affiliated with a Christian denomination. As the new century begins, of Kenya's 20-million-plus population, 6 million belong to the Roman Catholic Church. The Anglican Church of Kenya has almost 3 million members and the AFRICA INLAND CHURCH approximately 1.5 million members. The African Independent Pentecostal Church of Africa also has more than a million; it is now rivaled by the New Apostolic Church, which only arrived in the 1970s. Pentecostalism now counts adherents in the millions. Joining the Independent Pentecostal Church are the CHURCH OF GOD OF PROPHECY, the Kenya Assemblies of God, the Pentecostal Assemblies of God, and the Pentecostal Evangelistic Fellowship of Africa, all of which count their membership in the hundreds of thousands.

More than 100 African Initiated Churches exist; in addition, the missions were transformed into autonomous church bodies in the years after World War II, especially after Kenya was granted independence in 1963. Nairobi has emerged as an important African Christian center; it hosts both the All Africa Conference of Churches, affiliated with the WORLD COUNCIL OF CHURCHES, and the Association of Evangelicals of Africa, representing the WORLD EVANGELICAL ALLIANCE.

Ecumenical work manifested early in Kenya with the formation of the Alliance of Protestant Missions in 1918, the root organization of the present National Christian Council of Kenya. Kenyan-based churches that are affiliated with the council (and the World Council of Churches) include the Anglican Church of Kenya, the Kenya Evangelical Lutheran Church, the Methodist Church of Kenya, and the Presbyterian Church of East Africa. The largest of the evangelical churches, the Africa Inland Church, continues the mission established by the Africa Inland Mission (AIM) as its first effort in world evangelism. AIM International still supports several hundred personnel in the country.

In 1968, a year before Religious Rights were spelled out in the country's constitution, the government nationalized all of the mission-run primary schools. Church-sponsored religious classes are allowed in the schools, though students have the right to refuse such instruction.

See also AFRICA, SUB-SAHARAN.

Further reading: David B. Barrett, G. K. Mambop, J. MacLaughlin, and M. J. McVeigh, eds., *Kenya Churches Handbook: The Development of Kenyan Christianity, 1498–1973* (Kisumu, Kenya: Evangel Press, 1973); F. K. Githieya, *The Freedom of the Spirit: African Indigenous Churches in Kenya* (Atlanta: Scholars Press, 1997); Z. J. Nthamburi, ed., *From Mission to Church: A Handbook of Christianity in East Africa* (Nairobi, Kenya: Uzima Press, 1991).

Keswick movement

The Keswick movement in England has paralleled the HOLINESS MOVEMENT in the United States. It is centered on a yearly nondenominational conference held in Keswick in northern England.

Simultaneously with the growth of the Holiness movement in the United States, a similar phenomenon appeared in England, as Christians sought to promote personal holiness and a deeper experience of the Holy Spirit. It drew support from the visit of Walter and Phoebe PALMER during the years of the American Civil War, and from the 1873–74 ministry of fellow-Americans Robert Pearsall Smith and his wife, Hannah Whitall Smith (1832–1911). Hannah was the author of *The Christian's Secret of a Happy Life* (1870), the book most identified with the movement. Dwight L. MOODY made his first tour of the British Isles at about the same time.

The spiritual search prompted by the Smiths and others led to a proposal for a conference to "promote true holiness." The first such gathering convened at Broadlands, near Romsey (July 17–23, 1874). Subsequent gatherings were held at Oxford (Aug. 29–Sept. 7, 1874) and Brighton (May 29–June 7, 1875). At the Brighton convention,

Canon Harford-Battersby, vicar of St. John's Church (CHURCH OF ENGLAND) in Keswick, suggested his town as the sight of the next convention.

Since that original 1875 gathering at Keswick, a convention has been held every year, now attracting several thousand people. The Holy Spirit is formally recognized as the leader of the gathering, and no one was ever elected to chair the meetings. During his lifetime, Canon Harford-Battersby presided over the convention. Following his death, his place was assumed by Henry Bowker and then by Robert Wilson. Texts of the addresses given at the convention have been gathered and published in *The Keswick Week*.

Without accepting the perfectionism of the Wesleyan Holiness movement, the Keswick leadership preached the possibility of enjoying unbroken communion with God and victory over known sin. Keswick supporters teach that all Christians receive the Holy Spirit at the time of their initial regeneration, but most are not controlled by the Spirit. By abandoning their lives to Christ, the fullness of the Spirit can become experientially real.

Toward the end of the 1880s, the conventions began to include appeals for support for foreign missions and calls to the mission field. The first missionary sent and supported by the convention was Amy Carmichael (1867–1951), who in 1892 left for Japan and then in 1895 settled in southern India.

Beginning with Moody, various Protestant leaders, including G. Campbell Morgan, and later, John R. MOTT and Robert E. SPEER, have promoted Keswick, which became known for ignoring denominational labels. Meetings following a similar format (moving day by day through the major steps in Christian commitment) began to be held in locations across Great Britain, North America, and beyond. Albert Benjamin SIMPSON's CHRISTIAN AND MISSIONARY ALLIANCE was the North American group most identified with Keswick. As the Pentecostal movement spread to Europe, Keswick became a significant influence in its development. The movement continues to

Jessie Penn-Lewis (1861–1927), writer and leader of the Keswick movement *(Institute for the Study of American Religion, Santa Barbara, California)*

enjoy the support of the more conservative wing of the Church of England.

Further reading: C. F. Harford, *The Keswick Convention: Its Message, Its Method and Its Men* (London: Marshall Brothers, 1907); J. C. Pollock, *The Keswick Story* (London: Hodder & Stoughton 1964); Walter B. Sloan, *These Sixty Years: The Story of the Keswick Convention* (London: Pickering & Inglis, 1935); Hannah Whitall Smith, *The Christian's Secret of a Happy Life* (Westwood, N.J.: Fleming H. Revell Company, 1962), various editions.

Kim, Helen (1899–1970) *Korean Methodist educator and ecumenical leader*

Helen Kim was born in Inchon, South Korea, on February 27, 1899. Born GheeDeug, in English

Helen Kim (1899–1970), Korean Methodist educator *(Drew University Library)*

tion, World War II, and the Korean conflict. Under her leadership, it added a graduate school in 1952 and attained university status. By the end of her tenure in 1961, Ewha was the largest women's school in the world. During these years she became an international Christian leader of note, representing Korea at the WORLD COUNCIL OF CHURCHES, the INTERNATIONAL MISSIONARY COUNCIL, the General Conference of the Methodist Episcopal Church, and UNESCO. During the Korean conflict, she served as minister of public information in the Syngman Rhee cabinet.

Following her retirement, she turned her abilities toward evangelism and headed the 1965 Nationwide Evangelistic Campaign for Korea. Kim was repeatedly honored for contributions to the church and her country, including in 1963 the Order of Cultural Merit from the Republic of Korea. She died in Seoul on February 10, 1970.

See also KOREA, REPUBLIC OF (SOUTH); UNITED METHODIST CHURCH.

Further reading: Nolan B. Harmon, *Encyclopedia of World Methodism,* 2 vols. (Nashville, Tenn.: United Methodist Publishing House, 1974); Grace Kim, *Grace Sufficient,* ed. by J. Manning Potts (Nashville, Tenn.: The Upper Room, 1964); Gertrude Schultz, comp., *Women and the Way: Christ and the World's Womanhood; A Symposium* (New York: Friendship Press, 1938).

she was named after the female missionary who converted her family to Christianity. She graduated from Ewha College, the Methodist School in Seoul, in 1918. She taught at Ewha for four years before coming to the United States to attend Ohio Wesleyan University (1922–24) and Boston University (M.A., 1926). Upon her return to Korea, she was named dean of Ewha. She returned to the United States in 1930 and two years later became the first Korean woman to secure a Ph.D. (from Columbia University Teachers College).

In 1938, she succeeded Alice R. Appenzeller (1885–1950) as president of Ehwa. She led the school, the most prominent women's institution of higher learning in the region, through the country's most difficult years of Japanese occupa-

Kimbangu, Simon (1889–1951) *founder of the Kinbanguist Church*

Simon Kimbangu, an African Christian prophet and founder of the Church of Jesus Christ on Earth through the Prophet Simon Kimbangu (or Kinbanguist Church), was born in Nkamba in what was then the Congo Free State of Central Africa (later Belgian Congo and now the Democratic Republic of the Congo). He converted to the Baptist Church and was baptized in 1915. He had only a rudimentary education and could not read much of the Bible, which kept him from becoming a Baptist preacher.

In 1918, he began to have visions that announced a calling as a healer and a prophet. He tried to escape them, but in 1921 he began a public ministry of faith healing that garnered an immediate response. Large crowds attended him in his village, and people came from as far away as Leopoldville. The Belgian authorities became alarmed and feared that this movement could turn political and even revolutionary, and he was arrested.

By all accounts, Kimbangu preached a traditional orthodox form of Protestant Christian faith. He attacked polygamy and traditional Congolese religion and told followers not to participate in African ceremonies. He told them to refrain from palm wine, a popular alcoholic drink. He did make a place for the ancestors, important figures in African society.

Though he had preached obedience to authority, the court found him guilty and sentenced him to be executed. A protest by missionaries saved his life, but he spent the next 30 years in jail and died there on October 12, 1951. This date is observed annually as a memorial to the church's founder.

The church that developed from his brief three-month ministry became one of the largest of the AFRICAN INITIATED CHURCHES. When the Belgian authorities tried to suppress the movement, members took the persecution as part of their life in identification with Christ. The disruption of their main gathering point in Kimbangu's hometown had the effect of spreading the teachings into new areas. The church was finally recognized in 1959. In 1970, it was admitted to the WORLD COUNCIL OF CHURCHES.

See also AFRICA, SUB-SAHARAN.

Further reading: Allen H. Anderson, "Kimbanguist Church (Congo)/Église de Jésus Christ sur la terre par le prophète Simon Kimbangu" in J. Gordon Melton and Martin Baumann, eds., *Religions of the World: A Comprehensive Encyclopedia of Beliefs and Practices* (Santa Barbara, Calif.: ABC-CLIO, 2002); Adrian Hastings, *The Church in Africa: 1450–1950* (Oxford: Clarendon Press, 1994); Wyatt MacGaffey, *Modern Kongo Prophets: Religion in a Plural Society* (Bloomington: Indiana University Press, 1983); Marie-Louise Martin, *Kimbangu: An African Prophet and his Church* (Grand Rapids, Mich.: William B. Eerdmans, 1975); K. Gordon Molyneux, *African Christian Theology: The Quest for Selfhood* (Lewiston, N.Y.: Edwin Mellen Press, 1993).

King, Martin Luther, Jr. (1929–1968)
African-American preacher and civil rights leader

Martin Luther King, Jr., Baptist minister and leader of the Civil Rights movement in the United States in the 1960s, was born Michael King in Atlanta, Georgia, on January 15, 1929. His father was a prominent African-American minister and pastor of the Ebenezer Baptist Church in Atlanta. In 1933, the elder King had both his name and his son's name changed to Martin Luther King (after his father's two brothers). The younger King enrolled at Morehouse College at age 15. His call to the ministry came during his college years, and after graduation in 1948 he attended Crozier Theological Seminary in Chester, Pennsylvania, where he became the first African American elected as class president and was also his class valedictorian. At Crozier, he first encountered the nonviolent philosophy of the recently martyred Mahatma Ghandi (1869–1948).

King pursued graduate studies at Boston University and while there married Coretta Scott (b. 1927). He received his Ph.D. in 1955 and moved to Montgomery, Alabama, to serve as pastor of the Dexter Avenue Baptist Church.

Shortly after King's arrival in Montgomery, Rosa Parks was arrested for refusing to give up her seat to a white patron of the local bus system. The incident sparked a boycott of the city buses by African Americans, and the young pastor was named president of the Montgomery Improvement Association, a hastily formed organization to guide the boycott effort. Before the Supreme Court's ruling the next year quashing the segregation laws relative to the bus system, King's home was bombed. The success of the boycott led to the formation of the Southern Christian Leadership Conference (SCLC) with King as president. In 1958, his first book appeared, *Stride toward Freedom: The Montgomery Story.*

Starting in 1959, when he became associate pastor of his father's church in Atlanta, King devoted most of his time to the SCLC. In 1961, he joined a number of fellow clergy who seceded from the National Baptist Convention, U.S.A., over its refusal to support the Civil Rights movement; they founded the Progressive National Baptist Convention.

King led a new phase of the movement in Birmingham, Alabama, where he was arrested during a protest march. There he wrote one of his most memorable pieces, "Letter from a Birmingham Jail," later included in his book *Why We Can's Wait* (1964). Shortly thereafter, he led the 1963 march on Washington in support of new civil rights legislation. During the event, he gave his oft-quoted "I Have a Dream" speech, which helped inspire the landmark Civil Rights Act of 1964. As the movement grew, on January 3, 1964, he appeared on the cover of *Time* magazine as the Man of the Year, and in December received the Nobel Peace Prize.

In 1965, King led a ministers' march in Selma, Alabama, in which some 1,500 clergy participated. When several of the ministers were beaten, President Lyndon Johnson intervened and called for the passing of a Voting Rights Bill, which was signed into law before the year was out.

King decided to carry the movement to the urban North. However, the nonviolent tactics so effective in the South did not work well in Chicago. After a token victory, he withdrew. He wrote his next book, *Where Do We Go from Here, Community or Chaos?* to answer critics, most notably the "Black Power" movement.

King's opposition to the war in Vietnam threatened his alliances with the White House that had been so helpful to the movement. His work on poverty would cost him his life. On April 4, 1968, while in Memphis to support striking garbage collectors, King was assassinated. In what remains a controversial decision, James Earl Ray was convicted of his murder.

King was succeeded by a number of associates. Fellow Baptist minister Ralph Abernathy (1926–90) became the new head of the SCLC. Jesse Jackson (b. 1941), then a young minister, left the SCLC and for a generation was a major force in the continuing civil rights struggle. In 1977, Abernathy was succeeded by Joseph E. Lowery (b. 1924), who remained as leader through the 1990s.

Corretta Scott King emerged as a leader in her own right, largely though her speaking and writing. During the 1970s, she raised the money for the Martin Luther King, Jr. Center for Nonviolent Social Change, dedicated in Atlanta in 1981, and over which she served as president until 1995. Over time, her children have played a role in the center, her son Dexter Scott King succeeding her as head of the King Center.

In the decades since his death, King has become an international Christian figure inspiring a scope of efforts to liberate the poor, oppressed, and outcast of the world. While many follow his teachings, others have used him as the catalyst to develop new Christian approaches to social change in the varieties of LIBERATION THEOLOGY. Perhaps no others Christian leader so altered the course of both secular and religious history in the 20th century.

See also AFRICAN-AMERICAN BAPTISTS.

Further reading: Peter J. Albert and Ronald Hoffman, eds., *We Shall Overcome: Martin Luther King, Jr., and the Black Freedom Struggle* (New York: Pantheon Books, 1990); Lewis V. Baldwin, *There Is a Balm in Gilead: The Cultural Roots of Martin Luther King, Jr.* (Minneapolis, Minn.: Fortress Press, 1991); James A. Colaiaco, *Martin Luther King, Jr.: Apostle of Militant Nonviolence* (New York: St. Martin's, 1993); Martin Luther King, Jr., *Stride toward Freedom: The Montgomery Story* (New York: Harper & Row, 1958); ———, *Where Do We Go from Here: Chaos or Community?* (New York: Harper & Row, 1967); ———, *Why We Can't Wait* (New York: Harper & Row, 1964).

King James Version of the Bible

The Protestant Reformation, appealing as it did to biblical authority, spurred the development of better and more accurate translations of the Bible. As Protestantism gained ground in England, an initial English translation was completed by William TYNDALE (New Testament, 1525) and Miles COVERDALE (Old Testament, 1535). Coverdale's Bible became the basis of the 1539 Great Bible, an official translation issued by the British government in the name of King HENRY VIII. British Puritan exiles issued the infamous Breeches Bible (or Geneva Bible, 1560). The nickname came from the rendering of Genesis 3:7 in which Adam and Eve are said to have clothed themselves in "breeches" made from fig leaves. Anglicans issued the Bishops' Bible (1568) during the reign of ELIZABETH I.

By the end of the century, a consensus emerged that a new common translation was justified by the accrued linguistic knowledge, but a bill before Parliament to such an end was laid aside until the early years of King James I (r. 1603–25). At the Hampton Court Conference of 1604, a Puritan leader, John Reynolds (1549–1607), won the new king's approval to move forward. A committee of scholars from both Oxford and Cambridge Universities was chosen. They were then divided into work teams: 10 scholars at Westminster Abbey were assigned Genesis through 2 Kings (Old Testament), and seven others Romans through Jude (New Testament). From CAMBRIDGE UNIVERSITY, eight were assigned 1 Chronicles through Ecclesiastes (Old Testament), and seven others worked on the intertestamental APOCRYPHA. Seven Oxford scholars translated Isaiah through Malachi (Old Testament), and eight others worked on the Gospels, Acts, and Revelation (New Testament).

The finished product was to be sent to the king for his approval. There was some concern that James, known to favor Catholicism, would stop this project of Anglican and Puritan churchmen. Among the tactics to ensure his support was to render the Hebrew word *ob,* apparently a kind of pagan Canaanite medium, as *witch,* to take advantage of James's notorious support of the contemporary antiwitch craze in the British Isles. Thus came about the famous quote from Exodus 22: 18, "Thou shalt not suffer a witch to live."

Calvinist theology appears to have affected the translation. For example, in Psalm 8:5, the word *elohim,* commonly translated "God," was translated as "angels." Thus, "Thou has made him [man] a little lower than God," became "Thou has made him a little lower than the angels." The literal rendering of Psalm 8:5 seemed to some Protestants to challenge their affirmation about the sovereignty of God and the depravity of humanity.

These several problems aside, the King James Version was far superior in accuracy and style to those that preceded it. The finished copy dedicated to the king was presented to James and with his approval published in 1611. It would have a significant effect upon the development of post-Elizabethan English.

The King James Version put an end to any further attempts to translate the Bible into English until the 19th century, though some minor revisions were made in 1629, 1638, 1762, and 1769. The King James Version was the Bible of English-speaking Protestants for the next 300 years.

Eventually, the study of biblical texts, including the discovery of an increasing number of Greek texts older than those available to the King James scholars, and the obvious changes in the English language itself, prompted new attempts to translate the Bible. A new translation by some 50 scholars in England was begun in 1879 and published in 1885. An American group issued a similar revision in 1901. By this time, there were hundreds of Protestant churches, most of which did not participate in the revision activity. Many Christians rejected the modern language that replaced what had become the "sacred" and familiar language of the King James Version. Thus, in the 20th century, a number of DENOMINATIONS chose to continue to use the King James Version as their official translation.

Among those groups was the CHURCH OF JESUS CHRIST OF LATTER-DAY SAINTS.

In the Fundamentalist-Modernist debate, the King James Version became another divisive issue. In the mid-20th century, a number of prominent Bible scholars associated with the larger liberal Protestant denominations published the REVISED STANDARD VERSION OF THE BIBLE. Defenders of the King James Version complained about changes to familiar passages often used in Bible memorization exercises, and changes that were said to undermine essential Christian affirmations. Some Fundamentalist spokespersons have argued that the underlying Hebrew and Greek texts used by the translators of the King James Version are superior to the ones used by the modern versions. Some even believe that the *Textus Receptus,* upon which the King James Version was based, was inspired and inerrant. A small vocal group maintains that the English King James Version was itself divinely inspired and inerrant.

Defenders of the primacy of the King James Version include Bob Jones University; Henry Morris of the Institute for Creation Research; Jack Chick, founder of Chick Publications; Regular Baptist pastor David Otis Fuller; and Independent Baptist pastor Peter S. Ruckman.

The arguments for the special role of the King James Version can be traced to Benjamin G. Wilkinson (d. 1968), a Seventh-day Adventist theologian and college president. In 1930, he wrote *Our Authorized Bible Vindicated.* His attack on modern biblical scholarship was picked up in the 1950s by J. J. Ray and hence passed to Fuller and Ruckman in the 1970s. Fuller and Ruckman have forced Baptist Bible scholars to defend their use of more recently discovered texts and especially the Hort-Westcott text, a modern edited Greek text of the New Testament commonly used for Bible translation.

See also BIBLE TRANSLATION.

Further reading: The Interractive Bible "The King James Version Inspired?" Available online. URL: http://www.bible.ca/b-kjv-only.htm#bloodline. Accessed on March 15, 2004; Sakae Kubo and Wal-

ter Specht, *So Many Versions? Twentieth Century English Versions of the Bible* (Grand Rapids, Mich.: Zondervan, 1975); Jack P. Lewis, *The English Bible from KJV to NIV: A History and Evaluation* (Grand Rapids, Mich.: Baker Book House, 2nd ed., 1991); Bruce Metzger, *The Bible in Translation: Ancient and English Versions* (Grand Rapids, Mich.: Baker Academic, 2001); Peter Ruckman, *King James Onlyism versus Scholarship Onlyism* (Pensacola, Fla.: Bible Believers Press, 1992); F. H. A. Scrivener, *The Authorized Edition of the English Bible (1611), Its Subsequent Reprints and Modern Representatives* (Cambridge: Cambridge University Press, 1884).

Kitamori Kazoh (1916–1988) *Japanese Christian theologian of Pain of God theology*

Kitamori Kazoh was born in Kumamoto, JAPAN, in 1916. He grew up in a Christian context and graduated from both the Lutheran Theological Seminary in Tokyo and Kyoto Imperial University. He joined the faculty of Eastern Japan (later Tokyo Union) Theological Seminary in 1943 and remained there until his retirement in 1984. While teaching, he also served as pastor of a Kyodan (United Church of Christ) congregation and continued until 1986.

Kitamori is remembered for his articulation of a theology of CONTEXTUALIZATION (interpreting Christianity in a local cultural context), which he called the Pain of God theology. He first broached the subject in a 1946 volume, *The Theology of the Pain of God,* which went through 12 editions in his lifetime. An English edition appeared in 1965.

Kitamori rejected the Western notion that God was incapable of suffering. Building on Jeremiah 31:20, he believed the phrase "My heart is pained" suggests the essential nature of God. On the cross, God's pain overcomes his wrath and mediates between his love and the demands of justice. He critiqued Western theologies based largely on either God's love or the idea of election. A number of Western theologians have responded positively to his insights.

Kitamori died in Tokyo in 1988.

Further reading: Yasuo Furuya, *A History of Japanese Theology* (Grand Rapids, Mich.: William B. Eerdmans, 1997); Kitamori Kazoh, *The Theology of the Pain of God* (Richmond, Va.: John Knox Press, 1965); Carl Michalson, *Japanese Contributions to Christian Theology* (Philadelphia: Westminster Press, 1960); Scott W. Sunquist, ed., *A Dictionary of Asian Christianity* (Grand Rapids, Mich.: William B. Eerdmans, 2001).

Kivebulaya, Apolo (1864–1933) *Anglican missionary in Uganda*

Apolo Kivebulaya, an Anglican priest with the CHURCH OF ENGLAND in UGANDA, was an outstanding missionary and evangelist of the late 19th century. He was baptized in 1895, when he took the Western name Apolo. Soon afterward, he offered his services to Anglican missionaries as a catechist (unordained lay minister), and was sent in 1896 to Boga, a western Ugandan village. Though the tribal chief had requested a Christian teacher, he was offended by the denunciation of polygamy and traditional magical practices. Kivebulaya was blamed for the death of the chief's sister, and he was beaten by a mob and turned over to the British authorities for trial. He spent several months in jail before the charges were dropped. The manner in which he bore the experience won over the people of Boga, and eventually even the chief converted.

Settling in Boga, Kivebulaya expanded his ministry to include literacy training. He was ordained as a deacon in 1900 and as a priest three years later. In 1915, the border between Uganda and the Congo was changed, and suddenly Boga was in the Belgian Congo (now the Democratic Republic of the Congo). Kivebulaya remained at his post, and his parish remained attached to the church in Uganda. Eventually, the region became the site of a set of churches.

In 1922, Kivebulaya was named a canon, in recognition of his faithful and effective ministry. The work became the core of what in 1972 became a separate diocese, now part of the Church of Christ in the Congo—Province of the Anglican Church in the Congo.

Kivebulaya died on May 30, 1933.

See also AFRICA, SUB-SAHARAN.

Further reading: A. B. Lloyd, *Apolo of the Pygmy Forest 1923* (London: Church Missionary Society, 1937); Anne Luck, *African Saint: The Story of Apolo Kivebulaya* (London: SCM Press, 1963); M. Louise Pirouet, *Black Evangelists: The Spread of Christianity in Uganda 1891–1914* (London: Rex Collings, 1978).

Knox, John (c. 1514–1572) *leader of the Scottish Reformation and founder of Presbyterianism*

John Knox was born at Haddington, Scotland, prior to 1515. He attended school in Haddington, but there is no record of his having attended university. He managed to acquire a broad education in languages, law, and theology, and he was ordained as a priest in the Roman Catholic Church around 1536. He worked as a private tutor in the 1540s.

Knox was apparently present in 1546 when George Wishart, the first major exponent of the Reformation in Scotland, was arrested and burned at the stake in St. Andrews. He himself was by this time sympathetic to the Protestant cause and was happy to see Cardinal Beaton assassinated in retaliation for Wishart's death. He was also among those who took over St. Andrew's castle and held it for three months until it was captured by French forces. Knox was imprisoned for the next 19 months.

Released in 1549, Knox visited England, then in a Protestant phase under King EDWARD VI. Receiving a license to preach, he stayed for two years at Berwick and then became a chaplain to the king, though he turned down an offer to become bishop of Rochester. In 1554, he departed England as MARY I began her attempt to return England to Catholicism. He found a post as chaplain to British expatriates at Frankfurt and later at Geneva. In 1555, he returned to Berwick.

By this time, he had become a convinced follower of John CALVIN's doctrine and began to agitate on its behalf, his first public act being a letter to Mary of Guise, the queen regent in Scotland, asking tolerance for fellow Protestants. Before he returned to Geneva in 1556, he was summoned before the court in Edinburgh, condemned in absentia, and burned in effigy.

In 1558, he published his famous "First Blast of the Trumpet against the Monstrous Regiment of Women," an attack upon England's Queen Mary I, Mary of Guise, France's Queen Catherine de' Medici, and Mary Stuart. He followed with a "Brief Exhortation to England" calling for the acceptance of Calvinistic Protestantism. Then in 1559, soon after Mary I's death, he returned to Scotland and traveled around the country mobilizing the growing Protestant strength.

In Edinburgh on July 7, he was chosen minister of the Edinburgh Protestants. Two weeks later, the queen regent marched on the city. The Protestants were able to win a settlement while Knox moved to secure backing from Queen ELIZABETH I of England. Elizabeth did eventually come to Knox's aid, and the queen regent took refuge in Edinburgh castle, where she died in 1560. Mary Stuart, a decided Catholic, then assumed the throne.

When the Scottish Parliament met in August, it was firmly in the Protestant camp. It voted to accept the Confession of Faith that Knox had written, forbid celebration of the Mass, and withdraw any acknowledgment of the pope's authority. Knox and three assistants prepared the "First Book of Discipline," which detailed how the church was to be organized.

In 1566, following the murder of the queen's secretary, Knox found it prudent to retire for a period to Ayrshire, where he wrote his *History of the Reformation in Scotland*. He remained in Ayrshire during the momentous events that led to Mary's abdication in favor of her infant son, James, in 1567.

Knox spent the remaining years of his life consolidating the gains of the Reformation in Scot-

land. He preached regularly in Edinburgh at St. Giles Church until 1571, when he retired to St. Andrews. He died in Edinburgh on November 24, 1572.

See also UNITED KINGDOM.

Further reading: Ian B. Cowan, *The Scottish Reformation: Church and Society in Sixteenth-Century Scotland* (New York: St. Martin's, 1982); Richard L. Greaves, *Theology and Revolution in the Scottish Reformation: Studies in the Thought of John Knox* (Grand Rapids, Mich.: Christian University Press, 1980); John Knox, *History of the Reformation within the Realm of Scotland* (1584; reprint, Edinburgh: Banner of Truth Trust, 1994); Richard G. Kyle, *The Mind of John Knox* (Lawrence, Kans.: Coronado, 1984); W. Stanford Reid, *Trumpeter of God: A Biography of John Knox* (New York: Scribner, 1974).

Korea, Democratic People's Republic of (North)

The Democratic People's Republic of Korea was established in the northern half of the country at the end of World War II. A variety of Protestant groups from the Presbyterians and Methodists to the SEVENTH-DAY ADVENTIST CHURCH and the Swedenborgian movement had established work in the region before the war.

In 1946, shortly after its formation, the government began to suppress religion. A Christian League (Ki Dok Kyo Kyo Do Yen Mange) was established to mobilize Christian support for the new Marxist government, but as the Korean conflict came to an end, thousands of Christian joined the 2 million Koreans who escaped to the southern half of the country.

Harsh repression of all religion became the standard practice through the country for decades. Churches were taken over for secular purposes and ministers arrested. Protestant Christianity survived, however, and found representation in the Korean Christian Federation. Only in the 1980s was there any sign of relief. In 1983, the Korean Christian Federation was allowed to publish an edition of the Bible. Representatives of the WORLD COUNCIL OF CHURCHES were allowed to visit in 1985, and the following year members of the federation were allowed to visit the council in Geneva. The council is said to represent some 10,000 Christians, most of Presbyterian background. In 1997, four members attended a meeting of the WORLD ALLIANCE OF REFORMED CHURCHES.

At last report, there were only 25 Protestant ministers in North Korea. There is a Protestant seminary that is allowed to accept as many as nine students every three years. There are continuing reports of suppression of Christianity and arrests of leaders.

See also ASIA; KOREA, REPUBLIC OF (SOUTH).

Further reading: Jean-Jacques Bauswein and Lukas Vischer, eds., *The Reformed Family Worldwide: A Survey of Reformed Churches, Theological Schools, and International Organizations* (Grand Rapids, Mich.: William B. Eerdmans, 1999); A. D. Clark, *A History of the Church in Korea* (Seoul: Christian Literature Society of Korea, 1971).

Korea, Republic of (South)

The Republic of Korea is, along with the Philippines, one of the few Asian countries where Christianity has risen to a dominant position. As the 21st century began, Christians made up about 40 percent of the population, 80 percent of them Protestants. Buddhists and followers of the traditional Korean folk religion each make up some 15 percent.

Protestantism entered the country after the signing of the Amity Treaty with the United States in 1882, which abrogated an earlier law that banned Christianity. The first Protestant to take advantage of the new situation was Horace N. ALLEN (1858–1922), a Presbyterian physician. By saving the life of the queen's nephew, he set the stage for the arrival of the first ordained minister and missionary, Horace G. Underwood (1859–1916), also an American Presbyterian.

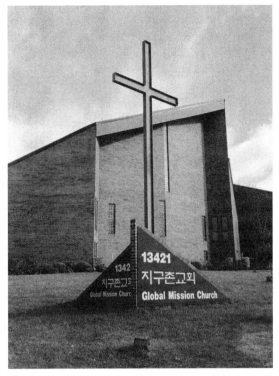

The Global Mission Church is a center of Korean Christian outreach in Wheaton, Maryland. *(Institute for the Study of American Religion, Santa Barbara, California)*

Over the next decade, Canadian and Australian Presbyterians established work, which in 1907 was merged with the American mission to form the Presbyterian Church of Korea. The Presbyterians enjoyed one of their great missionary successes in Korea, and the majority of Korean Protestants belong in one of the several Presbyterian churches.

Methodists arrived in 1884, followed by Anglicans in 1890 and BAPTISTS in 1895. The Methodists also enjoyed dramatic successes and today have around 1.3 million members. They also gave birth to the HOLINESS MOVEMENT, which has several churches that count their members in the hundreds of thousands. The Korean Baptist Convention (affiliated with the SOUTHERN BAPTIST CONVENTION) has almost a million members.

PENTECOSTALISM took off in Korea after the Korean conflict (1950–53), and has been the fastest-growing community ever since. It dates back to 1903, when the first of a series of revival movements swept through the Korean Protestant churches, characterized by an emphasis on receiving the Holy Spirit and yearnings for a deeper, more mature spiritual life. However, the Pentecostal movement that developed in Los Angeles in 1906 did not reach Korea until 1923, when Mary Bumsey was able to enter the country from Japan (then the occupying power). Bumsey founded the first Pentecostal church in 1932 at Yongsangku; she was joined by several other independent missionaries. They all ran afoul of the Japanese authorities and were deported as World War II loomed. By 1940, the four Pentecostal congregations that existed had several ordained Korean ministers that together carried the Pentecostal banner through the difficult war years. After the Korean conflict, several American Pentecostal groups sent missionaries—the ASSEMBLIES OF GOD, the CHURCH OF GOD (CLEVELAND, TENNESSEE), the CHURCH OF GOD OF PROPHECY, the INTERNATIONAL CHURCH OF THE FOURSQUARE GOSPEL, and the PENTECOSTAL HOLINESS CHURCH INTERNATIONAL. Today the Pentecostal community claims some 2.3 million members in the large DENOMINATIONS, and twice that many more in other groups who have had the defining experience of the movement—speaking in tongues as a sign of the reception of the Holy Spirit.

The Pentecostal movement has also produced one of the world's unique Christian phenomena, the YOIDO FULL GOSPEL CENTRAL CHURCH, believed to be the largest Christian congregation in the world. Starting with the Assemblies of God, Paul Yonggi Cho (b. 1936) began a congregation in Seoul in 1958. Four years later, he built a 1,500-seat center to accommodate the members. The church has subsequently grown to 700,000+ members who meet in a 10-story building on Yoido Island in central Seoul. The church and its leader, now known as David Yonggi Cho, have become international leaders; promoting the establishment of cell groups within congregations.

Following the disruption of the Japanese occupation and World War II, the Presbyterian Church reconstituted in 1949, but 10 years later it split into two factions. The more conservative faction, the Presbyterian Church of Korea (HapDong), aligned with American Fundamentalist leader Carl McIntire and his INTERNATIONAL COUNCIL OF CHRISTIAN CHURCHES. It is now the largest church body in the country. The more liberal faction, the Presbyterian Church of Korea (TongHap) is almost as big; each has more than 2 million members. The Presbyterian movement currently exists as some 95 denominations, more than 10 of which have at least 100,000 members. In addition, in 1967 the Christian Reformed Church of North America began work in Korea, and it now has more than 400,000 members.

The Presbyterian Church of Korea (TongHap) is a member of the WORLD COUNCIL OF CHURCHES, as is the Presbyterian Church in the Republic of Korea, the Anglican Church of Korea, and the Korean Methodist Church. Nationally, there is a spectrum of church councils ranging from liberal Protestant to separatist Fundamentalist. They include the National Council of Churches in Korea (aligned with the World Council of Churches), the Christian Council of Korea, the Korean Evangelical Fellowship (aligned with the WORLD EVANGELICAL ALLIANCE), the Conservative Christian Association of Korea, and the Council of Protestant Churches in Korea.

The very success of Christianity has led to the formation of a number of indigenous Christian movements. Of these, the Unification Movement (the Holy Spirit Association for the Unification of Christianity) founded by former Presbyterian Sun Myung Moon (b. 1920) has had the greatest impact. Moon created a synthesis of Protestantism and traditional Korean shamanism that became an international movement through the last decades of the 20th century.

Though dwarfed by the larger mainline Protestant groups, the JEHOVAH'S WITNESSES, the CHURCH OF JESUS CHRIST OF LATTER-DAY SAINTS, and the SEVENTH-DAY ADVENTIST CHURCH have made a respectable showing in South Korea, each with slightly more than 100,000 members.

See also ASIA; KOREA, PEOPLE'S REPUBLIC OF (NORTH).

Further reading: Jean-Jacques Bauswein and Lukas Vischer, eds., *The Reformed Family Worldwide: A Survey of Reformed Churches, Theological Schools, and International Organizations* (Grand Rapids, Mich.: William B. Eerdmans, 1999); A. D. Clark, *A History of the Church in Korea* (Seoul: Christian Literature Society of Korea, 1971); D. N. Clark, *Christianity in Modern Korea* (Lanham Md.: University Press of America, 1986).

Kramer, Hendrik (1888–1965) *Dutch missiologist and ecumenical leader*

The writings of Dutch Reformed minister/educator Hendrik Kramer dominated missiology (the study of missions) in the mid-20th century. Raised in Holland, partly at a church-sponsored orphanage, he attended Leiden University and received a Ph.D. in 1921. Already committed to a missionary career, at college he studied Indonesian languages and Islam, and in 1922 offered himself for service in what was then the Dutch East Indies. He moved there in 1922 under the auspices of the Dutch Bible Society with the twin tasks of overseeing Bible translations and working with converts from Islam. After 15 years in the Indies, he returned to Leiden as a professor of linguistics and the phenomenology of religions.

Kramer helped establish a seminary in Jakarta and became a major force in assisting the various missions to make the transition into autonomous churches. Under the influence of NEO-ORTHODOXY, he brought a new emphasis on the Bible to his missionary work. The work of theologians such as Karl BARTH and Emil BRUNNER underlay his 1938 classic study, *The Christian Message in a Non-Christian World*. In this and other writings, Kramer called for a clear biblical Christian witness in the face of other religions. In tune with Neo-Orthodox perspectives, he saw God's dealing with

humanity as distinct from what might be seen as natural human religious aspirations. These themes reappeared in his later books.

Upon his return to Holland in 1937, he became an active force for renewal in the Reformed Church and an ecumenist. In 1948, he left his teaching post to become the first director of the WORLD COUNCIL OF CHURCHES' Ecumenical Institute at the Chateau de Bossey near Geneva. During his later years, he promoted the new emphasis on the ministry of the laity, which matured in the decades immediately following his death.

Kramer retired in 1956 and died in 1965.

See also INDONESIA.

Further reading: Libertus A. Hoedemaker, "Hendrik Kramer, 1888–1965: Biblical Realism Applied to Mission," in Gerald H. Anderson, et al., eds., *Mission Legacies: Biographical Studies of the Modern Missionary Movement* (Maryknoll, N.Y.: Orbis Books, 1998): 508–15; Hendrik Kramer, *The Christian Message in a Non-Christian World* (London: Edinburgh House Press, 1938); S. Kulandrian, "Kramer Then and Now," *International Review of Missions* 46 (1957): 171–81.

Kubushiro Ochimi (1882–1972) *Japanese minister and women's rights leader*

Kubushiro Ochimi was born in Kumamoto Prefecture in JAPAN on December 16, 1882. After schooling in Japan, she attended the Pacific School of Religion in Berkeley, California, where she met and married Kubushiro Naokatsu. After stays in Seattle, Washington, and Takamatsu, Japan, they moved to Tokyo and began a joint ministry as founders of Tokyo Citizen's Church. Her husband died shortly afterward.

Kubushiro's career as an activist began several years later when she joined the Japan Women's Christian Temperance Union (WCTU). She began to work with Hayashi Utako on the problem of licensed prostitution in Osaka. Their work had little effect, and Kubushiro concluded that the problem of prostitution in Japan was directly related to women not being able to vote. She subsequently divided her time between continued work on the prostitution problem and attempts to obtain the vote for women. Her further church activity manifested in her attendance at the World Conferences on Mission and Evangelism sponsored by the INTERNATIONAL MISSIONARY COUNCIL at Jerusalem in 1928 and at Tambaram, near Madras, India, in 1938. Kubushiro and Kawai Michi wrote the first women's mission study book by non-Western Christians, *Japanese Women Speak: A Message from the Christian Women of Japan to the Christian Women of America* (1934). The booklet detailed, among other issues, the problems faced by Christian women in Japan for refusing to engage in Shinto worship (often identified with patriotism), their stance against Japanese aggression in CHINA, and their need for solidarity with Christian women in other parts of the world.

After the war (and an unsuccessful bid for the legislature), Kubushiro returned to the prostitution problem and finally was successful in getting a Prostitution Prohibition Law passed. She later served as president of the Japan WCTU. She was 83 when in 1966 she passed the examination for ordination in the United Church of Christ of Japan. Her autobiography appeared in Japanese posthumously.

Further reading: Michi Kawai and Ochimi Kubushiro, *Japanese Women Speak: A Message from the Christian Women of Japan to the Christian Women of America* (Boston: Central Committee on the United Study of Foreign Missions, 1934); Kikue Takahashi, "Kubushiro Ochimi," in Scott W. Sunquist, ed., *A Dictionary of Asian Christianity* (Grand Rapids, Mich.: William B. Eerdmans, 2001).

L

Lambeth Quadrilateral *See* Chicago-Lambeth Quadrilateral.

Latvia *See* Baltic states.

Laud, William (1573–1645) *Anglican church leader deposed by the Puritan Parliament*
William Laud was born on October 7, 1573, at Reading, Berkshire. He studied at St John's College at Oxford University and was ordained a priest in the Church of England in 1601. He found a mentor in Richard Neile, bishop of Rochester, and rose quickly, becoming a chaplain to King James I. In 1521, he was appointed a bishop while serving as chaplain to the marquess of Buckingham.

Laud presided at Charles I's coronation (1625). A close adviser to the king, he was rewarded by being made bishop of London in 1628, and archbishop of Canterbury in 1633.

Laud combined a Reformed theology highly influenced by Arminianism with a "high church" emphasis on liturgy and a desire for uniform worship throughout the realm. Puritans, who wanted to purify the church of "Romanish elements," found Laud too close to Roman Catholicism in practice. They especially opposed his attempts to impose a uniform liturgy across England, the British Isles, and the new colonies in North America.

Laud made broad use of the secular authorities to assist him in silencing Puritan critics. When in 1637 Laud had Puritans William Prynne, Henry Burton, and John Bastwick tortured, the Puritans turned them into martyrs. Laud met his most vigorous opposition in Scotland, where a form of Presbyterianism had become established. His attempt to enforce acceptance of a new Anglican prayer book met with staunch opposition. Scottish opposition to Laud was seen in London as opposition to the Crown; Charles went to war and lost, and found himself broke.

In response, Charles called Parliament back into session, but once summoned, Parliament took matters into its own hands. Oliver Cromwell was among the vocal critics of Laud, who in February 1641 was arrested and placed in the Tower of London. He was accused of assuming dictatorial power, bringing back popish superstition, and having caused the ruinous war with Scotland.

While Laud languished in prison, Parliament removed the remaining bishops of the Church of England from office (1642) and in 1643 called for an assembly of Puritan leaders to meet at Westminster and draw up plans to reform the church.

That assembly wrote the WESTMINSTER CONFESSION OF FAITH and other documents that became the defining statements of PRESBYTERIANISM.

Laud was tried in the House of Lords in March 1644. William Prynne, one of the men Laud had had tortured, served as his prosecutor. However, Prynne had a poor case, and Laud proved able in his own cause. The trial ended without a verdict. In November, the House of Commons passed a bill of attainder that condemned Laud by special decree. He was beheaded on January 10, 1645.

See also UNITED KINGDOM.

Further reading: E. C. E. Bourne, *The Anglicanism of William Laud* (London: S.P.C.K., 1947); Charles Carlton, *Archbishop William Laud* (London, Routledge & Kegan, 1987); W. H. Hutton, *William Laud* (London: Methuen, 1895); William Laud, *Works,* ed. by W. Scott and J. Bliss, 7 vols. (Oxford: John Henry Parker, 1847–60); Charles Hare Simpkinson, *The Life and Times of William Laud, Archbishop of Canterbury* (London: John Murray, 1894).

Lausanne Covenant

The Lausanne Covenant was a doctrinal statement adopted at the 1974 INTERNATIONAL CONGRESS FOR WORLD EVANGELISM that reaffirmed the need for world missionary effort. The statement, which also affirmed biblical INERRANCY, was a response to proposals by some Protestant leaders that the church in the West should refrain from sending more missionaries to other regions.

The covenant was written largely by John R. W. Stott (b. 1921), pastor of All Souls Church (Anglican) in London. The congress, which met in Lausanne, Switzerland, was a global meeting designed to mobilize Evangelical Protestants to even greater efforts in the world.

The covenant has proved a popular statement of Evangelical belief. It has been translated into more than 20 languages and adopted by a number of denominational bodies and PARACHURCH ORGANIZATIONS as their statement of belief.

See also EVANGELICALISM.

Further reading: Klaus E. Bockmuehl, *Evangelicals and Social Ethics: A Commentary on Article 5 of the Lausanne Covenant* (Downers Grove, Ill.: InterVarsity Press, 1979); C. Rene Padilla, *The New Face of Evangelicalism: An International Symposium on the Lausanne Covenant* (Downers Grove, Ill.: InterVarsity Press, 1976).

Law, William   (1686–1761) *theologian and writer whose ideas contributed to early Methodism*

William Law, a minister in the CHURCH OF ENGLAND who wrote several classics of Protestant spiritual literature, was born at King's Cliffe, Northamptonshire. He became a fellow of Emmanuel College, Cambridge, and was ordained in 1711.

When George I (of the House of Hanover) succeeded to the throne in 1714, Law felt unable to take the required oath of allegiance to the new Hanoverian dynasty. As a nonjuror, he was unable to work as a university instructor or a parish minister. He became a private tutor for historian Edward Gibbon. After 10 years he retired.

Denied access to pulpit and lecture hall, Law turned to writing; he produced a series of books including *Christian Perfection, the Spirit of Love, the Spirit of Prayer,* and, his most influential, *A Serious Call To a Devout and Holy Life* (1728). The thesis of the *Call* is that God, though he forgives disobedience, calls us to obedience and to a life completely centered in him.

Law's works were just being published as John WESLEY was maturing and launching METHODISM. He developed a great appreciation for Law's writings, especially his treatise on *Christian Perfection,* and recommended them to his preachers.

Law died on April 9, 1761.

Further reading: William Law, *The Life and Works of William Law,* 10 vols. (London: Thoemmes Continuum, 2000); ———, *A Practical Treatise upon Christian Perfection* (London: William & John Innys, 1726); ———, *A Serious Call to a Devout and Holy Life. Adapted to the State and Condition of All Orders* of *Christians* (London: William Innys, 1729); Arthur Keith Walker, *William Law: His Life and Work* (London: SPCK, 1973).

laying on of hands

Throughout church history the laying on of hands—the purposeful and symbolic touching of one Christian by another—has been used for a variety of purposes. It can be a formal public acknowledgment that the church is commissioning a member for service (for example, as a priest), or it can be used in devotion and prayer in the belief that the Holy Spirit moves through the hands to heal the body or empower the recipient.

The practice makes numerous appearances in the Bible. In Numbers 27:18–23, God commands Moses to lay his hands on Joshua in a public ceremony so that the people will follow him. In Acts 6:6, the church's first deacons are set apart for service by the laying on of hands in a public ceremony.

The laying on of hands commonly accompanies prayer for healing. Biblical examples include Jesus, who amid the crowds laid his hands on everyone brought to him and healed them (Luke 4:40), and Ananias, who was sent to lay his hands on Paul, who had been struck blind following his vision of Christ on the road to Damascus (Acts 9:17).

Over the centuries, the laying on of hands became a standard part of ordination rituals. The numerous biblical references to the practice made it quite acceptable to the new Protestant churches, and it is still used. Typical of the ordination prayer in many churches is one used in the Presbyterian Church of Aotearoa, NEW ZEALAND, which proclaims: "Send down your Holy Spirit upon your servant N, whom we, . . . by the laying on of our hands, ordain and appoint to the office of the holy ministry."

In the 20th century, the laying on of hands as a practice accompanying prayers for healing and empowerment has come to the fore within PENTECOSTALISM. The general public became familiar with the practice through its widespread presentation on television, beginning with the healing services of Oral ROBERTS in the 1950s. Pentecostals also use the laying on of hands in prayers for individuals to receive the BAPTISM OF THE HOLY SPIRIT. The biblical support is found in many passages in Acts such as 8:17, which mentions Peter and John placing their hands on some Samaritans who subsequently received the Holy Spirit.

The laying on of hands, especially in healing situations, is said to be frequently accompanied by a physical sensation of heat and of energy moving from one person to the other; these sensations are reported more often by the one praying for healing than the one for whom prayer is offered. Such experiences are not limited to Protestants or even Christians, but are commonly reported by people in many religious traditions, most notably the modern Western Esoteric tradition. This common experience has led some to search for a more mundane explanation for the sensations and the healing.

Various researchers have conducted experiments in an attempt to discover a spiritual healing power common to humankind. Canadian professor of gerontology Bernard Grad had Oskar Estabany, known for his healing touch, try to affect the growth of plants and the healing rate of laboratory mice, with spectacular results. Dolores Krieger, a nurse and member of the Theosophical Society, has also studied what she termed *therapeutic touch*, which has subsequently been taught in nursing schools. Some argue that any benefit is psychological, and is provided by the simple loving touch itself. At the same time, some conservative Christians have attempted to distance therapeutic touch from the healing practiced in Christian circles.

Further reading: David K. Blomgren, *Prophetic Gatherings in the Church: The Laying on of Hands and Prophecy* (Portland, Ore.: Bible Press, 1979); Delores Krieger, *Accepting Your Power to Heal: The Personal Practice of Therapeutic Touch* (Santa Fe, N.M.: Bear & Co., 1993); Edward D. O'Connor, *The Laying on of*

Hands (Pecos, N.M.: Dove Publications, 1969); Derek Prince, *Laying on of Hands* (Seattle: The Study Hour, n.d.); M. H. Shepherd Jr., "Hands, Laying on of Hands," *The Interpreter's Dictionary of the Bible,* vol. 2 (Nashville, Tenn.: Cokesbury, 1962): 521–22.

Leong Kung Fa (1787–1853) *early Chinese Protestant convert and evangelist*

Leong Kung Fa was born in a poor rural family near Canton (now Guangzhou), CHINA. As a printer, he was invited in 1815 by William Milne (1785–1822), from the Protestant mission in Canton, to accompany him to Melaka, Malaysia, where he wanted to found a college. Milne baptized Leong that same year, and together they began publishing the *Monthly Chinese Magazine.*

In 1819, Leong returned to China, where he began to distribute Christian literature in Chinese, leading to his arrest and beating. Robert MORRISON of the mission managed to free Leong, who rejoined Milne in Melaka. After Milne's death in 1822, Leong returned to China and helped Morrison print the Chinese Bible. In 1823, the LONDON MISSIONARY SOCIETY commissioned Leong as a lay evangelist. Morrison ordained him a minister in 1827, the first Chinese to receive clergy status as a Protestant. He developed an active ministry throughout Kwangtung Province.

Leong frequently ran afoul of Chinese laws against conversion to Christianity and distributing Christian literature. In 1834, a number of his associates in ministry were arrested, and Leong had to flee to Singapore. He returned in 1839. When Christianity gained legal status, he settled in Canton and pastored a small Chinese congregation.

Further reading: Brian Harrison, *Waiting for China: The Anglo-Chinese College at Malacca, 1818–1843, and Early Nineteenth-Century Missions* (Hong Kong: Hong Kong University Press, 1979); Richard Lovett, *The History of the London Missionary Society 1795–1895,* 2 vols. (London: Henry Frowde, 1899); Scott W. Sunquist, ed., *A Dictionary of Asian Christianity* (Grand Rapids, Mich.: William B. Eerdmans, 2001).

leprosy

In the context of the MEDICAL MISSIONS, Protestants developed specialized ministries to alleviate the physical and social suffering of leprosy (now known as Hansen's disease). In the 19th century, many of the thousands of Western missionaries were confronted with lepers (sufferers of leprosy) for the first time in their lives. At the time, it was incurable, highly contagious, and disfiguring—its victims appeared to be rotting away. Segregation was the more humane treatment in most countries—the alternative being periodic massacres.

Missionaries soon recognized that leprosy required a specialized ministry. Roman Catholics had established centers that welcomed those suffering with the disease, where they could live in relative safety among people who loved and cared for them. The first Protestant effort was the Mission to Lepers in INDIA, an agency established in Dublin, IRELAND, in 1874 by Wellesley Bailey. It operated as an interdenominational agency. Bailey's organization, now known as The Lepers Mission, inspired other agencies to form in different countries, such as the American Leprosy Missions founded in 1906.

In the 1870s, Armauer Hansen discovered the microbe that causes the affliction, and treatments were eventually developed. In 1966, the International Federation of Leprosy Associations was formed by religious and secular agencies under the auspices of the United Nations to work toward a world without leprosy. In the 1980s, a set of drugs was discovered that together can stop the progress of the disease. Since that time, the Leprosy Mission and other Christian agencies have focused on raising funds to get the medicine to those with the disease. Today, 70 percent of the 1 million active leprosy cases in the world are located in India, Myanmar, and Nepal. The rest are spread among some 90 other countries.

Further reading: William H. P. Anderson, "Christian Missions to Lepers," *International Review of Mission* 21 (1932): 264–71; Perry Burgess, *Born of Those Years, An Autobiography* (New York: Holt, 1951);

Alfred Donald Miller, *An Inn Called Welcome. The Story of the Mission to Lepers 1874–1917* (London: Mission to Lepers, 1965).

Leuenberg Church Fellowship

The Leuenberg Church Fellowship is an association of Protestant DENOMINATIONS that recognize one another's sacraments and allow any of their ministers to preach at any member church. The member churches are all active in the ECUMENICAL MOVEMENT and are members of the WORLD COUNCIL OF CHURCHES (WCC).

The fellowship originated in post–World War II dialogues between Lutheran and Reformed churches. The Waldensian Church (Italy) and the Church of the Czech Brethren (Czechoslovakia) were soon included in the conversations. By 1973, substantial progress had been made. A text of Leuenberg Agreements was published detailing the consensus, and the Leuenberg Church Fellowship was inaugurated.

The Leuenberg churches have come to a common affirmation on the sacraments, perhaps the most divisive issue among Protestants in the 16th century. Beginning with a reaffirmation of the basic faith statements that all of the churches had agreed upon since their formation on issues such as the Trinity and salvation in Jesus Christ, the fellowship achieved agreement about the practice and meaning of BAPTISM and the LORD'S SUPPER. Baptism, it states, is "administered in the Name of the Father and of the Son and of the Holy Spirit with water. In Baptism Jesus Christ irrevocably receives man . . . into his fellowship of salvation. . . . [and] calls him into his community and to a new life of faith." In the Lord's Supper, "the risen Jesus Christ imparts himself in his body and blood, given up for all, through his word of promise with bread and wine. He thereby . . . enables us to experience anew that we are members of his body."

By affirming that "Christ imparts himself" in the sacrament, the agreements allowed room for both Lutheran and Calvinist understanding of the nature of the Eucharist, though it discounted Free Church views that baptism and the Lord's Supper are ordinances performed because the Bible commands them and/or as memorials of Christ. Anglicans, too, have found the Leuenberg Agreements as yet incomplete.

Since its founding, the fellowship has been open to additional members, and a number of European churches have joined, notably the Methodists. In recent years, it has begun to reach beyond Europe to include several Lutheran churches in ARGENTINA. It was crucial in uniting Reformed/Presbyterian churches in Ethiopia with Lutherans in the Ethiopian Evangelical Church Mekane Yesus.

The Leuenberg Church Fellowship is headquartered in Berlin, Germany. As the new century begins, it reports 103 member churches and three additional cooperating and participating churches (the main Lutheran churches in SWEDEN, FINLAND, and ICELAND).

Further reading: Leuenberg Church Fellowship. Available online. URL: http://www.leuenberg.net. Accessed on June 15, 2003.

Lewis, C. S. (1898–1963) *Christian novelist, theologian, and lecturer*

Clive Staples (Jack) Lewis was an English professor who, after converting to Christianity, wrote widely popular fiction and nonfiction books reflecting and promoting Christian values and beliefs. Lewis is hailed as the exemplar of a Christian who successfully negotiated the world of secular academia.

Lewis was born on November 29, 1898, in Belfast, Northern Ireland. In 1908, following his mother's death, he was sent to school in England, where he soon announced his abandonment of religion. After service as an officer during World War I, Lewis attended University College, Oxford, where in 1923 he completed his studies in Greek and Latin literature, philosophy and ancient history, and English. Elected a fellow at Magdalen

College, Oxford, the following year, he remained to teach English language and literature for 29 years.

Lewis had an outstanding academic career. His 1936 volume, *The Allegory of Love: A Study in Medieval Tradition*, received the Gollancz Memorial Prize for Literature. His volume covering the 16th century for the *Oxford History of English Literature* was published in 1954 to great acclaim. In 1954, he was given the Chair of Medieval and Renaissance Literature at Cambridge, which may have occasioned his autobiographical *Surprised by Joy: The Shape of My Early Life* (1955).

Lewis recovered his faith in steps. He accepted the existence of God in 1929 and for the first time in many years offered a prayer. Two years later, following a lengthy conversation with fantasy writer J. R. R. Tolkien (himself a devout Christian), he accepted Jesus Christ as the son of God and reactivated his membership in the CHURCH OF ENGLAND. In 1933, he wrote his first bit of Christian fiction, *The Pilgrim's Regress: An Allegorical Apology for Christianity, Reason, and Romanticism.*

In 1938, Lewis published the first of a trilogy of science fiction novels that included speculation on Christian theology. For example, he explored original sin among extraterrestrials. One of his most famous works, *The Screwtape Letters,* a correspondence between a senior and a junior devil, treats serious questions of Christian behavior in a humorous context.

In 1942, Lewis gave a series of radio talks on the subjects "What Christians Believe" and "Christian Behavior." These, along with some other presentations, make up the small volume *Mere Christianity,* now considered one of the most readable presentations of the Protestant faith for lay people written in the 20th century. Lewis continued to write varied fiction and nonfiction, most notably the seven-volume *Chronicles of Narnia,* which has become a staple of children's literature.

Lewis's three-year marriage to Joy Davidman, a Jew by birth who had become a Christian after reading his books and who was suffering from cancer, inspired his 1961 book, *A Grief Observed.* Lewis died on November 22, 1963.

In the years since his death, Lewis's fame and reputation have grown immensely, and more than a hundred dissertations have been written about his books.

Further reading: R. L. Green and Walter Hooper, *C. S. Lewis: A Biography* (London: Collins, 1974); William Griffin, *Clive Staples Lewis: A Dramatic Life* (San Francisco: Harper & Row, 1986); Walter Hooper, *C. S. Lewis. A Companion and Guide* (London: Harper-Collins, 1996); Susan Lowenberg, *C. S. Lewis: A reference guide 1972–1988* (New York: Hall, 1993); J. D. Schultz and J. G. West Jr., *The C. S. Lewis Readers' Encyclopedia* (Grand Rapids, Mich.: Zondervan, 1998).

liberation theology

During the 20th century, various groups challenged the universality of traditional Christian theology. They suggested that established church theologies did not speak for the whole church, but only for the ecclesiastical and political leaders and those who supported them. They condemned theologians who found it relatively easy to support corrupt governments, oppression of the poor, colonial structures, and other institutionalized social injustices. Most crucially, they claimed, theology reacted blindly to the Nazi Holocaust.

Such critiques were very popular in Latin America. In the late 1950s, a new organization, Church and Society in Latin America, initiated primarily by Methodists and Presbyterians, began to analyze social and church structures from a Marxist perspective. Thinkers such as Emilio Castro (b. 1927), Julio de Santa Ana, Ruben Alves, and José Míguez Bonino, together with Roman Catholics such as Gustavo Gutiérrez and Juan Luis Segundo, reflected on the relationship between faith and poverty, and between the Gospel and social justice. They began to call for revolutionary change in how the church operated and for an end to unjust social patterns. They drew energy from the actions of Vatican II. Among

Liberation theologian Emilio Castro meets with South African president Nelson Mandela. *(Institute for the Study of American Religion, Santa Barbara, California)*

their early works were *A Theology of Human Hope* (1969) by Brazilian Presbyterian Ruben Alves and *A Theology of Liberation* (1971) by Peruvian Gustavo Gutiérrez. Within the Catholic Church, many priests associated with Maryknoll, the Catholic Foreign Mission Society of America, have identified with liberation theology; Maryknoll's press, Orbis Books, has published many of the movement's texts.

The liberation theologians asserted that genuine theological reflection had to begin with a commitment to the struggles of the poor. Their position drew heavily on passages in the Gospels in which Jesus spoke of the poor and other outcast groups. As liberation theology developed, it saw

liberation as the main theme of God's work in history: Christ's liberation of individuals from sin; the formation of a new humanity for a new society (the kingdom of God); and the liberation of the poor from oppression economically, politically, and socially.

Liberation theology found an international advocate in Uruguayan Methodist Emilio Castro, who became the general secretary of the WORLD COUNCIL OF CHURCHES in 1985. However, critics saw liberation theology as politicizing the church to an unacceptable degree. They said it led Christians to a too-hasty identification with violent revolutionary movements. Other critics were opposed to any use of Marxism, which they saw as an atheist philosophy that had produced communism, a far greater scourge than Latin American governments.

Liberation theologians have continued to evolve and remain a strong force in Latin America. They made common cause with emergent Protestant communities in Africa and Asia as well. In the United States in the 1970s, women and African Americans created new traditions of theological inquiry—BLACK THEOLOGY, FEMINIST THEOLOGY, and womanist theology.

Further reading: Ruben Alves, *A Theology of Human Hope* (New York: World, 1969); Emilio Castro, *Amidst Revolution* (Belfast: Christian Journals, 1975); Gustavo Gutiérrez, *A Theology of Liberation* (Maryknoll, N.Y.: Orbis Books, 1971); Arthur F. McGovern, *Liberation Theology and Its Critics* (Maryknoll, N.Y.: Orbis Books, 1989); Paul E. Sigmund, *Liberation Theology at the Crossroads* (New York: Oxford University Press, 1990).

Liberia

The modern nation of Liberia was a creation of the colonization movement in the United States, an effort to solve the slavery problem by transporting free blacks and then slaves to Africa. In 1821, the American Colonization Society purchased land previously part of SIERRA LEONE and founded the port city of Monrovia (named after former U.S. president James Monroe, a major backer). Unfortunately, the movement manifested little understanding of the variety in African cultures, and failed to foresee the difficulty of building a new society from people who had passed through slavery.

Christians were among the thousands of people who were transported to Liberia, as the new country was called. In 1822, Baptist missionaries Lott CAREY and Colin Teague (c. 1780–1839), who had been commissioned by the Richmond African Missionary Society, arrived to found the first Baptist congregation in the country (second in Africa only to the congregation in Freetown, Sierra Leone). The work eventually came under the care of the American Baptists, the Lott Carey Foreign

Missionary Convention, and finally the National Baptist Convention, U.S.A.

Methodist Episcopal Church missionary Melvin Cox (1799–1833) arrived in 1833; his death three months later heralded future missionary problems with the local environment. Transported slaves had their own troubles integrating into African society, so for several generations the work remained confined to Monrovia.

Presbyterians and Episcopalians soon arrived. Episcopal missionary John Payne (1815–74) survived the climate and opened work outside Monrovia. He became the first Anglican bishop in the country in 1851. Succeeding Payne in the episcopal chair was Samuel Ferguson (1847–1916), the church's first black bishop, who developed the church's educational system. The Lutherans were the last of the major groups to establish work in the 19th century.

Among the outstanding missionaries in Liberia was Alexander Crummell (1819–98), an African-American Episcopalian. Crummell moved to Liberia in the 1850s and became a Liberian citizen. He took a leading role in the evolving school system and was a professor at Liberia College for four years (1862–66). He was a major theorist of the Liberia project; he saw the country's role in God's redemptive purpose and looked toward a future of democracy, flourishing culture, and continental leadership. After a dispute with the Americanized leadership in Monrovia over his support for native Liberians, he returned to the United States in 1873.

Among 20th-century arrivals were the SEVENTH-DAY ADVENTIST CHURCH, the ASSEMBLIES OF GOD, and the PENTECOSTAL ASSEMBLIES OF THE WORLD. The relatively small Fire-Baptized Holiness Church of God made Liberia a major building block of its missionary program and built a substantial local following. The Church of the Lord (one of the ALADURA CHURCHES) is the largest of the AFRICAN INITIATED CHURCHES in Liberia.

In 1847, Liberia became an independent nation. Britain was among the first to recognize the new country, the United States waiting until the 1860s. Though remaining relatively poor, the country enjoyed a century of stability and participated in such international organizations as the League of Nations. However, a 1980 assassination of the president triggered civil conflicts that lasted more than 20 years. During the fighting, more than a million people were displaced, and another 300,000 fled the country. Church properties were looted and/or destroyed, personnel were killed, and humanitarian relief was blocked by the shifting lines of war. The negotiations leading to a restoration of stability in 1995 were credited to the country's Inter-Religious Council of Liberia, set up by the Liberian Council of Churches and the National Muslim Council of Liberia.

The Liberian Council of Churches, affiliated with the WORLD COUNCIL OF CHURCHES (WCC), includes about 15 DENOMINATIONS and PARACHURCH ORGANIZATIONS in Liberia. More conservative groups are part of the Evangelical Fellowship of Liberia affiliated with the WORLD EVANGELICAL ALLIANCE. In the effort to end the civil war, a notable coalition that included all segments of the Christian community came together with the help of Action by Churches Together (ACT) International, a global alliance of churches and relief agencies working with the WCC that assists people recovering from emergencies.

As the new century begins in Liberia, the largest Protestant churches are the Liberian Baptist Convention, the Liberian Assemblies of God, the Lutheran Church of Liberia, and the UNITED METHODIST CHURCH.

See also AFRICA, SUB-SAHARAN.

Further reading: D. Elwood Donn, *A History of the Episcopal Church in Liberia, 1821–1980* (Lanham, Md.: Scarecrow Press, 1992); Willis J. King, *History of the Methodist Church Mission in Liberia* (Monrovia: Methodist Church, 1950); J. R. Oldfield, *Alexander Crummel (1819–1898) and the Creation of an African-American Church in Liberia* (Lewiston, N.Y.: Edwin Mellen Press, 1990); Harold Vink Whetstone, *Lutheran Mission in Liberia* (Hartford, Conn.: Hartford Seminary Foundation, M.A. thesis, 1955).

Life and Work movement

The Life and Work movement of the early 20th century brought together ecumenically minded Protestant leaders dedicated to a Christian response to problems of war and peace and social justice. It reflected a sense of frustration that the churches had been unable or unwilling to work to prevent World War I, which had devastated European society.

Representative of some 90 churches gathered in Geneva in 1920 to plan for a conference that could work to make the peace permanent. Swedish Lutheran bishop Nathan Söderblom (1886–1931) emerged as the leading figure. His vision was that joint work on social concerns could be a step toward an international council of Protestant churches.

The initial gathering was held in Stockholm in 1925 under the name Universal Christian Conference on Life and Work. Both Orthodox and Catholic Churches were invited to participate. While falling short of solving the complex problems of postwar Europe, the conference did encourage a feeling that Christians could unite by rendering service to the world, while doctrinal discussions tended to divide them from one another.

Faced with the economic woes of Europe at the end of the 1920s and the rise of Nazism, movement leaders became aware that they lacked analytical tools to understand the phenomena. Fortunately, as work began for the next large gathering in Oxford, England, in 1937, the movement acquired dynamic new leadership in the persons of William TEMPLE (archbishop of York and future archbishop of Canterbury in the CHURCH OF ENGLAND) and J. H. Oldham (1874–1969), then secretary of the INTERNATIONAL MISSIONARY COUNCIL. They led an effort to clarify the theological basis of the churches' approach to society. The publications that flowed out of the 1937 conference were among the most influential Protestant documents on social ethics of the century.

The Life and Work movement became the driving force that culminated in its merger with the parallel movement FAITH AND ORDER, to produce the WORLD COUNCIL OF CHURCHES.

See also ECUMENICAL MOVEMENT.

Further reading: J. H. Oldham and Willem A. Visser't Hooft, *The Churches Survey Their Task: The Report of the Conference at Oxford, July 1937, on Church, Community and State* (London: Allen & Unwin, 1937); R. Rouse and Stephen Neill, eds. *A History of the Ecumenical Movement, 1517–1948* (Geneva: World Council of Churches, 1986); Willem A. Visser't Hooft, *The Genesis and Formation of the World Council of Churches* (Geneva: World Council of Churches, 1982).

Light of the World Church/Iglesia la Luz del Mundo

The Light of the World Church (in Spanish, Iglesia la Luz del Mundo) is a large JESUS ONLY PENTECOSTALS church based in Mexico with an international following. It was founded in Monterrey, Nuevo León, Mexico, in 1926 by Eusebio Joaquín González (d. 1964), later known as the Apostle Aarón. The church's official name is the Church of God, Column and Pillar of Truth, Jesus the Light of the World (La Iglesia de Dios, Columna y Apoyo de la Verdad, Jesús la Luz del Mundo), though popularly referred to in Mexico as the *aaronistas* (followers of Aarón).

González, a former soldier, was converted in 1926 by two itinerant "Jesus Only" Pentecostal lay preachers, José Perales and Antonio Muñoz, remembered today as Saul and Silas. Saul baptized González on April 6, 1926, and later prophesied, "Your new name will be Aarón and you will become known in all the world." By the end of the year, Aarón had founded a new church with headquarters in Guadalajara.

For the next eight years, Aarón traveled on foot with a cadre of followers throughout the countryside, forming small congregations wherever he met a response. In 1934, he opened the first temple of the Light of the World Church in Guadalajara.

The movement follows the non-Trinitarian "Jesus only" perspective, adding a belief that God has in the present age given the church a living apostle. Following Aarón's death in 1964, a new living apostle, Samuel Joaquín Flores, Aarón's son, assumed leadership of the church.

Aarón introduced a number of unique practices. Members participate in a daily 5:00 A.M. prayer service. Sunday worship is simple, but includes hymns that honor and praise Aarón as the church's First Apostle. At worship, women wear long white dresses and cover their heads, the sexes are separated, and no instrumental music is used. In 1952, Aarón founded the Colonia Hermosa Provincia, a self-supporting community outside Guadalajara. A large church was built along with a variety of commercial, medical, educational, and social services. Annually, the church's ordained pastors travel to the Mother Church in Colonia Hermosa Provincia (symbolic of Holy Jerusalem) on August 14, Aarón's birthday, for an annual celebration of the LORD'S SUPPER. Many laypeople also participate; in 1992, some 150,000 people attended. Among the first actions of Aarón's successor was the destruction of the stone wall around the community, signaling a new openness to the outside world.

By the 1990s, the church reported more than 4 million members in 22 countries.

In 1942, the Light of the World Church suffered a division, amid accusation that Aarón had misused church finances. A group of former church leaders formed the Good Shepherd Church (Iglesia El Buen Pastor). While not enjoying the same success as its parent organization, El Buen Pastor has spread through CENTRAL AMERICA and the Caribbean.

Further reading: Clayton Berg and Paul Pretiz, *Spontaneous Combustion: Grass-Roots Christianity, Latin American Style* (Pasadena, Calif.: William Carey Library, 1996); Renée de la Torre, "Pinceladas de una ilustración etnográfica: La Luz del Mundo en Guadalajara," in Gilberto Giménez, ed., *Identidades Religiosas y Sociales en México* (Mexico City: Instituto de Investigaciones Sociales de la Universidad Nacional Autónoma de México, 1996); Manuel J. Gaxiola, *La Serpiente y la Paloma: Historia, Teología y Análisis de la Iglesia Apostólica de la Fe en Cristo Jesús (1914–1994)* (Nacaulpan, Mexico: Libros Pyros, 1994); *La Luz del Mundo: Un Análisis Multidisciplinario de la Controversia Religiosa Que Ha Impacto a Nuestro País* (Bisques de Echegaray, Mexico: Revista Acadica para estudio de la Religiones, 1997).

limited atonement

Limited atonement is the Calvinist doctrine that Christ died to atone for the sins of only those whom God predestined to be saved. It conforms to an emphasis on the sovereignty of God and the depravity of humanity. Humans, in their depraved state, can do nothing to secure their own salvation; the faith by which some can respond to God's grace is itself a gift from God. Those who do not have faith are not among the elect.

The doctrine stands in opposition to the doctrine of universal atonement, which states that Christ died for all humans, even though the atonement becomes effective only when appropriated by faith. Methodists, for example, have generally argued for prevenient grace, a grace given to all that makes it possible for them to choose God after they have heard the Gospel message.

Limited atonement is also known as particular redemption and as such gives its name to the PARTICULAR BAPTISTS. The doctrine is most often associated with conservative Presbyterian, Reformed, and Baptist churches. A strong statement on limited atonement was made at the Reformed Synod of Dortrecht (1618–1619). It is one of a complex of doctrines that are known as the five points of Calvinism (TOTAL DEPRAVITY, UNCONDITIONAL ELECTION, irresistible grace, and the perseverance of the saints).

See also CALVINISM.

Further reading: Loraine Boettner, *The Reformed Doctrine Of Predestination* (Philadelphia: Presbyterian and Reformed Press, 1965); John Owen, *The Works Of John Owen,* 16 vols. (London: The Banner Of Truth Trust, 1963); David N. Steele and Curtis C. Thomas, *The Five Points of Calvinism: Defined, Defended, Documented* (Phillipsburg, N.J.: Presbyterian and Reformed Press, 1963).

literacy

Protestantism emerged as a religion of the book; the Bible was to be read and absorbed by every Christian. During the 16th century, a benchmark of the success of Protestantism in any country was the translation of the Bible into its spoken language. Once that was achieved, literacy no longer required learning foreign languages, and the new religion stimulated a vast increase in literacy. The publication of the Bible usually became an event of immense long-term cultural importance to many European nations.

As Protestantism left Europe, it encountered a number of nonliterary cultures. In North America at first, the more scholarly missionaries to the Native Americans began to reduce the languages they encountered to a written form and used it to translate the Bible. As early as 1661, John Elliot (1604–90) published a New Testament in Algonquian, with the Old Testament following two years later.

The experience of Puritans like Eliot also tied the work of BIBLE TRANSLATION to the larger concept of civilization. That is, the spread of Christianity was seen as an integral part of civilizing the non-European peoples of North America, the Caribbean, and subsequently the rest of the world. Civilization necessarily demanded literacy. To the present, the spread of Protestantism to new locations usually starts with the development of grammars and dictionaries for the languages encountered, the translation of Scripture, and the establishment of schools on a more or less Western model. Pioneering missionaries are often remembered not for their evangelistic success but their linguistic accomplishments.

By the beginning of the 20th century, it became obvious that those peoples without literacy would be swept aside by large economic and political forces. These peoples had to become literate not only to read the Bible, but also simply to survive.

The major figure promoting literacy in developing countries in the 20th century was Frank Laubach (1884–1970). Laubach came to the Philippines in 1915 under assignment from the AMERICAN BOARD OF COMMISSIONERS FOR FOREIGN MISSIONS. Over the next 15 years, he observed the processes of transforming people by introducing basic language skills. Even the very poor quickly picked up the basics and were effective in teaching their neighbors as well. Laubach refined this process into the "Each One Teach One" method of spreading literacy. He built teams to spread the method to countries throughout Asia, and in 1955 founded Laubach Literacy International. By the end of his life, he had introduced "Each One Teach One" in more than 100 countries.

Additional literacy programs have developed, such as Literacy & Evangelism International, which works with Christian groups to use the Bible in adult literacy programs and trains people in what is termed "literacy evangelism." Another was the Summer Institute of Linguistics, which grew out of the work of Wycliff Bible Translators. Wycliff leaders wanted to make sure that the Bibles they were producing were actually read and used.

By the end of the 20th century, the Bible had been translated into the languages spoken by 90 percent of the world's peoples. However, only about 50 percent of the world's population is as yet functionally literate.

Further reading: Carlo M. Cipolla, *Literacy and Development in the West* (New York: Penguin Books, 1969); Cushla Kapitzke, *Literacy and Religion: The Textual Politics and Practice of Seventh-Day Adventism.* Studies in Written Language and Literacy (Amsterdam/Philadelphia: John Benjamins, 1995); Frank Laubach, *Forty Years with the Silent Billion* (Westwood, N.J.: Fleming H. Revell, 1946); ———, *Toward World Literacy the Each One Teach One Way*

(Syracuse, N.Y.: Syracuse University Press, 1960); ———, Elizabeth Mooney Kirk, and Robert F. Laubach, *Laubach Way to Reading: Skillbook* (New York: New Readers, 1981).

Lithuania *See* BALTIC STATES.

liturgy

A liturgy is the ordered form of worship used by a church, including prayers, readings, and ceremonial acts such as the administration of the Eucharist/LORD'S SUPPER. Traditionally, Christian church liturgies were distinguished by the language in which they were spoken (Greek, Latin), the people with whom they are identified (Celtic, Slavic), the author (St. Chrysostom, Basil) and/or the doctrinal position assumed (Roman, Orthodox). With the Reformation, many theological and political issues began to shape church liturgy as well, especially in the new churches.

The shape and content of the liturgy became a crucial issue in England, where Catholics and Reformed Church adherents strongly disagreed over particular acts in the liturgy, in particular the Eucharist, as well as over the vestments worn by the officiating clergy. The compromise mandated by ELIZABETH I, known as the VIA MEDIA, had the effect of setting the Anglican liturgy as recorded in the BOOK OF COMMON PRAYER of the CHURCH OF ENGLAND.

Liturgy marks one area in which Protestantism is most clearly distinguished from Roman Catholicism and from Eastern Orthodoxy. The Roman Catholic Church tries to ensure a common liturgy that gives a certain sameness and familiarity to worship from one congregation to another. The same is true in the various Eastern Orthodox communions and the several Roman Catholic Eastern-Rite churches. Not so in Protestantism. Protestantism includes a bewildering variety of liturgies and forms of "nonliturgical" worship. The variations appeared in the 16th century and have grown steadily since.

Lutherans considered themselves a liturgical church, that is, a church that regularly proclaimed the Gospel and administered the Lord's Supper within a framework of an orderly pattern of worship. Its constituting documents, beginning with the AUGSBURG CONFESSION OF FAITH, treated a variety of liturgical issues, focusing on similarities and differences between Lutheran liturgy and the Latin-language liturgy commonly used in the Roman Catholic Church at the time. For example, the sacramental elements of bread and wine were both to be given to the people during the Lord's Supper, not just the bread. The Lutherans also added the use of German-language hymns, a first step in their eventual abandonment of Latin for Sunday worship.

In reforming the liturgy, Martin LUTHER rejected both the aspects of Catholic worship he considered contrary to the Bible and the extreme iconoclasm of his colleague Bodenstein of Carlstadt (1480–1541). Luther continued to refer to the Sunday service as a "mass," and while translating the service into German, retained some Latin. The existing sermon was made more important, with Sunday worship becoming a service of word and sacrament. Luther introduced his first revised liturgy in 1525. As it was passed to Lutheran churches in other lands, local leaders felt free to make changes and revisions.

The Reformed churches were not primarily concerned with liturgy. They continued using Roman Catholic liturgy, correcting it where required by theology and biblical precedent, simplifying it, and upgrading the level of congregational participation, in part through singing psalms. The most noticeable change was the translation into the language of the congregation.

Over the centuries, the liturgies of the Protestant churches underwent changes according to the demands of the times and the desires of various communities. Attempts to emphasize aesthetics sometimes conflicted with the needs of personal devotion and the intimacy of interpersonal communion. Some identified the ordered liturgy as the "letter" that killed the "spirit," and advocated more spontaneous forms of worship as found in the Free Churches and modern PENTECOSTALISM. The most extreme abandonment of liturgy occurred among the unprogrammed QUAKERS, for whom worship often meant sitting quietly awaiting a movement of the Spirit within the congregation.

The 20th century saw a movement among Protestant churches to revise the commonly used worship formats to make them more contemporary in language and more relevant in approach, without abandoning the essential affirmations of the church. Generally, Protestant churches do not demand that local congregations adopt uniform styles of worship. Many congregations follow suggested forms but adapt them with local changes and variations. Liturgical change in the late 20th century has often reflected the claim that the older liturgies do not resonate with the non-European Protestant majority, women, or various outsider communities.

In the Protestant and Free Churches, despite the wide variety of worship formats, some common elements generally appear in Sunday worship. They include the singing of hymns, readings from the Bible, communal prayers, and sermons. Protestant churches vary widely in the frequency of the Lord's Supper, from weekly to annually. Most churches, even those that have no set order for Sunday worship, use a liturgy for the Lord's Supper.

There has been a noticeable cross-fertilization of liturgical formats in the 20th century as a result of increased ecumenical contact. Among the more liturgically oriented churches, the use of various new forms of worship and prayer has become noticeable. Among the Free Churches, there has been a movement to explore and recover the centrality of liturgy that was undeniably present in the greater part of Christian history.

Further reading: Horton Davies, *Christian Worship: Its History and Meaning* (Nashville, Tenn.: Abingdon, 1957); Cheslyn Jones, Geoffrey Wainwright, Edward Yarnold, and Paul Bradshaw, eds., *The Study of Liturgy* (New York: Oxford University Press, 1992);

James F. White, *A Brief History of Christian Worship* (Nashville, Tenn.: Abingdon, 1993); ———, *Protestant Worship: Traditions in Transition* (Louisville, Ky.: Westminster/John Knox Press, 1987); William H. Willimon, *Word, Water, Wine and Bread* (Valley Forge, Pa.: Judson Press, 1980).

Livingstone, David (1813–1873) *legendary Scottish missionary and adventurer in Africa*

David Livingstone was born in Blantyre, Scotland, on March 19, 1813, into a deeply religious home. After completing his studies in medicine and theology at the University of Glasgow in 1838, he set his sights on a missionary career. He was inspired to choose Africa by Robert Moffat (1795–1883), a missionary who had first gone there in 1817. Livingstone joined Moffat and eventually (1845) married his daughter, Mary (1820–62).

Ordained by the LONDON MISSIONARY SOCIETY (LMS) in December 1840, Livingstone left for SOUTH AFRICA. He made his way to Kuruman, the most northerly LMS station there, and set out to establish work farther north. A crippling encounter with a lion, a disagreement with a fellow missionary, and drought caused Livingstone to move his base camp several times. He became convinced that his task was to open new territory to the missionaries who would follow him.

For the next quarter century, Livingstone conducted many wide-ranging exploratory excursions throughout South, East, and Central Africa, forging new routes connecting up the European colonies scattered along the continent's coasts. His triumphal visits back to England and his books made him a world-renowned celebrity. His lecture at Cambridge (1857) occasioned the founding of the Universities' Mission to Central Africa, for several generations an important missionary-sending agency.

In 1857, Livingstone severed ties with the LMS after criticism from some of its more conservative members, but in 1858 the British government appointed him consul at Quilimane, Mozambique, and commander of an expedition to explore East and Central Africa. In 1861, he helped six missionaries sent by the Universities' Mission establish their station near Lake Nyasa.

For a while in 1871, the outside world lost track of Livingstone's whereabouts. Henry M. STANLEY, a reporter for the *New York Herald*, found him and uttered the famous phrase, "Dr. Livingstone, I presume?" In a vain attempt to find the source of the Nile, Livingstone set out on what proved to be his last journey. He died at Chitambo, in present-day Zambia, on May 1, 1873. He was buried in Westminster Abbey.

Livingstone won legendary status among African missionaries. His adventures inspired many others to become missionaries, while those in the sending countries invoked his name to raise funds. His celebrity faded in the mid-20th century during a reappraisal and redirection of the missionary movement by most Protestant sending agencies.

See also AFRICA, SUB-SAHARAN.

Further reading: David Livingstone, *Missionary Travels and Researches in South Africa* (London: Murray, 1857); ———, *Narrative of an Expedition to the Zambesi and Its Tributaries, and of the Discovery of the Lakes Shirwa and Nyassa, 1858–1864* (London: Murray, 1865); George Seaver, *David Livingstone: His Life and Letters* (New York: Harper, 1957); Henry M. Stanley, *How I Found Livingstone. Travels, Adventures, and Discoveries in Central Africa* (London: Sampson Low, 1872); Sam Wellman, *David Livingstone: Missionary and Explorer* (Uhrichsville, Ohio: Barbour, 1995).

Local Church

The Local Church is an indigenous nondenominational Chinese Protestant body, also known as the Little Flock and the Assembly Hall Churches. The movement was founded in the late 1920s in Shanghai by Watchman NEE (1903–72). Raised a Methodist, Nee had had a gradual deepening of his Christian faith and had felt a call to the ministry. He also had come to feel that denominationalism was wrong and that there should be only one church (fellowship of believers) per locale (or city). His movement was designed to operate outside of denominational divisions.

Nee had also absorbed much from the Plymouth BRETHREN movement including DISPENSATIONALISM (a belief in successive historic-religious dispensations, or eras) and breaking bread (celebrating the LORD'S SUPPER) as a sign of Christian unity. He also associated with representatives of the KESWICK MOVEMENT, from which he learned of the higher Christian life.

The Local Church movement spread through the 1930s and survived the Japanese occupation, when fleeing believers spread the movement westward. After the Communist Revolution, Nee reassigned Witness Lee (1905–97), who had been largely responsible for the movement's growth in northern CHINA, to work in Taiwan among the many refugees there. Nee himself returned to Shanghai, where he was arrested (1952) and tried (1954) on a spectrum of charges. While the new government's antireligious animus was largely directed against foreign-led churches, Nee's theology was condemned as counterrevolutionary. He was sentenced to 20 years in prison, where he died in 1972.

The movement in China was persecuted for its refusal to merge into the single Protestant church set up by the government. During the years of the Cultural Revolution (1966–76), it was, like all churches, totally suppressed. The Local Church eventually reemerged, again refusing to associate with the state church. The movement grew and actually spun off splinter movements, known as the Shouters and the Eastern Lightning. The movement thrived in Hong Kong and Taiwan, and began to spread through Southeast Asia. In 1962, Witness Lee moved to the United States, learned English, and focused on growing the church outside Chinese-speaking communities.

The Local Church is organized congregationally, one congregation per city (though in larger cities the congregation holds more than one meeting). Each congregation selects its own leaders (ELDERS). Witness Lee established Living Stream Ministry to serve the congregations as the major

Witness Lee (1905–97), leader of the Local Church movement with British colleague and mentor T. Austin Sparks *(Living Stream Ministry, Anaheim, California)*

source of teaching. Several times a year, the ministry invites the leaders of the Local Churches together for continued training. It also oversees schools at which new coworkers and active laypeople are trained for special service, including evangelism. The Local Church is now the second-largest Protestant church in Taiwan. It has moved through the Chinese community in diaspora and far beyond to become a global movement.

The Local Church has encountered opposition from the Chinese government over attempts to circulate copies of Lee's translation of the Bible (in Chinese). Officials from the Local Church have been exploring ways to normalize their relationship with the present Chinese government and bring the church into the legal system.

Worldwide membership of the Local Church movement is estimated to be in excess of 1 million members, though the number within China is difficult to count. Living Stream Ministry is located in Anaheim, California. It is engaged in producing editions of the writings of Nee and Lee in a spectrum of languages. The church in Taiwan has assumed responsibility for publishing their writings in Chinese.

Further reading: *The Beliefs and Practices of the Local Church* (Anaheim, Calif.: Living Stream Ministry, 1978); Witness Lee, *The History of the Church and the Local Churches* (Anaheim, Calif.: Living Stream Ministry, 1991); ———, *Watchman Nee: A Seer of the Divine Revelation in the Present Age.* (Anaheim, Calif.: Living Stream Ministry, 1997); Watchman Nee, *The Collected Works*, 62 vols. (Anaheim, Calif.: Living Stream Ministry, 1994).

Lockhart, William (1811–1896) *pioneer medical missionary*

William Lockhart was born on October 3, 1811, in Liverpool. He took his medical training at Meath Hospital in Dublin and Guy's Hospital in London. He subsequently became a member of the Royal College of Surgeons (1834).

He applied to the LONDON MISSIONARY SOCIETY (LMS), and in 1838 sailed to Canton. He then located in Macau, where he opened a hospital. He eventually moved to Shanghai, where the largest community of Western missionaries was located, and opened a hospital there in 1842. He remained in Shanghai for the next 14 years.

In 1857, he returned to England for a visit, at which time he was named a fellow of the Royal College of Surgeons. He returned permanently in 1864 to become one of the directors of the LMS. In 1878, he became the first president of the Medical Missionary Association, and frequently wrote for its periodical, *Medical Missions at Home and Abroad.*

While in China, he had been outspoken on a variety of issues, including the binding of women's feet, a traditional Chinese practice. In his 1861 book, *The Medical Missionary in China*, he advocated the strict separation of the roles of preacher and physician. He died at Blackheath, England, on April 29, 1896.

See also MEDICAL MISSIONS.

Further reading: William Lockhart, *The Medical Missionary in China: A Narrative of Twenty Years' Experience* (London: Hurst & Blackett, 1861).

London Confessions of Faith

The London Confessions of Faith were composed by two groups of PARTICULAR BAPTISTS during the turmoil of 17th-century England. Though BAPTISTS consider themselves a noncreedal communion, and accept only the Bible as their doctrinal authority, they often still point to the London Confessions of Faith as a summary of the most important lessons that the Bible teaches.

Baptists were the most radical members of the Puritan movement in 17th-century England in their call for purifying the CHURCH OF ENGLAND. Two distinct groups emerged; one followed ARMINIANISM (which emphasized free will), while the other, the Particular Baptists, followed the Calvinist theology shared by Presbyterians and Congregationalists (which emphasized election). Particular Baptists emerged around 1630, and by 1644 there were at least seven congregations. In that year, representatives published a statement of faith that has come to be known as the First London Baptist Confession.

Often confused with the Arminian Baptists, the church was anxious to refute a number of false accusations that had been leveled against them. Article XXI affirmed "That Christ Jesus by his death did bring forth salvation and reconciliation only for the elect, which were those which God the Father gave him." They also wished to distinguish themselves from ANABAPTISTS, with whom they shared several important ideas.

The key paragraphs in the confession concerned the congregation, which is the focus of authority and the source of the ministry, and which is to be completely separated from the state. The London Confession stated that: "every Church has power given them from Christ for their better well-being, to choose to themselves meet persons into the office of Pastors, Teachers, Elders, Deacons . . . Baptists believe in legitimate state authority . . . while believing that the state does not have the right to impose any ecclesiastical order upon the local church."

During the years of the Commonwealth under Puritan Oliver CROMWELL, Baptists were able to survive in a relatively free environment. However, once a king was again placed on the throne and the episcopally led Church of England reinstated, the Baptists were among the groups that suffered the most, while the much stronger Presbyterians and Congregationalists were able to offer some resistance. In 1677, a group of Particular Baptists from England and Wales, called together by a circular letter, quietly met and produced a new confession of faith, this one designed to stress their unity with the other Puritan churches. This Second London Confession was published anonymously.

This Second London Confession was based consciously on the Presbyterian WESTMINSTER CONFESSION OF FAITH (1646) and the Congregationalist SAVOY DECLARATION (1658). It affirmed the authority of the Bible, the triune nature of God, the fall of humanity, and salvation in Christ by faith. The London Confession reinforced the Savoy stress on the key role of the local congregation. However, while Congregationalists left some role for assemblies beyond the local church, Baptists gave to such assemblies only the power of advising local churches.

Following the accession of King William and Queen Mary and the issuance of the Act of Toleration, London Baptists called for a general meeting of their fellow believers from across England and Wales. Some 107 congregations sent representatives to London. They formally adopted the Confession of 1677, which has since become the most frequently cited exposition of the Baptist position.

See also CREEDS/CONFESSIONS OF FAITH.

Further reading: Richard Belcher and Anthony Mattia, *A Discussion of the Seventeenth Century Particular Baptist Confessions of Faith* (Southbridge, Mass.: Crown, 1990); W. L. Lumpkin, *Baptist Confessions of Faith,* rev. ed. (Valley Forge, Pa.: Judson Press, 1969); H. Leon McBeth, *The Baptist Heritage: Four Centuries of Baptist Witness* (Nashville, Tenn.: Broadman Press, 1987); B. R. White, *The English Baptists of the 17th Century* (London: The Baptist Historical Society, 1983).

London Missionary Society

The London Missionary Society (LMS), founded in 1795, was one of the earliest and most active of the 19th-century Protestant missionary-sending agencies. It emerged out of the new awareness of the world produced by the voyages of Captain Cook. The immediate inspiration was the widely published letters written by William CAREY (1761–1834), who had just taken up his missionary post in India in 1793.

In December 1794, a group of ministers and laypeople, primarily from the Independent or Congregational Church but including Anglicans and Presbyterians, met to consider the idea of forming an interdenominational missionary society. In a short time, both the CHURCH OF ENGLAND and the Presbyterian Church established competing missionary structures, leaving the LMS with little interdenominational support.

The LMS chose the SOUTH PACIFIC as its initial target, and in September 1796 sent 13 men, five women, and two children to posts in Tahiti, Tonga, and the Marquesas. The initial cadre would be supplemented with missionaries to the Cook Islands, and eventually to most of the South Pacific island groups. These first missionaries established a pattern that would be followed through most of the 19th century. They mastered the local languages, trained early converts as teachers and congregational leaders, and focused their skills on translating and publishing the Bible.

After work in the South Pacific was well under way, the LMS expanded its work to CHINA. Robert MORRISON (1782–1834) was sent there in 1807; by 1817, the LMS had a missionary in far-off Mongolia as well.

For Africa, the LMS recruited from Scotland some of the most famous missionaries of all time, John Moffatt (1795–1883), John MacKenzie (1835–99), and David LIVINGSTONE (1813–73). Moffat pioneered work in SOUTH AFRICA beginning in 1817. MacKenzie later became the major advocate for British expansion throughout southern Africa (then controlled by Dutch and French settlers), and Livingstone explored the vast interior of the continent. During its peak years in the 19th century, the society supported some 250 missionaries at any given moment.

The LMS proved one of the most foresighted of the Protestant missionary agencies. Starting with its self-image as an interdenominational agency, it began to advocate for a cooperative approach to the mission field by the otherwise competing DENOMINATIONS. It pioneered amity agreements that cut down on duplication of efforts and competition by assigning defined territories to each group. These amity agreements would become the seeds from which the ECUMENICAL MOVEMENT would emerge in Europe and North America at the end of the century. Such agreements worked for several decades, until the growth of missions and the migration of their converts overran the old territorial boundaries.

World War II led to significant changes in the LMS. Many of the former colonial territories where the LMS operated became independent countries. CHINA, the single largest LMS missionary field, experienced a revolution that brought an antireligious and antiforeign regime to power. In several places, notably INDIA, attempts to create united Protestant churches were underway. The LMS responded to these changes in several ways. First, it went through a series of mergers, with the Commonwealth Missionary Society in 1966, and with the Presbyterian Board of Missions in 1977; the combined group was called the Council for World Mission (CMW). At the same time, the entire Protestant missionary enterprise was reorganizing itself to operate as a partner with the sister churches that had superseded the former missions.

A generation after its founding, the present CMW sees itself as a global cooperative endeavor involving 31 denominations headquartered in countries around the world. Missionaries, drawn from each of the cooperating churches, make themselves available to be sent anywhere as needed. The Council for World Mission maintains its headquarters in London, England.

See also CONGREGATIONALISM.

Further reading: Thomas Hiney, *On the Missionary Trail: A Journey through Polynesia, Asia, and Africa with the London Missionary Society* (New York: Atlantic Monthly Press, 2000); J. Herbert Kane, *A Global View of Christian Missions* (Grand Rapids, Mich.: Baker Book House, 1971).

Lord's Supper

No more contentious issue emerged among 16th-century Protestant reformers than that of the sacraments, those ceremonial events designed to serve as a sign of God's presence and confirmation of his promises in Jesus Christ to the community of the faithful. The reformers all agreed that Roman Catholicism had strayed from biblical truth in elevating seven such ceremonial events to a sacramental level, when they believed only two such events were biblically grounded—BAPTISM and the Lord's Supper. They also all agreed that Catholics erred in giving only the bread and not the wine to believers. However, beyond the demand for communion in both kinds, they could reach little agreement among themselves as to the nature of these two sacraments. Concerning baptism, they disagreed on both the mode of administering baptism (immersion, sprinkling, and so forth), and the designation of the appropriate subject (infant, adult). However, differences were much sharper concerning the Lord's Supper—they sharply disagreed over its very nature.

Among the first ideas proposed, by Ulrich ZWINGLI, was that the Lord's Supper was to be understood as a memorial meal. It was a ceremony instituted by Christ; believers were commanded to reenact the Last Supper of Christ with his apostles in order to keep his passion and death alive in their memory. Zwingli's view had the effect of stripping the Lord's Supper of any supernatural elements and turning what had traditionally been thought of as a sacrament into a mere ordinance. Zwingli's idea was initially adopted by the Reformed Church in SWITZERLAND, from where it passed to the Swiss Brethren and the majority of FREE CHURCHES, especially the MENNONITES and

Baptists. It has also become the belief of many in contemporary churches who either dissent from or do not understand the formal sacramental teaching of their denomination.

A contemporary statement of the Zwinglian understanding of the Lord's Supper is found in the "Baptist Faith and Message," a statement adopted by the SOUTHERN BAPTIST CONVENTION (the largest Protestant church in North America) in 1963: "The Lord's Supper is a symbolic act of obedience whereby members of the church, through partaking of the bread and the fruit of the vine, memorialize the death of the Redeemer and anticipate His second coming."

Martin LUTHER, in contrast to the rather secularized doctrine proposed by Zwingli, was determined to keep an understanding of the sacrament as close to the Roman Catholic doctrine as possible by affirming that Christ was truly present, not just symbolically represented, in the sacramental elements. However, he disagreed with the Roman Catholic notion of transubstantiation, which suggested that during the Eucharistic service, when the words of consecration were spoken, the substance (true reality) of the bread and wine was changed into the body and blood of Christ. He suggested instead a theory called CONSUBSTANTIATION, namely that the essence or substance of Christ was added to the elements of bread and wine. This belief retained the idea of the real presence of Christ while denying what Protestants thought of as the "magical" change.

A contemporary statement of the Lutheran position has been presented by the Wisconsin Evangelical Lutheran Synod in its statement, "We Believe": "We believe that those who partake of the Sacrament of the Lord's Supper receive the true body and blood of Christ, 'in, with and under' the bread and wine. . . . As we partake of His body and blood, given and shed for us, we by faith receive the comfort and assurance that our sins are indeed forgiven and that we are truly His own."

As the Reformation gained ground in the 1520s, Protestants of Zwingli's camp and those of Luther's attempted to work out a common confession that they could present to the secular authorities as representative of the Protestant position. However, they were unable to reach an acceptable compromise, and over time the two positions hardened.

A third, compromising position was offered in the 1530s by John CALVIN. He rejected Luther's concept of the real bodily presence of Christ in the bread and wine, but also rejected Zwingli's reduction of the sacrament to an imaginative re-creation of the Last Supper. He believed that a real communion with Christ was the essence of the Lord's Supper. Christ in his resurrected body was in heaven, but gives of himself spiritually through the Holy Spirit. His real presence is perceived by faith. Calvin thus retained the sacramental (sacred) element of the Lord's Supper, but in such a way that proved to his followers both more biblical in content and more acceptable to a modern consciousness.

In Calvin's tradition, the WESTMINSTER CONFESSION, written in the 1640s but still the standard of faith of most Presbyterian churches, affirms: "Worthy receivers, outwardly partaking of the visible elements in this sacrament, do then also inwardly by faith, really and indeed, yet not carnally and corporally, but spiritually, receive and feed upon Christ crucified, and all benefits of his death."

Calvin's teaching on the sacrament was passed from the continental Reformed churches to the British Puritans and hence became established in the Presbyterian and Congregationalist Churches. It was passed into the Anglican tradition during the reign of EDWARD VI (1547–53), and clearly stated in the Anglican Thirty-nine ARTICLES OF RELIGION (1563) issued during the reign of ELIZABETH I, from whence it passed to the Methodists in the 18th century. However, in the Free Churches the Zwinglian position dominated, and there has been a marked tendency in the older Reformation churches, as they have been separated from their role as inclusive state churches in the modern pluralistic world, to move from the Calvinist to the Zwinglian position.

In the 19th and 20th centuries, with the proliferation of Protestant Free Churches, great variation began to appear as new issues emerged concerning the Lord's Supper. DENOMINATIONS disagreed on the frequency of celebrating the Lord's Supper. The CHRISTIAN CHURCH (DISCIPLES OF CHRIST) traces its origin partly to the need for more frequent celebration of the sacraments on the American frontier: they celebrated weekly. Methodists tended to celebrate quarterly and at Christmas and Easter. Various Adventist groups such as JEHOVAH'S WITNESSES celebrate an annual Memorial Feast. The nature of the ritual accompanying the celebration of the Lord's Supper has also varied from the more elaborate ritual within Lutheran and Anglican churches to the very brief and minimalist ritual in most Free Churches. Within this context, the SALVATION ARMY has entered the ecumenical world with a unique position, that the life of the believer is sacramental in nature and that baptism and the Lord's Supper are not a necessary part of salvation and spiritual growth, and has dropped both practices.

Leaders of the ECUMENICAL MOVEMENT in the early 20th century rediscovered the role played by sacraments in dividing Protestants. Dialogue on the sacraments became a priority issue of the FAITH AND ORDER MOVEMENT beginning in 1910 and has continued as one of the more important issues in ecumenical deliberations. Agreements on the sharing of ministers among churches have largely depended upon finding an acceptable common statement on the sacraments. In this context, the Lutherans have played a crucial role as they looked to find common ground with Anglicans on the one hand and Calvinist churches on the other. Among the fruitful result of the sacrament discussions was the LEUENBERG CHURCH FELLOWSHIP.

See also SACRAMENTS/ORDINANCES.

Further reading: *Baptism, Eucharist and Minister 1982–1990. Report on the Process and Responses.* Faith and Order Paper No. 149 (Geneva: World Council of Church, 1990); G. C. Berkouwer, *The Sacraments,* translated by Hugo Bekker (Grand Rapids, Mich.: William B. Eerdmans, 1969); James O. Duke and Richard L. Harrison, *The Lord's Supper* (St. Louis: Council on Christian Unity, 1993); J. Gordon Melton, *The Encyclopedia of American Religions: Religious Creeds,* 2 vols. (Detroit: Gale Research, 1988, 1994); John Reumann, *The Supper of the Lord: The New Testament, Ecumenical Dialogues, and Faith an Order on Eucharist* (Philadelphia: Fortress Press, 1985).

Lumentut, Agustina (b. 1939) *church leader in Indonesia*

Agustina Lumentut was born into a Christian family at Rampi, Sulawesi, Indonesia. She grew up during World War II and the start of the Indonesian state. Her father was a prominent pastor in the Christian Church of Central Sulawesi, with its roots in the Reformed Church of the NETHERLANDS. At the age of 17, she began her studies for the ministry, a unique venture for a woman at the time. Her educational goals took her to AUSTRALIA and INDIA, and eventually to Trinity Theological College in Singapore.

She served in the Christian Church in Central Sulawesi for many years and built a reputation for her championship of the poor and underprivileged, her skills as a mediator, and for balancing the demands of preaching and pastoral leadership with the drive for social change. In the 1990s, Lumentut was elected as moderator of her denomination, the first female so recognized in all of Indonesia. She served for eight years, during which time she was also selected to serve on the central committee of the WORLD COUNCIL OF CHURCHES.

Following her years as moderator, she retired and has subsequently functioned as an ambassador at large for the church. In 1998, she represented the Christian Conference of Asia at the Synod of Asian Bishops (Roman Catholic) and addressed the synod during the visit of Pope John Paul II. She took the opportunity to call for the church to reorder its life to be ready to receive the gifts and graces of women.

Further reading: Margaret Kirk, *Let Justice Flow* (Delhi: I.S.P.C.K., 1997); Scott W. Sunquist, ed., *A Dictionary of Asian Christianity* (Grand Rapids, Mich.: William B. Eerdmans, 2001).

Luther, Martin (1483–1546) *founder of the Protestant Reformation*

By his 1517 appeal for debate on a set of issues faced by the Roman Catholic community in Germany, Augustinian monk Martin Luther inadvertently launched what would become Protestantism. His polemical and organizational talents enabled him to defy the powerful Roman Catholic Church and revolutionize the religious life of Europe and later on, the lives of millions of people around the world.

Luther was born on November 10, 1483, in Eisenben. He attended schools in Mansfield, Magdeburg, and Eisennach. In 1505, he earned his M.A. degree at the University of Erfurt, then entered the Augustinian Order. As a monk, he continued his education and was ordained a priest in 1507. His superiors recognized his abilities and sent him to WITTENBERG to prepare himself for a professorial career. He earned his bachelor's degree in theology in 1509 and a doctorate in 1512.

As a lecturer at the University of Wittenberg, in Saxony, he focused his teaching on the biblical book of Psalms (1513–15). He came to believe that salvation was best described as a new relationship with God, based upon faith in Christ and not upon any deeds of merit done by the individual. The individual, a sinner and hence undeserving of God's love, was nevertheless redeemed; out of that new relationship he tried to live a life in conformity to God's will. This new theological insight, combined with his continued study of the Bible, especially Paul's letter to the Romans, led to a personal experience of salvation, which he came to understand derived from God's forgiveness of his sin, which he received by faith alone.

Luther's personal experience of salvation and his new theological insights soon thrust him into

Statue of Protestant reformer Martin Luther (1483–1546) at Worms, Germany, where he made his famous statement, "Here I Stand" *(Institute for the Study of American Religion, Santa Barbara, California)*

the middle of public controversy. Johann Tetzel (1465–1519), a Dominican monk, had arrived in Saxony to sell INDULGENCES to raise funds for the erection of St. Peter's in Rome. The church in Luther's day believed that most people would have to spend some time after death in purgatory to atone for their sins through pain and suffering. Acts of goodness and piety by individuals in this life, however, cleansed one of sin and hence shortened time in purgatory. In addition, the church could grant "indulgences" or pardons that could reduce or even eliminate the time in purgatory, for oneself or for a loved one. Tetzel offered an indulgence to any church member in Saxony who contributed to St. Peter's. Luther saw the practice as a rejection of God's gracious act of granting salvation to the sinner.

Luther decided to raise the issue by calling for a public debate on the issue of indulgences, and on a set of additional topics, all of which grew out of his recent theological reflections. These issues were reduced to NINETY-FIVE THESES (debating points); legend has it that a copy was nailed to the door of the church at Wittenberg on October 31, 1517. Tetzel proposed a set of countertheses. Their actions led to a debate between Luther and another theologian, Johann Eck (1486–1543), in Leipzig in 1519. Luther invoked the authority of the Bible over the assertions of popes and the rulings of church councils, since the latter can err and have erred.

Luther was declared a heretic and excommunicated. However, he was protected from the power of the church by the authority of Frederick, the elector of Saxony. Frederick was protective of his university and its faculty, and he also opposed the movement of large sums of Saxon money to Rome. Luther used the time to produce three famous essays, all published in 1520, in which he expanded his thoughts. In *Appeal to the German Nobility,* he developed his understanding of the priesthood of all believers, an approach to church life that stripped some authority from parish priests (and which later came to be interpreted quite radically by some of Luther's followers). In *Babylonian Captivity of the Church* he opined upon the church's sacramental system. He argued that there were only two sacraments, BAPTISM and the LORD'S SUPPER, not seven as was commonly believed. He also argued that the cup of wine representing the blood of Christ should be given to all believers, not just to the clergy. Luther called the withholding of the cup from the laity the imprisonment of the Lord's Supper. He laid out his understanding of faith in God, salvation, and the Christian life in *The Freedom of the Christian Man.*

The broad circulation of Luther's ideas and essays led the emperor of the Holy Roman Empire,

the confederation of German states, to summon Luther to a meeting of the DIET OF WORMS, its governing body. Luther justified his position with an appeal to the Bible and to reason, but the diet rejected his approach and condemned him. However, by this time he had won significant support across northern Germany. With the protection of the civil authorities, Luther and his colleagues began to produce additional materials supporting his new perspective. This included a theological text written by Wittenberg colleague Philip MELANCTHON (1521), Luther's translation of the New Testament into German (1522), and a hymnal that included a number of hymns written by Luther (1524).

The progress of the Reformation was threatened when peasants in southern Germany rose up to protest their situation in life; they hoped to win support from Luther, thanks to his advocacy of the priesthood of all believers and the freedom of the Christian. However, even as Luther attempted to arbitrate their grievances, some of the peasants turned violent, and Luther turned against them. On May 15, 1525, 50,000 of them were massacred following their defeat in a battle at Frankenhausen.

Luther took a major personal step on June 13, 1525, when he put aside his monk's robes and married Catherine von Bora, thus signaling an end to clerical celibacy. The development of a uniquely Lutheran church occurred in the mid-1520s; the older Roman Catholic dioceses were dismantled and new church bodies established, bounded by the current borders of the many German states. For these churches Luther prepared the Longer and the Shorter Catechisms, the latter being the most used.

At this time, Luther came into conflict with the leader of the Reformation in Switzerland, Ulrich ZWINGLI. While agreeing on most issues, such as salvation by faith and the sole authority of the Bible, the two leaders sharply diverged on the issue of the Lord's Supper. Zwingli regarded the Lord's Supper as primarily a memorial meal, while Luther affirmed the real presence of Christ in the

sacraments, a position he termed CONSUBSTANTIA-
TION. Zwingli and Luther met at Marburg in 1529
in an attempt to work out their differences and
unite all of the Reformation adherents, but the
MARBURG COLLOQUY failed.

The failure at Marburg led directly to the
AUGSBURG CONFESSION OF FAITH, the statement of
faith of the Lutheran princes that was presented to
the diet in 1530. The confession is often seen as
the culmination of the first phase of the Reformation. Luther lived another 16 years, much of it
devoted to writing, even as his colleagues took the
lead in the ongoing battles with Catholic forces.
From 1533 to his death in 1546, he served as dean
of the theology faculty at Wittenberg.

During this period, Luther completed the German translation of the whole Bible (1534), and
compiled the confessional statement known as the
Schmalkald Articles (1537). He continued to
engage those who opposed the Reformation with
polemic writings. He wrote *Jews and their Lies* in
1543, an attack upon the Jewish community that
many have considered anti-Semitic; *Short Confession Concerning the Lord's Supper* (1544); and his
final attack on Roman Catholic authority, *Against
the Papacy at Rome Founded by the Devil* (1545).

In January 1546, Luther traveled to Eisleben
in what proved a vain attempt to settle a local dispute. While there, his health deteriorated. Unable
to return to Wittenberg, he died at Eisenben on
February 18, 1546.

Further reading: *Luther's Works (LW)*, ed. by Jaroslav
Pelikan and H. T. Lehmann (Philadelphia/St. Louis:
Fortress Press/Concordia, 1955–86) 55 vols; Roland
H. Bainton, *Here I Stand: A Life of Martin Luther*
(New York: Abingdon-Cokesbury Press, 1950);
Bernhard Lohse, *Martin Luther: An Introduction to His
Life and Work*, trans. by Robert C. Schultz (Philadel-
phia: Fortress Press, 1986).

Lutheran Church–Missouri Synod

The Lutheran Church–Missouri Synod is one of
the largest Lutheran bodies in the United States.

The relatively conservative church was founded
by Lutherans from Saxony who protested a forced
Lutheran-Reformed merger in that German state
in the early 19th century.

Some Lutherans in Saxony felt that the new
Evangelical Church compromised the Lutheran
confessions to which they were attached. In 1837,
a group of them arrived in the United States under
the leadership of Bishop Martin Stephan
(1777–1846). They settled in Perry County, Missouri (north of Cape Girardeau).

Soon after their arrival, the group dismissed
Stephan in favor of Carl F. W. Walther (1811–87).
In the face of the crisis, Walther affirmed the
authority of Lutheran orthodoxy and championed
congregational rights. As the group spread,

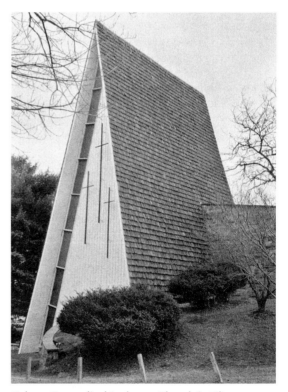

Calvary Evangelical Lutheran Church in Silver
Spring, Maryland, is affiliated with the Lutheran
Church–Missouri Synod. *(Institute for the Study of
American Religion, Santa Barbara, California)*

Walther settled in St. Louis as pastor of the believers there and opened a school that eventually became Concordia Theological Seminary. He founded a magazine, *Der Lutheraner,* in 1844, and then in 1847 founded the Missouri Synod as a fellowship of 16 congregations and 22 ministers. The synod reached out to German-speaking Lutherans across the United States. It emerged as the major defender of Lutheran confessionalism (that emphasized Lutheran orthodoxy) as opposed to the PIETISM (which emphasized personal devotion) that dominated Lutheranism in the eastern United States.

In the late 19th century, the Missouri Synod began what became an expansive world missionary program that at its height supported workers in 70 countries. Today, the church works in partnership with like-minded churches, some an outgrowth of its missionary endeavor, in some 40 countries, and supports around 300 full-time personnel around the globe.

The American church in 2003 reported 2.5 million members. Its headquarters are in St. Louis, Missouri. It is a member of the INTERNATIONAL LUTHERAN COUNCIL, but has rejected membership in the LUTHERAN WORLD FEDERATION and the WORLD COUNCIL OF CHURCHES.

See also LUTHERANISM.

Further reading: Walter A. Baepler, *A Century of Grace: A History of the Missouri Synod, 1847–1947* (St. Louis: Concordia Publishing House, 1947); Carl S. Meyer, *Moving Frontiers: Readings in the History of the Lutheran Church Missouri Synod* (St. Louis: Concordia Publishing House, 1986); E. Clifford Nelson, *The Lutherans in North America* (Philadelphia: Fortress Press, 1980); Eldon Weisheit, *The Zeal of His House: Five Generations of Lutheran Church-Missouri Synod History (1847–1972)* (St. Louis: Concordia Publishing House, 1973).

Lutheranism

Lutheranism, a movement founded by Martin LUTHER (1483–1546) in the early 16th century,

has in the 20th given birth to several hundred distinct Lutheran churches scattered in countries around the world. Though divided administratively and by national boundaries, they share a heritage based in Luther's experience of the grace of God and the saving faith it engendered, a faith provoked by his study of the Bible.

In 1517, Luther, then a professor of theology at the University at WITTENBERG, challenged church authorities over what he saw as the illegitimate practice of selling INDULGENCES. As a result of the acrimonious debates that followed, in which Luther asserted the authority of the Bible over that of the church and the pope, the pope denounced and eventually excommunicated Luther. Luther responded with three long essays in 1520 that essentially defined the doctrines of what became the new Lutheran Church.

Luther attacked the Roman Catholic doctrine of TRANSUBSTANTIATION, called for limiting the sacraments to two (BAPTISM and the LORD'S SUPPER) rather than the seven acknowledged by most Catholics, and championed the PRIESTHOOD OF ALL BELIEVERS. He later elaborated his basic principles of scriptural authority and salvation by grace through faith alone.

In 1521, Luther was condemned before the DIET OF WORMS, the secular body ruling the Holy Roman Empire, but he was supported by several German leaders. Those who stood with Luther founded the Lutheran or Evangelical Churches.

The Lutheran Reformation came to dominate the northern regions of Germany. Luther, not a systematic thinker, bequeathed to the next generation the task of compiling a systemic theological presentation of the Lutheran position. A number of documents were written and compiled to that aim, including Luther's own Small Catechism (1529) and Large Catechism (1529); the AUGSBURG CONFESSION OF FAITH (1530); Philip MELANCTHON's Apology for the Augsburg Confession (1531); the Treatise on the Power and Primacy of the Pope (1537); the Schmalkald Articles (1537); and the Formula of Concord (1577). Together with the three ecumenical creeds (Apostles',

Nicene, Athanasian), these documents were compiled into the *Book of Concord* (1580). Lutherans acknowledge the Bible as their only rule of doctrine and practice, but give special heed to the three ecumenical creeds, the Augsburg Confession, and Luther's catechisms as particularly accurate summaries of biblical truth.

With the confessional statements in hand, Lutheran scholars of the 17th century developed the theology to the point of dogmatism, in the opinion of some critics. During the 18th century, there was a reaction known as PIETISM. While not disregarding theology, Pietists placed more emphasis on personal religious experience and intimate church life. Today, Lutherans are characterized by their double emphasis upon word and sacrament, that is, to biblical authority and preaching coupled with liturgy and the sacrament of the Lord's Supper.

During the 19th century, Lutheran missionaries, many with Pietist backgrounds, and supported by missionary societies in Germany and Scandinavia, carried Lutheranism around the world. In the 20th century, most of the missions they founded matured into independent Lutheran churches. At the same time, Europe became the center of two world wars, the last of which was particularly destructive of Lutheranism in Germany. The effort to rebuild war-ravaged Europe became the catalyst for Lutherans to come together in a new ecumenical endeavor, the LUTHERAN WORLD FEDERATION (LWF). As the immediate issue of rebuilding Europe faded, the LWF emerged as the expression of Lutheran unity worldwide and launched a variety of international cooperative activities. The Lutheran World Federation has its headquarters in the same building that houses the WORLD COUNCIL OF CHURCHES. While most Lutherans are related through the federation, more conservative Lutheran bodies have formed the INTERNATIONAL LUTHERAN COUNCIL.

Further reading: E. Theodore Bachmann and Mercia Brenne Bachmann. *Lutheran Churches in the World: A Handbook* (Minneapolis, Minn.: Augsburg Press,

1989); J. H. Bodensieck, *The Encyclopedia of the Lutheran Church,* 3 vols. (Minneapolis, Minn.: Augsburg Press, 1965); Werner Elert, *The Structure of Lutheranism, Vol. I: The Theology and Philosophy of Life of Lutheranism, Especially in the Sixteenth and Seventeenth Centuries,* trans. by Walter A. Hansen (St. Louis, Mo.: Concordia, 1962); W. H. Arnold and C. George Fry, *The Way, The Truth, and the Life: An Introduction to Lutheran Christianity* (Grand Rapids, Mich.: Baker Book House, 1982).

Lutheran World Federation

The Lutheran church split into numerous organizational divisions in the 19th century, but some believers continued to harbor visions of reuniting the various segments of the community. World War I spurred the American churches, at least, to unite, as synods that had clung to the different European languages of their founders were motivated to Americanize. Once English became the common language, there remained little reason to remain separated.

In 1923, a World Lutheran Conference at Eisenach, Germany, brought together representatives from across Europe and North America for the first time. The conference highlighted the need for future theological discussions, mutual assistance, and joint efforts to address global problems. Subsequent gatherings were held in Copenhagen (1929) and Paris (1935). An initial gathering set for 1941 in the United States was prevented by the outbreak of World War II.

World War II influenced the world Lutheran community far more deeply than World War I. The universal recognition of the evils of Nazism altered the Lutheran self-image, in light of Germany's historical role as the birthplace of world Lutheranism. Europe was devastated and in need of massive help to rebuild. Lutheran missions in Asia and Africa were restless and ready to step forward as mature autonomous churches.

Immediately after the war, American Lutherans took the lead in planning for the rebuilding of Europe. First, though, work was required to heal the damage done by conflicting loyalties during the war. The process began just months after the war in Europe, as leaders of the established EVANGELICAL CHURCH IN GERMANY met with Lutheran leaders from across North America and Europe. The Stuttgart gathering initiated the process of drafting a constitution for what became the Lutheran World Federation (LWF), which first met in the summer of 1947.

The work to create the Lutheran World Federation paralleled similar efforts to create the WORLD COUNCIL OF CHURCHES (WCC), which held its first meeting in 1948 in Amsterdam. The formation of the Lutheran World Federation, soon to be joined by the WORLD METHODIST COUNCIL, reminded WCC leaders of the important continuing role of denominational families even as cross-denominational discussions took center stage.

The integral ties between the new federation and the WCC was illustrated when the federation established headquarters at the World Council of Churches' Ecumenical Building in Geneva, SWITZERLAND. The LWF's assembly meets every six years. Between assembly meetings, a council and executive committee oversee the work of its five program areas—theology and studies, mission and development, world service, finance and administration, and communication services. In 2003, it reported 136 member churches in 76 countries, representing approximately 62 million members.

Further reading: Lutheran World Federation. Available online. URL: http://www.lutheranworld.org; E. Theodore Bachmann and Mercia Brenne Bachmann, *Lutheran Churches in the World: A Handbook* (Minneapolis, Minn.: Augsburg Press, 1989); *Directory* (Geneva, Switz.: Lutheran World Federation, issued annually); E. Clifford Nelson, *The Rise of World Lutheranism* (Philadelphia: Fortress Press, 1982).

M

Mack, Alexander (1679–1735) *founder of the movement that came to be known as the Brethren*

Alexander Mack was born in Schriesheim, near Heidelberg, Germany, in 1679 to a prosperous mill owner who belonged to the local parish of the Reformed Church. Not formally educated, Mack was nevertheless an avid Bible student, which often led him to challenge the minister of his church.

Mack found new vitality in PIETISM, with its emphasis on personal religious devotion. Each individual, he now believed, needed a personal relationship to God. He called his fellow Christians to a life of honesty, integrity, and spiritual exercises like prayer, Bible study, and hymn singing.

Like all Pietists, Mack regularly met with a small group of like-minded seekers, but unlike most, he left his local parish. Following his father's death, he started holding services in what was now his mill. Challenged by the authorities, in 1706 Mack and his family moved to Schwarzenau near Marburg, where a sympathetic local ruler gave protection to Separatists.

Mack came to believe that true Christianity could only be found apart from the established church. Using Schwarzenau as a base, he visited many Pietist and other groups. From the MEN-NONITES he took the idea that BAPTISM should be performed not on infants, but on those old enough to understand. A New Testament church should be a disciplined community of baptized believers, not just the citizens of a particular parish. It should meet together as a moral community and be prepared to discipline wayward members. Unlike the Mennonites, he concluded that BAPTISM should be by immersion.

In 1708, Mack and seven followers rebaptized themselves in the Eder River. Chosen by lot, Mack was baptized first, and he then baptized the others. Since the act was illegal in most of Germany, they all agreed not to disclose his name. Each person was immersed three times (triune immersion) in the "name of the Father, and of the Son, and of the Holy Spirit."

The little group called itself the "Schwarzenau Baptists." They instituted several ordinances, including a LORD'S SUPPER that consisted of a meal, FOOT WASHING, and the sharing of bread and the cup. They believed that the church should be separate from the government, and appoint and ordain its own ministers. They were pacifists as well.

Over the next decade, the group grew and spread to other locations. To escape persecution, in 1719 the majority of the congregation at

Krefeld migrated to Germantown, Pennsylvania. Mack led the Schwarzenau group to the NETHERLANDS in 1720, and then to merge with the Germantown congregation nine years later, where he became leader. He was unable to prevent a schism when George Beissel left to found a communal group at Ephrata, Pennsylvania.

Mack died at Germantown on February 19, 1735. The largest group of his followers eventually became the Church of the BRETHREN. Among other successor groups are some who still keep the plain clothing once so noticeable among the Brethren; still others, such as the Grace Brethren, have identified with modern EVANGELICALISM.

Further reading: Freeman Ankrum, *Alexander Mack the Tunker and Descendants* (Scottdale, Pa.: Herald Press, 1943); Donald F. Durnbaugh, *Brethren Beginnings: The Origin of the Church of the Brethren in Early Eighteenth-Century Europe* (Philadelphia: Brethren Encyclopedia, 1992); Alexander Mack, *The Complete Writings of Alexander Mack*, ed. by William R. Eberly (Winona Lake, Ind.: BMH Books, 1991); William G. Willoughby, *Counting the Cost: The Life of Alexander Mack, 1679–1735* (Elgin, Ill.: Brethren Press, 1979).

MacKay, George Leslie (1844–1901)
pioneering Presbyterian missionary in Taiwan
George Leslie MacKay was born on March 21, 1844, in Zorra township near Woodstock, Ontario, where his parents had moved from Scotland. He attended Ontario Teachers' College in Toronto and began teaching school, but feeling a call to be a missionary, he dropped his work to attend Knox College (1865–68) and Princeton Theological Seminary (1868–71).

MacKay applied to the Mission Board of the Presbyterian Church of Canada and was chosen to be their first foreign missionary. He left for CHINA in 1871. He visited the missionary center along the China coast, but decided to begin work in Taiwan (then called Formosa). Since the American Presbyterians were active in the south, he moved to the northern part of the island and settled in

Tamsui, one of four ports that had been opened to foreigners in 1860.

He learned Taiwanese and began preaching, assisted by a young scholar and convert named Hoa. The first five Christians were baptized in 1873. Though not a physician, he learned enough medical skills to assist many people, and eventually opened a clinic. He became quite expert at extracting teeth, and reported pulling more than 20,000 in his first 20 years. Concerned about his inability to reach female Taiwanese, he decided to marry a Taiwanese woman as a means of identifying with his flock. In May 1878, he married Chang Tsung-Ming ("Minnie"). His wife became an assistant whose work brought immediate results.

Other missionaries came from Canada to assist him, but most lasted only a few years in the climate. MacKay began training local assistants. With money raised on his furlough in Canada in 1880, he began what became MacKay Memorial Hospital, now a large institution. Two years later, he founded what became Tam Kang High School and Taiwan Theological Seminary. In 1884, he opened the first school for girls in Taiwan.

At the end of 1893, MacKay returned home for a second furlough, when he was elected moderator of the Presbyterian Church of Canada (1894). He returned to Taiwan in 1895, where he died on June 2, 1901. MacKay oversaw the construction of some 60 chapels and raised up the most significant Protestant work in northern Taiwan prior to the entry of the hundreds of thousands of refugees from China following the Chinese Revolution.

See also CHINA: TAIWAN.

Further reading: George Leslie MacKay, *From Far Formosa: The Island, Its People, and Mission*, ed. by J. A. MacDonald (New York: Fleming H. Revell, 1896); R. P. Mackay, *Life of George Leslie Mackay, D.D. 1884–1901* (Toronto: Board of Foreign Missions, 1913); George A. Malcolm, *The Christian Layman in Formosa—One Hundred Years of Christian Witness* (Toronto: Toronto School of Graduate Studies, Knox College, Toronto, M.Th. thesis, 1965); Keith Marian, [pseudonym of Mary Esther MacGregor], *The Black-*

Bearded Barbarian (New York: Missionary Education Movement of the United States and Canada, 1912).

Maclay, Robert Samuel (1824–1907)
pioneer Methodist missionary in China, Japan, and Korea

Robert Maclay was born in Concord, Pennsylvania, on February 7, 1824. He attended Dickinson College and after graduating in 1845 was ordained as an ELDER in the Methodist Episcopal Church. The first Methodist missionaries arrived in CHINA in 1847; Maclay was part of the second group (that included Henry Hickok) sent out later that same year, arriving in China in 1848. The small group made Fuchow the center of their work. Maclay proved the natural leader and was appointed superintendent and treasurer, posts he held until 1872.

Through the 1860s, Maclay directed expansion up the Yangtze River, but then became interested in North China and in 1869 directed the opening of work in Beijing. In 1871, he co-authored a dictionary of the Fuchow dialect.

In 1871, church leaders in the United States responded positively to a letter he had written earlier suggesting that work be initiated in JAPAN. They chose him to lead it. Thus, he gave up his responsibilities in Fuchow and in 1873 moved to Tokyo. Maclay and his wife were one of five couples representing the Methodists in Japan. He was appointed superintendent of the mission and president of Ei Wa Gakko, a college that included the Philander Smith Biblical Institute and the Anglo-Chinese Academy.

In 1884, Maclay visited the king of KOREA and obtained permission for Methodist missionaries to enter the country. Presbyterian medical missionary Horace Newton ALLEN had opened the way with his medical work. Maclay did not return to Korea, but from Japan directed the work of Henry G. and Ella Appenzeller, the first of a team of missionaries who launched work in Seoul in 1885.

In 1888, Maclay returned to the United States and became dean of the Maclay College of Theology (now the Claremont School of Theology) (originally endowed by a relative, Charles Maclay). He retired five years later and died in 1907.

Further reading: Wade Crawford Barclay, *History of Methodist Missions,* 6 vols. (New York: Missions & Church Extension of The Methodist Church, 1950); Everett N. Hunt Jr., *Protestant Pioneers in Korea* (Maryknoll, N.Y.: Orbis Books, 1980); Robert S. Maclay, *Life among the Chinese* (New York: Carlton & Porter, 1861); Charles D. Stokes, *History of Methodist Missions in Korea, 1885–1930* (New Haven, Conn.: Yale University, Ph.D. diss., 1947).

Manz, Felix (c. 1498–1527) *martyr and cofounder of the Anabaptist movement*

Felix Manz was the illegitimate son of a Roman Catholic priest. He emerged in the 1520s in Zurich, Switzerland, where Ulrich ZWINGLI had carried out his historic reform of the church. By 1524, Manz and a small group of others, including George BLAUROCK and Conrad GREBEL, had reached the conclusion that the Reformation had fallen short, primarily by maintaining the practice of infant BAPTISM.

In Roman Catholic thought, baptism initiated one's entrance into the church and the Christian life. All citizens were baptized at birth and thenceforward considered part of the church and under its ministrations. Ideally, a person would follow the church's pattern for Christian growth, punctuated by various sacramental acts, the last being administered shortly before death. Manz and his cohorts found no basis for infant baptism in the Bible. Besides, they rejected the whole system of a state church in which all citizens, no matter their beliefs or patterns of behavior, were considered members. They envisioned a church composed only of adults who made a confession of faith and were willing to lead a disciplined Christian existence. Such a church would, of necessity, lead to a dramatic reordering of the relationship of church and state.

On January 17, 1525, a disputation on infant baptism was held before the city authorities, all of whom sided with Zwingli and his defense of the practice. The next day, Manz's group baptized one another at his home, thus launching the Anabaptist (rebaptizing) movement. They also began to visit their neighbors door-to-door, inviting them to join in. The authorities moved to stop their work, and the men had to flee.

Manz, Grebel, and Blaurock were arrested later in the year and sentenced to life imprisonment. However, the three escaped. Manz eluded authorities for about a year but was finally captured late in 1526. He was executed by drowning on January 15, 1527.

See also ANABAPTISTS.

Further reading: C. Arnold Snyder, *Anabaptist History and Theology: An Introduction* (Kitchener, Ontario: Pandora Press, 1995); J. Denny Weaver, *Becoming Anabaptist: The Origin and Significance of Sixteenth-Century Anabaptism* (Scottdale, Pa.: Herald Press, 1987); George H. Williams, *The Radical Reformation* (Kirksville, Mo.: Sixteenth Century Journal, 1992).

Marburg Colloquy

The Marburg Colloquy of 1529 was an unsuccessful attempt by the leaders of the fledgling Reformation to write a doctrinal statement that could appeal to all factions. It brought together leaders from Germany and SWITZERLAND, the two main countries where the reform movement had taken hold. Martin LUTHER and Ulrich ZWINGLI were the primary participants; others present included Philip MELANCTHON, Justus Jonas, Johann Brenz, Kaspar Cruciger, Andreas Osiander, Johann OECOLAMPADIUS, Wolfgang Capito, Martin BUCER, and Johannes Sturm. The gathering had been facilitated by Landgrave Philip of Hesse, and met at his castle.

The meeting tried to reconcile what appeared to be slight doctrinal differences between Luther and his colleagues on the one hand and Zwingli and his Swiss associates on the other. Quick con-

The church at Marburg, Germany, became the site of a colloquy between reformers Martin Luther and Ulrich Zwingli in 1592. *(Institute for the Study of American Religion, Santa Barbara, California)*

sensus was reached on 14 statements covering the nature of God, the person and work of Christ, justification by faith, and other basic issues. However, the sacraments remained in dispute.

Both sides agreed that the Catholic doctrine of TRANSUBSTANTIATION was incorrect. However, Luther still believed that Christ was *literally* present in the sacrament of the LORD'S SUPPER, while Zwingli interpreted the ceremony symbolically—for him, the elements of bread and wine *represented* Christ's body and blood. The colloquy failed to resolve the difference and thus failed to unite the Protestant cause. Lutheranism came to dominate Germany and Scandinavia, and the Reformed Church won out in Switzerland.

Several years later, John CALVIN offered a middle position between Luther and the now deceased Zwingli. However, the dividing line had already been drawn. The Reformed churches accepted Calvin's understanding that Christ was *spiritually* present in the sacrament, but the Lutheran position had already hardened. Sacramental theology would become the major issue dividing the two churches as they competed for members across Europe.

Further reading: Lowell C. Green, "What Was the True Issue at Marburg in 1529?" *The Springfielder,* 40 (1976): 102–06; Hermann Sasse, *This Is My Body: Luther's Contention for the Real Presence in the Sacrament of the Altar* (Minneapolis, Minn.: Augsburg, 1959); W. P. Stephens, *Zwingli. An Introduction to His Thought* (Oxford: Clarendon Press, 1992).

Marian exiles

The term *Marian exiles* refers to about 800 Protestants who fled England during the reign of MARY I (1553–58). Mary's attempt to reimpose Roman Catholicism on the CHURCH OF ENGLAND and the country included the arrest and execution of Protestant leaders. The majority of the exiles, mostly lay believers, settled in Germany at first, but they eventually gravitated to Holland and SWITZERLAND (several hundred in Geneva alone). There they absorbed the ideas of John CALVIN, whose *Institutes of the Christian Religion* had become the important statement of Reformed Church theology in both countries.

Among the more important of the exiles was John KNOX. After leaving Scotland, Knox settled in Frankfurt, Germany, as the chaplain to a group of British expatriates. When the community was taken over by Anglicans, he moved on to Geneva. While there, he wrote the "Brief Exhortation to England," an exposition in support of Calvin's perspective. With ELIZABETH I firmly on the throne in 1559, he returned to Scotland to lead a Geneva-style Reformation. The Church of Scotland was transformed into a Presbyterian church.

Peter Martyr Vermigli (1500–62) was another of the exiles. An Italian previously exiled from his homeland and sought by the Inquisition, Vermigli had come to England at the request of Thomas CRANMER to teach at Oxford. After fleeing once again, Vermigli moved first to STRASBOURG and then to Zurich. In 1561, he accompanied Theodore de BEZA to the Colloquy of Poissey, one of several peaceful attempts to reconcile Protestant-Catholic differences in France.

England could not ignore the returning exiles. Elizabeth, however, placed national unity as her most important goal. Her VIA MEDIA was an attempt to reconcile Reformed and Catholic practices so as to appeal to the broadest segments of the public. Her new BOOK OF COMMON PRAYER was an edited version of an earlier Protestant edition, but it dropped references that might seem to favor either Catholics or Protestants.

The great majority of Elizabeth's subjects accepted the *via media,* which allowed much scope for interpretation, but many of the Marian exiles would accept nothing less than the pure Calvinist ideal. These people founded the British Presbyterian Church and became the bedrock of PURITANISM, a broad movement that called for further purification of the Church of England. Their movement would enjoy its greatest success in the next century.

Further reading: K. R. Bartlett, "The Role of the Marian Exiles," in P. W. Hassler, ed., *The House of Commons, 1558–1603* (London: Her Majesty's Stationery Office, 1981); Dan G. Danner, *Pilgrimage to Puritanism: History and Theology of the Marian Exiles* (London: Peter Lang, 1999); C. H. Garrett, *The Marian Exiles, 1553–1558* (Cambridge: Cambridge University Press, 1938).

Marshman, Hannah (1767–1847) *first British woman missionary*

Hannah Marshman was born in Bristol, England, on May 13, 1767. Orphaned at the age of 11, she went to live with her grandfather. In 1799, she traveled with her celebrated husband, Joshua Marshman, to Serampore, INDIA. The mission station was founded there the following year upon the arrival of William CAREY. The Baptist Missionary Society did not approve of women missionaries, so Hannah decided to focus her attention unofficially on the women of East Bengal. At the time, women were subjected to various humilities, their rights were largely ignored, and they fell victim to regulations about which they were largely ignorant. Many of these women began to see Hannah as a person to whom they could turn in times of distress.

Hannah founded a girls' boarding school, a pioneering effort in the area that became a major source of income for the Serampore Mission. Hannah also took care of a number of orphans and destitute people. She died at Serampore on March 7, 1847, the last survivor of the original group.

Further reading: *The Bengal Obituary, or a Record to Perpetuate the Memory of Departed Worth, Being a Compilation of Tablets and Monumental Inscriptions from Various Parts of the Bengal and Agra Presidencies. To which is Added Biographical Sketches and Memoirs of Such as Have Pre-Eminently Distinguished Themselves in the History of British India, since the Formation of the European Settlement to the Present Time* (Calcutta, India: J. Thomas, Baptist Mission Press, 1848); Sunil K. Chatterjee, *Hannah Marshman: First Woman Missionary in India* (India, 1987); A. Christopher Smith, "The Legacy of William Ward and Joshua and Hannah Marshman," *International Bulletin of Missionary Research* 23 (1999): 120–29.

Martin, William Alexander Parsons
(1827–1916) *longtime American missionary in China*

Dominating the second generation of American missionaries in CHINA, W. A. P. Martin's career of over 60 years set him apart as a missionary extraordinaire. Martin was born in rural Indiana, the son of a Presbyterian minister. Following his graduation from New Albany Theological Seminary in 1849, he was ordained and married to Jan VanSant. In 1850, the couple moved to Ningpo, China, one of five treaty ports opened to Westerners in 1842 following the Opium War.

As an active Chinese-speaking minister he was strategically placed to comment on the Tai P'ing Rebellion of 1850, led by the messianic pretender Hung Hsuin-Chuan (or Hong Xiúquán). He urged the United States to back the revolt. Later, he helped write the Treaty of Tientsin; he was responsible for the clause, "Any person, whether citizen of the United States or Chinese convert, who, according to these tenets, peaceably teach and practice the principles of Christianity, shall in no case be interfered with or molested." The treaty also opened up new parts of China to Christian missionaries.

In 1862, Martin moved to Shanghai and the following year to Beijing. He taught at Tong Wen Kuan (interpreters' school) at the Imperial University. He edited the *Peking Magazine,* calling for reforms in Chinese society. He wrote articles for the *New York Times* interpreting China, as well as a number of books in both Chinese and English. In Chinese, his most important texts were the *Evidences of Christianity,* a comparative study of Christianity and other faiths, and a seven-volume set on natural philosophy. In English, he authored a number of lighter works on the history and culture of China. Historians have come to see his major contributions as opening China to missionary activity and interpreting China to the West.

Further reading: Ralph R. Covell, *W. A. P. Martin: Pioneer of Progress in China* (Washington, D.C.: Christian University Press, 1978); ———, "W. A. P. Martin (1827–1916): Promoting the Gospel through Education and Science," in Gerald H. Anderson, et al., eds. *Mission Legacies: Biographical Studies of the Modern Missionary Movement* (Maryknoll, N.Y.: Orbis Books, 1998): 183–89; William A. P. Martin, *A Cycle of Cathay* (New York: Fleming H. Revell, 1897); ———, *Siege in Peking* (New York: Fleming H. Revell, 1900); ———, *The Lore of Cathay* (New York: Fleming H. Revell, 1912).

Martyn, Henry (1781–1812) *pioneer Protestant missionary among Muslims*

Henry Martyn was born in Truro, Cornwall, England, of humble background. He was able to attend CAMBRIDGE UNIVERSITY, where he was influenced by Charles Simeon, the renowned minister of Trinity Church, and decided to be a missionary. He served with Simeon at Trinity briefly, and then accepted a commission as a chaplain with the East India Company, for whom he worked for four years, first at Dinapore (1806–09) and then at Cawnpore (1809–10).

While in India, he discovered his linguistic talents while working with Baptists on a Bible translation. He went on to complete a New Testament in Urdu, then rendered it into Persian, and supervised a translation into Arabic. His missionary focus on Muslims rather than Hindus explains his translation work in the most common Muslim languages. He also educated himself on Islam.

In 1810, suffering from tuberculosis, he moved to Persia (Iran), hoping the dry climate would assist his recovery. In light of what he learned there, he revised his Persian translation completely, eventually giving a copy to the shah. While in Iran, he engaged in a literary debate with Muslim clerics, the results of which were published in 1824 as *Controversial Tracts on Christianity and Mohammedanism.*

In 1812, only 32 years old, he died at Tocat. In his brief life he made a considerable impact on his contemporaries, especially the Armenians (who cared for his body after his death). His conciliatory approach to Muslims was followed by his 19th-century successors, though it was sometimes ignored in the changing environments of the 20th century.

Today, the Henry Martyn Trust promotes the world missionary movement, in part by supporting the Henry Martyn Centre, a library at Westminster College, Cambridge, focused on the study of missions and world Christianity.

See also MIDDLE EAST.

Further reading: Henry Martyn, *Christian India; or, An Appeal on Behalf of 900,000 Christians in India Who Want the Bible. A Sermon, Preached at Calcutta, on Tuesday, January 1, 1811, for Promoting the Objects of the British and Foreign Bible Society* (Calcutta, India: printed by P. Ferris, 1811); John R. C. Martyn, *Henry Martyn (1781–1812) Scholar and Missionary to India and Persia: A Biography* (Lewiston, N.Y.: Edwin Mellen Press, 1999); Jesse Page, *Henry Martyn of India and Persia* (London: Pickering & Inglis, n.d.); John Sargent Jr., *Memoir of the Rev. Henry Martyn, B. D.: Late Fellow of St. John's College Cambridge and Chaplain to the Honourable East India Company.* (Hartford: G. Goodwin and Sons, 1822); *Life and Letters of Henry Martyn,* Banner of Truth Trust, 1986); George Smith, *Henry Martyn* (London, Religious Tract Society, 1892).

Mary I, queen of England (1516–1558) *champion of Roman Catholicism in England*

Daughter of HENRY VIII and ruler of England for five tumultuous years (1553–58), Mary I was born on February 18, 1516. She was the only surviving offspring of Henry's brief marriage to Catherine of Aragon. While Henry awaited the birth of a son, Mary was generally recognized as the heir to the throne. However, once Henry moved to divorce Catherine, Mary also fell from his favor, although she enjoyed a brief respite after Catherine's death in 1536, when she signed a statement renouncing her Catholic allegiances.

In Henry's final will, she was named as second in succession to her half brother EDWARD VI (r. 1547–53). Following her father's death, she lived quietly away from London, though she defied the new Protestant governing council and continued to celebrate the Roman Catholic Mass in her home. The issue did not prevent her occasional formal visits to Edward.

Following Edward's death on July 6, 1553, Mary rallied her supporters and was acknowledged the new queen on July 19. Among her first actions, she executed Northumberland, Lord President of the Council, for his plot to enthrone Lady Jane Grey.

Step by step, Mary began reversing the religious changes of her father and her brother. She restored several Catholic bishops to their posts and removed the most outspoken Protestant ones. A few, including Nicolas Ridley, Miles COVERDALE, Hugh Latimer, John Hooper, and Thomas CRANMER, were arrested.

Following her coronation, Reginald Pole was named papal legate to deal with the problems of the country's formal excommunication. Parliament quickly reinstituted the Mass and repealed a spectrum of Protestant laws.

Mary decided to marry Philip of Spain, and she moved against those who had gone into open rebellion. The leaders of the revolt were executed and with them Lady Jane Grey. Whether Mary's half sister, ELIZABETH I, was implicated has never been made clear, but mercy was shown to her as well as to many others. On November 30, 1554, in a ceremony during which Mary, Philip, and all the members of Parliament knelt before him, Pole absolved England of its past anti-Roman actions. Over the next weeks, Parliament formally repealed the remaining anti-Roman laws, and Roman Catholicism once again became the dominant practice throughout the country.

Beginning in 1555, Mary turned on the Protestant leadership. In the remainder of her reign some 277 persons were burned at the stake for heresy, prominent among them Cranmer, Latimer, Hooper, and Ridley (Coverdale having escaped to the Continent). Mary might have succeeded in permanently returning England to the Catholic fold, were it not for her chronic dropsy (edema). She died on November 17, 1558. She was succeeded by her half sister, Elizabeth, who quickly asserted her own supremacy over the church and created what became Anglicanism.

The MARIAN EXILES, those Protestants who had fled Mary's wrath, returned to England following her death, and helped vilify her memory. She was later remembered throughout the English-speaking world as "Bloody Mary." The Protestant case against her was documented in the famous FOXE'S BOOK OF MARTYRS (1563).

See also UNITED KINGDOM.

Further reading: C. S. Knighton, *Calendar of State Papers, Domestic Series Mary I, 1553–1558* (London: Public Record Office, 1998); Theodore Maynard, *Bloody Mary* (Milwaukee, Wis.: Bruce Publishing, 1955); H. F. Prescott, *Mary Tudor* (New York: Macmillan, 1953).

mass movements

The mass conversion of entire populations, often out of all proportion to evangelistic activity, has now and then swelled the world Protestant community. Such mass movements were first recognized in India in the last half of the 19th century. In the 1860s, after decades of very slow progress, the Protestant churches suddenly began to receive large groups of converts from various ethnic-tribal groups, such as those inhabiting the hill country of northeast Bengal, and from the outcaste (Dalit) population. The initial movements, which occurred in every province of India and across the spectrum of Protestant groups, took missionaries by surprise. Over the next hundred years, mass movements accounted for up to 80 percent of Protestant growth in India. Approximately 1 million Dalits converted to Christianity before World War I. Mass movements into Sikhism and Islam also took place in the same era.

The churches had previously targeted high caste individuals for conversion. They believed that Christianity could end the caste system by converting the upper class of Indian society. Once Dalits converted in large numbers, the church was forced to reorient its work to serve the lowest levels of Indian society. As a result, it lost much of its support among other groups, and it became deeply involved in the very caste system it opposed.

The mass movements lifted Christianity into the spotlight in the 20th century. The Hindu majority believes that losses to Christianity have reduced its standing relative to the Muslim community, which counts far more adherents than the 5 percent of Indians who are Christian. Christians are also more frequently involved in class struggles against the Indian elite. Mass conversions have helped provoke the growing Hindu hostility against Christians in India, which has led to laws designed to hinder conversions. Among the early church leaders who tried to confront the problems of mass movements was Anglican bishop V. S. AZARIAH (1874–1945), who proposed a program of allowing caste structures to exist for a time, especially as the church was attempting to solidify the gains of a mass movement, with the goal of eventually eliminating them. The process of eliminating caste has proved much more difficult than Azariah imagined.

Further reading: Susan B. Harper, *In the Shadow of Mahatma: Bishop V. S. Azatiah and the Travails of Christianity in British India* (Grand Rapids, Mich.: William B. Eerdmans, 2000); Mark Laing, "The Consequences of the 'Mass Movements': An Examination of the Consequences of Mass Conversion to Protestant Christianity in India," *Church History Review* 35, 2 (December 2001): 94–104. Available online. URL: http://www.ubs.ac.in/Cms/Mass%20Movements.pdf; J. W. Pickett, *Christian Mass Movements in India* (New York: Abingdon Press, 1933); J. C. B. Webster, *The Dalit Christians: A History* (Delhi: ISPCK, 1992).

Mather family

The Mathers were one of the leading New England Congregationalist families of the 17th century. They offered theological and practical guidance to the church, when religion still played a key role in shaping the Massachusetts Bay Colony.

Richard Mather (1596–1669) was a self-educated teacher in Toxteth Park, near Liverpool. A convert to PURITANISM, he was ordained to the ministry in 1620 and became pastor of a Puritan flock in Toxteth Park. In 1633, he was silenced by the authorities for refusing to conform to the practice of the CHURCH OF ENGLAND. To avoid further trouble, he, his wife, Catherine, and their sons

Samuel, Timothy, and Nathaniel moved to New England, where two more sons were born, Eleazer and Increase.

Shortly after his arrival in 1636, Mather became pastor of the North Church in Dorchester, Massachusetts, the site of his ministry for the next 34 years. He emerged as a leading figure in the colony and was frequently invited to help settle disputes within the Congregational churches. He also became the editor of *Bay Psalm Book*, the first book printed in what would become the United States. He died in Boston on April 22, 1669.

Increase Mather (1639–1723) attended Harvard and Trinity College, Dublin, Ireland. He remained in Britain while the Puritan Commonwealth was in power but returned to New England in 1660 at the restoration of the monarchy. In 1661, he became pastor of the North Church, Boston, where he stayed for the rest of his life. In 1685, he was named president of Harvard. Increase was a defender of the Congregational system and resisted the attempts of British representatives, particularly Sir Edmond Andros (1637–1714), to bring Massachusetts into conformity with Anglican practice. In 1688, he presented Massachusetts's case in England and was able to obtain a new charter that, among other things, brought the separatists at Plymouth into the colony. Increase remained active during the Salem witchcraft trials, about which he wrote one book, *Cases of Conscience Concerning Evil Spirits* (1693).

Cotton Mather (1663–1728), the last of the leading lights of the family, was born and raised in Boston. He entered Harvard when only 11 and graduated at age 15. Overcoming a pronounced stutter, Cotton was ordained in 1685 and served with his father at North Church, Boston, eventually succeeding him in 1723. By continuous study, Cotton turned himself into one of the leading scholars of his era. His library of 450 volumes was the largest personal library in North America at the time.

In 1689, Cotton published his *Memorable Providences Relating to Witchcraft and Possessions* (1689), which served as a background for the trials at Salem. He first approved of the trials, but later worked actively to end them. However, he continued to pursue the subject in his next book, *Wonders of the Invisible World* (1693). By this time, public sentiment had turned against all who had been involved in the trials, and Cotton was sharply criticized by Robert Calef, the major voice of the post-trial skeptics.

Cotton's magnum opus, *Magnalia Christi Americana* (1702), was an ecclesiastical history of New England, which explored how God's will had been manifested in the colony. He was deeply interested in science and was the first native-born American to become a fellow of the Royal Society (1713). He supported smallpox inoculation when it was still controversial. He became one of the founders of Yale.

Further reading: Barry Richard Burg, *Richard Mather of Dorchester* (Lexington: University Press of Kentucky, 1976); Increase Mather, *Life and Death of Richard Mather* (Cambridge, Mass.: Harvard University Press, 1969); Robert Middlekauff, *The Mathers; Three Generations of Puritan Intellectuals, 1596–1728* (New York: Oxford University Press, 1971); Kenneth B. Murdock, *Increase Mather: The Foremost American Puritan* (Cambridge, Mass.: Harvard University Press, 1925); Kenneth Silverman, *The Life and Times of Cotton Mather* (New York: Harper & Row, 1984); Barrett Wendell, *Cotton Mather, Puritan Priest* (New York: Dodd, Mead, 1891; reprint, Cambridge, Mass.: Harvard University Press, 1925).

McPherson, Aimee Semple (1890–1944)
evangelist and founder of Foursquare Gospel Church

Aimee Semple McPherson was born on October 9, 1890, near Ingersoll, Ontario. Named Beth Kennedy, as a child she took the name Aimee Elizabeth. She was raised in the SALVATION ARMY.

She was 17 when she married Robert James Semple (1881–1910), an evangelist for the new Pentecostal movement. Three years later, though Aimee was pregnant, they left for Hong Kong to work with the fledgling Pentecostal church started by Alfred G. Garr (1874–1944). After her husband contracted typhoid fever and died, Aimee took her newborn back to the United States, where she joined with her mother as part of a traveling revival team. In 1912, she married salesman Harold Steward McPherson.

Aimee Semple McPherson launched her own career as a traveling evangelist in 1916, with Los Angeles as her base of operations. To supplement her work, she founded *The Bridal Call* periodical. Opposing her career, McPherson divorced her.

By 1923, she had built the 5000-seat Angelus Temple in Los Angeles and opened the Lighthouse of International Foursquare Evangelism (L.I.F.E.) Bible School. Accepting ordination from BAPTISTS, she then founded the INTERNATIONAL CHURCH OF THE FOURSQUARE GOSPEL. The "Foursquare Gospel" is derived from Albert Benjamin SIMPSON's "Fourfold Gospel," which emphasized Jesus as Savior, Sanctifier, Healer, and coming King. McPherson changed Sanctifier to Baptizer in the Holy Spirit, a reference to the unique Pentecostal teaching.

In 1924, McPherson became the first female to receive a Federal Communications Commission (FCC) license, which she used to start her own radio station, the first in America owned and operated by a religious institution. It took the call letters KFSG (Kalling Four Square Gospel). Her broadcasts gave her a new level of national fame, far beyond that achieved by her flamboyant services at Angelus Temple.

In 1926, McPherson disappeared for a month after swimming in the Pacific Ocean. The search for her body was front-page news until she reappeared in Mexico and claimed she had been kidnapped. While followers accepted the story, a more skeptical press speculated about an illicit affair. However, she was able to live down the scandal and continue building her institutions.

By the time McPherson died on September 27, 1944, there were more than 400 congregations attached to the Church of the Foursquare Gospel in North America and some 200 mission stations in countries overseas, many led by female minis-

son, *In the Service of the King: The Story of My Life* (New York: Boni & Liveright, 1927); ———, *The Second Coming of Christ: Is He Coming? How Is He Coming? For Whom Is He Coming?* (Los Angeles: Aimee Semple McPherson, 1921); ———, *This Is That* (Los Angeles: Bridal Call, 1919); Thomas, Lately, *Storming Heaven* (New York: William Morrow, 1970).

medical missions

Medical missions were health facilities and programs set up in Asian and African countries by Christian doctors and nurses from the West. The aim was to win local friends for the missionary enterprise, while expressing a Christian concern for the ill as inspired by the New Testament.

In the 1830s, Karl Gutzlaff (1803–51), a German serving with the Dutch Missionary Society, suggested that medical facilities be set up in CHINA to share Western medicine and Gospel literature. His idea led to the founding in 1838 of the Medical Missionary Society in China, with the backing of doctors, missionaries, businessmen, and some Chinese officials. Among the founders was Dr. Peter PARKER, a physician already in China with the support of the AMERICAN BOARD OF COMMISSIONERS FOR FOREIGN MISSIONS.

The medical missions raised serious questions from the start. Some missionaries wanted evangelistic goals to take precedence over medical work, and physicians had to guard the integrity of their calling. Some churches were slow in supporting the work due to longstanding doctrinal controversies. However, once established, the idea of medical missions gained ground and steadily expanded. China became the exploratory field, as various types of facilities (dispensaries, specialized hospitals, mental health services, and so forth) were opened and tested.

The idea was exported to India in the 1860s, with the CHURCH MISSIONARY SOCIETY opening the first facilities. In 1869, the Woman's Foreign Missionary Society of the Methodist Episcopal Church commissioned Clara SWAIN, who established her center in Bareilly in northern India the next year. The anti-Christian ruler of the region

Aimee Semple McPherson (1890–1944), Pentecostal healer and founder of the International Church of the Foursquare Gospel *(Library of Congress)*

ters. While she was by no means the first female ordained to the ministry, nor even the first to found a DENOMINATION, none before her were able to make such an impact on popular American religion or attain such an international presence. Her son, Rolf Kennedy McPherson, succeeded her as head of the church.

Further reading: Edith L. Blumhofer, *Aimee Semple McPherson. Everybody's Sister* (Grand Rapids, Mich.: William B. Eerdmans, 1993); Aimee Semple McPher-

was so impressed with her efforts that he donated land for a women's hospital, built in 1872. Swain's efforts opened new horizons for women missionaries. By the 1880s, medical missions had broad support among those Western Protestant churches that were committed to the world missionary endeavor.

The missions helped pave the way for the development of local medical establishments on a Western model. For example, the Medical Missionary Society in China (superseded in 1886 by the China Medical Missionary Association) published a professional periodical, trained local staff, and eventually opened the Peking Union Medical College. A decade earlier, Edith Brown opened the School of Medicine for Christian Women in India. China would retain the largest number of Protestant supported medical facilities until 1950, with India a close second.

After 1880, the missions expanded to other countries. A notable effort in Korea began in 1884 with the arrival of Presbyterian physician Horace Newton Allen. At the time, no missionaries were allowed in the country, but Allen's successful treatment of the queen's seriously wounded nephew during a palace revolt brought an end to exclusion. In Africa, the Church Missionary Society started pioneering efforts in the 1870s.

The number and scope of medical missions grew steadily throughout the 20th century. Outstanding efforts were initiated by Wilfred Thomason GRENFELL (1865–1940), who pioneered missions along the coast of Labrador, and Albert Schweitzer, who after writing a historical study of 19th-century BIBLICAL CRITICISM devoted his life to serving the people of Gabon, Africa. Schweitzer's hospital at Lambarene became world famous, and he won the Nobel Peace Prize in 1953.

In the mid-20th century, missionary theorist William Ernest HOCKING (1873–1966) argued cogently that evangelism should yield priority to medical and social work in the missionary endeavor. His idea gained support as postcolonial governments revived the old hostility to foreign missionaries. Indigenous leaders took charge of

the new churches that replaced the old missions, but trained medical professionals continued to be welcomed into most areas of the new countries.

As the 21st century begins, medical missions are a thriving part of church life. More agencies have joined the effort and personnel has increased. Efforts have focused on age-old scourges such as malaria and on the new pandemic of HIV/AIDS.

Further reading: Margaret I. Balfour and Ruth Young, *The Work of Medical Women in India* (London: Oxford University Press, 1929); Harold Balme, *China and Modern Medicine a Study in Medical Missionary Development* (London: United Council for Missionary Education, 1921); K. William Braun, *Modern Medical Missions* (Burlington, Iowa: Lutheran Literary Board, 1932); Ernest H. Jeffs, *The Doctor Abroad: The Story of the Medical Missions of the London Missionary Society* (London: Livingstone Press, 1934); John Lowe, *Medical Missions: Their Place and Power* (New York: Fleming H. Revell, 1886).

Melancthon, Philip (1497–1560) *leading theologian of the Lutheran Reformation*

As professor of Greek at WITTENBERG, Philip Melancthon became Martin LUTHER's intellectual right hand. It was Melancthon who formulated a systematic defense of the Lutheran position, and who wrote several of the Reformation's most important documents, especially the AUGSBURG CONFESSION OF FAITH.

Melancthon was born at Bretten, Unterpfalz (now Baden), on February 16, 1497. In 1507, he went to live with his grandmother Elizabeth, sister of the noted humanist Johann REUCHLIN. While studying Greek and Latin, he corresponded with Reuchlin, who persuaded him to change his name from Schwarzerd to its Greek equivalent, Melancthon. Two years later, the 12-year-old Melancthon entered the University of Heidelberg. He won his baccalaureate in 1511, but the university refused him a master's degree in 1512 because of his youth. He continued his studies at Tübingen, where he learned jurisprudence, mathematics, and medicine. In 1514, he was granted his master's degree and became an instructor at the university. Only then did he begin his systematic study of theology and the Bible. In 1518, the relatively new University of Wittenberg offered him the professorship in Greek, largely on the recommendation of Reuchlin.

Melancthon arrived at Wittenberg just as the debates over Martin Luther's NINETY-FIVE THESES were beginning. Under Luther's guidance, he continued his study of theology, which became the focus of his most popular lectures. In spite of his leading role in the shaping of the Reformation, he never accepted ordination, nor was he known to preach. However, his first treatise on theology was reprinted more than 100 times during his lifetime.

More conciliatory than Luther, Melancthon made an ideal coleader of the Lutheran movement, providing a diplomatic counterpart to Luther's blunt and often abrasive language. He participated in the 1529 MARBURG COLLOQUY, an attempt to unite Lutherans with Ulrich ZWINGLI and his Reformed Church followers from SWITZERLAND, but he stood by Luther in defense of the latter's stance on the LORD'S SUPPER. In the wake of this failure to attain Protestant unity, Melancthon became the principal author of the Augsburg Confession, a concise statement of the Lutheran position presented to the Imperial Diet (Reichstag) at Augsburg in 1530. The statement stressed that Protestants believed in the Universal Church and did not want to leave the Catholic fold, and it refrained from specifying the many Roman Catholic beliefs that Protestants rejected. However, when the confession failed to win Catholic approbation, Melancthon became a more forceful apologist for the full Lutheran position. The confession became the defining document of the emerging Lutheran Church.

Melancthon took the lead in introducing the Reformation to the states of Wurtemberg, Brandenburg, and Saxony. His role became even more central following Luther's death in 1546. He led the Lutheran opposition to the Augsburg Confession of Faith of 1548, when the diet at Augsburg tried to enact a temporary doctrinal settlement between Catholics and Protestants.

Melancthon's more conciliatory posture led him to assert that many Catholic practices were adiaphorous (neither good nor bad) and hence permissible. For example, he did not oppose Roman Catholic episcopal authority. Such concessions turned many Protestants against him, and he spent the last years of his life in almost continuous controversy with his colleagues.

Melancthon's early theological defense of the Lutheran position appeared in "Loci Communes," which was largely complete by the edition of 1535. By the end of his life, however, he had rejected some of Luther's important ideas, including CONSUBSTANTIATION in the elements of the Lord's Supper. In his final view, the elements facilitated a spiritual communion between Christ and the believer, a position not unlike that proposed by John CALVIN. After more than four decades teaching at Wittenberg, Melancthon died on April 19, 1560.

In the 1570s, there was a severe reaction against what was termed the Philippists or Crypto-Calvinists, and Luther's position on the Lord's Supper was reasserted in the FORMULA OF CONCORD of 1580. Melancthon's approach was largely rejected, and his historical status declined

Melancthon's position as a great leader was once again recognized in the 18th century. Since then, he has been particularly remembered for his biblical studies, especially on Paul's epistles, and his assistance in Luther's translation of the Bible. He was also the first theologian to construct a history of dogma and the first Protestant to write on theological method. His significant intellectual accomplishments in a variety of fields modeled the ideal of the learned Lutheran minister that has survived to the present. Many Lutheran institutions and churches participated in the Melanchthon Quinquennial in 1997, celebrating the 500th anniversary of his birth.

Further reading: Scott H. Hendrix and Timothy J. Wengert, eds., *Philip Melanchthon Then and Now*

(1497–1997): Essays Celebrating the 500th Anniversary of the Birth of Philip Melanchthon, Theologian, Teacher, and Reformer (Columbia, S.C.: The Eastern Cluster of Lutheran Seminaries, 1999); Clyde Leonard Manschreck, *Melanchthon, the Quiet Reformer* (New York: Abingdon Press, 1958); Philip Melancthon, *Melanchthon on Christian Doctrine: Loci Communes 1555,* ed. and trans. by Clyde L. Manschreck (New York: Oxford University Press, 1965); ————, *A Melanchthon Reader,* ed. and trans. by Ralph Keen (New York: Peter Lang, 1988).

Mennonites

The Mennonites emerged in the 1540s to consolidate and carry on the tradition of the Swiss Brethren and the first generation of ANABAPTISTS. The movement had been rocked by the martyrdom of most of its founders, the failed revolt led by Thomas Münzer (c. 1490–1525), the violence at Münster (1533), and the apocalyptic preachings of Melchior Hoffman (1500–45). At that critical juncture, Roman Catholic priest Menno SIMONS (1492–1561) converted to the Anabaptist faith and began to provide the movement with the steady and theologically sound leadership it needed.

Simons embraced the idea of the believers' church; only those who had experienced faith and were ready to live disciplined Christian lives could belong. In response to the Münster incident, he called for a life centered on love and nonresistance to evil, which to him implied complete pacifism. Within the church, the ban (disfellowshipping) became the means of exercising authority. Simons was able to locate havens for Mennonite believers in Holland, Germany, and DENMARK, which allowed the group to ride out the worst periods of persecution.

The Mennonites have produced several confessions of faith, of which the Dordrecht Confession of 1632 is the most authoritative. Originally written to unite the Dutch and Swiss Anabaptists, it also found approval among the AMISH, a strict branch of Mennonites that split off in Switzerland in the 1690s under the leadership of Jacob Amman. The confession affirmed traditional Christian doctrines of God, Christ, and salvation, but highlighted some distinctive practices such as the ordinance of FOOT WASHING and the separated life. Mennonites are not allowed to swear oaths or inflict pain, harm, or sorrow upon anyone; they are required to shun those who have been disfellowshipped.

Mennonites tended to be farmers and artisans. They tried to live quiet lives with as little contact with the secular government as possible. They often confronted crises when rulers tried to press them into military service, which led many of them to migrate to North America.

As the 21st century begins, there are an estimated 850,000 Mennonites in the world, the largest numbers in the United States, CANADA, and the Democratic Republic of the Congo. More than a third of all Mennonites now reside in Africa and Asia. In popular reference, the Mennonite label often covers the closely related Amish and Hutterites, and even the other classical pacifist churches, the QUAKERS and BRETHREN.

In the 20th century, an attempt began to build closer fellowship among the geographically scattered and doctrinally divided Mennonites. This resulted in the formation of the MENNONITE WORLD CONFERENCE. Mennonites have been prominent in efforts to bring world peace.

See also RADICAL REFORMATION.

Further reading: Cornelius J. Dyck, *An Introduction to Mennonite History* (Scottdale, Pa: Herald Press, 1993); Ross T. Bender and Alan P. F. Sell, eds., *Baptism, Peace and the State in the Reformed and Mennonite Traditions* (Waterloo, Ontario: Wilfred Laurier University Press, 1991); Leo Driedger, *Mennonites in the Global Village* (Toronto: University of Toronto Press, 2000); ————, and Donald Kraybill, *Mennonite Peacemaking: From Quietism to Activism* (Scottdale, Pa: Herald Press, 1994); C. Arnold Snyder, *Anabaptist History and Theology* (Kitchener, Ontario: Pandora Press, 1995)

Mennonite World Conference

The Mennonite World Conference (MWC) is an international fellowship of Christian churches that derived from the Swiss Brethren movement of the RADICAL REFORMATION. The groups in this tradition, which coalesced late in the 16th century as the Mennonite movement, are known for their belief in separation of church and state, their rejection of infant BAPTISM, their devotion to a simple Christian lifestyle, and their commitment to pacifism. Most groups have the word *Mennonite* in their name, but some do not, such as the Brethren in Christ.

The MWC comprises some 87 Mennonite and Brethren in Christ national churches from 48 countries around the world. The MWC provides a context for fellowship, cooperation, and mutual support. Gatherings and other events provide a time for learning, deepening faith, and calls to faithful living. Given that the majority of the member churches are no longer of European heritage, the MWC has reoriented itself to emphasize the Mennonite community as a single global congregation.

Efforts were made to found a worldwide Mennonite fellowship early in the 20th century. An international gathering was held in 1925 in SWITZERLAND to commemorate the first Anabaptist baptism in 1625. The third conference in 1936 marked the conversion of Menno Simons to Anabaptism. The mid-century transformation of mission churches into autonomous bodies created even more impetus toward cooperation. In the years since World War II, the periodic conferences evolved into a more permanent structure.

The MWC maintains offices in the United States, CANADA, FRANCE, and ZIMBABWE.

Further reading: Ross T. Bender and Alan P. F. Sell, eds., *Baptism Peace, and the State in the Reformed and Anabaptist Traditions* (Waterloo, Ontario: Wilfrid Laurier University Press, 1991); Diether Gotz Lichdi and Loretta Kreider, eds., *Mennonite World Handbook: Mennonites in Global Witness* (Carol Stream: Mennonite World Conference, 1990); C. Arnold Snyder, *From Anabaptist Seed* (Kitchener, Ontario/Scottdale, Pa.: Pandora Press/Herald Press, 1999).

Menno Simons   *See* SIMONS, Menno.

Messianic Judaism

Messianic Judaism is a Protestant movement that emerged in the last half of the 20th century among believers who were ethnically Jewish but had adopted an Evangelical Christian faith. Protestants had pursued efforts to evangelize Jewish people since the 19th century, but the JEWISH MISSIONS always assumed that converts would be integrated into the larger world of Gentile believers, and would abandon Jewish culture and language. Jewish evangelists, however, continued to use many Hebrew words and names, for example calling Jesus *Yeshua* and the Hebrew scripture *Tenach*. They would also refuse to pronounce the name of the deity and instead referred to G-d or Y—h.

By the mid-20th century, many ethnic Jewish believers had begun to think about culture as a separate category from faith. By the 1960s, a new effort to create a culturally Jewish Protestant Christianity emerged among individuals who began to call themselves Messianic Jews. Such individuals considered themselves to be fully Jewish (though Jewish communities tended to disown any Jew who converted to Christianity). They continued to maintain a Jewish lifestyle, by celebrating traditional Jewish holidays such as Passover and observing those customs that did not contradict the New Testament.

In 1975, the new movement captured control of the Hebrew Christian Alliance, one of the older organizations dedicated to evangelism among the Jewish population of America. The movement was influenced by Jews for Jesus, which is also interested in the Jewish cultural heritage, but unlike that organization, Messianic Jews form their own congregations, which they term synagogues. This development has most angered traditional Jewish leaders, who suggest that Messianic Jews deceive potential converts by implying that their synagogues still practice Judaism.

Messianic Jews have adopted an Evangelical Christian perspective (some from the Reformed tradition and some from the Pentecostal). They emphasize ESCHATOLOGY, especially the role of the

Jewish people in the end-time scenario. In the 1970s and 1980s, many of them joined in the speculation popularized by Baptist minister Hal Lindsey that the formation of the state of Israel in 1948 was the beginning of the last generation before Christ's return in 1988.

The Messianic movement has been strongest in the United States and CANADA, but has been exported to other countries with a significant Jewish presence, such as England, FRANCE, and ARGENTINA. Believers have had a number of confrontations with Israeli authorities as individuals have unsuccessfully tried to become Israeli citizens under Israel's Law of Return.

Messianic Jews have formed a set of congregational associations representing their various Jewish backgrounds (Orthodox, Reform) and Christian perspectives (Pentecostal, non-Pentecostal). The largest group is the Union of Messianic Jewish Congregations. Non-Pentecostal congregations have affiliated with the Fellowship of Messianic Jewish Congregations.

See also EVANGELICALISM; PENTECOSTALISM.

Further reading: Arnold G. Fruchtenbaum, *Hebrew Christianity: Its Theology, History, and Philosophy* (Washington, D.C.: Canon, 1974); Philip E. Goble, *Everything You Need to Know to Grow a Messianic Yeshiva* (South Pasadena, Calif.: William Carey Library, 1974); Carol Harris-Shapiro, *Messianic Judaism: A Rabbi's Journey through Religious Change in America* (Boston: Beacon Press, 1999); Paul Liberman, *The Fig Tree Blossoms: Messianic Judaism Emerges* (Harrison, Ark.: Fountain, 1976); David Rausch, *Messianic Judaism: Its History, Theology and Polity* (Lewiston, N.Y.: Edward Mellen Press, 1982).

Methodism

Methodism began as a movement to revitalize the 18th-century CHURCH OF ENGLAND, though it eventually emerged as an independent denomination of churches that spread widely in the British Isles and North America. The movement grew from the work of John WESLEY (1703–91), an Anglican minister who in 1738 had an intense religious experience that climaxed a period of personal religious searching. Together with his brother Charles WESLEY (1708–88), who had had a similar awakening, he began to found religious societies, groups that met informally for prayer, religious discussion, and spiritual nurturing in London and then throughout the British Isles. In his extensive travels in England and IRELAND, Wesley called people to a personal experience of the faith into which most of them had already been baptized. Those who assembled in the Methodist societies tried to grow toward holiness or perfection.

Wesley commissioned a number of lay preachers, who, though placed in charge of leading workshop, were not authorized to serve the SACRAMENTS, a practice reserved for the ordained ministry. Wesley did not want to break with the established church, and he urged Methodists to remain active in their parishes and receive the sacraments from their local priest.

Wesley inherited a Calvinist theological tradition mediated by British PURITANISM, but he adopted the variation developed by Dutch theologian Jacob Arminius (1560–1690), who rejected PREDESTINATION. Wesley taught that Christ had atoned for all humans, and God's grace had spread to everyone. This *prevenient* grace allowed anyone to respond to the Gospel of Christ, repent of their sins, and come to faith. The Wesleyan emphasis on the free grace of God became the basis of global evangelism. Wesley also developed a doctrine of holiness. The Christian's life should be structured toward the goal of growing in grace toward perfection in love, as evidenced by holy living and social action.

In the 1760s, Wesley sent preachers to the American colonies to organize societies. When the United States emerged as a new country without an established church, Wesley assumed the role of a BISHOP and ordained ministers who would create an independent American Methodist organization. In 1784, the American leaders organized the

Methodist Episcopal Church (now the United Methodist Church) and accepted ministerial orders from Wesley through his representative, Thomas COKE (1747–1814). British Methodists remained a fellowship within the Church of England until 1795 when, following Wesley's death, the Wesleyan Conference reorganized as a dissenting church.

Through the 19th century, both the Methodist Episcopal Church and the Wesleyan Conference experienced a number of schisms, and new Methodist bodies emerged. In the 20th century, however, the process was reversed, and a series of mergers resulted in the UNITED METHODIST CHURCH in the United States and the METHODIST CHURCH in Great Britain.

However, not all American Methodists affiliated with the United Methodist Church, especially AFRICAN-AMERICAN METHODISTS, who have been a vital part of the movement. At two points, early in the 19th century and immediately after the Civil War, large numbers of black Methodists left the predominantly white bodies that existed at the time to form such groups as the African Methodist Episcopal Church, the African Methodist Episcopal Zion Church, and the Christian Methodist Episcopal Church. The majority of African-American Methodists still remain separated from United Methodism, though merger talks have periodically been pursued.

John Wesley's doctrine of perfection gave birth to the HOLINESS MOVEMENT in 19th-century America. Adherents considered perfection not as a distant goal but as the norm of Christian life. In the 1880s, Methodist leaders criticized what they saw as an overemphasis on this particular theme, and many Holiness advocates began to leave and form independent Holiness churches. The Holiness movement itself later spawned PENTECOSTALISM.

Methodists were early participants in the Protestant world missionary movement. British and American churches founded missions on every continent. Since World War II, most of these mission churches have become autonomous.

A statue of John Wesley (1703–91), founder of Methodism, located in Washington, D.C. *(Institute for the Study of American Religion, Santa Barbara, California)*

Further reading: Nolan B. Harmon, ed., *Encyclopedia of World Methodism*, 2 vols. (Nashville, Tenn.: United Methodist Publishing House, 1974); Richard P. Heitzenrater, *Wesley and the People Called Methodists* (Nashville, Tenn.: Abingdon Press, 1995); John G. McEllhenney, ed., *United Methodism in America. A Compact History* (Nashville, Tenn.: Abingdon Press, 1992); Frederick A. Norwood, *The Story of American Methodism: A History of the United Methodists and Their Relations* (Nashville, Tenn.: Abingdon Press, 1974).

Methodist Church

The Methodist Church in Great Britain carries on the Methodist movement begun in the 1740s by

John WESLEY, a minister in the CHURCH OF ENGLAND. METHODISM grew out of Wesley's intense religious experiences, his MORAVIAN CHURCH contacts, and the Calvinist traditions of British PURITANISM.

Wesley launched Methodism as a movement within the Church of England. After the American Revolution, he took steps to organize American Methodists as a separate church, but always saw the British movement as an integral part of the Church of England. Methodist groups were organized as religious societies.

Through the years, Wesley called together his fellow preachers annually. This conference of ministers took control of the movement after Wesley died in 1791. Four years later, they authorized Wesleyan preachers to begin serving the SACRAMENTS, an act generally assumed to constitute a formal break with the Church of England. The Methodist Church became a new DENOMINATION with congregations in Great Britain and IRELAND.

The need to write a constitution for the new church led to its first schism in 1797, when a group seeking a more democratic POLITY broke away to form the Methodist New Connexion. Subsequent breaks occurred in 1837 and 1857. A Primitive Methodist Church was later formed, which adapted American style revivalism to the British setting. In the late 19th century, efforts were begun to reverse the pattern. In 1932, most of the Methodists in England merged into the presently existing Methodist Church.

British Methodists were in the forefront of the globalization of Protestantism in the 19th century. Thomas COKE (1747–1814), who had been sent to America to set up the new church, formulated a vision of a global missionary enterprise following a Caribbean visit. In 1794, he presented *A Plan of the Society for the Establishment of Missions among the Heathen*. He backed his idea with his own money and eventually his life. He died in 1814 on the way to India with a group of missionaries.

Jabez Bunting (1779–1858) took the lead in founding the Wesleyan Methodist Missionary Society and supported the initial missionary thrusts in the Caribbean, INDIA, and the South Seas. The Methodists also assumed leadership in the transformation of missions into autonomous churches in the mid-20th century.

The Methodist Church, headquartered in London, England, has some 380,000 members in England, Scotland, and Wales. It is a member of the WORLD COUNCIL OF CHURCHES and the WORLD METHODIST COUNCIL. Methodists in Northern Ireland united with Methodists in the Republic of Ireland in 1878.

Further reading: Rupert E. Davies and Gordon Rupp, eds., *A History of the Methodist Church in Great Britain,* 4 vols. (London: Epworth Press, 1965); Richard P. Heitzenrater, *Wesley and the People Called Methodists* (Nashville, Tenn.: Abingdon Press, 2001); John Munsey Turner, *Modern Methodism in England* (London: Epworth Press, 1997); Gordon Wakefield, *Methodist Spirituality* (London: Epworth Press, 1999).

Mexico

Mexico has long been a largely Roman Catholic country. However, in 1857 the country adopted a new constitution that limited the power of the Catholic Church and provided an opening for Protestantism. A few missionaries had already started work just south of the Rio Grande border with the United States. In 1852, for example, Congregationalist Linda Rankin extended her small work in Brownsville, Texas, into Matamoras across the border. In 1856, she associated this work with the American and Foreign Christian Union, a Protestant agency founded specifically to convert Catholics to Protestantism. Over the next few years, she opened a string of Protestant schools in Monterrey state.

In 1859, an independent Catholic church, not in affiliation with Rome, was opened in Mexico City as the Mexican Church of Jesus. Two years later, German expatriates opened a Lutheran church in Mexico City, which established ties with the Episcopal Church in 1868 and began to grow as the Episcopal Church of Jesus. BAPTISTS established an initial church in 1862, which prompted American Baptists to begin supporting a Mexican mission.

Some 15 American churches had set up multiple centers by 1900. The Presbyterians, who entered in 1872, had the most success; the National Presbyterian Church of Mexico today has more than a million members. Among groups who entered Mexico toward the end of the century, the CHURCH OF JESUS CHRIST OF LATTER-DAY SAINTS, the JEHOVAH'S WITNESSES, and the SEVENTH-DAY ADVENTIST CHURCH have received notable response. Like the Presbyterians, the Witnesses have more than a million members.

The year 1910 proved another turning point in Mexican Protestant history, as a new set of antichurch laws were instituted. While primarily aimed at the Roman Catholic Church, the laws also referred to Protestant churches, and a number of American groups withdrew their personnel. In 1917, the older DENOMINATIONS worked out a comity agreement to prevent competition and overlapping work. The agreement transferred some congregations from one church body to another in whose territory it was located. These transfers became a matter of intense anger on the part of many church members who were not consulted.

The AZUSA STREET REVIVAL occurred only hours from the Mexican border; undoubtedly, Mexicans who attended the revival meetings in Los Angeles were the first to bring the Pentecostal message to their homeland. Some converts affiliated with the ASSEMBLIES OF GOD as early as 1915. Besides the Assemblies, the CHURCH OF GOD OF PROPHECY, and the CHURCH OF GOD (CLEVELAND, TENNESSEE) have substantial work. Three independent indigenous Pentecostal churches are also noteworthy, the Church of God in the Mexican Republic, the Apostolic Church of Faith in Jesus Christ (JESUS ONLY PENTECOSTALS), and the LIGHT OF THE WORLD CHURCH (Iglesia la Luz del Mundo). The latter is controversial for its non-Trinitarian theology and its rapid growth. It now includes 4 to 5 million members scattered across Mexico, CENTRAL and SOUTH AMERICA, the United States, CANADA, SPAIN, and AUSTRALIA.

Though experiencing spectacular growth in the 20th century, by its end the Protestant community still represented less than 7 percent of

The oldest Methodist Church in Mexico City
(Institute for the Study of American Religion, Santa Barbara, California)

the Mexican population. However, it was large enough to support several ecumenical organizations, including the Evangelical Federation of Mexico, affiliated with the WORLD COUNCIL OF CHURCHES, the Pentecostal Fraternal Association, which includes the indigenous Pentecostal bodies, and the Confraternidad Evangélica Mexicana, affiliated with the WORLD EVANGELICAL ALLIANCE.

Further reading: D. J. Baldwin, *Protestants and the Mexican Revolution* (Chicago: University of Illinois Press, 1990); Kurt Derek Bowen, *Evangelism and Apostasy: The Evolution and Impact of Evangelicals in Modern Mexico* (Montreal: McGill-Queens University Press, 1996); John Wesley Butler and Francis J. McConnell, *History of the Methodist Episcopal Church* *in Mexico: Personal Reminiscences, Present Conditions, and Future Outlook* (New York: Methodist Book Concern, 1918); Wm. A. Ross, *Sunrise in Aztec Land: Being an Account of the Mission Work That Has Been Carried on in Mexico since 1874 by the Presbyterian Church in the United States* (Philadelphia: Presbyterian Committee of Publication, 1922).

Middle East

Christianity originated in the Middle East and has been present there in varying levels of strength throughout the centuries. When Protestants began thinking globally in the early 19th century, the region was Muslim territory with pockets of Christians and Jews, and was ruled by the Muslim Ottoman Empire.

The first Western Protestant presence in the Middle East came from England, thanks to the careers of three men, Henry MARTYN (1781–1812), Joseph WOLFF (c. 1795–1862), and Samuel ZWEMER (1867–1952). Martyn surrendered his Anglican parish to go to India as a chaplain with the East India Company. A linguist, he eventually translated the Bible into Urdu, Arabic, and Persian, and also studied Islam. His brief life culminated in his tour of Iran, where he engaged in polemical exchanges with Muslim scholars. His *Journals and Letters* were published in 1837, and he emerged in the public consciousness as a missionary pioneer and hero.

The son of a German rabbi, Joseph Wolff converted to Christianity, and with the support of the London Church's Ministry Among the Jews (CMJ), went to Jerusalem in 1821. As a result of his visit, the CMJ decided in 1823 to establish a permanent presence in Jerusalem, though it took a decade to accomplish that goal. Wolff spent the next 20 years traveling in the region, preaching and establishing small groups of converts. Building on Wolff's initial travels, a variety of churches arrived in the region, including the Church of Scotland (Jerusalem) and the AMERICAN BOARD OF COMMISSIONERS FOR FOREIGN MISSIONS (Lebanon). The CHURCH MISSIONARY SOCIETY (Anglican) had

previously arrived in EGYPT (1825), but it worked with the Coptic Orthodox Church rather than establish its own centers. These pioneering missions made very little progress at converting Muslims, drawing almost all of their support from former Jews, Catholics, and Orthodox Christians.

The slow spread of Protestant Christianity paved the way for Samuel Zwemer. A member of the Reformed Church in America, Zwemer was inspired by the work of Ion Keith-Falconer, who had established a center in Aden (Yemen) only to die two years later. Zwemer and a few associates founded the independent American Arabian Mission. In 1890, he settled in Aden and took over the Keith-Falconer mission. From that initial base, he traveled throughout the Arabian Peninsula, anchoring his work in clinics and hospitals in Bahrain, Kuwait, Muscat in Oman, and Basrah in Iraq. Alongside the medical centers, he opened bookrooms that distributed Bibles and Christian literature, since direct proselytizing was largely forbidden. He returned to the United States in 1929. Through his many books and editorship of *The Muslim World,* he did more than anyone in his era to champion the Protestant cause in the Middle East.

Protestant growth has been limited by the general hostility of local authorities to any evangelistic programs directed toward Muslims, and by the similar resistance of Orthodox and Catholic leaders to proselytization. However, a few Protestant groups have managed to emerge.

The most successful Protestant effort began in 1854 with the arrival of three Presbyterian missionaries in Egypt. What is now known as the Synod of the Nile of the Evangelical Church drew the great majority of its early converts from the Coptic Church. In 1869, a group of its members left to found the CHRISTIAN BRETHREN group in Egypt. Meanwhile, as Britain became more politically active in the region, an Anglican presence emerged, primarily to serve British expatriates.

The initial American Board mission in Lebanon was supplemented by later missions sponsored by American Reformed Presbyterians and Danish Lutherans. These three missions merged in the 1940s to form the National Evangelical Synod of Syria and Lebanon. Outreach among the Armenian Orthodox led to the Union of Armenian Evangelical Churches. Presbyterian work in Iran evolved into the Synod of the Evangelical Church of Iran.

In the 1840s, the CHURCH OF ENGLAND placed an Anglican bishop in Jerusalem, choosing former rabbi Michael Solomon Alexander (1799–1845). His successor, Samuel Gobat (1799–1879), redirected attention from the Jewish to the Arab community, and was the first to ordain Arabs as Anglican priests. Responsibility for Anglican work in the Middle East shifted over the next century as political changes dictated, with a significant movement of Anglican expatriates from Palestine following the creation of the modern state of Israel in 1948. In 1957, the diocese of Jerusalem was elevated in status to become an archdiocese. The work in Lebanon, Syria, and JORDAN became a separate diocese, as did the work in Egypt and the surrounding countries at a later date. In 1976, the Middle East became an autonomous province, the Episcopal Church in Jerusalem and the Middle East.

Today, Protestants constitute less than 1 percent of the population of the Middle East (from a Christian total of 7 percent). The largest percentage of Protestants may be found in Israel, but even there it is less than 2 percent. The Episcopal Church in Jerusalem and the Middle East, the Synod of the Evangelical Church of Iran, the National Evangelical Synod of Syria and Lebanon, and the Synod of the Nile of the Evangelical Church are all members of the WORLD COUNCIL OF CHURCHES and cooperate with the Middle East Council of Churches (which is dominated by the much larger Orthodox and Catholic participating bodies).

In the 20th century, a variety of Evangelical groups from the United States have begun small works in the region. Several groups have targeted Israel, motivated in part by theologies that stress the role of Israel in God's end-time plans. Others have focused on Muslim lands. Among the more notable of the Evangelical groups now operating are the CHRISTIAN AND MISSIONARY ALLIANCE (that started in Syria in 1921), the Lebanese Baptist Convention (related to the SOUTHERN BAPTIST CONVENTION), and the ASSEMBLIES OF GOD. MESSIANIC JUDAISM is growing slowly in Israel.

Beginning in the 1980s, the Middle East received renewed attention among Evangelical Protestants following the identification of the "10/40 Window" by Luis Bish, international director of the AD2000 and Beyond movement. The movement aimed to reach all the world's peoples that had not yet been evangelized. Bish noted that thousands of such peoples, having unique languages and cultures, lived between 10 degrees and 40 degrees north latitude; quite a few were found in the Middle East. While the AD2000 movement has been superseded, the 10/40 Window remains an important concept in Evangelical missiology.

See also SAUDI ARABIA.

Further reading: Gerald H. Anderson, Robert T. Cotte, Norman A. Horner, and James M. Phillips, eds., *Mission Legacies: Biographical Studies of Leaders of the Modern Missionary Movement* (Maryknoll, N.Y.: Orbis Books, 1998); David Barrett, *The Encyclopedia of World Christianity,* 2nd ed. (New York: Oxford University Press, 2001); Patrick Johnstone and Jason Mandryk, *Operation World, 21st Century Edition* (Carlisle, Cumbria, U.K.: Paternoster, 2001); J. Herbert Kane, *A Global View of Christian Missions* (Grand Rapids, Mich.: Baker Book House, 1971); J. Gordon Melton and Martin Baumann, eds., *Religions of the World: A Comprehensive Encyclopedia of Beliefs and Practices* (Santa Barbara, Calif.: ABC-CLIO, 2002); A. Scott Moreau, *Evangelical Dictionary of World Missions* (Grand Rapids, Mich.: Baker Book House, 2000).

Miller, William (1782–1849) *American religious leader who predicted Christ's return*

William Miller, whose teachings on the second coming of Christ prepared the way for the

SEVENTH-DAY ADVENTIST CHURCH and the JEHOVAH'S WITNESSES, was born on February 15, 1782, in Pittsfield, Massachusetts, and grew up in Washington County, New York. He had little formal education but was an avid reader of borrowed books. As a young man he was drawn to deism, which rejected many of the primry tenets of Christianity, but following his return from the War of 1812 he converted, affiliated with the BAPTISTS, and became a lay preacher. The attacks on Christianity by his deist acquaintances drove him to study the Bible in order to reconcile seeming contradictions. His study had an unpredicted consequence, leading him to a belief that Christ would soon return.

The keystone was Daniel 8:13–14, "Unto two thousand and three hundred days . . . then shall the sanctuary be cleansed" coupled with Daniel 9:24, "Seventy weeks [490 days] are determined upon thy people . . . to make an end to sins." He understood prophetic "days" as referring to mundane years, an idea based on biblical passages such as Ezekiel 4:6, "I have appointed thee each day for a year." Miller interpreted the second event ("an end to sins") to refer to Christ's resurrection in 33 C.E.; counting back 490 years to get Daniel's date, then adding forward 2,300 years, he arrived at the year 1843 for Christ's return ("the sanctuary be cleansed"). In 1832, he published his conclusions in the *Vermont Telegraph,* which led to a 64-page booklet the next year, *Evidences from Scripture and History of the Second Coming of Christ about the Year 1843.*

Miller toured the Northeast, expounding his ideas. While many ridiculed him, others responded favorably, and as the proposed date approached, a large Adventist movement emerged. Initially, Miller counseled supporters to remain in their local churches, but as the movement gained steam, and critics became more harsh, in the early 1840s the first Adventist congregations were founded.

Anticipation became focused on three specific days, March 21, 1843, March 21, 1844, and October 22, 1844. The failure of all three dates became known as the GREAT DISAPPOINTMENT. Some supporters responded by trying to find the error and recalculate. Others, notably Ellen G. WHITE, decided that the sanctuary being cleansed was in heaven, and that Jesus would soon appear to his followers. Her belief would become the foundation of the Seventh-day Adventist Church.

Miller published his own brief *Apology and Defense* in 1845. He admitted that he had been mistaken in his calculations, but he continued to travel and preach that Christ would return soon. He died on December 20, 1849. By then, he had lost control of the movement; more than a hundred Adventist DENOMINATIONS have arisen since, the Jehovah's Witnesses, the Seventh-day Adventists, and the WORLDWIDE CHURCH OF GOD being the most successful.

See also ADVENTISM.

Further reading: Everett N. Dick, *William Miller & Advent Crisis* (Brushton, N.Y.: TEACH Services, 1994); Joshue V. Himes, *Brief History of William Miller: the Great Pioneer in Adventural Faith* (Boston: Advent Christian, 1895); William Miller, *Apology and Defense* (Boston: Joshua Himes, 1845); ———, *Evidences from Scripture and History of the Second Coming of Christ about the Year 1843* (Brandon: Vermont Telegraph Office, 1833); Francis David Nichol, *The Midnight Cry; A Defense of the Character and Conduct of William Miller and the Millerites* (Takoma Park, Md./Washington, D.C.: Review & Herald Publishing, 1944); Ronald L. Numbers, *The Disappointed: Millerism and Millenarianism in the Nineteenth Century* (Knoxville: University of Tennessee Press, 1993).

Milton, John (1608–1674) *British Puritan poet*

John Milton was born on December 9, 1608, in London to a well-to-do family. His father was a scrivener (law writer) who also composed music. John Milton studied for the Anglican priesthood at Christ's College at CAMBRIDGE UNIVERSITY while writing poetry. After graduating in 1632, he dropped any plans for the ministry. He continued to write while pursuing studies in foreign languages and traveled across Europe. Among those he met was astronomer Galileo Galilei.

In 1639, Milton settled in London and opened a school. During the revolution and the Puritan Commonwealth, he dropped his poetic writing and focused on political pamphleteering, writing works advocating an end to BISHOPS, defending freedom of the press, and supporting the execution of Charles I. His position that the people had the right to depose and punish unjust rulers was echoed a century later in the founding documents of the United States. He assumed an official position in the Commonwealth government as secretary for foreign languages.

In 1642, Milton married for the first time. When his wife moved back to her former home after only a few weeks, Milton wrote his famous essays defending divorce. In another book, largely unknown today, he advocated polygamy as an alternative to divorce.

Milton became blind in 1651, which did not prevent his arrest as a leading supporter of the Commonwealth following the ascendancy of Charles II in 1660. While he spent only a short time in custody, upon release he found himself poverty stricken. In 1662, he moved to what is now Burnhill Row in London, where he resided for the rest of his life, dictating his most famous works, *Paradise Lost* and *Paradise Found*. *Paradise Lost*, based on the Genesis story of the Garden of Eden, concerns the fall of Satan and humanity. *Paradise Found* (1674), based on Luke 4:1–4, reflects on Christ's temptation leading to the end of Satan's reign. Both remain classics of English literature as well as statements of British PURITANISM, though Milton was always an independent thinker. He died at his family home in Buckinghamshire on November 8, 1674.

Further reading: Note: Milton studies have flourished in the 20th century, and entrance into both the primary texts and recent scholarly works is provided by John T. Shawcross, *Milton: A Bibliography for the Years 1624–1700* (1984) and Paul J. Klemp, *The Essential*

Milton: An Annotated Bibliography of Major Modern Studies (1989); John Broadbent, *John Milton: Introductions.* (Cambridge: Cambridge University Press, 1973); Cedric Brown, *John Milton: A Literary Life* (New York: St. Martin's, 1995); Douglas Bush, *John Milton: A Sketch of His Life and Writings* (New York: Macmillan, 1964); John Milton, *John Milton: The Complete Poems, Penguin English Poets,* ed. by John Leonard (London: Penguin, 1998); Don M. Wolfe, *Milton and His England* (Princeton, N.J.: Princeton University Press, 1971).

Mita's Congregation

Mita's Congregation is an indigenous Puerto Rican group that developed within the larger Pentecostal movement on the island. Juanita Garcia Pereza (1897–1970), during a long illness, had a revelation that God had chosen her as the dwelling place of the Holy Spirit. After she was healed, she carried out the command in her revelation that she found a church, organized to accord with the teachings of primitive Christianity. Pereza was subsequently seen by her followers as the instrument of God for healings. Pereza took the name Mita, meaning "Spirit of life."

Mita emphasized a triple message of love, liberty and unity. The God of love frees his people from sin and calls them to unite. Pereza is now honored as the promised Comforter mentioned in John 14:26. Because of its messianic beliefs about its founder, the church has been pushed to the fringe of the Pentecostal community; however, her impact was so great that following her death the Puerto Rican Senate suspended its meetings for three days.

Mita organized followers into an economic cooperative that now includes a set of agricultural, manufacturing, and retail businesses as well as social services. The apparent long-term goal is to create a totally self-sufficient community. The church also supports a school with classes from preschool through high school, a social service center, and a retirement home.

Mita's Congregation began to spread beyond Puerto Rico within a decade of its founding in

1940. In 1948, a minister was sent to work in the Spanish-speaking community of New York City. Under Mita's anointed successor (Teófilo Vargas Seín Aarón), the church has expanded across the United States to CANADA and into the CENTRAL and SOUTH AMERICAN countries that border on the Caribbean. In celebration of its 50th anniversary, Mita's Congregation opened a new house of worship in San Juan, Puerto Rico, with a seating capacity of 6,000.

Further reading: E. Camayd-Freixas, "The Cult of the Goddess Mita on the Eve of a New Millennium: A Socio-Anthropological Look at a Caribbean Urban Religion," *Latin American Issues.* Available online. URL: http://webpub.allegheny.edu/group/LAS/LatinAmIssues/Articles/LAI_vol_13_section_I.html. Accessed on February 15, 2004; J. Gordon Melton, *Encyclopedia of American Religions,* 7th ed. (Detroit: Gale Group, 2002).

Montgomery, Carrie Judd (1858–1946)
Pentecostalist healer and leader
Carrie Judd Montgomery was born in Buffalo, New York, in 1858. Her parents were members of the Episcopal Church, in which she was confirmed. Always a sickly child, she became an invalid following an accident. In 1879, however, she was healed through the ministry of an African-American Holiness woman, Elizabeth Mix. Montgomery wrote a book, *The Prayer of Faith* (1880), and began speaking in public about her experience. She began a periodical, *Triumphs of Faith,* in 1881 and continued editing it for the next 65 years. She became friends with Albert Benjamin SIMPSON and joined him in 1885 in the founding of the CHRISTIAN AND MISSIONARY ALLIANCE (CMA).

Montgomery transformed her Buffalo home into the Faith Rest Cottage, a place of prayer for the ill and her base for a wider healing ministry, practiced especially at HOLINESS MOVEMENT gatherings. In 1890, she moved to Oakland, California, and a short time later married George Simpson Montgomery (b. 1851), a prosperous businessman. In 1891, she

started a CMA congregation and worked closely with the SALVATION ARMY. Two years later, she opened the Home of Peace, the center of an expanding ministry that included an orphanage and school.

After hearing of the AZUSA STREET REVIVAL in Los Angeles, Montgomery began to pray for the BAPTISM OF THE HOLY SPIRIT with the accompanying sign of speaking in tongues. She actually received the baptism while visiting with a friend in Chicago in 1908. She began publicizing PENTECOSTALISM in her now widely circulated magazine. She opposed an exclusive emphasis on speaking in tongues to the exclusion of healing and other gifts of the spirit. Nevertheless, she became a charter member of the ASSEMBLIES OF GOD and in 1917 was ordained an assemblies minister.

Montgomery was cited by a number of Holiness and Pentecostal leaders as an influence on their life and ministry. Though she was not particularly active pressing the case for the ordination of women, she was a successful example that inspired many others. Montgomery published her autobiography, *Under His Wings,* in 1936. Her Home of Peace in Oakland survived her death and continues as a healing center to the present.

Further reading: Daniel E. Albrecht, "Carrie Judd Montgomery: Pioneering Contributor to Three Religious Movements." *Pneuma* 8 (Fall 1986): 101–119; Carie Judd Montgomery, *"Under His Wings": The Story of My Life* (Oakland, Calif.: Office of Triumphs of Faith, 1936); ———, with Donald W. Dayton, *The Life and the Teaching of Carrie Judd Montgomery* (New York: Garland, 1985).

Moody, Dwight L. (1837–1899) *widely popular and influential evangelist and revivalist*
Dwight Lyman Moody was born in Northfield, Massachusetts, on February 5, 1837, one of nine children. At the age of five, he was baptized in the local Unitarian church. He received only an elementary school education.

In 1854, Moody moved to Boston, where he attended a Congregational church. He was converted to Christianity by his Sunday school teacher and the next year joined the church. Moving to Chicago in 1856, he participated in various community activities, using several different churches as his base. He began his own Sunday school in 1858.

In 1860, Moody left his day job to go into the ministry full-time, and in 1861 became a city missionary for the YOUNG MEN'S CHRISTIAN ASSOCIATION. He was soon plunged into counseling with Union soldiers in the American Civil War. Meanwhile, his Sunday school grew into a church with its own building in 1863, which Moody served as a DEACON. In 1867, Moody, then president of the Chicago YMCA, built the first YMCA structure in America, and also held his first evangelistic preaching campaign in Philadelphia.

In 1869, on his first trip outside the United States, Moody met Henry Morehouse, a leader among the Plymouth BRETHREN who later introduced him to DISPENSATIONALISM, which Moody would help spread beyond the Brethren. In 1870, Ira D. Sankey (1840–1908) joined Moody in Chicago as music leader for his preaching services; Sankey helped develop the field of gospel music. Their future careers would be inseparable.

The great urban evangelistic campaigns that made Moody and Sankey famous across America actually began in the British Isles in 1873, at a meeting at the YMCA in York, England. Similar efforts followed in Sunderland, Newcastle (where Sankey introduced the first of his series of gospel songbooks), Edinburgh, Dundee, and Glasgow. In Edinburgh, he met biologist Henry DRUMMOND, who was greatly inspired by Moody's messages. After two more years of revivals in IRELAND and England, the pair returned to the United States, where Moody preached in Brooklyn, New York, and Philadelphia before returning to Chicago in 1876 to help dedicate his rebuilt church, burned in the fire of 1871.

Moody now traveled a great deal across America and England. He always drew large crowds and each campaign reported hundreds of converts, while hundreds of other nominal Christians testified to being energized and motivated to an active

Evangelist Dwight Moody (1837–99) was the most prominent Protestant spokesperson of the late 19th century. *(Library of Congress)*

Christian life. During summers at his old home in Northfield, Massachusetts, he founded several schools, including Northfield Seminary (now Northfield School for Girls) in 1879 and the Mount Hermon Massachusetts School for Boys in 1881. Later in the decade, he formed the Chicago Evangelization Society, which evolved into Moody Bible Institute.

Also at Northfield, in 1880 he began holding summer Bible conferences, which hosted pioneering student conferences. The college students Moody brought to Northfield created the STUDENT VOLUNTEER MOVEMENT in 1887.

Moody's last campaign was held in Kansas City, Missouri, in 1899. He died in Northfield on

December 22. His funeral service was led by C. I.
SCOFIELD, then the local Congregational pastor but
soon to become an influential promoter of dispensationalism via the notes he included in his
famous reference Bible.

Moody left behind an institutional legacy in
Chicago and Northfield that continues to the present, and influenced a number of people who went
on to become Protestant leaders in their own
right, from Fanny CROSBY to John R. MOTT. Moody
created the model followed by 20th-century evangelists from Billy Sunday to Billy GRAHAM. Ira
Sankey survived Moody and spent the last years of
his life as the president of Biglow and Main, a
large music publishing firm.

Further reading: Gamaliel Bradford, *D. L. Moody: A
Worker in Souls* (New York: George H. Doran, 1927);
James F. Findlay Jr., *Dwight L. Moody, American Evan-
gelist: 1837–1899* (Chicago: University of Chicago
Press, 1969); Dwight L. Moody, *New Sermons,
Addresses, and Prayers* (Cincinnati: Henry S. Good-
speed, 1877); ———, *The Overcoming Life and Other
Sermons* (New York: F. H. Revell, 1896); Wilbur M.
Smith, *Dwight Lyman Moody: An Annotated Bibliogra-
phy* (Chicago: Moody, 1948).

Lottie Moon, a pioneer female missionary with
the Southern Baptist Convention *(Southern Baptist
Historical Society)*

Moon, Charlotte "Lottie" (1840–1912)
prominent Baptist missionary in China

Possibly the most famous of the thousands of missionaries sent out by the SOUTHERN BAPTIST CON-
VENTION, Lottie Moon was a diminutive (4' 3")
woman who completed 40 years as a missionary
in CHINA. She was born in December 1840 in
Albemarle County. An uncle, James Barclay, had
been the first missionary to Jerusalem of the Disciples of Christ movement, but her family were
active BAPTISTS.

Lottie attended the Virginia Female Seminary
and the Albemarle Female Institute, from which
she received a M.A. in classics in 1861, making her
one of the most educated women in America at the
time. After the Civil War, she chose work as a
schoolteacher rather than marriage and homemak-

ing, and in 1872 became one of the first unmarried
women accepted for foreign service by the Southern Baptists. She moved to Tengchow and for the
next 40 years worked there and in Pingtu, teaching
children and evangelizing Chinese women.

Moon used her many celebrated letters home
to mobilize Southern Baptist women in America
to launch their own missionary efforts. Answering
her call, in 1888 a handful of women founded the
Woman's Missionary Union and instituted an
annual Christian offering for missions, named for
Moon in 1919. During its first century, it raised
more than $1 billion. The union is now the largest
Protestant organization for women in the world,
with a membership in excess of 1 million, as well
as the largest organized lay organization in the
Southern Baptist Convention.

Moon's letters to the Board of Baptist Foreign Missions helped push the group toward a greater utilization of female talent and led them to institute regular home furloughs for missionaries. She encouraged a greater identification with the target peoples, and criticized her fellow Baptists for their neglect of African Americans in the southern United States while they were sending missionaries to Africa.

Moon died on December 24, 1912, while sailing for a rare visit home.

See also ARMSTRONG, Annie.

Further reading: Catherine Allen, *The New Lottie Moon Story* (Nashville, Tenn.: Baptist Sunday School Board, 1980); Janet Benge, *Lottie Moon: Giving Her All for China* (WYAM Publishing, 2001); Irwin T. Hyatt Jr., *Our Ordered Lives Confess* (Cambridge, Mass.: Harvard University Press, 1976); Helen Albee Monsell, *Her Own Way: The Story of Lottie Moon* (Nashville, Tenn.: Broadman Press, 1958); Lottie Moon, *Send the Light: Lottie Moon's Letters and Other Writings,* ed. by Keith Harper (Macon, Ga.: Mercer University Press, 2002).

Moravian Church

The Moravian Church traces its history to John HUS (1373–1415), who tried to reform the church in Bohemia and Moravia a century before Martin LUTHER, and was burned at the stake for heresy. Hus's followers were known as the Unitas Fratrum (United Brethren) for two centuries. In 1620, the Habsburg rulers decided to destroy the remaining Hussite community and won a significant victory at the Battle of White Mountain on November 8 of that year. Many Hussites fled to Poland, but the

The interior of a Moravian church at Herrnhut *(Institute for the Study of American Religion, Santa Barbara, California)*

largest group eventually settled in the 1720s on the German lands of Count Nicolaus Ludwig von ZINZENDORF (1700–60), where they founded the town of Herrnhut.

At Herrnhut, Zinzendorf helped reorganize the community, which in 1727 accepted a new rule for ordering their common life. In 1735, they were able to secure episcopal orders from Daniel Ernest Jablonski (1660–1741), who received them from the Polish Moravians. Two years later, Zinzendorf was consecrated; in 1745, the CHURCH OF ENGLAND recognized the Moravian orders as legitimately apostolic.

At Herrnhut, the Moravians became aware of the new PIETISM movement centered on Halle, and found in it a spiritual resonance. The Moravians' pietism was later transmitted to John WESLEY, the founder of Methodism.

Moravians played a disproportionate role in creating the global Protestant missionary effort. In 1731, they encountered a slave named ANTHONY, who informed them of the deplorable living conditions of Africans in the Caribbean and their need for Christian nurture. A year later, John Leonhard Dober (1706–60) and David Nitschmann (1676–1758) left to begin work on St. Thomas. Missionaries were later sent to Greenland (1733), the British American colonies (1836), and SOUTH AFRICA (1737), and still later to Labrador, SOUTH AMERICA, and EGYPT. The Moravians were decades ahead of other churches in promoting the missionary enterprise.

Following Zinzendorf's death, the Moravians formed a General Synod as the highest authority in the church. As the church grew, it established semiautonomous provinces, the first in 1857: Europe, England, northern United States, and southern United States. Over the next century, additional provinces were established in JAMAICA, IRELAND, southern Africa, Suriname, Tanzania, and the eastern Caribbean. Each of these now exists as an autonomous body, and each is a member of the WORLD COUNCIL OF CHURCHES. The European Continental Province has its headquarters in the NETHERLANDS. There are approximately half a million Moravians worldwide.

Further reading: J. Taylor Hamilton and Kenneth G. Hamilton, *History of the Moravian Church: The Renewed Unitas Fratrum, 1722–1957* (Bethlehem, Pa.: Interprovincial Board of Christian Education, 1967); Edwin A. Sawyer, *All about the Moravians* (Bethlehem, Pa./Winston-Salem, N.C.: Moravian Church in America, 1990); John R. Weinlick, *Count Zinzendorf: The Story of His Life and Leadership in the Renewed Moravian Church* (New York: Abingdon Press, 1956); ———, *The Moravian Church through the Ages* (Bethlehem, Pa./Winston-Salem, N.C.: Moravian Church in America, 1996).

Morocco

Morocco has been a predominantly Muslim country for over a millennium. In 1912, it became a French protectorate, but it regained independence in 1956.

The North Africa Mission (now Arab World Ministries) introduced Protestantism to Morocco in 1884. It was joined by the Gospel Missionary Union in 1894 and the Emmanuel Mission Sahara in 1926. Following the declaration of the protectorate, the Reformed Church of FRANCE established work that continues as the Evangelical Church of Morocco.

Since 1956, Protestant and FREE CHURCH missionary efforts have met stiff resistance. A few groups were expelled, including the Gospel Missionary Union and the Emmanuel Mission Sahara. Most Protestants are expatriates. There are some 20 Protestant and Free Church groups with a total membership of around 4,000. The Evangelical Church of Morocco, the Anglican Church, the Roman Catholics, and several Eastern Orthodox churches have created the Morocco Council of Christian Churches, which is affiliated with the WORLD COUNCIL OF CHURCHES.

Further reading: David Barrett, *The Encyclopedia of World Christianity*, 2nd ed. (New York: Oxford University Press, 2001); Patrick Johnstone and Jason Mandryk, *Operation World, 21st Century Edition* (Carlisle, Cumbria, U.K.: Paternoster, 2001).

Morrison, Robert (1782–1834) *first Protestant missionary in China*

Of Scottish descent, Morrison was born on January 5, 1782, and grew up at Newcastle-upon-Tyne, England. He was apprenticed to a shoemaker but spent his leisure time reading religious texts. In 1803, he began a year at the Independent Academy at Hoxton, which prepared him to apply for support as a missionary by the LONDON MISSIONARY SOCIETY, which represented Congregationalists. After studying Chinese, he received his appointment to Canton.

The East India Company opposed the presence of Christian missionaries in territories it controlled and refused to transport Morrison to his station. Morrison sailed for the United States in 1807, where James Madison, then secretary of state, presented him with an introduction to the American consul in Canton. Christian merchants at Oliphant & Co. transported him the rest of the way to CHINA. Once in Canton, he worked as a translator for the East India Company; the job afforded him legal residence status and the time to complete a Chinese grammar and a translation of the New Testament, both published in 1814. Nevertheless, he had to operate discreetly, in light of a law against publishing books in Chinese. He lived a low-key existence and adopted local dress.

In 1820, Morrison helped found the Anglo-Chinese College at Malacca (where Milne then moved), both to continue the linguistic work and to train native evangelists who could work throughout the mainland without the legal restraints imposed on Europeans.

In 1821, Morrison completed his *Chinese Dictionary,* the six volumes of which were published by the East India Company. On a visit to England, he was elected a fellow of the Royal Society in 1824. He returned to China in 1826, where he continued his work at translating and publishing

The burial site of Robert Morrison (1782–1834), the first Protestant missionary in China *(Institute for the Study of American Religion, Santa Barbara, California)*

Christian literature in Chinese. He died at Canton on August 1, 1834.

Though Morrison made few converts directly after he baptized Tsai A-Ko (or Chai Agao), in 1814, his Bible, dictionaries, and other writings proved invaluable to the future army of missionaries who would arrive from a spectrum of Protestant groups, His gravesite in the Protestant cemetery in Macau remains a pilgrimage site.

Further reading: Maurice Broomhall, *Robert Morrison, a Master-Builder* (London: Livingstone Press, 1924); Robert Morrison, *A Dictionary of the Chinese Language,* 6 vols. (London: Black, Parbury & Allen, 1815–23); ———, *A Parting Memorial: consisting of miscellaneous discourses, written and preached in*

China; at Singapore; on board ship at sea, in the Indian Ocean; at the Cape of Good Hope; and in England; with remarks on missions, &c. &c. (London: W. Simpkin & R. Marshall, 1826); Murray A. Rubenstein, *The Origins of the Anglo-American Missionary Enterprise in China, 1807–1840* (Lanham, Md.: Scarecrow Press, 1996), ATLA monograph series no. 33.

Mott, John R. (1865–1955) *Methodist ecumenicist and missionary supporter*

John Raleigh Mott was born on May 25, 1865, in Livingston Manor, New York, but grew up in Postville, Iowa. His father, a lumber merchant, was elected the first mayor of the town.

Mott attended Upper Iowa University, a small Methodist preparatory school, but transferred to Cornell University. While there, he became an active leader in the local Young Men's Christian Association. He represented Cornell at the 1886

John R. Mott (1865–1955), missionary and ecumenical statesman *(Drew University Library)*

summer collegiate conference run by Dwight L. MOODY, and was among the hundreds of students who signed a commitment to work for world missions. Those students became the core of the STUDENT VOLUNTEER MOVEMENT (SVM).

Following his graduation in 1888, he became national secretary of the Intercollegiate Y.M.C.A. of the U.S.A. and Canada, and continued to work for the Y.M.C.A. for 50 years. During World War I, Mott served as general secretary of the National War Work Council.

Shortly after joining the Y.M.C.A. staff, Mott became chairman of the SVM executive committee. In 1895, with Karl Fries of SWEDEN, he organized the WORLD STUDENT CHRISTIAN FEDERATION (WSCF) and became its general secretary. He subsequently went on a two-year world tour and organized a number of national WSCF chapters. Thanks to his charismatic and effective leadership, he was chosen presiding officer of the World Missionary Conference in Edinburgh in 1910.

In 1900, Mott wrote possibly his most famous book, *The Evangelization of the World in This Generation.* His challenge to missionize the entire world, basic to the call of the Student Volunteer Movement, inspired a generation of Protestants to become missionaries or financial supporters.

In the years after World War I, Mott turned his attention from student work to the wider mission field and to ecumenism. In 1921, he was selected chairman of the International Missionary Council, which aimed to promote cooperation and planning among the growing number of sending agencies, and reduce the detrimental effects of competition. He worked closely with many of the new indigenous leaders of the churches that evolved from the old Western missions.

Mott was one of the founders of both the FAITH AND ORDER and LIFE AND WORK MOVEMENTS, the precursors to the WORLD COUNCIL OF CHURCHES (WCC), established in 1948. Mott's room at Oxford hosted the early morning prayer sessions in 1937 for the leaders who were drawing up plans for the future WCC. Many of those

George Müller built and maintained this orphanage in Bristol, England, in the 19th century. *(Institute for the Study of American Religion, Santa Barbara, California)*

in the room had first met Mott in the WSCF. Mott's lifetime of global work was acknowledged when he was named first honorary president of the WCC.

Mott died on January 31, 1955. He is most remembered today for aiding and celebrating the emergence of local leaders in the many new non-Western churches. After World War II, he also took the lead in bringing German and Japanese leaders back into the ecumenical fellowship.

Among Mott's many achievements was his persistent effort to preserve the historical records of the movements he aided. He helped found the Institute of Social and Religious Research and the Department of Social and Industrial Research of the International Missionary Council. His records have now been deposited at Yale University and elsewhere.

See also UNITED METHODIST CHURCH.

Further reading: Galen M. Fisher, *John R. Mott: Architect of Cooperation and Unity* (New York: Association Press, 1952); C. Howard Hopkins, *John R. Mott, 1865–1955: a Biography* (Grand Rapids, Mich.: William B. Eerdmans, 1980); John R. Mott, *The Decisive Hour of Christian Missions* (New York: Student Volunteer Movement, 1910); ———, *The Evangelization of the World in This Generation* (New York: Student Volunteer Movement, 1900); ———, *The World's Student Christian Federation* (n.p.: WSCF, 1920).

Müller, George (1805–1898) *influential leader of the Plymouth Brethren*

George Müller, whose example of living by faith became an inspiration to many across denominational lines, was born at Kroppenstaedt, Prussia, on September 27, 1805. As a young man, he attended the University of Halle, the center of German PIETISM, where he was converted to an active faith. He went to England to work with the London Society for Promoting Christianity among the Jews, but became involved with the emerging Plymouth BRETHREN movement. He resigned from his work in JEWISH MISSIONS and became a Brethren pastor in Teignmouth.

While at Teignmouth, Müller decided that he should not accept a salary but simply rely upon what God supplied through unsolicited freewill offerings. His life became legendary for the seemingly miraculously appearance of support in times of need. He moved to Bristol in 1832 to become pastor of Bethesda chapel. Two years later, he founded the Scriptural Knowledge Institution for Home and Abroad, which built day schools, SUNDAY SCHOOLS, and other educational facilities and supported missionary activity. Inspired by the example of Pietist leader A. H. Francke (1663–1727), Müller also founded the Bristol Orphanage Mission Work.

During his years at Bristol, Müller became quite famous in British Protestant circles. His church grew to more than 1,200 members, and several books were published by and about him. His story inspired many people to copy his pattern of living by faith. J. Hudson TAYLOR later built the CHINA INLAND MISSION on Müller's principles. At the age of 70, Müller turned over his affairs to his son-in-law and for the next 17 years made international missionary tours, on which he visited some 42 countries.

He died in Bristol on March 10, 1898.

Further reading: George Müller, *Answers to Prayer* (Chicago: Moody Press, 1984); ———, *Autobiography of George Müller, or A Million and Half in Answer to Prayer* (London: Nisbet, 1905); Mrs. George Müller, *Preaching Tours and Missionary Labours of George Müller (of Bristol)* (London: Nisbet, 1889); A. T. Pierson, *George Mueller of Bristol and His Witness to a Prayer-Hearing God* (Old Tappan, N.J.: Fleming H. Revell, 1899).

Murray, Andrew (1828–1917) *African educator, writer, and missionary supporter*

Andrew Murray was born in Graaff-Reinet, SOUTH AFRICA, on May 9, 1828. His father, a Scotsman, was a minister in the Dutch Reformed Church. Sent to England to attend school at the age of 10, he completed college in Scotland and pursued further work in theology and the Dutch language at Utrecht University in Holland. He was ordained at The Hague in 1848, then returned to South Africa. He served as pastor in Bloemfontein, Worcester, Cape Town, and finally Wellington, where he remained for 35 years.

Murray was cofounder of the University College of the Orange Free States (1856), the Stellenbosch Theological Seminary (1857), the Huguenot Seminary (for French-speaking Reformed pastors, 1874), and the Wellington Missionary Training Institute (1877). He also cofounded the South Africa General Mission (now the AFRICA EVANGELICAL FELLOWSHIP) and served as its first president from 1889 to his death in 1917.

Murray was a devoted follower of the KESWICK MOVEMENT and facilitated its introduction into South Africa. His many books are reflective of the Keswick emphasis on the higher life that is possible for a Christian, and have been read internationally. Murray died on January 18, 1917, in Wellington.

Further reading: J. du Plessis, *The Life of Andrew Murray of South Africa* (London: Marshall Morgan & Scott, 1919); Andrew Murray, *Andrew Murray Collection* (New York: Barbour, 1994), omnibus reprint edition; ———, *Believer's Secret of Living Like Christ* (Minneapolis, Minn.: Bethany House, 1985); ———, *The Holiest of All* (London: Nisbet, 1913); ———, *With Christ in the School of Prayer* (Old Tappan, N.J.: Fleming H. Revell, 1953), various editions.

music *See* HYMNS/MUSIC.

N

Nee, Watchman (1903–1972) *Chinese Christian founder of the Local Church*

Watchman Nee was born Ni Shu-tsu (Henry Nee) on August 4, 1903, in Swatow, Fukien, CHINA. He was raised in a Methodist family and baptized as an infant by an American Methodist bishop. He studied at the middle school of the CHURCH MISSIONARY SOCIETY (Anglican) in Foochow. In 1920, influenced by his mother's devotion to Dora Yu (1873–1931), an independent Methodist evangelist, he professed faith and assumed a new name, Ni To-sheng (or Watchman Nee). Following a call to the ministry, he moved to Shanghai, where Yu had established a school.

Nee made several symbolic breaks with his past including rebaptism by immersion (1921) and withdrawal from the METHODIST CHURCH (1922). He began to meet independently with fellow students to break bread (the LORD'S SUPPER). In 1923, he became associated with Margaret Barber (1866–1930), who introduced him to a host of British writers, most of whom were associated with the Plymouth BRETHREN, such as D. M. Panton (1870–1965), or the KESWICK MOVEMENT, such as Jesse Penn-Lewis (1861–1927) and Andrew MURRAY (1828–1917). Nee graduated from Trinity College in Foochow in 1924.

Through the mid-1920s, Nee began to work out a new understanding of Christian faith and practice, first published in *The Spiritual Man*

Watchman Nee (1903–72), the founder of the Local Church movement, as a young man in China *(Living Stream Ministry, Anaheim, California)*

(1928) and in several periodicals he edited. He also worked on a translation of Cyrus I. SCOFIELD's *Bible Correspondence Course,* a sign of his acceptance of the DISPENSATIONALISM of the Plymouth Brethren.

Crucial to Nee's thought was his concept of the church. Nee believed that denominationalism was wrong and hurtful to the church. He felt that there should be only one Christian congregation in each locale (city). He condemned and refused fellowship to those who continued to live within denominational barriers.

After founding several churches, in 1928 he established a congregation in Shanghai that became the most prominent congregation in the LOCAL CHURCH (also called Little Flock or Assembly Halls) movement. He also resumed publication of *The Present Testimony,* which became the main organ of the movement. Through the next two decades, he continued to grow the Local Church fellowship, despite the Japanese invasion and occupation of Shanghai.

In 1942, Nee (whose college degree was in chemistry) joined his brother in a business, over the opposition of his coworkers in the Shanghai church. At their request, he did not preach for the next six years, but resumed his ministry after a reconciliation in 1947. In 1952, he was arrested by the Communist government, and four years later brought before a public "accusation meeting" in Shanghai. He was sentenced to 20 years in prison, where he died on May 30, 1972.

Prior to his arrest, Nee had conveyed leadership of the movement to church leaders in Hong Kong and Taiwan, especially Witness Lee (1905–97), who eventually turned the Local Church into a worldwide movement based in the United States.

See also CHINA: HONG KONG; CHINA: TAIWAN.

Further reading: Angus I. Kinnear, *Against the Tide* (Fort Washington, Pa.: Christian Literature Crusade, 1973); Witness Lee, *Watchman Nee: A Seer of the Divine Revelation in the Present Age* (Anaheim, Calif.: Living Stream Ministry, 1991). (Also available in Chinese); Watchman Nee, *Collected Works,* 62 vols. (Anaheim, Calif.: Living Stream Ministry, 1994); ———, *The Normal Christian Church Life* (Washington, D.C.: International Students Press, 1969).

Neo-Orthodoxy

Neo-Orthodoxy emerged in Europe following the horrors of World War I, as a rejection of the liberal theology that had dominated German Protestantism for decades. The movement did not accept the 19th-century idea that humanity was progressing toward an ever more positive Christian future on earth. It found support from people who viewed the movement as a return to Protestant essentials.

The movement emerged in an intellectual climate dominated by the existentialism of Søren Kierkegaard (1813–55) and the dialectical philosophy of G. W. F. Hegel (1770–1831). For Kierkegaard, the simple straightforward statements of the Christian creeds or of typical theological works fell short of Christian truth, which was in fact not straightforward, but paradoxical. The believer holds apparently contradictory "truths" in tension. Hegel's dialectic saw truth emerging as opposites contended against each other to create a new synthesis.

Neo-Orthodoxy saw a variety of paradoxes in Christian faith—God as transcendent but self-disclosing, Christ as God and human; faith as both the gift of God but also the response of the individual. Reinhold NIEBUHR is famous for presenting Christian love as the impossible possibility. In struggling with these seemingly contradictory affirmations, theological truth emerges.

The Neo-Orthodox placed a new emphasis on the Bible and on the revealed Word of God, which takes on several meanings. The Word is primarily identified as Jesus, the Word made flesh. But the process of reading turns Scripture into the Word of God to the person reading the Bible, as God is encountered. The Word of God is also proclaimed in the witness of the church.

The movement is usually dated to Swiss theologian Karl BARTH's 1919 commentary on the Book of Romans. Within a few years, Barth found support from Emil BRUNNER, Friedrich Gogarten (1887–1968), and Eduard Thurneysen (1888–1977). Together they gave form to the new movement through the journal *den Zeiten,* founded in 1922. Their common ground was their affirmation of the transcendence of God (over against the liberal emphasis on God's imminence), the unique revelation in Jesus Christ, the authority of Scripture, and the sinfulness of mankind. Other exponents of Neo-Orthodoxy included C. H. Dodd (1884–1973) and Edwyn Hoskyns (1884–1937) in the UNITED KINGDOM; Gustaf Aulen (1879–1977) and Anders Nygren (1890–1978) in SWEDEN; H. Richard (1894–1962) and Reinhold Niebuhr in the United States; and Paul TILLICH, Dietrich BONHOEFFER, and Martin NIEMÖELLER in Germany.

With the rise of Nazism, many of the Neo-Orthodox became associated with the Confessing Church movement, and Barth was a major contributor to the BARMEN DECLARATION (1934). The Nazis tried to stamp out the movement; Tillich and Barth were forced to flee, Bonhoeffer was executed, and Niemöller imprisoned.

The movement peaked in the decades after World War II when it enjoyed a burst of support in North America, and through the ECUMENICAL MOVEMENT was carried to church centers worldwide. In the United States, it provided a home for disillusioned liberals, and was very attractive to conservatives who thought that FUNDAMENTALISM had run its course—for example, it found an amiable reception at Fuller Theological Seminary, America's leading Evangelical school.

Neo-Orthodoxy's prestige suffered somewhat when several of its supporters turned into the leading "Death of God" theologians of the 1960s. Within liberal Protestant circles, it has been partly replaced by various forms of LIBERATION THEOLOGY (many of which grew out of Neo-Orthodoxy). Within Evangelical circles, it has yielded place to theologians such as Cornelius van Til (1895–1987), who believed that Neo-Orthodoxy fell short of overcoming the problems of liberalism.

Further reading: Sydney E. Ahlstrom, ed., *Theology in America: The Major Protestant Voices from Puritanism to Neo-Orthodoxy* (New York: Bobbs-Merrill, 1967); Karl Barth, *The Epistle to the Romans,* trans. by Edwyn C. Hoskyns (New York: Oxford University Press, 1933); Emil Brunner, *Revelation and Reason,* trans. Oliver Wyon (Philadelphia: Westminster, 1946); William E. Hordern, *The Case for a New Reformation Theology* (Philadelphia: Westminster, 1959); Reinhold Niebuhr, *The Nature and Destiny of Man: A Christian Interpretation* (New York: Scribner, 1948); Cornelius Van Til, *The New Modernism: An Appraisal of the Theology of Barth and Brunner* (Philadelphia: Presbyterian & Reformed, 1947).

Netherlands

Luther's Reformation found support in the Low Countries (Belgium and the Netherlands) as early as the 1520s, but Charles V, the Holy Roman Emperor (and king of Spain), moved quickly to suppress it. Following the DIET OF WORMS, he imposed a death penalty on Lutheran supporters in his domains; the first executions occurred in 1523. Persecution did not, however, stop the appearance of the New Testament in Dutch in 1522. While LUTHERANISM was successfully repressed, ANABAPTISM grew, and beginning in the 1540s, the Reformed Church began to win support. The BELGIC CONFESSION of 1561, produced by Geneva-trained minister Guy de Brès, was accepted by a Dutch Reformed synod in 1566.

The emergence of strong support for the Reformed cause was one factor in the decision of Phillip II of Spain to send an army under the duke of Alva to enforce the anti-Reformation laws in 1567. Some 7,000 people were tried and executed. The disruption of normal life left the country in economic ruin. At this point, William of Nassau, prince of Orange (1533–84), emerged as leader of the anti-Spanish forces, and the Protestant cause in the Netherlands became identified with the drive to throw off Spanish rule. In 1581, the seven northern provinces declared their independence and the modern state of the Netherlands came into being. The Netherlands Reformed Church emerged as a unifying force in the new country.

Anabaptism had persisted in the Netherlands as well, despite a brief backlash following the disastrous communal experiment in Münster, which had been led by two Dutchmen, Jan Matthsy of Haarlem and Jan Beuckelsz. Menno SIMONS (1596–61) rescued the cause with his reformulation of Anabaptist principles, first publicized in the *Book of Fundamentals* in 1539 and refined in the next decade. His movement evolved into the Mennonite Church. The persistence of the MENNONITES as a nonestablished church helped make the Netherlands the most tolerant country in Europe over the next centuries.

A significant minority in the new state remained loyal to Catholicism. Over the next generation, efforts were made with a great deal of success to bring them into the Reformed camp. At the same time, a rift appeared in the Netherlands Reformed Church. Jacob Arminius (1660–1709) developed a form of CALVINISM that downplayed PREDESTINATION in favor of an emphasis on the free response of the individual to God's grace. His successor, Johan Wtenbogaerdt (1577–1644), was responsible for the Remonstrance (1610), the document that defined ARMINIANISM.

In response, the Reformed Church, with support from Reformed leaders in other countries, held the SYNOD OF DORT in 1618–19. The synod denounced the Remonstrants, promulgated the HEIDELBURG CATECHISM as the standard of faith, and reaffirmed the doctrine of predestination. The Remonstrants were able to return after a short period of exile, as Frederick Henry of Orange (r. 1625–47) opposed enforced uniformity. The new level of tolerance allowed the Remonstrants the opportunity to establish a seminary at Amsterdam and to open churches.

The Reformed Church, with state backing, remained the dominant religious force until 1795, when a French revolutionary army conquered the country and declared a separation of church and state. The Reformed Church never regained its privileged position. Though still the largest ecclesiastical body, when local rule returned with the fall of Napoleon, the Reformed Church faced a series of schisms in the 19th and 20th centuries that led to a multitude of dissenting DENOMINATIONS, some protesting the liberalization of the church and others declaring that it had not gone far enough. They included the Christian Reformed Church in the Netherlands (1869), the Reformed Churches in the Netherlands (1892), and almost a dozen smaller groups.

The Reformed Church in the Netherlands was taken by Dutch immigrants to such places as the United States, SOUTH AFRICA, and the various Dutch colonies. Indonesian converts to the Reformed faith migrated to the Netherlands in the 20th century and formed several Moluccan Reformed churches.

The Reformed Church became active in the ECUMENICAL MOVEMENT in the early 20th century and was a charter member of the WORLD COUNCIL OF CHURCHES (WCC); it was also active in the WORLD ALLIANCE OF REFORMED CHURCHES. The first general secretary of the WCC, W. A. Vissert HOOFT, was of Dutch Reformed heritage.

The small Lutheran contingent in the Netherlands was granted toleration in 1600. In 1633, they were able to purchase a building in Amsterdam. An association of congregations formed in 1605 evolved into the present Evangelical Lutheran Church in the Kingdom of the Netherlands.

The country's relative religious tolerance made it a refuge for various foreign dissenting groups such as the British Pilgrims, who later settled at Plymouth, Massachusetts, in 1620, and the MORAVIAN CHURCH, which settled permanently in the mid- 1700s. In the 20th century, as support for the Netherlands Reformed Church waned, a host of other Protestant groups emerged, among the more important being the SALVATION ARMY and the exclusive Plymouth Brethren.

The Netherlands Reformed Church, the Evangelical Lutheran Church in the Netherlands, and the Reformed Churches in the Netherlands are in discussions to form a United Protestant Church, to include some 2.7 million adherents. The churches are members of the LEUENBERG CHURCH FELLOWSHIP, designed to foster Lutheran/Reformed unity. In the meantime, the Roman Catholic Church, with almost 5.5 million members, has emerged as the largest church in the country, accounting for half the Christian community.

Further reading: Jean-Jacques Bauswein and Lukas Vischer, eds., *The Reformed Family Worldwide: A Survey of Reformed Churches, Theological Schools, and International Organizations* (Grand Rapids, Mich.: William B. Eerdmans, 1999); Maurice G. Hansen, *The Reformed Church in the Netherlands* (New York: Board of Publication of the Reformed Church in America, 1884); George Harinck and Hans Krabbendam, eds., *Breaches and Bridges: Reformed Subcultures in the Netherlands, Germany, and the United States* (Amsterdam: Vu University Press, 2000); E. G. Hoekstra and M. H. Ipenburg, *Wegwijs in religieus en levensbeschouwelijk Nederland. Handboek religies, kerken, stromingen en organisaties* (Kampen: Uitgeverij Kok, 2000).

Nevius, John Livingston (1829–1893)
missionary supporter of three-self independent churches

Nevius was born into a Presbyterian family in Seneca County, New York, on March 4, 1829. At the age of 15, he entered Union College in Schenectady. He graduated in 1848 and moved to Georgia to make his fortune. In 1850, he had a religious transformation and decided to enter the ministry. While studying at Princeton, he received the call to be a missionary in ASIA and was accepted for that role by the PRESBYTERIAN CHURCH. Following graduation and marriage, he and his wife left for CHINA in 1853.

Settling in Ningpo, they both learned Chinese, and Nevius began preaching and teaching in the local dialect. In 1856, he wrote a simplified catechism for new inquirers. In 1861, he moved to Chefoo in Shantung Province, where he began to suggest changes to the way missionary work was

organized. Apart from several visits back home, Nevius continued to evangelize, write, and train local leaders for three decades. Superintending a mission that extended hundreds of miles from Chefoo, he traveled to the various stations on horseback.

Nevius gradually developed a new missionary strategy, which he expounded in his 1886 book, *Methods of Mission Work*. He presented it at the second general missionary conference in Shanghai in 1889, and was invited to present it to Presbyterian missionaries in KOREA.

Nevis called for the rapid transformation of mission centers into self-propagating, self-governing, and self-supporting churches—hence the term THREE-SELF PRINCIPLES. The idea met stiff resistance at first, especially among those with implicitly racist assumptions about the suitability of Asians for leadership roles. Nevertheless, by the time Nevius died four years later, on October 9, 1893, his plan was already winning support. In Korea, each new missionary received a copy of his book, which is given partial credit for the spectacular expansion of Presbyterianism in Korea.

The effect in China was even greater. Today, the Three-Self Patriotic Movement of Protestant Churches in China, founded in 1954, with 20 million adherents is the largest Protestant body in the country.

Further reading: Samuel H. Chao, *John Livingston Nevius (1829–1893): A Historical Study of His Life and Mission Methods* (Pasadena, Calif.: Fuller Theological Seminary, Ph.D. diss., 1991); ———, *Practical Missiology: The Life and Mission Methods of John L. Nevius (1829–1893)* (London: Peter Lang, 1996); John Livingston Nevius, *China and the Chinese* (Philadelphia: Presbyterian Board of Publication, 1882); ———, *Methods of Mission Work* (Shanghai: American Presbyterian Missionary Press, 1886). ———, *The Planting and Development of Missionary Churches* (Philadelphia: Presbyterian & Reformed, 1958). Available online. URL: http://www.newchurches.com/resources/methodsofmission-Nevius.pdf; Helen Coan Nevius, *The Life of John Livingston Nevius* (New York: Fleming H. Revell, 1895); ———, *Our Life in China*

(New York: Robert Carter & Brothers, 1869); Roy E. Shearer, *Wildfire: Church Growth in Korea* (Grand Rapids, Mich.: William B. Eerdmans, 1966).

Newbigin, James E. Lesslie (1909–1998) *Indian bishop and ecumenical statesman*

James E. Lesslie Newbigin was born on December 8, 1909, at Newcastle-upon-Tyne, England. He attended Westminster College at CAMBRIDGE UNIVERSITY; following his graduation in 1936 he was ordained by the Church of Scotland and sent to INDIA as a missionary with the United Church of South India (formed by a union of Reformed and Presbyterian churches). He remained in Madras and helped found the new Church of South India, which resulted from the 1947 merger of the United Church with the Anglican and Methodist churches. He became the bishop of Madurai and Ramnad.

Newbigin attended the initial gathering of the WORLD COUNCIL OF CHURCHES, where he emerged as a major spokesperson for the new united churches in ASIA. In 1959, he was named head of the INTERNATIONAL MISSIONARY COUNCIL and continued in that post until the merger of the council with the World Council in 1961. He subsequently served as the associate general secretary of the World Council and director of its Commission on World Mission and Evangelism. In 1965, he returned to India to serve nine years as bishop in Madras. He retired in 1974 and returned to Birmingham, England.

Newbigin taught for five years at the Shelly Oaks Colleges and then took up a post as pastor of a small inner-city church. While there, he wrote three books on the claims of the church in a pluralist society: *The Other Side of 1984* (1983), *Foolishness to the Greeks* (1986), and *The Gospel in a Pluralist Society* (1989). Writing from a NEO-ORTHODOX position, Newbigin called upon Christians to share the Gospel with what he saw as a pagan Western culture. He also served a term as moderator of the General Assembly of the United Reformed Church (representing the several Presbyterian and Reformed traditions in England).

He died in London on January 30, 1998. His name now graces the Bishop Newbigin Institute for Church and Mission Studies in Madras.

Further reading: George Hunsberger, *Bearing the Witness of the Spirit: Lesslie Newbigin's Theology of Cultural Plurality* (Grand Rapids, Mich.: William B. Eerdmans, 1998); Geoffrey Wainwright, *Lesslie Newbigin. A Theological Life* (Oxford: Oxford University Press, 2000); Lesslie Newbigin, *Foolishness to the Greeks: The Gospel and Western Culture* (London: SPCK, 1986); ———, *The Gospel in a Pluralist Society* (London/Grand Rapids, Mich.: SPCK/Eerdmans, 1989); ———, *Signs amid the Rubble: The Purposes of God in Human History,* ed. and intro. by Geoffrey Wainwright (Grand Rapids, Mich.: William B. Eerdmans, 2003).

new measures

In the decades after the American Revolution, religious leaders, faced with a mostly unchurched public, sought innovative ways to attract people to Christian life. Preacher Charles Grandison FINNEY (1792–1875) introduced a series of such practices that came to be known as the "new measures."

REVIVALISM, introduced as far back as the 1740s, and CAMP MEETINGS had come to have an important role especially on the frontier. By the 1820s, Methodists, BAPTISTS and Cumberland Presbyterians had taken the lead in inviting frontier residents into the church. In that decade, Finney began holding revivals in New York and neighboring states, at which he aimed to lead believers through a crisis experience to repentance and acceptance of a new life in Christ. Taking a pragmatic approach, he refined a series of techniques that made him the leading evangelist of his era.

The "new measures" included protracted meetings, the anxious or inquirer's meeting, the anxious bench, and directed prayers for known sinners. Finney was also the first to allow women to offer verbal prayers in mixed gatherings. Protracted meetings were revivals with no set end date; they would continue nightly as long as results were obtained. Finney adapted and developed the Methodist practice of setting up an area where people unsure about the condition of their souls (that is, anxious about salvation) could be counseled toward further repentance. In his prayers, he would name specific individuals believed to be in need of and approaching a state of repentance.

Finley's measures, widely accepted on the frontier, provoked opposition from leaders of the organized Calvinist and Lutheran churches, many of whom believed that the timing of true revivals within Christianity as well as individual conversions were God's exclusive concern. Finney, influenced by Methodist ARMINIANISM, assumed that humans could turn and repent at any time. It was the evangelist's task to issue the call, in the belief that God would accept repentance. He denied that the new measures contradicted the Bible in any way, and called them effective tools in winning souls.

Among Finney's most important critics was German Reformed theologian John W. Nevin. He said that Finney had placed far too much emphasis on human action in the conversion process, downplaying the key Reformation principle of salvation by grace in favor of salvation by human endeavor. Despite criticism, Finney's new measures were widely adopted by the growing churches, though often modified over time. Finney's use of the anxious bench, for example, became the altar call so prominent in contemporary mass evangelistic meetings. The role of women in Finney's evangelistic meetings foreshadowed the changing status and role of women within the church.

Further reading: Several of Charles Finney's books, including his *Lectures on Revivals of Religion,* have been placed on the Internet by the Christian Classics Ethereal Library, URL: http://www.ccel.org/f/finney; Charles G. Finney, *An Autobiography* (New York: A. S. Barnes, 1876); ———, *Lectures on Revivals of Religion* (New York: Leavitt Lord, Boston Crocker & Brewster,

1835); Charles E. Hambrick-Stowe, *Charles G. Finney and the Spirit of American Evangelicalism* (Grand Rapids, Mich.: Eerdmans, 1996); Timothy L. Smith, *Revivalism and Social Reform: American Protestantism on the Eve of the Civil War* (Baltimore: Johns Hopkins University Press, 1980).

New Zealand

Christianity was introduced to New Zealand (or Aotearoa) from AUSTRALIA. The first Christian service was held in 1814 by Samuel Marsden, a CHURCH OF ENGLAND minister who resided in Sydney and had been placed in charge of the church's work throughout British settlements in the South Seas. He operated as a representative of the CHURCH MISSIONARY SOCIETY, one of the two early Anglican missionary-sending agencies. Marsden's sermon was immediately translated into Maori, the language of New Zealand's pre-European inhabitants, signaling the church's missionary intent.

Settlement began in the northern half of the country, and there the church first established itself. Permanent Anglican work began in 1819, with John Butler as first resident minister. METHODISM spread among the early settlers as well. John McFarlane, a Presbyterian, arrived in 1840, the year that Britain annexed New Zealand as a colony.

These Christian groups grew and expanded and were joined by additional DENOMINATIONS from the homeland. An Anglican bishop was consecrated in 1841. The first Baptist church opened its doors in 1851. In 1854, New Zealand's House of Representatives announced that it would treat all religious groups equally.

Missionaries found some success among the Maoris, who, while accepting Christianity, rejected European cultural patterns. In order to assert their allegiance to traditional ways, some Maori leaders formed independent groups that merged Christian and Maori elements. Between 1830 and 1860, some 20 such movements promoting a charismatic and millennial faith arose, with more following in later decades. Some of these churches were involved in the conflicts over land ownership between the Maori and newer settlers.

While the first denominations to arrive have remained the largest in the Protestant community, the majority of church members are scattered among the 50 or more later arrivals. The Ratana Church, a healing church founded in 1925, has become the largest group among Maoris. They established their headquarters in a new holy city, Ratanapa, where a large temple commemorates the church's founder, T. W. Ratana.

PENTECOSTALISM emerged rather late, when British healing evangelist Smith Wigglesworth (1859–1947) visited in 1922. In 1924, American evangelist A. C. Valdez Sr. (1896–1988) followed up on the enthusiasm Wigglesworth ignited, and his meetings became the catalyst for the formation of the Pentecostal Church of New Zealand. It soon fell victim to internal disagreements over POLITY; the largest faction is affiliated with the American-based ASSEMBLIES OF GOD. Pentecostal growth, largely associated with the CHARISMATIC MOVEMENT, has accelerated since 1980.

Many of the older Protestant churches are members of the National Council of Churches in New Zealand, which is affiliated with the WORLD COUNCIL OF CHURCHES. More conservative non-Pentecostal groups are affiliated with New Vision New Zealand, which is in turn a member of the Evangelical Fellowship of the South Pacific and the WORLD EVANGELICAL ALLIANCE. Pentecostal Churches have formed the Associated Pentecostal Churches of New Zealand.

See also SOUTH PACIFIC.

Further reading: Brian Colless and Peter Donovan, eds. *Religion in New Zealand Society,* 2nd ed. (Palmerston North, N.Z.: Dunmore, 1985); Allen K. Davidson, *Christianity in Aotearoa: A History of Church and Society in New Zealand,* 2nd ed., (Wellington: Education for Ministry, 1997); James E. Worsfold, *A History of the Charismatic Movements in New Zealand* (Bradford, West Yorkshire, U.K.: Julian Literature Trust, 1974).

Ng Choing Hui (1914–1988) *Taiwanese theologian and ecumenical leader*

Ng Choing Hue was born at Chiong-hoa, Taiwan, on August 20, 1914, the son of a minister. He was educated at Tokyo University (1934–37) and Westminster College in England (1938–41). After World War II, he returned to Taiwan, where as a native Taiwanese he faced discrimination from the Chinese Nationalist government.

In 1947, he was named principal of the Tainan Theological College, sponsored by the Presbyterian Church's southern synod, the first Taiwanese so honored. During two decades of leadership, he was elected twice as moderator of the Presbyterian Church of Taiwan.

In 1965, his leadership in the field of theological education led to an invitation to join the WORLD COUNCIL OF CHURCHES' Theological Education Fund, which he later came to head. While working with the fund, he and other Asian scholars took the lead in forming the South East Asia Graduate School of Theology. The new school aimed to explore the new theological task that Ng had named CONTEXTUALIZATION—communicating the Gospel to people in ways that are meaningful to their own cultural setting and existential context. Contextualization deals with every aspect of the work of the church from interpreting the Scripture to the lifestyle of the minister. The concept, which has been taken up by a wide variety of Protestants working in non-European countries, is considered Ng's major contribution to the Protestant movement.

The fund has promoted a variety of Asian theologies, such as the pain of God theology (JAPAN), water buffalo theology (THAILAND), third eye theology (CHINA), and Minjung theology (KOREA), as attempts at contextualization.

Ng was exiled from Taiwan by the government. In 1971, when Taiwan was expelled from the United Nations, Ng took the occasion to work with other Taiwanese exiles in forming a self-determination movement that would have significant effects within the country. In 1987, he was allowed to return to his homeland. He died in England on October 27, 1988.

See also CHINA: TAIWAN.

Further reading: S. B. Bevans, *Models of Contextual Theology* (New York: Orbis Books, 1992); Scott W. Sunquist, ed., *A Dictionary of Asian Christianity* (Grand Rapids, Mich.: William B. Eerdmans, 2001).

Niebuhr, Reinhold (1892–1971)
influential theologian and ethicist

Reinhold Niebuhr was born on June 21, 1892, in Wright City, Missouri. His father was a minister in the German Evangelical Synod and his mother the daughter of an Evangelical missionary. Reinhold's brother, Helmut Richard (1895–1987), would also become a religious scholar of note.

Niebuhr attended Elmhurst College near Chicago (1907–10), and then Eden Seminary, the denominational school at St. Louis, where he was introduced to the liberal Protestant thinking then popular in Germany, especially that of Adolf von HARNACK. In 1913, Niebuhr was ordained in the Evangelical Synod, but he continued his studies at Yale Divinity School (B.D., 1914) and Yale University (M.A., 1915).

For the next 13 years, Niebuhr served as minister of Bethel Evangelical Church in Detroit. His observations on the conditions of the workers in the expanding automobile industry challenged his views of capitalism and led to his first major book, *Leaves from the Notebook of a Tamed Cynic* (1929). For a time, he argued for socialism, but he eventually supported President Roosevelt's New Deal as a more just and realistic approach to labor's problems. This change accompanied his growing familiarity with Neo-Orthodox theology, which was replacing liberalism in Germany.

By this time, Niebuhr had begun his long tenure as a professor of applied Christianity (later renamed ethics and theology) at Union Theologi-

cal Seminary in New York City (1928–60). His move to what he termed a more realistic approach to Christian thinking manifested in his ethical treatise, *Moral Man and Immoral Society* (1932) and his monumental theological work, the *Nature and Destiny of Man*, published during World War II. The latter work, representing his Gifford Lectures, became an American appropriation of NEO-ORTHODOXY and placed Niebuhr in the center of the late 20th-century flowering of theological activity.

Niebuhr introduced the concept of love as the "impossible possibility." Love (Christian agape) is possible and exists in human encounters, but because of egoism, its historical and social expression always falls short of the ideal we know as the Kingdom of God.

While at Union, Niebuhr tried to demonstrate his attitude toward loving action and social concern through a life beyond the academic walls and the classroom. He frequently spoke on contemporary issues involving the cold war, and had almost a second full career in journalism. He served as editor of *The Christian Century* (1922–40), to which he added duties with *Radical Religion* (renamed *Christianity and Society*) (1935), *The Nation* (1938–50), *Christianity and Crisis* (1941), and the *New Leader* (1954–70).

Niebuhr died on June 1, 1971.

Further reading: Robert McAfee Brown, ed., *The Essential Reinhold Niebuhr: Selected Essays and Addresses* (New Haven, Conn.: Yale University Press, 1986); Richard Wightman Fox, *Reinhold Niebuhr: A Biography* (New York: Pantheon Books, 1985); Reinhold Niebuhr, *An Interpretation of Christian Ethics* (New York: Scribner, 1935); ———, *Leaves from the Notebook of a Tamed Cynic* (Chicago/New York: Wilett, Clark & Colby, 1929); ———, *Moral Man and Immoral Society* (New York: Scribner, 1932); ———, *The Nature and Destiny of Man: A Christian Interpretation,* vol. 1, *Human Nature;* vol. 2, *Human Destiny* (New York: Scribner, 1941, 1943).

Niemöller, Martin (1892–1984) *Lutheran bishop and opponent of the Nazi regime*

German Lutheran bishop Martin Niemöller was born on January 14, 1892, in Lippstadt, Westphalia, Germany, the son of a Lutheran minister. As a young man, he was a pioneer of the German submarine fleet and rose to command his own sub during World War I. He later wrote a popular book, *From U-Boat to Pulpit* (1934), describing the war experiences that drove him to study theology and become a Lutheran pastor.

He was initially attracted to the Nazi movement, but soon came to see it as a grave danger. As early as 1933, he organized the Pastors' Emergency League to protect fellow ministers from police action. The following year he helped organize a synod that adopted the BARMEN DECLARATION, largely written by his colleague Karl BARTH. It became the foundation statement for the Confessing Church, which opposed Hitler. Barth was driven out of the country, but Niemöller was for a while acceptable to the Nazis, who wanted to capitalize on his status as a naval hero.

He was first arrested in 1937, and eventually interned in a concentration camp, first Sachsenhausen and then Dachau. He was fortunate to escape execution in the final days of the war.

Niemöller resumed his ministerial career. He worked with surviving colleagues of the Confessing Church to lobby the EVANGELICAL CHURCH IN GERMANY (Lutheran) to produce a public statement of repentance for its complicity with the Nazis, and especially with the Holocaust against the Jews. In October 1945, the church's executive council issued the Stuttgart Confession of Guilt (Stuttgarter Schuldbekenntnis). Niemöller spoke widely of the Nazi era, frequently using the quote for which he has become famous, "First, they came for the socialists, and I did not speak out because I was not a socialist. Then they came for the trade unionists, and I did not speak out because I was not a trade unionist. Then they came for the Jews, and I did not speak out because I was not a Jew. Then they came for me, and there was no one left to speak for me."

The confession unleashed a storm of controversy within the church. Some of Niemöller's own ambiguous actions following his arrest were revealed, including an attempt to win clemency by identifying himself as an anti-Semite. In spite of these facts, he became head of the territorial church of Hesse and Nassau, one of the regional divisions of the Evangelical Church in Germany.

Niemöller's postwar efforts earned him the respect of the larger Protestant community. He served on the provisional committee that helped form the WORLD COUNCIL OF CHURCHES and was a member of its executive and central committees from its founding in 1948 to 1961, when he was selected as one of its six presidents. During his presidency, he also became well known for his advocacy of PACIFISM and reconciliation of East and West, leading to his efforts to bring the churches in Eastern Europe into ecumenical dialogues. In 1967, he received the Lenin Peace Prize from the Soviet Union.

Niemöller died on March 6, 1984.

Further reading: James Bentley, *Martin Niemöller* (Oxford: Oxford University Press, 1984); Clarissa Start-Davidson, *God's Man: The Story of Pastor Niemöller* (New York: Ives Washburn, 1959); Martin Niemöller, *Dachau Sermons* (London: Latimer House, 1947); ———, *Exile in the Fatherland: Martin Niemöller's Letters from Moabit Prison*, trans. by Ernst Kaemke, et al. (Grand Rapids, Mich.: William B. Eerdmans, 1986); ———, *Here Stand I!* (Chicago: Willett, Clark, 1937).

Nigeria

Nigeria, the most populous country in Africa, is about equally divided between Muslims and Christians. Of 45 million Christians, Roman Catholics number 12 million, with the remainder divided among the numerous Protestant churches.

The first Protestants to arrive were Methodist missionaries, who worked in the southwest among the Yoruba, one of the country's larger populations. The major figures were former slave Thomas Birch

FREEMAN (1809–90) and William DeGraft (and his wife), who settled at Badagry in 1842. The mission was an outgrowth of the British antislavery effort, as freed Nigerians returning to their homes requested Freeman's ministrations. Some of the freed slaves had been converted by CHURCH OF EN- GLAND missionaries prior to their return. To serve them, in 1842 CHURCH MISSIONARY SOCIETY (CMS) personnel established themselves in the towns of Lagos, Abeokuta, and Ibadan. The Anglicans had a great asset in Samuel CROWTHER (1807–91), a Yoruban who had been freed from slavery and edu- cated at the Anglican school in SIERRA LEONE.

In 1841, Crowther joined the Niger Expedi- tion, an exploratory trip to prepare for the destruction of the slave trade in the region. As a result of his performance on the expedition, Crowther was sent to England for further study and ordination. After settling in Abeokuta in 1842, he helped translate the Bible into Yoruban and was a significant evangelical force in building the church. In England, Harry Venn, head of the CMS, had Crowther consecrated as bishop of "the countries of Western Africa beyond the limits of the Queen's dominions." He developed an all- African church on the Upper Niger that could have been a model for all of Africa. Instead, Venn was pushed aside and Crowther was succeeded by a white bishop. The church had to wait another century for indigenization.

The Methodists and Anglicans were followed by Presbyterians (1846) and BAPTISTS (1850). The Baptists were the source of the first autonomous indigenous Protestant body, the Native Baptist Church, established in 1888.

Possibly the most important 20th-century addition to the Protestant community was the Sudan Interior Mission (now SIM International). Founded in 1893, it began work in northeastern Nigeria in 1935. By 1990, it reported more than 2 million members. It was rivaled in size among indigenous churches only by the Fellowship of Churches of Christ in Nigeria (Tarayar Ekklesiy- oyin Kristi a Nigeria or TEKAN). TEKAN was founded in 1954 as a federation of eight older mis-

sions, including four SIM works and the missions of the Church of the Brethren, the Dutch Reformed Church of South Africa, the Evangelical United Brethren (now the UNITED METHODIST CHURCH), and an independent indigenous Niger- ian church. Since its formation, three other churches have joined.

Today, the Anglican Church of the Province of Nigeria, with more than 17 million members, is by far the largest Protestant church. At least 12 other Protestant churches have as many as a million members. Among these are several relatively new AFRICAN INITIATED CHURCHES (AICs), including the Redeemed Christian Church of Jesus Christ and the BROTHERHOOD OF THE CROSS AND STAR. There are more than 1,000 separate AICs in Nigeria.

Some of the more important Nigerian AICs trace their history to the 1918 influenza epidemic. Judging the mission churches impotent in the face of the widespread illness, a number of independ- ent prayer groups emerged, and from them came the several ALADURA CHURCHES, the several Cheru- bim and Seraphim churches, and the Christ Apos- tolic Church.

As in most of Africa, PENTECOSTALISM has made a significant impact in Nigeria, beginning with the introduction of the ASSEMBLIES OF GOD and the Apostolic Church, a British body. Both have expe- rienced notable growth, and helped spread the Pentecostal experience among the AICs. The mil- lion-member Church of God Mission Interna- tional, founded in 1968, made an impact in western Nigeria through its Archbishop Benson Idahosa (1938–98), who became a leader in the International Communion of Charismatic Churches that includes churches in BRAZIL, the United States, and ITALY.

Ecumenically, the Christian Council of Nigeria includes those churches otherwise related to the WORLD COUNCIL OF CHURCHES (WCC) and the All Africa Conference of Churches. WCC churches based in Nigeria include the Church of the Brethren in Nigeria, the Church of the Lord Aladura, the Church of the Province of Nigeria, the Methodist Church Nigeria, the Nigerian Baptist

Convention, and the Presbyterian Church of Nigeria. More conservative churches have united in the Nigerian Evangelical Fellowship affiliated with the WORLD EVANGELICAL ALLIANCE. Several hundred of the AICs have joined the Nigeria Association of Aladura Churches.

See also AFRICA, SUB-SAHARAN.

Further reading: David Barrett, *The Encyclopedia of World Christianity,* 2nd ed. (New York: Oxford University Press, 2001); E. P. T. Crampton, *Christianity in Northern Nigeria* (London: Geoffrey Chapman, 1975); John B. Grimley and Gordon E. Robinson, *Church Growth in Central and Southern Nigeria* (Grand Rapids, Mich.: William B. Eerdmans, 1966); W. B. Webster, *The African Churches among the Yoruba, 1888–1922* (Oxford: Clarendon, 1964).

Niles, D. T. (1908–1970) *ecumenical leader from Sri Lanka*

Daniel Thambyrajah (D. T.) Niles was born into a Christian family in Jaffna, SRI LANKA, on May 4, 1908. He studied at the United Theological College in Bangalore, India (1927–33), and became the national secretary of the Student Christian Movement. He was ordained a Methodist minister in 1936 and served a district evangelist. Recognized as a talented young leader, in 1938 he was a major speaker and participant at the INTERNATIONAL MISSIONARY COUNCIL gathering at Tambaram, India. He became more widely known as the evangelism director for the World YMCA in Geneva (1939–40).

In 1941, he was the first full-time general secretary of the National Christian Council (India). During the war, he began to write about dialogues with non-Christian faiths. After the war, he served as a Methodist pastor while continuing his role on the world stage as an ecumenical spokesperson. He preached at the opening service at the first meeting of the WORLD COUNCIL OF CHURCHES (WCC) in 1948, and then became successively the chairperson of its youth department (1948–52) and executive secretary of its evangelism depart-

ment. His leadership with both the Methodist Church in Sri Lanka and the World Council continued through the mid-1960s.

In 1957, Niles became general secretary of the East Asia Conference of Churches. He held the post until 1968, when he was named the conference's chairperson. That same year, he was selected to head the Methodist Church of Sri Lanka, and elected as one of the presidents of the WCC.

Niles died in India on August 17, 1970. He is most remembered as an ecumenical strategist who helped structure the Protestant movement in southern Asia for the last decades of the 20th century.

Further reading: Christopher L. Furtado, *The Contribution of Dr. D. T. Niles to the Church Universal and Local* (Madras, India.: Christian Literature Society, 1978); D. T. Niles, *Brothers of the Faith* (New York: Abingdon, 1960); ———, *Buddhism and the Claims of Christ* (Richmond, Va.: John Knox Press, 1967); ———, *The Message and the Messenger* (Nashville, Tenn.: Abingdon, 1966); Glen Wagner Snowden, *The Relation of Christianity to non-Christian Religions in the Theologies of Daniel T. Niles and Paul Tillich* (Boston: Boston University School of Theology, Ph.D. diss., 1969).

Ninety-five Theses

The Protestant Reformation is traditionally traced to Martin LUTHER's Ninety-five Theses, or debating points, which he is said to have posted on the door of the parish church at WITTENBERG on October 31, 1517. The theses were Luther's first public expression of his developing theology; they were put forth in reaction to a church campaign to sell INDULGENCES throughout Germany. The action attributed to Luther of nailing them to the church door appears to be apocryphal.

According to accepted Roman Catholic teachings, average Christians would at the moment of death pass into purgatory. Here, they would make restitution for past sins through pain and suffering, so that they could finally enter heaven. However, the church could grant indulgences to any believer as a reward for acts of devotion; the indulgence would reduce or eliminate the term in purgatory, for the believer or a loved one. A representative of Rome, monk Johann Tetzel (1465–1519), was distributing indulgences in exchange for donations to finance the construction of St. Peter's in Rome. Tetzel's tactics enraged Luther, who challenged him, and through him Catholic theologians, to debate the issue.

The majority of the theses dealt with indulgences, but in so doing they raised many questions and doubts about purgatory, the authority of the pope, the SACRAMENT of penance, and the nature of Christian holiness. The theses struck a chord among Germans, many of whom resented the transfer of money from Germany to Rome. As the controversy raged, Tetzel's sales dropped significantly. Tetzel responded with a set of countertheses defending his actions and papal authority, arguing that those who sow doubt should be considered heretics.

The church called upon one of its prominent theologians, John Eck (1486–1543), to debate Luther. They met at Leipzig in 1519. Luther was forced into asserting his belief that the Bible overrode papal authority and that both popes and councils had made errors in the past. For these statements, Eck branded him a heretic and schismatic. The next year, Luther was excommunicated, and the Reformation went into full swing.

Further reading: Roland H. Bainton, *Here I Stand* (Nashville, Tenn.: Abingdon, 1950); Eric W. Gritsch, *Martin, God's Court Jester: Luther in Retrospect* (Philadelphia: Fortress Press, 1983); James M. Kittelson, *Luther the Reformer: The Story of the Man and His Career* (Minneapolis, Minn.: Augsburg, 1986); Theodore Tappert, ed. *Selected Writings of Martin Luther;* 4 vols. (Philadelphia: Fortress Press, 1967).

Norway

The Reformation came to Norway in 1537, following its acceptance by King Christian III of DENMARK (r. 1534–59), then sovereign of Norway as well.

Norway officially accepted LUTHERANISM in 1539, and those bishops who remained loyal to Rome were removed from their posts. The church was subsequently placed under the authority of the king, who confiscated Roman Catholic property.

At the end of 18th century, Norway was influenced by PIETISM, with its demands for personal faith and its questioning of church hierarchy. Hans Nielsen Hague (1771–1824), the primary exponent, organized a number of small informal groups for prayer and worship that unofficially competed with Sunday worship at established churches. While Hague's movement remained within the ecclesiastical structures in Norway, in America his followers established an independent synod that eventually merged into what is now the EVANGELICAL LUTHERAN CHURCH IN AMERICA.

Norway's constitution, adopted in 1814, affirmed freedom of religion though it retained Lutheranism as the official religion of the state; the king and more than half the members of the Council of State had to profess the official religion. (At the same time, Norway accepted an act of union with Sweden that continued until 1905.)

Non-Lutheran churches began to establish a presence in Norway early in the 19th century, beginning with the QUAKERS in 1818. Baptist work initiated in the 1850s led to the founding of the Norwegian Baptist Union. Other streams were METHODISM (1853), the SEVENTH-DAY ADVENTIST CHURCH (1887), the SALVATION ARMY (1888), and JEHOVAH'S WITNESSES (1891). Most of these churches came from North America, but the Mission Covenant (1850s) was a Free Church community from Sweden. The primary Free Church movement within the Church of Norway emerged late in the century under the leadership of Rev. Paul Peter Wettergren (1835–89), who called for acknowledgment of Jesus (not the king of Norway) as the only leader of the church and hence for a strict separation of church and state. His efforts led to the formation of the Evangelical Lutheran Free Church of Norway.

PENTECOSTALISM in Scandinavia had its beginning in Oslo, Norway. On a visit to New York in

1906, Thomas B. Barrett (1862–1940) experienced the BAPTISM OF THE HOLY SPIRIT. He shared his experience with readers of his magazine, *Byposten,* and began holding Pentecostal meetings in December. Word spread around Europe, and between visitors to Oslo and Barrett's own travels, Pentecostalism reached most European countries within a few years. In Norway, it was a loosely organized movement with each congregation constituting an autonomous organization. Eventually, the congregations joined in a loose fellowship called Pinesebevegelsen (or Pentecostal Revival). By the end of the 20th century, there were some 300 congregations. More than half the non-Lutheran Protestants in Norway are now affiliated with Pentecostal and Charismatic fellowships.

The Church of Norway has remained the state church, but it has suffered from the extreme secularization of the nation. Membership includes 96 percent of citizens, but church attendance is less than 5 percent. A law passed in 1953 introduced a number of democratic reforms into what was a staunchly hierarchical structure little changed from before the Reformation.

The Church of Norway is a member of both the LUTHERAN WORLD FEDERATION and the WORLD COUNCIL OF CHURCHES. Norwegian Methodists are an integral a part of the UNITED METHODIST CHURCH, also a council member. Several of the Protestant groups have formed the Norsk Frikirkerad (Free Church Council).

Further reading: Stanley M. Burgess and Eduard M. Van der Maas, eds. *International Dictionary of Pentecostal Charismatic Movements,* rev. ed. (Grand Rapids, Mich.: Zondervan, 2020); *The Church of Norway* (Hegdehaugen, Norway: Church of Norway Information Service, 1990); L. S. Hunter, *Scandinavian Churches: A Picture of the Development of the Churches of Denmark, Norway, Finland, Iceland, and Sweden* (London: Faber & Faber, 1965).

Ntsikana (c. 1780–1820) *early South African (Xhosa) convert, hymn writer, and preacher*

Ntsikana was born into an elite family. Besides learning to tend cattle and hunt, he became known for his singing, dancing, and speaking skills.

Ntsikana first learned of Christianity from Johannes T. van der Kemp (1847–1911), a missionary with the LONDON MISSIONARY SOCIETY, who worked among the Xhosa (1899–1900) without evident results. In 1816, missionary Joseph Williams settled near Ntsikana's home. By this time, Ntsikana had married twice, and inherited his deceased father's holdings.

A year before, Ntsikana had had a vision, during which he had spontaneously hummed a song that later became the first of his hymns. He began to organize worship services. Once Williams established his mission station, Ntsikana visited regularly, studying the Bible with him and his successor, John Brown Lee (1791–1871). Ntsikana died in Thwatwa in 1820.

Ntsikana's four hymns became a staple of Xhosa Christian hymnody. The hymn to the Great God is still sung almost two centuries later. He also inspired a later Xhosa hymn writer, John Knox Bokwe (1855–1922), who wrote a biography of Ntsikana.

See also SOUTH AFRICA.

Further reading: John K. Bokwe, *Ntsikana* (Lovedale, South Africa: Lovedale Press, 1914); Janet Hodgson, *Ntsikana's 'Great Hymn': A Xhosa Expression of Christianity in the Early 19th Century Eastern Cape* (Cape Town, South Africa: Centre for African Studies, University of Cape Town, 1980); Basil Holt, *Joseph Williams and the Pioneer Mission to the Southeastern Bantu* (Lovedale, South Africa: Lovedale Press, 1954); Richard Lovett, *History of the London Missionary Society, 1795–1895* (London: Henry Frowde, 1899); Ntsikana, *The Life of Ntsikana* (Lovedale, South Africa: Lovedale Press, 1902).

O

Obookiah, Henry (c. 1792–1818) *first Hawaiian convert to Christianity and mission activist*
Henry Obookiah was born on the big island of Hawaii around 1792. His family was killed in the internecine war that afflicted the islands in the late 18th century, but an uncle arranged for his training as a priest in the native religion. In 1808, he joined the crew of an American trading ship as a cabin boy, and was eventually put ashore in New Haven, Connecticut. There he met Edwin D. Dwight (son of Yale president Timothy Dwight [1752–1817]), who taught Obookiah to read and write. He also met Samuel J. Mills (1743–1833), the student who had become an advocate of foreign missions following the HAYSTACK PRAYER MEETING. Obookiah was living with the Mills family when in 1810 Samuel convinced Massachusetts Congregationalists to found the AMERICAN BOARD OF COMMISSIONERS FOR FOREIGN MISSIONS, the first American missions-sending agency.

In 1811, Obookiah moved to Andover, Massachusetts, where Mills was attending Andover Theological Seminary. After he converted the next year, he went to live in the home of a DEACON in Hollis, New Hampshire. By 1814, when he was living at the home of a minister at Goshen, Connecticut, he had begun to develop a written form of Hawaiian. In 1815, he joined the church at Torringford, Connecticut, and began to prepare himself to return to Hawaii as a missionary. He helped rally support for the founding of the Foreign Mission School, which opened in 1817 in Cornwall, Connecticut, and included in its first class several youths from INDIA, and some of Obookiah's fellow countrymen. Obookiah's presence led Mills and others to see Hawaii as a viable missionary target.

Obookiah himself was struck with typhus and died on February 17, 1818. Edwin Dwight quickly published Obookiah's memoirs, which became a potent force in recruiting missionaries; the first team sailed from Massachusetts for the islands in April 1819.

Further reading: Henry Obookiah, *The Memoirs of Henry Obookiah, a Native of Owhyhee, and a Member of the Foreign Mission School, Who Died at Cornwall, Conn., Feb. 17, 1818, Aged 26 Years* (New Haven, Conn.: Religious Intelligencer, 1818); LaReu W. Piercy, *Hawaii's Missionary Saga: Sacrifice and Godliness in Paradise* (Honolulu: Mutual, 1992).

Oceania *See* SOUTH PACIFIC.

Oecolampadius, Johann (1482–1531)
theologian and Reformation leader at Basel

Johann Oecolampadius (Hellenized form of Heusegen or candlestick) was born at Weinsberg, Swabia, Germany, in 1482. In 1499 he moved to Heidelberg to study theology and literature. After serving in several parish positions, he was appointed preacher at the cathedral of Basel (1515), and earned a doctorate in theology there in 1518. While in Basel, he became acquainted with noted humanist ERASMUS.

In December 1518, Oecolampadius moved to Augsburg. Although he associated with humanists who sympathized with Martin LUTHER, he tried to withdraw from the polemics by entering a monastery at Altomünster in 1520. The attempt was brought to an end by the publication of a confidential work that was favorable to Luther. Subsequent writings affirming the Protestant positions on confession to priests and the Eucharist forced him out of the monastery, and in 1522 he returned to Basel.

Oecolampadius used his Basel pulpit to defend Luther's ideas on JUSTIFICATION BY FAITH and the marriage of priests. In 1525, the council at Basel appointed him pastor at St. Martin's church. He agreed to refrain from introducing any innovations without the authorization of the council. However, he soon published a work aligning himself with Ulrich ZWINGLI, the reformer in Zurich who considered the Eucharist or LORD'S SUPPER to be merely a memorial meal.

In November 1525, Oecolampadius conducted the first celebration of the Lord's Supper with a new reformed liturgy that he had compiled. The council then decided to allow each local pastor to follow his own forms, whereupon the Protestants succeeded in purging the council of Catholics and seizing the cathedral and the remaining parishes still in Catholic hands. Oecolampadius was selected as the new pastor of the cathedral and head of the Protestant clergy of the city. He took the leading role in compiling the new ordinance favoring the Reformation that was promulgated by the council on April 1, 1529.

In October 1529, Oecolampadius joined Zwingli and Luther at the MARBURG COLLOQUY, an unsuccessful attempt to unite the Reformed and Lutheran wings of the Reformation. He had more success in 1531 when he helped Martin BUCER introduce Protestantism into Ulm, Biberach, and Memmingen. He also is given credit for helping to bring the Waldensians of northern Italy into the Reformation camp.

Oecolampadius died at Basel on November 24, 1531.

Further reading: Roland H. Bainton, *Studies on the Reformation* (Boston: Beacon Press, 1963); Akira Demura, *Church Discipline according to Johannes Oecolampadius in the Setting of His Life and Thought* (Princeton, N.J.: Princeton Theological Seminary, Ph.D. diss., 1964); Thomas A. Fudge, "Icarus of Basel? Oecolampadius and the Early Swiss Reformation," *Journal of Religious History* 21, no. 3 (1997): 268–84; Ernst Staehelin, *Briefer und Akten zum Leben Oekolampads* (Leipzig: M. Heinsius Nachfolger Eger & Sievers, 1927; reprint, New York: Johnson Reprint Corp., 1971).

Orange Order

The Orange Order, a fiercely partisan Protestant fraternity based in IRELAND, is dedicated to the memory of the 1690 Battle of the Boyne. In 1688, William II (of Orange) had driven James II from the British throne. Two years later, the staunchly Catholic James gathered an army of French and Irish in a bid to reclaim his crown. He was defeated on July 12 at the Battle of the Boyne (not far from Dublin). Irish Protestants from Derry joined in the effort.

In 1795, Protestant-Catholic conflict in County Armagh led to the formation of a Protestant fraternal lodge at Loughgall that drew on William of Orange for its symbolism. On July 12 of the following year, the first march by the new fraternity of Orangemen was held in Belfast. Lodges soon appeared in other communities across Ireland beset by Catholic-Protestant tensions. They drew most of their support from Presbyterians, and very little from Anglicans. Lodge activities over the next generation became the focus of a series of violent clashes between Catholics and Protestants, and in 1836 the British banned the Orange lodges.

Protestants, many of Scottish origin, reemerged as an organized force in the 1850s in defiance of British authorities. Over the next century, they opposed any attempts to return Ireland to Irish (and hence Roman Catholic) control. In 1912, northern Orangemen formed the Ulster Volunteer Force to fight against home rule. Nevertheless, the British in 1920 granted self-rule to the 26 counties that had a Catholic majority. Two years later, the Catholic counties declared their freedom as the Irish Free State, while the remaining six counties were reorganized as Northern Ireland and remained incorporated in the UNITED KINGDOM.

With the rise of an independent Irish state, the focus of the Orange Order, officially the Loyal Orange Institution of Ireland, was to prevent Ireland from absorbing the northern provinces. Catholic protests against discrimination in Northern Ireland in the 1960s provoked Protestant support for Ian Paisley (b. 1926), an Orangeman and founder of the ultraconservative Free Presbyterian Church (1951). Paisley believed that both political and ecclesiastical leaders were endangering the structures that kept Protestants in control.

The next 30 years were punctuated with clashes between Protestants and Catholics in Northern Ireland. Orangemen became known for their public demonstrations, often purposefully carried into Catholic neighborhoods. Catholics formed their own paramilitary groups to oppose the Ulster Volunteer Force and similar Protestant groups. British forces and local governments attempted to quell the violence. Significant progress was made in 1999 when the Good Friday Agreement led to the establishment of a new government for Northern Ireland, initially opposed by Paisley and the Orange Order.

The Orange Order spread internationally to CANADA (1818), AUSTRALIA (1845) and England. It now exists as two organizations, the larger Orange Order and the smaller Independent Loyal Orange Institution, with which Paisely is associated.

Further reading: J. Brown, M. W. Deware, and S. E. Long, *Orangeism: A New Historical Appreciation* (Belfast: Grand Orange Lodge of Ireland, 1967); Tony Gray, *The Orange Order* (London: The Bodley Head, 1972); C. C. O'Brien, *Ancestral Voices: Religion and Nationalism in Ireland* (Chicago: University of Chicago Press, 1995); Hereward Senior, *Orangeism in Ireland and Britain, 1795–1836* (London: Routledge & Kegan, 1966).

Oriental Mission Society

The Oriental Mission Society (now OMS International) was founded in 1901 by HOLINESS missionaries Charles E. Cowman (1864–1924), and his wife Lettie B. Cowman (1876–1960), members of the Pilgrim Holiness Church (now a constituent part of the WESLEYAN CHURCH). The Cowmans supported the model proposed by Methodist bishop William Taylor, who aimed to found self-sufficient indigenous churches in the mission field. As they were preparing for missionary service, the couple met Japanese student Juji Nakada (1870–1936) at Moody Bible Institute in 1897–98. He became a cofounder of OMS and was largely responsible for Japan becoming the first field of operation. In Chicago, they also encountered E. A. Kilbourne (1865–1928), a telegrapher, who became the fourth cofounder of OMS.

Nakada returned to JAPAN in 1898, and the Cowmans joined him in 1901. Kilbourne arrived in 1902. Nakada and the Cowmans established a center where they held services every evening and trained coworkers during the day. Kilbourne founded a periodical, *Electric Messages*. By 1912, they had developed enough support to launch an expansive effort called the Every Creature Crusade. Over the next six years, workers with the mission attempted to contact every home in Japan with some Gospel literature. As the work grew, they expanded their operation to CHINA and KOREA.

Following the death of her husband in 1924 and then Kilbourne in 1928, Lettie Cowman became the president of OMS and led it for the next 21 years. She retired in 1949. Her devotional book, *Streams in the Desert* (1925), has become a Holiness classic.

The early work evolved into the Japan Holiness Church. Since World War II OMS has expanded into more than 30 countries and is no longer focused exclusively on ASIA.

Further reading: Lettie B. Cowman, *Charles E. Cowman: Missionary Warrior* (Los Angeles: Oriental Missionary Society, 1928); ———, *Streams in the Desert* (Los Angeles: Oriental Missionary Society, 1925); R. D. Wood, *In These Mortal Hands: The Story of the Oriental Missionary Society: The First 50 Years* (Greenwood, Ind.: OMS International, 1983).

Orthodox-Protestant dialogue

The Protestant movement began as dissent within the Roman Catholic Church, which is still the major focus of Protestant relations with the rest of Christendom. At first, Protestants had little contact with Orthodox Christians. A dialogue initiated by Lutheran theologians at the University of Tübingen with the Ecumenical Patriarchate in Constantinople toward the end of the 16th century did not achieve much agreement and had no follow-up. The Counter-Reformation further separated the two streams, by placing Catholic-controlled lands (such as POLAND) between Protestant and Orthodox countries.

In the 19th century, Protestants, till then confined to northern and western Europe and North America, launched a worldwide missionary program. Increasingly, they found themselves working in traditionally Orthodox lands or in juxtaposition with minority Orthodox communities in ASIA and the MIDDLE EAST. In INDIA, Protestants encountered the Mar Thomas churches; in the Muslim lands of North Africa (including Ethiopia) and the Middle East, they sought converts primarily among traditionally Orthodox

peoples, rather than Muslims. Missionaries also arrived in eastern Europe, and although their primary targets were Jewish communities, they sought Orthodox converts as well.

The CHURCH OF ENGLAND played a particular role in the Protestant encounter with Orthodoxy, based on its centuries-old concern about the legitimacy of its BISHOPS. Roman Catholics insisted that the Anglicans had broken the legitimate line of succession from Christ's apostles, ever since the reform of ordination rites under EDWARD VI. Pope Leo XIII (1810–1903) reiterated this charge in 1896.

In the 19th century, the Anglicans began to turn to Orthodox Churches, whose relations with Rome had also been disrupted over the centuries, for recognition of its orders. In spite of missions that were bringing Orthodox believers into the Church of England, cordial relations were established. Among the high points was a statement issued by the Ecumenical Patriarchate in 1922 stating that "the practice in the Church affords no indication that the Orthodox Church has ever officially treated the validity of Anglican Orders as in doubt, in such a way as would point to the reordination of the Anglican clergy as required in the case of the union of the two Churches." Similar statements have been issued by other Orthodox churches throughout the 20th century. In reaction, some Anglicans came to think of themselves as Western-rite Orthodox.

Relations between the Orthodox and Protestants suffered after the Russian Revolution, when many Orthodox churches found themselves under an antireligious totalitarian government. Many in the West questioned the legitimacy of the Orthodox leadership, especially in the official Russian Orthodox Church. Many ethnic communities in America formerly under Russian Orthodox leadership left to establish a full array of ethnic Orthodox denominational bodies.

Early in the 20th century, the Ecumenical Patriarchate indicated a desire to enter into dialogue with other Christian churches. As early as 1920, Orthodox churches were invited to participate in the LIFE AND WORK and the FAITH AND ORDER conferences, the precursors for the WORLD COUNCIL OF Churches (WCC), and in 1927 Orthodox leaders attended the first Faith and Order conference. When the WCC was formed in 1948, the Ecumenical Patriarchate, the Church of Greece, and the Church of Cyprus were among the charter members; most of the other major Orthodox bodies joined later on. In addition to those Eastern churches in communion with the Ecumenical Patriarchate (Russian, Greek, Antiochean, Romanian, Bulgarian, and so forth), the WCC eventually attracted those churches that continued ancient Orthodoxy and did not affirm the Chalcedonian statement on the nature of Christ. These non-Chalcedonian bodies include the Syrian, Armenian, Coptic, and Ethiopian churches. Over the years, a number of Orthodox leaders have served as president of the World Council.

The Orthodox Church sees itself in direct continuity in faith and practice with the first-century Apostolic church. It rejects doctrinal looseness and entered ecumenical dialogue with the understanding that the goal is full unity of faith, though it accepts that diverse Christian communities can cooperate on mutually agreed upon projects and offer one another support, assistance, and new experiences.

The Russian Orthodox Church was accepted into ecumenical circles in the early 1960s, with the support of mainstream Protestants. Conservative church leaders in the West had accused the Russian Church leadership of being either dupes or collaborators with the Communist authorities. However, in subsequent decades, a spirit of cooperation has ensued.

Toward the end of the 1990s, new issues have challenged Protestant-Orthodox relations. The Orthodox always criticized Protestants for a variety of reasons: their lack of an episcopate (apart from Anglicans), their doctrinal differences, and their views on the Eucharist. Since the 1970s, the ordination of women and the role of homosexuals in church life have joined the list of controversial

topics. Even earlier, Orthodox leaders faced opposition in their own communities for affiliating with churches that reject many of the essential Orthodox doctrines and practices.

In 1998, at the General Assembly in Harare, the WCC appointed a Special Commission on Orthodox Participation. In 2002, the WCC Central Committee adopted the commission's recommendations, including the development of a new decision-making process, a reform of the council's system of representation, a new framework for conducting common prayer, and the initiation of studies aimed at elucidating fundamental differences between Orthodox and Protestant churches.

Following the Harare Assembly, two Orthodox churches withdrew from the World Council, citing among other issues the council's willingness to consider questions of homosexuality. Other Orthodox leaders countered with public statements of support for the council.

Just as liberal Protestantism has evoked a conservative counterpart, so Orthodoxy has developed a similar conservative wing. The conservatives oppose participation in the ECUMENICAL MOVEMENT and any accommodation to communist governments; they refuse to adopt the Western (Gregorian) calendar. Old calendar churches exist in Greece, Romania, and Russian expatriate communities worldwide.

Further reading: Faith and Order Commissions, *The Orthodox Church and the Churches of the Reformation (1975) A Survey of Orthodox—Protestant Dialogues* (Geneva: World Council of Churches, 1965); Lutheran-Orthodox Joint Commission, *Lutheran-Orthodox Dialogue. Agreed Statements 1985–1989* (Geneva: Lutheran World Federation, 1992); John Meyendorff and R. Tobias, eds., *Salvation in Christ: A Lutheran-Orthodox Dialogue* (Minneapolis, Minn.: Augsburg, 1992).

Oxford movement

The Oxford movement was a revitalization movement within the CHURCH OF ENGLAND in the

1830s, which aimed to revive the church's Catholic roots in order to keep it from becoming just another Protestant sect. Among the events that contributed to the movement were passage of the Catholic Relief Act of 1829, which allowed Catholics to worship openly in England, and the 1833 sermon by John Keble (1792–1866), preached at St. Mary's church in Oxford, entitled "National Apostasy." Keble criticized the country for turning away from God; he charged that the Anglican Church was no longer the prophetic voice of God, but rather a mere institution of society. The sermon drew much popular response and was reprinted widely.

Keble's sermon had a particular effect on three who heard it delivered: Edward Pusey (1800–82), Hurrel Froude (1803–36), and John Henry Newman (1801–90). They joined others to discuss Keble's ideas; the movement took on organizational life at a conference at St. Mary's church in Hadleigh, Suffolk, in 1835. Over the next decade, the group developed their ideas in a series of tracts, and they became known as the Tractarians.

The Oxford movement accepted the Reformation Church of England as a valid part of the universal Catholic Church, but defined it more in terms of its pre-Reformation life. They explored medieval English church LITURGY, DOCTRINE, and practice. One tract tried to reconcile the 39 ARTICLES OF RELIGION with the documents promulgated by the Council of Trent, which had defined Roman Catholic practice in opposition to the Reformation.

The Oxford movement came to a rather abrupt end in 1845, when Newman and a number of other leaders formally converted to Catholicism. For the rest of his long life, Newman would be an effective advocate for Catholicism in the English-speaking world. He and his colleague Henry Edward Manning (1807–92) were both named cardinals.

Though relatively short lived, the Oxford movement succeeded in strengthening the high-church factions already present in the Church of England. Since the 1840s, these Anglo-Catholics have periodically proposed initiatives for reconciling the Church of England with Roman Catholicism. These efforts culminated in 1960, when Archbishop of Canterbury Geoffrey Fisher met with Pope John XXIII. The spirit of the Tractarians was also exported through the ANGLICAN COMMUNION. In the United States, the movement initially found its greatest support in New York. However, it encountered major hostility as well. Opponents of Oxford teachings were able to force the resignation of Bishop Henry Onderdonk (1789–1858), while his brother Bishop Benjamin T. Onderdonk (1791–1861) was tried on trumped-up charges and suspended from office. Both the Onderdonks had supported the Oxford cause.

The contemporary renewal of interest in formal liturgies in ecumenical Protestantism can be traced to the Oxford movement. The movement can also take some credit for the openness demonstrated by the Roman Catholic Church since Vatican II toward Anglicans and the other members of the WORLD COUNCIL OF CHURCHES.

Further reading: Yngve Brilioth, *Evangelicalism and the Oxford Movement* (Oxford: Oxford University Press, 1934); R. W. Church, *The Oxford Movement: Twelve Years, 1833–1845,* ed. by Geoffrey Best (Chicago: University of Chicago Press, 1970); Peter B. Nockles, *Oxford Movement in Context: Anglican High Churchmanship, 1760–1857* (Cambridge: Cambridge University Press 1994); Stephen Thomas, *Newman and Heresy: The Anglican Years* (Cambridge: Cambridge University Press, 1991).

P

pacifism

Pacifism, an ideological opposition to violence and war, emerged at the time of the Reformation and became the opinion of the majority of the groups of the Radical Reformation. As early as 1527, the SCHLEITHEIM ARTICLES devoted seven paragraphs to the Christian's relationship to the sword, defined as the coercive power of the state to punish the wicked to the point of death. The Christian was to withdraw from any use of the sword. The Dordrecht Confession (1632) was more concise, disavowing the use of force to protect believers from their enemies.

The development of pacifism among MENNONITES and later groups such as the German BRETHREN, QUAKERS, and other Free Church communities, was in part a reaction against two violent episodes, the campaigns of Thomas Münzer (c. 1490–1525) and the communal experiment at Münster in Germany. In 1524, Münzer, a former Catholic priest, concluded that he had a right to assume the authority of a prince for the purpose of carrying out God's will. He led an army against the German princes who supported Martin LUTHER. Before his defeat in 1525, his army destroyed a number of monasteries and castles.

Then in 1534–35, a group of dissidents took power in the city of Münster, Westphalia. A communal society was instituted and increasingly bizarre rules set in place. Unable to resolve the situation by more peaceful means, Catholic forces under Philip of Hesse finally overran the city and executed its leaders. The incident at Münster was very much in the mind of Jacob Hutter (d. 1536), founder of the Hutterites, when he wrote in 1535, "sooner than strike our enemy with the hand, much less with the spear, or sword, or halbert, as the world does, we would die or surrender life."

Pacifism among Christian groups draws upon the New Testament admonition to follow a path of love toward one's neighbor (Luke 10:25–28; I Corinthians 13) as well as passages against retaliation (Matthew 5:38–48; I Thessalonians 5:15). The early church was pacifist, and soldiers who converted were told to find another occupation. A radical change came with Constantine (c. 280–337) and the identification of Christianity with the ruling authorities. Just one year after Constantine gave Christianity legal status in the Roman Empire, the Council of Arles (314) threatened to excommunicate those who refused to engage in combat. A century later (following the Barbarian sack of Rome), Augustine (354–430) developed the theory of a "just war," which has remained the standard position of the Christian church in the intervening centuries.

Prior to the 20th century, Protestant pacifism was largely confined to the older Peace Churches, the Mennonites, Hutterites, Amish, Brethren, and Quakers, who were often persecuted for refusing to cooperate with the war plans of various rulers. They were the foundation for William PENN's Commonwealth of Pennsylvania. Quaker control led numerous European pacifist sectarian groups to migrate to Pennsylvania, which gives a unique flavor to the religious life of some Pennsylvania counties (especially Lancaster) to the present.

In the 20th century, the Peace Churches took on a more proactive stance. They pushed for new laws recognizing conscientious objector status in many countries. When World War I began, the Hutterites faced a conscription crisis in the United States; as a result of government pressure to join the armed forces, they abandoned their land and moved to the more accommodating atmosphere in Canada. Peace Churches have also been active in developing programs that promote peace and nonviolent means to resolve conflicts. The development of a new intelligensia by the Peace Churches has led to a renewed respect for the pacifist position even by Protestant leaders who disagree with the position.

Following World War I, there was a noticeable emergence of pacifism within the SOCIAL GOSPEL movement. The desire to prevent war took on organizational form in 1914 with the founding of the FELLOWSHIP OF RECONCILIATION (FOR) in Europe and soon after in the United States. The list of Protestant pacifists in the 1920s and 1930s reads like a who's who of liberal Protestant leadership: A. J. Muste (1885–1967), Kirby Page (1890–1957), and Harry F. Ward (1873–1966), to mention but a few. The abandonment of pacifism by ethicist Reinhold Niebuhr, who adopted the position as a result of World War I and abandoned it as World War II began, became a major event in the development of Protestant thought.

New bastions of pacifism emerged in some unexpected places. There has been a pacifist strain among American sectarian groups, the SEVENTH-DAY ADVENTIST CHURCH being a notable example.

Alexander Campbell (1788–1866), Dwight L. MOODY, and John Alexander Dowie (1847–1907) also identified themselves with pacifism. In the 19th century, a number of Quakers close to the HOLINESS MOVEMENT spread pacifist ideas to some of its adherents. Pacifism in the early 20th century Pentecostal groups has been traced to Charles Fox PARHAM, whose wife was a Quaker, and Ambrose J. Tomlinson (1865–1943), a Quaker who became the leader of the CHURCH OF GOD (CLEVELAND, TENNESSEE). British Pentecostal pioneers Donald Gee (1891–1966) and Howard (1891–1971) and John Carter (1893–1981) were also pacifists, and pacifist sympathies were visible in the early Pentecostal organizations across Europe.

World War I proved a crisis for Pentecostals. African-American bishop Charles H. Mason (1866–1961), head of the CHURCH OF GOD IN CHRIST, for example, was jailed for his pacifist leanings. Meanwhile, independent Pentecostal congregations scurried to create pan-congregational associations that could approach the United States government on behalf of their draft-age members. Though still present, there has been a significant erosion of support for pacifism in the decades since the end of World War I.

Though pacifism lost much of its support in the wake of the Japanese attack on Pearl Harbor and with the emergence of the more realistic theology of NEO-ORTHODOXY, it still found expression in such organizations as the World Conference of Religions for Peace, which had among its founders United Methodist bishop John Wesley Lord (b. 1902), and experienced a resurgence in the 1960s, inspired by the nonviolent strategies for social change generally associated with Mahatma Gandhi. While attending Crozer Theological Seminary, Martin Luther KING Jr., was first exposed to pacifism in both its liberal Protestant form of teacher A. J. Muste, and its Indian form in his writings on Gandhi. He developed a new synthesis of pacifist thought to support a program of nonviolent protest that led to the passing of the Civil Rights Acts of the 1960s, and to his repudiation of the American involvement in Vietnam.

Since his assassination in 1968, King's disciples have attempted to perpetuate his nonviolent philosophy of social change. It has been challenged within the African-American community by leaders who have suggested that the potential of King's approach has been exhausted. A strain of pacifism also continues in organizations such as the Fellowship of Reconciliation, which makes common cause with the Peace Churches as new issues emerge. Support peaked in the 1970s during the last years of the Vietnam War, but has since been able to garner only marginal support.

Further reading: Peter Brock and Nigel Young, *Pacifism in the Twentieth Century* (Syracuse, N.Y.: Syracuse University Press, 1999); Clyde L. Manschreck, *A History of Christianity* (Englewood Cliffs, N.J.: Prentice Hall, 1964); Geoffrey Nuttall, *Christian Pacifism in History* (Oxford: Basil Blackwell, 1958); J. C. Wenger, *Pacifism and Biblical Nonresistance* (Scottdale, Pa.: Herald Press, 1968); Walter Wink, ed., *Peace Is the Way: Writings on Nonviolence from the Fellowship of Reconciliation* (Maryknoll, N.Y.: Orbis Books, 2000); John Howard Yoder, *Nevertheless; a Meditation on the Varieties and Shortcomings of Religious Pacifism* (Scottdale, Pa.: Herald Press, 1971); ———, *The Politics of Jesus: Vicit Agnus Noster* (Carlisle, U.K./Grand Rapids, Mich.: Paternoster Press/William B. Eerdmans, 1994).

Pal, Krishna (1764–1822) *first Baptist convert in India and Indian missionary*

Krishna Pal was born in Birra Gram in Bengal, and was raised as a Hindu. He eventually became a guru (teacher) and had taught for some 16 years before meeting Dr. John THOMAS of the Serampore mission established by William CAREY. Pal had broken his arm, and Thomas set it for him. Converted to Christianity, he was baptized by Carey on December 28, 1800.

Shortly after his BAPTISM, Pal erected a chapel and continued to work directly with the missionaries for the next few years. In 1804, they sent him to Calcutta (where they themselves were not allowed access) as a missionary. He worked there for five years and then traveled around the region, settling in English Bazaar for six years and then returning to Calcutta, where he died on August 22, 1822.

Pal's success prepared the way for other Indian Christian leaders, first as unordained missionaries, then as ordained ministers, and finally as leaders of established denominations.

Further reading: *The First Hindoo Convert: A Memoir of Krishna Pal: A Preacher of the Gospel to His Countrymen More Than Twenty Years* (Philadelphia: American Baptist Publication Society, 1852). Available online. URL: http://www.wmcarey.edu/carey/krishna_pal/krishna-pal.htm; Eleanor Jackson, "From Krishna Pal to Lal Behari Dey: Indian Builders of the Church in India or Native Agency in Bengal 1800–1880." Available online. URL: http://cp.yahoo.net/search/cache?p=%22Krishna+Pal%22+Eleanor+jackson&ei=UTF8&n=20&fl=0&url=xxYXiLD5pyAJ:www.multifaithnet.org/mfnopenaccess/research/online/drafts.htm. Accessed on January 11, 2004; "Short Account of the Conversion and Baptism of Kristno Paul," in *The American Baptist Magazine, and Missionary Intelligencer,* New Series, vol. 1, no. 2 (March 1817): 65–67.

Palau, Luis (b. 1934) *Argentinian evangelist*

Luis Palau was born on November 27, 1934, in Buenos Aires. He had a personal conversion to Christ at age 12. Six years later, he began preaching on weekends while making his living working in a bank. Around 1957, Palau and several associates organized an independent tent evangelism and radio ministry in ARGENTINA. After he heard Billy GRAHAM speak on the radio, the evangelist became his career role model.

Palau received his basic education through Saint Alban's College in Argentina, part of the Cambridge University Overseas Program. In 1960, he traveled to the United States for graduate study at Multnomah School of the Bible, a conservative Evangelical school in Portland, Oregon.

In 1961, Palau affiliated with Overseas Crusades (now OC International), a missionary agency supported by the CHRISTIAN BRETHREN, and launched a ministry to Spanish-speaking communities. He was able to meet Graham the next year and served as a Spanish translator during his crusade in Fresno, California. The next year he was ordained and sent by OC International to Bogotá, Colombia. There he began a radio ministry that continues to the present as *Luis Palau Responde* and *Cruzada,* heard across Latin America. In 1966, he held his first large-scale public preaching event, in Bogotá. Others have been held periodically at locations around the world. His crusade in London (1984–85) attracted a cumulative attendance of more than half a million people. His ministry has been assisted by his fluency in both Spanish and English.

In 1967, he was named OC's Latin America field director. An outstanding orator, he put together an international team of men and women to assist in his expansive evangelistic campaigns. By 1971, the Luis Palau Evangelistic Team emerged as a separate division within OC International, then on October 1, 1978, Palau and his team left OC to form an independent organization. Soon afterward, the first issue of *Continente Nuevo,* a magazine for Spanish-speaking ministers, appeared. The Luis Palau Evangelistic Association has its international headquarters in Portland, Oregon, and subsidiary offices in Miami, Guatemala City, and London.

As the new century began, Palau visited the Peoples Republic of CHINA, leading preaching services at three churches. He was also a keynote speaker at Billy Graham's *Amsterdam 2000* event attended by some 10,000 evangelists. Palau remains one of the most well known Christian leaders in the world.

Further reading: Ellen Bascuti, *Luis Palau, Evangelist to the World* (Uhrichsville, Ohio: Barbour, 2000); Luis Palau, *Calling America and the Nations to Christ* (Nashville, Tenn.: Thomas Nelson, 1994); ———, *It's a God Thing* (Garden City, N.Y.: Doubleday, 2001); ———, *Where Is God When Bad Things Happen?* (Garden City, N.Y.: Doubleday, 1999).

Palmer, Phoebe (1807–1874) *Holiness teacher and women's rights advocate*

Phoebe Palmer was born Phoebe Worrell in New York City on December 18, 1807, and grew up in the Methodist Episcopal Church (now an integral part of the UNITED METHODIST CHURCH). She had a conversion experience early in life, but was not satisfied in her relationship with God for many years.

In 1827, she married Walter C. Palmer (1804–83). They joined the Norfolk Street Church, which they felt needed strengthening. Beginning in 1835, Phoebe held women's meetings on Tuesday afternoons at her home (with Walter's encouragement). These meetings took on new meaning after 1837, when Pheobe experienced what Holiness people call sanctification or the second blessing. She felt that she had been perfected in love. The Palmers emerged as leaders

Phoebe Palmer, Methodist laywoman and Holiness evangelist *(Drew University Library)*

in the burgeoning HOLINESS MOVEMENT within the METHODIST CHURCH.

Palmer's Holiness beliefs led her to charitable work among the poor and the imprisoned. In 1850, she took the lead in founding the Five Points Mission to assist people trapped in the city's slums. She began to write articles for Timothy Merrit's periodical, *Guide to Holiness,* the movement's chief organ, as well as her first books.

Throughout the 1850s, the Palmers made annual tours of the eastern United States and CANADA, visiting Methodist CAMP MEETINGS and initiating their own Holiness revivals, helping to stimulate a revival that swept through Methodism in 1857. The Palmers spread Holiness teachings in England from 1859 to 1863 (as the Civil War raged in America). Upon their return, Walter purchased the *Guide to Holiness* and installed Phoebe as its editor, a post she held for the rest of her life. Once the war ended, the Holiness movement swept the Methodist church at every level. It was given institutional form by the National Association for the Promotion of Holiness, organized in 1867.

During the last decade of her life, Phoebe was a dominant force in the movement. She wrote several more books and was outspoken on a variety of issues from fair wages for domestics to temperance. Outside the Holiness movement, she is most remembered for her advocacy of women's rights in the church. She was frequently called upon to justify her career, which she did in her book *Promise of the Father,* which relied on her reading of the second chapter of Acts. From the fact that the BAPTISM OF THE HOLY SPIRIT was for both men and women, she argued that women had the power and obligation to testify about the Lord.

Phoebe continued her evangelistic, literary, and social work until her death on November 2, 1874. Walter continued to publish the *Guide to Holiness* until his death in 1883.

Further reading: Melvin E. Dieter, *The Holiness Revival of the Nineteenth Century* (Metuchen, N.J.: Scarecrow Press, 1980); Phoebe Palmer, *Promise of the Father* (Boston: H. V. Degen, 1859; reprint, Salem, Ohio: Schmul, 1981); ———, *The Way of Holiness with Notes by the Way,* 2nd ed. (New York: Lane & Tippett, 1845); Richard Wheatley, *The Life and Letters of Mrs. Phoebe Palmer* (New York: W. C. Palmer, Jr., 1876); Charles Edward White, *The Beauty of Holiness: Phoebe Palmer as Theologian, Revivalist, Feminist, and Humanitarian* (Grand Rapids, Mich.: Zondervan, 1986).

parachurch organizations

Protestantism has been carried forward through its primary structure, the DENOMINATION, whether established by the state or independently, which provides the context for the life of worship and service of the average Christian.

In the 18th century, secondary religious organizations began to emerge to provide new services that extended the work of the denominations. At first, these parachurches called attention to new areas of concern that were not being met by the churches. Among the first such organizations, the SOCIETY FOR PROMOTING CHRISTIAN KNOWLEDGE and the SOCIETY FOR THE PROPAGATION OF THE GOSPEL IN FOREIGN PARTS (SPG), educated Christians in England about the needs of the British American colonies in North America and, as the empire grew, in other parts of the world. The Naval and Military Bible Society was the first organization devoted to publishing and distributing copies of the Bible as a means of evangelism.

In the 19th century, the number of such organizations expanded rapidly. Leading the way were the missionary societies. For the loosely organized BAPTISTS in England, the Baptist Missionary Society championed the cause of world missions in the face of a majority that opposed such ministry. The American Board of Commissioners for Foreign Missions, though at heart a Congregationalist body, provided the means for other denominations to contribute to the missionary cause until their own churches could organize mission boards. The parachurch idea was especially attractive to congregationally organized denominations that wanted to avoid the trappings of more centrally controlled groups led by bishops or elders.

Many parachurch organizations of the early 19th century were used to organize support across denominational lines for various moral crusades—the destruction of slavery, Sabbath observance, SUNDAY SCHOOLS, temperance, women's rights, peace, and so forth. Some of these organizations were exclusively Christian, such as the New England Tract Society and the Woman's Christian Temperance Union, while others such as the Society for the Promotion of Temperance and the American and Foreign Anti-Slavery Society included many non-Christians in their membership.

By the end of the 19th century, the largest number of parachurch organizations were providing services for churches within the congregationally organized denominations—the Plymouth Brethren, the Churches of Christ, the Disciples of Christ, various Baptist denominations, and the independent Holiness churches. They were soon joined by a host of organizations serving PENTECOSTALISM and the Fundamentalist movement. Parachurch organizations included publishing concerns, healing homes, schools, orphanages, and a variety of evangelistic and missionary agencies. Organizations such as the Standard Publishing Company, the Oriental Missionary Society, Asbury College, and GIDEONS INTERNATIONAL became large, permanent parts of the Protestant community.

The most visible parachruch organizations were the nondenominational missionary groups that added so much to the spectacular growth of Protestantism from the mid-19th century to World War II. Often inaccurately referred to as FAITH MISSIONS, because of the faith policies articulated by the CHINA INLAND MISSION, these groups were able to mobilize Christians from denominations that lacked their own missionary programs, and target geographical areas that denominational programs had not yet reached.

The number of parachurch organizations has continued to grow in the West. In some cases, they have developed new types of ministry, such as Youth for Christ, the Institute for Church Growth, and the International Society for Frontier Missiology.

Increasingly, parachurch organizations have also been founded to spur reforms in the denominations themselves. Within almost all the larger denominations there now exist a spectrum of organizations designed to push the denomination in one direction or another. Conservative organizations such as the Good News Movement in United Methodism or the Biblical Witness Fellowship in the United Church of Christ attempt to call their churches back to traditional standards from which they are seen to have drifted. At the same time, a variety of organizations promoting gay rights and abortion rights have attempted to move denominations to adopt what they see as prophetic positions. There are also interdenominational parachurch organizations such as the Religious Coalition for Reproductive Choice and the Traditional Values Coalition that aim to pressure more than one denomination to adopt their perspectives.

Professional and scholarly associations have constituted another major parachurch sector since the late 19th century. The former provide fellowship, support, and opportunities for action for Christians in almost every imaginable occupation, including physicians, lawyers, athletes, and others. The scholarly associations have provided Christian scholars with similar resources, especially in the face of the secularization of the American Academy of Religion, which has moved away from theology and biblical studies to religious studies as its major focus. The American Scientific Affiliation and the Evangelical Theological Society are the most well known of the Christian scholarly parachurch organizations.

Parachurch organizations have sometimes been criticized for competing with denominational ministries for sparse church funds, for spending too large a percentage of their finances on overhead, for masking theological divergences from the giving public, and occasionally for providing a haven for fraud.

Further reading: H. Wayne House, *Christian Ministries and the Law: What Church and Parachurch Leaders Should Know* (Grand Rapids, Mich.: Baker

Book House, 1992); K. Wilmer Wesley and J. David Schmidt, with Martyn Smith, *The Prosperous Parachurch: Enlarging the Boundaries of God's Kingdom* (San Francisco: Jossey-Bass, 1998); Jerry W. White, *The Church & the Parachurch: An Uneasy Marriage* (Portland, Ore.: Multnomah Press, 1983).

Parham, Charles Fox (1873–1929)
founder of modern Pentecostalism

Charles Fox Parham was born in Muscatine, Iowa, on June 4, 1873. He grew up in Kansas, where he became a SUNDAY SCHOOL teacher and then a licensed minister in the Methodist Episcopal Church (now an integral part of the UNITED METHODIST CHURCH). After preaching for several years, he left the Methodists in 1894 to become an independent evangelist. In 1896, with his wife, Sarah Thistlewaite, he opened Bethel, a healing home, in Topeka, Kansas. He eventually lost control of his home, and in 1900 moved across town and opened a new Bethel, where students could reside and learn from his evangelistic experience.

Late in 1900, departing for an evangelistic trip, he asked his students to search Scripture for citations about the BAPTISM OF THE HOLY SPIRIT. Among Methodist HOLINESS people, the baptism was associated with their experience of sanctification, a second act of grace, which God worked among believers to make them perfect in love. The students discovered that speaking in tongues seemed to be the sign of the baptism. On New Year's Eve, the group began to pray for the baptism, and in the morning hours of January 1, 1901, Agnes Oznam (1870–1937) became the first person in modern times to successfully pray for the baptism and actually speak in tongues. The connection between the baptism of the Spirit with speaking in tongues became the distinguishing feature of PENTECOSTALISM. In the context of his Holiness background, Parham presented the baptism of the Holy Spirit as a third work of grace in the life of a believer who had already experienced sanctification.

Parham introduced this new teaching, which he called Apostolic Faith, into Holiness circles in Kansas and neighboring states, and eventually moved to Houston, Texas, where he opened a Bible school. In 1905, William J. SEYMOUR, a black Holiness minister formerly with the African Methodist Episcopal Church, audited his classes, although Texas segregation laws forced him to listen to the lessons from outside the classroom.

In 1906, Parham helped Seymour move to Los Angeles, where he had been invited to be pastor of a small church. Seymour was soon presiding over the three-year-long AZUSA STREET REVIVAL, which became a national and then international phenomenon. Parham eventually split with Seymour over issues of church practice as well as charges of sexual impropriety brought against Parham.

Alienated from the mainstream of the Pentecostal movement, Parham returned to the Midwest and settled in Baxter Springs, Kansas, to teach in a small Bible school and preach in nearby communities. A set of congregations grew up around his ministry, which later became an association that continues to be known as the Apostolic Faith. After Parham's death on January 29, 1929, his wife wrote a biography defending Parham's character.

Further reading: James Goff, *Fields White Unto Harvest: Charles Fox Parham and the Missionary Origins of Pentecostalism* (Fayetteville: University of Arkansas Press, 1988); Charles F. Parham, *A Voice Crying in the Wilderness* (1944; reprint, Charles F. Parham, 1902); ———, *The Everlasting Gospel* (Baxter Springs, Kans.: Charles F. Parham, 1911); Robert L. Parham, ed., *Selected Sermons of the Late Charles F. Parham and Sarah E. Parham, Co-Founders of the Original Apostolic Faith Movement* (Baxter Springs, Kans.: Robert Parham, 1941); Sarah Parham, *The Life of Charles Fox Parham* (Baxter Springs, Kans.: Sarah Parham and Tri-State Printing, 1930).

Paris Evangelical Mission Society

The Paris Mission (officially the Société de missions évangéliques de Paris) is the missionary arm of the Reformed Church of FRANCE. It originated early in the 19th century as some French Protestants gathered to pray for and help support the pioneering European missionary-sending agencies such as the BASEL MISSION and the LONDON MISSIONARY SOCIETY. A separate agency for the French-speaking world was formally organized in 1822; soon the Paris Mission had affiliated branches in Holland, ITALY, and French-speaking SWITZERLAND. The society accepted support on an interdenominational basis, but found its greatest support from members of the several Reformed churches.

The Paris Mission sent missionaries to SOUTH AFRICA in 1829, and they opened work in Lesotho and Zambia. The mission's choice of fields was largely dictated by the growth of the French colonial empire. As the French assumed authority in areas previously evangelized by British, American, and German missionaries, the government introduced Roman Catholicism and moved to restrict or suppress Protestant missionary enterprises. Survival often meant handing control to the Paris Mission. In this way, the mission acquired work in Tahiti and other South Pacific islands, and African centers in Madagascar, GABON, Togo, and Cameroon. It, of course, also pioneered its own work in other, unevangelized areas that came under French control.

After World War II, the Paris Mission worked to facilitate the rapid transformation of its missions into autonomous churches. Having completed that process in 1971, the Paris Mission voted itself out of existence. It passed its remaining resources to the Département Francais d'Action Apostolique, a missionary agency serving several French Protestant DENOMINATIONS, and the Communaute Evangélique d'Action Apostolique, an international communion of 47 churches working in French-speaking lands. Both organizations are based in Paris.

Further reading: Jean Bianquis, *Les origines de la Société des Missions Evangéliques de Paris, 1822–1829,* 3 vols. (Paris: Societe des Missions Evangeliques, 1930–35); A. Scott Moreau, ed. *Evangelical Dictionary of World Missions* (Grand Rapids, Mich.: Baker Book House, 2000).

Parker, Peter (1804–1888) *pioneer medical missionary in China*

Peter Parker was born in Framingham, Massachusetts, in 1804, and raised within the Congregational Church. He graduated from Yale University in 1831, but stayed on to win degrees in theology and medicine (1834). Ordained a Presbyterian minister in January 1834, he left for CHINA a month later with the support of the AMERICAN BOARD OF COMMISSIONERS FOR FOREIGN MISSIONS. He settled in Canton, where in 1835 he opened an ophthalmic (and general) hospital. While treating a wide range of conditions, Parker specialized in diseases related to the eye. Among other firsts, he introduced anesthesia to China.

In 1838, Parker led in forming the Medical Missionary Society in China. When forced out of China during the Opium War (1840–42) he used the time to advocate for MEDICAL MISSIONS within the Protestant community in North America and Europe.

He returned to China with his wife (incidentally the first Western female allowed to reside in China). In 1844, he began to work part time to help U.S. Attorney General Caleb Cushing negotiate the first treaty between China and America. His diplomatic foray cost him his relationship with the American Board in 1847, but he continued to work as a doctor and as the American Commissioner and Minister to China.

In 1857, Parker returned to the United States, where he remained for the rest of his life. He eventually reconciled with the American Board, and was named a corporate member. He died in January 1888.

Further reading: Eugene M. Blake, "Yale's First Opthalmologist—The Reverend Peter Parker, M.D.," *Yale Journal of Biology and Medicine* 1931, 3(5): 387–396; T. R. Colledge and Peter Parker, *Address and Minutes of Proceedings of the Medical Missionary Society Canton, China 1838* (Canton: Office of the Chinese Repository, 1838); Edward C. Gulick, *Peter Parker and the Opening of China* (Cambridge, Mass.: Harvard University Press, 1973); Edward H. Hume, "Peter Parker and the Introduction of Anesthesia into China," *Jour-*

nal of the History of Medicine 1 (October 1946): 670–674; George B. Stevens, The Life, Letters, and Journals of the Rev. and Hon. Peter Parker, M.D., Missionary, Physician, Diplomatist, The Father of Medical Missions and Founder of the Ophthalmic Hospital in Canton (Boston/Chicago: Congregational Sunday-School and Publishing Society, 1896).

Parr, Katherine (c. 1513–1548) sixth wife of HENRY VIII and Protestant convert

Katherine Parr, sixth wife of HENRY VIII, played an important role in the development of Protestantism in England. Katherine's mother was a lady-in-waiting to Catherine of Aragon, the mother of MARY I, and Katherine was raised in the royal nursery. Henry married her in 1543.

It appears that she was converted to Protestantism by Thomas CRANMER. She used her position in the royal household to ensure that her stepchildren (later EDWARD VI and ELIZABETH I) were educated by Protestant tutors. She also wrote two works of Protestant piety, Prayers or Meditations (1545) and The Lamentations of a Sinner (published in 1547, after Henry's death). In March 1547, she married Thomas Seymour and became involved in his family's attempt to control affairs in England during Edward's reign. She died in childbirth in 1548.

During her brief period as Henry's wife, Parr was able to provide patronage for a number of Protestant leaders, such as Miles COVERDALE and Hugh Latimer, who would later play major roles in the triumph of Protestantism. Coverdale attained fame for his Bible translation, and Latimer was martyred by Mary I.

Further reading: Mary Luke, The Early Modern Englishwoman: A Facsimile Library of Essential Works Printed Writings, 1500–1640: Katherine Parr, part 1, vol. 3 (Menston, U.K.: Scolar Press, 1996); Anthony K. Martienssen, Queen Katherine Parr (New York: McGraw-Hill, 1974); Janel Mueller, "A Tudor Queen Finds Voice: Katherine Parr's Lamentation of a Sinner," in The Historical Renaissance, Heather Dubrow and

Richard Strier, eds. (Chicago: University of Chicago Press, 1988): 15–47.

Particular Baptists

At the start of the 17th century, British BAPTISTS split into General Baptists and Particular Baptists. The former group taught the doctrine of general atonement, that Christ had died for all and that anyone who turned to him in faith would be saved. The Particular Baptists taught the idea of particular atonement, that Christ died only for the elect whom God foreknew and predestined to turn to faith. These two groups existed side by side through the 18th century, until a modified form of the Particular perspective developed by Andrew FULLER became the dominant theological stance of the Baptists.

The Strict Baptists emerged among Particular Baptists in England in the early 19th century. They practice what is termed closed communion, meaning that they limit participation in the LORD'S SUPPER to those who have been baptized as adults by immersion. While many Baptists practice closed communion, the primary group that retains the strict label is the Strict and Particular Baptists of England (who have a small branch in the United States).

Further reading: H. Leon McBeth, The Baptist Heritage: Four Centuries of Baptist Witness (Nashville, Tenn.: Broadman Press, 1887).

Peace See PACIFISM.

Peace of Augsburg See AUGSBURG, PEACE OF.

Penn, William (1644–1718) Quaker leader and advocate of religious freedom

William Penn was born in London, England, on October 14, 1644. He was raised as a member of the CHURCH OF ENGLAND. His early life showed little direction, but after hearing Thomas Loe preach, he became a member of the Society of Friends (QUAKERS). This landed him in prison on several occasions as he began to speak out for personal and religious liberties. He quickly rose in the small movement and in 1677 traveled with founder George FOX to Holland.

About this time, Penn wrote a charter for some British Quakers hoping to settle in New Jersey. The "Concessions and Agreements" document included provisions for the right to a jury trial and freedom from imprisonment for debt, and it forbade capital punishment. More than 800 Quakers migrated to New Jersey.

In 1681, he called in a debt owed his father by the king. The king granted him a charter to what became Pennsylvania (and Delaware). Penn hoped to recoup his finances by selling tracts of land. He also hoped to make of Pennsylvania an experiment in self-governance. He attracted enough investors to keep him afloat, but his "holy experiment" made a decisive mark on history. Penn constructed a legal framework that included many of the same rights previously written into the document for the New Jersey colonists. He arrived in Pennsylvania in 1682 and made treaties with various native peoples.

Penn spent most of the rest of his life in England, mired in the ups and down of royal politics. He lost control of Pennsylvania for a while, but he managed to reinstitute provisions of his initial charter in 1699, placing essential powers in the hands of the legislative assembly.

Penn died in 1718, leaving his sons in control of Pennsylvania for the next generation.

Though Penn was unable to enjoy most of the fruits of his labors, he created one of the most religiously liberal governments of his time. The success of the colony's pluralistic life helped inspire the Bill of Rights of the United States Constitution and its groundbreaking experiment with religious liberty.

Further reading: Genevieve Foster, *The World of William Penn* (New York: Scribner, 1973); Jean R. Soderlund and Richard S. Dunn, eds., *William Penn*

and the Founding of Pennsylvania: 1680–1684 (Philadelphia: University of Pennsylvania Press, 1999); William Penn, *No Cross No Crown* (1669; reprint, Shippensburg, Pa.: Destiny Image, 2001); ———, *The Political Writings of William Penn,* ed. by Andrew R. Murphy (Indianapolis, Ind.: Liberty Fund, 2002); ———, *William Penn on Religion and Ethics: The Emergence of Liberal Quakerism,* 2 vols., ed. by Hugh S. Barbour (Lewiston, N.Y.: Edwin Mellen Press, 1991).

Pentecostal/Filadelfia Church (Sweden)

PENTECOSTALISM came to SWEDEN in 1907 from Norway, and the first church was formed in 1913. It grew significantly, and by the end of the 20th century had become the largest FREE CHURCH movement in the country, with more than 90,000 members. Somewhat unique within the Pentecostal world, Swedish Pentecostalism developed as an ultra-congregational movement with none of the organizational structure generally associated with denominational life. Missionary programs, educational efforts, social services, and communication are all handled by organizations owned jointly by the several Pentecostal congregations. These organizations include the International Broadcasting Association, which supports IBRA Radio, an extensive international network of Christian radio stations; the International Center of the Pentecostal Mission, which prints and distributes Bibles and other Christian literature in different languages; PMU Interlife, a social service agency; and four schools that provide secondary and some college education.

The Swedish Pentecostal churches support missions around the world. The first missionaries, Samuel and Lina Nystrom, arrived in BRAZIL in 1916. Today, some 400 missionaries serve worldwide in more than 50 countries.

Further reading: Lauri Ahonen with J. E. Johannesson, "Sweden," in Stanley M. Burgess and Eduard M. Van der Maas, eds. *International Dictionary of Pentecostal Charismatic Movements* (rev. ed., Grand Rapids, Mich.: Zondervan, 2000).

Pentecostalism

Pentecostalism, which emphasizes the gifts of the Holy Spirit such as speaking in tongues, emerged at the start of the 20th century as a revitalization of the HOLINESS MOVEMENT in the United States. The Holiness churches had followed the doctrine of sanctification, an act of God that they believed made each believer perfect in love. Sanctification would come as a second blessing after the believer had already been justified, or graced by faith into a saving relationship with Christ. The believer's first subjective experience of sanctification was often called the BAPTISM OF THE HOLY SPIRIT. With time, some adherents felt that the movement was focusing too much on strict behavioral codes as evidence of the sanctified life.

The Pentecostal movement was presaged by episodes where the gifts of the Holy Spirit, including speaking in tongues, had appeared, as for example among early members of the CHURCH OF JESUS CHRIST OF LATTER-DAY SAINTS, or at the ALBURY CONFERENCES in England. The more immediate precursors were the KESWICK MOVEMENT, with its search for empowerment and Christian victory, and the Fire-Baptized movement, almost all of whose followers became Pentecostals.

Modern Pentecostalism is traced to a Bible school in Topeka, Kansas, founded by former Methodist minister Charles F. PARHAM (1873–1929). During a prayer session seeking the baptism of the Holy Spirit, one of the students, Agnes Oznam (1870–1937), began to speak in tongues.

Within a short time, Parham and the other students also received the baptism, and they began to spread the news through the Holiness community in Kansas and nearby states. Parham opened another Bible school in Houston, where an African-American Holiness preacher, William J. SEYMOUR, picked up the teachings. Seymour took the movement to Los Angeles, where he led the historic three-year AZUSA STREET REVIVAL. News of the revival spread like wildfire around the world, and within a decade Pentecostalism was a global movement.

The Stone Church, a large Pentecostal congregation in Toronto, Canada *(Institute for the Study of American Religion, Santa Barbara, California)*

The original Pentecostal teachings offered a third experience of God's grace to Holiness believers, who had already experienced faith in Christ and sanctification (holiness). Among Holiness Pentecostals, sanctification was considered a prerequisite for the baptism of the Holy Spirit. This understanding is held by such groups as the CHURCH OF GOD (CLEVELAND, TENNESSEE), the CHURCH OF GOD IN CHRIST, and the INTERNATIONAL PENTECOSTAL HOLINESS CHURCH.

Soon after the Pentecostal teachings emerged, William H. Durham (1873–1912), a Baptist minister from Chicago, rejected the Holiness teachings and claimed that the baptism of the Holy Spirit was available to every believer quite apart from any experience of sanctification. This perspective was called the "finished work," meaning that Christ had completed his salvific work on Calvary and all of the benefits were available to all at any moment. Durham's perspective appealed to those attracted to Pentecostalism from other than Methodist or Holiness backgrounds. It would undergird the teachings of groups such as the ASSEMBLIES OF GOD.

Several years later, still another stream emerged in the movement, the JESUS ONLY PENTECOSTALS. Jesus Only ministers rejected the orthodox Christian doctrine of the Trinity. From their reading of the Bible, which does not mention the Trinity, they concluded that Trinitarianism was close to tri-theism (belief in three gods). They stressed instead the Oneness of God. They rejected the baptismal formula derived from Matthew 28:19, in the name of the "Father, and of the Son, and of the Holy Ghost"; instead they baptized in the name of Jesus alone, as used throughout the Book of Acts. They concluded that Jesus was the name of the singular God. The Oneness or Jesus Only Pentecostals founded such groups as the UNITED PENTECOSTAL CHURCH, INTERNATIONAL and the PENTECOSTAL ASSEMBLIES OF THE WORLD.

Within a very few years, the Pentecostal movement took root in the UNITED KINGDOM, Scandinavia, Africa, and Latin America. In Scandinavia, Pentecostals became the largest Christian denomination outside the state churches. The South African Apostolic and Zionist churches helped spread Pentecostalism throughout sub-Saharan Africa (*see* AFRICA, SUB-SAHARAN). Spanish-speaking attendees at the Azusa Street revival took the movement to MEXICO and CENTRAL AMERICA. In the last half of the 20th century, it would become the major religion contesting the hegemony of Roman Catholicism throughout Latin America. The largest Christian congregation in the world is the Pentecostal YOIDO FULL GOSPEL CENTRAL CHURCH, a Pentecostal church in Seoul, Korea.

In the 1960s, a wave of Pentecostal experience spread through the older Protestant churches and among Roman Catholics, bringing about a revitalization even more extensive than that of the first decade of the century. This wave of spiritual empowerment is referred to collectively as the CHARISMATIC MOVEMENT.

Pentecostals have found some international fellowship through the PENTECOSTAL WORLD FELLOWSHIP.

Further reading: Stanley M. Burgess and Eduard M. Van der Maas, eds. *International Dictionary of Pentecostal Charismatic Movements* (rev. ed., Grand Rapids, Mich.: Zondervan, 2002); Walter J. Hollenweger, *Pentecostals: The Charismatic Movement in the Church* (Minneapolis, Minn.: Augsburg, 1972); Harold D. Hunter, *Spirit Baptism: A Pentecostal Alternative* (Washington, D.C.: University Press of America, 1983); Vinson Synan, *The Century of the Holy Spirit: 100 Years of Pentecostal and Charismatic Renewal, 1901–2001* (Nashville, Tenn.: Thomas Nelson, 2001).

Pentecostal World Fellowship

The Pentecostal World Fellowship emerged at the end of the 20th century. It was the latest step in a long process of unifying believers who shared the experience of the BAPTISM OF THE HOLY SPIRIT and the resulting manifestations of the gifts of the Spirit (I Corinthians 12).

The initial outpouring of PENTECOSTALISM that began with the AZUSA STREET REVIVAL in 1906 brought hopes that all Christians would soon be united. Instead, new divisions emerged not just between Pentecostals and non-Pentecostal Christians, but among Pentecostals themselves. The movement soon split into HOLINESS, FINISHED WORK, and JESUS ONLY factions, and DENOMINATIONS began to spring up across the United States. All attempts to find some means of expressing unity had only limited success until after World War II.

Shortly after World War II, European leaders called for a World Pentecostal Conference to be held in Zurich, SWITZERLAND, in May 1947. The gathering gave birth to a periodical, *Pentecost,* and named Donald Gee (1891–1966) as its editor. Gee, together with David J. du PLESSIS (1905–87), had been largely responsible for planning the conference.

Similar conferences have been held at approximately three-year intervals at locations on every continent, symbolizing the movement's rapid global growth. In 1961, the conference was first identified as the Pentecostal World Conference. In 2001, at Los Angeles, the name Pentecostal World Fellowship was adopted.

Many of those attending the conferences have resisted any proposal that might appear to give the conference itself any undue powers. Generally, each conference chooses a secretary and advisory committee to plan the next conference, and a presidium to preside at the various sessions. Leadership of the conference has been shared by some of the most famous names in the movement, including Petrus Lewi Pethrus (1884–1974, Sweden), W. E. McAleister (1880–1953, Canada), and Thomas F. Zimmerman (1912–91) of the ASSEMBLIES OF GOD, who chaired the conferences for over two decades.

Donald Gee edited *Pentecost* until his death in 1966. A new editor, Percy Brewster (1908–80), was appointed in 1970, and the periodical renamed *World Pentecost,* but it was discontinued in 1999.

The Pentecostal World Fellowship defines itself as a cooperative association of Pentecostal churches and groups committed to furthering the Gospel. It is designed to promote fellowship, cooperation, and mutual support among its member bodies and organizations. It has adopted a brief statement of faith that affirms the authority of the Bible, the TRINITY, the deity of Christ, the human need for regeneration by the Holy Spirit, and the baptism of the Holy Spirit with the evidence of speaking in tongues.

With the change of name in 2001, the fellowship has also taken on some specific tasks within the larger Pentecostal world, including the encouragement of cooperation on the mission field, speaking for the Pentecostal community to governments on behalf of persecuted believers, generating humanitarian assistance in selected places, and helping to build worldwide prayer networks.

The fellowship has headquarters in Springfield, Missouri, where the Assemblies of God is also headquartered. Its 2004 president was Thomas Trask (b. 1936), who is also general superintendent of the Assemblies of God. It has been a catalyst for the formation of regional structures such as the Pentecostal Fellowship in North America (1948) and the Pentecostal European Fellowship, founded in 1987 by the merger of two older fellowships.

See also ECUMENICAL MOVEMENT.

Further reading: Cecil M. Roebeck, Jr., "Pentecostal World Conference," in Stanley M. Burgess, and Eduard M. Van der Maas, eds., *International Dictionary of Pentecostal Charismatic Movements* (rev. ed., Grand Rapids, Mich.: Zondervan, 2002); Vinson Synan, *The Century of the Holy Spirit: 100 Years of Pentecostal and Charismatic Renewal 1901–2001* (Nashville, Tenn.: Thomas Nelson, 2001).

Peoples Temple

The short-lived Peoples Temple, founded in 1955 by Rev. Jim Jones (1931–78), is best known for its tragic end, when 900 members (and a party accompanying Congressman Leo J. Ryan [1925–78]) died in a massive act of murder-suicide in GUYANA on November 17, 1978. The subsequent use of the Peoples Temple as the model of a "cult" has obscured its previous history.

As a young minister in Indianapolis, Indiana, Jim Jones emerged as a messenger of social change with an emphasis on the church's concern for the poor and outcast. To some African Americans in the city, he offered hope, brotherhood, and socialism. His message came out of the SOCIAL GOSPEL MOVEMENT of the early 20th century. In 1964, Jones was ordained in and brought his church into the Christian Church (Disciples of Christ). The Christian Church was a member of the National Council of Churches and the WORLD COUNCIL OF CHURCHES, and the association gave Jones access to the ecumenical world of liberal Protestantism. The congregation moved to Ukiah, California, in 1965, and actively participated in the ecumenical activities of the California Council of Churches. In the mid-1970s, the Peoples Temple impressed the more socially active in the American Protestant community, and several denominational bodies held it up as a model of socially aware Christianity.

The Disciples of Christ, as a liberal, non-creedal (without a formal statement of belief), and loosely organized body with a congregational POLITY, was and remains home to a wide spectrum of belief. A number of its ministers prior to World

War II saw socialism as the practical expression of the kingdom of God on earth; in the 1970s they embraced LIBERATION THEOLOGY, a form of theology in dialogue with Marxism. As such, when Jones began to speak on such themes, his message resonated with one wing of contemporary Protestant church life.

By the early 1970s, the Peoples Temple was holding Sunday services in several California cities, with a remnant in Indiana. In 1972, Jones leased land in rural Guyana and started a farming community. Over the next few years, however, the temple became the object of several government criminal investigations. Former members filed complaints that they had been attacked, or that children under the temple's care were being abused. By 1977, the lawsuits and media exposés convinced Jones to move to the site in Guyana, eventually bringing more than 900 followers to settle there. Meanwhile, the congregations in California continued to gather regularly.

In light of these challenges, the group's leadership became ever more doubtful that the temple had a future. The visit of Congressman Ryan, even though conducted on outwardly friendly terms, seemed to be the final threat. Ryan and his companions were murdered, and nearly all the members died in a massive episode of murder and suicide. The deaths represent a case of what is termed revolutionary suicide.

After the deaths, the members still in California moved to dissolve the temple formally. People who lost family members and close friends in Guyana and former temple members still gather annually to remember and mourn.

Though called a cult, the Peoples Temple came from within the mainstream Protestant community. The tragedy in Guyana has joined similar incidents in other religious communities as an object of consideration by those who would prevent similar occurrences in the future.

Further reading: David G. Bromley and J. Gordon Melton, *Cults, Religion and Violence* (Cambridge: Cambridge University Press, 2002); John R. Hall, *Gone From the Promised Land: Jonestown in American Cultural History* (New Brunswick, N.J.: Transaction Books, 1987); Mary McCormick Maaga, *Hearing the Voices of Jonestown* (Syracuse, N.Y.: Syracuse University Press, 1998); Rebecca Moore, *Sympathetic History of Jonestown: The Moore Family Involvement in People's Temple* (Lewiston, N.Y.: Edwin Mellen Press, 1985); Catherine Wessinger, *How the Millennium Comes Violently: From Jonestown to Heaven's Gate* (New York: Seven Bridges Press, 2000).

perfectionism

There has always been an optimistic viewpoint within the Christian community that believers have the power to respond to the highest ideals of the faith. Various movements have taught that Christians could approach or attain at least some degree of perfection in this life. Those searching for completeness and wholeness in their response to God, beyond mere observance of a moral code of conduct, have generally drawn inspiration from a few biblical passages, especially the words attributed to Jesus, "Be ye therefore perfect, as your Father which is in heaven is perfect" (Matthew 5:48).

Some Christian theologians, such as Augustine (354–430), have denied the possibility of human perfection in this life, due to the continuing influence of the Fall. Others, such as Pelagius, disagreed; they charged that the church had become morally corrupt after it abandoned the biblical ideal of perfection.

The first reformers tended to agree with Augustine. To Martin LUTHER and John CALVIN, sin always remained a reality for believers. However, as Protestantism blossomed, with its emphasis on the Bible and its teachings, leaders arose who again explored the possibilities of perfection. In the 17th century, PIETISM advocated a search for holiness through a life built around prayer and devotion. John WESLEY in the 18th century was the first to articulate a full-blown doctrine of Christian perfection.

Wesley believed that Christians, after experiencing a justifying encounter with God in Christ, would begin to grow in grace and love. Eventually, they would reach a second critical moment when by the work of the Holy Spirit they became perfect in love. This was a lifelong process, and only a few reached perfection in this life. Wesley himself never professed to have done so, though a few other Methodists did. In the face of some who claimed perfection, Wesley issued a revised edition of his classic statement, *A Plain Account of Christian Perfection*. He explained that Christian perfection was not absolute, did not imply sinlessness, was capable of being lost, was not to be equated with the perfection of angels, and did not preclude further growth in grace.

METHODISM became for a period the largest religious group in the United States, but perfectionism was not at first its main appeal. Then, in 1839, Timothy Merrett (1775–1845) launched the periodical *Guide to Christian Perfection*. At first a lone voice in the Methodist Episcopal Church, Merrett gradually gained a following, which took on the attributes of a movement following the conversion of Phoebe PALMER, a lay leader in Manhattan. Palmer's parlor became the center of a revival that swept through the Methodists of New York just prior to the Civil War. Phoebe and her husband, Walter C. Palmer (1804–83), purchased Merritt's periodical; as the *Guide to Holiness* it became the focus of the movement, which expanded rapidly throughout the Methodist community.

In 1839, after reading Wesley's Plain Account, Congregationalist minister Charles G. FINNEY experienced sanctification. Already a prominent evangelist, Finney integrated Wesley's teaching into his own life's work, which included a search for social holiness. From his chair of theology at Oberlin College, Finney was a champion of the antislavery cause and a pacifist during the Mexican war (1846–48). His Oberlin associate Asa Mahan (1799–1889) wrote the *Scriptural Doctrine of Christian Perfection* (1844), which influenced many non-Methodists to adopt perfectionist ideals.

Wesley had emphasized a life of gradual improvement. Palmer and her associates, who created the HOLINESS MOVEMENT, believed that the Holy Spirit could operate on the believer immediately to bring sanctification. Holiness leaders counseled believers to make the search for perfection their top priority, and to expect the Holy Spirit to honor their search. The sanctified life became the norm, not the goal.

One fascinating outgrowth was the perfectionist colony of Oneida, New York, established by John Humphrey Noyes (1811–86). Following his conversion in 1831, Noyes came to believe that Jesus had completed his salvific work; after conversion, the believer was free from sin and could live the perfect life. To that end, he created a communal society in which each member renounced personal property and any binding personal relationships. Each male was married to each female and vice versa. Sexual contact was regulated to prevent couples from developing relationships that might detract from communal life. The Oneida colony worked for a generation, but finally gave way to social pressures.

By the 1880s, the Holiness movement was a national phenomenon. It was strongest within Methodism, where several of its advocates were elected BISHOPS. One notable adherent was Frances WILLARD, president of the Woman's Christian Temperance Union, the largest women's rights group of its time. Numerous CAMP MEETINGS strengthened the followers' identification with the movement.

As the movement peaked in the 1880s, criticism mounted. Church leaders often had trouble controlling the autonomous camp meetings. Some Methodists challenged Holiness from a theological perspective as well. They said it created two classes of church members; furthermore, some "sanctified" members were obsessed with rote observance of strict moral codes, or did not even lead the exemplary life they professed. Meanwhile, many Holiness people began to leave the Methodist Church to form Holiness churches, some of which grew into global DENOMINATIONS, including the CHURCH OF THE NAZARENE, the WESLEYAN CHURCH, the SALVATION ARMY, and the CHURCH OF GOD (ANDERSON, INDIANA).

At the beginning of the 20th century, the Holiness movement provided the foundation for PENTECOSTALISM. Pentecostal churches that have integrated sanctification and holiness into their theology are the CHURCH OF GOD (CLEVELAND, TENNESSEE), the CHURCH OF GOD OF PROPHECY, the INTERNATIONAL PENTECOSTAL HOLINESS CHURCH, and the CHURCH OF GOD IN CHRIST. These churches have joined those of the Holiness movement in teaching perfectionism around the world.

Some psychologists and social critics claim that 19th-century perfectionist religious ideals have been translated into secular terms, finding expression in the American emphasis on material success. They consider perfectionism to be a pathological state in which the individual tries to attain excessively high and unrealistic goals. Others have argued for a more balanced response, noting that the ideal of perfection can motivate people to great achievement. Some Holiness spokespersons have drawn sharp distinctions between their perfectionism and the behaviors cited by critics.

Further reading: Miriam Adderholdt-Elliott, *Perfectionism: What's Bad about Being Too Good* (rev. ed., Minneapolis, Minn.: Free Spirit, 1999); Samuel Chadwick, *The Call to Christian Perfection* (Kansas City, Mo.: Beacon Hill Press, 1943); Robert Newton Flew, *The Idea of Perfection in Christian Theology: An Historical Study of the Christian Ideal for the Present Life* (London: Oxford University Press, 1934); William Edwin Sangster, *The Path to Perfection: An Examination . . . of John Wesley's Doctrine of Christian Perfection* (London: Epworth Press, 1984); Charles Edward White, *The Beauty of Holiness: Phoebe Palmer as Theologian, Revivalist, Feminist, and Humanitarian* (Grand Rapids, Mich.: Zondervan, 1986).

Philippines

Thanks to centuries of Spanish rule, Roman Catholicism is the faith of 80 percent of the Philippine people. After the United States assumed control around 1900, missionaries could enter the country to begin wooing Catholics to Protestant churches.

Before that could happen, a revolt broke out demanding independence. Rebel leader Emilio Aguinaldo (1869–1964) appointed Gregorio AGLIPAY (1860–1940) as leader of the church (i.e., the Roman Catholic community) in areas under their control. Roman Catholic authorities excommunicated Aglipay, but he became a national hero. He organized his followers as the Philippine Independent Church. In 1906, the courts forced him to give up all Roman Catholic property, and he had to rebuild from scratch.

The first American Protestant missionary was Presbyterian James B. Rogers, who arrived in April 1899. Methodists soon followed; they enjoyed great success, until faced with two schisms, the first by supporters of Philippine independence. Within a few years, missionaries from the Church of the United Brethren, the Christian Church (Disciples of Christ), and the Congregationalists (through the AMERICAN BOARD OF COMMISSIONERS FOR FOREIGN MISSIONS) also arrived.

The Episcopal Church sent missionaries in 1902, who targeted some of the many minority groups that other churches had ignored, such as the Chinese community in Manila.

Meanwhile, Aglipay had been able to rebuild the church, though he lost much support from those loyal to their local parishes. He had also given up belief in the Trinity. Thus he developed a relationship with the American Unitarian Association (now the Unitarian Universalist Association) and continued that relationship until his death in 1940. His successors reasserted their orthodox Trintarian faith and reached out to the Episcopal Church, the group closest to them in faith and practice. Negotiations brought the Philippine group into alignment with the Anglican tradition by 1948, when Episcopal bishops consecrated the new leadership of the Philippine Independent Church.

Since World War II, the Philippines has experienced a radical religious pluralism, from extremist Islam to spiritualism. The whole spectrum of Protestant and FREE CHURCH movements from the

West is represented. A controversial group, the IGLESIA NI CRISTO (one of several with that name) now claims more than a million and a half members and has developed an expansive outreach overseas. It was founded by Felix Manalo (1886–1963), who in 1904 left the Catholic Church to become a Methodist. He began a period of religious seeking in several churches, including the SEVENTH-DAY ADVENTIST CHURCH. He left the Adventists in 1913 and started the Church of Christ. Over the years, Manalo developed some dissenting ideas, including a rejection of the Trinity. He won a following among Catholics. His church now claims that Manalo was the fifth angel spoken of in Revelation 7:2.

The Japanese occupying authorities had forced Protestant bodies into one church during World War II. In 1948, those who wished to continue as one church, including Presbyterians and Congregationalists (who had merged to form the United Evangelical Church before the war) and the United Brethren and Disciples of Christ (previously united in the Evangelical Church), formed the United Church of Christ in the Philippines. It had almost a million members at the start of the 21st century.

PENTECOSTALISM began organizing in the 1920s following the arrival of an ASSEMBLIES OF GOD missionary, Benjamin H. Caudle. He was followed by a wave of Filipinos who had become Pentecostals in the United States and came home to spread the movement. The Assemblies grew steadily over the years and is the largest of the Pentecostal bodies today. It is closely followed, however, by the UNITED PENTECOSTAL CHURCH, INTERNATIONAL, the Church of God (Ecclesia Dei), the INTERNATIONAL CHURCH OF THE FOURSQUARE GOSPEL, and the CHURCH OF GOD (CLEVELAND, TENNESSEE).

A variety of non-Pentecostal evangelical groups have found a high level of success, including the CHRISTIAN AND MISSIONARY ALLIANCE, the LOCAL CHURCH, and the Seventh-day Adventists. In 1974, a group of evangelical leaders created the "Dawn 2000" movement, aimed at planting 50,000 evangelical churches in the country by 2000. Evangelical Christianity was the fastest-growing segment of the religious community in the last two decades of the 20th century; the largest Evangelical community is the Jesus is Lord Fellowship, led by a former politician, Eddie Villanueva. By the end of the century, it had more than 250,000 members and was active in more than 25 countries.

Among indigenous groups, the largest, apart from the Iglesia ni Cristo, is the Crusaders of the Divine Church of Christ, which has also become an international body. Of the older bodies, the UNITED METHODIST CHURCH, the Philippine Episcopal Church, and the Convention of Philippine Baptist Churches continue to maintain a substantial following.

Philippine Protestants cooperate in three primary ecumenical organizations, the National Council of Churches in the Philippines affiliated with the WORLD COUNCIL OF CHURCHES, the Philippine Council of Evangelican Churches affiliated with the WORLD EVANGELICAL ALLIANCE, and the Philippine Council of Fundamental Evangelical Churches, representing the most conservative groups.

See also ASIA; SOUTH PACIFIC.

Further reading: Gerald H. Anderson, ed., *Studies in Philippine Church History* (Ithaca, N.Y.: Cornell University Press, 1969); *Church Profiles: Basic Information on Member Churches and Associate Members* (Quezon City: National Council of Churches in the Philippines, Research and Documentation Office, 1989); C. Sabato, *Philippine Church History* (Manila: Salasianam 1990); M. Wourms, *The J. I. L. [Jesus Is Lord] Love Story: The Church without a Roof* (El Cajon, Calif.: Christian Services, 1992).

Pietism

Pietism began as a movement within German LUTHERANISM in the 17th century that emphasized a personal faith in God and Christ. Pietists opposed what they saw as a sterile Lutheran Church, content with mere verbal confessions of belief in Lutheran tenets while tolerating a disregard for the Christian life among the general population.

A statue of A. H. Francke, one of the founders of Pietism *(Institute for the Study of American Religion, Santa Barbara, California)*

One of the first Pietists who tried to breathe life into Lutheranism was pastor Johann Arndt (1555–1621), author of *True Christianity* (1605). Arndt was influenced by a variety of mystical texts. While orthodox in belief, he came to feel that the Christian life involved right living and the union of the soul with God. Arndt in turn influenced Philip Jacob Spener (1635–1705) and August Hermann Francke (1663–1727). From the 1660s, Spener held informal meetings, called Collegia Pietatis, in his home in Frankfurt, Germany, for prayer, Bible study, and discussion of the previous week's sermon. In 1675, he published a new edition of Arndt's book with his own lengthy preface, later published separately as the *Pia Desiderata*. *Pia*

Desiderata laid out a program for further reform of the church (including changes in the education of ministers) that would help members experience a personal faith and live an upright and moral life.

The publication of *Pia Desiderata* caused such a storm of protest that Spener was forced out of his ministeral post in Frankfurt. He eventually continued a fruitful ministry in Berlin. By this time, he had found a major disciple in Francke, as well as other followers from across German-speaking Europe. In 1694, he founded the university at Halle, where Francke was installed as a professor. It became the center of Pietism in the following century.

Spener also influenced Count Nicolaus Ludwig von ZINZENDORF (1700–60), who studied with Francke at Halle. In the 1720s, Zinzendorf made his estate a haven for Czech Protestant exiles and took an active role in their reorganization as the MORAVIAN CHURCH. Zinzendorf's own Jesus-centered mysticism shaped Moravian life.

Halle graduates and Pietists Barthoemew Ziegenbalc (1682–1719) and Heinrich Plütschau (c. 1677–1747) were the first missionaries to Tranquebar, the Danish settlement in India. The Danish-Halle Mission, established in 1706, is considered the pioneering first step in the great expansion of Protestantism through global missionary work. The Moravians undertook a missionary program of their own, initially directed toward Africans in the Caribbean and the British American colonies. Through the Moravians, Pietism was passed to METHODISM founder John WESLEY and to George WHITEFIELD, who brought it to America in the years of the first GREAT AWAKENING (1740s). Whitefield in turn spread Pietism to Presbyterian minister and theologian Jonathan EDWARDS, among others.

In the centuries since the founding of the university at Halle, much of Lutheran history has been played out in the tension between Pietists and confessionalists, with confessionalists questioning the orthodoxy of the Pietists, and Pietists accusing the confessionalists of loosing the essence of faith that church dogma was intended to convey. In the 19th century, American confessionalism was championed by Charles Porterfield Krauth (1823–83) and embodied in the LUTHERAN CHURCH–MISSOURI SYNOD and the Wisconsin Evangelical Lutheran Church. Pietism, by making doctrine second to personal faith, tended to minimalize the difference between Lutheran and Reformed church theologies and prepared the way for the merger of the two churches where they were both influenced by Pietism, notably in Prussia. In Germany, Pietism also inspired new movements such as the BRETHREN.

Spreading to Scandinavia, Pietism led to the creation of the Mission Covenant Church of Sweden and the Evangelical Free Church. Internationally, Pietism had its greatest expression in Methodism, which spread from England and the United States into most of the world, and gave birth to both the HOLINESS MOVEMENT and PENTECOSTALISM, the most vibrant expression of Pietism as the 21st century begins.

Further reading: Dale Brown, *Understanding Pietism* (Grand Rapids, Mich.: Eerdmans, 1978); Peter C. Erb, ed., *Pietists: Selected Writings* (New York: Paulist Press, 1983); Kenneth Collins, "John Wesley Critical Appropriation of Early German Pietism." Available online. URL: http://wesley.nnu.edu/WesleyanTheology/theojrnl/26-30/27.3.html; Gary R. Sattler, *God's Glory, Neighbor's Good: A Brief Introduction to the Life and Writings of August Hermann Francke* (Chicago: Covenant Press, 1982); F. Ernest Stieffler, *The Rise of Evangelical Pietism* (Leiden: Brill, 1965).

Plymouth Brethren *See* BRETHREN.

Poland

The Protestant cause in Poland has taken an unusual course. At the time of the Reformation, Poland had a weak central government unable to unify its various language and religious groups. Whatever religion the nobles favored could dominate in their lands.

Among the early converts to LUTHERANISM was a Dominican named Samuel, a preacher at the Posen cathedral. One of his colleagues at the cathedral, Jan Seklucyan, composed a Protestant confession of faith, published hymnbooks, and completed successively the first Polish translations of the four Gospels (1551), the New Testament (1552), and the entire Bible (1563). Lutheranism was followed by CALVINISM and Anabaptism. Followers of John HUS, persecuted in their native Bohemia, found some protection in neighboring Poland. In the 1570s, anti-Trinitarians made a place for themselves in Krakow.

In 1555, Polish King Sigismund II Augustus (d. 1572) granted religious freedom to all Protestants, including the anti-Trinitarians. Protestantism flourished during his reign, and some 900 congregations are known to have existed. Some Protestants attained high posts in the government. There were attempts to unite the various Protestant factions into one Evangelical church, but Sigismund preferred to keep the various factions under his control by playing one against the other. Then, under the influence of Catholic bishop Stanislav Hosius (d. 1579), one of the presidents of the Council of Trent, he invited the Jesuits to Poland to try to reverse Protestant gains. Stephen Báthory, who after a period of instability succeeded Sigismund, also favored the Jesuits, though he reaffirmed religious liberty.

During Bathory's regime, the non-Trinitarian reformers under Faustus Socinius (1539–1604) established a flourishing center at Krakow. For a generation it was the major dissemination point for the Socinians' anti-Trinitarian literature.

However, as the century drew to an end, the Jesuits proved effective. They established a college in Hosius's diocese at Braunsberg (Ermland) and an academy in Vilnius (Lithuania). Within a generation, most of Poland and Lithuania returned to Catholicism. Protestantism survived only in what is today Latvia, in several urban centers such as Danzig (present-day Gdansk), and in the Duchy of Prussia (southeast of Danzig).

By the early 17th century, Protestantism in all its forms had been marginalized. SOCINIANISM was destroyed in Poland, but Lutherans (Evangelical

Church of the Augsburg Confession) and Calvinists (Evangelical Reformed Church of Poland) survived; in the 18th century, both again began to grow. Steady growth continued in the 19th century, though the Protestants never challenged the Roman Catholic hegemony over the people and culture.

No other Protestant and FREE CHURCH bodies appeared until the early 20th century, when the JEHOVAH'S WITNESSES (1906) and the SEVENTH-DAY ADVENTIST CHURCH (1912) arrived, as well as the first Pentecostal churches. The Methodists and BAPTISTS began small works in 1922. Various independent factions merged in 1946 to form the present United Evangelical Church of Poland. The non-Catholic churches suffered significantly during World War II. It is estimated that approximately 30 percent of all their pastors died in concentration camps.

After World War II, Protestant efforts were stifled by the officially atheist Communist government. Protestants returned largely to a survival mode. However, when freedom of religion returned in the 1990s, Protestantism revived. Nevertheless, it represents less than 1 percent of the population. As the new century begins, the largest non-Catholic groups are the Jehovah's Witnesses and the Lutherans.

See also LITHUANIA; RUSSIA.

Further reading: A. Korbonski, *The Church and State in Poland after World War II* (Washington, D.C.: Council for Soviet and East European Research, 1994); A Piekarski, *The Church in Poland: Facts, Figures, Information* (Warsaw: International Publication Service, 1978); A. Tokarcyzk, *Five Centuries of Lutheranism in Poland* (Warsaw: Interpress, 1984).

polity

A church's polity is its form of government. Like the words *politics, police,* and *policy,* the word is ultimately derived from the ancient Greek *polis,* which evokes both the order and the community of the ancient city state. As Protestantism developed, especially during the Puritan controversies in England, three forms of church polity were recognized—episcopal, presbyterian, and congregational. Over time, additional variations were introduced.

EPISCOPAL POLITY

As the name implies, episcopal polity is based upon the authority of the BISHOP (*episcopos,* overseer), originally the leading Christian ELDER in a given city. By the time of Ignatius, at the beginning of the second century C.E., evidence shows a single bishop as the head of each local church; Ignatius likens the one bishop to the one God, whose representative he was. From the city, the bishop's authority reached out to the surrounding countryside. The bishop's headquarters was almost always the central city of the territory over which he presided (the diocese), and bishops came to be called by the city name, rather than the district or province name (hence, the pope is referred to as the bishop of Rome). The bishops of the larger dioceses came to be seen as archbishops and/or metropolitans.

In the fourth century, when Christianity aligned with the Roman government, the church began to acquire secular authority. Constantine, for example, granted the church some judicial powers. Over the centuries, the authority of bishops increased as all rival religions were pushed to the fringe of society. The centralized authority of the church in the West came to be focused on the diocese and bishop of Rome.

Some Protestants found the episcopal system acceptable. In England under HENRY VIII, where the anti-Catholic cause revolved around the authority of the pope within England, the early reformers did not question the authority of bishops. The new CHURCH OF ENGLAND simply transferred the pope's authority to the archbishop of Canterbury (under the king's supervision).

Episcopal polity assumed that the bishops' power was derived from Christ through his apostles, the original bishops, by a process of laying on of hands—ordination. This is termed *apostolic succession.* The church came to be defined as those individuals, congregations, priests, and so forth, who were in communion with the bishops. In this system, bishops should be able to trace their lineage back to one of the apostles, although modern scholarship maintains that such lineages cannot be accurately traced in the first two centuries after Christ.

As Protestantism developed, a legitimate apostolic succession became a prized possession for those favoring some form of episcopal polity, including the Lutherans, the Anglicans, and the Moravians. However, it was not always available. Following the American Revolution, after John WESLEY failed to gain Anglican episcopal orders, he improvised. Declaring that he had for some time done the work of a bishop in raising the Methodist movement, he assumed episcopal authority and designated two "superintendents" with authority to organize the now independent American branch of the movement. American Methodists allowed Wesley's superintendents to pass episcopal authority on to Bishop Francis ASBURY. In effect, the church replaced apostolic authority with Wesley's charismatic authority.

A number of newer Protestant groups, especially in the HOLINESS and Pentecostal tradition (both ultimately traced to Methodism), have chosen to adopt an episcopal form of church government, but without succession. They simply designate leaders as bishops and define their powers in the denomination's constitution. These churches consider their bishops legitimate and expect them to be shown proper etiquette.

PRESBYTERIAN POLITY

John CALVIN, founder of the Reformed Church in Geneva in the mid-16th century, argued that there was no biblical justification for a separate order of ministry called bishops. Bishop was just another name for elder. He argued for a church ruled by elders or *presbyters* (Greek for old man), hence the name Presbyterian. In his system, there were two kinds of leaders—teachings elders or ministers, and ruling elders, laypeople who cared for the temporal affairs of the church. Elders carried

out their functions in a system of ruling bodies, decision making being seen as a corporate rather than individual matter.

Within the Reformed tradition, the name given to the gathering of elders varies from country to country and from denomination to denomination. In American Presbyterianism, for example, the elders at each local church constitute a session. Representative ruling elders and teaching elders in a region together constitute a presbytery. Three or more presbyteries may come together in a synod. The larger Presbyterian bodies have a national gathering, the general assembly. The decisions at each level are binding on those below it.

The Reformed or Presbyterian churches saw themselves ideally as exclusive state churches, aligned with the government. This actually occurred in several Swiss cantons, one German state, the NETHERLANDS, and Scotland. Calvin's polity spelled out the church-state relationship, including the duties of the magistrate to order society and keep sinful behavior in check. The magistrate also had the duty of supporting the church and backing its efforts to perform its divine mandate. Under the Puritan Commonwealth in England in the mid-17th century, an attempt was made to impose a presbyterial system on England. Outside of these countries, however, Presbyterianism has always had to develop in a pluralistic setting, without the benefit of backing from the government, and often in the face of state hostility.

CONGREGATIONAL POLITY

In England and New England, immediately after the Westminster Assembly of 1645 published its "Form of Presbyterian Church Government," presbyterian polity was challenged by a dissenting group, the Congregationalists. This group shared Calvin's Reformed theology with the Presbyterians, but opted for a polity centered on the local church. Their position was offered in two documents, both released in 1648, the SAVOY DECLARATION in England and the CAMBRIDGE PLATFORM in

New England. In both cases, the authors argued that the basic form taken by the visible church in the biblical text is the local church. As the Savoy Declaration notes, "To each of these churches thus gathered . . . he [Christ] hath given all that power and authority, which is any way needful for their carrying on that order in worship and discipline, which he hath instituted for them to observe."

In the congregational system, there was room for synods and other pan-congregational gatherings, but their role was largely advisory. Their authority came for their wisdom and the power of social pressure. The Congregationalists, just like those favoring episcopal or prebyterial polities, saw themselves ideally as the state church of the nation (or of the colony, in New England). They expected close cooperation from the magistrates, who were to support the church by providing civil order and prosecuting those who actively opposed the church, such as blasphemers and heretics.

The Puritans, who began to emerge during the Elizabethan era, all supported Reformed theology, and all agreed that the church should remain coterminus with the nation and aligned with the government. They disagreed as to polity, with groups supporting all three forms.

THE FREE CHURCH CHALLENGE

A fourth possible polity was proposed at the very start of the Reformation among the ANABAPTISTS. They argued against the assumption that all citizens should be defined as Christian at birth, and that the church was coterminus with the state. To them, the church consisted only of those who as adults had come into a relationship with God, believed the Gospel, and committed themselves to Christ in BAPTISM. The church was thus a small gathering within the larger society under the otherwise secular state.

For Anabaptists, the essential goal was to develop a pure assembly of believers, purity defined as conformity to biblical behavior patterns and allegiance to the doctrinal consensus. In the absence of the magistrate, the only means of imposing discipline on misbehaviors or dissenters

was through SHUNNING (banning) and ultimately excommunication or disfellowshipping.

The early Anabaptists practiced a Free Church congregationalism, with charismatic individuals assuming the authority to carry out specific tasks, such as writing a statement of beliefs (the SCHLEITHEIM ARTICLES). During the era of persecution in the Netherlands, Menno SIMONS assumed the authority of a bishop, much as Wesley would do among the Methodists, and operated as the guiding force in the movement. Over the centuries, various Mennonite groups retained the office of bishop, but as time passed, most of its real authority was stripped away.

BAPTISTS, the most radical wing of the Puritan movement, departed dramatically from their fellow Puritans on polity issues. They rejected any ties to the state and opted for the congregation as the seat of authority. Any pan-congregational gathering could have only the authority it was specifically given by the local churches.

As the Baptist community developed, it reflected a spectrum of opinions on pan-congregational structure. The SOUTHERN BAPTIST CONVENTION accepted the idea that the convention could develop programs serving the whole membership, which were not subject to the dictates of any single congregation. The PRIMITIVE BAPTISTS held annual meetings for fellowship purposes only. The most radical branch, the CHURCHES OF CHRIST, rejected the idea of any churchwide conventions or gatherings. Those tasks that other DENOMINATIONS assign to such bodies, such as the publication of periodicals or the founding of colleges, are left to the initiative of individuals or local congregations.

TRANSITION TO THE MODERN WORLD

As Protestant churches moved into highly pluralistic countries and had to abandon even the hope of state-enforced domination, the nature of church polity changed. The authority that once rested with the state was now transferred to whoever owned the property. In the American Catholic Church, for example, all property in the diocese is invested in the bishop, who holds it in trust for the church.

In most of the larger episcopal or presbyterian denominations in the United States, property is held collectively by a judicatory, which owns it in trust for the denomination. In Congregationalist churches, both those of a Puritan Congregational background and those of an Anabaptist or Free Church background, local congregations own their own property; pan-denominational organizations may also own property, held in common for all of the congregations. For example, the LUTHERAN CHURCH–MISSOURI SYNOD is a denomination with a congregational polity. The synod is the child of the churches, but also exists as a corporate entity that owns a headquarters building and educational institutions, and controls a variety of agencies and boards, some of which also own property. On the other hand, in the Churches of Christ, there is no pan-denominational facility; periodicals, mission agencies, and schools are in the hands of individuals, private not-for-profit corporations, or local churches.

Today, many Protestant denominations have a mixed polity. Some groups that appear to have an episcopal polity are in fact congregational, with bishops serving as little more than office managers or administrative personnel. In almost no Protestant denomination with episcopal leadership is the diocese's property placed in the name of the bishop.

One popular model of polity appeared within PENTECOSTALISM in the mid-20th century: the five-fold ministry model. Based on Ephesians 4:11–14, it calls for the church to be organized around five orders—apostles, prophets, evangelists, pastors, and teachers. Apostles function as pan-congregational figures who reach that status after they help found and nurture multiple congregations. On close scrutiny, however, the five-fold ministry is usually a variation of Free Church CONGREGATION-ALISM with property ultimately in the hands of the local congregations and apostles exercising only whatever charismatic authority they possess.

Some modern Protestant groups believe that no exclusive polity design can be derived from the

Bible. Instead, organization should follow function. Whatever is needed and helpful for the fulfillment of the church's mission is acceptable. Evangelist Charles G. FINNEY began to develop such a position 150 years ago. A functional approach has been nurtured by the development of corporate law. In the United States, for example, corporations generally consist of a board, constituted of its officers (president, vice president, secretary, and treasurer) and additional members. The board may hire additional executives and support staff. In the 20th century, non-profit corporation models paralleled those of business corporations. Many churches have chosen explicitly to organize along the nonprofit corporation model instead of any traditional polity, thus facilitating their relationship to the Internal Revenue Service.

Further reading: David W. Hall and Joseph H. Hall, ed., *Paradigms in Polity: Classic Readings in Reformed and Presbyterian church government* (Grand Rapids, Mich.: William B. Eerdmans, 1994); James K. Mathews, *Set Apart To Serve: The Role of Episcopacy In the Wesleyan Tradition* (Nashville, Tenn.: Abingdon Press, 1985); Ross P. Scherer, ed., *American Denominational Organization: A Sociological View* (Pasadena, Calif.: William Carey Library, 1980); J. L. Shaver, *The Polity of the Churches,* 2 vols., 4th ed. (Grand Rapids, Mich.: Grand Rapids International, 1956); Conrad Wright, *Congregational Polity* (Boston: Skinner House Books, 1997).

Portugal

The complete dominance of the Roman Catholic Church in Portugal was first broken by the government when it gave permission to several expatriate communities to form congregations, the first being for German Lutherans (1763) and Anglicans (1843). Meanwhile, an independent missionary effort was initiated in 1838 by a Portuguese man who had converted while outside the country. British missionaries of several DENOMINATIONS became active in the last half of the 19th century. Finally, BRAZIL, a Portuguese-speaking former colony, became an additional route of Protestant entry.

A critical event in Protestant history occurred in 1871, when 11 Roman Catholic priests converted to Anglicanism. They founded the Igreja Lusitanian Catolica Apostolica Evangélica (Lusitanian Catholic Apostolic Evangelical Church) and subsequently obtained Anglican orders.

Official tolerance for non-Catholic religions was granted in 1933, though the primacy of the Roman Catholic Church was also guaranteed. Marriages by Protestant ministers were not recognized, and the purchase of property or erection of buildings was heavily taxed. Religious dissidents were subject to arrest. Significant changes occurred after the coup of 1974. These changes had been presaged by decades of problems between the government and the Vatican, especially over Portugal's refusal to give up its colonies.

The coup ended the close association between the Catholic Church and the state, and a number of religious dissidents, including Protestants, were freed from prison. While the primacy of the church was later reasserted, provisions for religious freedom have steadily improved. At the beginning of the new century, a law to broaden religious freedoms was under consideration.

Prospering most from the new atmosphere have been the SEVENTH-DAY ADVENTIST CHURCH, the JEHOVAH'S WITNESSES, and most of all two Pentecostal bodies. The UNIVERSAL CHURCH OF THE KINGDOM OF GOD came into Portugal in 1991 from Brazil and is now the only non-Catholic group to have more than 100,000 members. The Mana Christian Church, based in Lisbon, which practices speaking in tongues, casting out demons, and divine healing, has grown locally while developing work in more than 30 countries. Under the national and international leadership of APOSTLES and bishops, the Mana Church is a leading example of the cell church movement, which integrates new members via intimate groups for nurturing and discipling.

Several older Protestant churches have banded together in the Portuguese Council of Churches, which cooperates with the WORLD COUNCIL OF CHURCHES. Included in the council are the only two Portuguese-based churches that are members of the World Council, the Evangelical Presbyterian Church of Portugal and the Lusitanian Catholic Apostolic Evangelical Church.

See also SPAIN.

Further reading: David Barrett, *The Encyclopedia of World Christianity,* 2nd ed. (New York: Oxford University Press, 2001); G. C. Ericson, *A Short History of the Portuguese Evangelical Church.* (n.p., 1973).

postmillennialism

Most Reformation leaders followed the AMILLENNIALISM of St. Augustine (354–430), who interpreted the biblical millennium or kingdom of God allegorically. The kingdom was inaugurated by Christ's ministry, and it continues to exist alongside the worldly kingdom of Babylon; its full benefits will only be realized at some unknowable future date. However, Protestantism also contains two minority streams. PREMILLENNIALISM, which suggests that the kingdom is still to come, usually in the predictable or near future, has thrived in unhappy times; postmillennialism, which suggests that history is already advancing toward an era of peace and brotherhood, has thrived in more optimistic eras.

Daniel Whitby (1638–1725), a minister in the CHURCH OF ENGLAND and pastor of St. Edmund's Church, Salisbury, was an early postmillennialist. He suggested that the spread of Christianity throughout the earth presaged the gradual emergence of a reign of peace and brotherhood leading to a millennial kingdom on earth.

No special act of God was needed to bring this kingdom, save the influence of the Holy Spirit in the hearts of believers. The approach of the kingdom would be manifested in the downfall of the pope and of Islam, the return of the Jews to Palestine, the conversion of the world to Christian faith, the overcoming of evil in Christian society, and the spread of piety and holiness in people's lives.

The view was popularized in the mid-18th century by leaders such as Jonathan EDWARDS, who saw in the GREAT AWAKENING a step to the coming kingdom. Postmillennialism gained strength over the next century, though such traumas as the French Revolution and the American Civil War sapped that strength in certain countries and decades. Postmillennialism fed off several phenomena: the great social crusades of 19th-century America to stamp out slavery, alcohol abuse, and war, and to bring women into public life; the REVIVALISM of evangelists such as Charles G. FINNEY; and social experiments like the perfectionist colony at Oneida, New York. Its secular counterpart was the faith in progress that was confirmed by the rapid advance of technology.

Postmillennialism found new energy in the SOCIAL GOSPEL movement and the vision of equality offered by socialism. While such optimism was largely wiped out by World War I in Europe, it took World War II to destroy it in the United States.

After several decades in which little was heard from postmillennial voices, a new form arose in what has been termed the RECONSTRUCTIONIST MOVEMENT, advocated by a cadre of contemporary conservative Calvinist spokespersons. Reconstructionists marry postmillennial beliefs to a program for the reconstruction of society by way of a theonomic model. Aiming for a rule by God's law (theonomy), Reconstructionists look for the Mosaic law to be enacted as the law of the land, believing that it is God's purpose to bring all nations into subjection to Christ.

See also ESCHATOLOGY.

Further reading: Darrell L. Bock, ed., *Three Views of the Millennium and Beyond* (Grand Rapids, Mich.: Zondervan, 1999); Kenneth Gentry Jr., *He Shall Have Dominion: A Postmillennial Eschatology* (Tyler, Tex.: Institute for Christian Economic, 1992); Keith A. Mathison, *Postmillennialism: An Eschatology of Hope* (Phillipsburg, N.J.: Presbyterian & Reformed Press,

1999); Daniel Whitby, *Paraphrase and Commentary on the New Testament, With a Treatise on the True Millennium* (London: William Tegg, 1899); ———, *Six Discourses, concerning I. Election and Reprobation, II. Extent of Christ's Redemption, III. The Grace of God, IV. Liberty of the Will, V. Defectibility of the Saints, VI. Answer to Three Objections* (Worcester, Mass.: Isaiah Thomas, Jr., 1801).

Potter, Philip A. (b. 1921) *Methodist minister and ecumenical leader*

Philip A. Potter was born on August 12, 1921, in Roseau, Dominica. In 1944, he entered Caenwood Theological Seminary in Jamaica. After completing his training for the Methodist ministry, he became

Dominican Methodist Philip A. Potter has emerged in the 20th century as a leading ecumenical statesman. *(Institute for the Study of American Religion, Santa Barbara, California)*

a missionary to Haiti, symbolic of his commitment to the poor and oppressed of the world. After five years in Haiti, he moved to London to pursue postgraduates studies at London University. He worked on the staff of the Methodist Missionary Society, and became involved with the INTERNATIONAL MISSIONARY COUNCIL.

His leadership with the Student Christian Movement led to his involvement as an ecumenical leader. In 1948 and again in 1954, he was invited to address the assembly of the WORLD COUNCIL OF CHURCHES. He then successively became an executive with the WCC's Youth Department (1954), head of the World Student Christian Federation (1960), and director of the WCC's Division of World Mission and Evangelism (1967).

In 1972, Potter began a 12-year tenure as the general secretary of the World Council of Churches, succeeding Eugene Carson BLAKE. During this time, Potter became known for his insistence that Christian witness and action be unified, and that Christian action in the world was an outgrowth of personal spiritual life. After completing his years on the international stage, Potter moved to Jamaica to work with students at the University of the West Indies.

See also ECUMENICAL MOVEMENT.

Further reading: Michael N. Jagessar, "Full Life for All. The Work and Theology of Philip A. Potter: A Historical Survey and Systematic Analysis of Major Themes," *International Bulletin of Missionary Research* 22 (1998): 186; Konrad Raiser, "Celebrating an Ecumenical Pilgrimage: An Address to Honour Philip Potter on the Occasion of His 80th Birthday," *Ecumenical Review* (October 2001), Available online. URL: http://www.findarticles.com/cf_dls/m2065/4_53/8122 3349/p1/article.jhtml?term=; Pauline Webb, ed., *Faith and Faithfulness: Essays on Contemporary Ecumenical Themes* (Geneva: World Council of Churches, 1984).

predestination

Predestination is the belief that God has chosen or elected some for the gift of salvation, sometimes extended to include the idea that God chooses the rest of humankind for damnation. The most relevant biblical quote on the subject is Romans 28–30: "Whom he did foreknow, he also did predestinate to be conformed to the image of his Son, that he might be the firstborn of many brethren. Moreover whom he did predestinate, them he also called, them he also justified."

The doctrine was first developed by St. Augustine (354–430), who wrote against Pelagius. Pelagianism suggests that salvation comes from human endeavor. Augustine asserted that God had chosen, from the mass of humanity, some for salvation as a demonstration of his grace, leaving the rest as an illustration of his justice. Martin LUTHER, an Augustinian monk prior to the Reformation, affirmed Augustine's concept though it was not stressed by later Lutheran theologians.

Predestination was an important element in John CALVIN's doctrine of salvation. He proposed the notion of double predestination, that God chose the elect for salvation and those not elected for damnation. The aim was to assert that human salvation is solely a product of God's loving action to Christians.

Augustine, Luther, and Calvin did not find predestination incompatible with human free will, but later Protestants would. Among the most important critics of predestination was Dutch Reformed theologian Jacob Arminius, who reacted to the heightened emphasis on predestination in Calvinist thought as the 16th century progressed. At that time supralapsarianism was popular; it claimed that God's decrees of election were logically prior to his foreknowledge of the elect. Arminius picked up another line of Reformed thought and argued that God's foreknowledge preceded his decree; in other words, God predestined individuals based upon his foreknowledge of their faith.

ARMINIANISM was hotly debated in Holland and became the subject of the SYNOD OF DORT in 1618–19. Predestination was a key to the five points it voted in condemning Arminius's position. Unconditional election, it said, was essential to the doctrine of salvation by grace alone. The synod's findings would in effect divide Protestants of the Reformed camp into two communities, the Calvinists who affirmed Dort and the Arminians who rejected it.

The decisions at Dort were in effect ratified by the WESTMINSTER CONFESSION, the most influential statement of belief by English-speaking Calvinists. On the other hand, Arminians found their greatest champion in Methodism's founder, John WESLEY. Wesley argued that Christ had died for all, that "prevenient" grace had been shed abroad in the hearts of all humans, making them open to respond to the Gospel. REVIVALISM, especially as it was manifested in 19th-century America, was Arminian at heart.

As Moravians and Methodists pioneered the world missionary movement, Calvinists were slow to respond. Many had concluded that evangelism or missionary activity was pointless, in light of their understanding of salvation. However, by the end of the 18th century, even strictly Calvinist churches found themselves in contact with parts of the world where the Christian message was unknown. They found it necessary to develop a modified CALVINISM that not only allowed but supported and encouraged the global missionary enterprise. Leading the way in this effort was Baptist theologian Andrew FULLER (1754–1806), who, drawing on some themes from the Wesleyan movement, is credited with restating Calvinism, and stressing the responsibility of the individual believer to witness to the Gospel message.

Through the 19th and 20th centuries, Protestant theologians developed a spectrum of new theologies from the liberalism of Freidrich SCHLEIERMACHER to the NEO-ORTHODOXY of Karl BARTH and Emil BRUNNER to the FUNDAMENTALISM of Cornelius Van Til (1895–1987). Each one tried to restate the doctrine of predestination/election, retaining its central role in Protestant Christian thought.

Further reading: David Basinger and Randall Basinger, eds., *Predestination and Free Will: Four Views of Divine Sovereignty and Human Freedom*

(Downers Grove, Ill.: InterVarsity Press, 1986); Loraine Boettner, *The Reformed Doctrine of Predestination* (1968. rpt.: Phillipsburg, N.J.: Presbyterian & Reformed, 1992); Harry Buis, *Historic Protestantism and Predestination* (Phillipsburg, Pa.: Presbyterian & Reformed, 1958); Mark John Farrelly, *Predestination, Grace, and Free-will* (Westminster, Md.: Newman Press, 1964); Clark H. Pinnock, ed., *The Grace of God, The Will of Man: A Case for Arminianism* (Grand Rapids, Mich.: Zondervan, 1989).

premillennialism

Premillennialism is one of three major approaches to ESCHATOLOGY (the doctrine of the last things) in Christian theology. The concept of the millennium, the thousand-year reign of peace mentioned in Revelation 20:6–7, is a key to understanding Protestant thought about the destiny of humankind.

AMILLENNIALISM, the dominant view within Protestantism, views the verses figuratively and does not look for a literal millennium. POSTMILLENNIALISM sees humankind as already growing into the millennium, after which Christ will return to bring history to a culmination. Very popular in the 19th century, its optimism about the course of human history was essentially destroyed by the two world wars. Premillennialism sees Christ returning in the near future, as human life continues to deteriorate, after which he will establish and rule over the millennial kingdom.

Two forms of premillennialism were popularized in the 19th century, the Adventist view initially proposed by William MILLER, and DISPENSATIONALISM as developed by John Nelson DARBY and the Plymouth BRETHREN. While both views retain a large audience, the latter view has become by far the most popular as it was integrated into FUNDAMENTALISM in the 1920s.

Premillennialism assumes a somewhat literal reading of the Bible and attempts to reconcile all of its scattered eschatological passages. Dispensationalism has assumed that the next event in God's plan for humankind is the rapture, the events described in I Thessalonians 4:13–18. Christ will return to earth and take all living believers to meet him in the air. Following the rapture will be a seven-year period of tribulation (Matthew 24:21–22) in which those left behind will have a chance to come to faith. Of particular importance during the rapture will be the role of the Jewish nation and the end of Gentile times.

Following the tribulation, Christ will return to earth to establish his millennial kingdom. He will resurrect the believers who had died prior to the rapture, fight the battle of Armageddon, bind Satan, and establish his throne in Jerusalem. Christ will reign over the earth for a thousand years. Following the millennial reign, a second resurrection of all of the dead will occur, the wicked unbelievers will be judged and consigned to hell, and eternity will begin for the righteous.

Dispensationalist premillennialism spread with the Plymouth Brethren movement in the last half of the 19th century. Its acceptance by evangelist Dwight L. MOODY gave it an additional boost. One of Moody's associates, Cyrus I. SCOFIELD, incorporated the perspective into his very popular Reference Bible published in 1909. By the time the Fundamentalist controversy heated up in the 1920s, many BAPTISTS and Presbyterians had come to accept dispensationalism. It developed a growing following among Evangelicals through the last half of the 20th century. Dispensationalism has become particularly identified with several independent conservative Protestant schools—Moody Bible Institute, the Bible Institute of Los Angeles (Biola), and Dallas Theological Seminary.

As premillennism grew, a variety of alternatives were offered to the dominant view of the future history of humankind. For example, some suggested that the rapture would occur in the middle of the tribulation period and some that it would follow the tribulation. A variety of opinions have also been suggested concerning the role of the modern state of Israel, some seeing its establishment as a key end-time event.

Dispensational premillennialism has led some church leaders and writers to specialize in discerning the prophetic meaning of contemporary events. Among the most popular books to explore this theme was Baptist minister Hal Lindsey's *The Late Great Planet Earth.* Published in 1970, the book described events flowing from the founding of the state of Israel and predicted that the rapture would take place around 1988 (a generation of 40 years after that prophetic event). Lindsey had taken a step avoided by most premillennialists by actually predicting a specific date for the beginning of the future prophetic events. The continual failure of history to conform to predictions in the popular premillennial literature has been a significant factor in limiting its popularity.

Further reading: Mal Couch, ed., *Dictionary of Premillennial Theology* (Grand Rapids, Mich.: Kregal, 1996); Millard J. Erickson, *A Basic Guide to Eschatology: Making Sense of the Millennium* (Grand Rapids, Mich.: Baker Book House, 1998); Stanley J. Grenz, *The Millennial Maze: Sorting Out Evangelical Options* (Downers Grove, Ill.: InterVarsity Press, 1992); Hal Lindsey, *The Late Great Planet Earth* (Grand Rapids, Mich.: Zondervan, 1970); Jon R. Stone, *A Guide to the End of the World: Popular Eschatology in America: The Mainstream Evangelical Tradition* (New York: Garland, 1993).

Presbyterian Church (USA)

The Presbyterian Church (USA) was formed in 1983 by a merger of the United Presbyterian Church in the U.S.A. and the Presbyterian Church in the United States, thus healing a breach that had opened in the years prior to the American Civil War. Over the years since the Civil War, the United Presbyterian Church had participated in several mergers, each of which brought in a scattered segment. Included in its predecessor bodies are the first Presbyterian synods founded in what is now the United States.

Presbyterians, who constituted the largest segment of the Puritan movement in Great Britain, began to move to the American colonies in the 17th century, especially after the fall of the Com-

First Presbyterian Church, Salt Lake City, Utah *(Institute for the Study of American Religion, Santa Barbara, California)*

monwealth (1648–60) and the restoration of ANGLICANISM in the CHURCH OF ENGLAND. Most early congregations appeared in Connecticut, New York, Pennsylvania, and New Jersey. The first synod was formed in 1706. In the middle of the century, the movement was split for a time over the new REVIVALISM as practiced by George WHITE-FIELD and Jonathan EDWARDS.

Early in the 19th century, the supporters of revivalism and the new CAMP MEETINGS founded the Cumberland Presbyterian Church. The nonrevivalist majority of British Presbyterians persisted as the Presbyterian Church U.S.A. In 1906, most of the Cumberland Presbyterians reunited with the Presbyterian Church U.S.A.

Scottish Presbyterians, mostly from the factions that had split away from the established Church of Scotland, drifted into the American colonies in the middle of the 18th century. Different factions formed the Associate Presbyterian Church in 1753 and the Reformed Presbyterian Church in 1774. In 1782, these two churches merged to form the Associate Reformed Presbyterian Church, though one group stayed out of the merger and continued as the Associate Presbyterian Church. In 1822, the Associate Reformed

Presbyterian Church split into two factions, one in the north and one in the southern part of the country. In 1858, the continuing Associate Presbyterian Church and the northern faction of the Associate Reformed Church merged to constitute the United Presbyterian Church of North America.

In 1958, the main body of Scottish Presbyterians, the United Presbyterian Church of North America, and the main body of British Presbyterians merged to form the Presbyterian Church in the U.S.A. In 1983, that church, with its strength in the northern states, would merge with the Presbyterian Church in the U.S., primarily the southern church, to form the Presbyterian Church (U.S.A.)

During the early part of the 19th century, Presbyterians made common cause with Congregationalists on the American frontier, and in 1801 the two groups approved a plan of union to cut down on competition. After 1810, the two groups also cooperated in foreign missionary fields by their mutual support of the AMERICAN BOARD OF COMMISSIONERS FOR FOREIGN MISSIONS. That cooperation lasted until 1870, when the Presbyterians decided to create their own mission board. Mission churches created around the world that have matured into autonomous churches now operate in a partnership relationship with the Presbyterian Church (U.S.A.)

In 1967, the United Presbyterian Church in the U.S.A. caused considerable controversy when it adopted a new confession of faith. The controversy was reminiscent of the Fundamentalist controversy that shook the Presbyterians in the 1920s and 1930s. However, the church then published a new book of confessions that contained the Apostles' Creed, the Nicene Creed, several Reformed confessions, the Westminster documents, and the new confession of 1967. The adoption of such a broad confessional base communicated the fact that the church sees the Christian tradition in general and the Reformed tradition in particular as a living tradition to be understood in the light of both history and the contemporary situation.

The Presbyterian Church (USA) has its headquarters in Louisville, Kentucky. The church is organized on a presbyterial model. Its highest legislative body is the general assembly. Congregations are grouped into presbyteries and synods across the country. In 2000, it reported 2.5 million members. The church supports a number of colleges and theological seminaries. Women have been accepted into the ministry since 1956.

The Presbyterian Church (USA) is ecumenically oriented and is a member of the WORLD ALLIANCE OF REFORMED CHURCHES and the WORLD COUNCIL OF CHURCHES.

See also REFORMED/PRESBYTERIAN TRADITION.

Further reading: Randall Balmer and John R. Fitzmier, *The Presbyterians* (Westport, Conn.: Praeger, 1994); Wallace N. Jamison, *The United Presbyterian Story* (Pittsburgh, Pa.: Geneva Press, 1958); Park Hays Miller, *Why I Am a Presbyterian* (New York: Thomas Nelson & Sons, 1956); William J. Weston, *Presbyterian Pluralism: Competition in a Protestant House* (Knoxville: University of Tennessee Press, 1997).

Presbyterianism

Presbyterians represent that wing of the Reformed Church (which evolved from the teachings of John CALVIN) that developed in the English-speaking world. On the European continent, the Calvinist tradition retained the name "Reformed Church."

In England, the primary issues faced by the primary Reformed Protestant group, the Puritans, were ecclesiastical with the single most important issue being the organization of the CHURCH OF ENGLAND. The main body of Puritans argued or a Presbyterian POLITY with the church being led by presbyters (ELDERS) rather than BISHOPS.

The first success for Reformed Protestants in the British Isles was the mid-16th-century transformation of the church in Scotland into a Presbyterian body. For a time, in the middle of the 17th century, when the WESTMINSTER CONFESSION was issued by Puritan leaders during the Commonwealth, it appeared that England would also become dominated by a Presbyterian church. However, the process of Protestantizing the Church of England came to an end with the restoration of the monarchy in 1660.

The Westminster documents, especially the confession, remained the primary statement of Presbyterian faith. The earlier Scots Confession (1560) was also normative, while the Confession of 1967 (originally adopted by the United Presbyterians Church in the U.S.A.) and the BRIEF STATEMENT OF FAITH (a liturgical statement adopted at the time of the merger that produced the Presbyterian Church [USA]) are seen as contemporary restatements of the Presbyterian tradition. The more conservative Presbyterian bodies totally reject the newer confessions in allegiance to the Westminster documents.

The once solidly Presbyterian Puritans eventually divided over issues of polity, with Congregationalists advocating a congregational state church and BAPTISTS advocating a congregational polity and a separation of church and state. Presbyterians formed several churches in England, the majority of whom are now found in the United Reformed Church, which brought Presbyterians and Congregationalists together in 1972.

In Scotland, the Church of Scotland suffered several schisms in the 18th century and one in 1843 that produced the Free Church of Scotland. Most of the schisms have been healed, but the Free Church is still separate from the Church of Scotland. The largest Presbyterian group in Wales emerged in the 18th century from the preaching of Calvinist Methodist George WHITEFIELD.

In the 17th century, British and Scottish Presbyterianism were both transferred to North America. In CANADA, the majority of Presbyterians joined the Presbyterian Church of Canada, which in 1925 joined the merger that produced the United Church of Canada. In the United States, the various Scottish Presbyterian groups formed separate communities, the majority of which were consolidated into the United Presbyterian Church in 1858. British Presbyterians split into three prominent factions—the revivalist Cumberland Presbyterian Church, the Presbyterian Church in the United States (formed by the southern wing of the church at the time of the American Civil War), and the Presbyterian Church in the U.S.A. In 1983, these three churches completed a process of consolidation as the PRESBYTERIAN CHURCH (USA), though a minority of Cumberland Presbyterians continue as a separate body. In both Canada and the United States, a number of smaller Presbyterian bodies were created to represent conservatives unhappy with the perceived liberalism of the larger church; the largest is the Presbyterian Church in America. Several ethnic Presbyterian churches also exist, the largest ones serving Korean Americans.

In the 19th century, the Church of Scotland, the various American Presbyterian Churches, and British Presbyterians were among the primary participants in the world missionary thrust of Protestantism. Originally backing the LONDON MISSIONARY SOCIETY and the AMERICAN BOARD OF COMMISSIONERS FOR FOREIGN MISSIONS, the various churches later founded their own mission boards and seeded Presbyterians churches around the world. More than 25 Presbyterian churches are now members of the WORLD COUNCIL OF CHURCHES, and that many more are members via united churches of which they are now a part. Many are also members of the WORLD ALLIANCE OF REFORMED CHURCHES. Some Presbyterian bodies are members of the WORLD EVANGELICAL ALLIANCE, the INTERNATIONAL COUNCIL OF CHRISTIAN CHURCHES, and the WORLD COUNCIL OF BIBLICAL CHURCHES. Among the largest Presbyterian bodies that have refused membership in the World Council of Churches is the very conservative 2-million-member Presbyterian Church of Korea (HapDong).

See also REFORMED/PRESBYTERIAN TRADITION.

Further reading: Randall Balmer and John R. Fitzmier, *The Presbyterians* (Westport, Conn.: Greenwood Press, 1994); Jean-Jacques Bauswein and Lukas Vischer, eds., *The Reformed Family Worldwide: A Survey of Reformed Churches, Theological Schools, and International Organizations* (Grand Rapids, Mich.: William B. Eerdmans, 1999); Nigel M. de S. Cameron, ed., *Dictionary of Scottish Church History and Theology* (Edinburgh: T & T Clark, 1993); D. G. Hart and Mark A. Noll, eds., *Dictionary of the Presbyterian and Reformed Tradition in America* (Des Plaines, Ill.: InterVarsity Press, 1999);

James H. Smylie, *A Brief History of the Presbyterians* (Louisville, Ky.: Geneva Press, 1996).

Presbyters   *See* ELDERS.

Present Truth

Present Truth is the Christian doctrine that at particular moments in the life of the church certain special ideas need to be highlighted, along with the major teachings that are affirmed in every generation. The idea derives from 2 Peter 1:12: "Wherefore I will not be negligent to put you always in remembrance of these things, though ye know them, and be established in the *present truth.*" The term can also have a related meaning, that certain truths have been forgotten and need rediscovery today.

Those teachers who emphasize "Present Truth" usually affirm a form of DISPENSATIONALISM, the belief that God has presented different tasks to humans in different eras. The discovery of what God demands at present becomes an important part of Bible study. One must understand which passages particularly spoke to a past dispensation, and which speak to the present.

Teachers who emphasize the Present Truth often have a strong belief in the imminent second coming of Christ. The apostle Paul is seen as speaking Present Truth when addressing the church concerning marriage in I Corinthians 7: "In light of the soon appearance of Christ, it is better not to marry." Millennialist groups, from the early Adventists who followed William MILLER to the JEHOVAH'S WITNESSES, have often confronted the larger Christian community with the need to reorient their lives as Christ gets ready to appear. If such a dramatic change is to occur in the next few years, it would be proper to dedicate one's life to religious activity as opposed to following a career, raising a family, and building for future generations.

In both the Evangelical and Adventist tradition, editors have chosen *The Present Truth* as the title for periodicals, possibly the most prominent being that of James White, cofounder of the SEVENTH-DAY ADVENTIST CHURCH. Paul S. L. Johnson, who founded the Laymen's Home Missionary Movement with former followers of Charles Taze RUSSELL, used that same name for his movement's periodical. Representative of the Evangelical dispensationalist tradition are the books and other materials issued by Present Truth Publishers of Jackson, New Jersey.

Further reading: Ellen G. White, *Present Truth and Review and Herald Articles,* 6 vols. (Battle Creek, Mich.: Review & Herald, 1962); Jonas Wendall, *The Present Truth, or, Meat in Due Season* (Edenboro, Pa.: the author, 1870).

priesthood of all believers

In the first of his crucial essays of 1520, the "Appeal to the German Nobility," Martin LUTHER called upon the Christian leaders of Germany (all of them laypeople) to support his demand for reform; he supported his call with the idea of the priesthood of all believers. Luther suggested that all Christians were, by virtue of their BAPTISM, consecrated to act as priests; in fact, baptismal consecration was higher than the ordination offered by a BISHOP or pope. The congregation of such priests summons and appoints one of its number to act as worship leader, preacher, and speaker of God's forgiveness of sin. Such a person is a mere functionary. Falling back on I Corinthians 12, in which St. Paul spoke of the church as one body, Luther suggests that each church member engages in his/her own work the better to serve the whole.

Luther singled out the princes as possessors of the temporal authority to punish the wicked. If the leaders of the church had been guilty of wrongdoing (and Luther believed they had), then it was the Christian princes who should move against them.

Luther was not challenging the essential priestly role of ministers in serving the sacraments or hearing confession (part of the office of the keys for the binding and loosing of sins as mentioned in Matt. 16:19). At the same time, he challenged the exclusive right of ministers to priestly activities. As all are priests, each Christian can, for example, pray for others and teach others.

Once freed upon the Protestant constituency, however, the doctrine of the priesthood of believers took on a spectrum of connotations far beyond those intended by Luther. In their most extreme form, Protestants have argued for a thoroughgoing rejection of the ordained ministry in favor of a lay-led church. BAPTISTS have found the idea compatible with their understanding of the traditional sacraments as ordinances, and their rejection of any form of clericalism and sacerdotalism.

Within liberal Protestantism, the doctrine was used to affirm the role of the laity in ministry. This has led to the establishment of educational programs for laypeople, who often assume various professional and semiprofessional roles such as preaching, diaconal services, or teaching. Lay members are admonished to develop a personal ministry directed to serving either the congregation or the larger world.

Further reading: Cyril Eastwood, *The Priesthood of All Believers: An Examination of the Doctrine from the Reformation to the Present Day* (London: Epworth Press, 1960); Larry Richards and Gib Martin, *Lay Ministry: Empowering the People of God* (Grand Rapids, Mich.: Ministry Resources Library, 1981); Herschel H. Hobbs, *You Are Chosen: The Priesthood of All Believers* (New York: Harper & Row 1990); W. Norman Pittenger, *The Ministry of All Christians: A Theology of Lay Ministry* (Wilton, Conn.: Morehouse-Barlow, 1983).

Primitive Baptists

The Primitive Baptists (also called Hard-shell or Old School Baptists) emerged in the 1820s as Luther RICE (1783–1836) moved through the United States to organize support among American BAPTISTS for the new enterprise of foreign missions. The first gathering of the General Missionary Convention of the Baptist Denomination in the United States for Foreign Missions (generally called the Triennial Convention as it met every three years) was held in 1814; it expanded its concern three years later to include home missions and education. Several organizations were set up for these purposes, each of which received moneys from Baptist congregations and developed programs for all of them. Simultaneously, SUNDAY SCHOOLS gained a foothold; by the 1820s, Sunday schools were being organized by most Baptist congregations.

Not all Baptists were happy with foreign missions or Sunday schools. Theologically, their conservative Calvinist faith did not support efforts to convert the heathen either at home or abroad, the spread of faith being God's work alone. They also found no Scripture to support the idea of Sunday schools.

By 1827, the Kehukee Association of churches in North Carolina issued statements rejecting both missions and Sunday schools. Over the next decade, additional associations aligned with Kehukee, and individual churches withdrew from their local associations to create new anti-mission and anti-Sunday school associations. A number of Baptist ELDERS and members met at Black Rock, Maryland, on September 28, 1832, and published their Black Rock Address, which explained their intention to withdraw fellowship from those adhering to the new innovative practices.

The Primitive Baptist movement is conservative in its Calvinist faith and strictly congregational in POLITY. They tend to identify with one of three subgroups. The main body accept "conditional time salvation," meaning that while God predestined who would be among the elect, it was up to each person to manifest their salvation. The Absoluters suggested that God predestined all things. The Progressives, the last group to arrive on the scene, adopted a number of innovations rejected by the other two groups. The Primitive Baptists are strongest in the American South, and a fourth subgroup is defined solely by race. African-American Primitive Baptists organized the National Primitive Baptist Convention in 1907.

Primitive Baptist Churches form associations of churches in any geographical region, purely for fellowship purposes. Each association has a statement of faith that represents the agreed upon standard for a congregation's membership. Individual associations issue and receive letters from other associations of like mind.

Among the practices rejected by the Primitive Baptists was instrumental music, the spread of the organs in the 19th century being a sign of affluence in different churches. Within the churches, a form of hymn singing known as shaped note or Sacred Harp music identified with Primitive Baptists has enjoyed a revival in the last generation by those interested in folk music.

Because of its extreme congregationalism, it is difficult to get an accurate count of membership. Estimates run from 50,000 to 70,000.

Further reading: John G. Crowley, *Primitive Baptists of the Wiregrass South* (Gainesville: University of Florida Press, 1998); Beverly Bush Patterson, *The Sound of the Dove: Singing in the Appalachian Primitive Baptist Churches* (Urbana: University of Illinois Press, 1995); James L. Peacock and Ruel W. Tyson Jr., *Pilgrims of Paradox: Calvinism and Experience among the Primitive Baptists of the Blue Ridge* (Washington, D.C.: Smithsonian Institution Press, 1989); Albert W. Wardin, ed., *Baptists Around the World* (Nashville, Tenn.: Broadman & Holman, 1995).

Primitive Methodist Church

One of several factions in British METHODISM, the Primitive Methodists are remembered for their introduction of camp meetings into Great Britain and their use of female preachers. In 1805, the independent and eccentric Methodist preacher Lorenzo Dow traveled through Cheshire and Staffordshire in the English Midlands talking about the American CAMP MEETINGS he had attended. On hearing this account, Methodist layman Hugh Bourne (1772–1852) organized a camp meeting in 1807. The local Methodists disapproved, and Bourne was eventually disfellowshipped. Nevertheless, he continued his evangelistic work.

Meanwhile, another layman, William Clowes (1780–1852), had also begun independent evangelism for which he too was disfellowshipped. In 1811, the two men joined their work as the Soci-

ety of the Primitive Methodists. The name referred to the mention of "primitive methodism" by John WESLEY in his last talk in Cheshire in 1790.

By 1842, the group had some 80,000 members and 500 ministers; much earlier, though, the work became larger than Bourne and Clowes could handle and they called for volunteer lay speakers. A number of women stepped forward. Even though the main body of Wesleyan Methodists (now the METHODIST CHURCH) had officially ruled against female ministers, the Primitive Methodists put them to work, first in prayer and witness groups at the camp meetings and then in public preaching. In 1813, Sarah Kirkland (1794–1880) was recruited by Bourne as a salaried missionary to work in northern England. Through the next generation, some 100 women were recruited into the traveling ministry. In 1829, Ruth Watkins would be among the four missionaries sent to America to begin the Primitive Methodist Church in the United States. As the church evolved and became more oriented toward settled congregations and parish ministers, women gradually disappeared from the ranks of the preachers.

The American branch of the church was formally organized in 1840. Three years later, missionaries were sent to AUSTRALIA and NEW ZEALAND. Work subsequently began in West Africa (1870), South Central Africa, and southern Nigeria (1889).

In 1932, the Primitive Methodist Church in the UNITED KINGDOM joined the union of Methodist groups that produced the present Methodist Church. That union was effective for all of the overseas work except the United States, where the Primitive Methodists had formally separated from the British work and now survive as a separate DENOMINATION. The present Primitive Methodist Church in Guatemala is a result of missionary activity from the United States.

Further reading: Geoffrey Milburn, *Primitive Methodism* (London: Epworth Press, 2002); Julia Stewart Werner, *The Primitive Methodist Connexion: Its Background and Early History* (Madison: University of Wisconsin Press, 1984).

Princeton Theology

Princeton Theology is the general term used to encompass the work of several generations of 19th-century theologians at Princeton Theological Seminary. It was one of the most influential conservative schools of theology in America, remaining persistently loyal to the WESTMINSTER CONFESSION and its COVENANT theology.

Charles HODGE (1797–1878), one of the founders of Princeton Theology, defined his viewpoint in opposition to the prevailing teaching at Andover Theological Seminary. Andover accommodated CALVINISM to American REVIVALISM; it was also the center for the promotion of the Congregational Church's program that extended from world missions to domestic social reform. Hodge founded the *Biblical Repertory and Princeton Review,* the main voice of the Princeton faculty; starting in 1825, he edited it for more than 40 years. Hodge's colleagues included Archibald Alexander (1772–1851) and Samuel Miller (1769–1850).

The first generation of Princeton theologians were gradually replaced by Joseph Addison Alexander (1809–59), James Wardell Alexander (1804–59), and William Green (1825–1900). The third generation included Archibald Alexander Hodge (1823–1921), Benjamin B. Warfield (1851–1921), Francis L. Paton (1843–1932), and J. Gresham Machen (1891–1937).

The last generation of Princeton theologians attempted to turn back the tide of modernism that appeared to be engulfing the Presbyterian Church, and both Warfield and Machen emerged as defenders of the authority of the Bible against modernist BIBLICAL CRITICISM. As early as 1881, Warfield and A. A. Hodge wrote a defense of the INERRANCY of the Bible. Drawing on the work of Swiss professor Louis GAUSSEN (1790–1863), they also referred to the Bible's plenary inspiration and infallibility.

By the 1930s, the Princeton themes had been largely exhausted and the majority of theologians had passed from the scene without being able to leave their chairs to like-minded replacements. The last to survive was J. Gresham Machen, who challenged the drift, as he saw it, in the Presbyterian Church in his 1923 volume, *Christianity and Liberalism.* As debate continued, Machen became identified with FUNDAMENTALISM. Following the reorganization of the faculty in 1929, he resigned his post at Princeton to help found Westminster Theological Seminary. Four years later, he founded the Independent Board for Presbyterian Foreign Missions to counter the liberalism in church mission policies. In reaction, in 1936 the Presbyterians defrocked him. He then led in the founding of the Presbyterian Church of America (now known as the Orthodox Presbyterian Church), with which Westminster and the Independent Board eventually associated.

In its final stages, the Princeton Theology, which includes a form of POSTMILLENNIALISM, had to contend with DISPENSATIONALISM and PREMILLENNIALISM, which found wide support among Fundamentalists. However, its ideas find a continuing response among post–World War II Evangelicals, many of whom accepted Warfield's and Machen's explanations of biblical authority.

Further reading: Darrell Jodock, "The Impact of Cultural Change: Princeton Theology and Scriptural Authority Today," *Dialog* (1983): 21–29; Donald K. McKim, *The Authority and Interpretation of the Bible: An Historical Approach* (San Francisco: Harper & Row, 1979); Mark A. Noll, ed., *The Princeton Theology, 1812–1921* (Grand Rapids, Mich.: Baker Book House, 1983); Ernest R. Sandeen. "The Princeton Theology: One Source of Biblical Literalism in American Protestantism," *Church History* 31 (1962): 307–21; David F. Wells, *Reformed Theology in America: A History of Its Modern Development* (Grand Rapids Mich.: William B. Eerdmans, 1985).

Prokhanov, Ivan Stepanovich (1869–1935) *Russian and Soviet Evangelical leader*

Ivan Stepanovich Prokhanov was born in the Caucasus into a Molokan family. The Molokans were a Russian Free Church with many similarities to the BAPTISTS, but without the practice of BAPTISM.

He left the Molokans and was baptized in 1887. In 1893, he graduated from the St. Petersburg Institute of Technology in mechanical engineering.

As a student, he came into contact with the small circle of Free Church believers in the city, who traced their origins to the Christian BRETHREN. He started an underground publication, *Besseda* (Symposium), a Christian periodical designed to encourage Russian Free Church believers. In 1895, he went into exile to avoid arrest and studied theology in several locations in Europe, including Bristol College, a Baptist school in England. Returning to Russia in 1898, he was arrested and imprisoned on several occasions. However, he managed to get approval in 1901 to print an edition of an Evangelical hymnal.

In 1903, many among the believers in St. Petersburg decided to join with the Baptists in founding the Union of Evangelical Christians-Baptists. Prokhanov opposed the decision; in contrast to Baptists, he rejected formal ordination of ministers, favored open communion, and criticized what he saw as Baptist sectarianism. Prokhanov instead organized the All-Russian Union of Evangelical Christians, which greatly expanded after religious toleration was declared in 1905. In 1914, he established a Bible school in St. Petersburg to train leaders.

The All-Russian Union grew steadily, numbering some 8,500 members in 1914 and 30,000 by 1923. However, toward the end of the decade, with the rise of Joseph Stalin, the limited freedom of the Free Churches came to an end. After legal status was withdrawn from the churches in 1928, Prokhanov left Russia, never to return. He settled in the United States, appointing Peter Deyenka (1898–1987) representative of the All-Russian Union for the United States and Canada. Deyenka later became head of the Slavic Gospel Association; Prokhanov died in exile in 1935. The union survived, though battered by the government, and in 1944 merged into the Union Council of Evangelical Christians-Baptists, which survived through the remaining Soviet years and into post-Soviet Russia. In 1989, the council set up a Bible Institute of Evangelism and Mission, inspired and modeled on Prokhanov's original school in St. Petersbury.

See also RUSSIA.

Further reading: Steve Durasoff, *The Russian Protestants: Evangelicals in the Soviet Union, 1944–1964* (Rutherford, N.J.: Fairleigh Dickinson University Press, 1969); Ivan S. Prokhanov, *In the Cauldron of Russia* (New York: All-Russian Evangelical Christian Union, 1933); Albert W. Wardin, ed. *Baptists Around the World* (Nashville, Tenn.: Broadman & Holman, 1995).

providence of God

In Protestant theology, the providence of God refers to God's work as the preserver of creation, his continual interaction with created beings, and his direction of the universe to its predetermined end. While affirmed in Lutheran confessions, it has been more prominent in the Reformed tradition. All the early Reformed confessions include a separate paragraph on the subject. For example, the BELGIC CONFESSION asserted, "We believe that this good God, after he created all things, did not abandon them to chance or fortune but leads and governs them according to his holy will, in such a way that nothing happens in this world without his orderly arrangement."

Though the doctrine holds that God continues to direct the creation, that direction may be accomplished through a variety of means, such as natural law or the actions of humans. The doctrine was directed against the opinion, credited to the Epicureans, that chance rules the universe; it suggests instead that all things are working for the good. Refinements of the doctrine clarify that God is not the author of sin; sin and evil in God's good creation is the product of fallen humanity.

Protestant theology thus affirms the imminence of God in sustaining and directing creation along with his transcendence in creation and rulership. In making both affirmations it denies deism, which affirms God's creation but not his continued rule, and pantheism, which denies God's separateness and lordship over the created world.

The major difficulty within this doctrine for the Christian is the problem of evil. How can a good and powerful deity allow the amount of pain and suffering that is in the world? Numerous attempts have been pursued to answer the problem of evil. Traditionally, Christians have affirmed that evil must exist for freedom to be real, that is, if humans can love God, they must also be able to hate their creator. If they can do good, such actions would be meaningless if they were not also able to do evil. Christians also note the parallel with the natural world: when humans go against that law or ignore the world, disasters occur.

In the 20th century, Protestant theology has had its most severe crisis in affirming God's providence in the face of the Jewish Holocaust and Christian complicity in the death of so many under such senseless circumstances. The murder of 6 million Jews was compounded by the knowledge of other horrors: the murder of millions of others by the Nazis and the Communists, and other incidents of genocide from the massacres of the Armenians (1915–16) to more recent examples in Rwanda and Cambodia. For many people, these events made traditional solutions to the problem of evil untenable.

One reaction to the Holocaust was the so-called Death of God movement among theologians. These theologians were united more by the label than by any common theory, but they tended to agree with Baptist theologian William Hamilton (b. 1924) that the experience of God as transcendent reality had been lost over the last two centuries. Going even further, Episcopalian Paul Van Buren (1924–1998) suggested that traditional theism was intellectually untenable; in fact, it was meaningless.

The Death of God came and went quickly, but there were other theologies that challenged traditional language about God. In particular, LIBERATION THEOLOGY attacked what it called God-talk as a European elitist male enterprise.

In reaction to these radical formulations, most Evangelical theologians have reasserted a more traditional response to the problem of evil, while still wrestling with modern challenges. A good example is the Openness of God theology of Clark Pinnock (b. 1937). Meanwhile, even liberal Protestant theologians have been more cautious in their discussions of God's providence in the post-Holocaust world.

See also PREDESTINATION.

Further reading: Thomas Altizer and William Hamilton, eds., *Radical Theology and the Death of God* (Indianapolis, Ind.: Bobbs-Merrill, 1966); G. C. Berkouwer, *The Providence of God* (Grand Rapids, Mich.: William B. Eerdmans, 1952); Paul Helm, *The Providence of God* (Downers Grove, Ill.: InterVarsity Press, 1994); Douglas S. Huffman et. al. *God under Fire: Modern Scholarship Reinvents God* (Grand Rapids, Mich.: Zondervan, 2002); Clark H. Pinnock, Richard Rice, John Sanders, William Hasker, and David Basinger, *The Openness of God* (Downers Grove, Ill.: InterVarsity, 1994); John Sanders, *The God Who Risks: A Theology of Providence* (Downers Grove, Ill.: InterVarsity Press, 1998).

Psalms

For several centuries, the churches of the Reformed tradition followed the lead of John CALVIN in using the biblical book of Psalms as the only source for their hymnody. To make the Psalms accessible to contemporary congregations, they were recast into the most common meters of the day and set to popular tunes.

The first Protestant lyricist to adapt the Psalms was the poet Clement Marot (1496–1544), whose work Calvin used in his 1539 *Strasbourg Psalter.* Finding his work rejected in France, Marot fled to Geneva in 1542, where he worked for a time with Calvin on additional versions of Psalms. After Marot's death, Calvin worked with Theodore de BEZA, who in 1562 published a collection of all 150 Psalms. Beza's *Geneva Psalter* spread throughout the French-speaking Protestant world and was translated into Dutch (1566), German (1573), and English (1592). In the meantime, some of the more talented Protestant musicians worked on alternative tunes and arrangements that added variation and life to the Psalms.

An earlier English Psalter had been published by MARIAN EXILES in Geneva in 1556, using pre-Reformation texts by Thomas Sternhold and John Hopkins. *The Whole Book of Psalms,* which as the name suggests had all 150 Psalms arranged for singing, was republished in London; it became the common hymnal for British Puritans for the rest of the century. In Scotland, John KNOX developed his own English-language psalter after his return from Geneva.

All these efforts culminated in the 1696 publication of *A New Version of the Psalms of David, Fitted to the Tunes Used in Churches,* by Nicholas Brady and Nahum Tate. Tate, the poet laureate, dedicated the book to the king, and it was assumed by many to be an "official" volume. It took its place beside the 1556 volume; both competed for the favor of the dissenting churches.

In 1640, within a decade of settling in America, the Massachusetts Puritans produced their own psalter, *The Whole Booke of Psalmes Faithfully Translated into English Metre,* popularly known as the *Bay Psalm Book.* It was their first literary effort.

In the 18th century, there was no lack of writers who tried to perpetuate the tradition of Psalm singing by coming up with new revisions for use with contemporary songs. Nevertheless, Psalms increasingly fell by the wayside in favor of popular new hymns.

The first major blow to the dominance of the Psalms in the Reformed churches was delivered by Isaac WATTS. According to Watts, church songs should clearly present the Gospel that Christians actually proclaimed. The Psalms, however, were written centuries before the appearance of Christ, and expressed the Gospel only in anticipation. Rather than strictly adhering to a biblical text, Watts wanted Christian hymnody to manifest the feelings of Christian worshippers in relation to their savior.

Watts's breakthrough text was the 1707 collection *Hymns and Spiritual Songs,* which included some of his most popular songs such as "Alas! and Did My Saviour Bleed" and "When I Survey the Wondrous Cross." His songs created a new day for church music. As a bridge from the past, Watts also wrote new Psalm renditions, including "Our God, Our Help in Ages Past," based on Psalm 90, and "Joy to the World," based on Psalm 98.

Watts set the stage for the Wesleys. As Charles WESLEY'S thousands of hymns spread through the Methodist movement, they tipped the scale against Psalms in the Protestant churches. George WHITEFIELD republished the hymns for use by Americans in the GREAT AWAKENING, and Psalm singing noticeably declined. Only a few small conservative Presbyterian churches still use the psalter as their primary or only hymnbook.

See also HYMNS/MUSIC.

Further reading: Millar Patrick, *Four Centuries of Scottish Psalmody* (London: Oxford University Press, 1949); William Jensen Reynolds and Milburn Price, *A Survey of Christian Hymnody* (Carol Stream, Ill.: Hope, 1987); Erik Routley, *The Music of Christian Hymnody* (London: Independent Press, 1957); Richard R. Terry, *Calvin's First Psalter, 1539* (London: Ernest Benn, 1932).

Puerto Rico

The American takeover of Puerto Rico from Spain in 1898 allowed the introduction of Protestantism into the largely Roman Catholic land. Five churches arrived in 1899—the Lutherans, BAPTISTS, Disciples of Christ, Presbyterians, and United Brethen, followed by the Methodists and the CHRISTIAN AND MISSIONARY ALLIANCE in 1900 and the SEVENTH-DAY ADVENTIST CHURCH in 1909. The Baptists and the Adventists won the best response, with the latter creating a string of medical facilities. As of the beginning of the 21st century, fully a fourth of all foreign missionary personnel in Puerto Rico are connected with the Seventh-day Adventists.

The more important story, however, concerns PENTECOSTALISM. A number of Puerto Ricans who had converted to that faith in Hawaii and California in the first decade of the new century returned to the island in 1916 and founded the Pentecostal

Church of God. From that beginning, other groups emerged. Pentecostal missionaries from American denominations came to Puerto Rico, while Pentecostal missionaries from Puerto Rico began working in Spanish-speaking communities across America. Indigenous Puerto Rican groups include the Defenders of the Faith Church founded in 1931 and MITA'S CONGREGATION, which began a decade later. Prominent American-based churches on the island include the CHURCH OF GOD OF PROPHECY (1938), the CHURCH OF GOD (CLEVELAND, TENNESSEE) (1944), the ASSEMBLIES OF GOD (1957), and the UNITED PENTECOSTAL CHURCH, INTERNATIONAL (1962). Each group counts its membership in the tens of thousands, with the Pentecostal Church of God reaching above 100,000. The only other group to have a significant impact is the JEHOVAH'S WITNESSES, who have around 70,000 members.

See also CARIBBEAN; UNITED STATES.

Further reading: David Barrett, *The Encyclopedia of World Christianity,* 2nd ed. (New York: Oxford University Press, 2001); J. Gordon Melton, *Encyclopedia of American Religions,* 7th ed. (Detroit: Gale Group, 2002); Arthur C. Piepkorn, *Profiles of Belief: The Religious Bodies of the United States and Canada,* vol. III (San Francisco: Harper & Row, 1979).

Puritanism

Puritanism, as it name implies, was a movement dedicated to the purification of the CHURCH OF ENGLAND following the accession of Queen ELIZABETH I (r. 1558–1603). Elizabeth reversed the move to Roman Catholicism of her sister and predecessor, MARY I (r. 1553–1558). In its place, she articulated a *VIA MEDIA* between Catholicism and CALVINISM, which did not satisfy the most determined Protestants.

Puritans fell along a spectrum as to how much they wanted to change the church beyond the Act of Uniformity passed in 1559. Among the issues in question were clerical VESTMENTS; the refusal of some clerics to conform to the uniformity Elizabeth

demanded introduced the word *nonconformity* into the ecclesiastical vocabulary. A far greater issue was the organization of the Church of England. Puritans wanted to removed the BISHOPS and establish either a presbyterial or a congregational POLITY. In England, the Presbyterians were the larger party, but for most Americans, the Congregationalists who moved to New England in the early 17th century became the model of Puritanism.

Puritanism first gained some power in the early 1600s; among its accomplishments was the new translation of the Bible popularly termed the *KING JAMES VERSION.* They became strong enough to overturn King Charles I (r. 1625–1649) and seize control of the political apparatus in the mid-1640s. In 1645, they executed Archbishop of London William LAUD (1573–1645) and outlawed episcopacy. The following year, Parliament forbade the use of the Anglican BOOK OF COMMON PRAYER. The 1649 execution of Charles officially ushered in the administration of the Puritan Oliver CROMWELL (1599–1658) as Lord Protector.

In 1646–47, a gathering of Puritan clergy, called together as advisers to Parliament, wrote the Westminster documents, named for the meeting place at Westminster Abbey. The documents included the Westminster Directory of Worship, the Longer and Shorter Catechisms, and the WESTMINSTER CONFESSION; these works long remained the defining expression of the British Reformed tradition.

Puritanism eventually lost power, and in 1660 the Anglican episcopal hierarchy was put back in place. The Puritan groups survived as dissenting Christian minorities. Their writings, including such classic works as FOXE'S BOOK OF MARTYRS and John BUNYAN'S *The Pilgrim's Progress,* continued to exert significant influence on British life and culture.

Puritanism also remained a stream within the Church of England, though its leaders were less interested in the church's POLITY than in its spiritual health. They joined Calvinist reformers in seeking a life of moral earnestness, personal piety, and devotion. Under Puritan influence, many laymen built lives of self-reliance, frugality, industry, and energy. Such lives invigorated the secular sphere, and created many successful business entrepreneurs. The Puritans also developed a zeal for education; in the United States, they founded what remain some of the country's leading institutions of higher learning.

In the United States, the Puritan attachment to congregational self-government has often been seen as a source of modern democracy. In fact the pre-Revolutionary Puritans were an intolerant group, and their congregational system was not so democratic as it might first appear. It was primarily the Baptist strain in New England religious thought that contributed ideals of freedom that led to the Revolution, the Declaration of Independence, and the Bill of Rights.

Today, various churches that trace their roots to the British Presbyterians or the New England Congregationalists identify themselves as the contemporary bearers of the Puritan tradition.

See also REFORMED/PRESBYTERIAN TRADITION.

Further reading: Sacvan Bercovitch, *The Puritan Origins of the American Self* (New Haven, Conn.: Yale University Press, 1975); C. Gordon Bolam et al., *The English Presbyterians: From Elizabethan Puritanism to Modern Unitarianism* (Boston: Beacon Press, 1968); Patrick Collinson, *The Birthpangs of Protestant England: Religious and Cultural Change in the Sixteenth and Seventeenth Centuries* (New York: St. Martin's, 1988); Horton Davies, *The Worship of the English Puritans* (Westminster [London]: Dacre Press, 1948); Leon Howard, ed., *Essays on Puritans and Puritanism* (Albuquerque: University of New Mexico Press, 1989); Perry Miller, *The New England Mind: The Seventeenth Century* (Cambridge, Mass.: Harvard University Press, 1954).

Quakers

The Friends (or Quakers) movement represented the most radical wing of PURITANISM, the 17th-century attempt to "purify" the CHURCH OF ENGLAND. Founder George FOX (1624–1691) began to preach in 1647 after experiencing an inner illumination. Fox believed that revelation did not end with the Bible and was available to everyone; a believer could directly contact the living Spirit via an inner light. He opposed almost all forms of church hierarchy, ritual, or fixed LITURGY, and he was a pacifist.

Fox was arrested under the Commonwealth (1649–60) when his movement had hardly begun. Later, he began attracting followers, known as Friends. Their congregations were known as meetings. Rather than worship, they would quietly wait for the Spirit to speak to them. The messages and guidance they received was tested by the teachings and example of Jesus. While waiting, they were occasionally overcome by bodily movements, which gave them their popular name of Quakers.

Friends sought to lead simple lives. They did not wear colorful clothing, wigs, or jewelry, and they continued to use the familiar case (thee, thou) long after it disappeared from popular speech. They involved themselves in social causes including the abolition of slavery, prison reform, and most notably peace. Their PACIFISM regularly caused problems with the wider society whenever the country they lived in went to war.

In 1667, the Friends organized a set of monthly (congregations), quarterly (district), and yearly (national) meetings. Persecuted in England and then New England, Quakers found an early haven in Pennsylvania, founded by Quaker William PENN (1644–1718). The first Quakers arrived in Pennsylvania in 1682. Though never attracting a mass following, they slowly spread across North America.

They began to be organized in America in 1681, when a General Meeting of Friends was held in New Jersey. It evolved into the Philadelphia Yearly Meeting, which continues as the oldest Quaker association in North America. Other yearly meetings were organized across the country in the 19th century. The movement was hit by several schisms; one group called for a radical focus on the Inner Light, and another aligned itself with the HOLINESS MOVEMENT. Yearly meetings split and realigned, and three large national communities eventually developed: the FRIENDS UNITED MEETING, the Friends General Conference,

Sandy Springs (Maryland) Friends Meeting House dates to 1753. *(Institute for the Study of American Religion, Santa Barbara, California)*

and the Evangelical Friends International. Those favoring unity were eventually able to create an ecumenical social service organization, the FRIENDS WORLD COMMITTEE FOR CONSULTATION (FWCC).

In the late 19th century, Quakers began participation in the global Protestant missionary movement, and yearly meetings are now found on every continent. Their greatest success was in KENYA, where the East Africa Yearly Meeting of Friends became the largest Quaker association in the world. The organizational center of the Society of Friends remains in England, where the FWCC and the London Yearly Meeting are head-quartered.

Further reading: William Wistar Comfort, *The Quaker Way of Life* (Philadelphia: Blakiston, 1945); Wilmer A. Cooper, *Living Faith: A Historical and Comparative Study of Quaker Beliefs* (Richmond, Ind.: Friends United Press, 2001); George Peck, *What Is Quakerism? A Primer* (Wallingford, Pa.: Pendle Hill, 1988); *Quakers Around the World* (London: Friends World Committee for Consultation, 1994); Catherine Whitmire, *Plain Living: The Quaker Path to Simplicity* (Notre Dame, Ind.: Sorin Books, 2001).

R

Radical Reformation

The Reformation of the church in western and central Europe in the 16th century was dominated by Lutherans (based in Germany), Calvinists (based in SWITZERLAND), and Anglicans (based in England). Although most Protestants everywhere in Europe were associated with one of these three communions, those who thought that these movements had not gone far enough created a host of smaller churches and communities that often had a disproportionate influence on the wider movement. Many of these movements have survived in some form to the present day. The term *Radical Reformation* has come to designate this diverse group of new religious communities, especially since historian George H. Williams's (1914–2000) 1962 book of the same name.

The early groups, including the Swiss Brethren, the ANABAPTISTS, the MENNONITES, and the AMISH, gave birth to the Free Church tradition in Europe; they argued for a Christian community made up not of all citizens, but only of regenerated or baptized adult believers, free of any ties to the secular state. (Most Protestants, like Roman Catholics, believed that church authority should be integrated with the state.) Radical reformers also experimented with communalism (Hutterites), mysticism (Schwenckfelders), apocalypti-cism (Melchiorites), and theological innovation (SOCINIANISM).

The established Protestant churches opposed the radical reformers from the start and attempted to suppress their movement; their leaders were often arrested and even executed. Two episodes in particular stoked popular fears: the violent, destructive armed rebellion that radical Thomas Münzer (c. 1490–1525) led against the German Lutheran princes in 1524–25; and the disastrous experiment in utopian communal living in Münster, Westphalia, in 1535–36, which included such measures as a massive book burning and the legalization of polygamy.

In reaction to these events, the radical groups were severely repressed throughout Europe (even though most of them supported PACIFISM). Some movements such as the Swiss Brethren were completely destroyed or driven from their original homes. Continued repression against Free Church groups in the 17th century led many to flee to Pennsylvania, the colony established by British Quaker William PENN. The Society of Friends appeared in England as the most radical wing of the British Puritan movement and in the 17th century held a position analogous to that of the earlier radical reformers on the Continent.

Generally dismissed in earlier studies of Protestantism, the Radical Reformation has enjoyed new respect in the increasingly diverse world of Protestantism. Pioneering studies by Franklin H. Littell and George H. Williams have led to a reappraisal of its role in the development of Protestantism. The participation in the ECUMENICAL MOVEMENT of Brethren, Mennonite, and Quaker historians (including Harold S. Bender [1897–1962], Robert Friedmann [1891–1970], and John C. Wenger) has also helped disseminate this new evaluation.

Further reading: William R. Estep, *The Anabaptist Story* (Grand Rapids, Mich.: William B. Eerdmans, 1975); Franklin H. Littell, *The Anabaptist View of the Church* (Boston: Starr King Press, 1958); ———, *The Origins of Sectarian Protestantism.* (New York: Macmillan, 1964); George H. Williams, *The Radical Reformation* (Kirksville, Mo.: Sixteenth Century Journal, 1999).

Ramabai, Sarasvati Mary (c. 1858–1922)
Indian scholar, social reformer, and pioneer Pentecostalist

Sarasvati Mary Ramabai was thoroughly educated in the Hindu scriptures (and English) by her father, a social reformer. Following her parents' death in the famine of 1877, she and her brother became wandering pilgrims. She frequently impressed Hindu scholars with her knowledge. Ramabai, a high-caste Brahmin, married a low-caste man in Calcutta, where she was baptized a Christian before her husband's premature death.

In 1882, Ramabai presented the case for dispossessed women to the Hunter Commission, established to survey education in INDIA. Her presentation made its way to Queen Victoria, who responded by establishing several hospitals for women and financing the training of female physicians (a work already pioneered by Protestant missionaries). The next year, Ramabai and her young daughter visited England, where she was able to observe Christian social services among the poor. While there, she attended school and joined the CHURCH OF ENGLAND. In 1886, she accepted an invitation from the Episcopal Church to visit the United States, where she founded the Ramabai Association to support her Indian work.

Once back in India, Ramabai opened a home for widows in Bombay. The Ramabai Association became a supporter of her work among widows, especially minors. Her vision of serving dispossessed women and children was perceived by many of her contemporaries as too radical, but she persevered. In the 1890s, she acquired land at Khedgaon, where she established the Mukti Sedan, a farm and self-sufficient ashram community for widows and children. From that base, she established several orphanages and a home for former prostitutes. Each facility became a Christian evangelism center.

In 1905, before any word of PENTECOSTALISM had reached India, Ramabai's followers experienced a similar phenomenon. At a prayer service of some 500 women preparing to evangelize the villages, several reported bodily sensations that were interpreted as a BAPTISM OF THE HOLY SPIRIT; a few were SLAIN IN THE SPIRIT. The women became the center of a Christian revival over the next several years. The Christian community grew and offered even more community services, including a school that offered both academic and vocational training. Ramabai began work on a translation of the Bible into the local language, Marathi.

The work begun by Ramabai continues to the present as the Ramabai Mukti Mission, which supports an orphanage, a set of schools for different ages, a hospital, and a home for the "unwanted." Mukti Church, formally organized in 1899, now meets in a building that accommodates 2,000 worshippers. In 1989, the Indian government finally acknowledged Ramabai's work to raise the status and role of women in India by issuing a commemorative stamp with her likeness.

Further reading: Clementina Butler, *Pandita Ramabai Sarasvati: Pioneer in the Movement for the Education of the Child-Widow of India* (New York: Fleming H. Revell, 1922); Helen S. Dyer, *Pandita Ramabai: The Story of Her*

Life (London: Morgan and Scott, 1907); Mrs. Marcus B. Fuller, *The Wrongs of Indian Womanhood*, intro. by Pandita Ramabai (New York: Fleming H. Revell, 1900); Meera Kosambi, ed., *Pandita Ramabai Through Her Own Words: Selected Work* (Oxford: Oxford University Press, 2000).

Reconstructionist movement

The Reconstructionist movement emerged among conservative Reformed theological circles in the 1960s, aimed at reorganizing most social institutions on a Christian foundation. It took shape in 1965, when Rousas John Rushdoony founded the Chalcedon Foundation to help reverse what he saw as the growing control of society by secular HUMANISM. He argued that the "whole Word of God must be applied to all of life. It is not only our duty . . . to be Christian, but it is also the duty of the state, the school, the arts and sciences, law, economics, and every other sphere." Rushdoony was joined by a cadre of articulate intellectual supporters, including Gary North, Kenneth L. Gentry, Greg L. Bahnsen, and David Chilton.

Reconstructionists support Christian faith and biblical law as the standards by which Christians live their lives. They also try to develop the tools that Christians and Christian institutions can use to reconstruct the family, church, schools, work, the arts, economics, business, media, and the state.

Speaking for the foundation, Reconstructionist Andrew Sandlin has identified five components of the Reconstructionist perspective: CALVINISM, theonomy (that God's law as found in the Bible has not been abolished), presuppositionalism (assumes the truth of the Bible), POSTMILLENNIALISM, and dominion (that the godly should take dominion over the earth [Genesis 1:28]).

Despite its conservative views, Reconstructionism differs widely from those Protestant faiths that have adopted PREMILLENNIALISM and DISPENSATIONALISM. It draws instead on its Dutch Calvinist roots and on the teachings of Abraham Kuyper (1835–1920) and Cornelius Van Til (1895–1964), the two most prominent exponents of presuppositional theology. Van Till argued that the universe makes sense only after one accepts the existence of the Christian triune God and biblical revelation. Any perspective based upon the chance emergence of the universe by impersonal forces provides no base to explain either rationality or order.

Despite their powerful writings, Reconstructionists have won support from only a small segment of the conservative Calvinist community. Nevertheless, they have come under stinging criticism from a wide variety of both Christians and non-Christians, most of whom claim that Jewish/Mosaic law is not an appropriate basis for the reconstruction of contemporary legal systems.

See also RELIGIOUS RIGHT.

Further reading: David Chilton, *Paradise Restored: An Eschatology of Dominion* (Tyler, Tex.: Reconstructionist Press, 1985); Kenneth L. Gentry, *He Shall Have Dominion: A Postmillennial Eschatology* (Tyler, Tex.: Institute for Christian Economics, 1992); Thomas D. Ice, *Dominion Theology: Blessing or Curse?* (Portland, Ore.: Multnomah, 1988); Rousas John Rushdoony, *The Institutes of Biblical Law* (Philipsburg, Pa.: Presbyterian & Reformed, 1973).

Reformed Ecumenical Council

The Reformed Ecumenical Council (REC) is an international association of 39 conservative Reformed and Presbyterian church bodies from 25 countries, the most prominent being the Christian Reformed Church in North America. It has a combined membership of 10 million. The REC was founded in 1946 as the Reformed Ecumenical Synod, assuming its present name in 1988.

Member churches wish to present a united front in witnessing to their Reformed faith. They may express that consensus with any of the classic Reformed confessions. Confessional integrity is seen as essential, as it gives member churches a point of unity amid the diversity of their cultures.

The REC meets in assembly every four years. The assembly designates an executive committee with a permanent secretariat based in Grand Rapids, Michigan. Programs cover four major areas: human relations, mission and diakonia, theological education, and youth and Christian nurture.

See also ECUMENICAL MOVEMENT.

Further reading: Jean-Jacques Bauswein and Lukas Vischer, eds., *The Reformed Family Worldwide: A Survey of Reformed Churches, Theological Schools, and International Organizations* (Grand Rapids, Mich.: William B. Eerdmans, 1999); *Handbook* (Grand Rapids, Mich.: Reformed Ecumenical Council, 1997).

Reformed/Presbyterian tradition

The churches of the Reformed and Presbyterian tradition trace their shared history to the teachings and ministry of John CALVIN (1509–64) and the 16th-century Protestant Reformation in SWITZERLAND. Calvin, a Frenchman, assumed leadership of French-speaking Protestants following the publication of his systematic theology, the *Institutes of the Christian Religion* (1536). He directed the Protestant cause in Geneva, Switzerland, where exiles from all across Europe imbibed the teachings they would later share in their own countries.

Theologically, Calvin was close to Martin LUTHER, their major difference relating to Christ's presence in the LORD'S SUPPER. Luther's approach, termed CONSUBSTANTIATION, was more mystical than Calvin's view, that Christ's presence is spiritual and apprehended by faith. Underlying this difference was a more fundamental divergence in the reform program of the two men and the movements they launched. Lutherans tended to start with the church as it exists and remove whatever practice seemed clearly opposed by the Bible. CALVINISM took a more austere position, and tended to discard any practice not explicitly supported in the Bible. This had many ramification; for example, Reformed churches were more plain and unadorned than their Lutheran counterparts.

The Reformed movement radiated from the Calvin auditory adjacent to the cathedral in Geneva. *(Institute for the Study of American Religion, Santa Barbara, California)*

The Reformed Church spread from Switzerland to become the dominant force in Holland and a strong presence in FRANCE (where Reformed adherents were known as HUGUENOTS), HUNGARY, Transylvania, and some of the German states. As the Reformed movement spread to the British Isles, first to Scotland and then to England, the issue of church POLITY came to the fore. In the context of the episcopal VIA MEDIA of ELIZABETH I, British Calvinists set a goal of replacing BISHOPS with presbyters or ELDERS. Thus, Reformed churches in Scotland and England came to be called Presbyterian. English Congregationalists and BAPTISTS, Calvinist by theology, dissented from the Presbyterian consensus by calling for a congregational form of church governance.

Congregationalists and Presbyterians cooperated in their missionary endeavors in the 19th century, especially through the work of the AMERICAN BOARD OF COMMISSIONERS FOR FOREIGN MISSIONS and the LONDON MISSIONARY SOCIETY. In the 20th century, they formed several international cooperative agencies, especially the WORLD ALLIANCE OF REFORMED CHURCHES (which includes Reformed, Presbyterian, and Congregational bodies).

The Reformed/Presbyterian tradition defined its theological beliefs in a set of confessions issued in the course of the 16th and 17th centuries, the most important being the Gallican Confession (1559), BELGIC CONFESSION (1561), First and Second HELVETIC CONFESSIONS (1536, 1566), WESTMINSTER CONFESSION (1647–48), and Westminster (1647–48) and HEIDELBERG CATHECHISMS (1563). Reformed theology emphasized God's sovereignty; an important element was his election of his people to salvation through PREDESTINATION. This element was challenged by Jacob Arminius (1560–1609), a Dutch theologian; in response, the SYNOD OF DORT (1619) published a set of statements on predestination and related ideas that is now considered a core document of the tradition.

In the 20th century in the United States, the Reformed tradition was challenged by the new historical and scientific approach to BIBLICAL CRITICISM. American Presbyterians were forced to choose between FUNDAMENTALISM and Modernism in the 1920s and 1930s, as modernists took control of the larger bodies, especially those that merged to form the PRESBYTERIAN CHURCH (USA). That church, like other contemporary Reformed and Presbyterian churches, now see their faith as located within a historical and still evolving tradition and view authority of the other confessions as relativized by their historical context. More conservative Reformed and Presbyterian churches accept the authority of the older confessions as the valid interpretation of biblical teachings.

See also PRESBYTERIANISM.

Further reading: James H. Amylie, *A Brief History of the Presbyterians* (Louisville, Ky.: Geneva Press,

1996); Randall Balmer and John R. Fitzmier, *The Presbyterians* (Westport, Conn.: Greenwood Press, 1994); Jean-Jacques Bauswein and Lukas Vischer, eds., *The Reformed Family Worldwide: A Survey of Reformed Churches, Theological Schools, and International Organizations* (Grand Rapids, Mich.: William B. Eerdmans, 1999); Arthur C. Cochrane, *Reformed Confessions of the Sixteenth Century* (Philadelphia: Westminster Press, 1966).

Regular Baptists   *See* SEPARATE BAPTISTS.

Reichelt, Karl Ludvig   (1877–1952)
innovative evangelist in China

Karl Ludwig Reichelt was born on September 1, 1877, near Arendal, Norway, and raised in a lively pietist form of LUTHERANISM. A natural mystic, Reichelt developed an early calling to the mission field. Upon completing the Norwegian Missionary Society curriculum in 1903, Reichelt was ordained and almost immediately left for CHINA. He studied Chinese and then settled at Ninghsiang in Hunan Province. He made his first visit home in 1911, when he lectured and wrote about Chinese religion. His first book, *The Religions of China,* appeared in 1913.

Reichelt encountered Buddhism during his first sojourn in China. He found it backward and superstitious in practice, while richly appealing in spirituality. Unable to talk meaningfully to the monks, he later dedicated himself to mastering the means of communicating Christ to Buddhists.

Upon his return to China, he became a professor of New Testament at the Lutheran Theological Seminary at Shekow. He used his free time to master Buddhism, making numerous visits to nearby temples and monasteries. The first result was his 1923 book published in English as *Truth and Tradition in Chinese Buddhism.*

In 1922, with backing from the church, he founded a small community in Nanking, a Christian version of a Buddhist monastery. Buddhist monks would stay for a few days or longer, enjoy a relaxed atmosphere, and engage in discussions about Christianity. The center became famous throughout China as a meeting ground between the two faiths. In 1926, Reichelt separated his work from the Norwegian Missionary Society and reorganized as the Christian Mission to Buddhists.

Reichelt continued in Nanking until the bloody Nanking Incident of 1927, in which many people were killed as the city moved from Chinese to Japanese rulers. Looking for a more stable site, Reichelt moved his center to the New Territories in Hong Kong. Here, on top of a mountain, he built Tao Fong Shan or The Mountain of the Logos (Tao) Spirit. The fame of the Nanking center followed him, and monks from all over China made Tao Fong Shan a pilgrimage site. With those who had become Christians, he founded outposts at other Chinese centers. The work continued until the Japanese overran Hong Kong in 1941.

After the war, Reichelt retired to Norway and published his last book, a three-volume work on Buddhist monastic life (1947), the English version of which appeared in two volumes as *Meditation and Piety in the Far East* (1953) and the *Transformed Abbot* (1954). He returned to Hong Kong shortly before his death on March 13, 1952. Tao Fong Shan continues as a Christian center in Hong Kong, but the postwar situation has not allowed it to continue as Reichelt envisioned.

See also CHINA; CHINA: HONG KONG.

Further reading: Sverre Holth, *Karl Ludvig Reichelt and Tao Fong Shan* (Hong Kong: Tao Fong Shan Christian Institute, 1953); Karl Ludvig Reichelt, *Meditation and Piety in the Far East* (London: Lutterworth Press, 1953); ———, *Truth and Tradition in Chinese Buddhism: A Study of Chinese Mahayana Buddhism/Karl Ludvig Reichelt,* trans. from the Norwegian by Kathrina Van Wagenen Bugge (Shanghai, China: Commercial Press, 1927); Eric J. Sharpe, *Karl Ludvig Reichelt: Missionary, Scholar and Pilgrim* (Hong Kong: Tao Fong Shan Ecumenical Centre, 1984); Notto R. Thelle, "Karl Ludvig Reichelt, 1877–1952: Christian Pilgrim of the Tao Fong Shan," in Gerald H. Anderson, et al., eds., *Mission Legacies: Biographical Studies of the Modern Missionary Movement* (Maryknoll, N.Y.: Orbis Books, 1998): 216–24.

religious broadcasting

The beginning of religious broadcasting can be pinpointed to January 2, 1921, when the evening vesper services of the Calvary Episcopal Church in Pittsburgh, Pennsylvania, was aired on KDKA, the first radio station to receive a commercial license. The program was a success, and similar programs popped up on other stations around the country. In 1923, Aimee Semple McPHERSON became the first person to receive an FCC license to open her own religious station, KFSG, in Los Angeles. McPherson also became the first woman to deliver a sermon on the air. Two years later, Paul Rader (1879–1938), a minister with the CHRISTIAN AND MISSIONARY ALLIANCE in Chicago, moved to acquire his own station, WJBT. Over the next two years, some 50 religious stations came into operation. Most of these did not survive the formation of the Federal Radio Commission in 1927 and its regulation of the formerly chaotic radio world.

Christian radio ministries matured in the midst of the often bitter conflict between FUNDAMENTALISM and Modernism. Modernists used their majority in the Federal Council of Churches to try to control religious broadcasting. In the 1930s, they convinced the major national networks, NBC and CBS, to stop selling airtime to any religious groups, and instead offer free airtime to mainline Protestant, Catholic, and Jewish groups. Fundamentalist ministers and evangelists were limited to purchasing time on local radio stations and, in the late 1930s, the Mutual Broadcasting System.

Mutual devoted a significant amount of time to paid religious broadcasting after Charles E. Fuller signed the first contract for time in 1937. By 1942, Fuller's *Old Fashioned Revival Hour* was carried on 456 stations. Pressure on Mutual in the early 1940s to stop selling time was a factor in the formation of the National Association of Evangelicals (NAE) in 1942. One of its first actions was to create the National Religious Broadcasters in 1944. Nevertheless, Mutual caved in to the pressure and drove religious broadcasting back to the independent local stations, where it built an important presence.

After World War II, religious broadcasting ministries went international. A pioneering Christian radio effort had been established in 1931 in Quinto, Ecuador, when HCIJ, the "Voice of the Andes," went on the air. The postwar period saw the formation of the Far East Broadcasting Company (1945) in Manila, the Philippines, and the "The Voice of Tangiers" (Morocco, 1954), which evolved into Trans World Radio (1960). These three stations beamed Christian programming internationally in an increasing number of languages. The fall of the Berlin Wall in 1989 opened up new possibilities for broadcasting in the former Soviet Union.

In the early 1950s, television became the new medium for religious broadcasting. The National Council of Churches of Christ in the U.S.A., which succeeded the Federal Council in 1950, moved to pressure the new television networks to follow the exclusionary policies of the radio networks. Nevertheless, in 1953, Rex Humbard began televising services from his church in Akron, Ohio, and the following year Pentecostal evangelist Oral Roberts began his popular broadcasts, which included preaching and healing. Humbard and Roberts had as their major competition a Roman Catholic priest and later bishop, Fulton J. Sheen, who developed a prime-time television program, *Life Is Worth Living* (1952–58), that drew a large Protestant audience by avoiding exclusively Catholic topics.

In 1957, Billy GRAHAM began broadcasting his crusades on prime-time television, usually at the beginning or end of the annual television season. For more than 40 years, millions tuned in to listen to the singing of George Beverly Shea (b. 1909) and the oratory of Graham.

In 1959, little noticed at the time, Marion Gordon "Pat" Robertson purchased a television station in Portsmouth, Virginia, and several years later launched the Christian Broadcast

Chapel of the Air Ministries, Wheaton, Illinois
(Institute for the Study of American Religion, Santa Barbara, California)

Network (CBN). He gained a significant audience share after Jim and Tammy Faye Bakker began their appearances (1965). Robertson launched his *700 Club,* a Christian talk show, and through the 1970s other Christian stations linked with him. By the end of the decade, CBN had emerged as a genuine network. Programming expanded in the 1980s, when CBN was joined by the Trinity Broadcasting Network (TBN) and LeSea Broadcasting, both with bases in PENTECOSTALISM. Although religious broadcasting continued on the weekend on secular stations, more and more programs shifted to the religious networks.

At the same time, NBC and CBS moved to curtail the free time they had allotted to religious broadcasting. In any case, liberal Protestant churches had become increasingly skeptical about the use of television. Many leaders saw it competing with church attendance, and criticized the popular programs as slick and shallow. Others thought the financial resources that would be needed to build a real presence on television would be better placed in other ministries. Nevertheless, in 1988, a coalition of liberal Protestants and Catholics developed a new network, the Faith and Values Channel.

Christian television has given celebrity status to some of its leading figures—Robertson, Jerry

Falwell, D. James Kennedy, Robert Shuler, Jan and Paul Crouch—and helped make stars of many Christian musicians. It weathered a major storm beginning in the late 1980s with a set of scandals that drove a number of leading figures—including Jim Bakker, Jimmy Swaggert, Robert Tilton, W. V. Grant Jr., Larry Lea, and Peter Popoff—off the air. CBN and TBN recovered and today through the facilities of satellite and cable are broadcast around the world.

Religious broadcasting has been a welcoming medium for women in leadership roles. Beginning with Aimee Semple McPherson, such people as Evelyn Wyatt on radio and more recently Gloria Copeland, Anne Gimenez, Marilyn Hickey, and Joyce Meyer on television have found a means to reach an expansive audience with their ministries. Overall, however, both radio and television remain predominantly male domains.

In the 1980s, sociologist Jeffrey Hadden coined the term TELEVANGELISM to reflect how Evangelical and Pentecostal groups were using television as a primary arm of their outreach to the public. Scholars such as Hadden and leaders of the larger liberal Protestant churches also expressed concerns about the role of televangelists in creating and sustaining the RELIGIOUS RIGHT and promoting conservative political issues.

See also EVANGELICALISM.

Further reading: Ben Armstrong, *The Electronic Church* (Nashville, Tenn.: Thomas Nelson, 1979); Jeffrey K. Hadden and Charles E. Swann. *Prime Time Preachers: The Rising Power of Televangelism* (Reading, Mass.: Addison-Wesley 1981); Ben Armstrong and A. D. Shupe, *Televangelism* (New York: Holt, 1988); J. Gordon Melton, Philip Charles Lucas, and Jon R. Stone, *Prime Time Religion: An Encyclopedia of Religious Broadcasting* (Phoenix, Ariz.: Oryx Press, 1997).

Religious Right

The term *Religious Right* identifies a movement among conservative Protestants to advance their views about a variety of issues in American society through political activism. The movement drew strength in reaction to events such as Supreme Court decisions banning organized prayer at public schools and legalizing abortion; the rise of a visible gay/lesbian community and its drive to end discrimination; and the battle to have CREATIONISM taught in the public schools. Finding it difficult to enact their views into law, some conservative Christian leaders began to question the idea of SEPARATION OF CHURCH AND STATE, which their opponents continually cited. They claimed that separation violated the original intent of the country's founders to be a Christian nation.

Organizations devoted to each of these controversial issues had been in operation for years. In 1979, during Ronald Reagan's presidential bid, the first visible attempts were made to bring them all together and to mobilize conservative Christians (including Roman Catholics) for political activity. Three major groups were formed: the Moral Majority (led by fundamentalist Baptist minister Jerry Falwell [b. 1932]), the Religious Roundtable (led by Southern Baptist businessman Edward A. McAteer [b. 1927]), and Christian Voice. They launched campaigns to register conservative voters, developed a set of issues to present to constituencies, and brought religious and political leaders together for mutual support.

Though supportive of Reagan's generally conservative economic program, the group found little support from him as president on its most important agenda items. He nominated Sandra Day O'Connor to the Supreme Court over their objections on the abortion issue, and he offered only token support for a constitutional amendment on school prayer and for antiabortion legislation. Meanwhile, the Supreme Court made additional rulings against school prayer (1985) and creationism (1986).

In 1988, televangelist Pat Robertson decided to run for president. He was not helped by the financial scandal that involved his close associate, Jim Bakker, and spread to include popular preacher Jimmy Swaggart. Robertson's campaign fizzled in the Republican primaries. Also hit by the scandal, Jerry Falwell disbanded the Moral Majority in 1989. Partly in response, Robertson founded the Christian Coalition to continue the task of mobilizing the conservative religious community.

By the end of the 1980s, the Religious Right had become institutionalized as part of the American political scene. It includes such groups as the Traditional Values Coalition (1982) founded by Presbyterian Louis Sheldon, and the American Family Association headed by Methodist Donald E. Wildmon (b. 1938). The cause was also joined by Focus on the Family, founded in 1977 by psychologist James Dobson (b. 1936), which through the 1980s built a national audience on Christian radio.

The Religious Right scored some victories in the 1990s, such as the inclusion of its profamily plank in the 1992 Republican Party platform, the defeat of President Clinton's proposals on gays in the military and health insurance, and the passing of the Defense of Marriage Act by Congress in 1996. However, they could not prevent Clinton's reelection in 1996 or elect former Marine officer Oliver North to the U.S. Senate. The antiabortion movement was hurt by its violent fringe, and conservative House Speaker Newt Gingrich was ousted. By century's end, the Christian Coalition lost its tax exemption for its involvement in partisan politics.

Though still an active force in the Republican Party, the Religious Right has been weakened by its failure to have implemented most significant proposals into law, and its seeming inability to turn back continued gains by its opponents.

See also EVANGELICALISM.

Further reading: Leith Anderson, *Winning the Values War in a Changing Culture: Thirteen Distinct Values that Mark a Follower of Jesus Christ* (Minneapolis, Minn.: Bethany House, 1994); Stephen Bruce, *Conservative Christian Politics* (New York: Oxford University Press, 1998); Ralph Reed, *Active Faith: How Christians Are Changing the Face of American Politics* (New York: Free Press, 1996); Pat Robertson, with Bob Slosser, *The Plan* (Nashville, Tenn.: Thomas Nelson, 1989); Glenn H. Utter and John W. Storey, *The Religious Right,* 2nd ed. (Santa Barbara, Calif.: ABC-CLIO, 2001).

Remonstrants *See* ARMINIANISM.

Restoration movement

The term *Restoration movement* includes a set of American Protestant DENOMINATIONS that emerged on the American frontier early in the 19th century, often in rebellion against the rules and regulations of the many existing denominations, and aiming to "restore" the faith and practice of the New Testament church.

Among those who wished to return to the simplicity of the biblical church were three former Presbyterians: Barton Stone (1772–1884), Thomas Campbell (1763–1854), and his son Alexander CAMPBELL (1788–1866). Censured for participating in CAMP MEETINGS, Stone left the Presbyterian Synod of Kentucky and formed the independent Springfield Presbytery. In 1809, having concluded that a congregational POLITY was more biblical, the presbytery was dissolved and the group began to call itself simply the Christian Church. Meanwhile, the Campbells founded an independent church that united with the Red Stone Baptist Association in Pennsylvania. While agreeing on many points with the BAPTISTS, they rejected even the loose Baptist

The Church of Christ congregation in Washington, D.C., is a prominent church within the larger Restoration movement. *(Institute for the Study of American Religion, Santa Barbara, California)*

David Lipscomb provided leadership for the churches of the Restoration movement from this log cabin, now located on the campus of David Lipscomb University in Nashville, Tennessee. *(Institute for the Study of American Religion, Santa Barbara, California)*

congregational associations. The Campbells left the Baptists in 1830.

Both strains of the movement were committed to evangelism and to building Christianity in America, especially in the lands west of the Allegheny Mountains. The movement is associated with the origins of CAMP MEETINGS, though they quickly came to share their leadership with the Baptists, Methodists, and Cumberland Presbyterians. Alexander Campbell brought some unity to the movements through his travels, preaching, and writings. In 1830, he founded and for many years edited the widely read magazine *Millennial Harbinger.*

The Restoration churches hoped to unify the different denominations that made up the Protestant world. Toward that end, they chose to use no label other than Christian. In fact, however, they came to resemble Baptists in many ways. They eschewed infant BAPTISM, baptized only by immersion, and saw the LORD'S SUPPER as a memorial meal. Uniquely, they included the Lord's Supper as part of their regular Sunday worship.

The branches of the movement led by Barton Stone and by the Campbells came together in a loose association in 1832, but refused to set up any formal headquarters. The Campbells' publishing house and periodical served as visible points of unity for the movement.

In the years after the Civil War, the congregations in the North and South began to drift apart. The split was formalized in 1906, ostensibly over the use of instrumental music, which the southern congregations (which came to be known as the Churches of Christ) forbade, while the wealthier northern churches (which came to be known as the Christian Church [Disciples of Christ]) could afford to buy organs. Through the 20th century, the northern movement proved more open to pan-denominational structures, and was willing to identify with the Protestant ECUMENICAL MOVE-MENT and became a member of the WORLD COUN-CIL OF CHURCHES. However, many northern members objected to the new structures within the Disciples of Christ, especially the International Convention, which brought together a number of PARACHURCH ORGANIZATIONS. That led to a second formal break in 1968; the more conservative group left and subsequently became known as the Christian Churches and Churches of Christ.

Thus, since 1968, the Restoration movement has been composed of three separate branches, popularly known as the Independent Christian Churches, the Disciples of Christ, and the Churches of Christ. In addition, the very loosely organized "noninstrumental" Churches of Christ have spawned several subgroups that have added additional points to the standard Churches of Christ affirmations. One group has adopted PRE-MILLENNIALISM, another refuses to organize SUNDAY SCHOOLS, and still another has accepted the Pentecostal BAPTISM OF THE HOLY SPIRIT and speaking in tongues. Each subgroup is built around a periodical and publishing concern, and some support separate colleges and Bible schools.

The newest and most successful of the subgroups has been willing to tolerate a more centralized structure in order to carry out a plan for world evangelism. The INTERNATIONAL CHURCHES OF CHRIST has a headquarters in Los Angeles and no longer considers itself as part of the older Churches of Christ fellowship.

The larger branch of the Churches of Christ has found its own focus by supporting several schools such as Lipscomb University in Nashville, Tennessee, and Harding University in Searcy, Arkansas. It is also served by two prominent periodicals, *Firm Foundation* and the *Gospel Advocate*.

In spite of their hostility to structure, the churches of the Restoration movement were able to build and maintain vigorous foreign mission programs, often operating through autonomous missionary agencies drawing resources from

whichever congregations or individuals chose to support them. By the 1990s, the Churches of Christ reported some 14,000 congregations worldwide.

As the new century begins, the three main branches of the Restoration movement each has roughly 1 million members.

Further reading: D. Newell Williams, ed., *A Case Study of Mainstream Protestantism: The Disciples' Relation to American Culture, 1880–1989* (Grand Rapids, Mich.: William B. Eerdmans, 1991); Leroy Garret, *The Stone-Campbell Movement: The Story of the American Restoration Movement* (Joplin, Mo.: College Press, 1994); Lester G. McAllister and William Tucker, *Journey in Faith: A History of the Christian Church (Disciples of Christ)* (St. Louis: Bethany Press, 1975); Henry E. Webb, *In Search of Christian Unity, A History of the Restoration Movement* (Cincinnati: Standard, 1990).

Reuchlin, Johannes (1455–1522) *Hebraist whose biblical studies aided the Reformation*

Johannes Reuchlin was born at Pforzheim, Baden, Germany, on February 22, 1455. He studied at Freiburg, Paris, and Basel, where he also taught Greek and Latin. He then studied law at Orléans, and received a licentiate of law at Poitiers in 1481.

Reuchlin's trips to Italy in 1482 and 1490 strengthened his ties to scholars of the HUMANISM movement, while his 1498 visit with Italian Jewish scholars improved his mastery of Hebrew. Following his first trip, he became an important legal and political force in the court of Count Eberhard of Würtemburg. He later became counsel to the elector at Heidelberg.

In Stuttgart, as imperial judge of the Swabian Confederation (1502–12), he became involved in a bitter controversy with the semiliterate Johannes Pfefferkorn (1469–c.1521). A Jewish convert to Catholicism who had published an anti-Semitic work, Pfefferkorn in 1509 had appealed to the Holy Roman Emperor to have all Jewish books burned. Reuchlin had been active in introducing Hebrew to Germany, publishing a lexicon and grammar in 1506. Though he knew that the Dominican Order (which ran the Inquisition) was behind Pfefferkorn, Reuchlin stepped into the fray. Consulted by the emperor, he defended Jewish literature in general and argued that only a few books should be destroyed, and then only after judicial proceedings found them to be directly against the Christian faith. When he was summoned to appear before the Inquisition, Reuchlin appealed directly to the pope, who established a special commission to examine the charges leveled against him. The commission found him not guilty (1514). However, the decision was reversed a few years later, during the intense ideological struggles of the Reformation, and Reuchlin was ordered to keep silent. Reuchlin finished his outstanding career as professor at Ingolstadt (1520–21) and Tübingen (1521–22).

Reuchlin's primary contribution to the Reformation was his biblical studies, most specifically his efforts to make the Hebrew text of the Jewish Bible more generally available. For example, in 1512 he published a Hebrew text of the Psalms with an accompanying Latin translation.

He also developed an interest in the Kabbalah, the Jewish mystical system later associated with the Hassidic movement. During his last years, he wrote extensively on the subject, developing a Christianized version usually written as "Cabala." While few others shared his interest at the time, his writings became important in later centuries as Christian Cabala found an audience among Western esotericists.

Reuchlin died at Liebenzell on June 30, 1522. His great-nephew Philip MELANCTHON became Martin LUTHER's chief intellectual supporter.

See also BIBLE.

Further reading: Johannes Reuchlin, *Recommendation Whether to Confiscate, Destroy and Burn All Jewish Books: A Classic Treatise against Anti-Semitism, Studies in Judaism and Christianity* (New York: Paulist Pres, 2000); Erika Rummel, *The Case against Johann Reuchlin: Social and Religious Controversy in Sixteenth-Century Germany* (Toronto: University of Toronto Press, 2002); Lewis Spitz, "Reuchlin's Philosophy: Pythagoras and Cabala for Christ," *Archiv für Reformationsgeschichte* 47 (1956): 1–20.

Revised Standard Version of the Bible

By the late 19th century, Bible scholars concluded that the KING JAMES VERSION OF THE BIBLE, which enjoyed almost exclusive sway in the English-speaking Protestant world, needed to be revised. A group of British scholars began the task in 1870; their finished product was released in 1881 and 1885 as the Revised Version. A similar American group released an American Standard Version in 1901. The British edition was reprinted by unauthorized publishers who tampered with the text. To prevent similar tampering in America, the American Standard Version was copyrighted.

In 1928, the International Council of Religious Education (and by extension the churches that created and supported it) acquired the copyright of the American Standard Version. In 1935, the council authorized a further revision, based on the best contemporary biblical scholarship; 32 primary scholars and 50 advisers were engaged in the work. A New Testament was published in 1946. Four years later, the copyright on this new Revised Standard Version passed to the National Council of the Churches of Christ in the U.S.A., the education council's successor organization. The complete Bible was published the next year.

The Revised Standard Version Bible Committee is an ongoing body that meets at regular intervals. It now includes both Protestant and Catholic members who reside in Great Britain, Canada, and the United States. The committee's second edition of the New Testament was published in 1971. Many of the changes resulted from new scholarly insights on the text.

Improved ecumenical relations in the post–Vatican II era led to the inclusion of Eastern Orthodox scholars and eventually one Jewish scholar. In 1989, the committee published the New Revised Standard Version of the Bible. The new translation includes the APOCRYPHA (considered authoritative by Roman Catholic and Eastern Orthodox Christians, but not Protestants). Backed by the National Council of Churches, the new version also received the imprimatur of the American and Canadian Conferences of Catholic Bishops. The new edition tried to eliminate what it saw as the masculine bias of earlier translations, by replacing masculine nouns and pronouns when both males and females were indicated by the text.

The Revised Standard Version has been widely used in the larger Protestant bodies, especially after it was included in the popular Bible commentary, *The Interpreter's Bible.* However, it met with extensive criticism from the more conservative Protestant churches and spurred the creation of numerous competing translations.

See also BIBLE; BIBLE TRANSLATIONS.

Further reading: Oswald T. Allis, *Revised Version or Revised Bible? A Critique of the Revised Standard Version of the Old Testament* (Philadelphia: Presbyterian & Reformed, 1953); Jack P. Lewis, *The English Bible from KJV to NIV: A History and Evaluation* (Grand Rapids, Mich.: Baker Book House, 2nd ed., 1991); Bruce Metzger, *The Bible in Translation: Ancient and English Versions* (Grand Rapids, Mich.: Baker Academic, 2001); Peter J. Thuesen, *In Discordance with the Scriptures: American Protestant Battles over Translating the Bible* (New York: Oxford University Press, 1999); Luther A. Weigle, et al., *An Introduction to the Revised Standard Version of the Old Testament* (New York: Thomas Nelson, 1952).

revivalism

The term *revival,* in its most general sense, refers to a period of renewal within a Christian country or community during which many nonbelievers become believers, and many of the faithful find a new level of religious commitment. More narrowly, it refers to organized events, usually large communal gatherings where preaching, prayer, and singing are used to reawaken the attendees to a relationship with God in Jesus Christ.

The early Protestant era was a time of religious awakening for many people in Europe. It was carried out in a context in which nearly the entire population was considered to be Christian, having been baptized as infants and confirmed in their youth. In this context, revival meant an intensification of religious faith.

By the 18th century, the situation had changed considerably. In Europe, groups such as the MENNONITES and BAPTISTS believed that the true Christian church consisted only of adult believers who had professed faith and chosen to join a local congregation. In the American colonies, especially New England, a large percentage of the population had little or no connection to the established churches. In this context, revival could mean a renewal of religious faith, practice, and affiliation among the unchurched.

The Pietist movement in Germany and the Puritan movement in England stressed the need for personal faith and the work of the Holy Spirit among individuals. Both movements brought a revival of personal religious commitment. In Scotland and Ireland in the early 17th century, revivals were often accompanied by outward manifestations such as moaning and withering on the ground. The transition to a new form of revivalism emerged with the Wesleyan movement in England. John WESLEY traveled throughout the British Isles building communities of individuals who had experienced a renewal of faith such as his own. He saw his work as awakening Christians who already belonged to his own CHURCH OF ENGLAND, and, to a lesser extent, to the dissenting churches. The emphasis changed in America, where Wesley's Methodist followers worked to call people to an initial faith, especially Africans who had never been exposed to Christianity. The evangelization of African Americans helped reorient METHODISM from the task of awakening Christians to that of converting non-Christians.

Revivalism was transformed once again with the First GREAT AWAKENING, as George WHITEFIELD traveled the American colonies in the 1740s. Whitefield saw his task as spreading the Methodist awakening in America, using its new hymnody and preaching style. Jonathan EDWARDS, then a pastor in Northampton, Massachusetts, recorded many keen observations of the revival, especially the many physical manifestations that so disrupted the traditionally orderly worship in Congregationalist churches as well as his own theological reflections on the nature of revivals in general, trying to place them in the context of his Calvinist faith.

Once the United States became independent, and churches were disestablished, only a small minority of the public remained affiliated with a church. Religious activists needed to find effective methods to call people to faith and church membership. They were quickly found. Possibly the most fruitful method, at least on the American frontier, was the CAMP MEETING, in which people from across a sparsely populated region could come for a week or more of preaching, singing, prayer, and a general time out from normal activities to consider religion. Camp meetings emerged at the beginning of the 19th century and were a major aspect of revivalism for the remainder for the century.

Revivalism became the most important activity of Methodists and Baptists. When older denominations rejected revivalism, some of their members broke away and formed new denominations such as the Cumberland Presbyterian Church and the Disciples of Christ. Later in the 19th century, the drive to convert the nation was once more invigorated with the innovative and successfully evangelistic ministry of Charles G. FINNEY. Finney completed the theological transformation of revivalism from its origins in CALVINISM, with believers praying for God to act, to a perspective derived from ARMINIANISM, in which evangelists called on sinners to take the initiative and repent. Finney also is noteworthy for the introduction of a number of innovative techniques (the NEW MEASURES). This new era of churching the frontier has often been called America's Second Great Awakening, though it lacked the cohesion as demonstrated in the first Awakening of the 1740s.

Finney taught his students the techniques of conducting successful revival services. His *Lectures on Revivals of Religions* (1835) was long a standard handbook.

Rural camp meetings continued in the post–Civil War era; they played an important role in building the HOLINESS MOVEMENT. But a new form of evangelism appeared as well in the great urban crusades of Dwight L. MOODY. Aided by a team of professionals, Moody would lead a series of meetings in different cities including preaching, prayer, and the latest in gospel music. Moody's emphases would be carried forward by evangelists such as John Wilbur Chapman (1859–1918), Rodney "Gipsy" Smith (1860–1947), and former baseball player Billy Sunday (1865–1935).

While this new revivalism was primarily an American phenomenon, it was eventually introduced to the British Isles as well. Itinerant Methodist Lorenzo DOW introduced camp meetings there soon after they emerged in the United States; the PRIMITIVE METHODIST CHURCH took shape in that environment. Moody himself held some of his most memorable crusades in England and Scotland.

In the 20th century, revivalism went into a slow but steady decline in the larger Protestant churches, surviving primarily in the American South and among Holiness churches. Revivalist energy was now channeled into PENTECOSTALISM. Pentecostals adopted the camp meeting from the Holiness churches and became its last bastion. A number of independent evangelists kept Moody's techniques alive, if on a smaller scale. They ran tent revivals, touring the country to hold revivals at predetermined locations. Tent evangelism facilitated Holiness and Pentecostal growth through the mid-20th century. It was also exported to mission fields in Africa and South America.

Tent evangelism declined drastically after World War II, killed off by competition from outdoor movie theaters and then by air-conditioning. The end of tent evangelism, once the backbone of the ministry of such preachers as Oral ROBERTS, hastened the development of religious broadcasting. Revivalism survived and found a new life in the large civic auditoriums that appeared across America. They became major staged entertainment events, as typified by the urban crusades of Billy GRAHAM. The 21st century began with revivalism at a low ebb in most churches.

Further reading: Jonathan Edwards, *A Faithful Narrative of the Surprising Work of God* (Boston: James Loring, 1831); Charles G. Finney, *Lectures on Revivals of Religion* (New York/Boston: Leavitt Lord/Crocker & Brewster, 1835); W. G. McLoughlin, *Modern Revivalism: Charles Grandison Finney to Billy Graham* (New York: Ronald Press, 1959); George L. Mariott, *Religious Revivalism in America* (New York: Greenhaven Press, 1978); William Warren Sweet, *Revivalism in America* (Nashville, Tenn.: Abingdon, 1944); B. A. Weisberger, *They Gathered at the River* (Boston: Little, Brown, 1958); R. A. Torrey, *How to Promote and Conduct a Successful Revival, With Suggestive Outlines* (New York: Fleming H. Revell, 1901).

revocation of the Edict of Nantes   *See* EDICT OF NANTES.

Rhenish Mission

The Rhenish Mission, the popular name of the German-based United Rhenish Missionary Society (Rheinische Missions Gesellschaft), has been one of the most important Protestant missionary agencies since 1828. The society traces its origin to 1799, when 12 Lutheran laymen meeting at Elberfield founded the Bergische Bible Society and the Wupperthal Tract Society. The two organizations later merged with the Barmen Missionary Society (founded in 1815) to form the Rhenish Mission.

Namibia in southern Africa was the first field for the Rhenish Mission. As resources became available, work was initiated in Borneo (1830s) and CHINA (1846). These missions continue today in such structures as the Evangelical Lutheran Church in Southwest Africa and the Chinese Rhenish Church-Hong Kong Synod. Much of the Chinese mission was lost following the Communist takeover, but some congregations survive in association with the China Christian Council, the primary Protestant structure in China. In 1861, the work in Borneo spread to Sumatra, which survives today as the Batak Protestant Christian Church.

The society's work waxed and waned together with the German colonial enterprise, between the 1880s and the German defeat in World War I. The final blow was the German defeat in 1945 and the Chinese Communist revolution. What remained was gradually transferred to indigenous leadership.

In 1971, the Rhenish Mission merged with the Bethel Society, another German missionary organization, to form the United Evangelical Mission-Community of Churches on Three Continents. In the process of formation, the new society became more closely affiliated with the EVANGELICAL CHURCH IN GERMANY, and developed a new emphasis on social service ministries.

The United Mission is headquartered in Wuppertal, Germany.

Further reading: United Evangelical Mission. Available online. URL: http://www.vemission.org. Accessed on June 15, 2003; E. Theodore Bachmann and Mercia Brenne Bachmann, *Lutheran Churches in the World: A Handbook* (Minneapolis, Minn.: Augsburg Press, 1989).

Rice, Luther   (1783–1836) *founder of the first American Baptist missionary agency*

Luther Rice was born in Northborough, Massachusetts. As a young man he joined the Congregational Church and in 1807 enrolled in Williams College. While there, he met Samuel J. Mills (1783–1818) and other students with whom he shared a passion for foreign missions. In 1810, he followed them to Andover Theological Seminary, where he met Adoniram JUDSON. In 1812, he and Judson were commissioned by the newly formed AMERICAN BOARD OF COMMISSIONERS FOR FOREIGN MISSIONS to establish work in INDIA.

Luther Rice, who organized American Baptist support for foreign missions, speaks to the Baptists' Triennial Convention in the early 19th century. *(Southern Baptist Historical Society)*

The ship that took them to India carried several British Baptist missionaries, and the two converted to the Baptist faith. They were rebaptized by William Ward (1769–1823) soon after arriving in India. Rice immediately returned to America to rally the BAPTISTS to the missionary cause. He spent the next year traveling though the United States and organizing the first gathering of the General Missionary Convention of the Baptist Denomination in the United States for Foreign Missions (1814). This gathering became the catalyst for the formation of other national Baptist agencies to handle publishing and home missions, and became the core from which the AMERICAN BAPTIST CHURCHES IN THE U.S.A. would emerge. At

Rice's instigation, the convention also organized a college (now George Washington University).

Rice spent the remainder of his years traveling for the convention and the college, attending his last Triennial Convention in 1835. In the 21 years since its founding, the convention had come to support 25 missions and 112 missionaries. He died the next year on a fund-raising tour of the South.

Further reading: William A. Carleton, *The Dreamer Cometh: The Luther Rice Story* (Atlanta: Southern Baptist Convention, 1960); Edward B. Pollard and Daniel Gurden Stevens, *Luther Rice, Pioneer in Missions and Education* (Columbia, S.C.: Richbarry Press, 1995); James Barnett Taylor, *Memoir of Rev. Luther Rice* (Baltimore: Armstrong & Berry, 1841); Evelyn Wingo Thompson, *Luther Rice: Believer in Tomorrow* (Nashville, Tenn.: Broadman Press, 1967); Rufus W. Weaver, *The Place of Luther Rice in American Baptist Life* (Washington, D.C.: The Luther Rice Centennial Commission, 1936).

Ritschl, Albrecht (1822–1889) *Liberal German theologian*

Albrecht Benjamin Ritschl was born on March 25, 1822, in Berlin, the son of a cultivated Lutheran minister. He studied at Bonn, Halle, Heidelberg, and Tübingen, where he was influenced by the pioneering historical-critical work of Ferdinand Christian BAUR. Ritschl began his own professional career in 1839 at the University of Bonn, where he lectured in New Testament, history of doctrine, and later DOGMATICS. In 1864, he moved to the University of Göttingen, where he taught New Testament and systematic theology until his death in 1889.

Ritschl tried to ground his theology on the historical sources—most notably the Bible's narrative of Jesus and his work for human redemption. He reinterpreted traditional ideas of justification, reconciliation, and sin. He equated justification, which comes by faith in Jesus Christ, with the forgiveness of sins, through which humans gain ethical freedom and renew their fellowship with God. He understood Jesus' death not as a sacrifice for sins but as the end result of Jesus' obedience to his Father. Jesus is an ethical model, and Ritschl emphasized ethical action as opposed to metaphysical speculation. Salvation, in Ritschl's system, is not only individual, but social, symbolized in the ideal of the Kingdom of God. The community (church and society) becomes the place to express the new relationship with God.

Ritschl's optimistic theology found expression in his writings, notably the three-volume *Christian Doctrine of Justification and Reconciliation* (1870, 3rd edition in 1874); *Christian Perfection* (1874); and the *History of Pietism* (1880–6). The latter works deal with practical issues of living the Christian life and include a critique of the PIETISM he found early in his career at Halle.

Ritschl's thought came to dominate the generation prior to World War I in Germany and remained popular in North America through the 1930s. Its optimistic view of the world, however, was shattered by two world wars and gave way to NEO-ORTHODOXY through most of the Protestant theological community.

Further reading: Philip Hefner, *Faith and the Vitalities of History: A Theological Study Based on the Work by Albrecht Ritschl* (New York: Harper & Row, 1966); Darrell Jodock, *Ritschl in Retrospect: History, Community, and Science* (Minneapolis, Minn.: Fortress Press, 1995); Hugh Ross Mackintosh, *Types of Modern Theology: Schleiermacher to Barth* (London: Nisbet, 1937); David L. Mueller, *An Introduction to the Theology of Albrecht Ritschl* (Philadelphia: Westminster Press, 1969); Albrecht Ritschl, *The Christian Doctrine of Justification and Reconciliation: The Positive Development of the Doctrine,* trans. by H. R. Mackintosh and A. B. Macaulay (1874; reprint, Edinburgh: T. & T. Clark, 1902).

Roberts, Oral (b. 1918) *prominent Pentecostal healing evangelist*

Granville Oral Roberts was born in Pontotoc County, Oklahoma, on January 24, 1918. His father was a preacher in the INTERNATIONAL PENTECOSTAL HOLINESS CHURCH. At the age of 17,

Roberts developed tuberculosis but after some months of suffering, in July 1935, was healed of both the disease and the stuttering that had been a part of his life for many years. Roberts learned evangelism work from his father, and in 1936 was ordained as a Pentecostal Holiness minister. Through the early and mid-1940s he pastored several churches.

In 1947, Roberts held his first set of healing revival meetings in Enid, Oklahoma, and published his first book on the subject, *If you need Healing—Do These Things!* He subsequently established a headquarters in Tulsa, Oklahoma, issued the first copies of his magazine, *Healing Waters* (later renamed *Abundant Life*), and started a radio ministry. A capable orator, he had immediate success. His work emerged just at the time that a new emphasis on healing was emerging in American PENTECOSTALISM.

In 1951, Roberts threw his support to the FULL GOSPEL BUSINESS MEN'S FELLOWSHIP INTERNATIONAL, founded to help spread the Pentecostal message. Roberts addressed the first gathering of the group in Southern California.

In 1955, Roberts began a weekly Sunday morning television show that introduced the wider American public to Pentecostalism and to Roberts's healing ministry and made his name a household word. It also attracted controversy as many doubted his healing message. The show continued into the early 1980s. During this time, besides conducting an average of 15 healing crusades a year, Roberts wrote many books on healing and related Christian themes. His column appeared in hundreds of newspapers, and his magazine peaked at a quarter million subscribers. In 1968, he opened Oral Roberts College, which immediately took its place among the leading Pentecostal-related institutions of higher learning in North America. A decade later, it had grown to become Oral Roberts University.

In 1968, Roberts left the Pentecostal Holiness Church and joined the new UNITED METHODIST CHURCH. He subsequently pursued the course of study prescribed for those ministerial candidates who have not attended seminary, and was eventually granted ELDER's orders. The CHARIS-MATIC MOVEMENT was on the rise among Methodists, as thousands were enjoying their initial encounter with the Pentecostal experience. Roberts expanded his television work to include a series of prime-time television shows designed to attract a more secularized audience.

In the 1970s, Roberts began to groom his son Richard (b. 1948) to continue his ministry, though that effort received a setback in 1978 with Richard's widely publicized divorce. However, Richard remarried in 1980 and gradually assumed more duties in the television ministry. In 1993, Roberts celebrated his 75th birthday. He ceded the presidency of the university to Richard and was appointed chancellor.

Roberts's fame and interdenominational following in the last half of the 20th century was rivaled only by evangelist Billy GRAHAM (who spoke at the dedication of Oral Roberts College in 1967). Roberts was a major force in changing the image of Pentescotalism from the enthusiasm of uneducated "holy rollers" to a legitimate and attractive form of Christian piety.

See also REVIVALISM.

Further reading: David Edwin Harrell Jr., *Oral Roberts An American Life* (Bloomington: Indiana University Press, 1985); Oral Roberts, *The Miracles of Christ* (Tulsa, Okla.: Pinoak, 1975); ———, *Oral Roberts' Life Story As Told By Himself* (Tulsa, Okla.: Oral Roberts, 1952); Jerry Scholes, *Give Me That Prime-Time Religion: An Insider's Report on the Oral Roberts Evangelistic Association* (New York: Hawthorn Books, 1979).

Roman Catholic–Protestant dialogue

Protestantism originated as a schism within the Roman Catholic Church at the beginning of the 16th century, and the two communities struggled, often violently, for two centuries. Even when Christians in a particular country agreed to disagree, tension remained high wherever the two communities lived in close proximity, such as in IRELAND, where Anglican rulers attempted to gov-

ern a largely Catholic population, and FRANCE, where a Protestant minority sought to survive in a Catholic country.

The spread of religious freedom in the 19th and 20th centuries gradually converted conflict between the two communities into a war of words, though pockets of physical violence occasionally flared up. In the United States, the Know-Nothing movement of the 1850s included an anti-Roman Catholic element; Roman Catholics there responded by developing an openness to democratic structures and a willingness to participate in the wider society, unlike many of their coreligionists in Europe.

Until the 1960s, however, Roman Catholic–Protestant relations, though no longer violent, tended to perpetuate the hostility of the Reformation era. Each camp published large amounts of material condemning the other, theologically and behaviorally. Protestants were upset that Catholics did not recognize them as fellow believers destined to the same heavenly home. They also condemned the Catholic Church for holding onto what they considered un-Christian beliefs and practices, including the veneration of the Virgin Mary and the saints, purgatory, and INDULGENCES. The designation of papal infallibility in 1871 provided another issue between Catholics and Protestants. At the same time, Catholics chided Protestants for leaving the one true church established by Christ, for splitting into hundreds of DENOMINATIONS, and for being naïve about the authority of the church's tradition.

The possibilities of any reconciliation appeared gloomy as late as the mid-20th century. Vatican offices continue to oppose participation by local Catholics in ecumenical discussions. However, voices began to rise in the Catholic Church calling for some rapprochement. The emerging Protestant ECUMENICAL MOVEMENT that culminated in the formation of the WORLD COUNCIL OF CHURCHES provided a context in which Protestant voices eager to heal the Catholic breech found a forum.

The real change occurred with the election of Pope John XXIII (1958). His first pastoral letter (encyclical), *Ad Patri Cathedram* (1959), addressed Protestants as "separated brethren," a phrase that was a significant step in recognizing Protestants as legitimate partners in future dialogue. In 1960, he created the Secretariat of Christian Unity in the Vatican. In 1961, he formally received the archbishop of Canterbury, Geoffrey Fisher (1887–1972), and sent official observers to the World Council of Churches assembly in New Delhi. These initial actions presaged the dramatic events of Vatican II (1961–65). To begin with, official Protestant observers were given access to council leadership. The council went on to reject forced conversion of non-Christians and non-Catholic Christians and revised earlier directives concerning dialogue. The council declared that Catholics are united with both Protestants and Orthodox by a common BAPTISM and a common faith in Jesus Christ and the Gospel message.

After Vatican II, the whole atmosphere changed between Catholics and Protestants, and believers at every level of church life now engaged with one another. Groups gathered to share worship and music, to talk about commonalities, to discover mutual humanity, and to talk openly about the differences that remained. On the more formal level, Vatican officials at the Secretariat on Christian Unity and church leaders at the national and regional level began a series of dialogues with Protestants and Orthodox aimed at a future return to a unified Christianity. Working groups were established between the Vatican and the World Council of Churches and several of the larger global Protestant denominational families (Lutheran, Anglican, Reformed, and Methodist), which became institutionalized, as Catholics and Protestants now commonly sit together on ecumenical councils at the local and national level around the world.

Although little progress has been made toward organic unity between the Roman Catholic Church and specific Protestant communities, the changed relationship has had a marked effect upon the relationships between church members, especially in places where a high level of tension had persisted, notably Northern Ireland. Protestant-Catholic dialogue there was a key toward reducing the high level of violence in the 1980s and 1990s.

Fundamentalist Protestants have been the most reluctant to engage Roman Catholics; the last pockets of Protestant anti-Catholic literature emanate from their publishing houses. Evangelical Protestants, though less enthusiastic about dialogue with Catholics than mainline Protestants, have initiated conversations and report real progress in dealing with continuing points of misunderstanding and disagreement.

Further reading: John Armstrong, ed., *Roman Catholicism: Evangelical Protestants Analyze What Divides and Unites Us.* (Chicago: Moody Press, 1994); Robert McAfee Brown, *Observer in Rome: A Protestant Report on the Vatican Council* (London: Methuen, 1964); Karl Lehmann, Michael Root, and William Rusch, eds. *Justification by Faith: Do the Sixteenth-Century Condemnations Still Apply?* (New York: Continuum, 1997); Peter Toon, *Protestants and Catholics* (Ann Arbor, Mich.: Servant Books, 1983); Lukas Vischer and Harding Meyer, eds., *Growth in Agreement Reports and Agreed Statements of Ecumenical Conversations on a World Level* (Mahwah, N.J.: Paulist Press, 1984); Joseph W. Witmer and J. Robert Wright, eds., *Called to Full Unity: Documents on Anglican-Roman Catholic Relations 1966–1983* (Washington, D.C.: United States Catholic Conference, 1986).

Romania

The history of Protestantism in Romania is somewhat complicated due to the significant border changes that occurred over the centuries. Transylvania was an autonomous country under Turkish sovereignty when Protestantism emerged in the 16th century, but it later passed to first HUNGARY and then Romania.

LUTHERANISM entered Transylvania as early as the 1520s, followed by the Reformed faith a few decades later. Adherents of both groups worked together until 1564, when separate Reformed and

Lutheran churches were established. Both churches enjoyed their initial success among the German-speaking population, but then won support among Hungarian- and later Romanian-speaking people. By the end of the century, a new church was added to the mix, the anti-Trinitarian Unitarian Church.

The three churches survived through the changes that saw Transylvania transferred to the Habsburg Empire in the 18th century and then incorporated directly into Hungary in 1867. When Transylvania was transferred to Romania after World War I, the Protestant community became a distinct minority in a country dominated by the Romanian Orthodox Church. It was further weakened by the split between Lutherans of German heritage (now the Evangelical Lutheran Church of the Augsburg Confession) and those of Hungarian and Slovakian heritage (now the Evangelical Lutheran Synodical Presbyterial Church). In the meantime, various Free Churches began to establish work in the country. The first Baptist church was set up in 1856. They were joined by the CHRISTIAN BRETHREN (1903), the SEVENTH-DAY ADVENTIST CHURCH (1911), and JEHOVAH'S WITNESSES (1911). The first Pentecostal center opened in 1922, and three years later the Apostolic Church of God of Romania was organized.

All of the Protestant and Free Church groups showed some growth through the 1930s, but World War II and the subsequent establishment of an antireligious government brought severe suffering to the churches and to individual members and leaders. Many were arrested, and a significant portion of church property was confiscated for secular use. The last leader of the Communist regime was Nicolae Ceausescu (1918–89). His regime was brought down by a popular uprising sparked when in December of 1989 he ordered security forces to open fire on antigovernment demonstrators surrounding a Reformed Church in the city of Timisoara.

In the years following Ceausescu's execution, the older churches began to make their comeback, though church buildings were only slowly returned. The Reformed and Pentecostal churches vied for the greatest number of adherents within the Protestant community, with some 800,000 each. They were followed by the BAPTISTS, the Adventists, and the Christian Brethren, the only other groups to have more than 100,000 members.

During the 1990s, an array of Protestant and Free Church groups descended upon Romania, and Western-based Evangelical publishing houses printed millions of copies of the Bible in Romanian. Well over 100 groups have begun work in Romania, though most remain relatively small. The Jehovah's Witnesses have made a remarkable comeback. Prior to 1989, anyone could receive a 10-year prison sentence for attempting to spread Witness literature.

In spite of this activity, the country remains overwhelmingly Orthodox, with more than 80 percent of the population identifying themselves with the Romanian Orthodox Church.

The Reformed Church in Romania and the Evangelical Lutheran Synodical Presbyterial Church are members of the WORLD COUNCIL OF CHURCHES, and the latter church, along with the Evangelical Lutheran Church of the Augsburg Confession, are members of the WORLD LUTHERAN FEDERATION. However, there is no national council of churches. More conservative churches have organized the Romanian Evangelical Alliance, which belongs to the WORLD EVANGELICAL ALLIANCE.

Further reading: Nicolae I. Branzea and Stefan Lonita, *Religious Life in Romania* (Bucharest: Editura Paideia, 1999); Constantin Cuciuc, *Atlasul Religiilor și al Monumentelor Istorice Religioase din Romania* (Bucharest: Editura Gnosis, 1996); Patrick Johnstone and Jason Mandryk, *Operation World, 21st Century Edition* (Carlisle, Cumbria, U.K.: Paternoster, 2001).

Roma people

The Roma, popularly called Gypsies, are an ethnic group who left the Indian subcontinent about a thousand years ago. They appeared in southeastern Europe toward the end of the 13th century. Following a nomadic life, they were soon found throughout Europe and eventually reached the United States. They have not been a literary people, and their history and religion remain relatively unknown. During the Middle Ages, they adopted an overlay of Roman Catholicism, which concealed a magic-oriented religion.

The Roma have been objects of fear and distrust for centuries, valued as musicians and entertainers but branded as thieves and con artists. They were targeted by the Nazi Holocaust, and perhaps 250,000 to 500,000 were killed.

In the aftermath of World War II, a variety of Protestant ministries to the Roma have developed. In 1950, in Lisieux, France, a Roma boy was healed at an ASSEMBLIES OF GOD church, and news of the healing spread through the Roma community. The boy's older brother later became the first Roma Pentecostal preacher. The first Roma congregation was organized in Brittany by Clément Le Cossec in 1952. Similar incidents produced comparable results in GREECE, PORTUGAL, and the United States. A Roma Pentecostal convention was held at Brest, France, in 1954, and a Bible college was opened in 1963. PENTECOSTALISM has given birth to the Gypsy Evangelical Church, which in some countries has added the word *Philadelphia* to its name.

The first and for a number of years the only Roma church in the United States was at Texarkana, Arkansas. In 1962, it hosted the first national gathering of Roma Pentecostal Christians. American BAPTISTS have also been active among Gypsies. The Cooperative Baptist Fellowship (CBF), formed in the early 1990s by the moderate group within the SOUTHERN BAPTIST CONVENTION, selected the Roma people as one of their first missionary concerns. Charles T. and Kathie Thomas, CBF's first missionaries, built a ministry program around three teams: the Romany Team (Europe and Russia), the Banjara Team (India), and the Dom Team (Middle East and North Africa). Having discovered that INDIA was home to approximately half the world's 40 million Roma, the Thomases started the Banjara School of Evangelism, which trains indigenous pastors.

Gypsies For Christ, a British Pentecostal/Charismatic group based in the Woodford Christian Life Church, London, is an evangelical mission founded in 1975. A similar group, the Romani Gospel Waggon (sic), was created in 1990. The two organizations merged their efforts in 1993 and now concentrate their work in England, HUNGARY, and ROMANIA.

Further reading: Thomas, S. L., "Gypsies," *International Dictionary of Pentecostal Charismatic Movements*, rev. ed., eds., Stanley M. Burgess and Eduard M. Van der Mass (Grand Rapids, Mich.: Zondervan, 2002).

Russell, Charles Taze (1852–1916)
founder of the Jehovah's Witnesses

Charles Taze Russell was born on February 15, 1852, in Allegheny, Pennsylvania. Raised in the Congregational Church, he withdrew in 1869 when his minister could not resolve his religious doubts. In 1876, after reading a magazine published by Adventist Nelson Barbour (1822–1906), he became convinced that the end of the age was imminent and that humanity was then in a transition period called the harvest time. He himself decided that the end of the Gentile times would come in 1914. The following year he paid to publish Barbour's book, *Three Worlds and the Plan of Redemption*, which lays out a chronology of the end-time, and released his own booklet, *The Object and Manner of the Lord's Return*.

In 1878, Russell discovered what he believed was a basic flaw in his thinking. He decided that the Greek word *parousia*, commonly translated as *coming*, really means *presence*. He concluded that Christ had become present in 1874. This and other issues led to his break with Barbour and the other Adventists, and in 1879 he published the first issue of *Zion's Watch Tower and Herald of Christ's Presence*. Two years later, he founded the Zion's Watch Tower Tract Society as a corporate home for his ministry, which consisted largely of writing, publishing, and distributing his books. The writings present his restatement of traditional Christian teachings, especially his view of Christian history and the future. The first book of his six-volume magnum opus, the Millennial Dawn series, appeared in 1886.

Russell slowly built support. In 1900, a branch office was established in London to develop European distribution of the literature. In 1908, he moved his headquarters from Pittsburgh to Brooklyn, New York. By then he was a well-known, if controversial, Bible teacher, with a weekly newspaper column in hundreds of newspapers around the world. His writings were being translated into an increasing number of languages.

In 1914, when World War I broke out, many believed it signaled the end of Gentile times as Russell had predicted. Many were disappointed when the war ended without the dramatic changes they expected. After Russell's death on October 31, 1916, Joseph Franklin Rutherford (1869–1942) won a power struggle for control. He eventually reorganized the movement and in 1931 renamed it Jehovah's Witnesses.

Especially among conservative Protestants, Russell is criticized for his many departures from traditional Christian and Protestant affirmations including the Trinity and the deity of Christ. Russell accepted the view of Jesus Christ as a divine being less exalted than God, originally propounded by the fourth-century heretic Arius (c. 250–c. 336). Russell helped popularize the notion that those who did not accept Christ would be destroyed, rather than remaining alive in hell as many Protestants believe.

Further reading: Jerry Bergman, *Jehovah's Witnesses and Kindred Groups: A Historical Compendium and Bibliography* (New York: Garland, 1884); David Horowitz, *Pastor Charles Taze Russell: An Early American Christian Zionist* (New York: Philosophical Library, 1986); M. James Penton, *Apocalypse Delayed: The Story of Jehovah's Witnesses,* 2nd ed.

(Buffalo, N.Y.: University of Toronto Press, 1997); Charles Taze Russell, *The Divine Plan of the Ages.* Studies in the Scriptures, vol. 1 (1886; reprint, Rutherford, N.J.: Dawn Bible Students Association, n.d.); ———, *Pastor Russell's Sermons. A Choice Collection of His Most Important Discourses on All Phases of Christian Doctrine and Practice* (Brooklyn, N.Y.: International Bible Students Association, 1917).

Russia

As early as the 14th century, Orthodox church authority was challenged in Russia by proto-Protestant groups calling for a return to apostolic simplicity. During the Reformation, Protestants did not see Russia as a field for expansion, though LUTHERANISM did spread eastward to Lithuania and a variety of groups found their way to a relatively tolerant POLAND. As early as 1575, Czar Ivan the Terrible granted Lutherans the right to build a church near Moscow, and in 1652, the first Reformed congregation opened in Tula.

Catherine the Great (1729–96) actively recruited German settlers to help develop newly conquered territories, offering them various privileges, including freedom of religion. Both Lutherans and especially MENNONITES began to respond to her offers. In 1789, for example, 228 Mennonite families settled on the Dnieper River, north of the Black Sea, where a smaller group of Lutherans had already taken up residence. Mennonites and Lutherans both continued to arrive over the next 80 years. During this same period, the first Reformed and Lutheran congregations were founded by German immigrants who settled along the Volga River. In the 1870s, faced with the abandonment of the privileges that Catherine had granted, many of the Mennonites began to leave Russia for North America.

During Catherine's reign, another Protestant-like movement arose within Russian Orthodoxy. These believers found their program in the Bible, enlivened by revelations and charismatic gifts. Among these groups were the DOUKHOBORS and the Molokans. The Doukhobors rejected church ritual and took the Bible as their rule of life. Persecuted, they, like the Mennonites, began to migrate to Canada, where most now reside.

The most Protestantlike of the Russian sectarian groups were the Molokans, founded by Simon Uklein, a former Doukhobor who rejected their excesses. Molokans rejected all ritual (their name came from drinking milk during proscribed fast days), including BAPTISM and the LORD'S SUPPER, but became intense students of the Bible. Like the Mennonites, they were pacifists. In the early decades of the 19th century, following Russia's conquest of the Caucasus (Georgia, Armenia, Azerbaijan), many Molokans (and also some Doukhobors) relocated into the region.

A new wave of Protestantism came into Russia in the 19th century, with St. Petersburg as the primary disseminating point. In 1813, the British and Foreign Bible Society opened an office there and sent colporteurs throughout Russia distributing Bibles and preaching wherever possible. In the 1860s, the Bible was translated into spoken Russian (as opposed to the archaic Church Slavonic text used in the Russian LITURGY). It was circulated among Free Church groups and among the many wandering serfs who had been freed from the land in 1861.

In 1832, Johannes Bonekemper, a German-speaking pastor from Basel, SWITZERLAND, heavily influenced by PIETISM, settled at Rohrbach, to work in some of the German Lutheran parishes in the Black Sea region. He encouraged his congregation to meet in home groups for an hour (German *stunde*) for Bible study, prayer, and hymn singing. Soon this practice spread far beyond the territory to which he had been assigned, carried in part by migrant agricultural workers. Though Bonekemper encouraged people to remain in their former churches (even the Orthodox), the movement finally evolved into a separate movement known as Stundists. It experienced a second spurt of growth following the arrival of new Bibles after 1861.

On the heels of the Bible translation, BAPTISTS from Germany began to enter the country. In 1869, Johann Gerhard Oncken (1800–84), the father of the European Baptist Church, made a tour. Two years earlier, a Caucasus Molokan, Nikita I. Voronin (1840–1905), had accepted immersion and began evangelizing. In the 1880s, one of his converts, Valilii G. Pavlov (1854–1924), went to Hamburg, Germany, to study at Oncken's seminary. Voronin and Pavlov led many of the Molokans to become Baptists. The Baptists also moved among the Stundists and brought many to separate from their former Lutheran and Orthodox churches in the Ukraine. The first formally organized Baptist church was established in St. Petersburg in 1880, though it did not get a building until 1912.

During the last half of the 19th century, a spectrum of missionary-minded groups in the West turned their attention to Russia. Some targeted the large Jewish community. The Basel Mission (a Reformed society based in Switzerland) used the Reformed churches already established in the Volga Basin as a base of operation. In 1874, the Swedish Methodists launched work in FINLAND (then a part of the Russian empire), which became the base for moving on to St. Petersburg. The first Methodist church was organized in 1889.

St. Petersburg became the center of a new Protestant movement following the conversion of Countess Chertkova, occasioned by the death of her son. Her brother-in-law, Vasili Pashkov, was also converted, and he threw his wealth into the printing of Christian literature, including Russian Bibles, and in spreading his newfound faith among the Russian aristocracy. Arising in the same milieu was Ivan Stepanovich PROKHANOV (1869–1935), a former Molokan who in the 1880s became the founder and leader of the Union of Evangelical Christians. The union was very close to the Baptists in belief and practice, but more open on the question of baptism by immersion. Prokhanov was active in the BAPTIST WORLD ALLIANCE and emerged as a rival of the leader of the St. Petersburg Baptist community, Wilhelm Felter.

A new day arrived for Russian Protestants in 1905 with the declaration of religious tolerance by the government. In its wake, all of the Evangelical groups prospered and spread from St. Petersburg to other parts of the country. In 1907, for example,

Anna Eklund (1867–1949) came to St. Petersburg and organized a Methodist DEACONESS home. In 1911, Finland was designated as a new Methodist annual conference, with the Russian work listed as a district.

PENTECOSTALISM entered Russian in the person of Ivan Voronaev (1886–1943), a Russian Baptist pastor who received the BAPTISM OF THE HOLY SPIRIT in 1908 in New York. He began work in Siberia and then the Ukraine after World War I, and in 1924 founded the Union of Christians of the Evangelical Faith in Odessa. Pentecostalism swept through the Free Church communities over the next five years.

In 1928, the decade of postrevolutionary liberty enjoyed by Protestant groups came to a sudden halt when legal status was removed from all the churches. Repression became active, and much church property was confiscated. Among the first to suffer were the Methodists. The district superintendent withdrew, and care of the movement fell to Eklund, but by the end of the decade she, too, left the country, fearing for her life. The last Methodist BISHOP to visit the surviving group in 1939 effectively disbanded the work and advised the remaining members to affiliate with one of the other Protestant groups. The Lutheran Church in Russia was formally disbanded in 1938.

The Baptists, the Union of Evangelical Christians, and the Union of Christians of the Evangelical Faith all gained some reprieve from persecution when they joined the national defense against the Nazi invaders. However, in 1944, the first two of the groups were forced to merge, with Pentecostals being added to the merger in 1945. The Pentecostals were also forced to suppress speaking in tongues. The new Union of Evangelical Christians and Baptists became the major Protestant body in Russia in the remaining years of the Soviet Union. Some of the surviving Mennonites associated with the union in 1963.

Beginning in the 1930s, many Free Church groups went underground and did not come forward to join the 1944 union. About half of the Pentecostals stayed out of the union. During the post–World War II decades, some Western Christians targeted the Soviet Union with smuggled Bibles and other Christian literature. At the same time, the Russian Orthodox Church joined the predominantly Protestant WORLD COUNCIL OF CHURCHES.

The situation changed completely with the fall of the Soviet Union. During the 1990s, several Protestant churches (such as the Methodists) revived their work, while almost 100 churches and evangelistic associations launched efforts inside Russia. New indigenous Russian churches also sprang up. As the new century began, the entire Protestant spectrum was active within Russia, though most remain in limbo as to their legal status. The Russian parliament has attempted to take steps against so many foreign groups, which many believe are taking advantage of a period of vulnerability.

See also BALTIC STATES; CENTRAL ASIA.

Further reading: David Barrett, *The Encyclopedia of World Christianity*, 2nd ed. (New York: Oxford University Press, 2001); Steve Durasoff, *The Russian Protestants: Evangelicals in the Soviet Union, 1944–1964* (Rutherford, N.J.: Fairleigh Dickinson University Press, 1969); Albert W. Olema, *History of Evangelical Christianity in Russia* (Katy, Tex.: the author, 1983); M. Rowe, *Russian Resurrection: Strength in Suffering: A History of Russia's Evangelical Church* (London: Marshall & Pickering, 1994); Albert W. Wardin, ed., *Baptists Around the World* (Nashville, Tenn.: Broadman & Holman, 1995).

S

Sabbatarianism

In the Hebrew Bible (the Christian Old Testament), the Ten Commandments state "Remember the Sabbath day, to keep it holy." For the Jews, this command led to an elaborate weekly observance that began at sunset on Friday evening and continued for the next 24 hours. It included participation at communal worship, as well as refraining from anything that would be considered work, such as cooking, manual labor, and traveling more than a mile (i.e., to the synagogue and back home).

For most Christians, who believed that Christ's resurrection took place on a Sunday morning, the Sabbath commandment was reinterpreted as applying to Sunday. Believers who read the Bible literally and attempted to live by its precepts, however, would repeatedly face the issue of the proper Sabbath day. Most stayed with Sunday, but a minority reached a different conclusion.

The 16th-century ANABAPTISTS revived the issue. Oswald Glait and Andreas Fisher, both former Catholic priests, began to propagate Sabbatarianism (the belief that Saturday is still the Sabbath) around 1528 among Anabaptists in Moravia, Silesia, and Bohemia. Glait wrote a booklet on the subject, known today only from the refutation by Caspar Schewenckfeld (1487–1581).

By mid-century in England, as the Reformation spread, individual believers felt free to raise questions that arose from their Bible reading. They discussed the viability of keeping the seventh day (Saturday), the proper behavior for Sabbath rest, and the role of government in enforcing the Sabbath. After all, the Reformers were comfortable denouncing church tradition, and the Bible did not mention Sunday worship.

The first congregation organized around the idea of a seventh-day Sabbath was formed in 1617 in London under the leadership of John Trask. It was a Baptist church, and its Sabbatarianism was just one of many characteristic public departures from the norms of the CHURCH OF ENGLAND. By the end of the century, some 15 congregations existed. In America, immigrant Stephen Mumford (c. 1639–1707), who had joined the Baptist Church in Newport, Rhode Island, in 1664, left it in 1671 to open the first Seventh-day Baptist church in what would become the United States. Similar events took place in New Jersey and Pennsylvania, and the Sabbatarian Baptist movement slowly spread. The unique communal society that was formed at Ephrata, Pennsylvania, by Conrad Beissel (1690–1768) observed the Sabbath on Saturday. After its demise, a small German-speaking Sabbatarian Baptist movement persisted.

A national English-speaking organization for Sabbatarian Baptists appeared in 1801—the Seventh Day Baptist General Conference. A missionary society was formed in 1843, which sent its first missionaries to CHINA. During the 20th century, the General Conference has helped develop Seventh Day Baptist churches around the world. In 1965, the World Federation of Seventh Day Baptist Conferences was formed.

In 1840, Joseph Bates (1792–1872), a Seventh Day Baptist, introduced the practice to the Adventists, then in deep sorrow over Christ's failure to return in 1844. The practice spread among many Adventists, though the movement split as a result. In the 20th century, the SEVENTH-DAY ADVENTIST CHURCH has become the major force spreading Sabbatarianism among Christians in every country.

Smaller Sabbatarian groups also arose. By the 1980s, the Worldwide Church of God had become the second-largest Sabbatarian group in the world, but in the following decade, the church repudiated Sabbatarianism, which had been one of founder Herbert W. ARMSTRONG's (1892–1986) unique ideas. Breakaway Sabbatarians formed several new denominations.

The diverse Sabbath-keeping groups, which all faced the common problem of living in a social and legal context that recognized Sunday as a day of worship, banded together in 1943 to form the BIBLE SABBATH ASSOCIATION. It offers smaller Sabbatarian groups support and works to end discrimination against Sabbatarians in the workplace.

Further reading: Herbert W. Armstrong, *Which Day Is the Christian Sabbath?*, rev. ed. (Pasadena, Calif.: Worldwide Church of God, 1989); Samuele Bacchiocchi, *From Sabbath to Sunday: A Historical Investigation of the Rise of Sunday Observance in Early Christianity* (Berrien Springs, Mich.: Biblical Perspectives, 1977); *Directory of Sabbath-Observing Groups* (Fairview, Okla.: Bible Sabbath Association, periodically updated); Richard Nickels, *Six Papers on the History of the Church of God,* rev. ed. (Neck City, Mo.: Giving & Sharing, 1993).

sacraments/ordinances

The first generation of Protestants reexamined the Roman Catholic system of sacraments—the set of rites performed by the clergy for believers, which were seen as visible vehicles for delivering God's grace. Roman Catholics have seven sacraments. Ideally, a believer participated in five of them only once—BAPTISM, confirmation, marriage, ordination, and unction (now the anointing of the sick). The other two—the Eucharist (LORD'S SUPPER) and confession/penance (or reconciliation) would be received frequently throughout an adult's life.

The first issue before the reformers was the number of sacraments. In searching the Bible, they found justification for only two sacraments, baptism and the Eucharist or Lord's Supper, as

Minister and members of St. Mark United Methodist Church in Santa Barbara, California, prepare to serve the Lord's Supper. *(Institute for the Study of American Religion, Santa Barbara, California)*

they tended to call it. Marriage, confirmation, and ordination were indeed important ceremonial occasions, they agreed, but not genuine sacraments. The remaining sacraments, penance and prayer for the ill, were continued but on a more informal basis; the regular confession of one's sins to a priest was intensely criticized and eventually dropped by all Protestant groups.

All Protestants also reinterpreted the Eucharist, one of the two sacraments they did accept. Roman Catholics believed that during the ceremony, when the words of institution were pronounced, the invisible essence of the bread and wine were changed into the body and blood of Christ; this is called TRANSUBSTANTIATION. Lutherans believed instead in CONSUBSTANTIATION, which affirmed the real presence of Christ in the Eucharistic elements along with the bread and wine. Anglicans also affirmed the real presence, without officially declaring its nature. Calvinists on the other hand affirmed that Christ was present only spiritually, and received by faith.

Ulrich ZWINGLI, the reformer of Zurich, suggested another alternative—that the Eucharist was not a supernatural act, bur rather an ordinance to be performed as a biblical injunction. It assisted in assuring the faithful of the truth of their faith and became a sign of loyalty and belonging to the church. Calvin's position was an attempt to reconcile the Lutheran position with the radical desacralizing of Zwingli. Zwingli's position would be picked up by the ANABAPTISTS, who, in searching the biblical text, discerned another ordinance, foot washing, to be practiced along with the Lord's Supper as an act of humility.

The belief that the ordinances were to be followed as biblical precepts led some to reconsider the nature, proper time, and proper mode of baptism. The idea of the sacraments as ordinances was passed to the BAPTISTS and from them to various Adventist and Pentecostal groups.

Further reading: J. Gordon Melton, *The Encyclopedia of American Religions: Religious Creeds,* 2 vols. (Detroit: Gale Research, 1988, 1994); Charles L.

Quarles, "Ordinance or Sacrament: Is the Baptist View of the Ordinances Truly Biblical?" *Journal for Baptist Theology and Ministry,* vol. 1, no. 1 (Spring 2003): 47–57; Ronald F. Watts, *The Ordinances and Ministry of the Church: A Baptist View* (Toronto: Canadian Baptist Federation, 1986); James F. White, *The Sacraments in Protestant Practice and Faith* (Nashville, Tenn.: Abingdon, 1999).

Sacred Name movement

Members of the Sacred Name movement use the original Hebrew names and terms for the Lord, God, and/or Jesus in their translations, prayers, and/or church names. Since the start of the 20th century, Adventist churches have been concerned about the true name of the Lord. The origin of the question is not known, but its first important manifestation was the adoption of the name Jehovah by followers of Charles Taze Russell. In 1931, Russell's successor renamed his Bible student movement Jehovah's Witnesses.

By that time, Bible scholars had come to believe that in the Hebrew Bible (the Christian Old Testament), the Lord's name, spelled YHWH, was probably pronounced Yahweh (though Jews do not speak that name when reading the Scriptures). Some Christians now wanted to use that name in English translations wherever it was printed in the Hebrew text, and also to replace the English word *God* and even the Anglicized name Jesus with the Hebrew originals, Elohim and Yahshua. Many were particularly offended by the use of *God,* derived from the pagan German *Gott.*

In the 1930s, leaders in the CHURCH OF GOD (Seventh-day) began to use the Sacred Names exclusively. They formed the Faith Bible and Tract Society (1938), the Assembly of YHWH, a congregation in Michigan, and *The Faith,* a monthly periodical launched by Elder C. O. Dodd (1899–1955). One of the regular contributors to *The Faith,* A. B. Traina, began work on a Sacred Name Bible, which was published in installments as the New Testament (1950), the Old Testament (1963), and the complete *Holy Name Bible* (1980).

More recently several other Sacred Name Bibles have appeared.

The movement has remained relatively small and splintered as individuals disagreed over exactly how the names should be spelled. The largest group is the Assemblies of Yahweh founded by Jacob O. Meyer (b. 1934) in Bethel, Pennsylvania. Meyer began a radio ministry in 1966 and publishes two periodicals, the *Sacred Name Broadcaster* and the *Narrow Way*. The Assemblies fellowship includes more than 75 congregations in the United States and has affiliated members in more than 100 counties.

See also ADVENTISM.

Further reading: A. N. Dugger and C. O. Dodd, *A History of the True Church* (Jerusalem, Israel: the authors, 1968); Jacob O. Meyer, *The Memorial Name—Yahweh* (Bethel, Pa.: Assemblies of Yahweh, 1978); Richard Nickels, "Origin and History of the Sacred Name Movement." Available online. URL: http://www.giveshare.org/churchhistory/sacrednamehistory.html; A. B. Traina, *The Holy Name Bible* (Brandywine, Md.: Scripture Research Association, 1980).

St. Bartholomew's Day Massacre

The massacre of some 20,000 Protestants during the week following August 24, 1572, St. Bartholomew's Day, affected Protestant–Roman Catholic relationships for centuries afterward.

The prior generation had seen a civil war between Catholic and Protestants in FRANCE, but by 1572, a peace had been ostensibly negotiated. The massacre was instituted by the French king's mother, Catherine de Medici (1519–89), shortly after a peace-sealing wedding between the king's sister and Henry of Navarre, a prominent HUGUENOT. The first victims were Henry of Navarre's wedding party and the household of Admiral Gaspard de Coligny (1517–72), a statesman who had championed the Protestant cause. The massacre caught the Protestant community unprepared to defend itself, especially as the first deaths led to rioting and more indiscriminate killing. More than 8,000 people died in Paris, and within a week almost twice that many more were killed in the countryside. In Rome, Pope Gregory XIII struck a medal and ordered a mural painted to commemorate the occasion.

Further reading: Robert M. Kingdon, *Myths about the St. Bartholomew's Day Massacres, 1572–1576.* (Cambridge, Mass.: Harvard University Press, 1988); Robert Jean Knecht, *The French Wars of Religion 1559–1598* (New York: Longman, 1996); N. M. Sutherland, *The Massacre of St. Bartholomew and the European Conflict 1559–1572* (London: Macmillan, 1973).

Salvation Army

The Salvation Army is a Christian mission group with an outreach to the poor and to social outcasts. In 1865 William BOOTH (1828–1912), a former Methodist minister, and his wife, Catherine BOOTH (1829–90), opened what they called The Christian Mission in London's East Side. William also began a periodical, the *East London Evangelist.* As the work grew, he developed the idea of a team of workers organized on a military model. Thus was born the Salvation Army, the name formally adopted in 1878. Within two years, the work of the Army had spread across England, and the first centers opened in Scotland, IRELAND, AUSTRALIA, and the United States.

In 1890, William published his program of assistance and rehabilitation as *In Darkest England and the Way Out,* now a classic example of Christian social service. The Army encounters the public through its active program of social service, but it is actually structured as a church with congregations, Sunday services, and a belief structure, and its evangelical goals of bringing people to Christ run parallel with its social witness. The Army grew out of the Wesleyan HOLINESS tradition and continues the doctrinal outlook it inherited. Members are invited into a saving faith with Jesus Christ and are encouraged to look for and enjoy the life of entire sanctification. The most distinctive beliefs of the Army concern the SACRAMENTS. They do not consider the traditional two Protestant sacraments as necessity to either salvation or spiritual growth and thus do not practice them.

The Salvation Army's militarylike uniforms and disciplined life subject it to occasional ridicule. On the other hand its distinctive garb and regimen made it attractive to many and became a means of instant recognition for the general public. Those who join the full-time ministry become cadets; upon finishing their training, they are ordained as captains. Both men and women are accepted into all ranks of the Army. Above captain are the territorial commanders, commissioners, and the general, in charge of the entire corps of officers. At present (2004), the head of the Army is General John Larsson, who resides at the international headquarters in London.

Through the 20th century, the Army has expanded globally. As the new century began, it reported work in 190 countries through more than 15,000 centers. Over 25,600 men and women are commissioned officers, with another thousand in training. The army is a member of the CHRISTIAN HOLINESS PARTNERSHIP.

Further reading: Roy Hattersley, *Blood and Fire: William and Catherine Booth and Their Salvation Army* (New York: Doubleday, 2000); Norman H. Murdoch, *Origins of the Salvation Army* (Knoxville: University of Tennessee Press, 1994); Arch R. Wiggins, *History of the Salvation Army* (London: Thomas Nelson, 1968); Diane Winston, *Red-Hot and Righteous: The Urban Religion of the Salvation Army* (Cambridge, Mass.: Harvard University Press, 1999).

Samaritan's Purse

Samaritan's Purse in a worldwide Christian service organization dedicated to disaster relief and community development, especially, where children are involved. It was founded in 1970 by Robert "Bob" W. Pierce, founder of WORLD VISION, after he clashed with board members of the earlier group. Samaritan's Purse has much the same program as World Vision. Pierce died in 1978 and was succeeded by Franklin Graham, son of evangelist Billy GRAHAM.

As of 2002, Samaritan's Purse was at work in more than 100 countries. In the wake of the Iraq war of 2003, Graham entered into controversy concerning postwar rehabilitation plans. Christian organizations such as Samaritan's Purse are able to enter many countries by emphasizing practical assistance to people in need and keeping any evangelization efforts low key. However, as Samaritan's Purse was preparing to enter Iraq, Graham made several sharp widely reported anti-Islam remarks that called into question the group's work in Muslim countries.

See also FAITH MISSIONS.

Further reading: Franklin Graham, *Rebel with a Cause: Finally Comfortable Being Graham* (Nashville, Tenn.: Thomas Nelson, 1995); Franklin Graham and Jeanette Lockerbie, *Bob Pierce: This One Thing I Do* (Waco, Tex.: Word Books, 1983); Norman Rohrer, *Open Arms* (Wheaton, Ill.: Tyndale House, 1987).

Saudi Arabia

Sunni Islam is the only legally recognized religion in Saudi Arabia. Attempts by Protestants, primarily Samuel M. ZWEMER (1867–1952), to evangelize the Arabian Peninsula in the late 19th century met with little success. Today, Christian services are limited to expatriates and must be held completely in private.

There are several congregations in Dhahran, but most Christians meet in house churches. Anglicans are served by the Episcopal Church of Jerusalem and the Middle East. Other groups with members in Saudi Arabia include the CHURCHES OF CHRIST and the CHRISTIAN BRETHREN. Protestant expatriates come not only from Western Europe and North America, but also from other Arab lands, INDIA, and KOREA.

See also MIDDLE EAST.

Further reading: David Barrett, *The Encyclopedia of World Christianity,* 2nd ed. (New York: Oxford University Press, 2001); Patrick Johnstone and Jason Mandryk, *Operation World, 21st Century Edition* (Carlisle, Cumbria, U.K.: Paternoster, 2001).

Savoy Declaration

The Savoy Declaration was the doctrinal confession of those British Puritans who followed a congregational church POLITY.

On September 29, 1658, toward the end of the Commonwealth (when Puritans governed England), prominent Puritans who supported a congregational form of church organization (as opposed to the presbyterian polity advocated by most British Puritans) gathered for a synod at the Savoy Palace in London. The synod adopted a "Declaration of Faith and Order, Honored and Practiced in the Congregational Churches," popularly called the Savoy Declaration.

The new statement followed the WESTMINSTER CONFESSION but included a section on churches, which stated, "These particular churches thus appointed by the authority of Christ, and entrusted with power from him . . . are each of them . . . the seat of that power which he is pleased to communicate to his saint or subjects in this world, so that as such they receive it immediately from himself. Besides these particular churches, there is not instituted by Christ any church more extensive or catholic entrusted with power for the administration of his ordinances, or the execution of any authority in his name."

These three sentences essentially detail the rationale of congregational polity while denying the authority of BISHOPS, synods, and presbyteries. Along with the CAMBRIDGE PLATFORM, the declaration survives as one of the primary statements of CONGREGATIONALISM, and manifests its essential ties to the Calvinist theological tradition.

The Savoy Declaration later provided a rationale for the organization of Baptist churches.

See also CREEDS/CONFESSIONS OF FAITH.

Further reading: R. Tudur Jones, *Congregationalism in England 1662–1962* (London: Independent Press, 1962); *The Savoy Declaration of Faith and Order* (1656; reprint, London: Evangelical Press, 1971); Williston Walker, *The Creeds and Platforms of Congregationalism* (New York: Scribner/The Pilgrim Press, 1893, 1991).

Schleiermacher, Friedrich (1768–1834)
prominent German Protestant theologian

Friedrich Daniel Ernst Schleiermacher was born on November 21, 1768, at Breslau in Lower Silesia (now Wroclaw, Poland), the son of a Reformed minister. He took his first formal theological studies with the MORAVIAN CHURCH at Herrnhut, and then in 1787 studied with the Lutheran Pietist faculty at the University of Halle. In 1894, he was ordained and became pastor of a Reformed Church congregation in Berlin. He taught at Halle for three years (1804–07), then became a professor at the newly founded University of Berlin in 1810.

Schleiermacher's first theological task was a defense of religion in general and Christianity in particular against skeptical Enlightenment critics. In his 1799 volume, *On Religion: Speeches to Its Cultured Despisers,* he argued that religion began with a "sense and taste for the infinite," starting in feeling and belief with action coming later. He analyzed religious sentiments, which pointed to an infinite and eternal reality. In the end, he defined religion as a sense of absolute dependence upon the infinite.

In his later book, *The Christian Faith* (1821), Schleiermacher associated this sense of absolute dependence with a conscious intuition of God. Faith strengthens God-consciousness, and what we call sin obscures it. Schleiermacher departed significantly from traditional Protestant themes in arguing that Jesus Christ was fully human, but unique due to the strength and constancy of his God-consciousness. His redeeming work centered on imparting God-consciousness to believers.

Schleiermacher became the fountainhead of German liberal theology, which was dominant until the rise of NEO-ORTHODOXY following World War I. His work has enjoyed a certain revival in the post–Neo-Orthodox period as theologians have sought to merge the best of liberal and conservative themes.

Further reading: Keith W. Clements, ed., *Friedrich Schleiermacher: Pioneer of Modern Theology* (Philadelphia: Fortress Press, 1997); James O. Duke and Robert F. Streetman, eds., *Barth and Schleiermacher: Beyond the Impasse?* (Philadelphia: Fortress Press, 1988); Friedrich Schleiermacher, *The Christian Faith*, trans. by H. R. Mackintosh (Edinburgh: T & T Clark, 2001); ———, *On Religion: Addresses in Response to Its Cultured Critics,* ed. by Richard Crouter (Cambridge: Cambridge University Press, 1996); Stephen Sykes, *Friedrich Schleiermacher* (Richmond, Va.: John Knox Press, 1971).

Schleitheim Articles

The Schleitheim Articles were the first official confession of faith of the Reformation ANABAPTISTS. They were issued on February 24, 1527, by a group of Swiss BRETHREN in Schleitheim, Canton Schaffhausen, and were an attempt to state the basic beliefs that distinguished the persecuted movement from both the Protestants and Catholics. The document was officially titled the "Brotherly Union of a Number of Children of God concerning Seven Articles."

The articles called the Brethren to affirm believer's BAPTISM for adults only; the use of the ban on members of the fellowship who go astray; the sharing of the LORD'S SUPPER only with those in the fellowship; separation from "all popish and antipopish works and church services, meetings and church attendance, drinking houses, civic affairs, the commitments [made in] unbelief"; pastors to be men of good report; avoidance of the sword or the office of magistrate; and the avoidance of oaths, even in legal matters.

The primary author was Michael Sattler (c. 1495–1527). Before he was martyred a few months later, he managed to disseminate the document, which was translated into Latin and French within a few weeks. It remains a basic statement of Anabaptist belief and is recognized as authoritative by most MENNONITES.

See also CREEDS/CONFESSIONS OF FAITH.

Further reading: Michael Sattler, *The Legacy of Michael Sattler,* trans. and ed. by John H. Yoder. Classics of the Radical Reformation (Scottdale, Pa.: Herald Press, 1973); "The Schleitheim Confession of Faith," trans. by J. C. Wenger. *Mennonite Quarterly Review* 19 (1945): 243–53; Arnold Snyder, "The Schleitheim Articles in Light of the Revolution of the Common Man: Continuation or Departure?" *Sixteenth Century Journal* 16 (1985): 419–30; Sean Winter, "Michael Sattler and the Schleitheim Articles: A Study in the Background to the First Anabaptist Confession of Faith," *Baptist Quarterly* 34 (1991): 52–66.

Schmalkald League

The Schmalkald League was an alliance of German Protestant rulers ratified on February 27, 1531, at Schmalkald in Hesse-Nassau. In their pact, the rulers of Hesse, Saxony, Brunswick-Grubenhagen, Brunswick-Lünenburg, Anhalt, and Mansfeld stipulated that for the next six years any military attack upon one would be considered as against all. Their major fear was a Catholic force moving against them on religious grounds. They were soon joined by additional German rulers, and still more as Protestantism spread farther. DENMARK joined in 1538.

At a second meeting in 1535, the group extended the pact for an additional 10 years. In response, in 1538, several Catholic countries formed a Catholic League led by the Holy Roman Emperor. Only skillful negotiations prevented the outbreak of war at that time. In 1546, the emperor adopted a set of new measures aimed at suppressing the Protestant alliance, and the War of

Schmalkald ensued. The victorious Catholic forces captured and imprisoned both Elector John Frederick of Saxony and Landgrave Philip of Hesse, reinstated a number of Catholic prelates, and extracted a promise from the defeated rulers to attend and recognize the authority of the Council of Trent. The Schmalkald League was dissolved. However, war again broke out several years later, this time with Protestant forces gaining the upper hand and reversing the earlier Catholic provisions.

Further reading: Roland H. Bainton, *The Reformation of the Sixteenth Century* (Boston: Beacon Press, 1952); A. G. Dickens, *Reformation and Society in Sixteenth Century Europe* (London: Thames & Hudson, 1966); Harold J. Grimm, *The Reformation Era (1550–1650)* (New York: Macmillan, 1973).

Schwartz, Christian Friedrich

(1726–1798) *pioneer Lutheran missionary in India*
Christian Friedrich Schwartz was born in Sinnenber, Prussia, in October 1726. He grew up in a parish heavily influenced by PIETISM and was inspired by accounts of the DANISH-HALLE MISSION in INDIA. Benjamin Shultze (1689–1760) recruited the youthful Schwartz to assist in preparing a Tamil translation of the Bible. Schwartz was ordained to the ministry (1749), and arrived at Tranquebar in 1750.

He quickly mastered Portuguese, Persian, and several Indian languages, and began establishing schools and training Indian ministers. In 1763, he became military chaplain to one of the local rulers, which opened a whole region to Western-style schools.

In 1766, when his area came under British control, Schwartz placed his work under the sponsorship of the SOCIETY FOR PROMOTING CHRISTIAN KNOWLEDGE, an agency of the CHURCH OF ENGLAND, though he retained his LUTHERANISM. In subsequent decades, he was frequently engaged in peace negotiations between warring factions and in postwar relief. Not being British and familiar

with all the languages involved made him trustworthy to all sides. In 1787, the rajah of Tanjore named Schwartz guardian-teacher of his 10-year-old son and heir.

Schwartz started a major work in Tirunelveli when in the late 1770s he baptized a well-to-do Indian widow named CLORINDA. In 1785, she endowed a church building in Palamcottah, and Schwartz sent his assistant Sathiyanandan (c. 1752–1815) to pastor the church. Ordained in 1790, the latter began work among the Shanar community and oversaw one of the first MASS MOVEMENTS in Indian Christianity. While many of the Halle Mission converts became Anglicans, the Shanar church and its 20,000 members ultimately became the core of the Tamil Evangelical Lutheran Church, which in 1975 joined in forming the United Evangelical Lutheran Churches in India.

Schwartz died on February 13, 1798.

Further reading: Robert Eric Frykenberg, "The Legacy of Christian Fredrich Schwartz," *International Bulletin of Missionary Research* 23 (July 1999): 130–35; Daniel Jeyaraj, ed., *Christian Frederick Schwartz: His Contribution to South India* (Chennai: Lutheran Historical Archives, 1999); William H. Price, *The Life and Labors of the Rev. Christian Frederick Schwartz, the Great Lutheran Missionary to India* (Columbus, Ohio: Lutheran Book Concern, 1895); L. B. Wolf, ed., *Missionary Heroes of the Lutheran Church* (Columbia, S.C.: Lutheran Board of Publication, 1911).

Scofield, C. I.

(1843–1921) *Fundamentalist biblical scholar and early dispensationalist*
Cyrus Ingerson Scofield was born on August 19, 1843, in Lenawee County, Michigan. Having moved to Tennessee during his youth, in 1861 he fought for a year in the Confederate Army. After the war, he settled in St. Louis, learned law, and began a career in politics that ended in scandal, divorce, and drunkenness.

In 1879, Scofield had a conversion experience and subsequently was licensed to preach as a Congregationalist. In 1882, he accepted a call to pastor a church in Dallas, Texas, where he was ordained as a minister. After a successful decade in Texas, he cooperated with Dwight L. MOODY in an evangelistic crusade in the city. Moody invited him to teach at Bible conferences, including the one Moody personally sponsored at Northfield, Massachusetts.

It appears that Scofield initially absorbed DISPENSATIONALISM from Moody. Dispensationalism sees biblical history as divided into several periods, and interprets the Bible's prophetic passages as literal guides to future events. Scofield held to PREMILLENNIALISM, a belief in the imminent return of Christ.

In 1890, Scofield launched his own mission-sending agency, the Central American Mission, and began to offer a correspondence course teaching a dispensational approach to the Bible. In 1895, he moved to Northfield to pastor the Trinity Congregational Church and take charge of Moody's Northfield Bible Training School. In 1902, he began to write a study Bible with premillennial dispensationalist notes, a project funded by businessman John T. Pirie. The *Scofield Reference Bible* was published by Oxford University Press in 1908, with a second edition in 1917. Meanwhile, Scofield had returned to Dallas, and in 1908 led his old church out of the liberal Congregational Church. In 1910, he formally joined the Presbyterian Church, USA. He remained active in education via Bible schools, correspondence courses, and conferences until his death on July 24, 1921.

Scofield had become enormously influential within the Fundamentalist movement, and his writings retain their importance in the Evangelical movement that grew out of it in the 1940s. His Bible became the most popular study tool at Bible conferences and has continued to be used to the present, often in preference to a revised and updated edition issued in 1967 by several Evangelical scholars as the *New Scofield Reference Bible.*

See also FUNDAMENTALISM.

Further reading: William A. BeVier, *A Biographical Sketch of C. I. Scofield* (Dallas, Tex.: Southern Methodist University, M.A. thesis, 1960); Joseph M. Canfield, *The Incredible Scofield and His Book* (Ashville, N.C.: the author, 1984); Mal Couch, ed., *Dictionary of Premillennial Theology* (Grand Rapids, Mich.: Kregal, 1996); Arno C. Geabelein, *The History of the Scofield Reference Bible* (New York: Our Hope, 1943); Charles G. Trumbull, *The Life Story of C. I. Scofield* (New York: Oxford University Press, 1920).

Scotland   *See* UNITED KINGDOM.

Scranton, Mary Fletcher (1832–1909)
Methodist missionary in Korea

Mary Fletcher Scranton was born in December 1832. Little is known of her early life. In 1885, she, her son, Dr. William B. Scranton, and her daughter-in-law accepted an assignment to KOREA as missionaries. Mary became the first female Protestant missionary in Korea while William pioneered MEDICAL MISSIONS.

Upon her arrival in Seoul, she opened the first school for girls in Korea. The school would grow into one of the country's most prestigious institutions, Ewha Women's University, currently the largest all-female university in the world. Scranton spent the rest of her life expanding her school and working among the Methodist women in the country. Mary Scranton died in 1909.

Further reading: Marion Lane Canrow, *Our Ewha: A Historical Sketch of E.W.U., 1886–1956* (Seoul, Korea: Ewha Women's University Press, 1956); Anne B. Chaffin, *Fifty Years of Light: Women's Foreign Missionary Society of the Methodist Episcopal Church* (Seoul, Korea: YMCA Press, 1938).

Scudder, Ida Sophia (1870–1960) *pioneer medical missionary in India*

Ida S. Scudder carried on the family tradition started by her grandfather, John Scudder, a minister of the Reformed Church in America and the first American medical missionary. Scudder was born on December 9, 1870 and raised on the mission field in INDIA. Though she attended Northfield Seminary, the school founded by evangelist Dwight L. MOODY, she firmly set against becoming a missionary, until receiving a call one night during a 1894 visit to India. The call to the mission field took the form of three women who approached her to ask for help, all three of whom subsequently died giving birth for lack of a woman doctor who could assist them.

Scudder returned to study in the first class of Cornell University Medical School to admit women. She began her work out of her father's bungalow in Vellore, but had already initiated a fund-raising campaign to build a hospital. She moved into the new hospital in 1902, and by 1906 she was seeing as many as 40,000 patients a year; she gained an impressive reputation as a surgeon. She began to train nurses, her effort growing into the nursing school at the University of Madras. In 1909, she founded the first of her roadside dispensaries to treat patients in nearby rural communities. They grew into the Vellore Rural Unit for Health and Social Affairs.

In 1918, drawing together Protestant women of different denominations, she founded a small school to train women as physicians, and in 1923 she founded a large hospital in Vellore. Work proceeded smoothly for two decades, but the relatively isolated facility gradually fell behind the advancing medical field. In 1941, she returned to the United States to raise money and attract the personnel needed to upgrade the hospital. She succeeded, and both the college and the hospital expanded to provide quality medical services to southern India. Since World War II, it has operated with broad interdenominational support.

Scudder died in 1960 at age 90.

See also MEDICAL MISSIONS.

Further reading: Carol E. Jameson, *Be Thou My Vision* (Vellore, India: Christian Medical College Board, 1983); Mary Pauline Jeffrey, *Dr. Ida: India. The Life Story of Ida S. Scudder* (New York: Fleming H. Revell, 1918); Dorothy Clarke Wilson, *The Story of*

Dr. Ida Scudder of Vellore (New York: McGraw-Hill 1959); ———, "Ida S. Scudder, 1870–1960: Life and Health for Women of India," in Gerald H. Anderson, et al., eds., *Mission Legacies: Biographical Studies of the Modern Missionary Movement* (Maryknoll, N.Y.: Orbis Books, 1998): 307–15.

Selwyn, George Augustus (1809–1878)
Protestant pioneer in New Zealand and Melanesia

Selwyn was born at Hampstead, England, on April 5, 1809. He received his M.A. from St. John's College at CAMBRIDGE UNIVERSITY in 1834, and was ordained a priest in the CHURCH OF ENGLAND in 1834. In 1841, he accepted appointment as the first bishop of NEW ZEALAND. Selwyn learned Maori on the sea voyage, and began to develop a facility with languages that later enabled him to learn other island languages.

From his base at the Bay of Islands station of the CHURCH MISSIONARY SOCIETY (CMS), Selwyn traveled widely to organize the churches in his diocese, developing a structure similar to that of the church in England. His effort brought him into competition with the CMS. Its authority undermined, the CMS expelled Selwyn, and he moved to Auckland.

Selwyn refused to accept an extra diocesan church structure for the native Maori people, under CMS control. When he opened the College of St John the Evangelist (commonly known as St. John's College), native students shared classes and other activities with European students, provoking hostility from both settlers and clergy, some of whom boycotted the college.

In 1857, after extensive consultations, Selwyn called a constitutional conference that culminated in a Constitution of the Church of the Province of New Zealand. A unique act for its time, Selwyn offered both laity and clergy equal rights to manage the affairs of the church in New Zealand. He subsequently established several new dioceses and appointed new BISHOPS. He assumed the office of primate/metropolitan and held the first general synod in Wellington in 1859.

Selwyn accepted responsibility for the vast area of Melanesia, apparently assigned to him due to a clerical error, when the northern boundary of the New Zealand diocese was erroneously recorded as the 34th parallel north of the equator, instead of 34 degrees south. Selwyn began to travel through the region, gathering young people to be educated in New Zealand. In 1861, he consecrated John Coleridge Patteson (1827–71) as the first bishop of Melanesia.

Building up enemies in his quarter of a century as head of the New Zealand church, Selwyn was "asked" to give up his post at the 1867 Lambeth Conference, and he returned to England permanently the next year. Once in England, he introduced his ideas on lay leadership to his new Litchfield diocese, where he died on April 11, 1878. Four years after his death, Selwyn College at Cambridge University was founded in his memory and the Theological College in Dunedin, New Zealand, was named after him.

See also SOUTH PACIFIC.

Further reading: F. W. Boreham, *George Augustus Selwyn, D. D. Pioneer Bishop of New Zealand* (London: S. W. Partridge, 1911); Allan K. Davidson, *Christianity in Aotearoa: A History of Church and Society in New Zealand* (Wellington, N.Z.: Education for Ministry, 1997); W. E. Limbrick, *Bishop Selwyn in New Zealand 1841–68* (Palmerston North, New Zealand: Dunmore Press, 1983); H. W. Taylor, *Memoir of the Life and Episcopate of George Augustus Selwyn, D. D. Bishop of New Zealand, 1841–1869; Bishop of Lichfield, 1867–1878*, 2 vols. (London: William Wells Gardner, 1879).

Senegal

French rule allowed the introduction of Protestantism by the PARIS MISSION, representing the Reformed Church of France, but the only Protestant groups to survive in the difficult climate have been the ASSEMBLIES OF GOD (1956), the Lutherans (originating in a Finnish Lutheran missionary effort launched in 1974), and the New Apostolic Church (c. 1980). The latter group had by far the greatest success, with more than 10,000 converts by the end of the century. Many of the smaller Evangelical groups associate together in the Evangelical Fellowship of Senegal affiliated with the Association of Evangelicals of Africa and the WORLD EVANGELICAL ALLIANCE.

See also AFRICA, SUB-SAHARAN.

Further reading: David Barrett, *The Encyclopedia of World Christianity,* 2nd ed. (New York: Oxford University Press, 2001); J. Delcourt, *Historie Religieuse du Sénégal* (Dakar: Clairafrique, 1976); Patrick Johnstone and Jason Mandryk, *Operation World, 21st Century Edition* (Carlisle, Cumbria, U.K.: Paternoster, 2001).

Separate Baptists

The term *Separate Baptists* originated in New England in the middle of the 17th century when the Baptist movement split over the issue of REVIVALISM. As a result of the GREAT AWAKENING, the promotion of revivals became a popular activity among all the churches. Most BAPTISTS, however, opposed it, and those that accepted the new practice separated themselves from the main community of believers. The large body of antirevivalists became known as Regular Baptists. While most Baptists moved beyond this controversy, there remain in the United States several groups that retain the name Separate Baptists and Regular Baptists.

Further reading: H. Leon McBeth, *The Baptist Heritage: Four Centuries of Baptist Witness* (Nashville, Tenn.: Broadman Press, 1887).

separation of church and state

The Bill of Rights became part of the United States Constitution on December 15, 1791, including its famous First Amendment statement, "Congress shall make no law respecting an establishment of religion, or prohibiting the free exercise thereof." A decade later, on January 1, 1802, in a letter to the Danbury Baptist Association, President Thomas Jefferson penned his commentary to that phrase in which he introduced a metaphor explaining the intent of the First Amendment. Thus Jefferson, the author of the amendment, injected the idea of separation of church and state into the political discourse of the nation, the Christian West, and more recently the world community. Following the lead of Congress, all the states added phrases similar to the First Amendment to their constitutions.

In the United States, "separation of church and state" has been embodied not primarily in legislation, but in opinions of the Supreme Court. Among the Court's more famous rulings in this area was the 1947 case known as *Everson v. Board of Education,* in which the Court declared, "The First Amendment has erected a wall between church and state. That wall must be kept high and impregnable. We could not approve the slightest breach."

Over the years, various practices that some believed had breached the wall of separation were found acceptable by the Court (chaplains in the military and legislative bodies) and some not (government-funded census of religious groups). Over the years, Court cases have dealt with issues of religious proselytizing in various public settings (such as street corners, airports, and public schools), the funding of religiously sponsored universities with government research grants, government funding of parochial schools, and most recently, government funding of religious organizations to carry out charitable activities. In the 1950s, Congress added the phrase "under God" to the pledge of allegiance to the flag.

In the early 1960s, the Supreme Court handed down several rulings concerning prayers in public elementary and secondary schools. In most states, at the beginning of the day, classes held exercises that usually included a reading from the Bible, a brief prayer, and the pledge of allegiance to the flag. These rulings, most important in the cases of *Engle v. Vitale* and *Abington Township School District v. Schempp,* suggested that such prayers (and by implication, Bible readings) were not consistent with the First Amendment. State-sponsored religious exercises amounted to an establishment of religion, it decided, particularly in public schools, where the audience was required to attend.

These rulings angered many conservative Protestant Christians who had grown up with the practice. They opined that the Supreme Court had kicked God out of the public school. They were further angered by subsequent decisions that challenged public displays of religious symbols (crosses in public parks, Christian displays on government property, religious symbols in government emblems). Some conservative Christians began to question the whole idea of the separation of church and state, which had been a bedrock belief of most American Protestants.

American Christian arguments against the separation of church and state are generally based on the nonappearance of the phrase in legislative acts. Opponents charge the Supreme Court with making laws, thus breaching the separation of powers between the legislative and judicial branches of the government, an integral feature of American constitutional law. They also affirm that the United States was founded as a Christian country, and that the government was founded on Christian principles. Furthermore, in the post–World War II era, for the first time the majority of United States citizens were church members.

This opinion has been challenged by the emergent humanist and atheist communities, who argue that America is a secular nation and that the government should have nothing to do with religion, a form of separation popular in countries where the government has been somewhat hostile toward religion. In the case of FRANCE and CHINA, for example, laws were passed to keep religion from interfering with government. In the United States and the countries affected by the American legal heritage, on the other hand, the issue has historically been the reverse, a desire to keep government from interfering with religion. That different perspective has allowed a friendliness between the government and religious communities in the United States, which has led to repeated attempts to define the boundaries.

A new factor in recent decades is the emergence of Hindu, Buddhist, and Muslim communities among new immigrants, the first significant non-Christian religious communities other than Judaism.

Further reading: Tricia Andryszewski, *School Prayer: A History of the Debate* (Springfield, N.J.: Enslow, 1997); David Barton, *America: To Pray or Not to Pray* (Aledo, Tex.: Specialty Research Associates, 1994); Philip Hamburger, *The Separation of Church and State* (Cambridge, Mass.: Harvard University Press, 2002); John T. Noonan, *The Believer and the Powers That Are: Cases, History, and Other Data Bearing on the Relation of Religion and Government* (New York: Macmillan, 1987); Mary Segars and Ted Jelen, *A Wall of Separation* (Lanham, Md.: Rowman & Littlefield, 1998).

serpent handling

One biblical text rarely acted upon is Mark 16:18, where as part of the Great Commission to the church, Jesus notes that one of the signs of his apostles will be, "They will take up serpents and if they drink any deadly thing, it shall not hurt them." In the early Pentecostal movement, however, a few began to do just that. The rebirth of the practice has been traced to George Hensley (d. 1955), an independent Pentecostal preacher in rural eastern Tennessee. During an outdoor sermon, some people released rattlesnakes. Hensley was reported to have picked up the snakes while continuing to preach.

Soon afterward, Ambrose J. Tomlinson (1865–1943), head of the CHURCH OF GOD (CLEVELAND, TENNESSEE) invited Hensley to the annual meeting of the church, thus introducing the practice of handling snakes (and subsequently drinking poisons) into the movement. By 1914, the practice had spread throughout the CHURCH OF GOD, though only a very few people actually handled snakes.

During the 1920s, partly in response to public controversy, the Church of God withdrew its support for snake handling, and the practice was limited to some independent churches located in the Appalachian Mountains. It was carried into the Midwest and Gulf Coast states by Appalachian Pentecostals who moved away from their mountain homes in the last decades of the 20th century.

In the 1940s, snake handling saw some resurgence through the ministry of Raymond Harris and Tom Harden, who started the Dolly Pond Church of God with Signs Following in rural eastern Tennessee outside of Chattanooga. The death of a Dolly Pond church member in 1945 led to the banning of the practice in Tennessee in 1947 and North Carolina in 1948. The practice was again in the news in 1971 after three people died from snake bites and strychnine poisoning. Though the practice can still be found, and periodically new books and feature articles appear about it, its acceptance remains limited to a very small community.

See also PENTECOSTALISM.

Further reading: Fred Brown and Jeanne McDonald, *The Serpent Handlers: Three Families and their Faith* (Winston-Salem, N.C.: John F. Blair, 2000); Thomas Burton, *Serpent Handling Believers* (Knoxville: University of Tennessee Press, 1993); Dennis Covington, *Salvation on Sand Mountain: Snake Handling and Religion in Southern Appalachia* (New York: Penguin Books, 1995); David L. Kimbrough, *Taking up the Serpents: Snake Handling Believers of Eastern Kentucky* (Chapel Hill: University of North Carolina Press, 1995); Weston LaBarre, *They Take up Serpents* (New York: Schocken Books, 1969).

Servetus, Michael (1511–1553) *Spanish physician and theologian who was executed for his beliefs*

John CALVIN's consent to the persecution and execution of Michael Servetus for advocating heretical opinions has emerged as the major blot on his otherwise distinguished career. Servetus, a brilliant

Spanish intellectual and physician, was born at Villanueva de Sijena, Spain, and later studied law at Toulouse in FRANCE. He appears to have developed an interest in theology as a student; as early as 1530 he expressed his disbelief in the Trinity to Protestant reformer Johann OECOLAMPADIUS and publicized it in his book *Concerning the Errors of the Trinity* (1531). Facing disapproval, he moved to Lyon and then to Paris.

Servetus had begun his theological reflections by noting that Muslims and Jews considered the Trinity as an attack on the unity of God. He concluded that God was one, that Christ was not divine, and that the Holy Spirit was the name of God's power. He also concluded that the church should be reorganized as a community of those who believe, that infant BAPTISM should be replaced with believer's baptism, and that in the Eucharist believers could partake of divinity and participate in God. Such beliefs were heretical to Catholics and most Protestants, including Calvin.

While in Paris, Servetus studied medicine, and appears to have discovered the circulation of the blood long before its public discovery by William Harvey in the next century. He left Paris in 1538, following conflicts over his lecturing on astrology.

Servetus moved back to Lyon and then in 1544 was offered a position as the personal physician to the archbishop of Vienna. During these years, he operated under pseudonyms, though he kept up a confidential correspondence with Calvin. As early as 1546, he sent Calvin the manuscript of his book *Restitution of Christianity*, only published in 1553. It was the discovery of his authorship of this later book that led to his arrest in Vienna. However, he escaped and moved toward Italy. On his way, he stopped in Geneva, where he was recognized and arrested.

Servetus was subjected to a lengthy trial in which all his heretical opinions were aired. The court noted that his opinions not only attacked Christian orthodoxy, but also provided support for Muslims and Jews. He was condemned and burned at the stake in Geneva on October 27, 1553. Though not directly involved in the proceeding, Calvin is held responsible for Servetus's death, considering his unchallenged power at that time in Geneva.

Servetus did not raise up a community of believers nor participate in one, but he has in more recent years been seen as a precursor to the Unitarian beliefs of SOCIANISM.

Further reading: Roland H. Bainton, *Hunted Heretics* (Boston, Beacon Press, 1953); Michael Servetus, *Two Treatises on the Trinity*, ed. by Earl Morse Wilbur (Cambridge, Mass.: Harvard University Press, 1932); Earl Morse Wilbur, *A History of Unitarianism: Socinianism and Its Antecedents* (Cambridge, Mass.: Harvard University Press, 1945); George H. Williams, *The Radical Reformation* (Kirksville, Mo.: Sixteenth Century Journal, 1992).

Seventh-day Adventist Church

The Seventh-day Adventist Church is a global movement founded on the belief in the imminent return of Christ to earth. It is the primary heir to the ministry of William MILLER, a Baptist lay minister who emerged in the 1830s. After several years of Bible study, Miller came to believe that Christ would return around 1843, basing his claim on two passages in the book of Daniel. He published his views and traveled widely in the American Northeast lecturing on his ideas.

That Christ did not return as expected either in 1843, or in 1844, became known as the GREAT DISAPPOINTMENT for Miller's followers. While reactions varied, some suggested that the 1844 date had been correct. Jesus had indeed commenced his return at that time, but was delayed by a particular task, the cleansing of the heavenly sanctuary. He would come to earth soon, but the date was unknown.

James (1821–81) and Ellen G. WHITE were of that opinion. They drew more and more Adventists around them and in 1863 officially organized the Seventh-day Adventist Church, with 3,500 members in 125 congregations. As the name implies, the group had also adopted SABBATARIAN-

Among the many educational institutions founded by the Adventists is the Seventh-day Adventist Theological Seminary of Collonges-sous-Salève, France. *(Institute for the Study of American Religion, Santa Barbara, California)*

ism, the belief that Christians should observe Saturday as the day of rest. Over the years, Adventists advocated a variety of causes, including health reform, promoted through the Western Health Reform Institute (Battle Creek Sanitarium), founded in 1866. Dr. John Harvey Kellogg (1852–1943) joined the staff as the medical superintendent in 1876. His most famous innovation was flaked cereal, later the basis of two large cereal companies bearing the name of Kellogg's brother and of an employee named Post.

The Adventists in 1872 founded the first of what became an international network of seminaries and schools (from elementary through university). Today, the church sponsors more than 6,300 schools, 100 of them colleges, universities and graduate seminaries.

The church has been very active in global missionary work, anxious to spread the news of Christ's return. Within a decade of its founding, it commissioned J. N. Andrews for work in SWITZERLAND. Other early mission fields were AUSTRALIA

(1885), RUSSIA (1886), GHANA (1994), SOUTH AFRICA (1894), and JAPAN (1896). In the 20th century, the Adventists reached to every corner of the world. It is one of the very few religious bodies that has worshipping communities in more than 200 countries.

Since 1989, headquarters have been in Silver Spring, Maryland. In 2002, the church reported a world membership of 12 million in more than 51,000 congregations. Work is carried out in more than 800 languages.

The Seventh-day Adventist Church derived most of its theology from Baptist beliefs. It is a traditional Trinitarian faith based on the authority of the Bible, the only creed. Their statement of faith affirms the fall of humanity into sin and salvation by Christ. Peculiar to Adventists is the belief that prophecy is a gift of the Holy Spirit, and was a mark of the ministry of Ellen G. White. She is considered the Lord's messenger, and her writings are seen as a continuing and authoritative source of truth. The church affirms that humanity is now involved in the "great controversy between Christ and Satan." Satan rebelled against God, and introduced rebellion among humankind. Christ sends the Holy Spirit and angels to guide, protect, and sustain humans in their salvation.

See also ADVENTISM.

Further reading: Roy Adams, *The Sanctuary: Understanding the Heart of Adventist Theology* (Hagerstown, Md.: Review & Herald, 1994); P. Gerard Damsteegt, *Foundations of the Seventh-day Adventist Message and Mission* (Grand Rapids, Mich.: William B. Eerdmans, 1977); Erwin Gane and Leo Van Dolson, *This We Believe: An Overview of the Teachings of Seventh-day Adventists* (Nampa, Idaho: Pacific Press, 1993); George R. Knight, *Anticipating the Advent: A Brief History of Seventh-day Adventists* (Nampa, Idaho: Pacific Press, 1993); Gary Land, ed., *Adventism in America* (Grand Rapids, Mich.: William B. Eerdmans, 1986).

Seymour, William J. (1870–1922) *leader of Azusa Street revival and early Pentecostalist*

William Joseph Seymour was born on May 2, 1870, in Centerville, Louisiana. From 1890, he was associated first with METHODISM and then with a HOLINESS group, the Evening Lights Saints. He came to accept the Holiness emphasis on sanctification, an experience of God that allowed believers to be free of outward sin and perfected in love.

Living in Cincinnati with the Saints, he lost an eye to smallpox and decided to become a minister. He was ordained by the CHURCH OF GOD (ANDERSON, INDIANA). His travels led him in 1903 to Houston, Texas, where he met Charles Fox PARHAM and learned from him of the BAPTISM OF THE HOLY SPIRIT and speaking in tongues. He saw the baptism as an empowerment for those already sanctified.

In 1906, Seymour became the pastor of a small church in Los Angeles. When he tried to introduce his new ideas, he was locked out. He began to hold services in the home of Richard D. and Ruth Asberry on Bonnie Brae Avenue.

On April 9, the baptism experience occurred to two worshippers, Jennie Evans Moore (1883–1936, whom Seymour later married) and Edward Lee. Seymour received the experience on April 12. Crowds began to gather as the news spread, so the group moved to a former African Methodist Episcopal Church building, then being used as livery stable. Seating was arranged and a pulpit constructed from two boxes. Seymour found personal accommodations on the second floor.

A newspaper article criticizing the AZUSA STREET REVIVAL happened to appear on April 18, the day of the catastrophic San Francisco earthquake. Thousands of copies of a tract tying the earthquake to the revival were distributed; readers flocked to Azusa Street to the newly named Apostolic Faith Missions. Over the next three years, Seymour led three services a day. Most of the leaders of what would become the national and international Pentecostal movement made the pilgrimage to Los Angeles and received the baptism. Those in attendance included African Americans, Hispanics, and whites.

Following Seymour's marriage to Moore in 1908, dissident members Clara Lum (d. 1946) and Florence Crawford (1872–1936) took his mailing list and founded a rival church in Portland, Oregon. Seymour's center in Los Angeles never recovered. The revival came to an end, and Seymour was left as the pastor of a single congregation. His isolation deepened when the movement divided into black and white factions.

In 1911, William H. Durham (1873–1912), a white Baptist minister from Chicago, further split the Los Angeles Pentecostals by proclaiming his "Finished Work" views; he stated that anyone could received the baptism of the Holy Spirit, even if they had never been sanctified. The FINISHED WORK CONTROVERSY took more than 600 believers from the mission. In 1913, the mission was hit by a new controversy over the "Jesus Only" message. JESUS ONLY PENTECOSTALS, including many African Americans, rejected the Trinity and began to baptize people in the name of Jesus only. By 1915,

Seymour was left with only a minuscule following. However, that year he published a church manual, *The Doctrines and Discipline of the Azusa Street Apostolic Faith Mission of Los Angeles,* and he assumed the title of BISHOP. He began to travel the country, occasionally with Charles Harrison Mason (1866–1961), founder of the CHURCH OF GOD IN CHRIST, and founded a number of congregations, especially in Virginia.

Seymour died on September 18, 1922. His widow assumed control of the Los Angeles congregation and pastored it for the next few years; she died in 1936. The church building has not survived, and there is no visible remnant of Seymour's work in Los Angeles. The congregations Seymour founded in Virginia now make up the United Fellowship of the Original Azusa Street Mission.

White Pentecostal historians forgot about the African-American roots of the movement, and Seymour's role was obscured until the late 20th century, when white and black Pentecostals made efforts to heal their divisions. Scholars now consider Seymour important to the whole Pentecostal global endeavor. His emphasis on the imminent end of this order and the need for foreign missions, as well as his own self-effacing leadership that allowed the broadest participation in the Azusa Street revival are now seen as essential elements in shaping the course of PENTECOSTALISM.

Further reading: James T. Connelly, "William J. Seymour," in *Twentieth-Century Shapers of American Popular Religion,* ed. by Charles H. Lippy. (New York: Greenwood Press, 1989); 381–87; Iain McRobert, *The Black Roots and White Racism of Early Pentecostalism in the USA* (New York: St. Martin's, 1988); Douglas J. Nelson, *For Such a Time as This: The Story of Bishop William J. Seymour and the Azusa Street Revival: A Search for Pentecostal/Charismatic Roots* (Birmingham, U.K.: University of Birmingham, Ph.D. diss., 1981); Cheryl Sanders, *Saints in Exile: The Holiness-Pentecostal Experience in African American Religion and Culture* (New York: Oxford University Press, 1996).

Shee, Rebecca (1912–1991) *first woman minister among the Karen people*

Rebecca Shee was the first woman ordained to the ministry from among the Kayin (or Karen) people, the largest minority group in Myanmar (then Burma). Missionary work among the Kayin had been launched in 1827 by George Boardman. He converted Ko Tha Byu, who oversaw a mass movement to Christianity. Jonathan Wade (1798–1872) translated the Bible, schools were opened, and the Kayins became a largely self-supporting mission.

Shee grew up a Christian, attended the Paku Christian High School, and then the seminary at Insein (now Myanmar Institute of Theology). She completed her work in theology in 1940 and studied nursing. She worked as a nurse at the mission hospital at Gawgaligyi, and as housemother of an orphanage.

In 1958, Shee was sent by the Baptist Convention of Maynmar as an evangelist among the Kayin of neighboring Thailand. She and two colleagues opened a Bible school at Baw Keow. It would develop into the Center for Uplift of Hill Tribes, now located at Chiang Mai, Thailand.

Shee worked as an unordained missionary for many years, the only female evangelist commissioned by the Baptist Convention. In 1978, her work was recognized with ordination. Shee's achievements and dedication were a major inspiration for the next generation of Kayin women and helped improve their status.

Further reading: Clifford Kyaw Dwe, "Shee, Rebecca," in Scott W. Sunquist, ed., *A Dictionary of Asian Christianity* (Grand Rapids, Mich.: William B. Eerdmans, 2001): 758–59; Rebecca Shee, *The Life of Rebecca Shee* (1986).

Shi Mei Yi (1873–1954) *Chinese medical and educational missionary*

Shi Mei Yi (also known as Mary Stone) was born in 1873 to a Methodist minister father, who encouraged her to become a medical missionary. In 1896, she and another Chinese student, Kang

Cheng, became the first Chinese women to complete medical training in the United States. The pair returned to CHINA with the backing of the Woman's Foreign Missionary Society of the Methodist Episcopal Church. They opened a one-room hospital in Jiujing, where they treated thousands of outpatients.

Around 1900, they opened the Danforth Memorial Hospital with money from I. N. Danforth of Chicago. She became superintendent and took the lead in training nurses for a growing work that was treating almost 5,000 people a month. She also supervised a home for the disabled.

As a HOLINESS Methodist, Shi was growing uncomfortable with the liberal theological trends among the Methodists, and in 1920 she ended her relationship with the Woman's Board. She left Danforth and set up the independent Shanghai Bethel Mission. Over the next decade, she founded a hospital, a primary and secondary school, an orphanage, and an evangelistic training center, and she ran evangelistic campaigns around the country. Her training for nurses now included religious as well as medical education.

The work of the Bethel Mission suffered with the Japanese invasion in 1937. She returned to Shanghai briefly after World War II, but then moved to Pasadena, California, where she died in 1954. In 1958, the Bethel churches were integrated into the Church of Christ of China, though a Bethel Hospital survives in Hong Kong and the Bethel Mission of China continues in Pasadena.

Further reading: Charles Luther Boynton and Charles Dozier Boynton, eds., *1936 Handbook of the Christian Movement in China under Protestant Auspices* (Shanghai: Kwang Hsueh Publishing House, 1936); Connie Shemo, *The Medical Ministries of Kang Cheng and Shi Meiyu, 1872–1937* (Binghamton, NY: State University of New York, Ph.D. diss., 2001).

shunning

Shunning is a practice among MENNONITES of avoiding those who have been placed under the ban (disfellowshipped). It is a second level of separation and part of a strategy for winning an erring member back into full fellowship. It can be traced to the 1530s, when ANABAPTISTS needed a way to separate themselves from the radical communalists at Munster whose doctrinal errors, immorality, and violence had made Anabaptists a common object of derision.

In 1632, a paragraph on shunning was included in the Dordrecht Confession, one of the more important Mennonite statements of beliefs. According to Dordrecht, shunning includes refraining from eating, drinking, and holding similar intercourse with the shunned individual.

The Dordrecht Confession was not accepted by the Swiss Mennonites, but it became strongly identified with the AMISH. In America, only the more conservative Mennonite groups accepted it. The largest group, the Mennonite Church, recognizes Dordrecht but does not demand that either members or ministers individually subscribe to it; shunning is its most controversial provision.

Through the 20th century, shunning was quietly abandoned by most Mennonites, though it survives in a few small groups.

Further reading: Robert Bear, *Delivered unto Satan,* (Carlisle, Pa.: privately published, 1974); Donald Kraybill, *Old Order Amish: Their Enduring Way of Life* (Baltimore: Johns Hopkins University Press, 1993).

Sierra Leone

Both the country of Sierra Leone and its Protestant community emerged out of the 18th-century antislavery crusade in England. In 1784 William WILBERFORCE (1759–1833), a member of the British Parliament who belonged to an evangelical group within the CHURCH OF ENGLAND, was recruited to the antislavery cause. He joined with Thomas Clarkson (1760–1846), Granville Sharp (1735–1813), and others to found the Society for the Abolition of the Slave Trade in 1787. Among its first acts was the purchase of land in Sierra Leone for the settlement of repatriated slaves.

In 1792, the society brought the first pioneers to the colony, a group of some 1,100 Africans who had sided with the British during the American Revolution and had been resettled in Nova Scotia. Among the settlers were a number of Methodists and BAPTISTS. The 200 Methodists were led by Moses Wilkinson, a blind and crippled preacher, who organized the first Methodist church in Sierra Leone and led it until the British Methodists sent a minister, George Warren, and three schoolteachers in 1811. The arrival of British missionaries began an era of schisms, and four separate Methodist bodies emerged. With time, however, the groups reunited into a single church aligned with the Methodist Church in Great Britain. With the arrival and growth of American Methodist bodies, the Methodists eventually became the largest segment of the Protestant community.

The Nova Scotian Baptists were led to Sierra Leone by David George (1743–1810). Shortly after arriving in Sierra Leone, he built the first Baptist church building in Africa and organized the first Baptist congregation. Representatives of the Baptist Missionary Society from England arrived in Freetown in 1784, but were expelled three years later. A second Baptist congregation, composed primarily of Ibo people, was founded in 1838. The Baptist community struggled through the next decades, though receiving some input from the SOUTHERN BAPTIST CONVENTION just before the American Civil War. They were primarily confined to Freetown until the 1960s; it was not until 1974 that the Sierra Leone Baptist Convention was constituted.

The most expansive work by a Protestant group in Sierra Leone did not begin until the 1960s with the arrival of the German-based New Apostolic Church. With some 75,000 members by the end of the 20th century, it is the largest non-Catholic group in the country and larger than any of the individual Methodist groups. The Anglicans established work in Sierra Leone in 1804 and now have some 25,000 members.

Beginning in 1991, Sierra Leone has been the scene of a brutal civil war that has left thousands dead and 2 million displaced. The United Nations stepped in in 2002, though stability was not immediately achieved. Neighboring LIBERIA has also experienced civil strife, and at times the conflicts have spilled over between the two countries.

The older ecumenically oriented churches are members of the Council of Churches in Sierra Leone, which is affiliated with the WORLD COUNCIL OF CHURCHES. Of the locally based groups, only the Methodist Church of Sierra Leone is a full member of the World Council. The Evangelical Fellowship of Sierra Leone is the local affiliate of the WORLD EVANGELICAL ALLIANCE. The Protestant community remains small, constituting only about 7 percent of the population, which is mostly divided between Muslims (45 percent) and adherents of traditional African religions (40 percent).

See also AFRICA, SUB-SAHARAN.

Further reading: Joe A. D. Alie, *A New History of Sierra Leone* (New York: St. Martin's, 1990); Gilbert W. Olson, *Church Growth in Sierra Leone: A Study of Church Growth in Africa's Oldest Protestant Mission Field* (Grand Rapids, Mich.: William B. Eerdmans, 1969); Lamin Sanneh, *Abolitionists Abroad: American Blacks and the Making of Modern West Africa* (Cambridge, Mass.: Harvard University Press, 1999); Eric Wright, *Behind the Lion Mountains: The Methodist Church in Sierra Leone Today* (London: Cargate Press, 1962).

Simons, Menno (c. 1496–1561) *early Anabaptist leader*

Menno Simons was born in Friesland in the NETHERLANDS in 1496. He was 28 when he decided to enter the priesthood. After only rudimentary training, he was ordained, and by 1530 he was serving as a priest in Friesland. By this time, he had become influenced by the Sacramentalists, a Dutch-based reform movement launched by Cornelis Hoen. Hoen wanted to remove certain abuses in the Catholic Church and return to a biblical Christianity. He denied the doctrine of the "real presence" of Christ in the Catholic Mass. Simons confirmed the Sacramentalists' views

Menno Simons (1496–1561) took over leadership of the scattered followers of the Radical Reformation now known as Mennonites. *(Mennonite Library Archives, Bethel College, North Newton, Kansas)*

through his Bible studies, which led him to accept the authority of the Bible over that of the church.

Beginning around 1530, Melchior HOFFMANN introduced the Anabaptist idea of adult BAPTISM. He found support among Sacramentalists, including Simons. However, Simons rejected Hoffmann's apocalyptic notion that the New Jerusalem would soon appear. He denounced the Mechiorites as they came to be called, and became even more vocal after Hoffmann's arrest in 1533, and after the disastrous commune at Munster under Jan Matthijs and Jan of Leiden. The capture of Munster by Catholic forces in 1535 threatened all ANABAPTISTS, even though the majority of them had rejected the Munsterite course of action.

Simons stepped forward to assume leadership of the now floundering movement. He left his home and parish responsibilities and began to live an underground existence, moving quietly among Anabaptist communities, encouraging the fruitful and reclaiming Melchiorites. He began to write voluminously. As his efforts became known, a committee of Anabaptist leaders asked him to accept a more formal role as an ELDER/BISHOP. At this point, Simons withdrew from the Catholic Church, confessed his faith, and was rebaptized, possibly around January 1536. For almost 20 years, he, his wife, Geertruydt, and their children lived a mobile existence one step ahead of both Catholic and Lutheran authorities. In 1542, a reward was offered for his capture.

He found brief protection in east Friesland on the estate of Ulrich von Dornum, an unusually tolerant soul for his era. In 1543, however, east Friesland's ruler, Countess Anna of Oldenburg, responded to a request by the Holy Roman Emperor and issued a decree against the Anabaptists, who were for the first time called "Mennisten" or MENNONITES. Simons left east Freisland and continued his wandering.

Simons had to contend with unorthodox teachings among the Anabaptists, including spiritism and private revelations, which Simons considered fanatical and unbiblical. He opposed the followers of David Joris, who denied the necessity of building church communities during times of persecution. He also met with Anabaptist leaders to establish rules of church discipline. One such conference led to the promulgation of the 1554 Wismar Articles, which set rules concerning marriages between believers and unbelievers, settling disputes in court, and nonresistance.

At the end of 1554, Simons moved to Oldesloe, Holstein, finding protection from landowner Bartholomeus von Ahlefeldt, who resisted pressure to expel the Mennonites. In this haven, Simons penned his views on ecclesiology, the doctrine of the church. He accepted the goal of building a pure church of believers, and he advocated the use of the ban and the practice of avoidance to accomplish that end. Simons worked for consensus among strict and lenient colleagues. On the controversial question of SHUNNING between spouses, Simons in 1557 wrote that the marriage between Christ and the soul overrode in importance mere human relationships.

It is believed that Simons died at Wüstenfelde on January 31, 1561. He was buried there, though no one knows exactly where. In 1906, Mennonites placed a stone in a possible location. From the perspective of history, it is evident that Simons saved the Anabaptist movement from total destruction. The Swiss Brethren, the original Anabaptist group, entirely disappeared, as did those who espoused the Melchiorite notions. Many people lost their lives or were driven from their homes by authorities unable or unwilling to distinguish between the main body of the movement and its fringe elements that actively opposed secular rulers. Through his many writings, especially the *Foundation-Book* (1539–40), Simons molded the movement into a recognizable body that was finally not viewed as a threat to the established order.

See also RADICAL REFORMATION.

Further reading: John Horsch, *Menno Simons* (Scottdale, Pa.: Mennonite Publishing House, 1916); Cornelius Krahn, *Dutch Anabaptism: Origin, Spread, Life, and Thought (1450–1600)* (The Hague: Martinus Nijhoff, 1968); Menno Simons, *The Complete Writings*, trans. by Leonard Verduin (Scottdale, Pa.: Herald Press, 1956); Piet Visser and Mary Sprunger, *Menno Simons: Places, Portraits and Progeny* (Altona, Manitoba, Canada: Friesens, 1996); George H. Williams, *The Radical Reformation* (Kirksville, Mo: Sixteenth Century Journal, 1992).

Simpson, Albert Benjamin (1843–1919)
missionary activist and evangelist

Albert Benjamin Simpson was born on December 15, 1843, on Prince Edward Island, but grew up in Ontario. Accepting a call to the ministry in 1858, he attended Knox College in Toronto (1861–65). He subsequently served as a pastor in Hamilton, Ontario, Louisville, Kentucky (1874–80), and New York City. He developed a passion for evangelism and world missions, which prompted him to begin a periodical, *The Gospel in All Lands*, after moving to New York City in 1880.

In August 1881, Simpson was healed of a heart disorder under the ministry of Episcopal layman Charles E. Cullis (1833–92). In reaction, he soon came to identify as a BAPTIST (he was rebaptized by immersion) and to launch an independent evangelistic ministry. In 1882, he founded Gospel Tabernacle Church in New York City, where he held Friday afternoon meetings for consecration and healing. As the tabernacle grew, Simpson spun off several rescue missions, a healing home, and a training school. He also organized the Missionary Union for the Evangelization of the World.

At this time, he forged ties with the KESWICK MOVEMENT in England, reformulating the Keswick teaching as the four-fold gospel, a Christ-centered theology that emphasized Christ as Savior, Sanctifier, Healer, and Coming King.

In the mid-1880s, Simpson began to call for an alliance of Christians to promote world missions. In 1887, his followers voted to form two organizations, the Christian Alliance and the Evangelical Missionary Alliance. The latter agency immediately moved to send its first missionaries to China and India. Both alliances grew into national organizations over the next few years. By 1897, more than 300 missionaries had been commissioned and sent to various countries around the world. That same year, the Christian Alliance merged with the Evangelical Missionary Alliance to form the Christian and Missionary Alliance.

After 1906, Simpson lost some followers to PENTECOSTALISM, including leaders such as Carrie Judd MONTGOMERY. The last years of Simpson's life were marked by the slow but steady growth of the mission fields and the maturing of his association of congregations into a new denomination, the Christian and Missionary Alliance. Simpson died on October 29, 1919.

Further reading: Pat Dys and Linda Corbin, *He Obeyed God: The Story of Albert Benjamin Simpson*

(Camp Hill, Pa.: Christian Publications, 1986); David F. Hartzfeld and Charles Nienkirchen, eds., *The Birth of a Vision: Essays on the Ministry and Thought of Albert B. Simpson, Founder of the Christian and Missionary Alliance* (Beaverlodge, Alberta, Canada: Buena Book Services, 1986); Albert Benjamin Simpson, *A Larger Christian Life* (Uhrichsville, Ohio: Barbour, 1988); ———, *The Spirit-Filled Church in Action* (Harrisburg, Pa.: Christian Church, 1975); ———, *Wholly Sanctified* (New York: Christian Alliance, 1993).

Singapore

Singapore continues to play an important role in the development of the Protestant community in Southeast ASIA due to its history as a British colony, its present role as an economic powerhouse, and its extremely pluralistic religious community. Most of the population is of Chinese heritage, divided between Buddhists and followers of traditional Chinese religions. Malays (about 12 percent) are primarily Muslims. There is also an Asian Indian community who are Hindus. The Netherlands Reformed Church was brought to the region in the 17th century after the Dutch conquest of Malaysia, but Protestantism remained largely the preserve of European settlers prior to the 19th century.

The LONDON MISSIONARY SOCIETY (LMS) began an outreach in the area, using Malacca as a base of operations, in 1814. They were on the scene almost immediately when Sir Thomas Raffles (1781–1826) founded a trading post on Singapore in 1819. Over the next decades, the LMS, joined by the AMERICAN BOARD OF COMMISSIONERS FOR FOREIGN MISSIONS and the PARIS EVANGELICAL MISSIONARY SOCIETY, worked among the population evangelizing and setting up Western-style schools. Thus, the first generation of Protestant work was primarily in Presbyterian hands, and eventually the work was united into what is today the Presbyterian Church in Singapore.

The CHURCH OF ENGLAND sent a priest to Singapore in 1826 to serve the needs of British settlers, but did not begin to reach out to the native population until the 1850s, when missionaries with the SOCIETY FOR THE PROPAGATION OF THE GOSPEL IN FOREIGN PARTS arrived. The Plymouth BRETHREN arrived in 1856 and the Methodists in 1885, the only other groups to establish work in the 19th century.

Through the 20th century, a host of different groups have found their way to Singapore. PENTECOSTALISM, brought by the ASSEMBLIES OF GOD, has joined the Anglicans, Methodists, and Presbyterians as among the five largest Protestant bodies on the island. The BAPTISTS have about 10,000 members, divided between the Singapore Baptist Convention and the Faith Community Baptist Church.

The older and larger Singapore churches are members of the National Council of Churches, Singapore, which is affiliated with the WORLD COUNCIL OF CHURCHES. Many of the newer and more conservative churches are affiliated with the Evangelical Fellowship of Singapore, which is associated with the WORLD EVANGELICAL ALLIANCE. Like Hong Kong, Singapore has become an important center for missionary activity in the region and a number of PARACHURCH ORGANIZATIONS have used regional headquarters on the island as a launching pad for missionary outreach to nearby countries.

Further reading: Theodore R. Doraisamy, ed., *Forever Beginning: One Hundred Years of Methodism in Singapore*, 2 vols. (Singapore: Methodist Church in Singapore, 1985); Robert McLeish Greer, *A History of the Presbyterian Church in Singapore* (Singapore: Malaya Publishing House, 1956); *Singapore Church Directory* (Singapore: Singapore Every Home Crusade, issued annually): Bobby E. K. Sng, *In His Good Time: The Story of the Church in Singapore, 1819–1992* (Singapore: Graduates' Christian Fellowship, 1993).

Singh, Sadhu Sundar   *See* SUNDAR SINGH.

slain in the Spirit

Slain in the Spirit is the popular term for an experience in which the believer, often at a Pentecostal revival meeting or healing service, reports a sudden influx of energy (identified with the Holy Spirit) and an accompanying loss of motor functions leading to physical collapse. The phenomenon often appears during the LAYING ON OF HANDS by a healer or evangelist, but on occasion it occurs spontaneously or after being pointed to by the person conducting the service.

A variety of biblical accounts may be referring to this experience, such as the disciples of Jesus falling face down upon hearing the voice of God (Matthew 1:6), or Paul's experience on the Damascus road (Acts 9).

The experience of being slain in the spirit did not become particularly noticeable until the 1960s, when it appeared in meetings held by healing evangelists Kathryn Kuhlman (1907–76), Kenneth Hagin Sr. (1917–2003), and Charles and Francis Hunter (b. 1916). Most recently, it has been prominent in the meetings conducted by Benny Hinn (b. 1953), an evangelist who claims to carry on the ministry of Kathryn Kuhlman. It has also been a part of the revivals associated with the TORONTO BLESSING. Following the widespread televising of the phenomenon, it has spread within the Pentecostal/Charismatic world.

Critics of the phenomenon suggest that it is merely a learned behavior. Supporters, however, suggest that its spontaneous occurrence in many setting, the accounts of subjects themselves, and the changed lives that have followed it suggest that it cannot simply be reduced to a natural phenomenon.

See also CHARISMATIC MOVEMENT; PENTECOSTALISM.

Further reading: James A. Beverley, *Holy Laughter and the Toronto Blessing: An Investigative Report* (Grand Rapids, Mich.: Zondervan, 1995); Kenneth Hagin, *Why Do People Fall under the Power* (Tulsa, Okla.: Faith Library, 1980); Allen Spraggett, *Kathryn Kuhlman: The Woman Who Believes in Miracles* (New York: New American Library, 1970).

Smyth, John (c. 1570–1612) *founder of the Baptist movement in England*

John Smyth attended Christ's College, CAMBRIDGE UNIVERSITY, beginning around 1586 and received an M.A. in 1593. In 1600, he was named the CHURCH OF ENGLAND preacher for the city of Lin-

coln, but was dismissed two years later because of his indiscreet criticisms of the church and his nonconformist ideas. He later published two volumes of sermons and lectures delivered at Lincoln.

By around 1605, he had become minister of a Separatist congregation in Gainsborough on Trent. In 1607, the group decided to settle in the NETHERLANDS. Sometime in the next two years, he became an Anabaptist, accepting the idea of adult BAPTISM, though he did not suggest immersion as the only proper mode. His view on adult baptism split the congregation, especially after Smyth moved to join the MENNONITES.

Smyth died in 1612 before his examination by the Mennonites was complete. In the end, his group was accepted into the fellowship. Those who had broken with him returned to England. Under the leadership of Thomas Hewys, they founded the first Baptist congregation on British soil.

See also BAPTISTS; BAPTIST UNION OF GREAT BRITAIN.

Further reading: H. Leon McBeth, *The Baptist Heritage: Four Centuries of Baptist Witness* (Nashville, Tenn.: Broadman Press, 1887); Robert G. Torbert, *A History of the Baptists* (Philadelphia: Judson Press, 1950); W. T. Whitley, *The Works of John Smyth* (Cambridge: Cambridge University Press, 1915).

Social Gospel

The Social Gospel movement emerged in the late 19th century in the United States as a response to changes in urban America—the influx of non-English-speaking immigrants, industrialization and the resulting labor problems, and the rise of socialist thought. It was influenced by the emergence of sociology as a new tool to understand the human condition, and by a growing emphasis on the importance of the Kingdom of God in the message preached by Jesus. The kingdom was interpreted as a real possibility in the contemporary human community, as Christian ideals were applied in secular social settings. The identification of socialism as the best representation of a

Christian society bore fruit in the formation of the Society of Christian Socialists by W. D. P. Bliss in 1889.

Among the leaders of the new movement were Baptist scholar Walter Rauschenbusch (1861–1918), a professor at Rochester Theological Seminary, economist Richard T. Ely (1854–1943), and Congregationalist ministers Josiah Strong (1847–1916) and Washington Gladden (1836–1918). They denounced the excesses of laissez-faire capitalism and opted for a socialist vision. Traditional church leaders saw their work as an attack upon orthodoxy and the abandonment of evangelism in favor of moral endeavor.

The Social Gospel emphasized God's immanence, especially God's activity in the social process, and viewed Jesus as a moral exemplar working for social justice. It was a very optimistic form of social Darwinism, which heralded the evolution of society into a socialist Kingdom of God. Moral endeavor was transferred from personal ethics to efforts to make systemic changes in society that would produce an ever more equal and just social order.

The Social Gospel movement gained significant influence in liberal Protestantism in the early 20th century. The new Federal Council of Churches adopted a Social Creed soon after its formation in 1908, and many Protestant leaders adopted PACIFISM in the 1920s and 1930s. Among the leading Social Gospel advocates between the two world wars were Methodist Harry F. Ward (1873–1966) and African Methodist bishop Reverdy C. Ransom (1861–1959). The movement was largely destroyed by the horrors of World War II and the emergence of a more realistic picture of the human condition proposed by NEO-ORTHODOXY. A leading voice in calling for a revision of Social Gospel expectations was ethicist Reinhold NEIBUHR.

While the optimism of the Social Gospel could not be sustained, the movement left its mark in its pioneering of social ethics as an important element of Christian thinking, its championing of sociology as a tool in ethical awareness, its exploration of the social impact of sin, and its understanding of individual responsibility for the institutionalization of injustice in impersonal social structures. Among more conservative Protestants, the Social Gospel supported a set of moral crusades from temperance to Sabbath observance and missions (as a civilizing force in the world).

Further reading: Paul A. Carter, *The Decline and Revival of the Social Gospel: Social and Political Liberalism in American Protestant Churches, 1920–1940* (Ithaca, N.Y.: Cornell University Press, 1954); Susan Curtis, *A Consuming Faith: The Social Gospel and Modern American Culture* (Baltimore: Johns Hopkins University Press, 1991); Robert T. Handy, *The Social Gospel in America 1870–1920: Gladden, Ely, Rauschenbusch* (New York: Oxford University Press, 1966); Walter Rauschenbusch, *Walter Rauschenbusch: Selected Writings,* ed. by Winthrop S. Hudson. (New York: Paulist Press, 1984); Donald Cedric White, *The Social Gospel: Religion and Reform in Changing America* (Philadelphia: Temple University Press, 1976).

Society for Promoting Christian Knowledge

The Society for Promoting Christian Knowledge was one of the earliest Christian publishing ventures. It has played a major role in the spread of Protestant values in Britain, North America, and the missionary field.

In 1696, the bishop of London appointed Rev. Thomas BRAY, a priest of the CHURCH OF ENGLAND and author of a book of catechetical lectures, as an assistant (commissary) to survey the needs of the church in the American colonies. During the next several years, Bray began the process of recruiting ministers to serve in America. The effort broadened his preexisting concern for religious education. He found that the young ministers who were willing to relocate to the colonies lacked the resources needed for such pioneering ministry. Bray was also concerned about another issue—the vice and immorality that many believed was afflicting society, and which he attributed to ignorance of Christianity.

Bray proposed a comprehensive plan for public education to meet both needs. For those young ministers willing to take up a post in the American or Caribbean colonies, he proposed outfitting them with a set of basic books. To counteract vice, he proposed setting up libraries in every area served by the church, in both England and America. In 1698, he presented his idea to a small group of laymen shortly before traveling to Maryland, and together they founded the Society for Promoting Christian Knowledge (SPCK).

To meet its evolving goals, SPCK began publishing religious books, pamphlets, and tracts, soon emerging as the largest religious publishing house in England. To underwrite and distribute its publications, SPCK enlisted corresponding members, who would be sent packages of publications to sell or distribute. As their numbers grew, corresponding members formed district committees and established small book depots, some 400 in England alone in the 19th century. SPCK consciously strove to print a wide variety of texts on a range of subjects by many different authors.

Bray's libraries gave clergy and lay leaders access to the books they needed for parish work. Up until the American Revolution, SPCK shipped books to the American colonies to nurture the substantial network of libraries they had created, but even at the start its concern extended to other parts of the world; in 1709, it sent a printing press and a printer to Tranquebar in east India to support the work of the pioneering DANISH-HALLE MISSION.

As the British expanded their colonial system, SPCK assumed a support role for the missionaries sent out by the SOCIETY FOR THE PROPAGATION OF THE GOSPEL IN FOREIGN PARTS and the CHURCH MISSIONARY SOCIETY, by raising funds for church buildings, schools, and theological training colleges. It also recruited the chaplains who settled on the ships carrying personnel to the colonies. To this day, the group supports seminary libraries in Anglican jurisdictions worldwide, and supplies a start-up selection of books for their newly ordained Anglican priests.

The far-flung activities of SPCK have been transformed by the development of autonomous Anglican churches around the world. Among the new activities is a program in indigenous communication. SPCK has allocated funds to help set up publishing houses around the world, so that writers and theologians can publish locally, thus freeing them from their dependence on theological perspectives imported from Europe and North America, and promoting their participation in developing world perspectives on the faith.

As the 21st century begins, SPCK publishes under five imprints, and keeps more than 500 titles in print at any one time. Over the three centuries of its existence, it has published in excess of 30,000 titles. Included are translations of the BOOK OF COMMON PRAYER in more than 200 languages and dialects. SPCK Worldwide appraises the needs of the world ANGLICAN COMMUNION and annually makes grants that promote the education of Anglican clergy, the improvement of worship life, and communication of the Gospel.

SPCK is headquartered in London, England.

Further reading: Society for Promoting Christian Knowledge. Available online. URL: http://www.spck.org.uk; William O. Allen, *Two Hundred Years: The History of the Society for Promoting Christian Knowledge, 1698–1898* (New York: Burt Franklin, 1971); William D. Houlette, "Parish Libraries and the Work of the Reverend Thomas Bray," *Library Quarterly* 4 (October 1934): 588–609; Bernard C. Steiner, "The Reverent Thomas Bray and his American Libraries," *American Historical Review* 2 (1896–97): 59–75; Henry P. Thompson, *Thomas Bray* (London: SPCK, 1954).

Society for the Propagation of the Gospel in Foreign Parts

One of the oldest Protestant missionary agencies, the Society for the Propagation of the Gospel in Foreign Parts (SPG) was founded in England in 1701 in response to the report of Thomas BRAY (1656–1739) on the religious situation in the

American colonies. Bray had been in America for four years (1696–1700) as commissary for Maryland. He was concerned about the unmet educational needs of Church of England ministers serving in the colonies and the impact on their congregations. After returning to England, he convinced his colleagues to form a new society to focus upon the religious needs of English settlers overseas (primarily North America and the Caribbean), and the conversion to Christianity of the native populations there.

Bray obtained a royal charter and won the patronage of Archbishop of Canterbury Thomas Tenison (1636–1715), who lent Lambeth Palace in London for the society's first meeting. As it developed, SPG became identified with high-church elements, while the Church Missionary Society, founded a century later, was more representative of low-church evangelical Anglicans.

In its first century, the society focused on North America and the Caribbean. Among its first commissioned staff was a teacher for African-American children in New York City. In the 19th century, its work followed the far-flung movement of British entrepreneurs and soldiers in the ever-expanding network of colonies. Fortuitously, during the American Revolution most SPG personnel returned from North America, and the society found itself with the funds for a more diversified presence in additional parts of the world. Work was extended to India in 1818, soon followed by Africa, the Middle East, Malaysia, Japan, and Korea.

In the mid-20th century, SPG began to transform its work as former missions became independent Anglican jurisdictions within the Anglican Communion. The changes cost SPG significant popular support at home, and its income dropped. In 1965 and 1968, it merged with two other organizations, the Universities' Mission in Central Africa and the Cambridge Mission to Delhi, creating in the process the United Society for the Propagation of the Gospel. As the new century began, the United Society supports personnel in more than 20 countries and works with more than 50 Anglican church bodies worldwide.

The United Society is headquartered in London, England.

See also Anglicanism.

Further reading: United Society for the Propagation of the Gospel. Available online. URL: http://www.uspg.org.uk. Accessed on June 15, 2003; Charles Frederick Pascoe, *Two Hundred Years of the S.P.G.: An Historical Account of the Society for the Propagation of the Gospel in Foreign Parts, 1701–1900* (London: Society's Office, 1901); Henry Paget Thompson, *Into All Lands: The History of the Society for the Propagation of the Gospel in Foreign Parts, 1701–1950* (London: SPCK, 1951).

Society of Friends *See* Quakers.

Socinianism

Socinianism was an anti-Trinitarian movement that emerged during the 16th-century Reformation. Its name derived from the two Italian reformers who helped define it, Lelius Socinius (1526–62) and his nephew, Faustus Socinius (1539–1604), both natives of Sienna.

The movement began as a secret society in Venice that came to reject the doctrine of the Trinity, the almost universal Christian belief that the one God is expressed in the three persons of Father, Son, and Holy Spirit. Among the members was Lelius Socinius, a Catholic priest and acquaintance of other major reformers such as Heinrich Bullinger, John Calvin, and Philip Melancthon. When the society's views became known in the early 1550s, most of its members fled to Poland. Lelius settled in Zurich, though he stayed in contact with a circle of non-Trinitarians in Krakow. The Polish group suffered some divisions following Lelius's death in 1562, but was able to issue a catechism in 1574.

Giorgio Biandrata (1515–90), one of the leaders of the Venetian group, moved to Transylvania (then under Turkish Ottoman control). He became court physician to King John Sigismund, who in 1564 led the Transylvanian diet to adopt Calvinism as the state religion. Biandrata won over the leader of the Reformed (Calvinist) Church, Francis David, to his non-Trinitarian position. David thus became head of a Unitarian church centered in Transylvania, but he was soon imprisoned for his unique views. Unlike the Socinians, David no longer believed that Christ should be worshipped; in addition, his followers worshipped on the Sabbath rather than Sunday.

Meanwhile, Faustus Socinius was able to unite the Polish Unitarians. He was subsequently invited to Transylvania to try to moderate David's views. Socinius held that Christ, while not God, was the Promised Man, the Mediator of creation and thus the Mediator of regeneration. David refused to accept Socinius's view and died in prison.

The new center of Socinianism flourished at Racow, Poland. Faustus's revised catechism was published in Polish the year after his death (1605), and then in Latin four years later. Even as the Counter-Reformation gained strength in Poland, the Socinians established schools, held synods, and printed their own literature.

As Socinian literature found its way across Europe, in 1638 the Catholic authorities decided to suppress the movement, and on this issue Protestants agreed. Not only did the Socinians deny Christ's divinity, they also denied the real presence in the SACRAMENTS, original sin, hell, and infant BAPTISM. They taught that the Holy Spirit was an operation of God, the power of sanctification. One by one, Poland and other European governments moved to suppress the movement.

Socinianism was stamped out in Catholic countries by the Counter-Reformation. Protestants in England and Holland, where Socinians briefly emerged, were hardly kinder, though in England Socinian thought survived long enough to inspire what would become British UNITARI-ANISM in the next century.

Further reading: Marian Hillar, "From the Polish Socinians to the American Constitution," *A Journal from the Radical Reformation. A Testimony to Biblical Unitarianism* 3, 2 (1994): 22–57. Available online. URL:http://www.socinian.org/polish_socinians.html; Earl Morse Wilbur, *A History of Unitarianism,* vol. 1: *Socianianism and Its Antecedents* (Boston: Beacon Press, 1945); George H. Williams, *The Polish Brethren: Documentation of the History and Thought of Unitarianism in the Polish-Lithuanian Commonwealth and in the Diaspora, 1601–1685* (Atlanta: Scholars Press, 1980).

Sola Scriptura

One of the core ideas of the Protestant Reformation was that the BIBLE remained the sole authority for the teachings of the Christian church. The reformers needed an alternative authority in order to challenge the pope and his BISHOPS, who claimed that authority resided in the traditions of the church.

At first, when he challenged the pope in the NINETY-FIVE THESES, Martin LUTHER did not specifically raise the issue of a counter authority. But after he asserted, in his 1518 debate with Catholic theologian John Eck (1486–1543), that a church council had erred, the entire medieval church authority system was in doubt; Luther needed to firm up his position concerning the authority of the Bible. In 1520, in one of his three treatises, the *Appeal to the German Nobility,* he rejected any special authority of the pope to interpret Scripture and called on Christians to follow the Bible if the pope acted contrary to its dictates. Then, in his address to the DIET OF WORMS, he made a radical appeal to Scripture and to reason, and insisted that any refutations be based on them.

Luther's position implied that the Bible could be read and understood by the average person, and that it should become readily available to anyone in the church. After his appearance at Worms, Luther completed a translation of the Bible and saw to its publication. The first paragraph in the Formula of Concord (1580) stated what was by then the firm Lutheran doctrine: "We believe, teach and confess that the only rule and standard to which at once all dogmas and teachers should be esteemed and judged are nothing else than the prophetic and apostolic Scriptures of the Old and of the New Testament."

This affirmation was not meant to do away with church tradition entirely, or to reject the binding authority of the ancient church creeds. Such statements as the Apostles' Creed, the Nicene Creed, the AUGSBURG CONFESSION OF FAITH, and the FORMULA OF CONCORD set out the major teachings of the Christian church in a brief and straightforward fashion and are useful in refuting heresy. But by making the Bible the standard anyone could use to appeal against the authority of the church, Luther paved the way for the present reality, in which a multitude of interpretations has become the basis of a wide variety of separate Christian communities.

Further reading: Harold J. Grimm, *The Reformation Era* (New York: Macmillan, 1954); J. Gordon Melton, *The Encyclopedia of American Religions: Religious Creeds,* 2 vols. (Detroit: Gale Research, 1988, 1994); David Steinmetz, ed., *The Bible in the Sixteenth Century* (Durham, N.C.: Duke University Press, 1990).

South Africa

The settlement of Cape Town by the Dutch East India Company in 1652 provided the first opportunity for Protestantism to establish a foothold on the continent of Africa. The Reformed Church of the NETHERLANDS primarily served the colonizers, but it also began to spread among their African servants and slaves. The Reformed Church retained its privileged status even after the British arrived in 1795 and reorganized the local government as a British colony in 1806. By that time the MORAVIAN CHURCH had also set down roots (1737). It was the first to actively evangelize the local population, over the objections of the colonists.

The British takeover brought the CHURCH OF ENGLAND to the Cape and the LONDON MISSIONARY SOCIETY (Congregationalist) to the interior. The establishment of British authority throughout South Africa was achieved over the staunch resistance of the AFRIKANERS (settlers of Dutch background), culminating in the Boer War (1899–1902). The Union of South Africa became independent in 1934.

The London Missionary Society, the source of the present-day United Congregational Church, would be led in its early years by several illustrious missionaries, including Johannes van der Kemp (1747–1811), Robert Moffat (1895–1983) and David LIVINGSTONE. Within a generation they were joined by Methodists, BAPTISTS, Lutherans, and Presbyterians, giving the colony the same spectrum of Protestant churches found in England. Each church developed congregations among the British settlers and then reached out to local residents in the interior. Each of the churches split into two or more branches and denominational bodies as blacks and whites separated.

The Reformed Church splintered as well. Regional churches were established as Afrikaners settled the interior, beginning with the Transvaal in 1853. Differences over African evangelism and over schisms in the church back in the Netherlands caused additional splits. In 1881, black members were segregated into the Dutch Reformed Mission Church. Still other churches were set up through missionary activity in the different provinces. In 1962, the white Reformed churches merged to form the Dutch Reformed Church. In 1963 and 1994, the several Reformed churches serving the African community merged to form the Uniting Reformed Church in Southern Africa.

In 1895, the small Christian Catholic Church based in Zion, Illinois, established an outpost in Johannesburg. The church grew rapidly, primarily among Zulus. It was the vehicle in 1908 for the introduction of PENTECOSTALISM to South Africa. Almost the entire membership became Pentecostals, but they split over their relation to the Apostolic Faith Mission, which had initially brought the new teachings to Africa, resulting in two churches: the Apostolic and the ZIONISTS. As they spread across southern Africa, these two churches in turn became the parents of a set of Apostolic and Zionist churches (DENOMINATIONS). The largest today are the 7-million-member Zionist Christian Church, the largest Christian body in South Africa, and the Apostolic Faith Mission of South Africa.

The larger Reformed community, which includes about 9 percent of the country's residents, became deeply involved in the country's political struggles. In the 1940s, following independence from England, the Afrikaner National Party took control of the government, and the Reformed Church became an integral part of the apartheid system of racial segregation. By the 1960s, apartheid meant territorial segregation of blacks and a system of police repression.

As apartheid became more severe, the WORLD COUNCIL OF CHURCHES established the Cottesloe Consultation to look at the problem by its member churches within the country, causing the white Dutch Reformed Church and other white churches to resign. The predominantly African Dutch Reformed Mission Church, on the other hand, strongly denounced apartheid in 1974 and 1979, as did the WORLD ALLIANCE OF REFORMED CHURCHES, which suspended the Dutch Reformed Church of South Africa from membership in 1982.

Bolstered by international support, the Dutch Reformed Mission Church promulgated the BELHAR CONFESSION in 1986, a landmark in mobilizing South African churches against apartheid. Previously, the Institute for Contextual Theology brought together a group of church leaders to discuss apartheid as a theological issue; in 1985, they had issued the KAIROS DOCUMENT, which spoke of getting beyond apartheid through repentance and reconciliation. Both documents took on programmatic significance through the South African Council of Churches and its several general secretaries—most notably Desmond TUTU (1978–85), Beyers Naude (1985–88), and Frank Chikane (1988–95).

Desmond Tutu, as a bishop and then archbishop in the Anglican Church of the Province of South Africa, brought the largest of the older churches in South Africa into the antiapartheid cause. He was given the Nobel Peace Prize in 1984.

Today, the Protestant community in South Africa, with well over 100 denominations, claims about 75 percent of the population. The most important ecumenical associations are the South African Council of Churches (affiliated with the World Council of Churches) and the Evangelical Alliance of South Africa (affiliated with the WORLD EVANGELICAL ALLIANCE). South African members of the WCC include the Church of the Province of South Africa, the Council of African Instituted Churches, the Evangelical Lutheran Church of South Africa, the Evangelical Presbyterian Church of South Africa, the Methodist Church of South Africa, the Moravian Church in South Africa, the Presbyterian Church of Africa, the United Congregationalist Church of South Africa, the Uniting Presbyterian Church in Southern Africa, and the Uniting Reformed Church in Southern Africa. Meanwhile, the newer AFRICAN INITIATED CHURCHES have formed the African Independence Churches Association, the Assembly of Zionists and Apostolic Churches, and the Association of Pentecostal Ministers of South Africa.

See also AFRICA, SUB-SAHARAN.

Further reading: Johannes du Plessis, *A History of Christian Missions in South Africa.* (Cape Town, South Africa: Struik, 1911, 1965); C. F. Hallencreutz and M. Palmberg, *Religion and Politics in Southern Africa.* (Uppsala, Sweden: Scandinavian Institute of African Studies, 1991); P. Hinchliff, *The Anglican Church in South Africa* (London: Darton, Longman & Todd, 1963); Piet Naude, *The Zionist Christian Church in South Africa: A Case-Study in Oral Theology* (Lewiston, N.Y.: Edwin Mellen Press, 1995); J. Sales, *The Planting of the Churches in South Africa.* (Grand Rapids, Mich.: William B. Eerdmans, 1971).

South America

Most of South America had become dominantly Roman Catholic by the time Protestants began to develop their missionary programs. The exceptions were GUYANA and Surinam, which were under British and Dutch control, respectively.

As with most of the rest of the world, the Moravians took the lead in missionary activity. The Reformed Church of the NETHERLANDS had established a presence in Surinam in the 17th century, but its primary aim was to serve the Dutch settlers. The Moravians arrived in both Guyana and Surinam in 1738 (before the Dutch turned Guyana over to the British) with the idea of evangelizing the native population. They later extended their work to include the Maroons, former slaves who had escaped to the interior. As these two countries developed, a spectrum of Protestant groups arrived from England and Holland, and they emerged as Protestant enclaves.

The struggle to transform the South American lands from colonies to independent countries was accompanied by a level of anticlericalism and anti-Catholicism, since the Catholic Church tended to favor maintaining the colonial structures. This context provided a small opening for Protestant missionary efforts. The first to take advantage was James Thomson (1788–1854), an agent of the British and Foreign Bible Society. Arriving in Argentina in 1818, he traveled through a number of countries over the next eight years distributing Bibles and Protestant literature and founding Bible societies to continue the work when he moved on. Thomson was also a founder of schools. As an agent for the Lancastrian Educational Society, he established more than 100 schools that used the society's unique system of older students assisting younger ones. Unfortunately, as Thomson's work became better known, the Catholic clergy organized to destroy much of it. However, colporteurs, men like Thomson who carried Bibles and religious literature to be either sold or given away, were widely used in Latin America for several generations.

A next phase of Protestant life began with the immigration of non-Iberian Europeans, who brought their churches with them, including the Methodist (England), Waldensian (Italy), Lutheran (Germany and Scandinavia), Presbyterian (Scotland), Mennonite (Holland, Germany, Russia), and Baptist (Germany, France) churches. Some immigrant communities were quite large, such as the German Lutherans in BRAZIL, who numbered in the tens of thousands. They usually formed ghettolike communities, and most of their proselytizing was among their own ethnic group. For example, in 1824, representatives of the CHURCH OF ENGLAND and the Church of Scotland began work among English-speaking expatriates in Buenos Aires.

Outreach to the general population began in 1834 by American Methodists in Buenos Aires; the work spread four years later to Montevideo, Uruguay. Congregationalist David Trumbull (1819–89), a graduate of Princeton Theological Seminary, began work in Chile in 1845. With his first converts, English-speaking expatriates, he formed an interdenominational Union Chapel in Valparaiso. During his lengthy ministry, he opened work in other cities and assisted other missionaries to get started. In the end, he turned his work over to the Presbyterian Church.

In the 1850s, American Presbyterians launched work in Colombia (1856) and Brazil (1859). In Colombia, where they were for many years the only Protestant group, they became well known for the many schools and hospitals they founded and supported, though they were unable to translate their good works and good reputation into a substantial church membership. Three American Presbyterians arrived in São Paulo in 1859 and founded the Presbyterian Church in Brazil, which would over the next generation grow into a substantial body. From these beachheads, Protestantism grew, spread into the interior countries, and diversified. For example, as early as 1856, Methodists began to travel up the Platte River to Paraguay, though it took some time for permanent work to be established.

The coast of what was then Bolivia became the site of one of the most interesting and important Protestant missionary endeavors. William Taylor, a minister in the Methodist Episcopal Church, had developed a set of self-supporting churches in INDIA. Opposition to his methods drove him from his work, but he decided to spread his ideas to South America and arrived there in 1877. As the autonomous, self-supported churches were founded, he both recruited ministers from America and trained locals for leadership. In 1884, he was elected a BISHOP by the Methodist Episcopal Church and sent to Africa, but his efforts had far-reaching results in Chile.

Three major trends characterized South American Protestantism in the 20th century. First, the older churches continued to grow, though they sometimes split. Second, new churches would be added as additional North American and European churches began missionary work. One groundbreaking effort began in Ecuador in 1931 with the founding of HCJB ("Heralding Christ Jesus' Blessings"), the first Christian radio station outside the United States, by Clarence Jones and Reuben Larson, under the instigation of pioneer American radio preacher R. R. Brown (1885–1964). The station quickly developed programming in Quechua, an indigenous language of Ecuador, Bolivia, and Peru. As local churches sprang up without benefit of missionaries, the station received calls for assistance. As of the beginning of the 21st century, HCJB has grown into a significant operation offering programming in 40 languages from its 20 transmitters.

The third great trend has been the advent of PENTECOSTALISM, which experienced phenomenal growth, especially in the last half of the century. Among the first to accept the Pentecostal message in South America was Willis C. HOOVER (1856–1936), a Methodist minister with HOLINESS leanings, originally recruited by William Taylor. Hoover first heard of the BAPTISM OF THE HOLY SPIRIT in 1909, while he was pastoring the Methodist Church in Valparaiso. Soon his whole congregation accepted the new message and passed it to other Methodist churches. Expelled from the Methodist Church in 1911, Hoover and his followers reorganized as the Methodist Pentecostal Church, which become the parent of the

Methodist Bishop William Taylor started self-sufficient missions in Chile and Bolivia in the late 19th century. *(Drew University Library)*

Evangelical Pentecostal Church, the Pentecostal Church of Chile, and the Pentecostal Mission Church. Together the four churches have more than a million members.

Brazil has seen even greater Pentecostal growth. The movement arrived in 1910 from Chicago. Today the ASSEMBLIES OF GOD has become the largest non-Catholic group in Brazil, claiming a constituency of more than 14 million members. It is followed by the indigenous UNIVERSAL CHURCH OF THE KINGDOM OF GOD (with 4 million members) and several other churches with more than a million. It appears that many others who have received the baptism of the Holy Spirit have chosen to remain within their old churches, especially the Roman Catholic Church. The largest non-Catholic church in Colombia is the United Pentecostal Church of Colombia, a non-Trinitarian "Jesus Only" body.

South Americans from the older ecumenical Protestant groups helped originate LIBERATION THEOLOGY. Liberation theologians rejected what they saw as elitist European dominance in church life and thought, and claimed to identify with the largely poor membership of both Protestant and Catholic churches. The movement became a significant motivating force behind social action programs. It has also been exported to every continent and became a model for indigenous theologies as distinctive as BLACK THEOLOGY (in the United States) and Minjung theology (in KOREA).

As the 21st century begins, Protestantism claims the allegiance of some 20 percent of the population of South America, though religious boundaries remain fluid, as many believers maintain duel membership in Catholic and Protestant churches. The composition of the Protestant community varies greatly between countries. Liberal Protestantism is, for example, almost unrepresented in Ecuador, none of whose local churches is affiliated with the WORLD COUNCIL OF CHURCHES. In contrast, six such churches may be found in ARGENTINA, and five in Brazil; they cooperate with the Latin American Council of Churches, which ironically is headquartered in Quito, Ecuador.

Conservative Evangelical churches are served by the Latin American Evangelical Fellowship headquartered in Caracas, Venezuela, and affiliated with the WORLD EVANGELICAL ALLIANCE. In addition, several 19th-century American sectarian groups have done relatively well in South America; the SEVENTH-DAY ADVENTIST CHURCH, the JEHOVAH'S WITNESSES, and the CHURCH OF JESUS CHRIST OF LATTER-DAY SAINTS are among the few bodies present in every South American country, and have together won millions of supporters.

See also ECUADOR; FALKLAND ISLANDS.

Further reading: Gerald H. Anderson, Robert T. Cotte, Norman A. Horner, and James M. Phillips, eds., *Mission Legacies: Biographical Studies of Leaders of the Modern Missionary Movement* (Maryknoll, N.Y.: Orbis Books, 1998); David Barrett, *The Encyclopedia of World Christianity,* 2nd ed. (New York: Oxford University Press, 2001); Patrick Johnstone and Jason Mandryk, *Operation World, 21st Century Edition* (Carlisle, Cumbria, U.K.: Paternoster, 2001); J. Herbert Kane, *A Global View of Christian Missions* (Grand Rapids, Mich.: Baker Book House, 1971); J. Gordon Melton and Martin Baumann, eds., *Religions of the World: A Comprehensive Encyclopedia of Beliefs and Practices* (Santa Barbara, Calif.: ABC-CLIO, 2002); A. Scott Moreau, ed., *Evangelical Dictionary of World Missions* (Grand Rapids, Mich.: Baker Book House, 2000).

Southern Baptist Convention

The Southern Baptist Convention was an outgrowth of the sectionalism that split the United States over the issue of slavery and eventually led to the Civil War in 1860. Among BAPTISTS, the triennial convention on Baptist missions provided the arena for the struggle.

In the 1840s, Baptist leadership included both abolitionists and slaveholders, though the majority was moderately antislavery. At the 1844 triennial, the Georgia and Alabama delegations forced the issue by nominating a slaveholder as a home missionary and asking that slaveholders receive equal consideration as foreign missionaries. When both requests were denied, a breakaway convention was held in Augusta, Georgia in 1845, at which the Southern Baptist Convention was organized.

The Southern Baptist Convention departed from the antiorganizational precedent of Baptists by unifying the home and foreign missionary concerns under a single organization. The convention added other services over time. The convention's Foreign Mission Board was located in Richmond, Virginia, and the Domestic Missions Board in Marion, Alabama (and later moved to Atlanta, Georgia, where it remains). The Foreign Missions Board sent its first representatives to CHINA. That program continued to grow until the disruptions of the Civil War and the poverty that followed it.

Eventually, the number of boards and agencies multiplied, especially to meet SUNDAY SCHOOL and publishing needs. A common set of Sunday school materials proved a significant force in overcoming the intense congregationalism so characteristic of the Baptist community. In 1925, its agency budgets were all unified.

Doctrine was not at issue in the 1845 split and the Southern Baptists continued to affirm the two LONDON CONFESSIONS (1677 and 1689), the Philadelphia Confession (1742), and the New Hampshire Confession (1838). These principles were reaffirmed in the 1925 Baptist Faith and Message statement, slightly revised in 1963.

In the 1920s, many Southern Baptists supported the Fundamentalist cause, though the most strident supporters left the convention to form separatist DENOMINATIONS, the first being the World Baptist Fellowship founded by J. Frank Norris (1877–1952), a prominent and controversial Texas minister. Most Southern Baptists identified with the new Evangelical movement in the late 20th century, but the convention has refused to join any of the Evangelical ecumenical bodies.

In the 1960s, the more conservative elements in the movement began to protest the nontraditional opinions expressed by some teachers at convention-supported schools and seminaries. By the 1970s they developed a strategy to take control of the convention and of all its boards, agencies, and schools and to ensure a more conservative perspective, especially as related to the authority of the Bible and the infallible and inerrant Word of God. Their campaign was eventually successful. Convention "moderates" have reacted by forming the Cooperative Baptist Fellowship.

During this ideological struggle, Southern Baptists have passed several controversial position statements, including the rejection of ordained women ministers. A statement on the submission of women in marriage, passed in 1988, caused the greatest comment and led to the withdrawal of the convention's most famous member, former U.S. president Jimmy Carter.

In the 1960s, the Southern Baptists overtook the United Methodists as the largest Protestant

Headquarters of the Southern Baptist Convention, the largest Protestant body in the United States, located in Nashville, Tennessee *(Institute for the Study of American Religion, Santa Barbara, California)*

church in America and have continued to widen the gap since then. Two major factors are responsible: an emphasis on evangelism and growing individual churches, and a decision to expand into the northern and western parts of the nation. The latter decision was prompted by the need to follow members who had moved, and strengthened by a recognition that the Southern Baptists and American Baptists had so diverged in belief and practice that they no longer were sister denominations.

The Southern Baptist Convention has its headquarters in Nashville, Tennessee. It began the 21st century with approximately 16 million members. It sponsors a host of colleges, universities, and seminaries and maintains missionary personnel around the world. It is a member of the Baptist World Alliance, but has generally refrained from other ecumenical attachments.

Like other Baptist groups, Southern Baptists are organized congregationally. Individual Baptist churches can voluntarily affiliate with their state association and/or the national convention. Since the emergence of the Baptist Cooperative Fellowship, local churches, state associations, and schools have formed complex, shifting relationships to both the convention and the fellowship.

Further reading: W. W. Barnes, *The Southern Baptist Convention: 1845–1953.* (Nashville, Tenn.: Broadman Press, 1954); Joe Edward Barnhart, *The Southern Baptist Holy War* (Austin, Tex.: Texas Monthly Press, 1986); Jesse Fletcher, *The Southern Baptist Convention: A Sesquicentennial History.* (Nashville, Tenn.: Broadman & Holman, 1994); Bill Leonard, *Dictionary of Baptists in America* (Downer's Grove, Ill.: InterVarsity Press, 1994); Walter Shurden, *Not a Silent People: Controversies That Have Shaped Southern Baptists.* (Nashville, Tenn.: Broadman Press, 1972); Sladen A. Yarbrough, *Southern Baptists: A Historical, Ecclesiastical, and Theological Heritage of a Confessional People* (Brentwood, Tenn.: Southern Baptist Historical Society, 2000).

South Pacific

When in 1795 British Congregationalists and other Protestants created the LONDON MISSIONARY SOCIETY, the voyages of Captain Cook were still very much in their minds, and the South Pacific seemed the obvious target for the group's initial missionary effort. The fledgling society purchased a ship, the *Duff,* and recruited 30 missionaries, of whom four were ordained ministers. The party

In Honolulu, Hawaii, missionaries opened the first printing establishment to serve the churches in the South Pacific. *(Institute for the Study of American Religion, Santa Barbara, California)*

sailed on September 23, 1796. After seven months at sea, they landed in Tahiti, where 18 of the group remained, the others moving on to Tonga and the Marquesas. The first chapel was erected in 1800.

In 1812, King Pomare II converted to Christianity. He also paid to bring a printing press to Tahiti and built a large church. A stream of water from the mountains ran through the church, to be used for baptisms.

In 1820 the AMERICAN BOARD OF COMMISSIONERS FOR FOREIGN MISSIONS sent missionaries to Hawaii, which became the launching point for extended missionary activity throughout the South Pacific. British Methodists sent workers to Tonga in 1822 to revive the London Society's work, which had collapsed shortly after it began. John Lawry pioneered the work, followed by John Hutchinson and John Thomas, the latter remaining for 28 years.

Anglican work began with the arrival of chaplains to provide religious services to the Australian penal colony. In 1793, Rev. Samuel Marsden settled in AUSTRALIA, with authority over Anglican work in Tasmania and other British outposts. Marsden held the first Christian worship service in NEW ZEALAND in 1814. An Anglican priest arrived in 1819, as did a Methodist missionary. In 1823, an Anglican mission to the Aboriginal people was initiated.

In 1836, an Anglican diocese of Australia was finally established, followed several years later by another in New Zealand. The first bishop of New Zealand, George August SELWYN (1809–78) arrived in 1841 and began an expansive career. In 1850, Selwyn began work in the Solomon Islands. His own travels set the stage for John Patterson (1827–71), the first bishop of Melanesia, and his successor, John Selwyn (1844–98), Bishop Selwyn's son.

Europeans quickly came to rely on native converts, first as translators and then as unordained missionary preachers. Much early work focused on translating the Bible into local languages.

In some cases, European colonial rule proved disruptive. In Tahiti, for example, French control from 1842 led to the introduction of Roman Catholicism, which with government backing tried to suppress Protestantism. The London Society was forced to abandon its work, which survived under the auspices of the PARIS MISSION. British and American colonial governments proved more supportive.

Through the 20th century, the South Pacific became a laboratory of missionary methodology. Secular scholars criticized the missionaries for destroying native religion and culture and their economic base, a criticism developed in James Michener's 1959 novel *Hawaii,* inspired in part by the diary of early missionary Mercy Partridge Whitney. In the 20th century, missionary agencies reevaluated their history and worked to build indigenous leadership and make the transition to autonomous national churches.

As the new century began, more than 20 South Pacific Protestant churches are members of the WORLD COUNCIL OF CHURCHES and cooperate regionally as members of the Pacific Council of Churches headquartered in Fiji. More conservative churches have affiliated with the WORLD EVANGELICAL ALLIANCE and the Evangelical Fellowship of the South Pacific, based in New Zealand.

See also FIJI ISLANDS; FRENCH POLYNESIA; PHILIPPINES.

Further reading: Jean-Jacques Bauswein and Lukas Vischer, eds., *The Reformed Family Worldwide: A Survey of Reformed Churches, Theological Schools, and International Organizations* (Grand Rapids, Mich.: William B. Eerdmans, 1999); Nolan B. Harmon, *Encyclopedia of World Methodism,* 2 vols. (Ashville, Tenn.: United Methodist Publishing House, 1974); J. Herbert Kane, *A Global View of Christian Missions* (Grand Rapids, Mich.: Baker Book House, 1971); Albert Wardin, ed., *Baptists Around the World* (Nashville, Tenn.: Holman, 1995).

Spain

Roman Catholic domination of Spanish life actually increased in the Reformation era. Such events as HENRY VIII's treatment of his first wife, Catherine of Aragon, the defeat of the Spanish Armada (1588), and Protestant resistance to Spanish rule in the NETHERLANDS strengthened Spaniards in their national-religious identification, which was further solidified by the emergence of a Catholic-oriented reform led by Spaniards such as Ignatius Loyola (1491–1556), founder of the Jesuits, and the mystics St. John of the Cross (1542–91) and St. Theresa of Avila (1515–82).

Protestantism was first introduced in the 1830s by Plymouth BRETHREN and in the mid-1850s by Luis de Usoz y Rio, who began to quietly distribute Bibles and Protestant materials he received from Scottish sources. Several evangelists such as Francisco de Paula Ruet and Manuel Matamoras operated out of a base in British-controlled Gibraltar. The arrest and trial of Matamoras in 1860 became an issue throughout Europe, as Spain expelled all known Protestant leaders.

However, in 1868 Spain passed a constitutional provision that guaranteed religious tolerance. Almost immediately, Protestant groups emerged, primarily in the south, and formed the Iglesia Reformade Española (later known as the Iglesia Christiana Española, and since 1890 the Iglesia Evangélica Española). It held its first national assembly the next year. The original organization contained a broad range of Protestant opinions, which the leadership tried to reconcile in a confession of faith. However, in 1880 the church split when those favoring an Anglican stance formed the Iglesia Española Reformada Episcopal. Plymouth Brethren and BAPTISTS also formed visible organizations at the end of the 1860s.

The status of Protestant groups waxed and waned as periods of secularization alternated with reaffirmations of special ties to Rome. Protestant churches operated under a set of discriminatory regulations. Several groups, such as the JEHOVAH'S WITNESSES, which came into the country following World War I, carried on a completely clandestine operation. Nevertheless, the community expanded slowly and new groups were introduced, most notably the SEVENTH-DAY ADVENTIST CHURCH and Pentecostals (from Sweden).

In 1967, a new Law on Religious Liberty replaced the 1853 Concordat with the Vatican. The new law, which still acknowledged the primacy of the Catholic Church, reflected the decisions of the Second Vatican Council. Liberty was granted to law-abiding groups that showed proper respect for the Catholic Church. Further liberalization occurred in 1978, when the new constitution stated that the country henceforth had no official religion. Marriage was removed from Catholic control, and freedom to change one's faith was guaranteed.

Today, there are more than 50 Protestant and Free Church groups, which together constitute less than 3 percent of the population. Some baptized Roman Catholics participate in Protestant groups without becoming formal members. PENTECOSTALISM has grown spectacularly in the last generation and more than half of all Protestants can be found in the several larger Pentecostal bodies—the Philadelphia Church, the ASSEMBLIES OF GOD, and a spectrum of groups introduced from Latin America.

See also PORTUGAL.

Further reading: Directorate of Religious Affairs (Dirección General de Asuntos Religiosos), Ministry of Justice, Spain. Available online. URL: http://www.mju.es/asuntos_religiosos/index.html; *Guía de Entidades Religiosas de España (Iglesias, Confesiones y Comunidades Minoritarias)* (Madrid: Dirección General de Asuntos Religiosos, Ministerio de Justicia, 1998); Marcelino Menéndez y Pelayo, *Historia de los Heterodoxos Españoles,* 3 vols., 3d ed. (Madrid: Consejo Superior de Investigaciones Científicas, 1992); D. G. Vought, *Protestants in Modern Spain* (South Pasadena, Calif.: William Carey Library, 1973).

speaking in tongues *See* BAPTISM OF THE HOLY SPIRIT.

Speer, Robert Elliott (1867–1947)
Presbyterian leader and missionary statesman
Robert Elliott Speer was born on September 10, 1867, in Huntingdon, Pennsylvania, into a devout Presbyterian family. He entered the College of New Jersey (Princeton) in 1885. As a college student influenced by evangelist Dwight L. MOODY, he committed his life to foreign missions. He entered Princeton Theological Seminary in 1890 but left after a year to work for the Board of Foreign Missions of the Presbyterian Church, where he made his mark during an 1896 world tour. From his involvement with the STUDENT VOLUNTEER MOVEMENT, Speer became an early advocate of ecumenism, feeling that theological disputes distracted from the church's mission and its role in solving problems between governments.

Speer helped organize the 1920 missionary conference in Edinburgh. The same year he began a four-year term as president of the Federal Council of Churches (in the United States) and in 1927 was moderator of the PRESBYTERIAN CHURCH (USA). He took a distinctive position during the Fundamentalist-Modernist struggle of the 1920s, opposing both sides on the grounds that the debate was distracting from the missionary cause.

Viewed as a Modernist, Speer became the target of Fundamentalist criticism. In 1929, he rebuffed J. Gresham MACHEN's attempts to have the Board of Foreign Missions bar missionaries who did not meet Fundamentalist standards for orthodoxy. In 1933, Machen again charged the board with tolerating Modernists, and when the Presbyterian Church's assembly backed the board, Machen founded the Independent Board of Presbyterian Foreign Missions. By 1936, he was suspended from the ministry and left to form an independent body, the Orthodox Presbyterian Church. Speer's defense of the traditional work of evangelism as the core of the missionary endeavor, which brought him into conflict with the Fundamentalists, also led him to criticize the famous *Rethinking Missions* by William E. HOCKING, who advocated a significant transfer of missionary energy into social service.

After nearly half a century with the mission board, Speer retired in 1937. He would be remembered not only for his leadership of Presbyterianism in American during a time of change, but also for his early advocacy of racial justice and the rights of women within the church. Speer authored more than 60 books covering not only missions but international relations and christology.

Further reading: John F. Piper, Jr., *Robert E. Speer: Prophet of the American Church* (Louisville, Ky.: Geneva Press, 2000); Robert E. Speer, *The Finality of Jesus Christ* (New York: Fleming H. Revell, 1933); ———, *Foreign Missions and Christian Unity* (New York: Laymen's Missionary Movement, 2001); ———, *Of One Blood, A Short Study of the Race Problem*. (New York: Council of Women for Home Missions and Missionary Education Movement of the United States and Canada, 1924); W. Reginald Wheeler, *A Man Sent from God: A Biography of Robert E. Speer* (New York: Fleming H. Revell, 1956).

Spener, Philip Jacob *See* PIETISM.

spiritual warfare

The term *spiritual warfare* refers to the use of New Testament military imagery to describe the struggles of the Christian life, from simple resistance to sin to fights against demonic forces. Basic references include Ephesians 6:12, which states, "For we wrestle not against flesh and blood but against . . . the rulers of the darkness of this world, against spiritual wickedness in high places." The appropriate response for the Christian is to "Put on the whole armor of God . . . Stand therefore having your loins girded with truth, and having on the breastplate of righteousness; and your feet shod with the gospel of peace; above all, taking the shield of faith." Such passages of "spiritual warfare" have been used throughout Christian history to inspire a life of piety and holiness.

At times, the term refers to a special ministry of casting out demons in imitation of Jesus and the apostles, part of the healing ministry of the church. While exorcisms have always been present in Christianity, they were a fringe enterprise by the 19th century. In the 20th century, secular psychology offered nonsupernatural explanations of what had been called demon possession.

However, deliverance ministry, specializing in freeing people from demonic influence and possession, has made a significant return in the contexts of spiritual healing and PENTECOSTALISM. Much of the impetus came from the mission field and the encounter with polytheistic and magical faiths. Simultaneously, spiritualism, fortune-telling, astrology, and other esoteric practices were on the rise in the West, even in a secular context.

Exorcisms made a significant comeback in the 1970s with the rise of the CHARISMATIC MOVEMENT. Among leading early spokespersons was Win Worley (d. 1994), pastor of Hegewisch Baptist Church in Chicago, a Pentecostal congregation. Worley wrote no fewer than 11 books and released more than 50 booklets, audiotapes, and videotapes on the subject. Literally hundreds of deliverance ministries have been founded in more recent years. Within these ministries, there has been a tendency to move beyond prayer for people facing dysfunctional mental and spiritual conditions; a whole range of negative life conditions, bad habits, and sinful behaviors are seen as signs of demon possession.

The rise of deliverance ministries raises serious issues for conservative Christians, especially the basic question of whether a Christian who has been delivered by the grace of God can ever be possessed. Pentecostal scholars and leaders have also criticized the ministries for placing too much emphasis on secret knowledge of the demonic world, distracting attention from Christ's healing power.

In the 1980s, the notion of territorial spirits entered the deliverance world, apparently from Latin America. Some evangelists talked about powerful demons who ruled over certain regions or territories and whose main goal was hindering people from coming to faith in Christ. In the 1970s, Frank Peretti (b. 1951) wrote two popular books, *This*

Present Darkness (1986) and *Piercing the Darkness* (1989), that treated battles with territorial spirits. A new picture of the spiritual world became popular, in which the devil assigned demons to different tasks: presiding over territories, assisting magicians and sorcerers, and possessing individuals.

In 1990, John Dawson wrote a popular treatment of the idea, *Taking Our Cities for God: How to Break Spiritual Strongholds* (1990). Fuller Theological Seminary professor Peter C. Wagner (b. 1930) also identified with the new movement in his volume *Engaging the Enemy: How to Fight and Defeat Territorial Spirits* (1991). Wagner has gone on to write several books promoting what has become known as Strategic Level Spiritual Warfare (SLSW). Adherents practice spiritual mapping by assembling information on a particular region, including the status of Christianity, any historical events that might have caused trauma, the dominant philosophies and religions, and different groups that pose spiritual opposition. All these factors become the focus of directed prayer.

Further reading: Ray Beeson, *Strategic Spiritual Warfare: An Interactive Workbook* (Nashville, Tenn.: Thomas Nelson 1995); John Dawson, *Taking Our Cities for God: How to Break Spiritual Strongholds* (Lake Mary, Fla.: Creation House, 1990); Peter C. Wagner, *Breaking Strongholds in Your City: How to Use Spiritual Mapping to Make Your Prayers More Strategic, Effective and Targeted* (Ventura, Calif.: Regal Books, 1993); ———, *Engaging the Enemy: How to Fight and Defeat Territorial Spirits* (Ventura, Calif.: Regal Books, 1991); Win Worley, *Conquering the Hosts of Hell: An Open Triumph* (Lansing, Ill.: Hegewisch Baptist Church, 1977).

Spurgeon, Charles Haddon (1834–1892)
conservative British Baptist leader and theologian

Charles Haddon Spurgeon was born on June 19, 1834, at Kelvedon, Essex, England. His father and grandfather were both Congregationalist ministers. He experienced a personal conversion to Christ at age 15. His own study of the Bible soon convinced him that there was no biblical basis for

Spurgeon's Tabernacle, where Charles Spurgeon (1834–92) preached in London *(Institute for the Study of American Religion, Santa Barbara, California)*

infant BAPTISM and at age 16 he was baptized by immersion.

He preached his first sermon at age 17 and three years later, in 1854, became pastor of New Park Street Church in London. His oratorical skills attracted large crowds to his Sunday services. On the Day of National Humiliation that followed the Indian Mutiny, Spurgeon addressed a crowd of 23,000, possibly the largest religious gathering in the history of the country. In 1861, his congregation built the Metropolitan Tabernacle, where he preached for the rest of his life.

In 1856, Spurgeon opened a Pastor's College to train Baptist leaders. He started his own magazine, *Sword and Trowel,* and his weekly sermons were published as the *Metropolitan Tabernacle Pulpit* and widely reprinted in several languages.

Spurgeon rose to prominence as Protestants were dealing with the new findings of biology and geology and with modern BIBLICAL CRITICISM, which he opposed. In another disturbing development, the British Baptist Union in 1873 dropped its former doctrinal statement to pave the way for a planned union of General Baptists (who favored ARMINIANISM) and PARTICULAR BAPTISTS (who backed strict CALVINISM).

In 1887, Spurgeon charged that the union was on the "down grade," in a state of moral and doctrinal decay. He claimed that there had been a decline in prayer meetings in the churches, that ministers had developed worldly habits such as attending the theater, and that unorthodox beliefs were being preached from Baptist pulpits, denying the Trinity, affirming universal salvation, and denigrating the authority of the Bible. Spurgeon's early articles provoked a defensive reaction from members of the union, and in November 1887, he and his Metropolitan Tabernacle withdrew.

Spurgeon refused to build another Baptist association, and few churches left the union, but he managed to keep the "down grade" controversy alive until his death on January 31, 1892. In the years since his death, Spurgeon has been admired as a leading modern exponent of Calvinism. His writings and sermons are still in print, the Metropolitan Tabernacle remains as a large London congregation, and the *Sword and Trowel* continues to appear regularly.

Further reading: Ernest W. Bacon, *Spurgeon: Heir of the Puritans* (London: George Allen & Unwin, 1967); Lewis Drummond, *Spurgeon: Prince of Preachers* (Grand Rapids, Mich.: Kregel, 1992); Charles Haddon Spurgeon, *C. H. Spurgeon Autobiography,* 2 vols. (Edinburgh: Banner of Truth Trust, 1962); ———, *Lectures to My Students* (Grand Rapids, Mich.: Zondervan, 1975).

Sri Lanka

The Dutch who held sway on Sri Lanka (formerly Ceylon) introduced the Reformed faith in 1642, but Dutch ministers made little effort to evangelize the largely Buddhist population. The British took over in 1796 and soon established colonial rule over the whole island.

The British conquest of Sri Lanka coincided with developing interest in INDIA as a missionary target among Anglicans, Methodists, and BAPTISTS in England. Ceylon was a convenient stopping place on the way to Calcutta and India's east coast. At that time, the East India Company, which controlled India by royal charter, was hostile to missionary activity. Ceylon, on the other hand, was relatively open to missionaries.

As the Anglican Church expanded, most Reformed Church members joined the CHURCH OF ENGLAND or the Roman Catholic Church. The LONDON MISSIONARY SOCIETY (Congregationalist) established work there in 1804, but as India opened it shifted personnel to the mainland and by 1818 had totally abandoned the island. The CHURCH MISSIONARY SOCIETY arrived in 1818.

The Baptists entered in 1812, when James Chater was forced out of Burma by war. He published a Ceylonese grammar in 1815. The first British Methodists, unable to settle in India, settled in Ceylon in 1814. They founded what remains one of the largest Christian communities on the island.

American Congregationalists arrived in 1816 with support from the new AMERICAN BOARD OF COMMISSIONERS FOR FOREIGN MISSIONS. They focused their work among the Tamil (Hindu) population in the northern part of Ceylon. Jaffna College, opened in 1823, was the first school to present Western-style education.

A few additional churches, such as the SALVATION ARMY, arrived later in the century. Today more than 50 DENOMINATIONS are at work in Ceylon, PENTECOSTALISM leading the way through the efforts of the ASSEMBLIES OF GOD and the INTERNATIONAL CHURCH OF THE FOURSQUARE GOSPEL.

The older Protestant churches are associated together in the National Christian Council of Sri Lanka, affiliated with the WORLD COUNCIL OF CHURCHES. Though the churches of the island have been active ecumenically, and produced a world-class leader in the person of D. T. NILES, they have not followed their Indian colleagues in creating a United Church. The Congregationalists did become a part of the Church of South India (formed in 1947) and now exist as its Jaffna Diocese. Meanwhile, the WORLD EVANGELICAL ALLIANCE established its regional affiliate, the Evangelical Fellowship of Asia, in Dehiwala, just south of Colombo, Sri Lanka's capital, and has organized a local affiliate, the Evangelical Alliance of Sri Lanka. The Protestant community in Sri Lanka includes about 2.5 percent of the population, which remains overwhelmingly Buddhist.

See also ASIA; INDIA.

Further reading: S. Douglas Franciscus, *Faith of Our Fathers: History of the Dutch Reformed Church in Sri Lanka (Ceylon)* (Colombo, Sri Lanka: Pragna Publishers, 1983); Donald Hoke, ed., *The Church in Asia* (Chicago: Moody Press, 1975); J. T. Small, *A History of the Methodist Church in Ceylon, 1814–1964* (Colombo: Wesley Press, 1971); G. P. V. Somarantna, *The Events of Christian History in Sri Lanka: A Chronology of Christianity in Sri Lanka* (Sri Lanka: Margava Fellowship of Sri Lanka, 1998); ———, *Origins of the Pentecostal Mission in Sri Lanka* (Sri Lanka: Margava Fellowship of Sri Lanka, 1996).

Stanley, Henry Morton (1841–1904)
Anglo-American journalist and explorer of Africa

Henry Stanley, who followed up on the New York *Herald's* quest to find missionary David LIVINGSTONE, with whom contact had been lost, eventually would share fame with the subject of his quest. He wrote a best-selling book and added the phrase "Doctor Livingstone, I presume!" to the popular culture.

Stanley was born John Rowlands at Denbigh, Wales, the illegitimate son of John Rowlands and Elisabeth Parry. He received a modest education at St. Asaph Workhouse, beginning at the age of five. In 1857, he ran away to sea, eventually landing in the United States. Still in his teens, he was adopted by a merchant who gave him the name by which he was later known. He became a newspaper reporter and in that capacity traveled to Turkey as a correspondent in the year immediately after the American Civil War.

Then in 1869, he accepted a commission to locate David Livingstone, who was exploring Central Africa, seeking the headwaters of the Nile and Congo Rivers. The expedition began almost two years later in East Africa. After a series of setbacks (desertion by his bearers, disease, and problems with various tribal conflicts) he located Livingstone near Lake Tanganyika in Ujiji on November 10, 1871. The pair subsequently explored the northern end of Lake Tanganyika. Stanley then returned to the United States and published his best-selling *How I Found Livingstone* (1872).

Stanley was also deeply affected by his encounter with Livingstone, and following the missionary's death in 1873 decided to continue his exploratory work. His legacy would be mixed, and his rather successful explorations would lead to the furtherance of European colonialism.

Setting out in 1874, Stanley first explored Lake Victoria, establishing it as the second-largest freshwater lake in the world. He also traced the Congo River from its source to its mouth, which set up further exploration to survey the wealth of the Congo Basin and verify that the residents could accommodate European efforts to bring them into a modern "civilized" state. Stanley's travels led directly to the establishment of the Congo Free State. In 1877, Stanley traveled the 800 miles of the Iruri River, a Central African river that joins the Congo near present day Kisangani. He continued exploring the Congo in the employ of King Leopold of Belgium until 1884.

Upon his return to the West, Stanley became a popular writer and lecturer, eventually settling in England. In 1888, he went to Africa again, this time to search for Emin Pasha (1840–92), a German explorer who in 1878 had become the governor of the southernmost province of the Egyptian Sudan. His territory had been cut off from the outside world by a revolution in the Sudan, and Stanley set out to find him. Succeeding, Stanley convinced Pasha to accompany him to Mombasa, on the Kenyan coast.

Stanley lived his last days as a celebrity in the UNITED KINGDOM, North America, and AUSTRALIA. He sat in Parliament for several years and was knighted in 1899. He died in London on May 10, 1904.

See also AFRICA, SUB-SAHARAN.

Further reading: Byron Farwell, *The Man Who Presumed: A Biography of Henry M. Stanley* (New York: Holt, 1957); Frank McLynn, *Into the Dark Continent: The Travels of Henry Morton Stanley* (London: The Folio Society, 2002); Henry M. Stanley, *The Autobiog-*

raphy of Sir Henry Morton Stanley, ed. by his wife, Dorothy Stanley (Boston: Houghton Mifflin, 1909); ———, *How I Found Livingstone: Travels, Adventures and Discoveries in Central Africa, Including an Account of Four Months' Residence with Dr. Livingstone* (New York: Scribner/Armstrong, 1872); ———, *Through the Dark Continent: Or, the sources of the Nile around the Great Lakes of Equatorial Africa, and Down the Livingstone River to the Atlantic Ocean.* (New York: Harper & Brothers, 1878).

Stockton, Betsy (c. 1796–1865) *first female African-American Protestant missionary*

Betsy Stockton was born in slavery at Princeton, New Jersey. Through several transactions, she became the property of Ashbel Green (later president of the College of New Jersey), who freed her on her 20th birthday. She remained as a hired servant. About this time, she experienced a conversion and was admitted to membership in the Presbyterian Church.

Stockton also felt a call to the foreign mission field, with Africa as her chosen target. A few years later, she was invited to accompany Rev. Charles Stewart and his wife to Hawaii under the sponsorship of the AMERICAN BOARD OF COMMISSIONERS FOR FOREIGN MISSIONS. The board accepted her, but only as a "Christian friend" under the care of the board. Once the ship carrying her to Hawaii left America, she was treated as an equal by the other missionaries. Upon landing in Maui in 1822, she established a school, the first in the islands.

Stockton's work was played down by the American Board, somewhat nervous about commissioning a single black female. In 1825, she returned to the United States and worked as a servant for the couple she had served in Hawaii. In 1837, she picked up her teaching career. She settled in Princeton around 1840 and helped lead the black members of First Presbyterian Church to establish an African-American congregation in 1846.

Stockton died on October 24, 1865, in Princeton, where she had taught school for 25 years.

Further reading: John A. Andrew III, "A. D. Recalls: Betsy Stockton, Early Missionary to Hawaii," *A. D.* (March 1976): 30; ———, "Betsy Stockton: Stranger in a Strange Land," *Journal of Presbyterian History* 52 (Summer 1974): 157–66.

Strasbourg

Soon after its appearance in Germany and SWITZERLAND, Protestantism found strong support in the Free Imperial City of Strasbourg in Alsace. Strasbourg had been a publishing center since 1459.

As early as 1522, the city council, which had in the past proved its independence of the resident Catholic BISHOP, confiscated an anti-Lutheran volume. It acted to maintain civil peace while conservatives and reformers fought for support among the people. As reformers attempted to introduce changes, they, too, had to obtain the council's approval.

The full acceptance of Protestantism was somewhat delayed by the spread of the Peasants War to Alsace. During the next several years, Martin BUCER held a variety of public debates with the ANABAPTISTS, who had found a home in Strasbourg after being driven from Switzerland. Only in 1534, after many disputations, did the council make a final choice for LUTHERANISM over the Catholic and Anabaptist alternatives.

Martin Bucer, Wolfgang Capito (1478–1541), and Caspar Hedio (1494–1552) had led the Protestant cause in the city. Bucer took a mediating position between Martin LUTHER and Ulrich ZWINGLI. He presented a compromise alternative to the AUGSBURG CONFESSION OF FAITH in 1530, termed the "Confessio Tetrapolitana," but soon withdrew it in favor of the Lutheran document. In 1536, two years after the council's acceptance of the reformers, Strasbourg adopted a unique state church organization with pastors (who preached), doctors (who taught), presbyters/ELDERS (who together with the pastors were responsible for public morale), and DEACONS (who handled charitable efforts). John CALVIN, who lived in Strasburg

(1538–41) during his brief exile from Geneva, found this POLITY to accord with his own proposals in his 1536 *Institutes of the Christian Religion,* and he copied it upon his return to Geneva.

During the Schmalkaldic War (1546–47), when Catholicism briefly reasserted it dominance throughout much of Germany, Strasbourg was forced to submit to a number of demands by the Holy Roman Emperor, including the reinstitution of Catholic religious services. Martin Bucer and other prominent Protestant leaders fled the city. Bucer spent his last years in England.

In 1551, the city accepted the Augsburg Interim, an attempt by the Holy Roman Emperor to mediate the Lutheran and Catholic positions. The interim was superseded by the PEACE OF AUGSBURG in 1555, which allowed local choice on religion (between Lutheran and Catholic faith).

Protestantism remained dominant until the 1681 annexation by Louis XIV's France. From that time, two distinct trends have been evident: the rise of French over German, and the rise of Catholicism over Protestantism. The Protestant heritage has survived in the region in two churches, the Reformed Church of Alsace and Lorraine, and the Church of the Augsburg Confession of Alsace and Lorraine. Alsace and Lorraine have the largest Protestant minorities of any region in present-day FRANCE.

Further reading: Jean-Jacques Bauswein and Lukas Vischer, eds., *The Reformed Family Worldwide: A Survey of Reformed Churches, Theological Schools, and International Organizations* (Grand Rapids, Mich.: William B. Eerdmans, 1999); G. R. Elton, *The New Cambridge Modern History,* vol. 2 (Cambridge: Cambridge University Press, 1990); D. F. Wright, *Martin Bucer: Reforming Church and Community* (Cambridge: Cambridge University Press, 1994).

Strauss, David Friedrich (1808–1874)
German theologian and historian

David Friedrich Strauss was born on January 27, 1808, in Ludwigsburg (near Stuttgart), Germany. He attended a seminary (1821–25) at Blaubeuren,

where he met Ferdinand Christian BAUR, the most important influence on his life. Strauss completed his studies at the University of Tübingen and became a Lutheran pastor at Kleiningersheim.

In 1832, Strauss became an assistant lecturer in the theological college at Tübingen, but ceased lecturing the next year in order to concentrate on a biographical study of Jesus. His book, *The Life of Jesus Critically Examined,* appeared in the fall of 1835 and immediately turned him into one of the most controversial persons in Germany. The negative response destroyed his academic career. He moved back to Stuttgart as a freelance writer. In the third edition of his book, he made a number of concessions to his critics, but these were removed in the fourth edition.

Strauss's *Life* tried to find a third way of understanding biblical miracles, especially the stories that are so integral to the Gospel accounts of Jesus. Strauss rejected what he termed the literal supernatural approach, but also rejected the rationalist approach, which saw the miracle stories as misunderstandings of mundane events, such as Jesus appearing to walk on water but actually walking on rocks just beneath the surface.

For Strauss, the events described in the miracle stories never really happened. Instead, they are messages about the spiritual significance of Jesus, using imagery from the cultural milieu of the time and place. Thus, one could point to the account of God feeding the children of Israel with manna in the desert (Exodus 16:13–36) to make a claim that Jesus is the bread of life who regularly feeds his people with spiritual food. While Strauss seemed to retain some spiritual value for the text, his approach was unacceptable to traditional believers. It undercut Christianity as a faith in an incarnate Jesus whose actions provide salvation for humanity. At the time, while widely read, Strauss proved too extreme even for liberal Protestants, who, led by Friedrich Schleiermacher, were trying to redefine Christianity as something other than a salvation-oriented religion.

Strauss's writings were later viewed as an important step in pushing forward the critical study of Gospel texts as other than simple historical accounts. While subsequent biblical scholars continued to disagree on just how historical the Gospels are, after Strauss it was impossible ever again to approach the text with the former naiveté.

In the early 1840s, Strauss withdrew from the theological arena and wrote on various biographical and historical topics. He tried to make a comeback in 1864 with his *Life of Jesus for the German People,* somewhat in the vein of popular pious books on the subject. It was attacked by the reviewers as was his next book, *The Old Faith and the New* (1872). He died in February 1874.

See also BIBLICAL CRITICISM.

Further reading: Edwina G. Lawler, *David Friedrich Strauss and His Critics: The Life of Jesus Debate in Early Nineteenth-Century German Journals.* American University Studies, series VII, Theology and Religion, vol. 16 (New York: Peter Lang, 1986); Albert Schweitzer, *The Quest of the Historical Jesus* (New York: Macmillan, 1968); David F. Strauss, *The Christ of Faith and the Jesus of History: A Critique of Schleiermarcher's Life and Jesus* (Philadelphia: Fortress Press, 1977); ———, *The Life of Jesus Critically Examined* (Philadelphia: Fortress Press, 1972); ———, *The Old Faith and the New: A Confession,* (London: Asher, 1873).

Strict Baptists *See* PARTICULAR BAPTISTS.

Student Volunteer Movement

The Student Volunteer Movement is a fellowship that had a significant impact upon world Protestantism by motivating young adults from across denominational lines to become foreign missionaries. It dates to 1886, when founder Robert P. Wilder (1863–1938) attended one of Dwight L. MOODY's summer conferences of college students at Mount Hermon, Massachusetts.

Wilder was the son of a Presbyterian missionary, Royal Wilder, who had been sidelined by poor health. Robert himself eventually attended college at Princeton, where he founded the Princeton Foreign Missionary Society. At the Mount Hermon Conference, Wilder convinced 100 attendees to sign a statement indicating their willingness to go abroad. He began to travel to different college campuses to recruit students for missionary service.

The Student Volunteer Movement (SVM) emerged in stages over the next years. Among his early recruits to the missionary cause were fellow Presbyterian Robert SPEER (1867–1947) and Samuel ZWEMER (1867–1952), a minister in the Reformed Church in America. The keystone of the SVM program was a pledge it asked students to sign: "We are willing and desirous, God permitting, to become foreign missionaries." By the time that the SVM held its first conference in 1891, it had recruited some 6,000 young people for the mission field.

In 1891, Wilder graduated from the seminary and was ordained. By this time, one of the original hundred from Mount Hermon, John R. MOTT (1865–1955) had become a charismatic leader in the SVM. Mott, national secretary of the Y.M.C.A. (*see* YOUNG MEN'S CHRISTIAN ASSOCIATION), became the chairman of SVM's executive committee and the effective American leader. He used his position with the Y.M.C.A., SVM, and later the WORLD STUDENT CHRISTIAN FEDERATION to spread the missionary vision. Wilder departed to spend a year recruiting students and building the SVM in England and Scandinavia, and then to settle in INDIA as a Presbyterian missionary.

Mott adopted as the SVM motto, "The Evangelization of the World in This Generation." Many recruits believed that by the time their ministry ended in the mid-20th century the Christian message would have been presented to every individual on earth. Mott spoke of the need for 20,000 laborers to evangelize the world. Church leaders rallied to support SVM as they accepted the idea that the students might be able to move the church into many unevangelized areas.

Most of the students recruited by the SVM were actually sent out by the mission boards of the Methodist, Baptist, Presbyterian, and Congregational churches. Thousands of others became advocates of the missionary cause in churches across America. SVM leadership helped found the World Student Christian Federation, did much of the preliminary work for the 1910 World Missionary Conference at Edinburgh, and provided the leadership for the early stages of the ECUMENICAL MOVEMENT.

SVM declined after World War I. Mott focused on ecumenical work. In 1919, Wilder became general secretary of the SVM. Against his own desires, he oversaw the group's transformation to meet a widespread critique of missions among Protestant churches. Many were concerned more for social justice than evangelism in the countries in which SVM worked, while others wrote that missionaries needed to honor the cultures among which they labored. Those who championed the older and simpler missionary approach became the minority, and the number of missionary recruits dropped considerably. The SVM officially disbanded in 1969.

Further reading: Ruth E. Braisted, *In This Generation: The Story of Robert P. Wilder* (New York: Friendship Press, 1941); John R. Mott, *The Decisive Hour of Christian Missions* (New York: Student Volunteer Movement, 1910); ———, *The Evangelization of the World in This Generation* (New York: Student Volunteer Movement, 1900); Robert P. Wilder, *The Great Commission: The Missionary Response of the Student Volunteer Movement in North America and Europe: Some Personal Reminiscences* (London: Oliphants, 1936).

Sudan Interior Mission

The Sudan Interior Mission (SIM), one of the early independent FAITH MISSIONS, began in 1893 when Walter Gowans (1868–94), Rowland Bingham (1872–1942), and Thomas Kent (d. 1894) set their sights on being the first Christian missionaries in the Sudan region of West Africa. They began work in NIGERIA, where Gowans and Kent both succumbed to the climate and died in 1894. Bingham returned to his home in Toronto, Ontario, to regroup. With new backing, he was able to estab-

lish an initial station in Nigeria in 1902; from there efforts spread to Niger, Ethiopia, and Upper Volta (Burkina Faso). From Ethiopia, SIM personnel were finally able to reach today's country of Sudan in 1936. Subsequently efforts spread to BENIN, the Central African Republic, Cote d'Ivoire, ERITREA, Ghana, GUINEA, KENYA, LIBERIA, Malawi, SENEGAL, SOUTH AFRICA, and Togo.

Meanwhile, in SOUTH AMERICA, an independent work that began in Bolivia in 1907 by a New Zealand couple evolved into the Andes Evangelical Mission. The mission grew to include work in Chile, ECUADOR, Paraguay, Peru, and Uruguay. This movement merged with SIM in 1982. Seven years later, SIM absorbed the work of the International Christian Fellowship in BANGLADESH, CHINA, INDIA, Mongolia, Nepal, the Philippines, and Pakistan. Finally, after a century of working primarily in Central Africa, in 1998, SIM joined with the AFRICA EVANGELICAL FELLOWSHIP, which brought with it work in ANGOLA, Botswana, GABON, Madagascar, Mauritius, Reunion, Mozambique, Namibia, Swaziland, Tanzania, Zambia and ZIMBABWE.

The Sudan Interior Mission changed its name in the 1980s to Serving in Mission; it is now known globally as SIM International. As the new century began, SIM supported personnel in more than 40 countries. Much of its older work has matured into autonomous churches such as the Sudan Interior Church in Sudan and the Evangelistic Church of West Africa in Nigeria.

Further reading: Rowland Brigham, *Seven Sevens of Years and a Jubilee: The Story of the Sudan Interior Mission* (Toronto: Evangelical Publishers, 1943); J. du Plessis, *A History of Christian Missions in South Africa* (Cape Town, South Africa: C. Struik, 1911, 1965); W. H. Fuller, *Run While the Sun Is Hot* (New York: Sudan Interior Mission, 1967).

Sundar Singh, Sadhu (1889–1929) *Indian Christian missionary and theologian*

Sundar Singh was born in the Rampur, Punjab, on September 3, 1889, to a Sikh mother, but as a youth he read widely in the literature of other faiths as well. He learned yoga and in his teens made the vows of a *sanyassin* (the renounced life) and began wandering through India as a *sadhu*, or holy man.

He interrupted his wandering life to attend college in Calcutta. A British colleague introduced Sundar Singh to the Bible and Christianity, but he cared for neither and became openly hostile after his graduation. However, after burning a Bible before his father, he had a transforming vision of Jesus Christ while praying in his bedroom. On his 16th birthday, in 1905, he was baptized at St. Thomas Anglican Church in Simla; however, rather than joining the congregation he decided to continue his role as a *sadhu* and wear the saffron robe of one living on the charity of others. Over his father's condemnation, he became a wandering, celibate Christian evangelist. His only possession was a New Testament. He was convinced that he could best introduce Christianity to his fellow countrymen as a *sanyassin*.

For a few months, Sundar Singh studied at the St. John School of Theology in Lahore, but then resumed his travels across the Punjab and into Afghanistan. Those who knew him dubbed him the "apostle of the bleeding feet." In 1914, while preaching in Nepal, he was arrested and thrown into a well to die for spreading another religion. He escaped and when recaptured was expelled from the country.

Sundar Singh traveled throughout India and Sri Lanka. Between 1918–19 he visited Malaysia, Japan, China, western Europe, Australia, and Israel (1920–22). His travels made him famous, at least among Western Christians. He won many friends by his effort to live a Christlike life. He continued traveling through the 1920s. Then in 1929 he set off for Tibet and was never seen again.

Sundar Singh provided a new pattern for the Indian appropriation of Christianity, one appreciated by Indians who had rejected European Christian forms. He opened Christians to the rich heritage of the Indian religions, providing a new way for the church to indigenize. Through per-

sonal meetings, correspondence, and books he influenced a number of prominent Christian leaders, from British writer C. S. Lewis to Indian bishop Aiyadurai Jesudasen Appasamy. Among Sudar Singh's books on Christian spirituality and living are: *At the Master's Feet* (1922), *Reality and Religion* (1923), *Search After Reality* (1924), *Spiritual Life* (1925), *Spiritual World* (1926), *Real Life* (1927), *With and Without Christ* (1928), and *Life in Abundance* (1980).

Further reading: C. F. Andrews, *Sadhu Sundar Singh: A Personal Memoir* (London: Hodder & Stoughton, 1934); A. J. Appasamy, *Sundar Singh: A Biography* (London: Lutterworth Press 1958); Sadhu Sundar Singh, *The Complete Works of Sundar Singh* (Madras, India: Christian Literature Society, 1986); ———, *Visions of Sadhu Sundar Singh of India* (G. Dahle, 1926; reprint, Minneapolis, Minn.: Osterhus, n.d.); B. H. Streeter and A. J. Appasamy, *The Message of Sadhu Sundar Singh: A Study in Mysticism on Practical Religion* (New York: Macmillan, 1921).

Sunday schools

Beginning as a small ministry of an English newspaperman in the late 18th century, Sunday schools became in the 20th century one of the major structures for passing Protestant teachings from one generation to the next. Robert Raikes (1735–1811) began the movement in 1780 in response to the widespread employment of children in British factories, mines, and other businesses for long hours six days a week. Sunday became a day for rowdiness that for many youths became a prelude to a life of crime. Owner of the *Gloucester Journal*, Robert Raikes at first considered the problem a social nuisance. He wanted to give the young people an education and a sense of moral involvement in society.

Raikes decided to set up a school on Sundays, the only day many children were free. He paid for four female teachers to teach the children to read. With the assistance of a local pastor, Rev. Thomas Stock, Raikes had soon enrolled some 100 children in these schools. They met from 10 A.M. to 2 P.M. for reading lessons and then received instruction in the catechism at church through the late afternoon.

Observers believed the school was soon working a marvelous transformation on the pupils. City leaders noticed a drop in the local crime rate. Raikes mobilized public support and used his printing press to publish needed school materials. By 1785, Londoners formed a Sunday school society to assist the cause. By 1786, the first such school was opened in Virginia; soon similar schools were functioning throughout the United States. The first in Canada opened in 1811.

The movement got a significant boost in 1817 with the founding of the Sunday and Adult School Union of Philadelphia, which in 1824 evolved into the American Sunday School Union, a national organization designed to found Sunday schools in needy communities and distribute literature to the teachers and their pupils. Beginning in 1844, the movement received the support of most Protestant DENOMINATIONS and spread to every part of the growing country.

In the last half of the 19th century, with the introduction of child labor laws and the spread of elementary public education, the nature of Sunday schools changed. They became primarily an instrument to instruct the next generation in the Bible, church teachings, and religious piety. For many churches, it was where children had their first religious experiences.

Among the leaders in this transformation was Methodist John Heyl Vincent (1832–1920). As a pastor, Vincent developed a variety of innovative educational techniques including the use of normal (teacher training) classes. His Sunday school teacher training spread through the Methodist Episcopal Church in the 1860s. In 1866, he published the first periodical of Sunday school lessons. His work led in 1872 to an interdenominational Uniform Lesson Plan. He soon became active in the Chautauqua movement, an early adult education effort based at Chautauqua Lake, New York, where he established a Sunday School Institute that offered two weeks of intensive leadership training.

Church Sunday schools were particularly important in the United States, where the separation of church and state kept religious education out of the public schools (a major structure for passing the faith in most European countries). The Sunday school (now generally called the church school in most denominations) has continued to evolve but remains a solid part of congregational life.

An initial World Sunday School Convention was held in London in 1889, out of which came the World's Sunday School Association, which evolved into the World Council of Christian Education in 1947. In 1971, the council merged into the WORLD COUNCIL OF CHURCHES' Office of Education. The broad acceptance of the Sunday school and the acceptance of denominational responsibility for publishing Sunday school literature made the American Sunday School Union obsolete. In 1974, it reorganized as the American Missionary Fellowship and reoriented its program to the evangelizing of unchurched persons in the United States.

PRIMITIVE BAPTISTS rejected Sunday schools as an unbiblical modern innovation. A variety of Mennonite groups rejected them as well.

Further reading: Frank Booth, *Robert Raikes of Gloucester* (Surrey, U.K.: National Christian Education Council, 1980); Anne M. Boylan, *Sunday School: The Formation of an American Institution, 1790–1880* (New Haven, Conn.: Yale University Press, 1990); John T. McFarland and Benjamin S. Winchester, eds., *The Encyclopedia of Sunday Schools and Religious Education,* 3 vols. (New York: Thomas Nelson, 1915); Leon H. Vincent, *John Heyl Vincent: A Biographical Sketch* (New York: Macmillan, 1925); Anne S. Wimberly, *Soul Stories: African American Christian Education* (Nashville, Tenn.: Abingdon Press, 1994).

Swain, Clara (1834–1910) *Methodist missionary*

Clara Swain was born in Elmira, New York, on July 18, 1834. While teaching school, she read correspondence from a female physician noting the need for more women doctors. She moved to Philadelphia to attend the Women's Medical College.

Methodist Clara Swain (1834–1910) pioneered medical missions in India. *(Drew University Library)*

In 1869, women in the Methodist Episcopal Church (now a constituent part of the UNITED METHODIST CHURCH) organized the Woman's Foreign Missionary Society, with the idea of extending the Gospel "to women by women." While still studying medicine, Swain heard of the society's plans to send a doctor to INDIA and applied for the position. She was selected and became one of the two first female missionaries commissioned by the society, the other being Isabella THOBURN.

Swain arrived in Bareilly, India, on January 20, 1870, and immediately went to work. Within the first year, she treated more than 1,300 patients and trained a number of women to assist her. Apart from a three-year furlough (1876–80), she remained at Bareilly until 1884. That year she

traveled to Khetri State in Rajputana to treat the Rani Saheba. Her treatment worked, and she was offered a position at court to attend to the health of the women and, in her spare time, operate a clinic and a girls' school. She seized the opportunity to work where Christianity was otherwise not present, without any expense to the society. She stayed in Rajputana for the next 12 years until she retired due to ill health in 1896.

Swain died on Christmas Day, 1910, in Castile, New York. The work she began in Bareilly as a clinic for women and children evolved into the Clara Swain Hospital, the oldest and largest Methodist hospital in India.

See also MEDICAL MISSIONS.

Further reading: Wade Crawford Barclay, *History of Methodist Missions,* vol. 3, *Widening Horizons, 1845–1895* (New York: The Board of Missions of the Methodist Church, 1957); Dana L. Robert, ed., *Gospel Bearers, Gender Barriers: Missionary Women in the Twentieth Century* (Maryknoll, N.Y.: Orbis Press, 2002); Dorothy Clarke Wilson, *Palace of Healing The Story of Dr. Clara Swain, First Woman Missionary Doctor, and the Hospital She Founded* (New York: McGraw-Hill, 1968).

Sweden

In 1520, the Danish king Christian II (1481–1559) entered Stockholm with his army and beheaded many members of the Swedish nobility. In response, Gustavus Vasa (1523–60) led a revolt that overthrew the Danes. Gustavus Vasa took the throne of an independent Sweden as Gustav I.

Gustav's actions coincided with the rise of the Reformation. The new Lutheran faith had an extra attraction for Gustav, as he confiscated the Catholic Church's many property holdings to pay the debts incurred in the Danish war.

In several steps through the 1520s, LUTHERANISM gained dominance: the king became head of the church; Lutheran dogma was formally endorsed; the New Testament was translated into Swedish; and a new Swedish LITURGY replaced the old Latin one. The spread of Lutheranism culminated in 1634, when a new constitution required all Swedes to adhere to the AUGSBURG CONFESSION OF FAITH.

In 1741, recognition was granted to the Anglican and Reformed (Calvinist) Churches, which primarily served expatriates living in Stockholm. In 1781, the government issued an Edict of Toleration that extended some degree of religious freedom to all who professed Christianity. The edict provided cover for the many Free Church movements that had either emerged in the country or were introduced from abroad, primarily England or the United States. Swedes began to migrate to North America in the 17th century, and by the 19th century, Americans of Swedish descent formed a sizable portion of the American Lutheran community. Swedish Americans formed several Lutheran SYNODS that have subsequently merged into the Evangelical Lutheran Church in America.

The most important of the 19th-century movements to emerge in Sweden was the Mission Covenant Church, which grew out of a revival movement initiated by Karl Olof Rosenius (1816–68). Rosenius organized people into conventicles, informal groups outside of the control of Lutheran authorities, which placed emphasis on a personal religious life. He also developed a new hymnody. Independent congregations emerged through the middle of the century, and in 1817 they established a formal organization as a new DENOMINATION. Many followers of Rosenius joined the Swedish migration to America and became the source of the Evangelical Free Church and the Evangelical Covenant Church in America.

Other groups began to populate the religious landscape, including Methodists (1826), BAPTISTS (1848), and the SALVATION ARMY (1882). The Free Church movement had a rather inauspicious beginning in 1830, when English Methodist George Scott got permission to build a "revivalist" church, Methodist in belief and practice, that remained within the Church of Sweden; Scott also began a periodical, *Pietisten*. Several years later, while in the United States, he made some comments interpreted as insulting to Swedes and was banned from the country.

PENTECOSTALISM was introduced in 1907 from Norway. The first congregation was organized in 1913. The Pentecostal congregations eschewed pan-congregational structures, but have been able to accomplish a significant amount of work with an informal fellowship. Swedish Pentecostal missionaries have, for example, been in the forefront of the spread of Pentecostalism around the world. Lewi Pethrus (1884–1974) was the most dominant voice of the movement. A Baptist who converted under the ministry of Thomas B. Barrett (1862–1940), he was for many years the pastor of the Philadelphia Church in Stockholm.

The Mission Covenant Church and the Pentecostal movement are the largest Protestant groups outside of the Church of Sweden, between them claiming as much as 10 percent of the Christian community.

Through the 20th century, significant changes have occurred in the Church of Sweden, though it retained its dominant position in society. Each person whose parents are not a member of another religious body is automatically entered on the church rolls. The church continues to assume some responsibility for the Swedish population as a whole, performing most marriages and burials. Since the introduction of a new law on religious freedom in 1951, an individual may formally withdraw from membership. While few have taken that option, several million have indicated in various surveys that they no longer consider themselves Christian and have adopted an agonistic or atheist outlook and lifestyle. The Lutheran Church of Sweden counts some 65 percent of the population as affiliated.

Through the century, the church was able to offer important leadership to the Lutheran community internationally. Several Swedish Lutheran church leaders have become widely known for their contributions to theology and ecumenism, most notably Bishop Nathan Soderblom (1886–1931), Anders Nygren (1890–1978), Gustav Aulen (1879–1978), and Archbishop Erling Eidem (1880–1972). The Swedish church was influential in the formation of the WORLD COUNCIL OF CHURCHES in 1948, and in 1968 hosted the council's fourth meeting at Uppsala. Nygren served as the first president of the LUTHERAN WORLD FEDERATION.

Further reading: L. S. Hunter, *Scandinavian Churches: a Picture of the Development of the Churches of Denmark, Norway, Finland, Iceland, and Sweden* (London: Faber & Faber, 1965); R. Murray, ed., *The Church of Sweden: Past and Present,* trans. by N. G. Sahlin (Malmo, Sweden: Alhrm, 1960); Anders Nygren, ed., *This Is the Church* (Philadelphia: Muhlenberg Press, 1952; Swedish ed., 1943); Margareta Skog, ed., *Det religiösa Sverige* (Orebro: Bokförlaget Libris, 2001).

Switzerland

Switzerland was one of the two countries where the Reformation began and from which it spread. The call for reform began in Zurich, where Ulrich ZWINGLI (1484–1531) had in 1518 been called as the people's priest for the Grossmünster or Great Church, the center of the canton's religious establishment. Under Zwingli, the Reformation spread through German-speaking cantons, though after his untimely death in 1531, the center shifted to Geneva, where John CALVIN (1509–64) took the leading role in developing French-speaking Protestantism. Calvin also offered a viable compromise interpretation of the sacraments between Zwingli's acts of remembrance and Martin LUTHER's almost Catholic sacramentalism. Calvin's solution, which affirmed Christ's spiritual presence in the sacrament, unified the various segments of Swiss Protestantism.

In the 1520s, the German-speaking cantons of Zurich, Bern, Basel, and Schaffhouse become predominantly Protestant. In the 1530s, French-speaking Neuchâtel and Geneva were added to the Protestant camp. The single Italian-speaking canton remained Roman Catholic. Geneva's peculiar role in the development of Protestantism was further accented in 1559, when Calvin founded the Academy for the training of pastors and other church leaders. It quickly developed an international student body.

Switzerland remained split between Protestant and Roman Catholic establishments at the start of the 19th century, but the country later became radically pluralistic. From the beginning of the Reformation, Switzerland had been home to dissenting Protestant Free Church groups, initially the Swiss BRETHREN and then the MENNONITES. Later the AMISH movement was begun by a Swiss Mennonite, Jacob Amman (b. c. 1644). However, serious challenges to the authority of the Reformed Church did not take place until the 19th century. Switzerland was one of the first lands into which the Plymouth Brethren movement spread, founder John Nelson DARBY having resided in the country for several years in the 1830s. It now exists in both its exclusive and open (CHRISTIAN BRETHREN) branches. The Baptist Union dates to the 1840s.

The Reformed Church had always existed as a set of different churches, one in each canton (whether the established or a minority church). In the 19th century, these churches began to cooperate more closely, resulting in the present Federation of Swiss Protestant Churches. It now includes the 22 cantonal Reformed Churches, the Evangelical-Methodist Church of Switzerland, and the Free Church of Geneva. The HELVETIC CONFESSION (1558) serves as a common statement of faith. In the 19th century, the Swiss became heavily involved in the worldwide Protestant missionary endeavor through such groups as the Basel Mission, founded in 1815. The first major break in Protestant unity in Switzerland occurred in the Canton of Vaud, where a group of Reformed ministers and members left in 1846 in protest against state intrusions into church life.

In the 20th century, a spectrum of Protestant and Free Church groups settled in Switzerland, the JEHOVAH'S WITNESSES and the Pentecostals being possibly the largest. The ASSEMBLIES OF GOD (based in the United States) now report some 25,000 members, just behind the Fellowship of Pentecostal Free Churches. Both groups were founded in the 1960s. In 1919, the Jehovah's Witnesses suffered a schism that led to the formation of the Friends of Man under Alexander Freytag (1870–1947), which has remained the largest Free Church group in the country. As many as 100 additional Protestant and Free Church groups now have congregations in Switzerland, some serving expatriate communities.

Following World War II, Switzerland took on an additional significant role in the Protestant world when the headquarters of the WORLD COUNCIL OF CHURCHES was located in Geneva. The WCC's presence further attracted the LUTHERAN WORLD FEDERATION and the WORLD ALLIANCE OF REFORMED CHURCHES to locate their headquarters and the WORLD METHODIST COUNCIL to place its European office in the same building. Although the WORLD EVANGELICAL ALLIANCE chose to locate its regional headquarters in London, it has affiliated members among the many Swiss Free Churches that organized locally into the Schweizerische Evangelische Allianz.

Switzerland divides almost equally among residents with Protestant and Catholic sympathies, with some 44 percent of the population in each group. The remaining population adheres to Eastern Orthodox Christian or non-Christian groups.

Further reading: Jean-Jacques Bauswein and Lukas Vischer, eds., *The Reformed Family Worldwide: A Survey of Reformed Churches, Theological Schools, and International Organizations* (Grand Rapids, Mich.: William B. Eerdmans, 1999); Claude Bovay, *L'évolution de l'appartenance religieuse et confessionnelle en Suisse* (Bern: Office Fédéral de la Statistique, 1997); Pamela Johnson and Robert W. Scribner, *The Reformation in Germany and Switzerland* (Cambridge: Cambridge University Press, 1993); Lukas Vischer, et al., *Ökumenische Kirchengeschichte der Schweiz* (Freiburg-Basel: Paulusverlag-F. Reinhardt, 1994).

synod

The term *synod* describes a wide variety of gatherings of church leaders for the purpose of developing policy on church life. As such, synods may be occasional and informal, or regularly held legislative bodies that create and maintain the legal structure of a church or denomination. The latter is usually the case among Protestant churches that have synods. In some churches, as with the LUTHERAN CHURCH–MISSOURI SYNOD, the highest legislative body of the church is its synod. It exists as a creature of the member congregations and has charge over the church's various national boards and agencies. As such, it is analogous to, for example, the General Conference of the UNITED METHODIST CHURCH, or the General Council of the UNITED CHURCH OF CANADA, or the General Assembly of the CHURCH OF GOD OF PROPHECY.

Within the Reformed tradition, the synod (or classis) is an intermediate structure between the presbytery, a set of congregations in close geographical proximity, and the national (or international) assembly. Typical of the Reformed tradition, the Presbyterian Church in Canada's many congregations were as of 2003 organized into 46 presbyteries, which in turn have constituted eight synods. The eight synods come together annually for the meeting of the general assembly.

The CHURCH OF ENGLAND describes itself as an episcopal body (with more than 108 BISHOPS), but it is governed by its General Synod, a delegated body that includes both laity and clergy from each diocese. The General Synod meets semi-annually to legislate on matters before the church. Other Anglican jurisdictions around the world have similar synodal structures.

See also CONSISTORY; POLITY.

Further reading: Joan S. Gray, *Presbyterian Polity for Church Officers* (Louisville, Ky.: Geneva Press, 1999); Edward Le Roy Long, Jr., *Patterns of Polity: Varieties of Church Governance* (Cleveland, Tenn.: Pilgrim Press, 2001); A. D. Mattson, *Polity of the Augustana Lutheran Church* (Rock Island, Ill.: Augustana Book Concern, 1952); J. L. Schaver, *The Polity of the Churches* (Chicago: Church Polity Press, 1947).

T

Taylor, James Hudson (1832–1905)

founder of the China Inland Mission

James Hudson Taylor was born at Barnsley, Yorkshire, England, on May 21, 1832. His father was a pharmacist, but also a Methodist local preacher. Hudson had a conversion experience at age 15 and a call to full-time Christian service. He went on to study medicine at the London Hospital, with CHINA already in mind as his field of work.

Lacking formal theological training or any other university credentials, he was turned down when he first applied to mission agencies in the early 1850s. He was also sickly. However, the newly formed and inexperienced China Evangelization Society gave him the opportunity.

Taylor spent six years (1854–60) in Shanghai, Swatow, and Ningpo. In the meantime, the China Evangelization Society disbanded, and Taylor was forced to find alternative sources while continuing as an independent missionary. During his last years in this first stay in China, he became head of a hospital in Ningpo.

Illness forced his return to England in 1860, where he translated the New Testament into the Ningpo dialect, finished his medical training, and wrote his first book, *China, Its Spiritual Need and Claims* (1865). He completed his stay by founding the CHINA INLAND MISSION (1865) and raising the first group of missionaries to go out under its auspices. In 1866, with 16 missionaries and his wife, he returned to China.

As executive director of his new agency, Taylor spent his time moving around the countryside coordinating the work of his growing staff of missionaries, and returning home to secure new recruits and raise funds. In 1888, he opened offices in North America (where he found an ally in evangelist Dwight L. MOODY) and in 1890 in AUSTRALIA. He also cooperated with missionary agencies in Europe, which sent missionaries to work under Taylor's direction. He wrote several books, including: *Union and Communion* (1893); *A Retrospect* (1894); *Separation and Service* (1898); and *A Ribbon of Blue, and other Bible Studies* (1899).

In 1900, he began to shift his responsibilities to Dixon Edward Hoste (1861–1946) and settled in SWITZERLAND. He died on a visit to China on June 3, 1905. At the time of his death, the China Inland Mission oversaw more than 900 missionaries (including wives) scattered across the country.

Like other Christian organizations working in China, the mission was thoroughly disrupted by the exile of its missionaries in 1950–51. With

James Hudson Taylor (1832–1905), founder of the China Inland Mission *(Institute for the Study of American Religion, Santa Barbara, California)*

China closed, it redirected its efforts to other countries, initially in Southeast Asia, and reorganized itself as the Overseas Missionary Fellowship (or OMF International).

See also FAITH MISSIONS.

Further reading: Cyril James Davey, *On the Clouds to China: The Story of Hudson Taylor* (London: Lutterworth Press, 1964); Marshal Broomhall, *The Man Who Believed in God: Hudson Taylor* (London: Hodder & Stoughton, 1936); Grace Stott, *Twenty-Six Years of Missionary Work in China . . . With a Preface by the Rev. J. Hudson Taylor* (London: Hodder & Stoughton, 1904); James Hudson Taylor, *A Retrospect* (London: Morgan & Scott, 1894); ———, *Union and Communion* (1893, rpt., Minneapolis, Minn.: Bethany House, 1971).

televangelism

Televangelism refers to the use of television by many evangelists to spread their message and win supporters. It came into its own in the 1970s, and revolutionized RELIGIOUS BROADCASTING.

Prior to that time, with few exceptions, religious programming on television had been limited to modest shows on weekends, usually Sunday mornings, with primarily a local or regional reach. The huge growth in the number of TV stations and improvements in technology created opportunities for independent ministers from nonmainstream DENOMINATIONS, which had previously been denied access to the networks.

In the 1960s, Pat Robertson (b. 1930) founded the Christian Broadcast Network, and in the 1970s a growing number of stations linked to CBN. Satellites and cable made it possible to cover the country with relatively inexpensive programs. With networks like CBN, soon joined by Trinity Broadcasting Network, programming could go on every day and at all hours. Both the opportunity and the need to fill 24 hours a day with programming led to the development of talk-show formats (the initial model being Robertson's *700 Club*) and the inclusion of news coverage from a Christian perspective.

The heightened presence of religious (specifically conservative Protestant) programming on television attracted widespread attention by the end of the 1970s. It became a national issue after popular television minister Jerry Falwell (b. 1932) allied himself with political activists to found the Moral Majority, in hopes of bringing alienated conservative Christians into the political process. Falwell aimed at countering legal abortions, the growing visibility of homosexuals, the abandonment of prayer in public schools, and other "liberal" phenomena.

The initial success of the Moral Majority, then the primary organization of the RELIGIOUS RIGHT, attracted scholars to examine religious broadcasting on television. Sociologist Jeffrey Hadden (1936–2003) coined the term *televangelism* in 1981. In the meantime, there was a parallel growth in Christian radio, with hundreds of new stations syndicating new national programs.

In spite of complaints that its political aspects were breaching the wall of separation between church and state, the world of televangelism grew tremendously in the 1980s. In 1988, Pat Robertson ran for the Republican presidential nomination. His failure to attract support happened to coincide with the start of a series of scandals when Robertson associate Jim Bakker (b. 1940) was accused of adultery and major financial mismanagement, the very successful Jimmy Swaggart (b. 1935) was accused of sexual misconduct, and several lesser scandals were aired. Falwell dissolved the Moral Majority. Though superseded by a new Christian Coalition, the political clout of the televangelists never returned to its pre-1988 level.

Nevertheless, Christian television survived the temporary loss of financial support and emerged in the mid-1990s stronger than ever. As the new century began, both CBN and TBN had adapted successfully to cable television; both were broadcast worldwide via cable and satellite.

Measuring the size of the Christian television audience is difficult; measuring its usefulness as an evangelism tool is even more so. However, there is little doubt that it supplies weekday religious entertainment for millions of dedicated conservative Christians and that it has, in secular terms, added a diversity of ideas to the popular culture.

Until the 1990s, the televangelism phenomenon was largely confined to the United States. In the 1990s, however, its international potential was being exploited. Cable has enabled religious broadcasting to reach countries that otherwise block such programs from broadcast stations, often government owned. Among the more recent additions, in January 2004 the SEVENTH-DAY ADVENTIST CHURCH began broadcasting to Europe via a new satellite vehicle, the Hope Channel.

Further reading: Steve Bruce, *Pray TV: Televangelism in America* (London: Routledge, 1990); Jerry D. Cardwell, *Mass Media Christianity: Televangelism and the Great Commission* (New York: University Press of America, 1984); Jeffrey K. Hadden and Charles E. Swann, *Prime Time Preachers: The Rising Power of Televangelism* (Reading, Mass.: Addison-Wesley, 1981); ———, and Anson Shupe, *Televangelism: Power and Politics on God's Frontier* (New York: Henry Holt, 1988); Stewart M. Hoover, *Mass Media Religion: The Social Sources of the Electronic Church* (Newbury Park, Calif.: Sage, 1988).

Temple, William (1881–1944) *Anglican theologian and church leader*

William Temple was raised in the CHURCH OF ENGLAND; his father, Frederick Temple, served as bishop of London (1885–92) and archbishop of Canterbury (1892–1902). After studying at Oxford, Temple taught philosophy there at Queen's College (1907–10), during which time he was ordained a priest. In 1908, he became headmaster of Repton School and four years later began a lengthy tenure as rector of St. James Piccadilly, a large church in central London. While at St. James, he wrote the first of his several books, *Mens Creatrix* (1917). He was a strong advocate of greater self-governance for the Church of England and won a partial victory in 1919 when the church's assembly was established.

Temple was named bishop of Manchester in 1921, archbishop of York in 1929, and archbishop of Canterbury in 1942. He wrote his most important book while at York, *Nature, Man, and God* (1934), originally delivered as the Gifford Lectures at the University of Glasgow.

Temple's ecumenical career began in 1924 with his chairmanship of the Conference on Christian Politics, Economics and Citizenship that met in Birmingham, England. In 1928, he drafted the statement accepted by the Jerusalem Missionary Conference. He went on to chair the 1937 FAITH AND ORDER CONFERENCE in Edinburgh in 1937, where it was decided to found the WORLD COUNCIL OF CHURCHES. The next year he was elected chairman of the first provisional conference to create the WCC.

Temple died during World War II.

Further reading: F. A. Iremonger, *William Temple, Archbishop of Canterbury, His Life and Letters* (Oxford: Oxford University Press, 1948); William Temple, *Christus Veritus* (London: Macmillan, 1924); ————, *Mens Creatrix* (London: Macmillan, 1917); ————, *Nature, Man and God* (London/New York: Macmillan/St. Martin's, 1934).

The Evangelical Alliance Mission (TEAM)

The Evangelical Alliance Mission, one of the early independent FAITH MISSIONS, was founded in 1890 as the Scandinavian Alliance Mission of North America. It grew out of the ministry of Fredrik Franson (1852–1908), who was born and raised in SWEDEN. A capable student, he became fluent in several languages prior to his migrating at the age of 17. He became a farmer in Nebraska. During a period of illness, he began the search for salvation that led him to the Baptist Church, in which he was baptized at the age of 20. Several years later, having become interested in evangelism, he moved to Chicago and joined Dwight L. MOODY's church.

In 1875, Franson set out as an evangelist among the Swedes of Minnesota. He then spent several years in Utah before returning to Nebraska in 1880. The next year, he was ordained by the Evangelical Free Church. He then worked in Europe for the rest of the decade. Responding to the call of Hudson TAYLOR for people to go to CHINA, Franson developed a plan to form missionary sending agencies in different European countries. By 1890, he had founded six such agencies, including the Danish Mission Confederation, the Swiss Alliance Mission, the Finnish Alliance Mission, and the Swedish Alliance Mission, which continue to the present.

Back in the United States in 1890, Franson held an initial Bible and missionary course for individuals who were desirous of missionary service. This course occasioned the formation of the Scandinavian Alliance Mission. Hundreds of missionaries were sent out to ASIA, Africa, and SOUTH AMERICA. Impressed by the work of Hudson Taylor and George MÜLLER, Franson built the alliance on similar principles of faith in God's support for the work.

TEAM headquarters in Wheaton, Illinois *(Institute for the Study of American Religion, Santa Barbara, California)*

Franson died in 1908, but the work he started has continued, and as the new century began, TEAM supported more than 800 active missionaries scattered in some 22 different countries.

Further reading: Vernon Mortenson, *God Made It Grow: The History of T.E.A.M.* (Pasadena, Calif.: William Carey Library, 1994); Edvard P. Torjesen, *Fredrick Franson: A Model for Worldwide Evangelism* (South Pasadena, Calif.: William Carey Library, 1983); David B. Woodward, *Aflame for God: Biography of Frederick Franson, Founder of the Evangelical Alliance Mission* (Chicago: Moody Press, 1966).

Thoburn, Isabella (1840–1901) *early Methodist missionary in India*

Thoburn was born near St. Clairsville, Ohio, on March 29, 1840. Her brother, James Thoburn, went to INDIA as a missionary in 1859 and once there began to encourage his sister to join him.

Isabella began her adult life as a schoolteacher. She responded favorably to the idea of going to India, but waited until she could receive the approval of the church. She was in correspondence with the women who founded the Methodist Woman's Foreign Missionary Society and was at the top of the list when they began to commission missionaries for service abroad. Thoburn and Clara SWAIN, the first two missionaries authorized by the society, arrived in Bombay (now Mumbai) in 1870.

Thoburn went immediately to her post in Lucknow. Three months after her arrival, she opened a girl's school in the Lucknow bazaar. The following year, the society purchased a seven-acre estate, formerly a palace, for her use. She turned the palace into a boarding school. Thoburn worked in Lucknow for more than three decades, concentrating much of her educational and evangelizing efforts among the women of the zenanas (harems).

On visits home, Thoburn traveled across the country, speaking on behalf of the Indian mission. She also served for a year (1887–88) at the DEACONESS house and taught in the Chicago Training

Isabella Thoburn (1840–1901), a pioneer female missionary in India *(Drew University Library)*

School, both organized by Lucy Rider Meyer (1849–1922), who pioneered deaconess activity in Methodism.

Upon her return to India, she discovered that her boarding school had evolved into a Girls' High School (1887). At her suggestion, it soon added a college department, and later a teachers' course and a kindergarten (1893). Thoburn picked up her duties as principal and also began a semimonthly Hindi-language newspaper, *Rafiq-i-Niswan* (*Woman's Friend*). Meanwhile, her brother, James, had been named India's first Methodist bishop in 1888.

In 1895, the Indian government granted Thoburn a charter for a full woman's college. Lucknow Woman's College opened in 1896 as the first Christian institution of higher education for women in ASIA. She headed the college and her efforts thereafter were largely devoted to its development and support. Thoburn died in Lucknow on September 1, 1901. The college she founded was renamed in her honor in 1903. It would later became the woman's college of Lucknow University.

Further reading: Marjorie A. Dimmitt, *Isabella Thoburn College* (Cincinnati: World Outlook Press, 1962); William F. Oldham, *Isabella Thoburn* (Chicago, Jennings & Pye, 1902).

Thomas, John (1796–1881) *pioneer Methodist missionary to the South Pacific*

John Thomas was born in Worcester, England, and became a blacksmith. Converted by Methodist preaching, he felt a call to the mission field after reading about Henry MARTYN. Thomas traveled to Tonga (then called the Friendly Islands) in 1826, arriving as part of a company that included himself, a Tasmanian, a British associate, James Hutchinson, and their wives. He remained in Tonga for 25 years.

Thomas learned the language quickly, made friends with the chief and leaders of the people, and engaged in evangelism. His work had an initial success in 1831, when Chief Taufa'ahau, who ruled one of the northern Tongan islands, and his wife accepted BAPTISM. Later, Taufa'ahau, who took the name Siaosi or George at his baptism, united the Tongan Islands under his leadership through a series of wars. Thomas participated in his enthronement in 1845 as the first king of all Tonga. He also supported the king's policy of sending Tongan missionaries to Fiji and Samoa.

Thomas remained in Tonga until 1850. He then returned to England for four years before going back to Tonga when the mission was transferred to the Australian Methodists. He remained in Tonga another six years and then retired to England.

See also SOUTH PACIFIC.

Further reading: Shalamit Decktor Korn, "After the Missionaries Came: Denominational Diversity in the Tonga Islands," in J. Boutilier, D. Hughes, and S. Tiffany, eds., *Mission, Church, and Sect in Oceania*, ASAO Monograph 6 (Ann Arbor: University of Michigan Press, 1978); Sarah Farmer, *Tonga and the Friendly Islands* (London: Hamilton, Adams, 1855).

three-self principles

The three-self principles were an early statement of the view that Protestant missions in non-Christian countries should aim to be independent of the mother churches in Europe or the New World. This idea became the majority view in the second half of the 20th century, as mission churches became indigenized all over the world.

The idea was originally advanced by three prominent Protestant missionaries—Henry Venn (1796–1873), Rufus Anderson (1796–1880), and John L. NEVIUS. For more than 30 years, Venn served as the honorary secretary of the CHURCH MISSIONARY SOCIETY (1841–72). Venn believed missionaries should aim to set up local churches that would be "self-governing, self-supporting, and self-extending." As an Anglican, he opposed setting up missionary dioceses, or naming bishops, before a local following had developed. He argued that foreign missionaries should quickly turn over control to local leadership.

Operating as an executive for the AMERICAN BOARD OF COMMISSIONERS FOR FOREIGN MISSIONS in Boston, Rufus Anderson arrived at essentially the same ideas as Venn. He argued for a focused and purposeful missionary program whose only goal was the creation of a scriptural, self-propagating Christianity. Missionaries were to seek the conversion of the lost, organize them into churches, train a competent local ministry, and lead the congregations to a stage where they became self-propagating. Any other activities were superfluous and even distracting. By the end of the 1860s, he was clearly articulating the three-self principles.

John Nevius was a Presbyterian missionary who further developed the three-self idea while working in CHINA and KOREA. The key to making the three-self principles work, he believed, was teaching converts to become a witness for Christ among their neighbors and coworkers. The building of local leaders meant that churches would not be dependent on foreign funds for their survival and growth.

Churches were often reluctant to give control of their missions to local leaders. But with the decolonization and other changes brought by World War II, the idea became unavoidable. During the war, many churches had been forced into self-sufficiency; most of them demonstrated their readiness for self-governance. After the war, the end to colonization was frequently accompanied by the transformation of missions into autonomous churches.

As a philosophy, the three-self principles survived most visibly in China. The Communist government expelled all foreign missionaries in 1950, and in 1954 forced the Protestant churches to merge into a single body, the Three-self Patriotic Movement of Protestant Churches in China. Ostensibly formed to break church reliance on foreign money, influence, and leadership, the movement was actually designed to train leaders in patriotism (support for the government) and to facilitate communication between the government and the Christian community. In 1966, as the Cultural Revolution began and the government attempted to destroy Christianity, the Three-self Movement was disbanded. It was reorganized in 1980. Its main role is to articulate new government policies regarding religion. On a more positive note, it has helped foster the sense that the contemporary Chinese Protestant church is an indigenous body and no longer a branch of a foreign institution.

Further reading: Gerald H. Anderson, ed., *Mission Legacies: Biographical Dictionary of Christian Missions* (Grand Rapids, Mich.: Eerdmans, 1998); Scott W. Sunquist, ed., *A Dictionary of Asian Christianity* (Grand Rapids, Mich.: William B. Eerdmans, 2001); Philip L. Wickeri, *Seeking Common Ground: Protestant Christianity, the Three-Self Movement and China's United Front* (Maryknoll, N.Y.: Orbis Books, 1988).

Ting, K. H. (Ding, Guangxun) (b. 1915)
Protestant church leader in Communist China

K. H. Ting was born in Shanghai in 1915, the son of a banker and grandson of an Anglican priest. He attended St. John's University in Shanghai and received a B.D. (1942) and M.A. (1948) at Union Theological Seminary in New York City. He was ordained a priest in 1942. He pastored the International Church in Shanghai during the Japanese occupation. Returning to the West after the war, he was for a period the student secretary of the Student Christian Movement in Canada and worked for the WORLD STUDENT CHRISTIAN FEDERATION in Geneva.

Ting returned to CHINA in 1951, shortly after Western missionaries had been expelled. The postrevolutionary government in China moved swiftly to consolidate the various Protestant DENOMINATIONS into a single body that was structured through several organizations, including the three-self patriotic movement. Ting was elected to its first national committee in 1954. In 1962, he was named president of the Nanjing Union Theological Seminary, previously sponsored by a variety of denominations.

During the Cultural Revolution, when all public religious practice was banned, Ting and his wife, Kuy Siu-may, were kept under close observation in modest quarters where they had been relocated. He and several other faculty members were for a time engaged by the government in translating documents, and he worked on a new English-Chinese dictionary.

In the late 1970s, as the Cultural Revolution died out and religious activity was once again tolerated, Ting emerged into prominence. He attended the Third Assembly of the World Conference on Religion and Peace, held at Princeton, New Jersey, in 1979. In 1981, he resumed leadership of the reopened Nanjing Theological Seminary. He was elected president of both the revived three-self movement and the China Christian Council. He led in the creation of the *Chinese Theological Review* in 1985, and that same year became president of the Amity Foundation, a new

Christian organization created to embody a variety of good works, from education, to social and health services, to rural development across China.

In 1995, Ting retired as leader of the China Christian Council and the three-self movement. In 2000, the Amity Foundation presented Ting Amity's 25-millionth copy of the Bible.

Further reading: Alan Hunter and Kim-Kwon Chan. *Protestantism in Contemporary China* (Cambridge: Cambridge University Press, 1993); K. H. Ting, "A Call for Clarity: Fourteen Points from Christians in People's Republic of China to Christians Abroad," *China and Ourselves* 24, 1 (February, 1981); ———, *A Chinese Contribution to Ecumenical Theology: Selected Writings of Bishop K. H. Ting,* ed. by Janice and Philip Wickeri (Geneva: WCC Publications, 2002); ———, *No Longer Strangers: Selected Writings of K. H. Ting* (Maryknoll, N.Y.: Orbis Books, 1989).

total depravity

The doctrine of total depravity is a perspective within Protestantism about the consequences of humanity's fall into sin. All Christians believe that humans are fallen, but they disagree over the nature and extent of the state. Within the Calvinist tradition, the prevailing view is that humanity has been so corrupted that individuals cannot of themselves make any decision or do any act that would lead them to believe the Gospel and manifest faith in Christ. God has chosen to save some individuals and offers his grace to them. That grace, being irresistible, leads to faith and response in those who receive it.

From the viewpoint of total depravity, the image of God, in which humans were created (Genesis 1:26), has almost completely disappeared and needs total regeneration. Other Christian viewpoints maintain that the image of God still remains to some degree; while humans need God's assistance to believe, that assistance is available to all.

The doctrine of total depravity enabled CALVINISM to maintain its Reformation faith that salvation was the work of God, not of humanity. Not even faith itself, or any human response to the message of salvation, could be seen as a human contribution to God's saving work.

Total depravity is part of a complex of doctrines affirmed by Calvinists, including unconditional election, LIMITED ATONEMENT, irresistible grace, and the perseverance of the saints, that are collectively known as the five points of Calvinism.

Further reading: A. W. Pink, *Gleanings from the Scriptures, Man's Total Depravity* (Chicago: Moody Bible Institute, 1969); David N. Steele and Curtis C. Thomas, *The Five Points of Calvinism: Defined, Defended, Documented* (Phillipsburg, N.J.: Presbyterian & Reformed Press, 1963).

transubstantiation

Transubstantiation refers to the change in the elements of bread and wine into the body and blood of Christ during the Eucharist, according to Roman Catholic belief.

Christian doctrine has presented various explanations of Christ's presence in the sacraments, especially in the Eucharist, which most Protestants term the LORD'S SUPPER. In the centuries immediately preceding the Reformation, the concept of transubstantiation was introduced, and by the 16th century it had become the dominant theory within the Roman Catholic Church.

In Catholic doctrine, when the words of institution (consecration) are spoken, the substance of the bread and wine are changed into the substance of Jesus Christ, such that the LITURGY of the Mass reenacts the actual crucifixion of Christ. The idea is most easily explained in terms of Aristotle's philosophy. In looking at any object, according to Aristotle, one could distinguish between its substance and its accidents. That is, if one looked at a chair, the substance was what made it a chair. Chairs, however could have many attributes (accidents)—color, texture, size, number of legs, general appearance. In like measure, bread may have many accidents—color, taste, texture—all of which can be distinguished from its substance, its breadness. During the Mass, Catholics believe that when the words of institution are spoken, though the accidents remain unchanged, the substance of bread becomes the substance of the body of Christ. The priest's authority to officiate at the Mass when such change occurs derives ultimately from Christ; it was conveyed through the apostles to the successive bishops of Rome (the popes), and through them to the bishops of the Roman Catholic Church.

Protestants rejected transubstantiation as well as the idea that the Mass was a new sacrifice of Christ, but they disagreed as to what actually did happen during the Lord's Supper, Martin LUTHER suggested the idea of CONSUBSTANTIATION, by which he was able to keep the idea of a real presence, but hoped to remove the magical element implied if the priest caused the change by pronouncing the words of institution. Protestants in the tradition of Ulrich ZWINGLI tended to suggest that the Lord's Supper was simply a memorial meal. John CALVIN attempted to mediate the two positions by suggesting that Christ was present spiritually in the elements and perceived by faith.

In England in the 16th century, Protestants claimed to notice a similarity between a common phrase used by jugglers and conjurers, "hocus pocus," and the words of institution in the Latin Mass, "Hoc est corpus" (this is my body). In the 1690s, Archbishop of Canterbury John Tillotson (1630–94) tied the two phrases together as part of an anti-Catholic polemic, the implication being that the Mass was so much nonsense.

Further reading: Adolf Adam, *The Eucharistic Celebration: The Source and Summit of Faith* (Collegeville: The Liturgical Press, 1994); Louis Bouyer, *Eucharist: Theology and Spirituality of the Eucharistic Prayer,* trans. by C. U. Quinn (Notre Dame, Ind.: Fides, 1968); *Lutherans and Catholics in Dialogue: IV: Eucharist and Ministry* (Published jointly by Representatives of the U.S.A. National Committee of the Lutheran World Federation and the Bishops' Committee for Ecumenical and Interreligious Affairs, 1970).

Trans World Radio

Trans World Radio broadcasts Christian programs to most of the world, through a series of powerful, strategically placed transmitters. It grew out of the concern of Paul Freed (1918–96), a worker for Youth for Christ, about the situation of Protestants in Spain in the 1950s. Having documented persecution from Catholic authorities under the regime of Francisco Franco (1892–1975), he raised funds to start a radio station in Tangiers, Morocco, to broadcast into Spain. It opened in 1954 as the Voice of Tangiers, and quickly expanded to other countries far beyond Spain. By the end of the decade it was reaching ROMANIA, HUNGARY, and even the Soviet Union.

In 1959, Tangiers came under the control of the Muslim-led Moroccan government, which closed down the station. The station moved its operation to Monaco and changed its name to Trans World Radio. As the station grew, the number of languages in which programming was offered steadily increased. It was eventually heard across Europe, North Africa, and the MIDDLE EAST. A network of studios emerged in different countries to produce shows that were taped and flown to Monaco for broadcast.

In the 1970s, Trans World opened a facility on the island of Bonaire, off the Venezuelan coast, to broadcast programming to SOUTH AMERICA and the CARIBBEAN, and in 1978 began broadcasting to the Indian subcontinent from SRI LANKA. An additional facility was opened on Guam to reach into CHINA.

As the 21st century began, the facilities built around Trans World's 13 primary transmitting sites and satellite hook-ups reach about 80 percent of the world's population. The station broadcasts more than 1,800 hours of Christian programming a week to more than 160 countries in some 180 languages.

See also RELIGIOUS BROADCASTING.

Further reading: Ben Armstrong, *The Electronic Church* (Nashville, Tenn.: Thomas Nelson, 1979); Norah Freed, *Cupped Hands: on Trans World Radio*

From Monte Carlo (London: Trans World Radio, 1981); Paul E. Freed, *Towers to Eternity: the Remarkable Story of Trans World Radio as Told by Its Founder* (Cary, N.C.: Trans World Radio, 1994).

True Jesus Church

The True Jesus Church is a Sabbatarian Pentecostal church founded in CHINA early in the 20th century. SABBATARIANISM had been introduced into China in 1847 by missionaries of the Seventh-day Baptists Church (who centered their work on Shanghai) and was given further impetus by Seventh-day Adventists arriving in 1888. PENTECOSTALISM was introduced in 1907, when Alfred A. Garr and his wife, Lillian Garr, arrived in Hong Kong and began preaching among Congregationalists. The movement quickly became indigenous, and within a few years Mok Lai Chi became its effective leader. A few years later the first Pentecostals reached Shanghai.

Among the first people to find their way to the Shanghai Apostolic Faith Church was Lin-Shen Chang (d. 1935), a Presbyterian DEACON, who began a quest for the BAPTISM OF THE HOLY SPIRIT. This did not occur during his initial period of study with the congregation, but later in the year at home. At the same time he began to speak in tongues, he received a revelation about observing the Sabbath.

Several years later, Paul Wei (d. 1919), associated with the LONDON MISSIONARY SOCIETY (Congregationalist) in Beijing, became seriously ill; he regained his health through the prayer and LAYING ON OF HANDS at the local Pentecostal fellowship. Subsequently, while praying at his home, he, too, received the baptism of the Holy Spirit and spoke in tongues. The experience led him to found a house church. During a subsequent time of fasting, Wei received an additional revelation about water baptism, that it should be in the name of Jesus Christ alone, "head bowed in the living water." At this time, one segment of the larger Pentecostal movement had also come to believe in baptism by the name of Jesus alone, the JESUS

ONLY PENTECOSTALS. The Pentecostal Assemblies of the World (PAW) had accepted this idea, which meant abandoning traditional teachings about the Trinity. PAW had begun sending missionaries to China in 1914.

Wei began preaching services under the name International Reformed Jesus True Church. In 1917, the name was shortened to True Jesus Church. The next year, Lin-Shen Chang made his way to the True Jesus Church, where he met Paul Wei and convinced him that the church should observe the seventh-day Sabbath. Today, Wei, Chang and another early worker, Barnabas Chang, are seen as the founders of the True Jesus Church. Paul Wei died in 1919, and Lin-Shen Chang later defected from the movement, leaving Barnabus Chang as leader.

As the church developed, other unique elements were added to its Sabbatarian "Jesus Only" perspective. It accepted the two ordinances of BAPTISM and the LORD'S SUPPER, but also the third ordinance of FOOT WASHING. It taught that baptism, done in response to God's command, cleanses the believer of sin, a position known as baptismal regeneration. The regenerating power of baptism was confirmed in the accounts of healing miracles that occurred to people as they were baptized. The proper mode of baptism is full immersion while the believer's head is bowed. Only those who have been baptized can receive the Lord's Supper, or Holy Communion.

Within the True Jesus Church, speaking in tongues usually occurs as a group act, with all engaging in prayer at the same time. Those speaking in tongues often vibrate or move under the influence of the Spirit, though in an orderly manner. The primary function of tongues is self-edification, hence there is no need to limit the number who speak.

The True Jesus Church spread quickly in China, and reached Hong Kong, Taiwan (then under Japanese control), SINGAPORE, and Malaysia before the end of the 1920s. In the 1930s, missionaries began work in JAPAN, KOREA, INDONESIA, and even Hawaii.

Like all Chinese churches, the True Jesus Church was disrupted by the changes in government following the revolution of 1949. Within China, the church was merged into the Church of Christ of China, though keeping a somewhat distinctive presence as its members gathered on Saturday rather than on Sunday. Then the entire church was suppressed in 1966 during the Cultural Revolution. In 1967, church leaders from the other countries met in Taiwan for the first World Delegates Conference, which accepted the task of coordinating the movement outside of China. An international headquarters was established in Taichung, Taiwan, where a seminary was opened. The headquarters was subsequently moved to California in 1985, and four regional evangelical centers were established to coordinate the work in different parts of the world—America, Europe, northeastern Asia, and Southeast Asia.

As the 21st century began, the True Jesus Church reported a membership of 1.5 million in 29 countries. The majority of them still reside within the People's Republic of China, where they are part of the single Protestant church under the leadership of the China Christian Council. The True Jesus Church is the third-largest Protestant church in Taiwan.

See also CHINA: TAIWAN.

Further reading: F. F. Chong, *One True God* (London: TJC Press, 1998); *Q & A on the Basic Beliefs* (Garden Grove, Calif.: True Jesus Church, Department of Literacy Ministry, 2000); Murray A. Rubinstein, "Evangelical Spring: The Origin of the True Jesus Church on Taiwan, 1925–1926," *Society for Pentecostal Studies Annual Papers* (1986); John Yang, *Essential Biblical Doctrines* (Garden Grove, Calif.: Word of Life, 1997).

Tsizehena, John (c. 1840–1911) *early Protestant convert and evangelist on Madagascar*

John Tsizehena had his first exposure to Christianity through missionaries sent by the CHURCH MISSIONARY SOCIETY. While seriously ill, Tsizehena had a deathbed vision of Christ followed swiftly by his recovery. The event solidified his commitment to the growing Anglican community.

At a later date, Tsizehena moved to the northern region of Madagascar, which was not connected to the Anglican community at the time. He began evangelizing in the region, without any formal commissioning. As he gathered converts into a congregation at Namakia, he instituted Anglican liturgical formats following the order of the BOOK OF COMMON PRAYER. As the work grew, he identified himself as the Rt. Rev. Lord Bishop of the North and made some clerical and even episcopal clothing to identify his role in the community. He also recruited other evangelists to expand the work, and as the "bishop" took it upon himself to baptize believers and ordain ministers. For services not included in the prayer book, he composed his own liturgies.

Shortly after the turn of the century, Tsizehena began negotiations with Anglican officials concerning the integration of his "diocese" into the larger Anglican community in Madagascar. Those negotiations were successfully consummated, and Tsizehena's church now forms one of the three dioceses on the island, all of which belong to the Church of the Province of the Indian Ocean.

See also AFRICA, SUB-SAHARAN.

Further reading: B. A. Bow, "John Tsizehena: A Self-ordained Malagasy Bishop," *Journal of Religious History* (Australia) (December 1976): 158–72; A. Scott Moreau, ed. *Evangelical Dictionary of World Missions* (Grand Rapids, Mich.: Baker Book House, 2000).

Turkmenistan

Turkmenistan became independent with the breakup of the Soviet Union in 1991. A traditionally Muslim land, Turkmenistan received Eastern Orthodox Christianity over the century of Russian rule.

Protestantism entered Turkmenistan in the 1890s. A Baptist, I. K. Savl'ev, and a Mennonite, F. S. Ovsyannikov, moved from RUSSIA to Ashkhabad, the Turkmen capital. They founded the new village of Kuropatkinsky nearby and built the first Baptist church. After several decades of peaceful existence, the small church was targeted by Soviet officials in the 1930s. The movement survived, however, and experienced a small revival in the 1990s, though there are only three congregations. They have been joined by Adventists and Pentecostals, who enjoyed a brief period of growth in the mid-1990s.

Through the 1990s, the government had shown itself hostile to all religious groups apart from Islam and Russian Orthodoxy. In 1996, it passed a law requiring religious communities to have 500 members before they could apply for registration, but officials have been reluctant to allow Protestant groups of whatever size to register. Protestants have been subject to discrimination and even persecution. Their meeting houses have been vandalized, and a few, such as the Adventist church in Asigabad, destroyed. Private homes used for worship have been confiscated and individual Protestants have been fined, imprisoned, beaten, and deported for continuing to practice their faith. In 1999, Shageldy Atakov, a Baptist pastor, was sentenced to four years in jail.

Various U.S. government agencies have warned of a deteriorating situation for religious liberties and have urged Congress to apply sanctions.

See also CENTRAL ASIA.

Further reading: David Barrett, *The Encyclopedia of World Christianity,* 2nd ed. (New York: Oxford University Press, 2001); Patrick Johnstone and Jason Mandryk, *Operation World, 21st Century Edition* (Carlisle, Cumbria, U.K.: Paternoster, 2001); Albert W. Wardin, ed. *Baptists Around the World* (Nashville, Tenn.: Broadman & Holman Publishers, 1995).

Tutu, Desmond (b. 1931) *Anglican leader who helped overturn apartheid in South Africa*

Desmond Tutu was born on October 7, 1931, at Klerksdorp, Transvaal. He was educated at Pretoria Bantu Normal College and the University of South Africa and became a high school teacher.

However, he pursued studies in theology and was ordained to the priesthood in 1960.

Tutu continued his education in England (1962–66), receiving divinity and theology degrees from Kings College, CAMBRIDGE UNIVERSITY. Returning to his homeland, he taught theology at the Federal Theological Seminary in Alice and at the University of Botswana, Lesotho and Swaziland. On a second visit to England, he served for three years as the associate director of the Theological Education Fund of the WORLD COUNCIL OF CHURCHES.

Starting in the 1970s, he began to break down many of the barriers keeping black people out of church leadership in SOUTH AFRICA. In 1975, he was the first black appointed dean of St. Mary's Cathedral in Johannesburg. The next year, he was elected as a bishop and served two years as head of the diocese of Lesotho. In 1978, he became the first black general secretary of the South African Council of Churches (SACC).

Tutu turned the SACC into his forum and used his position there (1978–85) to speak out against apartheid and assist the victims of the South African system. Though many of the all-white churches withdrew, SACC became a singularly important voice of South African Christianity. Attempting to silence him, the South African government denied him the right to travel internationally, but relented in the face of international criticism. In 1984, Archbishop Tutu was given the Nobel Peace Prize in recognition of his fight against racism.

Following the disintegration of the apartheid system, Tutu was showered with a series of honors. In 1985, he was elected bishop of Johannesburg and the following year became archbishop of Cape Town. In 1987, he became president of the All African Conference of Churches and a fellow of Kings College.

Through the 1990s, Tutu was a principal voice of reconciliation during the process of government changes that brought President Nelson Mandela to office in South Africa. In December 1995, Mandela appointed Tutu to chair the Truth and Reconciliation Commission in South Africa.

Archbishop Desmond Tutu (1931–   ) (far right) has emerged as an international spokesperson for the liberation of people in every country. *(Institute for the Study of American Religion, Santa Barbara, California)*

Tutu retired from the office of archbishop of Cape Town in 1996. He remains a voice calling for cooperation between the various segments of South African society and for an end to the violence and corruption that continues to haunt the country in the post-apartheid era.

Further reading: Shirley du Boulay, *Tutu, Voice of the Voiceless* (London: Penguin Books, 1989); Dickson Mungazi, *In the Footsteps of the Masters: Desmond M. Tutu and Abel T. Muzorewa* (Westport, Conn.: Greenwood Press, 2000); Buti Tlhagale, *Hammering Swords into Ploughshares: Essays in Honor of Archbishop Mpilo Desmond Tutu*, ed. by Buti Tlhagale and Itumeleng Mosala (Grand Rapids, Mich.: William B. Eerdmans, 1986); Desmond Tutu, *Crying in the Wilderness: The Struggle for Justice in South Africa*, ed. by John Webster. (Grand Rapids, Mich.: William B. Eerdmans, 1982); ———, *The Rainbow People of God: The Making of a Peaceful Revolution*, ed. by John Allen (New York: Doubleday, 1994).

25 Articles of Religion *See* ARTICLES OF RELIGION.

Tyndale, William (c. 1494–1536) *English Reformation scholar and Bible translator*
William Tyndale was born in Gloucestershire, United Kingdom, probably in 1494. He won a B.A. in 1512 from Magdalen Hall (now part of Hertford

College) at Oxford University and his M.A. three years later. He appears to have been ordained a Roman Catholic priest around 1521. Fluent in several languages including Greek and Latin, Tyndale was also quite conversant with the Bible. As the Reformation on the Continent proceeded, he followed it closely and came to agree with its major ideas.

Tyndale decided to translate the BIBLE into English and make it available to everyone. To that end, he left England for Germany and in Hamburg spent time with some prominent Jews, mastering Hebrew. His English New Testament was published in 1525–26, much to the ire of King HENRY VIII, at the time still a staunch Catholic in belief and practice. Copies of Tyndale's New Testament were smuggled into England, his work being the first English Bible translated from the original Greek.

Tyndale went into hiding, but continued his translation work, the next goal being the Pentateuch. From 1527 through the mid-1530s, he was assisted by another British exile, Miles COVERDALE. The Pentateuch appeared in 1530, followed by the book of Jonah the following year. Also appearing in 1530 was *The Practice of Prelates,* a volume that criticized Henry VIII's divorce. Henry asked the Holy Roman Emperor to have Tyndale arrested and sent back to England.

In 1534, as Henry separated from the Catholic Church, Tyndale came out of hiding and settled in Antwerp, Belgium. He continued his translating and also began to preach in what was still largely Catholic territory. Eventually, his location was discovered by a British spy, and he was arrested and confined in a castle near Brussels. Tried for heresy/treason (the two charges being at times indistinguishable), he was condemned and on October 6, 1536, executed by strangulation before his body was burned at the stake. Coverdale carried on a Tyndale's work and brought out a complete English Bible in 1538.

See also BIBLE TRANSLATION.

Further reading: David Daniell, *William Tyndale: A Biography* (New Haven, Conn.: Yale University Press, 1994); A. G. Dickens, *The English Reformation,* 2nd ed. (University Park: Pennsylvania State University Press, 1992); Donald Dean Smeeton, *Lollard Themes In the Reformation Theology of William Tyndale* (Ann Arbor, Mich.: Edwards Brothers, 1986, vol. VI, Sixteenth Century Essays and Studies); *Tyndale's New Testament.* William Tyndale's 1534 translation, in modern spelling, ed. by David Daniell (New Haven, Conn.: Yale University Press, 1989); *Tyndale's Old Testament. William Tyndale's 1531 Translation of Genesis to 2 Kings, in Modern Spelling,* ed. by David Daniell (New Haven, Conn.: Yale University Press, 1992).

U

Uchimura Kanzo (1861–1930) *prominent Japanese evangelist*

Uchimura Kanzo was born in Tokyo on March 23, 1861. While studying at the Sapporo Agricultural School, he became a Christian and was baptized in 1878 by Methodist missionary Merriman Colbert Harris (1846–1921). Following his graduation in 1881, he took a government job. As a Christian layman, he helped found the Sapporo Independent Church and the Sapporo Y.M.C.A. (*see* YOUNG MEN'S CHRISTIAN ASSOCIATION).

In 1884, Uchimura went to the United States. He had an intense religious experience while studying at Amherst College and entered Hartford Seminary, where he studied for a year. Upon his return to JAPAN, he taught school for several years. He became well known in the 1890s for his Japanese books, such as *Comfort for the Christian Believer* and *Spirit of Mission Work,* and articles, especially "Why I Became a Christian" (later translated into English).

In 1897, he moved to Tokyo. Uchimura held to a conservative Evangelical faith, but remained intensely independent. He advocated his own brand of Christianity called Mukyokai (nonchurch movement), and for many years led a weekly Bible study class in his home. With two colleagues, Nakata Juji and Kimura Seimatsu, he founded the Second Coming of Christ movement in 1919. In 1922, he founded World Missionary Cooperation, which sent evangelists to CHINA, Taiwan, and the South Sea islands.

In 1926, he started an English-language periodical, *The Japan Christian Intelligencer,* which widened his already broad influence in religious circles in Japan. Two years after his death on March 28, 1930, a set of his collected works began to appear. His epitaph is often quoted, "I for Japan; Japan for the World; The World for Christ; And All for God."

Further reading: Hiroshi Miara, *The Life and Thought of Kanzo Uchimura* (Grand Rapids, Mich.: William B. Eerdmans, 1997); Kanzo Uchimura, *The Complete Works of Kanzo Uchimura, vol. 7, Essays and Editorials* (Tokyo: Kyobunkwan, 1973), text in Japanese and English; ———, *The Diary of a Japanese Convert* (New York: Fleming H. Revell, 1895).

Uganda

Uganda became the target of European religious concern in the 1860s, when missionary explorer David LIVINGSTONE first visited. On his famous trip to locate Livingstone, reporter Henry STANLEY took note of the slow movement of Islam southward from the Sudan into Uganda, and upon his return to the West he alerted the Protestant leadership of that fact. The Anglican CHURCH MISSIONARY SOCIETY (CMS) responded quickly and had missionaries on the ground by 1877. They found the way already prepared for them by Dallington Maftaa, an African commissioned as a missionary by Livingstone.

Alexander M. Mackay (1849–90) led the CMS team; within two years, all his colleagues perished from the climate. Mackay established close relations with King Mutesa of Buganda, who wanted British help to stop the encroachments from the north. But after Mutesa died, his successor, Mwanga, came to resent Christian opposition to some of his rulings, and he had at least 250 Anglicans and Catholics killed. A Muslim coup in Buganda in 1888 forced MacKay from the country.

About that time, the European powers allotted Uganda to British control as a protectorate. British authority was established on the ground in 1893. In the succeeding years, Anglicans vied with Catholics for religious influence in Uganda. By the end of the 20th century, each community numbered between 7 and 8 million members, accounting for about two-thirds of the country's residents. Both faiths saw schismatic groups emerge. Former Anglicans founded the Society of the One Almighty God (1914) and the Chosen Evangelical Revival (1967). Catholics lost members to the Maria Legio of Uganda in the 1960s and to the Movement for the Restoration of the Ten Commandments in the 1990s. The latter group came to a violent end in a tragic mass murder in 2001, the exact circumstances of which remain unknown.

A wide variety of groups appeared in Uganda throughout the 20th century. The SEVENTH-DAY ADVENTIST CHURCH began work in 1926, and the SALVATION ARMY in 1931. PENTECOSTALISM came in 1935 through the efforts of the Pentecostal Assemblies of Canada; the several Pentecostal churches count a total of several million adher-

ents. AFRICAN INITIATED CHURCHES from KENYA, such as the AFRICAN ISRAEL CHURCH, NINEVEH, have also become an important element in Uganda's religious life.

The Anglicans have formed a Joint Christian Council that includes Catholics and Orthodox. It is affiliated with the WORLD COUNCIL OF CHURCHES.

Uganda became independent of Britain in 1963. In 1971, a military officer, Idi Amin (c. 1925–2003), instituted a brutal dictatorship that negatively affected all religions for the remainder of the decade. In 1973, Amin accused some 28 Christian DENOMINATIONS of subversive activity and banned them from the country. Some of them sought protection through the Anglican Church, and others went underground. Amin's government killed or exiled some 400,000 people. In 1977, the Anglican archbishop was murdered, it is believed by Amin personally. The bloody purge of the preexisting Anglican leadership ended only with Amin's overthrow in 1979, when the religious situation gradually returned to normal.

See also AFRICA, SUB-SAHARAN.

Further reading: W. B. Anderson, *Christianity in Contemporary Africa: Uganda* (Kampala, Uganda: Department of Religious Studies and Philosophy, Makerere University, 1973); E. T. Rutiba, *Religions in Uganda, 1960–1990* (Kampala, Uganda: Department of Religious Studies, Faculty of Arts, Makerere University, 1993); John V. Taylor, *The Growth of the Church in Uganda. An Attempt at Understanding* (London: SCM Press, 1958); A. D. T. Tuma and P. Mitibwa, *A Century of Christianity in Uganda, 1877–1977* (Nairobi, Kenya: Uzima Press, 1978).

unconditional election

Unconditional election means that those elected by God for salvation cannot do anything of their own will to advance or hinder that choice. Together with the concepts of TOTAL DEPRAVITY, LIMITED ATONEMENT, irresistible grace, and the perseverance of the saints, it is one of the "five points of CALVINISM." It is intimately connected with the idea of PREDESTINATION.

According to Calvinism God, in his plan for human salvation, predetermined and foreknew exactly who would receive his grace and as a result turn in faith and believe in Christ. The SYNOD OF DORT proclaimed that "Election is the unchangeable purpose of God."

From its inception, Protestantism has been identified with the view that God's saving grace is separate from all human efforts to do good or to merit salvation. It rests in part on Paul's Epistle to the Romans 8:29–30: "For whom he did foreknow, he also did predestinate to be conformed to the image of his Son." The formulation of the doctrine of unconditional election and its four related Calvinist points was an attempt to preserve that view as the new church grew.

Those Christians who have opposed the doctrine often charged that it denies human free will and hence human responsibility. If nothing we can do either wins or loses God's favor, they say, then nothing that we do really matters. Many of these critics believe that God elected humanity in general; the duty of individuals is to act upon that election and make it effective in their life.

The doctrine of unconditional election carries with it a set of corollary beliefs: (1) from among fallen humanity, God has arbitrarily chosen to save a fixed number; (2) election is made quite apart from any merit associated with the individuals so chosen; (3) one so chosen cannot reject that election. A minority of Calvinists add another corollary: God has decreed that those left unchosen have been selected for damnation. Those who supported ARMINIANISM specifically rejected that view.

Further reading: Loraine Boettner, *The Reformed Doctrine of Predestination* (Philadelphia: Presbyterian & Reformed Press, 1965); John Owen, *The Works of John Owen,* 16 vols. (London: The Banner of Truth Trust, 1963); David N. Steele and Curtis C. Thomas, *The Five Points of Calvinism: Defined, Defended, Doc-* umented (Phillipsburg, N.J.: Presbyterian & Reformed Press, 1963).

Unitarianism

The word *unitarian* means one who believes in the oneness of God; historically it refers to those in the Christian community who rejected the doctrine of the Trinity (one God expressed in three persons). Non-Trinitarian Protestant churches emerged in the 16th century in ITALY, POLAND, and TRANSYLVANIA. One of the early Unitarians, Michael SERVETUS (1511–53), was martyred for his opinions. The Unitarian SOCINIANS grew strong for a period in Poland, but were eventually engulfed by the Counter-Reformation. Socinian publications appear to have made their way to England, where they inspired English non-Trinitarian writing and the founding of a few independent Unitarian congregations among the Puritans.

Prior to the 19th century, those espousing a non-Trinitarian form of Christianity encountered intense hostility. The Trinity and the divinity of Jesus Christ are foundational to Christianity. However, in the 19th century, a new Unitarian movement emerged that found some important support from intellectuals and a more tolerant public.

This new impulse is generally attributed to William Ellery Channing (1780–1842), a Congregationalist minister, though he was not the first to discuss non-Trinitarian ideas. In 1805, for example, the appointment of Henry Ware to a position at the Harvard Divinity School prompted some strict Trinitarians to withdraw and found a new seminary at Andover. A decade later, concern over Unitarian departures from orthodoxy prompted Rev. Jedediah Morse (1761–1826) to write a pamphlet, "Are You of the Christian or the Boston Religion?" A more liberal minister issued a rejoinder, "Are you a Christian or a Calvinist?"

Following his graduation from Harvard in 1798, Channing underwent a spiritual and theological struggle that led him through skepticism about Christianity to a reformulated theology that did not include the Trinity. He also questioned the doctrines of total depravity and believers' election to salvation. In 1803, he became pastor of the Federal Street Church (Congregational) in Boston, but he did not publicly announce his alignment with non-Trinitarian Congregationalists until 1819, when he laid out his beliefs in the ordination sermon for a young minister.

The sermon elevated Channing to the informal position of leader of the Unitarians. It provoked many Congregational churches across New England to hold votes and split over the issue of the Trinity. In most cases, the minority party withdrew from the congregation and formed a separate church. In this manner, Unitarian Congregational churches appeared, first in New England and then in other parts of the country. In 1825, a convention of Unitarian congregations was held, which founded the American Unitarian Association.

The association, especially in the 20th century, became home to increasingly radical approaches to religion. Attempts were made to formulate a universal religion apart from specifically Christian beliefs and practices. Some members accepted intellectualized forms of other traditional religions and eventually nontheistic religious perspectives (most notably HUMANISM).

In 1961, out of a recognition that Unitarianism and UNIVERSALISM had evolved along similar paths and reached largely the same conclusions about religion and the religious life, the American Unitarian Association and the Universalist Churches of America merged to form the Unitarian Universalist Association (UUA). The UUA has by now eliminated all evidence of its Protestant roots and no longer considers itself a specifically Christian organization.

Further reading: John Buehres, *The UUA Pocket Guide* (Boston: Unitarian Universalist Association, 1999); David B. Parke, *The Epic of Unitarianism* (Boston: Unitarian Universalist Association, 1980); John Sias, *100 Questions That Non-members Ask about Unitarian Universalism* (Nashua, N.H.: Transition, 1994); Robert B. Tapp, *Religion among the Unitarian Universalists: Converts in the Stepfather's House* (New York/London: Seminar Press, 1973).

United Church of Canada

The United Church of Canada (UCC) continues the traditions of the Methodists, Presbyterians, and Congregationalists in Canada. It was formed in 1925 by the merger of the Methodist Church (Canada, Newfoundland, and Bermuda), the Congregational Union of Canada, the Presbyterian Church in Canada, and the General Council of Union Churches of Western Canada. A minority of the Presbyterians did not accept the merger and continued under the former name. The UCC was an early expression of ecumenism; hopes of further consolidation toward a united Protestant church in Canada never materialized.

The articles of faith included in the 1925 Basis of Union represented the consensus beliefs of the merging bodies. A new "Statement of Faith" was approved in 1940, and a brief "New Creed," adaptable for liturgical use, was approved in 1968. In 2000, the General Council asked the Committee on Theology and Faith to prepare a statement acknowledging both the theological diversity of the church and the pluralistic world in which it operates. The church is solidly in the liberal Protestant camp, and accepts modern BIBLICAL CRITICISM.

The church is divided into regional conferences that meet annually, and district presbyteries that have oversight of congregations in their area. The structure features elements from the three uniting churches, balancing the demands of CONGREGATIONALISM and presbyterian POLITY. The UCC continues to work with churches around the world that derived from its historic missions, providing funds and personnel for a spectrum of projects.

The UCC was the first denomination in Canada (and among the earliest in the world) to ordain women (1936). In 1980, Lois Wilson became the first woman moderator. It also led the way in liberalizing rules on the remarriage of divorced persons (early 1960s) and in 1988 began ordaining gay and lesbian persons.

The UCC is the largest Protestant body in Canada, with some 660,000 confirmed members. In recent surveys, more than 3 million Canadians identify themselves as affiliated with it. Church headquarters are in Etobicoke, Ontario. The UCC helped organize the Canadian Council of Churches (1944) and was a charter member of the WORLD COUNCIL OF CHURCHES in 1948. It is also a member of the WORLD ALLIANCE OF REFORMED CHURCHES and the WORLD METHODIST COUNCIL.

See also WOMEN, ORDINATION OF.

Further reading: Steven Chambers, *This Is Your Church: A Guide to the Beliefs, Practices and Positions of the United Church of Canada,* 3rd ed. (Toronto: United Church Publishing House, 1993); Shirley Davy, *Women Work & Worship in the United Church of Canada* (Toronto: The United Church of Canada, 1983); John Webster Grant, *The Canadian Experience of Church Union* (London: Lutterworth Press, 1967); Peter Gordon White, ed. *Voices and Visions: Sixty-five*

Years of the United Church of Canada (Toronto: United Church Publishing House, 1990).

United Church of Christ

The United Church of Christ (UCC) is an American denomination founded in 1957 by the merger of the Congregational Christian Churches and the Evangelical and Reformed Church. It embraces perhaps the most diverse set of traditions of any American denomination, including New England Puritan CONGREGATIONALISM, the frontier RESTORATION movement, German LUTHERANISM, and German Reform (CALVINISM).

The UCC sees itself primarily as a continuation of the Puritan Congregationalism of early New England. Their congregational POLITY was developed in Massachusetts in intimate relationship with the

Missionaries of the American Board established a number of churches in Hawaii, including this one, the Hau'ula Congregational Church, in rural Oahu. *(Institute for the Study of American Religion, Santa Barbara, California)*

local government, and the Congregationalists remained the established church in Massachusetts into the early 19th century. Nevertheless, due to their congregational polity (local autonomy), the church became home to a broad spectrum of theological opinions. Unitarianism grew within its ranks but eventually split off into its own body. In the late 19th century, Congregationalists took the lead as spokespersons for various liberal causes from the SOCIAL GOSPEL to a theological accommodation to evolution. The denomination was eventually organized as the National Council of the Congregationalist Churches.

Early in the 19th century, the Massachusetts Congregationalists took a leading role in the global spread of Protestantism by founding the AMERICAN BOARD OF COMMISSIONERS FOR FOREIGN MISSIONS. It survives today as the UCC Board of Global Ministries, which maintains contact with the many former mission churches founded by the American Board.

In the post–Revolutionary War era, the Restoration movement emerged in different parts of the country. It encompassed groups of churches that shared a congregational polity and an aversion to denominational labels. They called themselves simply Christian churches. Unlike the Congregationalists, they had no tradition of government ties. In 1833, representatives from many of these churches held a convention, which is generally considered the start of the Christian Church as a denomination. It was this church that in 1931 merged with the National Council of the Congregationalist Churches to become the General Council of the Congregational Christian Churches.

The Evangelical Synod of North America was an immigrant import of the church created by King Ludwig of Prussia in 1817 by merging the Lutheran and Reformed Churches in his realm. One resource the church drew upon to make the union work was PIETISM, a form of Lutheran thought that emphasized personal devotion over strict doctrinal proscriptions. Pietism in Prussia

also produced a new burst of energy for Bible and missionary societies.

The same Pietist spirit had produced the Basel Missionary Society, which sent almost 300 ministers to German-American communities in the Midwest beginning in the 1830s. In 1840, a group of these ministers met in St. Louis and formed the German Evangelical Church Society of the West, which over the next decades evolved into the Evangelical Synod of North America.

The Reformed Church in the United States traced its history to colonial Pennsylvania. While most of the people who accepted William PENN's invitation to settle there belonged to Free Church groups, thousands of people identified with the German-speaking Reformed Church also arrived. In the 1730s, Michael Schlatter (1716–90) roamed through Pennsylvania at the behest of the Dutch Reformed Church in New York to help the scattered German churches form a network. His work bore fruit in 1747 with the formation of the Reformed Ministerium of the Congregations of Pennsylvania, which evolved into the Reformed Church in the United States.

In 1934, the Evangelical Church and the Reformed Church united to create the Evangelical and Reformed Church, which soon began negotiations to merge with the Congregational Christian Churches. Despite opposition on the Congregational side, the merger was completed in 1957.

The United Church incorporates elements of both Congregationalism and Presbyterianism. The General Synod is the highest policy-making body. The church has affirmed its standing in the Reformed theological tradition, though the 1959 statement of faith is open to interpretation. The church is one of the most socially liberal denominations and was the first American church to ordain openly gay and lesbian ministers.

The church is headquartered in Cleveland, Ohio. As the new century began, it reported 1.4 million members. It is a member of the WORLD COUNCIL OF CHURCHES and the WORLD ALLIANCE OF REFORMED CHURCHES. In 1995, its Board of World Ministries merged with the Division of Overseas

Ministries of the Christian Church (Disciples of Christ), to create a new Board of Global Ministries serving congregations in both churches. The merger was a sign of the communion between the two groups that had been growing for several decades.

Further reading: David Dunn, et al., *A History of the Evangelical and Reformed Church* (Philadelphia: Christian Education Press, 1961); Louis H. Gunnemann, *The Shaping of the United Church of Christ* (New York: Thomas Nelson, 1971); ———, *United and Uniting* (Cleveland, Ohio: Pilgrim Press, The United Church Press, 1987); Douglas Horton, *The United Church of Christ* (New York: Thomas Nelson, 1962); J. William Youngs, *The Congregationalists* (Westport, Conn.: Greenwood Press, 1988).

United Kingdom

Protestantism gained its first foothold in the British Isles thanks to King HENRY VIII's search for a male heir. His divorce of the Catholic Catherine of Aragon brought a break with the pope and the Roman Church. The many English nobles and churchmen leaning toward Protestantism, including Archbishop of Canterbury Thomas CRANMER, used the opportunity to push Henry and the newly independent CHURCH OF ENGLAND in their direction.

It was under EDWARD VI (r. 1547–53) that Protestantism took firm hold within the church. After a brief Catholic restoration under MARY I (r. 1553–58). ELIZABETH I (1558–1603) gave to the British church its unique stance, the VIA MEDIA between Catholicism and CALVINISM. The Church of England would have BISHOPS, a vernacular LITURGY (as found in the BOOK OF COMMON PRAYER), and a distinctly Calvinist flavor in its formal statement of faith. This compromise faith became known as ANGLICANISM, which was imposed on Wales and Ireland as well.

Events had developed differently in Scotland, where John KNOX led the Scottish church to adopt the Reformed faith and POLITY he had absorbed as

St. Paul's Cathedral, London, is a leading center of Anglicanism. *(Institute for the Study of American Religion, Santa Barbara, California)*

an exile in Geneva. The Church of Scotland became Presbyterian, and those who aligned themselves with the Church of England remained in the minority, eventually forming a Scottish Episcopal Church.

The church under Elizabeth and her successors faced continual pressure from PURITANISM, supported by Calvinists who sought to abolish the episcopacy in favor of a Presbyterian polity (with a few advocating CONGREGATIONALISM). The Presbyterians came to power in the 1640s under Oliver CROMWELL and the Commonwealth. Anglican order, belief, and practice were replaced with the system embodied in the WESTMINSTER CONFESSION OF FAITH and the two Westminster catechisms.

The shifts in British religious life, however, came to an end with the return of a king to rule England in 1660 and the restoration of Anglicanism, which subsequently remained the dominant faith in England and Wales. Puritan dissent survived in the Presbyterian, Congregational, and Unitarian Churches. Congregationalism would find its strongest support in Wales.

During the 1600s, another dissenting group appeared, the BAPTISTS. They favored adult BAPTISM and rejected any attempt to tie the church to the state. The most radical movement, however, was the QUAKERS, whose members insisted on following their Inner Light along with Bible teachings.

Some dissenting groups, unable to make headway in England, relocated to the new British settlements overseas, most notably the Congregationalists in Massachusetts and the Quakers in Pennsylvania. Simultaneously, the Anglican Church began an organized effort to provide services for its members outside of England, leading to the formation of the first two international missionary organizations at the end of the 17th century, the SOCIETY FOR THE PROPAGATION OF THE GOSPEL IN FOREIGN PARTS and the SOCIETY FOR PROMOTING CHRISTIAN KNOWLEDGE, both of which continue to supply personnel and literature to Anglicans worldwide.

Puritanism had sought to infuse a personal faith in its followers; their leaders periodically launched efforts to revive faith in what they saw as spiritually dead churches. Various efforts through the 17th century culminated in the careers of the WESLEY brothers, John and Charles, and their singular effort to revive the nation in the mid-1700s through the Methodist movement.

METHODISM was intimately connected with the MORAVIAN CHURCH, and from it absorbed an interest in foreign missions. In the 1770s, Methodist preachers were dispatched to the British American colonies, where after the American Revolution an independent Methodist Church arose in the new United States. Thomas COKE, who John Wesley sent to America to set up the new church, pioneered a vision of a world missionary movement.

Coke presented his plan for a global mission to his Methodist colleagues in 1784; its enactment turned Methodism into a global presence.

A few years after Coke, in 1792, William CAREY helped found the Baptist Missionary Society to send missionaries overseas. Eventually, a set of denominational missionary agencies arose, from the LONDON MISSIONARY SOCIETY (1796), which worked among several Calvinist churches, to the CHURCH MISSIONARY SOCIETY (1799, Anglican). In the middle of the 19th century, independent faith missions, such as the CHINA INLAND MISSION, began to form. England became the most important center for the global spread of Protestantism through the 19th century.

In IRELAND, support for Catholicism became identified with the aspiration of the Irish to throw off British rule. Catholicism was legalized in 1829, and the Church of Ireland (Anglican) was disestablished in 1869. Through the 1870s, most church parishes reverted to Catholicism and the Church of Ireland became a minority church. Even in Protestant Northern Ireland, Anglicans fell behind the Presbyterian Church, which had grown strong from Scottish migration into the region.

Throughout the 20th century, the Church of England, its Anglican sister, the Church of Wales, and the Presbyterian Church of Scotland formed a structure that blanketed the United Kingdom with a Protestant Christian presence, though surveys have shown a steady decay of support. The old dissenting churches that originated in the Puritan and Methodist movements also seemed to be loosing membership. At the same time, England became home to the wide spectrum of Protestant and Free Church organizations so identified with the United States. Numerous small Christian communities—HOLINESS, Pentecostal, Adventist, and Evangelical—emerged. In addition, a variety of groups from former British colonies (especially JAMAICA and NIGERIA) also entered the country. Methodism was by no means the last of the revival/revitalization movements to emerge in Great Britain. The Christian story was dotted with efforts such as the ALBURY CONFERENCES, the KESWICK MOVEMENT, the 1905 revival in Wales that heralded the arrival of PENTECOSTALISM, and the CHARISMATIC MOVEMENT of the late 20th century. Each of the revivals produced new Protestant denominations.

In a countertrend, the older British churches were enthusiastic supporters of the ECUMENICAL MOVEMENT. The various Methodist groups formed in the 19th century reunited in the METHODIST CHURCH in 1932; Presbyterian and Congregational churches merged in stages into the Reformed Church of the United Kingdom; and most of the schismatic Scottish Presbyterians rejoined the Church of Scotland. Besides these three churches and the Church of England, no less than a half-dozen more UK-based churches are members of the WORLD COUNCIL OF CHURCHES. Other unity efforts include the Churches Together in Britain and Ireland, Churches Together in England, and the Afro-West Indian United Council of Churches.

Evangelicals are also active in England. The Evangelical Alliance of the United Kingdom adheres to the European Evangelical Alliance (with which it shares headquarters in London) and through it to the WORLD EVANGELICAL ALLIANCE.

As the new century began, the Church of England (and its sister Anglican churches) retained the allegiance of some 44 percent of the public in the United Kingdom. Roman Catholics approached 10 percent with the remaining Protestants making up about 12 percent. There is a significantly high nonreligious community (about 11 percent), though it is not as large as other European countries such as Denmark and the Czech Republic. At the same time, the Church of England and other older churches carry a large number of nonpracticing Christians on their rolls.

Further reading: D. W. Bebbington, *Evangelicalism in Modern Britain: A History from the 1730s to the 1980s* (London: Unwin Hyman, 1989); Peter Brierley, *"Christian" England: What the English Church Census Reveals* (London: MARC Europe, 1991); *The Church of England Yearbook* (London: Church Publishing House, published annually); Grace Davie, *Religion in Britain since 1945* (Oxford: Blackwell, 1994); Sheridan Gilley and W. J. Sheils, eds., *A History of Religion in Britain: Practice and Belief from Pre-Roman Times to the Present* (Oxford: Blackwell, 1994); Roy Kerridge, *The Storm Is Passing Over: A Look at Black Churches in Britain* (London: Thames & Hudson, 1995); Paul Weller, ed. *Religions in the UK: A Multi-Faith Directory* (Derby, U.K.: University of Derby/Inter Faith Network for the United Kingdom, 1993).

United Methodist Church

The largest Methodist body in the world, and the original parent of many other Methodist churches around the world, the United Methodist Church was formed in the United States in 1968 by the merger of the METHODIST CHURCH with the Evangelical United Brethren. Both had been the products of earlier mergers.

METHODISM in America can be traced to immigrants who came from the British Isles in the 1760s. Baltimore, Leesburg (Virginia), New York City, and Philadelphia emerged as the first centers of activity. Originally conceiving his movement as a revitalization effort within the CHURCH OF ENGLAND, John WESLEY moved to create an independent Methodist Church in the United States after the American Revolution. He dispatched several superintendents with authority to ordain ministers; the new church took the name Methodist Episcopal Church. At the founding conference in 1784, the ministers selected Francis ASBURY (1745–1816) as their first bishop.

Beginning with just a few thousand members, the church became the largest religious body in the country within a few decades, despite facing a number of schisms. Many AFRICAN-AMERICAN METHODISTS left the church to found the African Union Church (now the African Union Methodist Protestant Church), the African Methodist Episcopal Church, and the African Methodist Episcopal Zion Church. Today, the latter two churches

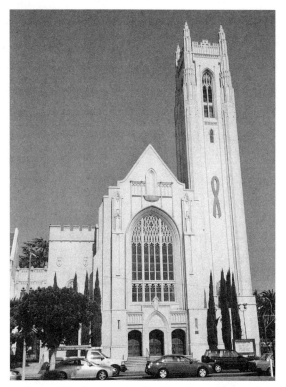

Hollywood United Methodist Church, Hollywood
California *(Institute for the Study of American Religion,
Santa Barbara, California)*

each have more than a million members. In 1830, a group rejecting episcopal leadership formed the Methodist Protestant Church.

In 1844, a crisis developed when a bishop from Georgia was discovered to be a slaveholder. The church divided into two jurisdictions, which became known as the Methodist Episcopal Church (MEC) and the Methodist Episcopal Church, South (MECS). The bulk of the African-American members still in predominantly white Methodist organizations were slaves in the Deep South. Following the Civil War, the southern church facilitated the movement of these members into an autonomous Colored Methodist Episcopal Church, now the Christian Methodist Episcopal Church.

During the early 20th century, both the MEC and MECS became staunch members of the Fed-

eral Council of Churches and felt the ecumenical pressure to overcome their division. In 1939, joined by the Methodist Protestant Church, they merged to form the Methodist Church.

During its formative years, Methodist thought and practice influenced many German-speaking Americans, most of whom had either a Lutheran, Reformed, or Mennonite background. The result was two new Methodistlike denominations, the Evangelical Association and the United Brethren in Christ. These two groups, having dropped the remnants of their German-speaking past early in the 20th century, merged in 1946 to form the Evangelical United Brethren.

The United Methodist Church retains the doctrinal statements of both the Methodist Episcopal Church and the Evangelical United Brethren. They include the affirmations of early Christianity and of the Protestant Reformation, and the Twenty-five ARTICLES OF RELIGION sent by John Wesley to America, which were taken directly from the Anglican Thirty-nine Articles of Religion. The founding churches that constituted the United Methodist Church were all identified with liberal Protestantism and its emphasis on ecumenism, social action, and a modern recasting of theological affirmations.

The United Methodist Church retains its episcopal POLITY. Adult members of each church elect the local officers; they also choose one or more delegates to the regional annual conference, consisting of all ordained ministers in a given area and an equal number of lay delegates. Annual conferences are grouped into five regional jurisdictions that meet to elect BISHOPS. The bishop presides over the annual conference, and in consultation with the district superintendents appoints ministers to their posts for the next year. The annual conference elects a designated number of ministerial and lay delegates to the quadrennial General Conference, the highest legislative body in the church.

Since its founding in 1968, the United Methodist Church, like most liberal Protestant denominations, has experienced a significant loss of membership, moving from 11 million to

8.3 million in 2002. Of the larger Protestant groups, it is spread most evenly across the United States, with at least one congregation in more than 95 percent of the counties in the country. Most of its former mission affiliates have become fully autonomous churches, but it still retains a membership across Europe, Africa, and Asia.

Further reading: Richard P. Heitzenrater, *Wesley and the People Called Methodists* (Nashville, Tenn.: Abingdon Press, 1995); Anna Ledbetter and Roma Wyatt, eds., *World Methodist Council, Handbook of Information, 2002–2006* (Lake Junaluska, N.C.: World Methodist Council, 2003); John G. McEllhenney, ed., *United Methodism in America: A Compact History* (Nashville, Tenn.: Abingdon Press, 1992).

United Pentecostal Church, International

The United Pentecostal Church, International (UPCI) is the largest denominational body of non-Trinitarian or JESUS ONLY PENTECOSTALS. The Jesus Only perspective emerged in Los Angeles in 1913, and by 1918 won over the Pentecostal Assemblies of the World.

In 1924, most white members of the church withdrew to found three different organizations. After a series of further splits and mergers, the majority of white Oneness or Jesus Only groups merged in 1945 to form the United Pentecostal Church. With its growth worldwide, it more recently added the word *international* to its name.

The UPCI holds most of the beliefs of PENTE-COSTALISM, but differs in that it believes in the One God, whose name is Jesus, and baptizes members in the name of Jesus, rather than in the name of the "Father, Son, and Holy Spirit." The church also practices FOOT WASHING as an ordinance. The church is officially pacifist (*see* PACIFISM) and recommends conscientious objection to its members.

The UPCI is congregational in POLITY, but has developed a national and international organiza-tion that carries out tasks such as education nd foreign missions. Oneness missionaries were already active outside of the United States by 1945, but since the formation of the UPCI, the church has made missions a priority. By 2004, it was active in 170 nations serving some 3 million members in 28,000 church centers.

As of 2004, the UPCI reported 4,142 churches, 8,801 ministers, and a constituency of a half million in North America. The international headquarters is at Hazelwood (suburban St. Louis), Missouri.

Further reading: David K. Bernard, ed., *The Oneness of God* (Hazelwood, Mo.: Word Aflame Press, 1997); Arthur L. Clanton and Charles E. Clanton, *United We Stand, Jubilee Edition* (Hazelwood, Mo.: Word Aflame Press, 1995); Ford Foster, *Their Story: 20th Century Pentecostals* (Hazelwood, Mo.: Word Aflame Press, 1986).

United States of America

The United States is the largest predominantly Protestant country in the world. That dominance began with the establishment of colonies along the Atlantic coast by British, Swedish, and Dutch settlers. The initial settlements brought with them the CHURCH OF ENGLAND and Puritan CONGREGA-TIONALISM in the British colonies, the Church of Sweden (Lutheran) in Delaware, and the Reformed Church of the Netherlands in New York and New Jersey.

As the British took control of the land, a Con-gregationalist establishment dominated New England, though a dissenting minister, Roger WILLIAMS, left Massachusetts to establish Rhode Island, where he helped found the first Baptist congregation in the colonies and allowed broad religious liberties. Farther south, William PENN, a member of the Society of Friends, created a colony in which the beleaguered sectarian groups from across Europe were welcome. Not only QUAKERS, but MENNONITES and BRETHREN made Pennsylvania their home. With the exception of Pennsylvania,

ANGLICANISM came to dominate in the colonies south of New England, at least among the ruling elite. As the British took over Delaware and New York, the Lutheran and Reformed Churches were disestablished, while Roman Catholics were pushed out of power in Maryland, where Lord Baltimore had tried to create a Catholic haven of religious freedom.

The great majority of colonists were not religious. They represented the most alienated groups of European society, including former residents of debtor's prison, disinherited sons seeking opportunity, and failures seeking a new start. Then, in the 1740s, the evangelist George WHITEFIELD toured the colonies and helped spark the GREAT AWAKENING, a wide wave of spiritual enthusiasm that swept many people into the existing churches while providing a sense of national unity. It was the first intimation of America's future religious character, in comparison with Europe.

The War for American Independence (1776–81) led to dramatic changes in the religious community. Two denominations existed in strength in the new country, the Congregationalists in New England and the Anglicans in the southern colonies. Anglicanism was closely identified with England, but there was no support south of New England to establish Congregationalism as the new American church. The leading figures in the revolution, such as Thomas Jefferson, George Washington, and Benjamin Franklin, were pragmatic politicians as well as deists. They had little attachment for the various churches (though Washington was a regular attendee at his local Anglican parish and Franklin shared his wealth with several religious communities in Philadelphia), and they feared the power of an established church. As a result, they came to support a bold new experiment—a country without a state religion. They left the option for individual states to establish a state religion, though most did not. Only Massachusetts continued its Congregational establishment for a while; by the early 19th century, every state had an antiestablishment clause in its constitution.

When the United States was born, most of the several hundred Native American nations remained intact, though some had been destroyed by disease and war brought by the Europeans. Congregationalist John Eliot (1604–90) had founded the first mission to Native Americans and created the famous towns of "praying Indians" in Massachusetts. In the 1700s, the MORAVIAN CHURCH sent missionaries to the colonies specifically to woo the Indians, and indeed future Methodist founder John WESLEY originally came to Georgia in the 1730s in part to preach to the Indians. A variety of churches opened missions among Native Americans in the 19th century, but their efforts were undermined by their identification with the U.S. government, with its record of treaty violations and Indian "removals" to barren lands in the West.

Following the American Revolution, slavery expanded in the South, and antiblack legislation was adopted by most free states. Most slaves became Christians, initially within the existing churches of European origin. The country fought a civil war in the 19th century (1860–65) that ended slavery but did not prevent the passage of "Jim Crow" laws to segregate and discriminate against blacks. American religious life was strongly shaped by racial issues, both in its race-based Protestant denominational patterns and in the struggles to free slaves and protect free blacks. Both abolitionism and the 20th-century Civil Rights movement were ideologically and organizationally based in Protestant churches.

When George Washington was inaugurated the first president in 1789, there were some 17 religious groups among those of European origin: 15 Protestant denominations, the Roman Catholic Church, and Judaism. Church of England parishes quickly reorganized to become the Protestant Episcopal Church in the U.S.A. (now simply the Episcopal Church). Most of the country's early presidents were members.

Congregationalists soon found Reformed allies against Anglican domination. Presbyterians began moving to the United States following the Restoration of the monarchy in England in 1660, and in even larger numbers as a result of problems in the Church of Scotland beginning in the 18th century. Together, the various groups of Puritan origin came to dominate higher education, founding many of the most respected universities, such as Harvard, Yale, and Princeton. Throughout the 19th century, the majority of the nation's leading theologians came from one of these churches, from Jonathan EDWARDS (1703–58) to Timothy Dwight (1752–1817) and Horace Bushnell (1802–76).

As the nation expanded westward, BAPTISTS, Methodists, and Roman Catholics showed the most growth, leaving the formerly dominant Congregationalists and Anglicans behind in the eastern states. The Baptist and Methodist Churches were minuscule at the time of the American Revolution, but their programs of evangelism and their ability to place ministers in the emerging communities won them many followers among the largely unchurched and irreligious settlers. A Second Great Awakening occurred in the early 19th century as waves of religious excitement and activity passed across the frontier. REVIVALISM and CAMP MEETINGS survived right through the 20th century. By the 1830s, the Methodists had become the largest church in the nation, though the Baptists surpassed them later in the century. Frontier religion produced the Cumberland Presbyterians and the RESTORATION MOVEMENT led by Barton Stone (1772–1844) and the CAMPBELLS, Thomas (1763–1854) and Alexander (1788–1866). The movement produced three new "nondenominational" DENOMINATIONS, the Churches of Christ, the Christian Church (Disciples of Christ), and the Churches of Christ and Christian Churches.

In the 1840s, the Methodists divided over the issue of slavery, leaving the Roman Catholic Church the largest single ecclesiastical body in America. While the American religious community remained decidedly Protestant, the Catholic Church has remained the largest single organization, claiming between 20 and 25 percent of the public among its members. The church grew both by evangelizing the public, steady immigration

from Catholic countries in Europe and more recently Latin America, and the annexation of former French and Spanish territories.

The number of religious groups multiplied in each decade of the 19th century, in part thanks to continued immigration. Without a controlling state church, factionalism thrived. Innovation also fueled a continuing number of new religious movements. The CHURCH OF JESUS CHRIST OF LATTER-DAY SAINTS, the CHURCH OF CHRIST, SCIENTIST, and the Unity School of Christianity grew up on the edge of the Protestant community, using traditional Christian language but pouring very different content into it. Following the death of their founder, the Latter-day Saints relocated to the Rocky Mountain region. They became the majority body in Utah and the surrounding states, and retain that dominance to the present. By the end of the 19th century, there were more than 300 Protestant and Free Church denominations.

Another major new movement was launched when William MILLER (1782–1849) publicized his view that Christ would return in 1843. Though his prophecy failed, it inspired several of the most successful religious groups of the 20th century, including the SEVENTH-DAY ADVENTIST CHURCH and the JEHOVAH'S WITNESSES.

With the end of slavery, African Americans were free to develop their own religious institutions. In the early 19th century, two independent groups that would later become large national bodies had been established—the African Methodist Episcopal Church and the African Methodist Episcopal Zion Church. After the Civil War, the scattered AFRICAN-AMERICAN BAPTISTS began to organize nationally, and by the end of the century, they had formed the National Baptist Convention of the U.S.A., out of which three additional national organizations would form: the National Baptist Convention of America, the Progressive National Baptist Convention of America, and the National Missionary Baptist Convention of America.

The introduction of so many divisions within the religious community ensured that no one religious organization would dominate. Some Protestants, however, deplored the disunity and joined with other Protestants worldwide in seeking to reunite via the ECUMENICAL MOVEMENT. Their efforts resulted in 1908 in the Federal Council of Churches, which included most of the older and larger denominations. They also promoted the merger of many closely related church bodies within the Lutheran, Presbyterian/Reformed, and Methodist family of denominations.

While one group envisioned a united Protestantism, another group disapproved of the theological drift it discerned among the ecumenicists, who were trying to respond to the social and intellectual challenges of contemporary culture. Modernists had absorbed German BIBLICAL CRITICISM, which questioned the authorship and authenticity of the Old Testament. They were also willing to modify Christian beliefs in light of scientific claims about the age of the earth and the origin of humans. Conservatives accused church leaders of rejecting the fundamentals of the faith, including the authority of the BIBLE, the Trinity, the deity of Christ, and the doctrine of creation. That concern would be focused in the 1920s in the arguments over the biblical account of creation in Genesis, which the Fundamentalists (as they had come to be known) insisted should be taken literally.

The controversy between FUNDAMENTALISM and Modernism split the American Protestant community into three factions, which remain to the present. The largest group, which gained control of most of the major denominations, was the Modernists, who sought to restate traditional faith within the contemporary context. The Fundamentalists focused on reaffirming traditional theological ideas and called on like-minded Christians to leave the denominations where apostasy reigned. The tendency of the third group, composed of theological conservatives who saw the value of participating in the existing church bodies and remaining in dialogue with the broader culture, came to be called EVANGELICALISM.

These three groups eventually organized their own ecumenical bodies, the National Council of Churches of Christ in the U.S.A., the National Association of Evangelicals, and the American Council of Churches. Internationally, these three groups would associate, respectively, with the WORLD COUNCIL OF CHURCHES, the WORLD EVANGELICAL ALLIANCE, and the INTERNATIONAL COUNCIL OF CHRISTIAN CHURCHES.

The process of merging closely related churches continued under the aegis of the National Council (formed in 1950). During the late 20th century, a number of the largest churches in America were formed by the new unions: the UNITED CHURCH OF CHRIST (1957), the UNITED METHODIST CHURCH (1968), the PRESBYTERIAN CHURCH (USA) (1983), and the EVANGELICAL LUTHERAN CHURCH IN AMERICA (1988). The largest Baptist churches, the SOUTHERN BAPTIST CONVENTION and the AMERICAN BAPTIST CHURCHES IN THE UNITED STATES, had drifted to opposite ends of the theological perspective and have not seriously considered merging.

The churches of the Eastern Orthodox tradition were barely present in the United States until the mid-19th century, when they were swelled by immigration. In the years since World War II, they have joined the National Council of Churches and had a workable if shaky alliance with liberal Protestants. The ORTHODOX-PROTESTANT DIALOGUE has provided an important new element affecting the development of American Protestantism.

Next to the Fundamentalist-Modernist split, by far the most important development in American Protestantism was the emergence of the HOLINESS churches, PENTECOSTALISM, and the CHARISMATIC MOVEMENT. In the last decades of the 20th century, the Charismatic movement surged in the United States both within and outside of the Roman Catholic Church and the large Protestant churches, while Pentecostalism exploded in size in South America and Africa. The Charismatics have led a swing back toward a more conservative form of Protestantism as the 21st century begins.

As America emerged as the wealthiest country in the world, and Protestants developed a global missionary ethos, the United States contributed to the global spread of Protestantism in ways only partially understood. Beginning with the formation of the AMERICAN BOARD OF COMMISSIONERS FOR FOREIGN MISSIONS, which drew support from the older Puritan churches, most denominations large and small have established mission boards and sent missionaries around the world. By the end of the 19th century, many nondenominational missionary-sending agencies had also arisen. These missions founded and nurtured numerous church bodies in almost every country of the world and transformed Protestantism into a truly global faith. In the 20th century, the missionary effort drew new strength from the Pentecostal movement, which joined the world missionary endeavor from the moment of its emergence in America. The CHURCH OF GOD IN CHRIST, the ASSEMBLIES OF GOD, the CHURCH OF GOD (CLEVELAND, TENNESSEE), and the CHURCH OF GOD OF PROPHECY have become vast international fellowships.

Finally, throughout the 20th century, the same innovative impulses that gave birth to the Jehovah's Witnesses and Christian Science, continued to produce new American forms of Christianity. These groups often considered themselves part of the Protestant community, but were largely pushed aside because of doctrinal or behavioral unacceptability. Included would be groups that denied essential traditional doctrines, such as the non-Trinitarian Apostolic or JESUS ONLY PENTECOSTALS. The adoption of nontraditional sexual mores pushed such groups as the Children of God (now known as The Family) to the fringe, while the UNIVERSAL FELLOWSHIP OF THE METROPOLITAN COMMUNITY CHURCHES, serving the lesbian-gay-bisexual-transgender community, was denied entry into the National Council of Churches.

By the end of the 20th century, there were more than 1,000 Christian denominations operating in the United States, the overwhelming majority of them Protestant, representing about half the total population. The largest percentage are Baptists, and the Southern Baptist Convention is the largest single denomination, almost twice as large as it closest rival, the United Methodist Church. Following behind are the Presbyterian Church (USA), the Church of God in Christ, the Evangelical Lutheran Church in America, the National Baptist Convention of the U.S.A., the National Baptist Convention of America, the African Methodist Episcopal Church, the Progressive National Baptist Convention, the National Baptist Missionary Convention of America, and the Episcopal Church. More than 20 other Protestant denominations have around a million members. Collectively, these large denominational bodies show every sign of continuing to dominate American religion in the next generations.

See also AFRICAN-AMERICAN METHODISTS.

Further reading: Catherine Albanese, *American Religion and Religions,* 2d ed. (Belmont, Calif.: Wadworth, 1992); Winthrop S. Hudson, *Religion in America,* 6th ed. (New York: Scribner, 1998); Martin E. Marty, *Pilgrims in Their Own Land* (Boston: Little, Brown, 1984); J. Gordon Melton, *Encyclopedia of American Religions,* 7th ed. (Detroit: Gale Research, 2002); ———, *The Encyclopedia of American Religions: Religious Creeds,* 2 vols. (Detroit: Gale Research, 1988, 1994); Larry G. Murphy Jr., J. Gordon Melton, and Gary L. Ward, eds., *Encyclopedia of African American Religion* (New York: Garland, 1993); Mark A. Noll, et al., eds., *Eerdmans' Handbook to Christianity in America* (Grand Rapids, Mich.: William B. Eerdmans, 1983); Daniel G. Reid, Robert D. Linder, Bruce L. Shelley, and Harry S. Stout, eds., *Dictionary of Christianity in America* (Downers Grove, Ill.: InterVarsity, 1990); Peter Williams, *America's Religious Traditions and Culture* (New York: Macmillan, 1990).

Unity School of Christianity/ Association of Unity Churches

Unity, the most outwardly Christian of the several New Thought groups, began in Kansas City, Missouri, in 1889, when its cofounders, Myrtle (1845–1931) and Charles Fillmore (1854–1948), created an organization to embody what they called "practical Christianity." Several years earlier,

Myrtle had been healed from tuberculosis after attending a lecture on mental healing in 1886. The couple had accepted ordination in 1891 from Emma Curtis Hopkins, head of the Christian Science Theological Seminary in Chicago.

The Fillmores launched their new movement with a periodical, *Modern Thought* (later *Unity*), and a prayer ministry, the Society for Silent Help (later Silent Unity), whose round-the-clock prayer ministry has been well known far beyond New Thought circles. In 1903, they incorporated the Unity Society of Practical Christianity (later the Unity School of Christianity). Its extensive output of periodicals, books, and pamphlets attracted metaphysical teachers, and congregations began to emerge. The various centers and congregations were organized in 1966 into the Association of Unity Churches (AUC), which cooperates with the Unity School. The association ordains and supervises ministers, sanctions churches, and coordinates the movement's expansion. As of 2001, there were nearly 1,000 ministries and 57 affiliated study groups in 64 countries. Unity has a strong presence in Africa, with some 50 groups in NIGERIA. Unity School remains the heart of the movement from facilities near Kansas City, Missouri. Its daily devotional guide, *The Daily Word*, has 1.3 million subscribers.

Unity uses the BIBLE as a primary text, with a Christian Science-like allegorical interpretation. Charles Fillmore authored a New Thought classic, the *Metaphysical Bible Dictionary* (1931). His writings and H. Emilie Cady's *Lessons In Truth* (1894) set the basic perspective for the movement.

Unity affirms that the basis of reality is mental (not material) and that mental states determine material conditions. Characteristic of New Thought as a whole, Unity affirms God as Mind. Though formerly describing itself as nondoctrinal, a number of foundational teachings consistently reappear in its literature: (1) the absolute goodness of God and the unreality of evil; (2) the innate divinity of humanity; (3) the omnipotently causative nature of consciousness; and (4) the

freedom of individuals in matters of belief. Unity's recasting of Christian doctrine as an idealistic philosophy has made it unacceptable to most Protestants, though it has had some influence on popular American Christianity, especially in the positive thinking espoused by Norman Vincent Peale (1898–1993) and Robert Schuller (b. 1926), both ministers and former presidents of the Reformed Church in America.

Unity School is headed by a self-perpetuating board of directors and its current president, Connie Fillmore Bazzy, the founders' great-granddaughter.

Further reading: Marcus Bach, *The Unity Way* (Unity Village, Mo.: Unity Books, 1982); Charles Braden, *Spirits in Rebellion: The Rise and Development of New Thought* (Dallas, Tex.: SMU Press, 1963); H. Emilie Cady, *Lessons in Truth* (Unity Village, Mo.: Unity Books, 1975); James Dillet Freeman, *The Story of Unity* (Unity Village, Mo.: Unity Books, 1978); Neal Vahle, *The Unity Movement: Its Evolution and Spiritual Teachings* (Philadelphia: Templeton Foundation Press, 2002).

Universal Church of the Kingdom of God

The Universal Church of the Kingdom of God began in July 1977, when Edir Macedo (b. 1945), a new Pentecostal believer in Rio de Janiero, Brazil, decided to set up an independent chapel and become an evangelist. His broadcasts from radio stations in Rio and São Paulo brought success, and Macedo created his own radio stations and daily newspapers, culminating in 1990 with the purchase of the TV Record network. His church, the Universal Church of the Kingdom of God (Igreja Universal do Reino de Deus, IURD), thus commands a vast media empire that now reaches Europe and Africa. The church has grown to more than 6 million members scattered in more than 45 countries. The TV Record network has emerged as the primary competitor of TV Globo, which has become the church's most vocal critic.

The Universal Church of the Kingdom of God center in downtown Atlanta, Georgia *(Institute for the Study of American Religion, Santa Barbara, California)*

Meanwhile, the church has been growing rapidly in Portugal and in southern Africa.

The Universal Church follows the teachings of other Brazilian Pentecostal churches, but has absorbed some influences from the Word of Faith movement and has become an integral part of the Deliverance movement of the last generation by its preaching of SPIRITUAL WARFARE. Macedo teaches that demons are the cause of most illnesses, unhappiness, and poverty. The church regularly offers exorcisms to counter their effects. Macedo has also included an element of anti-Catholicism in his teachings, and was forced into an official apology to Catholic Church leaders in 1995 when Sérgio Von Helder, the Universal Church's bishop for São Paulo, kicked a statue of the Virgin Mary during a TV show.

Worship is noisy and spontaneous. Services are usually held in former movie theaters. In Hollywood, California, the church purchased the historic One Million Dollar Theater on Hollywood Boulevard and converted it into a church center.

Further reading: E. Macedo, *Aliança com Deus* (Rio de Janeiro: Editora Gráfica Universal, 1993); ———, *Apocalipse hoje* (Rio de Janeiro: Editora Gráfica Universal, 1990); ———, *Vida com abundância* (Rio de Janeiro: Editora Gráfica Universal, 1990); Anders Ruuth, *Igreja Universal do Reino de Deus. Gudsrikets Universella Kyrka, en brasiliansk kyrkobildning* (Stockholm: Almqvist & Wiksell International, 1995).

Universal Fellowship of Metropolitan Community Churches

The Universal Fellowship of Metropolitan Community Churches (MCC) grew out of the experience of its founder, Troy D. Perry (b. 1940), as a homosexual man in the Protestant church. Licensed as a Baptist preacher, Perry was drawn to PENTECOSTALISM and became an evangelist for the CHURCH OF GOD (CLEVELAND, TENNESSEE). He later married, but an early homosexual encounter led to his dismissal from the church. He became a member of the CHURCH OF GOD OF PROPHECY, and worked as a pastor in Southern California.

Over the next few years, he came to accept his homosexuality, ended his marriage, and left the Church of God of Prophecy. In 1968, following a period of reflection on his call to the ministry and his sexual orientation, he began a church serving the homosexual community in Los Angeles, the Metropolitan Community Church, the first congregation of what would soon be a new DENOMINATION. The movement would enjoy great success as the gay movement developed through the 1970s. The Universal Fellowship of Metropolitan Community Churches emerged in 1974.

The church adopted a simple statement of beliefs drawn from the Apostles' and Nicene Creeds, which places it squarely in the Protestant theological tradition. It affirms the Trinity, the BIBLE as the word of God, the incarnation of God in Jesus Christ, and justification by grace through faith in Jesus Christ. The church believes that the

Bible does not condemn homosexual relationships, and that God is accepting of them. The church has been open to LIBERATION THEOLOGY and feminist approaches to the Bible, and advocates reading the Bible from the perspective of oppressed gay and lesbian people.

The MCC has seen itself as a safe haven for those rejected by other religious communities, especially those who identify themselves as lesbian, gay, bisexual, or transgender (LGBT). It works for LGBT rights and opposes homophobia. MCC developed a massive response to HIV/AIDS, promoting education and assistance for HIV-affected people across the United States and around the world.

The fellowship's headquarters are in West Hollywood, California. It currently has some 40,000 members in 300 congregations in 18 countries. It is ecumenically oriented, though its attempts to join the National Council of Churches have been rebuffed. The fellowship is the largest of more than a dozen gay-affirming denominations, most others being limited to a few congregations.

Further reading: *AIDS: Is It God's Judgment? A Christian View of Faith, Hope and Love from Metropolitan Community Church* (Los Angeles: Metropolitan Community Church, n.d.), 6-page leaflet; Troy D. Perry, *Don't Be Afraid Anymore* (New York: St. Martin's, 1990); ———, *The Lord Is My Shepherd and He Knows I'm Gay: The Autobiography of the Reverend Troy D. Perry* (Los Angeles: Nash, 1972); ———, with Thomas L. P. Swicegood, *Profiles in Gay and Lesbian Courage* (New York: St. Martin's, 1991); Nancy Wilson, *Our Tribe: Queer Folks, God, Jesus, and the Bible* (San Francisco, Calif.: Harper San Francisco, 1995).

Universalism

In Protestant theological discourse, Universalism holds that all humans will eventually become heirs of the salvation offered in Christ, some immediately after death and others after a period of recompense for their sin. Universalism arose out of the belief that the love of God was incompatible with a belief in eternal torment in hell. Universalists found support from biblical scholars who suggested that eternal torment/punishment was not clearly taught in the BIBLE, but first appeared in the second century in the writings of Justin Martyr and Ignatius of Antioch.

Modern challenges to the doctrine of eternal punishment took one of two approaches. One suggested that sinners would be annihilated in hell, rather than face conscious torment. Among popular exponents of this idea was Charles Taze RUSSELL (1852–1916), founder of what today is known as the JEHOVAH'S WITNESSES. However, Universalism proper does not just deny eternal torment, but believes that all souls will eventually enter heaven.

Through the centuries, individuals have occasionally voiced the belief, and a few small groups like the Schwenckfelders included it as part of their affirmations. It did not take on organizational form until the 18th century in America.

Rev. John Murray (1741–1815) was the founder of what became the Universalist Church in America. An English Methodist minister, he was won over to Universalism by John Rilley, a former Methodist minister who had been excommunicated. Migrating to America in 1770, Murray was invited to pastor a small group of like-minded believers in New Jersey. After a period, he began to travel among the cities of the eastern seaboard. On January 1, 1779, a fellowship of Universalists in Gloucester, Massachusetts, signed *Articles of Association* that created an Independent Church of Christ. The following year, Murray became its pastor. Other Universalist churches emerged, and in 1785 they held their first convention. In 1793, a more formal organization was created as the General Convention of Universalists.

The convention's beliefs were laid out in the Winchester Profession of Faith, adopted at Winchester, New Hampshire, in 1803. They affirmed belief in God, the authority of the Bible, the leadership of Jesus Christ, and the certainty of just retribution for sin. They also professed belief that

God, whose nature is love, will restore the whole family of humankind. Two years later, a young Universalist minister, Hosea Ballou (1771–1852), published *A Treatise on the Atonement,* which rejected the doctrine of the Trinity. From that time, UNITARIANISM would become more common among Universalists than Trinitarianism.

Though unordained, as early as 1811 women preached to Universalist congregations, starting with Maria Cook. In 1863, Universalist Olympia Brown (1835–1926) became the first woman ordained as a minister in the United States.

In 1961, the Universalist Churches of America united with the American Unitarian Association to form the Unitarian Universalist Association.

The vision of the two organizations had by this time largely converged.

See also WOMEN, ORDINATION OF.

Further reading: A. L. Bressler, *The Universalist Movement in America, 1770–1880* (New York: Oxford University Press, 2001); Russell E. Miller, *The Larger Hope: The First Century of the Universalist Church in America, 1770–1870* (Boston: Unitarian Universalist Association, 1979); John Murray, *The Life of Rev. John Murray, Preacher of Universal Salvation, written by himself; with Notes and Introduction* (Boston: Francis & Munroe, 1816); George Hunston Williams, *American Universalism* (Boston: Beacon Press, 1971).

V

vestments

Over the centuries, A complex set of vestments, or clothing, was developed for Christian priests when officiating at the Mass and in their daily movements. Different garments were prescribed for DEACONS, priests, and BISHOPS. All Reformation churches criticized Roman Catholic practice on the proper garb for ministers, but the Reformed Church was particularly severe.

As early as 1523, Ulrich ZWINGLI called for the abolition of priestly vestments in his Reformed Church in Zurich. Expensive materials such as silk and gold were rejected for ministerial garb among Swiss reformers, who considered the demands of modesty and order. In Geneva, a form of dress adapted from what had been priests' outdoor garb, a black gown worn over a cassock, became the accepted clothing for officiating at worship and has evolved today into what is know as the Geneva gown.

Martin LUTHER saw vestments as a matter of lesser importance. They were permitted but did not convey any special virtues.

England saw intense controversy over vestments as Catholics, Anglicans, and Presbyterians vied for control of the church. During the reign of EDWARD VI, Bishop John Hooper was arrested for adopting a Zwinglian position against vestments.

During ELIZABETH's reign, the 1559 Act of Uniformity demanded the continuance of traditional priestly garb. When Matthew Parker (1504–75), the archbishop of Canterbury, demanded strict conformity to the act, 37 London ministers refused, the majority of those holding pulpits.

The opposition party in what was later called the vestiarian controversy was defeated, but they added a new term to British religious life, *nonconformists*. Eventually, English Protestants across the spectrum (with the exception of high-church Anglicans) adopted a more simple dress.

As a whole, Free Church ministers (i.e. those not in the CHURCH OF ENGLAND) wore the same clothes as laypeople, even for leading worship services. The adoption of a distinctive clerical dress was often more a matter of money than of liturgical considerations. However, Protestants did occasionally allow their anti-Catholic polemics to draw analogies between feminine dress and Catholic priestly garb.

In the late 20th century, in the context of the ECUMENICAL MOVEMENT, more traditional clerical garb has been revived by Protestants as part of the spirit of cordiality at gatherings of ministers of different faiths. Traditional priestly garb has also been revived by those involved in the liturgical revivals that have periodically arisen within

Protestantism. Among recent efforts was that begun in 1946 by the Order of St. Luke, an organization operating within the UNITED METHODIST CHURCH and dedicated to exploring and reviving liturgical worship within that church.

Smaller DENOMINATIONS and ordered communities have often developed distinctive dress both for worship and daily wear. These vary from the simple dress of the QUAKERS to the monastic dress of communal groups such as the Ephrata Cloister of 17th-century BAPTISTS in Pennsylvania. The purpose of such dress, however, is primarily to identify believers within the larger social context, rather than to fulfill a sacred or liturgical purpose.

Further reading: Mary Ann James, *Liturgical Dress, An Analysis of Purpose and Function* (Nashville, Tenn.: Vanderbilt University, M.A. thesis, 1986); Janet Mayo, *A History of Ecclesiastical Dress* (London: Batsford, 1984); Arthur Carl Piepkorn, *Survival of the Historic Vestments in the Lutheran Church after 1555* (St. Louis: Concordia, 1958); John H. Primus, *The Vestments Controversy: An Historical Study of the Earliest Tensions within the Church of England in the Reigns of Edward VI and Elizabeth* (Kampen: Theological University of the Reformed Churches in the Netherlands, diss., 1960).

via media

The *via media,* or middle way, was the set of beliefs and practices imposed by Queen ELIZABETH I (1533–1603) on the CHURCH OF ENGLAND early in her reign, as a compromise between the Protestant supporters of her brother, EDWARD VI (r. 1547–53), and the Catholic supporters of her sister, MARY I (r. 1553–58), whose reigns had been torn by religious controversy and violence. The middle way was the foundation of the Anglican tradition; it is the basis for the rejection by some Anglicans of the Protestant label.

Elizabeth moved slowly in transforming familiar Catholic worship patterns, but she almost immediately banned the elevation of the host, a highly symbolic act supportive of the real pres-ence of Christ in the LORD'S SUPPER and most offensive to Protestants. She moved to revise the statement of faith, approving the 39 ARTICLES OF RELIGION still used by the Church of England and its daughter bodies. Thus, while the basic Sunday worship retained a Catholic flavor, the official statement of belief was highly Calvinist and contained a number of specifically anti–Roman Catholic statements. Richard Hooker's (c. 1553–1600) massive *Of the Lawes of Ecclesiastical Politie* (1594–97) is often seen as the major defense of the *via media* written during Elizabeth's reign.

In response to her decrees, Elizabeth was excommunicated in 1570 by Pope Sixtus V (1521–90). When, from the opposite end of the spectrum, some Puritan ministers refused to wear VESTMENTS and demanded the elimination of BISHOPS in favor of presbyters (ELDERS), Elizabeth deprived them of their positions and the income that went with them. The most vigorous protesters, such as Thomas CARTWRIGHT (1535–1603), were forced into exile and/or jailed. This led to the solidification of the Presbyterians and Congregationalists as separate communities apart from the Church of England.

Thanks to Elizabeth's long reign, the ANGLICANISM of the *via media* was able to survive the onslaughts of later Catholic kings and of Puritan dictator Oliver CROMWELL (1599–1658). A low-church Evangelical wing did eventually develop within the ANGLICAN COMMUNION, as well as an Anglo-Catholic high-church wing favoring movements toward Roman Catholicism.

Further reading: Paul Avis, *Anglicanism and the Christian Church* (Minneapolis, Minn.: Fortress Press, 1989); Richard Hooker, *Of The Lawes of Ecclesiastical Politie,* 4 vols., W. Speed Hill, ed. (Cambridge, Mass.: University of Harvard Press, 1977); William L. Sachs, *The Transformation of Anglicanism: From State Church to Global Communion* (New York: Cambridge University Press, 1993); Andrew Wingate, et al., eds., *Anglicanism: A Global Communion* (London: Mowbray, 1998).

Visser't Hooft, Willem A. (1900–1985)
ecumenical statesmen

Willem A. Visser't Hooft was born in Haarlem, the NETHERLANDS, on September 20, 1900. While attending the University of Leiden, he was drawn into the STUDENT CHRISTIAN MOVEMENT and was inspired by meeting John R. MOTT to see the church as a global mission. His faith was further shaped by his reading of Karl BARTH and adoption of NEO-ORTHODOXY.

Visser't Hooft joined the staff of the YMCA, (*see* YOUNG MEN'S CHRISTIAN ASSOCIATION) in Geneva. Before long, he was general secretary of the WORLD STUDENT CHRISTIAN FEDERATION. In 1938, he became secretary of the WORLD COUNCIL OF CHURCHES (WCC), at the time still in the process of formation. He retained that post until his retirement in 1966.

Visser't Hooft traveled widely for the cause of ecumenism and was applauded after World War II for his efforts to keep Christians in contact with one another across the battle lines. He wrote a number of books that called on the church to free itself from unworthy entanglements and prepare to face the onslaught of modern secular society. He also wrote his *Memoirs* and a history of the WCC, both of which remain important historical documents. He remained active in ecumenical discussions from his retirement in 1968 until shortly before his death on July 4, 1985.

See also ECUMENICAL MOVEMENT.

Further reading: Robert C. Mackie and Charles C. West, ed., *The Sufficiency of God: Essays on the Ecumenical Hope in Honor of W. A. Visser't Hooft* (Philadelphia: Westminster Press, 1963); Willem A. Visser't Hooft, *The Genesis and Formation of the World Council of Churches* (Geneva: World Council of Churches, 1982); ———, *Has the Ecumenical Movement a Future?* (Atlanta: John Knox Press, 1974); ———, *The Kingship of Christ* (New York: Harper, 1948); ———, *Memoirs* (London/Philadelphia: SCM Press Westminster Press, 1973).

W

Wang Ming-tao (1900–1991) *Chinese evangelist and three-self exponent*

Wang Ming-tao was born in 1900 in Beijing. He was raised in a Congregational church under the guidance of the London Missionary Society. Following a serious illness, he pledged to enter the ministry. He received no theological training, but he had a good speaking voice and had absorbed a conservative Bible-oriented belief system.

As a young minister in the 1920s, he advocated the three-self principles as originally suggested by John Nevius—the church in the mission field must be self-propagating, self-governing, and self-supporting. He began a small home meeting that over the years grew into the Christian Tabernacle in Beijing. He insisted that each member manifest a visible spirituality. There were some 570 members at the time the Communists took over.

The Christian Tabernacle advocated a simple worship and lifestyle that relied on the Bible for direction. There was an emphasis on the practical appropriation of Christianity. A popular periodical, *Spiritual Food,* spread the church's message.

Wang espoused the complete separation of church and state. He was able to hold his position after the Japanese takeover in the 1930s, but did not fare as well after the Chinese revolution. His indigenous congregation, independent of Protestant missionaries from its inception, was just what the new government said it wanted. However, Wang's refusal to back the new government by joining the three-self patriotic movement landed him in jail in 1955. He was briefly released, but then once more put in prison, where he remained until 1979, when new policies on religion allowed his release.

Further reading: Lyall Leslie, *Three of China's Mighty Men.* (Kent, U.K.: Hodder & Stoughton/Overseas Missionary Fellowship, 1980); John D. Woodbridge, ed., *Ambassadors for Christ: Distinguished Representatives of the Message throughout the World* (Chicago: Moody Press, 1994).

Warneck, Gustav (1834–1910) *leading German Protestant missiologist*

Gustav Warneck was born on March 6, 1834, in Naumburg. After completing his studies at the University of Halle (1855–58), he became a tutor and counselor at a nearby school. He wished to become a missionary, but poor health prevented his acceptance. He served as a parish minister (1862–71, 1874–96) and worked for the Rhenish Mission in Barmen (1871–74). During his pastorate at

Dommitzsch, he completed his doctorate at Jena (1871).

Warneck began to build his reputation as a scholar of the missionary enterprise. In 1874, he started a journal, *Allegemeine Missions-Zeitschrift,* which he edited for the next 37 years. In 1879, he wrote a study on the interaction of mission and culture, published in Scotland in 1883 as *Modern Missions and Culture: Their Mutual Relations.* However, he is most remembered for his *Evangelische Missionslehre,* whose five volumes appeared between 1887 and 1905. It presented a comprehensive survey of the theory of missiology, and became the foundation upon which future study developed.

Warneck criticized John R. MOTT and the STUDENT VOLUNTEER MOVEMENT for perpetuating what he considered a superficial and naïve approach. He challenged popular notions that the world could be evangelized in a single generation, or that missionary activity could have an effect on the timing of Christ's return. He also criticized those who evangelized without thinking about the additional task of making disciples of converts. At the same time, he championed the work of the various independent missionary agencies that had appeared, especially in Germany, for picking up the task that the older Reformation churches had neglected.

Warneck retired in 1908 but continued to write until his death on December 26, 1910. Warneck's writings had considerable influence in Europe, but had less impact in England and North America, since little was translated. Ideas that have caught on are his proposal for regular international missionary conferences and for a central committee to provide continuity for missionary agencies. He lived to see the famous missions conference at Edinburgh in 1910, which ultimately led to the INTERNATIONAL MISSIONARY COUNCIL (1921).

Further reading: Hans Kasdorf, "Gustav Warneck, 1834–1910: Founder of the Scholary Study of Missions," in Gerald H. Anderson, Robert T. Cotte, Nor-man A. Horner and James M. Phillips, eds., *Mission Legacies: Biographical Studies of Leaders of the Modern Missionary Movement* (Maryknoll, N.Y.: Orbis Books, 1998), 272–82; Gustav Warneck, *Evangelische Missionslehre,* 5 vols. (Gotha: Frederich Andreas Perthes, 1887–1905); ———, *Modern Missions and Culture: Their Mutual Relations,* trans. by Thomas Smith (Edinburgh: James Grammell, 1883).

Watts, Isaac (1674–1748) *father of modern Protestant hymnody*

Isaac Watts was born in Southampton, England. His father was a Puritan DEACON who had at times been imprisoned for nonconformist beliefs. Isaac received an education that included Greek, Hebrew, and Latin. He turned down a university scholarship to study for the Anglican ministry, instead attending a small Puritan school, and later joining a Congregationalist church.

Watts began to write HYMNS as a young man, and his church in Southhampton became the site for testing them out. In 1699, he was chosen assistant pastor of a church in London and was ordained in 1702. In 1712, he was forced to retire for health reasons. He moved into the home of Sir Thomas Abney, and the Abneys served as Watts's patrons for the remaining 36 years of his life.

Watts wrote a number of popular books, but he is most remembered for his collections of hymns: *Hymns and Spiritual Songs* (1707); *Divine Songs for Children* (1715), the first children's hymnbook; and *Psalms of David* (1719). He wrote more than 600 hymns, some of which are still popular, such as "When I Survey the Wondrous Cross," "Joy to the World," "O God Our Help in Ages Past," and "Alas and Did My Savior Bleed."

Watts is not as well known for his non-Trinitarian views. In 1719, he voted against requiring Independent ministers to adhere to the doctrine. He argued that the idea of the Trinity was a limited attempt to explain the mystery of the Godhead. He suggested that the human soul of Jesus had been created before the world and only later united with the Logos principle in the Godhead.

He also argued that the Holy Spirit was not a person in the same literal sense as God the Father and God the Son.

Watts also floated a proposal to unite Congregationalists and the BAPTISTS; the former would abandon infant baptism and the later baptism by immersion. In spite of his questionable doctrinal stands, Watts's two didactic manuals, the *Catechisms* (1730) and *Scripture History* (1732) were widely used by Puritans for the next century, and his hymns remain popular to the present.

Watts set the stage for the prolific hymn production of Charles WESLEY (1707–88), his younger contemporary. Watts's hymns help break the mode of using only PSALMS as the text for hymns, though several of his more popular hymns were, in fact, rephrased Psalms, such as "Joy to the World" (Psalm 98) and "O God Our Help in Ages Past" (Psalm 90).

Further reading: Selma L. Bishop, *Isaac Watts' Hymns and Spiritual Songs (1707): A Publishing History and a Bibliography* (Ann Arbor, Mich.: Pierian Press, 1974); Arthur Paul Davis, *Isaac Watts: His Life and Works* (New York: Dryden Press, 1943); Jane Stuart Smith and Betty Carlson, *Great Christian Hymn Writers* (Wheaton, Ill.: Crossway Books, 1997); Isaac Watts, *Hymns and Spiritual Songs* (Southampton, U.K.: Mayflower Christian Books, 2003).

Wesley, Charles (1707–1788) *hymn writer and cofounder of Methodism*

Charles Wesley was born on December 18, 1707, the 18th child of Samuel and Susannah Wesley. In 1726, he entered Christ Church, Oxford. While there, he organized a group of religiously serious students called the Holy Club, a distinctive name in the secularized atmosphere at Oxford. His brother John WESLEY was a subsequent leader of the group; in 1732, future evangelist George WHITEFIELD joined the group as well. The three became close friends.

After graduating from Oxford, in 1735 Charles went to the newly established American colony of

Charles Wesley (1707–88) wrote more than 3,000 hymns, many still widely used in Protestant churches. *(Drew University Library)*

Georgia as secretary of Governor James Oglethorpe; John also spent time there, though both returned soon after. While there, they met with a group of Moravians, who introduced them to the idea of a personal faith in Christ. After some struggle with his faith, on May 21, 1738, Charles found peace with God, three days prior to his brother's more famous "heart-warming" experience at the Aldersgate religious society.

In response to his own experience, Charles wrote the first of his more than 6,000 hymns, describing himself as "A slave redeemed from death and sin, A brand plucked from eternal fire!" He also helped his brother preach and set up the religious societies that became the core of the Methodist movement. An initial collection of his hymns was published in 1739.

Charles married and settled in Wales in 1749, but continued to preach until 1756. In 1771, he moved to London to provide oversight to the Methodists, especially during his brother's extended travels.

Many of Charles Wesley's hymns have been forgotten, but a few became world famous, such as "O, For a Thousand Tongues to Sing," "Hark the

Herald Angels Sing," "Love Divine, All Love's Excelling," and "Christ the Lord Has Risen Today." His hymns have been featured in the various editions of Methodist hymnals to the present; they became identified with METHODISM, and then with Protestantism in general as it spread around the world.

Charles Wesley died in London on March 29, 1788.

Further reading: S. T. Kimbrough Jr., ed., *Charles Wesley: Poet and Theologian* (Nashville, Tenn.: Abingdon/Kingswood, 1992); John R. Tyson, *Charles Wesley: A Reader* (New York & Oxford: Oxford University Press, 1989, 2001); Carlton R. Young, *Music of the Heart: John and Charles Wesley on Music and Musicians* (London: Stainer & Bell, 1995).

Wesley, John (1703–1791) *founder of Methodism*

John Wesley was born on June 17, 1703, at Epworth, England, the 15th of 19 children born to Samuel and Susannah Wesley. His father was an Anglican priest. His mother was a Puritan, notable for her learning. Both John and his brother Charles WESLEY attended Oxford University.

While at Oxford, Wesley took over leadership of the Holy Club, an organization of religiously seeking students established by Charles. After graduation, on a voyage to America, Wesley had his first encounter with members of the MORAVIAN CHURCH, who pressed him on his personal religious life. On his return to England, he began attending informal services at several lay-led religious societies in London. At one such society meeting on Aldersgate Street on May 24, 1738, he had what he termed a "heart-warming experience" that is generally seen as the founding event of the Methodist movement. The movement took shape when he broke with the Moravians the following year, and the first "Methodist" religious societies began to form. Within each society, members were invited into smaller intimate groups called classes.

John Wesley (1703–91), founder of Methodism *(Drew University Library)*

Another Oxford classmate, George WHITEFIELD, had a similar pilgrimage and had begun preaching in Bristol. Before leaving for a tour of America, he turned his work over to Wesley. It became the first major extension of the movement outside of London. Over the next decades as the movement expanded, Wesley traveled around England periodically visiting the many Wesleyan societies. He regularly preached two or three times a day and kept a daily journal.

Wesley wrote numerous books and edited hundreds of others to educate the lay preachers who had emerged to serve the movement. In 1744, he began to hold conferences for the preachers; the published minutes became an important guide for the developing movement.

Prominent among Wesley's writings was a set of sermons that covered the basic teachings of METHODISM; collected, they became an essential statement of the movement's doctrines. Wesley developed a unique concept of the ideal Christian life. The true Christian would move through life steadily growing in grace. He should aim at a separation from sin, until he became perfected in love, a goal that might not be fully achieved in this life.

Methodism spread throughout the British Isles as a movement within the CHURCH OF ENGLAND, and Wesley made no attempts to build church structures or his own hierarchy. But after the American Revolution, when all but one of the preachers he had sent to work there returned to England, and Wesley was unable to get organizational help from the Anglican authorities, he made a decision that in effect turned the American movement into a separate church. In 1784, he himself assumed the office of BISHOP and "set aside" two men, Thomas COKE (1747–1814) and Richard Whatcoat, to be Methodist superintendents, and commissioned them to set up American Methodism as an independent movement. After Wesley's death, the movement organized as a separate church in England.

In England, Wesley's movement had developed a unique place. Following both his Anglican and Puritan roots, Wesley kept the movement within the established church, and followed the Calvinist theology of Jacob Arminius (1560–1609), which had rejected the PREDESTINATION so central to John CALVIN. Wesley preached that the free grace of God was immediately available to any who would turn and accept it. Meanwhile, he and George Whitefield had parted company over CALVINISM, and Whitefield went on to develop a form of Methodism that would later merge into the Presbyterian Church.

In his 40 years of travel throughout the British Isles, Wesley delivered more than 40,000 sermons. He remained active until close to the end of his life on March 2, 1791. Among his last works was a letter to William WILBERFORCE (1759–1833) supporting his work to end slavery.

In 1976, the Abingdon Press began the most recent attempt to publish Wesley's works. To date some 20 volumes have been issued.

Further reading: Frank Baker, *John Wesley and the Church of England* (Nashville, Tenn.: Abingdon,

1970); V. H. H. Green, *John Wesley* (London/New York: University Press of America, 1987); Richard P. Heitzenrater, *Wesley and the People Called Methodists* (Nashville, Tenn.: Abingdon, 1995); John Wesley, *John Wesley's Sermons: An Anthology,* ed. by Albert C. Outler, et al. (Nashville, Tenn.: Abingdon, 1991).

Wesleyan Church

The Wesleyan Church was founded in 1968 by the merger of two American HOLINESS denominations, the Wesleyan Methodist Church and the Pilgrim Holiness Church.

The Wesleyan Methodist Church was born in the crucible of the conflict over slavery in the Methodist Episcopal Church (MEC). The MEC had been strongly antislavery at its founding, but had gradually moderated its views as the practice spread in the South. The rise of abolitionism encouraged some Northern members to demand a stronger stand. Most of the church was against slavery, but also opposed its immediate end.

The crisis came to a head in the 1840s and eventually split the church when Northern members were unwilling to allow a slaveholder to become a BISHOP. Nevertheless, abolitionists became the object of attack throughout the MEC, and resolutions against abolitionism were passed in many conferences. In reaction, former MEC ministers Orange Scott (1800–47), Lucius Matlack (1816–83), and Luther Lee (1800–89) founded the Wesleyan Methodist Connection in 1843. Besides its strong stand against slavery, the group became identified with the emerging Holiness movement in American Methodism and added a statement on Wesleyan sanctification to the Methodist ARTICLES OF RELIGION (otherwise adopted whole).

One of the first Holiness associations to form outside the MEC was the Holiness Christian Church (1889), which grew to become the International Apostolic Holiness Church. In 1922, that group, under the leadership of Martin Wells Knapp (1853–1901), merged with another Holiness group, the Pilgrim Church of California, founded in 1917 by Seth C. Rees (1854–1933), to form the Pilgrim Holiness Church. Over the next half century, additional groups would merge into both the Wesleyan Methodist and the Pilgrim Holiness Church.

Some of the constituent churches had begun missionary work quite early. In 1889, the Wesleyan Methodists sent George and Mary Lane Clarke and a small group of missionaries to SIERRA LEONE.

Today (2004), the Wesleyan Church has a worldwide membership of approximately 270,000 in some 3,600 churches located in 40 countries, about half of which are in North America. Headquarters are in Indianapolis, Indiana. The church sponsors an international radio ministry, *The Wesleyan Hour.* It is a member of the CHRISTIAN HOLINESS PARTNERSHIP.

Further reading: Keith Drury, *Holiness for Ordinary People* (Indianapolis, Ind.: Wesley Press, 1994); Lee Haines and Paul William Thomas, *An Outline History of the Wesleyan Church* (Indianapolis, Ind.: Wesley Press, 1985); Ira Ford McLister and Roy S. Nicholson, *History of the Wesleyan Methodist Church* (Marion, Ind.: Wesley Press, 1959); Paul Westphal Thomas and Paul William Thomas, *The Days of Our Pilgrimage* (Marion, Ind.: Wesley Press, 1976).

Westminster Confession

As Puritan's rose to power in England in the 17th century, Parliament called a group of Puritan clergy to Westminster Abbey to make proposals for the further reform of the CHURCH OF ENGLAND. The group met from 1643 to 1648 and produced a series of documents including a Confession of Faith (designed to replace the Thirty-time ARTICLES OF RELIGION), the Larger and Shorter Catechism, the Directory for Public Worship (designed to replace the Anglican prayer book) and the Form of Church Government (which affirmed a Presbyterian POLITY).

While the Westminster documents were adopted by the Presbyterian Church of Scotland,

they were far less directly influential in England. They were largely discarded after the Restoration, which returned episcopal authority to the Church of England and the prayer book to church pews. The Congregationalists and BAPTISTS each produced statements competing with Westminster (Savoy Declaration and the LONDON CONFESSION OF FAITH), which in effect became the sole possession of the remnant Presbyterian Church. However, from Scotland and Britain, the Westminster documents were passed to North America and then to Presbyterian churches around the world by missionaries. Today, they remain the most cited confessional documents of the Reformed faith globally.

The Confession of Faith remains the most important of the documents. It is a lengthy document of 33 chapters, which affirms, in detail, the BIBLE as the Word of God, the Trinity, PREDESTINATION, salvation by Christ, the perseverance of the saints, the church as the total number of the elect, the two sacraments of BAPTISM and the LORD'S SUPPER, and the return of the souls of the deceased to God immediately after death. Throughout the document, the sovereignty of God, the authority of the Bible, and its proper interpretation are affirmed.

In Chapter XX, "Of Christian Liberty, and Liberty of Conscience," the Westminster divines made an important statement about human liberty in the political arena: "The requiring of an implicit faith, and an absolute and blind obedience, is to destroy liberty of conscience, and reason also."

Through the years, Presbyterian SYNODS have debated the binding authority of the Westminster Confession. One decisive statement was made in 1967 by the United Presbyterian Church in the U.S.A. (now a constituent part of the PRESBYTERIAN CHURCH [USA]). By adopting the contemporary Confession of 1967 and placing it alongside the Westminster Confession and other documents from the early Christian church, the United Presbyterians relativized the authority of Westminster. In contrast, more conservative bodies, such as the Presbyterian Church of America, affirm the continuing authority of the confession in the contemporary world.

See also CREEDS/CONFESSIONS OF FAITH.

Further reading: Benjamin Warfield, *The Westminster Assembly and Its Work* (New York: Oxford University Press, 1931); Samuel William Carruthers, *The Everyday Work of the Westminster Assembly* (Philadelphia: Published jointly by the Presbyterian Historical Society [of America] and the Presbyterian Historical Society of England, 1934); John Richard De Witt, *Jus Divinum: The Westminster Assembly and the Divine Right of Church Government* (Kampe: J. H. Kok, 1969); John H. Leith, *Assembly at Westminster: Reformed Theology in the Making* (Richmond, Va.: John Knox Press, 1973); Robert S. Paul, *The Assembly of the Lord: Politics and Religion in the Westminster Assembly and the "Grand Debate"* (Edinburgh: T. & T. Clark, 1985).

Wheatley, Phillis (c. 1753–1784) *first published African-American woman poet*

Phillis Wheatley was born in West Africa, probably in what is now Gambia, and after being enslaved was transported to Boston, Massachusetts, and purchased in 1761 as a servant by John and Susannah Wheatley. She was trained as a personal maid to Mrs. Wheatley and lived in the family residence.

Encouraged by the Wheatleys, Phillis learned to read and write. Impressed by her comprehension of complicated BIBLE passages, the Wheatley's in 1770 sponsored Phyllis's membership in the Old South Church, soon to become a center of revolutionary activity. Wheatley had already written some of her many poems with Christian themes. For example, "To the University of Cambridge" called upon students to avoid sin and follow Christ. The year she joined the church she wrote a poem on the occasion of the death of evangelist George WHITEFIELD. Her poems made her a local celebrity.

In 1773, the Wheatleys freed Phillis and sent her to England in hopes of restoring her health. In England, she was received by the countess of Huntington, George Whitefield's patron. Phillis also had the opportunity to publish her book, *Poems on Various Subjects: Religious and Moral*. She returned to Massachusetts and worked for her former masters until their deaths in 1774 and 1778. She continued to write until close to her death, but a bad marriage and the need to work to support her children lessened her output. She died on December 5, 1784.

Wheatley's works were later used by abolitionists to defend the idea of native talents and capabilities of black people. Her fame has waxed and waned, but she has most recently been rediscovered by spokespersons of womanist theology, a movement devoted to highlighting the voices of black women as they confront a racist and sexist community.

Further reading: Shirley Graham, *The Story of Phillis Wheatley* (New York: J. Messmer, 1949, 1966); William Henry Robinson, *Critical Essays on Phillis Wheatley* (Boston: G. K. Hall, 1982); Phillis Wheatley, *The Collected Works of Phillis Wheatley*, ed. by John C. Shields (New York: Oxford University Press, 1989).

White, Alma (1862–1946) *Holiness leader and first female bishop in modern times*

Alma Birdwell White was born on June 16, 1862, in Louis County, Kentucky. At the age of 16, she had a conversion experience and accepted Christ during a Methodist revival meeting.

At the time of her conversion, White also professed a call to the ministry, which Methodist ministers refused to accept. She turned instead to teaching, but eventually married a Methodist ministerial student in Montana. She used her husband's status to begin holding unofficial revival meetings in the relatively tolerant atmosphere of the Rocky Mountains. Her success, however, soon brought condemnation from Methodist authorities on her husband and herself.

In 1901, the couple left the Methodist Episcopal Church (now an integral part of the UNITED METHODIST CHURCH) and founded a new HOLINESS denomination, the Methodist Pentecostal Union, later renamed the Pillar of Fire. Alma became its bishop and Arthur her assistant. She received the donation of a tract of land in Zarephath, New Jersey, which became the church's headquarters and the location of their college. It also became the base of their radio ministry in the 1920s.

White supported a number of unpopular causes, not the least being the rights of women, on whose behalf she founded a periodical, *Women's Chains*. She also became a vegetarian. Less to her credit, she was anti-Catholic, a position that led her to support the Ku Klux Klan in the 1920s.

During her four decades of leadership White built the Pillar of Fire into a national DENOMINATION. Following her death on June 26, 1946, she was succeeded by her two sons. Now known as the Pillar of Fire, International, the church has affiliated congregations in England, INDIA, Malawi, LIBERIA, NIGERIA, and Costa Rica.

Further reading: Susie Cunningham Stanley, *Feminist Pillar of Fire: The Life of Alma White* (Cleveland, Ohio: Pilgrim Press, 1993); Alma White, *Looking Back from Beulah* (Denver, Colo.: Pentecostal Union, 1902; reprint, Zarephath, N.J.: Pillar of Fire, 1951); ———, *Radio Sermons and Lectures* (Denver, Colo.: Pillar of Fire, 1936); ———, *The Story of My Life and the Pillar of Fire,* 6 vols. (Zarephath, N.J.: Pillar of Fire, 1919–34); ———, *Women's Ministry* (London: Pillar of Fire, n.d.).

White, Ellen G. (1827–1915) *cofounder of Seventh-day Adventist Church*

Ellen Gould Harmon White was born on November 26, 1827, at Gorham, Maine. She was raised as a Methodist, and in 1842 had a conversion experience and joined the church. At just that time, enthusiasm was sweeping the country over William MILLER's predictions about Christ's imminent return. Ellen's family identified with the movement, were disfellowshipped by the Methodists, and then had to suffer through the GREAT DISAPPOINTMENT when the predictions were not fulfilled.

Ellen was one of those who rallied the discouraged Adventists. She told audiences that Christ had indeed returned in 1844, but had immediately moved into the heavenly sanctuary, which he was now cleansing. As soon as that task was completed, he would appear visibly.

Ellen soon met James White (1821–81), and they married in 1846. From their encounter with Seventh-day Baptists, they introduced SABBATARIANISM to the Adventist community. For the next two decades, Adventism would remain a very fluid movement. White influenced the process with her advocacy of Sabbath worship and then her emergence as a visionary and prophetess. The periodical her husband founded became her mouthpiece, and she wrote many pamphlets and books. In 1851, the couple moved to Battle Creek, Michigan, which became the center of the movement coalescing around Ellen White.

The SEVENTH-DAY ADVENTIST CHURCH was formally organized in 1863. As the leader of the church for 50 years, she wrote 25 books and some 200 shorter works. She was revered as a biblical interpreter and a prophet/visionary. Her prophetic works are still considered authoritative within the church, though opinion differs as to how they should be used. She imparted her missionary zeal to the church, which carried it into more than 200 countries as the 21st century began.

White died on July 16, 1915 at St. Helena, California.

A controversy surfaced in the late 1970s, when the Adventist scholar Ronald L. Numbers wrote a book suggesting purely mundane explanations for the supposed supernatural experiences that underlay the prophecies. A number of books subsequently appeared defending White.

Further reading: Francis D. Nichol, *Ellen G. White and Her Critics* (Takoma Park, Md.: Review & Herald Publishing, 1951); Ronald L. Numbers, *Prophetess of Health: A Study of Ellen G. White* (New York: Harper & Row, 1976, rev. ed., Knoxville: University of Tennessee Press, 1992); Ellen G. White, *Early Writings of Ellen G. White* (1882; reprint, Washington, D.C.: Review &

Herald Publishing 1945); ———, *The Great Contro-versy Between Christ and Satan* (1911; reprint, Mountain View, Calif.: Pacific Press Publishing, 1950); ———, *Life Sketches of Ellen G. White.* (1915, reprint, Mountain View, Calif.: Pacific Press Publishing, 1943).

White, William (1748–1836) *first presiding bishop of the Episcopal Church in America*

William White was born in Philadelphia, Pennsylvania, on April 4, 1748. His family was relatively wealthy and young William studied English, Latin, and theology. In 1770, he traveled to England, where he met with the archbishop of Canterbury, who approved his request for ordination. Ordained that year, he began to serve the bishop of London in his responsibilities for the American colonies.

He soon returned to Philadelphia, married the mayor's daughter, and served as assistant minister of two churches, then became priest of the merged congregations shortly thereafter. When the American Revolution broke out, most of the Anglican clergy remained loyal to England and returned home. White and the other Philadelphia Anglican clergy were fierce patriots and remained at their posts. He left the city at the time of the British occupation in 1777.

After the American victory, White accepted responsibility for rebuilding the CHURCH OF ENGLAND. For that purpose, he believed, a BISHOP was needed, but that was not a simple matter. The British authorities had never appointed one, unwilling to establish an autonomous seat of authority in the colonies, and the new citizens of the United States now staunchly opposed the reimposition of British patterns on church life, including bishops.

In 1784, White and representatives from the other Anglican churches in Philadelphia called for a general convention of Anglicans to meet in that city. When the delegates met in 1785, they organized themselves as a "general convention." They selected White as the chair and appointed committees to draw up a constitution and to suggest appropriate changes in the prayer book, reflecting the new political situation.

At this gathering, White wrote to the bishop of London, requesting that episcopal orders be passed to the now independent American brethren. After some delay, the bishop of London granted the request, and in 1786 White and Samuel Provoost (1742–1815) sailed for London to be ordained. Since the pair could not take the oath of allegiance to the British authorities, Parliament had to pass a special enabling act. In 1787, White and Provoost were consecrated by the archbishops of York and Canterbury in Lambeth Palace, the headquarters of the Church of England.

Given his newfound authority, White was invited to assume the office of chaplain to the United States Congress. He continued to hold that post, among his other duties, until Congress began to meet in New York. As the Episcopal Church revived, White became a fixture in the multiple altruistic organizations that formed over the next generation. Among the structures he helped organize and lead were societies specializing in BIBLE distribution, aid to prisoners, and service to the hearing and seeing impaired.

White wrote several books, including his *Lectures on the Catechism* (1813); *Comparative View of the Controversy between the Calvinists and the Arminians* (2 vols., 1817); and the *Memoirs of the Protestant Episcopal Church in the United States of America* (1820; 2d ed., 1835). White died on July 17, 1836, leaving behind a thriving church organization.

Further reading: Robert Prichard, *A History of the Episcopal Church* (Harrisburg, Pa.: Morehouse, 1991); W. H. Stowe, et al., *The Life and Correspondence of Bishop William White* (New York: Morehouse-Gorham, 1937); William White, *The Integrity of Christian Doctrine and the Sanctity of Christian Practice United in Christian Preaching* (New York, 1811); ———, *Memoirs of the Protestant Episcopal Church in the United States of America* (Philadelphia: S. Potter, 1820; rev. ed; New York: Swords, Stanford, 1836); Bird Wilson,

Memoir of the Life of Right Reverend William White (Philadelphia: James Kay, 1939).

Whitefield, George (1714–1770) *popular evangelist in Britain and America*

George Whitefield was born in Gloucester, England, on December 16, 1714. Feeling a call to preach, at the age of 17 he finished his grammar school education and in 1732 entered Pembroke College, Oxford. There, in 1733, he met John and Charles WESLEY, and underwent a conversion in 1735. He finished his decree after serving for a period as an ordained DEACON in the CHURCH OF ENGLAND.

In 1738, at the urging of John Wesley, then in Georgia, Whitefield made the first of many trips to the American colonies, where he founded a school for girls in Savannah. Back in London, he was ordained an Anglican priest in 1739. When he preached, overflow crowds attended. Finding many doors closed because of his identification with the Wesleys, he began to preach in the open air.

In 1839, before leaving for America again, he introduced John Wesley to field preaching outside of Bristol, which led to a major expansion of the Methodist movement. Meanwhile, Whitefield landed in Philadelphia, and after a stop in New York, he worked his way south. In Charleston, South Carolina, he founded an orphanage with money he had raised in England. He completed his trip with a stop in New England, where he preached to thousands in Boston and, on four occasions, at Jonathan EDWARDS's church in Northampton, Massachusetts (October 17–20). His stay started a wave of revival that lasted more than a year.

Back in England in 1741, he found that while he had been drifting toward CALVINISM, Wesley had become an exponent of ARMINIANISM. The two men separated amicably. Whitefield made his headquarters at a London edifice named the Moorfields Tabernacle and emerged as the leader of the Calvinist wing of the Evangelical Awaken-

ing. He continued to travel through Great Britain for the next few years and in 1743 became moderator for the Calvinist Methodists in Wales, a position he retained for many years.

Whitefield's third trip to America, starting in 1744, lasted four years. What became known as the GREAT AWAKENING had spread from New England to the middle and southern colonies. Crowds attended Whitefield's sermons everywhere he went; he became one of the first persons widely known in all the very different British colonies. He returned several times during his life and is credited with helping to bring a sense of unity to the future United States.

Back in England in 1752, Whitefield was appointed a chaplain to the Countess of Huntingdon Connexion, a Calvinist Methodist fellowship. In 1756, he opened the Whitefield Congregational Chapel on Tottenham Court Road in central London. When in London, he would preach there as well at the Moorsfield Tabernacle.

He preached his last sermon at Exeter, New Hampshire, in 1770, and died the following day. His death was widely mourned on both sides of the Atlantic.

One of the great orators of his century, Whitefield is known to have preached on literally thousands of occasions, using a fairly small repertoire of sermons. The several groups to which he was attached survive today as component parts of the United Reformed Church in the United Kingdom.

See also REVIVALISM.

Further reading: Arnold A. Dallimore, *George Whitefield: The Life and Times of the Great Evangelist of the Eighteenth Century*, 2 vols (Carlisle, Pa.: Banner of Truth Trust, 1989); John Gillies, ed., *Memoirs of Rev. George Whitefield: An Extensive Collection of His Sermons and Other Writings* (Middletown, Conn.: Hunt & Noyes, 1838); J. B. Wakely, *The Prince of Pulpit Orators: a Portraiture of Rev. George Whitefield, M. A.* (New York: Nelson & Phillips, 1871); George Whitefield, *George Whitefield's Journals [1714–1745]* (London: Banner of Truth Trust, 1960).

Wilberforce, William (1759–1833) *pioneering voice in the abolition of slavery in the West*

William Wilberforce was born into a relatively wealthy family in Hull, Yorkshire, England, in 1759. At the age of 17, he entered St. John's College at CAMBRIDGE UNIVERSITY, where he made a valuable friend in future prime minister William Pitt. That friendship partially influenced his decision to enter politics.

Wilberforce stood for Parliament in Hull in 1779. He entered the House of Commons to support the government of his college friend, William Pitt, which he did without much distinction.

Meanwhile, in 1784, he experienced a conversion and became associated with the so-called Clapham Set, a zealous group of young Anglicans with Methodistlike sympathies associated with John Venn (1759–1813), the rector of Clapham Church in London. Wilberforce's new spiritual life led him to consider issues of social reform, and he responded favorably when Lady Middleton asked him to use his influence in Parliament to help end the slave trade. Pitt urged Wilberforce to become his point man on the slavery issue in the House of Commons. He delivered his first speech on the subject on May 12, 1789, and quickly emerged as one of the leading voices in the still relatively small antislavery movement. He found himself alienated from many of his Tory colleagues, who did not believe that ending slavery was economically feasible or desirable.

The antislavery movement became a crusade for Wilberforce. After a stinging defeat of his bill to end British participation in the slave trade in 1791, he worked for 16 years until that vote was finally and decisively reversed. Having outlawed the slave trade, the next issue was granting freedom to those who remained in slavery. Wilberforce backed away from that step, as he believed the slaves were not yet prepared for freedom, needing education and training for the life ahead. In 1823, he joined in the work of the newly formed Society for the Mitigation and Gradual Abolition of Slavery. He died on July 29, 1833, just a month before Parliament passed the Slavery Abolition Act that ended slavery throughout the vast British Empire.

Further reading: Leonard W. Cowie, *William Wilberforce, 1759–1833, a Bibliography* (London: Greenwood Press, 1992); Garth Lean, *God's Politician: William Wilberforce's Struggle* (London: Darton, Longman & Todd, 1980); Robert Isaac Wilberforce and Samuel Wilberforce, *Life of William Wilberforce,* 5 vols. (London: John Murray, 1838); William Wilberforce, *A Practical View of the Prevailing Religious System of Professed Christians in the Higher and Middle Classes of this Country Contrasted with Real Christianity* (London: Cadell Davies, 1797); ———, *An Appeal to the Religion, Justice, and Humanity of the Inhabitants of the British Empire in Behalf of the Negro Slaves in the West Indies* (London: J. Hatchard, 1823).

Willard, Frances (1839–1898) *feminist leader of the Women's Christian Temperance Union*

Frances Elizabeth Willard was born on September 28, 1839, in Churchville, New York, and grew up in Janesville, Wisconsin, where the family joined the Methodist Episcopal Church. Her parents, both teachers, made sure that Frances and her sister, Mary, received a good education. Frances was motivated through much of her life to be like her brother, who as a Methodist minister was educated, could vote, and could preach.

At age 17, Willard entered Milwaukee Female College, then continued her studies at Northwest Female College and Garrett Biblical Institute, both sponsored by the Methodists at Evanston, Illinois. She graduated as her class valedictorian.

Frances began a teaching career; in 1871, she became president of the Evanston College for Ladies. She introduced some startling educational changes designed to create more autonomous female graduates. Criticism led her to come out publicly in favor of the new women's movement. Her career at the college came to an end in 1873, when Charles Fowler became president of Northwestern University. Fowler, who had been briefly engaged to Willard, moved to

Home of Frances Willard (1839–98) in Evanston, Illinois, adjacent to Northwestern University and the headquarters of the Women's Christian Temperance Union *(Institute for the Study of American Religion, Santa Barbara, California)*

end Evanston College's independence and strip Willard of her presidential powers.

Leaving her academic post, Willard became active in the Association for the Advancement for Women as its national vice president. Seeing the possibilities in the antisaloon crusade that was sweeping the Midwest, she became the national corresponding secretary of the Woman's Christian Temperance Union (WCTU), and pushed the union to back women's suffrage. Then in 1879, she attained the presidency of the union and kept it for the rest of her life, sustained by the annual vote of the national convention.

In 1880, Willard announced the "Do-Every-thing Policy," which would involve the WCTU with a wide variety of issues relevant to the status and role of women—from hiring women police to dealing with female offenders to rescu-ing teenagers from prostitution. As the union expanded, Willard's prominence increased. In 1888, she was one of the first group of women elected as delegates to the Methodist Episcopal Church's General Conference, but was denied her seat, with Charles Fowler, now a BISHOP, help-ing to block her way, Willard was particularly targeted because of her recent new book, *Women in the Pulpit.*

Willard was effective on the suffrage question in Illinois, which in 1913 adopted her proposal for "Home Protection." As a step toward full suffrage, the plan would allow women to vote on all issues that directly affected the home, with alcohol abuse at the top of the list.

Willard died on February 17, 1898. She was widely honored in death; the state of Illinois donated a statue to the U.S. Capitol's Statuary

Hall, the only woman so honored. The WCTU backed away from Willard's feminist programs in the decades following her death when their primary cause triumphed with the Prohibition amendment. Her role in the women's movement was largely forgotten until revived in the late 20th century by Evangelical women seeking role models for their own efforts to escape male-dominated ecclesiastical structures.

See also WOMEN, ORDINATION OF.

Further reading: Carolyn D. Gifford, ed., *Writing Out My Heart: Selections from the Journal of Frances E. Willard, 1855–96* (Urbana: University of Illinois Press, 1995); Anna Gordon, *The Beautiful Life of Frances Willard* (Chicago: Woman's Temperance Publishing Association, 1898); Richard W. Leeman, *Do Everything Reform: The Reform Oratory of Frances E. Willard* (Westport, Conn.: Greenwood Press, 1992); Ray Strachey, *Frances Willard Her Life and Work* (New York: Fleming H. Revell, 1913); Frances Willard, *Glimpses of Fifty Years* (Chicago: H. J. Smith, 1889).

Williams, George (1821–1905) *founder of the YMCA*

George Williams was born at Dulverton, Somerset, England, on October 11, 1821. As a young man he entered the business world; however, a sudden conversion experience changed his life. He became concerned for the lot of the laboring classes. With his new motto, "It is not how little but how much we can do for others," the 20-year-old Williams launched an effort to improve the lives of shop assistants, whom he saw as little more than slaves working 14 to 16 hours a day. He became a leader in what was termed the "early-closing movement." As he became a successful businessman and employer, he led by example. Williams also became an example in Christian philanthropy, annually giving away as much as a third of his income. He was active in a number of Christian organizations such as the CHURCH MISSIONARY SOCIETY, the British and Foreign Bible Society, and the Religious Tract Society.

In the summer of 1844, William took the lead in a series of discussions that led to the founding of the YOUNG MEN'S CHRISTIAN ASSOCIATION (YMCA). The goal of the organization was to mobilize young men to help nurture the spiritual life of their peers. The YMCA quickly moved from a concern with exclusively spiritual matters to issues of education and general problems facing young adult males. The original association developed branches throughout London's West End and soon jumped to Leeds, Manchester, Liverpool, Exeter, Bristol, Plymouth, and Hull. During the 1850s, the movement spread internationally to AUSTRALIA, FRANCE, INDIA, and North America. In 1855, the World's Alliance of Young Men's Christian Associations was formed. It took shape as an association of centers concerned with evangelization, cooperative spirit, and improving the lot of young men through changing social conditions and education.

Williams remained active in the association for the rest of his life. In 1880, he gave money for the purchase of the headquarters, then two years later led in forming an association of the British YMCAs, over which he presided until his death. Queen Victoria knighted him in 1894 on the occasion of the association's 50th anniversary. He died on November 6, 1905, shortly after addressing the World YMCA Jubilee gathering. He was subsequently buried in St. Paul's Cathedral, London.

Further reading: Clyde Binfield, *George Williams and the YMCA. A Study in Victorian Social Attitudes* (London: Heinemann, 1973); C. P. Shedd, et al., *History of the World Alliance of Young Men's Christian Associations* (London: SPCK, 1955); J. E. Hodder Williams, *The Life of Sir George Williams, Founder of the YMCA* (New York: Eaton & Mains, 1906).

Williams, John (1796–1839) *pioneer missionary to the South Pacific*

John Williams was born at Tottenham High Cross, London, England, in 1796 and apprenticed to an ironmonger as a youth. He joined the Moorfields

Tabernacle, a church established by George WHITEFIELD in the previous century, and in 1814 offered himself to the LONDON MISSIONARY SOCIETY (LMS) as a missionary for the South Seas. He was ordained a Congregationalist minister and married shortly before sailing.

After a long trip, he arrived at Moorea in the Society Islands in 1817. He settled in Huahine in 1818 but left in a disagreement with certain LMS policies and launched work on Raiatea. He learned the language, and in 1821 purchased a schooner, the *Endeavour,* to extend his missionary work to other islands. He introduced Protestantism to the Hervey Islands and visited the islands of Rurutu and Rimatara in 1823.

In 1827, Williams visited Raratonga, in the southern Cook Islands, and while there translated part of the BIBLE into Rarotongan; he also built a new boat, the *Messenger of Peace,* to further extend his work. While in Tonga, in 1830 he negotiated an important agreement with the British Methodist leadership on a division of labor to prevent competition among the different missionary agencies then at work in the Pacific region. In 1834, he sailed to England, where he oversaw the publication of his Rarotongan New Testament by the British and Foreign Bible Society. He took the opportunity to publish an account of his work, speak widely on the mission cause, and raise the funds to buy a new ship.

Williams returned to the South Seas and continued to found new LMS mission stations. In 1839, while traveling in the New Hebrides, he landed at Erromanga in what is now the nation of Vanuatu. The island's residents attacked his group, and he was among those killed.

Williams was widely revered as a martyr for the missionary cause. Over the years, no fewer than seven LMS mission ships were named after him.

See also SOUTH PACIFIC.

Further reading: Cecil Northcott, *South Seas Sailor: the Story of John Williams and His Ships* (Fort Washington, Pa.: Christian Literature Crusade, 1965);

Basil Mathews, *John Williams the Shipbuilder* (London: Humphrey Milford, 1915, 1947); John Williams, *Narrative of Missionary Enterprises in the South Sea Islands* (London: John Snow, 1839).

Williams, Roger (c. 1603–1683) *Puritan champion of freedom of religion*

Roger Williams was born in London around 1603. His father, James Williams, was a well-to-do tailor. Williams studied at Pembroke College, CAMBRIDGE UNIVERSITY, where he received a scholarship based on his facility with the classical languages. He graduated in 1627.

After leaving Cambridge, Williams was ordained in the CHURCH OF ENGLAND and became the chaplain to a wealthy family. By this time, he had become alienated from the Church of England and increasingly identified with the Puritan Independents. He left England with his wife and arrived in Boston, Massachusetts, early in 1631. He worked as a Puritan (Congregational) minister in Salem and Plymouth, but soon ran into conflict with fellow ministers, both on theological issues and on his advocacy of Free Church ideals.

He was brought before the Salem Court on several occasions for his "diverse, new, and dangerous opinions." Among his most controversial ideas was his suggestion that the land now occupied by the British colonists belonged to the Native Americans, not the king. He also refused to serve any congregation that recognized the Church of England (a touchy issue as most Puritans still wanted to reform the Church of England, rather than separate from it). Possibly the ultimate heresy was his opposition to enforced religious uniformity in New England in favor of what he termed "soul-liberty," by which he would grant each colonist a liberal freedom of opinion on religious matters. In 1635, he was deported from Massachusetts. Rather than return to England, he headed south and found refuge among native people. He purchased land from the Narragansett people and in 1636 founded the colony of Rhode Island and the future city of Providence.

In the summer of 1643, Williams traveled to England to obtain a charter for Rhode Island, so as to keep the Puritans from taking over the settlement. The charter provided corporate status for Providence, Newport, and Portsmouth. Because of the political turmoil in England and the change in regimes, Williams had to return to England in 1651 to renew the charter; after the restoration of the monarchy, his colleague John Clarke (1609–76) finally obtained a royal charter for Rhode Island in 1663. In the meantime, Williams worked on his first important book, *Key into the Languages of America,* published in London in 1643. With its appearance, he was recognized as an authority on the native peoples.

While in England in 1643, Williams published the first of a series of pamphlets concerning religious liberty and related issues of church-state relations, *The Bloody Tenant of Persecution.* His belief that true religion had to be freely adopted and conversion should never be coerced led him to invite Jewish refugees to settle in peace in Newport. His ideas on the SEPARATION OF CHURCH AND STATE were the seed for the First Amendment religious freedoms enshrined in the United States Constitution.

Williams is generally looked upon as the founder of the first Baptist Church in America. He had been rebaptized in 1639 and became the leader of a small group, but withdrew from the church after only a few months and afterward considered himself a "Seeker." He remained a dedicated Christian, but had doubts about how the church should be organized. The group he formed, however, continues to this day as the First Baptist Church of Providence.

Roger Williams died at Providence in 1683.

Further reading: Samuel Brockunier, *The Irrepressible Democrat, Roger Williams* (New York: Ronald Press, 1940); Edwin S. Gaustad, *Liberty of Conscience: Roger Williams in America* (Grand Rapids, Mich.: William B. Eerdmans, 1991); Glenn W. LaFantasie, ed., *The Correspondence of Roger Williams* (Providence, R.I.: Brown University Press,

1988); Perry Miller, *Roger Williams, A Contribution to the American Tradition* (Indianapolis, Ind.: Bobbs-Merrill, 1953); Roger Williams, *The Bloody Tenant of Persecution for Cause of Conscience,* Richard Groves, ed. (Macon, Ga.: Mercer University Press, 2001).

Winter, Ralph D. (b. 1924) *Evangelical missiologist and mission supporter*

Ralph D. Winter was born in 1924. A Presbyterian, he graduated from both Princeton Theological Seminary (BB.D.) and Cornell University (Ph.D.). While serving 10 years as a missionary in Guatemala (1956–66), Winter began implementing some of his innovative ideas, through his Theological Education by Extension movement. He wanted to decentralize theological education and pastoral training, locating programs where church leaders could remain connected to their own culture and community.

In 1966, Winter moved to Pasadena, California, to accept a position at the School of World Mission at Fuller Theological Seminary. Over the next decade, he and his wife, Roberta Winter, founded a set of structures to meet what they saw as the pressing need for the global extension of the church: the William Carey Library (a publishing house, 1968), the American Society of Missiology (1974), the International Society of Frontier Missiology (1986), the United States Center for World Mission (1976), and the William Carey International University (1977).

In 1974, Winter alerted the Lausanne Congress on World Evangelism to the existence of many peoples who had yet to receive a Christian missionary or see a BIBLE in their own language. The effort to reach the unreached peoples, (defined by their distinct languages and cultures rather than nationhood) gave birth in the next decade to AD 2000 and Beyond, which encouraged cooperative Evangelical churches to establish a church for every unreached people by the year 2000. It first received significant attention at the international missions conference at Manila in 1989.

Among the new ideas generated by the A.D. 2000 Movement was what came to be known as the "10/40 Window," a region identified by Luis Bish, AD2000's international director. The 10/40 Window includes the area of North Africa, the Middle East, and Asia between 10 degrees and 40 degrees north latitude where, Bish asserted, 95 percent of the world's least evangelized people are found.

Simultaneously, Winter encouraged the idea of people adoption. It was institutionalized in the Adopt-A-People Clearinghouse founded in November at the U.S. Center for World Missions, which matches local churches with unreached peoples. The clearinghouse mobilized a number of missionary agencies and compiled significant research on different people groups. It has recently merged its efforts with that of the Bible League based in Crete, Illinois.

Apart from his missiology work, Winter and his wife have produced a series of Bible study books anchored by the Word Study New Testament, designed to facilitate the mastery of the New Testament for those with little or no knowledge of the biblical languages, Greek and Hebrew.

See also FAITH MISSIONS.

Further reading: Ralph D. Winter, *Protestant Mission Societies: The American Experience* (Pasadena, Calif.: William Carey Library, 1979); ———, *Theological Education by Extension* (Pasadena, Calif.: William Carey Library, 1970); ———, *The 25 Unbelievable Years 1945–1969* (Pasadena, Calif.: William Carey Library, 1970); ———, *The Word Study New Testament* (Pasadena, Calif.: William Carey Library, 1978); Ralph D. Winter and Steven C. Hawthorn, eds., *Perspectives on the World Christian Movement: A Reader* (Pasadena, Calif.: William Carey Library, 1992).

Wittenberg

Wittenberg, a city in Saxony-Anhalt in east central Germany, is the site where the Reformation began. Its new university hired Martin LUTHER for its faculty, and he nailed his NINETY-FIVE THESES to the

Martin Luther reputedly nailed the Ninety-five Theses to the church door at Wittenberg, Germany, thus beginning the Protestant movement. *(Institute for the Study of American Religion, Santa Barbara, California)*

doors of the still standing Castle Church on October 31, 1517. Luther remained in Wittenberg to direct the Reformation for the rest of his life. Wittenberg printer Hans Lufft (1528–84) issued the first edition of Luther's German Bible in 1534.

Many of the city's historical sites survived the wars that have ravaged the region. Visitors may see Luther's home (a museum); the graves of Luther and fellow reformer Philip MELANCHTHON in the Castle Church; the 14th-century parish church where Luther preached; and the spot where Luther burned a papal bull condemning his doctrines.

The city has periodically become a focus of ceremonial activities. In 1922, it was the site where the German state churches agreed to establish the present EVANGELICAL CHURCH IN GERMANY. Located in the officially atheist Communist East Germany for more than four decades, it has gained a new importance since the unification of Germany as a pilgrimage site for Lutherans and other Christians. The 2002 meeting of the council of the LUTHERAN WORLD FEDERATION (LWF) opened with a worship service in Wittenberg's Castle Church.

Further reading: Home page of Lutherstadt-Wittenberg. Available online. URL: http://www.wittenberg.de; James M. Kittelson, *Luther the Reformer: The Story of the Man and His Career* (Minneapolis, Minn.: Augsburg, 1986); Steven Ozment, ed., *Reformation Europe: A Guide to Research* (St. Louis: Center for Reformation Research, 1982).

Wolff, Joseph (c. 1795–1862) *Jewish convert who led missions to Jews*

Joseph Wolff was born in Weilersbach, Bavaria, Germany, the son of a rabbi. As a youth, he left his family and converted to Catholicism; Jesuit missionary Francis Xavier became his role model. Baptized in 1812 in Prague, Wolff pursued studies at Vienna and then at the University of Tübingen, where he studied Middle Eastern languages and absorbed Protestant leanings.

In 1817, he enrolled at the Propaganda Fide College in Rome, but was expelled when his Protestant beliefs were uncovered. Traveling around Europe, he met Robert HALDANE, who invited him to England, where he formally converted to the CHURCH OF ENGLAND. He also came to know people associated with the London Jew's Society (LJS). With the society's sponsorship, he attended CAMBRIDGE UNIVERSITY and studied under Charles Simeon (1759–1836), who influenced a number of students to become missionaries.

After two years at Cambridge, in 1821 Wolff headed for the MIDDLE EAST under LJS sponsorship. Based on his early reports, the society accepted his recommendation to open a perma-

nent mission center in Jerusalem. He traveled from Egypt to Iran (Persia) as the society's emissary, preaching when he could to Jewish audiences. In 1826, he returned to England, where he met Lady Georgina Walpole, whom he married in 1827.

Returning to the Middle East in 1828, Wolff continued his pioneering work in JEWISH MISSIONS, and also began a quest to locate the fabled Ten Lost Tribes of Israel. His quest took him to Jewish communities from Armenia to southern India.

In 1837, he traveled to the United States, where he was ordained an Anglican priest in 1838. He settled in England as a parish priest in Linthwaite, Yorkshire, and then, from 1845, at Ile Brewers, Somerset. His parish life was interrupted in 1843, when he traveled to Bokhara in present-day Uzbekistan to assist two British officers in what became a hair-raising adventure and the subject of a best-selling book. He died in England on May 2, 1862.

Further reading: Hugh Evan Hopkins, *Sublime Vagabond: The Life of Joseph Wolff, Missionary Extraordinary* (London: Churchman, 1984); H. P. Palmer, *Joseph Wolff. His Romantic Life and Travels* (London: Heath Cranton 1935); Joseph Wolff, *Narrative of a Mission to Bokhara* (London: John W. Parker, 1864); ———, *Researches and Missionary Labours among the Jews, Mohammedans, and Other Sects* (London: the author, 1835); ———, *Travels and Adventures of Joseph Wolff*, 2 vols., (London: Saunders, Otley, 1860–61).

women, ordination of

During the 1970s, the issue of the full ordination of women as professional clergy swept through Christendom. All the major Protestant bodies were forced to consider it, if only, in some cases, to reaffirm the traditional practice of barring women.

The question was in part a deferred inheritance of the Reformation, which abolished most female religious orders, one of the few arenas in which women could exercise some religious leadership. By the beginning of the 19th century, the first waves of feminism, coupled with the need for preachers for the emerging revivalist movements, created a new environment for the rise of female leadership.

The first group to make room for women in the ministry appears to have been the Society of Friends in both England and America. In 1666, Margaret Fell, wife of Quaker founder George Fox, penned her manifesto: *Women's Speaking Justified, Proved and Allowed by the Scriptures, all such as speak by the Spirit and Power of the Lord Jesus.* Though QUAKERS did not ordain ministers of either sex, they allowed both men and women to assume preaching duties, as the movement of the Spirit abided among women as well as among men. The success of female Quaker preachers later provided a model for Methodists.

The PRIMITIVE METHODIST CHURCH, an offshoot of the Wesleyan movement, brought American-style CAMP MEETINGS to England. Allowing women to assist in its revivals was in a sense an extension of the enhanced role METHODISM assigned to laypeople in general. Women began as prayer leaders, then became exhorters, and finally preached. Since most meetings were held outdoors and preaching was done without a reading stand, the objections of those who might have been offended if a women stood behind a pulpit were eased.

In 1813, the Primitive Methodists recruited 19-year-old Sarah Kirkland (1794–1880) as a full-time salaried missionary. Following her marriage in 1818, both she and her minister husband were appointed to work at Hull. Eventually, more than 100 women were employed throughout England as ministers (traveling preachers). One of these women preachers, Ruth Watkins, was later part of the initial contingent of Primitive Methodist preachers sent to America in 1829.

Within the more established Protestant denominations, the issue surfaced only with the rise of the 19th-century women's rights movement. The demand for women's ordination was part of the general drive for women's admission to colleges and professional positions. At the very first women's rights gathering, at the Wesleyan Methodist Church in Seneca Falls, New York, in 1848, one of the grievances aired was that "with only a few exceptions, women were not allowed to participate in the affairs of the church." In 1852, Lydia Sexton became the first woman to receive a license to preach—from the Church of the United Brethren (a Methodistlike body of German extraction, now a constituent part of the UNITED METHODIST CHURCH).

In 1853, Antoinette Brown BLACKWELL (1825–1921) became the first woman to be ordained a fully recognized minister. She served as pastor of the Congregational Church of South Butler, New York. Congregationalists practice local church autonomy; each congregation ordains its own ministers, and Brown did not need approval from a judicatory. Brown's ordination sermon was preached by Rev. Luther Lee, one of the founders of the Wesleyan Methodist Connection.

A decade later, Olympia Brown (1835–1926) was ordained by the St. Lawrence Association of Universalists, the first woman to be ordained by a church judicatory. One other church, the Advent Christian Church, had authorized the ordination of women by that year, but had not yet acted on its decision.

Throughout the last two decades of the 19th century, a spectrum of churches began to ordain women, the most important being the Northern Baptist Convention (now the AMERICAN BAPTIST CHURCHES U.S.A.) and the Christian Church (Disciples of Christ). The CHURCH OF GOD (ANDERSON, INDIANA) introduced female ministers to the HOLINESS movement, though it was already exposed to outstanding female leadership in the person of Phoebe PALMER (1807–74), who in 1860 had penned her support of female ministers, *Promise of the Father.* Catherine BOOTH (1829–90), the wife of the founder of the SALVATION ARMY, wrote one of the early books advocating women's ordination, and the Army joined the list of churches with female ministers (officers, in their case).

In the same era, the drive for ordination received an unintended boost from the new DEA-CONESS movement, which amounted to a reintroduction of an ordered female community into Protestantism. The modern movement was founded by Theodore Fliedner and his wife, Friedericke Munster, who opened the first deaconess motherhouse in Germany in 1836. The movement spread through the European Lutheran churches. In 1884, seven deaconesses arrived in Philadelphia to manage the German hospital. The spread of a Lutheran deaconess movement in America inspired Lucy Rider Meyer (1849–1922) to found the Methodist deaconess movement in Chicago. The Episcopal Church had instituted a deaconess order even earlier, and in 1855 the bishop of Maryland formally "set apart" two women for their new ministry. That act is now seen as the beginning of the drive for ordination in the worldwide ANGLICAN COMMUNION.

Many more Protestant DENOMINATIONS opened the door to women ministers in the 20th century, though few were actually allowed to walk through that door. For example, in 1939 the METHODIST CHURCH approved legislation allowing women in the ordained ministry, but many of those ordained were the widows of ministers in a specialized ministry, which the wife continued after his death. One sign of continued exclusion was the emergence of several new denominations created and led by women—most notably the Pillar of Fire (Alma WHITE) and the INTERNATIONAL CHURCH OF THE FOURSQUARE GOSPEL (Aimee Semple McPHERSON).

A more successful effort to open the remaining denominations to women's ordination, and to ensure equal treatment of women ministers where they existed, began in the 1970s. In 1972, for example, the new United Methodist Church passed extensive legislation to improve the status and role of women at every level of church life. With the exception of the conservative SOUTHERN BAPTIST CONVENTION, most of the other large Protestant groups followed suit.

Much of the publicity concerning women was focused on the Episcopal Church. Like their fellow Anglicans around the world, Episcopalians had worked hard to cultivate legitimacy alongside the Roman Catholic and Eastern Orthodox churches, none of which had female priests nor seemed inclined to accept them. On the other hand, as a member of the burgeoning ECUMENICAL MOVEMENT (both the WORLD COUNCIL OF CHURCHES and the National Council of Churches of Christ in the U.S.A.), the Episcopal Church was closest to the other liberal Protestant bodies that were already allowing women to be ordained. The church also had to face growing internal support to ordain women.

The issue reached a crisis point on July 29, 1974, when 11 female DEACONS were ordained to the priesthood by three BISHOPS, two of whom were retired and the other of whom had resigned his post. The church's sitting bishops subsequently labeled the ordinations invalid. That action was reversed in 1976 by the next General Assembly, which regularized the ordinations. Bolstered by the earlier ordination of women in Hong Kong and by the Canadian church's approval of ordination for women, the Episcopal Church had finally accepted the practice as a reality. By the end of 1977, more than 100 women had been ordained Episcopal priests.

In 1978, the bishops of the worldwide Anglican Communion gathered for the Lambeth Conference and approved in principle the ordination of women. Since then, most Anglican churches around the world have ordained women. At the same time, a dissident movement of traditionalists emerged in the United States; it set up new jurisdictions that rejected women priests along with a host of other recent changes. Traditionalist bodies soon appeared in England, Canada, and Australia. The gap between the traditionalists and the Anglican Communion has widened over the succeeding decades, but the traditionalists have been unable to agree among themselves and are now divided into more than 50 small denominations.

While women were entering the ministry, parallel efforts were made to open high-level lay positions in the various denominations to women, and to appoint female bishops in the episcopally led churches. In the 1890s, two women, first Alma White (1862–1946) and then Emma Curtis Hopkins (1853–1925) assumed the role of bishop, but they had both founded their own churches. In the 1980s, attention turned to the United Methodist Church and the Episcopal Church, where women were already serving as ministers.

The United Methodists elected Marjorie Swank Matthews (1916–86) a bishop in 1980. She served but one quadrennial term, but a number of others soon followed her. With the 1984 election of Leontine T. C. KELLY (b. 1920), the first African-American female bishop, it was felt that all the barriers had been broken, at least in principle. In 1989, the Episcopalians elected their first female (and African-American) bishop, Barbara C. HARRIS. The following year, Penelope Jamieson was consecrated as bishop of Dunedin in the Anglican Church in NEW ZEALAND. The years since have been marked by initial ordinations and consecrations in Anglican churches around the world, with the last pockets of opposition found in southern Asia and central Africa. There were 11 female bishops in attendance at the last Lambeth Conference in 1998. While the CHURCH OF ENGLAND has ordained women since 1994, they had not elected a female bishop as of 2003.

The Southern Baptist Convention remains the largest Protestant body in North America that staunchly rejects ordination of women at the denominational level. However, being congregationally organized, local Southern Baptist churches may ordain women without reference to the convention. As of 2003, there were an estimated 1,600 ordained Southern Baptist women ministers, though only about 100 served as congregational pastors. However, as recently as 2000, the convention passed additional legislation against churches ordaining or hiring female ministers. Some ministers, such as Anne Graham Lotz, the daughter of popular evangelist Billy GRA-HAM, have become evangelists and now speak regularly to large audiences across the United States.

Further reading: Janet Wilson James, ed., *Women in American Religion* (Philadelphia: University of Pennsylvania Press, 1980); Edward C. Lehman Jr., *Women Clergy: Breaking through Gender Barriers* (New Brunswick, N.J.: Transaction Books, 1985); J. Gordon Melton with Gary L. Ward, eds., *The Churches Speak on Women's Ordination* (Detroit: Gale Research, 1991); Geoffrey Milburn, *Primitive Methodism* (London: Epworth Press, 2002); Paula D. Nesbitt, *The Feminization of the Clergy in America: Occupational and Organizational Perspectives* (New York: Oxford University Press, 1997); Carl J. Schneider and Dorothy Schneider, *In Their Own Right: The History of American Clergywomen* (New York: Crossroad, 1997); Barbara Brown Zikmund, Adair T. Lummis, and Patricia M. Y. Chang, *An Uphill Calling: Ordained Women in Contemporary Protestantism* (Louisville, Ky.: Westminster John Knox, 1998).

World Alliance of Reformed Churches

The World Alliance of Reformed Churches traces its history to 1875, when 21 Reformed and Presbyterian churches from Europe and North America united under the somewhat unwieldy name: the Alliance of the Reformed Churches Throughout the World Holding the Presbyterian System. Over the next century, some of the original members merged with one another to form new united churches. At the same time, many of the missions they had created around the world matured into new autonomous Presbyterian and Reformed DENOMINATIONS, which were welcomed as sister churches into the alliance.

Meanwhile, in 1891 the Congregational churches, most of whom shared the British Puritan heritage with the Presbyterians, formed their own ecumenical body, the International Congregational Council. However, two of the council's most important members, the National Council of Congregational Christian Churches (in the United States) and the Congregational CHURCH OF EN-

GLAND and Wales merged with non-Congregational Reformed Church bodies, in 1957 and 1972 respectively. The American Congregationalists merged with the Evangelical and Reformed Church to form the UNITED CHURCH OF CHRIST and the British Congregationalists merged into the United Reformed Church.

Such mergers suggested that the shared Reformed theological heritage was felt to be more important than differences in POLITY between CONGREGATIONALISM and Presbyterianism. In confirmation, the Alliance of the Reformed Churches and the International Congregational Council merged in 1970 to form the World Alliance of Reformed Churches.

In 1946, the Alliance of Reformed Churches, anticipating the formation of the WORLD COUNCIL OF CHURCHES (WCC), moved its headquarters to Geneva, Switzerland. Most of its member churches are also members of the WCC, and the two organizations work closely together.

Like its sister organizations, the LUTHERAN WORLD FEDERATION and the WORLD METHODIST COUNCIL, the World Alliance keeps alive concerns that grow directly out of its allegiance to a particular theological heritage. The alliance promotes theological dialogues, facilitates communication and programs of mutual cooperation among its members, and publishes various items, including a periodical, *The Reformed World.*

The alliance focused much of its attention on South Africa in the 1980s. In 1982, the alliance suspended the membership of two South African Reformed bodies until they brought their policies in line with the alliance's antiapartheid stance. One church left the alliance altogether, while the other maintained a dialogue and was received back into full membership in 1997.

In 2003, the alliance reported 218 member churches in more than 100 countries.

See also ECUMENICAL MOVEMENT.

Further reading: World Alliance of Reformed Churches. Available online. URL: http://www.warc.ch; Jean-Jacques Bauswein and Lukas Vischner, eds. *The*

Reformed Family Worldwide: A Survey of Reformed Churches, Theological Schools, and International Organizations (Grand Rapids, Mich.: William B. Eerdmans, 1999).

World Council of Biblical Churches

The World Council of Biblical Churches, originally organized in 1987 as the Council of Bible Believing Churches International, was founded by former members of the INTERNATIONAL COUNCIL OF CHRISTIAN CHURCHES (ICCC). The ICCC was founded by separatist Fundamentalist Protestant churches from different DENOMINATIONS that rejected what they saw as the liberal theological consensus of the WORLD COUNCIL OF CHURCHES, and renounced any contact with like-minded believers who remained within the allegedly apostate churches. The ICCC was represented in the United States by the American Council of Christian Churches (ACCC).

The separatists found their primary spokesperson in Presbyterian minister Carl McIntire (1906–2002), who had founded the ACCC in 1941, and the ICCC several years later. When the ACCC removed McIntire from its board, the ICCC expelled the ACCC. American Fundamentalists who had broken with McIntire had no international agency to work with until 1987, when they founded the Council of Bible Believing Churches. The council seeks to use its united voice to address the issues affecting Fundamentalist Christians globally.

The council believes in the infallibility and INERRANCY of the BIBLE and the importance of complete separation from heresy and apostasy. The World Council of Churches and its member churches and the WORLD EVANGELICAL ALLIANCE and its member churches are viewed as tainted organizations that must be completely shunned. The council opposes the modern Pentecostal/ Charismatic movement.

See also ECUMENICAL MOVEMENT.

Further reading: Jerry Falwell, *The Fundamentalist Phenomenon.* Garden City, N.Y.: Doubleday, 1981.

World Council of Churches

The World Council of Churches is the largest global Protestant ecumenical organization, which began the 21st century with some 340 member churches (DENOMINATIONS) based in 120 nations and representing approximately 400 million church members. While commonly seen as a Protestant fellowship, it is more accurately perceived as a fellowship of Christians who are not part of the Roman Catholic Church, as it included Eastern Orthodox churches as an integral part of its fellowship from the outset.

The ECUMENICAL MOVEMENT that produced the World Council began in the 19th century. Protestant leaders from around the world, especially those involved in the global missionary endeavor, were acutely aware of the splintering of the

First Methodist Church, Evanston, Illinois, hosted the 1954 assembly of the WCC. *(Institute for the Study of American Religion, Santa Barbara, California)*

Protestant movement into hundreds of denominations, which was an embarrassment in the missionary field. These leaders called for new organized expressions of Christian unity. An initial step was a set of agreements to head off direct competition on the mission field. Early in the 20th century, large international conferences were held around major issues dividing the churches under two broad areas of concern: FAITH AND ORDER (theological and ecclesiastical issues) and LIFE AND WORK (the mission and activity of the church in the world).

In 1933, American theologian William Adams Brown suggested to William TEMPLE, then the archbishop of York in the CHURCH OF ENGLAND, that a spectrum of international Protestant groups should launch a conversation regarding their possible future together. Temple acted upon the suggestion, and in 1937, he and others proposed the idea of a World Council of Churches. The idea was placed on hold as the world went to war, though World War II became for many an added motivation to form the World Council.

The initial gathering of the World Council of Churches took place in 1948 in Amsterdam, the NETHERLANDS. Over the next half century, its membership grew significantly, and its geographical center shifted from Europe and North America to Asia and Africa as the original members granted autonomy to former mission churches around the world.

The council describes itself as "a fellowship of churches which confess the Lord Jesus Christ as God and Saviour according to the scriptures and therefore seeks to fulfill together their common calling to the glory of the one God, Father, Son and Holy Spirit." Its Protestant membership is dominated by churches representative of Reformation and Puritan origins, though it also includes such 20th-century Christian expressions as the AFRICAN INITIATED CHURCHES. Few HOLINESS or Pentecostal churches have applied for membership, and the more theologically conservative Protestant organizations have rejected the council and formed competing global fellowships, such as the EVANGELICAL WORLD ALLIANCE and the INTER-NATIONAL COUNCIL OF CHRISTIAN CHURCHES, which have far smaller memberships.

From its beginning, Orthodox churches have formed an important segment of the council's membership, though their location in lands under dictatorial atheist regimes occasioned much controversy. Both the council and these churches, especially the Russian Orthodox Church, were accused of being instruments of Communist propaganda. Those accusation were largely put aside after the fall of the Soviet Union and the related Marxist governments in Eastern Europe. In the 1990s, the Orthodox churches began to serve another role, as critics of the council's liberal theological and liturgical innovations and its involvement in controversial social issues. In the late 1990s, some of the more conservative Orthodox churches resigned from the council in protest.

The World Council is headquartered in Geneva, Switzerland, and governed ultimately by a General Assembly. It develops program through four internal administrative groupings: (1) Issues and Themes, (2) Relationships, (3) Communication, and (4) Finance, Services, and Administration. Above all, the council promotes dialogue among its member churches, between member churches and the Roman Catholic Church, and between its members and the world's other major religions. It extends this endeavor through a set of affiliated regional, national, and local councils. It has also built important alliances with the global Protestant family communions such as the WORLD METHODIST COUNCIL, the ANGLICAN COMMUNION, the WORLD ALLIANCE OF REFORMED CHURCHES, the Ecumenical Patriarchate, and the LUTHERAN WORLD FEDERATION.

The World Council's relationship to the Roman Catholic Church (RCC) has evolved significantly. A major breakthrough in amity occurred as a result of the Second Vatican Council. The council built close working relationships with the Pontifical Council for Promoting Christian Unity, the primary Vatican II structure to conduct ecumenical dialogue. A WCC/RCC joint working group now meets annually, and the WCC Faith and Order Commission has invited Roman Catholics to join as full voting members.

Further reading: Michael Kinnamon and Brian Cope, eds., *The Ecumenical Movement: An Anthology of Key Texts and Voices* (Geneva: World Council of Churches, 1997); Nicholas Lossky et al., eds., *Dictionary of the Ecumenical Movement* (Geneva/Grand Rapids, Mich.: WCC Publications/William B. Eerdmans, 1991); Conrad Raiser, *To Be the Church: Challenges and Hopes for a New Millennium* (Geneva: World Council of Churches, 1997); Ans J. van der Bent, ed., *Handbook of Member Churches: World Council of Churches* (Geneva: World Council of Churches, 1982); *Yearbook* (Geneva: World Council of Churches, issued annually).

World Evangelical Alliance

The World Evangelical Alliance (formerly the World Evangelical Fellowship) traces its history to the Evangelical Alliance, founded in London in 1846 by delegates from more than 50 different Christian denominational bodies. The original organization was an association of individuals. It adopted a statement of belief that included affirmation of the authority of Scripture, the need and right of individual interpretation, the Trinity, human depravity, and salvation through Jesus Christ. The alliance quickly found international support and spread to all the Protestant-dominated countries of Europe and North America, and as far as Turkey and INDIA. The United States branch did not open until 1867.

In Europe, the alliance remained a vital organization, but its work in America was largely superseded by the Federal Council of Churches (formed in 1906), which in 1944 finally inherited the alliance's few remaining corporate assets. The alliance in America had divided during the Fundamentalist-Modernist controversy of the early 20th century. In 1942, more conservative Protestants founded the National Association of Evangelicals.

In the years following World War II, American Evangelical leaders began to seek an international network. On August 5–11, 1951, a call was issued for a meeting of interested persons at Woudschiten, near Zeist, the Netherlands. Those gathered founded the World Evangelical Fellowship (WEF). Brief doctrinal and purpose statements were adopted. Within two years, 12 national Evangelical fellowships from various parts of the world had affiliated with WEF. By the 1990s, the WEF had grown into a global network. It currently has more than 120 affiliated national/regional alliances, 104 organizational ministries, and six specialized ministries.

In 2001, the fellowship voted to change its name to World Evangelical Alliance (WEA). It is currently headed by an International Executive Council, with leadership drawn from all parts of the world. Seven regional alliances coordinate the activity of national bodies in their region.

The WEA operates in the middle of the spectrum between the separatist Fundamentalist INTERNATIONAL COUNCIL OF CHRISTIAN CHURCHES and the liberal Protestant WORLD COUNCIL OF CHURCHES.

See also ECUMENICAL MOVEMENT.

Further reading: World Evangelical Alliance. Available online. URL: http://www.worldevangelical.org; David M. Howard, *The Dream That Would Not Die: The Birth and Growth of the World Evangelical Fellowship, 1846–1986* (Exeter, U.K.: Paternoster, 1986); W. Harold Fuller, *People of the Mandate* (Carlisle, U.K./Grand Rapids, Mich.: Paternoster/Baker Book House, 1996).

World Methodist Council

The World Methodist Council, the primary agency providing fellowship between the many Methodist churches around the world, traces its origins to 1881, when the first of the Ecumenical Methodist Conferences assembled in London, England. These conferences aimed to overcome the splits in the movement, primarily those in North America that had separated Methodists both regionally and racially. Also, British and American relations had been strained by two wars (1776 and 1812) and by the British government's pro-South views during the American Civil War. The first conferences included attendees primarily from North America and Britain. They were especially important to African-American Methodist leaders, who had few others opportunities for ecumenical contacts.

The conferences continued to meet every 10 years until 1941, when the meeting was cancelled due to World War II. In the meantime, the larger predominantly white Methodist bodies in the United States—Methodist Episcopal Church, Methodist Episcopal Church, South, and Methodist Protestant Church—united in 1939. Earlier, the British Methodists had overcome much of their own splintering with a merger in 1932 that created the METHODIST CHURCH.

While splintering and merging at home, both the United Methodist Church and the Methodist Church had created international presences through their expansive missionary programs. Like most Western Protestant groups, after World War II they began elevating their mission churches into autonomous bodies. Ecumenism within the Methodist family was now redirected toward maintaining close ties between the older Methodist bodies in the West and the newer churches being formed around the world. Symbolic of that transformation, the group was renamed the World Methodist Council in 1951. It soon acquired a permanent secretariat, and headquarters at Lake Junaluska, North Carolina. Since the 1950s, the World Methodist Conferences have met at five-year intervals.

The council also has a European office in the WORLD COUNCIL OF CHURCHES headquarters in Geneva, Switzerland. Its ongoing program covers a spectrum of educational, evangelistic, and worship concerns. It supports exchanges of clergy and laity, and facilitates scholarship and theological reflection through the quinquennial Oxford Institute of Methodist Theological Studies. Churches from more than 108 countries are served by the council.

Further reading: Nolan B. Harmon, *Encyclopedia of World Methodism*, 2 vols. (Nashville, Tenn.: United Methodist, 1974); *World Methodist Council, Hand-*

book of Information (Lake Junaluska, N.C.: World Methodist Council, 2003).

World Student Christian Federation

The World Student Christian Federation (WSCF), one of the key global Protestant ecumenical organizations, was founded in 1895 at Vadstena Castle in SWEDEN. Prominent among the founders were American Methodist John R. MOTT (1865–1955) and Swedish student leader Karl Fries. Fries became its first president and Mott its general secretary.

Mott had earlier proposed that Christian students from different countries form autonomous fellowships to mobilize youth for mission and ecumenical tasks. WSCF became the means of linking these national fellowships internationally.

At the national and local levels, Student Christian movement groups brought together students of diverse Protestant backgrounds, called them to a variety of full-time service, and funneled their energy into a spectrum of endeavors. In the early 20th century, WSCF recruited many future pastors and missionaries and became the training ground of Christian ecumenical leaders. W. A. VISSER'T HOOFT, WSCF general secretary in 1932, went on to become the first general secretary of the WORLD COUNCIL OF CHURCHES. Global leaders who began with the Student Christian movement would include such notables as William TEMPLE, D. T. NILES, and Philip POTTER.

The movement has been deeply affected by the split between liberal and Evangelical Protestant leaders. In 1910, Inter-Varsity Fellowship was established by former WSCF members in England who wanted to operate out of a more conservative theological consensus. As other similar national organizations were formed, in 1947 representatives came together to create the INTERNATIONAL FELLOWSHIP OF EVANGELICAL STUDENTS that now mirrors WSCF worldwide.

The WSCF now covers more than 100 countries. Following the formation of the World Council of Churches, it established headquarters in Geneva. In 1972, it went through a major structural change reflecting the shift of Protestant strength to Asia and Africa. Most work moved from Geneva to six regional offices around the world.

The WSCF General Assembly meets quadrennially. Each region conducts its own regional assembly, is headed by a regional committee, and maintains a regional office.

The work of the WSCF is conducted in close cooperation with other bodies, especially the YOUNG MEN'S CHRISTIAN ASSOCIATION (YMCA), the YOUNG WOMEN'S CHRISTIAN ASSOCIATION (YWCA), the International Movement of Catholic Students, and the World Council of Churches.

See also ECUMENICAL MOVEMENT.

Further reading: C. Howard Hopkins, *John R. Mott* (Grand Rapids, Mich.: William B. Eerdmans, 1979); Ruth Rouse, *The World's Student Christian Federation: A History of the First 30 Years* (London: SCM, 1948); C. Howard Hopkins and Stephen Neill, eds., *A History of the Ecumenical Movement, 1517–1948* (Geneva: World Council of Churches, 1986).

World Vision

World Vision is a Christian missionary organization that has specialized in relief and development work and service to the overall missionary movement among Evangelical Christians. It was founded in 1950 by Robert "Bob" W. Pierce (1914–78), a minister in the Church of the Nazarene, in response to the plight of children orphaned by the Korean War. It began with a child sponsorship program, which was carried to other countries, first in ASIA and then in Africa and SOUTH AMERICA.

In the 1960s, it expanded its work to include relief efforts following natural disasters. A subsidiary agency, World Vision Relief Organization, delivered food grants from the U.S. government and merchandise donated by large corporations. Pierce resigned in 1967 over objections to his management style. He later founded SAMARITAN'S PURSE, an organization with goals similar to World Vision.

During that period, World Vision leaders were also considering ways they could help the burgeoning Evangelical missionary endeavor. Under the leadership of Ted Engstrom and Ed Dayton, the Missions Advanced Research and Communications Center (MARC) was opened, to apply computers to rationalize the somewhat chaotic world of global missions, with its hundreds of independent agencies. MARC compiled a mission handbook, including key data about North American-based sending agencies, and about unreached peoples, as defined in the LAUSANNE COVENANT. MARC subsequently established an office in Europe, which began compiling data on the state of European Christianity.

In the meantime, World Vision enlarged its own work in developing countries with a new focus on breaking the cycle of poverty in defined communities. It began with vocational and agricultural training programs and funds to seed small businesses, and evolved into more expansive community development programs aimed at self-sufficiency. Thus, when famine struck in Ethiopia, World Vision sent massive assistance to alleviate the immediate problem, and as the famine receded, created programs to help survivors rebuild their lives and restore land most affected by drought.

In 1995, World Vision, today the largest Christian relief agency in the world, moved its headquarters to suburban Seattle, Washington. One of the most respected of mission agencies, it continues both its relief and development programs and its cutting-edge research on the missionary enterprise. MARC has pioneered consciousness-raising efforts among missionary personnel about the living conditions of the people they are trying to evangelize, including problems of HIV/AIDS, war, child exploitation, and hunger. As World Vision has expanded, so has MARC, which in 2003 changed its name to World Vision Resources.

As of 2003, World Vision was working in more than 100 countries.

See also FAITH MISSIONS.

Further reading: Richard Gehman, *Let My Heart Be Broken . . . With the Things That Break the Heart of God. The Story of World Vision and Dr. Bob Pierce* (New York: McGraw-Hill, 1960); Minnette Northcutt and Dotsey Weliver, eds., *Mission Handbook: U.S. and Canadian Christian Ministries Overseas* (Federal Way, Wash.: World Vision Resources, 2004) regularly updated.

Worldwide Evangelization Crusade/WEC International

The Worldwide Evangelization Crusade (now WEC International) grew out of the life of its founder, Charles Thomas "C. T." Studd (1860–1931). Studd was born into wealth; his father was converted to Christianity during the visit of Dwight L. MOODY and Ira Sankey to England in 1877, and C. T. himself experienced a saving faith in Christ the following year. He let the experience lapse until it revived six years later when he heard Moody preach.

Studd decided to go as a missionary to CHINA and applied to the CHINA INLAND MISSION. He left England in 1885. Once in China, he adopted Chinese dress, learned the language, and otherwise tried to absorb Chinese ways. He was in China when he reached his 25th birthday and inherited a considerable sum of money; he proceeded to give most of it away. Moody and George MÜLLER were among the recipients. Studd remained in China for 10 years, leaving in 1894 for reasons of health. He later toured the United States on behalf of the STUDENT VOLUNTEER MOVEMENT.

In 1900, Studd and his family went to south India, where he served for six years as pastor of a church in Ootacamund. Following their return to England in 1906, he came to believe that he should go to Central Africa. Against doctors' advice, and without sponsorship, he left for the continent in 1910. Back in England the following year, he founded the Heart of Africa Mission, somewhat modeled on the China Inland Mission. He returned to the Belgian Congo (now the Democratic Republic of the Congo) in 1913 and worked there for the rest of his life.

Studd was not a capable mission organizer, but his reputation and his organization were saved by his son-in-law, Norman Grubb (1895–1993). In 1920, Grubb moved to the Belgian Congo and stayed for seven years. He returned to England to take charge of the World Evangelization Crusade. By the time he retired in 1965, some 800 missionary personnel were working with the WEC. Grubb also founded Christian Literature Crusade (CLC), a sister organization to the WEC.

The original work in the Congo is now known as the Church of Christ in the Congo-Community of Christ in the Heart of Africa. WEC churches also play an important role in Equatorial Guinea and Guinea-Bissau.

Norman Grubb identified with the KESWICK MOVEMENT and attended many of its conventions. The CLC has helped keep in print the writings of Andrew MURRAY, Hannah Whitall Smith, Jesse Penn-Lewis, and Watchman NEE.

See also AFRICA, SUB-SAHARAN; FAITH MISSIONS.

Further reading: Edith Buxton, *Reluctant Missionary* (London: Lutterworth Press, 1968); Norman P. Grubb, *C. T. Studd: Cricketer and Pioneer* (Atlantic City, N.J.: World-Wide Revival Prayer Movement, 1937); ———, *The Deep Things of God* (Fort Washington, Pa.: Christian Literature Crusade, 1958); ———, *God Unlimited* (Fort Washington, Pa.: Christian Literature Crusade, 1962); Eileen Vincent, *C. T. Studd and Priscilla: United to Fight for Jesus* (Kent, U.K.: STL Books, 1988).

Wycliffe, John (c. 1330–1384)
pre-Reformation English church reformer

John Wycliffe (or Wyclif) was born in Hipswell, near Richmond, Yorkshire, England. As a young man, he attended Balliol College at Oxford, and he remained in that city for the rest of his life. His intellectual accomplishments were noticed by King Richard II (r. 1377–99), who appointed him first a chaplain and then rector at Lutterworth.

In the 1360s and 1370s, Wycliffe won a reputation as a popular preacher against papal authority. He was condemned by Pope Gregory XI in 1377, and summoned before the bishop of London. However, he had such strong support at Oxford and in the king's court that he was not arrested.

Wycliffe continued to argue against papal authority and for the BIBLE as the only source of truth. Like Martin LUTHER 150 years later, these premises led him to the conclusions that the popes and councils were not infallible, and that papal decrees derived any authority they might have from their conformity to Scripture. He also challenged Catholic doctrines concerning TRANSUBSTANTIATION and purgatory.

Wycliffe argued that parish priests should operate as the people's servants, not their rulers. In 1380, he organized a band of "poor priests," known as the Lollards, who traveled from their center in Oxford to preach around the country. The bishop of London responded by barring Wycliffe from preaching. In 1382, he was condemned by the archbishop of Canterbury.

As attacks by church authorities mounted, Wycliffe remained among his supporters at Oxford. During this time, he completed a translation of the Bible into English, though it was not published, and summarized his ideas in a book, *Trialogues.*

After Wycliffe died in 1384, church authorities suppressed his writings as much as possible. However, a generation later his ideas were still alive and being spread by the Lollards. In 1415, after condemning to death another popular reformer, John HUS, the Council of Constance ordered Wycliffe's body exhumed and burned together with his books. The order was carried out in 1428.

Once Protestant hegemony was established in England in the 16th century, Wycliffe came to be seen as an important precursor of the Reformation. His New Testament was finally published, in a limited edition, in the 18th century, and his entire Bible was published in the middle of the 19th century.

Further reading: David Fountain, *John Wycliffe. The Dawn of the Reformation* (Southampton, U.K.: Mayflower Christian Books, 1984); A. Kenny, *Wyclif* (Oxford: Oxford University Press, 1985); ———, ed., *Wyclif in His Times* (Oxford: Clarendon Press, 1986); Douglas C. Wood, *The Evangelical Doctor* (Welwyn, U.K.: Evangelical Press, 1984); John Wyclif, *Select English Works of John Wyclif,* 3 vols. ed. by T. Arnold (Oxford: Oxford University Press, 1869–71).

Y

Yoido Full Gospel Central Church

The Yoido Full Gospel Central Church in Seoul, Korea, the largest Christian congregation in the world, emerged as part of the vision of its pastor, David Yonggi Cho (b. 1936). Cho, a former Buddhist, recovered from an apparently fatal case of tuberculosis after converting to Christianity. He later experienced a call to the ministry, and after attending the Full Gospel Bible College in Seoul of the Pentecostal ASSEMBLIES OF GOD, he began a new church in Seoul. Four years later, he moved the congregation into a 1,500-seat revival center, and he was named general superintendent of the Assemblies of God in Korea. Meanwhile, his own pastorate continued to grow with a team of associate pastors and a host of home cell groups. The church has pioneered cell church ministry, which has been the source of much of its worldwide popularity. The church also became known for its use of female leaders at all levels.

In 1973, a large new church was begun on Yoido Island in Seoul and completed in time to host the 10th Pentecostal World Conference. Church membership hit 100,000 in 1979. In the 1980s, the church building was enlarged to accommodate 25,000 people at multiple services throughout the day each Sunday. As the new century began, membership reached around 700,000. Besides the main sanctuary on Yoido Island, there are 24 independent satellite churches and 16 dependent satellite sanctuaries. Pastors trained at Yoido have founded 62 additional independent churches.

In 1992, Cho became chairman of the executive committee of the World Pentecostal Assemblies of God Fellowship (now the World Assemblies of God Fellowship). Cho was praised for his innovations, but often criticized for his theology, which appeared close to the Word Faith movement with its emphasis on positive confession. He teaches that the spoken word can release the power and presence of Jesus. In praying, the believer should visualize needs and be specific in requests. Cho presented his ideas in several books, some of which have been translated into English and other languages.

The church has built a global ministry program, sending out 300 missionaries by the beginning of the new century. More than half of these were sent to North America, which has returned to its earlier position as an object of missionary concern. Others are scattered across more than 25 countries of SOUTH AMERICA, Europe, and CENTRAL ASIA. The church also sponsors the International Theological Institute, which supports the training and dispatching of evangelists.

See also KOREA, REPUBLIC OF (SOUTH).

Further reading: Paul Yonggi Cho, *The Fourth Dimension* (Plainfield, N.J.: Logos International, 1979); ————, *More than Numbers: Principles of Church Growth* (Gainesville, Fla.: Bridge-Logos, 1983); ————, *Successful Home Cell Groups* (Plainfield, N.J.: Logos International, 1981); Nell Kennedy, *Dream Your Way to Success: The Story of Dr. Yonggi Cho and Korea* (Gainesville, Fla.: Bridge-Logos, 1980).

Young Men's Christian Association

The Young Men's Christian Association (YMCA) was founded in 1844 by George WILLIAMS (1821–1905), a young layman in London, England, in response to the conditions in which many workers his own age lived, either on the streets or in overcrowded rooms at their place of work. He organized a group of men to create the YMCA, which aimed to provide a decent place to live and a Christian environment for young men in the hours apart from work, including opportunities for BIBLE study and prayer. By the end of the decade, there were some 20 Ys scattered across Great Britain. In 1851, the first YMCAs opened in both Canada and the United States. The first YMCA serving African Americans opened in Washington, D.C., in 1853.

By 1854, an international convention was held in Paris. It adopted the so-called Paris Basis, which limited membership to active members of Protestant churches, but deliberately ignored the denominational differences and social barriers that divided people, sometimes rigidly, in secular society.

Originally, local Ys were run by volunteers. However, as the movement grew, paid staff were added. The Ys became involved in evangelistic work in the cities and service to those called to war, notably the American Civil War.

In the 1880s, Ys began putting up buildings that included such additional facilities as gyms and swimming pools, auditoriums, and even bowling alleys. Residence halls with hotel-like facilities were also added. As early as 1866, the New York Y had accepted as its purpose: "The improvement of the spiritual, mental, social and physical condition of young men." This idea evolved into the YMCA symbol, a red triangle with the words *spirit, mind, body.*

During the last half of the 19th century, evangelist Dwight L. MOODY, who had started with the YMCA, became a great influence in setting its direction. However, the organization's greatest achievements are associated with Methodist layman John R. MOTT (1865–1955), who became national secretary in 1888, right after graduating from Cornell University.

Mott fostered the movement internationally by sending hundreds of YMCA secretaries overseas to create new organizations, and then turn them over to local leaders. During World War I, Mott set up military canteens to assist servicemen. After the war, he directed war relief efforts for refugees and prisoners of war on both sides. Y. C. James Yen, a YMCA worker in FRANCE, developed a simplified Chinese alphabet that became a major force in overcoming illiteracy in CHINA. Mott used his position in the YMCA and its resources to aid the development of a variety of organizations such as the WORLD STUDENT CHRISTIAN MOVEMENT and the STUDENT VOLUNTEER MOVEMENT. After World War I, the YMCA provided important support for the emerging ECUMENICAL MOVEMENT.

In the 1930s, the YMCA movement aligned itself with a variety of social service agencies to respond to the changing urban environment. Bible classes were now being replaced with general educational programs, including vocational training. A variety of free services were offered. The YMCA again became involved in World War II. Internationally, it developed programs to serve prisoners of war. In the United States, it joined a number of other organizations to form the United Service Organization (USO) and pioneered programs to send celebrities overseas to entertain the troops.

By this time, the YMCA had to a considerable extent become secularized. People of all religions were accepted into its programs, as were women.

As the new century began, the YMCA in the United States, with its 2,400 centers, remains the largest not-for-profit service organization in the country. Each center is encouraged to respond to the perceived needs locally, and thus there is great variation from one Y to another. There are active YMCAs in 120 countries around the world.

Over the years, the YMCA has nurtured a variety of programs that became substantial organizations in their own right, including: the Camp Fire Girls, the Boy Scouts, the Toastmasters Club, and GIDEONS INTERNATIONAL. In 1915, Carter G. Woodson met with three associates at the Wabash Area Y in Chicago to found the Association for the Study of Negro Life and History.

See also YOUNG WOMEN'S CHRISTIAN ASSOCIATION.

Further reading: Young Men's Christian Association. Available online. URL: http://www.ymca.net; John R. Mott, *The Addresses and Papers of John R. Mott, The Young Men's Christian Association* (New York: Association Press, 1947); Clarence Prouty Shedd, et al., *History of the World's Alliance of Young Men's Christian Associations,* with a foreword by John R. Mott (London: SPCK, 1955); William Howard Taft, ed., *Service With Fighting Men: An Account of the Work of the American YMCA in the World War,* 2 vols. (New York: Association Press, 1922).

Young Women's Christian Association

What would later became known as the Young Women's Christian Association (YWCA) began in the 1850s as a set of disconnected efforts in England and the United States to assist young unmarried women, especially working girls who had migrated from the countryside to the cities. In England, several homes for young women and some all-female prayer unions were established. Among the first was Lady Mary Jane (Mrs. Arthur) Kinnard's boarding home in London, and Miss Emma Roberts Prayer Union in Barnet. Robart's group began to use the name "Young Women's Christian Association," borrowed from the already existing YOUNG MEN'S CHRISTIAN ASSOCIATION. Over the next decades, other boarding homes and prayer groups formed around the country.

Similar works emerged in New York and Boston in 1859 and 1860, respectively. Mrs. Marshall O. Roberts of New York City formed what is generally credited with being the first YWCA under the name Ladies' Christian Union. The name Young Women's Christian Association was first used in Boston in 1866. The association in New York City provided a boarding home for young women as early as 1860; one opened in Boston in 1868. In the 1870s, the New York YWCA pioneered in job training, which included the first typewriting instruction for women and the first sewing machine classes. The work in Boston spread to college and university campuses. The first exclusively campus group emerged at Illinois State Normal University (now Illinois State University at Normal, Illinois) in 1873. By 1890, there were more than 100 YWCAs across the United States.

In 1877, Robarts and Kinnard met and effected a union of their work under the name, "The London Young Women's Institute Union and Christian Association" with the goal of "prayer and work on behalf of Young Women of all classes." Step by step, the organization developed around six centers, each with its own officers: London, England and Wales, Scotland, Ireland, Outside of Great Britain, and Colonial and Missionary.

In 1894, representatives from Great Britain, the United States, SWEDEN, and NORWAY met to form the World YWCA. Its first international conference in London in 1898 drew 300 representatives from 20 countries. The various YWCAs in the United States did not create a national body until 1906. In 1912, a national headquarters was opened in New York City, where it has remained.

Beginning as strictly a women's organization, the YWCA has responded to the Civil Rights movement and to feminism. Its current programs serve girls and young women of all religious, ethnic, and racial backgrounds. The 1958 national convention in the United States voted to work for greater inclusiveness in YWCA leadership, membership, programs, and services. As early as 1965, an Office of Racial Justice was established at the national level. Today, the Y sees itself as an organization run by women for women with the goal of improving the status and role of women and eliminating racism.

International headquarters of the YWCA are now located in Geneva, Switzerland. There are more than 100 national chapters serving some 2 million members.

Further reading: Marion O. Robinson, *Eight Women of the YWCA* (New York: National Board of the YWCA, 1966); Mary S. Sims, *The Natural History of a Social Institution: The Young Women's Christian Association* (New York: Woman's Press, 1936); ———, *The Purpose Widens, 1947–1967* (New York: Woman's Press, 1969); Judith Weisenfeld, *African American Women and Christian Activism: New York's Black YWCA, 1905–1945* (Cambridge, Mass.: Harvard University Press, 1997).

Z

Zimbabwe

The LONDON MISSIONARY SOCIETY (Congregationalists) established the first work in what is now Zimbabwe among the Zulus in 1859, but the work was limited. In 1888, the British government allocated some land in the area to the Universities Mission to Central Africa, a group that had arisen in direct response to David LIVINGSTONE's appeal for attention to the African interior. It became the base for a mission to both the Zulu and Shona peoples.

British Methodists arrived two years later, and along with their America colleagues (who came in 1896), METHODISM thrived. The British worked primarily among the white settlers and the Americans among the native Africans. The American work, still attached to the United Methodist Church as its Zimbabwe Conference, later played an important role in the political life of independent Zimbabwe. Abel Muzorewa (b. 1925), the first Zimbabwean consecrated a BISHOP, briefly served as the country's prime minister in a failed attempt to build a biracial postcolonial government. In the 1990s, the United Methodists founded the Africa University in Mutare.

The SALVATION ARMY arrived soon after the Methodists; their work expanded greatly in the 20th century, then rivaling that of the two Methodist groups. Also arriving in the 1890s were the SEVENTH-DAY ADVENTIST CHURCH and the Central African Christian Mission (affiliated with the American-based Churches of Christ and Christian Churches), which both did well.

A host of additional Protestant missionary groups fanned out across Zimbabwe in the 20th century, but none of them have had the response of the AFRICAN INITIATED CHURCHES, especially the African Apostolic Church of Johane Maranke, the Zion Christian Church, the Zion Apostolic Churches, and the Zimbabwe Assemblies of God Africa. PENTECOSTALISM came to Zimbabwe in the 1920s through the two Zion churches, based in SOUTH AFRICA. The Zion Christian Church has now become the largest Protestant body in the country, and the only one with more than a million members.

Johane Maranke (1912–63), who had received revelations in dreams and visions, at first worked with the leaders of the two Zionist churches. In 1932, he was told by a voice that he was to be "John the Baptist, an apostle." He was to preach and teach observance of Old Testament laws (including SABBATARIANISM). Founding his African Apostolic Church, he began a ministry throughout Zimbabwe and neighboring countries. It is now the second-largest church in Zimbabwe. The

594

Zimbabwe Assemblies of God Africa was founded by former members of the Apostolic Faith Mission, another South African Pentecostal body, which began work in several Zimbabwean urban centers in 1959. This newer church has now become the third-largest Protestant body in Zimbabwe.

Many of the older Protestant churches in Zimbabwe are associated in the Zimbabwe Council of Churches, affiliated with the WORLD COUNCIL OF CHURCHES, including the Church of the Province of Central Africa (Anglican), the Evangelical Lutheran Church of Zimbabwe, the Methodist Church of Zimbabwe, the Reformed Church of Zimbabwe, and the United Church of Christ of Zimbabwe, all of whom are members of the World Council in their own right. More conservative churches are members of the Evangelical Fellowship of Zimbabwe and the WORLD EVANGELICAL ALLIANCE. Larger than either the council or the fellowship, however, is the Conference of African Initiated Churches. Zimbabwe reports a majority of its residents as Christian (about 68 percent), most of them members of the Protestant communities. The rest remain affiliated with traditional African religions.

See also AFRICA, SUB-SAHARAN.

Further reading: M. L. Daneel, *Zionism and Faith Healing in Rhodesia: Aspects of African Independent Churches* (The Hague: Mouton, 1970); C. F. Hallencreutz and A. Mayo, eds., *Church and State in Zimbabwe,* vol. 3: *Christianity South of the Zambesi* (Gweru, Zimbabwe: Mambo Press, 1988); C. J. M. Zvobgo, *History of Christian Missions in Zimbabwe* (Gweru, Zimbabwe: Mambo Press, 1996).

Zinzendorf, Nicolaus Ludwig von
(1700–1760) *Moravian leader*

Nicolaus Ludwig von Zinzendorf was born on May 26, 1700, in Dresden. His ancestors had left Austria after converting to Protestantism, and his parents identified with PIETISM; the founder of the Pietist movement, Philipp Jakob Spener (1635–1705), was the boy's godfather. Zinzendorf was educated at the Pietist center at Halle before attending the University of Wittenberg.

Zinzendorf abandoned early ambitions to be a diplomat and decided instead to become a Christian landowner, dedicating his life to the people on his land according to Spener's principles. He was already giving thought to abandoning the Lutheran Church in favor of FREE CHURCH associations when he encountered the Moravians. He offered his land as an asylum from their persecutions and founded the settlement of Herrnhut for them on his estate, Berthelsdorf. He imposed some discipline on the rather scattered group, and convinced the authorities that he was not harboring a heterodox group. Through 1727–28 he worked to create a common order of worship and organization for the reconstituted MORAVIAN CHURCH.

Zinzendorf oversaw (and financially supported) the pioneering missionary work that the group undertook in the 1730s. They sent missionaries to the West Indies (1732), Greenland (1733), and the North American Indians (1735). His financial resources were depleted in the 1740s, and in 1750 the group's leaders established a financial board to oversee their far-flung activities. Zinzendorf remained active for another decade, until his death on May 9, 1760. His son-in-law John de Watteville succeeded him as leader of the Herrnhut community.

Zinzendorf left behind a number of texts of his sermons. He also wrote nearly 2,000 hymns, many published by the Moravians and some by John WESLEY for use by the Methodists.

Further reading: George W. Forell, *Zinzendorf: Nine Public Lectures on Important Subjects in Religion* (Iowa City: University of Iowa Press, 1973); Arthur J. Freeman, *An Ecumenical Theology of the Heart: The Theology of Count Nicholas Ludwig von Zinzendorf* (Bethlehem, Pa.: Moravian Church in America, 1998); A. J. Lewis, *Zinzendorf the Ecumenical Pioneer* (London: SCM Press, 1962); John R. Weinlick, *Count Zinzendorf* (New York: Abingdon Press, 1956).

Zionists

The Zionist churches of SOUTH AFRICA have been a major instrument facilitating the entrance of PENTECOSTALISM in Africa. In 1895, a representative of the Christian Catholic Church founded by John Alexander Dowie (1847–1907) of Zion, Illinois, began work in Johannesburg. The work expanded suddenly in 1903, when Peter L. le Roux (a student of Keswick minister Andrew MURRAY) joined the Johannesburg work. He brought with him three African evangelists (Daniel Nkonyane, Muneli Ngobesi, and Fred Lutuli) and some 400 people who lived in the eastern Transvaal. With the arrival of Daniel Bryant in 1904, the following took off, and within a short time included some 5,000 members.

In 1908, a group of Pentecostals, fresh from the AZUSA STREET REVIVAL, arrived in Johannesburg. They converted the leadership of the group to Pentecostalism, but the group disagreed over affiliation with the Apostolic Faith Mission (AFM) of the new arrivals. Le Roux affiliated with the AFM, which became the parent of one lineage of Pentecostal churches. The others remained to constitute the continuing Zionist movement. These two movements, virtually identical in belief and practice, continued to interact over the years.

In 1910, Daniel Nkonyane left the AFM to form the Apostolic Holy Spirit Church in Zion, and afterward founded the first of a number of "Zion cities" based loosely on the community at Zion, Illinois. Then in 1917 Elias Mahlangu founded the Zion Apostolic Church of South Africa, the ultimate source for the Zion Christian Church established in 1925. The latter group would go on to become the largest church in South Africa, with some 5 million members.

The Zionist and Apostolic churches adhere to traditional Pentecostal beliefs, especially concerning the BAPTISM OF THE HOLY SPIRIT. They are distinguished from other Pentecostal bodies in South Africa by certain practices, including BAPTISM by immersion in running water using the triune name, unique healing rituals, and the conspicuous white clothing worn by most members.

Pentecostalism in the Zionist and Apostolic modes spread to ZIMBABWE in the 1920s. The Zion Christian Church in that country now has more than a million members, and other Zionist and Apostolic churches are active as well.

See also AFRICA, SUB-SAHARAN.

Further reading: Allen H. Anderson, *Zion and Pentecost: The Spirituality Experience of Pentecostal and Zionist/Apostolic Churches in South Africa* (Pretoria: University of South Africa Press, 2000); M. L. Daneel, *Old and New in Southern Shona Independent Churches,* 2 vols. (The Hague: Mouton, 1971).

Zwemer, Samuel Marinus (1867–1952)
Reformed missionary to the Middle East

Samuel M. Zwemer was born on April 12, 1867, in Vriesland, Michigan. After receiving degrees from Hope College (1887) and New Brunswick Theological Seminary (1890), he was ordained a minister in the Reformed Church by the Pella, Iowa, classis.

While still a student, Zwemer and fellow student James Cantine decided to become missionaries to Muslims, inspired by Ion Keith-Falconer's small (1856–87), brief mission in Aden, Yemen. Unable to find any sponsoring agency, they founded their own American Arabian Mission. In the mid-1890s, the Reformed Church relented and agreed to sponsor the mission. Traveling to the MIDDLE EAST in 1890, Zwemer studied Arabic in Beirut and then settled in Aden, where the Church of Scotland had adopted the Keith-Falconer mission. Zwemer replaced the former missionary and helped found a hospital. With Reformed Church help, other hospitals were opened in Bahrain, Kuwait, Muscat in Oman, and Basra in Iraq. Maintaining the hospitals and their bookrooms for distributing BIBLES and Christian literature became the mission's main work.

In Iraq in 1896, Zwemer met Amy Elizabeth Wilkes, an Anglican missionary, whom he soon married. They initially settled in Bahrain, where Zwemer wrote his first book, *Arabia: Cradle of*

Islam (1900). In 1911, he would became the founding editor of *The Moslem World,* a quarterly journal, which he continued to edit for the next 37 years. Zwemer moved around the Arabian Peninsula until 1913, when he moved to Egypt, where he lived until 1929.

In 1929, Zwemer returned to the United States, acknowledged by all as the foremost authority on Christian missions to Islam. He became a professor of history of religions and Christian missions at Princeton Theological Seminary, where he would remain until 1939. He died in New York City on April 2, 1952, still struggling with the problems of evangelizing the Muslim world.

Further reading: J. Christy Wilson, *Apostle to Islam: A Biography of Samuel M. Zwemer* (Grand Rapids, Mich.: Baker Book House, 1952); Samuel M. Zwemer, *Across the World of Islam* (New York: Fleming H. Revell, 1939); ———, *Arabia: The Cradle of Islam* (New York: Fleming H. Revell, 1900); ———, *The Cross-Above the Crescent: The Validity, Necessity and Urgency of Missions to Moslems* (Grand Rapids, Mich.: Zondervan, 1941); ———, *Evangelism Today: Message Not Method* (New York: Fleming H. Revell, 1944).

Zwingli, Ulrich (1484–1531) *founder of the Reformation in Switzerland*

Ulrich (or Huldrych) Zwingli was born at Wildhaus, Switzerland, on New Year's Day in 1484, the son of a district official in the Duchy of Toggenburg. Zwingli attended the universities at Berne, Vienna, and Basel, and received his master of theology degree at Basel in 1506. He subsequently became the parish priest at Glarus.

His broad education had included an emphasis on the humanities, and he continued his study of Greek and the ancient classics, along with the early Christian writers. His public activity started with service as a chaplain for the Swiss army during the campaigns of 1513 and 1515. He made a name for himself as a staunch defender of Catholicism and the authority of the pope.

Statue in Zurich of Ulrich Zwingli (1484–1531), founder of the Reformation in German-speaking Switzerland *(Institute for the Study of American Religion, Santa Barbara, California)*

In 1518, he moved to Zurich, where he had been chosen the people's priest (lead priest at the cathedral) for the Grossmünster, or Great Church. Thanks to his correspondence with ERASMUS, his knowledge of Martin LUTHER's activities, and his own experiences, he had by then come to believe that the church needed to be reformed. He expressed his views in a series of sermons on the Gospel of Matthew, which are generally cited as the spark that ignited the Swiss Reformation.

Zwingli wanted to simplify worship, first by removing statues from church buildings, as well as any other objects that did not have a biblical justification. He supported only two SACRAMENTS, BAPTISM and the LORD'S SUPPER. He denied the real presence of Christ in the Lord's Supper and spoke of the rite as a celebration and memorial of Christ's death and resurrection. He did believe that during the meal Christ was spiritually present, uniting the believers. He also came to emphasize the sovereignty of God and the doctrine of election, a belief that God had chosen the elect to salvation even before the creation of the world.

As a first step toward reform, Zwingli issued his own list of debating points, the 67 Theses. He convinced the city council of Zurich to hold a public debate on January 29, 1523, with the understanding that all decisions would be made with the BIBLE as the sole authority. When supporters of the Roman Catholic Church drew upon the church's teachings and traditions to argue their case, the council regarded their arguments as irrelevant. It gave Zwingli authority to make his proposed reforms in both theology and church life.

Among the changes he made was to abandon priestly celibacy, which he argued was frequently violated. From 1522, the marriage of priests became common in Zurich; Zwingli himself married in 1524. In 1525, the Mass was abolished and replaced with a Zwinglian service of the Lord's Supper.

In the eight years following his ascendancy at Zurich, Zwingli helped spread the Reformation throughout the German-speaking cantons of Switzerland, enjoying the most success at Berne and Basel. He met opposition on two fronts. First, Lutherans opposed his low-church approach to the sacraments. They held to a doctrine of the real presence of Christ. The failure of Martin Luther and Zwingli to reach a theological agreement at the MARBURG COLLOQUY in 1529 resulted in the continued division of Protestants into two camps, of which the Swiss were by far the smaller and weaker. Second, Roman Catholics opposed the spread of the Reformation, and in the late 1520s war broke out. The small Protestant force was defeated, and Zwingli was killed at the second battle of Karpel on October 11, 1531. Following his death, the fulcrum of the Swiss Reformation moved from Zurich to French-speaking Geneva, where John CALVIN soon emerged as its leader.

Further reading: E. J. Furcha and H. Wayne Pipkin, *Prophet, Pastor, Protestant: The Work of Huldrych Zwingli after Five Hundred Years* (Allison Park, Pa.: Pickwick, 1984); H. Wayne Pipkin, *A Zwingli Bibliography* (Pittsburgh, Pa.: Clifford E. Barbour Library, Pittsburgh Theological Seminary, 1972); G. R. Potter, *Zwingli* (Cambridge: Cambridge University Press, 1976); W. P. Stephens, *The Theology of Huldrych Zwingli* (Oxford: Clarendon Press, 1986); ———, *Zwingli. An Introduction to His Thought* (Oxford: Clarendon Press, 1992).

BIBLIOGRAPHY

Anderson, Gerald H., Robert T. Cotte, Norman A. Horner, and James M. Phillips, eds. *Mission Legacies: Biographical Studies of Leaders of the Modern Missionary Movement.* Maryknoll, N.Y.: Orbis Books, 1998.

Bachmann, E. Theodore, and Mercia Brenne Bachmann. *Lutheran Churches in the World: A Handbook.* Minneapolis, Minn.: Augsburg Press, 1989.

Bainton, Roland. *Here I Stand.* New York: Abingdon-Cokesbury, 1950.

Baker, D. *Reform and Reformation: England and the Continent.* Oxford: Oxford University Press, 1979.

Balmer, Randall. *Encyclopedia of Evangelicalism.* Louisville, Ky.: Westminster John Knox Press, 2002.

Barbour, Hugh. *The Quakers.* New York: Greenwood Press, 1988.

Barbour, Hugh, and Arthur O. Roberts. *Early Quaker Writings, 1650–1700.* Grand Rapids, Mich.: William B. Eerdmans, 1973.

Barrett, David. *The Encyclopedia of World Christianity.* 2d ed. New York: Oxford University Press, 2001.

Bauswein, Jean-Jacques, and Lukas Vischer, eds. *The Reformed Family Worldwide: A Survey of Reformed Churches, Theological Schools, and International Organizations.* Grand Rapids, Mich.: William B. Eerdmans, 1999.

Beaver, R. Pierce. *American Protestant Women in World Missions.* Grand Rapids, Mich.: William B. Eerdmans, 1980.

Beeke, Joel R. *A Reader's Guide to Reformed Literature: An Annotated Bibliography of Reformed Theology.* Grand Rapids, Mich.: Reformed Heritage Books, 1999.

Bender, Harold S. *Two Centuries of American Mennonite Literature, 1727–1928.* Goshen, Ind.: The Mennonite Historical Society, 1929.

Benedetto, Robert, Darrell L. Guder, and Donald K. McKim. *Historical Dictionary of the Reformed Churches.* Metuchen, N.J.: Scarecrow Press, 2000.

Bergendoff, Conrad. *The Church of the Lutheran Reformation.* St. Louis: Concordia Publishing House, 1967.

Bergman, Jerry. *Jehovah's Witnesses and Kindred Groups: An Historical Compendium and Bibliography.* New York: Garland, 1984.

Bissio, Roberto Remo, et al. *Third World Guide 93/94.* Montevideo, Uruguay: Instituto del Tercer Mundo, 1992.

Bodensieck, Julius, ed. *The Encyclopedia of the Lutheran Church,* 3 vols. Minneapolis, Minn.: Augsburg Publishing House, 1965.

Bolshakoff, Serge. *Russian Nonconformity.* Philadelphia: Westminster Press, 1921.

Brackney, William H., ed. *Baptist Life and Thought: 1600–1980.* Valley Forge, Pa.: Judson Press, 1983.

Brackney, William H. *Historical Dictionary of the Baptists.* Metuchen, N.J.: Scarecrow Press, 1999.

Bradley, James E., and R. A. Muller. *Church History: An Introduction to Research, Reference Works and Methods.* Grand Rapids, Mich.: William B. Eerdmans, 1995.

Brasher, Brenda E. *The Encyclopedia of Fundamentalism.* New York: Routledge, 2001.

The Brethren Encyclopedia. 2 vols. Philadelphia: The Brethren Encyclopedia, 1983.

Bull, Malcolm, ed. *Apocalypse Theory and the End of the World.* Oxford: Blackwell, 1995.

Bundy, David D. *Keswick: A Bibliographical Introduction to the Higher Life Movements.* Wilmore, Ky.: B. L. Fisher Library, Asbury Theological Seminary, 1975.

Burgess, Stanley M., and Eduard M. Van der Maas, eds. *International Dictionary of Pentecostal Charismatic Movements,* rev. ed. Grand Rapids, Mich.: Zondervan, 2002.

Cameron, Nigel M. De S. *The Dictionary of Scottish Church History and Theology.* Downers Grove, Ill.: InterVarsity Press, 1993.

Cameron, Euan. *The European Reformation.* Oxford: Oxford University Press, 1991.

Casey, Michael W., and Douglas A. Foster, eds. *Stone-Campbell Movement: An International Religious Tradition.* Knoxville: University of Tennessee Press, 2002.

Chadwick, Owen. *The Reformation.* Harmondsworth, U.K.: Penguin, 1991.

The Church of England Yearbook. London: Church Publishing House, published annually.

Cochrane, Arthur C., ed. *The Reformed Confessions of the Sixteenth Century.* Philadelphia: Westminster Press, 1966.

Couch, Mal, ed. *Dictionary of Premillennial Theology.* Grand Rapids, Mich.: Kregal Publications, 1996.

Cross, F. L., ed. *Oxford Dictionary of the Christian Church.* 3d ed. New York: Oxford University Press, 1997.

Dayton, Donald W. *The American Holiness Movement, A Bibliographic Introduction.* Wilmore, Ky.: B. L. Fisher Library, Asbury Theological Seminary, 1971.

———, David W. Faupel, and David D. Bundy, eds. *The Higher Christian Life: A Bibliographical Overview.* New York: Garland, 1985.

Dieter, Melvin Easterbury. *The 19th-Century Holiness Movement.* Kansas City, Mo.: Beacon Hill Press of KC, 1998.

Directory—*Handbuch.* Geneva: Lutheran World Federation, issued annually.

Dollar, George W. *A History of Fundamentalism in America.* Greenville, S.C.: Bob Jones University Press, 1973.

Durnbaugh, Donald F. *The Believer's Church.* New York: Macmillan, 1968.

Durnbaugh, Donald F. *Fruit of the Vine: A History of the Brethren, 1708–1995.* Elgin, Ill.: Brethren Press, 1997.

Eggenberger, Oswald. *Die Kirchen Sondergruppen und religiösen Vereinigungen.* Zürich: Theologischer Verlag, 1994.

Ehlert, Arnold D., comp. *A Bibliographic History of Dispensationalism.* Grand Rapids, Mich.: Baker Book House, 1965.

Elwell, W., ed. *Evangelical Dictionary of Theology.* Grand Rapids, Mich.: Baker Book House, 2002.

The Encyclopedia of Southern Baptists. 3 vols. Nashville, Tenn.: Broadman Press, 1958.

Estep, William R. *The Anabaptist Story: An Introduction to Sixteenth-Century Anabaptism.* Grand Rapids, Mich.: William B. Eerdmans, 1996.

———. *Renaissance and Reformation.* Grand Rapids, Mich.: William B. Eerdmans, 1986.

Ferm, Vergilius. *Pictorial History of Protestantism.* New York: Philosophical Library, 1957.

Fister, Douglas A. *Encyclopedia of the Stone-Campbell Movement.* Grand Rapids, Mich.: William B. Eerdmans, 2004.

Furniss, Norman F. *The Fundamentalist Controversy, 1918–1931.* New Haven, Conn.: Yale University Press, 1954.

Gassmann, Günther, with Duane H. Larson and Mark W. Oldenburg. *Historical Dictionary of Lutheranism.* Metuchen, N.J.: Scarecrow Press, 2001.

Glazier, Stephen. *The Encyclopedia of African and African American Religion.* Boston: Routledge, 2001.

Gonzalez, Justo L. *A History of Christian Thought: From the Protestant Reformation to the Twentieth Century.* Nashville, Tenn.: Abingdon Press, 1987.

Greaves, Richard L., ed. *Triumph over Silence: Women in Protestant History. Contributions to the Study of Religion.* Westport, Conn.: Greenwood Press, 1985.

Green, Vivian. *The European Reformation.* Sutton Pocket Histories. Gloucester, U.K.: Sutton Publishing, 1998.

Grimm, Harold J. *The Reformation Era.* New York: Macmillan, 1954.

Gritsch, Eric W. *Fortress Introduction to Lutheranism.* Minneapolis, Minn.: Fortress Press, 1994.

Hamilton, J. Taylor, and Kenneth G. Hamilton. *History of the Moravian Church.* Bethlehem, Pa.: Interprovincial Board of Christian Education, Moravian Church in America, 1983.

Handbook. Grand Rapids, Mich.: Reformed Ecumenical Synod, 1997.

Harmon, Nolan B. *Encyclopedia of World Methodism.* 2 vols. Nashville, Tenn.: United Methodist Publishing House, 1974.

Hart, D. G., and Mark A. Noll, eds. *Dictionary of the Presbyterian and Reformed Tradition in America.* Des Plaines, Ill.: InterVarsity Press, 1999.

Hilderbrand, Hans J. *Christendom Divided: The Protestant Reformation.* Chichester, U.K.: Corpus, 1971.

———. *Encyclopedia of Protestantism.* New York: Routledge, 2003.

———, ed. *The Oxford Encyclopedia of the Reformation.* 4 vols. New York: Oxford University Press, 1996.

———. *The Reformation: A Narrative History Related by Contemporary Observers and Participants.* Grand Rapids, Mich.: Baker Book House, 1981.

Hillerbrand, Hans J., and Jon Woronoff. *Historical Dictionary of the Reformation and Counter-Reformation.* Walnut Creek, Calif.: Rowman & Littlefield, 2000.

Hoke, Donald, ed. *The Church in Asia.* Chicago: Moody Press, 1975.

Holl, K. *The Cultural Significance of the Reformation.* New York: Meridian, 1959.

Hollenweger, Walter J. *Pentecostalism: Origins and Developments Worldwide.* Peabody, Mass.: Hendrickson, 1997.

Hostetler, John A. *Amish Life.* Scottdale, Pa.: Herald Press, 1959, 1983.

———. *An Annotated Bibliography on the Amish.* Scottdale, Pa.: Mennonite House, 1951.

Introvigne, Massimo, PierLuigi Zoccatelli, Nelly Ippolito Macrina, and Verónica Roldán. *Enciclopedia delle Religioni in Italia.* Leumann, Torino: Elledici, 2001.

Johnstone, Patrick, and Jason Mandryk. *Operation World, 21st Century Edition.* Carlisle, Cumbria, U.K.: Paternoster, 2001.

Jones, Charles Edwin. *Black Holiness: A Guide to the Study of Black Participation in Wesleyan Perfectionist and Glossolalic Pentecostal Movements.* Metuchen, N.J.: American Theological Library Association/Scarecrow Press, 1987.

———. *The Charismatic Movement: A Guide to the Study of Neo-Pentecostalism with Emphasis on Anglo-American Sources.* Philadelphia: Scarecrow Press, 1995.

Jones, Rufus M. *Spiritual Reformers of the Sixteenth and Seventeenth Centuries.* Boston: Beacon Press, 1914.

Kane, J. Herbert, *A Global View of Christian Missions.* Grand Rapids, Mich.: Baker Book House, 1971.

Kaplan, Jeffrey, ed. *Encyclopedia of White Power: A Sourcebook on the Radical Racist Right.* Walnut Creek, Calif.: AltaMira Press, 2000.

———. *Radical Religion in America.* Syracuse, N.Y.: Syracuse University Press, 1997.

Kostlevy, William C. *Historical Dictionary of the Holiness Movement.* Metuchen, N.J.: Scarecrow Press, 2001.

Keith, John H. *An Introduction to the Reformed Tradition.* Atlanta: John Knox Press, 1977.

Landes, Richard, ed. *Encyclopedia of Millennialism and Millennial Movements.* New York: Routledge, 2000.

Lindsay, Thomas M. *A History of the Reformation.* New York: Scribner, 1920.

Lossky, Nicholas, et al., eds., *Dictionary of the Ecumenical Movement.* Geneva/Grand Rapids, Mich.: WCC Publications/William B. Eerdmans, 1991.

Lumpkin, W. L. *Baptist Confessions of Faith.* Chicago: Judson Press, 1959.

McBeth, H. Leon. *The Baptist Heritage: Four Centuries of Baptist Witness.* Nashville, Tenn.: Broadman Press, 1887.

McGrath, Alister E. *The Intellectual Origins of the European Reformation.* Oxford: Oxford University Press, 1987.

———. *Life of John Calvin: A Study in the Shaping of Western Culture.* Oxford: Basil Blackwell, 1990.

McKim, Donald K., with Daniel F. Wright, eds., *Encyclopedia of the Reformed Faith.* Louisville, Ky./Edinburgh: Westminster and John Knox Press/St. Andrew Press, 1992.

McNeill, J. T. *The History and Character of Calvinism*. Oxford: Oxford University Press, 1954.

Magnuson, Norris A. *American Evangelicalism: An Annotated Bibliography*. West Cornwall, Conn.: Locust Hill Press, 1990.

Maltby, William S. ed. *Reformation Europe: A Guide to Research II*. St. Louis: Center for Reformation Research, 1992.

Marty, Martin E., ed. *Varieties of Protestantism*. Munich/New York: K. G. Saur, 1992.

Melton, J. Gordon. *Encyclopedia of American Religions*. 7th ed. Detroit: Gale Group, 2002.

———. *The Encyclopedia of American Religions: Religious Creeds*. 2 vols. Detroit: Gale Research, 1988, 1994.

———, and Martin Baumann, eds., *Religions of the World: A Comprehensive Encyclopedia of Beliefs and Practices*. Santa Barbara, Calif.: ABC-CLIO, 2002.

The Mennonite Encyclopedia. 4 vols. Scottdale, Pa.: Mennonite Publishing House, 1955–59.

Mildenberger, Friedrich. *Theology of the Lutheran Confessions*. Philadelphia: Fortress Press, 1986.

Moreau, A. Scott, ed. *Evangelical Dictionary of World Missions*. Grand Rapids, Mich.: Baker Book House, 2000.

Murphy, Larry, G., J. Gordon Melton, and Gary L. War. *Encyclopedia of African American Religion*. New York: Garland, 1993.

Neill, Stephen, *Anglicanism*. London: A. R. Mowbrays, 1977.

———. *A History of Christian Missions*. Rev. 2d ed. New York: Penguin Books, 1990.

Nichol, Francis D. *The Midnight Cry*. Washington, D.C.: Review & Herald Publishing Association, 1944.

Noel, Napoleon. *The History of the Brethren*. 2 vols. Denver: W. F. Knapp, 1934.

Noll, M. ed. *Confessions and Catechisms of the Reformation*. Grand Rapids, Mich.: Baker Book House, 1991.

Oberman, H. A. *Forerunners of the Reformation: The Shape of Late Medieval Thought*. Philadelphia: Fortress Press, 1981.

———. *The Dawn of the Reformation*. Edinburgh: T & T Clark, 1986.

Ozment, Steven E., ed. *Reformation Europe: A Guide to Research*. St. Louis: Center for Reformation Research, 1982.

Parker, T. H. L. *John Calvin: A Biography*. Philadelphia: Westminster Press, 1975.

Pauck, Wilhelm. *The Heritage of the Reformation*. Oxford: Oxford University Press, 1961.

Payne, Wardell J. *Directory of African-American Religious Bodies*. 2d ed. Washington, D.C.: Howard University Press, 1996.

Pickering, Hy. *Chief Men among the Brethren*. London: Pickering & Inglis, 1918.

Poewe, Karla O., ed. *Charismatic Christianity as a Global Culture*. Columbia: University of South Carolina Press, 1994.

Quakers Around the World. London: Friends World Committee for Consultation, 1994.

Raitt, J., ed. *Shapers of Religious Traditions in Germany, Switzerland, and Poland 1500–1600*. New Haven, Conn.: Yale University Press, 1981.

Reid, Daniel G., et al., eds. *Dictionary of Christianity in America*. Downers Grove, Ill.: InterVarsity Press, 1990.

Russell, C. Allyn. *Voices of American Fundamentalism*. Philadelphia: Westminster Press, 1976.

Ryken, Leland. *Worldly Saints: The Puritans As They Really Were*. Grand Rapids, Mich.: Academic Books-Zondervan, 1986.

St. Clair, Michael. *Millennial Movements in Historical Context*. New York: Garland, 1992.

Schmidt, Martin. *John Wesley, A Theological Biography*. 2 vols. New York: Abingdon, 1963–73.

Springer, Nelson P., and A. J. Klassen. *Mennonite Bibliography, 1631–1961*. 2 vols. Scottdale, Pa.: Herald Press, 1977.

Steimer, Bruno. *The Dictionary of the Reformation*. London: Herder & Herder, 2004.

Stoeffler, F. Ernest. *German Pietism During the Eighteenth Century*. Leiden: E. J. Brill, 1973.

Sunquist, Scott W., ed. *A Dictionary of Asian Christianity*. Grand Rapids, Mich.: William B. Eerdmans, 2001.

Sweet, Leonard I. *The Evangelical Tradition in America*. Macon, Ga.: Mercer University Press, 1984.

Synan, Vinson, ed. *The Century of the Holy Spirit: 100 Years of Pentecostal and Charismatic Renewal.* Nashville, Tenn.: Thomas Nelson, 2001.

Thernstrom, Stephan, ed. *Harvard Encyclopedia of American Ethnic Groups.* Cambridge, Mass.: Belknap Press of Harvard University Press, 1980.

Tucker, Ruth A. *From Jerusalem to Irian Jaya: A Biographical History of Christian Missions.* Grand Rapids, Mich.: Zondervan, 1983.

Van der Bent, Ans J., ed. *Handbook/Member Churches/World Council of Churches.* Geneva: World Council of Churches, 1985.

Verduin, Leonard. *The Reformers and Their Stepchildren.* Grand Rapids, Mich.: William B. Eerdmans, 1964.

Walker, Williston. *The Creed and Platforms of Congregationalism.* Philadelphia: Pilgrim Press, 1960.

Ward, Kevin, and Brian Stanley. *The Church Missionary Society and World Christianity, 1799–1999.* Richmond, Surrey, U.K.: Curzon Press, 2000.

Wardin, Albert W., ed. *Baptists Around the World.* Nashville, Tenn.: Broadman & Holman, 1995.

Weber, Timothy P. *Living in the Shadow of the Second Coming.* New York: Oxford University Press, 1979.

Westin, Gunnar. *The Free Church Through the Ages.* Nashville, Tenn.: Broadman Press, 1958.

Wingate, Andrew, et al., eds. *Anglicanism: A Global Communion.* London: A. R. Mowbrays, 1998.

Whale, John. *The Anglican Church Today: The Future of Anglicanism.* London: A. R. Mowbrays, 1988.

Williams, George H. *The Radical Reformation.* Philadelphia: Westminster Press, 1962.

Williamson, William B., ed. *An Encyclopedia of Religions in the United States: One Hundred Religious Groups Speak for Themselves.* New York: Crossroads, 1992.

Winter, Ralph, and Steve Hawthorne, eds. *Perspectives on the World Christian Movement: A Reader.* 3d ed. Pasadena, Calif.: William Carey Library, 1999.

World Methodist Council, Handbook of Information. Lake Junaluska, N.C.: World Methodist Council, 2003.

Yrigoyen, Charles, Jr., and Susan E. Warrick, *Historical Dictionary of Methodism.* Metuchen, N.J.: Scarecrow Press, 1996.

INDEX